THE WORLD AT ARMS

THE WORLD AT ARMS

THE READER'S DIGEST ILLUSTRATED HISTORY OF WORLD WAR II

Published by
The Reader's Digest
Association Limited
LONDON
NEW YORK · SYDNEY
MONTREAL · CAPE TOWN

THE WORLD AT ARMS
was edited and designed by
The Reader's Digest Association Limited,
London

Editor: Michael Wright, MA
Art Editor: Bob Hook

First Edition

Printed in America

The typefaces used for the text in this book are Plantin Light, Helvetica and Modern

Illustrations: Inside front cover: conscripts sign on, 1939.
Page 1: US troops land on 'Utah' beach on D-Day.
Pages 2–3: German bomber over London, 1940.
Pages 4–5 (clockwise from top left): through the wire at El Alamein, 1942; HMS *Kipling* on patrol; Himmler and Hitler watch manoeuvres; British poster, 1945; British surrender at Singapore, 1942; Nazi party poster for rally, 1938; French Resistance question suspected collaborator; Russian poster, 1942 (comparison with 1812); Mussolini and other fascists in 'march on Rome', 1922; German Tiger tank; Churchill with Tommy gun.
Page 6 (top to bottom): Allied merchant seamen rescued; Italian-American poster, 1942 ('This is the enemy'); *Saturday Evening Post* cover, 1943; group of Chindits.
Inside back cover: VJ Day, Times Square, New York.

Contributors

The publishers wish to express their gratitude to the following who, as contributors or consultants, assisted in the preparation of *The World at Arms*

Consultant editor

John L. Pimlott, PhD, BA
Deputy Head, Department of War Studies
Royal Military Academy, Sandhurst

Major contributors

Duncan Anderson, MA, DPhil
Senior Lecturer
Department of War Studies
Royal Military Academy, Sandhurst

Neil Ardley, BSc, FRSA

Robin Cross
Former editor
The History of the 20th Century

Christopher Dobson

William Escombe
Military historian

William Fowler, MA, DpJ, AIExpE
Army editor, *Defence* magazine

William Geldard

Eric J. Grove, MA
Naval historian and defence consultant

Tim Healey, MA

James S. Lucas

John Man, BA, DipHistPhSc

Barbara Matthews

Charles Messenger, MA
Military historian and defence analyst

Eric Morris, MA, MBIM
Consultant political analyst and military historian

Robert Stewart, MA, DPhil
Historian

Elise K. Tipton, PhD
Lecturer in East Asian Studies
University of Sydney

David Ward

H. P. Willmott, MA, FRHistS
Senior Lecturer
Department of War Studies
Royal Military Academy, Sandhurst

John W. Young, BA, PhD, FRHistS
Lecturer in International History
London School of Economics

Consultants

John R. Bullen, BA, MA, PhD
Curator
Department of Exhibits and Firearms
Imperial War Museum

Terry C. Charman, BA
Research Assistant
Department of Printed Books
Imperial War Museum

Diana Condell, MPhil
Curator
Department of Exhibits and Firearms
Imperial War Museum

Lt Commander James Goldrick, BA, MLitt
Royal Australian Navy

Lt Colonel David Horner, MA, PhD
Joint Services Staff College
Canberra, Australia

Map artists

Eugene Fleury

Gary Hincks

Malcolm Porter

Illustrators

Mick Gillah

Paul Hannon

Ivan Lapper

The publishers would like to thank the following for their special assistance:

Vere Dodds

Carina Dvorak

Andrew Kerr-Jarrett, MA

Alfred LeMaitre, MA

Judith Taylor, MA

The publishers also wish to thank the following members of the staff of the Imperial War Museum for their kind assistance in providing facilities for research:

Dr Alan Borg
Director General

Dr Gwyn Bayliss
Keeper, Department of Printed Books

Jane Carmichael
Keeper, Department of Photographs

Special thanks are also due to Lt Colonel L.M.B. Wilson, MBE, of The Queen's Regimental Museum; Brigadier J.M. Cubiss, CBE, MC, of The Prince of Wales's Own Regiment of Yorkshire; and Alastair Forsyth of Southampton City Museums.

CONTENTS

ECCO il NEMICO

POST
BILLION-DOLLAR PLANE BUILDER
A Gay Short Story
THANKSGIVING

When you go home
Tell them of us and say
For your tomorrow
We gave our today

INSCRIPTION ON THE BRITISH
2ND DIVISION MEMORIAL AT KOHIMA

PART ONE

WORLD WAR II was an earth-shaking drama in five Acts, played out on a stage as immense as the planet itself, and touching upon millions of lives.

The prologue took place in the Thirties, when Hitler cowed the democracies and extended the boundaries of his malign power through a gangster-like combination of bluff and bullying.

Act One opened with a crash – the Nazi onslaught on Poland. Britain and France, after years of appeasing the dictators, stood by their promises to the Poles and declared war – after which very little happened.

Then, in the spring of 1940, the storm howled again as Norway, the Low Countries and France succumbed to the jackboot, the Stuka and the panzer. But one triumph eluded Hitler: saved by the miracle of Dunkirk, Britain stood defiant and alone.

Switching his malevolence to the east, and invading Russia in Operation 'Barbarossa', was to prove Hitler's costliest mistake. Even so, by the late autumn of 1942, his empire stretched from the shores of the Atlantic to the burning sands of Egypt; from Greece to Leningrad and beyond, to the Arctic wastes ●

TERRITORIAL ACQUISITIONS		
1	Saarland to Germany	Jan '35
2	Rhineland remilitarised by Germany	Mar '36
3	Austria to Germany	Mar '38
4	Sudetenland to Germany	Oct '38
5	Teschen to Poland	Nov '38
6	Southern Slovakia to Hungary	Nov '38
7	Bohemia/Moravia to Germany	Mar '39
8	Ruthenia to Hungary	Mar '39
9	Memel to Germany	Mar '39
10	Albania to Italy	Apr '39
11	Parts of Finland to USSR	Mar '40
12	Bessarabia and N. Bucovina to USSR	Jun '40
13	Dobruja to Bulgaria	Sep '40
14	Transylvania to Hungary	Sep '40

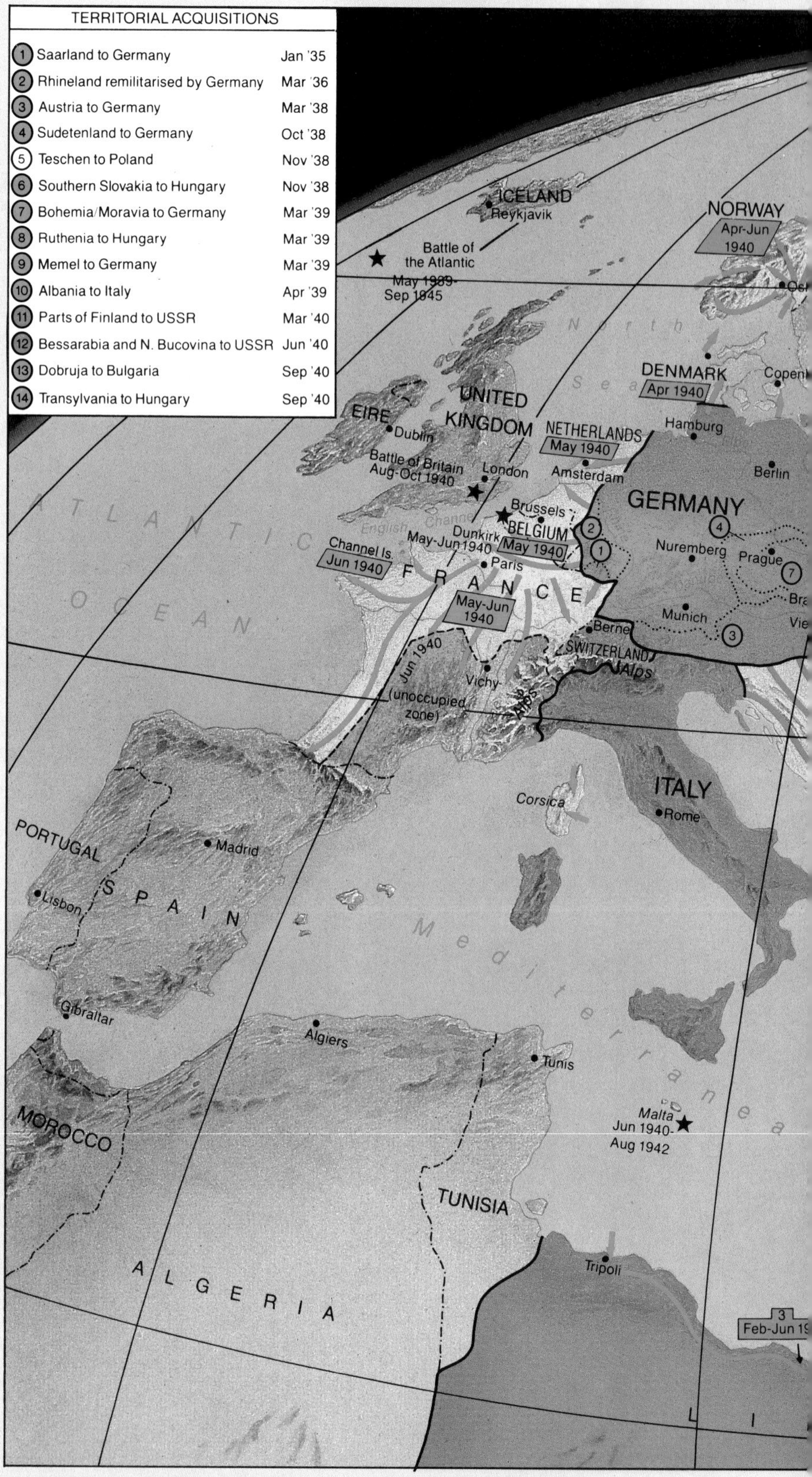

THE REICH RAMPANT

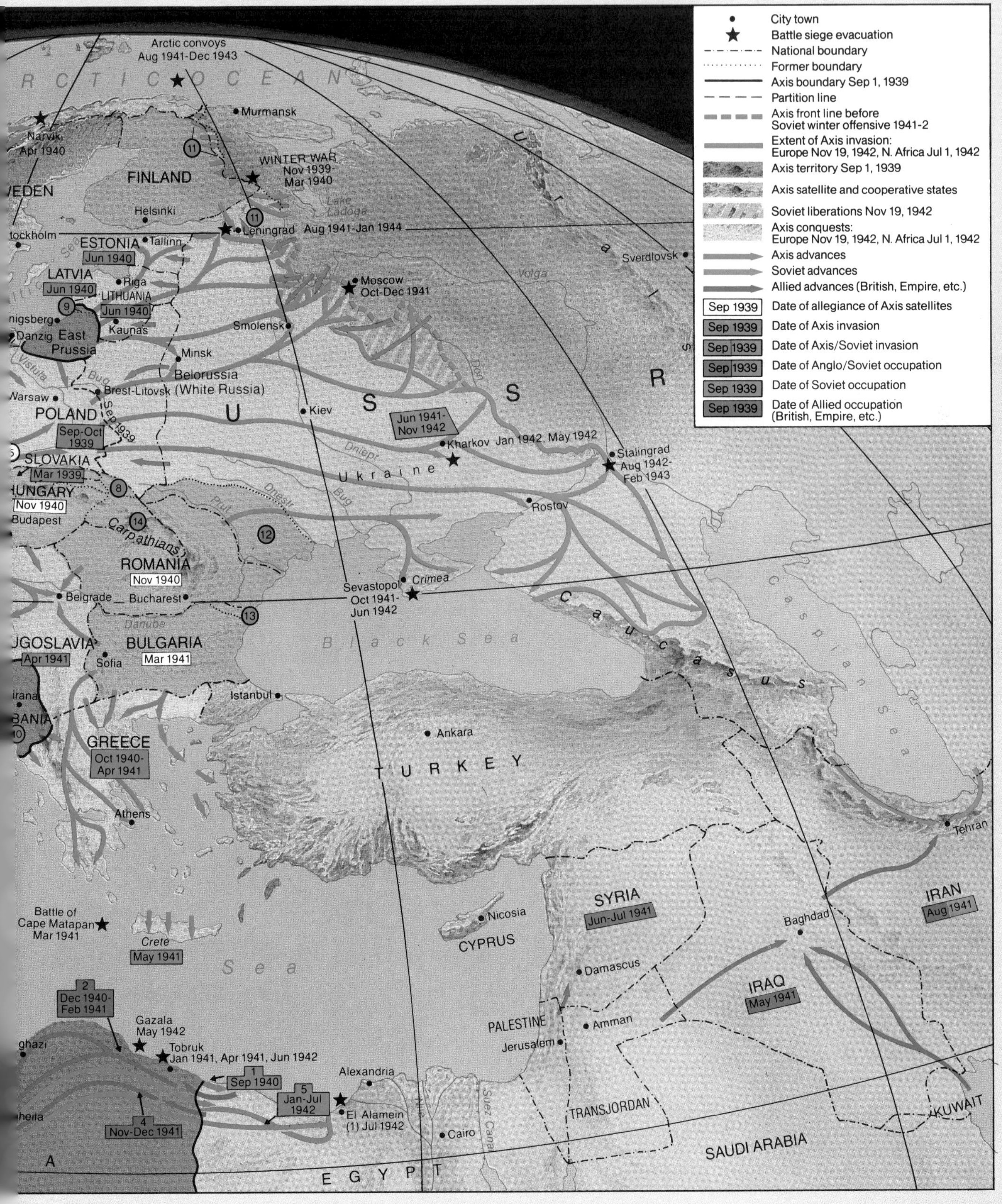
City town
Battle siege evacuation
National boundary
Former boundary
Axis boundary Sep 1, 1939
Partition line
Axis front line before Soviet winter offensive 1941-2
Extent of Axis invasion: Europe Nov 19, 1942, N. Africa Jul 1, 1942
Axis territory Sep 1, 1939
Axis satellite and cooperative states
Soviet liberations Nov 19, 1942
Axis conquests: Europe Nov 19, 1942, N. Africa Jul 1, 1942
Axis advances
Soviet advances
Allied advances (British, Empire, etc.)
Sep 1939 Date of allegiance of Axis satellites
Sep 1939 Date of Axis invasion
Sep 1939 Date of Axis/Soviet invasion
Sep 1939 Date of Anglo/Soviet occupation
Sep 1939 Date of Soviet occupation
Sep 1939 Date of Allied occupation (British, Empire, etc.)
Arctic convoys Aug 1941-Dec 1943
RCTIC OCEAN
Murmansk
Narvik Apr 1940
WINTER WAR Nov 1939-Mar 1940
FINLAND
VEDEN
Helsinki
Lake Ladoga
Leningrad Aug 1941-Jan 1944
tockholm
ESTONIA Jun 1940
Tallinn
LATVIA Jun 1940
Riga
LITHUANIA Jun 1940
nigsberg
Danzig
East Prussia
Kaunas
Moscow Oct-Dec 1941
Smolensk
Minsk
Belorussia (White Russia)
Vistula
Bug
Warsaw
Brest-Litovsk
POLAND Sep-Oct 1939
Sep 1939
U S S R
Kiev
Jun 1941-Nov 1942
Don
Volga
Ural
Sverdlovsk
Kharkov Jan 1942, May 1942
Stalingrad Aug 1942-Feb 1943
Dniepr
Ukraine
Rostov
SLOVAKIA Mar 1939
HUNGARY Nov 1940
Budapest
Dnestr
Prut
Carpathians
ROMANIA Nov 1940
Crimea
Sevastopol Oct 1941-Jun 1942
Belgrade
Bucharest
Danube
Caucasus
Caspian Sea
Black Sea
UGOSLAVIA Apr 1941
BULGARIA Mar 1941
Sofia
Istanbul
irana
BANIA
Ankara
TURKEY
GREECE Oct 1940-Apr 1941
Athens
Tehran
Battle of Cape Matapan Mar 1941
Crete May 1941
Sea
SYRIA Jun-Jul 1941
Nicosia
CYPRUS
Baghdad
IRAN Aug 1941
Damascus
IRAQ May 1941
2 Dec 1940-Feb 1941
Gazala May 1942
Tobruk Jan 1941, Apr 1941, Jun 1942
PALESTINE
Amman
Jerusalem
ghazi
1 Sep 1940
Alexandria
5 Jan-Jul 1942
El Alamein (1) Jul 1942
Nile
Suez Canal
TRANSJORDAN
KUWAIT
heila
4 Nov-Dec 1941
Cairo
SAUDI ARABIA
A
EGYPT

1: STORM CLOUDS OVER EUROPE

Some historians see the 1920s and 30s as an interlude in a conflict lasting from 1914 to 1945.

The legacy of Versailles

The treaty that formally ended World War I was signed in the splendour of the Château of Versailles' great Hall of Mirrors on June 28, 1919. Its prime aim was to prevent Germany from ever again disturbing the peace of Europe – yet its very harshness would give Hitler an excuse to prepare for war.

HISTORY IN THE MAKING At last, after months of ruthless negotiations, the Versailles treaty is being signed. Some Allied officers wait phlegmatically, but others cast dignity aside to peer in at the ceremony.

WORLD WAR I – the 'Great War' – was meant to be the 'war to end all wars'. The Allies – among them, France, Britain and its empire, Italy, Russia (until early 1918), Japan and (from 1917) the USA – were ranged against the Central Powers – Germany, Austria-Hungary, Bulgaria and Turkey. Britain and the United States claimed that the war was fought to make the world 'safe for democracy'. After the armistice that brought fighting to an end in November 1918, the victors had one overriding objective – to lay down peace terms that would stop Germany from dominating Europe again.

Under the treaty signed at Versailles at the end of the Paris peace conference, the Allies laid the entire responsibility for the war on Germany, which was to be almost totally disarmed forever. Its army was to have no more than 100 000 men, its navy only six warships above 10 000 tonnes and no submarines. It was forbidden any military aircraft. The German west bank of the Rhine was to be occupied by Allied troops – and, under the 'reparations clauses', Germany was to pay for all the losses and damage suffered by the Allied nations during the war.

The treaty also deprived Germany of large parts of its territory and population, radically redrawing the map of central Europe in the process. Poland, for example, which had not existed as an independent state since 1795, was re-created. It incorporated territory taken from Germany, including the 'Polish Corridor', a narrow strip extending to the Baltic near Danzig (now Gdansk) and cutting off East Prussia from the rest of Germany. Danzig itself, whose population was almost entirely German, was included within the frontiers of Poland but made a self-governing free city under the protection of the newly created League of Nations.

In the west, Alsace-Lorraine (which the Germans had seized from France in 1871) was returned to the French. The rich industrial province of the Saarland was to be governed by the League of Nations for 15 years, after which a plebiscite would decide its future. Meanwhile the French would administer its coalfields. Germany was also deprived of all its colonies in Africa, in the Pacific and in China. The treaty took away from Germany about 13 per cent of its prewar territory, 10 per cent of its population, 75 per cent of its iron ore and 25 per cent of its best-quality coal.

GERMAN RESENTMENT

From right to left of the political spectrum, the German people resented the Versailles treaty. Even moderate politicians denounced it as a 'document of hatred and delusion' and 'a peace of violence'. The moderates had particular cause to feel cheated. For two years, US President Woodrow Wilson had declared that the Allies were not at war with the German people, only with the Kaiser ('Emperor') Wilhelm II and the Prussian militarists of his army. The Kaiser had abdicated at the end of the war and, despite a Communist uprising in January 1919, a new democratic republican government had been set up, with its seat initially at the city of Weimar.

Yet at Versailles the Germans found themselves treated as severely as if they were still ruled by right-wing nationalists. Their delegates, headed by the haughty Foreign Minister, Count Brockdorff-Rantzau, were not even given a place at the negotiating table. When, near the end, they were finally given a hearing, the Count delivered a rasping, insolent speech without bothering to rise from his chair; in it he refused to admit sole German responsibility for the war. The speech was described by Wilson as 'the most tactless I have ever heard', and left Allied leaders red-faced with fury. But there is no doubt that it reflected German resentment.

The moderates also suffered from Wilson's high-minded refusal to have dealings with the German High Command. This simply allowed the militarist and anti-democratic right wing to distance itself from the armistice of November 1918 and the treaty terms – and to blame both on the left and centre politicians of the new Weimar Republic. The armistice was after all signed while Germany's army still occupied foreign territory and presented an unbroken front to the west.

The German right could denounce the treaty as a *Diktat*, and brand the Weimar leaders as the 'November criminals', by whom Germany had been 'stabbed in the back'. Nothing so assisted Adolf Hitler and other right-wing politicians in the coming years as to be able, when anything went wrong, to point the finger at Versailles and blame their democratic opponents.

DANGERS AHEAD

In practice, Germany's continental neighbour France bore the burden of trying to enforce the Versailles treaty. But France was too weak to carry the burden alone – as, for example, when Nazi Germany began to rearm during the 1930s. The USA and Britain, whose leaders felt little of France's natural fear of Germany, rarely gave France the backing it needed.

Moreover, the pre-1914 balance of power, with Russia and France aligned against Germany and Austria-Hungary, no longer existed. To the east everything was uncertain. A series of treaties, with Austria (in September 1919), Bulgaria

(November 1919), Hungary (June 1920) and Turkey (August 1920), was creating a clutch of new Slav states, such as Czechoslovakia and Yugoslavia. These emerged partly as a result of the high principles of national self-determination, pushed by Wilson. But none of the new states was powerful enough to counterbalance Germany, while the new Soviet Union, abject anyway after the country's crushing defeat during the war, was too absorbed in its revolutionary politics.

Further dangers were created by the large German minorities in several of the new states, notably Czechoslovakia. 'I cannot conceive of any greater cause of future war,' wrote British premier David Lloyd George during the Paris peace conference, 'than that the German people, who have certainly proved themselves one of the most vigorous and powerful races in the world, should be surrounded by a number of small states, many of them consisting of people who have never previously set up a stable government for themselves, but each of them containing large masses of Germans clamouring for re-union with their native land.'

Many hoped that the League of Nations, a predecessor of the United Nations set up under the Versailles treaty, would help to keep the peace. Members of this international body pledged mutual protection against aggression, arbitration over disputes and a three-month delay before taking any military action after such arbitration. However, Germany was excluded until 1926 and the US Senate overrode Wilson's determination to join – a portent of two decades of US isolationism, ended only when the Japanese attacked Pearl Harbor.

THE MARK COLLAPSES

In April 1921, the Allies fixed the total sum to be paid by Germany in reparations – a colossal 200 million gold marks (about US$40 000 million). Rather than agree to pay, the German government of the day resigned – but a new government was soon forced to acquiesce. Faced with the resulting vast budgetary deficits, the government simply printed more money. The result was inflation on a scale never equalled before or since. Before the war a little over 4 marks had been equivalent to US$1. By the beginning of 1922, there were 162 paper marks to the dollar, by the end of the year 7000.

In December 1922, the French government declared Germany in default with its reparations payments – and in the following month French and Belgian troops occupied Germany's industrial heartland, the Ruhr valley, taking over control of its mines and railways.

The effect on the German economy was catastrophic, as the German government urged the Ruhr people to show passive resistance and printed yet more money. By November 1923, one US dollar was worth an astonishing 4 200 000 million marks. Businesses were bankrupted throughout the country and thousands of workers were thrown onto the streets. People's lifetime savings were wiped out. That month, however, a new chancellor, Gustav Stresemann, and the Reichsbank president, Dr Hjalmar Schacht, started a currency reform. They replaced 1 million million old marks with one new Rentenmark, later renamed the Reichsmark.

This and other measures brought an impressive recovery. Inflation dropped; business began to prosper again and unemployment fell. In 1924 the Dawes plan, devised by an international committee under the American Charles Dawes, provided Germany with a foreign loan of 800 million Reichsmarks (US$190 million). Five years later another committee under Owen Young reformed the system of reparations payments.

HOPE AT LOCARNO

At the same time, international relations seemed increasingly hopeful. In 1925, the European powers met at Locarno in Switzerland, and for the first time since the war Germany was given an equal place at the negotiating table.

Agreements that emerged included treaties guaranteeing Germany's 1919 borders with France and Belgium. But for Germany the most important agreements were its 'arbitration' treaties with Poland and Czechoslovakia. These laid down rules for settling border disputes between Germany and the other two countries – for no postwar German politician accepted as permanent the eastern borders drawn at Versailles. The *Drang nach Osten*, or 'pull to the east', was part of every German's vision for the future.

By agreeing to arbitration, the other European powers were effectively agreeing that Germany's claims to lands to the east (the *Lebensraum*, or 'living space', that Hitler later made much of) were negotiable. It was, in fact, the first step in the appeasement of Germany. Nonetheless, for a few years the 'spirit of Locarno' seemed to hold out the promise of an era of secure European peace.

That promise evaporated in October 1929, when the world's financial markets crashed and the still fragile edifice of German democracy was loosed from its shallow foundations.

BARTER VIEWING Children waiting outside a picture house in Berlin in 1923 each clutch the price of a ticket – two briquettes of coal (*2 Presskohlen*). The most devastating inflation ever had made money in Germany virtually worthless. Middle-class people suddenly found themselves paupers. City streets were thronging with unemployed workers.

The dictators take power

After the abject failure, in November 1923, of the Nazis' attempted coup d'état in Munich, their leader Adolf Hitler seemed set to disappear from the pages of history. In fact, though, the Munich Putsch was just a beginning – and within ten years the Austrian-born former corporal had become Germany's democratically elected chancellor.

PARTY STALWARTS Two of Hitler's lieutenants, the gaunt-faced Rudolf Hess and bespectacled Heinrich Himmler, stand with armed supporters at barricades in central Munich during the attempted 'Beer Hall' Putsch.

GERMANY IN NOVEMBER 1923 was in chaos. The inflation that had been growing steadily since the Great War was completely out of control. In Berlin, a single loaf of bread cost 201 000 million marks. The streets of Germany's cities were thronged with unemployed workers, and hitherto prosperous middle-class people were suddenly made paupers as money lost nearly all value. Throughout the country extremists of right and left were calling for the overthrow of the central German government in Berlin and for a new revolutionary government in its place.

On the evening of November 8, an unusually large and influential crowd filled Munich's largest beer hall, the *Bürgerbräukeller* ('Citizens' Beer Hall'). It included the commander of the army in Bavaria, General Otto von Lossow, and the state's police chief, Colonel Hans von Seisser. They had gathered to hear a speech by the right-wing head of Bavaria's state government, Gustav von Kahr, on the moral justification for dictatorship. Lossow, Seisser and Kahr were the state's most powerful men. Also present was Adolf Hitler, leader of the National Socialist or Nazi party, one of the many far-right political groups that had sprung up in post-war Bavaria.

Suddenly, at 8.30 pm, shortly after Kahr had begun his speech, one of Hitler's lieutenants, Hermann Göring, burst into the hall. He was followed by 25 armed, brown-shirted supporters – members of the Nazis' stormtrooper force, the *Sturmabteilungen* or SA. Hitler jumped onto a chair and fired a shot at the ceiling. 'The national revolution has begun,' he shouted. 'This hall is occupied by 600 heavily armed men. No one may leave the hall.' He then forced Kahr, Lossow and Seisser into another room.

For several months Hitler had been calling on Kahr and his colleagues to support him in overthrowing Germany's republican government. He now informed the three men that he and his ally, the Great War veteran General Erich Ludendorff, had already formed a new German government, with Hitler as dictator. Influenced by Mussolini's march on Rome the year before (see box), he demanded support for a similar march on Berlin and in installing the new regime.

The Munich, or 'Beer Hall', Putsch was soon over. Hitler's three captives agreed to back him, but once released alerted Berlin. The next day Hitler, Ludendorff and a column of supporters marched through Munich. At the Feldherrnhalle war memorial in the centre, they encountered a police cordon. A shot was fired (nobody knows by whom) starting a shoot-out which left three police officers and 16 Nazis dead.

One police shot very nearly changed the course of history. A demonstrator marching arm in arm with Hitler was mortally wounded, dislocating Hitler's shoulder as he fell. Ludendorff, like the general he was, marched proudly on. But he was alone. Hitler picked himself up and fled, only to be arrested two days later.

THE LESSONS OF DEFEAT

The Nazis' bid to seize power in Munich collapsed because they failed to win the support of either the army or rich conservatives in whose eyes Hitler was simply an unkempt, unemployed upstart. Munich, however, made him a nationally known figure. At his trial for treason afterwards, he took the offensive. 'I alone bear the responsibility,' he proclaimed. 'If I stand here as a revolutionary, it is as a revolutionary against revolution. There is no such thing as high treason against the traitors of 1918.' He was given the minimum sentence of five years' imprisonment – yet was released after nine months. Hitler used the time profitably, dictating the first chapters of his political testament *Mein Kampf* to the ever-faithful Rudolf Hess.

Hitler had two supreme political virtues: patience and resilience. Nor did he ever fail to draw profitable lessons from defeat. His setback, he decided, was the 'wise finger of Providence' pointed at him. Henceforth, he would follow a legal, electoral strategy to gain power.

By 1928, however, Germany seemed to have set its foot on the road back to prosperity, and old enemies such as France and Britain were showing at least an understanding of its problems: at Locarno (p. 11) they had accepted Germany's right to feel disgruntled about its borders with Poland and Czechoslovakia. Hermann Müller, the moderate Social Democratic Chancellor, was emboldened to proclaim that the foundations of the Weimar Republic were 'unshakable'. Good times for Weimar meant bad times for the infant Nazi party. In the 1928 Reichstag elections it won only 3 per cent of the vote and only 12 seats.

Then, in October 1929, the New York stock market on Wall Street crashed. Recession followed in the USA, as banks and businesses throughout the country failed and millions of workers lost their jobs, then spread to the rest of the world. The recession hit Germany's still fragile economy particularly hard. Unemployment, for example, rose from just 1.3 million in the month before the crash to over 6 million by the beginning of 1932. The chancellor at the time was the centre-right Heinrich Brüning. He was a 46-year-old bachelor, a devout Roman Catholic with the look of a monk, authoritarian but entirely lacking the charisma to inspire and lead the nation out of the crisis.

The depression provided an ideal breeding ground for the spread of the Nazi virus. Feeding on fear, Nazi propaganda blamed the country's woes on the Communists, Socialists, 'Versailles criminals' – and above all the Jews. In 1931 the Nazis forged an alliance with the right-wing Nationalist party, led by Alfred Hugenberg. The Nationalists had the support of industrial and big business magnates – and an efficient party

NATIONAL SOCIALISTS: NAZI PARTY ORGANISATION

A Munich locksmith, Anton Drexler, founded the Nazi party in 1919 as the German Workers' Party. He wanted it to fuse socialism and German nationalism. Hitler joined in September and soon took over leadership. The party grew rapidly and was renamed the *Nationalsozialistische Deutsche Arbeiterpartei* ('National Socialist German Workers' Party') – Nazi for short. Hitler chose as its symbol the swastika, an ancient religious sign.

In 1921 Hitler's devoted lieutenant Ernst Röhm created a 2000-strong paramilitary force of stormtroopers – the *Sturmabteilungen*, or SA, also known as 'Brownshirts'. They kept order with their fists at Nazi meetings, disrupted those of opponents and kept the party in the public eye. Most recruits were unemployed, social misfits, disaffected former servicemen or thugs. By 1934, membership had risen to 2 million, but was severely purged in June of that year (see box, p. 18).

In 1929 Heinrich Himmler took over command of Hitler's personal bodyguard, the *Schutzstaffel* (SS) or 'Protection Squad', and expanded it considerably. SS recruits had to have a Nordic appearance and unmixed German ancestry back to 1750. By 1933 they numbered 50 000 men.

The SS developed a number of subsections during the early 1930s. These included the SD (*Sicherheitsdienst* or 'Security Service'), under the ruthless Reinhard Heydrich, responsible for dealing with the regime's opponents; and the *Totenkopf* ('Death's-head') guards, who staffed the concentration camps. Members of the Gestapo (*Geheime Staatspolizei*, or 'Secret State Police'), set up by Hermann Göring, were also usually SS members.

STANDARD-BEARER A Brownshirt from Munich holds his Nazi banner proudly aloft. 'Germany awake', it reads.

organisation and newspapers. At last the Nazis could reach a truly nationwide audience.

In the Reichstag elections of 1930, after a campaign soured by ugly street fighting between the Nazis and Communists, the Nazis gained 107 seats, becoming the Parliament's second largest party. 'Never in my life,' wrote Hitler later, 'have I been so well disposed and inwardly contented as in these days.' Communist successes in the elections (they won 4.5 million votes and 77 seats in the Reichstag) also delighted Hitler. The Bolshevik threat, much played upon by Nazi propaganda, brought money flowing into the party coffers from industrialists.

CONQUEST OF THE STREETS

In the following years Nazi-inspired violence on the streets of German cities grew worse and worse – fanned by a massive propaganda campaign, which in its skill, cunning, lies and sheer frenzy was unprecedented in world history. 'The conquest of the streets,' wrote the Nazis' propaganda chief, Josef Goebbels, 'is the characteristic feature of modern politics.' On October 13, 1930, the day the new Reichstag met for the first time, there were violent outbursts of anti-Semitism on Berlin's streets: windows of Jewish shops were smashed and Jews were taunted and attacked. In the first nine months of 1931, 45 people were killed in Prussia alone in street clashes, mostly in Berlin, between Nazis and Communists.

Nazi belligerence was carried into the Reichstag as well. Here the proceedings of the debating

MAN OF PARTS An urbane *Duce* performs on the violin. Italian music critics on the make often commended his technique, but others were less benign. Though a figure of fun to many foreigners, especially in his later years, Mussolini held power for more than two decades, restored law and order in Italy, and did much to put its economy on a firm footing.

NAZI SIDEKICK Mussolini liked to talk grandiosely of restoring imperial Roman greatness. But few outside Italy were deceived. A Soviet cartoon of 1936 shows him firmly subordinated to Hitler.

MUSSOLINI – EUROPE'S FIRST FASCIST RULER

Unlike the middle-class Hitler, Benito Mussolini (1883-1945) had truly humble origins. He was the son of an outspokenly socialist blacksmith from central Italy. His early career was as a socialist journalist, but he broke with the party after advocating Italian entry into World War I; the Socialists favoured neutrality. 'It is blood,' he said, 'that moves the wheels of history.' He joined the army and rose to the rank of corporal.

In 1919 Mussolini founded the Fascist party – so named from its *fasci di combattimento* ('combat groups') – and in 1921 was elected to the Italian parliament. He announced that he spoke from 'the benches of the extreme right, where formerly no one dared to sit'. At the same time, blackshirted supporters created a reign of terror in the streets. Postwar Italy was already suffering from acute economic, social and political unrest.

On October 28, 1922, Mussolini (*Il Duce*, 'the leader', to his followers) told a rally of supporters in Naples that he would lead them in a 'march on Rome', seize control of the government and 'hand over to the king and army a renewed Italy'. In fact, he arrived in Rome by train – wearing a bowler hat. On October 30, he was given dictatorial powers, under King Victor Emmanuel, for a year. Within six years he had turned Italy into a totalitarian state.

chamber were frequently brought to a halt as Nazi deputies, brown-shirted and decorated with swastikas, hooted down opponents and hissed disrespect for Socialist, Communist and Jewish members. The National Socialists made no pretence of being a democratic political party. 'If today our strategy employs among its different weapons that of Parliament,' Hitler told a rally of cheering supporters at Munich in 1931, 'that is not to say that parliamentary parties exist only for parliamentary ends. For us Parliament is not an end in itself, but merely a means to an end.'

This extra-parliamentary dimension of Nazism was its attraction for many voters. Nazism was much more than a political party; it was a movement, whose aim was to embrace the entire German *Volk* ('people') in a national rebirth. It offered so-called Aryan men and women (defined by the Nazis as white, particularly Nordic, non-Jews) a glorious vocation to lead mankind. Implicit in this vision was the eventual abolition of all parties other than the Nazi party.

NAZI CHANCELLOR

Real breakthrough came for the Nazis in 1932. In presidential elections that year, Hitler was roundly beaten by the incumbent, 85-year-old Great War hero Field Marshal Paul von Hindenburg, but in a Reichstag election in July, the Nazis won 230 seats, making them the largest party in Germany. In August, President Hindenburg invited Hitler to serve as vice-chancellor under the right-wing Franz von Papen. The President and his fellows of the traditional nationalist right felt that Hitler's aims were, after all, little different from their own, if spoken more stridently. They did not understand (or failed to predict the consequences of) the Nazi party's savage anti-Semitism.

Hitler, however, refused the offer. He wanted the chancellorship itself, or nothing. Then, in a second Reichstag election in November, the Nazis suffered a setback: they won only 196 seats. Concluding that the Nazi tide was ebbing, and therefore less dangerous, Hindenburg decided to approach Hitler again. This time he offered the Nazi leader the chancellorship. But Hitler wanted sweeping extra powers, which the President had no intention of giving him. The conservative General Kurt von Schleicher became chancellor instead. 'This year has brought us eternal ill-luck,' a despondent Goebbels wrote in his diary. 'The past was sad, and the future looks dark and gloomy; all chances and hopes have quite disappeared.'

But power was, in fact, just around the corner for the Nazis. In January 1933, Schleicher was forced to resign and, at this crucial moment for the Weimar Republic, Hindenburg once more offered Hitler the chancellorship. This time the Nazi leader accepted immediately. It was January 30. But even now the President limited Hitler's authority: in a cabinet of 12 the Nazis had only three seats, while independent and Nationalist ministers held the other nine. Hindenburg hoped that power would tame the Nazis and that gradually their strident, hate-filled rhetoric would fade away.

At five that afternoon, Hitler presided over his first cabinet – and, contrary to Hindenburg's calculations, Nazi rhetoric, far from fading, was about to blossom. Later that night he stood with Hindenburg on the balcony of the Chancellery, watching a torchlight procession march past. Germany had found the chancellor to lead it to power – and to disaster.

GOEBBELS – SHOWMAN TO THE LAST

A club foot kept Paul Josef Goebbels (1897-1945) out of World War I. He spent most of the war at Heidelberg University, where he gained a doctorate with a thesis on an obscure German romantic dramatist, Wilhelm von Schütz.

Goebbels joined the Nazi party in 1926 and became its chief intellectual and a master of propaganda. In 1926, he was appointed Nazi *Gauleiter* (district leader) in Berlin and in 1927 he founded the party's Berlin newspaper, *Der Angriff* ('The Attack'). He was largely responsible for building up the Nazi power base, until then mostly concentrated in Bavaria, in the German capital.

When Hitler came to power, Goebbels became Minister of Public Enlightenment and Propaganda, controlling the press, radio, publishing, theatre and cinema. He shared Hitler's fanatical belief in the 'spiritual struggle' against the Jews, and was the instigator of *Kristallnacht* (p. 18).

Always a showman, Goebbels faced the war's last throes with unbent pride and unbowed spirit. 'Gentlemen,' he told a propaganda ministry meeting in April 1945, 'in a hundred years' time they will be showing a fine colour film describing the terrible days we are living through. Do you not wish to play a part in that film? . . . Hold out now, so that a hundred years hence the audience does not hoot and whistle when you appear on the screen.'

PROPAGANDA GENIUS Josef Goebbels' inestimable gift to the Nazi party was his understanding of mass psychology. This was shown in the mounting of numerous hysterical rallies, precision street marches and torchlight parades that brainwashed a nation.

HITLER – THE MAKING OF A CHANCELLOR

The characteristics that marked Adolf Hitler (1889-1945) as an adult were already apparent in his schooldays. One teacher later remembered him as a 'gaunt, pale-faced youth . . . arrogant and bad-tempered'. He 'demanded of his fellow pupils their unqualified subservience, fancying himself [as a] leader'.

Hitler was born into comfortable circumstances in the small Austrian town of Braunau on the Bavarian border. His father, whose original name was Schicklgruber, was a customs official of the Austro-Hungarian Empire. He sent Adolf to good schools, where he failed to distinguish himself.

He left school at 16 and in 1908 arrived in Vienna. He tried being an artist, slept in dosshouses and made ends meet as a casual labourer. In Vienna, where anti-Jewish feeling was rampant, he developed his virulent anti-Semitism. In 1913, Hitler moved to Munich and joined the 16th Bavarian Reserve Infantry at the start of the Great War. His future Nazi colleague Rudolf Hess was in the same regiment.

War came to Hitler, he said, 'like a redemption from the vexatious experience of my youth . . . In a transport of enthusiasm, I sank down on my knees and thanked Heaven from an overflowing heart'. Four dangerous years on the Western Front as a runner (he was made a lance-corporal in 1914 and was wounded in the leg in 1916) earned him the Iron Cross, First Class – an unusual honour for an NCO. The shock of Germany's defeat in 1918 gave him a permanent 'hatred for the originators of this dastardly crime', the democratic politicians.

In 1919, Hitler joined the tiny German Workers' (later Nazi) Party, and within two years was officially party leader. After the failed Munich Putsch (p. 12), he spent nine months in prison. There he dictated his only book, *Mein Kampf (My Struggle)*, a turgid outpouring of anti-Semitism and extreme German nationalism, to his faithful follower and fellow prisoner Hess.

From 1925 to 1929, Hitler consolidated his hold on the party, while posters and continual speaking tours made him familiar throughout Germany. His style of oratory – in which he used simple, repeated points, vicious invective against his enemies and a tone of rising hysteria – was extremely successful. His Austrian accent, the plainness of his dress and the Iron Cross he frequently wore gave him the image of a simple patriot.

Once power came to him, he took hold of it more firmly than almost any politician before or since. From then until his death in 1945, Hitler's story was Germany's story, just as the Nazi party and the German state became one.

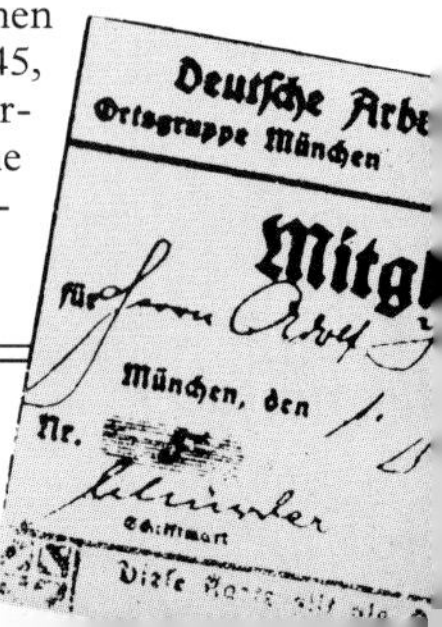

SIGNED UP The future Führer's party card.

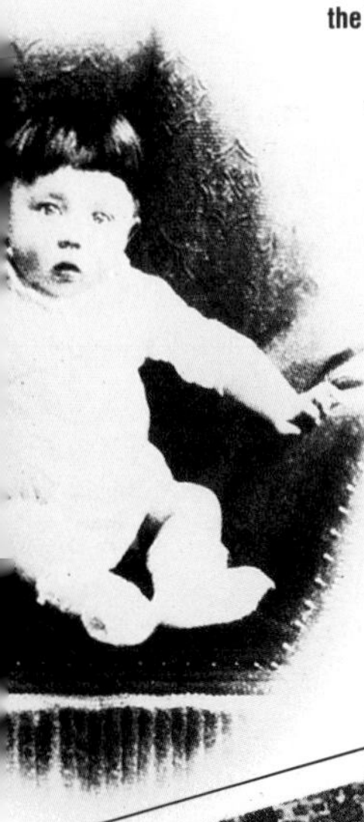

Familien-Nachrichten.

Vom 3. bis 10. Jänner.

Geburten: Am 6. Jänner Josef Huber, Wirthskind.

Trauungen: Am 7. Jänner Josef Eichinger, Fleischhauer und Karo lina Kofler, Fleischauerswittwe; Alois Hitler, k. k. Zollamts-Offizia und Klara, geb. Pölzl; Valentin Pali, Bahnschlosser und Julie, geb Fischer.

Sterbfälle: Am 5. Jänner Maria Scheinast, Faßzieherskind, 5 Wo chen alt, Wasserkopf; Anna Toppler, Taglöhnerskind, 3 Jahre alt an Wassersucht. Am 7. Jänner Josef Huber, Wirthskind, 2 Tag alt, an Lebensschwäche.

BABY ADOLF The first photograph and the birth announcement in a local paper.

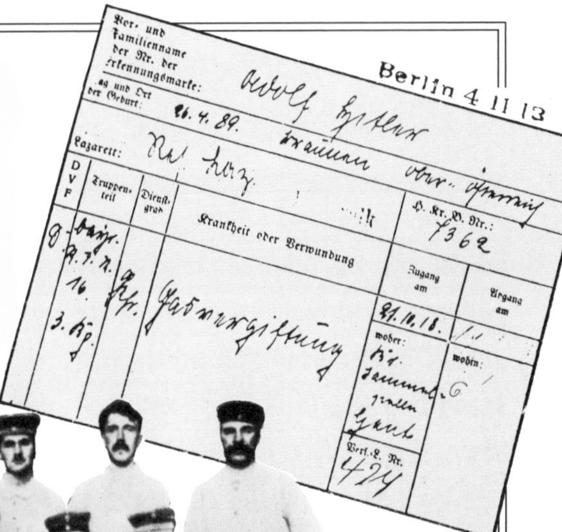

Vor- und Familienname der Nr. der Erkennungsmarke: Adolf Hitler

Berlin 4 11 13

Tag und Ort der Geburt: 20. 4. 89. Braunau

Lazarett:

Truppenteil	Dienstgrad	Krankheit oder Verwundung	H. Kr. B. Nr.: 7362
			Zugang am
			Abgang am
			woher:
			wohin:
			Verl.-L. Nr. 424

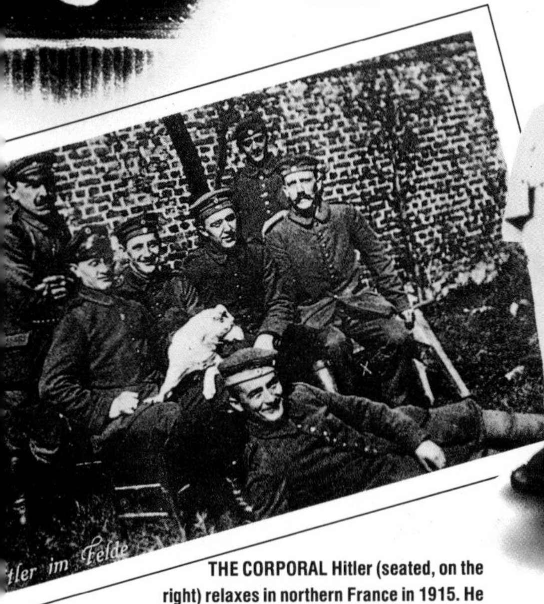

THE CORPORAL Hitler (seated, on the right) relaxes in northern France in 1915. He forfeited Austrian citizenship to join the German Army.

GASSED Poison gas briefly halted Hitler's war exploits in 1916. Army records register his disablement. He stands, capless at the back, with other field hospital inmates.

Preis 15 Pfennig

Der Nationalsozialist

Hitler frei!

Parteigenossen! Parteigenossinnen!

REPOSE AND ACTION A relaxed-looking Hitler reads in Landsberg prison. A party paper greets his release in December 1929. Five years later he grasps a flag bloodied in the Munich Putsch. He poses (right) in his beloved Bavarian woods.

The road to war

Hitler was a man of volatile temperament, but he showed remarkable patience in waiting for power. Once handed it, he moved with astonishing speed first to eliminate opposition at home, then in foreign policy to start righting the humiliations of Versailles.

FOR TEN YEARS since the failure of the Nazis' attempt to seize power by force at Munich in 1923, Hitler had played the parliamentary game. Within months of becoming chancellor on January 30, 1933, he had transformed hitherto democratic Germany into a dictatorship, imposed through terror disguised by skilful propaganda.

His first step was to persuade President Hindenburg to dissolve the Reichstag and call fresh elections. Rather than submit to the strait-jacket of an alliance with more moderate parties, Hitler was determined to get an outright majority. In the campaign that led up to the elections on March 5, the German people experienced for the first time the barbarity of Nazi rule. Opposition newspapers were suppressed, opposition political meetings disrupted by Nazi stormtroopers and their speakers beaten up. The terror was made worse by the Communists who were using similarly violent tactics.

Hermann Göring, the Nazi minister of the interior for Prussia, which comprised two-thirds of Germany, carried out a ruthless purge of the Prussian police force. He replaced large numbers of its senior officers with Nazis and drafted 30 000 SA and SS members into an auxiliary police force. In effect, he delivered the police force into the hands of thugs.

A few days before polling, Göring made quite clear Nazism's utter contempt for normal political decencies and its merciless determination to destroy all opposition. 'I don't have to worry about justice,' he told a rally at Frankfurt. 'My mission is only to destroy and exterminate, nothing more . . . I shall use the power of the state and the police to the utmost . . . but the struggle to the death, in which my fist will grab your heads, I shall lead with those down there – the Brownshirts [the SA].'

TERROR ON THE STREETS

The combination of terror on the streets and the genuine appeal of Nazi propaganda brought the Nazis 288 seats and their Nationalist allies 52. Together, the two parties had won more than half the votes – in an election that was legal, though with its campaign of intimidation hardly free. And with the Communists banned after being blamed for a fire that destroyed the Reichstag on February 27, the Nazis had a clear majority even without the support of the Nationalists. (Hitler cunningly delayed banning the Communists until after the election, to split the left-wing vote.)

BOOKS BURN Brownshirts and students in Berlin in 1933 gleefully consign to the flames publications considered undesirable by the Nazis. These ranged from the works of the Jewish psychiatrist Sigmund Freud to the novels of Thomas Mann.

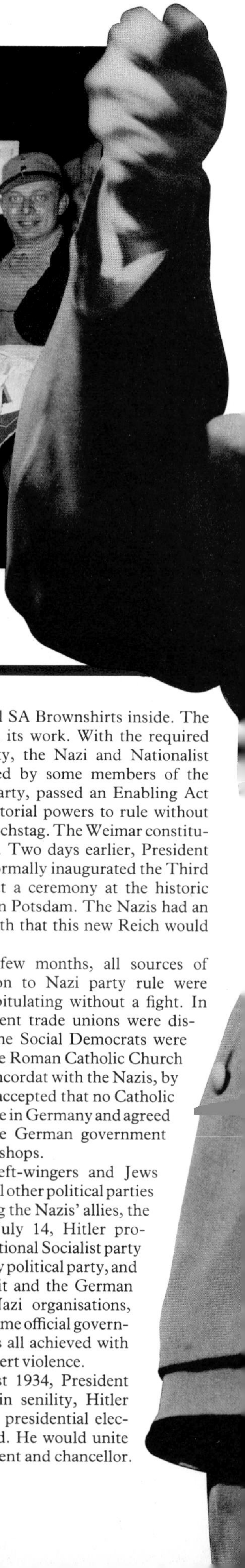

GRIM VIGILANCE A Berlin policeman and a member of the Nazi auxiliary police force (right) patrol the German capital's streets during the election of March 1933.

When, on March 23, the newly elected deputies arrived to take their places in Berlin's disused Kroll Opera House (the Reichstag's meeting place after the fire) they had to walk through cordons of SS guards outside the building, and past rows of armed SA Brownshirts inside. The threat of force did its work. With the required two-thirds majority, the Nazi and Nationalist deputies, supported by some members of the Catholic Centre party, passed an Enabling Act giving Hitler dictatorial powers to rule without reference to the Reichstag. The Weimar constitution was in tatters. Two days earlier, President Hindenburg had formally inaugurated the Third *Reich* ('Empire') at a ceremony at the historic Garrison Church in Potsdam. The Nazis had an almost mystical faith that this new Reich would last for 1000 years.

Over the next few months, all sources of potential opposition to Nazi party rule were crushed, many capitulating without a fight. In May, all independent trade unions were disbanded. In June the Social Democrats were banned. In July, the Roman Catholic Church made a historic Concordat with the Nazis, by which the Vatican accepted that no Catholic party should operate in Germany and agreed to consult with the German government when appointing bishops.

Thousands of left-wingers and Jews were arrested and all other political parties dissolved, including the Nazis' allies, the Nationalists. On July 14, Hitler proclaimed that the National Socialist party was Germany's only political party, and in December that it and the German state were one. Nazi organisations, such as the SS, became official government forces. It was all achieved with remarkably little overt violence.

When, in August 1934, President Hindenburg died in senility, Hitler announced that no presidential elections would be held. He would unite the offices of president and chancellor.

PRETEXT FOR CLAMP-DOWN Berlin's theatrically grandiose Reichstag building blazes on the cold, snowy night of February 27, 1933, less than a month after Hitler became chancellor. Finding in the burning edifice a young Dutch Communist, Marinus van der Lubbe, clutching incriminating oiled rags, the Nazis claimed the outrage as proof of a Communist revolutionary plot. The next day, Hitler published a decree 'for the protection of the people', which suspended all guarantees of civil liberties. In the following days, left-wing leaders were summarily arrested and the Communist party outlawed. Van der Lubbe – probably a lone protester against the Nazis – was gruesomely beheaded in September 1933.

From now on the *Reichswehr* (German Army) would swear a personal oath of loyalty to the *Führer* ('Leader'), as Hitler liked to be known.

By this time the German people were thoroughly intimidated by, for example, the burning of books regarded as undesirable and the anti-Semitic outpourings of the Nazi party's youth arm, the Hitler Youth. In a referendum, more than 38 million voted in favour of Hitler's new status, just over 4 million against. Germany had become a totalitarian state.

At the same time, the Nazis' obsessive anti-

SERRIED RANKS Banner-bearing SS men from throughout the Third Reich parade at Nuremberg in 1935. Rallies such as this, with their hypnotic chanting of '*Sieg heil*' ('Hail victory'), helped to cow the German people.

Jewish campaign was getting into its stride. It began in 1933 with a boycott of Jewish shops and businesses and the dismissal of Jews from the civil service. Then the Nuremberg Laws of 1935 denied Jews basic rights of German citizenship, such as the right to vote, and forbade them to marry outside their own kind – in order to preserve the 'racial purity of the state'.

With the systematic anti-Jewish violence of *Kristallnacht* in November 1938 (see box), the campaign intensified. Two days later, a fine of 1000 million Reichsmarks (US$250 million) was imposed on the Jews for damage done during the violence; it was levied by confiscating 20 per cent of the property of each Jew. A few days after that, all Jewish children were expelled from German schools. The horrors of the 'final solution' were drawing ever closer.

VERSAILLES OVERTHROWN

Having consolidated Nazi rule at home, Hitler had meanwhile turned his attention to foreign policy – in which his avowed aims were to undo the humiliations of the Versailles treaty (p. 14) and re-establish German supremacy in Europe. He launched an ambitious rearmament programme – secret until 1935 – and began creating an air force, using the state airline to train pilots.

At the international disarmament conference in the autumn of 1933, when it became clear that France was not prepared to disarm, Germany walked out and Hitler announced that Germany would withdraw from the League of Nations. In January 1935, the German people of the Saarland voted in a League of Nations plebiscite to rejoin Germany. In March the next year, Hitler flouted Versailles by sending two divisions of German troops into the Rhineland.

The guardian of the Versailles settlement, the League of Nations – which had already shown its impotence the previous autumn, in its reaction to Mussolini's invasion of Ethiopia (see box) – simply resolved that no violation of the treaty had taken place and so effectively tore it up.

Later in the same year, the Spanish Civil War (see box), helped to strengthen Hitler's most important and lasting foreign alliance – with Mussolini's Italy. In October, the two dictators signed an agreement in Berlin to provide joint military support for the Spanish Nationalists.

'This Berlin-Rome connection,' Mussolini announced a few days later, 'is not so much a diaphragm as an axis, around which can revolve all those states of Europe with a will towards collaboration and peace.' The following month Germany signed the Anti-Comintern Pact with Japan to fight the spread of Communism. A year later Italy also signed this pact, completing the Rome-Berlin-Tokyo Axis.

THE GREATER REICH

Meanwhile, Hitler was laying the ground for his next major goal – the unification of what he regarded as the ethnic Germans of eastern Europe with the German Reich. These included 6 million people living in Austria and 3 million in the Sudetenland in western Czechoslovakia.

The annexation of Austria (the *Anschluss* or 'joining') came first. In 1934, a group of Austrian Nazis had attempted a coup in Vienna, during which they had shot (probably by mistake) the chancellor, Engelbert Dollfuss. The coup was quickly put down, but the Austrian Nazi party, supported by Germany, continued to grow.

In February 1938, Dollfuss's successor, Kurt von Schuschnigg, was forced by Hitler to take several Nazis into his cabinet; the alternative, Hitler informed him, was a German invasion. But in March, as Hitler's intention to incorporate Austria into Germany became increasingly clear, Schuschnigg openly defied him. He announced a plebiscite to allow the Austrian people to say whether they wished to remain independent.

Two days later, on March 11, the Nazis closed the frontier between Austria and Germany, and German troops massed on the border. The same day, Göring delivered an ultimatum: the plebiscite was to be postponed and the Austrian Nazi leader, Arthur Seyss-Inquart, installed as chancellor by 7.30 that evening, or the order to invade would be given.

Neither of the twin democracies, Britain and France, was prepared to go to the defence of Austria and therefore ignored Schuschnigg's appeals for help. He had no choice but to cancel the plebiscite and resign. Seyss-Inquart took his place as chancellor, then requested German troops to enter the country. On March 13, the new chancellor decreed Austria out of existence – and himself out of a job. Hitler was now chancellor of Greater Germany.

NIGHT OF THE LONG KNIVES

By 1934 the Nazi stormtroop force, the SA or Brownshirts, had become dangerously powerful, and Hitler decided to destroy it. In the early hours of Saturday, June 30, SS officers under orders from Göring and Himmler burst into a hotel at the Bavarian lake resort of Bad Wiesee, where SA leader Ernst Röhm and a group of his men were spending the weekend. The SS men dragged Röhm away to Stadelheim Prison in Munich, where he was shot the next day. Other SA officers were shot on the spot.

The slaughter continued elsewhere on the Sunday. The Berlin SA leader, Karl Ernst, was seized but died loyally, shouting 'Heil Hitler'. Other scores were settled when radical Nazis, such as Gregor Strasser, and prominent anti-Nazis were eliminated. Hitler later told the Reichstag that 58 had been 'executed' and that another 19 'lost their lives', but other estimates of the dead exceed 400.

SA chief Ernst Röhm

THE NIGHT OF BROKEN GLASS

When a 17-year-old Polish Jew shot Ernst vom Rath, a German Embassy official in Paris, in November 1938, he gave the Nazis a pretext for an orgy of anti-Jewish violence. Vom Rath died on November 9. Later that night, Nazi Propaganda Minister Josef Goebbels sent signals to waiting SA and SS squads throughout Germany to begin 'spontaneous' acts of violence against Jews and Jewish property.

In the next 24 hours, over 7000 Jewish businesses were destroyed, nearly 200 synagogues burned and 76 razed to the ground. Nearly 100 Jews were killed and 36 severely wounded. More than 30 000 were arrested and sent to concentration camps. After *Kristallnacht* (literally 'Crystal night', or 'Night of Broken Glass', from the smashed windows of Jewish businesses) increasing numbers of Jews began to flee Germany, despite strict emigration restrictions.

TRIUMPHAL ENTRY Enthusiastic crowds at Freiburg in the Rhineland greet reoccupying German troops in March 1936. Hitler was ready to pull back if Britain and France intervened, but he took a gamble and got away with it.

ITALIAN INVASION OF ETHIOPIA

'I ask the great powers, who have promised the guarantee of collective security to small states over whom hangs the threat that they must one day suffer the fate of Ethiopia: What measures do they intend to take?' In these words the exiled Emperor Haile Selassie of Ethiopia (Abyssinia) appealed to the League of Nations at Geneva on June 30, 1936.

The previous October, Mussolini, anxious for imperial glory, had ordered the invasion of Ethiopia from Italian Somaliland. Forces under Marshal Pietro Badoglio crushed the poorly equipped Ethiopians – using poison gas in the process – and by May 1936 Italy had formally annexed the country. Haile Selassie fled to exile in Britain.

The invasion was a fatal blow to the standing of the League of Nations. It voted to penalise Italy with economic sanctions, but they were ineffectual. (Mussolini later admitted that an effective oil embargo would have forced him to withdraw within a week.) Four days after Haile Selassie's appeal, the League Council voted to end the sanctions. Mussolini had defied international opinion and got away with it. His German ally Hitler did not fail to take note.

Next it was the turn of Czechoslovakia, where since 1933 a Nazi puppet, Konrad Henlein, and his Sudeten German Party had been demanding autonomy for the German communities in the west of the country. During the Anschluss, Göring had promised the Prague government on his word of honour that it had not 'the least reason to feel any anxiety'. However, the following September, Hitler made an inflammatory speech in Nuremberg demanding that the Sudeten Germans be allowed to decide their future for themselves. The speech was followed by widespread disorder in Czechoslovakia. Pro-German demonstrations took place, particularly in Eger and Karlsbad, though the Czechoslovak government restored order through martial law.

In the crisis that followed, three men were ranged against Hitler – the British and French prime ministers, Neville Chamberlain and Edouard Daladier, and the Czechoslovak president, Eduard Beneš. All three were prepared to yield to Hitler's demands – though only Chamberlain believed, sincerely, that Hitler could be trusted to act in good faith. Beneš did not want to risk all of Czechoslovakia for the non-Czechoslovak part of it. The British and French leaders had some sympathy with the Sudeten Germans' desire for national self-determination, but more importantly wished to preserve the peace at least until their armies were prepared for war. Only belatedly had they begun to rearm with modern weapons.

'PEACE FOR OUR TIME'

'How horrible, fantastic, incredible it is,' Chamberlain told the British people in a radio broadcast on September 27, 'that we should be digging trenches and trying on gas-masks here because of a quarrel in a faraway country between people of whom we know nothing.'

Two days later, he flew to Munich to confer with Hitler, Daladier and the Italian leader, Mussolini. Just after midnight that night, they signed an agreement giving Hitler nearly 30 000 km (11 500 sq miles) of Czechoslovak territory. The next day, Chamberlain had another meeting with Hitler in which the two leaders agreed on their determination 'to continue our efforts to remove possible sources of difference and thus to contribute to assure the peace of Europe'.

On his return to London, Chamberlain had reassuring words for the British. 'There has come back from Germany to Downing Street peace with honour,' he told them. 'I believe it is peace for our time.' In the House of Commons, Winston Churchill spoke more darkly. 'England,' he growled, in the voice that was shortly to rouse the nation's patriotic spirit, 'has been offered a choice between war and shame. She has chosen shame – and will get war.'

DRESS REHEARSAL FOR BLITZKRIEG

With the outbreak of civil war in Spain in July 1936, the rest of Europe began to have a sickening foretaste of the kind of 'total war' that it too was shortly to experience. In the first days of the war, General Francisco Franco, *caudillo* ('leader') of the Nationalists – who were rebelling against a weak left-wing Republican government – appealed to Germany for help.

Officially, the major European powers had agreed not to intervene. But on July 29, the Nationalists received 20 German bombers and six fighters. Fascist Italy also sent fighters. More followed the next summer. These were faster, with greater range and firepower than aircraft simultaneously supplied to the Republicans by the Soviet Union. As a result, the Nationalists were able to win control of the skies. The last major Republican stronghold, Madrid, fell in March 1939.

Foreign intervention probably had little influence on the war's eventual outcome. But the strafing and bombing of Republican strongholds by Nationalists and foreign fliers – most devastatingly the Basque town of Guernica – in which hundreds of civilians lost their lives, helped to erode support in the democracies for the current policy of appeasing the Fascist powers. Also important were the reports sent home by thousands of Republican sympathisers who descended on Spain, such as the writers George Orwell and Ernest Hemingway.

GERMANS IN SPAIN Luftwaffe fighter pilots, flying for Franco's Nationalists, study Spanish maps. Nazi Air Minister Hermann Göring welcomed an opportunity 'to prevent the further spread of Communism, [and] to test my young Luftwaffe in this or that technical respect'.

Daily Herald

SATURDAY, OCTOBER 1, 1938 — No. 7061 — ONE PENNY

MR. CHAMBERLAIN DECLARES "IT IS PEACE FOR OUR TIME"

5,000 British Troops Will Be Sent To Sudetenland

PRAGUE'S DAY OF SORROW

TO a frenzied welcome from tens of thousands of Londoners, Mr. Neville Chamberlain came home last night and announced to all the world: "I believe it is peace for our time."

GERMANS WILL MARCH AT NOON

From a Window at No. 10

BUT— Poles Rush Ultimatum

BY OUR OWN CORRESPONDENT

WARSAW, Friday night.

WITHIN 24 hours of one threat of an immediate war on the Czechs being averted, Poland tonight handed a new ultimatum to Prague.

Woman's Fair Olympia Nov. 2nd–26th 1938

Easy on the tongue FRANKLYN'S MILD TOBACCO 8d

"BLACK & WHITE"

BACK FROM MUNICH Headlines greet Chamberlain's return from meeting Hitler. At 10 Downing Street the premier greets wildly cheering crowds. He came back triumphantly waving the piece of paper containing his agreement with Hitler.

2: BLITZKRIEG – SITZKRIEG

When Poland fell, Britain and France went to war – but then nothing much happened.

Steps towards the abyss

Sincerely but naively, the leaders of the democratic nations of Europe hoped that the agreement signed at Munich on September 30, 1938, had bought lasting peace. Within a year this illusion was rudely shattered.

NAZI JACKBOOTS marched into Czechoslovakia on the morning of Saturday, October 1, 1938. With a speed and organisation that betrayed lengthy planning, Hitler was acting on the terms of the Munich pact signed in the early hours of the previous day.

This gave Germany the Sudetenland – the largely German-speaking border area of Czechoslovakia's two western provinces, Bohemia and Moravia. Other areas were given to Poland and Hungary on November 20, costing Czechoslovakia a third of its population and large parts of its industry. President Eduard Beneš resigned on October 5 rather than accept these losses. His successor, Emil Hacha, was left to preside over the disintegration of Czechoslovakia into a federation of squabbling self-governing provinces: Slovakia, Ruthenia and what was left of Bohemia and Moravia. Within months, even that federation was torn apart.

On March 14, 1939, Slovakia declared its independence under the protection of Germany. This brought Hacha hurrying to Berlin to prevent the dismemberment of his country – but in vain. German forces moved into Bohemia-Moravia on March 15, and the next day Hitler proclaimed the region a German protectorate. 'Independent' Slovakia, under its pro-German president, the priest Josef Tiso, remained a German puppet state until 1945. Ruthenia, with Hitler's agreement, was handed over to Hungary.

DEATH OF MUNICH ILLUSIONS

Hitler had broken the promise given at Munich and shown that he could not be trusted, but the other Munich signatories could do nothing. Britain was shocked, and in Parliament even Prime Minister Neville Chamberlain's Conservative party colleagues were critical of him. Chamberlain weakly protested to Berlin, but refused to consider stronger action on the grounds that Britain had no treaty with Czechoslovakia.

With Austria and Czechoslovakia now in his hands, Hitler turned his attention to Poland. It was intolerable to him that the German province of East Prussia on the Baltic was separated from the rest of the Reich by a corridor of land that gave Poland its only sea access at Danzig (Gdansk). On March 21, he stepped up demands that Danzig be restored to Germany and that Germany be allowed to build road and rail links to East Prussia across Polish territory. Poland refused.

Two days later, Hitler scored a notable success on the other side of East Prussia. Threat of force made Lithuania hand back to Germany the Memel district which the Germans had been compelled to cede after World War I. Fearing now that Germany would use force to seize Danzig, the Polish Government warned Hitler that any attempt on the city would mean war. On March 31, Britain promised Poland immediate military aid if Germany made any move that the Poles 'considered it vital to resist with their national forces'. This was a positive stance at last, and it deterred Hitler, at least temporarily, from making any further moves against Poland – but it also meant that the decision on whether and when Britain should go to war would depend on what Poland did. France already had a similar agreement with Poland.

PACTS BETWEEN DICTATORS

Farther south, the German successes had reawakened Mussolini's ambitions to expand into the Balkans. On April 7, Good Friday, he sent 100 000 troops into Albania and annexed it. With Romania and Greece now clearly under threat from Italy, Britain and France on April 13 gave them the same guarantees that they had given Poland; Yugoslavia, which also bordered Albania, had a pro-Axis government at this time. In May, Britain ordered limited conscription in belated recognition of how serious the European situation had become. (Full conscription of all men aged 18 to 41 did not come until September.)

Hitler saw the Italian Fascists' aims as similar to his own, and he believed that they must both inevitably go to war with Europe's democracies. On May 22, he and Mussolini signed the so-called Pact of Steel, guaranteeing to support each other in any future war. Italy had made it a condition that there should be no war for two or three years – but this was a useless insistence. Hitler's plans for invading Poland were already prepared.

For the next three months, there were no more positive steps towards war. The Western Allies were tentatively discussing pacts with the Russians, but Hitler beat Britain and France to an agreement – and stunned the world – when Foreign Ministers Vyacheslav Molotov and Joachim von Ribbentrop signed a non-aggression pact in Moscow on August 23 (see box, *Unlikely allies*).

The Nazi-Soviet pact removed the traditional German fear of having to wage war on two fronts. Hitler immediately gave orders to his generals that they were to attack Poland at dawn on August 26 – but, at the last, Britain caused him to delay.

The pact had brought pressure from Britain, the USA, France and Pope Pius XII for Germany

STALIN – THE MAN WHO BUILT A SOVIET EMPIRE

The supreme ruler of the Soviet Union had been born to a drunken and violent Georgian shoemaker, and trained for the priesthood in the Tiflis seminary. Ironically, Joseph Vissarionovich Dzhugashvili (1879-1953), who was expelled from the seminary in 1899 for rebelling against the church's inflexible authority, would stamp his own even more inflexible authority on one of the world's largest nations.

He quickly became a Marxist revolutionary and was repeatedly imprisoned and exiled by the tsarist regime. He adopted the name Stalin (from the Russian for 'steel'). After the 1917 Revolution, he emerged as a close confederate of Vladimir Ilich Lenin, leader of the revolution and head of the Soviet government.

A partly paralysed left arm made Stalin unfit for service in World War I, so he was free to devote himself to amassing power in the Communist party. He became its general secretary in 1922 and its leader when Lenin died in 1924. Stalin had his great rival Leon Trotsky expelled in 1927 and later murdered, and gradually removed other potential rivals and opponents. Jail, deportation and death eliminated them all, until there was no one left to challenge his absolute control.

When the Germans invaded his country in 1941, Stalin was utterly shocked and saw no one for several days. Then he rallied, roused the people with inspired speeches, took personal day-to-day control of the armed forces and gradually, after the initial reverses, welded together a formidable fighting machine.

The long-term Soviet advantage was his constant aim. He was determined to bring all eastern Europe under his control to serve as a defensive buffer for the USSR. At Allied conferences the squat, pockmarked, non-intellectual Stalin looked unimpressive. But he was a wily negotiator. Britain's Foreign Secretary Anthony Eden wrote: 'If I had to pick a team for going into a conference room, Stalin would be my first choice . . . He never stormed, he was seldom even irritated. Hooded, calm, never raising his voice . . . he got what he wanted.'

After the war, Stalin continued to rule by terror. When he was safely dead many of his policies and methods were discredited, but his ruthless control and purpose had enabled the USSR to shrug off the disasters of 1941 and achieve vast territorial gains.

UNLIKELY ALLIES

As the war clouds gathered, Stalin was desperate for allies. Hitler made no secret of his hatred of the Bolsheviks or of his desire for *Lebensraum* ('living space') in eastern Europe. When Czechoslovakia was taken over by the Nazis, it was like a gun pointing at the Soviet heart.

Stalin turned first to Britain and France. But negotiations dragged on and Stalin began to look elsewhere. Any ally was better than none. Stalin made encouraging signals and Hitler responded by sending his foreign minister, Ribbentrop, to make a deal with Stalin under the noses of the Anglo-French mission still in Moscow.

During the night of August 23/24, Ribbentrop and Soviet Foreign Minister Molotov signed a ten-year non-aggression pact. In its secret clauses, Hitler and Stalin agreed to divide Poland. Stalin was also to have a free hand in Finland, Estonia, Latvia and the Romanian province of Bessarabia. Lithuania would be in the German sphere of influence. The pact also gave the Soviet Union time to prepare for war and a buffer of foreign soil between itself and Germany.

But for independent Poland the signing of the pact was the death knell.

CLINCHING THE DEAL Molotov signs the Nazi-Soviet pact, watched by Ribbentrop (far left) and Stalin (centre).

THE SOVIET HAMMER

As a 15-year-old schoolboy Vyacheslav Mikhailovich Skriabin (1890-1986) fought in the 1905 Russian Revolution in Kazan. He joined the Bolshevik party the following year, later changing his name to Molotov ('the hammer').

After the 1917 Revolution, he rose to the Politburo, where he was a dedicated supporter of Stalin. Molotov was made foreign minister in May 1939, in time to negotiate non-aggression pacts with Germany (August 1939) and Japan (April 1941). After the German invasion of Russia, later in 1941, he became a member of the five-man State Defence Committee responsible for the conduct of the war.

Molotov often travelled abroad to negotiate with the Western Allies, sometimes with Stalin. At the major Allied conferences, the two made a formidable partnership. Molotov took the role of the hard man, beside whom even Stalin seemed a moderate and subtle negotiator.

to settle its differences with Poland by negotiation. But Chamberlain also warned Hitler that the pact made no difference to Britain's responsibility to Poland, and Britain converted the guarantee given to Poland in March into a formal alliance. This went against all Hitler's calculations. He had not believed that the Western Allies would go to war for Poland's independence. He had got his own way so far by threats, but he was prepared to carry them out – unlike Mussolini, whose nerve was the first to crack. On August 25 he told Hitler that his country was not yet ready for war, and proposed an international conference instead.

Hitler made the gesture of asking the Poles to send an emissary to Berlin to settle the Danzig question. The Polish ambassador went to see Ribbentrop on August 31, but it was obvious that Poland was not going to yield to the German demands. The next day Hitler gave his armies the final signal for invasion at dawn on September 1. What all Europe had dreaded for the previous 20 years was about to happen.

HITLER'S SALESMAN

Talkative charm and contacts abroad elevated Joachim von Ribbentrop (1893-1946) to the post of German foreign minister. He served as a cavalry officer in World War I, then worked as a champagne salesman during the 1920s, marrying into a wealthy champagne-making family. He took the nobleman's 'von' through adoption by a distant aunt.

When Ribbentrop joined the Nazi party in 1932, Hitler made him first adviser on foreign policy and then an ambassador at large. He was ambassador in London for two years, and became foreign minister in 1938. He signed the Pact of Steel with Italy and the Nazi-Soviet non-aggression pact.

Ribbentrop gave sound advice to Hitler that attacking Poland would bring Britain to war but too late to help Poland. Once the war started, he was heeded less and less. He was arrested by the British in June 1945, tried at Nuremberg, convicted of war crimes and hanged.

Lightning strikes Poland

Hitler's orders went out just after noon on August 31, 1939: Poland was to be invaded at dawn the next day. The world was about to witness a new form of warfare – *blitzkrieg*, or 'lightning war'.

THE BARRIERS ROSE, and German panzers and motorised infantry moved across the Polish frontier at 4.45 on the morning of Friday, September 1. If a time can be so precisely set, then World War II began nine minutes earlier, when the Luftwaffe – led by Stuka dive-bombers – attacked Polish communication centres and airfields. The Germans hoped to catch the Polish Air Force on the ground, but the Poles had prudently moved most of their planes to subsidiary airstrips. Yet these aircraft gave the Germans very little trouble, for they were slow and clumsy. The Luftwaffe's main problem was fog, which made its targets hard to find.

The Poles were not totally unprepared. German war propaganda and the signing of the Nazi-Soviet Pact were warning enough. Moreover, Polish Intelligence – which first broke the German Enigma codes – knew in considerable detail the line-up of German forces on its borders. But Hitler was still sensitive enough about world opinion to make the effort to fake a pretext for his attack on Poland.

Late on August 31, news reports subsequently stated, men wearing Polish uniforms raided a radio station, customs post and forestry camp near Gleiwitz in the far south-eastern corner of Germany (now Gliwice in Poland). At 11 pm, a voice in broken Polish interrupted a Radio Gleiwitz programme with a call to Silesians – the people of the border region – to take up arms against the Nazis.

The 'raiders' were not Poles, but SS men acting on the orders of Reinhard Heydrich, deputy head of the Security Service. To complete the plan a fake counterattack was needed – and some bodies. These were provided by concentration camp inmates, already condemned to death. Dressed in Polish uniforms and killed with lethal injections, they were hauled to the scene and shot as they lay on the ground to provide evidence of an exchange of fire. The following day their bodies were displayed to the world's press to support the story of Polish 'aggression'.

LINE-UP FOR BLITZKRIEG

The German plan depended above all on speed, for Hitler wanted to crush the Poles while the world held its breath – and before Britain and France were in a position to honour their obligations by attacking his western front.

Poised for the invasion were about a million men. At dawn on September 1, the Poles found themselves attacked from three directions at once (see map, p. 24). In the north, General Fedor von Bock launched his Fourth Army from Pomerania in the west and his Third Army from East Prussia in a huge pincer movement. Their objective was to cut off the Polish Corridor – the stretch of Polish territory between the two parts of Germany – at its base, then swing south to attack Warsaw, the Polish capital. Farther south, under General Gerd von Rundstedt, the Eighth and

FORCING THE FRONTIER German infantrymen remove a wooden barrier on the Polish border on September 1, 1939. From first light that morning about a million of Hitler's troops, in 41 infantry and 14 panzer and motorised divisions, began to pour into Poland. Nothing could stop them. The Poles had about as many infantry but little armour, and their defences were thinly stretched.

A NEW KIND OF WAR

Blitzkrieg – 'lightning war' – was the key to Germany's successes on land during the first half of the war, and speed was the essence of blitzkrieg. Aircraft, tanks and motorised infantry were the tools that made it feasible.

The thinking behind blitzkrieg was not German. Two British theorists, Maj General J.F.C. Fuller and Captain Basil Liddell Hart, conceived it in response to the stalemate and carnage of World War I. They argued that the internal combustion engine had transformed the pace of battle and needed new strategies. Destroy the enemy's brain, not the body, they said: make sudden concentrated attacks on the headquarters and communications, not on the mass of the army.

The western democracies did not take up these ideas, but the Germans were more open. General Heinz Guderian was a major force behind their new battle plans.

In practice, after probing for the enemy's weak spots, the tanks of a panzer division surged ahead, bypassing the strong points, not tackling them head on, to penetrate deep behind the enemy's defences and cut up the troops into separate pockets. Air power made a pre-emptive strike to destroy the enemy air force and Ju87 Stuka dive-bombers went with the tanks to give bombing cover and act as swift, highly manoeuvrable artillery. Slow-moving conventional artillery and infantry – only a fraction mechanised – followed up to crush the pockets.

Blitzkrieg notched up rapid successes for the Germans. Only much later in the war were effective countermeasures developed – mainly by the Russians. In 1941-2 they retreated too rapidly for the Germans to get behind them. And then, at Kursk in 1943, they showed how complex, deep defences could break the impetus of a blitzkrieg attack.

SAVAGE FIGHTING Members of the elite SS Liebstandarte Adolf Hitler – originally the Führer's bodyguard – fight off a fierce Polish counterattack near the Bzura river west of Warsaw. By mid-September, the bulk of the Polish armies were sealed into a series of pockets, unable to break free for the relative safety of south-east Poland.

LOST LEADER

Wladyslaw Sikorski (1881-1943) was in Paris when Poland was overrun. A former Polish Prime Minister (in 1922-3) and Defence Minister (1923-5) and an army general, he soon formed a Polish provisional government and took command of Polish forces who had fled to France. When France fell, Sikorski moved to London, where he soon got on close terms with Churchill. He persuaded many countries to give aid to the Polish Underground, and when Germany turned on the USSR he reached an agreement with the Russians to reinstate his country's pre-1939 borders and free the thousands of Poles seized in 1939.

These prisoners were Sikorski's downfall. He was determined that they should be found, but the ensuing wrangles irritated Churchill and infuriated Stalin. After a quarrel with Stalin over the bodies found at Katyn (see box, *Echoes from the forest*), the Soviet dictator broke off all dealings with Sikorski and set up his own puppet Polish government. Within weeks Sikorski was dead, killed when his plane crashed while taking off from Gibraltar.

Tenth Armies struck east from Silesia for Warsaw, and the Fourteenth pushed east for Cracow (Krakow) and Lwow (Lvov).

Marshal Edward Smigly-Rydz, the Polish Commander in Chief, had decided to spread the bulk of his armies along the 2800 km (1750 mile) western and northern frontiers. What leavings he could scrape together he positioned as reserves in front of Warsaw. He had about as many infantry as the Germans, but their line was too thinly stretched to fight off a sharply concentrated attack. Once the Germans had penetrated it, there were not enough reserves behind the line to counterattack. The only stronger defensive line was that of the Vistula and San rivers – and to dig in here meant conceding from the outset the richest industrial and agricultural regions of Poland. Moreover, the Poles were sadly unprepared for the age of mechanised warfare. Only one of their 12 cavalry brigades was armoured and they had very few additional light tanks.

HORSEMEN AGAINST TANKS

In the event, the panzers, supported by the Stukas, were soon breaking through the Polish defences. Rains might have slowed the Germans, but on ground baked hard by a hot summer the tanks travelled with ease and the Luftwaffe readily found makeshift airstrips. In desperation, Polish cavalrymen on horses attacked the panzers with lances and sabres. The air force, starved of fuel as the Germans blew up roads, railway lines and bridges, could do little to help.

On the third day the two German northern armies met across the base of the Polish Corridor, and Bock's troops headed towards Warsaw. Rundstedt's Army Group South was also making good progress. By September 4, tanks of the Tenth Army were more than 80 km (50 miles) inside Poland's frontier, the Poznan region that bulged west into Germany was cut off and the Fourteenth Army was sweeping eastward along the northern edge of the Carpathian Mountains.

SHIFTING THE BLAME 'England! This is your work', a wounded Polish soldier cries out to British premier Neville Chamberlain in a Nazi poster. He points to the unburied dead and smouldering ruins of Warsaw, devastated by 11 days of German bombardment. With tortuous logic, Hitler tried to transfer responsibility for the tragedy to the foreign powers who encouraged the Poles to resist.

POLAND'S TROOPERS Polish cavalrymen had just lance, carbine and sabre to pit against the mechanised might of Hitler's panzers. Their attacks were brave – but completely futile.

During the brief campaign, Hitler toured the front line speaking hearteningly to the troops from an open car or a hillock. Contact with his fighting men always boosted Hitler, but the sight of Poland confirmed his poor opinion of the country. It seemed to belong to another century. The untended, ramshackle countryside was dotted with filthy wooden sheds, the homes of labourers who came out, cowed and bedraggled, to stand beside the dusty, rutted roads while the Führer whirled across the flat, treeless land.

All these German advances isolated the Polish armies from one another and made coordinated counterattacks all the more difficult. A young German officer wrote that the proceedings were 'so like a manoeuvre that we could hardly believe this was really war; it all seemed too well-ordered and familiar'. Yet lack of combat experience meant that not everything went according to plan. Units hesitated, made unauthorised local withdrawals and fired on their own troops. Commanders were nervous that their tanks were getting far ahead of the foot-slogging infantry, leaving gaps through which the Polish troops could withdraw and regroup.

Nevertheless, on September 11, when Smigly-

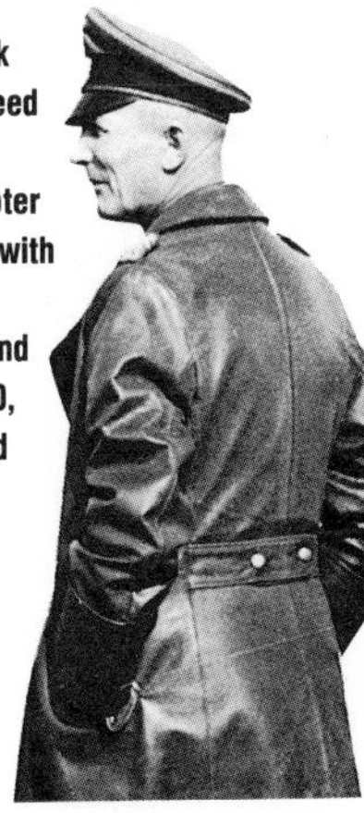

TOUGH FATALIST Fedor von Bock (1880-1945) often spoke of the need for sacrifice in war – earning the nickname ***Der Sterber*** ('the accepter of death'). A World War I veteran with the coveted ***Pour le Mérite***, he commanded army groups in Poland and the Low Countries in 1939-40, then in Russia. He was now a field marshal. However, after incurring Hitler's wrath with unauthorised moves outside Moscow in 1941 and again in the Caucasus in 1942, he was sacked from active service. He died in an Allied air raid.

ECHOES FROM THE FOREST

Horrible discoveries were made in the Katyn Forest near the Russian city of Smolensk in the spring of 1943. By then the USSR had joined the Allies and the Poles taken prisoner in 1939 should have been freed. But thousands – mainly officers – were never found. The mystery was mentioned in newspapers, and peasants around Smolensk, in German hands since Hitler's invasion of Russia, reported what they knew.

Daily during the early months of 1940, they had seen men spilling out of railway wagons and being driven into the Katyn Forest. There were tales of Polish prisoners, of Russians with picks and spades, of gunshots. In 1942, slave labourers working for the Germans had uncovered a dead, uniformed Polish officer.

The Germans investigated. They found seven mass graves of Polish officers, hands bound, all shot in the back of the head. An international team of scientists decided that they had been killed in spring 1940, when the Russians controlled the area.

The Soviet Union denied any part in the massacre, but General Sikorski's Polish government-in-exile in London asked the Red Cross for another inquiry. Apparently outraged, Stalin broke with Sikorski and set up his own Polish puppet government. The dead – about 4500 – were probably men who refused to accept Communist indoctrination. The fate of another 11 000 who disappeared is still unknown.

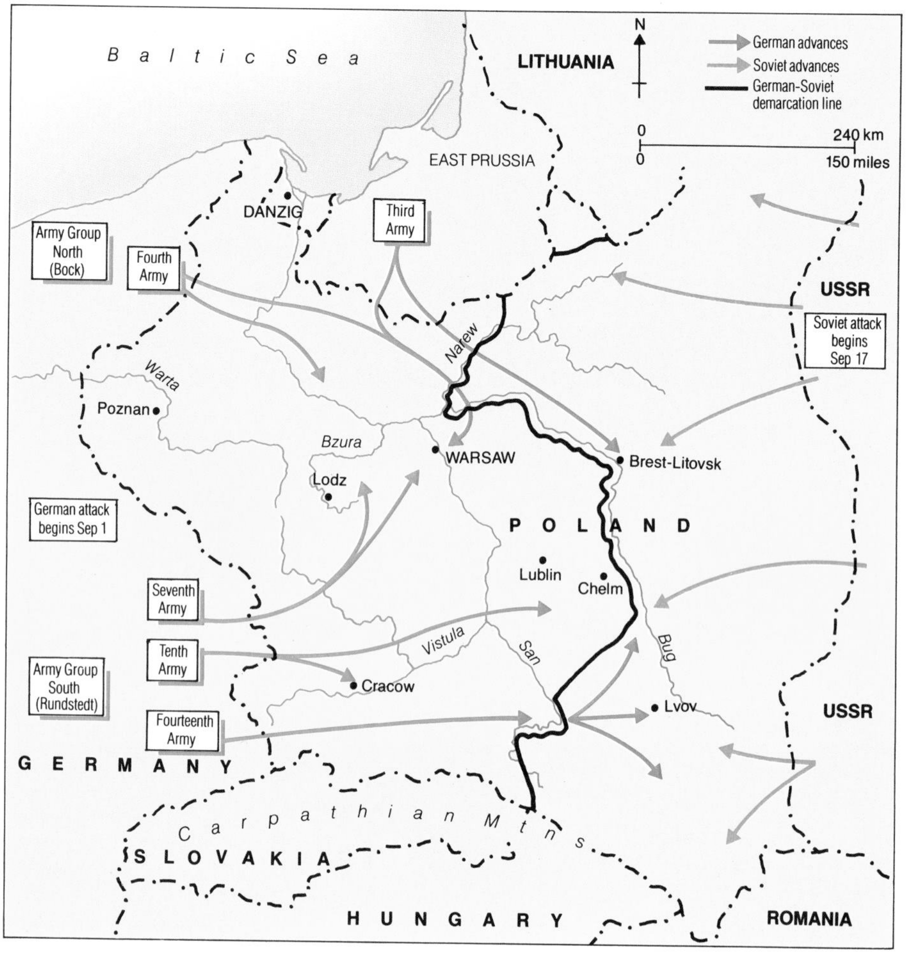

UNSTOPPABLE The Germans' lightning advance across Poland in September 1939 was remorseless. By the 16th they had reached Warsaw; by the end of the month it had fallen. Slower infantry mopped up pockets of resistance. On the 17th, the Russians invaded eastern Poland.

Rydz finally ordered his armies to withdraw towards south-east Poland, it was too late. Most of them were inextricably trapped.

THE ORDEAL OF WARSAW

The Germans had Warsaw surrounded by September 16 and were demanding its surrender. Although refusal brought on saturation bombardment from both air and artillery – the Germans had no time for siege tactics – it was September 27 before the capital capitulated.

After Brigadier Erwin Rommel visited the city on October 2, he wrote to his wife: 'There is hardly a building not in some way damaged . . . The people must have suffered terribly. For seven days there has been no water, no power, no gas, and no food . . . The mayor estimated there are 40 000 dead and injured . . . The people are probably relieved that we have come and that their ordeal is over . . . The field kitchens are besieged by starving, exhausted people.'

Polish hopes of saving anything were dashed when Russian troops invaded from the east – acting on a secret clause of the Nazi-Soviet Pact. At 5 am on September 17 the Soviet army crossed the border and took the Poles completely by surprise. They had no defence since all their troops, apart from a sprinkling of border guards, were fighting the Germans in the west. On that first day, the Red Army was able to advance 96 km (60 miles) unopposed. One of the Russian officers, Georgi Antonov, wrote later that as the Russians passed through the villages the people, 'awakened by shots and the rumbling of tanks, looked out at us from their windows frightened and distraught, unable to understand what was happening . . . not suspecting that this was the arrival of their liberators'. Their commanders had impressed on them that they were liberators, not conquerors, freeing the Poles from oppressive landowners.

On the second day, the Russians met some Polish troops and had to fight hard in the towns. There, the local people were apathetic, waving and raising their hats to the Russians, but Ivanov noticed that 'they did it with some indifference as if our arrival did not concern them'. By September 21, the Russians reached the Bug river, the demarcation line agreed with the Germans, but they found that some Germans had already crossed it. There were scuffles between the armies before the line was established. Ivanov's unit suffered two men killed and in reply killed 15 Germans in a sabre charge.

All that the Poles could now aim for was time – time to get as many fighting men as possible to France to continue the fight. About 10 000 Poles escaped. The number of Polish dead is uncertain, but 694 000 were taken prisoner by the Germans and 217 000 by the Red Army. The Germans lost 10 761 men.

When the last Polish resistance was crushed during the first days of October, the conquerors shared out the country as agreed in August – except that the province of Lublin was annexed by Germany. East of the Bug the Russians, determined that Communism would rule the country, moved the Polish intelligentsia and the upper classes to camps deep within Russia. Many were never heard of again. In the west, there began brutal rule by the Gestapo and SS – and six years of terror for Poland's large Jewish population.

Throughout the battle for Poland, the far-off Western Allies could do little, but the next German blows would fall on them.

A MIND OF HIS OWN It was Johannes von Blaskowitz (1878-1948), commander of the German Eighth Army, who received the Polish surrender at Warsaw. Later, as commander of the occupying army in Poland, then Commander in Chief East, he was horrified at SS atrocities. He complained and was dismissed by Hitler, infuriated at his 'Salvation Army methods'. In 1944, Blaskowitz commanded Army Group G in southern France. He was again dismissed, then transferred to the Netherlands, after making a withdrawal. In 1945, he signed the German surrender in the Netherlands. While awaiting trial for minor war crimes at Nuremberg, he committed suicide.

No going back

Diplomacy and appeasement did not stop Hitler. Now the promises to Poland had to be honoured.

IN BRITISH HOMES, families clustered anxiously around wireless sets on a sunny Sunday morning and heard the thin, cool voice of Prime Minister Neville Chamberlain: 'This morning, the British Ambassador in Berlin handed the German government a final note, stating that unless the British government heard from them by 11 o'clock that they were prepared at once to withdraw their troops from Poland, a state of war would exist between us. I have to tell you now that no such undertaking has been received, and that consequently this country is at war with Germany . . . it is evil things that we shall be fighting against – brute force, bad faith, injustice, suppression and persecution; and against them I am certain that the right will prevail.' It was 11.15 am on September 3, 1939.

Unlike 25 years before, the outbreak of war was not greeted with patriotic hysteria. People could remember only too well the awful carnage of 1914-18, and were fearful of the threat of mass bombing. Instead the situation was accepted soberly, with the realisation that Hitler was a cancer within Europe which must be eradicated before peace could be achieved.

The Prime Minister had merely expressed his grief at Poland's fate, not promised direct action. In truth it was already too late to help Poland. When the violation of Britain's ally started two days earlier, the British government knew within three hours, but their reaction was curiously muted. They were in a wait-and-see mood, hoping that Mussolini would make a move to restrain Hitler. When the cabinet met just before midday on September 1, they ruled out any immediate military action and once again discussed ways of pacifying Hitler.

Yet the government had made some preparation for war. Reservists had been called back to the forces on August 24, the same day that the Air Raid Precautions (ARP) organisation was alerted. Evacuation of children, expectant mothers and the disabled from the cities began on September 1, and that night blackout was imposed. Streets were unlit, public entertainments closed, and no glimmer of light was to show at houses, shops or offices in case it helped German planes to locate a target. The gas-masks that had been issued to everyone a year before were now to be carried everywhere. Most ordinary people were convinced now that war was inevitable – indeed they were ahead of their government.

Poland's allies spent a second day in talking. Both the British and French governments eventually agreed that, if Hitler would withdraw from Poland, they would support Mussolini's proposed conference to alter the terms imposed on Germany at the end of World War I.

Hitler, knowing that Poland would be his if the Allies kept talking just a little longer, let false word leak via a German journalist that he would leave Poland alone if he could have Danzig (Gdansk) and the Polish Corridor. Chamberlain and his cabinet grasped this straw eagerly, but the mood of Parliament and people was now running against them. Late that night a group of prominent Conservatives in Parliament, led by the Chancellor of the Exchequer, Sir John Simon, and the Secretary of State for War, Leslie Hore-Belisha, gave a warning to the Prime Minister. If he did not declare war they would vote against him in the House of Commons.

Chamberlain gave in. At 9 am on September 3 the British government sent an ultimatum to Hitler, giving him two hours to agree to withdraw from Poland. When no reply came, Britain was at war with Germany. On Saturday, the French government had ordered its troops to prepare for war, but Foreign Minister Georges Bonnet still hoped that a peaceful solution might be found. France issued an ultimatum at noon on September 3. When it expired at 5 pm that afternoon, France was also at war.

THE EMPIRE BACKS BRITAIN

Australia and New Zealand took the same attitude as in 1914 and assumed that they were at war once Britain was. Australian Prime Minister Robert Menzies broadcast to his people an hour after Chamberlain, at 9.15 pm local time: 'It is my melancholy duty to inform you officially that, in consequence of a persistence by Germany in her invasion of Poland, Great Britain has declared war on her and that, as a result, Australia is now also at war . . . There can be no doubt that where Britain stands, there stand the people of the entire British world.'

New Zealand's Prime Minister Michael Savage shared these loyal feelings: 'We arrange ourselves without fear beside Britain. Where she goes, we go; where she stands, we stand.'

Canada and South Africa – both with sizable non-British minorities who wanted no involvement in a 'European war' – took a different attitude. The Canadian Parliament held a three-day debate in Ottawa before it voted (with only one dissenter) to declare war on September 10. The South African Prime Minister, General Barry Hertzog, wanted to keep his country out of the war, and some of his countrymen were Nazi sympathisers. Hertzog resigned when his cabinet and Parliament voted against him. The pro-British General Jan Smuts, who took his place, declared war on September 6.

Eire, still a member of the British Commonwealth, declared itself neutral – as did other nations around the world, including Italy, Japan and the USA.

THE KING'S APPEAL TO EMPIRE

King George VI started his war diary on September 3, 1939, and every day for the duration he noted down what had happened and what he thought about it. Part of his first entry recalled the outbreak of World War I, when he was at sea as an 18-year-old midshipman: 'Everyone was pleased that it had come at last. We had been trained in the belief that war between Germany and this country had to come one day, and when it did come we thought we were prepared for it. We were not prepared for what we found a modern war really was, and those of us who had been through the Great War never wanted another.

'Today we are at war again . . . the country is calm, firm and united behind its leaders, resolved to fight until Liberty and Justice are once again safe . . .

'The PM came to see me in the evening. He was very upset but very calm that all his work of the past months had been of no avail to keep the peace of the world . . . I broadcasted a message to the Empire at 6 pm.'

For the second time that day, families gathered around their wireless sets. 'For the sake of all that we ourselves hold dear,' said the King, 'and of the world's order and peace, it is unthinkable that we should refuse to meet the challenge . . . To this high purpose I now call my people at home and my peoples across the seas. I ask them to stand firm and united in this time of trial.'

The endless overture

Europe was officially at war, but it was an unreal war, a phoney war – to the Germans *Sitzkrieg*, an 'armchair war'. The stage was set, but no epic drama opened in Europe except in the snows of Finland. In the South Atlantic, however, heroism and tragedy flared in the Battle of the River Plate.

AIR-RAID SIRENS wailed in London within minutes of Neville Chamberlain's declaration of war to the nation. An unidentified aircraft had been located on radar, and many civilians panicked, expecting air attacks as soon as the war began. Two flights of RAF fighters were scrambled before the intruder was found to be a French civilian light aircraft. The false alarm typified the next seven months – getting geared up with nowhere to fight. Only a few violent incidents erupted during a lengthy war of words and watching.

The RAF had the swiftest access to the enemy, but most RAF targets risked killing civilians and bringing massive German retaliation. Naval targets at sea did not hold this risk but the RAF had little success in striking them. One hour after Britain entered the war, Flying Officer Andrew MacPherson took off from RAF Wyton, Huntingdonshire, in a Blenheim light bomber to check on shipping in the Schillig Roads, the approaches to the big *Kriegsmarine* (German Navy) base at Wilhelmshaven. However, he could not report back from the air because his radio froze up, and by the time he got back to base an attack that day was out of the question.

The next day RAF Bomber Command launched three daylight raids against shipping in the Schillig Roads. They damaged one German ship slightly and lost seven of their 29 planes – not an endeavour worth repeating. Leaflet raids, the only alternative, were pursued more enthusiastically. On the first night of the war, more than 5 million leaflets showered onto German cities to tell the citizens the evils of their leaders. By the end of the month 18 million leaflets had been dropped. Neither pilots nor public were impressed by this role for their air force.

ACTION AT SEA

On the ground, there was much scurrying and preparation but little action: hardly a shot was fired in anger until the following spring. Only at sea was there constant activity. On the very day Britain declared war, the British liner *Athenia*, bound for Canada from Liverpool, was sunk by the German submarine *U-30* in the eastern Atlantic. The U-boat's skipper, Lt Commander Fritz-Julius Lemp, had mistaken the liner for an auxiliary cruiser. Among the 112 passengers who died were 28 US citizens. Any British hopes that this loss would bring the United States into the war were quickly dispelled by President Roosevelt, who knew that the majority of his nation would not support it.

The British immediately instituted a rudimentary convoy system for protection and set about hunting down the U-boats. *U-39* was the first to be sunk, on September 14, but then came two early disasters when the aircraft carrier HMS *Courageous* was sunk with the loss of 518 lives on September 17 and, even more dramatically, the sinking of the battleship *Royal Oak* in Scapa Flow on October 14 (see box).

Reluctant to tackle the much stronger Royal Navy head-on, Hitler had forbidden the Kriegsmarine to attack British warships, and decided instead to use his own surface warships and U-boats to throttle the life from Britain's merchant fleet. His small battleships or battlecruisers *Scharnhorst* and *Gneisenau* sank the armed merchant cruiser *Rawalpindi* in the North Sea on November 23. His pocket battleship *Deutschland* sank two vessels in the Atlantic. His other pocket battleship *Graf Spee* was a positive plague.

Graf Spee had left Wilhelmshaven for the South Atlantic before war broke out. As soon as Captain Hans Langsdorff received Hitler's orders, he began attacking and sinking British merchant vessels in the South Atlantic and Indian oceans. In late November, when his engines began to give trouble, he decided to make for the South American coast for one final flurry of activity before steaming home to Germany.

Langsdorff had sunk nine vessels by early December, and the Royal Navy organised several task forces to scour the Atlantic for this menace. One of them, consisting of four cruisers based in the Falkland Islands, was under the command of Commodore Henry Harwood. Deducing from the last messages put out by Langsdorff's recent victims that he was heading for South America, Harwood decided to concentrate his ships off the River Plate. Sure enough, on December 13 Langsdorff approached and spotted the smoke of *Cumberland*, *Exeter*, *Ajax* and the New Zealand-manned *Achilles*. Believing them to be convoy escorts – mere destroyers which his six 280 mm (11 in) guns could blow out of the water – Langsdorff went for the attack. He blotted from his mind the strict instructions he had received not to tangle with enemy warships.

SETTING A TRAP

Harwood dispatched *Cumberland* for an urgently needed refit, then split his remaining force. *Exeter* with its 8 in (203 mm) guns was sent to draw *Graf Spee*'s fire while the other two got in close enough to attack it with torpedoes. *Graf Spee* blasted away at *Exeter* and, when the others were sighted, swung to fire at them too. Both *Exeter* and *Ajax* were grievously damaged. *Exeter* was soon listing, holed below water, burning fiercely, without forward gun turrets and without telephones or radio transmitter. Only two of *Ajax*'s eight guns were able to fire and all its radio aerials had been felled when a shell brought down the main topmast.

'We might just as well be bombarding her with bloody snowballs,' Harwood snapped in frustration. He was about to withdraw when to his astonishment Langsdorff put up a smokescreen and headed westward, running for port. *Graf Spee* too had been damaged – by 17 shell hits; its captain thought pessimistically that his vessel could not make the passage home without putting into port immediately for repairs. Harwood shadowed *Graf Spee* until, late that evening, it anchored outside the port of Montevideo, in Uruguay. But because of the country's neutrality and the terms of international law, the pocket battleship was allowed only temporary sanctuary.

How could Harwood prevent it from putting to sea again? By guile and deception. A sham order for fuel oil was leaked to the Germans with the assistance of the British naval attaché in Montevideo, Henry McCall. Langsdorff was fooled into believing that the fuel was for strong reinforcements that had joined Harwood.

Huge crowds gathered in Montevideo on Sunday, December 17, after radio reports said *Graf Spee* would sail that day. When the ship steamed from the harbour early in the evening, the excited crowd expected to have a grandstand view of a sea battle. But 5 km (3 miles) out the ship stopped, tugs and boats fussed round it and the

PIERCING THE 'IMPENETRABLE'

Lt Commander Gunther Prien's mission was proving unexpectedly simple. It was the night of October 13/14, 1939, and, helped by one of the highest tides of the year, his submarine *U-47* had managed to enter the Royal Navy's nearly impregnable anchorage at Scapa Flow, in Orkney. Although on the surface, *U-47* had not been detected.

Prien headed for the main anchorage. It was a moonless night, though the aurora borealis was bright, and ideal for a surface attack. At one point a car's dim headlights – in fact Robbie Tullock's taxi – shone straight at him. Prien thought that he had been spotted but decided to press on.

Finding no targets in the main anchorage, with rain clouds gathering and visibility worsening, Prien turned back along the coast into Scapa Bay. Here he spotted what he took to be two battleships. In fact, there was only one: World War I veteran *Royal Oak*. At 1.04 am, Prien sent three torpedoes hissing from *U-47*'s bow tubes from 3000 m (3300 yds).

His exultation turned to chagrin when only one torpedo struck and exploded with little effect against the battleship's bow. Now, thought Prien, all hell will be let loose. Firing a fourth torpedo, he turned to make his escape. But nothing happened. At 1.16 am he swung *U-47* around for another strike. Three more torpedoes sped from its bows; this time all three struck.

'There is a loud explosion, roar and tumbling,' Prien wrote in his logbook. 'Then come columns of water, followed by columns of fire, fragments fly through the air.' Within 15 minutes *Royal Oak* rolled slowly over onto its side, then slid beneath the waves, taking with it 833 men. *U-47* made it back to the open sea and a hero's welcome in Germany. The crew were flown to Berlin, where a grateful Führer awarded Prien the Knight's Cross.

RALLYING TO THE COLOURS Twenty-year-old London conscripts (top) queue outside King's Cross Employment Exchange in June 1939. Two months earlier, Prime Minister Neville Chamberlain had announced limited conscription. Once war broke out, the British Empire also responded enthusiastically to the call to arms. Australian 'digger' veterans of the Great War, having rejoined their regiments, march through Melbourne (above). They will take on duties at home, freeing younger men to serve with the Australian Imperial Force in Europe and elsewhere. A poster (right) calls for recruits for the RAAF. Service overseas was voluntary for Australians, but New Zealand sent conscripts abroad – as did Canada after a fierce debate in 1944. South Africa had no conscription. The Indian Army was the Empire's biggest, with over 2 million men by 1945.

crowd fell silent. Suddenly smoke poured from *Graf Spee*; with a blaze of light and an ear-splitting boom, it blew up. Rather than risk letting the ship and its equipment – which included an early form of radar – fall into enemy hands, the Germans had scuttled it with its own torpedoes, rigged to explode in the ammunition magazines after the crew had been taken off.

Three nights later, Langsdorff shot himself in Buenos Aires. His farewell letter said: 'I am quite happy to pay with my life for any possible reflection on the honour of the flag.' But he might also have had in mind the court-martial he would face at home for disobeying the order not to engage enemy warships.

In Britain, starved of good war news, the Battle of the River Plate was greeted as a famous victory, and Commodore Harwood and his men became overnight heroes.

FINDING THE FRONT

While the Royal Navy was getting the glory, the priority for the army was to move the British Expeditionary Force (BEF) of four infantry divisions across to the Continent. Under the command of General Lord Gort – a distinguished guardsman with a first-class fighting record in World War I and a Victoria Cross – an army of more than 150 000 men crossed the Channel to France during the second half of September, taking with them 24 000 vehicles and supplies of fuel, ammunition and food.

On the Franco-Belgian border – Belgium was still neutral – they took up a spartan, morale-testing existence in a cold, soggy autumn. A young platoon commander recorded: 'The men lived in barns and stables and slept on straw which was never more than two inches thick. They only received three blankets apiece, and as the buildings were full of holes were swept by icy draughts. They had to wash in water drawn the night before in large tubs, with the result that there was never less than an inch, sometimes two inches, of ice in the morning. Our work did not keep us warm either. We were widening a stream, which entailed standing in water most of the day.'

The aim was to prepare for the threat of a German attack westward within weeks of Poland's collapse. Allied leaders agreed that Hitler would not attack the French Maginot Line of fortifications immediately across his border, but would strike farther north, disregarding Belgian neutrality. In fact several of Hitler's generals were arguing that such an attack on central Belgium was too predictable and would meet strong defences. They wanted to attack through the Ardennes in southern Belgium, where, the Allies thought, the thickly wooded hills and narrow roads and bridges would reduce Hitler's tanks to a vulnerable crawl.

The arguments forced Hitler into repeated postponements. While he delayed, the Allies amended their plans. Rather than wait for the Germans to come to them, they would advance to the Scheldt or the Dyle (Dijle) river, which provided better natural obstacles to defend. The problem was that Belgium was still vehemently neutral and would not even allow in reconnaissance parties. Nevertheless some movement came into the Allies' preparations with constant practice of the move up to the Belgian frontier. One British divisional commander, Maj General Bernard Montgomery, caused some dismay by insisting on practising withdrawal too.

As the weeks rolled by, 1939 ended in inac-

A FIERY GRAVE The burning *Graf Spee*, scuttled by its own crew, settles to the bottom in the River Plate off Montevideo on December 17, 1939. A surprisingly cheerful Captain Langsdorff and his men are borne by tug across the river to Buenos Aires, where they face internment. The 16 000 tonne pocket battleship was still ablaze three nights later when Langsdorff took his own life.

SEASON'S GREETINGS British Tommies, in rounded tin helmets, exchange Christmas drinks with their French counterparts on the Maginot Line in December 1939. They had already spent three cold, damp, cheerless months on the line – and would have to wait nearly five more before seeing any action on their front.

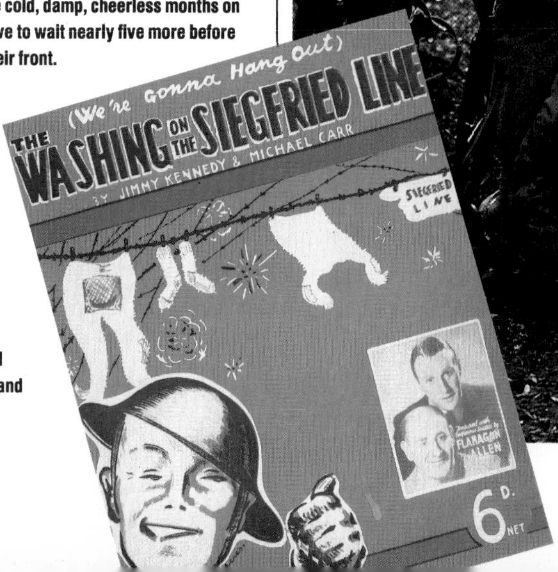

COMPLACENT A new popular song expressed British self-confidence and contempt for the Nazis' military effectiveness.

tivity, apart from the odd patrol action in the no-man's-land between the Maginot and Siegfried lines. At home, the blackout reigned, bomb shelters were dug, anti-aircraft guns were in place and searchlights played in the skies. But the expected clouds of German bombers did not appear over British and French cities.

In Britain relief mingled with impatience, both tempered with wry humour. 'We're gonna hang out the washing on the Siegfried Line', sang the British scornfully. But people overlooked the efficiency with which Hitler's army had marched into Poland and underestimated the might of the German war machine, which was to be launched into western Europe. Most of the children evacuated from London on the outbreak of war were brought back after a few months because of this spirit of false optimism, only to face the full onslaught of the Blitz. In France, scarred by the sufferings of 1914-18, many people hoped that Hitler's delay was a sign that fighting could be staved off indefinitely.

The hard winter made an attack before spring seem increasingly unlikely. On the German side there was another reason for postponement. A German light aircraft had made a forced landing in Belgium on January 10, 1940. On board was a liaison officer carrying the complete *Fall Gelb* ('Plan Yellow'), as the German attack plan was code-named. Hitler prudently revised his plan, at last falling in with those generals who wanted to thrust through the Ardennes.

While Hitler planned, there was a sequel to the Battle of the River Plate, far away in Norway, that helped decide his next move. During the night of February 15/16, 1940, *Graf Spee*'s former supply ship *Altmark* was chased and trapped in Jössing Fiord, near Stavanger, by the British destroyer *Cossack*. Among *Altmark*'s 'cargo' were 299 prisoners, British merchant seamen from the crews of *Graf Spee*'s victims. With the cry 'The Navy's here', *Cossack*'s crew boarded *Altmark* and freed the men.

This violation of a neutral country's territorial waters provoked strong protests to the British government from Norway – a country whose strategic position was attracting growing attention from both the Allies and Germany.

The winter war in Finland's snows

For once winter did not favour the Russians. On the frozen lakes and within the deep, tree-clothed gullies that divide Finland from Russia, snow was already thick by the last day of November 1939. That day the USSR embarked on the 'Winter War' against its tiny neighbour (until 1917 part of the Russian Empire) to enforce territorial demands made the previous month. It found the going remarkably tough.

The Russians, who could call on almost inexhaustible supplies, attacked with more than a million men – over three times as many as the whole Finnish Army. They also had over 1500 tanks (and later brought up more), while the Finns had only a few obsolete ones, and 3000 planes against the Finns' fewer than 200 antique flying machines. But the Red Army's morale was low after Stalin's purges of senior officers in the 1930s.

The Finns also had two valuable weapons to thwart the Russians: they were mobile and resourceful. Their ski patrols glided close to Soviet tanks, forced on the wooded slopes to use the few roads, and picked them off. Many tanks broke down in the abnormally extreme cold, and they were all ludicrously vulnerable to makeshift bottle bombs. The Finns hurled some 70 000 rag-stoppered bottles filled with petrol, paraffin and tar at the Russian tanks. These Molotov Cocktails – named in irony after Stalin's Foreign Minister – left many immobilised.

The Finns stopped the invaders along most of their frontier. But in the south the Russians eventually broke through. Marshal Semyon Timoshenko, commanding Soviet forces in the border region of Karelia, issued orders on February 1, 1940, to begin a saturation bombardment of the line of earthworks and pillboxes that defended Finland's border across the Karelian isthmus between Lake Ladoga and the Gulf of Finland. This was the Mannerheim Line, named after the brilliant Finnish Commander in Chief, a former cavalry officer in the Tsar's army, Baron Carl von Mannerheim.

The line gave way after two weeks under the barrage, and the invaders poured through. By the end of the month, the Russians had advanced up the isthmus almost to its most important town, Viipuri (now Vyborg). On March 5 the Finns negotiated for peace, and the war ended when the Treaty of Moscow was signed on March 12. With considerable loss of face and at an estimated cost of 200 000 men, about 700 aircraft and 1600 tanks, the Russians had got what they wanted.

All the territories assigned to their sphere of influence in the secret clauses of the Nazi-Soviet Non-aggression Pact were now safely under control – half of Poland had been seized, Estonia, Latvia and Lithuania had been forced to accept Soviet garrisons; finally, Finland had become a buffer protecting Leningrad, Murmansk and the north-western Soviet Union. The Red Army also benefited: Timoshenko was given the job of reorganising it – especially the training and discipline of recruits – to put right the defects shown up in Finland.

Finland, meanwhile, had suffered 25 000 dead and yielded all that it had refused to the Soviet demands of October 1939 and more: the Karelian isthmus, the shores of Lake Ladoga, the heights around Salla, a 30-year Russian lease on the Baltic port of Hanko and a promise to build a railway from Murmansk towards the Gulf of Bothnia. Nonetheless, a chastened Moscow refrained from seizing the whole country or installing a puppet regime.

In 1941, Finland allied itself with Germany, mainly to fight again for its lost territories. But in 1944, with Germany facing defeat, Mannerheim, now Finnish president, made a separate peace with the Soviet Union. Most of the losses of the Winter War became permanent, but Mannerheim managed to keep his country free of Soviet occupation. When he retired as president in 1946, he was the hero of his countrymen.

UNDER STALIN'S WING Friendship with Stalin gained Semyon Timoshenko (1895-1970) rapid promotion in the Red Army. Although a Stavka member, he lost much of his influence after 1942.

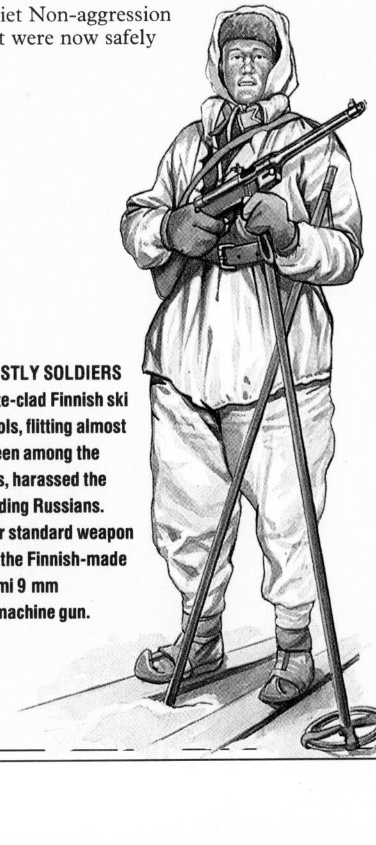

GHOSTLY SOLDIERS White-clad Finnish ski patrols, flitting almost unseen among the trees, harassed the invading Russians. Their standard weapon was the Finnish-made Suomi 9 mm submachine gun.

FÜHRER'S ESTEEM Hitler valued the support of Marshal Mannerheim.

3: STORMS IN SPRING

The Phoney War was shattered, as Denmark, Norway, the Low Countries and France all fell.

Germany's great gamble in the snow

Norway and Denmark were both neutral, but their geographical importance made neutrality one of the first casualties of the war, as Germany gambled almost all of its surface fleet in a daring combined operation.

SNOW SQUALLS danced across the icy waters of Ofoten Fiord as ten German destroyers steamed towards the north Norwegian port of Narvik in the early hours of April 9, 1940. The little town slept, and only the coastal defence vessel *Eidsvold* saw the grey shapes approaching, and fired a single warning shot.

The leading destroyer, *Wilhelm Heidkamp*, called on *Eidsvold* to surrender. Its captain refused and trained his guns on the Germans. Moments later three torpedoes tore *Eidsvold* apart. As the destroyers moved towards the harbour, *Eidsvold*'s sister-ship *Norge* opened fire. Two more torpedoes sent it to the bottom of the fiord. The Norwegian death toll was 276.

Narvik was of considerable strategic importance to Hitler. Germany was importing some 10 million tonnes of iron ore a year from Sweden, and much of it went by rail to Narvik for shipment by sea. Both Norway and Sweden were neutral, but Winston Churchill, then Britain's First Lord of the Admiralty, advocated laying a minefield inside Norwegian territorial waters to sever this vital lifeline. He even suggested landing British troops in Norway.

Reluctantly, Prime Minister Neville Chamberlain agreed. Norwegian waters would be mined on April 5, and troops landed at Narvik, Trondheim, Bergen and Stavanger a few days later. Britain had already encroached on the country's neutrality in February, when the Royal Navy destroyer *Cossack* chased the German supply ship *Altmark*, carrying 299 British prisoners of war, into Norway's territorial waters and rescued them. The Norwegian government had protested vigorously but fruitlessly.

The Germans meanwhile were reading British naval codes – not that they needed to, for the possibility of an action as urged by Churchill was being openly discussed in British and French newspapers – and were already preparing to mount their own invasion. British Intelligence and air reconnaissance reported large concentrations of warships in Germany's Baltic ports, but Admiral Sir Charles Forbes, Commander in Chief Home Fleet, said they were 'of doubtful value' and perhaps only a move in the war of nerves. And so, blindly, Royal Navy minelaying vessels entered Norwegian waters on April 8.

On the way, they had run into a violent storm, and the destroyer *Glowworm* was forced to turn away to search for a man washed overboard. Racing back to rejoin the main force, it crossed the path of the German assault group heading for Trondheim, and in the murky gloom encountered the destroyer *Bernd von Arnim*. Unaware that the German warship was part of a larger force, *Glowworm* went into action.

The German destroyer, its decks crammed with troops, was getting the worst of it when the heavy cruiser *Admiral Hipper* intervened. At almost point-blank range, *Hipper*'s guns savagely punished *Glowworm*. Crippled and on fire, the British destroyer made smoke and limped away, pursued by *Hipper*.

For a time the quarry was elusive, but suddenly, as the smoke cleared, *Hipper*'s crew saw *Glowworm* reappear on their starboard bow at close range, heading straight for them and intent on ramming. It was a desperate and only partly successful counterattack. The destroyer ground into the cruiser's hull and tore away 40 m (130 ft) of its armour belt. *Hipper* hove to, to assess the damage. It was serious – but not serious enough to stop it reaching Trondheim. As for *Glowworm*, it was already doomed and as it drifted away an explosion split it open.

Before it sank it radioed a warning that a German fleet was at sea. Among survivors picked up by *Hipper* was *Glowworm*'s captain, Lt Commander Gerard Roope, but as he climbed aboard he fell back into the sea exhausted, and was lost. He was awarded a posthumous VC.

FIVE-FINGER EXERCISE

The German operation against Norway was masterminded by Grand Admiral Erich Raeder, Commander in Chief of its navy. It was one of the most daring gambles in the history of naval warfare, mounted in the face of massive British naval superiority. Almost the entire German surface fleet was committed to forming five assault groups, and had the Royal Navy been in the right place at the right time, they might have been annihilated. Certainly few if any of the assault groups would have reached their objectives – Narvik, Trondheim, Bergen, Kristiansand and the capital Oslo – at widely separated points along Norway's 2500 km (1550 mile) coastline.

The five-pronged attack, calling for close inter-service cooperation, was under the command of General Nikolaus von Falkenhorst. On April 7 and 8, the assault groups, laden with troops, left their home ports on the North Sea and Baltic and steamed north. The entire assault force, including some paratroops to attack Oslo, consisted of only about 10 000 men.

In the darkness and snow of early morning, Commodore Paul Bonte, in *Wilhelm Heidkamp*, and Maj General Edward Dietl, commanding the

SMOKING DEFIANCE The crippled destroyer *Glowworm*, seen from the deck of a German warship, lays a smoke screen before turning to ram the heavy cruiser *Admiral Hipper* in Norwegian waters off Trondheim.

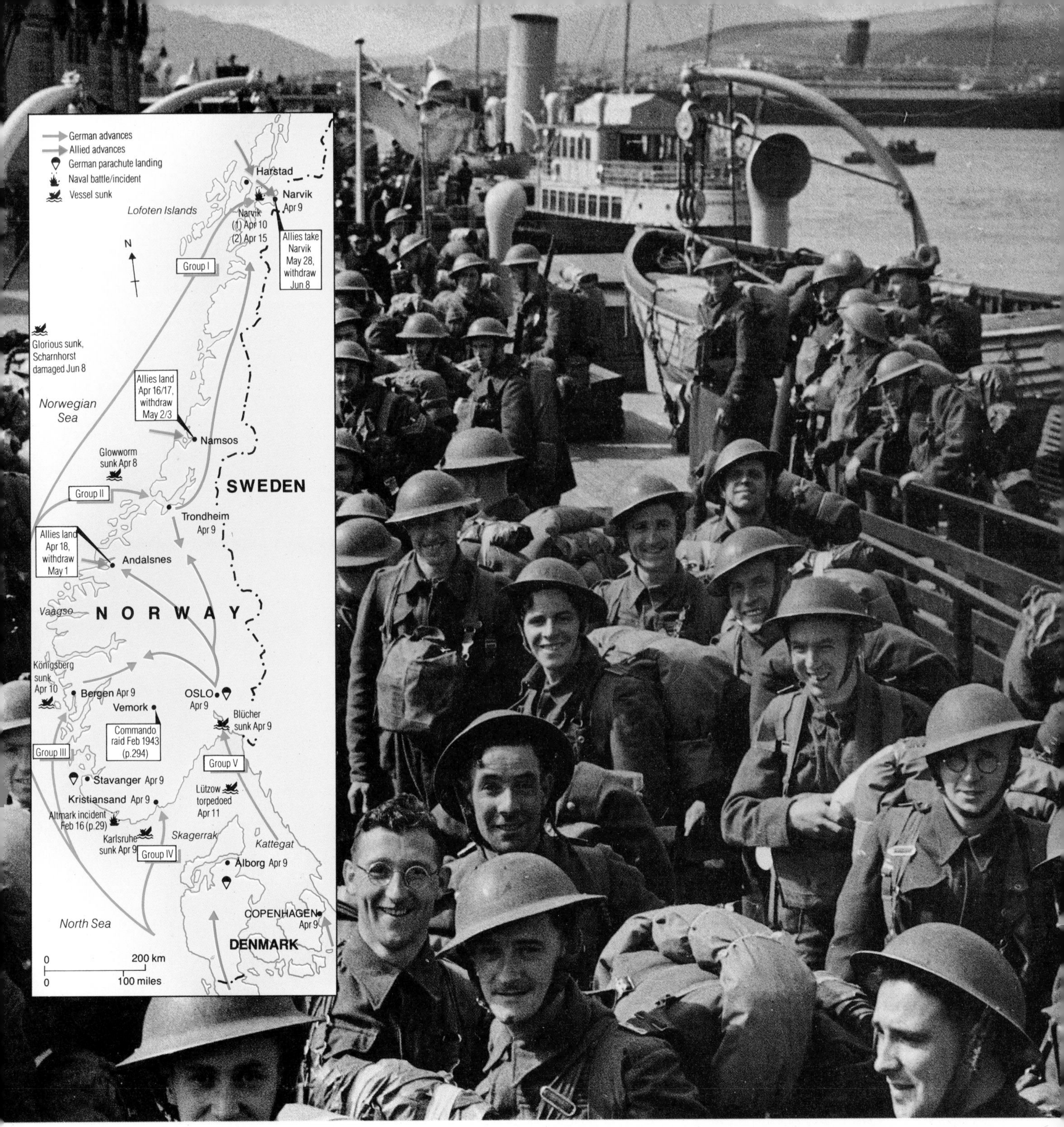

HOME AGAIN With smiles that scarcely reflect the failure of the Norwegian campaign, evacuated British soldiers land at Greenock. Despite successes on land and at sea, the Allies were outmanoeuvred by Raeder's many-pronged attack, and Denmark and Norway came under German rule.

3rd Mountain Division, were well satisfied with the progress of Group I along the fiords towards Narvik. At 5.15 am the assault group entered Narvik harbour dead on time and, having dealt with *Eidsvold* and *Norge*, landed with no resistance. Colonel Konrad Sundlo, commandant of the small Norwegian garrison, was a friend and follower of the Nazi-sympathiser Vidkun Quisling and had ordered his men not to resist.

At Trondheim, *Hipper* steamed ahead of its four destroyers, exchanged a few shots with defence batteries at the fiord entrance, but met no other opposition. Much the same happened at Bergen, though shore batteries there managed to damage the cruisers *Königsberg* and *Bremse* before being overcome. A sea fog hampered the Kristiansand landing, and shore batteries held off the attackers for a while. But as the fog cleared and the Germans moved in, the defenders held their fire, thinking the vessels were French.

Only at Oslo did the Germans meet stiff opposition and suffer a bloody nose. The heavy cruiser *Blücher*, with Vice Admiral Oskar Kummetz and Maj General Erwin Engelbrecht of the 163rd Infantry Division on board, entered Drobak Narrows, which were guarded by the guns and torpedoes of Oscarsborg fortress. At point-blank range the fortress's 205 mm (8 in) and 280 mm (11 in) guns opened fire, setting the cruiser ablaze and damaging its steering. Almost stationary, *Blücher* now lay at the mercy of torpedoes, and two launched by troops on shore wrecked its engines and set fire to the magazine. It soon capsized and sank, with the loss of 1000 men.

The ships following turned back, landing their troops lower down the fiord, and it was left to the Luftwaffe to save the day. Though delayed by fog, a battalion of paratroops seized Oslo's airport and marched boldly into the city. By the evening of April 9, all the key points in Norway had been captured, but the resistance in Oslo Fiord had allowed the royal family and most of the government to escape by train north to Hamar. Quisling, never a Member of Parliament, proclaimed himself prime minister in a new pro-German government – without telling the Germans. His name became synonymous with treachery.

DENMARK OVERRUN

The Germans struck at Denmark simultaneously with their attacks on Norway, and succeeded with even greater ease. When three German troopships sailed into Copenhagen's peaceful and unprotected harbour at 5 am on April 9, bewildered Danes offered no resistance. German troops also poured across Denmark's land frontier. Resistance cost 13 Danish lives and was quickly called off by the government to avoid pointless casualties. Airborne troops seized the airfield at Ålborg in the north. In Denmark, unlike Norway, a non-Nazi coalition government was allowed to hold power after the German invasion. King Christian X stayed with his people.

Once in Denmark, the Germans had easy access to the short sea routes to Norway, essential for the supply and reinforcement of their new occupying forces there. Moreover, Danish air bases gave them control of the Skagerrak and Kattegat, the waters leading to the German Baltic ports.

The British, as ill-prepared for the German attack as the Norwegians and Danes, could see that southern Norway was lost, but the centre and north were still vulnerable to a counterattack – and worth taking to deny their iron ore deposits to the Germans. The German forces in Narvik and Trondheim, more than 1600 km (1000 miles) from home, had to be supplied and reinforced by sea, so the Royal Navy went into action.

ROYAL NAVY DRAWS BLOOD

On the night of April 9, the British submarine *Truant* spotted the light cruiser *Karlsruhe* off Kristiansand and torpedoed it, damaging it so badly that the Germans had to sink it. Farther south, *Spearfish* torpedoed and crippled the pocket battleship *Lützow* and, on the 10th, Fleet Air Arm Skuas operating from Scapa Flow in Orkney dive-bombed and sank the cruiser *Königsberg*. So began a mauling of the German surface fleet that, while not decisive, was to inflict losses from which the Germans never recovered.

While submarines and aircraft were harrying the Germans, the Home Fleet, under Admiral Forbes, was steaming north. In the vanguard was the 2nd Destroyer Flotilla – *Hotspur*, *Havock*, *Hunter* and *Hostile*, led by Captain Bernard ('Wash') Warburton-Lee in *Hardy*. As the mists and snow flurries cleared on the morning of April 10, Warburton-Lee took his flotilla into Narvik's Ofoten Fiord and surprised the Germans completely. One of *Hardy*'s torpedoes wrecked the *Wilhelm Heidkamp*, killing Commodore Bonte. Two more sank *Anton Schmitt*. Gunfire damaged *Diether von Roeder* and *Hans Lüdemann*.

Warburton-Lee then turned to escape, but unknown to him the remaining German destroyers were hidden in inlets off the fiord. Now they emerged to cut off the British retreat. Almost immediately *Hardy* was forced onto the shore, damaged beyond repair, and Warburton-Lee was killed. *Hotspur* was hit, went out of control and collided with *Hunter*, already badly mauled by German fire. *Hunter* rolled over and sank. But *Havoc* and *Hostile*, which escaped almost unscathed, covered *Hotspur*'s retreat to the open sea, and damaged two German destroyers.

Despite the loss of *Hardy*, *Hunter* and Warburton-Lee (who received a posthumous VC), this first battle of Narvik had been a victory for the gallant 2nd Flotilla, with two enemy destroyers sunk and four damaged. And they claimed another victim – the supply ship *Ravenfels*, carrying ammunition. It failed to answer a challenge, was raked with gunfire by the British destroyers and blew up.

Three days later the battleship HMS *Warspite* – originally bound for the Mediterranean but hastily switched north by the Admiralty – and nine destroyers sailed into Ofoten Fiord to finish off the devastation. First a Swordfish reconnaissance plane from *Warspite* bombed and sank *U-64*. Then *Warspite*'s massive guns fired point-blank into the destroyer *Erich Köllner* – and sank it. Other German ships fought to the last with astonishing bravery. They damaged the destroyers HMS *Eskimo*, *Punjabi* and *Cossack*, and when they could fight no more ran themselves aground so that their crews could get ashore to fight another day.

Around 2000 German sailors escaped in this way and streamed into Narvik, spreading alarm and despondency among the German troops there. The mayor of Narvik, Theodor Broch, described a scene on the evening of April 13: 'Bands of Germans continued to drift through the town and up into the Fagernes Mountains . . . Their dark rows stood out against the snow like curving snakes.' The thoroughly demoralised Germans were fleeing the assault by a British landing force that they felt sure would follow the rout at sea. Vice Admiral William Whitworth signalled from *Warspite* that same evening: 'I recommend that the town be occupied without delay by the main landing force.'

Unfortunately the British landing force, under Maj General Piers Mackesy, consisted of just half a battalion of Scots Guards, with the remainder of the 24th Guards Brigade to follow two days later. Admiral of the Fleet Lord Cork and Orrery, commanding the fleet off Narvik, wanted a direct assault on the town. Mackesy, unaware that the Germans were in disarray, wanted to land at Harstad, on an island to the north-west of Narvik, where there were no Germans. He got his way and the first troops went ashore on the afternoon of April 14.

But the swastika still flew over Narvik, and the opportunity for a swift capture had passed. Maj General Dietl had brought his men down from the mountains, and combined them with the beached sailors to mould a solid defence force.

Farther south, an Allied attempt to capture Trondheim was also a dismal failure. British, French and Polish troops – 13 000 of them against a mere 2000 Germans in Trondheim – were landed at Namsos and Andalsnes, to the north and south. The troops were ill-equipped for war in snow and ice, and had only limited air support. They came under heavy dive-bombing by Luftwaffe Stukas. At Andalsnes, German mountain troops counterattacked in force. Maj General Sir Adrian Carton de Wiart, at Namsos, reported that the situation was hopeless, and on May 1 and 2 the men were evacuated.

NORWAY FIGHTS ON

The withdrawal of the Allied forces left only Mackesy's group, near Narvik, on Norwegian soil – and the anti-Nazi Norwegians. After the initial shock of the German landings, the Norwegian Army had regrouped under the command of Maj General Otto Ruge, and continued to fight hard in the remote mountains. During April, Mackesy was reinforced by French and Polish troops, and on May 13 they linked up with the Norwegians in the mountains near Narvik. Lt General Claude Auchinleck took over from Mackesy.

By May 28, Dietl's force was so weakened by Allied and Norwegian attacks that an assault on Narvik became possible. After a naval bombardment, men of the French Foreign Legion and a battalion of Norwegians stormed the town and drove the Germans into the hills. Narvik rejoiced, but the victory was to be short-lived. The withdrawal from Trondheim had freed the German mountain troops there to move north in support of Dietl – and events in another theatre of war now intervened with dramatic effect.

On May 10, Hitler had begun his blitzkrieg on the Low Countries, and Allied troops in Norway were needed to counter the threat to France and Britain. The withdrawal began on June 4, but Ruge remained with his men and later agreed an armistice with Dietl, who treated him honourably and allowed his soldiers to disband. King Haakon VII and his government escaped from Tromsø in the cruiser HMS *Devonshire* on June 7.

The Germans now tried to cut off the Allied retreat by sea, and on June 8 the battleships *Scharnhorst* and *Gneisenau* lay in wait off the coast for a convoy carrying 10 000 men. Their attention was diverted when the aircraft carrier HMS *Glorious* and its escorting destroyers *Ardent* and *Acasta* appeared on the horizon.

Glorious was transporting Gladiator and Hurricane fighters back home from Narvik. Its commander, Captain Guy D'Oyly-Hughes, wrongly assuming that the carrier was in no danger, was not flying reconnaissance patrols and none of his fighters or torpedo bombers were ready for action. Virtually defenceless, *Glorious* was an easy target. Desperately the destroyer escorts tried to swathe the carrier in a smoke screen, but the Germans had its range and bearing, and their 280 mm (11 in) guns set it ablaze. It sank two hours later.

Ardent and *Acasta* turned to attack with torpedoes, but *Ardent* was stopped in its tracks and sunk. *Acasta* too was mortally wounded, but Leading Seaman Carter, manning a torpedo tube, was determined to hit back. Though his fellows at the tube had been killed when a shell hit *Acasta*'s engine room, and Carter was knocked out briefly, he scrambled back into the control seat. 'I see those two ships,' he recalled later. 'I fired the remaining torpedoes, no one told me to, I guess I was raving mad.' One of his torpedoes struck *Scharnhorst* aft, killing 48 men and disabling its rear turret. Carter jumped over *Acasta*'s side and was picked up. The two German battleships headed back to Trondheim, and the British convoy sailed on unmolested.

So the fighting ended with Norway in German hands. Hitler was assured of his iron ore and had won naval and air bases from which to operate against Britain – a brilliant reward for Raeder's daring and imaginative campaign. For the Allies it was a chapter of muddle and confusion – all the more tragic when weighed against the gallantry of individual fighting men.

'In the name of God, go!'

After the failure in Norway, Prime Minister Neville Chamberlain was swept from office and Churchill became Britain's warlord, promising 'blood, toil, tears and sweat' . . . but ultimate victory 'however long and hard the road'.

DEFEAT IN NORWAY spelt the end for Neville Chamberlain as Britain's Prime Minister. He had done his duty as he saw it. He had kept Britain out of a war with Hitler in 1938, when the country was totally unprepared, and had reluctantly led it to war a year later, when at least the RAF had the modern Spitfire and Hurricane fighters. Cheered when he returned from meeting Hitler at Munich in September 1938 with the promise of 'peace in our time', he was now accused of being the great appeaser.

He never looked a war leader and the nation fretted that he was not the man for the job. Chamberlain believed that an economic blockade of Germany was Britain's 'main weapon' and on April 4, 1940, he told his Conservative party central council that Hitler had 'missed the bus'.

The Norwegian fiasco showed who had been left behind. When he entered the House of Commons on May 7 for a debate on Norway, the Prime Minister was greeted with shouts of 'Missed the bus!' He made a lacklustre speech defending himself. Admiral of the Fleet Sir Roger Keyes, a World War I hero and Tory MP, entered the packed House in full uniform, six rows of medal ribbons on his chest. His pedigree thus established, he made a devastating attack upon the conduct of the Norwegian campaign.

The *coup de grâce* came from another Tory, Leo Amery, who told his leader: 'This is what Cromwell said to the Long Parliament when he thought it was no longer fit to conduct the affairs of the nation: "You have sat too long for any good you have been doing. Depart, I say, and let us have done with you. In the name of God, go!" '

It was a dramatic moment. All MPs knew that once Amery had uttered what Winston Churchill later described as 'those terrible .words', Chamberlain was finished. But Churchill's own position was ambiguous: friends wanted him to succeed Chamberlain, but as First Lord of the Admiralty he was just as responsible as Chamberlain for the Norwegian campaign. Churchill met the situation head-on: 'I take my full share of the burden,' he said. He supported Chamberlain in the debate, but all present knew that Churchill expected to be the next Prime Minister.

When the vote was taken a government majority of 213 was slashed to 81 – revealing that now many of Chamberlain's own party lacked confidence in him. Uproar followed. Two MPs stood and sang *Rule Britannia* while others chanted 'Go! Go! Go!' as Chamberlain left.

RESIGNED A sad Chamberlain leaves 10 Downing Street on May 10, 1940, the day he resigned office. Churchill's hour had come.

CHURCHILL KEEPS QUIET

But who would succeed him? There was much manoeuvring behind the scenes, and Churchill was by no means the automatic choice. He had left the Tories to join the Liberals in 1904, only to return in 1924. Moreover, he was blamed for the Gallipoli disaster in World War I. Many politicians preferred Lord Halifax, the Foreign Secretary, but the dynamic Churchill had caught the public imagination. Would he serve under Halifax?

Friends advised Winston to stay silent if asked the question directly. Then, two days after the Commons debate, Chamberlain called a meeting at 10 Downing Street which was to settle the future of Britain and, ultimately, of the world. There was Chamberlain, grey with strain and soon to be struck down with a fatal illness; the ebullient Churchill, striving to restrain himself; Halifax, the perfect diplomat; and David Margesson, the Conservative Chief Whip. Chamberlain asked 'whom (he) should advise the King to send for' after his own resignation. They waited for Churchill to say he would serve under Halifax – who was also the King's choice. But he said nothing. A seemingly interminable silence was finally broken by Halifax himself.

Realising that he could not win without Churchill's active support, he politely excused himself, saying that as a peer, with no right of entry into the House of Commons, he would find it difficult to wage the war. Chamberlain resigned next day and the King, having first put forward Halifax's name, summoned Churchill and asked him to form a government. That was May 10, the day the German panzers crashed into Belgium, the Netherlands and Luxembourg.

PULLING TOGETHER

Churchill's appointment as Prime Minister signalled not only new leadership at the top in Britain but new political unity in face of the Nazi threat as Labour and the Liberals joined Churchill in the Cabinet and its committees. Labour leader Clement Attlee was effectively Deputy Prime Minister and often ran the government when Churchill was abroad. The bluff trade unionist Ernest Bevin became Minister of Labour, organising the work force and directing who had to work where, and Liberal leader Sir Archibald Sinclair was Secretary of State for Air. Thus the coalition National Government represented the whole of the nation at war.

THE WARLORD WHO INSPIRED A NATION

Three days after becoming Prime Minister, Winston Spencer Churchill (1874-1965) told the Commons: 'I have nothing to offer but blood, toil, tears and sweat,' but he promised 'victory, however long and hard the road may be.' This speech was the first of many that inspired the country. After Dunkirk, with invasion seemingly inevitable, Churchill vowed: 'We shall fight on the beaches, we shall fight on the landing grounds, we shall fight in the fields and in the streets, we shall fight in the hills; we shall never surrender.' And at the height of the Battle of Britain he paid his immortal tribute to the RAF: 'Never in the field of human conflict was so much owed by so many to so few.'

The British loved that unmistakable voice coming from their wireless sets, with its growling inflections and snarled references to 'the Narzies'. And they loved, too, his two-fingered V-for-victory sign, the no-nonsense siren suit, the massive cigars and the bulldog look.

Churchill surrounded himself with able men, but men who would bend to his will. He made himself Minister of Defence, and thereby became effective warlord – and a ruthless 'hirer and firer' of generals and admirals. His judgments were seldom wrong, and brought to the fore such architects of victory as Montgomery, Cunningham and Alexander.

In his conduct of the war he sometimes gambled outrageously and made a few costly mistakes – such as the attempt to capture the Dodecanese islands in 1943. However, he knew the need to keep on the offensive, and once said 'Safety first is ruin in war'. He saw the importance of defeating the Germans in North Africa, and weakened Britain's defensive forces by sending reinforcements there – a gamble that paid off handsomely.

When the Soviet Union and USA entered the war, Churchill developed a strange love-hate relationship with Stalin, who he admired but did not trust. But he struck up a warm friendship with Roosevelt. It was a friendship which survived Roosevelt's taunt that 'Churchill has a hundred ideas a day, and only four of them are any good' (to which Churchill replied that the remark came ill from a man who never had any ideas at all!).

When D-Day came, Churchill wanted to sail with the invasion fleet, but the King dissuaded him. However, as the Germans retreated he made many visits to the front – a constant worry for those responsible for his safety. When the war in Europe ended, Winston enjoyed the accolades he so richly deserved. Addressing a large crowd in Whitehall he announced: 'This is your victory.' The crowd responded: 'No, it is yours.' But two months later he was defeated at the polls. The British, who had adored him as their war leader, just did not see him as the man to win the peace.

EARLY DAYS Home life, even with his adored American mother Jennie and younger brother Jack, was not happy – nor were schooldays at Harrow (far-right). Despite the low opinion of his MP father Lord Randolph Churchill, Winston was an MP by 1900, Home Secretary in 1911, then First Lord of the Admiralty. Sacked in 1915 after the Dardanelles failure, he went to war in France (below, in helmet).

WAR WORK Churchill saw action as soldier and war reporter (right) in India, Egypt and South Africa by 1900. Lloyd George (below with Churchill) made him Minister of Munitions in 1917. As premier himself in 1940, Churchill saw too well the damage wrought by war.

Germany smashes west

Hitler found a way past the 'impregnable' French Maginot Line, once again catching the Allies on the hop. Then a small but crucial Allied counterattack halted him – and gave the British time to organise a great escape.

GLIDERS WERE THE KEY – and it was Hitler who spotted it. German planners – preparing for the campaign that would, in the spring of 1940, take their armies in six weeks of brilliant attacking warfare through Belgium and the Netherlands, drive the British out of mainland Europe and subjugate France – were puzzling over a dangerous problem: how to deal with Belgium's fort of Eben Emael.

Most people considered the fort impregnable. It had heavily armoured turrets for its two 120 mm (4½ in) and six 75 mm (3 in) guns, a multitude of anti-aircraft guns, a buried command post and barracks, massive concrete walls, and machine, flak and anti-tank guns covering the approaches. But the Germans had to capture it, for its guns could pound enemies some 20 km (12 miles) away, and reach almost to the German frontier (see map, p. 37).

Gleefully, the Führer pointed out the answer to Maj General Kurt Student, commanding the 7th Airborne Division: 'The top is like a meadow. Gliders can land on it.' Thanks to this simple observation, the Nazis' blitzkrieg in the west got off to a flying start.

DARING, SPEED AND SECRECY

As dawn broke on May 10, Junkers Ju52 transports towed a swarm of 42 gliders aloft. A special force of 424 men, under Captain Walther Koch, had been training for months in great secrecy. The assault itself would rely on daring, speed and the first wartime use of the potent armour-blasting hollow explosive charges.

Eleven gliders, carrying 85 parachute sappers under Lieutenant Rudolf Witzig, would assault the fort; the remainder, led by Koch, would seize the nearby bridges at Veldewezelt, Vroenhoven and Kanne. The first two bridges were captured as planned, machine-gun sections parachuted in and the way opened for the advance of the German Sixth Army, commanded by General Walther von Reichenau. At Kanne, however, the defenders blew up the bridge and then took heavy toll of the glider troops.

At Eben Emael, one glider was forced down, but the others, with 78 men, swooped silently down to land on top, completely surprising the defenders. Sappers ran to their targets carrying about 2.5 tonnes of explosives. Hollow charges destroyed the gun emplacements; explosives were pushed through gun slits and down gun barrels, defence posts were wiped out by a shower of grenades. The shattered garrison retreated into the depths of the fort and called for help, but the only infantry available was an hour's march away. It set out, only to be bombed by Stukas.

By the following day, the fort was a shambles. The Germans were exploding charges down the lift shafts. Choking fumes from broken barrels of chloride of lime – used in the toilets – filled corridors. The garrison had suffered more than 80 casualties, but still numbered many times more men than the Germans. However, most of these men were gunners, with no heart for hand-to-hand fighting. Around midday the great steel doors were opened and the 1100 men surrendered. The Germans had lost just six men killed and 15 wounded in removing the greatest obstacle on the road into Belgium.

DUTCH TRICKED

If surprise led to the fall of Eben Emael, subterfuge secured the bridge over the Maas river at Gennep, south of Nijmegen on the Dutch border. Just before dawn on May 10, Dutch soldiers guarding the bridge saw men in Dutch uniform, apparently escorting a party of German deserters, coming towards them. As the group reached the bridge they opened fire on the real Dutch soldiers, overpowered them, and seized the bridge. Actions such as this, by specially trained German troops – mainly from the commando-style Brandenburg Detachment – helped to open the way west for the advancing panzers.

Meanwhile, other paratroops of Student's 7th Airborne Division, supported by General Albert Kesselring's *Luftflotte* (Air Fleet) 2, seized key points in Rotterdam and the Waalhaven airport, and the 22nd Infantry Division, commanded by Maj General Graf von Sponeck, landed at airfields around The Hague. The Dutch woke that morning to the crackle of rifle fire in their cities. Except in the air, the German forces were always fewer than the defenders, and relied for their success on surprise.

Student said later that his limited manpower meant that he had to concentrate on the bridges at Rotterdam, Dordrecht and Moerdijk, which carried the main north-south route across the mouth of the Rhine. He had to take them before the Dutch could blow them up, and hold on until mobile ground forces arrived. One ruse he used to convince the Dutch that he was landing in great strength was to drop dummy paras. Student took the bridges at a cost of 180 casualties.

Sponeck, with one parachute battalion backed by four air-transported regiments, planned to race into The Hague after seizing the airfields, capture leading Dutch officials and demand the capitulation of the country from Queen Wilhelmina. He flew in after his paratroops had surprised the airfield defenders and, mindful of his royal mission, was wearing his full dress uniform. Things did not work out quite as planned. The Dutch I Corps counterattacked and drove the Germans from the airfields. Sponeck was wounded, his dress uniform ruined and over 1000 German paratroops forced to surrender. By nightfall they were being shipped off to England to sit out the war in prison camps.

That, however, was the sum total of Dutch success on the first day of Hitler's western blitzkrieg. Bombers pounded Rotterdam and The Hague, and Stukas took out strongpoints holding up the German advance as the 9th Panzer Division rumbled along the road to Rotterdam.

MAGINOT LINE BYPASSED

While world attention focused on the Low Countries, the Germans – unseen except by some startled French cavalry scouts – were also engaged on a much more dangerous move against the British and French armies. Seven panzer divisions totalling 2270 tanks, self-propelled guns and armoured vehicles, rolled around the northern end of the Maginot Line – on which the French relied to keep out the Germans – and drove almost unopposed through Luxembourg and into the wooded hills of the Belgian Ardennes. This area was only lightly screened by French cavalry, because French military thinking held that the region's narrow roads could not accommodate a large armoured force. Even when French airmen reported a build-up of armour, their warnings were ignored. All eyes, all expectations were concentrated farther north.

Acting on prewar arrangements with Belgium, the cream of the French Army and the seven divisions of General Lord Gort's British Expeditionary Force (BEF) hurried east on May 10. They planned to occupy positions from Moerdijk in the north along the Dyle (Dijle) river to Sedan in the south, to face what they thought would be the main German assault – a classic 'right hook' to outflank them to the north and cut them off from the Channel ports.

And the Germans had intended doing just that in their original blitzkrieg plans, code-named *Fall Gelb* ('Case Yellow'). Hitler, fearful that the longer he waited, the stronger the Allies would be, wanted to attack on November 25, 1939, but bad weather delayed the start five times. Finally a favourable forecast saw the attack set for January 17, 1940. Meanwhile, an accident had occurred which would change the course of the war.

On January 9, Major Hellmuth Reinberger, of the airborne operations planning staff, was called to a conference at Luftflotte 2 headquarters in Cologne. Instead of going by train, Reinberger got a lift in a light plane flown by Major Hönmanns. Against standing orders, Reinberger carried secret papers about 'Case Yellow'. Bad weather closed in and Hönmanns strayed over the

DRESSED FOR DEFEAT
French Army uniform had changed from light blue to khaki since World War I, but its design was virtually the same. The infantryman (right) still wore *pantalons golf* (knee breeches) with puttees above stout boots. Blue chevrons and red numbers on khaki collar patches showed his unit in the infantry. His Lebel rifle and leather ammunition pouches were World War I issue. The steel helmet was stamped in one piece, with a ridge fixed on the crown and back to deflect blows in close combat. New equipment and slightly altered uniforms were being issued in 1940, but France fell before all troops got them.

Belgian frontier. Then the engine failed and he put down south of Antwerp. Reinberger tried to burn the documents but enough survived to alert the Belgians. They warned the Dutch, and the French Army was alerted.

Hitler was furious. Göring said later: 'The Führer rebuked me frightfully, as the C-in-C of the unfortunate courier, for having allowed a major part of our western mobilisation and the very fact of such German plans to be betrayed. Look what a ghastly burden on my nerves it is to know that in the Führer's view my Luftwaffe officers have thrown this, the German people's mortal struggle, into jeopardy.' Indeed, Hitler almost sacked Göring, who had to dismiss Lt General Hellmuth Felmy, commander of Luftflotte 2 – opening the way for Kesselring.

The Germans had no option but to postpone the attack yet again. However, the delay was to win them the Battle of France. For they now built a radical new element into their plans. Hitler had always wanted a more southerly thrust to trap the Allies as they advanced into the Low Countries, but had been told that it was impossible. Maj General Erich von Manstein, Chief of Staff in Field Marshal Gerd von Rundstedt's Army Group A, saw the opportunities offered by a massive armoured sweep through the Ardennes to strike the French at Sedan. Against much opposition he persuaded Hitler that the main thrust should be through Luxembourg and southern Belgium. From there the Wehrmacht would capture not just part of the Channel coast, but could deliver a blow so devastating that the fall of France would surely follow.

THE SICKLE SWEEPS

Hitler was delighted and ordered a new plan to be drawn up. It decreed that Rundstedt's Army Group A would have seven of Germany's ten panzer divisions – the greatest armoured force yet assembled. All told, 45 divisions would advance through the Ardennes. The plan was known as *Sichelschnitt* ('Cut of the Sickle') – and so it proved. As they raced through the wooded hills virtually unnoticed on the brilliant morning of May 10, their only real obstacles were massive traffic jams building up behind the lead units. Colonel Günther Blumentritt, Rundstedt's chief of planning operations, who watched the advance, commented: 'Like a great phalanx they stretched back for 160 km [100 miles], the rear rank lying 80 km [50 miles] east of the Rhine.'

They presented an unmissable target for an air attack – so the Germans had clouds of Messerschmitt Me109s patrolling above. But no Allied planes appeared; most of them had been thrown into the battle of the Low Countries, suffering horrific losses. Nor were there any roadblocks, with anti-tank gunners ready to pick off leading panzers and stall the column. In fact all that faced Rundstedt's massed tanks were four French light cavalry divisions and two cavalry brigades, with 300 tanks and armoured cars. Behind them were poorly trained and equipped reservists.

So the first day of the blitzkrieg ended with the Dutch and Belgian armies in confused retreat, and the French and British advancing to face the Germans in the Low Countries, while the *Sichelschnitt* started its deadly sweep through the Ardennes. Hitler, learning that the Allies were walking into his trap, was overjoyed.

The German successes on May 10 and the days following owed much to the use of the Luftwaffe as a battlefield force. Stuka dive-bombers were used as mobile artillery, fighters cut down Allied aircraft that interfered, and Dornier and Heinkel bombers blasted vulnerable rear areas.

The Dutch lost most of their airfields and 62 out of 125 aircraft; the tiny Belgian Air Force suffered equally heavy losses. The French and British discovered that their obsolescent bombers could not survive against German fighters and flak, massed to defend important targets. Out of 32 single-engine Fairey Battle light bombers sent to attack the German columns that first day, 13 were shot down and all the rest damaged. They achieved nothing. And Me110 fighters shot down five out of six Bristol Blenheims which attacked the captured Dutch airfield at Waalhaven. However, the RAF's Hurricane fighters had performed well, claiming 42 enemy aircraft shot down for the loss of four Hurricanes. French fighter pilots, equipped mainly with Morane-Saulnier 406 fighters, fought bravely, but their planes were no match for the Me109s. French fighter squadrons also lost 37 planes on the ground in Luftwaffe raids.

UNSTOPPABLE Buoyed up by easy victories at the Maas and Rhine crossings, the Germans advanced confidently through Holland. Even the massive defences of Fort Eben Emael (inset) barred the way to Belgium for only a day.

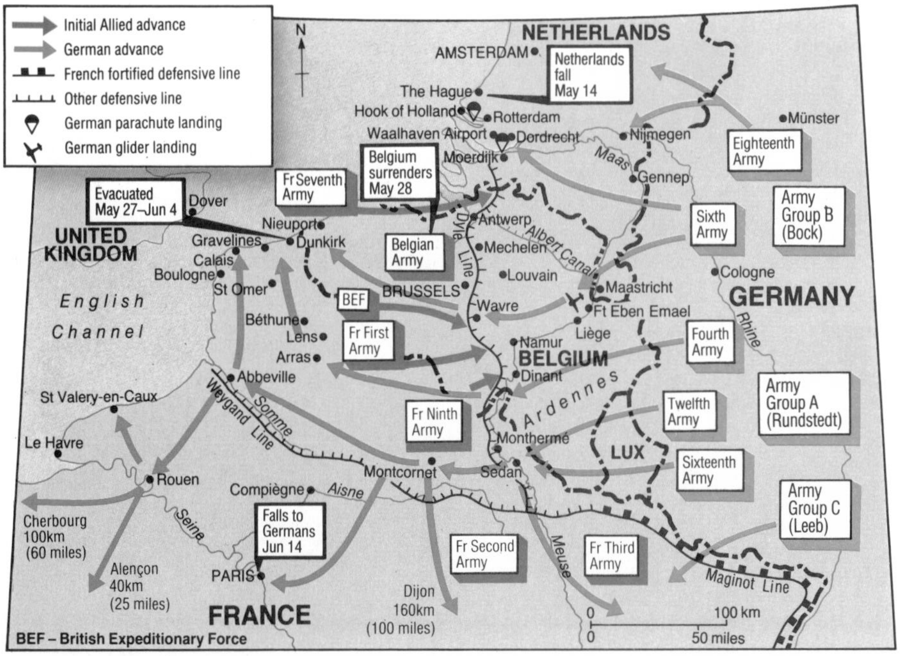

ALLIES OUTWITTED **With deceptive feints and crushing attacks, the Germans seized the strongpoints that gave entry to the Low Countries. While the British and French prepared for an advance near the coast, the panzers thrust through Sedan and overran northern France.**

The following day developed just as the Germans had planned. The BEF occupied its positions along the Dyle; Maj General Bernard Montgomery, settling his 3rd Division in at Louvain, reported that all had 'gone like clockwork'. He had arrived so promptly that the Belgians mistook his men for German paratroops and opened fire, wounding a private.

North of Montgomery, French General Henri Giraud's Seventh Army had raced along the coast towards Antwerp to support the Dutch, but as both Dutch and Belgian armies fell away before the German panzers, the French flank became dangerously exposed. South of the BEF, General Georges Blanchard's French First Army swung round towards Wavre, with the right of his line resting on Namur. There some protection would come from General André Corap's Ninth and General Charles Huntziger's Second Armies, which were covering the Ardennes.

Meanwhile, the German panzers, led by blitzkrieg expert Lt General Heinz Guderian, continued towards Sedan. London and Paris still had not appreciated the strength of their advance. Winston Churchill's first Cabinet meetings as premier were concerned with the Low Countries; not a word was said about the Ardennes.

RAF WINS TWO VCs

On May 12, volunteers were called for from No 12 Squadron (unofficially known as 'The Dirty Dozen') to crew six Fairey Battles in an attack on the Albert Canal bridges west of Maastricht captured by Koch's glider troops. The German Army was now pouring over them. The Belgian Air Force had already lost ten Fairey Battles in a previous unsuccessful attack. Now the whole of No 12 Squadron volunteered, so the first six crews on the duty roster were chosen. Only five flew, because one plane had mechanical troubles.

Two of the slow, vulnerable Battles, flown by Flying Officer Norman Thomas and Pilot Officer T.D.H. Davy, attacked the Vroenhoven bridge with 250 lb (115 kg) bombs. Greeted by a curtain of flak, Thomas and his crew of two were shot down and captured. Davy, his aircraft riddled with holes, limped home and crash-landed. They missed the bridge. Meanwhile, Flying Officer Donald Garland, Pilot Officer I.A. McIntosh and Sergeant Fred Marland attacked the Weldwezelt bridge at low level. One bomb hit the bridge but all three Battles were shot down. McIntosh and his crew were taken prisoner; the others died. Garland and his observer, Sergeant Thomas Gray, were posthumously awarded the Victoria Cross; unfortunately there was no award to their air gunner, Leading Aircraftman Lawrence Reynolds, who was just as brave – and just as dead.

By May 13 the Dutch were almost beyond resisting, and Queen Wilhelmina was resigned to fleeing her country. That night the Belgian forces were ordered back to a short line between Antwerp, Louvain and Wavre.

SPECIAL TASK FORCE **Waffen-SS units were first formed in 1933 as Himmler's elite force, charged with guarding the Führer and performing special tasks. It grew into a motorised, well-equipped 'parallel army' that aroused resentment in the regular Wehrmacht. By 1945 almost a million men – guards from the concentration camps, policemen, even enthusiasts from occupied countries – had been recruited into the Waffen-SS. One of its crack divisions was the *Totenkopf* ('Death's Head'), for whom the SS badge of a skull beneath an eagle (as on the major's cap, right) was particularly apt. Even before the war, the Waffen-SS began to wear the camouflage that became their trademark.**

ASSAULT ON SEDAN

During the day the Germans had emerged in strength from the Ardennes. Lt General Ewald von Kleist, commanding two panzer corps of Army Group A, allowed the impatient Guderian to unleash his three panzer divisions across the Meuse near Sedan, without waiting for the infantry to catch up. The panzers struck on a 2.5 km (1½ mile) stretch just west of Sedan, where the river bent in a way that left the French defenders overlooked on all sides by Germans on the opposite bank. Not only were the Germans able to fire down on the French, but woodland shielded their preparations from French eyes.

Stukas dived in soon after midday and rained down bombs until nightfall, concentrating on artillery positions of the French 55th Division. 'Eighty Eights' – high-velocity 88 mm ack-ack guns converted into battlefield artillery – picked off the French bunkers. Sergeant Prümers of the 1st Panzer Division saw the Stukas in action: 'We can see the bombs very clearly . . . a regular hail of bombs that whistle down on Sedan and the bunker positions. Each time the explosion is overwhelming, the noise deafening. Everything becomes blended together: along with the howling sirens of the Stukas in their dives, the bombs whistle and crack and burst.'

Late in the afternoon, Guderian sent his men across the river. First over were assault engineers and panzer grenadiers – the infantry integral to panzer divisions – whose rubber boats and inflatable rafts came under shellfire. Some boats were destroyed, but about a dozen engineers got across and took cover against a bunker wall. Any counterattack would have wiped them out – but no counterattack came.

Infantry of the 'Grossdeutschland' Regiment were then ferried over and attacked the surviving French positions. Some of the French fought to the last man, others broke and ran. The collapse started among the elderly reservists of the 55th Division when artillery officers panicked under

FATHER OF THE PANZERS

While commanding a humble motor-transport battalion in the small Reichswehr of 1929, Heinz Guderian (1888-1954) was spurred by other military theorists' work to develop his own concept of massed tank divisions, coordinated by radio, spearheading a lightning assault. His ideas found favour, and the first *panzer* (armoured) division was formed in 1935. Two years later he published an influential textbook, *Achtung! Panzer!* and became Chief of Mobile Troops in 1938. He was a corps commander in the campaigns in Poland, the Low Countries and France, then brilliantly led Panzer Group II – later Second Panzer Army – in the invasion of Russia. However, Hitler sacked him in 1941 for making a timely withdrawal against orders. He never held field command again, though Hitler gave him the title Chief of Staff in 1944.

Stuka attack, destroyed their guns and fled the field, leaving the division's infantrymen unprotected. Guderian said later of the crossing: 'I was now anxious to take part in the assault across the Meuse . . . I went over in the first assault boat. On the far bank of the river I found the efficient and brave commander of the 1st Rifle Regiment, Lieutenant Colonel Balck, with his staff. He hailed me with the cry: "Pleasure-boating on the Meuse is forbidden." I had in fact coined the phrase myself during training . . . since the attitude of some of the younger officers had struck me as too light-hearted. I now realised that they had judged the situation correctly.'

The German build-up went on remorselessly. Brigadier Erwin Rommel's 7th Panzer Division crossed a weir downstream from Dinant and found a gap between the French 5th Motorised Division and the 18th Division. A counterattack failed because of poor coordination between French tanks and infantry. By the evening of May 13, Rommel's engineers were building pontoons across the river. But as the 6th and 8th Panzer Divisions tried to cross at Monthermé they met a hail of bullets from machine-gunners of the 42nd Colonial Demi Brigade. The German tanks lined up along the river bank and picked off the machine-gun nests one by one. A rifle battalion then stormed across and, after a further fierce fight, took Monthermé.

By nightfall the French 55th Division had lost 500 dead and had broken. The 71st Division, which had arrived to join in the battle, was being torn apart. Eighty field guns had been lost and the Germans were across the Meuse in strength. The rout had started.

The French High Command went to pieces as the news filtered back from the battlefield. A staff officer described the scene when General Joseph Doumenc, Commander of Land Forces, arrived to see General Alphonse Georges, Commander of the North-East Front: 'The atmosphere is that of a family keeping vigil over a dead member. Georges rises briskly and comes up to Doumenc. He is terribly pale: "Our front has been pushed in

BLITZKRIEG GENERAL

Erich von Manstein (1887-1973) masterminded the plan that gave Germany its lightning victory in the west in 1940. He witnessed in World War I the futility of slogging, inconclusive battles, and it was he who talked Hitler into the daring thrust through the Ardennes into France. In 1941-2 he conducted Eleventh Army's conquest of the Crimea – and was equally impressive in retreat. His brilliant Caucasus counteroffensive of 1942 saved Army Group Don from annihilation, and he made a fighting retreat to the Donets to form a strong front there.

Hitler admired Manstein's abilities, but had a personal aversion to him – possibly suspecting that Manstein, who was adopted as a child, had Jewish blood. Manstein was not afraid to dispute military matters with Hitler. He did so once too often in 1944, and was sacked. In 1949 he was tried as a war criminal. His sentence of 18 years in jail was later cut to 12 – and he was freed in 1953.

RAIDERS SWOOP Screeching Stuka dive-bombers (right) and rumbling heavy bombers hurled destruction at any defences that could resist and delay the panzer sweep westward. To escape the bombardment, terrified townsfolk bundled as much as they could onto carts and made off into the countryside (below right), abandoning home and livelihood. German troops rifled whatever they had left behind, including the stocks in the wine cellars (below).

at Sedan. There have been some failures . . ." He falls into an armchair and a sob stifles him. It was the first man that I had seen weep in this battle. I was to see many others, alas!'

HOLLAND FALLS

May 13 also saw an extraordinary Irish Guards expedition to the Netherlands, just as resistance collapsed there. Lt Colonel Joseph Haydon, commanding the under-strength, half-trained 2nd Battalion, plus a company of the Welsh Guards, went to the Hook of Holland, where they met a Royal Marines landing party. Haydon had orders to move his troops towards The Hague 'with the object of safeguarding the Dutch Government and restoring the situation in the capital'. Away to the south-east, Rotterdam could be seen burning. Docks at the Hook of Holland were under constant air attack as the Guardsmen watched diamonds from Amsterdam being loaded on a British ship.

Then their orders were changed – the Guards were now to stay put, hold the port and keep open the road to The Hague. Suddenly a fleet of large black cars appeared and braked sharply by the quay. Out of one stepped Queen Wilhelmina. Protesting that she wanted to go to an overseas Dutch island, she was taken on board the destroyer HMS *Malcolm* and carried to England. The Dutch government and the diplomatic corps followed soon afterwards.

With their exit, Haydon's mission ended, but his force remained another day, under mounting air attacks. Refugees flooded into the Hook, only to be bombed by Stukas. The battalion chaplain, Father John Stonor, recalled later: 'The morning I can only remember as a confused kaleidoscope of horrors. I found myself facing an endless stream of refugees from poor Rotterdam. Some of them were pushing dead relatives or children on handcarts and perambulators, and every now and again a German plane would swoop down and machine-gun some more.' Father Stonor himself was a strange sight as he knelt to give absolution to the badly wounded. The crown of his steel helmet had vanished, leaving only the brim 'like a collapsed halo'. When the force sailed for Dover that night, they left behind 11 Irish Guardsmen killed in the strafing.

DRIVE FROM THE MEUSE

On May 14, too, Montgomery's 3rd Division had their first encounter with the Germans sweeping through Belgium. The panzers were driven off but the action was irrelevant, because Guderian was pushing so strongly that the BEF was in obvious danger of being outflanked. Indeed his advance was so rapid that the German High Command told him to halt, worried that he would be cut off by a counterattack before supporting infantry arrived. However, he talked Kleist into letting him mount a 'reconnaissance in force' – in effect, continuing his advance.

Rommel wrote later of the sweep from the Meuse: 'Civilians and French troops, their faces distorted with terror, lay in the ditches, alongside hedges and in every hollow beside the road . . . Always the same picture, [other] troops and civilians in wild flight down both sides of the road . . . a chaos of guns, tanks and military vehicles . . . inextricably entangled with horse-drawn refugee carts . . . By keeping our guns silent and occasionally driving our crosscountry vehicles alongside the road, we managed to get past the column without great difficulty. The French troops were completely overcome by surprise at our sudden appearance, laid down their arms and marched off to the east . . . Nowhere was any resistance attempted.'

Churchill was woken at 7.30 am on May 15 by a despairing telephone call from French Premier Paul Reynaud. He told Churchill: 'We are beaten; we have lost the battle . . . the road to Paris is open.' He talked of 'giving up the struggle', and pleaded for more British help. Next day, Churchill flew to Paris and met Reynaud, National Defence Minister Edouard Daladier and General Maurice Gamelin, the French Commander in Chief. Gamelin explained the desperate military situation and Churchill then asked, *'Où est la masse de manoeuvre?'* ('Where is the strategic reserve?'). Gamelin shrugged and said simply: *'Aucune'* ('None').

'Outside in the garden of the Quai d'Orsay [the French Foreign Ministry],' wrote Churchill in his memoirs, 'clouds of smoke arose from large bonfires, and I saw from the window venerable officials pushing wheelbarrows of archives onto them. Already therefore the evacuation of Paris was being planned.'

The next day, the French attempted their only real counterattack when Colonel Charles de Gaulle led the hastily assembled 4th Armoured Division towards Montcornet, about 160 km (100 miles) north-east of Paris. He gained some 34 km (21 miles) and took a number of prisoners before Stukas, against which he had no defences, forced him back. He attacked again on May 19 and got within 1.6 km (1 mile) of Guderian's advanced headquarters. Again Stukas drove him back. Now Guderian began driving north-west for Abbeville and the Channel.

'BACK TO THE SEA'

It was on the 19th that Gort made the first move that was to lead to the Dunkirk evacuation. He reported to London that the French First Army on his right had disintegrated, so he would base himself on Dunkirk to 'fight it out with my back to the sea'. Alarmed, Churchill sent General Sir Edmund Ironside, Chief of the Imperial General Staff, to France to report on the situation and urge Gort to counterattack south. So far the British forces were intact, having suffered only about 500 casualties. However, the danger to a thrust south lay in the possible collapse of the Belgians and French on their flanks.

Nevertheless, on May 21, two tank battalions and two battalions of Durham Light Infantry under Maj General Harold Franklyn, supported by the French 3rd Light Mechanised Division, hit the 7th Panzer and SS *Totenkopf* ('Death's Head') Divisions near Arras, 100 km (60 miles) south-east of Calais.

A concentrated attack by 74 tanks and determined infantry caught the Germans on their long, extended flank, and there was panic – some SS troops ran away and Rommel thought that five Allied divisions were attacking him. The British Matilda tanks' heavy armour could absorb a lot of punishment, and it was not until the German 88s came into action that they were stopped. Stukas were also called down and, after a nine-hour battle, the British were forced to retreat. The Germans had suffered 700 casualties and lost 20 tanks. But the Durhams, too, had been badly mauled and 46 British tanks were lost.

Although this was a minor incident in the campaign, it was important because it was exactly what the German High Command had feared might happen, and it put a temporary brake on Guderian's run for the coast. It may also have influenced Hitler's decision not to risk his panzers in an all-out assault on Dunkirk – the boggy terrain near the coast was not good tank country anyway, and Rundstedt (whose counsel he valued) wanted to regroup them for the drive south to Paris. Furthermore, Göring had requested that the Luftwaffe be allowed to finish off the trapped British and French – for there was little Gort could do but make a fighting retreat towards the Channel.

On May 23, Lt General Alan Brooke, commander of BEF's II Corps, noted in his diary: 'Nothing but a miracle can save the BEF . . . The German armoured divisions have penetrated to the coast, Abbeville, Boulogne and Calais have been rendered useless. We are therefore cut off from our sea communications [and] beginning to be short of ammunition.'

The following day Hitler visited Rundstedt's headquarters at Charleville, on the Meuse, and forbade Guderian to pass the line running through Lens, Béthune, St Omer and Gravelines, stopping him when he could have reached Dunkirk in a day. It was a miraculous escape for the British – and another was in the making. Even while urging Gort to fight his way south, Churchill had ordered that 'as a precautionary measure, the Admiralty should assemble a large number of small vessels in readiness to proceed to ports and inlets on the French coast.' The scene was set for the epic of Dunkirk.

RUNDSTEDT, THE GREAT SURVIVOR

An aloof Prussian aristocrat, Karl Rudolph Gerd von Rundstedt (1875-1953) had made a great impression on Hitler, who called him from retirement in 1939 to command Army Group A in Poland and later in France, where his armies spearheaded the breakthrough at Sedan. In 1941 he commanded Army Group South in the drive through the Ukraine, but was sacked in Hitler's purge of the Eastern Front generals that December. The Führer called Rundstedt back in July 1942 to take over the defence of the west, but sacked him again when the Normandy landings wrongfooted the Germans. His final recall came in December 1944, to lead the Ardennes offensive. Rundstedt retired for good when it failed.

His cynical attitude – he thought privately that trying to resist the Normandy landings was hopeless – made him suspect among his fellow officers, but he was a resourceful and flexible leader, adept at exploiting the talents of gifted subordinates such as Guderian and Manstein. However, he also influenced Hitler's decision to halt Guderian's panzers before Dunkirk – which allowed the British Expeditionary Force to escape.

The miracle of Dunkirk

Seemingly, only a miracle could save the British Expeditionary Force from annihilation. It came when Britain's 'Skylark Navy' put to sea – little ships that once ran pleasure trips now sailed on a life-or-death mission to Dunkirk.

GRACIE FIELDS began its last voyage on Wednesday, May 29, 1940. The 400 tonne Red Funnel Line paddle-steamer was named after the popular Lancashire singer and comedienne, who launched it in 1936. It had been a pleasure and ferryboat before the war, but in 1939 it was requisitioned as a minesweeper. Now it was one of the hundreds of 'little ships' helping to evacuate the remnants of the British Expeditionary Force (BEF) from Dunkirk. It had already made one successful return trip between England and France on May 28. This time it was crammed with troops picked up from the beach at La Panne on the Belgian border when a Luftwaffe bomb hit it amidships. Clouds of steam enveloped the ship but it kept on moving at 6 knots (11 km/h) in a circle – for the rudder was jammed at an angle. Even so, two Belgian barges managed to get alongside and took off all the troops they could carry.

Then the minesweeper HMS *Pangbourne* arrived on the scene. It was already holed on both sides by near misses that had killed 13 men, but it too got alongside *Gracie Fields*. It took off 80 men, then began to tow the paddler towards the White Cliffs of Dover. But *Gracie Fields* was shipping water and began to sink. *Pangbourne* took off its remaining crew and slipped the towrope. Finally abandoned, *Gracie* sank in the early hours of the 30th, but its crew and all the troops it rescued reached England – 750 out of over one-third of a million who escaped to fight another day.

The saga of *Gracie Fields* was one among many heroic stories that turned a crushing military defeat into a psychological victory and gave the British the will to fight on. It also helped to make the name Dunkirk a poignant symbol of British determination and improvisation. Yet only four days earlier General Sir Edmund Ironside, Chief of the Imperial General Staff, had viewed the prospect with dismay. He noted in his diary on May 25: 'The final debacle cannot be long delayed . . . It cannot mean the evacuation of more than a minute proportion of the BEF and the abandonment of all the equipment . . . Horrible days to have to live through.'

HOLDING THE LINE

On May 22, fresh from rescuing Queen Wilhelmina of the Netherlands, the 2nd Battalion Irish Guards had been ordered to embark again for the Continent with a battalion of Welsh Guards. This time their task was to hold back Hitler's panzers at Boulogne while a defensive ring was thrown around Dunkirk, 65 km (40 miles) north-east – for it was already obvious that the Battle of France was as good as lost after only 12 days, and that an evacuation would be necessary.

The Guardsmen took up positions around Boulogne on May 23 and fought until their Bren-gun barrels overheated and warped. They held out for two days but were gradually forced back to the harbour, where they held the quay under a rain of bullets and shells. When two destroyers arrived to take them off, a naval officer reported: 'The courage and bearing of the Guardsmen were magnificent, even under a tornado of fire with casualties occurring every second.' The destroyers came alongside, blasted the German tanks 'like cartwheels' from the quay and the Guardsmen scrambled on board. The Irish had lost over 200 men killed and the Welsh about the same. Two Welsh companies were cut off, and were still fighting two days later.

Meanwhile, three battalions from the Rifle Brigade and other rifle regiments, plus an anti-tank battery, had been sent on a similar mission to Calais. Supporting them were the 3rd Royal Tank Regiment, eight anti-tank guns and a mixed bag of 800 Frenchmen who earned fame as the 'Volunteers of Calais', choosing to fight rather than be evacuated. Again, the riflemen reached Calais just in time, on the 23rd – but even so they would not have succeeded if men of the 1st Searchlight Regiment had not snatched up guns and helped to fight off the Germans.

Three days of bloody, hand-to-hand fighting through the streets of Calais followed. The British refused a call to surrender, and their commander, Brigadier Claude Nicholson, circulated a message from Churchill: 'The eyes of the Empire are upon the defence of Calais and HM Government are confident you and your gallant regiment will perform an exploit worthy of the British name.'

And so they did. Panzer commander Lt General Heinz Guderian himself described their fight as 'heroic, worthy of the highest praise'. By the time they were finally overrun on the evening of May 26, they had bought precious time for Operation 'Dynamo', the great evacuation. The gallant Brigadier Nicholson was taken prisoner and died later in a prisoner-of-war camp.

ON THE BEACH British and French soldiers wait to be rescued from Dunkirk. Men wade out, neck deep, to a ship. *The Daily Mirror* proclaimed the soldiers' return.

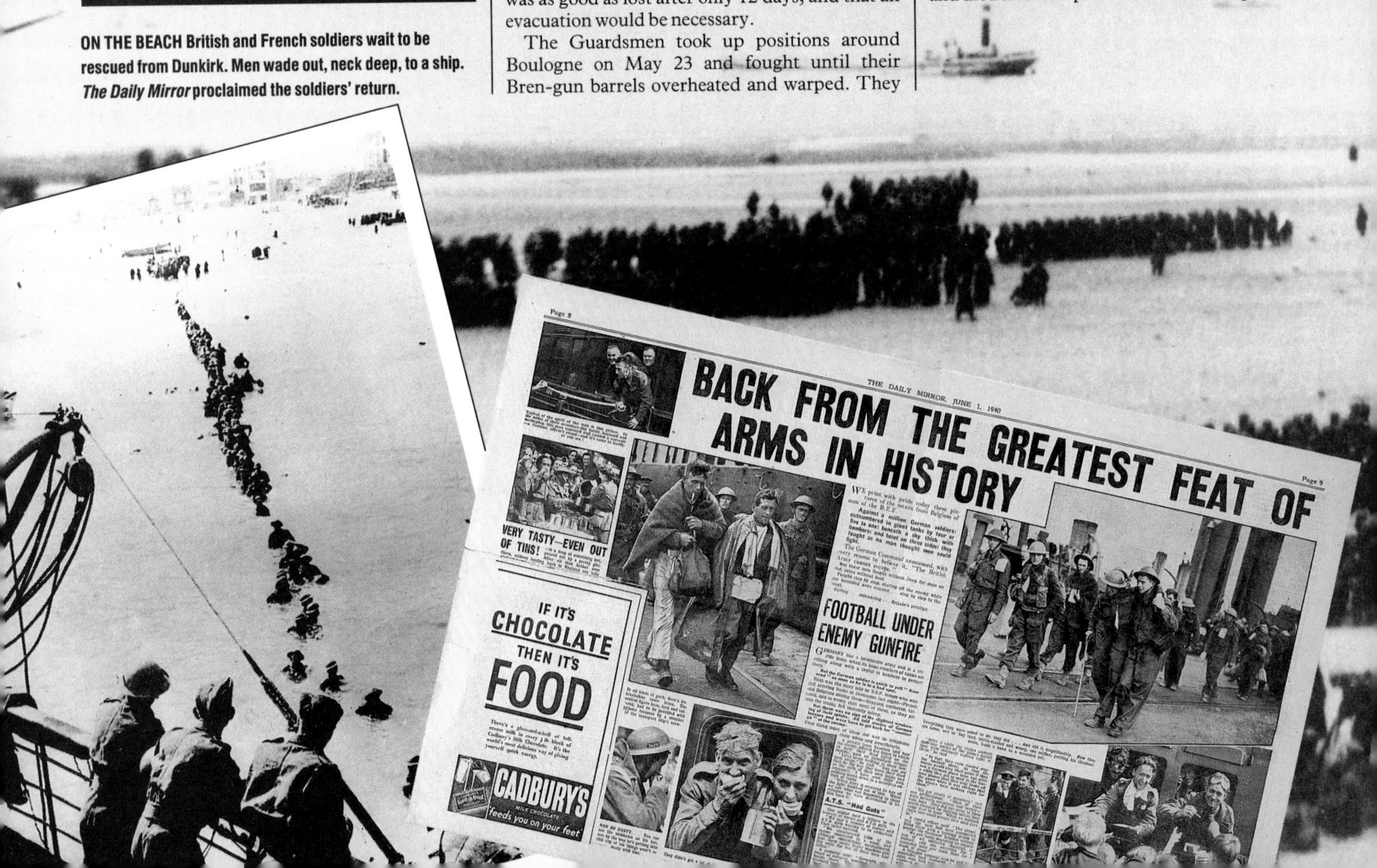
THE DAILY MIRROR, JUNE 1, 1940

BACK FROM THE GREATEST FEAT OF ARMS IN HISTORY

VERY TASTY—EVEN OUT OF TINS!

FOOTBALL UNDER ENEMY GUNFIRE

OFF THE BEACHES

At 7.57 pm on May 26 Vice Admiral Bertram Ramsay, Flag Officer Commanding Dover, had received an Admiralty signal at his headquarters deep beneath Dover Castle: 'Operation Dynamo is to commence.' He had had less than a week to prepare, and on the first day only 7669 troops were brought out. It became clear that the rescue boats, destroyers, paddle-steamers, and passenger ferries that Ramsay had commandeered would not be able to use Dunkirk harbour. This was now a smoking, flaming hell of screaming Stukas and artillery fire. With only the harbour's East Mole usable, men would have to be taken off the beaches either side of the town.

But the ferries could not get in close enough in the shallow water. So Ramsay commandeered virtually anything in southern England that could float and was over 9 m (30 ft) long – cabin cruisers, fishing boats, barges. He put naval officers in charge and sent them into the beaches, often with their civilian crews. So was born the legend of the little ships that saved an army.

And units of that army were still pouring into Dunkirk – bone-weary, almost out of ammunition and hungry. Maj General Bernard Montgomery's 3rd Division had secured its own 'rations on the hoof', driving cattle along with the troops. Others had nothing but what they could scrounge from deserted farmhouses. With the BEF came remnants of the French First Army.

The Belgian King Leopold capitulated on May 28, leaving the BEF's eastern flank wide open. But by then there was a tight Allied line around Dunkirk. Isolated units struggled along roads jammed with refugees, and under constant Stuka attack, to find sanctuary of a sort within this perimeter. But now Guderian, set free from an earlier order of Hitler's not to push on to Dunkirk, began pressing hard against the defences, while Göring's Luftwaffe reduced the town to a flaming shambles.

Monty's corps commander, Lt General Alan Brooke (later Lord Alanbrooke), recorded his 3rd Division's movement to safety: 'Our own guns were firing . . . whilst German artillery was answering back, and the division was literally trundling slowly along in the darkness down a pergola of artillery fire . . . It was an eerie sight which I shall never forget.'

Once on the beaches, lorries and other heavy equipment were destroyed; some lorries were driven into the sea to form an improvised 'mole'. Long, snake-like queues of men stood in patient lines, scattering under air attack, then reforming. Over all hung a pall of black, oily smoke from burning vehicles and equipment.

WHERE'S THE RAF?

Overhead, Stukas wheeled and dived. Men who still had rifles and ammunition took pot shots at them, grumbling: 'Where's the RAF?' In fact the airmen were fighting an all-out war high above their heads. Every squadron of Fighter Command except three in Scotland had been thrown in to protect the beaches, and between May 27 and June 4, when the evacuation ended, they lost 99 aircraft over Dunkirk. The Luftwaffe lost 132.

However, the men suffering on the beaches knew nothing of this. One Spitfire pilot, Flt Lieutenant Alan Deere, who had been shot down 25 km (15 miles) outside Dunkirk, made his way to the mole to board a destroyer. There he was stopped by a major, who told him: 'For all the good you are doing, you might as well stay on the ground.' Once on board, he met stony silence. 'Why so friendly? What have the RAF done?' he asked. 'That's just it,' someone replied. 'What *have* they done?'

Back on the beaches, the soldiers enjoyed one bit of luck – the soft sand absorbed much of the shock of the Stukas' bombs. But often they were walking into a sea whipped to a white froth by machine-gun bullets.

Once on board ship the ordeal was far from over, as the *Gracie Fields* story illustrates. As well as bombers, E-boats (fast torpedo boats) were also prowling. The destroyers HMS *Wakeful* and *Grafton* were torpedoed with over 1000 men lost, and HMS *Montrose* was badly damaged. Altogether seven French destroyers and torpedo boats, and six British destroyers and 24 smaller warships were sunk during 'Dynamo', along with one in every four of the 665 small boats. But they continued to run the gauntlet to pick up men in numbers nobody had ever dared hope for.

The Guards Brigade formed the British rearguard, and amid the chaos the Guardsmen turned out for duty washed, shaved and fully kitted. By June 1 the perimeter was being held by the gallant French of the XVI Corps, and Churchill was anxious to rescue as many of them as possible. On the night of June 2/3, the remaining 4000 British and over 20 000 Frenchmen were evacuated, and on the next and final night another 26 175 men – mostly French – were taken off. Early on June 4, the last defenders of Dunkirk surrendered. By then, 338 226 officers and men, 139 097 of them French, had been carried to England.

There, as trainloads of weary, defeated troops rolled through the burgeoning countryside, they were treated not as a beaten army, but as homecoming victors, welcomed by housewives offering tea, sandwiches and cigarettes. Britain rejoiced. True, its tanks and guns still littered northern France, but the men were home. Churchill had to warn Parliament that wars are not won by evacuations, but he later wrote: 'There was a white glow, overpowering, sublime, which ran through our Island from end to end . . . and the tale of the Dunkirk beaches will shine in whatever records are preserved of our affairs.'

IT'S GOOD TO BE BACK! Two returning soldiers of the British Expeditionary Force are given a light by a FANY – a member of the First Aid Nursing Yeomanry.

The Swastika flies over Paris

Churchill strove to save France from final humiliation, but defeatism gripped both politicians and military leaders. They wanted peace at any price. It was left to an obscure army officer to raise the proud flag of Free France in London.

CALL TO ORDER Cruising through the streets of Paris in their loudspeaker cars, the new overlords broadcast instructions to the stunned and sullen citizens.

WHEN THE GUNS fell silent around Dunkirk, Hitler turned his attention to the rest of France. He was obsessed with the prize that eluded the Germans in World War I – Paris. He was determined that this time there would be no mistakes.

The failure of the Allied Supreme Commander, General Maurice Gamelin, to stem the German advance led French Prime Minister Paul Reynaud to replace him on May 20, 1940, with the elegant 73-year-old General Maxime Weygand, summoned from commanding the French forces in Syria. Weygand set up a line along the Somme river to hold the panzers, and his hastily formed defence groups – especially Colonel Charles de Gaulle's makeshift 4th Armoured Division – had a brief success in attacking German bridgeheads across the river.

Not all the British Expeditionary Force (BEF) had been evacuated from Dunkirk. The 51st Highland Division had remained in front of the Maginot Line and now, north of Rouen, faced the Germans. Brigadier Erwin Rommel's 7th Panzer Division came at them on June 5, the day after Dunkirk fell, and they fought hard. However, by June 11, because Weygand had refused them permission to withdraw across the Seine while there was still time, most of the Highlanders had been driven into the Havre peninsula along with French troops. About 46 000 British and French soldiers were taken prisoner.

Lt General Sir Alan Brooke, knighted for his services in France and sent back there to form a new BEF, found under his command the desperately understrength 1st Armoured Division, which was striving to hold up panzers storming towards Rouen and the Seine Valley. There was, too, a scratch force of nine infantry battalions scraped together by Brigadier Archibald Beauman – many of whose men had never used a rifle. Finally, Brooke was amazed to find that he also had nearly 100 000 assorted engineers, signallers, medical staff, service corps and other ancillary troops strung out across France.

TOO LATE FOR WEYGAND

Maxime Weygand (1867-1965) was 73 when he became the French Supreme Commander on May 20, 1940. He tried vigorously to create a new defensive front south of the Somme, but he was too late. His First Army and the British Expeditionary Force were already cut off, and his line broke on June 5.

After Paris fell, he advised Prime Minister Paul Reynaud to seek an armistice. Weygand became Minister of National Defence under Pétain and then High Commissioner in French North Africa. In November 1941, he resigned. Later he was recalled, then arrested by the Germans and held in Germany until the war ended. Afterwards he was tried by the French for treason and acquitted.

Churchill, determined to keep France in the fight, sent reinforcements – the 52nd Lowland and 1st Canadian Divisions. They landed at Cherbourg and Brest and hurried towards the fighting. But even as they arrived, the French Army began crumbling under the hammer blows of the panzers and Stukas. Some units still fought bravely, even brilliantly. General Jean de Lattre de Tassigny counterattacked the German XXIII Corps on the Aisne river, wiped out its bridgehead and took 1000 prisoners. General Henri Olry's Army of the Alps in south-eastern France fought off not only the German XVI Panzer Corps, but two Italian armies (for the Italian dictator Benito Mussolini had declared war on France and Britain on June 10, hoping to snatch some juicy titbits).

Many more French units, however, simply faded away in face of the panzers, and both the French government and its High Command were riddled with defeatism.

PARIS ABANDONED

On June 10, with the Germans across the Loire river and Rouen fallen, the French government abandoned Paris without a fight and moved to Tours, 210 km (130 miles) to the south-west. On the morning of June 14, the weary but triumphant German Army entered the undefended capital and the Nazi swastika flag was raised on the Eiffel Tower. Veterans of World War I wept as the Germans marched stern-faced down the Champs Elysées. On that same day the French government moved on to Bordeaux and Brooke went to see Weygand at his headquarters at Briare, on the Loire, finding him 'wizened and tired with a stiff neck from a car smash on the previous evening'. Weygand told him of plans to make a stronghold

PARIS SHAMED German horse artillery trample on French pride as they clatter down the cobbled avenue from the Arc de Triomphe, shrine of France's unknown soldier.

SAVIOUR OF FRANCE

Flown to England after the fall of France, Charles de Gaulle (1890-1970) broadcast an appeal for support to his people, saying that France had lost a battle, but not the war. A few weeks later he was sentenced to death as a traitor by a Vichy French military court.

The Allies found him difficult to deal with, for he was a single-minded patriot. But his personal bravery was legendary, and the Free French Army that he led fought gallantly in many theatres of war. De Gaulle's reward came in August 1944, when he entered liberated Paris to the adulation of the people. He headed the provisional government after the liberation, and was prime minister again in 1958. He was president from 1959 to 1969.

ONE AIM Victory for France was de Gaulle's obsession.

in Brittany. But he had neither men nor guns to do so – and Brooke knew it.

So, just two days after returning to France, Brooke had again to think about getting his troops back to England. After a furious argument on the phone with Churchill, Brooke won the day. In the second evacuation, Operation 'Ariel', some 136 000 British troops got away, along with 20 000 French, Belgians and Poles. They were only just in time. German tanks raced into Cherbourg on June 18; Brest and St Nazaire fell the next day. The escape was not, however, without tragedy. On June 17, nearly 3000 troops and civilians died when the liner *Lancastria* was bombed and sunk as it sailed from St Nazaire.

PEACE AT A PRICE

That was the first of many days that Britain would fight alone, for France was out of the war. The night before, Reynaud had resigned, to be succeeded by Marshal Philippe Pétain, the 'hero of Verdun'. But there would be no heroics from Pétain this time. In the early hours of June 17 he sued for peace. Churchill had done his best to keep France in the war, making five trips there to stiffen resolve in the face of increasing recriminations from Reynaud, who demanded what Britain could not give – its remaining squadrons of fighters. These were too precious to risk.

Churchill had made one grand gesture on June 16: at the suggestion of de Gaulle – who had flown to London on the 14th seeking ships to evacuate French troops to North Africa – he offered France union with Britain. 'The Union,' he declared, 'will concentrate its whole energy against the power of the enemy, no matter where the battle may be. And thus we shall conquer.' De Gaulle relayed the offer to an elated Reynaud, but it was coldly received by his cabinet and Reynaud collapsed, physically and mentally exhausted. Next day Pétain replaced him.

Pétain was determined on peace and Churchill, realising this, agreed that if the French would send their fleet immediately to British ports, he would let them off their promise not to negotiate with Germany.

On June 20, Pétain sent a delegation to negotiate with the Germans. Hitler, determined to humiliate the French, insisted on holding the meeting in the same railway carriage at Compiègne where Marshal Foch had accepted the German surrender in 1918. When the French entered the carriage on June 21 they found the Nazi leaders already there: Hitler, Ribbentrop, Hess, Göring, Keitel and Raeder.

Hitler himself handed each delegate a copy of his armistice terms, then left the carriage. He felt he had won the war. France was beaten, Britain would soon come to terms, then he could turn his attention to Russia. After he left it was made plain to the French that there could be no discussion of the armistice document. The French insisted on consulting their government, but the following afternoon they received a brutal ultimatum: they had precisely one hour; if they had not signed by then, the panzers would roll again. Grey-faced, the chief French delegate, General Charles Huntziger, signed. Next day the French were flown to Rome, to repeat the whole humiliating process before Mussolini.

France was now at peace, but at what cost! Pétain ruled a truncated nation from the small spa town of Vichy. The Germans occupied all the northern and western parts of the country, including Paris and the Channel and Atlantic coasts. France's only air force was in the colonies and its navy was immobilised. It was the fate of the navy which concerned Britain. If Germany or Italy gained control of it, Britain's position would become infinitely more dangerous. This concern eventually led to the Royal Navy attacking the French ships in North Africa.

Vichy rapidly became a dictatorship under Pétain, whose determination to 'save France' developed into collaboration with the Germans. Never had France known such shame. Yet this terrible hour saw the sudden elevation of the man who would salvage French pride. De Gaulle, the tall, prickly tank commander, was now in Bordeaux as Under Secretary for National Defence. On June 17 he went to the airport to see off Churchill's representative to Reynaud, Maj General Edward Spears. As they shook hands through the open door of the small plane, Spears simply yanked a not unwilling de Gaulle on board.

Churchill had already decided that here was the future 'constable of France' – and had heard that de Gaulle would be at risk from Nazi sympathisers if he remained in Bordeaux.

THE OLD MAN OF VICHY

Traitor or patriot? Opinions still differ about Henri Philippe Pétain (1856-1951). A World War I hero at the age of 60, he was later prominent among those keen to have the Maginot Line built.

In May 1940 he became Premier Paul Reynaud's deputy, taking over when Reynaud resigned. Pétain made an armistice that allowed him to govern southern France from Vichy. His deputy, Pierre Laval, wanted alliance with Hitler, but Pétain had no wish to fight Britain and sacked him in December 1940. Hitler made Pétain reinstate Laval in 1942; from that time, Vichy France collaborated with Germany and Pétain was powerless. The Germans occupied Vichy France in 1942, and took Pétain back to Germany when they retreated in 1944, but he returned voluntarily to be tried for treason in 1945. Convicted and sentenced to death, he was reprieved by President de Gaulle and given a life sentence.

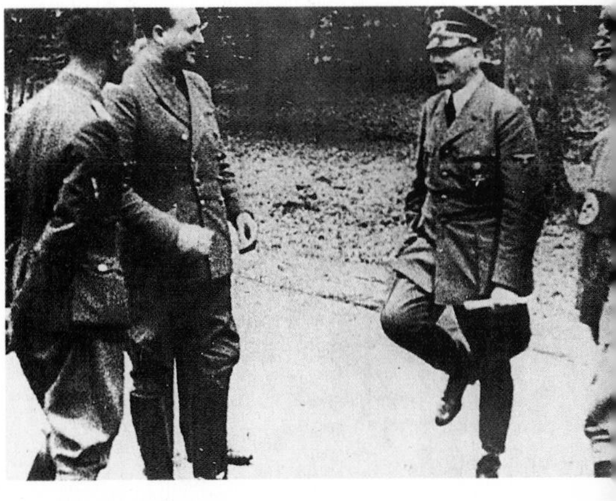

JOY UNCONCEALED Hitler vigorously makes a point to his colleagues at Compiègne, where France capitulated. Allied propagandists multiplied and joined the shots to show Hitler gleefully dancing on the grave of French freedom.

4: BRITAIN STANDS ALONE

Hitler's forces wheeled to obliterate Britain – now the only threat to his iron grip on Europe.

Victory of the Few

For nearly nine centuries the Channel had stood, in Shakespeare's words, as 'a moat defensive . . . against the envy of less happier lands'. If the Führer was to invade Britain, he needed control of that moat – but first, this meant dominating the skies over the Channel . . .

GUNNER'S EYE VIEW Lying in the transparent nose of a Heinkel, a German bomb-aimer/gunner could only watch his escorting fighters swirling above to fend off the thrusts of RAF pilots. They aimed to make a target of him before he dropped his bombs on the airfield that was his target.

BRITAIN'S CRITICAL BATTLE for survival began in earnest just 18 days after the fall of France. Soon after 1 pm on Wednesday, July 10, 1940, radar stations along the south-east coast detected German aircraft assembling behind Calais. A flight of Hurricane fighters took off from RAF Biggin Hill, south-east of London, to protect the target – for nobody doubted that a convoy in the English Channel was the target. The large convoy of coasters steaming west from Dover to Dungeness was a juicy morsel for the bombers of General Albert Kesselring's *Luftflotte* (Air Fleet) 2.

Seven Hurricanes and eight Spitfires were ordered up from Manston, Kent, as reinforcements, and nine Hurricanes from Croydon. As the fighters climbed, their controllers back in the sector operations rooms at Hornchurch, Essex, and Biggin Hill, Kent, radioed them that the ships were already being bombed. But they did not prepare the pilots for what they came upon a few moments later – a sky full of German aircraft.

There were 120 of them – far more than the Luftwaffe had ever before sent against British targets. They flew in three tiers, with Dornier Do17s bombing the convoy, path-clearing twin-engine Messerschmitt Me110s escorting the Dorniers, and nippy single-engine Messerschmitt Me109s high above, providing top cover. Despite the odds, the RAF fighters attacked, some going for the bombers, others for the Me110s.

The 109s came screaming down, but after a brief snapping and snarling 'dogfight' the Germans had to withdraw. Only one of the 150 bombs they dropped had found a target and sunk a ship. All but one of the 'Hurris' and 'Spits' returned safely; they claimed three 'kills'. The lost Hurricane sank in the Channel after colliding with a Dornier, which also crashed. Another 'kite' crashed on landing but the pilot, Sergeant R. Carnall, walked away from the 'prang'. The war in the air had already acquired its own language.

New Zealand-born Flt Lieutenant Alan Deere was another who had a narrow escape, on the previous day. Flying from Manston on his fourth convoy patrol of the day, his flight of Spitfires broke up a formation of about a dozen Me109s and separated to take them on. Deere hurtled at one of them. The next moment the Messerschmitt 'was on top of me, a terrifying blur which blotted out the sky ahead. Then we hit. The force of the impact pitched me violently forward onto my cockpit harness, the straps of which bit viciously into my shoulders. At the same moment, the control column was snatched abruptly from my gripping fingers. In a flash it was over; there was clear sky ahead of me and I was still alive . . . With smoke now pouring into the cockpit I reached blindly for the hood release toggle . . . Again and again I pulled at the toggle but there was no response . . . I was trapped. There was only one thing to do; try to keep the aircraft under control and head for the nearby coast . . .

'Through a miasmatic cloud of flame and smoke the ground suddenly appeared ahead of me . . . then the aircraft struck the ground . . . Fortunately the straps held fast as the aircraft ploughed its way through a succession of splintering posts before finally coming to a halt on the edge of the cornfield . . . frantic with fear, I tore at my harness release pin. And then, with my bare hands wielding the strength of desperation, I battered at the Perspex hood which entombed me. With a splintering crash it finally cracked open.'

FIRST ROUND: *KANALKAMPF*

For the next month, any ships that moved around Britain's south-east coast had droning Dorniers and howling Stuka dive-bombers homing in on them amid clusters of attendant fighters. Dover – now on the frontier of the free world – was forced to experience the harsh taste of modern aerial warfare. This *Kanalkampf* ('Channel Battle') was the opening round of the German fight to open the way for Operation 'Sea Lion' (see box), Hitler's proposed seaborne invasion of Britain.

Field Marshal Hermann Göring, the Nazis' Air Minister and Luftwaffe chief, had set off the *Kanalkampf* on June 30 when he ordered an aerial blockade of Britain. During the following week, Luftwaffe aircraft taking off from captured airfields in France, Belgium and the Netherlands made tentative raids and reconnaissance flights over Britain, while regrouping after the effort and losses of defeating France. The heavy, meticulously planned assaults did not begin until July 10, but by then RAF Fighter Command had fought off a dozen raids, had 13 pilots killed and lost 18 fighters. Göring had assigned General

Albert Kesselring's Luftflotte 2 to the bases east of the Seine, facing the fighters of Air Vice Marshal Keith Park's No 11 Group in the south-east corner of England. Another powerful air fleet, Luftflotte 3 under General Hugo Sperrle, was west of the Seine, facing Park's western sector and Air Vice Marshal Sir Christopher Quintin Brand's No 10 Group in the West Country.

Harbours and shipping were the Germans' main targets – with strikes at the defending fighter planes a welcome bonus. The Luftwaffe pilots were confident – and with good cause. They had swept the skies clean of their enemy in all their campaigns so far. They respected the Hurricanes and Spitfires, but believed that Britain had few of these potent fighters left, whereas just across the Channel they had 760 fighters, 1300 bombers and some 300 of the Stuka dive-bombers which had wrought such havoc in Poland and France.

What the Luftwaffe did not realise was that one of their principal weapons was already lost – surprise. Not only had decoded signals revealed their plans, but Britain's radar system could also pick up approaching raiders.

EARLY WARNING

Around Britain's coast 90 m (300 ft) steel masts had sprouted – the 'ears' of the RDF (radio direction finding) stations. These were the links forming the Chain Home radar system devised by Robert Watson-Watt and his team of scientists – 'boffins' in the jargon of 1940 – at the National Physical Laboratory in Teddington, Middlesex. Radio signals sent out from the masts bounced back from objects in the sky and were picked up by receivers at the radar stations and displayed as blips on cathode-ray tubes in the receiver huts. The blips heralded a raid, and indicated its height, bearing, distance and strength.

Details of the raid were telephoned to a 'filter room' where the raid was plotted with markers on a board along with all other RDF reports, to give an overall picture of the positions, friendly and enemy. The 'filtered' information was passed on to the main Fighter Command Operations Room and to the group operations room and sector operations room in the area where the raid was expected. (The Fighter Command groups were divided into several sectors, and a sector was controlled from its key airfield. A sector generally had several airfields, each home for up to five squadrons, generally of 10-16 aircraft each.)

In all these 'ops' rooms the WAAFs (Women's Auxiliary Air Force members) plotted the moves and controllers watched the overall picture of the fighting develop. It was the controller's message that wakened the young men dozing in their deckchairs in the hot summer sun and sent them running to their aircraft where their mechanics waited to buckle them in. The controllers 'talked' the fighter pilots to the correct height and guided them until the leader spotted the 'bandits'.

LEARNING THE HARD WAY

When the *Kanalkampf* phase of the battle came to an end on August 11, the seabed off Kent and Sussex was littered with wrecked ships and aircraft. Both sides claimed victory. The Germans pounded the convoys until they forced the British ships to keep out of the Straits of Dover in daylight. The Royal Navy withdrew from Dover to Portsmouth. But the Germans had not succeeded in wearing down Fighter Command. The pilots had gained experience and the controllers had honed their skills. The Luftwaffe had lost nearly 300 aircraft, the RAF 150.

Hard lessons had been learned. The Germans, for example, found that the Junkers Ju 87 Stuka could not live against a Spitfire or a Hurricane, and that the Me110 could not be regarded as a front-line day fighter despite its long range. The RAF discovered that the slow and cumbersome Boulton Paul Defiant two-seater fighter – which had all its four guns in a turret operated by a gunner – was a sitting duck; it was withdrawn from the main battle, although it was still pressed into service in desperate moments.

The advantage of fighting over home territory had also become plain. Any Germans shot down over England were lost, while British pilots, if they survived, could fold up their parachute and take a taxi back to their airfield to fly again. British pilots running short of fuel could land on a number of airfields, whereas the Germans had

Operation 'Sea Lion' – the invasion that never happened

'Since England, in spite of her hopeless military situation, shows no signs of being ready to come to an understanding, I have decided to prepare a landing operation against England and, if necessary, to carry it out. The aim of this operation will be to eliminate the English homeland as a base for the prosecution of the war against Germany, and, if necessary, to occupy it.' Thus ran Adolf Hitler's Führer Directive No 16. It was not until July 16, 1940, three weeks after the surrender of France, that he signed it. He hesitated for two main reasons: he did not believe that Britain could fight on alone; and his army was not ready.

Grand Admiral Erich Raeder, Commander in Chief of the *Kriegsmarine* (German Navy), had been half-heartedly planning an amphibious invasion for eight months. Hitler showed little interest until, much to his surprise, Britain turned down his proposals that it should recognise Germany's current position in Europe and he would leave the British Empire alone.

Hitler based Directive No 16 on a memorandum from General Alfred Jodl, head of the High Command's operations staff, and named the plan Operation *Seelöwe* ('Sea Lion'). It would need about 260 000 men, 62 000 horses and 34 000 vehicles. To get them across the Channel – together with everything from ropes and camping stoves to carrier pigeons and life jackets – barges and lighters were strengthened with iron plates and concrete, and wooden platforms were slung between motorised pontoons. It all had to be done in just four weeks: the invasion target date was August 15.

The Luftwaffe was moved up to airfields in northern France. Its commander, Field Marshal Hermann Göring, boldly claimed that in four days he would smash the air defences of southern England and in four weeks the RAF would be wiped from the skies.

The troops would be able to stroll ashore unopposed, taking the Kent and Sussex beaches so that the men of General Gerd von Rundstedt's Army Group A could land and overrun Britain.

Detailed plans were made for military government based on six regions. A 'special search list' named 2300 peers, MPs, trade unionists, journalists and others who could lead dissent; they would be rounded up at once. The economy and art treasures would be stripped, able-bodied males interned and ordinary households robbed of anything useful to Germany's war effort.

With the RAF showing no sign of being 'wiped from the skies', the target date for 'Sea Lion' was moved to September, then to October, and finally to the next spring – by which time Hitler's mind was on the Eastern Front.

HOME ARMY A week after a government appeal in May 1940, 250 000 men had joined the LDV (Local Defence Volunteers). The number doubled by July when they were renamed the Home Guard. Few had uniform or rifle then. Sporting guns, golf clubs or broom-handles had to do. The unpaid men watched public buildings, roads, railways, factories and coasts for enemy troops or infiltrators.

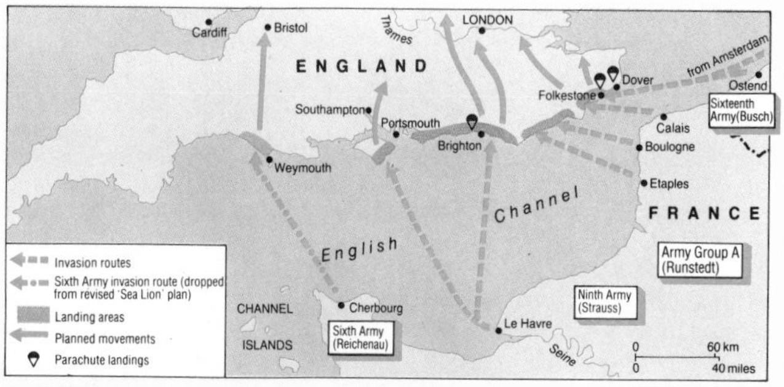

TAKEOVER BID With the south-east seaports captured in the first assault by 90 000 men, the invaders could ship in a further 170 000 troops to swarm over the Home Counties and set up a Nazi government in London.

RIVALS IN THE SKY

Supermarine Spitfire

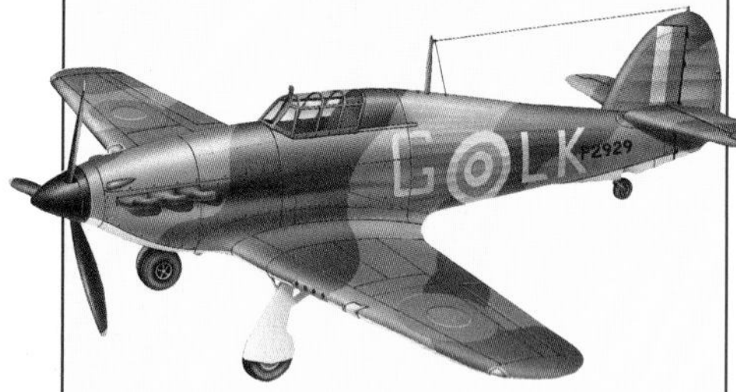

Hawker Hurricane

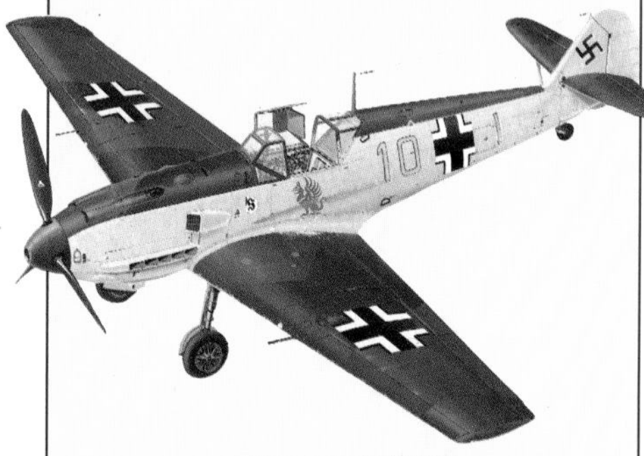

Messerschmitt Me109

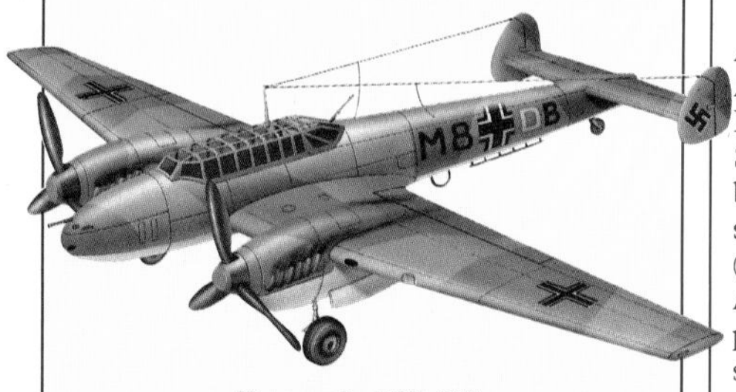

Messerschmitt Me110

When it appeared in 1935, the Me109 became the pacesetter for all new fighters, a slender 550 km/h (342 mph) single-seater monoplane with two machine guns and two cannon. Britain's first answer, in 1937, was the sturdy Hurricane, slower than the Me109 but easy to handle. Its glamorous companion, the Spitfire (1938), could reach 563 km/h (350 mph), and was slim, manoeuvrable and armed with eight machine guns. The Battle of Britain showed up the Me109's great drawback – a range of only 660 km (410 miles). Its raiding partner, the Me110, was designed as a long-range fighter but was slow, hard to handle and unable to match the British duo's agility; it later succeeded as a night fighter.

constantly to keep an eye on their fuel gauges.

The short range of the Me109 – 660 km (410 miles) in early versions – was its chief handicap, but if extra discardable fuel tanks (drop-tanks) were fitted, the pilots hated them. They were not armoured, and just one of the RAF's De Wilde incendiary bullets would blow tank and pilot to eternity. So it was common for Me109 pilots to limp across the Channel with near empty tanks. If such easy prey fell to a marauding Spitfire, the pilot's only hope was that a Heinkel He59 floatplane would soon pick him up.

Each Luftwaffe pilot had a survival kit of an inflatable dinghy, flares, sea dye, and a bright yellow inner helmet. A number of British pilots were lost with only their 'Mae West' inflatable life jackets to float in and, until late August 1940, no organised air-sea rescue service to look for them.

The lesson about tactics, first learned in France, was driven home: the German *Schwarm* ('swarm') formation was superior to the British 'vic'. In the close-spaced inverted V of the vic, the wing men were so concerned with holding position and avoiding collision that they could scan only a small arc to the side. The *Schwarm* or 'finger four' formation had two leaders flying between and slightly ahead of two wing men and all were widely spaced. The wing men could scan to the side and behind, the formation had a fourth firing unit and it could break into two pairs for a pursuit. It was soon copied by the RAF.

Another advantage to the Germans was that they could concentrate their aircraft to deliver two or three blows simultaneously. The RAF fighters had to be ready for an attack anywhere in Britain and could not be concentrated for maximum effect. Air Vice Marshal Richard Saul, for example, itching to get his pilots into the big battles in the south, had to keep the fighters of No 13 Group in the north of England and Scotland ready for attacks from Luftflotte 5, based in Norway and Denmark.

SECOND ROUND: *ADLERANGRIFF*

As the battle moved into its second round in August, Air Chief Marshal Hugh Dowding's RAF Fighter Command had 749 Hurricanes and Spitfires to take on the Luftwaffe's 702 Me109s backed up by 227 Me110s. Göring had at last settled on Tuesday, August 13, as *Adlertag* ('Eagle Day'), the start of the *Adlerangriff* ('Eagle Attack'). This would sweep the RAF – supposedly reeling from the *Kanalkampf* – out of the sky and bring Britain to its knees.

Göring prepared the way with softening-up attacks on August 12. They were aimed at Manston, Lympne and Hawkinge, the forward airfields near the Kent coast. For the first time, the radar stations strung along the south and east coasts were also to be targets – at the insistence of General Wolfgang Martini, a Luftwaffe signals expert who understood what the masts were.

Low-level attacks peppered the airfields with bomb holes, which were quickly filled in – pilots took off from grass, not hard runways – and there was some damage to buildings (*continued on p. 50*)

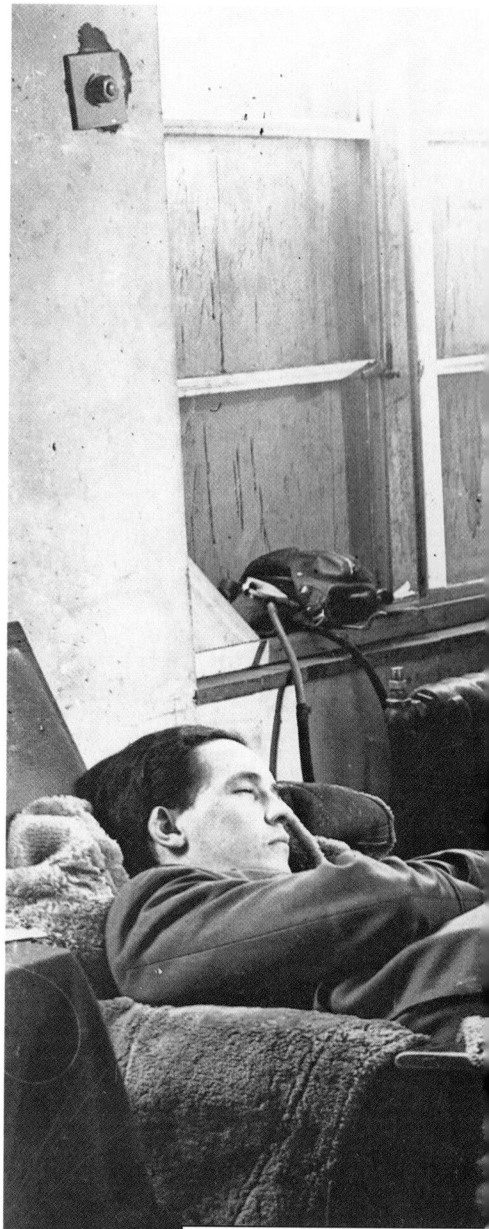

LULLS IN THE FEVER In the nerve-stretching, seemingly endless wait for the urgent command that triggered the scramble for the planes and the skies (inset), pilots toyed with a book or a game of cards to blot out thoughts of the dogfights to come, of close shaves – and of comrades who shared the waiting yesterday but never would again.

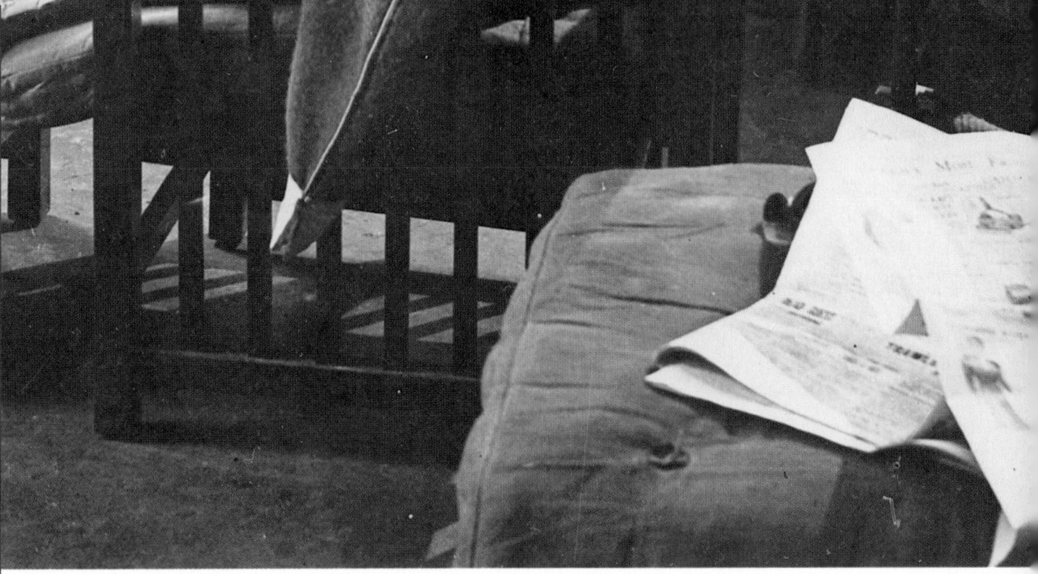

BATTLE OVERVIEW The WAAFs clustered at the 'ops' room table slide counters across the map to mark the progress of raiders and defenders. The controller sitting above saw the raid coming, ordered squadrons into the air and radioed directions to them during the battle. Sometimes their chief, Dowding (right), and sometimes Churchill himself paid a visit. The main Fighter Command operations room kept track of the overall picture in the groups and sectors, and of the state of individual airfields and radar stations (see map below).

A SAVIOUR UNTHANKED

The young Hugh Dowding (1882-1970), no great scholar, was steered by his kindly headmaster father to enter the army. By 1913 he had learned to fly in his spare time. When World War I began, he flew with the Royal Flying Corps in France and commanded 16 Squadron. He was introspective, abstemious and ten years older than most other fighter pilots – who nicknamed him 'Stuffy'.

In the 1930s, as a senior Air Ministry staff officer, Dowding brought in, against much opposition, the monoplane Hurricane and Spitfire fighters and was closely involved with Robert Watson-Watt's development of radar. His seniority and experience should have made Dowding Chief of Air Staff, but he was a dour man with a sharp tongue who made enemies easily. He was given Fighter Command, but received several dismissal notices because of his age – only to be reprieved. His last reprieve came only five days before the Battle of Britain began.

Although his prudent use of the small number of pilots available proved successful, Dowding was harshly criticised as too cautious. Once the battle was won he was asked to vacate his office in 24 hours. All Churchill's attempts to find Dowding a senior post were scotched by the Air Ministry. His only rewards were winning the battle, the admiration of his young pilots – 'Dowding's Chicks' – and, after an insulting lapse of three years, a peerage.

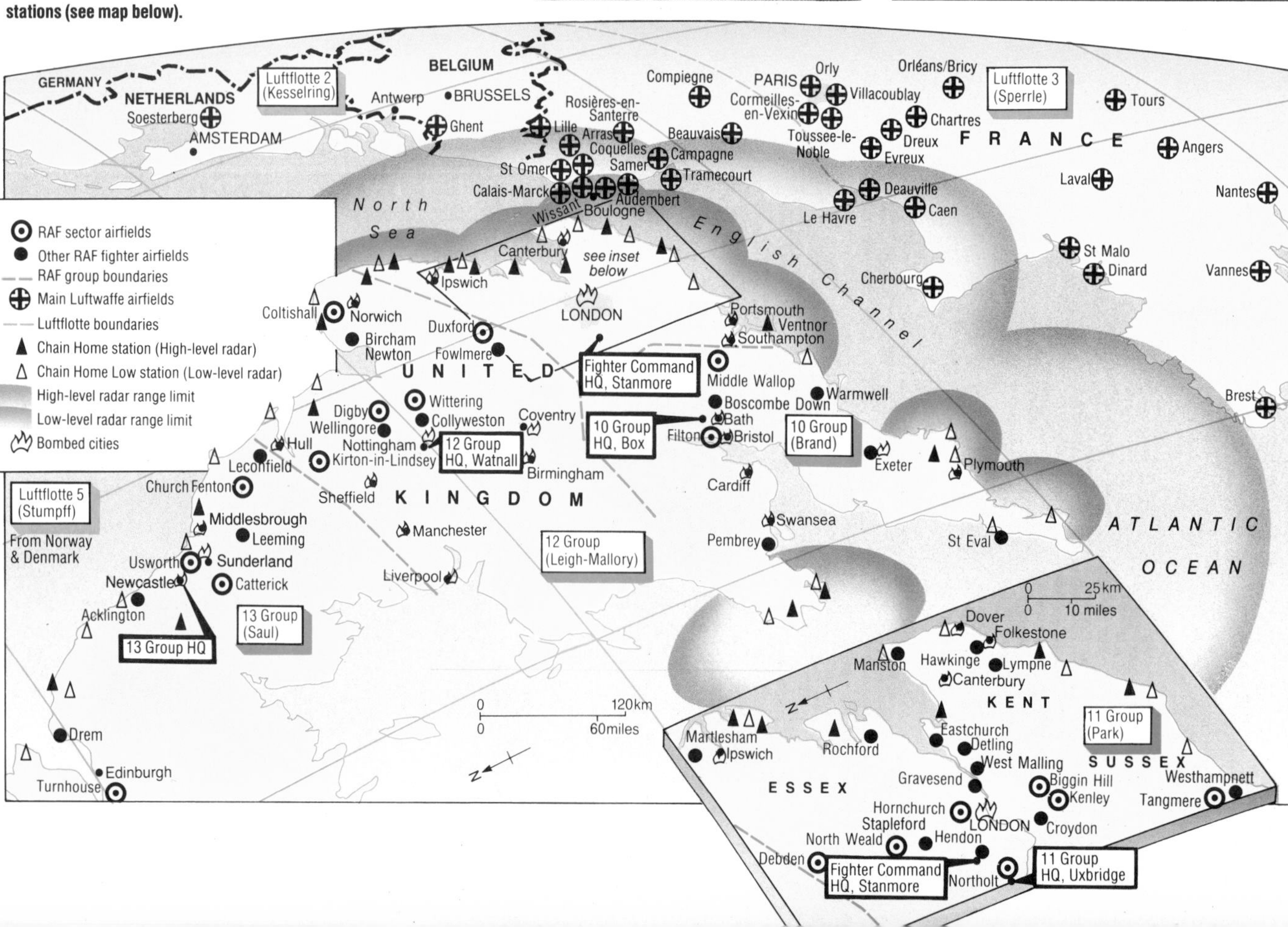

Sky-high heroes

The hunting instinct and a willingness to get in close to enemy planes were qualities shared by 'aces' of all nationalities in the Battle of Britain.

The Luftwaffe and RAF pilots all looked absurdly young. Photographs show them lounging in the sunshine, smoking pipes, writing letters and reading while they waited for the call to action. In the evening there was beer and schnapps for the Germans, beer and whisky for the British and their allies. Energetic horseplay and legions of admiring girlfriends were part of their lives. Even when the battle began in earnest, life on the airfields remained much as before for the Germans. They were an elite, living off the best food and wine France could provide. They were not under attack. But the RAF pilots often returned to an airfield that was a smoking ruin.

As the fighting grew more furious, pilots on both sides became desperately tired. As many of their friends were killed, horseplay gave way to a gallows gaiety in the face of death.

The best known ace was Douglas Bader, but the battle's top RAF scorers were the Czech Josef František, and Eric Lock (16 kills) who was killed in August 1941. Among the survivors were the South African former seaman Adolphus 'Sailor' Malan, who shot down 35 before the war was over, and James 'Ginger' Lacey, credited with 28. Also in the long list of heroes were Richard Hillary, dreadfully burned but saved by plastic surgery to fight again before he was killed in 1943; Peter Townsend, who achieved a different fame from his romance with Princess Margaret; and the New Zealanders Colin Gray and Alan Deere (three kills).

Foremost among the German *Experten* was Adolf Galland, who shot down 57 RAF fighters during the battle and had a war total of 104. His great rival was Werner Mölders (with 20 kills). Helmut Wick (56 kills) survived until November 1940.

'DOLFI' GALLAND (above) He lived, and was a guest at RAF battle reunions.

JOSEF FRANTIŠEK (below) He died, but downed 17 German planes first.

WERNER MÖLDERS (above) Died 1941; 55 kills in all.

COLIN GRAY (above) New Zealander with 13 kills.

PETER TOWNSEND (left) He shot down five planes.

JAMES LACEY (above) A battle survivor who downed 28 in all.

LEGLESS WONDER Douglas Bader (1910-82; fourth from right) lost both legs in a fighter crash in 1931 but proved he could still fly and rejoined the RAF in 1939. His skill impressed his 242 Squadron of Canadian pilots (right); he claimed ten Battle of Britain 'kills' and 13 others. Bader crashed in France in 1941, was captured, and was sent to Colditz Castle after escape attempts. He won the DSO, DFC, *Légion d'Honneur* and *Croix de Guerre*. His postwar work for the disabled won him a knighthood.

and equipment, but the airfields remained operational. More serious was the damage to the radar chain. The Ventnor station on the Isle of Wight was so badly damaged that it was out of action for nearly two weeks, but others escaped serious damage because their latticework towers were little harmed by near misses.

The August 12 attacks should have achieved more but, inexplicably, Göring ignored Hitler's orders to concentrate on 'the flying units, ground organisation and supply installations of the RAF' and instead targeted docks and shipping as well. Then *Adlertag* dawned with south-east England covered in thick cloud. Göring ordered a postponement, but some squadrons never received the order, while others got it when they were already in the air. So the morning's battles developed haphazardly, with aircraft searching for each other in the cloud.

Keith Park in the south-east fed his No 11 Group squadrons frugally into the fray – a frustrating exercise for the pugnacious New Zealander. He longed to take on the Luftwaffe with his full force, but he knew the main battle was still to come and refused to be drawn, even though the German Me109s chased across Kent and Sussex trying to lure Park into a costly battle.

The weather cleared a little in the afternoon and *Adlerangriff* was relaunched. The airfields of southern England were hammered. On the ground, the people of Kent and Sussex kept life ticking over in their shops and offices, or worked on in orchards and wheatfields. They looked up at the scribbling vapour trails and hurtling black blobs swooping and spiralling seemingly at random like bluebottles just before they die. Sometimes a blob would take shape as it fell; sometimes, heart-stoppingly, its shape splintered into fragments. The engines screamed and machine guns chattered high above, and at times it seemed to be raining cartridge cases.

In the ops rooms the WAAFs listened to the pilots' excited cries and too often, unbearably, heard them shrieking as they burned to death in the cockpits of shattered planes.

As the long *Adlertag* ended with the frenzy of the battles replaced by the droning of the night bombers, both sides licked their wounds. It had been a day of intense effort. The Luftwaffe had flown nearly 1500 sorties, the RAF 700. A number

MATCH FOR GÖRING From the French coast the Luftwaffe commander Hermann Göring (left, centre) trains his binoculars on the intransigent target across the Channel. Dowding's fighter pilots were outwitting him in their agile Spitfires (above), and by late September tired crews, such as No 249 Squadron at North Weald, Essex (below), could smile again.

of airfields had been hit, but none was put out of action. Far from knocking out the RAF, the day's fighting had cost the Luftwaffe 46 aircraft against the RAF's 13. Seven British pilots had died.

STRETCHED TO THE LIMIT

Next day, Wednesday, bad weather and the need to recover from *Adlertag* kept most of the German squadrons on the ground. Even so, the Luftwaffe lost 27 planes and the RAF 11. Thursday, the 15th, brought the heaviest day's fighting of the whole battle. Aircraft rose to the attack from airfields stretching from Brittany to Norway, in an attempt to overwhelm Britain's defences. Soon the fighting ranged from Tyneside all down the east coast and along the south coast to Devon.

Saul's No 13 Group in the north was first into action. He reacted boldly, sending five squadrons – almost all he had – into battle against 63 He111s and 21 Me110s of Luftflotte 5, an air armada stacked up in three waves. Saul's pilots dived out of the sun, harrying and breaking up the Luftwaffe formations to such good effect that many of the bombers dropped their loads into the sea. When it was all over, Saul's pilots had knocked down 15 without losing a single plane themselves.

Meanwhile, Air Vice Marshal Trafford Leigh-Mallory, commander of No 12 Group in the Midlands, sent a squadron of Spitfires and half a squadron of Hurricanes against 50 unescorted Ju88 bombers approaching from Denmark. The fighters shot down seven Junkers but the unprotected force was not wiped out, as it could have been, and enough of them got through to bomb Great Driffield aerodrome in Yorkshire.

In the south, the pilots of Park's and Brand's groups were having a torrid time, for the bombers were heavily escorted by Me109s. Crashed aircraft littered the south coast, some plunging into soft farmland at such speed that they disappeared. Many of the bombers got through to their targets, the airfields and aircraft factories.

When the raids died away at 5 pm – it was said that the Luftwaffe flew office hours – the Germans had flown nearly 1800 sorties and lost 90 aircraft. The British had flown nearly 1000 sorties and lost 42 fighters.

The battle was resumed with equal ferocity the next day, Friday, August 16. Winston Churchill, unable to contain his excitement, spent the afternoon in No 11 Group's operations room at Uxbridge. When the fighting died away, the Prime Minister was driven to his country home, Chequers, with Maj General Hastings ('Pug') Ismay, his chief representative on the Chiefs of Staff Committee. Ismay recalled later that Churchill's first words were: 'Don't speak to me; I have never been so moved.' After about five minutes he leaned forward and said: 'Never in the field of human conflict has so much been owed by so many to so few' – words that would become famous when Churchill repeated them in a House of Commons speech four days later.

It was on that Friday that Flt Lieutenant James Nicolson of 249 Squadron won Fighter Command's only Victoria Cross of the war. He was 'bounced' (caught off guard) by an Me109 while patrolling in a Hurricane over Southampton and within seconds his plane was on fire. Hit in the head and half-blinded, he was about to bale out when the 109 flashed past him. At that moment revenge was sweeter than safety; he followed the Messerschmitt down, got it in his sights and pressed the gun button until the 109 hit the sea. As Nicolson pulled back on the stick, he noticed for the first time that his hands were on fire. Everything was white-hot. He baled out, the cold air slicing agonisingly into his burns. When another 109 flew towards him, he slumped in his harness, playing dead. The German plane flew off, but a new danger arose: the local Home Guard opened fire on the descending pilot. Although Nicolson survived this brush with death, he was killed in 1945 in the Far East.

SPIRITS FLAG

Legends of courage multiplied as Dowding's dwindling pilots fought on through the summer. Among the Luftwaffe, too, there were many daring exploits. The German fliers were uncrushable fighters, eager young pilots who went on their missions singing: *'Wir fliegen gegen England . . .'*

We fly against England,
How red the roses bloom.
We fly against England,
And with us flieth doom!

As the battle continued through August, it seemed that Göring might indeed wear down Fighter Command. It was running out of pilots, even though Poles, Czechoslovaks, Frenchmen and seven Americans had joined in – flying alongside Commonwealth pilots such as the New Zealander Alan Deere, the South African 'Sailor' Malan, and a whole squadron of Canadians. There were Fleet Air Arm and bomber pilots, even test pilots who volunteered.

The training time had to be slashed until 18-year-olds were going into combat with only ten hours on single-seat fighters. Many of them died before they learned how to fight. The pilots were also worn out. Dowding rotated exhausted squadrons to quiet sectors and fed in fresh young men, but the relief was short and partial.

The German air crews were equally exhausted – and short of planes, as intercepted signals showed. Morale began to slump as many bombers were shot down and others limped home with dead and wounded men aboard. The attackers no longer sang on the way to England, but they kept on bombing the airfields. Göring had given orders on August 18 for the fighters to stay with the bombers. Previously, fighters allowed themselves to be drawn away by the RAF fighters or lost their bombers in bad weather; there was no radio communication between bombers and fighters, and they could not link up again. Each bomber was now given two fighters to protect it (which curtailed the fighters' freedom of action). Fewer bombers came, but it was much harder for the RAF to get at them. There were now days when the 109s shot down more planes than they lost.

On the ground in Britain the situation was just as serious. Of No 11 Group's airfields, Manston was out of action except for emergency landings; West Malling, Lympne and Hawkinge were just holding out; Tangmere, Kenley, Biggin Hill, Hornchurch and Debden were severely damaged. The survival of Fighter Command was on a knife edge. If the Luftwaffe had then inflicted similar damage to the operations rooms or telephone systems of other groups, the intricate structure of the whole command would have crumbled.

Fighter Command was not helped by internal conflicts. Leigh-Mallory's No 12 Group squadrons always seemed to arrive late to guard Park's airfields when his squadrons had been sent off to intercept German formations over the Channel. Leigh-Mallory also questioned Air Chief Marshal Dowding's tactics. Like the legless fighter ace Douglas Bader, he favoured the 'big-wing' tactic of meeting the attackers with four or five massed squadrons rather than pecking at them with small groups of fighters. On the first few occasions the big wing was used it was not successful. It was slow to assemble, unwieldy in action and committed too many of the RAF's scarce resources to a single action. Leigh-Mallory claimed that the big wing had turned back German raids, but it was just as likely that the raiders were ready for turning back anyway, because his group's area was at the limit of the 109s' range.

CHANGE OF PLAN

As August passed, Göring was confident enough to assure Hitler that a few more days of concentrated attack on Fighter Command would enable Operation 'Sea Lion' to go ahead. On August 24 he initiated a new ruse. The Luftwaffe made a feint attack to draw the RAF, then made the real attack when the fighters were refuelling.

But on the same day there occurred one of those unplanned incidents that change the course of battles – even of history. In order to increase the pressure on the RAF, Göring had ordered his bombers to work at night as well as 'office hours', attacking targets all over Britain. One target – London – was forbidden because of fear of retaliatory strikes at German cities. That night a flight of He111s lost their way to their targets – aircraft factories at Rochester and Kingston and oil refineries at Thames Haven. They dropped their bombs over the City of London. It was the excuse Churchill was awaiting. On the following night 81 British bombers made for Berlin and half found the target. This attack enraged the Nazi leaders, who had believed Berlin would never be touched. The city was hit four more times in the next ten days, and on September 4 Hitler threatened that if British attacks continued, 'we will raze their cities to the ground'.

Three days later, on a hot Saturday afternoon, the Luftwaffe obeyed the *(continued on p. 54)*

'The world's on fire'

Saturday, September 7, 1940. The Luftwaffe turns its attacks from RAF bases to London. That first night of the Blitz killed or wounded nearly 2000, but their sacrifice was a turning point.

THE FAINT DRONE grew to a deafening thunder and the sunlit afternoon sky filled with menace as hundreds of bombers flocked over London's East End. People came out to stare: could they be 'ours'? Not so. They were the slender Dorniers and chunky Heinkels expected a year before, but now a terrifying surprise. In the moments before the bombs dropped, people were transfixed. Then their world changed.

Years later Len Jones, 18 years old in 1940, recalled how 'bombs began to fall, and shrapnel was going along King Street, dancing off the cobbles . . . the suction and compression from the high explosive blasts just pulled and pushed you . . . you could actually feel your eyeballs being sucked out . . . The suction was so vast, it ripped my shirt . . . I couldn't get my breath, the smoke was like acid . . . And these bombers just kept on and on; the whole road was moving, rising and falling.'

Many East Enders were killed in an instant. After an hour the bombardment stopped, then the next onslaught began just after 8 pm. Waves of planes – 318 of them altogether – kept up the attack until 4.30 am on Sunday.

That afternoon, the Luftwaffe Commander in Chief, Reichsmarschall Hermann Göring, had stood with Field Marshal Albert Kesselring on the cliffs at Cap Blanc Nez, just south-west of Calais. They watched the stream of bombers, escorted by over 600 fighters, roar north-westward to deal death and destruction principally to London's docks.

But the severe damage to the terraces of small houses behind was no accident. The death and injury of civilians, Hitler hoped, might force Churchill to sue for peace. At least it would cause confusion before the Germans invaded. Equally important, Hitler saw the raid as vengeance for the RAF's bombing of Berlin

CRASH COURSE The inexperienced fire-fighters of Saturday noon changed within days into veteran, expert, exhausted heroes. Most of them were auxiliaries, many with other jobs. They fought to contain unprecedented fires, limit destruction, keep open escape routes and rescue trapped victims.

two weeks before. And Göring believed that in the raid the British would lose 'the tiny remainder of their fighters'.

They were both wrong. By switching the attacks from the vital RAF airfields, Göring had thrown away his chance of winning the Battle of Britain. Not that it seemed like that when the bombs poured down. More than 300 tonnes crushed a wide swathe of east London. 'Send all the pumps you've got,' pleaded one fire officer. 'The whole bloody world's on fire.'

All fire-fighters had been alerted when intercepted German signals revealed an attack was coming – but there was little enough the inexperienced firemen could do: after a dry summer, the Thames had fallen and they had difficulty getting their pumps to work.

During those hours of terror, the RAF lost 42 planes, the Luftwaffe 63. When morning came the fires were still burning, Union Jacks were planted in the rubble, and signs on the doors of shattered shops announced 'Business as usual'. But life was not to be as usual for months – or ever again for some. Thousands of homes had been destroyed and some 450 people had died. They were only the first.

1 It is 10 pm on Saturday night, and the raid is at its height. Tower Bridge survives this and all the successive nights of the Blitz, though many other London landmarks will disappear before the war's end. Down river from the bridge the docklands are illuminated by more than 1000 fires. Already they are out of control, and civilians and fireman are dying under seas of flame and fallen rubble.

BOMBED OUT Thousands of dazed survivors returned next morning to collapsed or unsafe homes. They found disproportionate comfort in saving a few possessions and huddling with them in the middle of the street away from falling masonry, and in recounting the night's experiences to neighbours. A rest centre became their refuge during the days or weeks of trudging to find another home.

2 A flight of Heinkel He111s, having dropped their bombs on Surrey Commercial Docks, fly up-river before turning to head for their bases near Calais. They are part of the horde that keep coming until dawn.

3 Searchlights rake the sky to pinpoint the raiders and hold them in a beam long enough for anti-aircraft gunners to sight and fire at them; only two or three German planes are downed by flak during the whole night.

4 Pillars of smoke in the glowing sky guide the German bombers to the docklands. The fires still raging from the afternoon raid light up every detail of their targets.

5 London Docks erupt. Barrels of rum explode from smashed warehouses, drums of paint flare to white heat and melting rubber billows black, choking smoke. Blazing sugar cascades over the wharves and floats aflame on the water. Swarms of rats flee blazing buildings.

6 Water jets, puny sprays against the inferno, arch from the fireboats that work up the creeks and along the burning wharves. At London Docks the task is hopeless; the heat forces the boats back to the Surrey shore – and even that far away their paint blisters.

7 Barrage balloons lift a forest of steel cables over London. Clearly visible in the radiant sky, they are not the hazard they are meant to be – yet they force bombers to fly at a height that lessens their accuracy.

8 The biggest fire of the night is at the Surrey Commercial Docks. Fences, telegraph poles, barges, warehouses, even the wooden blocks surfacing the roads are burning. Embers as big as a man's head whirl off to start new fires many streets away. Beyond, flames engulf the West and East India Docks.

9 The dockland parish of Rotherhithe, and Limehouse and Wapping across the Thames, suffer the worst casualties of the night. Whole streets disappear. Fathers, mothers and children are crushed beneath their falling homes, or burned, or slashed by flying glass.

'SMILING ALBERT' Commending some of his wounded airmen, Albert Kesselring, commander of Luftflotte 2, lives up to the affectionate nickname coined by his pilots. Men and leaders alike respected his astute judgment, but it let him down when he backed Göring's shift of bombing from airfields to cities. The shift enabled the RAF to survive.

Führer's personal orders and made the attack on London that was to change the course of the Battle of Britain (see feature, p. 52). It was a fatal mistake. The terror and slaughter of civilians, the destruction of docks, railways and factories were shocking losses, but not decisive. Who ruled the air over Britain was what mattered. When the Luftwaffe suddenly shifted its attacks from the airfields to London, the RAF were able to fill in the holes, repair the equipment, reconnect the communications, and draw breath.

The fighting in the air went on just as fiercely, with the Hurricanes and Spitfires hurling themselves at the endless bombing formations that droned towards the capital. Until now Londoners had thrilled at the scores chalked up on the newspaper placards, as if a test match was in progress. Now they were no longer spectators, they were in the middle of it. The scores were grossly exaggerated; the Air Ministry gave accurate figures for British losses, but the pilots mistakenly claimed many more kills than they actually achieved. With several pilots squirting their guns at the same crippled enemy, each one might claim the victory.

Similarly the Luftwaffe heavily exaggerated the number of RAF fighters they shot down. The German bomber pilots grew cynical about these claims. If the figures were true, no Hurricanes or Spitfires could be left in action, yet they were still harrying the bombers. The RAF's losses were indeed severe. In the first week of September, Fighter Command lost 185 aircraft against the Luftwaffe's 225. On September 7, the day the London Blitz began, the RAF lost 42 planes, destroyed or badly damaged, and – more seriously – had 17 pilots killed or wounded.

MAKE-OR-BREAK DAY

Clearly the battle could not continue at such a pitch; it must soon be won or lost. The climax came on Sunday, September 15, a fine still day. Kesselring mustered all his force to make two attacks on London while Sperrle attacked Portland and Eastleigh, near Southampton, to keep Brand's pilots busy in the west. The blips began to show on the radar sets at 10.50 am as the formations gathered over the French coast. Churchill chose this day to visit Park's headquarters at Uxbridge. Down there, 17 m (50 ft) underground, all was quiet efficiency. High above Kent 100 Luftwaffe bombers escorted by some 400 fighters were heading for London.

Park was ready for them. His young pilots had enjoyed a comparatively easy week, their exhaustion had eased and their zest had returned. Park put up 11 squadrons (roughly 100 planes) to slash at the German formations. Brand sent a Spitfire squadron to guard Park's western flank, and Leigh-Mallory dispatched his big wing of five squadrons, commanded by Bader, to meet the Germans over London. The fight raged all the way from the coast. Park put up six more squadrons, leaving only four in reserve.

The biggest clash came just before midday, as four squadrons of Hurricanes attacked the bombers head-on, breaking up their formations, while Bader led his fighters against the escorting Messerschmitts. Whirling dogfights swooping over the brilliant autumn sky drove off some of the escort, yet still the Germans flew on over the south-eastern suburbs – though no longer in tight groups. When the bombs came down, they were scattered too widely for maximum effect. At last the Germans turned for home, and the RAF men landed to refuel and rearm.

While Park's men were wolfing down sandwiches at their scattered bases and their planes were hastily made ready again, another 150 German bombers were gathering in north-east France to renew the attack in the afternoon. This time Kesselring sent in fighters ahead of the Heinkels and Dorniers, hoping to brush aside the defenders. They did not succeed, but while they engaged RAF pilots in individual combat the bombers got as far as east London. Park asked Leigh-Mallory for three of No 12 Group's squadrons to be put at his disposal, and when Churchill asked him: 'What other reserves have we?' Park replied: 'There are none.'

'The odds were great,' Churchill wrote, 'our margins small; the stakes infinite.' But the bombers were met by a massive attack from Bader's big wing of 60 Hurricanes and Spitfires. The unnerved German pilots peeled off to left and right, and again the scattered bomber formations hurriedly dropped their loads over east and south-east London. They did considerable damage, but nowhere near as much as they would have done had the armada remained intact.

As the last stragglers made off across the Channel and the 'all clear' siren sounded, the newsboys started to yell the score: 185 to 26. After the war the number of German aircraft lost in combat that day was whittled down to 57. It did not matter; the British people knew immediately that Fighter Command was not finished and never would be. Dowding's parsimonious strategy had won – just. More important, the German pilots – who had been told for weeks that the RAF was down to its 'last 50 Spitfires' – and their commanders knew it, too.

From that day's victory, honoured ever since on Battle of Britain Day, the Germans realised that they would not gain supremacy in the air, there could be no easy invasion of Britain, there could be no swift end to the war. Although the raids continued through October, they would not achieve their purpose. The 3080 young men – the Few – of Fighter Command had thwarted Hitler's plan. Two days later Hitler told Grand Admiral Raeder, Commander in Chief of the German Navy, that he had decided to postpone Operation 'Sea Lion' indefinitely.

GÖRING – SUPREME PRETENDER

While his diplomat father served abroad, the young Hermann Göring (1893-1946) lived in a castle near Nuremberg owned by his mother's Jewish lover; Nuremberg, Jews and large estates were to be interwoven throughout Göring's life.

During World War I Göring became a fighter ace who shot down 22 planes and won the highest award of the Kaiser's Germany, the *Pour le Mérite*. Afterwards he was a commercial pilot in Denmark and Sweden. When he met Hitler in 1921, he became a fervent supporter. He was badly wounded by police preventing a Nazi march in 1923, and became addicted to the morphine prescribed for his pain.

He became a member of the Reichstag in 1928, and was soon leader of the Nazi party there and President of the Reichstag. When Hitler became Chancellor in 1933, Göring was soon prime minister of Germany's strongest state, Prussia. He quelled democracy through the Gestapo, which he established, and the concentration camps which he set up. Next he became Air Minister, Commander in Chief of the Luftwaffe, and overall head of the Nazi economy.

Vain and self-indulgent though he was, Göring also possessed a magnetic charm that made him popular not only with other Nazis but also among foreign diplomats. He acquired vast wealth, estates and art treasures, and in July 1940 took the special rank of *Reichsmarschall* ('Imperial Marshal'). When war came, he was named Hitler's successor.

For all his position and charm, the Reichsmarschall was powerless to press his own plans against Hitler's opposition. Unable to convince his Führer that Germany needed more fighters, not bombers, he lost face when the Luftwaffe allowed the British to escape at Dunkirk and then lost the Battle of Britain. When Operation 'Sea Lion' was called off, he went away to sulk on his hunting estate. He became more dependent on morphine and unstable in his moods, which roused resentment in the other Nazi leaders.

When the Luftwaffe failed to get supplies to the Sixth Army, struggling at Stalingrad in 1942-3, Göring was further disgraced. Even so, he declared that he was taking over as the Third Reich crumbled in 1945. Hitler ordered his arrest, but it was the Allies who took him. At the Nuremberg Trial the over-confident, adroit chief representative of Nazism was found guilty of war crimes and sentenced to death. The night before he was to hang he poisoned himself.

CARTOONIST'S DREAM Göring liked to be known as 'the Iron Man', but his pilots nicknamed him 'Fatty'.

Defiant cities survive the ordeal of the Blitz by night

Since Hitler could not occupy Britain, he would savage it. Germany's bombers aimed first to pulverise centres of war production, but before long any target – military or civilian – seemed legitimate. To the British public who suffered the Blitz it signalled that 'We're all in it now'.

LONDONERS became troglodytes, 20th-century cave-dwellers seeking shelter in whatever safe niches a metropolitan landscape could offer. As soon as night fell, thousands upon thousands disappeared into underground stations, public shelters or cramped metal tunnels in their own gardens, setting up camp and not emerging until dawn and the last all-clear sounded.

Night after night, the melancholy rise and fall of the warning siren heralded the throbbing engine beat of the bombers. It was the night bombers that now carried the main German attack. Britain's night fighters – Defiants, Hurricanes, even Gladiator biplanes and Blenheim light bombers – hunted them blindly and, not surprisingly, could do little to foil the raids.

Searchlights would weave their patterns and suddenly come together in a cone, pinning a bomber against the night sky like a silver moth as the ack-ack shells blinked redly all round it. Then, with a disdainful dip of its wings, it would be gone, leaving the lights to hunt in vain.

As the lovely summer of 1940 drifted into an unsettled autumn, the Luftwaffe's daylight raids did not come to a sudden end. Small formations of fast Junkers Ju88 bombers escorted by ten times their number of fighters made lightning attacks. Some lone fighter-bombers made nuisance raids; and on October 28, more than 450 bomb-carrying Messerschmitt Me109s and Me110s made a mass attack on targets in London and the south-eastern counties (21 were shot down for the loss of one British fighter). But the great battles of September 15 had proved that RAF Fighter Command would not be beaten. Luftwaffe chief Hermann Göring abandoned the battle, and in mid-November went on a long leave.

Among the attackers, briefly, were Italians, sent by Mussolini to Belgium. The pilots had no experience of fighting in such poor weather as afflicted Britain. Their fighters, Fiat CR42 bi-

FLYING THE BEAMS

The first German radio-guidance system for night bombers in the Blitz was *Knickebein* ('Crooked Leg'). A giant transmitter directed two narrow, slightly overlapping beams at the target. A pilot who 'flew the beam' along the overlap heard a continuous tone in his earphones. If he strayed to right or left, he heard short Morse dots or long Morse dashes and adjusted accordingly. Another signal cutting across the beam gave the cue to drop the bombs.

Dr R.V. Jones of Air Intelligence fathomed the system and devised countermeasures. Detector planes scanned each night for beams (called 'Headaches'). When they located one, a false beam (an 'Aspirin') was put out in that area giving loud Morse dashes. The German pilots adjusted course, lost touch with the real beam and never found the target.

Similar false signals ('Bromides') interfered with the more refined *X-Gerät* ('X Apparatus') system. In this, three signals crossing the main beams were linked to a device that calculated speed and distance. When it showed that the plane was at the target, it released the bombs. The next German development, *Y-Gerät*, was thwarted by intercepting and retransmitting the signal in such a way that the bombers dropped their bombs too soon, over open country.

SERENE SURVIVOR Floating above fiery chaos, the dome of London's St Paul's Cathedral inspires belief that evil Nazi ambitions will not defeat order, beauty and eternal values.

HOME COMFORTS Lovingly applied plaster and tiles and a neat roof garden imposed normality on the corrugated iron tunnel of an Anderson shelter sunk in a damp hole. It was the family bedroom that withstood all but a direct hit.

planes, were too slow and inadequately armed and armoured. Their sturdy Fiat BR20 Cicogna bombers were obsolescent by Battle of Britain standards. Before November was out, Mussolini stopped the raids. In all, the Italians flew 1071 sorties for the loss of 20 men and eight planes.

CIVILIANS IN THE FRONT LINE

What developed after the terrible night of September 7/8, when the London Blitz began, was systematic destruction by night in Britain's cities. London, Southampton, Plymouth, Bristol, Liverpool, Hull, Coventry, Derby, Leicester, Sheffield, Birmingham, Manchester, Glasgow and Belfast were among the cities that suffered. The targets were centres making armaments, aircraft and steel, and ports and naval docks.

Although the provincial cities shared the terror inflicted on London, none of them suffered such prolonged ferocity; two or three consecutive nights of bombing at a time were more common for them. For London, September 7/8 was only the first of 57 consecutive nights of bombardment – and there were many more after the first 57.

On Sunday, September 8, the second night, every railway line into the capital from the south was hit, but even so people got to work the next day. A young Tooting woman hitched a lift on a lorry and then walked to her insurance office in the City. Still working among rubble, soot, falling tiles, tilting doorways and flamethrowing gas mains were the weary firemen; she crunched over glass to give them her sandwiches.

Often the day's work was to clean up damaged, dust-laden furniture and sort out the blast-strewn files, books and other paraphernalia of commerce. As the nights drew in, shops and offices closed early; people wanted to get home or out of the target area altogether before the nightly siren. Many did not make for the shelter when the sirens sounded. Instead they huddled in a cupboard under the stairs or under a sturdy dining table.

The huddlers clung to vestiges of normality. When a Manchester ten-year-old heard his father say, 'That's a Jerry. I can tell by the engine', he later recalled: 'I duly took my cup of tea and squatted between the table legs with my back to the wall. Just as I had settled comfortably the plane dropped a land mine. There was a tremendous explosion.' The huge land mines, usually weighing 725 kg (1600 lb), floated down on parachutes to demolish whole areas of houses. These were truly terror weapons.

In the first half of September, 2000 civilians were killed and about 8000 wounded, 80 per cent of the casualties being in London – and the toll rose steadily. In the third week of September, 1500 civilians were killed, 1300 of them in London. During the whole of the month, 6954 civilians were killed, most of them in London.

After one of his periodic visits to badly bombed areas, Churchill wrote: 'In all my life I have never been treated with so much kindness as by the people who have suffered most. One would have thought that I had brought them some fine substantial benefit which would improve their lot in life . . . when we got back into the car a harsher mood swept over this haggard crowd. "Give it 'em back", they cried, and "Let *them* have it too".'

Through the nights when fires raged, masonry fell, landmarks vanished, buses were swallowed by craters and firepumps were useless because of damaged water mains, the ARP wardens, firefighters, heavy rescue squads and UXB (unexploded bomb) squads worked in the utmost danger. They dug out casualties and tended the wounded, knowing that it would all be there to do again the next night.

BOFFINS TO THE RESCUE

The defence of the cities at first fell almost entirely to Lt General Sir Frederick Pile's Anti-Aircraft Command, commonly called the Ack-Ack. Its batteries of 3 in (76.2 mm), 3.7 in (94 mm) and 4.5 in (114 mm) guns were supported by searchlights whose beams probed the night sky for enemy planes, and by barrage balloons that made the bombers fly high and lose accuracy. The Ack-Ack's problem was the same as the RAF's: it had no sure way of finding the bombers and no way of firing accurately in the dark.

Pile gathered his forces around major targets to create a barrage of fire whose very sound and fury lifted the spirits of those under attack. A Londoner, a boy of 12 during the Blitz, recalled how 'mobile gun units would roar up the road, clamp down, and fire a few salvos before rushing off elsewhere. I don't think they ever shot any enemy planes down, but it helped morale.'

In the pipeline were two inventions that were to replace the Ack-Ack's hopeful barrage by precision shooting. These were radar sets, code-named 'George' and 'Elsie', that enabled crews to aim their guns and searchlights accurately.

The RAF boffins were also working to devise an air-to-air radar set small enough to fit into night fighters. These AI (Aircraft Identification) sets, code-named 'Smellers', were eventually to make the skies over Britain risky for the night bombers, but at the start of the Blitz the first cumbersome sets could fit only in the Blenheim – which was too slow to catch the German bombers even when the 'Smellers' picked them up.

During the first months of the Battle of Britain, the Germans used radio direction beams to guide the bombers towards their target (see box, *Flying the beams*). One sophisticated system, *X-Gerät* ('X Apparatus'), was fitted in an elite unit, *Kampfgruppe* (Battle Group) 100 or KG 100, which led raids. A pathfinder from KG 100 dropped incendiaries which lit the target for the bombers that followed with high explosives. With such pinpoint' raids, the Luftwaffe severely damaged the Spitfire factory at Castle Bromwich on the night of August 13/14, and temporarily stopped production of the first true night fighter, the Beaufighter, at Bristol on the morning of September 25.

But the British scientists countered the German beams, and German accuracy deteriorated so much that only a fifth of their bombs fell in the target area. A simpler expedient – fires lit as if by incendiaries, far from likely targets – also led the bombers astray on many occasions.

LIVING IN A NIGHTMARE

No device saved Coventry on the night of November 14, 1940. Three main forces of bombers streamed in over Lincolnshire, Portland and Dungeness – 439 of them in all, and all heading for Coventry's arms factories. Decoded German signals had suggested some big raid and even revealed its code name – *Mondlichtsonate* ('Moonlight Sonata'). But the Enigma-coded message that revealed Coventry as the target was not deciphered in time that night, and although the beam the raiders were flying was located, the jamming signal was misdirected.

In any case the night was so clear and bright that the targets were plain to see. The city's defenders failed woefully. Coventry had 40 anti-aircraft guns reinforced by light guns and mobile batteries, and 120 sorties were flown by night fighters, some of them Beaufighters using the latest 'Smellers'. Only one German plane was lost – it just crashed mysteriously.

At 7.20 pm ten pathfinder aircraft of KG 100 dropped more than 1000 incendiaries in the centre of the city, and the bombers homed in to tear out its heart with 511 tonnes of high-explosive bombs, 50 land mines, and up to 30 000 incendiaries. Groups of German bombers targeted particular factories, but most of the factories were set among residential areas. In all, 60 000 buildings were damaged, including 111 factories (12 of them producing aircraft), 600 shops, 28 hotels, 121 offices and all the city's railway lines. The destruction of Coventry Cathedral became a symbol of German brutality. The raid killed 568 civilians and injured 1256.

The scenes in Coventry were similar to those in other bombed cities, with flames roaring out of control, once proud buildings collapsing into untidy heaps of rubble, the rescue services working desperately to reach people trapped in the ruins of their homes and the mangled, burnt human remains. What made the Coventry raid different was the attack's sheer intensity, brought about by the accuracy that the first large-scale use of the pathfinder pinpointing technique made possible. It was that intensity which gave Coventry its particular horror. Thousands fled. The army wanted to impose martial law, and an official report quoted a survivor as saying 'Coventry is finished'. And yet, soon afterwards, production at Coventry's factories actually rose.

The week after this attack, Birmingham arms factories were the target. Some 900 civilians were killed and almost 2000 injured. Three weeks later, six Birmingham churches, 11 schools, two cinemas, a hospital and a crowded air-raid shelter were hit. The raids were becoming indis-

DAILY ROUND A London milkman crunches over rubble to his customers – typical in his dogged resolve not to give in to the enemy.

RISING TO THE CHALLENGE The heart of Coventry (above), and of its citizens, was ripped out by the ferocious raid of November 14, 1940, when thousands of incendiaries and hundreds of tonnes of high explosives cascaded from the moonlit sky. Dented morale soon rose again. Workers whose arms and aircraft factories were the main targets of the raid soon restored, even increased, production. Workers everywhere were eager to contribute, not least the women who not only took on civilian jobs but ran gun batteries and had charge of barrage-balloon sites (right).

criminate. In one of the December raids on Sheffield, fire engines were hampered because so many streets were blocked by trams welded to their rails by the fierce heat of the fires.

Just before Christmas, 250 bombers raided Manchester and Liverpool. In Manchester five hospitals, three hotels, a theatre, 20 churches, a block of shops, two large air-raid shelters and 11 railway bridges were hit. While the raid raged, families in their coal-house shelters sang hymns to drown the sounds of screaming bombs.

Many children witnessed horrifying sights. A Liverpudlian never forgot the moment when, as a mere six-year-old, she saw 'a parachute and a land mine. The parachute was stuck on the school railings and a man pulled the parachute and the school blew to pieces, and so did the man.' A Merseyside girl leaving the shelter for home one morning, found 'there was no home. All that was left was a pile of bricks. We had nowhere to live except the shelter, and that was to be our home for six months. We had our meals at different relations.' Even worse, dead were being brought from nearby houses: 'They were put in bags and then in large bins. It was very frightening.'

Homelessness became a huge problem. During the Blitz, London alone had varying degrees of damage to more than a million homes. In Hull, a frequent target, 87 000 homes had some damage and only 6000 had none. Over the whole country, nearly 4 million of the 13 million homes were damaged and 200 000 completely destroyed.

On the night of December 29/30, 1940, after a Christmas lull, a force of 130 aircraft attacking London dropped mainly incendiary bombs, and the whole area between St Paul's Cathedral and the Guildhall was a sea of blazing buildings. The water supply failed and engineers blew up buildings to create a fire break. Fortunately, bad weather sent the bombers home after three hours. Even though decoded German signals foretold the huge raid, whole office blocks burned out that night because they were locked up with nobody on duty. Within three weeks it became compulsory in most urban areas to have a fire-watcher on duty to put out incendiaries or to call for help.

THE LUFTWAFFE PULLS OUT

Gradually, however, the defenders began to knock down the bombers. Flying the new radar-equipped Beaufighters, RAF pilots and their radar operators were able, as Churchill said, to 'claw the Hun out of the sky'. The Beaufighter had four cannon and six machine guns, and its radar could pick up an aircraft at 7 km (4 miles) and track it until it could be seen. Most successful of the new breed of night-fighter 'aces' was Flt Lieutenant John 'Cat's-Eyes' Cunningham of 604 Squadron, who claimed 15 German aircraft in ten months of 1940-1.

On May 10, London suffered its most damaging attack of 1941. During 541 sorties the Germans killed more than 1400 civilians, destroyed 5000 houses and made 12 000 people homeless, some of them for the second or third time. The glow of the fires lit the London sky for three days. But the Luftwaffe lost 14 aircraft. Their losses were increasing and Britain was not collapsing. Hitler's attention was turning to the USSR, and planes were going east for Operation 'Barbarossa'.

The raid of May 10 was the last of the night Blitz – though bombing raids continued sporadically almost to the end of the war. In March and April 1942, York, Exeter, Canterbury and Bath were heavily bombed in the so-called 'Baedeker Raids' made on beautiful, historic cities in retaliation for the RAF's bombing of Lübeck and Rostock.

The battle for Britain was in effect won, however – and won not by improvisation or luck but by careful planning, by skilful use of resources, by technological advances, and above all by the courage of ordinary citizens and of the young men who waged war in the skies.

5: WHO RULES THE WAVES?

Shipping was Britain's lifeblood; all would be lost unless the convoy routes stayed open.

Hunting the hunters

Merchant shipping moved more safely in guarded convoys – a lesson Britain learned in World War I. But now the convoys faced new menaces, including the U-boat 'wolf packs', magnetic mines and air attacks. When the Americans entered the war, they spurned the convoy system at first – but learned better.

CONVOY SC7 was nearly home, its 35 ships – carrying mainly timber from Nova Scotia to the Clyde – huddled together like sheep while the Royal Navy sloops HMS *Fowey* and *Scarborough* and the corvette *Bluebell* scurried back and forth along the convoy's flanks like sheepdogs. As darkness approached on that night of October 16, 1940, the convoy was about 800 km (500 miles) north-west of Ireland, and just before midnight Lt Commander Heinrich Bleichrodt spotted its shadowy outlines from the conning tower of his submarine, *U-48*.

Slowly and silently Bleichrodt manoeuvred his boat to within 1.8 km (just over a mile) of the unsuspecting convoy, and then radioed its position, course, speed and size to the German Navy's U-boat headquarters at Lorient, in occupied France. This was the procedure devised by the U-boat fleet commander, Admiral Karl Dönitz – the 'wolf pack' technique whereby other U-boats could be quickly directed towards a target and carry out a mass attack. But Bleichrodt decided not to wait for his fellow 'wolves', and while still on the surface fired a salvo of three torpedoes at the convoy. Two found their mark, and the night sky was rent with flames as the French tanker *Languedoc* exploded, while the British merchantman *Scorseby* lurched violently and sent its deck cargo of pit props tumbling into the sea. Both sank within minutes, and Bleichrodt moved away, aware that dawn was fast approaching.

His decision to stay on the surface as long as possible, however, was almost his undoing. By now the convoy was within range of air cover provided by RAF Coastal Command, and shortly after daylight a Sunderland flying boat caught *U-48* on the surface. Desperately Bleichrodt crash-dived, but not before two bombs from the Sunderland had rocked the sub with violent shock waves. And there was more to come: within minutes depth charges from *Scarborough* forced Bleichrodt to dive in order to avoid destruction.

Meanwhile the U-boat staff at Lorient had been busy, and six more submarines were on their way to join *U-48*, which because of its enforced dive had lost contact with the convoy. At dusk on the 17th, Lt Commander Heinrich Liebe in *U-38* was patrolling alone when he spotted the convoy and immediately radioed Lorient. Now the wolf pack could be directed into the path of the convoy, which had gained the additional protection of the sloop *Leith* and corvette *Hartsease*. Liebe stalked the convoy until dark, managing to damage the freighter *Carsbreck* with a torpedo.

The successes of *U-48* and *U-38*, however, were nothing compared with the carnage yet to come, when the wolf pack was to act in unison. Lt Commander Engelbert Endrass in *U-46* began the massacre at 8.15 pm on October 17, his torpedoes finding the Swedish freighter *Convallaria*. Then the British freighter *Beatus* and the Dutch steamer *Boekolo* were hit by torpedoes from *U-123*, commanded by Lt Commander Karl-Heinz Möhle. Frantically the escort vessels ploughed back and forth in the darkness in search of the attackers, their asdic submarine-detecting equipment useless against the U-boats that were on the surface. In the middle of the convoy Lt Commander Otto Kretschmer in *U-99* was picking off his targets like sitting ducks.

Kretschmer wrote in his diary: 'Three destroyers, line abreast, approach the ship, searching the vicinity. I went off at full speed on a south-westerly course and very soon regained contact with the convoy. Torpedoes from other boats exploding all the time. The destroyers are at their wits' ends shooting off star shells to comfort themselves and each other . . . I am now beginning to pick them off from the stern of the convoy.'

When dawn came convoy SC7 was no longer a convoy, but a mass of sinking, burning and broken ships under a heavy pall of black smoke from burning wood and oil. In the heaving sea black-faced men clung to life rafts or tried to clamber onto oil-soaked timbers.

Of the convoy's 35 ships only 15 survived – and of the seven U-boats that had savaged the convoy not one was lost. As the submarines slipped quietly away from the scene, Lorient radioed to say that another convoy, HX79, was approaching. Four of the U-boats headed for HX79, and the carnage began all over again.

SAFETY IN NUMBERS

In 1917, at the height of World War I, German U-boats (*Unterseeboote*, or 'undersea boats') operating a 'sink without warning' policy sent so many merchant ships to the bottom that defeat stared Britain in the face. Only the introduction of the convoy system saved the day. Ships in convoy could move only at the speed of the slowest vessel, but they were protected by heavily armed escort ships. Moreover, the convoys sailed in a 'zigzag' pattern, changing course at prearranged intervals which made it hard for prowling submarines to find them. And when radio intelligence gave warning of the presence of U-boats, convoys could be diverted to avoid them. It was a brave U-boat commander who would dare to attack a convoy, and those that did were either sunk or usually only able to achieve a single attack.

At the outbreak of World War II, however, it was believed that Germany would not engage in a sink-on-sight policy for fear that it would bring the USA into the war as it had in 1917. The Admiralty planned to use its anti-U-boat forces in hunting groups rather than as convoy escorts – unless unrestricted submarine warfare broke out.

There had been improvements to anti-submarine techniques during the interwar years. The most effective anti-submarine weapon had, in fact, been developed during World War I. It was the depth charge, a dustbin-sized canister, packed with high explosives, triggered by a device that reacted to the change in pressure as the depth charge sank through the water. Then had come the development of asdic, which took its name

PRELUDE TO AMERICA'S WAR

The USA became involved in the Battle of the Atlantic long before the Japanese attack on Pearl Harbor. In July 1941, American marines took over Britain's bases in Iceland when the British troops there were needed for duty in North Africa, and the US Navy began providing limited convoy escorts – especially for goods supplied under the 1941 Lend-Lease Act (p. 174).

In an incident on September 4, a British aircraft attacked *U-652*, after notifying USS *Greer*, which was nearby. The U-boat, thinking the strike had come from the US destroyer, attacked the American ship, which replied with depth charges. Neither vessel was sunk, but it was inevitable that a more serious incident could not be far off.

On September 17 five American destroyers took over the escort of convoy HX150. A month later the US destroyer *Kearney* was torpedoed, though not sunk, while escorting convoy SC48. Then the inevitable happened: on October 31, USS *Reuben James* was sunk by *U-562* while escorting convoy HX156, and 115 US seamen died. Although American public reaction was surprisingly muted – most people still wanted to keep out of the war – a reluctant United States was steadily inching towards involvement.

VALIANT *VANOC* The destroyer HMS *Vanoc* plunges through the Atlantic on convoy duty, its charges spread across the horizon. Well past its prime – it had seen service in World War I – *Vanoc* did stout work with the convoys.

from the Anti-Submarine Detection Investigation Committee. It was a sonar device which bounced sound waves off a submerged submarine's hull, and by a series of 'pinging' signals could accurately detect its distance and direction. Many in the Royal Navy considered, therefore, that the submarine problem had been solved.

But the convoy defences had many weaknesses. Asdic was effective in detecting submerged submarines, but it could not remain in contact throughout an attack. Worse, it was useless when the U-boats were on the surface – and the small low outline of a submarine was almost invisible at night. RAF Coastal Command had few long-range aircraft, and crews were trained to search for surface raiders, not submarines. In the early days, too, British anti-submarine bombs had an embarrassing tendency to bounce on the water and explode, so bringing down the aircraft that had dropped them.

As the Royal Navy took up its war stations in August 1939 it was decided to introduce convoys immediately along the east coast of Britain. Ocean shipping, however, would sail alone until the Germans showed their hand. This Hitler seemed to do on the very first day of the war. The *Kriegsmarine* (German Navy) had only 57 U-boats in service at the time, and they were indeed under instructions not to sink unarmed merchantmen without warning. One boat, however – Lt Commander Fritz-Julius Lemp's *U-30* – mistook the British liner *Athenia* for an armed merchant cruiser and sank it without warning off the Scottish coast. Of 1400 passengers, 112 died.

The incident helped the British Admiralty to make an important strategic decision. It convinced them that the Germans had begun unrestricted submarine warfare, and ocean-going convoys were introduced immediately for ships of between 9 and 15 knots (17 and 28 km/h). Slower ships had to take their chances alone, although casualties were so severe that the slow 'SC' convoys were introduced in August 1940. Faster ships were thought to be relatively safe, but unless they were very speedy, like the liners *Queen Mary* and *Queen Elizabeth* – both capable of 30 knots (55 km/h) – they were still very much at risk.

THE 'HAPPY TIME'

After the *Athenia* incident Hitler strictly forbade U-boats to attack any more liners, but the German Prize Regulations – which *(continued on p. 62)*

RESCUED FROM ICY WATERS **Two British officers from a torpedoed merchant vessel cling, bare-handed and barefooted, to a wooden life raft. They are lucky; they were spotted and are being picked up by a US Coast Guard cutter. A seaman with them is being hauled on board.**

LIFE UNDER THE OCEAN WAVE A crewman relaxes in the forward torpedo compartment of *U-552*, nicknamed the 'Red Devil' boat. Commanded by Erich Topp, it sank nearly 200 000 tonnes of Allied shipping, the war's third highest score. Men on board another Type VII U-boat (inset) work on the torpedo tubes. A third boat – *U-29* – leaves Lorient (below), to the sound of a German band. Based on a Finnish design, the Type VII ('Sea Wolf') was the mainstay of Germany's submarine fleet. The first were built in the mid-1930s and a second batch of ten enlarged VIIB boats in 1938-9. These had a two-shaft diesel/electric power system, giving the boats a surface speed of 17 knots (31 km/h) and 8 knots (15 km/h) submerged. They could stay submerged for 18 hours while cruising at 4 knots (7.5 km/h). The VIIBs were followed by the 863 tonne Type VIIC, of which 593 were built between 1940 and the end of the war. They had four 533 mm (21 in) torpedo tubes forward and one aft, and carried 14 torpedoes. Armament varied, but a typical VIIC U-boat late in the war might have had a 37 mm (1.45 in) gun on the forecastle and two twin 20 mm (0.8 in) anti-aircraft guns.

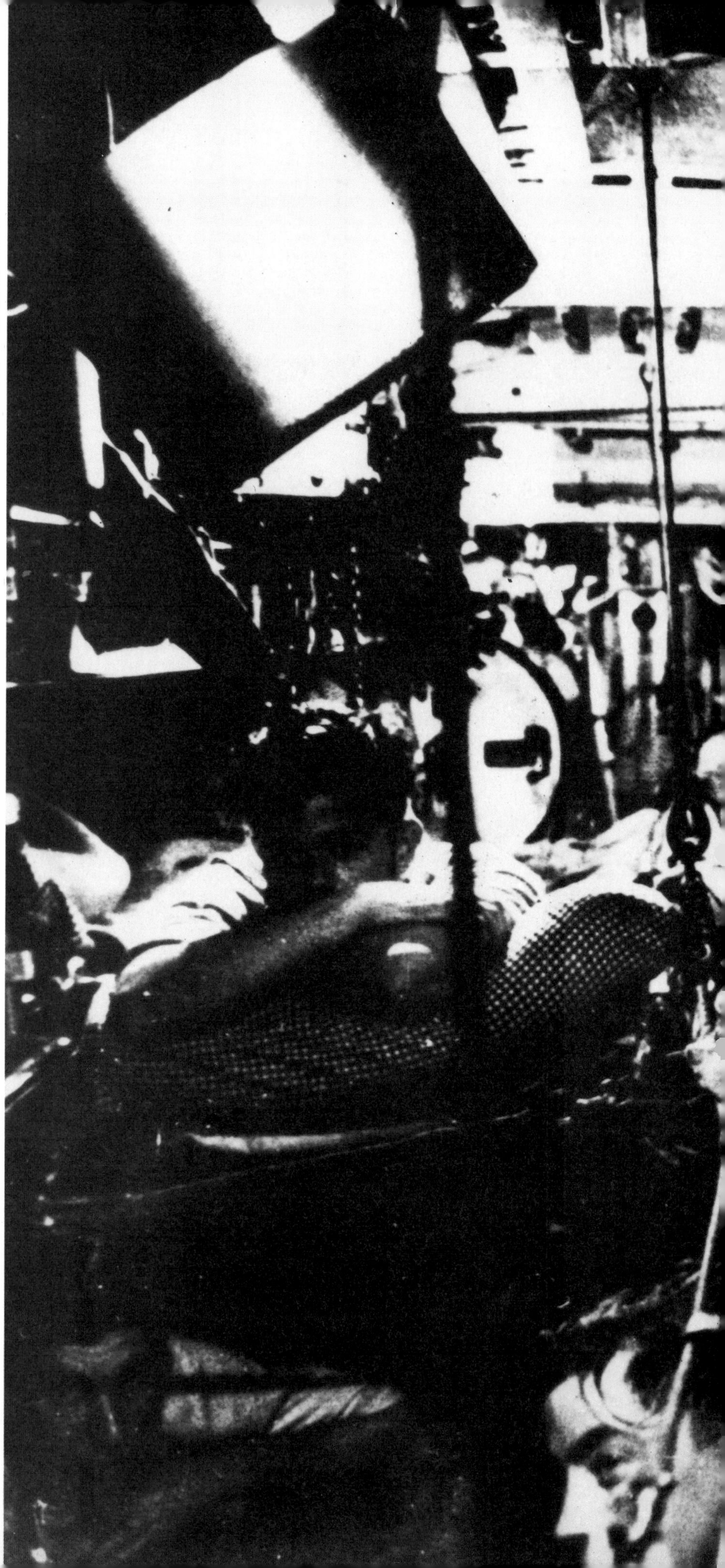

HERO OF SCAPA FLOW *U-47* commander Gunther Prien (1908-41) is dressed with the casualness on which German submariners prided themselves – shabby reefer jacket, leather trousers, cork-soled shoes. Prien's achievement of penetrating Scapa Flow and sinking the battleship *Royal Oak* in October 1939 was one of the war's greatest naval feats. His career ended on the night of March 7/8, 1941, when *U-47* was sunk while attacking convoy OB293. He is credited with sending 28 merchant ships to the bottom.

Rosmarie

RADAR: THE ANSWER TO THE SURFACED SUBMARINE

When radar was fitted to British escort vessels in 1941, it completed a ship's capacity to spot a U-boat. An attacker could be detected whether on the surface or, by the use of asdic, submerged. The first radar, Type 286, could detect a submarine up to 2.8 km (1¾ miles) ahead. Its first success was when HMS *Vanoc* accounted for *U-100* in March 1941. Later types could spot targets as small as a periscope in all directions, and surfaced U-boats at up to about 9 km (5¾ miles). Similar sets were mounted in aircraft; the ASV (air to surface vessel) Mk 3 radar helped aircraft to become the main means of sinking U-boats in 1943.

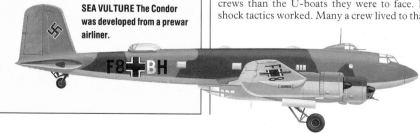

FLOWER POWER 'A corvette would roll on wet grass', wrote the author Nicholas Montsarrat. These sturdy little vessels – named after flowers – were built in large numbers before and during the war, but were poorly suited to ocean work and unpopular with crews. They were, however, the mainstay of the convoy escorts. They were lightly armed, with a single 4 in (102 mm) gun on the forecastle and light anti-aircraft weapons amidships. Their main weapons were 40 depth charges, later increased to 72, fired from launchers or dropped over the stern. Based on a whale-catcher design, with a top speed of only 16.5 knots (30.5 km/h), the 'Flower' corvettes were only replaced by the much improved 'Castle' class in 1943.

governed attacks on merchant ships – were continually revised to allow greater freedom to the U-boat commanders. In late 1939 a less restricted submarine campaign began against Allied and neutral shipping. The scene was set for what came to be known as the Battle of the Atlantic.

Most of the subs' victims were ships sailing alone. Coastal vessels also faced a new menace, the magnetic mine (see box). Not only merchant ships fell foul of the submarine menace; before 1939 was out the Royal Navy had lost the fleet carrier HMS *Courageous* on anti-submarine patrol and then one of its largest warships, *Royal Oak*.

The U-boats sank many unescorted vessels in the early weeks of 1940, and sinkings peaked at 45 ships in February. But submarines could gain successes against convoys only at their dire peril. In January 1940, convoy OA80, sailing in bad weather and escorted only by a single sloop, was attacked by *U-55*. Two ships were sunk, but two destroyers and a Sunderland flying boat came to the convoy's aid and so harried the submarine that its commander scuttled his boat.

The invasion of Norway by Germany in April 1940 kept both the Kriegsmarine and the Royal Navy fully occupied, and brought about a lull in the Battle of the Atlantic. But when France fell two months later the U-boats returned to their main task of attacking the Atlantic convoys – and now they had the use of the French ports on the Bay of Biscay and a command centre at Lorient.

German U-boat commanders called the period from July to October 1940 the 'happy time'. During those four months, 217 merchant ships, mostly sailing independently, were sunk. Like the fighter pilots of World War I, U-boat commanders became 'aces', with men like Kretschmer, Liebe, Wolfgang Luth and Gunther Prien becoming household names in Germany. On August 17 Hitler – inflamed by Churchill's dogged refusal to capitulate – declared a total blockade of the British Isles. He directed that all shipping of whatever nationality, apart from a few specified Irish ships, was to be sunk on sight.

The aces made their reputation by picking off ships as they made their own way after leaving a convoy at its dispersal points, straggled away from convoys or sailed their own lonely courses. Since the invasion of Britain was a real threat, the Royal Navy could not divert resources from home waters to extend anti-submarine protection. What little protection it could provide was limited by inadequate training, while the U-boat force was growing in strength and experience. It was these two factors that encouraged Dönitz to send his wolf packs into action against the convoys – beginning with the ill-fated SC7.

THE CONDOR THREAT

Nicknamed the 'scourge of the Atlantic', the Focke Wulf Fw200 Condor was a long-range (3530 km; 2206 mile) reconnaissance and bomber aircraft. A gondola fitted to the underside of the aircraft carried a forward-firing 20 mm cannon and 1750 kg (3857 lb) of bombs. Two gun mountings, each carrying twin machine guns, were fitted on top of the fuselage – one forward, one aft.

Condors went into service in 1940 in their dual role as bombers and convoy spotters for the U-boats. Communications with the U-boats were poor at first, and navigational errors sometimes led the U-boats the wrong way, but the aircraft were highly successful in their bombing role, sinking 11 ships in 1940 and crippling the liner *Empress of Britain*, later finished off by a U-boat. Sometimes it was the U-boats that called up the Condors to attack a convoy, rather than the other way round, and in February 1941 a submarine spotted convoy HG53 outward-bound from Gibraltar and called up six Condors which sank five ships.

The threat was met by the introduction of escort aircraft carriers, by fitting anti-aircraft guns to Allied merchant ships and by the use of long-range fighter aircraft. CAM ships (Catapult Aircraft Merchantmen) were another effective, though expensive, defence against the Condors. These ships carried a Hawker Hurricane fighter which could be launched from the deck by catapult, but after his mission the pilot had either to ditch his aircraft in the sea close to the CAM or parachute from it. In either case the aircraft was lost.

SEA VULTURE The Condor was developed from a prewar airliner.

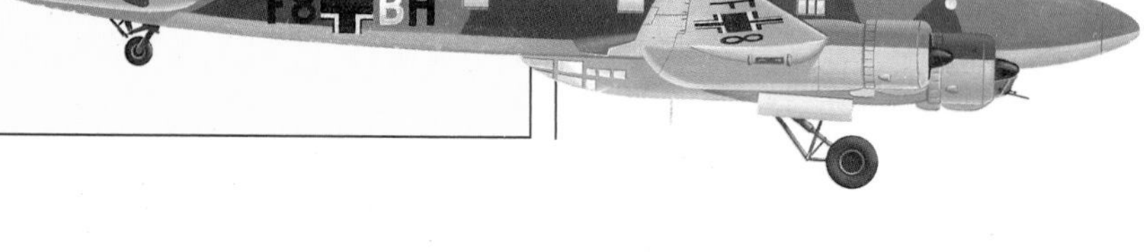

HOLDING THE THREAT

The mass night attacks of the wolf packs caught the convoy escorts almost totally unprepared. Apart from the uselessness of asdic against U-boats on the surface, there were no proper communications between escort vessels other than signal lamps using Morse code, sirens and flags. (Escorts were fitted with radio telephones only after November 1940.) Often the escort ship commanders did not know one another and were not briefed on tactics.

That began to change in July 1940 when the fire-eating Commodore Gilbert O. Stephenson was put in charge of a training base – HMS *Western Isles* – at Tobermory on the Hebridean island of Mull. Known variously as 'Monkey', the 'Terror of Tobermory' and 'Lord of the *Western Isles*', Stephenson struck greater fear into the hearts of his trainee escort commanders and their crews than the U-boats they were to face. But shock tactics worked. Many a crew lived to thank the commodore for his insistence on the highest standards of efficiency.

Other factors that helped turn the tide against the U-boat threat were the development of surface radar, which enabled escort vessels to spot surfaced U-boats at night (see box), and the breaking of the code used by the U-boats to send signals to Lorient. The first breaks into the code were made in March 1941, and in May the British captured Lemp's *U-110*, complete with its Kriegsmarine version of the Enigma code machine. The Government Code and Cypher School at Bletchley Park devoted one of its computers to naval work, and German signals could usually be decoded within 36 hours – sometimes immediately. Controllers could thus route convoys away from impending U-boat attacks, and even when such attacks occurred the better equipped and better trained escorts were able to exact a heavy toll.

Soon the U-boat aces began to disappear. Prien was killed while attacking convoy OB293 on the night of March 7/8, 1941 – blown into oblivion by the destroyer HMS *Wolverine*. A few weeks later Lemp spotted convoy HX112, and his radio signal to Lorient resulted in four other boats racing to the scene, including Lt Commander Joachim Schepke in *U-100* and Kretschmer in *U-99*. Despite the escort of five destroyers and two corvettes, Kretschmer got into the centre of the convoy and sank five ships.

Shortly afterwards depth charges from HMS *Walker* and *Vanoc* swept *U-100* to the surface, where the sub was picked up on radar – the first time this had been achieved. Schepke and most of his crew died when *Vanoc* rammed *U-100* and sank it. Now *Walker*, under Captain Donald MacIntyre, picked up *U-99* on asdic. Seven depth charges went over the side, and moments later *Vanoc*'s searchlight revealed *U-99*'s conning tower as it lifted out of the water. A message flashed from the conning tower came out as 'We are sunking'. It was the end of the war for Kretschmer – Germany's most famous ace – as he and most of his crew were taken prisoner.

THE MENACE OF MAGNETIC MINES

German magnetic mines were fired by a change in magnetism caused by the passage of a ship above them. Every steel ship has a magnetic field, and this triggered the mine's detonator. There were several types of magnetic mines, some moored just below the sea surface like conventional mines and others that were laid on the sea bottom. One type, the LM series, was laid by being dropped from the air by parachute, and it was one of these that enabled the Royal Navy to find an effective answer to the menace.

In November 1939 a type LM mine landed on the mudflats at Shoeburyness in the Thames Estuary. The mine was defused by Lt Commander John Ouvry, who calmly went about his task while talking to colleagues on shore through a throat microphone; he described each phase of the operation so that, should he make a mistake and be blown to eternity, the next man to disarm a mine would know what not to do.

Through Ouvry's courageous efforts – which won him the DSO – the mine gave up its secrets and the answer was found. Ships were 'degaussed' – their magnetic fields neutralised – by fitting a cable around the hull and passing an electric current through it.

COVER FROM THE AIR

Despite these British successes the wolf packs continued to be a threat, especially in areas where air escort was still unavailable. One way of providing air cover was to use escort carriers, and the first to go into service was HMS *Audacity*, which was converted from a captured German merchantman. Its main role was dealing with the Focke Wulf Fw200 Condor maritime bomber (see box, *The Condor threat*).

Audacity was a strange-looking vessel, with no superstructure and a short flight deck carrying six American-built Grumman Martlet fighters (the British name for the Wildcat). Nevertheless it soon proved its usefulness against both aircraft and submarines – so much so that Dönitz ordered it to be sunk. The end came in December 1941, when it was ordered to escort convoy HG76 sailing from Gibraltar to Britain.

The 32 merchant ships had a massive escort: no fewer than 16 warships led by Commander F.J. ('Johnnie') Walker in the sloop HMS *Stork*. Walker had his own ideas on how to deal with a submarine attack, and on the morning of December 17 he was able to put them into practice. *Audacity*'s planes made the first sighting, a U-boat on the surface some 37 km (23 miles) away. Walker sent five ships in hot pursuit, and the submarine, *U-131*, hastily crash-dived – but not hastily enough, and a corvette plastered it with ten depth charges and forced it to the surface again. The sub's anti-aircraft guns brought down one of the Martlets. But intense fire from the 4 in (102 mm) guns of the attackers eventually sank it.

The next day the escort made its second kill, depth-charging *U-434*, and the convoy steamed on intact. But there were more dangers to come. In the early hours of the 19th a tremendous explosion lit up the dawn sky. HMS *Stanley* – one of the old four-stack destroyers given to Britain by the USA in 1940 in exchange for military bases in the Caribbean – had been hit by torpedoes from *U-574* which had been shadowing the convoy. Walker raced to the destroyer's assistance, and immediately picked up an asdic contact at close range. Depth charges hurtled from *Stork*'s launchers in a blistering pattern, and suddenly *U-574* surfaced only 180 m (200 yds) ahead of the sloop.

Then began a desperate chase. The U-boat turned in a tight circle, with the sloop close behind – so close that *Stork*'s guns could not be depressed low enough to keep the U-boat in their sights. Three times pursued and pursuer circled, until Walker rammed the submarine, then unleashed a salvo of depth charges. *Stanley* was avenged.

On December 21, three more U-boats moved in. One, *U-567*, was commanded by Endrass – since the capture of Kretschmer, Germany's top U-boat ace. He was about to play his last trump. After sinking a ship carrying iron ore, *U-567* was bombarded by depth charges from the sloops *Deptford* and *Stork*, and sank without trace. In the meantime *Audacity* was patrolling the starboard flank of the convoy, and crossed the path of *U-751*. The U-boat's first torpedo hit the carrier's engine room, and two more fired at point-blank range blew off its bows and sent the first British escort carrier to the bottom. But, happily for the convoy, it was now within range of air cover provided by Coastal Command Liberators.

These American-built long-range bombers were to play a decisive role in the battle to rule the Atlantic waves. Together with the later mass-produced escort carriers they were able to give convoys full air cover. The days when the wolf packs could roam the seas at will were numbered – though the Americans' entry into the war offered them some rich pickings for a while.

KRETSCHMER: THE 'ONE-SHOT' ACE

A single torpedo fired at point-blank range was the hallmark of Otto Kretschmer (1912-), a technique he perfected while commanding *U-23* and then *U-99*. It made him Germany's top U-boat ace, sinking 44 ships – a total of more than 250 000 tonnes. He preferred to operate on the surface at night, the method used by the wolf packs, though most of his score was made by hunting down lone targets. His most notable victims were the armed merchant cruisers *Petroclus*, *Laurentic* and *Forfar*, sunk in November and December 1940.

Kretschmer's activities came to an abrupt end in March 1941, when he was captured after being sunk while attacking convoy HX112. Held as a prisoner of war first in Yorkshire and then in Canada, he impressed his captors by his modesty, courtesy and self-confidence. In Canada he masterminded an unsuccessful escape attempt by several prisoners. After the war he helped to rebuild the navy of the Federal German Republic, in which he reached the rank of admiral.

SECOND 'HAPPY TIME'

On the night of January 13/14, 1942, Lt Commander Reinhard Hardegan of *U-123* realised a lifetime ambition. 'I always wanted to see New York,' he told his crew, 'and now this is our opportunity.' He made the teasing claim that he could see the dancers on the roof of the Hotel

A CAPTAIN COURAGEOUS

Frederick John Walker (1897-1944) was one of the Royal Navy's most successful convoy escort commanders. Knowing that the U-boats preferred to attack on the surface and at night, Walker, who commanded 36th Escort Group, concentrated on bringing the maximum amount of firepower against the U-boats, so forcing them to submerge where they could be detected by asdic and destroyed by depth charges. His successes earned him promotion to captain, the DSO and Bar and the awe of the U-boat commanders. While later leading 2nd Escort Group, in HMS *Starling*, Walker sent six U-boats to the bottom during one patrol in January and February 1944. He was a workaholic and died soon afterwards of a stroke. He was buried at sea.

Astor! It was the New York skyline, still lit up as in peacetime, that enabled him to pick off two tankers off Long Island. Weather reports from US commercial radio stations also helped his activities. Obviously the USA, on its home front at least, was acting as if it was not at war at all.

The Germans were quick to take advantage, and five large Type IX U-boats arrived off America's eastern seaboard. The 'happy time' had come again, and with it a new crop of aces. Hardegan was the first. Three days after his successes off New York he reached the busy shipping lane off Cape Hatteras, 600 km (375 miles) to the south. Within 90 minutes he sank an American tanker and a small freighter. The following night he brought *U-123* to the surface, and from the conning tower watched ship after ship sail by with lights blazing. An old freighter, *City of Atlanta*, was his first victim, but now he had only two torpedoes left, and there were eight ships out there. Hardegan turned his gun on a big tanker, *Malay*, set it on fire, then went after another victim. But then *U-123* broke down. Hardegan waited patiently while repairs were carried out – with the U-boat still on the surface. When his boat got under way again, Hardegan picked up a radio message from *Malay* which had also managed to get going. As *U-123* moved to finish it off, Hardegan sank a Latvian freighter with his penultimate torpedo, before using the last to send *Malay* to the bottom.

After returning home for more torpedoes, Hardegan came back and between mid-March and late April sank 11 more ships. Meanwhile, Hardegan's fellow U-boat commanders were also having a field day, sinking 40 ships in the western Atlantic alone in January 1942. In February the U-boats moved south, where the bright lights of Miami still blazed for the tourists. Now the tourists were treated to the spectacle of ships being sunk only a few kilometres offshore.

'MILCH COW' SUBS

To increase the range of U-boats, the Germans introduced supply submarines, nicknamed 'milch cows', in 1942. They could carry over 430 tonnes of fuel oil as well as the 206 tonnes they needed themselves. Their range was over 17 000 km (10 600 miles). First in service was *U-459*, fuelling small Type VII submarines north-east of Bermuda in April and May. Another five were operational by August. 'Milch cows' were protected against air attack by two 37 mm guns and one 20 mm – but all but one were sunk wholly or partly from the air. *U-490* was the last, going on patrol in May 1944 and being sunk only six weeks later. The Germans also used four large minelaying submarines – *U-116* to *U-119* – as tankers. All were sunk in 1942-3.

HUNTERS BECOME VICTIMS

Against British advice, the Americans started submarine-hunting patrols and used decoy ships – though both methods had been tried and found useless by the Royal Navy. The sub-hunters themselves became victims of the U-boats. A destroyer was sunk at the end of February. The American Chief of Naval Operations, Admiral Ernest King, refused to introduce convoys, on the grounds that he lacked escort ships for the job.

The British were furious at so much shipping being lost. The U-boat menace in the eastern Atlantic had by now been contained, yet ships that had safely crossed the ocean were being sunk within sight of port. A particularly sad loss was the tanker *San Demetrio*, heroically saved in November 1940 (p. 65), only to be torpedoed off the American coast in March 1942. To persuade the Americans to adopt the convoy system, Britain offered them corvettes, anti-submarine trawlers, plus two experienced convoy officers.

The Americans accepted the ships, but obstinately refused to be told how to use them. However, in April they introduced a scheme called the 'Bucket Brigade' – groups of ships were escorted from port to port by day, staying in protected anchorages by night. This made for slow progress, but it developed into a proper convoy system and the U-boats moved south to the Caribbean and the Gulf of Mexico, aided by 'milch cow' tanker submarines (see box).

In May the losses along America's coast fell to five, and to three in July. In the Gulf of Mexico, however, 41 ships were sunk in May. But in July a system of interlocking convoys was set up; ships sailed in convoy from Trinidad to New York, linking there with the Atlantic convoy system. Sinkings in the Gulf fell, then ceased altogether. The second 'happy time' was over.

SHIPS THAT SPELLED LIBERTY

In the dark days following the fall of France, the outcome of the Battle of the Atlantic depended on a grim equation: could the Allies build merchant ships faster than the U-boats could sink them? They could and did – thanks to American know-how. In May 1941, as part of Lend-Lease, Roosevelt ordered 2 million tonnes of merchant shipping to be built. The shipyards of Delaware, the Great Lakes, Mississippi and West Coast went to work with a will. Standardised designs allowed ships to be prefabricated in sections, for quick assembly at the yards.

Most famous and numerous of these designs was the freighter known as the 'Liberty ship'. Thousands rolled down the slipways under the guidance of men like the dynamic industrialist Henry J. Kaiser. The first Liberty ship took 244 days to build, but once the design was mastered the time was cut to only 42 days – though on one occasion a ship was completed in less than five. In 1942, 646 freighters, including 597 Liberty ships, slid off American launchways. By July 1943, Allied shipbuilding as a whole outstripped the number of U-boat sinkings. The flow of supplies across the Atlantic was saved.

LIBERTY PARADE Identical 'Liberty ships' are given final touches in a California dockyard.

Menace of the surface raiders

The Royal Navy had no doubt that it would prevail against Germany's surface fleet. But on the way to victory the British admirals had some nasty surprises.

ERICH RAEDER, Grand Admiral and Commander in Chief of the *Kriegsmarine* (German Navy), had no illusions about the strength of his adversaries. 'Our surface forces,' he wrote on the day Britain declared war on Germany, 'can do no more than show that they know how to die gallantly.'

He was speaking in the knowledge that the German fleet was heavily outnumbered. Two small battleships (*Scharnhorst* and *Gneisenau*), three pocket battleships, seven cruisers (with another about to enter service), 21 destroyers and 13 torpedo boats made up a pitifully small fleet against the might of the Royal Navy. Britain began the war with 12 battleships, three battlecruisers, seven aircraft carriers, 60 cruisers and 184 destroyers. There would be no question this time of mounting the kind of challenge which, in 1916, had led to a full-scale clash of fleets at the Battle of Jutland. The German surface warships would play the risky role of hit-and-run raiders.

POCKET POWER

But Raeder did have some aces up his sleeve in the form of the *Panzerschiffe* ('armoured ships', or 'pocket battleships'): *Admiral Scheer*, *Admiral Graf Spee* and *Deutschland*. Built in the mid-1930s and the world's first major warships powered by diesel engines, they proved ideal for attacking commercial shipping. They were more powerful than anything they could not outrun, and could outrun almost anything they could not outgun. Only the three British battlecruisers and two French battlecruisers of the *Dunkerque* class were their superior in both speed and firepower. Their six 280 mm (11 in) guns, top speed of 28 knots (52 km/h) and range of almost 40 000 km (25 000 miles) made them a formidable threat.

Deutschland and *Graf Spee* were both in the Atlantic when war was declared, and *Graf Spee* immediately went into action south of the Equator with conspicuous success, sinking nine merchant ships in the space of four months. Flushed with his success, *Graf Spee*'s skipper, Captain Hans Langsdorff, headed for the estuary of the River Plate off South America to attack a convoy due to leave Montevideo. Instead he was met by the British cruisers *Exeter*, *Ajax* and the New Zealand-manned *Achilles* – and the result was victory for the Royal Navy in the Battle of the River Plate, when Langsdorff scuttled his ship.

Deutschland, operating in the North Atlantic, made little impact, sinking only two merchant ships. On its return to its home port of Kiel, Hitler ordered its name to be changed to *Lützow*, apparently worried that German morale would suffer should a ship bearing the name of the Fatherland be sunk. He had every right to be, for *Lützow* was repeatedly crippled by the British. The submarine *Spearfish* torpedoed and damaged it during the Norwegian campaign, and in the Battle of the Barents Sea on December 31, 1942, *Lützow* and the cruiser *Hipper* were beaten off when they attacked a British convoy. The failure cost Raeder his job. He was replaced by Grand Admiral Karl Dönitz, who already commanded the U-boat fleet.

Admiral Scheer made it into the Atlantic in November 1940, soon to encounter convoy HX84 protected by a single escort, the British armed merchant cruiser *Jervis Bay*. Bravely, *Jervis Bay* made a direct attack on the pocket battleship, even though its 6 in (152 mm) guns were no match for *Scheer*'s firepower. Undaunted and with most of its guns put out of action by *Scheer*'s salvoes, *Jervis Bay* closed to within 2 km (about 1 mile) of its attacker before being sunk, winning time for the convoy to scatter. Its commanding officer, Captain Edward Fogerty Fegen, who went down with the ship, was awarded a posthumous VC. Although *Scheer* raced after them into the twilight, it succeeded in sinking only five of the convoy's 35 ships before the rest escaped into the darkness. Another – the tanker *San Demetrio* – was set on fire, and then began another tale of heroism (see box).

HEAVYWEIGHT MARAUDERS

Germany's two battleships, *Scharnhorst* and *Gneisenau* – usually classed as battlecruisers by the British – roamed the North Atlantic during the early months of 1941, but on the only two occasions when they encountered convoys they were deterred by the 15 in (380 mm) guns of the two British battleships acting as escorts. They were, however, able to sink 22 unescorted ships, 14 of them in the space of two days.

After returning to Brest, in France, and being persistently harried by RAF bombing attacks, both ships – along with the cruiser *Prinz Eugen* – made a daring dash back to Germany through the English Channel in February 1942. They were attacked by some old British destroyers, a mixed bag of torpedo boats and six Fleet Air Arm Swordfish aircraft – all of which were shot down. But the battleships suffered damage by mines, and *Gneisenau* was later bombed in its dock in Kiel in February 1942 and never went to sea again.

The cruiser *Hipper*, plagued by engine trouble for much of its career and with a limited range, also sailed in February 1941, and after sinking a lone ship came across convoy SLS64. Seven of the 19 convoy ships were sunk.

In all, the German Navy's surface raiders sank 54 ships between November 1940 and March 1941, but their success was nothing compared with that of the 'secret raiders' – armed merchant ships posing as neutral merchantmen. Nine such marauders sank 130 ships altogether. *Atlantis* was the most notorious of them all (see box).

In May 1941 the battleship *Bismarck* went to sea, accompanied by *Prinz Eugen*. *Bismarck* was the pride of the Kriegsmarine, capable of taking on the best that the Royal Navy could offer, and for the first time German warships were ordered to engage the enemy fleet if attacked. The ultimate outcome, however, was a crushing blow for Hitler (see feature, p. 66), who decided not to risk any more of his capital ships in the Atlantic. Besides, there were other tempting targets – the convoys through the Arctic Ocean to Russia.

SAGA OF SAN DEMETRIO

'She was the only thing we could see in all the wide circle of ocean, and she looked good . . . And besides, she was our own ship.' Those words, written by Able Seaman Calum MacNeil, one of the survivors of the blazing tanker *San Demetrio*, summed up the spirit of the men who courageously reboarded this potential time-bomb and brought it safely home.

The ship, carrying 12 000 tonnes of aviation fuel in its tanks, was set on fire by *Admiral Scheer* on November 5, 1940. It could have exploded at any time, and the crew took to the lifeboats leaving the tanker to its fate. The following day one of the lifeboats, carrying 15 men, was still near the ship which had not stopped burning but was otherwise intact. With no other vessel in sight, the survivors chose to reboard the tanker rather than drift in the Atlantic with little chance of rescue.

They brought the blaze under control and repaired the engines. Chief engineer Charles Pollard got the ship under way and second officer Hawkins used an atlas to navigate. *San Demetrio* dropped anchor in Rothesay Bay, Scotland, on November 16.

THE SECRET RAIDERS

Remembering the World War I successes of disguised merchant raiders – notably *Möwe* and the incredible three-masted windjammer *Seeadler* – Grand Admiral Erich Raeder saw a way to supplement his inadequate navy. Nine merchantmen, disguised to look like neutral or Allied ships, were packed with guns and torpedo tubes and given free rein to roam far and wide in search of their prey. One, *Kormoran*, was intercepted off Shark Bay, Western Australia, in November 1941 by the cruiser HMAS *Sydney*, and in a slogging battle the two ships sank each other. All 645 men aboard *Sydney* were lost, but 315 of the 400-strong crew of *Kormoran* made it to the Australian coast.

Perhaps the most famous of the merchant raiders was *Atlantis*. With a formidable but odd collection of armaments, including guns from an ancient training ship, it captured or sank 22 ships – British and others – on a 176 000 km (110 000 mile) trip right around the world beginning in March 1940. It was eventually destroyed by the British cruiser *Devonshire* in November 1941, while posing as a British merchantman. Captain Bernhard Rogge and most of his crew were picked up by a U-boat they had been about to refuel.

Most of the raiders – which could change their appearance with collapsible funnels and dummy deck cargoes – came to an untimely end. The last of them was the motor ship *Michel*, formerly Polish, which sailed from Germany in early 1942 and sank 18 ships before being sent to the bottom by an American submarine.

SINK THE BISMARCK!

When the most powerful battleship in the world set out to destroy British convoys, it was the prelude to the greatest naval chase of the 20th century.

THE STEEP SIDES of Norway's Kors Fiord dwarfed the Martin Maryland plane with Royal Navy markings as it probed its way beneath the low cloud. Visibility was appalling that day – May 22, 1941 – as Commander Geoffrey Rotherham tried to track down Germany's formidable new battleship *Bismarck*, last seen near Bergen on the south-west coast of Norway.

For Rotherham to make a sure observation, the plane had to fly perilously close to the cliffs, coming under a vicious barrage of fire from the German anti-aircraft batteries guarding nearby Bergen dockyard. But he saw all he needed, and signalled back to base: *Bismarck* had sailed.

The British Admiralty had been only too aware that *Bismarck* was ready – but when, how, and where would it strike? The concern was well justified. The Commander in Chief of the Kriegsmarine, Grand Admiral Erich Raeder, was eager to get the new battleship into action. His plan – code-named *Rheinübung* ('Exercise Rhine') – was to cut off Britain's lifeline by crippling the already battered merchant convoys that carried crucial supplies of raw materials, food and troops across the North Atlantic.

Prinz Eugen – a new heavy cruiser of over 19 000 tonnes and with a speed of 32 knots (59 km/h) – accompanied *Bismarck* out of Gdynia (Gotenhafen) on the Baltic coast of occupied Poland on May 18. Two days after they set sail, a neutral Swedish cruiser spotted them in the Skagerrak, the passage between Norway

OPPOSING ADMIRALS Lütjens (above), German fleet commander, was told Tovey (right), Home Fleet commander, had his ships anchored in Scapa Flow. But they were already out on the prowl.

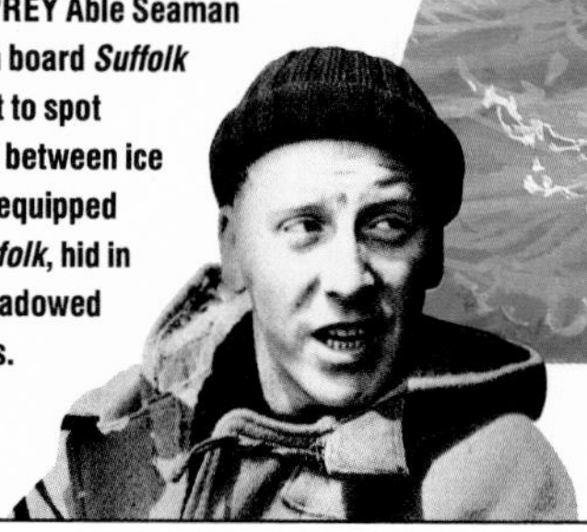

SIGHTING THE PREY Able Seaman Alfred Newall, on board *Suffolk* (above), was first to spot *Bismarck* edging between ice floes. The radar-equipped *Suffolk*, with *Norfolk*, hid in fog banks and shadowed the German ships.

HMS HOOD One of the only three survivors when *Hood* exploded was Seaman Tilburn. The battle-cruiser's fatal flaw was its thin deck armour, vulnerable to heavy shells plunging from a height. *Hood's* outdated weapons were removed and in 1939-40 it was given seven twin 4 in (102 mm) guns, five multiple rocket launchers, three multiple pom-poms, four sets of multiple machine guns and four 21 in (533 mm) above-water torpedo tubes. The navy's prestige warship had fired its guns only once in anger (at Mers El Kébir in June 1940) before it was sunk by shells fired from *Bismarck*.

and Denmark; the information was leaked to the British by Swedish intelligence. Flying Officer Michael Suckling provided more evidence on May 21, when a photograph taken from his Coastal Command Spitfire revealed the pair anchored in Kors Fiord. Rotherham confirmed next day that *Bismarck* was on its way to the Atlantic. The British Home Fleet was put on the alert, and the hunt was on.

The Germans had their own reconnaissance aircraft in the air. On May 20 they had observed the three largest warships of the Royal Navy's Home Fleet – *King George V*, *Prince of Wales* and *Hood* – together with the aircraft carrier *Victorious*, battlecruiser *Repulse* and six cruisers, safely at anchor in Scapa Flow, the Orkney naval base guarding Britain's northern approaches. On May 22 a pilot reported seeing the four big ships still there. The German surface fleet commander, Admiral Günther Lütjens, thought that *Bismarck* had got clean away. They were both mistaken.

Admiral Sir John Tovey, Commander in Chief of the Home Fleet, had ordered *Hood* and *Prince of Wales* to put to sea in the early hours of the 22nd and he followed with *King George V* and *Victorious* within 24 hours. While the cruisers *Manchester* and *Birmingham* watched the Iceland-Faeroes gap, two heavy cruisers, HMS *Suffolk* and *Norfolk*, patrolled the Denmark Strait between Iceland and Greenland. It was there on May 23 that *Suffolk* sighted *Bismarck* and *Prinz Eugen* edging south.

DEATH OF A GIANT

As soon as he learned *Bismarck*'s course, Vice Admiral Lancelot Holland set course to intercept it with his heavyweights, *Hood* and *Prince of Wales*. A strong wind from the north had dispersed the worst of the fog by the early hours of May 24, as the two British ships closed in on their prey.

Prinz Eugen's long-range radar had given plenty of warning of the British approach, and the Germans were ready to attack. Lütjens had craftily placed *Prinz Eugen* ahead, leaving *Bismarck* relatively free to judge *Hood*'s range and unleash its own fire with deadly accuracy.

There can be no certainty about what happened next. Perhaps *Hood*'s armour was penetrated. Perhaps its unprotected torpedoes exploded; they were enough to break the ship's back. But the end came spectacularly, only eight minutes after the start of the action, just after 6 am. *Prinz Eugen*'s gunnery officer, Commander Jasper, described

1 Encased in specially strengthened armour with decks up to 120 mm ($4\frac{3}{4}$ in) thick, the new 50 000 tonne German battleship *Bismarck* is at large in the Atlantic ready to strike at the convoys of merchant ships supplying Britain. The swift heavyweight, with a normal speed of 29 knots (54 km/h), has earlier been caught by British ships and damaged by *Prince of Wales*.

2 Just before 8 pm on the rain-soaked gusty evening of May 26, 15 Swordfish torpedo bombers from the carrier *Ark Royal* swoop at *Bismarck*. If they can slow it further, British warships could catch up and engage it.

3 Holed two days before by *Prince of Wales*, *Bismarck* is trailing an oil slick and sailing bow down with seawater surging over the deck. With its speed cut, the ship is still over 1000 km (620 miles) from St Nazaire.

4 Eight menacing 380 mm (15 in) and twelve 150 mm (5.9 in) guns bristle from *Bismarck*, as well as 105 mm (4.1 in) ack-ack guns and a host of closer-range armament. The battleship has the latest radar gun-aiming gear.

5 Two open-cockpit Swordfishes dash at *Bismarck* from the starboard quarter. They plummet down to skim the heaving water, and finally fly so low that fire from *Bismarck*'s guns passes over them. One of the biplanes delivers a crippling torpedo before it banks and climbs.

6 Below water near its stern *Bismarck* is pierced by the Swordfish's torpedo. The explosion damages the steering gear and the maimed giant careers in circles; then, with rudder jammed, it heads NNW. On that course it makes easy prey for British warships, which will gather to pound *Bismarck* to destruction.

the scene: 'There was an explosion of quite incredible violence . . . Through huge holes opened up in the grey hull, enormous flames leapt up from the depths of the ship . . . and blazed for several seconds through an ash-coloured pall of smoke [which formed] two billowing columns . . . Below them formed a kind of incandescent dome.'

Ordinary Signalman Albert Briggs, one of just three survivors from *Hood*'s crew of 1420, described his experience after *Hood* had listed 25 degrees to port: 'I got out of the starboard door . . . the water by that time had got level with the compass platform. I do not remember anything more then until I found myself on the surface. The bows of the *Hood* were vertical in the water about 50 yards away and I was looking at the bottom of the ship.'

Hood was ripped in half, and within minutes the entire ship had been engulfed by the sea. *Prince of Wales*, now alone with jammed turrets and considerable shell damage, withdrew. But two shells from *Prince of Wales* had holed *Bismarck* and broken its fuel lines, reducing its speed. Lütjens decided to make for St Nazaire in German-occupied France for repairs. He left *Prinz Eugen* to continue its raiding patrol and headed south.

TENSION BUILDS

Admiral Tovey then threw the full weight of the Home Fleet into the chase; from now on *Bismarck* was to have no rest. *Suffolk* shadowed at extreme radar range, accompanied by *Norfolk* and the damaged *Prince of Wales*. Fairey Swordfish torpedo bombers, antiquated-looking but sturdy, took off from the carrier *Victorious* hoping to further retard *Bismarck*'s progress; but in the thick, low cloud, only one torpedo inflicted damage, and that was minimal. At the same time the Gibraltar-based Force 'H' – led by the carrier *Ark Royal* – was heading north.

Then, alarmingly, early on May 25, the British lost the scent. In a feverish search, Swordfish swept the northern seas, and *Suffolk* and *Norfolk* scoured the south-west – but both drew blanks. *Bismarck* seemed to have vanished and the chance of bringing it to action lost. But then a depressed Admiral Lütjens sent home a long signal with *Bismarck*'s telltale signature; this gave Allied direction finders an excellent fix. Soon after this code-breakers at Bletchley Park deciphered a personal message from a senior Luftwaffe officer in Athens, whose nephew was serving on *Bismarck*. He wanted to know where the ship was bound, and British code-breakers deciphered the answer.

The following morning, May 26, Catalina flying boats from RAF Coastal Command knew where to concentrate their search. Through a break in the clouds, a US Navy pilot on loan to the RAF, Ensign Leonard Smith, saw *Bismarck* and signalled its bearings back to the fleet.

But a vital 31 hours had been lost, and the German ship was now way ahead and approaching the Bay of Biscay and safety. Much of the Home Fleet, including *Prince of Wales*, had turned back because it was short of fuel. In a desperate last-ditch attempt to halt it, a Swordfish strike was launched from the pitching, spray-washed decks of *Ark Royal* on the afternoon of May 26. Thick layers of cloud meant the aircrew were attacking blind; when their radar picked up a ship in the expected vicinity of *Bismarck*, the diving planes released 14 torpedoes. None found their mark – luckily, for the target ship turned out to be the British cruiser *Sheffield*.

Just before 8 pm a second flight homed in on *Bismarck* and came under fierce fire. Two torpedoes out of 13 struck the battleship, and one of them – the Germans later described it as a thousand-to-one chance – completely wrecked *Bismarck*'s steering.

Condemned and exhausted, the ship's company watched a wave of British destroyers appear on the horizon. The accuracy of *Bismarck*'s fire kept the five ships of the 4th Destroyer Flotilla at bay, and of the 16 torpedoes fired by the Allies, none hit their target. But throughout that long night, the beleaguered German ship was constantly harassed.

THE FINAL BLOW

Tovey chose his two most powerful and well-armoured battleships to deliver the final blow: *King George V*, the fleet flagship and fully worked-up sister-ship to *Prince of Wales*, and *Rodney*, with its huge 16 in (405 mm) guns – the biggest in the British fleet. They were supported by the cruisers *Norfolk* and *Dorsetshire*. Just after 8.45 am on May 27, the British ships at last homed in on their quarry.

Hundreds of shells smashed into *Bismarck*, and within two hours all that remained was the blackened, skeletal hull of a once mighty ship, consumed within by an inferno of flame. That it was still afloat was remarkable. As the British fleet halted the action and turned for home, *Dorsetshire* fired the last three British torpedoes that finally sank *Bismarck*.

Lieutenant Burkard von Müllenheim-Rechberg, the senior survivor, later wrote of the sinking: 'We all snapped our hands to our caps, glanced at the flag, and jumped . . . In the water we were pushed together in a bunch, as we bobbed up and down like corks. We swam away from the sinking ship as hard as we could to escape her suction.' They looked back to see *Bismarck*'s bow rearing out of the water and its captain, Ernst Lindemann, struggling towards the stern – 'which was becoming more level as the ship lay over. There he stopped and raised his hand to his white cap. The *Bismarck* now lay completely on her side. Then slowly, slowly, she and the saluting Lindemann went down.'

It was 10.39 am. Over 2000 crew members went down with *Bismarck*. *Dorsetshire* picked up 110 survivors, but a U-boat warning sent it scuttling away, leaving nearly 300 German sailors to the relentless sea. Churchill interrupted House of Commons business to announce that *Hood* had been avenged, and MPs erupted into loud cheers.

SPARING ITS VICTIMS The British cruiser *Dorsetshire* picks up survivors from *Bismarck* after launching the three torpedoes that finished off the battleship. As it heeled over, its surviving crew saluted their dead comrades and then abandoned ship. *Dorsetshire* hauled up 110 Germans before a U-boat drove it off. Others were left in the chill Atlantic; more than 2000 of the battleship's crew died.

The coldest war

Storms, sub-zero temperatures and pack ice made the convoy runs to northern Russia bad enough. The German Navy and Luftwaffe did all they could to make things worse, and a decision by an ailing British First Sea Lord led to tragedy.

WITHIN TWO MONTHS of Hitler's invasion of the Soviet Union in June 1941, British convoys began the perilous task of taking supplies and raw materials to the hard-pressed Russians. The Germans controlled the Baltic, and they and the Italians made the route through the Mediterranean and Black Sea too hazardous. So the main route at first had to be through the Arctic Ocean – picking a way between the pack ice and German-held Norway – to Archangel and the ice-free port of Murmansk. (Supplies also went via the Persian Gulf and overland through Iran, but they could not at first match the tonnage carried by ships. However, by 1943 the safer overland route had begun to take the lion's share.)

The first convoy to Russia sailed in August 1941. Regular convoys, prefixed PQ for the outward journeys (probably after Commander P.Q. Edwards, who planned them) and QP for the homeward, began the following month. At first only the weather, which could be foul even in summer, posed problems. But as 1942 came, Hitler's blitzkrieg had been blunted, and the Germans began to take a serious interest in the convoys that were carrying planes, tanks, guns and other war supplies to Stalin. They began by beefing up their Norwegian-based naval forces with more U-boats, the battleship *Tirpitz*, the pocket battleship *Admiral Scheer* and the heavy cruiser *Prinz Eugen*, along with every available destroyer and torpedo boat. *Prinz Eugen* was torpedoed en route and put out of action by the submarine HMS *Trident*, but the threat to the convoys remained serious.

On March 5, convoy PQ12 was spotted by a Focke-Wulf Condor long-range reconnaissance plane, and *Tirpitz*, escorted by three destroyers, sailed to intercept. But it in turn was spotted by the submarine *Seawolf*. Under the command of Admiral Sir John Tovey in the battleship *King George V*, a force including the battlecruiser *Renown* and aircraft carrier *Victorious* set out to try a repeat of the *Bismarck* victory.

Remembering how *Bismarck* had first been crippled by air-launched torpedoes, Tovey sent six Fairey Albacore aircraft on a reconnaissance to fix *Tirpitz*'s position, followed by a strike of 12 torpedo-carrying Albacores. This was, he told the crews, 'a wonderful chance which may achieve most valuable results. God be with you'. Unfortunately, the slow Albacores could not launch an effective attack, and two were lost to anti-aircraft fire. Nevertheless the Germans were unnerved by the attack on their last large battleship, and *Tirpitz* was ordered back to its Norway base.

Now the offensive against the convoys was stepped up with U-boats, aircraft and lighter surface forces. Not that the U-boats had been idle – a group of three had attacked convoys PQ7 and PQ8 on January 2 and 17, 1942, claiming a freighter and the escort destroyer HMS *Matabele*. Only two of *Matabele*'s crew of 200 were saved from the icy waters, cold enough to kill a man within minutes. Convoy PQ13 was the first to sail after the German Naval Staff's decision to launch the three-pronged attacks, and particularly bad weather scattered the ships over 240 km (150 miles) of ocean. On March 28 two fell prey to Junkers Ju88 bombers, and the next day three German destroyers sank a Panamanian ship.

But now the weather worsened. Icy winds whipped the sea into a heaving mass, and the big, somewhat top-heavy German destroyers wallowed in the turmoil. They were caught by three escort ships: the cruiser *Trinidad* and the destroyers *Fury* and *Eclipse*. One German destroyer was sunk but the others got away, damaging *Eclipse* in the process. During the exchange *Trinidad* suffered the indignity of being hit by one of its own torpedoes, which reversed course in the icy sea as the extreme cold affected its steering. U-boats accounted for two more of PQ13's ships.

TANKS AWAY! On their way to the Red Army, Matilda tanks are loaded aboard a ship for convoy PQ2 in October 1941. This convoy reached Archangel without loss, but later the route became much more hazardous. (Below) Merchant captains are briefed at a convoy conference.

As winter ended, the convoys no longer enjoyed the cover of long dark nights. Casualties began to mount and the First Sea Lord, Admiral Sir Dudley Pound, warned the War Cabinet of the dangers of continuing the convoys. Churchill, however, was under strong pressure from both Roosevelt and Stalin to keep them going. Sir Dudley's misgivings were confirmed by what happened to PQ14 and QP10. Sixteen of PQ14's 24 merchant ships and two escorts had to return to Iceland after ice damage, and one merchantman was sunk by a U-boat. Four ships of QP10 were sunk. Then the Royal Navy lost one of its biggest cruisers, HMS *Edinburgh*, in a U-boat attack on the westbound convoy QP11.

Edinburgh, carrying a cargo of gold bullion, was hit twice by torpedoes from *U-356*, and with its stern blown off turned back to Murmansk for repairs. With the cruiser out of the way, the Germans sent three destroyers, *Z-24*, *Z-25* and the older *Hermann Schoemann*, into the attack. But they were tenaciously held at bay by the aptly named destroyer *Bulldog* and succeeded only in sinking a straggling Russian merchantman. The three Germans were then ordered to seek out and finish off *Edinburgh*.

They caught up with it and two escorting destroyers on the morning of May 2. Crippled or not, *Edinburgh* still had plenty of fight in it, and with superb gunnery fatally damaged *Hermann Schoemann*. But a salvo of torpedoes finished off the cruiser and it was abandoned. Fearful that its valuable cargo should fall into German hands, the escorting destroyer *Foresight*, though badly damaged itself, sent *Edinburgh* to the bottom. QP11 suffered no more losses, but while the German destroyers were dealing with *Edinburgh*, PQ14 was suffering a new form of attack. In the half-light of early morning, six Heinkel He115 twin-engine seaplanes swooped down and sank three merchantmen with torpedoes.

AIR THREAT

It was plain to the Admiralty that air attacks constituted a very serious threat, and when PQ16 sailed on May 21 – the biggest convoy yet, with 35 cargo ships – it was escorted by *Empire Lawrence*, a CAM ship (a merchantman carrying a catapult-launched aircraft) and all ships towed barrage balloons to discourage low-level air attacks. The first attack came from Ju88 bombers and Heinkel He111 torpedo aircraft. *Empire Lawrence* launched its Hurricane, which shot down an He111 and damaged another, but was itself accidentally shot down by an American merchant ship. The convoy, however, was unscathed – though the next day a ship was sunk by a U-boat.

The Germans' main attack came from the air on May 27. Ju88s sank four ships, including *Empire Lawrence*, which was carrying explosives and went up like a bomb. Later that day another ammunition ship, *Empire Purcell*, was bombed and blew up. Further attacks were beaten off when the convoy was reinforced by Soviet destroyers, six Russian-based British minesweepers from the Kola Inlet and Hurricanes of the Red Air Force, and the surviving ships made port safely in Murmansk and Archangel. The minesweepers had been in Russia since regular convoys began, to cover them at the eastern end of their voyages. Convoy QP12, which had left for home on May 21, had a relatively safe passage, a Hurricane from the CAM ship *Empire Morn* shooting down a shadowing aircraft. Sadly the Hurricane pilot died when his parachute failed to open.

The Germans were not too pleased with the results of the attack on PQ16 – 108 aircraft sorties had managed only six sinkings. They decided to revert to using big ships for the attack on the next convoy. These would work in two groups – *Tirpitz* and *Admiral Hipper* (which had replaced *Prinz Eugen*) in one group, *Admiral Scheer* and *Lützow*, which had arrived in May, in the other. They called the plan *Rösselsprung* ('Knight's Move'); ironically it was a knight, Sir Dudley Pound, who helped the plan to succeed without the big ships firing a shot.

CONFUSION OVER PQ17

The ships of convoy PQ17 gathered in Hvalfiord, Iceland, in late June – 35 merchantmen, three rescue ships and two fleet tankers. They would be escorted by six destroyers, four corvettes, three minesweepers, four armed trawlers and two anti-aircraft ships, all under Commander Jack Broome in the destroyer HMS *Keppel*.

There was also a covering force, commanded by Rear Admiral Louis Hamilton, consisting of the cruisers HMS *London*, HMS *Norfolk*, USS *Tuscaloosa* and USS *Wichita* and three destroyers, which would stay close to the convoy for part of its journey. Also in support was the main body of Tovey's Home Fleet, the battleships HMS *Duke of York* and USS *Washington*, the carrier *Victorious*, two cruisers plus more destroyers. Two British submarines gave close support to the convoy, and two patrol lines of British, Free French and Russian submarines lay in wait off northern Norway.

Intelligence reports and decoded German radio signals had forewarned the Admiralty of German intentions – and with PQ17 in the offing, the scene was set for a major showdown between Germany's big ships and the Allied navies. The convoy sailed on June 27, and six days later came the first attack from the air. Seven He115s dropped torpedoes. No hits were scored and one aircraft was shot down. Two days later a lone He115 roared out of the fog and torpedoed an American Liberty ship. The biggest air attack came when 23 He111s came in from two directions while Ju88 bombers tried to divert the attention of the escorts. Four aircraft were shot down, and the convoy lost one ship sunk and one abandoned. Broome was well satisfied with his escorts – as long as the convoy kept together he could protect it from air and submarine attacks.

Broome's confidence was not shared by the Naval Staff in London. Conflicting reports as to the whereabouts of the German ships had created confusion. Were they still at their base in Altenfjord in Norway or had they put to sea? Intercepted and decoded German signals were inconclusive. At 8.30 pm on July 4, Pound called a meeting of senior staff officers concerned with PQ17. With no certain knowledge of the movements of the German force a decision had to

be made on whether the convoy should continue on course or be ordered to scatter.

Vice Admiral Henry Moore, Vice Chief of Naval Staff, argued that if the convoy was to scatter it should do so that evening, as there would be a lack of sea room the next day. Pound leaned back in his chair and closed his eyes. Then he picked up a signal pad and said: 'The convoy is to be dispersed.' He personally drafted a signal ordering the convoy to disperse and proceed to Russian ports. But as soon as the signal had been sent, Moore realised that the word 'disperse' was ambiguous: the ships might fall into disorganised groups, offering good targets to the enemy. To escape the German force the convoy would have to scatter, every merchant ship making its own way to safety, and Broome would have to decide what to do with the escorts. Moore now drafted a new signal: 'MOST IMMEDIATE . . . Convoy is to scatter.'

The two conflicting signals, coming in quick succession, followed an order to Hamilton to withdraw his covering force to the south-west. Broome ordered the convoy to scatter and then, thinking that Hamilton's force was about to tackle the German battle group, took his destroyers to join it. But all they found was empty sea.

BIRDS OF PREY Torpedo-carrying Heinkel He111s attack a ship of the ill-fated convoy PQ17. U-boats and planes took a heavy toll after a tragic error over an order. The searing cold was another powerful adversary. After an icy night, a signalman (below left) tests his lamp. And three heavily wrapped men (below) stand beside icicle-encrusted gear.

AT THE U-BOATS' MERCY

Rösselsprung had got off to a bad start, when *Lützow* and three destroyers ran aground on July 2, while *Tirpitz*, the two remaining cruisers, nine destroyers and two torpedo boats were held back at Altenfjord until it could be confirmed that there was no aircraft carrier nearby. Confirmation came on the morning of July 5, when it was learned that not only were the British fleet and its carrier withdrawing, but also the convoy's escort was doing the same.

Tirpitz and its accompanying warships set sail with high hopes, but were soon spotted by a Russian submarine, and then by a British aircraft. This gave the Germans cold feet once more – like Tovey, Admiral Raeder was not certain of his enemy's whereabouts, and the threat of the Allied fleet and its carrier could not be ruled out. Raeder ordered his ships back to port, and the great confrontation never came about.

Meanwhile, PQ17 had been left to the mercy of the U-boats. *U-703* sank the freighter *Empire Byron* after five attempts. Then the toll began to mount steadily – eight more ships sunk by U-boats, six more by aircraft and another six by the combined attacks of aircraft and submarines. The 24 ships lost took with them 430 tanks, 210 aircraft, 3350 other vehicles and 100 000 tonnes of general cargo; 153 sailors died.

Pound had made one of the saddest errors of the war. Even if the powerful German battle squadron had attacked, the toll could hardly have been worse. In fact, given the Germans' persistent nervousness about confronting even much weaker convoy escorts, they may well not have attacked at all – or only halfheartedly. There was also a tragic aftermath. The homeward-bound convoy QP13, which had escaped the attention of U-boats while they were attacking PQ17, lost itself in the mist and storms of the Denmark Strait, and ran into an Allied minefield. Five ships and one escort vessel sank.

Tovey was determined that there would be no repeat of PQ17, so he sent an exceptionally powerful destroyer escort with the next convoy, PQ18, plus the escort carrier *Avenger*. The convoy sailed in September and was heavily attacked, losing 13 ships to U-boats and aircraft – but at the cost to the Germans of three U-boats and 22 planes. Raeder – under orders from Hitler not to risk his surface ships unduly – called off a planned attack on the returning QP14. But then there was a lull in the Arctic as the Royal Navy concentrated on supporting the North African 'Torch' landings. When the convoys resumed in December, strong, close destroyer escorts would be the rule, with cruisers in support and the Home Fleet's capital ships as distant cover.

SAD SIR DUDLEY

Early in 1942, Chief of the Imperial General Staff Sir Alan Brooke described Admiral Sir Dudley Pound at chiefs of staff meetings as being like 'a parrot asleep on his perch'. In truth, Alfred Dudley Pickman Rogers Pound (1877-1943) was never really fitted for the tremendous role of First Sea Lord. He gained the position when his predecessor, Sir Roger Backhouse, resigned shortly before dying of a brain tumour.

Pound had joined the Royal Navy as a cadet in 1891. At the Battle of Jutland, in World War I, he commanded the battleship *Colossus*. He was promoted rear admiral in 1926 and became Second Sea Lord in 1932. Three years later, he was promoted to full admiral and Commander in Chief of the Mediterranean Fleet, where he stayed until he took over from Backhouse as First Sea Lord in 1939.

Pound's strategies during the war were not without success. They led to the sinking of *Graf Spee* and *Bismarck* and to victories such as that off Cape Matapan in the Mediterranean. He oversaw the naval elements of the 'Torch' landings in November 1942 and the Allied landings on Sicily. He also opposed the fatal decision to send *Prince of Wales* and *Repulse* to the Far East. But from as early as 1940 Pound started to show signs of ill health and his powers of concentration began to fail. He was, in fact, seriously ill when he made the fateful PQ17 decision. In September 1943 he resigned; he died a month later of a brain tumour – like his predecessor.

6: THE NEW ROMAN EMPIRE

Benito Mussolini's dreams of emulating the Caesars were embarrassingly short-lived.

Fighting over the 'Italian lake'

When Mussolini brought Italy into the war in June 1940, he bragged of making the Mediterranean an 'Italian lake'. But Britain's forceful Admiral Sir Andrew Cunningham had other ideas. By the start of 1941, the Mediterranean could more fairly be known as 'Cunningham's Pond'.

ITALY HAD BEEN AT WAR less than a month when it suffered its first sharp reprimand at the hands of the Royal Navy. Mussolini was to claim the skirmish as a splendid victory, ignoring the fact that his ships had turned tail. The overture to the action came on July 7, 1940, when a British submarine spotted a powerful Italian naval force escorting a military convoy to Libya, Italy's North African colony.

Admiral Sir Andrew Browne Cunningham, commanding the British Mediterranean Fleet on board the battleship *Warspite*, had been itching to hear just such news. With three battleships, the aircraft carrier *Eagle* and an escort of cruisers and destroyers, Cunningham immediately headed west from the eastern Mediterranean. By dawn on the 9th, he was just 230 km (145 miles) east of the Italians, now heading home again, and by midday was close enough to dispatch a wave of Swordfish torpedo bombers to spot the enemy. But the aircraft were too slow to find the speeding battleships. He also sent ahead his fast cruisers.

When *Neptune* made contact the two fleets were just off the Calabrian coast, near the toe of Italy. Soon the first shots were exchanged, causing no damage. Then *Warspite* hove in view of the enemy. Italian shells burst on either side of the battleship, but left it unharmed. *Warspite*, however, had an ultra-modern fire control computer to direct its 15 in (380 mm) guns, and scored a hit on the thinly armoured Italian flagship, *Giulio Cesare*, at a range of more than 21 km (13 miles); the flagship kept going, but at reduced speed.

This precision flabbergasted the Italians, who promptly turned tail and made off behind a smoke screen. Italian land-based bombers mounted a high-level attack on Cunningham's fleet but did negligible damage. Indeed, the Italian strikes were as dangerous to their own ships as to the British. Crews untrained in maritime operations and in bombing moving targets could not even identify the ships, let alone hit them – none of which stopped Mussolini from claiming victory. For Cunningham the action had been disappointingly inconclusive.

BALANCE OF SEA POWER

In the war's first months the Allies had ruled supreme in the Mediterranean. The French fleet was unopposed from Gibraltar to Malta – and Cunningham's fleet from Malta to Suez. Oil supplies could pass through undisturbed from the Middle East, and British communications with India were secure.

Then all changed. First came Italy's entry into the war on the Axis side on June 10, 1940. Jutting right into the central Mediterranean, Italy was in a perfect position to sever Britain's sea routes. It had a large, modern fleet and, though without aircraft carriers, the *Regia Aeronautica* (Italian Air Force) had strategically placed air bases on Sardinia, Sicily, the little island of Pantellaria between Sicily and Tunisia, and in the Italian-ruled Dodecanese group off south-western Turkey. In late June, France's capitulation to Hitler made Britain's position in the Mediterranean still more precarious.

From as early as May 1940, when Italy began to look threatening, the British started to divert shipping around the Cape of Good Hope – and for a while considered abandoning the Mediterranean altogether. Instead, though, they set about reorganising their forces. Cunningham transferred his main base to Alexandria from Malta – dangerously exposed to attack from Sicily, 95 km (60 miles) to the north. And a smaller fleet known as Force 'H', under Vice Admiral Sir James Somerville, was based at Gibraltar to replace the French. Malta was maintained as a base for raids against Italian convoys to Libya.

At the same time, the British had another, extremely distasteful, task – to make sure that France's Mediterranean Fleet did not fall into Axis hands. This was accomplished on July 3, when Force 'H' attacked the French North African base at Mers El Kébir near Oran (see box, '*A hateful decision*'). At Alexandria, Admiral Cunningham managed diplomatically to secure the disarmament and immobilisation of France's Eastern Mediterranean Squadron. French warships in British ports were seized. These actions soured relations with the French, including those who continued to resist Germany. But fortunately for Britain, the Vichy government kept its promise to keep its ships out of German hands and scuttled the remains of its fleet after Hitler occupied all France in 1942.

Cunningham, meanwhile, had decided to seek out and destroy the Italian fleet. His action off Calabria on July 9 was followed on July 19 by a bigger success, when a force including the Australian cruiser HMAS *Sydney* sank the Italian cruiser *Bartolomeo Colleoni* off northern Crete. In August he was considerably strengthened by the arrival of the brand-new carrier *Illustrious* (equipped with all the latest technology, including radar), the battleship *Valiant* (also with radar) and two anti-aircraft cruisers.

BY NIGHT TO TARANTO

But the pride of the Italian fleet – its six battleships, supreme of which were the brand-new 42 000 tonne *Littorio* and *Vittorio Veneto* – was remarkably elusive. After July 9 their commanders were under strict orders to avoid full-scale confrontations with the British. Cunningham came close to a fleet action in September when he was escorting a troop convoy to Malta, but covering the vulnerable troops had priority – especially as the Italians had four battleships to his two. The Italians did not attack, nor was anything seen of them in October when another

troop convoy was run to Malta. Finally, the British decided to hit them in their base at Taranto, just inside Italy's heel.

Cunningham revived a plan first suggested five years before, when Britain seemed close to war with Italy after Mussolini's invasion of Ethiopia: his carriers prepared to launch a daring night-time air strike against Taranto. They first chose the night of October 21/22 (the anniversary of the Battle of Trafalgar), when a full moon would help their aircraft to find their targets. But after a fire aboard *Illustrious* the date had to be put back to November 11/12 – a night of three-quarters moon. They also meant originally to use both *Illustrious* and *Eagle*, but at the last minute the elderly *Eagle* had to be pulled out because of battle damage. In the end, just 21 lumbering Swordfish biplanes were available for the attack.

At 8.35 pm on November 11, the first wave of 12 Swordfishes began to take off from *Illustrious*, stationed off the Greek island of Cephalonia (Kefallinia), some 275 km (170 miles) south-east of Taranto. Just under 2½ hours later the leading aircraft, piloted by Lt Commander Kenneth ('Hooch') Williamson and navigated by Lieutenant Norman ('Blood') Scarlett, was approaching the Italian base when the sky ahead erupted suddenly with ack-ack fire. The Italians had been alerted by their sound detectors, which ruined any chance of surprise.

The attackers carried on undeterred. As flares dropped by two Swordfishes bathed the harbour in a weird golden light, six other torpedo-bearing planes swooped down for the attack. Flying just above the wave tops, weaving around the lethal steel cables of barrage balloons and swerving wildly from side to side to avoid savage enemy fire, they let loose their torpedoes. Within minutes, all was devastation. One torpedo, launched by Williamson and Scarlett, hit and sank the battleship *Conte di Cavour*. Two more damaged *Littorio*. Two Swordfishes bombed the fuel stores and four others dropped their loads on ships and the seaplane base. The seaplane hangars were set on fire. An hour later, torpedoes from the second Swordfish strike hit *Littorio* once more and another battleship, *Caio Duilio*.

'None of us really thought we would come out of it alive', confessed one of the raiders later. In fact, only two Swordfishes were lost. Both crew members of one were killed, but Williamson and Scarlett in the second managed to swim ashore and were taken prisoner. Meanwhile, the chaos left by the intrepid airmen from *Illustrious* was spectacular. Three of the Italian battleships were out of action, one permanently and two for months to come. The same night, British cruisers sank three Italian ships heading for Brindisi.

As the surviving Italian battleships withdrew ignominiously to Naples, the British felt secure enough to move a small troop convoy from Gibraltar to Alexandria. It was covered by Force 'H', which on November 27 drove off two enemy battleships off Cape Spartivento, Sardinia.

On the other side of the world, the Japanese Navy's Commander in Chief, Admiral Isoroku Yamamoto, studied accounts of the successful British raid on ships in harbour with close interest, even sending officers to visit Taranto. The fruits of their studies would be seen just over a year later – at Pearl Harbor.

BITTER ENCOUNTER Royal Navy shells explode in the French naval base of Mers El Kébir on July 3, 1940. The bombardment began at 5.54 pm, after the French rejected Somerville's appeals for a peaceful disarmament.

'A HATEFUL DECISION'

Just before 6 pm on July 3, 1940, a British naval force under Vice Admiral Sir James Somerville opened fire on French ships moored at Mers El Kébir in France's North African colony Algeria. In the ensuing bombardment, the British blew up one old French battleship, disabled another as well as the modern fast battlecruiser *Dunkerque,* and killed more than 1200 French seamen. *Dunkerque*'s sister-ship *Strasbourg* got away, with five destroyers, to Toulon in unoccupied southern France.

Just over ten days earlier, France had capitulated to Hitler – leaving Britain with the question: What would become of the French fleet? It was the world's fourth-largest after those of Britain, the USA and Japan. In Axis hands it would transform the balance of power at sea and greatly increase the risk of an invasion of Britain.

France's ships were carefully dispersed among overseas bases. The Vichy government vowed not to let the Germans or Italians use them, but that was not good enough for Churchill's new government in London, which decided on June 27 that French ships must be neutralised – or sunk. Churchill called this 'a hateful decision, the most unnatural and painful in which I have ever been involved'.

A week later Somerville's force appeared off Mers El Kébir, which had the largest concentration of French ships. Vice Admiral Marcel Gensoul was given the choice of joining the British, disarming or scuttling. He refused all these options and Somerville had to open fire after postponing the deadline several times.

In Berlin, meanwhile, Hitler was increasingly worried. Before his planned invasion of the Soviet Union the next summer, he wanted a secure southern flank – but his ally Mussolini was proving quite unreliable. *Il Duce* could not contain the British at sea or in North Africa, and his invasion of Greece, launched in October, was another fiasco. In late October Hitler met Spain's dictator, General Francisco Franco, but failed to get him to enter the war and join in an Axis attack on Gibraltar.

OLD FAITHFUL The plodding Fairey Swordfish biplane carried a single torpedo at 225 km/h (140 mph). But it proved a fine aircraft, robust and durable, that showed its worth at Taranto. This daring raid on warships in harbour changed the face of naval warfare.

ENTER THE LUFTWAFFE

Then in December Hitler sent *Fliegerkorps X* (X Flying Corps) to Sicily. This specially trained anti-ship bomber force crippled *Illustrious* in a 6½ minute attack on January 10, 1941. The carrier, which had been covering convoys to Malta and Greece, had to limp back to Malta before making a slow, painful journey through Suez, around the Cape and across the Atlantic for a complete refit in the USA. It was replaced in the Mediterranean by *Formidable*. On January 11, the cruiser *Southampton* was sunk and its sister-ship *Gloucester* damaged. Fliegerkorps X also made a series of devastating raids against Malta, and Cunningham told London that no more convoys could be risked in the Mediterranean until the fleet had more air cover. By March a small convoy was able to reach Malta safely, but two of its ships were sunk on arrival.

In March Italy's Rear Admiral Angelo Iachino was dispatched with a formidable raiding force, including the battleship *Vittorio Veneto* but no air cover, to intercept British and Commonwealth troops being ferried from North Africa to reinforce the Greeks – in anticipation of Hitler's expected invasion of Greece and Yugoslavia. At the same time, members of the Italian navy's special assault units (see box, *Raids of the human torpedoes*) made a daring raid on Suda Bay in Crete with six motor launches carrying explosives. The British cruiser *York* was crippled.

Aggressive as ever, Cunningham decided to ambush the Italians off the island of Gavdhos, just south of Crete. Making sure that he was seen – so that Axis spies in Alexandria would hear of his movements – he left *Warspite*, ostentatiously armed with his golfing gear, and checked in for the night at the local golf club. But as soon as darkness fell he slipped back on board and a few hours later *Warspite*, with the battleships *Valiant* and *Barham*, the carrier *Formidable* and nine destroyers, slid silently out to sea. Off Gavdhos, they would link up with a cruiser and destroyer force (including the Australian cruiser *Perth*) under Vice Admiral Henry Pridham-Wippell.

AMBUSH AT MATAPAN

The Italian and British fleets first made contact south of Gavdhos early the next morning (March 28). Pridham-Wippell tried to lead the Italians towards the main fleet. At around 11 am, however, a strike by six Albacore torpedo bombers and two Fulmar fighters from *Formidable* so worried Iachino that he started to withdraw north-west towards Taranto. The battle became, in Cunningham's words, 'a pursuit'.

Neither side scored a hit, however, until the afternoon, when a further air strike from *Formidable* led by Lt Commander John Dalyell-Stead attacked *Vittorio Veneto*. Dalyell-Stead was shot down – but not before he had dropped a torpedo which made a large hole in the Italian battleship's port side. It juddered to a halt, but picked up speed again and escaped. In further British air strikes at 7.25 pm the heavy cruiser *Pola* was severely damaged.

By now darkness was falling, with the Italians in full retreat. Cunningham proposed a night pursuit. When some officers demurred, he accused them of being 'a pack of yellow-livered skunks!' After 9 pm came the opportunity he had been longing for. Pridham-Wippell's cruiser *Ajax* – off the southernmost tip of the Peloponnese, Cape Matapan (Cape Tainaron) – reported picking up a large, motionless vessel on its radar. Cunningham's ships immediately began to converge on the stricken vessel.

It was *Pola* – and just at that moment two more Italian cruisers, *Fiume* and *Zara*, were approaching with four destroyers through a light mist to rescue it. Without radar, they were quite unaware of the presence nearby of Cunningham's ships. The British battleship *Valiant*, however, soon picked them up on its radar. Suddenly, at 10.30 pm, as the unsuspecting Italians were closing up on *Pola*, several dazzling searchlights were pinned upon them, followed seconds later by devastating, almost point-blank fire. Men on the three British battleships had allowed them to get within 3500 m (3800 yds) before letting rip their broadsides.

This was the end of *Fiume, Zara* and the destroyer *Alfieri*. Cunningham recalled later that the ships were soon 'nothing but glowing torches and on fire from stem to stern'. Later another Italian destroyer, *Carducci*, was sunk. Early the next morning British sailors boarded *Pola*, found many of the surviving crew roaring drunk, and took them off before sinking the ship.

The Battle of Cape Matapan had cost Cunningham's fleet Dalyell-Stead's plane and its three-man crew. It had cost the Italians five ships and 2400 seamen. Never again would Mussolini's fleet challenge British naval domination of the Mediterranean. A few weeks later, however, the devastation Hitler's Luftwaffe could cause would be seen only too clearly off Crete. Until the Luftwaffe left for the Russian campaign, the Mediterranean was to be virtually closed to British shipping. Malta was kept going – just.

CUNNINGHAM: NELSONIC FIGHTER AND LEADER

From earliest youth, Andrew Browne Cunningham (1883-1963) loved the sea – and when his father asked him if he would like to join the navy, his reply was unhesitating. 'Yes, I should like to be an admiral.' 'ABC' was the outstanding British naval leader of World War II, often compared by historians to Nelson. Sturdy and weatherbeaten, with penetrating blue eyes, he was every inch a fighter. He entered the navy in 1897, and served in the Boer War and on destroyers in World War I. He was given command in the Mediterranean in June 1939, and led Allied naval forces during the 'Torch' landings of 1942 and the invasions of Sicily and the Italian mainland in 1943. Reaching the top as First Sea Lord, he retired a viscount in 1946.

RAIDS OF THE HUMAN TORPEDOES

On the night of December 18/19, 1941, six members of the Italian navy's special assault unit – known as the 'Sea Devils' – did more damage to the British Mediterranean Fleet than all the rest of Mussolini's ships had managed in 1½ years of war. They crippled two battleships, a destroyer and a fuel tanker, all berthed in Alexandria harbour.

They used human torpedoes, or *maiali* ('pigs'), developed before the war. Around 6 m (20 ft) long with its detachable warhead, each torpedo had a crew of two who sat astride it in frogmen's suits. They would approach a target with just their heads bobbing above the waves, then submerge, clamp the warhead below the target's keel, set a time fuse and make off.

The raid on Alexandria was their most spectacular success. A submarine released three torpedoes with their crews, led by Commander Luigi Durand de la Penne. When British destroyers appeared out of the night, the Italians sneaked into the harbour with them. De la Penne and Chief Diver Emilio Bianchi got through anti-torpedo nets protecting the battleship *Valiant*. Then, close to its target, their torpedo stuck in cables and mud. They set the time fuse and swam to a buoy. The other torpedo crews also reached their targets – the battleship *Queen Elizabeth* and the tanker *Sagona*. At dawn all three ships were wracked by violent explosions, and the destroyer *Jervis* was also damaged. The six Italians were taken prisoner.

The British developed their own human torpedo, the 'Chariot', which they used widely in the Mediterranean.

North Africa: Italian ambitions sink in the sand

To Benito Mussolini in the summer of 1940, Egypt seemed a rich prize ready to be plucked from the faltering hands of the British. The Italian Army in North Africa had a ten to one numerical superiority. A walkover seemed certain.

IL DUCE'S ORDERS to his North African commander, Marshal Rodolfo Graziani, were clear: 'The loss of Egypt will be the *coup de grâce* for Great Britain, while the conquest of that rich country, necessary for our communications with Ethiopia, will be the great reward for which Italy is waiting. That you will procure it, I am certain.'

Graziani was not so sure. True, in June 1940 some 300 000 Italian troops in Cyrenaica (north-east Libya) faced a mere 30 000 British and Empire troops in Egypt, under General Sir Archibald Wavell, whose leadership qualities Churchill was already beginning to doubt. Also, the Italians were, on paper, far better equipped, with 1811 guns, 339 light tanks, 8039 trucks and 151 front-line aircraft, while the British were short of all types of equipment and ammunition. But Graziani knew that, should anything go wrong, there would be little time for fresh supplies to reach him. He was disposed to delay his attack until the Germans invaded Britain.

The British had already shown their fighting qualities in sorties behind the Italian lines with armoured cars and motorised infantry. They had ambushed Italian lorries on the coast road and on June 13 even attacked Fort Capuzzo, just over the Libyan border, and took 200 prisoners. These incursions had convinced many of Graziani's troops that their enemy might be fewer in number but was far better armed.

Bullets from the British armoured cars could pierce the armour of the Italian light tanks with ease. And there were disturbing reports about the Matilda, the most heavily armoured tank then in service; Graziani knew that he had no answer to it. Then there was the summer heat, often reaching 50°C (122°F). Every factor suggested to Graziani that he should postpone an assault, at least until autumn. But by September, Mussolini would allow him to delay the attack no longer.

PROUD FEATHERS The Italian forces in North Africa included the Bersaglieri, whose insignia was the distinctive plume of cockerel feathers worn in the helmet. This elite corps of riflemen was founded at the time of the unification of Italy during the 18th and 19th centuries. Like the British Brigade of Guards, the Bersaglieri were considered the 'cream' of the infantry. Though they wore standard tropical dress in the desert, the Bersaglieri were better equipped than the other Italian infantry regiments. The standard issue weapon was a Mannlicher-Carcano M91, 7.35 mm carbine fitted with a folding bayonet.

At first the invasion was surprisingly easy. Six Italian divisions, supported by plenty of artillery and swarms of aircraft, moved east and the British fell back. On September 17, having advanced 95 km (60 miles) in four days, Graziani's army stopped, sat down in the desert, and began to construct a line of fortified camps. These lavish encampments extended from Sidi Barrani, on the coast, 80 km (50 miles) inland. Graziani intended to concentrate on improving his supply lines until the cool of winter, then advance again. But he did not get the chance. In mid-September, Wavell received reinforcements from Britain, including 154 tanks, 48 anti-tank guns, 20 Bofors anti-aircraft guns and 48 25-pounder field guns.

THE BRITISH COUNTERATTACK

Maj General Richard O'Connor, commander of the British Western Desert Force, sent out reconnaissance patrols into the desert from his base at Mersa Matruh. They discovered that, while the Italian camps were well protected with mines and defensive earthworks, there were huge unprotected gaps in between. In the case of Rabia and its neighbour Nibeiwa, the gap was some 25 km (15 miles) wide. In an audacious move code-named Operation 'Compass', O'Connor planned to send the 4th Indian Division supported by 50 Matilda tanks stealthily through the gap to assault the camps from the rear. Meanwhile, his 7th Armoured Division would block the coast road behind the enemy at Buq Buq.

On December 9, at dawn, he struck at Nibeiwa, where the garrison was plunged into chaos by a short 72-gun artillery bombardment. Before they could rally, the Matildas of the 7th Royal Tank Regiment swept into the camp, knocking out 25 Italian tanks before their crews could get to them and blasting the artillery and infantrymen at close range. Two battalions of British infantry, transported by lorries to the camp perimeter, charged with bayonets and grenades. General Pietro Maletti, the Italian forward commander, was found dead in his pyjamas, machine gun in hand.

In the afternoon, similar assaults took the Tummars and Point 90 camps, between Nibeiwa and the sea. Sidi Barrani, on the coast, was bombarded by Royal Navy ships on the night of December 8/9, and fell on the 10th; the Italians abandoned the camps farther south and west of Nibeiwa. The 7th Armoured Division reached Buq Buq on December 11 after sweeping through the desert south of the Italian line. With their line of retreat blocked, 38 300 Italians surrendered, including four generals.

The spectacular success of 'Compass', originally intended simply as a raid on the Italian camps, inspired O'Connor to push on. He was delayed when the 4th Indian Division was ordered to East Africa to reinforce the campaign against the Italians in Eritrea, and by abortive schemes for an expedition to Greece. But in late December he advanced, the 6th Australian Division (which replaced the Indians) following the coast road, the 7th Armoured again sweeping through the desert to outflank the enemy.

DESERT DISCOURSE Generals O'Connor (left) and Wavell discuss tactics near Bardia. Richard O'Connor (1889-1981) was a scholarly man whose imagination produced highly unconventional plans. He led his men from the front, keeping his tactical headquarters near the front line, and often reconnoitred behind enemy lines. He was captured by the Germans on one such trip in April 1941, but escaped when Italy capitulated in 1943 and fought in Normandy. He used to wear an Italian medal won in 1918.

The Italians held two fortresses, at Bardia (Al Bardi), 25 km (15 miles) into Libya, and Tobruk; mines, anti-tank ditches and a double line of concrete bunkers ringed them both. The Commandant of Bardia, Lt General Annibale Bergonzoli, proudly accepted an order from Mussolini to 'fight to the last'. His fortress was taken in three days of hard fighting, from January 3-6, 1941. The RAF and Royal Navy bombarded the town; Australian sappers lifted the mines and blew in the sides of the anti-tank ditches; then the Matildas appeared, leading the infantry through the wire and bunkers.

The British tanks raced on to El Adem, 20 km (12 miles) south of Tobruk. Tobruk fell on January 22, victim to the same tactics as Bardia. O'Connor then prepared to move on to Benghazi, another 385 km (240 miles) west. But on February 3 the Italians began to evacuate Cyrenaica. Graziani had decided to abandon Benghazi and the green, settled hills of Jebel Akhdar. He would make a stand at Sirte, the gateway to the western province of Tripolitania.

THE RACE TO BEDA FOMM

O'Connor was determined not to let the Italians escape. He ordered the 7th Armoured Division, at Mechili 160 km (100 miles) west of Tobruk, to cross the trackless waste south of the Jebel and intercept them. This meant driving across 240 km

GRAZIANI – THE RELUCTANT WARRIOR

Long experience taught Rodolfo Graziani (1882-1955) the hazards of desert warfare. He made his military reputation in Libya in the 1930s, and was Commander in Chief of the southern front during the Italian invasion of Ethiopia in 1935-6. He served as Viceroy of Ethiopia in 1936-7, and was a committed Fascist and ruthless governor. The use of mustard gas by his forces and his brutal reprisals against Ethiopian rebels earned him a sinister reputation. It led to permanent unrest in Ethiopia and an assassination attempt against him in Addis Ababa in February 1937. Mussolini made him Army Chief of Staff in 1939.

Graziani's cautiousness as Military Governor of Libya in 1940 infuriated Mussolini, who dismissed him in the spring of 1941. A court of inquiry reprimanded him after the North African defeat, but Graziani remained a loyal Fascist. In 1943 he became Minister of Defence in Mussolini's rump state in northern Italy. The Americans captured and imprisoned him in 1945.

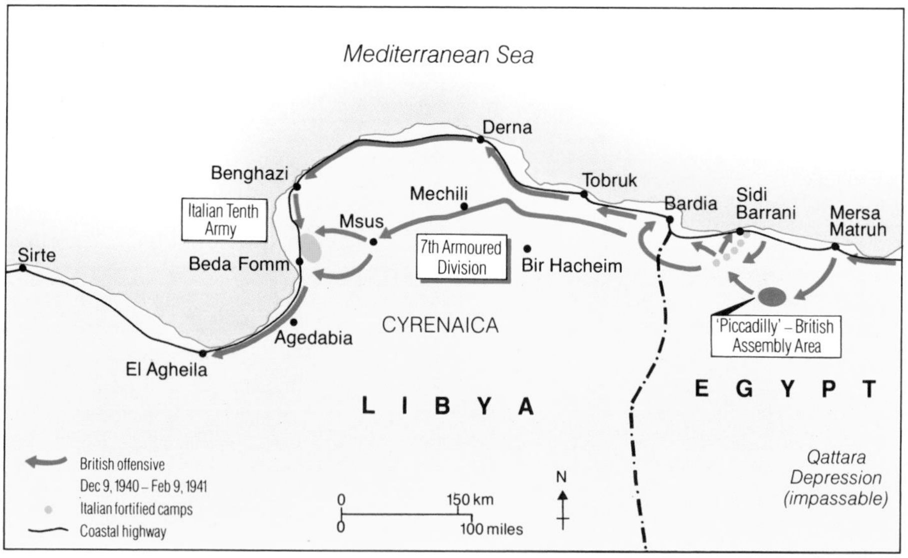

SEE HOW THEY RAN The British offensive began with a thrust from Mersa Matruh through the undefended gap between Rabia and Nibeiwa, to take Bardia and Tobruk. Then the Italians were in full flight through Cyrenaica.

(150 miles) of desert reckoned impassable by the Italians and shunned even by the Bedouin.

The 7th Armoured sent a force of armoured cars, lorried infantry and artillery ahead of the main body. They reached the coast road at Beda Fomm, 100 km (62 miles) south of Benghazi, at noon on February 5; half an hour later the retreating Italian column appeared from the north.

The battle lasted until the dawn of February 7. The Italians tried time and time again to push through the roadblock or break into the desert, fighting hard and bravely and losing 80 tanks. But they arrived in random penny packets and could not concert their efforts. The British forces were reinforced as more tanks arrived from the race across the desert. Some fired on the flank of the enemy column, others attacked the rear, and it was increasingly compressed and confused.

In one last effort, 30 Italian tanks drove straight down the road; one reached the officers' mess tent of the Rifle Brigade, but all were stopped. The Italians surrendered. On February 7, Australian troops entered Benghazi and the next day El Agheila, at the head of the Gulf of Sirte. In less than two months, O'Connor's forces had advanced 800 km (500 miles), destroyed ten Italian divisions, and taken two fortresses, 130 000 prisoners, some 400 tanks and over 800 guns. British casualties were less than 2000.

O'Connor had a plan to exploit his success, to conquer Tripolitania. He had Wavell's support, but Churchill believed that it was more important to send help to Greece, now under threat from the Germans as well as the Italians. On February 12 he ordered Wavell to reduce the army in Cyrenaica to a minimum and send all available troops to Greece. The same day, General Erwin Rommel landed in Tripoli with the first elements of the Afrika Korps.

FESTIVE BOARD A group of British officers celebrate the capture of Sidi Barrani with a well-earned meal, washed down with plenty of Italian wine.

FIASCO AT DAKAR

In the summer of 1940, Free French leader General Charles de Gaulle won Churchill's approval for a bid to set up a Free French movement in French West Africa. De Gaulle reckoned to land unopposed at Dakar, to 'liberate' the Vichy-governed colony. Eleven ships with 6900 British and French troops set sail on August 31, escorted by the battleships HMS *Barham* and *Resolution*, the carrier *Ark Royal*, four cruisers and 16 destroyers.

Far from being unopposed, they met fierce resistance when they reached Dakar on September 23. De Gaulle's broadcast appeals for peaceful surrender were ignored, and emissaries sent ashore were seized. Threats of attack by the British naval force were answered by accurate gunfire from shore batteries and the 47 000 tonne battleship *Richelieu* and other French naval units in the harbour. *Barham*, two cruisers and two destroyers were hit; *Resolution* was torpedoed by the submarine *Bévéziers* and badly damaged. The landing attempt was abandoned on Churchill's orders.

An African empire lost

The first Axis-occupied territory to be liberated by the Allies in World War II was Ethiopia. In 1941 British armies toppled Mussolini's East African empire, created by the seizure of Ethiopia in 1935-6 and British Somaliland in 1940.

EVEN WORSE than Monte Cassino – that was to be the verdict of British troops who fought in both that Italian battle and the bloody struggle to take the Eritrean town of Keren early in 1941. The Keren battle followed a modest push to take a small border town. The British ended up shattering what Churchill called 'Mussolini's dream of an African Empire built by conquest . . . in the spirit of ancient Rome'.

The Italians had built up an East African army of more than 250 000 since invading Ethiopia (Abyssinia) in 1935, but 182 000 of them were Askari (native) troops of dubious reliability, and much of their equipment was obsolete. However, they considerably outnumbered the British forces in the region and enabled the Italians to strengthen their defences by capturing border posts in Kenya and the Sudan in July 1940 and to seize British Somaliland and its port Berbera in August. But then the Italian Viceroy in East Africa, the Duke of Aosta, ordered a halt, intending to wait for Axis victory in Europe. British deception schemes persuaded him that he faced a much stronger enemy than he really did; as a result he let the initiative pass to the British.

An attempt by Brigadier William Slim to recapture the Sudanese-Ethiopian frontier towns of Metema and Gallabat failed in November 1940. Then, on January 19, 1941, Maj General William Platt's 4th and 5th Indian Divisions launched an attack near the northern Sudan-Eritrea border. The Sudanese town of Kassala, seized by the Italians the year before, was the major objective. But, unknown to Platt, the Italian commander in Eritrea, General Luigi Frusci, was expecting a much larger offensive and had already pulled his forces out of Kassala.

After bloody encounters at Barentu and Agordat, inside Eritrea, the Italians fell back still farther until by the beginning of February Platt was over 160 km (100 miles) deep in Eritrean territory. Then the British realised that they could take the whole of Eritrea. General Sir Archibald Wavell, British Commander in Chief Middle East, ordered Platt to push on. Wavell was particularly anxious to capture the Red Sea port of Massawa (Mitsiwa), which threatened supply routes to his Middle East forces.

STALEMATE AT KEREN

Near the town of Keren, however, the Italians stuck. They could not have hoped for a better defensive position. West of the town, blocking the path of the pursuing British, stood a massive, steep-sided escarpment of almost sheer rock, stretching north-south for hundreds of kilometres and rising in places to nearly 1800 m (6000 ft) above sea level. There was only one way through it – the narrow, winding Dongolaas Gorge. Frusci's men blew up part of a cliff to block the road through the gorge, closed a railway tunnel with wagons full of rocks, and established forts on all the surrounding peaks.

On February 2, Platt's men started arriving at the foot of the escarpment. Over the next ten days, they made a series of brave frontal assaults – but to little avail. In this fighting the defenders had all the advantages. They just watched and waited in their high eyries – while below, under a baking sun, the attackers toiled painfully across the dry, scrubby plain, then up the rocky mountainsides. The Italians simply dropped hand grenades on the attackers at the last moment. By February 12, the British had gained a single narrow foothold on the escarpment – a ridge taken by Cameron Highlanders on the battle's first day.

A month's lull then followed. Platt's men toiled to bring up supplies, one company from each battalion acting as porters. Each man was allowed 1 pint (600 ml) of water per day. Indian reinforcements also arrived. Meanwhile, the RAF established air superiority. They bombed Keren, Massawa and the Eritrean capital Asmara. They also dropped propaganda leaflets over the Italian lines. Addressed to Askari troops and bearing the lion seal of the exiled Ethiopian Emperor Haile Selassie, they appealed to them to desert to the British. Over 1500 did so.

THROUGH THE GORGE

On March 15, a British artillery barrage opened the battle's second round. It was the 'hottest, most still and sultry day of the campaign', recorded the official historian. 'As the great guns blazed off in the oppressive valley, they were answered by the crash of thunderstorms in the highlands above.'

At first it seemed that this too would end in stalemate, despite the attackers' ingenuity. One British officer, Viscount Corvedale, son of the former Prime Minister Stanley Baldwin, tried to demoralise the Italians by broadcasting passages from Verdi operas over loudspeakers – interspersed with news of Italian defeats in Libya. But it seemed of little use. After three days' fierce hand-to-hand fighting, often with rifle butt and bayonet, Platt's men had captured only one important point – Dologorodoc peak to the south of Dongolaas Gorge, taken on the night of March 16/17. To make matters worse, Platt was under

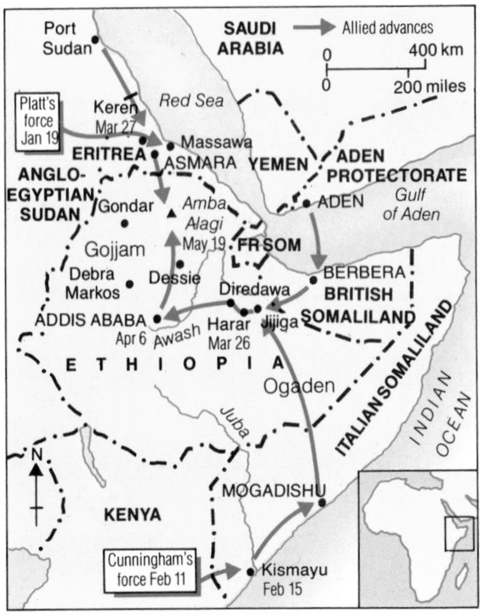

HARD GOING The conquest of Italian-held Eritrea, Ethiopia and Somaliland was the first absolute British success of the war. The terrain was tough and tricky. Southern penetration of Ethiopia involved hard desert marching. In the north, the Red Sea port of Massawa was a major goal.

PLATT: TESTY AND EXACTING

William Platt (1885-1975) was not an easy officer to serve under. He was active, aggressive, testy and exacting. His relations with fellow officers – and civilian administrators – were often explosive. Yet he was a superb trainer of troops, particularly Africans, in whose abilities he had immense faith.

Platt joined the army in 1905. He learnt his trade on the North-West Frontier of India and on the Western Front in World War I. He was promoted major general in 1938 and the next January arrived in the Sudan as *Kaid*, commander of British and Sudanese forces there. After Italy entered the war he made skilful use of minimal resources to defend Sudan from vastly superior Italian forces in Ethiopia. After the conquest of Ethiopia, Platt became British Commander in Chief East Africa.

LITTLE BIG MAN

With his soft voice, ruddy complexion and ready smile, Alan Cunningham (1887–1983) looked more like a prosperous business executive than a professional soldier. A small man, he commanded attention by his energy and drive.

Cunningham, born in Dublin, was the younger brother of Admiral of the Fleet Sir Andrew Cunningham. A gunner by training, he served in France in World War I. He was General Officer Commanding Kenya when Italy entered World War II in 1940, and was put in charge of Britain's East African Forces. His rapid advance through British Somaliland and Ethiopia in early 1941 was highly successful, but his lack of experience in armoured warfare showed when he became Eighth Army Commander in North Africa and allowed Operation 'Crusader' to stall. He was relieved of his command and spent the rest of the war in regional commands in Britain.

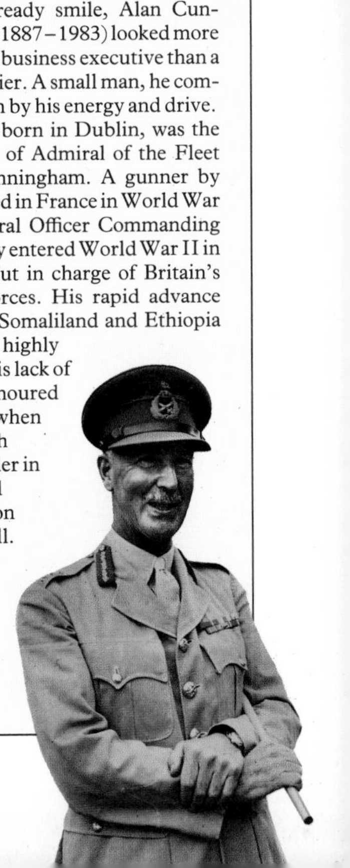

RIVER TO CROSS South Africans of Cunningham's force get their vehicles across a pontoon bridge on the Juba river in Italian Somaliland. Cunningham's troops met only occasional opposition on the way to Mogadishu, the territory's capital.

VICTORY PIPER Scottish soldiers march through Asmara, Eritrea. A dog decides to have its day, too.

increasing pressure from Wavell, who wanted his men back in Egypt as soon as possible. A simultaneous British and Free French attack led by Brigadier Harold Briggs from Port Sudan towards Keren was no more successful.

Then came a ray of hope. During fighting on March 17, Indian engineers had managed to creep forward to the road blocks in the Dongolaas Gorge. These could be cleared in 48 hours or less, they reported. On the 25th, Indians and Highland Light Infantry set off down the gorge, crossed the road blocks and held positions on either side all that afternoon and the following day as the sappers got to work.

The Italians, meanwhile, were at last beginning to waver. Since March 17, they had thrown no fewer than seven counterattacks against Dologorodoc. But despite these and an incessant bombardment from higher Italian-held peaks, Dologorodoc's defenders held on. At the same time, British artillery and air bombardments were taking a heavy toll. In just five days Frusci lost over 1000 men killed and 2300 wounded.

At dawn on March 27, the Dongolaas road blocks were finally cleared, and Matilda tanks of the Royal Tank Regiment with Bren-gun carriers pushed through towards Keren. They met no resistance. Frusci had already withdrawn his men. At the same time, Briggs' Anglo-French force broke through from the north.

The battle of Keren had cost the Italians 3500 dead, while Platt lost over 500 dead and 3000 wounded. On April 1 Asmara was taken, then on April 8 Massawa. The way was now clear to head south into the heart of Ethiopia.

CUNNINGHAM'S ADVANCE

At the same time, Ethiopia was being overrun from the south. On February 11, an army under Lt General Alan Cunningham had crossed the frontier from Kenya into Italian Somaliland (now part of Somalia). His troops included Nigerians, men from the Gold Coast (Ghana), East Africans of the King's African Rifles and South Africans.

ROYAL RETURN Haile Selassie rides through Addis Ababa in triumph – exactly five years after Italian troops marched in.

Like Platt, Cunningham started with a limited objective – to take the Somalian port of Kismayu (Kismaayo). But, like Platt, he was soon thrusting deeper and with unexpected speed into Italian-ruled territory. His troops took Kismayu on February 15, began to cross the Juba river to the north-east on February 17 and just over a week later had reached Italian Somaliland's chief port and capital, Mogadishu. During the advance, they had had only brief encounters with Italian troops, commanded by Maj General Carlo de Simone, and captured intact vast supply dumps.

Cunningham now decided to pursue de Simone's retreating men north into Ethiopia. He cabled Wavell for permission – and got it. For almost a month, his troops marched across the bone-dry Somalian plain, through Ethiopia's Ogaden desert as far as the town of Jijiga in the foothills of the central Ethiopian highlands. Nigerian troops entered Jijiga unopposed on March 17. At the same time, more British troops from Aden were landing at Berbera and retaking British Somaliland.

By now de Simone's troops were in the small city of Harar, high on the edge of Ethiopia's stark central plateau, 70 km (44 miles) west of Jijiga. This plateau forms a perfect natural fortress. Rising as high as 4500 m (some 15 000 ft) above sea level and stretching for hundreds of kilometres in all directions, it is rutted by countless plunging chasms and deep gorge-like valleys. Between Jijiga and Harar alone were two easily defended passes at Marda and Babile.

In the Marda Pass, Cunningham's men met serious opposition for the first time on March 21. At the end of a day of heavy fighting, Nigerian troops had captured only one hill. By next morning, however, Marda's defenders had withdrawn. More and more of the Italians' Askari troops were deserting. At Babile, Italian artillery managed to delay the Nigerians for $2\frac{1}{2}$ days. But on March 26 they entered Harar unopposed.

Retreating ever westwards, de Simone pulled his remaining troops out of the railway town of Diredawa on March 28. Later that night British officers in Harar received a frantic telephone call from Diredawa's Italian chief of police. He implored them to occupy the town as soon as possible. With the Italian troops gone, the Ethiopians there had gone wild – looting, raping and killing Italian civilians in bloody revenge for earlier Italian atrocities. South African troops arrived the next day.

RETURN TO ADDIS ABABA

By now Cunningham had decided to push on to the Ethiopian capital Addis Ababa, 335 km (210 miles) to the west. But both he and the Italians were anxious to prevent scenes there similar to those at Diredawa. On March 30, the RAF dropped a message for the Duke of Aosta, asking for his cooperation in protecting the city's 18 000 Italian women and children. The British also hoped that he might surrender. Aosta promised Italian cooperation, but did not surrender. On the evening of April 3, he left Addis Ababa. Three days later, British troops entered the capital. Once more they had been urged on by Italian police faced with rampaging Ethiopians.

In a little less than eight weeks, Cunningham's men had covered 2700 km (1700 miles). They had routed an army many times their size, losing just 135 men killed and 310 wounded. On May 5, exactly five years after the invading Italians had first entered Addis Ababa, Emperor Haile Selassie returned in triumph to his capital – a small yet supremely dignified figure, in British Army greatcoat and outsized pith helmet. A delighted Churchill sent his congratulations: 'It is with deep . . . pleasure that the British nation and Empire have learned of Your Imperial Majesty's welcome home . . . Your Majesty was the first of the lawful sovereigns to be driven from his throne and country by the Fascist-Nazi criminals, and you are the first to return in triumph.'

Haile Selassie was accompanied by Lt Colonel Orde Wingate, whose tiny Gideon Force (see box) had been tying down large numbers of Italian troops in the north-western Gojjam province.

A MOUNTAIN FASTNESS

But the battle for Ethiopia was by no means over. After leaving Addis Ababa, the Duke of Aosta and his men had headed north to Amba Alagi, a mountain stronghold near the Eritrean border. Here they joined the remains of Frusci's army from Eritrea to make a force of 7000 men. Their position was redoubtable. The peak of Amba Alagi itself rises to 3446 m (11 305 ft) above sea level and is encircled by others almost as high. The terrain between the peaks is broken by dizzy precipices and razor-sharp ridges. In the east the mountains descend sheer to the coastal plain.

Italian engineers fortified the peaks, laid down kilometres of barbed wire and dug countless machine-gun pits. They had plenty of ammunition and food – including foie gras and Chianti – and abundant fresh spring water. From Rome, Mussolini's instructions were clear: 'Resist to the last limit of human endurance.' There were other Italian armies in Ethiopia under General Pietro Gazzera south-west of Addis Ababa and under Lt General Guglielmo Nasi in a remote defensive position at Gondar in the north-west.

On May 3, a force of mostly Indian troops under Maj General Ashton Mayne – veterans of Keren – began attacking Amba Alagi from the north. A straightforward frontal assault was out of the question – so Mayne chose a ruse. He sent a small force to attack the Falagi Pass through the eastern sector of the mountains. Early on May 4, however, he planned to deliver his principal blow in the west. Falagi was not taken, but the ruse worked. The Italians moved troops east.

The attack in the west began before light the next morning. Advancing with astonishing speed, Indian troops had driven the Italians off three peaks by 8 am. Before dawn the next day, they had taken another peak, immediately below Amba Alagi. Here, though, they came to an abrupt halt. The only possible route onto Amba Alagi itself was along a narrow ridge, flanked by precipices and barred by impenetrable barbed wire.

Checked in the west, Mayne switched the main attack to the Falagi Pass – first confusing the Italians still further with an attack in the south-west. On May 8, Lt Colonel Bernard Fletcher took Falagi, then pushed west, until he too was checked. At this point, South African and Ethiopian reinforcements arrived from Addis Ababa – having been held up by fierce fighting with an Italian rearguard near the town of Dessie (Dese). They broke the stalemate by taking a peak called Triangle after heavy fighting.

Aosta's men were now surrounded and being pounded day and night by British artillery. They had held on with gallantry and skill for nearly two weeks, but their morale was breaking. They could no longer bring wounded men back from forward positions for treatment. Several ammunition dumps had gone up in flames; even their precious Chianti store had been hit. On May 19, Aosta surrendered. Awarded full honours of war by respectful foes, his little army marched into captivity past a British guard of honour with bagpipes playing.

Mopping-up operations in Ethiopia took more than six months to complete, but the surrender of Aosta sealed the fate of Mussolini's short-lived East African empire.

FEW AGAINST MANY

While British armies were invading Ethiopia from north and south in early 1941, a strange little force had entered Gojjam province from the Sudan. Led by the eccentric Lt Colonel Orde Wingate – later to achieve fame as Chindit leader in Burma – it consisted of Sudanese and Ethiopian Patriot (anti-Italian) troops with British and Australian officers and NCOs. Accompanying it was the exiled Ethiopian Emperor Haile Selassie.

Wingate christened his little army – never more than 1700 strong – 'Gideon Force', after the Old Testament hero who with 300 defeated 15 000. 'A thousand resolute and well-armed men,' he claimed, 'can paralyse, for an indefinite period, the operations of a hundred thousand' – and so it proved. Combining daring with bluff, Wingate's men drove the Italians from Bure in March and then drove a force of 12 000, plus thousands of Ethiopian warriors, from Debra Markos. Later Wingate chased after a group of about 10 000 Italian troops retreating to their last stronghold of Amba Alagi. Both sides ran out of food and their clothes were reduced to tatters in bitterly cold weather before the Italians surrendered on May 19. Gideon Force had taken over 15 000 prisoners in all, and had tied down vastly superior forces.

AOSTA: OFFICER, GENTLEMAN AND PRINCE

'The Duke of Aosta is dead. With him disappears the noble figure of a prince and an Italian, simple in his ways, broad in outlook, humane in spirit.' So wrote Mussolini's son-in-law and Foreign Minister, Count Galeazzo Ciano, in his diary in March 1942.

Brave, distinguished and tall – nearly 2 m (6 ft 7 in) – Aosta (1898-1942) served in World War I, commanded the Camel Corps in Libya, switched to the Italian Air Force, and in 1937 was appointed Viceroy of Italian East Africa in succession to Marshal Rodolfo Graziani, whose brutal regime had provoked bloody revolts. Aosta released many detained Ethiopians and introduced liberal reforms.

He was a devoted admirer of Britain, where he was partly educated, and of France – and regretted his country's entry into the war. After the surrender at Amba Alagi, he went as a prisoner of war to Kenya, where he died of tuberculosis.

Defiance in the Balkans

Mussolini thought that Greece would be a walkover when he invaded in October 1940. It was not – only intervention by Hitler subdued the Greeks. The Yugoslavs, who also defied the Führer, paid in blood for their presumption.

IT WAS 3 O'CLOCK in the morning when the Greek dictator, General Ioannis Metaxas, standing in his dressing gown and slippers, received Mussolini's ultimatum. His situation may not have been dignified, but his answer made up for that. '*Ochi!*' – 'No!' – he snapped at Count Emmanuele Grazzi, the Italian minister in Athens.

In the ultimatum, delivered on the morning of October 28, 1940, Mussolini accused the Greeks of collaborating with the British by allowing them to use Greek ports and airfields for refuelling their ships and aircraft. He demanded that Italian troops should also have access to certain unspecified 'strategic points' within Greek territory. The ultimatum expired at 6 am. 'I could not make a decision to sell my own house on a few hours' notice,' Metaxas told Grazzi. 'How do you expect me to sell my country?'

At 5.30 am, without waiting for the ultimatum to expire, Mussolini's troops began to pour over the frontier from Italian-occupied Albania into the mountains of north-western Greece. By 10 am, the Italian dictator was able to greet Hitler jubilantly at the railway station in Florence. 'Führer,' he cried, 'we are on the march! At dawn this morning our Italian troops victoriously crossed the Albanian-Greek frontier!'

ITALIAN FIASCO

Il Duce was crowing too soon. For months he had cherished ambitions of a purely Italian military success. Having occupied Ethiopia in 1936 and Albania in 1939, he now felt that Greece would make a glorious, and easy, prey. For the attack he had 162 000 men in Albania under General Count Sebastiano Visconti Prasca.

But Mussolini's calculations were mistaken. In the first place, the weather was against him. Heavy icy rains turned Greek mountain roads into little more than boggy tracks, and later in the winter came deep snow and bitter temperatures as low as −30°C (−20°F). Then the Greek Army, commanded by General Alexandros Papagos, proved to be supremely skilled and effective. It was small, with no more than 150 000 men, no tanks, little air support, a bare handful of anti-tank and anti-aircraft guns and few trucks. But the Greeks kept to the mountain-tops, in altitudes of nearly 1500 m (5000 ft), where their skill and knowledge of the terrain more than compensated for a lack of equipment. Particularly deadly were their crack Evzone troops – tough highland infantrymen who also provided the royal guard.

In early November an Evzone force trapped the elite Italian 'Julia' Alpine Division in a series of gorges in the northern Pindus mountains. For four desperate days the Italians tried to escape – but to no avail; they lost 13 000 men killed. After this disaster, Mussolini replaced Visconti Prasca with General Ubaldo Soddu – but it made no difference. In late November, the Greeks crossed the Albanian border and trapped the Italian Ninth Army in the mountain town of Koritsa (Korcë). After a savage eight-day battle they took 2000 prisoners. The Greeks also received limited British air and naval support – when for example,

THRUST AND COUNTERTHRUST Mussolini invaded Greece from Albania in October 1940. But the Greeks struck back and drove his men from much of Albania. Then the Germans invaded Greece and Yugoslavia, and were unstoppable.

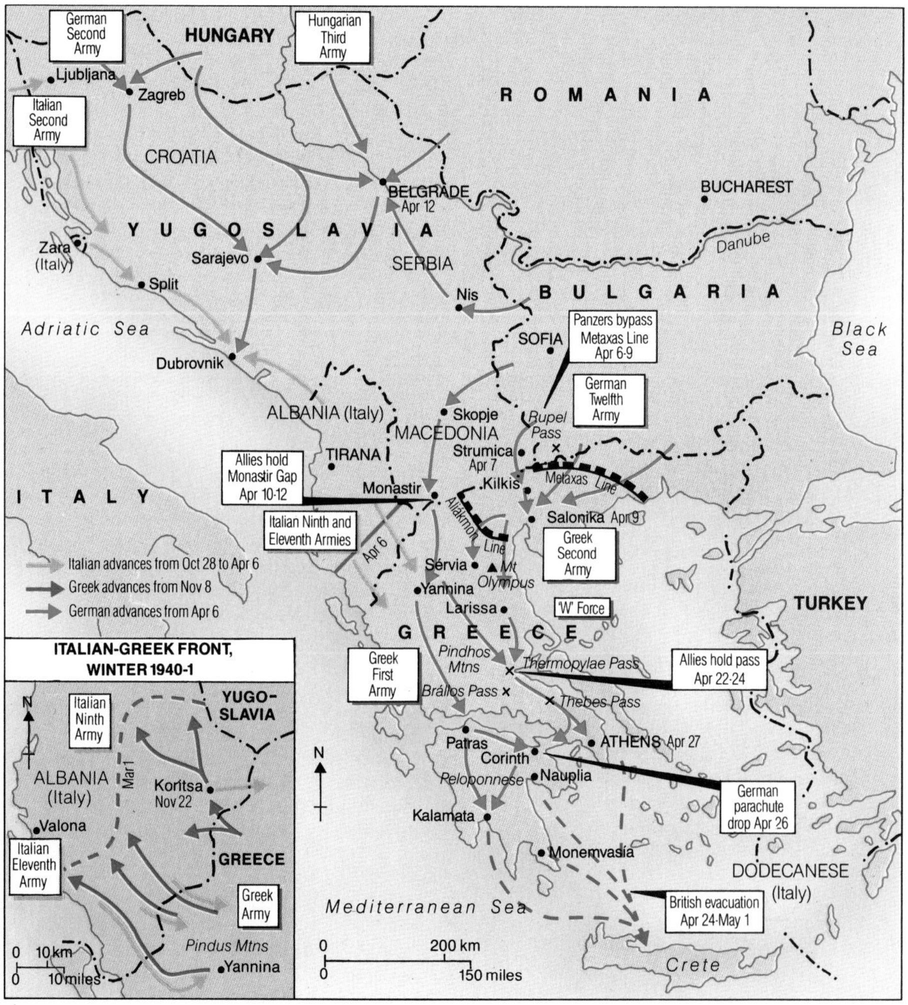

PATRIOT AND REALIST

Ioannis Metaxas (1871-1941) was not an obvious ally for the British. He was a dictator with distinct Fascist sympathies whose followers used the stiff-armed salute. But he was also a Greek patriot who met Mussolini's ultimatum with a decisive 'Ochi!' – 'No!'. The Greeks still celebrate Ochi Day on October 28.

Metaxas, a former Chief of the Greek General Staff, and an ardent royalist in politics, was appointed premier with dictatorial powers by King George II in 1936. He was ruthless in suppressing opposition, but also pushed through social and economic reforms. Knowing his country's vulnerability from the north, Metaxas tried desperately to keep it out of the war, and even after Mussolini's unprovoked invasion refused large-scale British aid for fear of precipitating a German attack. He died – of a heart attack due to diabetes and overwork – just over two months before the German attack he had so feared.

IL DUCE'S DREAM Motorised Bersaglieri – elite Italian riflemen – pour into Greece (left), traditional black cockerel feathers sweeping from their helmets, at the start of the Italian invasion. Mussolini later views the front (above); General Ubaldo Soddu stands on the left. The *Duce* hoped for a triumph to rival Hitler's victories, but met humiliation.

the Royal Navy bombarded the Albanian port of Valona (Vlorë) – under Britain's 1939 undertaking to guarantee Greece's independence.

On November 23, the last Italian troops were pushed from Greek soil – and by mid-January 1941, the Greeks had occupied a quarter of Albania in a stunningly successful counter-offensive. On March 9, Soddu launched another attack on Greece – but it failed as abjectly as the earlier one, with 12 000 casualties in a month.

HITLER'S ANGER

In Berlin, Hitler watched Italy's humiliation with mounting disgust. He had always opposed Mussolini's Balkan schemes, for with the planned invasion of the USSR he wanted no disturbances farther south. As early as November 4, 1940, he ordered a start on plans for a more effective German invasion of Greece (code-named 'Marita') the following spring.

At the same time, he was strengthening his position throughout the Balkans. Already, in October, the Romanian dictator General Ion Antonescu, under pressure from the local Fascist Iron Guard, had invited German troops into his country. Then Hitler began forcing the Balkan states to adhere to the Axis powers' Tripartite Pact. Antonescu and Admiral Miklós Horthy's Hungarian government signed in November and the Bulgarians in March 1941. When Bulgaria signed, German troops marched in – right up to the Greek frontier in the south.

The Yugoslavs, however, dared to resist. On March 25, 1941, the government of the Regent, Prince Paul – uncle of the 17-year-old King Peter II – reluctantly adhered to the Pact. This pleased the generally pro-German Croats – the second largest of Yugoslavia's many national groupings – but infuriated the larger, mostly pro-British

FOOD'S UP Italian prisoners of war line up for midday rations of bread and meat doled out by Greek guards.

SKILLED COMMANDER

After Metaxas' death, one man, above all, kept the Greeks fighting – the Commander in Chief, Alexandros Papagos (1883-1955). But Papagos also knew when to accept defeat – and it was he who finally advised the British to withdraw from Greece.

Papagos first saw action in the Balkan Wars against Turkey (1912-13). Thereafter he rose rapidly, serving briefly as Minister of War in 1935. As Chief of General Staff under Metaxas, he was responsible for modernising the Greek Army before the war, and was the architect of the spectacular Greek victories over the Italians in 1940-1.

During the German occupation, Papagos stayed in Greece, until deported to Dachau concentration camp in 1943. He was liberated by the Americans in 1945. In the Greek Civil War of 1946-9, he was once more Commander in Chief, directing the fighting against Communist guerrillas. He later turned to politics, modelling himself on the French soldier-statesman Charles de Gaulle, and was a generally popular Prime Minister from 1952 until his death.

UNFLAPPABLE GIANT

When with much misgiving the British War Cabinet decided to send an expeditionary force to Greece in 1941, they were unanimous in choosing its commander. Of the men available, only Sir Henry Maitland Wilson (1881-1964) had the right skills. He was an experienced soldier, popular with his colleagues and with a calmly reassuring yet authoritative manner. An immense height and bulk had long earned him the affectionate nickname 'Jumbo'.

Maitland Wilson first saw action in the Boer War. In World War I he was a highly regarded staff officer and, by the outbreak of World War II, a lieutenant general commanding British troops in Egypt. After the Italians were driven out of Cyrenaica early in 1941, he was appointed military governor there.

After Greece, Wilson directed Allied campaigns in Iraq, Iran and Syria. In 1943 he became British Commander in Chief Middle East, then in January 1944 Allied Supreme Commander Mediterranean. Later that year he was promoted field marshal and took on the crucial liaison post of head of the British military mission in Washington. 'I can find only one officer with the necessary credentials and qualities,' Churchill told him, 'namely, yourself.' The post suited Wilson's administrative and diplomatic talents, and he stayed in Washington to the end of the war.

Serbian group. On the night of March 26/27 a coup led by Air Force General Dušan Simovic, a Serb, overthrew the Regent and proclaimed the young King old enough to rule in his own right. There was wild rejoicing by the largely Serbian population of Belgrade.

In fact, Yugoslavia had signed its own death warrant. In a blind fury Hitler ordered immediate preparations for 'the destruction of Yugoslavia militarily and as a national unit . . . [to be] carried out with pitiless harshness'. Operation *Strafe* ('Punishment') was to coincide with 'Marita'.

GERMANY STRIKES

Hitler's savage vengeance took the Yugoslavs completely by surprise. In the early hours of Palm Sunday, April 6, the clear skies over Belgrade were darkened by German bombers. They dropped their lethal loads, then sped home. More bombers followed in wave after devastating wave for two days. By Monday evening the city was reduced to little more than rubble. The death toll was put at 17 000.

At the same time, Axis troops – Germans, Italians and Hungarians – under General Maximilian von Weichs were invading overland. Supported by Stuka dive-bombers, they crashed through the brave but ineffectual Yugoslav front-line infantry. Throughout Holy Week, they thrust from north, south and east on Belgrade, some troops covering up to 70 km (over 40 miles) a day. On Easter Saturday, April 12, the capital's mayor surrendered to SS Captain Fritz Klingenberg, who had raced ahead of the rest of his corps to take the city.

Five days later, the last units of the Yugoslav army capitulated. Operation 'Punishment' had lasted just 12 days. At a cost of 151 killed, 15 missing and 392 wounded, the Germans had netted 254 000 prisoners – though many Yugoslavs escaped. British aircraft bore King Peter and his government to exile in London.

The Greeks, meanwhile, proved a tougher foe. At 5.15 am on Palm Sunday, German troops began to cross the mountainous frontier from Bulgaria into north-eastern Greece. The Greeks – already mobilised and experienced – had the advantage here of the fortified Metaxas Line. Creeping across ground still patchily covered with snow, the Germans – from Field Marshal Wilhelm List's Twelfth Army – had to fight dear for every metre. Troops trying to cross the Nestos (Mesta) river lost 700 men in three days' fighting. Another regiment lost a quarter of its number in the Rupel Pass. At forts at Istibey and Kelkayia the Germans had to bring up flamethrowers and smoke generators to force out the defenders.

Farther west, the German 2nd Panzer Division under Lt General Rudolf Veiel had struck west from Bulgaria into Yugoslavia. Before dusk on Palm Sunday they took Strumica, then at first light on Tuesday crossed into Greece. They had better success than their comrades to the east, and that evening swept into the outskirts of Greece's second city, Salonika (Thessaloniki). This was the end of the battle in eastern Greece. All Greek forces east of Salonika – 70 000 in all – were cut off, and they surrendered the next day.

Farther south, the Luftwaffe had also crippled Piraeus, the port of Athens. In a raid on Palm Sunday evening, a chance bomb hit a British freighter, SS *Clan Fraser*, carrying 250 tonnes of explosives. It set off an explosion which sank 11 small ships and maimed several larger ones. Only five out of 12 berths remained usable.

BRITAIN INTERVENES

But the Greeks were not defending their homeland single-handed. During the Italian invasion Metaxas had welcomed British air and naval support, but firmly declined offers of assistance on the ground. In January 1941, however, he died – and his successor, Alexandros Koryzis, was much more interested in British help.

In February, top-ranking British and Greek leaders – including British Foreign Secretary Anthony Eden and the Greek King George II – met near Athens. Here, despite the protests of hard-pressed British army and navy commanders, they laid plans for the transfer of some British and Empire troops in North Africa to Greece. The British government hoped to achieve in Greece a morale-boosting land victory that would also impress the still neutral Americans.

The 57 000-strong expeditionary force (officially 'W' Force) consisted of Australian, New Zealand and British troops under Lt General Sir Henry Maitland Wilson. They began arriving on March 7, and built up rapidly despite Italian attacks on the convoys. By the end of March, most of 'W' Force was in position in northern Greece on the Aliakmon Line.

A mood of tremendous optimism filled the Greeks. It 'was a time of rejoicing', remembered the novelist Olivia Manning. 'The British troops were coming in in force now, filling the streets with new voices, and the spring warmth and

A FORETASTE OF CRETE

Defeated Anzac and British troops streaming south across the Isthmus of Corinth had to pass the tiniest of bottlenecks – a single road and rail bridge across the Corinth ship canal. This was all that linked the near-island of the Peloponnese to the rest of mainland Greece. Just before dawn on April 26, General Maitland Wilson crossed the bridge with his staff. By now most of his men were over – many already evacuated, others waiting hidden on beaches farther south. Engineers had laid demolition charges and once the last troops were across, the bridge would be blown up. A small, mostly Australian force was left to guard it.

At about 7 am, these men suddenly heard an ominous drone from the north. Minutes later they were savagely bombarded by German dive-bombers and ground-attack fighters. Then came more aircraft, and the skies north and south of the canal filled with parachutes; eerily silent gliders crashed to the ground.

Men from the gliders rushed for the bridge, took it, and went frantically to work to remove the explosives – but to no avail. During an Australian counterattack it collapsed – no one is sure why. Later that day the Germans took Corinth, while farther west SS men crossed the Gulf of Corinth in small boats to Patras.

The attack on Corinth gave the Allies a foretaste in miniature of what they were to face in Crete – heavy preliminary air attacks followed by glider-borne troops going for the main target, with paratroops coming in to support. Yet, as Crete showed, they failed to heed its lessons.

HOLDING THERMOPYLAE

For three heroic days in 480 BC, the Spartan King Leonidas with just 300 soldiers held the narrow pass between the sea and high cliffs at Thermopylae against the vast invading armies of King Xerxes of Persia. In 1941, Anzac and British forces similarly held Thermopylae for three crucial days against Axis troops – while their fellows of the British expeditionary force were evacuated farther south. The pass where Leonidas made his stand was held by New Zealand and British troops, while inland a mountain pass at Brallos was held by Australians. In a respite before the battle the Allied soldiers soaked themselves in the same hot sulphur springs used by Leonidas's men.

The first attack, against Brallos, came on April 22. It was successfully beaten off. Two days later the Germans tried to send a mixed force of tanks and infantry through the coastal pass – but the defenders were ready and waiting. They held their fire until the panzers were within easy range, then let loose with artillery and machine guns. Within minutes none of the 19 tanks, according to an official German report, was 'in going order and only two were still able to shoot'.

That night the Allied soldiers withdrew to another pass farther east, just south of Thebes. There again they halted the Germans, until April 26. Then they made a final withdrawal to Porto Rafti and Rafina, east of Athens, from where Royal Navy destroyers carried them to Crete.

HANDS ALOFT Yugoslav soldiers surrender to Germans. Some 300 000 managed to evade capture, however, many escaping to the mountains and forests from where they kept up an increasingly effective anti-German resistance.

flowers came with them . . . The Greek forces were taking fresh heart and everyone waited for . . . the victories to start again.'

But their hopes were soon dashed. On April 8, Maitland Wilson received reports that List's right wing was heading across southern Yugoslavia for Monastir (now Bitola). These troops included the crack SS 'Leibstandarte Adolf Hitler' Division. Wilson immediately detached men to defend the densely forested Monastir Gap, through which they had to pass.

The Germans took the town the next day and immediately pressed south for the gap. Here, in blinding snow, sleet and a whirling fog that sometimes reduced visibility to as little as 45 m (50 yds), a joint Australian, New Zealand and British force held back the Germans for three days until the night of April 12/13. Among the action's many heroes were men of the Royal Horse Artillery who covered their comrades' retreat by staying at their 25-pounders until enemy tanks and infantry were within 370 m (400 yds).

Meanwhile, the rest of Wilson's troops had withdrawn to a new defensive line around Mt Olympus. In the high Servia Pass, west of Olympus, New Zealanders stopped an attack by Austrian troops and took 168 prisoners. But Wilson's forces were hopelessly outmatched. On April 18, the Germans broke around east of Olympus to take Larissa, while others broke through to the west. Wilson's army – numb with cold and mindless with fatigue – withdrew through the mountains towards Athens.

Events moved fast over the next few days. Prime Minister Koryzis, sunk into deepest despair, committed suicide on April 18. The next day, the Allied commanders – Greek, British and Commonwealth – agreed that 'W' Force should evacuate mainland Greece. 'You have done your best to save us,' said Papagos. 'We are finished. But the war is not lost. Therefore save what you can of your army to help win elsewhere.'

On April 20, the Greek First Army – which had withdrawn from Albania in the face of a new Italian offensive – surrendered at Yannina. The following day, the commanders of Greek forces in the west, against the wishes of Papagos, signed a capitulation to the Germans. A touchy Mussolini insisted on a further surrender ceremony two days later in the presence of an Italian emissary. The same day, the RAF flew the Greek King and his government to Crete.

During this time, Maitland Wilson and his men started leaving Athens, to a poignant send-off. Thousands of Athenians, some in tears, others cheering and throwing flowers, lined the streets as they left. The defeated soldiers trudged wearily to small ports such as Rafina to the east and Megara to the west of Athens and to Nauplia (Navplion), Monemvasia and Kalamata (Kalamai) on the Peloponnese – from where the Royal Navy would evacuate them to Crete and North Africa. Meanwhile, a rearguard of Anzac and British troops held passes at Thermopylae, then Thebes, to cover their retreat (see box). The Germans reached Athens on April 27.

The evacuations lasted from April 24 to May 1. Helped by cloudy, moonless nights, they were remarkably successful – despite a setback at Corinth (see box, *A foretaste of Crete*). The Royal Navy force under the Canadian-born Rear Admiral Harold Baillie-Grohman skilfully saved nearly 51 000 men, at the cost of four transports and two destroyers. Only at Kalamata were a large number of men – around 7000 – left behind. Of these, several remained in hiding, then escaped.

SWASTIKA OVER THE ACROPOLIS The Germans raise their flag in Athens on April 27, 1941. Days earlier the Athenians had watched the British expeditionary force depart. 'You will be back,' they shouted. 'We'll be waiting for you.'

British plans for a morale-boosting victory had gone disastrously awry. As well as the men captured at Kalamata, Maitland Wilson had lost 900 killed and 1200 wounded; since Mussolini's invasion, the Greeks had lost 70 000. The Germans had lost only just over 4500 men. But some good did emerge. In the United States, public opinion was shocked by Hitler's actions and started to run in favour of the Allies.

Crete falls to German paras

History's first airborne invasion came out of a clear blue sky over Crete on May 20, 1941. During the next ten days, 22 000 Germans drove more than twice their number of Allied troops from the island – though at terrific cost.

MORNING BROKE COOL but sunny over Crete's northern shore. Shortly before 6, the New Zealand, Australian, British and local troops of the island's garrison began to hear the low, ominous drone of aircraft approaching over the sea from the north. Most dashed for trenches cleverly concealed amid golden barley fields, vineyards and picturesque almond and olive groves. A few manned anti-aircraft guns.

Soon the aircraft were upon them – and for a few minutes the early morning peace was shattered by the screaming, nerve-tearing sirens of Stuka dive-bombers, the roar of exploding bombs and the rattle of bullets. Then the aircraft departed and peace returned. Another early morning 'hate' – a daily bombing and strafing raid by German aircraft from bases on the Greek mainland – was over. The Allied soldiers tucked into their breakfast. It was May 20, 1941, and Crete was the last part of Greece that the Allies still held.

Then, just before 8 am, New Zealand troops around the western village of Maleme once more heard the roar of aircraft. Leaving their breakfast, they gazed north, where, remembered one, a 'long black line as of a flock of migrating birds' appeared over the horizon. Gradually the whole northern sky filled with planes – 'from as far east to as far west as could be seen, from horizon to horizon', recalled another New Zealander. He scarcely exaggerated, for the Luftwaffe threw well over 1000 aircraft against Crete that day.

First came the bombers, dive-bombers and fighters. They concentrated particularly on the Maleme airfield, silencing its anti-aircraft guns until just one remained. 'This went on firing some time,' recalled a survivor, 'till a host of Stukas and Me109s fastened on it and shot and blasted it out of existence.' A brief silence followed. Then the sky filled with white and speckled green parachutes – 'flowering like bubbles from a child's pipe but infinitely more sinister', as one defender remembered them. At the same time, the first troop-carrying gliders slid silently to the ground.

HUNTERS FROM THE SKY

In late April 1941, as the German invasion of mainland Greece drew to its victorious close, Hitler and his generals began to make plans for invading Crete as well. Crete occupies a key strategic position in the centre of the eastern Mediterranean and has in Suda Bay (Kolpos Soudhas) – just west of Khania (Canea), then the island's capital – the Mediterranean's largest natural harbour. This was used by the Royal Navy as an important refuelling base.

The capture of the island by the Germans would deprive the British of this base, exclude them from the Aegean and threaten the Mediterranean convoy route between Malta and Alexandria. Its three airfields, at Maleme, Rethimnon (Retimo) and Heraklion (Iraklion), would also make bases for attacks on Allied positions in North Africa. In Allied hands, they could be used by bombers to hit Hitler's chief source of oil, the Ploesti oilfields in Romania. With his planned strike against the USSR drawing near, Hitler wanted no threat to these.

On April 21, General Kurt Student, father of the *Fallschirmjäger* ('Hunters from the sky') – the Luftwaffe's elite airborne troops – met Hitler in eastern Austria and proposed an invasion using airborne troops on an unprecedentedly large scale. Reluctantly at first, Hitler assented.

According to the plan eventually agreed, a morning lift would drop 3000 men, under Maj General Eugen Meindl, for the main attack around Maleme and Khania in the west. In the afternoon, a second wave would drop 1500 men at Rethimnon and 2600 at Heraklion. More troops would be dropped and airlifted in the next day, to be supported by amphibious landings that night bringing in tanks, heavy weapons and still more troops. The plan for Operation *Merkur* ('Mercury') was Student's pride and joy. 'He had devised it,' recalled one of his officers, 'struggled against heavy opposition for its acceptance and had worked out all the details . . . He believed in it and lived for it and in it.'

Student did not anticipate serious opposition – for German intelligence put the Allied garrison on Crete at a mere 5000 men. In fact, there were 32 000 Anzac and British soldiers alone, supported by Greek and Cretan irregulars – well over 40 000 men in all. Their commander, appointed just three weeks before the invasion began, was a New Zealand World War I hero, Maj General Bernard Freyberg, VC.

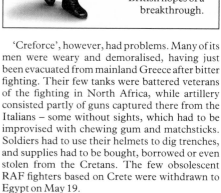

'Creforce', however, had problems. Many of its men were weary and demoralised, having just been evacuated from mainland Greece after bitter fighting. Their few tanks were battered veterans of the fighting in North Africa, while artillery consisted partly of guns captured there from the Italians – some without sights, which had to be improvised with chewing gum and matchsticks. Soldiers had to use their helmets to dig trenches, and supplies had to be bought, borrowed or even stolen from the Cretans. The few obsolescent RAF fighters based on Crete were withdrawn to Egypt on May 19.

Communications too were unreliable. There were few radios – and these were erratic. During the battle, Freyberg and his officers would have to rely on field telephones, runners and dispatch riders – all highly vulnerable where an enemy has control of the skies. On the other hand, Freyberg had the advantage of accurate intelligence. Using decoded German signals, London was able to give him a good picture of Student's plans. He also had the advantage of a friendly local population.

LIKE SHOOTING DUCKS

At first on May 20 all went remarkably well for Freyberg's men. The flimsy canvas and wood-built German gliders came in so low that the defenders could fire right into them with their

AIRBORNE GENERAL

'It sounds all right but I don't think it's practicable.' That was Hitler's initial lukewarm reaction to the plans of Kurt Student (1890-1978) for the airborne invasion of Crete. But the enthusiastic Student, one of Hitler's favourite generals, soon won him over.

Student was committed heart and soul to airborne warfare. A World War I fighter pilot, he later joined the fledgling Luftwaffe. When, in 1938, its chief, Hermann Göring, decided to set up a parachute infantry force, he chose Student to command it. Under Student the force expanded eventually to about 4500 men, and troop-carrying gliders were also developed. Student's men played a key role in the attacks on Norway and the Netherlands in 1940. After Crete, airborne operations were strictly limited – but Student's force continued to grow, its men used in Russia, Italy and France as elite, highly trained infantry. At the time of the Allied airborne attack on Arnhem in September 1944, Student happened to be commanding Army Group H in the Netherlands; and it was he who skilfully directed the German counterattacks that smashed British hopes of a breakthrough.

BOXER PARA Former world heavyweight boxing champion Max Schmeling, now a para, crouches, stick grenade in one hand, a Schmeisser MP-40 machine pistol in the other. His 'bone sack' paratroop smock, worn over his ordinary uniform, has the Luftwaffe eagle on the breast. A cloth band around his helmet has pockets for camouflage greenery. Dysentery prevented Schmeling from seeing much action on Crete, but Göring, thinking that the popular ex-boxer had played a hero's part, awarded him the Iron Cross.

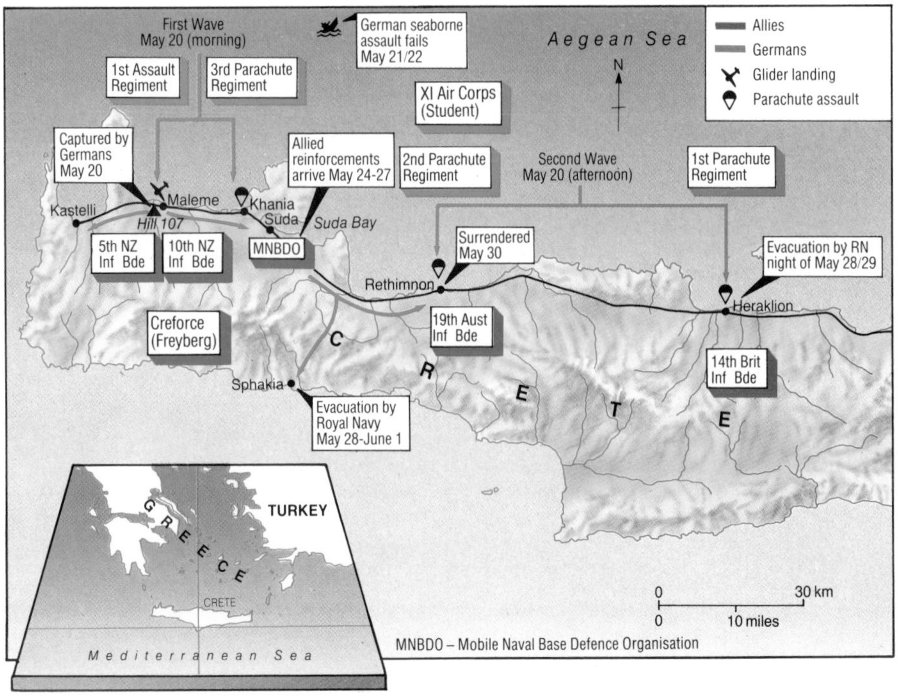

TWO-PHASE ASSAULT General Student's plans were for troops to be dropped at four places on Crete's north coast, and in two phases – around Maleme and Khania in the morning, at Rethimnon and Heraklion in the afternoon. In the event, it was the troops at Maleme who gained a secure foothold and the island was conquered from there.

small arms and many of the troops inside were dead before they even hit the ground. Other gliders landed on rocks or against terraced mountain sides and broke up on impact, killing their occupants.

The paras meanwhile fared no better, many falling directly over New Zealand positions – to be picked off one by one as they drifted helplessly down. It was 'like the opening of the duck shooting season in New Zealand', thought one defender. The German commander, Meindl, was badly wounded in the chest soon after landing.

Many paratroops who landed at the little fishing port of Kastelli, west of Maleme, were massacred by Cretan irregulars, clad in traditional scarlet-sashed costumes and wielding curved knives, flintlocks and axes. Two hundred of these men were later shot by the Germans for alleged 'atrocities' during this action.

SURRENDER The end comes for a group of British soldiers, rounded up by German paras. But they and Crete's other defenders had fought like tigers. 'I had never expected such bitter fighting,' wrote one German officer of the invasion's first day, 'and we began to despair of ever gaining our objectives or indeed of surviving at all.'

The afternoon attacks on Rethimnon and Heraklion were even less successful. In just an hour, 1500 paratroops at Rethimnon were reduced to 1000 men in small, scattered groups, while at Heraklion, transport aircraft had to come in singly because of delays at Athens, caused by dust kicked up by the aircraft on the earth and grass runway. This plight made them easy targets for the British and Australian defenders, who shot many down in flames with their paratroops still inside. The German commander of these troops, Brigadier Wilhelm Süssmann, was killed before he even reached Crete, when his glider crashed on a small island south of Athens.

By the end of the day, 40 per cent of Student's assault force was either dead, wounded or taken prisoner. Nonetheless, some Germans did survive – and at Maleme, a large number managed to establish themselves in the dried-up bed of the Tavronitis river and to launch an offensive towards the Maleme airfield.

'Today has been a hard one,' Freyberg that night cabled his commanding officer in Egypt, General Sir Archibald Wavell. He went on: 'We have been hard pressed. So far, I believe, we hold aerodromes at Heraklion and Maleme . . . Margin by which we hold them is a bare one, and it would be wrong of me to paint an optimistic picture. Fighting has been heavy and we have killed large numbers of Germans. Communications are most difficult.'

THRIVING IN THE FIRE OF WAR

'I would have been happier,' Rommel once said, 'if [Freyberg] had been safely tucked up in one of our prison camps instead of still fighting us.' Churchill likened Bernard Freyberg (1889-1963) to the mythical salamander that 'thrived in the fire of war'. He was a New Zealand dentist who joined the British Army in World War I and ended it a brigadier, with the VC, two bars to his DSO, and the French *Croix de Guerre*. He stayed in the army afterwards, despite a medical board trying to discharge him.

In 1939, Freyberg took command of the New Zealand Expeditionary Force, and moulded it into a highly professional little army. It played a key role in North Africa, then Italy, where its men led the attack on Monte Cassino. But the New Zealanders were not sticklers for military minutiae. Montgomery once remarked to Freyberg that they did not salute much. 'Oh,' came back the reply, 'if you wave to them, I expect they'll wave back.' After the war, Freyberg was made a peer and Governor-General of New Zealand.

GALLANT SUPPORT: NAVAL ACTIONS OFF CRETE

'Navy must not let Army down,' signalled Admiral Sir Andrew Browne Cunningham to his fleet at the height of the battle for Crete. 'No enemy forces must reach Crete by sea.' Scarcely a handful did – but the cost paid by Cunningham's forces was enormous. Almost all the damage was inflicted by planes of the Luftwaffe.

The first loss, at dawn on the battle's second day, May 21, was the destroyer *Juno* sunk by German aircraft off eastern Crete. The first major action came that night, when a force under Rear Admiral Irvine Glennie intercepted off Suda Bay a fleet of commandeered Greek caïques (fishing boats) bearing 2300 German reinforcements. Glennie sent packing the Italian escort destroyer *Lupo* and sank several caïques. The rest turned tail. Around 800 Germans were killed.

Farther east, another fleet of caïques appeared off Heraklion early the next morning, supported by Luftwaffe dive-bombers. A force under Rear Admiral Edward King turned it back, but later that day German bombers sank the destroyer *Greyhound* and the cruisers *Gloucester* and *Fiji*. The day after, destroyers under Captain Lord Louis Mountbatten turned back yet more caïques, but Stukas later sank *Kashmir* and Mountbatten's own ship *Kelly* off southern Crete; *Kelly*'s story was made into the film *In Which We Serve* by the actor-playwright Noël Coward. After this there was a lull until May 26, when Cunningham sent a force with the carrier *Formidable* to attack a key Luftwaffe base on the island of Scarpanto (Karpathos), between Crete and Rhodes. The attack did little damage – but German bombers savaged the destroyer *Nubian* and *Formidable*, which only just made it back to base, Alexandria in Egypt.

The next day London authorised Crete's evacuation. At Sphakia, from where troops in western Crete were evacuated, losses were light. But taking off troops from Heraklion on the north coast was considerably more dangerous. This unenviable task was entrusted to Rear Admiral Henry Rawlings.

On the evening of May 28, while still on the way to Heraklion, a German bomb damaged the steering gear of Rawlings' destroyer *Imperial* off eastern Crete. Later that night its steering failed completely and the ship had to be abandoned and sunk off Heraklion. Early the next morning, as Rawlings' ships headed home again laden with evacuated soldiers, the Luftwaffe struck once more. They sank the destroyer *Hereward* and crippled *Decoy* and the cruiser *Dido*. Then a bomb crashed through the upper structures of Rawlings' flagship, *Orion*. It exploded on a deck crowded with soldiers, killing 260 and wounding 280 more. The battered force staggered back to Alexandria with Rawlings himself badly wounded.

MAORI WARRIOR A Maori private, ammunition pouches slung over his shoulders, holds his Lee-Enfield rifle, and wears the traditional New Zealand 'lemon-squeezer' hat – so called from its shape. The 28th (Maori) Infantry Battalion – successor to the Maori Pioneer Battalion of 1914-18 – was formed just after the outbreak of war. Most officers and all men were Maoris.

POINT OF NO RETURN

But even as Freyberg was sending this cable, the battle for Crete was passing its turning point. This was the loss of a small hill, known to the military as Hill 107, that commanded the Maleme airfield from the south. All day, the New Zealand commander in the area, Lt Colonel Les Andrew, had been worried by the German build-up and attack from the Tavronitis. He sent frequent pleas for help to his commanding officer, Brigadier James Hargest. But a counterattack organised by Hargest was tied down by German dive-bombers as it formed up to the south-east of the airfield.

That evening Andrew decided to launch his own counterattack. He could spare only a pathetically small force of some 40 men but sent two Matilda tanks with them. The attack – launched at 5.15 pm – was a disaster. One tank had to turn back almost immediately with a jammed turret; the other broke down later in the thick of the enemy. The little force had to retreat, with only three men returning not wounded.

A dour South Islander, and like Freyberg a World War I veteran with the VC, Andrew was not a man to panic. But his situation was increasingly serious. German troops were closing in from both north and south, and at 6.45 pm the Luftwaffe struck with a brief but devastating bombardment. Andrew had lost all touch with his own outlying units, and radio contact with Hargest was erratic. He felt desperately exposed.

At 8.30 pm, he got through to Hargest and informed the brigadier that he would have to withdraw. Hargest, in common with Freyberg and most of the senior Allied commanders, was expecting a major German attack from the sea that night. Preoccupied with this, he failed to appreciate the importance of Hill 107 and agreed to Andrew's withdrawal. The seaborne attack never came – but by dawn the Germans, exhausted and running dangerously low of ammunition, found to their surprise that they had taken the hill unopposed. They effectively controlled the airfield.

A few hours earlier, it had seemed to Student in Athens that his forces faced inevitable defeat – with some of his senior officers even talking of abandoning 'Mercury'. But now all was transformed. He decided to send all available troops to Maleme. The rest of Crete, in his own words, 'would have to be rolled up from the west'. That day aircraft carrying 650 German mountain troops landed at Maleme and 550 more paras were dropped there – though some fell above positions held by Maori troops and suffered heavy losses.

The following night, May 21/22, a Royal Navy force under Rear Admiral Irvine Glennie intercepted a fleet of commandeered Greek fishing boats transporting a further 2300 mountain troops to Crete (see box). But the same night a counterattack against Maleme failed miserably. The force Freyberg assigned to the attack was too small – and started late. After a brief skirmish with the Germans, dawn broke. The Luftwaffe's total control of the skies made daytime operations impossible, and the attack had to be called off.

Freyberg had lost his last opportunity to drive the Germans from Crete. On May 22, another 2000 mountain troops landed at Maleme accompanied by Maj General Julius Ringel, who took over command from the wounded Meindl. Over the next few days, the situation grew steadily worse for the Allies. On May 24, the Greek King George II, who had been flown to Crete from Athens just over a month earlier, was evacuated by a British destroyer to Egypt.

On the night of May 24/25, German troops pushing east from Maleme linked up with a regiment of paras trapped since the first day of the invasion in a valley south-west of Khania, known as Prison Valley. All that now stood between the Germans and the island's capital was a small,

UPHAM, VC AND BAR

On the night of May 21/22, 1941, a small New Zealand force was attacking the Germans at Maleme. One machine-gun nest was causing particular trouble when 2nd Lieutenant Charles Hazlitt Upham (1908-), a peacetime sheep farmer from New Zealand's South Island, appeared out of the dark. Advancing fearlessly, firing his pistol and lobbing hand grenades, he so rattled the gunners that his men were able to destroy the position with ease. Later, between May 22 and 30, Upham was wounded by two mortar shells, received a bullet through his foot and caught dysentery, yet carried on leading his men.

For such exploits on Crete, Upham won the VC. A year later, now a captain, he won the bar to his VC at El Ruweisat Ridge near El Alamein. Despite two serious wounds, he insisted on leading his men into battle. A machine-gun bullet broke his arm, but he managed to destroy a German tank and several machine guns with grenades. He was captured and imprisoned until 1945.

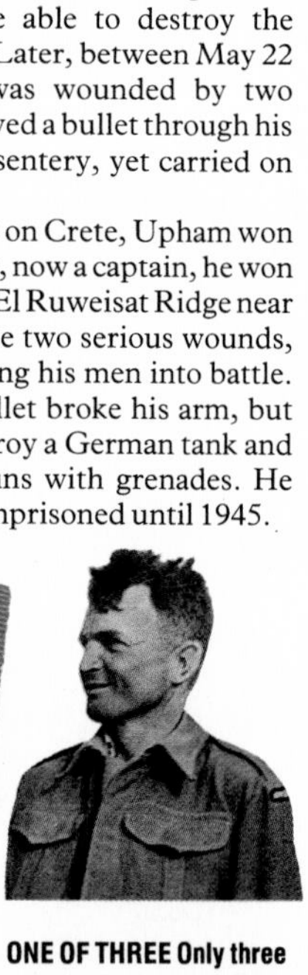

ONE OF THREE Only three men have ever won the VC twice. Upham was the only one in World War II.

hastily assembled New Zealand force under Colonel Howard Kippenberger, on high ground around the village of Galatas. Early the next morning, Student himself arrived in Crete.

Throughout the morning and afternoon of May 25, German artillery and aircraft pounded Galatas mercilessly until it was enveloped in a dense, blinding pall of smoke, dust and exploding bombs. Then, at 4.30 pm, German soldiers appeared out of the smoke and fell upon the defenders, machine guns blazing. Forced to retreat, the New Zealanders ran straight into fire from Stukas wheeling and diving overhead. From all directions, bullets flew so thick and fast that officers had to yell at the top of their voices to make themselves heard. Kippenberger, meanwhile, weaved fearlessly among his men, exhorting and encouraging them, and making sure that they retired in good order. Another hero was 2nd Lieutenant Charles Upham (see box) who, among many notable deeds that day, led his platoon in a sudden counterattack which temporarily forced the Germans to fall back.

At 8.30 pm, reinforced by British Hussars with two tanks, Kippenberger launched a counterattack from a ridge just east of Galatas. As his men reached the village's outskirts, they broke into a run and let forth a spontaneous, blood-curdling yell – a 'deep-throated wild beast noise', one of them called it later. Then, slowly but surely, alley by alley, house by house, they drove the astonished Germans from the village. Most of the inhabitants had fled to the hills.

But the Allies were in no position to consolidate this victory, and a little after midnight the order came for Kippenberger's men to withdraw eastwards. Their action had simply delayed the German advance. 'From a military point of view our position is hopeless', Freyberg informed Wavell the next day – and on May 27, London sent permission for him to prepare for evacuation. The same day, the Germans captured Khania.

RETREAT

For the Allied troops in western Crete there was now a slow, painful retreat across baking hot, rocky plains, through the high White (Levka) Mountains, under skies patrolled by German dive-bombers, to the small south-coast port of Sphakia – from where Royal Navy ships would evacuate them to Egypt. Commandos under Brigadier Robert Laycock landed at Suda Bay at night on May 23/24 and 26/27 to cover the retreat.

The decision of the Mediterranean Fleet's Commander in Chief, Admiral Sir Andrew Browne Cunningham, to take on the evacuation was a brave one – for German air power made naval actions even south of Crete dangerous. 'We cannot let them down,' he signalled his fleet. 'It takes the Navy three years to build a ship. It would take 300 years to rebuild a tradition.' Between May 28 and June 1, his ships saved 18 000 men. Of the 5000 left on Crete, some managed to escape in small craft, others surrendered and about 500 fled into the mountains to fight with the Cretan partisans. The troops at Heraklion, meanwhile, were evacuated on the night of May 28/29, but orders to prepare for evacuation never got to those at Rethimnon. When German troops reached Rethimnon from the west, they found 500 of their comrades besieged in an olive oil factory by over 1500 Australian and Greek troops. Another 700 lay dead.

During the battle for Crete over 1700 Anzac and British troops were killed, a similar number wounded and nearly 12 000 taken prisoner. The Royal Navy lost nine ships sunk and others were crippled, including the cruiser *Orion* (see box). German losses were also high – nearly 2000 men killed and the same number missing. They also lost 220 out of nearly 500 transport aircraft.

'The day of the parachutist is over,' Hitler told Student firmly when he heard of these casualties. 'The parachute arm is a surprise weapon and without the element of surprise there can be no future for airborne forces.' But he was wrong. Although the Germans abandoned large-scale airborne operations, their enemies did not. Just over three years later, on D-Day, Hitler would find this weapon used effectively against himself.

As for the German garrison on Crete, it found itself somewhat out on a limb. It was too far from North Africa to affect the war there, and it did not prevent the USAAF from bombing Ploesti twice.

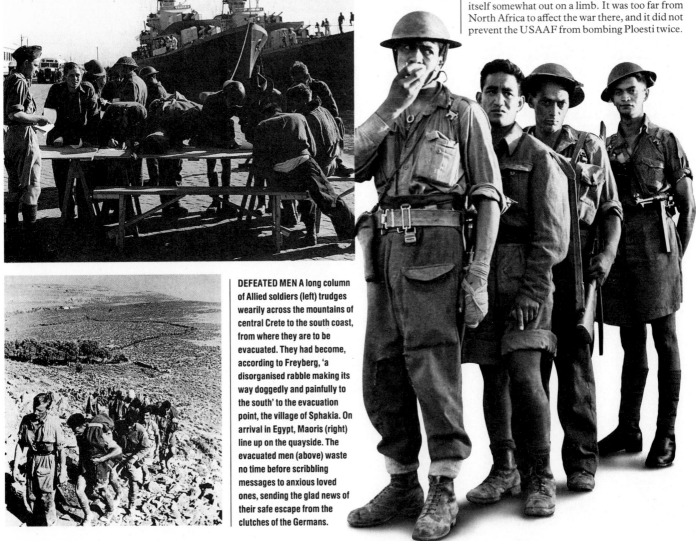

DEFEATED MEN A long column of Allied soldiers (left) trudges wearily across the mountains of central Crete to the south coast, from where they are to be evacuated. They had become, according to Freyberg, 'a disorganised rabble making its way doggedly and painfully to the south' to the evacuation point, the village of Sphakia. On arrival in Egypt, Maoris (right) line up on the quayside. The evacuated men (above) waste no time before scribbling messages to anxious loved ones, sending the glad news of their safe escape from the clutches of the Germans.

7: SUN, SAND AND SEA

While rival armies duelled over desert sands, Malta stood firm against the Axis onslaught.

A Desert Fox goes hunting

With the Italians beaten in Libya, the Axis powers needed a man of military genius to swing the tide of war back in their favour. They found one in Lt General Erwin Rommel, who soon earned the nickname 'the Desert Fox'.

STUKAS SWOOPED out of the sky like plummeting vultures, while on the ground tanks and motorised infantry of the Afrika Korps swept along the coast road towards Agedabia. Among those on the receiving end of the attack was Sergeant Jake Wardrop, of the 5th Royal Tank Regiment, who thought it was a 'real how d'ye do'. He wrote in his diary: 'We sat behind a ridge and waited until they came, then popped up and let loose. There seemed to be nothing in front but tanks coming on, but we kept firing and they slowed down and finally halted and shot it out stationary.'

The date was April 1, 1941, a date with a deadly irony, for the British had been fooled – and not for the last time – by the man who came to be known as 'the Desert Fox'. Lt General Erwin Rommel, in command of the newly formed Deutsches Afrika Korps, had been ordered not to start his offensive until his forces were up to strength – an order which had been intercepted and decoded by the British. But the headstrong German decided to seize the initiative with a surprise attack on the overstretched Allies, and it worked.

Rommel had arrived in Tripoli in February 1941, and came under the nominal authority of General Italo Gariboldi, the Italian Commander in Chief in North Africa. But he retained complete operational command and in reality answered only to Berlin. His orders were to recapture Cyrenaica, the eastern region of Libya, and its chief town, Benghazi, which had been taken swiftly from the Italians by Lt General Richard O'Connor at the beginning of the year.

Making unpredictable moves came naturally to Rommel. On March 24, within a few weeks of arriving in Africa, he launched the surprise attack with his 5th Light Division and Italian motorised infantry from his position 145 km (90 miles) west of the port of El Agheila.

Rommel divided his mechanised units into three columns. On the first day one column easily overran El Agheila, then pursued the retreating British along the coast road to take Agedabia on April 2. Rommel's men then rolled into Benghazi and beyond, to Barce and Derna, during the first week of April. Meanwhile, the second tank column headed inland, taking petrol dumps at Msus and Mechili on April 7, before bursting out onto the coastal plain at Gazala, about 64 km (40 miles) west of Tobruk. The third column, led by Lt Colonel Count von Schwerin, was sent in a wide outflanking move through Ben Gania to Mechili and Derna. Their task was to trap British units trying to evacuate Cyrenaica.

On the night of April 6, the Germans took their most eminent prisoners so far: O'Connor, commander of British troops in Egypt, and another senior commander, Lt General Philip Neame, VC. The two men were surprised by a German motorcycle patrol when their car got lost near Derna, and were sent to captivity in Italy.

On Good Friday, April 11, Rommel took Bardia, and four days later Sollum, as he bypassed Tobruk and pushed relentlessly east towards Egypt and the Suez Canal. It seemed as if nothing and no one could halt his advance. Many crews of the 2nd Armoured Division abandoned their tanks and joined in the headlong retreat. In the meantime, brigades of the 9th Australian Division, under the resolute command of Maj General Leslie Morshead, gathered inside the fortified Tobruk perimeter. 'There'll be no Dunkirk here,' declared Morshead, who was to command the Tobruk garrison until October 22. 'If we should have to get out, we shall fight our way out. There is no surrender and no retreat!'

Lt General Sir Noel Beresford-Pierse was brought from East Africa to take over command of the Western Desert Force on April 11. He positioned his men along a new and strung-out defence line near the Egyptian-Libyan frontier. Infantry and armour were deployed in 'boxes', with minefields and barbed *(continued on p. 90)*

SPRINGTIME FOR HITLER German troops have good cause to smile as they relax after capturing the fort of El Agheila in late March 1941. Their new commander, Erwin Rommel, was already justifying the faith Hitler had shown in him.

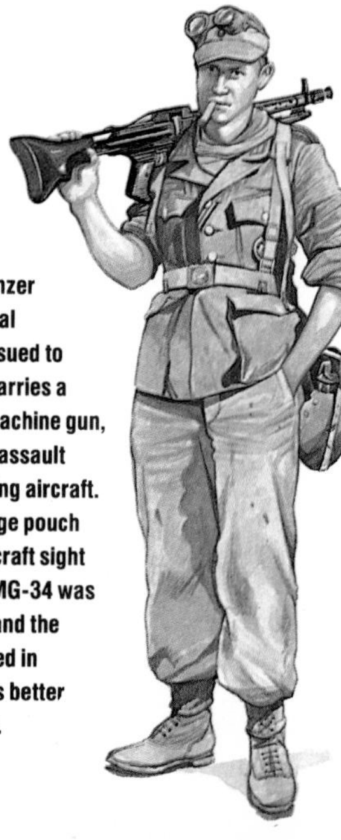

DESERT FIGHTER This panzer grenadier wears the tropical uniform and peaked cap issued to Afrika Korps infantry. He carries a general-purpose MG-34 machine gun, which could be used as an assault weapon or against low-flying aircraft. Attached to his belt is a large pouch which contains an anti-aircraft sight and maintenance kit. The MG-34 was a precision-built weapon, and the sturdier MG-42 – introduced in Tunisia early in 1943 – was better suited to desert conditions.

ROMMEL, 'THE DESERT FOX'

'I sniff through the country like a fox', said Erwin Rommel (1891-1944) referring to his instinctive 'feel' for new terrain and for his opponent's weak points. And before he had long been in North Africa his opportunism and daring earned him the nickname 'the Desert Fox'.

Rommel (above, left) was born at Heidenheim in south Germany, and became an officer cadet in 1910. He saw front-line action as a junior officer in France and Italy in World War I, when he was awarded the *Pour le Mérite*, Imperial Germany's highest decoration for bravery, for capturing more than 9000 Italian soldiers in just over two days. He stayed in the army, and in 1937 his lectures at the Infantry School in Dresden formed the basis of a classic military textbook, *Infanterie Greift An* ('Infantry Attacks').

At the outbreak of World War II, Rommel was a major general in command of the troops guarding Hitler's headquarters. In 1940 he was given command of the 7th Panzer Division – his first experience of tank warfare – and soon proved his flair in leading the breakthrough to the Channel ports during the invasion of France. He won the Knight's Cross for his personal bravery, and in February 1941 Hitler appointed him commander of the new Afrika Korps in Libya.

Despite some reverses, by the summer of 1942 he had, in a series of highly mobile armoured battles, driven the Allied forces almost 1000 km (600 miles) back to within 95 km (60 miles) of Alexandria, and he was promoted field marshal – at 50, the youngest in the German Army. The Press in Germany hailed him as a national hero and dubbed him 'the People's Marshal'. He was said to be unbeatable. Even Churchill, in May 1942, raged to his War Cabinet: 'Rommel, Rommel, what else matters but beating him?' But after his shock defeat at El Alamein by Lt General Bernard Montgomery and the Eighth Army in October his star went into decline. He was sick with jaundice and exhausted, and after his forces were driven back to Tunis in March 1943 he was sent on leave.

He briefly commanded German forces in northern Italy, but in November 1943 Hitler sent Rommel on a special mission to inspect the Atlantic Wall defences. And in January 1944 he was given command of Army Group B in France, covering the Channel coast from the Dutch-German border to the Loire river. He improved the defences but disagreed with his superior, Field Marshal Gerd von Rundstedt, on where best to position the panzers. He was badly wounded when a British fighter strafed his staff car on July 17, 1944, and shortly afterwards his name was associated with the army officers' plot to assassinate Hitler – although Rommel took no active part. He was given the choice of taking poison or facing trial by the People's Court – and almost certain execution.

For his family's sake, he chose poison and died on October 14. But his fame and popularity were such that the truth about his death was not publicised until after the war. He received a state funeral, officially having 'died of his wounds'.

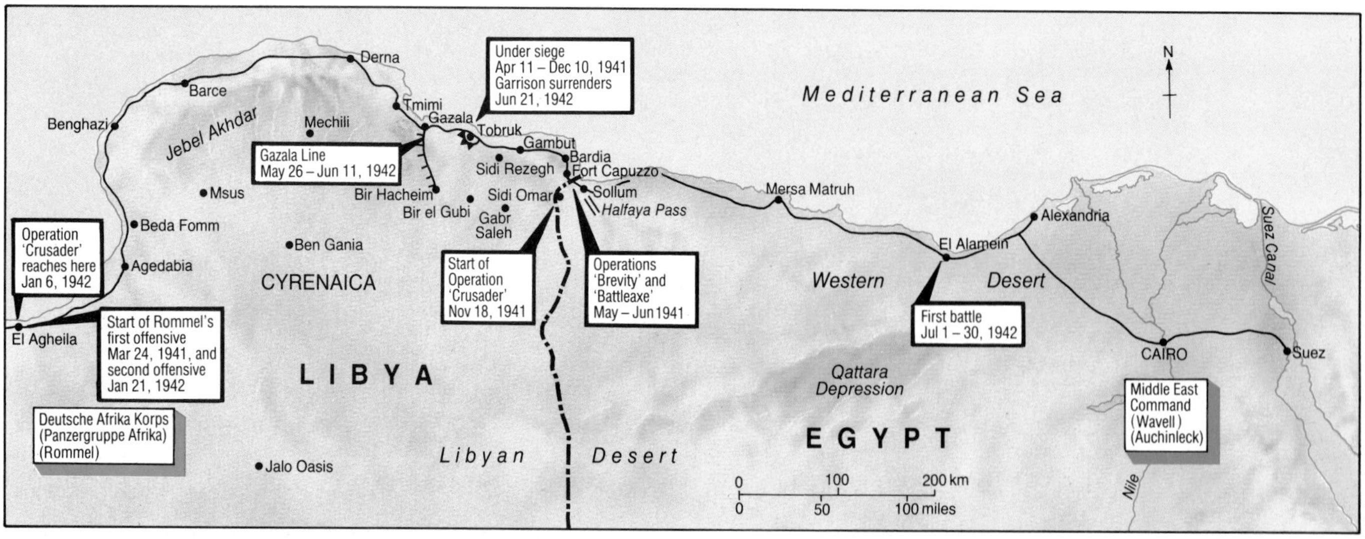

DUELLING GROUND Across pitiless terrain, Allied and Axis forces battled grimly in 1941-2. The names of remote villages were written into history, and the key fortress of Tobruk became linked for ever with the Desert Rats.

wire facing any likely Axis attack. Mobile 'Jock columns' of infantry, armoured cars and field guns – named after Colonel 'Jock' Campbell – were formed, and harassed the Germans like packs of terriers. After the capture of Addis Ababa in Ethiopia, Indian and South African reinforcements were rushed to Egypt.

TOBRUK BESIEGED

To the Allies, the fortress of Tobruk – about 120 km (75 miles) west of the frontier with Egypt – was the dominant factor in the 15 month phase of the North African campaign which became known to Allied troops as the 'Benghazi Handicap', from the way the opposing armies chased each other to and fro across the desert. Tobruk's importance lay in its deep-water harbour, where one ship unloading 5000 tonnes of cargo was worth more than a dozen convoys of trucks.

By April 11, Rommel had encircled Tobruk's 50 km (30 mile) long perimeter. This was based on the old Italian defences, which included a 9 m (30 ft) anti-tank ditch and about 70 strongpoints; these were repaired and added to. There were two lines of defence – an outer 'Red Line' and an inner 'Blue Line' – between which was a minefield covered by barbed wire. The 23 000-strong garrison included almost 15 000 Australians, some 500 Indian troops and the rest British.

The Afrika Korps began its drive on Tobruk that same day, April 11, with a series of reconnaissance thrusts by panzers and German and Italian infantry. Rommel decided on a major assault on a part of the southern perimeter in the early hours of the 14th, Easter Monday.

Pounded by artillery and air bombardment from Stukas, the defences gave way as German assault pioneers and Mark II and Mark III panzers moved in. The leading panzer battalion fought its way about 3 km (2 miles) inside the perimeter before it was stopped. The Australians turned the Italian coastal guns around to point inland and – with British 25-pounders joining in – destroyed 16 out of 38 German tanks. The rest were forced to withdraw.

After the Italian Ariete armoured division had suffered a defeat – with more than 800 men surrendering to the Australians – the Afrika Korps made a do-or-die attack on April 30. Stukas dive-bombed the Allied positions and then panzer grenadiers and assault pioneers rushed the south-western corner of the Tobruk defences at night. But the Allied garrison had been forewarned by their intelligence service, and although the Germans got a toehold on the outer defences, their losses were great. On May 4, Rommel called off the attack, though his troops retained a 3 km (2 mile) deep salient near Fort Pilastrino for the rest of the siege.

The failure to capture Tobruk – the forward base Rommel so badly needed for his proposed drive into Egypt – was the Wehrmacht's first major reverse of the entire war.

Encouraged by Rommel's unexpected setback, British troops advanced from their defensive line in western Egypt and drove the Germans and Italians back towards the strategically important Halfaya Pass, whose twisting road crossed the 215 m (700 ft) high escarpment running south-east from the port of Sollum towards Egypt. So far, some 300 German tanks had been destroyed and the 38 000 Axis casualties were more than twice those of the Allies.

In May, Churchill sent a fast convoy code-named 'Tiger' to Egypt with 50 Hurricane fighters and almost 400 tanks, hoping for the speedy destruction of the Afrika Korps and the permanent relief of Tobruk.

MORSHEAD: CHIEF 'RAT'

Leslie Morshead (1889-1959), who commanded the Tobruk garrison for nearly seven months of its long siege, was a Sydney schoolteacher before he volunteered for the Australian Imperial Force in 1914. In 1939 he went to war again as a major general commanding the 9th Australian Division. After the relief of Tobruk, Morshead – a no-nonsense disciplinarian – and his division featured prominently in both battles of El Alamein. Then they transferred to the Far East. Morshead directed the drive against the Japanese in New Guinea. He was knighted and promoted lieutenant general.
In 1944 he was given command of all Australian forces in New Guinea, and later of operations against the Japanese in Borneo.

'BREVITY' AND 'BATTLEAXE'

The opening move by General Sir Archibald Wavell, Commander in Chief Middle East, was to launch Operation 'Brevity', signalling the start of Round Two of the Benghazi Handicap. On May 15 he sent a force of 29 cruiser tanks against the Italians at the border fortress of Fort Capuzzo to seal the Axis forces' desert flank. At the same time, 24 Matilda tanks and supporting infantry attacked the Germans, who had repositioned themselves in the Halfaya Pass. After two days of scrappy fighting the Germans withdrew from the pass, and both sides paused to regroup. On May 26, Rommel craftily sent two armoured battle groups totalling 160 tanks with infantry support towards the frontier.

Fearing that the Germans would outflank and then attack them from behind, the British fell for the feint and beat a general retreat. Seizing his opportunity, Rommel turned his main power on the pass, which he retook after a short, sharp engagement. He then fortified it with artillery and 88 mm anti-tank guns. Soon Halfaya would earn its British nickname of 'Hellfire Pass'.

Rommel had won the opening encounter of the Handicap's second round, but Wavell soon retaliated. On June 15 he launched a new offensive, Operation 'Battleaxe', using the tanks brought in by 'Tiger'. The plan was for the heavy tanks and part of the 4th Indian Infantry Division to attack Halfaya Pass, while elements of the 7th Armoured Division with lorried infantry in support covered the left flank. Meanwhile, other columns from the 7th Armoured Brigade and 7th Armoured Division support groups would advance on Hafid Ridge and Fort Capuzzo. Rommel was warned by Intelligence and moved in the newly arrived (*continued on p. 92*)

LIFE OF THE 'RATS'

German propaganda dismissed the Tobruk garrison as 'rats in a trap'; the men themselves were soon proudly calling themselves the 'Rats of Tobruk' – a name that caught on throughout the British Empire.

Once they had repulsed the first German assaults in April, the biggest problem for the besieged men was boredom – closely followed by the dust that blew almost continuously through the battered town, and by the recurring plagues of flies and fleas.

'The desert fleas are famous,' wrote an anti-aircraft battery sergeant, 'and ours were obviously in the pay of the enemy. How we cursed them on nights when the moon was late up and we hoped to catch a couple of hours' sleep before the inevitable procession of night-bombers started. The fleas marched up and down our twitching bodies until we thought we would go crazy . . . And we needed the hours of sleep, for when the moon was up we would get mighty little rest. Twenty-one alarms in a night was our record.'

Other bugbears were the lack of fresh food and the shortage of drinking water. To combat the lack of vitamin C – and the desert sores that resulted – the troops took vitamin tablets. Some fresh water was distilled by the men themselves, using their own ingenious stills made from old petrol drums. But it was difficult to remove the medicinal taste of the purifying chlorine in the water in the main tanks, which the Italians had erected. 'Do not bother to try to make coffee,' wrote one of the garrison. 'Just heat the water. The result will look like coffee anyway . . . and taste like sulphur, which every drink out here does!' Water – for all purposes – was restricted to 6 pints (3.4 litres) a day per man.

The beleaguered troops ate mainly bully beef – prepared in a variety of forms from rissoles to hash – augmented by tinned stew and canned fruit, plus the inevitable Army-issue 'dog biscuits'. These basics were sometimes supplemented by fish caught (or stunned with hand grenades) in the harbour. Morale was kept up by listening to BBC news broadcasts and hearing the stirring chimes of Big Ben. Living quarters in the town were reasonably good: they ranged from timber-shored rooms in stone houses, and deep, bombproof tunnels drilled by the Italians, to sturdy shelters made of slabs of concrete from bombed-out houses, wood and sandbags.

The soldiers had their own ways of combatting the conditions. Amateur 'bookies' catered for a love of gambling, taking bets on whether ships would safely sail in or out of port, and there were also stage entertainments. But the greatest attraction of all was probably the troops' own newspaper, the *Tobruk Truth*, which the Aussies nicknamed 'The Dinkum Oil' – Australian slang for 'the honest truth'. In spite of enemy air raids and long-range bombardments, the paper came out every day with items of local interest, the latest war news (courtesy of the BBC) and readers' contributions.

DESERT REPORT Australian newsman Chester Wilmot plays back a recording to a gun crew.

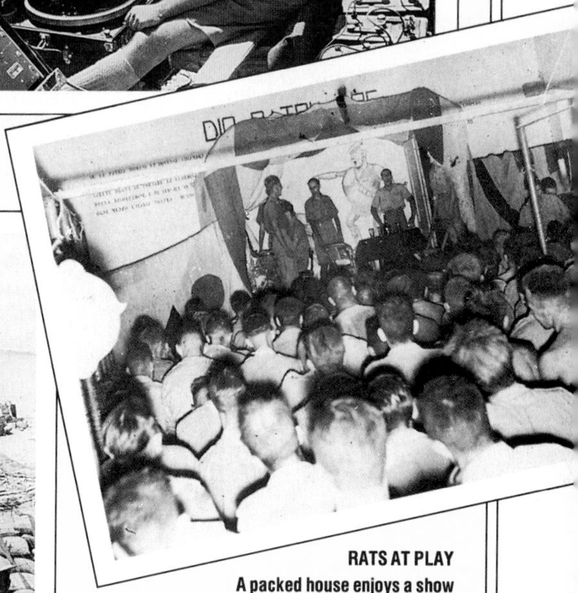

RATS AT PLAY A packed house enjoys a show in an improvised theatre.

STUKA ALERT Ack-ack gunners at the ready.

MAKING DO Ironing, darning and making rissoles relieve boredom.

TROUBLE IN ASIA MINOR

At the beginning of May 1941, Nazism suddenly raised its head in Asia Minor. Soldiers of the Iraqi Army laid siege to the British Embassy in Baghdad, the capital, and attacked the large British air base at Habbaniyah, 80 km (50 miles) to the west – a vital link in the air route to India. British forces defending the airfield drove off the attackers, and units of the 10th Indian Division, under Maj General William Slim, quickly relieved the embassy. The prime minister, Rachid Ali – a Nazi sympathiser – was ousted and a pro-British government established.

In neighbouring French-ruled Syria, the Vichy presence threatened British-controlled Palestine and pro-British Transjordan (present-day Israel and Jordan) – and thus the Suez Canal. A worried Churchill ordered an expeditionary force to 'liberate' Syria and Lebanon. On June 8, 1941, British, Indian and Australian troops, together with a token Free French contingent, crossed into Lebanon from Palestine and Transjordan, led by Lt General Sir Henry Maitland Wilson.

Their prime objective was the Lebanese capital Beirut, but 30 000 Vichy troops dug in along the coast road resisted fiercely. The Syrian capital, Damascus, fell on June 21, 1941, and after a month of savage hostilities the Allies battled their way into Beirut. General Henri Dentz, the Vichy Governor and Commander in Chief, negotiated a ceasefire through the American consul general. It was signed on July 14, and gave the Allies the right to occupy Syria and Lebanon.

One more Middle Eastern country still caused the Allies worries: Iran. Not only did it supply much of Britain's oil, but after the German invasion of the USSR in June 1941 it was a vital route for supplying Britain's new ally. So in August, British and Russian troops quickly and almost bloodlessly occupied the country, forestalling any Nazi plans.

TAKEOVER Indian soldiers guard an Iranian oil refinery which must not fall into German hands.

PASSAGE FROM INDIA The slogan chalked on the side of a lorry carrying men of the 4th Indian Division recalls that Indian troops here fought for the British before – against rebellious tribesmen in the mountains of their homeland.

15th Panzers alongside the Italian Brescia and Trieste infantry divisions.

The battle was a bruising affair, and both sides sustained heavy casualties. The Halfaya garrison fought hard, and that evening the 8th Panzer Regiment was badly mauled while charging British tanks positioned hull-down around Fort Capuzzo. On the morning of the 17th the British faced a renewed German thrust and withdrew from the fort, putting up a fierce rearguard action and keeping Rommel's forces at a reasonably safe distance. Even so, the British lost 91 tanks against the Germans' 25. More than 120 British troops were killed, almost 600 were wounded and some 260 were reported missing. The German losses were 93 killed, 350 wounded and 235 missing.

The pause that followed signalled the end of the Handicap's second round. The Afrika Korps had recaptured most of the territory gained by O'Connor in his brilliant campaign the previous year, but its success was far from total. Tobruk still held out, denying Rommel the use of its harbour and forcing him to divert troops to contain it. Nevertheless, Hitler was pleased enough to promote Rommel full general in command of the newly created Panzergruppe – later Panzerarmee – Afrika. This put him in charge of all the Axis troops in the battle areas, while the Afrika Korps itself was taken over by Lt General Ludwig Crüwell.

For the British the campaign had fallen short of the decisive victory on which Churchill had gambled. Wavell was removed as Commander in Chief and exchanged jobs with General Sir Claude Auchinleck, previously Commander in Chief India. 'The Auk' set about rebuilding the Allied forces as a new coherent unit, the Eighth Army, and restoring morale. Lt General Sir Alan Cunningham, fresh from his successes in Ethiopia, became its commander.

INSIDE THE FORTRESS

With both armies preoccupied in building up their strength and positions, there now followed a five-month lull in the desert war before the final two rounds of the Benghazi Handicap. Meanwhile, in the besieged fortress of Tobruk, the garrison went about its daily life (see box) ever alert to the threat of further attacks. Morshead's Australian brigades had suffered over 3000 casualties in the April fighting, and his government demanded that the men be withdrawn and reunited with other Australian units in Egypt.

In audacious night operations under the noses of Axis guns, most of the garrison was replaced by fresh troops – Indians, South Africans, Poles and British. Starting in the moonless nights of mid-August, fast Allied vessels audaciously carried in not only new troops – including a whole tank battalion – but also food and other supplies in what was called the 'spud run'. Slipping into berth in total darkness between the rusting hulks of sunken Italian ships, the transports quickly unloaded and were on their way back to Alexandria or Mersa Matruh within the hour.

After several months of relative calm, German attacks increased. Tobruk survived a mass attack by 100 dive-bombers at the beginning of September, and beat off German tank attacks throughout October. On October 19, the siege entered its eighth month. It would be two more months before relief finally came – but six months after that Tobruk would fall to Rommel in a single day's fighting.

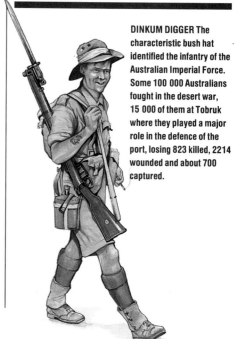

DINKUM DIGGER The characteristic bush hat identified the infantry of the Australian Imperial Force. Some 100 000 Australians fought in the desert war, 15 000 of them at Tobruk where they played a major role in the defence of the port, losing 823 killed, 2214 wounded and about 700 captured.

Crusade to relieve Tobruk

November and December 1941 saw some of the fiercest fighting of the North African war – culminating in the Allied relief of Tobruk. Rommel, deprived of reinforcements, managed his retreat with great skill, and by the New Year was preparing to launch a counteroffensive against the Eighth Army.

HARDENED DESERT RATS had never experienced weather like this before. On November 17, 1941, the heavens opened and for two days the Western Desert, lashed by torrents of rain, became a sea of mud as British armour and other vehicles churned their way forward to do battle with General Erwin Rommel and the Afrika Korps. Both sides had planned a winter offensive, but the British, who knew of the German intentions to capture the besieged port of Tobruk through decoded German signals, attacked first. They aimed to destroy Rommel's panzers and raise the siege, which had now lasted seven months.

The winter battle – representing Round Three of the to-and-fro desert war the troops nicknamed the 'Benghazi Handicap' – began on November 18, when the elements of the British 7th Armoured Division clashed with the combined strength of the 15th and 21st Panzer Divisions for possession of Sidi Rezegh, a small but tactically vital airstrip which held the key to Tobruk. Named after the tomb of an Arab martyr, Sidi Rezegh lay just 16 km (10 miles) south-east of the Tobruk perimeter. It was the place chosen by Lt General Sir Alan Cunningham, commander of the newly formed British Eighth Army, for a decisive confrontation with the massed might of Axis armour under Lt General Ludwig Crüwell, who had taken over as commander of the Afrika Korps on Rommel's promotion to overall chief of *Panzergruppe* (Panzer Group) Afrika – to be renamed Panzerarmee Afrika in January 1942.

ODDS IN FAVOUR

Operation 'Crusader' was the code name of the ambitious British plan to advance the massed armour of XXX Corps in a wide sweeping move to the village of Gabr Saleh, 65 km (40 miles) south-east of Sidi Rezegh, and lure the Axis forces into a deadly tank battle. Meanwhile, infantrymen of XIII Corps, with a tank brigade in support, were to tie down the German defences around the Egyptian coastal village of Sollum, near the Libyan border 110 km (70 miles) east of Tobruk, and Sidi Omar, 50 km (30 miles) south of Sollum. As soon as the enemy's armour was destroyed, the Allied infantry would move up to relieve Tobruk – squeezing the Axis forces between themselves, the port and the victorious tanks of XXX Corps.

Numerically, the odds were in the Allies' favour. XXX Corps had 453 cruiser tanks – 287 Crusaders and 166 Stuarts. These significantly outweighed the 272 tanks of the 15th and 21st Panzers, 96 of which were unfit for battle. The British also had another 135 tanks in the 1st Army Tank Brigade attached to XIII Corps. Half were Matildas and half Valentines – the new, fast, but not very well armed infantry tanks.

The action started quietly enough at dawn on November 18, when in driving rain the infantry and tanks of XIII Corps crossed the frontier from Egypt into Libya and advanced on the enemy's forts stretching from Sidi Omar to the coast. Cunningham travelled with XXX Corps headquarters as the three armoured brigades drove north towards their objectives. The 7th Armoured Brigade, with the division's Support Group in attendance, drove for Sidi Rezegh, and the recently formed 22nd Armoured Brigade headed for Bir el Gubi. The 4th Armoured Brigade Group occupied the ground between the two corps at Gabr Saleh.

But Rommel – who had just returned from Rome, where on November 15 he had celebrated his 50th birthday with his wife – did not react as Cunningham expected. From his advanced headquarters at Gambut, midway between Tobruk and the Libyan frontier town of Bardia, the 'Desert Fox' concentrated on planning his attack on Tobruk and at first dismissed the reports of strong British forces advancing to Gabr Saleh, regarding the move as a mere diversion.

ITALIAN LINES HOLD

The next day, November 19, the 22nd Armoured Brigade clashed with the armour of the Italian Ariete Division at Bir el Gubi. This was the British brigade's first battle, and it showed. Regiments of Yeomanry and Hussars in their Crusaders charged the Ariete, destroying 34 of the enemy tanks but losing 25 of their own in the minefield and to enemy artillery. Another 30 Crusaders broke down and the brigade had to withdraw having lost half of its tanks.

Meanwhile, as planned, the British 7th Armoured Brigade headed north and seized Sidi Rezegh. The Italian defenders were caught by surprise. Many of their aircraft were destroyed on the ground by the charging Crusaders and 19 were captured intact. The British tried to make contact with forces attempting to break out of Tobruk, but the Italian infantry along the perimeter, well led and in strong defensive positions, held firm.

Rommel was by now concerned at the reconnaissance reports and intelligence assessment, and he alerted the panzers. *Kampfgruppe* (Battle Group) Stephan – named after its leader, Lt Colonel Fritz Stephan – with some 85 tanks supported by artillery and anti-tank guns, skirmished with the Stuart tanks of the 4th Armoured Brigade at Gabr Saleh. There followed the first large-scale tank battle of the desert war, a confused affair in which both sides claimed victory. In truth the British lost 23 tanks while the panzers withdrew with few losses.

At last aware of what the British were up to, Rommel cancelled his own offensive against Tobruk and turned to deal with this more immediate threat. He ordered the 15th and 21st Panzers to concentrate at Gabr Saleh and then head west to attack Sidi Rezegh. Even though that was exactly where Cunningham had wanted the decisive tank encounter, Rommel was the better prepared for it, for the British had only one brigade, the 7th Armoured, against the combined force of the Afrika Korps.

Although the British 4th and 22nd Armoured Brigades hurried separately to the scene, they were too late to prevent the near destruction of the 7th. And armoured counterattacks led by Colonel 'Jock' Campbell (see box) in his open car resulted only in further punishing losses. Even so, his gallantry and daring at Sidi Rezegh won him the Victoria Cross. The fighting ended on November 22 with the Germans back in possession of the airstrip and the 7th Armoured Brigade reduced to about ten battle-worthy tanks.

SUNDAY OF THE DEAD

But for the Allies there was far worse to come. On Sunday, November 23 – Remembrance Day in pre-Nazi Germany – Crüwell led his forces in a

THE MAN WHO INVENTED THE 'JOCK COLUMNS'

Waving a blue scarf from his open staff car to direct his tanks, Colonel John ('Jock') Campbell of the Royal Horse Artillery led his unorthodox 'Jock columns' against Rommel's forces at Sidi Rezegh airstrip on November 21, 1941. Halting only to get out and help service the guns, Campbell led from the front until he stopped an enemy bullet. He refused medical treatment and was later awarded the Victoria Cross for his bravery.

His four hastily formed mobile columns each consisted of a company of about 120 lorried infantry, a troop of three or four 25-pounder field guns, some armoured cars or light tanks, together with signals and other support. They first went into action in Egypt in September 1940, when they harassed the communication lines of the advancing Italians.

Despite their success at Sidi Rezegh, the columns were used mainly to patrol the desert and as a rearguard defence. They were usually outgunned by the enemy, and the infantry received little protection in their canvas-topped vehicles. Never more than a temporary arrangement, the columns were phased out after Campbell was killed in a vehicle accident near Halfaya Pass on March 5, 1942.

drive to link up with the Ariete Division at Bir el Gubi. Thrusting through the gap between XXX Corps at Gabr Saleh and XIII Corps at Sollum, he found his way barred by the 5th South African Infantry Brigade. In some of the fiercest fighting of the whole desert war – involving the use of rifles, bayonets and hand grenades – the South Africans refused to give ground and died where they stood. Their vehicles were blown up or left on fire and their headquarters overrun.

The remains of the 22nd Armoured Brigade were also caught in the gap. Together with its artillery and 34 surviving tanks, the division could muster 100 guns. Deciding to brush them aside, Crüwell formed his tanks and armoured vehicles – including 160 panzers and 100-odd M13s of the Ariete Division – into line abreast and charged. He quickly found that he had seriously underestimated the British troops' morale and fighting qualities. They fought back like demons, and Crüwell lost some 70 tanks. Even so, the British were eventually forced to withdraw.

By now, the plain around the airstrip was a fog of smoke and dust as it dried after the rains of the previous week. Some 3400 of the South Africans were either dead or captured, and isolated units of tanks and guns were stranded among the widespread destruction and carnage. Lieutenant Cyril Joly, a tank commander in the 4th Armoured Brigade, later wrote a graphic, first-hand account of the scene at Sidi Rezegh:

'It was a frightening and awesome spectacle – the dead and dying strewn over the battlefield, in trucks and Bren-carriers, in trenches and toppled over in death, others vocal with pain and stained by red gashes of flowing blood or the dark marks of old congealed wounds. Trucks, guns, ammunition, odd bits of clothing were smouldering or burning with bright tongues of fire. Here and there ammunition had caught fire and was exploding with spurts of flame and black smoke. Tanks of all kinds – Italian, German and British – littered the whole area.'

Scanning the wide plain below Sidi Rezegh, Rommel reasonably felt that the battle was going his way. 'Visibility was poor,' he recorded, 'and many British tanks and guns were able to break away to the south without being caught. But a great part of the enemy force still remained inside. Twilight came . . . and hundreds of burning vehicles, tanks and guns lit up the field of the *Totensonntag* [Sunday of the Dead].'

Fighting continued in and around Sidi Rezegh for the next 24 hours, with both sides suffering heavy losses in men and armour. By then Cunningham felt that defeat was imminent – and his loss of confidence brought General Sir Claude Auchinleck, Commander in Chief Middle East, to the front in a decisive effort to stop the rot. His decision not to retreat from Sidi Rezegh proved vital to the Allied cause. And Rommel's hopes of a speedy and sweeping victory were dashed by the confused scrapping at the airstrip. He had neither the manpower nor the resources for a prolonged engagement – and the capture of Tobruk was still his immediate priority.

DASH TO THE WIRE

On November 24, Rommel met Crüwell near Tobruk and received an optimistic report about the situation at Sidi Rezegh. According to Crüwell, most of the British forces there had been destroyed, and he sought permission to return and finish off the job. All that stood between the Afrika Korps and Cairo were the Indian, Australian and New Zealand infantry divisions and a few shattered remnants of the once powerful

DAVID AND GOLIATH Rommel called his panzers, seen below advancing on a reconnaissance patrol, the 'hard core of the motorised army'. And a hard core they proved to be, with their speed, manoeuvrability and firepower. The British answer was the 2-pounder anti-tank gun (inset), a highly mobile weapon but lacking the punch to penetrate the panzers' 30 mm ($1\frac{1}{4}$ in thick) armour.

armoured brigades. Rommel agreed, and later that day gathered together the 106 remaining tanks of the Afrika Korps and the Ariete Division and tried to repeat the tactics that had proved so successful the previous summer. Driving a captured British armoured command vehicle nicknamed *Mammut* ('Mammoth'), he led his men eastwards through the desert in a rapid thrust towards the Egyptian frontier.

This time, however, the ploy failed. Instead of running, as Rommel had anticipated, the Allied infantry divisions simply allowed the enemy through their lines. Then they reformed and pulverised the Axis supply formations, which followed in the rear. Rommel spent four crucial days out of touch with his forward headquarters at Gambut. What became known as his 'dash to the Wire' – the 640 km (400 mile) long belt of barbed wire along the Egyptian-Libyan frontier – added greatly to Rommel's glamorous appeal, but it did nothing for his reputation as a mature battlefield commander.

While this was going on – on November 26 – Auchinleck abruptly replaced Cunningham as commander of Eighth Army with Maj General Neil Ritchie, his own chief of staff. At 44, Ritchie was the youngest general in the British Army and was trusted not to 'lose his nerve', as Cunningham was deemed to have done. Indeed, Cunningham went straight into a Cairo hospital, suffering from mental exhaustion.

Orders immediately went out to the 2nd New Zealand Division, under World War I hero and veteran of Crete Maj General Sir Bernard Freyberg, VC, to push along the coast to take Belhamed, Sidi Rezegh and El Duda – and relieve the beleaguered Tobruk garrison.

LIFTING THE SIEGE

Since the evacuation of Maj General Leslie Morshead and his men the previous autumn, the troops holding Tobruk had been commanded by Maj General Ronald Scobie. He and his British 70th Division landed in the port as part of the replacement for the besieged Australians. But the new garrison was not prepared to sit back during the last few days of November, while the oncoming New Zealanders were exposed to a battering from the German armour.

Thousands of defenders crammed into jeeps, Bren-gun carriers and lorries, and fought their way south-eastwards through the Axis lines. Some of the garrison travelled in groups on foot, first of all intent on helping to drive the Italians of the Trieste Division from a ridge at El Duda, 8 km (5 miles) north-west of Sidi Rezegh. By mid-afternoon on November 26, the last enemy had been beaten off the ridge.

The New Zealanders were now just 6 km (4 miles) to the east. That evening their 19th Battalion with tanks in support linked up with the Tobruk garrison at El Duda. Meanwhile the New Zealanders' 6th Battalion went in with bayonets against the Italians on the Sidi Rezegh ridge. The Italians were wiped out as a fighting unit and by morning the ridge was in New Zealand hands.

But it was not over yet. Rommel, refusing to give up, gathered pockets of his troops who were all but lost in the dust storms that shrouded the area and in a series of stinging attacks returned to the offensive. His tanks attacked the 4th and 6th New Zealand Brigades and fighting raged for three days until, by December 1, both sides had suffered heavy losses and were dispirited and tired. The New Zealand division was so battered that it retired from the fray. Some of the German units were in no better shape. Since the battle had begun on November 18, Rommel's forces had suffered more than 4000 casualties and lost 170 armoured fighting vehicles. The situation was stalemate when the Allies launched a final, concerted thrust.

The Eighth Army, with massive support from the RAF, tenaciously fought for every patch of ground between Sidi Rezegh and Tobruk. Left with only 40 serviceable tanks, Rommel decided to give up the fight and retreat through Cyrenaica (eastern Libya). Before long the German and Italian troops abandoned their positions. They streamed westwards past Tobruk, fired at and bombed along the way.

On December 10, the relieving troops at last entered the fortress port of Tobruk, more than seven months after the siege had begun. The following day Prime Minister Winston Churchill triumphantly announced the fact in the House of Commons, declaring: 'The enemy, who has fought with the utmost stubbornness and enterprise, has paid the price of his valour, and it may well be that the second phase of the Battle of Libya will gather more easily the fruits of the first than has been our experience . . . so far . . . I will go so far on this occasion as to say that all the danger of the Army of the Nile not being able to celebrate Christmas and the New Year in Cairo has been decisively removed.'

ROMMEL'S RETREAT

So far, the winter campaign had not gone Rommel's way. Unlike Auchinleck and Ritchie, he had received no reinforcements whatsoever – not even a single tank – to replace his losses. In addition, he was constantly beset by a shortage of fuel. Since the beginning of November the RAF Desert Air Force and Royal Navy had done more than their share to cripple the Axis forces in North Africa – including the destruction of 16 ships carrying some 60 000 tonnes of supplies. British air attacks by planes based on the island of Malta also took their toll of German and Italian supply ships, which ran a constant gauntlet of bombs between Sicily and the Axis-held port of Tripoli, in western Libya.

END OF THE CRUSADE On a rubble-strewn plain outside Tobruk, infantrymen of the 2nd New Zealand Division link up with tanks of the Tobruk garrison that have fought their way through the Axis lines besieging the town. The siege has lasted seven months.

Rommel's supply situation would have been even more precarious during the struggle to relieve Tobruk had it not been for the Allies' 'generosity'. Many of the relieving troops were in the habit of withdrawing each evening into defensive encampments – a common tactic by Eighth Army. With the battlefield free, German and Italian engineers had the opportunity to recover and repair what tanks they could, and they looted those – their own and the British – which could not be salvaged.

Throughout the rest of December, Rommel and his men methodically retreated westwards, thwarting each British outflanking attempt with great skill. At the beginning of 1942 Derna, Barce and then Benghazi fell to the British forces. The only effective resistance came from the Afrika Korps under Crüwell, which stubbornly stood its ground at Beda Fomm, 100 km (60 miles) south of Benghazi, while the bulk of the Germans and Italians beat an orderly retreat to the coastal town of El Agheila – where Rommel had started his long drive towards Tobruk nine months earlier.

Now it was the turn of the Allied forces to be thinly stretched across a long communications line from the Egyptian frontier to Benghazi – a straight-line distance of 450 km (280 miles). In addition, the outbreak of war against Japan meant in the short term diverting some Allied troops and resources from North Africa to the Far East. This gave fresh hope to Rommel, who was resting and regrouping his forces in readiness for a counteroffensive – with Tobruk once again his main objective.

Exploits of the desert raiders

The 'phantom major' and Popski . . . just two of the very individual 'freelances' of the desert.

MEN NOTED for unusual bravery and unorthodox methods led the numerous 'freelance' fighting groups that shot up enemy camps and installations, destroyed planes on the ground and generally created havoc behind enemy lines. They moved in from the desert – often under cover of darkness – and after striking withdrew as rapidly and eerily as they had arrived.

The most spectacular of the raiders, the Special Air Service (SAS), was formed in the summer of 1941 by Lieutenant David Stirling, a Scots Guards officer nearly 2 m (6 ft 6 in) tall. He sold the idea of a special raiding group – to go in ahead of a major offensive or drive – to General Sir Claude Auchinleck, Commander in Chief Middle East. It was based on the recently disbanded Middle East Commando.

The SAS's first operation – by parachute-drop on the night of November 16, 1941 – was a disaster. Gale-force winds, driving rain and poor visibility prevented the Bombay transport planes from reaching their target – five enemy airfields in the Gazala region, where it was planned to destroy aircraft on the ground – and one stray British plane was shot down. Two of the crew and one parachutist were killed; the rest were captured. Only 22 officers and men made their way to a rendezvous point where the lorries of the Long Range Desert Group (LRDG) waited to whisk them away.

From then until they got their own vehicles in summer 1942, Stirling and his men used the LRDG to ferry them to and from their objectives. Operating from Jalo Oasis about 190 km (120 miles) south-east of El Agheila, they derailed trains, hijacked trucks, mined roads and destroyed arms and supply depots. Their biggest successes came in December 1941, when in a two-week period they wrecked a total of 90 Axis planes standing on their strips.

The following year the 60 remaining SAS men and six officers formed the nucleus of a fully fledged regiment – the 22nd Special Air Service Regiment – whose winged-dagger badge and motto, 'Who Dares Wins', were both created by Stirling. At one time it incorporated the Special Boat Section (SBS) – a group of saboteurs including frogmen and canoeists.

By 1942 the 27-year-old Stirling was known on German radio as the 'phantom major'. He was promoted lieutenant colonel, and Churchill described him as 'the mildest mannered man that ever scuttled ship or cut a throat'. The Germans were jubilant when a unit specially formed to hunt down the SAS captured Stirling near the Mareth Line in January 1943. Rommel admitted that the group had 'caused us more damage than any other British unit of equal strength'.

After four escapes from an Italian prison camp, Stirling sweated out the rest of the war at Colditz Castle. Meanwhile, his former comrades – led now by Captain Blair ('Paddy') Mayne – continued their audacious raids and by the end of the desert war had destroyed at least 250 enemy planes on the ground.

The SAS often shared the bases of the Long Range Desert Group, whose open-topped Chevrolet trucks – some of them painted pink and green – became one of the sights of the desert. Generally recognised as the aristocrats of desert raiders, the LRDG had been formed in 1940 primarily as a reconnaissance/intelligence group operating from advanced desert bases. It was headed by Brigadier Ralph Bagnold, who between the wars had led weekend motoring expeditions across the Libyan Desert.

Initially, the LRDG provided the Allies with valuable information about the movements of Italian troops in Libya. But the patrols sometimes went for weeks in the desert without encountering anyone. They were later used to destroy ammunition and fuel depots and attack enemy camps.

Another celebrated British raiding force of the time was Popski's Private Army. It was founded and led by Major – later Lt Colonel – Vladimir ('Popski') Peniakoff, a Belgian engineer of Russian parentage who had worked in Egypt. He loved driving solo through the sands of North Africa and became a self-taught expert in desert navigation. When war broke out he joined the British Army and was commissioned in the commando-like Libyan Arab Force.

He wanted to join the Long Range Desert Group, but was considered too eccentric even for that unconventional outfit. Instead, he was talked into forming his own independent raiding unit – the smallest in the British Army. It initially consisted of five officers and 18 other ranks, who dashed about the Libyan Desert in armed jeeps and trucks wrecking military installations, planes and petrol dumps behind the Axis lines. The unit – which grew at times to about 120 men – had its own shoulder flashes and badges, and its odd title became official.

Finally, there was the Special Interrogation Group (SIG) made up mostly of Palestinian Jews and anti-Nazi Germans who were chosen to penetrate enemy defences wearing uniforms of the Afrika Korps. The unit set out on its first raid behind Rommel's lines in June 1942. But the men were betrayed by a German prisoner recruited into the force. The mission was a disaster, with most of the group killed.

In spite of the glamour and effectiveness of these raiders, the British high command never really appreciated their worth. Gradually they were phased out or moved to other theatres.

The Germans and Italians had their own special groups in the Middle East. The Brandenburgers' Afrika Kampanie consisted of some 60 men – mainly English-speaking, and including some South Africans of German descent. One of their operations was an attempt to find a British trans-African military supply route, which turned out to be non-existent.

WORRIER WARRIORS Back from a raid, SAS men (above) are greeted by Lt Colonel David Stirling – on the right. Another man who harried the enemy in the desert was the eccentric Vladimir Peniakoff (right) – 'Popski', of Private Army fame.

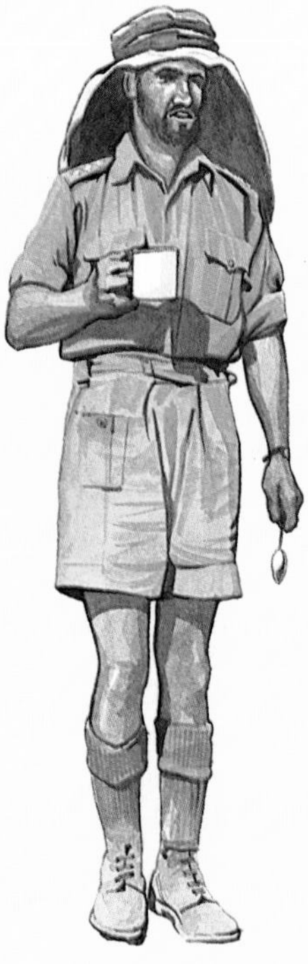

NOMAD LOOK The desert raiders tended to develop sartorial styles of their own. Here an officer of the Long Range Desert Group sports an Arab headdress along with conventional tropical uniform and casual desert boots.

The island that refused to die

The Italians and Germans did their best to blow Malta off the map and starve it into submission. The British warships and aircraft based there wreaked havoc among Axis ships and planes trying to supply North Africa.

MASONRY FELL in an ear-splitting thunder as successive plane-loads of high-explosive bombs crashed on the buildings of Valletta, capital of the beleaguered island of Malta. People could see only a few paces ahead through the thick yellow dust that choked the streets and seeped into air-raid shelters carved in solid rock.

The dust – swirling from the ruins of the city's limestone buildings – filled the mouths and noses of sheltering islanders, making them gasp, splutter and wheeze. There was nothing to do but huddle together and pray. It was April 1942, the worst month in the seemingly endless Axis air raids that rocked and blasted Malta, making it the most frequently bombed place of the entire war. This was the month that inspired King George VI to award the island the George Cross.

Strategically, Malta held a vital place in the narrows of the Mediterranean. A British possession with three airfields and a great naval dockyard in Valletta's Grand Harbour, it lay only 90 km (55 miles) south of Sicily. It was an ideal launching pad for air and sea strikes against ships carrying fuel and supplies for the Italian and later German forces in North Africa.

It was for these reasons that the Italians and Germans set out to bomb Malta into submission – and then seize it for themselves. Rommel wanted to invade it, but a proposed airborne and parachute invasion, code-named 'Hercules', did not get beyond the planning stage. Meanwhile, Malta's Governor and Commander in Chief, Lt General Sir William Dobbie, promised that his men would fight until the enemy was defeated.

The first bombing raid on Malta was made by the *Regia Aeronautica* (Italian Air Force) on June 11, 1940 – the day after Italy declared war. Ten Savoia-Marchetti SM79 three-engined bombers flew from Sicily and attacked Valletta and the surrounding area, including the airfield at Hal Far on the southern tip of the island. Altogether that day, eight separate air attacks took place involving some 40 bombers escorted by a dozen fighters. In the last raid, early in the evening, the planes attacked naval installations in Valletta's dockyard – where the block-shaped, limestone buildings were virtually fireproof and could survive everything except direct hits. Civilian casualties were inevitably high, and the enemy hoped this would have a demoralising effect on the Maltese. But they had counted without the islanders' spirit, which helped them to withstand these attacks and some 3340 more to come.

SEA HERO Malta, familiar to generations of Royal Navy men, played a major part in Britain's mastery of the seas. Men like this captain, dressed in regulation tropical whites, found themselves in the thick of fierce air and sea combat from the time Italy entered the war in June 1940.

FAITH, HOPE AND CHARITY

The Royal Air Force chiefs had already decided that Malta could not be adequately defended, and had neglected to strengthen it. When Italy declared war the island had only 42 anti-aircraft guns, instead of a promised 172, and not a single operational fighter aircraft, though four squadrons of Hurricanes had been promised.

Four Gloster Gladiator biplane fighters were found in crates in a Fleet Air Arm store. Hastily assembled, they were flown by seven pilots in relays. One Gladiator was soon badly damaged in action and written off; but the remaining three – affectionately nicknamed 'Faith', 'Hope' and 'Charity' – took on the Italian planes for the next three weeks, when four Hurricanes were flown in to help them. By then the Gladiator pilots had become local heroes, with their photographs in shop windows and crowds cheering as they gamely rose to the attack. The Gladiators gave a good account of themselves against Italian bombers, and on July 13 Flt Lieutenant George Burges was awarded the DFC for six victories.

For the rest of the year the Italian air raids continued regularly but usually inaccurately. By December 1940 the raids were by as many as 70 or more bombers, gallantly opposed by no more than eight or nine British fighters.

THE LUFTWAFFE STEPS IN

On December 10, Hitler stepped up the air offensive and sent the Luftwaffe's crack *Fliegerkorps X* ('X Flying Corps', equivalent to an RAF group), commanded by Lt General Hans Geissler, to Sicily. His mission: to gain control of the central Mediterranean skies so that Rommel's newly formed Afrika Korps could be transported to Libya in safety and then kept supplied with fuel, ammunition and food. Geissler's squadrons of level bombers and Stuka dive-bombers – whose crews were specially trained in anti-shipping strikes – soon showed their skill. One of the Stukas' first victims – in January 1941 – was the aircraft carrier HMS *Illustrious*, which was hit six times and crippled.

THE SAGA OF 'SCREWBALL' BEURLING

George 'Screwball' Beurling (1922-48) – a Canadian with the RAF – was posted to Malta on June 8, 1942. In his first week of operations Beurling, flying a Hurricane, shot down nine enemy bombers. By the end of October, he was the island's leading fighter pilot, with 29 kills to his credit.

Rejected by the Royal Canadian Air Force in 1940, Beurling, who came from Quebec, became a sergeant-pilot in the RAF. He earned the nickname 'Screwball' because he broke formation to attack every enemy aircraft in sight. Shot down and badly wounded in Malta, he was soon back in action, now commissioned and holding the DSO, DFC, DFM and Bar. He finally joined the RCAF, but left it in June 1944 after a disagreement over his service future. On May 20, 1948, he was killed in a crash while taking off from Rome to join the new Israeli Air Force.

The following month saw the arrival of Messerschmitt Me109 fighters in Sicily. Malta's Mark I Hurricanes were outclassed and outnumbered. Altogether, the Axis had some 400 planes at its disposal while Malta, even with reinforcements, had only 16 Hurricane fighters, 16 Wellington bombers, 12 Fairey Swordfish biplane torpedo bombers, and a few American-made Martin Maryland light bombers.

Even so, the island's air commander, Air Vice Marshal Hugh Lloyd – who took over from Air Vice Marshal Forster Maynard in May – did not lose hope. Day and night he spent his entire time between Malta's three airfields – Hal Far, Luqa and Takali – overseeing improvements and extensions to the runways and defences. From June to December 1941 there was a comparative lull in the bombing, as some of Geissler's planes were transferred elsewhere. This allowed the British to replenish Malta with more Hurricanes.

New squadrons of Blenheim IV bombers and Beaufighters were also flown in and soon began to hound Axis shipping and make night raids on Italian ports. They were so successful that in October 1941 some 63 per cent of the Afrika Korps' much-needed supplies were sunk, and the following month Rommel's men received only about 30 000 out of an expected 70 000 tonnes of oil, rations, shells and small-arms ammunition. This severely restricted German effectiveness in North Africa just as the Allies were about to launch a new offensive, Operation 'Crusader'. The Italian Foreign Minister, Count Ciano, told Hitler that the convoys had to be halted because 'the British on Malta are slaughtering us!'

BLACK WINTER

Meanwhile, Maltese civilians were suffering dreadful hardships. Their response was typical of their nerve and initiative. They built sandstone shelters and blessed the fact that the island was virtually treeless, without wooden structures to act as targets for incendiary bombs.

The air raids began again, with a new intensity, on December 22, 1941 – the start of the island's aptly named 'black winter'. By then, the annihilation of Malta had been entrusted to Field Marshal Albert Kesselring's *Luftflotte* (Air Fleet) 2, jointly with the Regia Aeronautica. As well as taking to the shelters, many of Malta's inhabitants virtually lived in vast natural caves beneath Valletta, but hundreds were buried alive in hits on offices and homes. A blackout was enforced and fuel shortages and food rationing added to the privations.

The New Year began with a prolonged assault by enemy bombers. At the end of February 1942 the island's remaining Wellingtons were withdrawn by the RAF, and by the beginning of March there were only eight serviceable Hurricanes left. Then, on March 7, a consignment of 15 Spitfires was flown in from the aircraft carrier HMS *Eagle*. The fighters gave the island's defences a long overdue boost, but they were not enough to lessen the frequency and savagery of the attacks. On April 20 a further 47 Spitfires flew into Malta from the American carrier USS *Wasp*. Just as they did so an air raid began. The fighters had so little fuel left that they had no choice but to land and become sitting ducks as ground crews struggled to refuel them. The result was a shambles, as 30 of the new Spitfires were destroyed or damaged by German bombers before they could take off again.

By now as many as 300 German and Italian bombers were taking part in a single raid. Buildings were reduced to rubble; whole streets were obliterated; towns and villages were mercilessly pounded. Even Dobbie, a strong man, eventually suffered physical and mental exhaustion, and in May was replaced by the tough and aggressive General Lord Gort, VC, who had commanded the British Expeditionary Force (BEF) in France in 1939-40, and had then been Governor of Gibraltar.

On May 9, Gort was cheered by news that some 60 more Spitfires had flown in from *Wasp* and *Eagle*. This time the planes were refuelled and armed for action before German bombers could blast them on the ground. They were flung straight into the fray. One pilot, Denis Barnham, wrote: 'One lives here only to destroy the Hun . . . living conditions, sleep, food, have gone by the board . . . It makes the Battle of Britain . . . seem like child's play.'

AGAINST ALL ODDS

But these reinforcements alone were not enough to save Malta, which was desperately short of food, ammunition and aviation fuel. Kesselring told Hitler: 'The aerial attack on Malta has, I feel, eliminated Malta as a naval base.' His confidence was shared by Rommel, who captured Tobruk and its stockpile of stores and fuel on June 21.

Rommel had already seized the formerly British-held airfields in Cyrenaica – so depriving Allied convoys to Malta of bases for much-needed air cover. Indeed, in mid-June, two major supply convoys – one from Egypt and the other from Gibraltar – were badly mauled. Of 17 merchant ships, ten were sunk, five turned back to port, and only two got through to Valletta. In desperation, some vital supplies were smuggled in by submarine and fast-flying transport planes in July; and 59 Spitfires were brought in by HMS *Eagle* on two trips. The minelayer HMS *Welshman*, one of the fastest warships afloat, made night runs from Gibraltar, carrying ammunition. At the end of July there were 80 serviceable fighters in Malta – with an average of 17 a week shot down or too badly mauled to fly again.

On August 2 the biggest convoy ever sent to Malta left Britain. In it were 14 large, fast merchantmen carrying food, fuel and ammunition. They were escorted by the battleships *Nelson* and *Rodney*, the carriers *Eagle*, *Indomitable* and *Victorious*, three anti-aircraft cruisers and 14 destroyers. The convoy – codenamed 'Pedestal' – reached the Strait of Gibraltar on August 10. There, it was joined briefly by the carrier *Furious*, from which 38 Spitfires took off for Malta – one was lost. That night *Furious* turned back to Gibraltar, but the convoy was joined by the heavy cruisers *Kenya*, *Manchester* and *Nigeria*, the anti-aircraft cruiser *Cairo* and 11 more destroyers. Lying in wait were 21 Italian and German submarines, 784 enemy aircraft, 23 torpedo boats and the Italian fleet.

Early on the morning of August 11 the convoy was spotted by an enemy submarine about 80 km (50 miles) south of the island of Ibiza. Soon *Eagle* was under attack by the German submarine *U-73*. Four torpedoes struck home and within ten minutes the carrier went down with about 200 of its crew. *U-73* picked up some survivors.

For the next two days the convoy was attacked relentlessly. *Indomitable* was hit on its flight deck, leaving *Victorious* the only carrier operational. *Manchester* was crippled by Italian torpedo boats and then scuttled; nine merchantmen were sunk; and the oil tanker *Ohio* was repeatedly hit and set on fire. Frenziedly, its crew fought the blaze and finally managed to get it under control. Even so, the tanker was dangerously close to sinking and to keep it afloat it was lashed, decks awash, between two escorting destroyers, *Penn* and *Ledbury*. Then the minesweeper *Rye* took it in tow.

Ohio's survival and onward progress became a symbol of the convoy's doggedness and refusal to give in. By August 13, the escort ships were down to their last rounds of ammunition. They had succeeded in shooting down 66 enemy planes and sinking two U-boats. Later that day, against all the odds, three of the surviving cargo ships reached Malta and a fourth, *Brisbane Star*, limped in next morning. They brought some 32 000 tonnes of general supplies. And the gallant *Ohio* was finally towed into Valletta's Grand Harbour – to cheering crowds – on the afternoon of August 15 bearing its invaluable cargo of 11 500 tonnes of kerosene, petrol and aviation fuel.

There was now enough food and fuel to continue the struggle, and air attacks gradually grew less fierce as enemy planes were diverted to help Rommel in North Africa. However, the blitz on Malta resumed on October 11, in Axis efforts to protect supplies being shipped to the Afrika Korps before the main battle of El Alamein. In eight days of savage fighting, the RAF on Malta shot down 42 enemy planes for the loss of 27. But this was enough for the Germans. On October 18 Kesselring called off all daylight raids.

By mid-November there was only about two weeks' food left on the island. Another – perhaps final – convoy was called for, so four merchantmen escorted by cruisers and destroyers set out from Egypt on November 17. This time none of the freighters was lost and three days later they sailed triumphantly into Grand Harbour. Malta's ordeal was over. But 1540 civilians had been killed and 1846 severely injured, while the RAF lost 547 planes in the air and 160 on the ground.

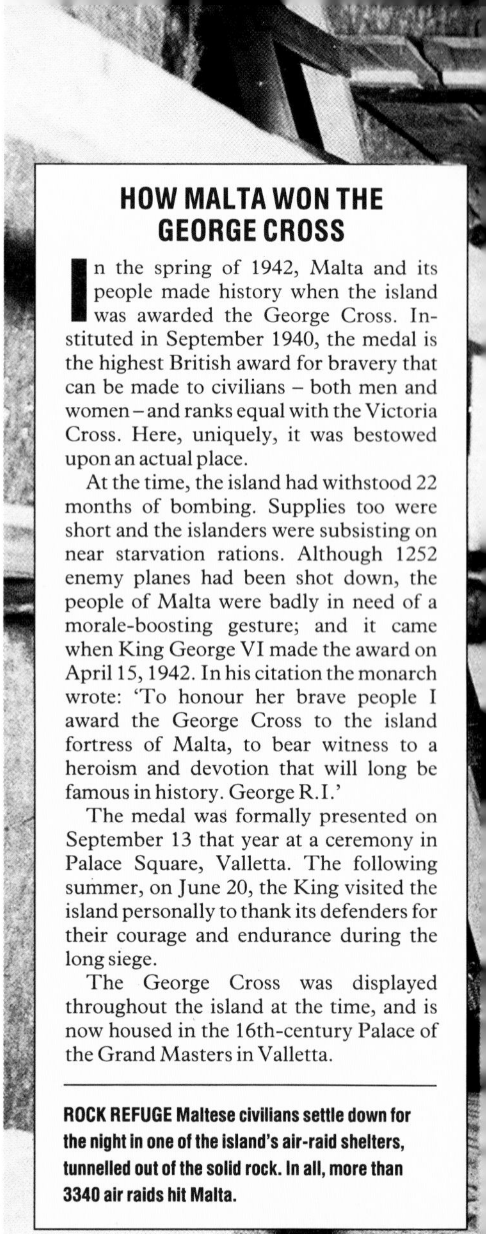

HOW MALTA WON THE GEORGE CROSS

In the spring of 1942, Malta and its people made history when the island was awarded the George Cross. Instituted in September 1940, the medal is the highest British award for bravery that can be made to civilians – both men and women – and ranks equal with the Victoria Cross. Here, uniquely, it was bestowed upon an actual place.

At the time, the island had withstood 22 months of bombing. Supplies too were short and the islanders were subsisting on near starvation rations. Although 1252 enemy planes had been shot down, the people of Malta were badly in need of a morale-boosting gesture; and it came when King George VI made the award on April 15, 1942. In his citation the monarch wrote: 'To honour her brave people I award the George Cross to the island fortress of Malta, to bear witness to a heroism and devotion that will long be famous in history. George R.I.'

The medal was formally presented on September 13 that year at a ceremony in Palace Square, Valletta. The following summer, on June 20, the King visited the island personally to thank its defenders for their courage and endurance during the long siege.

The George Cross was displayed throughout the island at the time, and is now housed in the 16th-century Palace of the Grand Masters in Valletta.

ROCK REFUGE Maltese civilians settle down for the night in one of the island's air-raid shelters, tunnelled out of the solid rock. In all, more than 3340 air raids hit Malta.

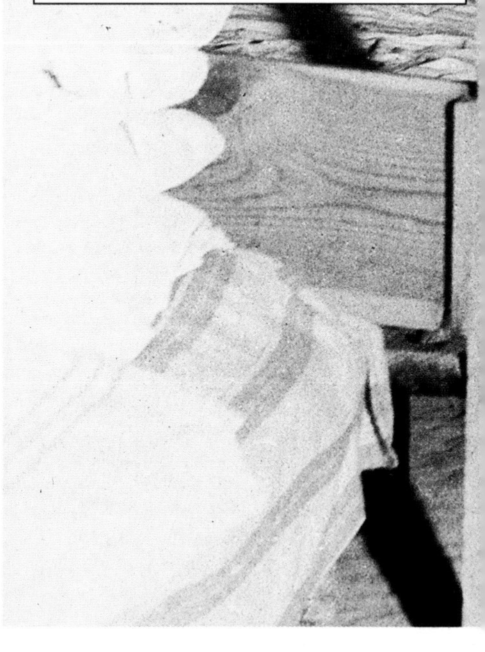

FOR GALLANTRY The courage of the rock-firm islanders was rewarded with this George Cross in April 1942. The medal shows St George killing the dragon.

CHEERED HOME Troops welcome the c
Melbourne Star in Valletta's Grand Har
Operation 'Pedestal'.

Rommel rebounds to take Fortress Tobruk

The capture of Tobruk after the bruising battles of the Gazala Line made Rommel Germany's new folk hero – and cost Britain's youngest general his command.

A LULL in the fighting in the Libyan Desert marked the first five months of 1942, as General Erwin Rommel built up the strength of the German and Italian forces under his command and prepared for a final, all-out assault on the fortress port of Tobruk. He welcomed the breather as he was desperately short of supplies – especially fuel and ammunition – owing to attacks on his supply ships by the Royal Navy and Malta-based RAF bombers.

The British Eighth Army held the Gazala Line, running south from the coastal village of Gazala. Consisting of extensive minefields and barbed wire, the line relied on some half-dozen strongholds, or 'boxes', each about 3 km (2 miles) square. The most important of them was the fortress village of Bir Hacheim, garrisoned by the Free French Brigade. Tobruk itself was now held by the 2nd South African Division, part of Lt General William ('Strafer') Gott's XIII Corps, which was also responsible for the northern sector of the Gazala Line. Lt General Willoughby Norrie's XXX Corps held the southern sector.

The British had superior firepower to the Germans. Lt General Neil Ritchie, commander of Eighth Army, had 850 tanks against Rommel's 560 – of which only 332 were panzers. Most of Ritchie's tanks were Matildas, Valentines and Stuarts, but he had taken delivery of 167 of the new high-sided American Grant tanks armed with 75 mm (2.95 in) guns. These were capable at last of taking on the panzers.

Rommel's coming offensive was part of an elaborate plan mapped out at conferences with Hitler and Mussolini in April and May 1942. The intention was to capture Tobruk and push the British back to the Egyptian frontier before launching a major attack on Malta in June. On January 21, Rommel had already launched a counteroffensive from El Agheila, to which the British had driven him back during 'Crusader'. By May his advanced formations were near Tmimi. From here he planned a frontal infantry assault to keep the British busy while the Afrika Korps' panzers delivered the main attack as a sweep around the Gazala Line's southern end.

BRITAIN'S YOUNGEST GENERAL

Great things were expected of Neil Ritchie (1897-1984) when, in November 1941, he was given command of the Eighth Army. He had served with the Black Watch in World War I, and at the beginning of World War II was chief of staff to Lt General Sir Alan Brooke in France and Belgium. He was noted for the levelheadedness he displayed during the Dunkirk evacuation. Early in 1941 he went to the Middle East, at first as deputy chief of staff to General Sir Claude Auchinleck, before being made Britain's youngest army commander.

But Ritchie's lack of command experience let him down, and he was sacked after the fall of Tobruk. However, he led with distinction the British XII Corps in north-west Europe after D-Day.

IN THE FIELD Generals Ritchie and Auchinleck (left) study a map at advanced headquarters during the British offensive in Libya in 1941.

INTO THE CAULDRON

At 3.30 pm on May 26, General Ludwig Crüwell, with a few tanks and light infantry, and supported by Stuka dive-bombers, led the Italian X and XXI Corps forward in a sandstorm to attack the northern sector of the Gazala Line. It was a feint. Rommel led the 15th and 21st Panzer and 90th Light Divisions, plus the Italian Ariete and Trieste Divisions, in a swing around Bir Hacheim. The Trieste failed to take Bir Hacheim, but Rommel pressed on with the main attack, smashing two boxes held by Indian troops.

The British 4th Armoured Brigade moved to cover the Indians' withdrawal and clashed with the panzers in a bruising encounter. The battle now developed into an untidy and confused affair, and on May 28, Rommel realised that the momentum of the attack had been lost, at least for the time being, so he decided to go over to the defensive. He concentrated his mobile forces into a defensive crescent – some 25 km (15 miles) long and 5 km (3 miles) wide – which would soon be known by the British as 'the Cauldron', from its relentless heat and the fierce fighting there.

Though surrounded by the enemy and with his back against the British minefields, Rommel still remained confident that his massed artillery would destroy any British armour before it could get at his panzers. But there were two problems which could not wait. First, his forces in the Cauldron were running low on fuel and ammunition. However, Rommel managed to take in supplies, personally leading a convoy from the south. Later, German sappers cleared a path through the minefield. The second problem was the discovery that 150th Brigade Group box was right in the middle of the Cauldron.

On May 30, leaving his artillery on the perimeter to keep the British tanks at bay, Rommel turned the full weight of his armour on this box. The British held off six assaults, though their losses were heavy and ammunition nearly exhausted. On June 1 the German tanks swept forward behind a relentless Stuka bombardment, and the gallant force was overwhelmed.

ATTACK ON BIR HACHEIM

Rommel next turned his attention to the French at Bir Hacheim. On June 3 the Trieste and 90th Light Divisions began their assault. The fort was defended by some 3600 men, including members of the French Foreign Legion, under General Pierre Koenig. They were determined men.

Despite suffering heavy casualties, German sappers worked under cover of artillery fire and smoke screens clearing lanes through the minefields. For a week the Luftwaffe directed almost nonstop raids on Bir Hacheim, making some 1300 sorties in all. Attempts by Ritchie's armoured brigades to hack their way into the Cauldron to relieve the pressure on the French all failed. On the morning of June 8, Rommel's 90th Light Division made yet another drive to capture the fort, and its spearheads got within a few hundred metres of their objective. But once more dogged French resistance halted the advance.

Later that night the German sappers again cleared lanes through the mines – and in the morning, after an air and artillery bombardment, the infantry stormed the French defences head-on. Yet again the attack was beaten back. 'This was a remarkable achievement on the part of the French defenders,' Rommel recorded, 'who were now completely cut off from the outside world. To tire them out, flares were fired and the defences covered with machine-gun fire throughout the following night. Yet when my storming parties went in the next morning, the French opened fire again with undiminished violence. The enemy troops hung on grimly in their trenches and remained completely invisible.'

Three times Rommel called on Koenig – a veteran of the French colonial wars – to surrender. And three times Koenig contemptuously rejected the offers. So, on June 10, the Afrika Korps attacked Bir Hacheim under cover of heavy air and artillery bombardment, and succeeded in penetrating the main northern defences. The French furiously defended every foxhole and nest. Sensing victory, Rommel sent in the 15th Panzer Division with orders to 'finish off' Bir Hacheim the following day.

But Koenig still had a trick left up his sleeve. The German ring around the fort had not been completely sealed; there was a gap in the western section. Under cover of darkness, Koenig and some 2700 of his men broke through and disappeared into the desert – where they were picked up by a fleet of British trucks. When Rommel's forces finally swarmed into Bir Hacheim early on June 11, they found only about 300 French soldiers there, many of them wounded. Some 600 of their comrades had died.

In the meantime, the battle of the Cauldron had swung against the British. Rommel's artillery had inflicted crippling losses on the attacking forces and they were in no state to withstand a series of counterattacks. On the afternoon of June 5, Rommel unleashed his panzers. They attacked east out of the Cauldron, causing 6000 Eighth Army casualties and destroying 150 tanks.

The initiative clearly lay with Rommel, who had carefully husbanded his own tanks. The German commander concentrated his efforts first on destroying the remaining armour of XXX Corps. In a series of actions between June 10 and 13, he repeated the tactic of drawing British tanks on to his gun line and then sending in his own panzers to complete the destruction. In this way he broke out of the Cauldron. Those British infantry units that stood in his way were systematically bombarded and forced to withdraw. The 201st (Guards) Motor Brigade put up a stout defence of 'Knightsbridge' box, but they too were forced to retreat.

By June 13, Ritchie was facing up to the prospect of defeat. The Commander in Chief Middle East, General Sir Claude Auchinleck, unaware of the true condition of Eighth Army, ordered Ritchie to fight all the way and hold Rommel west of Tobruk. Ritchie's inclination was to allow Tobruk to be besieged and fall back towards the frontier. As a result there was confusion and delay. The Germans increased the pressure again as a rolling thunder of tank and artillery fire hit the remaining British positions at Gazala, and on June 14 Ritchie had no alternative but to order a retreat.

It was a crushing defeat for the Eighth Army. 'Rommel is out-generalling Ritchie', commented General Sir Alan Brooke, Chief of the Imperial General Staff, in London. For his part, Rommel expressed admiration for his opponents. 'The Guards Brigade evacuated Knightsbridge that day,' he wrote later, 'after it had been subjected all morning to the combined fire of every gun we could bring to bear. This brigade was almost a living embodiment of the virtues and faults of the British soldier – tremendous courage and tenacity combined with a rigid lack of mobility.'

He then once more turned his gaze towards Tobruk, which he planned to attack while his troops were riding high on their recent victories and Allied morale was correspondingly low.

NEGLECT AT TOBRUK

A state of confusion over the defence (or abandonment) of Tobruk reigned in the first half of 1942. As early as February Auchinleck had issued orders stating: 'It is not my intention to continue to hold it once the enemy is in a position to invest it effectively. Should this appear inevitable, the place will be evacuated and the maximum amount of destruction carried out in it.'

As a result, the port's double ring of defences had been badly neglected. The main anti-tank ditch had become choked with sand; many mines had been taken up and used at Gazala; tanks and

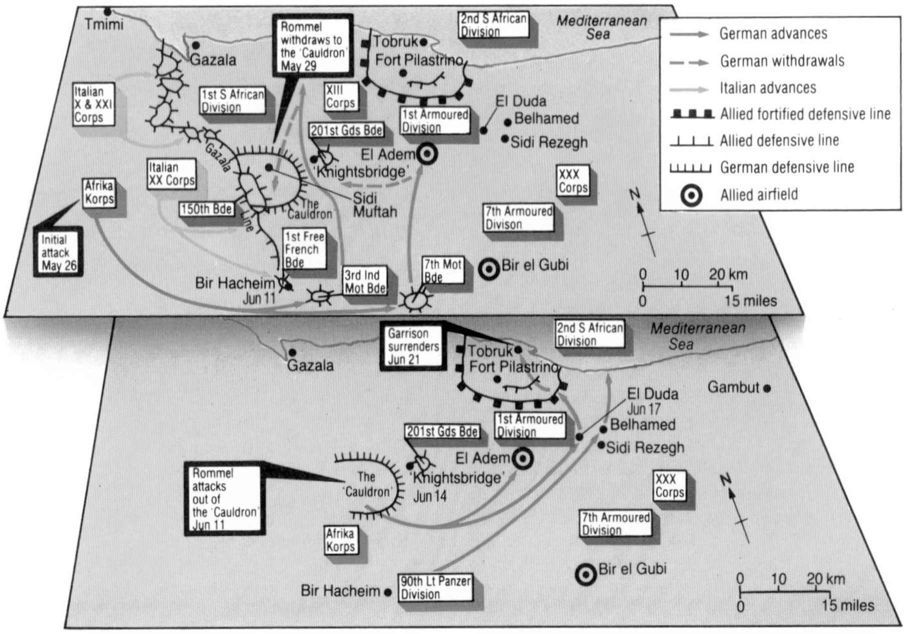

THE FOX'S MOVE 'Desert Fox' Rommel attacked the Gazala Line in late May. Then, after breaking out of the Cauldron, he swept north to attack and capture fortified Tobruk.

COUNTDOWN TO A KNOCKOUT In a narrow concrete bunker, the seconds tick away as German shock troops stand by for a night attack on Tobruk. The infantry were the vanguard of the assault, engaging in bitter hand-to-hand fighting before the tanks rolled in. The attack from the south-east took the defenders by surprise.

Daily Express

"Rommel massed all his six divisions and fell on Tobruk . . ." Alan Moorehead, in Cairo despatch this morning, tells first full story of the last stand

WHY TOBRUK FELL: OUTGUNNED AND OUTNUMBERED 3 TO 1

THEY HAD NO AIR COVER

2 JAP SHIPS HIT

"The need is— Second Front with no delay"

'TOBRUK BRINGS IT NEARER'

CAUSE FOR CONCERN As Rommel's tanks entered Tobruk the newspapers at home told the grim story. Churchill called it a 'shattering and grievous loss', and faced a vote of no confidence in the House of Commons, which he won 475 to 25.

lorries had driven through and enlarged gaps in the rusting coils of barbed wire. The defences were particularly dilapidated in the south-eastern sector, defended by the 2nd Cameron Highlanders plus several Indian units. Even so, Ritchie decided to hold a defensive line running from the western perimeter of Tobruk to the fortified airfield of El Adem.

By the beginning of June the 35 000-strong garrison – over half of them now South Africans – was under the command of Maj General Henry Belsazar Klopper, a former farmer in the Orange Free State. He had little experience of battle conditions, but at the age of only 39 was regarded as a name for the future. Most of his men came from the 2nd South African Division, and altogether they had enough food and ammunition to withstand a siege of up to 90 days.

Amazingly enough (and for reasons which have never been explained) Churchill knew nothing of Auchinleck's indecision over Tobruk: whether to defend it to the last man, or evacuate it and save as many of the defenders' lives as possible. After the fall of Bir Hacheim, the premier later wrote: 'Tobruk glared upon us, and, as in the previous year, we had no doubt that it should be held.' As for the victorious Rommel, he had no doubt about his intentions towards the port. 'To every man of us,' he wrote afterwards, 'Tobruk was a symbol of British resistance, and we were now going to finish it for good.'

On June 15, as the Axis forces closed in on the port, Churchill's concern increased. He wired Auchinleck: 'Presume there is no question in any case of giving up Tobruk.' To which Auchinleck replied: 'Ritchie is putting into Tobruk what he considers an adequate force to hold it.'

ROMMEL'S TRUMP CARD

In the meantime, Klopper – completely out of his depth – panicked and turned to Ritchie for advice. It turned out to be the worst thing he could have done. Ritchie told him to strengthen the south-western defences – where, he was assured by Intelligence, Rommel would direct his main thrust. Accordingly, Klopper moved the 6th South African Infantry Brigade to the area and hastily transferred mines from the already weakened south-eastern sector. Everything was set for Rommel to play his trump card – an attack from the south-east.

On June 17, Rommel's men captured the outlying forts of El Duda and Belhamed, and overran the airfield at nearby El Adem. The Afrika Korps also seized British supply depots between the border town of Bardia and Tobruk. On June 16, Rommel drove to the Via Balbia – the main road between Tobruk and Gazala – to see the aftermath of the fighting.

'Evidence of the British defeat could be seen all along the road and verges,' he recorded. 'Vast quantities of material lay on all sides, burnt-out vehicles stood black and empty in the sand. Whole convoys of undamaged British lorries had fallen into our hands, some of which had been pressed into service immediately by the fighting troops, while others were now awaiting collection by the salvage squads.'

By June 18 the Axis forces had surrounded Tobruk, and German artillerymen – to their amazement – came across ammunition dumps and arms depots abandoned by them during the winter campaign of 1941-2. Two days later – at 5.20 am on June 20 – the Axis assault on Tobruk began with a massed artillery and air attack in the south-east. Under cover of heavy gunfire, several hundred Stukas and Junkers Ju88 bombers blasted the proposed break-in point. The planes operated a shuttle service from the airfield at El Adem, and Rommel launched his main land drive from El Duda. Once the defensive minefields had been well hammered, German and Italian storm parties drove a wedge into the fort's defences.

By 8 am the German sappers had bridged the fort's anti-tank ditch. Waves of tanks of the 21st Panzer Division then drove over the positions held by the 2nd/5th Mahrattas. The Indians' centre company was virtually wiped out in a futile last stand, but even so the survivors and the Cameron Highlanders fought back savagely, before being the last to surrender.

SITUATION 'SHAMBLES'

There was little more organised resistance. The panzers fanned out and drove on towards the harbour, while the 90th Light Division mopped up in the rear, and assault parachutists sprayed the streets with submachine-gun bullets.

Meanwhile, at his headquarters in underground caves at Fort Pilastrino, Klopper and his staff were in a state of confusion and despair. They could not decide whether to fight on or try to break out, and some of them were for immediate surrender. 'Only by surrendering can you preserve the cream of South Africa's manhood!' cried one of the officers.

Still Klopper could not make up his mind. He got in touch with Ritchie by radiotelephone and told him that the situation was a 'shambles'. Further resistance would only result in fearful casualties. What was he to do? Ritchie was no great help. 'Every day and hour of resistance materially assists our cause,' he told Klopper. 'I cannot tell the tactical situation and must therefore leave you to act on your own judgment regarding capitulation.'

So Klopper called his staff officers together for the last time. 'I'm sorry, boys,' he told them, 'but we will have to pack up. It would be foolish to carry on. I propose to surrender, in order to save useless bloodshed.' He set about burning code books and destroying wireless sets. He ordered harbour installations to be destroyed – and the whole port shuddered as lighters, field guns and ammunition dumps were blown up. Vast amounts of fuel and stores were burnt and Tobruk was covered by a pall of thick, black smoke.

As Klopper evacuated his headquarters, the Axis troops pouring into Tobruk bypassed Fort Pilastrino in their eagerness to reach the town proper. Then at 5 am the following day – a Sunday – Rommel himself drove triumphantly into the port in his open staff car. Goggles pushed up and scarf flapping at his neck, he was the epitome of the victorious military commander. 'Practically every building of the dismal place was either flat or little more than a heap of rubble,' he wrote later, 'mostly the result of our siege in 1941.'

A few hours later, on the Via Balbia – lined with blazing vehicles and Allied prisoners of war – he encountered Klopper, who formally announced the surrender of Tobruk, and soon a white flag was hoisted over Fort Pilastrino. The moment they saw it the men of the 6th South African Infantry Brigade – who had spent the night digging in and reinforcing their positions in the unattacked western sector – gave a great moan of anguish and despair. They felt betrayed by their commanders, who had sent them no orders whatsoever. Rommel told a band of captured Allied officers later: 'Gentlemen, you have fought like lions and been led by donkeys!'

NATIONAL PRIDE

The defenders' grief was echoed by Churchill, in Washington conferring with Roosevelt. The premier called the loss of Tobruk 'one of the heaviest blows I can recall during the war'. Roosevelt's immediate response was to dispatch 300 powerful Sherman tanks to North Africa.

The fall of Tobruk yielded Rommel a rich haul of food, armour and supplies – including 5000 tonnes of provisions, over 2.25 million litres (500 000 gallons) of petrol and more than 2000 serviceable vehicles. More importantly, he had gained a vital port and opened the way to Egypt.

And he had achieved all this at relatively little cost. Since May 26, the Germans had suffered 3360 casualties or about 15 per cent of the Afrika Korps' fighting strength, and the Italians probably suffered even less. More disturbing for Rommel was the 300 officer casualties; nevertheless, it was the high point of his career. Hitler immediately promoted him field marshal – at 50 the youngest in the Wehrmacht – and the German newspapers hailed him as 'invincible'. North Africa, they declared, was his for the taking.

It seemed so, as Rommel resumed his push towards Egypt. Ritchie was trying to regroup the remains of his shattered, retreating Eighth Army with the idea of stopping Rommel at Mersa Matruh, about 350 km (220 miles) east of Tobruk. Auchinleck now stepped in to stop the rot, sacking Ritchie and moving into the desert to take personal command of the Eighth on June 25. He decided that Mersa Matruh could not be defended – and as Rommel duly took the town there was panic in Cairo, where the British Embassy and Middle East High Command burned their archives ready for evacuation.

At Alexandria, Allied warships put out to sea, for the place Auchinleck had chosen to make his stand to save Egypt was only about 100 km (60 miles) to the west – a settlement, little more than a halt on the coastal railway, called El Alamein.

PROPAGANDA COUP

The capture of Tobruk was acclaimed by the German propaganda machine as a personal triumph for Rommel. Speaking from the battlefield, Captain Alfred Berndt, a Propaganda Ministry official, told radio listeners back home: 'Field Marshal Rommel's tactics, of attacking from the east one day, turning up from the west the next, and other surprise movements, outwitted the enemy. His success in Libya was due to two things: he personally made the reconnaissances and directed all the battles, and he showed the greatest swiftness in changing his decision . . . as new possibilities of success arose.

'During the battle for Tobruk he changed his decisions no fewer than ten or twelve times, thus driving his staff officers to the verge of madness. Yet events proved this was the only way to meet the strategy of the enemy. Before the . . . campaign opened, the field marshal spent many days in his reconnaissance car. For two days he explored the Bir Hacheim area, and thus knew all the details like his own pocket.'

The battle that saved Cairo

After racing across the desert, Rommel's Afrika Korps was only a few days' advance away from Cairo. Then came the first battle at El Alamein.

ON JUNE 29, 1942, Mussolini mounted a white charger and rode it through the streets of Derna, Libya. It was a dress rehearsal for what Field Marshal Erwin Rommel had promised him would be his triumphal entry into Cairo. But, as with so many of *Il Duce*'s dreams, the reality turned out to be rather different. His plans and Rommel's came to grief some 240 km (150 miles) short of Cairo, near a rocky rise on the coast called El Alamein. About 65 km (40 miles) to the south of Alamein lies the desolate and trackless waste of soft sand known as the Qattara Depression, and it was between these two points that the British Eighth Army made its last-ditch stand against the Afrika Korps.

Despite Rommel's confidence, the odds were now in favour of the British, for although weakened and under strength they held the best defensive position along the entire North African coast: the sea on one side and the Qattara Depression on the other meant it was exceedingly difficult to outflank. Only a frontal attack could break through their line.

Most of the troops under General Sir Claude Auchinleck, Commander in Chief Middle East and now also field commander of the Eighth Army, were stationed in a number of strongly fortified positions, called 'boxes' because of their all-round defence. The largest, the Alamein box, lay on the coast and was garrisoned by the 3rd South African Infantry Brigade. The Deis el Shein box, defended by the 18th Indian Infantry Brigade, was at the western end of the Ruweisat Ridge. Farther inland was the 6th New Zealand Brigade in the box at Bab el Qattara. Two other New Zealand brigades acted as a 'backstop'. On the verge of the Qattara Depression was the 9th Indian Infantry Brigade at Naqb Abu Dweis.

There was no 'Alamein Line' as such but rather a series of static positions astride the most obvious lines of advance and between which mobile columns of lorried infantry, armoured cars and artillery patrolled. 'The Auk' positioned the 1st Armoured south of Ruweisat. The 7th was sent farther south, beyond Deir el Munassib. Between them they had about 155 tanks. He guessed that Rommel would bypass the El Alamein box rather than waste time on a direct assault. To counter such a move, he positioned two more South African brigades between the Alamein perimeter and the Ruweisat Ridge.

Early on July 1, Rommel opened his offensive, sending the 90th Light Division of only 2000 men to bypass the Alamein box. But they went too far north, stumbled into a minefield and came under heavy artillery fire from the Alamein defences. The more lightly defended Deir el Shein box was overcome by the 15th and 21st Panzer Divisions.

Rommel then sent the Italian Ariete Division to occupy ground east of the Bab el Qattara box. But New Zealand infantry routed them with a bayonet charge, and they were also hit by tanks. On July 4 the Afrika Korps made one final effort. On the south ridge of Deir el Shein the panzers encountered the 1st Armoured Division, and were driven back. Both sides suffered losses, and the British also withdrew.

'AUK' ON THE OFFENSIVE

Rommel's advance had been blunted; now it was the British turn to attack. On July 10 a devastating artillery bombardment softened up the Italian Sabratha Division, positioned along the coast, for an assault by Australian infantry. With bayonets fixed they charged the Italians, who broke and ran. The next day a similar fate befell the Trieste Division at Tel el Eisa. Rommel had to move part of his 164th Infantry Division to fill the gap.

On July 14, Auchinleck went on the attack along the Ruweisat Ridge. By then he had nearly 400 tanks in fighting order against Rommel's 30. The Allied attack was intended to be a night-time set-piece battle, with brigades of New Zealand infantry detailed to punch holes in the enemy lines – and so let in the tanks. The infantry brigades secured their objectives along the ridge but the tanks of the 22nd Armoured Brigade waited until daylight before moving forward. The Germans counterattacked furiously and 4th New Zealand Brigade, badly exposed and isolated, was overrun.

Both sides were suffering from exhaustion, lack of adequate food and a general slump in morale. Auchinleck had been deliberately aiming to destroy Rommel's weakest links – the Italian divisions – and they could no longer be counted on. Reinforcements were still awaited. In addition, the Afrika Korps had used up all its artillery ammunition. Informed by his codebreakers, Auchinleck decided to launch a final night attack.

It began on July 21 with a thrust to break through Rommel's defences near the coast. After a good start, things began to go wrong. Once again the armoured brigades failed to give adequate support to the already tired infantry. And some armour ran into ambushes. In one such incident near Deir el Shein, 87 Valentine tanks were destroyed or badly damaged.

The infantry lost all trust and confidence in their armour. Rommel's mine belts and cleverly sited anti-tank guns had turned the scales and the Eighth Army, having suffered 13 000 casualties since July 1, was exhausted. By the end of July the fighting had petered out on both sides.

Hitler still had faith in Rommel and his ability to conquer Egypt, and the Desert Fox received badly needed reinforcements and supplies. But Auchinleck's understandable refusal to fight on was seen by Churchill as a grave sign of weakness. It was time, the Prime Minister decided, for an Eighth Army leader with the killer touch – one who could bring an all-out victory.

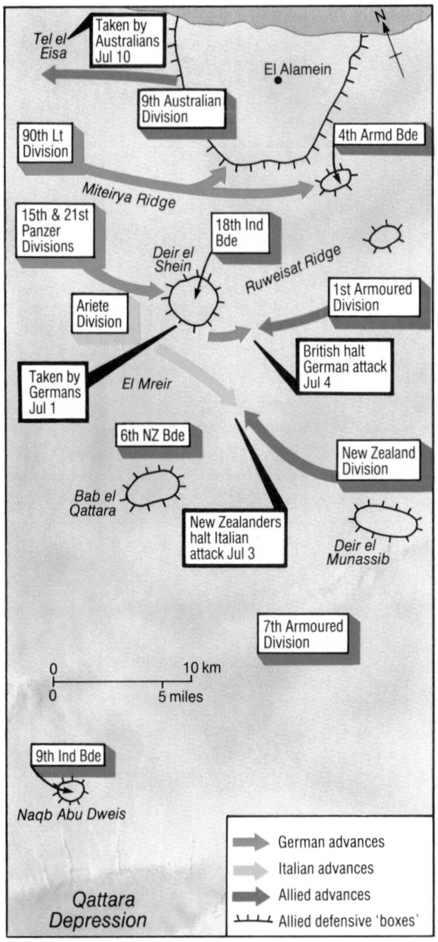

SANDS OF GLORY Under a scorching desert sun, the Allies halted Rommel's drive for the Nile. Key clashes around the Alamein box and Ruweisat Ridge pre-echoed the huge second Battle of Alamein four months later.

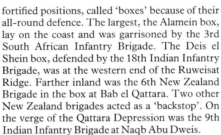

THE MAN THEY CALLED 'THE AUK'

A tall, imposing figure with a jutting jaw, sandy hair and piercing blue eyes, Claude Auchinleck (1884-1981) was affectionately known to all his troops in the Middle East as 'the Auk'.

He was born in India and learned his trade in the Indian Army, which he joined in 1904. In World War I he fought against the Turks in the Middle East, and between the wars was one of the Indian Army's youngest commanders. In World War II, he masterminded the withdrawal of the British forces from northern Norway in June 1940, then organised southern England's defence forces. He then returned to India as Commander in Chief of the Army; and in June 1941 he took over as Commander in Chief Middle East from General Sir Archibald Wavell.

After the fall of Tobruk, he took direct field command of the Eighth Army and halted Rommel's advance at El Alamein. But he was sacked by Churchill, and returned to India in June 1943 as Commander in Chief, a job he held until India gained independence in 1947.

8: HITLER STRIKES EAST

The greatest attack in history was a brilliant success, but contained the seeds of its own failure.

'Barbarossa': the day the world held its breath

When Hitler unleashed his forces against the Red Army, the German juggernaut rolled over and through the Russian defences. Its success owed as much to Russian unreadiness as to German strategic brilliance and military might.

GERMAN TANKS and other vehicles, their headlights masked into narrow beams, eased into the central Polish forest of Pratulin. There the men camped, a few kilometres short of the Bug river – since September 1939 the German frontier with the Soviet Union in this central sector of occupied Poland. Across the river stood the huge old fortress of Brest-Litovsk (today the Soviet city of Brest).

The men had strict orders to remain silent and hidden, that night of June 19/20, 1941, and all the following two days. At 10 pm on the 21st, they were ordered on parade, to learn that their small unit – the 3rd Battalion, 39th Panzer Regiment, itself part of the 17th Panzer Division – was just one tiny cog in the greatest military machine ever assembled. To north and south, more than 3 million men, 600 000 vehicles, and 3350 tanks were massed along a 2000 km (1250 mile) frontier from the Baltic to the Black Sea. Hidden in forests, pastures and cornfields, isolated by enforced radio silence and sleepless with tension, they waited for the moment to attack.

BUILD-UP TO 'BARBAROSSA'

For Hitler, the impending assault was to be the culmination of a long-standing obsession. He wanted Russia's industries and agricultural lands as *Lebensraum* ('living space') for Germany. He would exterminate and enslave the 'degenerate' Slavs. He would obliterate their 'Jewish Bolshevist' government before it could turn on him. His 1939 pact with Stalin and the subsequent division of eastern Europe were meant only to win time to prepare for war.

As soon as Germany had conquered France, Hitler looked east. Insisting that Britain was as good as defeated, he determined to finish off the Soviet Union as soon as possible, before it could build up its armed forces. Right now was the time. 'We have only to kick in the front door,' he told his staff, 'and the whole rotten edifice will come tumbling down.' His generals warned him of the danger of fighting a war on two fronts and of the difficulty of invading such a vast country as the Soviet Union – but he simply overruled them. He made agreements with both Finland and Romania to place German troops there, and set about creating an Eastern Front. In December 1940 Hitler made his final choice of battle plan.

He gave the huge operation a suitably portentous name: 'Barbarossa' ('Redbeard'), the nickname of the crusading 12th-century Holy Roman Emperor, Frederick I. The campaign would open in May 1941 and proceed in great thrusts by three army groups: Army Group North would secure the Baltic; Army Group South would seize the agricultural, coal-rich, oil-rich lands of the Ukraine and Caucasus; and Army Group Centre would drive for Moscow. All the Soviet Union west of a line from Archangel to Astrakhan would be drawn into the Reich.

GRIM REAPER A Panzer III anti-tank tank gives support to infantry as the Germans advance across cornfields into Russia. These 19 tonne tanks with 50 mm (2 in) guns were more than a match for the lightly armoured Russian BT-7s.

In the event, military developments in the Balkans delayed 'Barbarossa' by five weeks. The delay was to prove fatal to Hitler's hopes, although at the time it did not seem important. The Red Army would still be conquered long before winter, he thought. By mid-June, the build-up was complete: 148 divisions, 80 per cent of the German Army, stood ready, aided by 14 Romanian divisions, 22 Finnish, three Italian and one Slovakian. No wonder that Hitler boasted: 'When Operation Barbarossa is launched, the world will hold its breath.'

THE SLEEPING GIANT

As Hitler's orders were read to his concealed men, Russian commanders were totally unprepared – despite many signs and warnings – for the impending attack. Official Soviet policy insisted that such a thing was an impossibility. In reality, though, Stalin was less optimistic. He was sure that war with Germany was inevitable sometime, and in spring 1941 had admitted privately that 'a German attack in the near future is not to be ruled out'. But his armies were in no state to withstand an assault: 35 000 of its senior officers had been purged in 1937-8 to ensure the unquestioning loyalty of the remainder; all but 1500 of its 24 000 tanks were obsolete, and only 27 per cent of them were in full working order; the 170 divisions in the west were spread thinly to cover newly occupied areas of eastern Europe.

Stalin planned a steady build-up of strength over the next year, but for the time being was determined not to provoke Hitler to attack. The terms of his pact with Germany were to be followed meticulously. Between February 1940 and June 1941, the Russians sent Germany 1.5 million tonnes of grain and 2 million tonnes of oil products in exchange for German goods. The trains carrying the supplies continued to run until the very last moment – the last crossed the border in the early hours of June 22. Russian reconnaissance planes were not to provoke the Germans by being too intrusive. As a result, dozens of warnings went unheeded.

Richard Sorge, a brilliant and reliable Russian spy in Tokyo, warned the Kremlin of the coming invasion in May. German officials in the Soviet Union packed their possessions and sent their families home. As the day of 'Barbarossa' approached, warnings became more insistent. On June 18, a member of the 'Lucy' spy-ring in Switzerland sent complete plans for the invasion. The same day, a German soldier defected to the Russians in the western Ukraine, insisting that the invasion was set for four days' time, at dawn on Sunday, June 22. The local commander passed the information to Moscow, but Stalin dismissed it as 'provocation'.

STORM UNLEASHED

On the night of June 21/22, on the border between German and Soviet-held territory, there was silence as German soldiers wrapped rifles, gas masks and bayonets in blankets to deaden sound. The only noise – remembered by all Germans along the banks of the Bug that night – was the croaking of frogs. As the hands of synchronised watches reached 3.15 am it was as if a switch had been thrown. The silent, shadowy western horizon exploded into the thunder and lightning of countless artillery barrages from over 7000 guns. Tracers stitched lines across trees, fields and rivers. Mortar bombs screamed down.

Along the 800 km (500 mile) length of the Bug, assault parties dashed across bridges, overwhelming surprised Russians before they could detonate demolition charges. Others in rubber dinghies built pontoon bridges. At Pratulin, the 17th Panzer Division had no bridge, but they did have an extraordinary secret weapon: an underwater tank. Developed for the invasion of Britain, these machines, with all joints sealed and 3 m (10 ft) 'snorkel' breathing pipes, could drive straight across the riverbed. Eighty of them came streaming out of the Bug without meeting opposition.

The Luftwaffe had already been busy. Small groups of Heinkel He111 bombers dropped mines in the Black Sea and Baltic at 2 am. Then, three to a target, they bombed Soviet airfields with fragmentation bombs to cause maximum confusion at the precise moment of the ground attack. As the Germans advanced, the Luftwaffe bombed and strafed ahead of them, smashing roads, blasting tank parks, blowing up fuel stores, machine-gunning Russian planes before they could get into the air. By midday, the Russians had lost 1200 aircraft, most of them on the ground; the Germans just ten.

By the afternoon, German armoured formations – motorcycles, tanks, armoured cars, half-track infantry carriers – were driving forward on undamaged roads 32 km (20 miles) into the countryside. Behind the lead German units came the tanks – Mark III and IV panzers – and behind them again trucks full of infantry. One unit – LVI Corps in the north – advanced 80 km (50 miles) before dusk. A German lieutenant commented: 'The Russian defences might have been a row of glass-houses.'

DON'T FIRE ON THE GERMANS!

The Russian defences – stretched in a thin line with no depth and few reserves – broke in confusion. Far from being ordered to counter-attack, commanders found that their standing orders not to provoke the Germans were confirmed. When General Dmitri Pavlov in Minsk reported to Moscow the bombing of every major city in his area – Bialystok, Grodno, Lida, Brest-Litovsk – Marshal Semyon Timoshenko, Commissar of Defence and one of Stalin's oldest aides, telephoned Pavlov's subordinate, Lt General Ivan Boldin: 'Comrade Boldin, remember that no action is to be taken against the Germans without our knowledge. Will you please tell Pavlov that Comrade Stalin has forbidden the opening of artillery fire against the Germans.'

'But how is this possible?' Boldin yelled. 'Our troops are in full retreat. Whole towns are in flames. People are being killed all over the place.' Timoshenko interrupted to remind him of the rules about limited aerial reconnaissance. When Boldin insisted on using artillery, infantry and anti-aircraft guns, Timoshenko would only repeat: 'No – only reconnaissance of no more than 60 km [35 miles] over German territory.'

It was a ludicrous response. Most Soviet planes had already been destroyed on the ground by the Luftwaffe, and the Germans were far into Soviet-held territory. Later, towards evening, at the headquarters of the Russian Tenth Army outside Bialystok, its commander, Maj General K.D. Golubev, drew shakily on a cigarette and muttered to Boldin: 'The frontier guards are fighting well, but few of them are left and we have no means of supporting them. So the Nazis advance, insolently, marching upright, behaving like conquerors. And that's on the very first day of the war! What'll happen after that?'

HESS'S STRANGE PEACE BID

If Stalin needed proof that leaks of plans for 'Barbarossa' were attempts to force a confrontation between Germany and the USSR, he found it in a sensational incident in May 1941, when Hitler's deputy Rudolf Hess crash-landed in Scotland on a bizarre solo peace mission.

Hess (1894-1987) was one of the Führer's oldest comrades, who helped Hitler write *Mein Kampf* while the two men were held in prison after the Munich Putsch. He was named Deputy Führer in 1933 and third (to Göring) in the Nazi hierarchy in 1939. Knowing that Hitler saw the Soviet Union rather than Britain as Germany's real enemy, Hess dreamed up a scheme in 1941 to make peace with Britain – and thereby boost his now waning prestige.

On Saturday, May 10, he piloted a twin-engine Messerschmitt Me110 with long-range fuel tanks to Scotland. South of Glasgow, after an astonishing 1450 km (900 mile) flight, he bailed out, allowing his plane to crash in a field. A Scottish farmer turned him over to the Home Guard. Giving his name as 'Alfred Horn', Hess insisted on seeing the Duke of Hamilton, whom he claimed to have met at the 1936 Olympic Games in Berlin. He revealed his true identity to the Duke, who passed on his message to Churchill: Germany was on its way to winning; if Britain made peace now, it could keep its empire. Hitler knew nothing of his mission, but he – Hess – knew exactly what Hitler wanted.

Churchill refused to see Hess and never took the offer seriously. In Germany, Hess was declared to be a 'deranged idealist'; Hitler ordered him to be shot if he ever returned. But Stalin saw it all as part of an anti-Soviet plot. Hess was held as a prisoner of war, then tried for war crimes at Nuremberg after the war. He spent the rest of his life in Spandau Prison, Berlin.

DAILY NEWS
FINAL
HESS QUITS HITLER, FLIES TO SCOTLAND
No. 3 Nazi Lands by Chute
Pals—to The End

PAGE ONE NEWS Rudolf Hess makes headlines in a New York newspaper. The USA was still neutral.

He might well have asked. The only response from the Soviet General Staff was as ludicrous as Timoshenko's to Boldin: '1: Troops . . . will attack the enemy and destroy him . . . where he has violated the Soviet frontier. [Without] special authorisation, ground troops will not cross the frontier line. 2: Reconnaissance and attack aircraft will locate the concentration areas of enemy aircraft and . . . ground forces. Bomber and ground-attack aircraft will destroy . . . the aircraft on enemy aerodromes and will bomb the main . . . ground forces. Aviation strikes will be mounted to a depth of 100-150 km [60-90 miles] in German territory. Königsberg and Memel will be bombed. No flights over Finland and Romania . . . without special authorisation.'

By the end of the day, there was little left with which to strike: 1489 Russian aircraft had been destroyed on the ground. Planes took off into almost certain death: 322 were shot down. Troops on the ground had no information from reconnaissance aircraft. By nightfall, three infantry divisions had simply vanished.

Everywhere, German troops had resounding successes. In the north, General Erich von Manstein, commanding LVI Panzer Corps, punched a hole 160 km (100 miles) wide towards Leningrad. In the centre, the Germans destroyed half of the Russian tanks, and the bulk of three Soviet armies – Third, Fourth and Tenth – were about to be surrounded. Only in the south was Russian resistance effective – not that the Germans were slowed for long.

One thing puzzled the Germans: the astonishing bravery of the Russian soldiers. They simply refused to surrender. A captain of the 18th Panzer Division wrote: 'There was no feeling, as there had been in France, of entry into a defeated nation. Instead, there was resistance, always resistance, however hopeless.' A few Germans were beginning to sense that, while Bolshevism might be a rotten edifice, Russian nationalism certainly was not. The door had been burst open, but the building would not collapse as easily as Hitler had predicted.

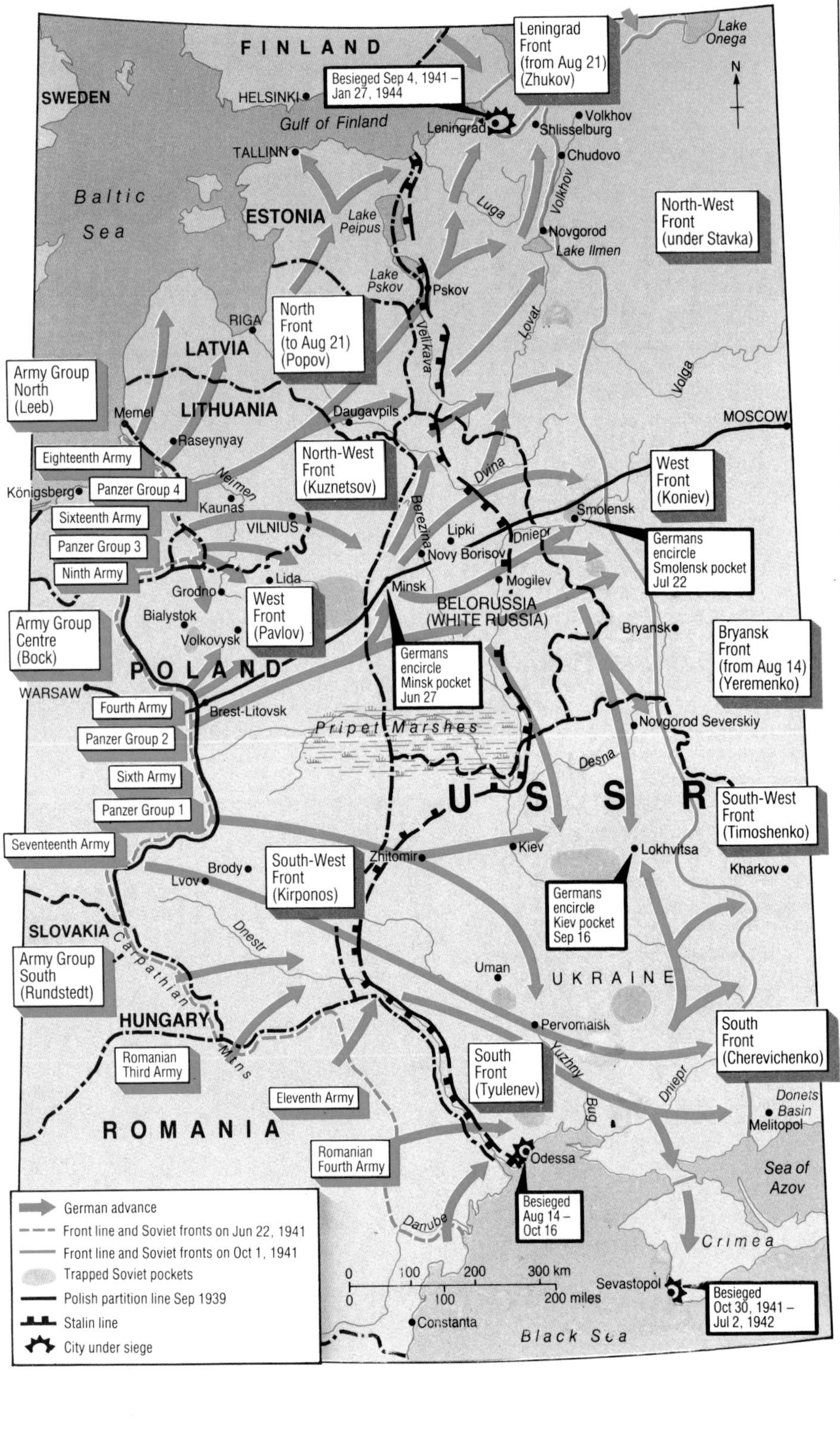

BIGGEST BLITZKRIEG In three great thrusts, Hitler's assault on the Soviet Union rapidly conquered huge areas, surrounding one after another of Stalin's armies. Only in the south, where the attack began nine days later, was there strong initial resistance.

A LESSER EVIL

'If Hitler invaded hell,' Churchill told his secretary, John Colville, on the day before 'Barbarossa', 'I would make at least a favourable reference to the Devil in the House of Commons.' It was in this spirit that Western leaders, including the strongly anti-Communist British premier, threw their support behind the Soviet Union when Germany invaded.

The next day, June 22, Churchill repeated his sentiments in a national broadcast. 'No one has been a more consistent opponent of Communism than I have,' he said, 'but all this fades away before the spectacle that is now unfolding . . . Any man or state who fights on against Nazidom will have our aid.'

The American attitude was similar, but material aid was slow in forthcoming. A British military mission to Moscow led to a mutual-assistance pact, but the Russians insisted that Britain open a second front in the west. Churchill said that such action would be suicidal. He could only send 200 American fighters, supplied under Lend-Lease. In Washington, the Soviet ambassador submitted a US$2000 million list of wants. Roosevelt could not oblige but ordered all possible help.

In August 1941, Soviet and British troops jointly seized Iran, opening another route for aid apart from the Arctic convoys and ships across the Pacific to Vladivostok. In 1942 Lend-Lease was extended to the Soviet Union, but aid picked up substantially only in 1943. All the time Stalin pressed for military assistance in the form of a second front – to be opened by 'superhuman' effort. 'Unfortunately,' Churchill commented laconically, 'these attributes are denied us.'

A major blunder: Hitler halts the march on Moscow

In the drive to Moscow, brilliant pincer movements led to hopes of a quick victory – until Russian resistance, and Hitler's own orders, brought the German armies up short. The pause was to prove fatal to the Führer's ambitions.

JUNE 30, 1941, was a day of celebration at the German High Command headquarters near Berlin. It was the 57th birthday of the Chief of the General Staff, General Franz Halder. His superior, Field Marshal Walther von Brauchitsch, the Wehrmacht's Commander in Chief, had sent red roses and strawberries to decorate the immaculate breakfast table. Later, as a special sign of favour, the Führer himself came to tea, at which an SS adjutant set down a silver flagon of cream.

There was good reason for rejoicing. The invasion of the Soviet Union, Operation 'Barbarossa', had been launched eight days previously, and had been a resounding success. Field Marshal Fedor von Bock's Army Group Centre was well on its way to Moscow.

During the previous week, two tank forces – General Hermann Hoth's Panzer Group 3 and General Heinz Guderian's Panzer Group 2 – had leaped forward through waving grasslands and wheatfields towards Minsk, 320 km (200 miles) east of the German-Soviet border through occupied Poland (see map, p. 106). Trapped inside the two fast-moving claws were three Russian armies, the Third, Fourth and Tenth.

Guderian was astonished by the speed of his advance, which at one stage led to a narrow escape. Two days after the attack, he was returning to his command post when he found himself in the midst of Russian infantry. 'I ordered my driver . . . to go full speed ahead and we drove straight through the Russians; they were so surprised by this unexpected encounter that they did not even have time to fire their guns. All the same, they must have recognised me because the Russian press later announced my death; I felt bound to inform them of their mistake by means of the German wireless.'

By June 26, both Guderian and Hoth were approaching the Belorussian (White Russian) capital Minsk. So certain were they of success that they suggested pushing on another 300 km (190 miles) east to seize Smolensk, halfway to Moscow. Hitler, afraid of spreading German forces too thinly, told them to take Minsk first.

Behind them, while some troops besieged the old border fortress of Brest-Litovsk (now Brest), German infantry of Fourth and Ninth Armies were completing a double-pincer movement of their own on a miscellaneous collection of Soviet troops under Lt General Ivan Boldin around Bialystok and Volkovysk. In Minsk, General Dmitri Pavlov, commander of the West Front (Army Group), made an effort to save his colleague. Unaware of the speed of the advancing German panzer groups, he sent his reserves westward, leaving Minsk almost undefended.

Hoth reached a point north of Minsk on June 26, and he and Guderian met, encircling the city, the next day. On the 28th the German infantry also met around Bialystok. Two days earlier, after a devastating bombardment that almost blew the place to bits, the 7000 Russians in Brest-Litovsk had surrendered. By July 9, when Minsk finally fell, the Germans had taken some 324 000 prisoners, 3300 tanks and 1800 field guns in the Bialystok-Minsk pocket. No wonder Hitler was happy to offer Halder his congratulations. If the tanks could manage another pincer movement to take Smolensk – an ancient fortress, and key to the road to Moscow – there seemed no reason why German troops should not be in the Soviet capital before the end of the summer, as planned.

Only a few battered remnants of Boldin's force managed to escape, arriving behind the Russian lines two months later – though some others formed partisan groups behind the German lines. Pavlov escaped from Minsk to establish new headquarters in Mogilev, 160 km (100 miles) to the east. It did not save him: he was called to Moscow to explain the catastrophe, and was promptly shot, along with his chief of staff, Maj General V.E. Klimovskikh, and chief signals officer, Maj General A.T. Grigoriev.

ON TO SMOLENSK

Guderian – 'Fast Heinz' as he was known – was as usual eager to move on at once, and ordered his panzers to get ready to cross the Dniepr river. Field Marshal Gunther von Kluge, who had just been given command of a new Fourth Panzer Army that included both Hoth and Guderian, told him to wait for the infantry to catch up. Guderian, by inclination and training, wanted to grab the chance to press on rapidly to Smolensk, 320 km (200 miles) to the east. Kluge reluctantly gave him the go-ahead. 'Your operations,' he muttered testily, 'always hang by a thread!'

Once again, Guderian advanced rapidly, and was matched by Hoth's tanks to the north. Smolensk fell on July 16, only one week later, and the two panzer groups met on July 22, trapping another two Russian armies. Despite a number of desperate Russian counterattacks from the south and east against Guderian's and Hoth's forces, the tanks retained control of their areas until the infantry arrived on July 27 to mop up the huge pocket of Russian troops – another 310 000 men, 3200 tanks and 3100 guns. Resistance in the pocket continued for nine more days.

The prisoners were marched off to internment camps in interminable columns. As one German soldier, Benno Zieser, wrote: 'We suddenly saw a broad, earth-brown crocodile slowly shuffling down the road towards us. Prisoners of war. Russians, six deep. We couldn't see the end of the column. As they drew near the terrible stench which met us made us quite sick . . . We made haste out of the way of the foul cloud which surrounded them, then what we saw transfixed us where we stood, and we forgot our nausea. Were these really human beings, these grey-brown figures, these shadows lurching towards us, stumbling and staggering, moving shapes at their last gasp, creatures which only some flicker of the will to live enabled to obey the order to march?'

Could there be any Russians left to offer resistance? Most ordinary German soldiers thought not. East of Smolensk, German troops put up numerous hand-painted signs: 'To Moscow'. They, along with their leaders, believed total victory was near.

THE GIANT AWAKENS

However, there had already been signs that the Soviet Union would not fall easily. The day after the invasion, a new Soviet high command – known as *Stavka* – was established. Two weeks later, three new commanders were appointed to sectors opposite the German army groups: Marshal Kliment Voroshilov (North-West Front), Marshal Semyon Timoshenko (West Front) and Marshal Semyon Budenny (South-West and South Fronts). Orders went out to set up workers' battalions, home-guard units and guerrilla operations behind enemy lines.

But the heart of Russian opposition to the Germans came from the Russian soldiers themselves. As Hitler wrote to Mussolini, they fought with 'truly stupid fanaticism . . . with the primitive brutality of an animal that sees itself trapped'. As a result, in the opening weeks of Operation 'Barbarossa', the Germans lost some 100 000 men – as many as the Wehrmacht had lost in all the war's previous campaigns combined.

There were three principal reasons for Russian determination: fear of their own masters, hatred of German ruthlessness and unalloyed patriotism. Quite simply, there was nothing to be gained by surrender. Russian soldiers captured by the Germans were usually declared by Stalin to be traitors, as if sullied by contact with the enemy. If they escaped and returned to their own lines, they were considered suspect and were likely to be shot. Stalin even imprisoned his own daughter-in-law when his son, Yakov, was captured. She was not released for two years, by which time Yakov had died in captivity – either by his own hand after his name was used in German propaganda or shot by his captors, according to different stories. For officers, failure was tantamount to treachery, and they were punished accordingly, as Pavlov discovered.

Hitler himself was in part responsible for Russian 'fanaticism'. In what was termed the Commissar Decree, he had ordered that all Red Army commissars – the political officers who worked alongside military officers – were to be executed. Often, the term 'commissar' came to mean simply 'Russian'. Special SS units known as *Einsatzgruppen* ('task forces') worked full-time killing Jews, while the Gestapo dealt with prisoners of war and civilians.

For ordinary Russians, however, fear of the Germans and their own political masters combined with a genuine love of 'Mother Russia'. Amazingly, it was Stalin himself who was able to tap the depths of this affection. On July 3 he made his first public statement since the invasion. Though he had previously been ready enough to treat his people as traitors unless they were slaves to his will, he now addressed them fulsomely as 'comrades, citizens, brothers and sisters, fighting

COMRADE COMMISSAR Red Army political commissars were Stalin's watchdogs, who kept an eye on army commanders to see that they did not falter in their duties. The commissars – Communist party officials – had enormous powers, and could countermand an officer's order even under combat conditions. Many an officer was shot by his commissar for refusing to obey his orders. This dual command system played a part in the Red Army's early setbacks, and was abolished in 1942, when commissars switched to non-military duties. They acted as welfare officers, giving morale-boosting lectures and dealing with soldiers' problems.

men of our army and our fleet'. He spoke of a 'national patriotic war . . . for the freedom of our motherland', and called for a scorched-earth policy that would not leave 'a single railway engine, a single wagon, a single pound of grain' for the enemy. His words acted as a genuine inspiration, and Russian people responded.

The Russians well knew the advantages of their climate and thickly forested landscape. In the vast Bialowieza Forest of Poland and the soggy expanses of the Pripet (Pripyat) Marshes, to the south of Minsk, no tanks could operate and there was ample cover for small groups. Here, Russian troops were already showing the skills that would serve them well later, infiltrating German positions through dense forest, communicating by imitating animal cries.

'Their positions, not on the forest edge, but deep inside, were superbly camouflaged,' wrote one German. 'Their dugouts and foxholes were established with diabolical cunning, providing a field of fire only to the rear. From the front and from above they were invisible. The German infantrymen passed them unsuspecting, and were picked off from behind.'

What the Russians really needed was time to make better use of their country's huge resources, time to mobilise more of the 16 million men of military age, and time to gain experience.

BROWBEATEN BRAUCHITSCH

Of Prussian aristocratic stock, Walther von Brauchitsch (1881-1948) served on the German General Staff throughout World War I. He was a major general and Inspector of Artillery during the Weimar Republic, and was appointed Commander in Chief of the Wehrmacht in 1938. He was promoted field marshal after the fall of France.

Fortunately for Russia, Brauchitsch lacked the moral strength to oppose Hitler, who easily browbeat him. Twice, in December 1940, when 'Barbarossa' was still in the planning stage, and again in July 1941, Hitler rejected his arguments for giving priority to a centre drive on Moscow. In November 1941, Brauchitsch suffered a serious heart attack; finding himself bypassed by Hitler, who issued orders directly to army commanders, he offered his resignation. In fact, Hitler dismissed him on December 17 with the contemptuous observation that he was 'a vain, cowardly wretch and a nincompoop'. Arrested by the Allies on his estate in Schleswig-Holstein at the end of the war, Brauchitsch died awaiting trial.

ARMOURED CONFRONTATION

The potential danger to the German forces if this were ever to happen became apparent in a small but dramatic incident near the village of Lipki, roughly halfway between Minsk and Smolensk, in early July. Here Guderian's spearhead was met by 100 Russian tanks, including a massive 52 tonne KV-2 and a number of the sleek new T-34s, making their first appearance in this area. The Germans had nothing to match either machine, and their anti-tank shells simply bounced off the Soviet tanks.

However, the Germans discovered that the Russians were slow to reload and had no idea how to fight in formation, and so they were able to manoeuvre their tanks in among the Russian machines – close enough to shoot the tracks off them. Later, Maj General Walther Nehring, commander of the 18th Panzer Division, stared in amazement at an abandoned KV-2. It had 11 direct hits, none of which had penetrated the armour. Guderian himself came across three T-34s abandoned undamaged after they got stuck in marshy ground. Clearly, if the Russians were given time to become expert in handling their machines, their opposition could become truly formidable.

For the moment, Russians resorted to close combat to stop the German tanks, using charges attached directly to unarmoured spots on the tanks. They also employed an improvised weapon consisting of two bottles, one of phosphorus (which burst into flames on contact with air) and the other of petrol; sometimes, a fuse would be used instead of phosphorus. When thrown at a tank, the glass would break, releasing flaming petrol to flow inside, setting the machine on fire. The Russians had first been on the receiving end of these 'Molotov cocktails' during the 1939 Winter War against the Finns. They now used them to good effect against their own enemies.

At Smolensk the growing strength of Russian resistance first became really effective. The city had considerable symbolic significance. It was there that Napoleon's Grande Armée had won the victory that opened for him the way to Moscow in 1812; and it was there, three months later, that he was defeated.

Though Smolensk itself quickly fell to the German blitzkrieg, the Russians established a strong front some 30-40 km (20-25 miles) to the east. By now German tanks were showing the strains of the fast, gruelling advance. And the Russians for the first time deployed a terrifying new weapon: multi-barrelled batteries that fired rocket-propelled mortars with devastating effect. The Russians nicknamed them *Katyushas* ('Little Kates') and the Germans *Stalinorgeln* ('Stalin organs') because of the sound they made.

The Smolensk Line, protected by its Katyushas and its battalions of scratch reserves, established a shield – albeit a thin one – behind which the Russians could regroup and organise the defence of Moscow.

DISPUTE OVER TARGETS

Hitler chose this moment to intervene. He had never fully agreed with his generals' eagerness to take Moscow – he saw it as a 'geographical expression', not the Russian nerve-centre – and had long hankered after the rich resources of the

FOR THE LOVE OF HOLY RUSSIA Inspired by a fanatical love of their Motherland, the Russian soldiers fought back with a ferocity that astonished the Germans, who had expected them to run like rabbits, and their crude but effective 'Molotov cocktails' (right) were the terror of the panzer crews. During lulls in the fighting, morale was boosted by news read out to the soldiers, such as the group of Twentieth Army men (right, below) seen resting in a forest in the Smolensk area in the summer of 1941.

Ukraine. On July 23 he ordered a delay in the attack towards Moscow until the Smolensk pocket had been cleared. Then, on July 30, he ordered Hoth to turn north to help take Leningrad, and Guderian to join the advance on Kiev, in the Ukraine.

Guderian protested bitterly. A quick strike now, he believed, would burst through the Smolensk Line and lay Moscow at Hitler's feet. Hitler went to the front himself on August 4, spoke to the commanders at Army Group Centre's headquarters at Novi Borisov and confirmed his orders. Hoth complied, but Guderian sent off only a few units, paying little more than lip service to Hitler's orders. The Führer insisted. On August 21, an order from Armed Forces Headquarters declared: 'The essential target to be achieved before winter is not the capture of Moscow but the conquest of the Crimea and the Donets coal and industrial basin.'

Brauchitsch reluctantly accepted the order. There were indeed a number of worrying aspects to Army Group Centre's advance: exhausted foot-soldiers trailing 160 km (100 miles) behind the tanks; the panzers themselves 320 km (200 miles) away from their depots; partisans emerging and vanishing again into trackless forests; torn-up dirt roads that would turn to mud in rain. It would be hard indeed to support another huge leap forward.

Guderian would have none of it, and his superiors Halder and Bock agreed with him. On August 23, still incensed at Hitler's change of mind, Guderian went with Halder and Bock to Hitler's headquarters in Rastenburg to plead his case in person as an expert in tank warfare. He pointed out that he was only 350 km (220 miles) from Moscow, yet he was now being asked to undertake a 1000 km (600 mile) diversion. He received an icy rebuff.

It was settled: there would be an advance on Moscow – but only after Kiev had fallen.

The drive to Leningrad

A three-month sprint, slowed by muddled German leadership and Russian tenacity, left Leningrad within the Germans' reach, but not within their grasp.

ORDERS WERE TERSE and to the point. 'Forward!' commanded the field marshal. 'Don't stop for anything! Never let the enemy consolidate!' Wilhelm Ritter von Leeb, commanding Army Group North, was winding up his men for a spectacular dash.

The plan was to race through the Baltic states of Latvia, Lithuania and Estonia, cross four major rivers, force a way through the easily defensible 200 km (125 mile) gap between Lakes Peipus (now Chudskoye) and Pskov and Lake Ilmen – and finally take Leningrad (see map, p. 106). But Leeb knew that Russian forces were thinly spread throughout the vast area; there could be none of the huge encirclements that would net so many prisoners farther south. Speed and surprise were of the essence; the Russians had to be defeated in a matter of weeks.

Initially, the advance was easier than Leeb had any right to expect. The Russians, it turned out, were totally unprepared for defensive action. General Fyodor Kuznetsov, commander of the North-West Front (Army Group), had only two understrength armies to defend the frontier. Army Group North had the Sixteenth and Eighteenth Armies and General Erich Hoepner's Panzer Group 4. Easy going – or so it seemed.

RESISTANCE AND DELAY

At Raseynyay (Raseiniai), just 60 km (40 miles) into Lithuania, one element of Hoepner's force – Lt General Georg-Hans Reinhardt's XLI Panzer Corps – ran into trouble, in the shape of some 200 super-heavy Russian tanks. These cumbersome monsters – 43 tonne KV-1s and 52 tonne KV-2s – had 80 mm (3 in) armour plating. The Germans complained that their shells simply bounced off.

Reinhardt's men managed to immobilise the Russian tanks only by engaging them closely enough to blow their tracks off or stick high-explosive charges to vulnerable parts. By June 26, the Russians had lost most of their tanks. Only then, after a four-day delay, was Reinhardt free to drive on to the broad Dvina river, 300 km (185 miles) from his starting point and the greatest obstacle between the border and Leningrad.

The other spearhead of Panzer Group 4, LVI Panzer Corps under General Erich von Manstein, advanced quickly enough into Latvia, heading for Daugavpils (Dvinsk). 'Keep going! Keep going!' Manstein urged. On June 26, 8th Panzer Division's advance vehicles and motorcyclists roared towards a bridge over the Dvina, which they knew would be wired for demolition.

Fearing that the Russians would blow the bridge if attacked directly, a platoon of 30 Brandenburgers – commando-style German special forces – wearing Russian uniforms drove in four captured Russian trucks through the enemy's lines. The trucks were waved on by retreating Russians, but on the bridge itself they were stopped by a Russian guard. The Germans leaped out, some opening fire on the surprised Russians, while others ran to disarm the demolition charges. The 3rd Motorised Division, meanwhile, captured a second bridge over the Dvina. Manstein's panzers rolled across in safety, and by evening Daugavpils was in German hands. They were a third of the way to their goal.

MUDDLE AT THE TOP

Manstein now had an opportunity to punch straight ahead for Leningrad. But he was some 100 km (60 miles) ahead of Reinhardt, let alone the main infantry forces, which as late as June 26 were still crossing the Neimen, the first of the major river obstacles. Manstein was ordered to stay put until the others caught up.

This delay allowed the Russians precious time to pull together reserves and reinforcements, and prepare defence lines. Meanwhile, the German infantry of the Sixteenth Army moved ponderously up on the right, drained increasingly by the summer heat. One soldier wrote: 'The sweat, the flies and the dirt from dusty tracks – hardly roads – became part of life. After a while you didn't bother even to brush the insects away.'

Even so, by July 2, Reinhardt's tanks were across the Dvina some 60 km (40 miles) downriver from Manstein, and both tank corps were ready to advance. They set off again, on diverging tracks, Manstein north-east for Novgorod, and Reinhardt north for Pskov, moving slowly now through wooded, swampy lowlands.

By mid-July both corps had reached the Luga river – the last major natural obstacle before Leningrad – having covered almost 800 km (500 miles) in three weeks. Some units lower down the river were only 100 km (60 miles) from the city.

For a time, the panzers were stuck, while

ANTI-HITLER GENERAL

Erich Hoepner (1886-1944) was a fine soldier, and also a bitter political opponent of Hitler. In 1938, when commander of the 3rd Panzer Division, he became involved in a plot to remove the Führer. The scheme came to nothing with Hitler's triumph at Munich later that year. Thereafter, Hoepner pursued his military career with professional zeal.

A tank warfare expert, he consistently favoured a bold, armoured thrust to seize Leningrad during the 1941 advance, until Hitler ordered him to join Army Group Centre to attack Moscow instead. His panzers led the assault until winter stalled them. Following the Soviet counterattack in January 1942, Hoepner prepared to withdraw some of his units. Hitler, wrongly thinking the withdrawal had already been made without permission, had him court-martialled and cashiered.

Deeply enmeshed in the 1944 Bomb Plot, Hoepner was among those hanged on Hitler's orders. Had the plot succeeded, he could well have become Army Commander in Chief.

NOT SO MUCH AN ALLY

Ever since the four-month 'Winter War' of 1939-40 (p. 29), Finland had been smarting over its lands lost to the USSR. In planning 'Barbarossa' the Germans saw a way of offering the Finns a chance to regain those lands and also play a useful role in the assault. In the far north, two Finnish divisions joined troops under General Nikolaus Falkenhorst facing the Soviet Fourteenth and Seventh armies. In the south, the Finnish Karelian Army under General Erik Heinrichs – with an added German division – would drive south from the Finnish border on both sides of Lake Ladoga.

In May 1941 the Finns agreed to the plan, and on July 1 a major Finnish attack drove back the Soviet troops north of Lake Ladoga. On August 27 they cut the Leningrad railway and by September 1 had reached the old frontier east of the lake. Then they stopped. Field Marshal Carl von Mannerheim, Finland's Commander in Chief, claimed that his army lacked artillery and bomber strength, but in reality he had achieved his aims – recovery of the 1939 frontier – and intended to go no farther.

The Germans were furious. Army Group North had taken Shlisselburg (now Petrokrepost) at the southern tip of Lake Ladoga, and less than 65 km (40 miles) separated Finns and Germans. Closing that gap would have completed a ring around Leningrad. But Mannerheim was adamant. 'Finland is not interested in annexing any part of Russia', he said. Restoring the borders, and national pride, had cost the Finns 25 000 dead and more than 50 000 wounded. Their contribution to 'Barbarossa', however, was negligible.

MOTORISED SOLDIERS Two SS panzer grenadiers (motorised infantry) make for Leningrad. The man in the sidecar uses a Mauser MG-34 'Spandau' machine gun – with the later MG-42, one of the war's classic German machine guns. The driver has a Schmeisser machine pistol. Motorcycle troops headed lightning German attacks.

leaders bickered about the best way to proceed. Should the tanks plunge ahead – and would that leave them exposed and under-supplied? Or should they wait for the Sixteenth Army infantry, now depleted by demands for help from Army Group Centre? Things were not helped by Hitler's indecision over priorities – Moscow, Leningrad and/or the Ukraine.

As time passed, Soviet defences strengthened. The people of Leningrad struggled to complete kilometre after kilometre of earth walls and anti-tank ditches. The opportunity for a rapid German victory trickled away.

LENINGRAD IN SIGHT!

On the Baltic coast, the German Eighteenth Army swept on without meeting serious resistance. Latvia, Lithuania and Estonia had all been occupied by the Soviet Union the previous year; many people welcomed the Nazis as liberators. The Russians mobilised 25 000 civilians to build a defensive line around the Estonian capital and port of Tallinn, an important Soviet naval base. The Germans began their attack on August 19. The Russians, supported by naval guns, held them off for nearly a week, but then they broke through. Most Russian troops and ships escaped.

Meanwhile, inland, the Germans had renewed their offensive towards Leningrad. On August 8, in streaming rain, Leeb's men broke out of their bridgeheads across the Luga. Slowly, rushing reinforcements back and forth to counter strong Soviet resistance, the Germans moved northwards. One prong, advancing north-east along the Volkhov river, took Novgorod on August 16, and then Chudovo four days later. A second prong, on their left, approached to within 50 km (30 miles) of Leningrad by August 31, before turning south to trap 20 000 Russian prisoners.

The first German shells fell on Leningrad on September 1. Soon afterwards, the first panzers reached the city's defences. Slowly, other forces arrived, putting a cordon across the south of Leningrad from the Gulf of Finland in the west to Lake Ladoga in the east. Relying on Finnish forces to block the city to the north, Leeb's 'final' attack began on September 9. Within two days, his troops had taken heights only 12 km (7½ miles) from the city, and could see its gleaming cupolas.

They were so near – and yet so far. On September 6, Hitler had ordered that the assault on Moscow should now have priority. Leningrad was to become a side show, to be besieged and starved into submission. On September 17, Leeb's panzers started to head south. Army Group North had a stranglehold on Leningrad, but lacked the strength to finish the job.

LENINGRAD'S WOMEN SET TO By mid-July 1941, civilians and soldiers had built 160 km (100 miles) of anti-tank obstacles, trenches and strongpoints around Leningrad.

PANZER WORKHORSE The only German tank to remain in service throughout World War II was the sturdy Panzer IV; by 1945 some 9000 had been produced. This medium tank – weighing roughly 20 tonnes – was originally designed to go into battle in support of lighter anti-tank, or machine-gun armed, tanks. It was armed with a 75 mm (2.95 in) gun and two machine guns, one in the turret beside the 75 mm, one in the front of the hull. The Panzer IV did stout service in Poland and France, but in Russia met its match in the Soviet T-34. The German tank's excellent basic design, however, meant that it could be updated to meet this challenge. Later versions were given much more powerful long-barrelled 75 mm guns, and their armour plating was considerably toughened – to a thickness of 80 mm (3.2 in) in some parts. Thus equipped, the Panzer IV became, in its turn, an effective anti-tank tank, the only German one able to hold its own against Allied counterparts. Later Panzer IVs had a crew of five, a speed of up to 40 km/h (25 mph) and a range of 210 km (130 miles).

LENIN'S CITY 'DIGS A GRAVE FOR FASCISM'

Hitler claimed that, once encircled, Leningrad would 'fall like a leaf'. But the city had a fierce pride. It endured for almost 900 days.

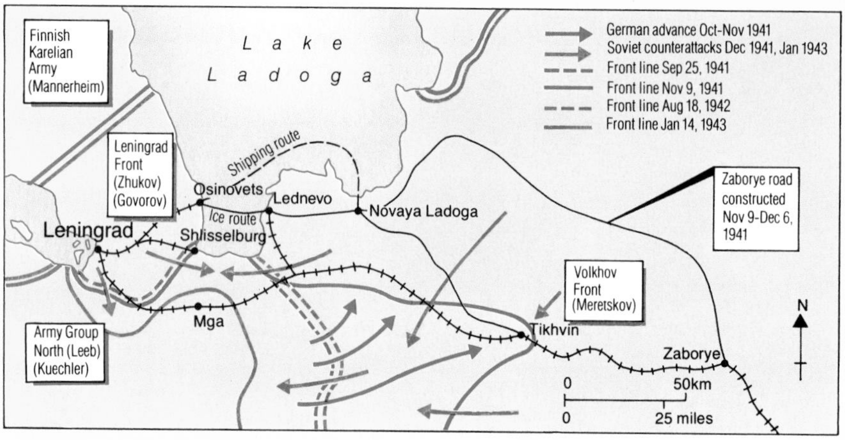

ANDREI ZHDANOV, Leningrad's Communist party secretary, faced his gaunt, red-eyed party colleagues. It was August 20, 1941, and German troops of Field Marshal Ritter von Leeb's Army Group North had just overrun Leningrad's outer defences. To the north, the Karelian Army of Hitler's Finnish ally was advancing down between Lake Ladoga and the sea. It seemed that only the citizens themselves could save the city – once Russia's capital and cradle of the Revolution. 'We must teach people in the shortest possible time the methods of street fighting,' insisted Zhdanov. 'We must dig Fascism a grave in front of Leningrad.' The next day, massive posters appeared in the streets, proclaiming: 'The enemy is at the gates!'

Over the following days, the German grip tightened inexorably. By early September, the railway stations of Shlisselburg (now Petrokrepost) – 30 km (20 miles) away – and Mga were in German hands. With 300 000 Germans to the south and the Finns just to the north, the city was cut off from the rest of the country except by boat across Lake Ladoga. The roads into Leningrad were crammed with a hopeless tide of refugees.

But just as the city seemed about to fall, the German momentum flagged. Hitler decided that his prime objective should be Moscow, justifying his change of plan with chilling logic. To take Leningrad would mean feeding almost 3 million people through the winter. A winter siege, on the other hand, would starve at least a million to death, damaging Russian morale far more severely – and at far less cost – than a successful assault.

This change of tactics coincided with a tougher Soviet stance. On September 9, Stalin dispatched General Georgi Zhukov to put Leningrad on a war footing. Factories, bridges and public buildings were mined, ready to be blown up if the Germans penetrated the city. Streets were blocked with wire, the city sown with anti-tank obstacles, buildings protected with fire points and pillboxes. By October 7, when Zhukov was recalled to Moscow, Leningrad was ready to fight to the end.

BITTER COLD AND STARVATION

It seemed that the end might not be far off. The city's inhabitants needed 1000 tonnes of food a day to survive. But by November it was receiving less than half that amount, all of it carried by rail from Tikhvin, 210 km (130 miles) east, then ferried across Lake Ladoga.

On November 9, Tikhvin itself fell to Leeb's troops. The only link to the outside world now was a single, vulnerable airfield at Novaya Ladoga. Zhdanov at once issued a decree: a road would be cut in a wide arc through the virgin forest north of Tikhvin for trucks to bring supplies to Novaya Ladoga from Zaborye, 80 km (50 miles) farther east.

Food and fuel shortages rapidly turned the city into a hell. On November 20, the rations, already scanty, were cut to a record low: manual workers received 250 g (9 oz) of bread daily, while others received just half that – one-sixth of the amount needed for a healthy diet. People hunted cats, dogs, rats and sparrows for food. Horses were killed.

Weakened by hunger, people succumbed to any disease. 'It is so simple to die,' one inhabitant, Yelena Skryabina, noted in her diary. 'You just begin to lose interest then you lie on the bed and you never get up.' The dead lay where they fell, frozen solid beneath the drifting snow. At best, engineers blasted mass graves in the frozen ground.

Worst of all, some people turned to cannibalism. Corpses were seen with their fleshy parts cut away, and in the market, traders sold patties said to be of human meat. Many feared that to venture out would be to risk a violent death at the hands of their starving compatriots. Anyone who looked well fed was the object of deepest suspicion.

THE CITY RALLIES

The cold that brought so much suffering also offered the city its only hope. As soon as the waters of Lake Ladoga froze enough, supplies could be carried across the ice from the east.

Astonishingly, the forest road was finished in less than a month. By early December a narrow track, crudely surfaced with branches, linked the lake to the railway line at Zaborye. Manhandled by skeletal volunteers through

THE RACE TO SAVE THE HERMITAGE

When Germany invaded the Soviet Union on June 22, 1941, Joseph Orbeli knew instantly what his first duty must be. As curator of The Hermitage, in Leningrad – one of the world's greatest art collections – he had to evacuate all the great treasures to a safer place.

Three government ministers came from Moscow to oversee the packing. They watched as Rembrandt's *Holy Family* and his massive *Return of the Prodigal*, Madonnas by Leonardo da Vinci and Raphael, wonderful sculptures, and crown jewels, all disappeared under wraps. Nine days after the invasion, a 31-wagon train, equipped with an armoured car and two anti-aircraft batteries, left the city with more than 500 000 of the finest works.

Orbeli had been planning the operation since 1939, and another 23 train wagons carrying 700 000 more objects left Leningrad on July 20, bound for Sverdlovsk in the Urals. But on August 30 the order came to stop. The Germans had captured Mga, cutting off the last safe rail link to the east. Orbeli could only move his remaining treasures to the cellars.

snowdrifts and up impossible gradients, trucks could manage no more than 40 km (25 miles) a day. Fortunately, the city did not have to rely on the road alone. On December 9, Tikhvin was recaptured, and the ice of the lake thickened. Trucks began the run from Tikhvin to the shore, then across the ice.

By January 1942, as many as 400 trucks a day were shuttling back and forth over Ladoga's ice-road to the city. They also helped by carrying out refugees – easing the plight of those left behind.

But the spring thaw would bring a new problem: epidemics spreading from the thousands of rotting corpses. In March, 300 000 Leningrad citizens went to work cleaning the city. Slowly it regained signs of vitality. When the ice melted, a pipeline laid across the floor of the lake pumped in fuel as boats resumed operations. In August – in an event which seemed to symbolise the city's resurrection – the bomb-damaged Philharmonic Hall reopened with a performance of Shostakovitch's Seventh Symphony.

The worst was over. But it would take another two years for the Germans to be driven back completely. In January 1943, a massive assault by the armies of the Leningrad and Volkhov Fronts (Army Groups) recaptured Shlisselburg, thus reopening a direct if narrow rail link to the city along what came to be called the 'corridor of death'.

The final offensive to relieve Leningrad opened on January 13, 1944. On the 27th, streams of red, white and blue rockets marked the city's liberation. After 890 days, it was free. But the toll had been terrible. According to some experts, 1.5 million people, civilian and military, had died during the siege.

HOME FRONT HEROINES The women of Leningrad braved air raids and shelling to act as ambulance drivers and medical orderlies during the siege.

DESPERATE MEASURES At the height of the siege, the only water supply was from the Neva river.

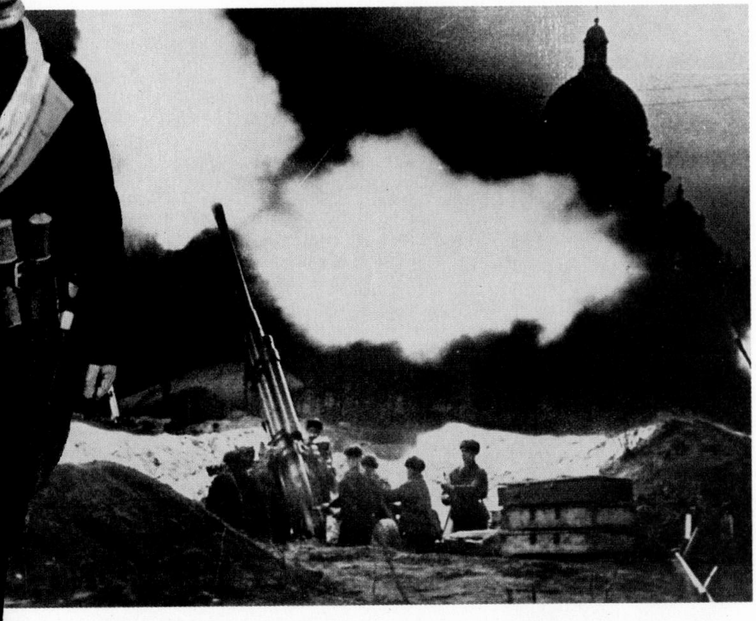

DEFIANT CITY Young Russian soldiers were ready for street fighting, and in the shadow of St Isaac's Cathedral anti-aircraft guns fought off incessant air attacks.

ANGEL OF MERCY A first-aid instructor tends a wounded man on the Leningrad front.

Kiev falls, as panzers surge through dust and mud

After a hard-fought advance, the Germans, aided by Stalin's own catastrophic errors of judgment, secured much of the Ukraine by taking Kiev. In doing so, they took some of the largest bags of prisoners in the history of warfare.

TOO HOT OR TOO WET – it always seemed to be one or the other in the Ukraine, that summer of 1941. In the sun, tank-tracks ground the baked earth to powdery, flour-fine dust that clogged machinery, clothing, eyes and mouths alike. Thunderstorms laid the dust and brought relief from the heat, but turned roads into axle-deep quagmires. As the German Army Group South advanced, the going grew increasingly tough. To cap it all, they found the Russians to be a formidable force: their 1 to 1.5 million soldiers outnumbered the Germans two to one, and they had 2400 tanks – albeit mostly obsolete – against the Germans' 600. It would take all Field Marshal Gerd von Rundstedt's strategic brilliance to win through.

He had two forces along the Soviet frontier: a northern one in Poland and a southern one in Romania (see map, p. 106). The northern force – the Sixth and Seventeenth Armies plus General Ewald von Kleist's Panzer Group 1 – was strong and reliable. But the southern force, responsible for advancing along the Black Sea coast, had just a single German army – the Eleventh – with two less reliable, under-equipped Romanian armies and a Hungarian corps. Their advance was planned to start on July 1, nine days after the initial 'Barbarossa' assault, when the Russian reserves would, the Germans hoped, have been pulled away to oppose the northern attack.

EARLY RESISTANCE

Rundstedt did not get off to a good start. The Russians retreated, but did so methodically, resisting the German advance with mechanised forces and frequently leaving suicide squads as rearguards, making the Germans fight for every kilometre. Nevertheless, cracks did begin to appear in the retreating Soviet line. Near Brody, Rundstedt managed to drive a dangerous wedge between the Soviet Fifth and Sixth Armies, which a furious four-day counterattack failed to close. Another breach – 32 km (20 miles) across – opened up farther south between the Sixth and Twenty-Sixth Armies. Around Lvov, where the Russians tried desperately to stem the German tide, there were eight days' savage fighting, during which the Soviet 22nd Motorised Corps lost 119 tanks. The city fell on June 29.

Belatedly, on June 30, the Soviet South-West Front (Army Group) commander, General Mikhail Kirponos, ordered his troops to pull back to the fortifications the Germans called the Stalin Line, marking the pre-1939 frontier. In the event, the Stalin Line proved no great deterrent – the pillboxes and anti-tank barriers had not been strengthened since the frontier moved west – and by July 9, Sixth Army and Panzer Group 1 had broken through towards the town of Zhitomir.

That day, Maj General M.I. Potapov's Fifth Army, pushed back northwards into the Pripet (Pripyat) Marshes by the German advance, emerged from the forests and bog-lands in an attempt to sever Kleist's panzer spearhead from the slower-moving infantry. At the same time, the Soviet Sixth Army attacked from the south. The attacks failed, but they did slow the German advance. It took two weeks for Kleist to smash a way through to clearer ground beyond Zhitomir and prepare the way for Rundstedt's armies to strike at the strategic heart of the Ukraine.

The prize was Kiev, the Ukrainian capital and the third largest city in the Soviet Union. Road and rail links to the east made it also the key to the industrial region of the Donets Basin, which produced 60 per cent of Russia's coal and 30 per cent of its iron ore.

The Russians meanwhile were desperately organising their own response. The new commander of the South-West Front, Marshal Semyon Budenny – appointed with the reorganisation of the fronts on July 10 – was not the man for the job. An old-fashioned former cavalry sergeant major with handle-bar moustaches, his main qualification was unswerving political loyalty to his old colleague Stalin. Just in case, though, the burly, abrasive Nikita Khrushchev, Budenny's political watchdog, was at hand to make sure the dictator's wishes were observed. His wishes in this case were that Kiev be held.

OTHER OPTIONS

For the Germans, Kiev might be the prize, but it would also need a massive concentration of arms to take it. Better to bypass it, isolate it and take it later. Meanwhile, there were other possibilities. The railway system, vital for the deployment of Russian troops, came together at another major junction: Uman, with links south to the Crimea. Rundstedt saw that slicing between Kiev and Uman would give him three options: to drive on eastwards, swing north to isolate Kiev, or turn south to surround Uman. The choice was dictated by events farther south, where Eleventh Army and the Romanians were advancing towards Odessa on the Black Sea. Budenny ordered some of his southern forces to hold Odessa, and the rest to concentrate at Uman. The prize of capturing this valuable communications centre and at the same time destroying a large Russian force beckoned Rundstedt.

So, when Kleist's tanks surged forward in heavy rain between Kiev and Uman, they turned south. A Russian counterattack, consisting largely of trucks crammed with infantry driving flat-out at German tanks until blown up by direct hits, proved hopeless. On August 3, Kleist's leading units linked up with Seventeenth Army on the Bug river, some 80 km (50 miles) beyond Uman. Over the next five days, the noose tightened around Uman as the German infantry marched across rough terrain under a fierce sun. The Russians delayed their withdrawal too long, and the Germans trapped three armies – over 100 000 men – with 300 tanks and 1100 guns. The roads lay open to the Dniepr, with its great bend bellying eastwards into the rest of the Ukraine.

Kleist drove on rapidly, his men exhilarated and for a while carefree. There was almost no resistance, for the Russians – while leaving large forces to defend Kiev – were now putting all their efforts into building up defences beyond the Dniepr and pulling back industrial equipment beyond reach of the Germans.

Meanwhile, on the Black Sea coast, the Romanian Fourth Army had arrived outside the great naval port of Odessa and by August 14 were besieging it. The siege was to last nine weeks – until October 16, when the garrison was withdrawn by sea to bolster the defences of Sevastopol in the Crimea. An estimated 350 000 civilians and valuable military equipment were also evacuated from Odessa. During the siege, the Romanians suffered over 100 000 casualties.

BUDENNY'S LUCK

A veteran of the Russo-Japanese war of 1904-5, Semyon Budenny (1883-1973) served as a Tsarist cavalry NCO in World War I. After the Revolution he met Stalin in Tsaritsyn (later Stalingrad). He commanded cavalry in Poland in 1919 and in the 1920 Civil War.

Created a marshal in 1935, he owed his advancement to political reliability and long-standing devotion to Stalin. His bluff manner was accentuated by a large handle-bar moustache and the pair of mahogany-butt revolvers that dangled ostentatiously from his hips. He was a hard drinker.

Within a month of being appointed Commander in Chief of all operations in the south on July 10, 1941, he was taken by surprise by Guderian's drive towards Kiev. When counterattacks failed and it became clear that Kiev would be lost, Budenny asked permission to retreat. Stalin promptly transferred him to command the Reserve Front; he had been in operational command for just under two months.

NO QUARTER GIVEN Street fighting (above) was a new experience for the Germans, who were forced to move cautiously against determined resistance. In open country (left) the Russians even used their own dead as 'planks'.

TIME OUT Two travel-stained German dispatch riders find time for a break during Army Group South's advance across the dusty Ukrainian plain in the summer of 1941.

RENEGADE RED

Andrei Vlasov (1900-46) had peasant origins, and was drafted into the Red Army in 1919. In 1938 he went to China as a military adviser, and on his return to the Soviet Union the following year he reorganised the 99th Infantry Division. During Operation 'Barbarossa' he distinguished himself as commander of IV Mechanised Corps at Kiev and then commanded Twentieth Army.

Promoted lieutenant general, Vlasov led the Second Assault Army to relieve Leningrad in January 1942. Though surrounded in the Volkhov Marshes, Stalin ordered him to fight to the last man. To Vlasov this was madness and, already disillusioned by the prewar purges, he determined to 'rid his country of Stalin's system of terror'. After he was taken prisoner in July he started to raise a patriotic 'Russian Army of Liberation' among his fellow Russian prisoners, inevitably supplying Josef Goebbels with useful propaganda. After the war the Americans returned him to Moscow, where he was hanged for treason in August 1946.

GUDERIAN ORDERED SOUTH

Once securely established along the great bend of the Dniepr in late August, Kleist began to create a number of bridgeheads across the river. Then, when he was joined by other units freed by the fall of Uman, he was ready to turn on Kiev. But he would need help. That help could only come from Army Group Centre, still embroiled in the advance on Moscow.

There, finally, a long wrangle had been resolved about whether to assault Moscow straight away or later. On August 24, Hitler confirmed a decision to delay the assault until the flanks were secured. In the south, this meant the immediate destruction of the Russian armies in the Kiev area, seizure of the Crimea – to secure Army Group South's flank and capture the naval base of Sevastopol – and then the capture of the Donets Basin. General Heinz Guderian's Panzer Group 2, which had spearheaded the advance towards Moscow, was ordered south to join up with Kleist.

Guderian was appalled to be deprived of his prize when it seemed almost within his grasp, and made his feelings plain in a meeting with Hitler. But the Führer would not be moved and Guderian had to bend. 'I did not then think it would be right,' he explained later, 'to make an angry scene with the head of the German State when he was surrounded by his advisers.' By mid-August he was heading for Kiev through a desolate region of forest and scrub parallel to the Desna river.

Guderian was not the only one who believed that Moscow was the Germans' only true objective. Stalin, too, was convinced of it, interpreting Guderian's southward swing as a massive outflanking movement. He gave General Andrei Yeremenko, commander of the Bryansk Front to the south of Moscow, reinforcements on the understanding that he would 'stop that scoundrel Guderian'. Yeremenko agreed, and he harried the Germans' flanks from the forests and marshes beyond the Desna river, holding in reserve enough troops to stop Guderian in his tracks when he turned towards Moscow. But Guderian made no attempt to turn, and Yeremenko's forces remained largely unused.

Towards the end of August, Guderian was approaching the Desna river at a point where it turned westward towards Kiev, blocking the way into the Ukraine. The Desna there was sprawling, swampy and up to 900 m (1000 yds) wide, and Guderian had to get across if he was to join up with Kleist. Ahead, beyond the ancient town of Novgorod Severskiy, lay two long wooden bridges. If the bridges could be taken, it would save days of work and fighting.

On August 26, a dawn attack – heavy artillery to flatten anti-tank obstacles, followed by tanks and motorcycles driving through the city's defensive lines – impelled the Russians to blow up one of the bridges. Before they could detonate explosives fixed to the second bridge, however, a small detachment of German armoured infantry-carriers from the 6th Panzer Division roared through the town under cover of thick dust-clouds, overwhelmed the guards and tore out the charges.

The gateway southwards stood open. Kiev had become a salient jutting into German-held territory, a salient containing five armies about to be snipped off by Guderian and Kleist.

APOCALYPSE AT KIEV

Too late the local Russian commanders saw the danger. On September 13, Budenny requested permission to withdraw eastwards, but Stalin would not hear of it, and removed him. Rather than admit failure by ordering withdrawal, Stalin had just written off some 750 000 men. Potapov, the captured commander of the Soviet Fifth Army, later told Guderian: 'An order from the highest quarters – this means Stalin – instructed us to turn back, and fight in accordance with the slogan: "Stand fast, hold out, and if need be die".'

Commanders in Kiev made one last effort to make Stalin see sense. On September 14, Maj General M.P. Tupikov, Chief of Staff of the South-West Front, reported to Moscow: 'The beginning of the catastrophe about which you know is a matter of a couple of days away.' To no avail; in Moscow, General Boris Shaposhnikov – Chief of the General Staff since General Georgi Zhukov was removed on July 29 for advocating abandoning Kiev to strengthen Moscow's defences – dismissed the report as 'panicky'.

It was not panicky; it was the truth. Guderian's progress southwards in early September had been slowed to walking-pace by heavy rain that turned the dusty roads to knee-deep sludge, but on September 16 the tanks of the two panzer groups, fighting their way through Russian supply columns still heading into Kiev, met at Lokhvitsa, 195 km (120 miles) east of the city.

The next day, Marshal Semyon Timoshenko, who had taken over from Budenny, ordered that the corridor to the east be kept open to allow a retreat. Only towards midnight on September 17 did Stalin himself authorise withdrawal, but it was far too late by then: there was no corridor to the east, and no escape.

The outcome was catastrophic. Trapped against the 800 m (½ mile) wide Dniepr, Russian infantry and horses wheeled in confusion, herded about like sheep by the oncoming German tanks and constantly harried by the Luftwaffe. Others, dug in, died where they lay, many with Stalin's supposedly inspiring words ringing in their ears through loudspeakers. As one eyewitness wrote: 'There is something diabolical, and at the same time terribly naive, about these soldiers who fight to the death . . . about the final gestures, the stubborn, violent gestures of these men who died so terribly lonely a death on this battlefield, amid the deafening roar of the cannon and the ceaseless braying of the loudspeaker.'

The city of Kiev fell on September 19, and a week later it was all over. The battlefield around the city was a jumble of burned-out trucks, fire-blackened, twisted tanks, enormous mounds of small arms, rifles stacked 10 m (30 ft) high, rows of field guns with their breeches blasted out, and everywhere tangled corpses. The Germans claimed to have captured 655 000 prisoners (one-third of the total Red Army strength at the opening of 'Barbarossa'), 884 armoured vehicles and 3718 guns.

There seemed nothing to stop them. How much longer could the Russians possibly endure such losses? Even as the battle for Kiev ended, Hitler ordered the next great strike – Operation *Taifun* ('Typhoon') to Moscow – and Guderian hastened northwards once more.

FINAL ADVANCE

In the south, Rundstedt was equally determined not to allow the Russians much respite. A quick dash across the 200 km (120 miles) dividing the Dniepr from the Sea of Azov would trap more Russians between Kleist's panzers and Eleventh Army, advancing along the Black Sea coast.

The plan worked perfectly. The panzers attacked on September 30, and a week later they linked up with the Eleventh Army. In the pocket behind them lay 106 000 Russian troops, 212 tanks and 700 guns. After Rundstedt's infantry had finished mopping up, the Eleventh turned back south to the Crimea, pushing the Russians into the fortress-city of Sevastopol and leaving Rundstedt to continue his advance eastwards to Rostov, at the mouth of the Don.

But by now the summer was over. Autumn rains once again turned roads to mud, and there was no heat left in the sun to dry them out. By mid-October the Germans, harassed by partisans and the Red Air Force – reorganised and massively strengthened since June – and slowed by cloying mud, were making less than 3 km (2 miles) a day. Then, outside Rostov, they came up against an ingenious collection of obstacles, mines and fortifications. Baulked there, Rundstedt tried to outflank the defenders with an assault along the coast. The Germans made it on November 20, but only briefly, holding the city for eight days until a Soviet counterattack drove them out again.

Farther north, Rundstedt had at least managed to take the great industrial city of Kharkov on October 24, using two armies of infantry – the Sixth and Seventeenth – in pincer movements to the north and east of the city. But this time there was no great haul of prisoners and weapons; Stalin did not intend to turn Kharkov into another Kiev, and had ordered the city to be abandoned.

Army Group South, its supply lines overstretched, its troops exhausted and with more and more vehicles breaking down, could do no more, but for Hitler it was not enough. When Rundstedt announced his intention to withdraw in the south behind the Mius river, some 65 km (40 miles) west of Rostov, Hitler commanded him to stand fast. Instead the field marshal offered his resignation and the Führer accepted. It made no difference: the withdrawal went ahead anyway; winter now locked the front solid, and attention was concentrated on the immense battles already engulfing the approaches to Moscow.

A German typhoon batters Moscow – then freezes

Hitler thought Moscow was his for the taking. But he had reckoned without his greatest opponents: 'General Winter' and the implacable Russian fighting spirit.

HITLER BOASTED on September 6, 1941: 'Today begins the last – the great – battle of this year.' Kiev had not yet fallen, but he gave the orders for Operation *Taifun* ('Typhoon') – an attack on Moscow that was intended to be as swift and as devastating as the code name he gave it implied.

Fifteen Russian infantry armies – 800 000 men – were in position along Moscow's first line of defence, which protected the approaches to the city. Within it, three other lines ringed the capital (see map, p.122). However, Stalin's troops were ill-equipped and had just 770 tanks and 364 aircraft in support. It appeared that the Russians were at the end of their tether and victory was Germany's for the taking, but Hitler had not reckoned with the treacherous weather that soon threatened to destroy his armies by disabling their transport and cutting off their supplies. It was the mud of autumn and 'General Winter' that were to become the real enemies. And it was survival, not triumph, that was to become the real issue.

Farther west, the Russian armies grouped to form a primary shield of combat troops – a huge front line, 400 km (250 miles) long, behind which was another defensive line. The aggressive Marshal Ivan Koniev commanded West Front (Army Group) in the north, and General Andrei Yeremenko the armies of Bryansk Front in the south. The advancing Germans kept to their well-tried blitzkrieg tactics, as Field Marshal Fedor von Bock's Army Group Centre aimed to knock out the cities of Vyazma and Bryansk by cutting them off in pincer movements by fast-moving tanks, before pursuing the remaining Russians right into Moscow itself.

DEVASTATING ASSAULT

The attack opened in fine autumn weather on October 2. Two days before the main assault, the tanks of General Heinz Guderian's Second Panzer Army (as Panzer Group 2 had been renamed) doubled back from the Ukraine and took Orel, 120 km (75 miles) behind the Russian front line. Their arrival on October 3 so surprised the Russians that the town's trams were still running as the tanks rolled in. Three days later, Guderian's leading tank units emerged from the surrounding forests into Bryansk, 350 km (220 miles) south-west of Moscow. At the same time, the German Second Army attacked from the west, trapping three Soviet armies. Only a few Russians escaped, including a wounded Yeremenko.

To the north, General Hermann Hoth's Third and General Erich Hoepner's Fourth Panzer Armies tore through the Russian lines around Vyazma, isolating that city and trapping another five Soviet armies. Altogether, the two pockets yielded over 663 000 Russian prisoners, plus 1242 tanks and 5412 guns. Almost all Moscow's primary shield, and the defensive line behind it, had been lost. Koniev was blamed for the debacle and demoted. The legendary 'trouble-shooter' General Georgi Zhukov – only ten weeks earlier removed by Stalin as Chief of the General Staff – was brought back to save the capital.

On October 14, Hoth crossed the Volga at Kalinin, cutting the Moscow-Leningrad railway, capturing a bridge over the Volga and establishing himself just 110 km (70 miles) north of Moscow. Panic swept the city itself, now abandoned by many government departments (see box). By the end of the month, Guderian's leading units were approaching the industrial city of Tula, 190 km (120 miles) south of Moscow, ready to enter the capital from the rear.

But the Germans had already tasted stubborn Soviet resistance. On October 10 at Borodino – the key to the city's first line of defence – the Germans faced a horrifying combination of tanks, rockets and burly well-equipped Siberian troops, all backed by minefields, barbed wire and pillboxes. Furious assaults by the 10th Panzer and 2nd SS Panzer Divisions, sometimes fighting hand to hand with spades and rifle-butts, finally opened the way towards the second defensive line that ran through Mozhaisk. By October 30, the Germans had broken through the Mozhaisk Line along its entire length and there were no further combat defences between them and Moscow.

THE ADVANCE BOGS DOWN

Now, however, Mother Russia had a new and powerful ally: the weather. In the last week of October, glorious sunshine gave way to rain and sleet; rivers flooded, roads became knee-deep in mud, and fields turned into quagmires. Tracks and wheels churned the ground into an axle-deep glue as the Germans struggled to bring up supplies. Mud sucked the boots off marching men and mired supply wagons. Trucks by the thousand stuck and stalled for want of fuel, while horses wallowed up to their bellies. Railways were destroyed by retreating Russians and by partisan bands behind the German lines. And this was only the climate's opening skirmish.

It was imperative for Zhukov to stall the Germans until 'General Winter' could unleash the full spectrum of its terrible forces, for the Russians were in little better shape. Just 382 tanks remained to protect Moscow, only half of them in working order. The 4th Armoured Brigade defending Tula, however, had 45 wide-tracked T-34s that could travel nimbly over the sodden terrain, firing their 76.2 mm (3 in) weapons – which could cripple a German panzer with a single shot. Lowering clouds protected Russian railways from German bombers, allowing supplies and reinforcements to be pushed to the front, while German vehicles crowded the slimy, cratered roads, where the Russians defended every junction with pillboxes.

But perhaps the greatest force in Zhukov's favour was the implacable fighting spirit of his soldiers. This had little to do with Communist inspiration. The Russians had for so long been used to suffering that they had little to lose by fighting to the death – particularly if the alternative was likely to be a political commissar's bullet. To the Germans, the Russians' stolid, often suicidal determination had about it something unnervingly primeval. Gradually, the advance slowed to a crawl of 16 km (10 miles) a day, then five, then two – no faster than Napoleon's foot-soldiers in 1812. Guderian's attack on Tula, well defended by T-34s and anti-tank ditches, bogged down in bitter house-to-house fighting.

On the night of 6/7 November, the first frosts hardened the ground, offering the Germans one last chance to get moving. A conference of chiefs of staff at Army Group Centre on November 13 dismissed the idea of digging in for a desolate winter, and supported Bock's view that now was

WEHRMACHT WAGON TRAIN The tanks of Hitler's panzer divisions which sped into Russia in the blitzkrieg of 1942 relied heavily on horse-drawn transport for supplies. When the autumn rains came, the wagons bogged down in mud.

the time to attack – as Hitler himself wanted. Guderian was to take Tula, and loop around beyond Moscow from the south, while other units attacked from the north and west. And so, on November 15, German forces embarked on their final lunge towards Moscow.

Two days later, when Hoepner's V Corps infantry advanced on Klin, 110 km (75 miles) north-west of the city, the Germans were astonished to be confronted by men of the 44th Mongolian Cavalry Division charging towards them over the snow, brandishing sabres. Shells and machine guns turned the charge into a bloody mess of horses and riders. Only 30 of the 2000 horsemen survived – but the unyielding Russian spirit had again made its mark.

One by one, outlying villages fell, and by November 28, Moscow was ringed at a distance of 32 km (20 miles) from the Kremlin. Germans standing at a suburban bus station joked about catching a bus to see Stalin, while on high ground officers peered through field-glasses at buildings in the city centre.

'GENERAL WINTER' STRIKES

But that was as far as they got. The cold at last began to take its toll, and the end that seemed so near slipped out of reach. All too often, the Germans did not have the equipment to survive, let alone fight. Some units had only a quarter of their ammunition supply. The first shipment of coats for the Third Panzer Army provided a single overcoat per tank crew. A food consignment for the Fourth Army consisted of a trainload of frozen wine in broken bottles. One -40^0C (-40^0F) night spent in tight, nail-studded jackboots could cripple a man for life. Machine guns froze, oil turned to sludge, batteries died and engines had to be kept running, draining fuel supplies. In one village, the Germans heated bricks in the stoves and rushed them outside to place them against the locks of their guns.

This was a battle that could not be won. On December 1, Kluge launched a final attack along the Minsk-Moscow highway. On the night of December 5, the attack was called off. Even Guderian was forced to admit defeat. 'We have seriously underestimated the Russians, the extent of the country and the treachery of the climate,' he wrote to his wife. 'This is the revenge of reality.'

THE GOBLIN AT MOSCOW'S GATES

The boundless energy displayed by Hermann Hoth (1895-1971) earned him the nickname 'the Goblin'. It was an energy he applied skilfully in command of Panzer Group 3 (later redesignated Third Panzer Army) during Operation 'Barbarossa', and in the dash to Moscow that took him to within sight of the Soviet capital.

Hoth served in World War I, commanded a division in 1936 and was promoted to general after leading XV Panzer Corps in Poland and France. In 1942 he assumed command of Fourth Panzer Army and led the unsuccessful operation to relieve the Sixth Army beleaguered in Stalingrad. The following year he took part in the battles of Kursk and Kharkov, but on December 10, 1943, Hitler dismissed him for defeatism, after he conducted a fighting withdrawal. After the war he stood trial at Nuremberg for war crimes and was sentenced to 15 years' imprisonment, but served only six.

MUSCOVITES PREPARE TO DEFEND THEIR CITY

As the winter of 1941 approached, Moscow's citizens had no idea that an attack was imminent. Newspapers and the radio directed public attention to Leningrad and the Ukraine. Only in early October, when the Germans were just 100 km (60 miles) from the city, did Russian leaders take any action.

Volunteer civilian units were sent to plug gaps in the front line. A rearguard 11 700 strong of workers' battalions was formed, and 17 000 women stepped in as medical orderlies. Workers and machinery were loaded into railway wagons for the long haul to the hinterlands beyond the Urals, where new factories were being set up out of reach of the Germans. But small plants remained to produce guns, mortars and rifles for Moscow's defenders.

To secure the city, Muscovites were mobilised to build defensive lines – outside the city along the Nara river, and along the inner and outer boulevards. Some 450 000 civilians (many of them women and children) built 100 km (60 miles) of anti-tank ditches and 8000 km (5000 miles) of trenches by mid-November. Often they had to light fires to thaw the ground before they could dig. 'Our backs ached, and at times we could hardly lift the tools,' a survivor recalled later. 'Some, old and exhausted, simply lay down and died.'

As the Germans approached, the city was seized by terror. On October 16, as German planes bombed and strafed, the city all but collapsed. Looters raided empty apartments as tens of thousands stampeded stations to cram aboard the last east-bound trains.

A state of emergency was declared on October 20, and by the end of the month 2 million people had been evacuated, including Government officials and diplomats. To boost morale, Stalin refused to leave the Kremlin and roused his people with a defiant speech at the October Revolution parade on November 7. Moscow was prepared for the worst – but winter made sure the worst never happened.

RED ALERT Imminent disaster threatened Moscow and anti-aircraft gunners took to the rooftops.

9: CLASH OF THE TITANS

After five months of German advances, the most powerful armies on earth met face to face.

Winter saves Moscow

The tidal wave of the German advance had lost momentum when it broke against the outskirts of Moscow. Then the Red Army struck back in two massive counter-attacks. The spring of 1942 brought an exhausted, precarious stalemate.

A SMALL PATROL of German motorcyclists, members of the 62nd Panzer Engineer Battalion, probed forward on December 2, 1941, along the road leading into Moscow from the north. They reached Khimki, some 8 km (5 miles) from the outskirts of the city and a mere 23 km (15 miles) from the Kremlin. After riding around the town, terrifying the locals, but without a shot being fired, the motorcyclists sped back to their base. That was the closest any of Hitler's troops came to Stalin's lair. Thereafter, the German assault ground to a halt, stopped by Russia's two great assets – 'General Winter' and an almost endless supply of manpower.

Already, the snow had arrived. Soon, temperatures dropped to −40°C (−40°F), and out in the open any wind would chill exposed skin well below that. Guns refused to fire, engines would not start and men froze. The Germans could not bring forward enough winter clothing because of a critical shortage of rail transport.

One soldier ironically recorded using German leaflets intended for the Russian troops to pad his boots: 'I remember trying for a week to keep warm on a proclamation that "Surrender is the only sane and sensible course".' The only answer was to pile on more clothes and never take them off, a sure recipe for disease and infestation.

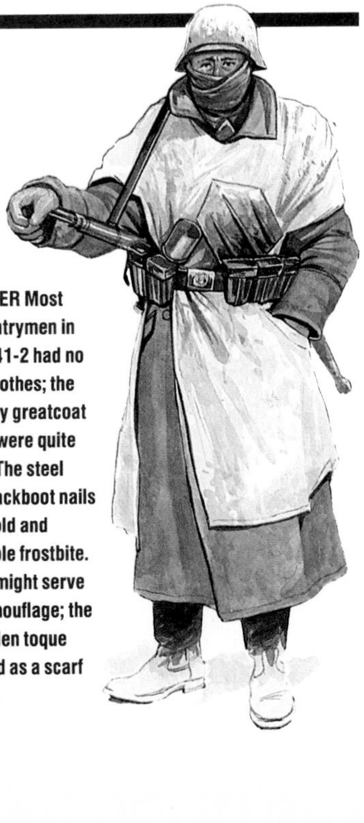

COLD INVADER Most German infantrymen in Russia in 1941-2 had no real winter clothes; the ordinary army greatcoat and uniform were quite inadequate. The steel helmet and jackboot nails conducted cold and caused terrible frostbite. Torn sheets might serve for snow camouflage; the tubular woollen toque could be used as a scarf or balaclava.

Meanwhile, the Russians had been preparing. There was no alternative to counterattack, if Moscow was to be saved. Besides, as General Georgi Zhukov, Commander in Chief of the Red Army's West Front (Army Group), assured Stalin: 'The Germans are suffering from physical and mental exhaustion.'

He had the men for an attack. Reinforcements had come from eastern Siberia, where Stalin had been nervously expecting a further Japanese attack from its puppet state of Manchukuo (Manchuria). But the top Soviet agent in Tokyo, Richard Sorge, had sent news that the Japanese were preparing for war against the United States and had no intention of taking action against the Soviet Union. So well-equipped, winter-trained troops – more than 30 divisions in all – were transported west along the Trans-Siberian Railway to join the able-bodied men conscripted into the Red Army from cities and rural areas, from factories and fields. By early December, Zhukov had 578 000 men in position near Moscow.

The Russians knew the dangers of their own climate. A Russian lieutenant recorded in his diary: ' "You know, Comrade Lieutenant," one of my men said to me yesterday, "when one gets really cold one becomes indifferent to freezing to death or being shot. One only has one wish – to die as quickly as possible." That is the exact truth. The cold drains the men of the will to fight.' Those from Siberia, in particular, were well prepared for the conditions. In their white winter gear and thick boots, they could lie out in the open for hours or days; their snow houses were lined with branches and roofed with tarpaulins.

ATTACK AND ENCIRCLE

Zhukov's plan for Moscow's salvation was simple. The Germans had two vulnerable salients jutting into the Soviet line north and south of the city, the remnants of their earlier attempt to encircle the city. Soviet troops would pinch these out, and then launch a more general encirclement of the German Army Group Centre.

On December 5 and 6, the Russians attacked along a 960 km (600 mile) front stretching from its northern point only 160 km (100 miles) from Leningrad to Kursk, 400 km (250 miles) south of the capital (see map, p. 122). Within days, it was clear that the attacks were achieving extraordinary successes, mainly because of the tremendous 'do-or-die' spirit of the Russian soldiers. Sacrifices were sometimes quite deliberate. Zhukov's commanders made widespread use of men in dark clothing from punishment battalions to lead white-camouflaged troops into battle in order to draw German fire.

All along the front, German armies were fragmented into thousands of isolated units. If they had food, they were short of fuel to cook by. Without fuel, they had to saw at deep-frozen butter and hack with axes at the bodies of horses. Of the 113 000 frostbite cases, over 14 000 needed amputation. The medal struck later for those who took part in this campaign was known in the ranks as the 'Order of the Frozen Meat'.

On December 8, Hitler accepted the need to call off the German offensive against Moscow, and nine days later agreed to a straightening of the line – a euphemism for retreat. Yet when General Heinz Guderian, commander of Second Panzer Army facing the southern part of Zhukov's attack, flew to East Prussia to describe the conditions and insist on further withdrawal, Hitler ranted at him that the troops must dig in.

But by the end of December the Russians had recaptured virtually all the territory lost since October. Guderian was fired on December 24. He was not the only one to go. Hitler had begun by dismissing his overall commander in chief, Field Marshal Walther von Brauchitsch, himself assuming direct command of the German Army on December 19. Two field marshals, Wilhelm Ritter von Leeb (commander of Army Group North) and Fedor von Bock (Army Group Centre), were relieved (the latter because of ill-health) and another, Gerd von Rundstedt (Army Group South), was transferred to the west. A total of 35 other corps and division commanders were removed over a period of five days.

Zhukov had not only saved Moscow, but had

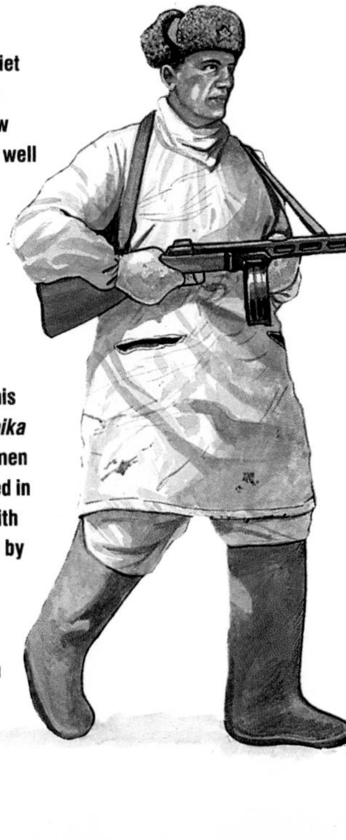

SNUG SIBERIAN Soviet troops switched from Siberia to the Moscow front were especially well equipped against the weather. This man wears *valenki* (boots of compressed felt) and a 1940 issue fur cap. He has a white cotton camouflage oversuit and under this would wear a *telogreika* – a quilted suit. The men from Siberia sheltered in snow houses lined with branches and topped by tarpaulin. Weapons were winterised with low-temperature oil. This man has a PPSh submachine gun.

driven the enemy back 80 km (50 miles) out of the two salients north and south of the capital. The myth of German invincibility had been shattered.

Early in the New Year, determined to follow up these initial successes, Stalin asserted: 'Now is the best moment to launch a general offensive.' Despite Zhukov's protest that such an ambitious plan would spread Soviet forces too thinly, he ordered an all-out attack along a 1600 km (1000 mile) front from Lake Ladoga to the Black Sea.

But the December assaults had taken a tremendous toll. The five armies of General Ivan Koniev's Kalinin Front, in the sector north of Zhukov, for instance, had only some 35 tanks left, and its rifle divisions were down to little more than 3000 men each rather than their full strength of 8000. In Zhukov's West Front, armoured brigades scarcely numbered 20 tanks each, and few artillery regiments had more than a dozen guns.

On the other hand, by retreating, the Germans had been able to regroup nearer to established bases. In their advance the previous year, they had turned major towns – Demyansk, Rzhev, Vyazma, Bryansk, Orel and Kursk – into fortress-towns, 'hedgehogs' bristling with fortifications. In the next Russian assault, which opened on January 7, 1942, not one of these towns fell. Now it was the Germans who occupied secure positions and the Russians who were out in the cold, far from their bases, on a vastly extended front.

THE ATTACKS FALTER

In the north, although the Russians failed to break through to Leningrad, they did for a while look close to victory at Demyansk. There, halfway between Moscow and Leningrad, they closed around the German II Corps – part of Sixteenth Army – almost trapping its 96 000 men. The

ZHUKOV – PEASANT WITH A SCHOLAR'S BRAIN

Georgi Zhukov (1896-1974), the hero of Moscow's defence, served as a cavalry NCO in the tsar's forces and later joined the Red Army. As a lieutenant general in 1939 he led the defeat of the Japanese at Nomonhan in Mongolia.

In January 1941 he became Stalin's Chief of General Staff. He lost his post when he advocated a withdrawal from Kiev in July. After briefly rallying forces in besieged Leningrad, he was brought back to save Moscow, where he inflicted the first major reverse on the Germans. Promoted to the rank of marshal and appointed Deputy Supreme Commander, he organised the attack that relieved Stalingrad and destroyed Hitler's Sixth Army. Further successes culminated in the capture of Berlin in May 1945.

Zhukov – known as *Zhuk* ('the Beetle') – had all the coarseness and brutality of his peasant background. But he was a careful student of military history and learned rapidly from experience. He served in 1955-7 as Minister of Defence.

MARCH OF DEFEAT German infantrymen – victims of 'General Winter' – retreat across the open plains near Moscow, their despair shown in their frozen faces (inset). A hardy dog – perhaps a lucky dog by the men's standards – watches them pass by.

attack faltered, however, when the Luftwaffe began an airlift that enabled II Corps to hold out. Over the next ten weeks up to 150 flights a day ferried in 65 000 tonnes of supplies and lifted out 34 500 wounded. The men in the Demyansk pocket were relieved in the last week of April.

In the central sector due west of Moscow, the most bitterly contested area was around Vyazma, which lay in German-held territory some 225 km (140 miles) from the capital. This area, which controlled the main road and rail links from Moscow to Smolensk and the Belorussian capital Minsk, was held by Army Group Centre. Stalin planned a pincer movement to trap the whole group. Four armies, anchored by General Mikhail Yefremov's Thirty-Third, drove due west towards Vyazma, while the Twenty-Ninth and Thirty-Ninth Armies swept down from the north to trap the Fourth Panzer and Ninth Armies. Meanwhile, other Soviet armies carried out similar movements farther to the north and south.

At first the advance there, as elsewhere, went well, before stalling in battles that sent the front line undulating back and forth. By January 27, the Soviet Twenty-Ninth Army had almost reached the Minsk-Smolensk-Moscow road, trapping General Walther Model's Ninth Army in a tongue of territory 80 km (50 miles) across and 200 km (125 miles long). Model counterattacked instantly, turning the tables on the Twenty-Ninth and killing 27 000 men.

In early February, Yefremov reached the outskirts of Vyazma, where he was to be joined by other Russian units. On February 18-22, some 7000 paratroops were dropped behind enemy lines south of Vyazma to link up with groups of partisans already operating in the area and disrupt German communications. The drop was a disaster. The Germans killed most of the men.

As the offensive ran out of steam, Stalin began to juggle commanders and armies in an attempt to keep the action going. On the Moscow front, he switched the First Shock Army and Sixteenth Army to the northern and southern flanks, thus weakening the thrust of Maj General Andrei Vlasov's Twentieth Army just north of Vyazma.

When Zhukov objected to the moves, saying that Stalin was prejudicing the attack on Vyazma, Stalin retorted: 'Don't protest. You have plenty of troops – just count them.'

TO THE GATES AND BACK The German 1941 offensive took them within sight of Stalin's capital – but the weather and a massive counterattack pushed them back.

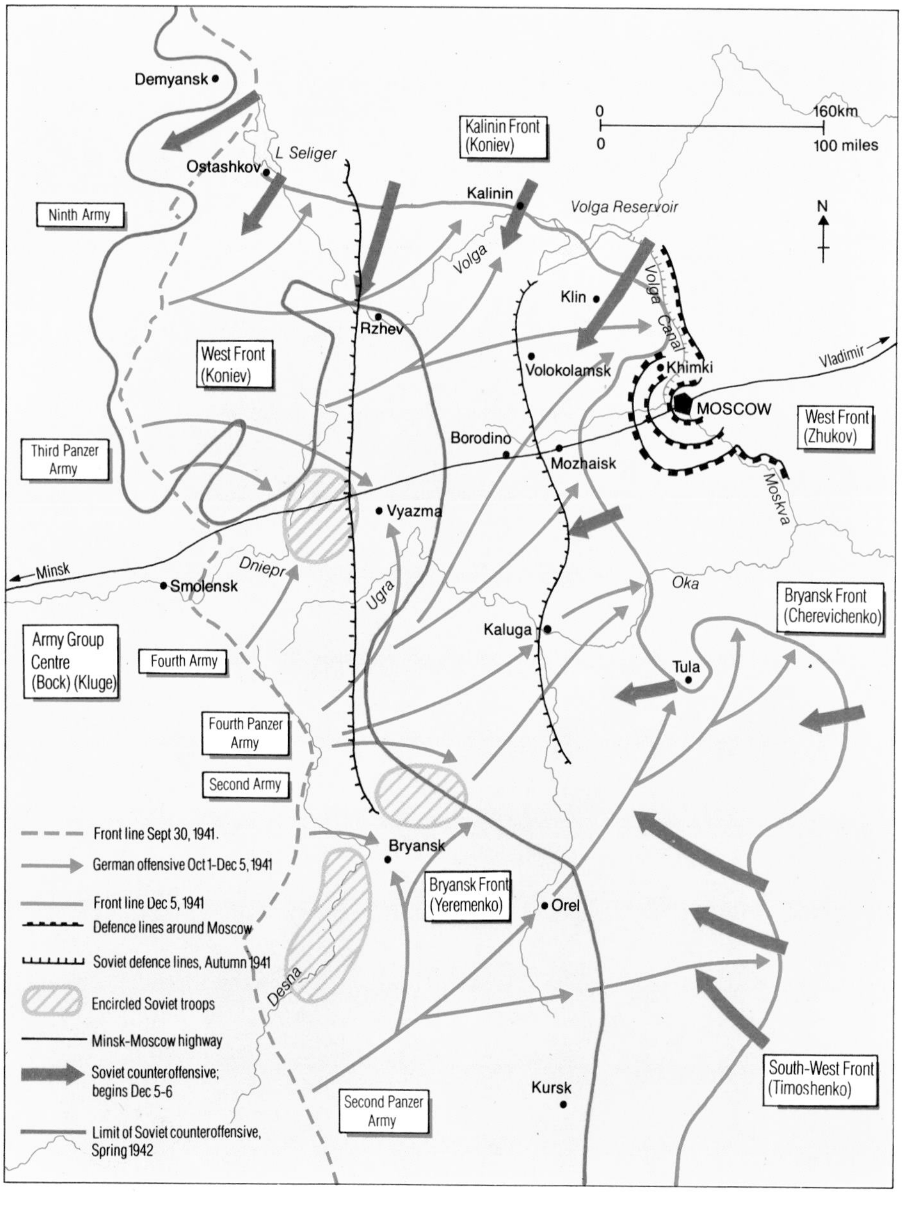

SHORT OF SUPPLIES

But Zhukov – since February 1 put in overall command of Kalinin and Bryansk Fronts as well as his own West Front – did not have enough of anything to ensure further advances. He complained that lack of artillery shells – he never received even one-third of what had been promised – 'makes it impossible to conduct the artillery offensive'. German strongpoints could not be destroyed before Russian attacks began.

By early March the Germans had established a firm defensive line from Rzhev in the north, through Vyazma to Orel in the south. The Soviet thrusts petered out. Yefremov never did manage to take Vyazma. He found himself cut off, and it was all he could do to prevent his own army's annihilation. In March, severely wounded and facing capture, he shot himself.

The first Russian counteroffensive of the war had not fulfilled Stalin's ambitions, yet it was by no means a failure. It had cost the Germans over 500 000 dead and wounded, 1300 tanks, 2500 guns and 15 000 vehicles. Moscow had been saved, and 11 000 other Russian towns and villages liberated. The front had been pushed back between 145 and 290 km (90 and 180 miles).

Moreover, the Russian partisans, tucked into forest lairs behind enemy lines, had meanwhile become a hardened force. Large bands, sometimes under regular Red Army officers, continually attacked isolated posts and lines of communication. They were a thorn in the Wehrmacht's side for the rest of the war.

THE AVENGERS 'Beat the enemy mercilessly', urges a poster rallying Russians to the partisans, who harried the Germans throughout the war. In winter, men on skis often attacked German supply and troop trains.

Russia's agony at Kharkov

A Soviet counterattack near Izyum early in 1942 drove a wedge into German-held territory south of Kharkov. As in the north, the Germans held the advance – but then went on to deal the Russians a stunning blow.

TANK MAN Khaki overalls worn over the uniform was the working dress of the Soviet tank major, who was also armed with a 7.62 mm Tokarev automatic pistol. A black cloth helmet later replaced the leather padded helmet worn until 1942. Although Russian tanks outnumbered the German panzers in 1941, it was not until 1943 that they were organised into tank brigades. These were combined into tank corps, consisting of three brigades with a motorised rifle brigade and support units, and operated much in the same way as German panzer divisions.

IN THE WINTER of 1941-2, while huge battles raged around Moscow, Soviet commanders in the south were focusing their attention on Kharkov. This great industrial city, the USSR's fourth largest, lay some 400 km (250 miles) east of Kiev. It had been captured by Hitler's troops the previous October, and Germany's occupation of the Ukraine depended on holding it.

Marshal Semyon Timoshenko, commander of the Red Army's South-West Front (Army Group), planned a classic pincer movement to regain Kharkov. The Russian Sixth Army would drive westward past the small provincial town of Izyum, on the Donets river 115 km (70 miles) south-east of Kharkov, and then wheel north. Meanwhile Thirty-Eighth Army would head west across the Donets farther to the north. The two prongs would embrace and reclaim the city. (For locations, see map, p. 251.)

On January 18, 1942, the Russians struck. Though Thirty-Eighth Army – the northern arm of the pincer – could force its way forward only about 5 km (3 miles), the Sixth had immediate success, advancing nearly 32 km (20 miles) in four days. 'We sped forward,' one Russian wrote exultantly, 'slowed only by the terrain.'

But the speed of that advance was deceptive. On either side of Izyum, two towns – Balakleya and Slavyansk – were held fast by German and Austrian infantry. The strength and determination of their resistance astonished the Russians. In 11 days of fighting for one small village, Cherkasskoye, the 1000 German defenders lost half their number, killing 1100 of the enemy before the Russians finally won.

Slowly, in temperatures down to −50°C (−58°F), Timoshenko's men secured the isolated villages and farms. By the end of January, when the Germans finally stemmed the tide, the Russians were left holding a vulnerable pocket 88 km (55 miles) deep by 110 km (70 miles) wide on the west bank of the Donets south of Kharkov. But German forces firmly held the territory on either side of the salient.

SECOND DRIVE

Kharkov remained Stalin's primary objective. In April 1942 – in spring sunshine and with the ground now dried and firm after the thaw – he ordered Timoshenko to try again. In another pincer movement, Sixth Army would strike north from the salient to Kharkov, while the Twenty-Eighth and Thirty-Eighth attacked from the north-east and south-east. In all, the attacking forces totalled 640 000 men and 1200 tanks.

Simultaneously, however, the Germans under Field Marshal Fedor von Bock were looking to eliminate the Izyum salient. In an operation code-named 'Fridericus', German armies – Sixth to the north, Seventeenth and First Panzer to the south – would drive in close to the river and nip the salient at its root. Their strength was almost exactly equal to that of the Russians.

It was Timoshenko who made the first move, on May 12, six days before Bock's planned attack. Soviet troops broke through the German defences north and south of Kharkov. But already the Germans were prepared for action – not a counterattack, but their own assault. One Russian at least saw the danger – Timoshenko's bouncy political commissar, Nikita Khrushchev, who was all for calling off the advance on Kharkov to contain this new threat. But when he telephoned Moscow for permission, Stalin refused even to speak to him. Georgi Malenkov, one of Stalin's aides, relayed the leader's response. 'Stalin ordered, "Leave things as they are",' wrote Khrushchev later. 'And what was the result? The worst one could expect.'

SURROUNDED

There was only one thing Bock could do: launch at least part of Operation 'Fridericus' anyway, and hope that the assault would force the Russians away from Kharkov. On May 17, General Ewald von Kleist's First Panzer Army drove up into the Soviet Ninth Army, with immediate success. It routed the Russians and had precisely the effect Bock intended: the Soviet forces, within sight of Kharkov, were ordered to break off, turn south and crush the German advance. Too late. Already the damage was beyond repair. On May 23, Kleist's panzers and the German Sixth Army met across the base of the salient. The Russian Sixth and Fifty-Seventh armies were trapped.

The only safety for the trapped Russians lay in a retreat eastwards across the Donets. That retreat was horrific. Arms linked, primed with vodka, yelling 'Urra! Urra!', lines of Russians threw themselves against chattering German machine guns, bludgeoning and bayoneting in their attempts to reach safety. In their desperation, they even made use of dogs trained to run beneath enemy vehicles. Strapped to their backs the dogs carried explosive charges primed with trigger rods. When they made contact, the charges exploded, blowing both dog and target to smithereens. But German infantrymen soon learned to shoot dogs on sight, and this gruesome expedient achieved little.

In all, some 70 000 Russians were killed – among them three generals. Another 200 000 were captured, and the Russians lost almost all their armour. Total German losses were 20 000. For the Russians it was a horrifying reversal; for the Germans, a famous victory. Hitler was free to launch his next big offensive south and east towards Stalingrad and into the Caucasus.

DREADNOUGHT OF THE RUSSIAN PLAINS Even Germany's tank expert Heinz Guderian grudgingly admitted that Russia's 32 tonne T-34 was 'the best tank in the world'. Armed with a 76.2 mm cannon and two machine guns, it had a top speed of 50 km/h (32 mph) and could cover 300 km (185 miles) without refuelling. Its wide tracks kept it going over the mud and snow that often bogged down the German panzers.

Sevastopol's 247 day siege

For eight months of 1941-2, the Crimean port of Sevastopol – home of the Soviet Black Sea fleet – withstood besieging German forces. Its heroic defenders – seamen as well as soldiers – tied down an entire German army.

A FORMIDABLE SIGHT confronted the troops of General Erich von Manstein's Eleventh Army besieging Sevastopol in late 1941. A rock of a city at the south-western tip of the Crimea, Sevastopol is a natural fortress – a mass of steep cliffs backed by mountainous peaks – and by 1941 it had been reinforced by three heavily fortified lines. The first was a 3 km (2 mile) deep zigzag of trenches, anti-tank obstacles and mines. The second was a line of heavy fortifications, strengthened in the south by a third section. This was the Zapun Line, a maze of mortar pits, machine-gun posts and artillery emplacements. Behind these defences, a dozen massive concrete bunkers guarded the port city's northern approaches. In command was Vice Admiral Filip Oktyabrskii.

No wonder that when German troops swept into the Crimea in October 1941, Sevastopol was the one part of the peninsula that they failed to take. It had withstood a siege for 11 months during the Crimean War in 1854-5, and was ready to do so again. Even so, a second German attack in December 1941 pushed back the defenders – who had been reinforced in late October by troops evacuated across the Black Sea from Odessa – to within 8 km (5 miles) of the city's centre. That winter, Sevastopol was battered by ceaseless artillery barrages and bombing raids. To escape the pounding, most of the inhabitants moved into underground shelters and caves just outside the city, but within the defensive lines.

CAPTURING KERCH

Help seemed briefly at hand in the last days of December, when strong Soviet forces from the Caucasus managed to land and establish a beach-head near Kerch on the German-held eastern tip of the Crimean peninsula. But severe winter weather, as well as German counter-attacks, prevented Lt General D.T. Kozlov's newly created Crimean Front from moving westwards to relieve Sevastopol. In April, Kozlov attempted another drive west from his Kerch stronghold, but ran into newly reinforced units of Manstein's Eleventh Army and stopped dead.

By now Manstein was anxious to eliminate the Russians at Kerch, then Sevastopol, in time to release his troops to take part in the German spring advance into the Caucasus. But to assault the well-entrenched Kerch positions head-on would spell disaster. So Manstein resorted to cunning. On May 8, three German divisions with dive-bomber support pierced the outer defences of the Kerch peninsula – a huge water-filled ditch 3 m (16 ft) deep and 10 m (33 ft) wide. The assault was a feint. The real attack came from German assault boats driving straight into the ditch from the south.

Soviet forces staged a desperate Dunkirk-style retreat across the Kerch Strait, separating the Crimea from the Caucasus to the east, but by May 17 more than 170 000 Russians had been captured, along with 250 tanks and 1100 artillery pieces. An angry Stalin sacked Kozlov.

In Sevastopol, the citizens had emerged from their caves, hoping that relief was near. They now returned to their refuges, fearing the worst. They could no longer expect outside help. Although the defenders numbered more than 100 000 fighting men with 600 guns, they had only 38 tanks and 55 aircraft. Manstein, on the other hand, had twice as many men supported by 600 aircraft. Offshore, the Germans also had enough fast vessels, operating from captured Crimean bases, to harass Russian ships trying to supply Sevastopol.

FINAL ASSAULT

On June 2, the Germans brought up their heaviest artillery, including the railway-mounted 800 mm (31.5 in) 'Dora', one of the largest guns ever built, which could lob 5 tonne shells more than 45 km (28 miles) or 7 tonners 38 km (23½ miles). For the next five days, explosive and incendiary shells rained down on the city, killing thousands.

Then, on the morning of June 7, a wave of German and Romanian troops attacked the outer line of defence from the north and south-east. It took them two days to reach the first of the forts. To penetrate the most threatening – nicknamed 'Maxim Gorky I' by the Germans – the attackers used Röchling bombs, 1 tonne shells that burrowed into rock or concrete before exploding. The shells cracked open the fort like a nut, but even then German infantry had to fight for every metre of its labyrinthine passages.

By June 20 the northern forts had fallen. Only the 1 km (little more than ½ mile) wide Sevastopol Bay lay between them and Sevastopol proper on the bay's southern shore. East of the city rose an 800 metre (½ mile) long stretch of cliffs, into which was dug an arms factory doubling as a haven for wounded and refugees. Even as the Germans attacked, however, the whole cliff exploded, burying thousands of people. Rather than surrender, several groups of Russians had blown themselves up. The Soviet Navy, meanwhile, did its best to help the defenders. Warships braved the German blockade to bring in some 3000 reinforcements, and submarines delivered 4000 tonnes of supplies and carried off the wounded.

But with the cliffs to its east taken, Sevastopol could not hold on for long. On July 1, German artillery started bombarding the inner city, forcing the Russian defenders back to the very tip of the peninsula, Cape Khersones. Submarines evacuated the Russian leaders, leaving the rest to their fate. One officer was told by his superior: 'We trust you to die here. The wounded are being withdrawn to Khersones. Cover them – until the last man, the last metre, the last breath.'

On July 3, 1942, the last of the Russians surrendered. They had been reinforced during the course of the siege and lost tens of thousands dead and wounded. Almost 100 000 went into captivity. Sevastopol had endured for 247 days, battered into ruins by over 46 000 tonnes of shells. It was a heroic defeat, for the defenders had kept the whole German Eleventh Army occupied.

HIVE OF INDUSTRY In the caves, cellars and tunnels that honeycombed Sevastopol, the besieged citizens set up factories to manufacture the shells and mortars that kept the defenders fighting.

Into the Caucasus – but Hitler's 'genius' begins to crack

In the summer of 1942, Hitler launched a massive drive to the south and east – Operation *Blau* – intended to seize Russia's oil and wheat. His armies thrust deep into the Caucasus. But he had made a fatal error.

DAWN IN SOUTHERN RUSSIA on June 28, 1942, was heavy, with clouds threatening a rainstorm for the Soviet troops dug into the grasslands east of the city of Kursk. No rainstorm came. Instead, with a din like a thousand thunderclaps, German artillery bombarded the Russian lines. Then, on either side of Kursk, hordes of Germans burst through the dazed Russians.

One Russian army – the Fortieth – took the full impact of General Hermann Hoth's Fourth Panzer Army, and broke within 48 hours. Three others reeled back in disarray. Amid clouds of dust raised by advancing German tanks and the billowing smoke of burning buildings, they sought meagre cover in shallow hollows and scattered farms. There was nothing the Russians could do to stem the advance. 'They fire their guns like madmen,' wrote one exhilarated German sergeant, 'but they don't hurt us!'

Ahead lay the immediate German objective: the industrial town of Voronezh, strategically placed on the Don river, controlling road, rail and river traffic into central Russia from the west and south. Farther south lay the parts of the Ukraine not already in German hands, open for the taking. Beyond that again lay the oil-rich Caucasus, Hitler's prime target in this offensive.

OPTIMISTIC LEADERS

Both sides had had weeks to prepare for action. Earlier, in the spring of 1942 at the end of the Red Army's winter offensive, the combatant armies had paused in a respite forced upon them by exhaustion and the thick, clinging mud of the spring thaw. The two leaders used the break to devote themselves to longer-term plans.

By then, Stalin had recovered from the shock of 'Barbarossa' and was positively buoyant. In Moscow talks with the British Foreign Secretary, Anthony Eden, he said he was convinced the Germans would be incapable of a spring offensive. In March he had himself planned offensives in three areas: Leningrad, Kharkov and Sevastopol. Despite failures in all three attacks, he still asserted that the Fascists had reached their limit, while the Red Army, its strength growing, would soon begin operations to seize the initiative from the Germans.

Hitler was equally optimistic. True, his initial objectives in the USSR had not been achieved. But his army had survived the bitter winter – the coldest of the century – with its battle line intact, holding the cities of Rzhev, Vitebsk, Vyazma, Smolensk, Bryansk, Orel, Kursk and Kharkov against all the fury of the Red Army, whose assaults had been repulsed. Now he could finish off the USSR by using the same areas as springboards for a further advance.

The optimism of the two leaders was not reflected in the mood of their troops. The exhausted Red Army soldiers had fought for months on the poorest of rations. They had seen the draught horses that pulled the guns dying for lack of fodder and guns falling silent for want of ammunition. Now they had lost heart, and foresaw a German summer offensive with resigned pessimism.

The German soldiers were hardly less disheartened. Those at the front knew that units were under strength. Harsh experience had taught them that the Russian Army was much stronger, much better armed and had more reserves than anyone had guessed. Yet they believed they had superior military ability.

OKW – the German High Command – realistically counted only eight divisions out of 160 in the field as fit for a full offensive; 48 could take limited action; 73 were suitable only for defence; 29 were so badly depleted they would not even be able to defend themselves for long; and two were incapable of any action at all. Altogether, the Wehrmacht and Waffen-SS were short of half a million men. The Chief of the General Staff, General Franz Halder, advised against a major summer campaign in the south. He said the army should instead build for an all-out attack in 1943.

PLANNING FOR *BLAU*

To any leader lacking Hitler's messianic self-confidence, such arguments might have meant something. He, however, knew what he wanted: a summer campaign to seize the oil of the Caucasus, the grain of the Ukraine, and the industrial output of the Don. 'My generals know nothing of economic warfare', he said, dismissing Halder's proposals out of hand.

Having himself assumed supreme command of the German Army in December 1941, he was determined to assert his authority by imposing his

BLUE OFFENSIVE Early success carried Hitler's armies through Voronezh and across the Don. A concentrated attack towards Stalingrad could have driven the Red Army from the city. Instead Hitler dispersed his forces and strung them out too far in a hasty bid to grab the whole oil region.

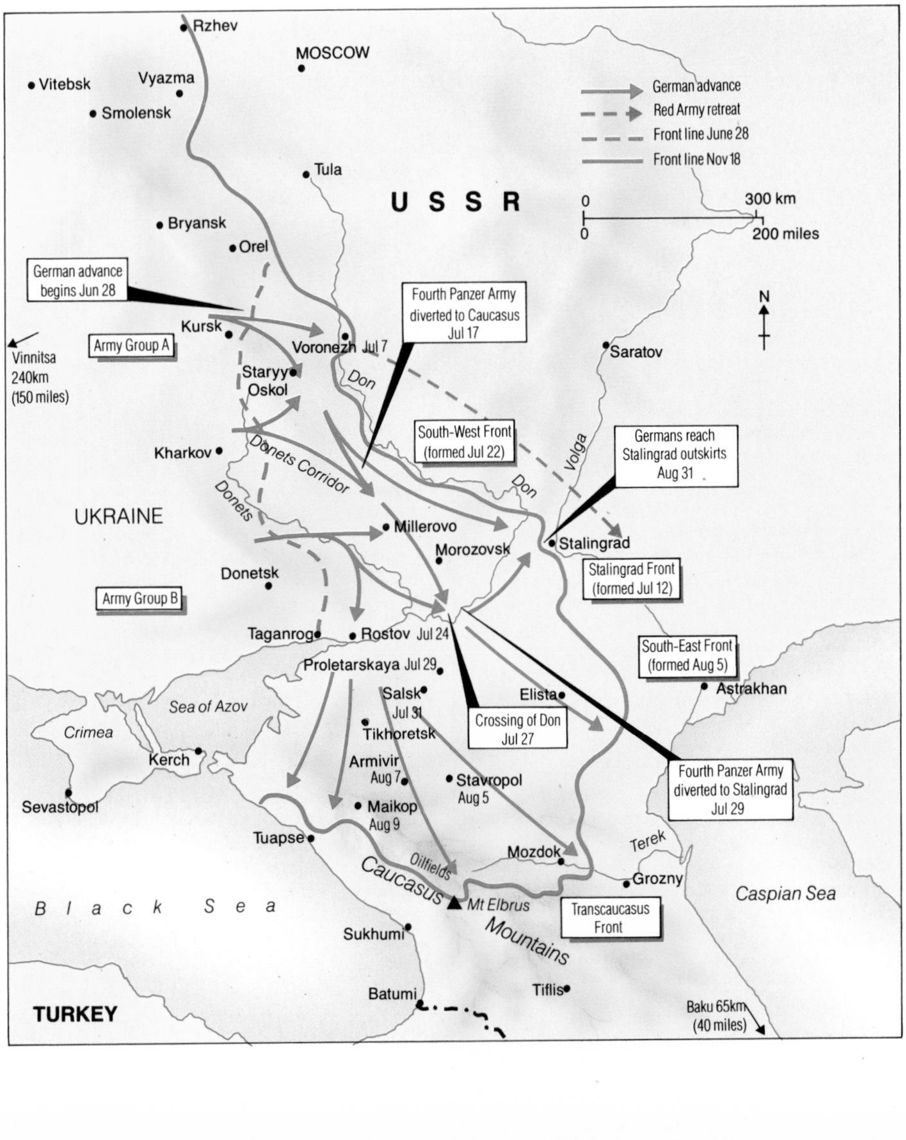

own battle plans. He did so in Führer Directive No 41 of April 5, 1942 – one of the war's most crucial strategic plans.

Hitler was prudent enough to realise that his three army groups on the Eastern Front could not all attack at once. In an offensive he code-named Operation *Blau* ('Blue'), he decided to concentrate on the south, to win the economic prizes.

The Führer proposed a two-pronged offensive, flinging one arm eastwards towards the Stalingrad area (not the city itself – that was a later development) to destroy Soviet forces between the Don and Volga rivers, and then a second down into the Caucasus. He ignored the advice of his strategists that the two prongs would be too far apart to support each other and asserted they would split the Soviet forces, which would thus be unable to stop either thrust.

Hitler laid out his incredibly detailed plan for a series of four blows – first down the west bank of the Don, next farther west, and then towards Stalingrad to protect the final strike into the Caucasus. To realise this grand scheme, Hitler ordered a huge mobilisation programme – transfers from rear echelons to the front, 51 more divisions from Germany's allies, plus units from Army Groups Centre and North. In the end, Field Marshal Fedor von Bock's Army Group South contained almost half of all Germany's Eastern Front forces – nine of the 19 panzer divisions, four of the ten motorised divisions, and 93 of the 189 infantry divisions.

It was a huge and ambitious build-up. Even Halder was won over; he saw German forces sweeping beyond the Caucasus into Iraq and Iran and linking up with Rommel's Afrika Korps.

Both Hitler and Stalin were, however, living in something of a dream world. Hitler refused to accept figures indicating the strength of Russian military forces. Stalin was convinced that Moscow was Hitler's target, and he was blind to all else (see box, *The strange case of the Reichel papers*).

BRILLIANT ATTACK

After *Blau*'s dramatically successful opening on June 28, German troops drove fast towards the Don in a classic armoured thrust. Two days later, Sixth Army headed north in a pincer movement to Voronezh. Only in the second week of July, when no offensive against Moscow had materialised, did Stalin take defensive action. By that time, the armies of Marshal Semyon Timoshenko's South-West Front (Army Group) were in disarray. Reluctantly, Stalin told Timoshenko to pull back into defensive positions on the Don bend, if that was the only way to escape encirclement, but then to stand firm at the Volga. When units of Sixth Army duly linked up with Fourth Panzer Army, sealing a large pocket of territory around Staryy Oskol, south-east of Kursk, they found that they had trapped hardly any Russians.

Voronezh played a key role in the Russian retreat. The rapid German advance established a bridgehead across the Don there. In one dramatic incident, the Russians attempted to dynamite the bridge over which they had been retreating. A German sergeant waded through the chin-high water and snatched the burning fuse away moments before it set off the 55 kg (120 lb) charge. Once across, however, the Germans found Voronezh crammed full of Soviet troops. The Germans wavered. Should they attack the city, or bypass it and cut off the other retreating Russians? Hitler changed his mind several times before authorising the attack. It took the Germans almost two weeks to capture the city – time enough for the Russians to retreat in good order.

Slowly, Timoshenko's men hauled back to the narrow corridor of land between the Don and Volga. Stalingrad itself (now Volgograd) was to be held at all costs. A new Stalingrad Front was established, with three new armies – Sixty-Second, Sixty-Third and Sixty-Fourth. Initially the front was given to Marshal Timoshenko, but he did not last long. Within two weeks, he was replaced by General V.N. Gordov.

The Germans continued to advance. They took Millerovo, controlling the railway southwards from Voronezh. Rostov, the major industrial complex at the mouth of the Don, fell by July 24 after heavy street fighting.

CHANGE OF PLAN

Hitler, unaware of Stalin's orders not to give more ground, declared he was on his way to a great victory. 'The Russians are in full flight! They're finished! They're reeling from the blows we have dealt them!' In fact, his assessment was merely wishful thinking. At both Millerovo and Rostov, the Germans captured few prisoners and not much equipment. The Russians were not broken, but withdrawing to safety.

The Führer's belief that *Blau* was as good as won – which Halder found 'grotesque' – led him to make disastrous changes of plan. He transferred five divisions of Field Marshal Erich von Manstein's Eleventh Army from the Crimea (where they had just captured Sevastopol) to Leningrad. He also moved two crack divisions – the SS Panzer 'Leibstandarte' and the 'Grossdeutschland' Motorised Infantry – to France, arguing that an Allied invasion there was imminent. The moves drastically reduced German strength in the southern part of the Eastern Front.

Hitler also extended the scope of the advance into the Caucasus. Originally, the German objective had been limited to the taking of the oil town of Maikop in the west. Now he wanted to push forward two prongs to encompass the whole oil-bearing region, from the Black Sea port of Batumi to Baku on the Caspian Sea.

In addition, Hoth's Fourth Panzer Army, originally part of the dash towards Stalingrad with Sixth Army, was ordered south 350 km (220 miles) to fight off Russian resistance at the Don. This move slowed Sixth Army's advance on Stalingrad, with disastrous consequences.

As it happened, by the time General Ewald von Kleist's First Panzer Army reached the Don east of Rostov, there were virtually no Russians defending the river. Those who had not been trapped in Rostov were already withdrawing eastwards. The two German forces met in mid-July to form a massive sledgehammer, but with nothing to crush. As Kleist commented later: 'Fourth Panzer Army could have taken Stalingrad without a fight at the end of July, but it was diverted to help me in crossing the Don. I did not need its aid, and it simply got in the way.'

Then, just as the first of Hoth's panzers crossed the Don on July 29, Hitler changed the orders again, sending Hoth back towards Stalingrad.

Kleist, once across the river, accelerated

THE STRANGE CASE OF THE REICHEL PAPERS

Shortly before Operation *Blau* was launched, Hitler's plans were revealed to Stalin – but prejudice led Stalin to ignore the evidence.

Eleven days before the German attack, the commander of XL Panzer Corps, General Georg Stumme, briefed his three divisional commanders. When asked for a written summary, the genial Stumme flouted Hitler's orders and provided one. It made abundantly clear the intention to attack the Ukraine and the Caucasus, not – as Stalin asserted – Moscow.

Two days later, Stumme was entertaining fellow officers at his headquarters in Kharkov when he received disturbing news. The chief of operations of 23rd Panzer Division, a Major Reichel, had taken off that afternoon on a reconnaissance flight over the division's deployment area, taking Stumme's summary and maps with him. He had not returned.

Within an hour, news came that Reichel's Fieseler Storch light plane had been seen landing at Nezhegol, close to Russian lines. The next morning a German patrol found the aircraft, empty, with no documents aboard. It had a bullet-hole in the fuel tank. Nearby were two fresh graves. Presumably the Russians had Reichel's papers.

They had. They knew the German order of battle and where the Germans would strike first. Yet when Stalin was shown the plans, he simply dismissed them out of hand as 'planted evidence'.

Stumme's report of the loss caused consternation. Should the starting plans for *Blau* be altered? In the end, Hitler decided that it was too late to change things. Stumme was court-martialled and imprisoned – but returned to favour. Dispatched to North Africa, he took over command of Axis forces from Rommel in September 1942 – only to die of a heart attack the following month when his car was attacked.

PANZER PIONEER BROUGHT LOW

The first panzer group ever formed was put under the control of Ewald von Kleist (1881-1954) on May 10, 1940, and bore his name. He led the panzers in the invasion of the Low Countries, a masterly display of swift armoured warfare that won Kleist the Knight's Cross. His high reputation was sustained by capturing Belgrade in the Balkans campaign and Kiev in the successful early phase of the Russian campaign. He was promoted field marshal in 1943.

His fortunes turned as the advance in the USSR slowed, and finally Hitler dismissed him at the end of March 1944 for the retreat from the Ukraine and for his view that Germany should withdraw entirely from the Soviet Union.

Kleist was captured the following year by the Americans, tried in Yugoslavia for war crimes and sentenced to 15 years in jail. Four years later he was handed over to the Russians and died in a Soviet prison.

DEADLY HARVEST German infantry stalk warily through ripening maize where Soviet tanks (top) and pillboxes are waiting for them. It was the late summer of 1942 in the foothills of the Caucasus and the German advance on the Soviet oilfields had been halted. They were to stay there all through a bitter winter.

southwards. By August 9, his leading units could see the oil derricks of Maikop. The Germans took the town quickly, only to find that all the oil installations had been put out of action by the retreating Russians. However, Kleist expected to take Baku within two or three weeks.

He was helped considerably by many of the local people, who had been unwilling subjects of Russia under both Tsars and Bolsheviks, and welcomed the Germans as liberators. (After the war, Stalin exacted terrible revenge, banishing whole communities to Siberia.)

So fast was the advance that it no longer seemed ludicrous to dream of grand strategic conquests: of winning Turkey for the Axis, of undermining the Allied position in Iran, of cutting the southern supply line to Stalin by way of the Gulf, even of crossing the Nile into North Africa.

STRETCHED TOO FAR

But in fact the Germans had before them an almost impossible task. Their front and their supply lines were lengthening daily. To grab both the Black Sea and Caspian coasts was an immense challenge. Not only did they propose to tackle the icy heights of the Caucasus Mountains, but they intended to create a huge pocket at least 640 km (400 miles) across at its leading edge, and double that in depth – a front of 4000 km (2500 miles) in all. Drained by the scorching sun and the vast steppes, the Germans were weakening.

Moreover, unbeknown as yet to Kleist, the Russians had made a dramatic response to the German advance. During August and September, 90 000 civilians had been put to work to dig defences for key cities and mountain passes. The Russian commander of Transcaucasus Front, General Ivan Tyulenev, described their labour: 'People worked until they nearly collapsed, with bloody rags around their blistered hands. Sometimes they had little or nothing to eat for days, but they still went on with the work, even at night . . . By the beginning of autumn about 100 000 defence works were built, including 70 000 pillboxes and other firing points. Over 800 km (500 miles) of anti-tank ditches were dug, 320 km (200 miles) of anti-infantry obstacles were built, as well as 1600 km (1000 miles) of trenches.'

As a result, the German advance was stopped short. In the west, Kleist's panzers never reached Tuapse, the key to control of the Black Sea coast. In the south, they failed to cross the forbidding 4000 m (13 000 ft) passes leading through the Caucasus Mountains. In the east, they were unable to break out of a bridgehead established across the Terek river, near Mozdok, hardly more than halfway to Baku. There they stayed, locked in position through the autumn and winter.

Only later would the consequences of Hitler's decisions become apparent. The main German priority should have been the destruction of the massed Soviet forces before the Volga. The great Prussian 19th-century military theoretician Karl von Clausewitz had understood as much when he wrote: 'It is not by conquering one of the enemy's provinces . . . but by seeking out the heart of enemy power . . . that we can strike him to the ground.' But Hitler was convinced he was a far greater military genius than Clausewitz.

He was not. By dispersing his armies, by allotting them objectives hundreds of kilometres apart instead of concentrating them to defeat the Red Army, he laid the foundations for Germany's eventual defeat.

PART TWO

ACT TWO of the world drama began on December 7, 1941, when Zeros and torpedo bombers streaked out of a dawn sky to attack the American base at Pearl Harbor, Hawaii. Now the United States was in the war, and all the principal protagonists were on stage.

The surprise attack, described by President Roosevelt as 'a date that will live in infamy', was only the beginning. In a string of dazzling victories, Japanese forces swept through the western Pacific and south-east Asia. Hong Kong fell, Malaya was overrun, Singapore capitulated, the Dutch East Indies and the Philippines were conquered. The myth of white supremacy was dealt a blow from which it was never to recover.

The juggernaut from the Land of the Rising Sun rolled through Burma to put India in peril, and island-hopped to New Guinea to threaten Australia. A quarter of the globe was controlled from Tokyo.

But in attacking Pearl Harbor, Japan had provoked the mightiest of the democracies. And a fatal flaw in the plan was that the victory was not complete: the US aircraft carriers, at sea on the day of the attack, lived to fight another day. Nemesis was on the way, and its first loud knock on the door came at the Battle of Midway ●

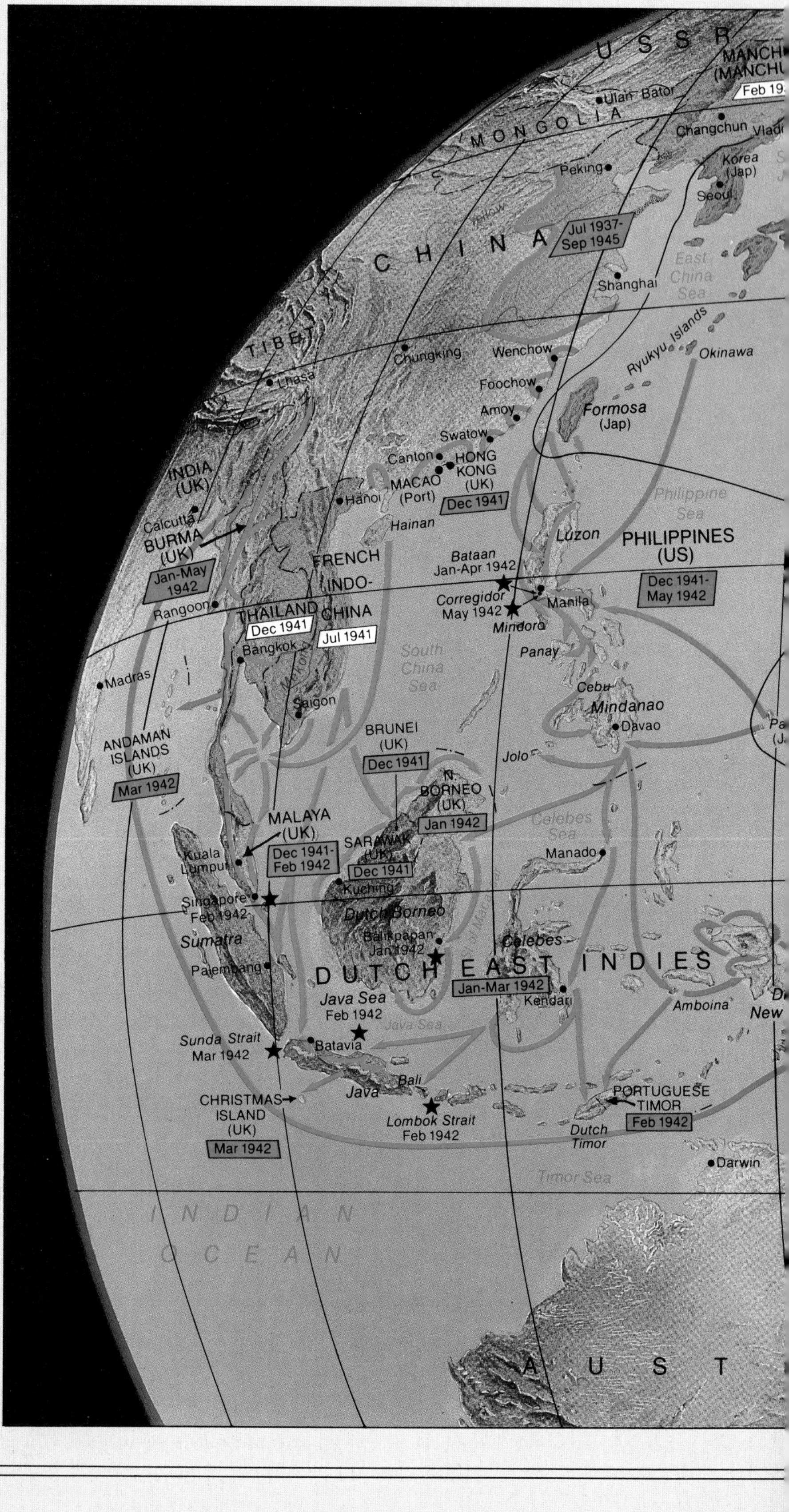

THE JAPANESE JUGGERNAUT

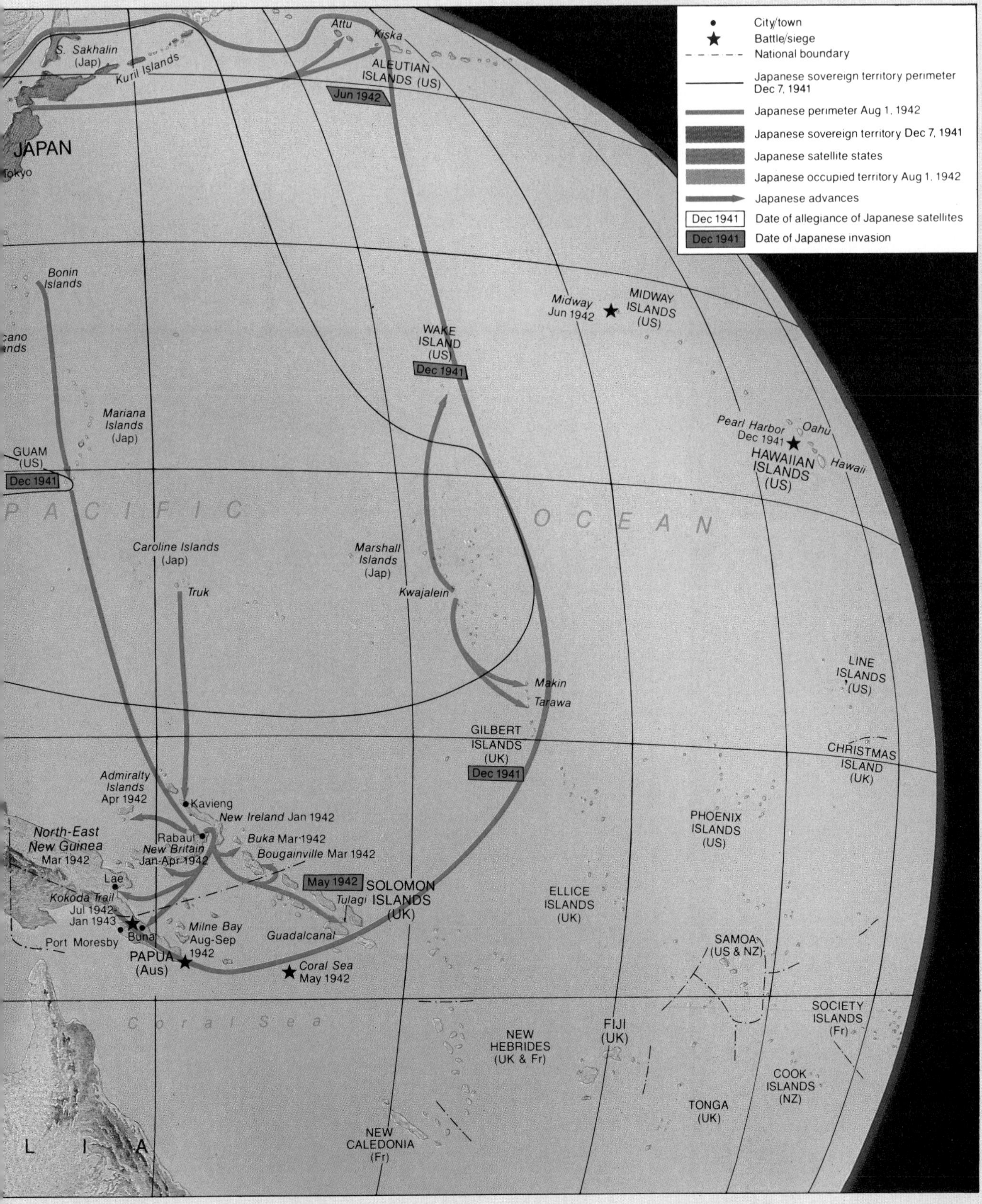

City/town
Battle/siege
National boundary
Japanese sovereign territory perimeter Dec 7, 1941
Japanese perimeter Aug 1, 1942
Japanese sovereign territory Dec 7, 1941
Japanese satellite states
Japanese occupied territory Aug 1, 1942
Japanese advances
Dec 1941 Date of allegiance of Japanese satellites
Dec 1941 Date of Japanese invasion
S. Sakhalin (Jap)
Kuril Islands
Attu
Kiska
ALEUTIAN ISLANDS (US)
Jun 1942
JAPAN
Tokyo
Bonin Islands
Mariana Islands (Jap)
GUAM (US)
Dec 1941
WAKE ISLAND (US)
Dec 1941
Midway Jun 1942
MIDWAY ISLANDS (US)
Pearl Harbor Dec 1941
Oahu
Hawaii
HAWAIIAN ISLANDS (US)
PACIFIC OCEAN
Caroline Islands (Jap)
Truk
Marshall Islands (Jap)
Kwajalein
Makin
Tarawa
GILBERT ISLANDS (UK)
Dec 1941
LINE ISLANDS (US)
CHRISTMAS ISLAND (UK)
Admiralty Islands Apr 1942
Kavieng
New Ireland Jan 1942
North-East New Guinea Mar 1942
Rabaul
New Britain Jan-Apr 1942
Buka Mar 1942
Bougainville Mar 1942
Lae
May 1942
SOLOMON ISLANDS (UK)
Tulagi
Kokoda Trail Jul 1942-Jan 1943
Buna
Port Moresby
Milne Bay Aug-Sep 1942
Guadalcanal
PAPUA (Aus)
Coral Sea May 1942
PHOENIX ISLANDS (US)
ELLICE ISLANDS (UK)
SAMOA (US & NZ)
Coral Sea
NEW HEBRIDES (UK & Fr)
FIJI (UK)
SOCIETY ISLANDS (Fr)
COOK ISLANDS (NZ)
TONGA (UK)
NEW CALEDONIA (Fr)

10: EMPIRE OF THE RISING SUN

Prosperity had doubled Japan's population – then the Great Depression savaged its economy. The country's powerful militarists saw a simple solution to its problems: expand by conquest.

Bright morning that turned into a sinister night

The young Emperor Hirohito took the imperial name of *Showa* – 'Bright Peace' – when he came to the throne in 1926, and Japan seemed set on the road to Westernisation. But with the 1930s came the *kurai tanima* – 'dark valley' – as modern Japanese call it, when blind militarism drove the nation to war.

VICTORY OVER RUSSIA in 1904-5 made Japan the first Asian country in modern times to defeat a great European state in war. It startled other European powers, won admiration in east Asian colonial territories and raised Japanese national pride to a new height. The Japanese had much to be proud of. In the few decades since 1867, when the reforming Emperor Mutsuhito (who took the reign name *Meiji* – 'enlightened rule') ascended the throne, Japan had been transformed. Once a semi-feudal state ruled by *shoguns* (military leaders) and the warrior *samurai* caste, it was by 1905 an industrialised nation with a Diet (parliament), cabinet government and multi-party politics. In 1918 for the first time a commoner became prime minister – the liberal-minded Takashi Hara.

A number of liberal measures were introduced in the 1920s, and in 1924 the army was cut by four divisions. For a while it was possible to openly express 'dangerous thoughts' – even Marxist and anti-imperial ones. 'Marx boys', radical socialist youths, appeared in universities, and in Tokyo youngsters took up the *Moga* ('modern girl') and *Mobo* ('modern boy') style, aping 'Roaring Twenties' Westerners of the 'flapper' era.

However, nationalist conservative groups, centred on the armed services, resented bitterly the Westernisation of Japanese society and the extension of democracy. They even opposed Western sports, dancing and music, and became dangerously restive: Hara was stabbed to death by a right-wing fanatic in 1921. But in 1926, the pro-Western Hirohito became emperor. He was a keen marine biologist and the first member of the imperial family to travel abroad – he was even photographed in plus fours playing golf with the Prince of Wales (later Edward VIII). Although regarded by most Japanese as a 'living god', he favoured progress towards democracy.

In foreign affairs, meanwhile, Japan proceeded with caution, under the influence of the liberal Baron Kijuro Shidehara, dominant politician of his time, who became foreign minister in 1924.

Japan is a country ribbed with mountains, with less than a quarter of the land flat enough for agriculture and an acute shortage of mineral resources. One of the keys to understanding Japan's history in modern times is that in order to support an expanding population it desperately needed vital raw materials such as coal, iron and oil. And there were only two ways to win these: either by trade or by military conquest.

Before and during World War I – which it fought on the side of Britain and the Allies – Japan was aggressively expansionist. In 1910, for example, Korea was annexed, and in 1915 China was presented with the so-called 'Twenty-One Demands', which would have reduced that nation to little more than a Japanese vassal state. The Chinese rejected these. But they could not stop Japanese troops taking over an area previously held by Germany – the Shantung (Shandong) peninsula, in north-east China. (Japan had already annexed Formosa, or Taiwan, in 1895.)

However, under Shidehara's influence, Japan withdrew troops from Shantung and from the northern half of Sakhalin island, claimed by Russia. It evacuated the area in 1925 in exchange for rights to extract oil and coal there. The Japanese, however, stayed in Korea. At the Washington Disarmament Conference of 1921-2, Japan promised to keep a smaller navy than either Britain or the USA, with only three battleships to every five for the British or US navies.

PRESSURES FOR EXPANSION

As a major world trading nation, Japan had by far the highest standard of living in Asia, but from the late 1920s, cracks began appearing in this prosperity – particularly in the countryside. In 1927 a financial crisis forced 36 banks to close. Two years later the Wall Street Crash, followed by the Great Depression, struck Japan like the rest of the world. Silk farming (a mainstay of the rural economy) was hard hit when American demand for silk collapsed. This coincided with poor rice harvests, and caused acute hardship in rural areas.

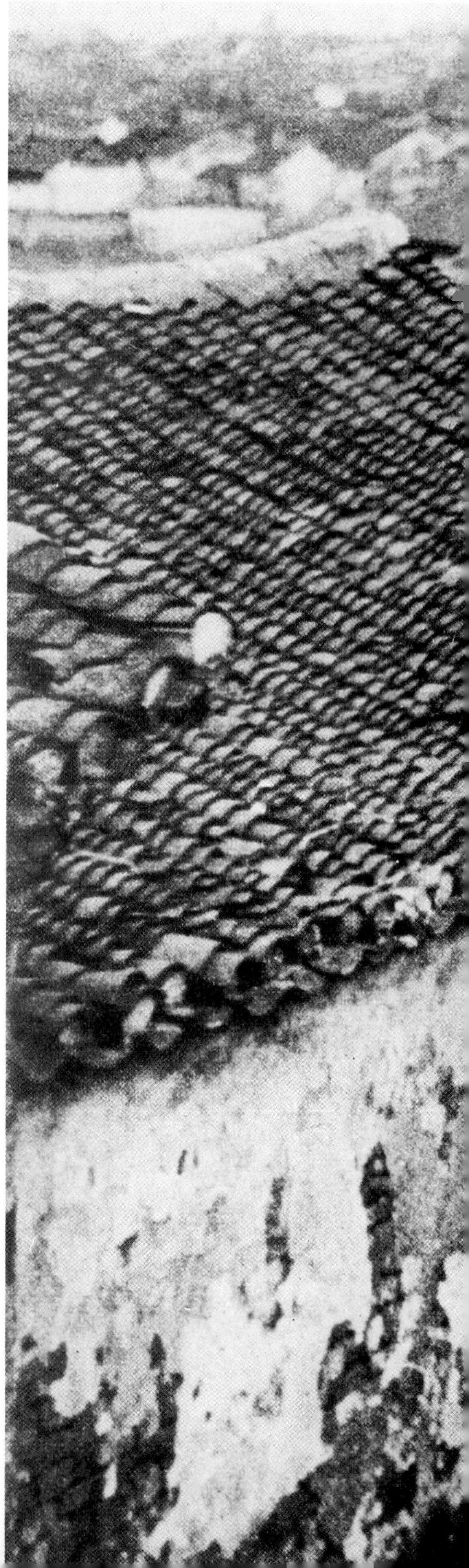

THE CONQUERORS Japanese cavalrymen ride down a rocky road in a Manchurian village in 1931. Some houses display Japanese flags as a sign of welcome – or fear. Manchuria was conquered in three months of 1931.

Other problems resulted from Japan's increasing population – which had grown from 34 million in 1872 to nearly 56 million in 1920.

One answer seemed to be a return to aggression. Especially attractive was Manchuria, just across the sea in north-east China, where Japan already had a railway, iron works, coal mines and other holdings. Here were vast open spaces where Japanese colonists could settle and grow food.

Chief advocates of expansion were the right-wing militarists. Army and navy officers, many of them from the impoverished countryside, and their supporters attacked the parliamentary parties and big business – which they accused of corruption and greed. They sought a return to rule by the Emperor and military leaders, contrasting corrupt politicians with *samurai* warriors of old, with their code of loyalty, self-discipline, bravery and simple living. They found ready allies in ultra-nationalist societies such as the *Kokusuikai* ('National Purity Society'), and the terrorist *Ketsumeidan* ('League of Blood').

As these forces gained in influence, so Japan's democratic freedoms were threatened. In 1928 thousands of Marxists were arrested and imprisoned under a repressive new anti-Leftist law, which made it a crime to form an organisation aimed at destroying the private property system. In 1930 the naval chiefs, with public backing, fought savagely to block the London Naval Treaty – a further disarmament pact signed by Japan, Britain, the USA, France and Italy. It included an agreement limiting Japanese naval

strength to less than 70 per cent of the USA's. The navy lost this battle, but a few weeks later Prime Minister Yuko Hamaguchi was shot and wounded by a nationalist youth. The act was symbolic: the victory of the so-called 'old liberals' in signing the London treaty would be their last. Hamaguchi died of his wounds a year later.

THE MUKDEN BOMB

In late August 1931, word began to reach Shidehara that nationalist Japanese Army officers stationed in north-eastern Manchuria were plotting to seize Mukden, the capital, and bring the province under Japanese rule. They had no support from the government – though some senior General Staff officers were sympathetic. Shidehara went straight to Hirohito, who ordered the War Minister, General Jiro Minami, to put a stop to the plot.

Minami, whose sympathies lay with the plotters, deliberately entrusted Hirohito's instructions for his commander in Manchuria to a well-known nationalist, General Yoshitsugu Tatekawa, who took his time about getting there. Instead of flying to the Manchurian capital, Mukden (now Shenyang), he went by slow boat and train. Arriving on September 19, he met a Japanese colonel and went to a geisha house – with the Emperor's letter still in his pocket. A few hours later a bomb exploded on the Japanese-controlled South Manchurian Railway. Chinese saboteurs were blamed, but almost certainly the Japanese themselves were the culprits. The Japanese commander of the Korean Army, General Senjuru Hayashi, ordered his troops into Mukden, and took it in 24 hours. So began the Japanese invasion of Manchuria.

The Japanese had been involved there since the Russo-Japanese War, after which Russia transferred its rights and privileges in southern Manchuria to Japan. These included a lease of the coal and iron-rich Kwantung region, and the right to run the South Manchurian Railway from Port Arthur (Lushun) north-east to Changchun. The railway company also operated iron works, coal mines and a bureaucracy to administer the surrounding zone. The Japanese troops stationed there were known as the Kwantung Army.

The Mukden affair acutely embarrassed the Japanese government. It accepted a League of Nations resolution calling on Japanese troops to return to the railway company zone. But by now relations between army and government had almost broken down. The army simply ignored the government and by the beginning of 1932 had conquered the whole province of Manchuria and parts of Mongolia.

When the League of Nations recommended a withdrawal of Japanese troops and restoration of Chinese sovereignty over the province, Japan's reaction was to quit the League. Its sole concession to international opinion was to instal the last Chinese Emperor, Pu Yi, as puppet governor and later emperor of a new 'independent' Manchurian state, Manchukuo. Shidehara meanwhile had been driven from office by the militarists – he re-emerged as a key figure in postwar Japan and was briefly prime minister.

A COUP THAT FAILED

In February 1936 rumours spread that the Japanese Army's 1st Division, a hotbed of ultra-nationalism, was to be transferred from Tokyo to Manchuria. In its ranks were adherents of the *Kodo-ha* ('Imperial Way Faction') bent on overthrowing the elected government and advancing northwards against the Communist Soviet Union. Some *Kodo-ha* hotheads decided to strike while they had the chance. In a blinding blizzard just after midnight on February 26/27, 1500 soldiers and junior officers – but with high-ranking support – left their barracks.

They woke up leading politicians and army officers loyal to the constitution, murdering several of them, including two former prime ministers. The furious Emperor declared martial law, filled the streets with loyal troops and called on the mutineers to surrender. 'They are trying to pull a silk rope round my neck', he said. After four tense days the rebels gave in and at a secret court martial 13 were sentenced to death.

Kodo-ha was discredited and the army was now controlled by the rival *Tosei-ha* ('Control Faction'), which advocated an advance against China.

BOMBS ON SHANGHAI

When a Shanghai mob killed two Japanese – said to have been Buddhist monks – in January 1932, a Japanese marine force stationed there took prompt revenge. The incident was almost certainly engineered by the Japanese – to distract international attention from their invasion of Manchuria and to give the navy an opportunity for action.

Resistance by the Chinese Nineteenth Route Army in Shanghai was, however, more than the Japanese had bargained for. What began as skirmishing developed into intense fighting. Army reinforcements had to be sent to help the marines and a fierce aerial bombardment was launched on Chapei, the thickly populated Chinese section of Shanghai. Deadly fighting went on for six weeks.

The so-called Shanghai Incident gave the world a frightening glimpse of the destructive efficiency of modern warfare. Newsreel cameramen were there, and in cinemas all over Europe and America, people were horrified by the spectacle of massive air raids on near-defenceless civilians. There was widespread admiration for the outgunned Chinese resisters.

CITY'S AGONY Smoke billows from a bombed Shanghai station. (Inset) Japanese sailors attack.

ENTERING THE DARK VALLEY

Two further incidents during 1932 showed Japan's changing mood. In January, Japanese planes bombed Shanghai in savage reprisal after a Chinese mob murdered two Japanese in the city (see box). News of the bombings brought wild public rejoicing in Japan. Then in May a gang of naval officers gunned down the moderate Prime Minister, Tsuyoshi Inukai, who had tried to curb the military's power. His assassins behaved like heroes at their trial, won public applause for their patriotism and escaped capital punishment.

Inukai was the last party political prime minister. One of the most powerful men in the new government was the War Minister, General Sadao Araki, and until the end of Japan's war against the West, the military remained a decisive influence. The country had entered what modern Japanese call the *kurai tanima* ('dark valley'), a time of increased repression and censorship at home and aggression abroad. In February 1936 a group of young army officers tried to set up an even more thoroughgoing military rule, but their attempted *coup* was rapidly put down (see box).

Japan's armies, meanwhile, were gradually taking over more and more of northern China – until by 1935 they had conquered an area extending south from the Great Wall to within 24 km (15 miles) of Peking (Beijing). The Chinese put up a heroic guerrilla resistance, but were finally unable to withstand the superior, disciplined Japanese forces. The Japanese also used subversive tactics – such as large-scale smuggling of opium, morphine and heroin, sold cheaply to the Chinese to enfeeble and demoralise them.

No foreign power came to China's aid. Only the United States could have done so – but isolationism ran strong there, and the country was trying to disengage itself from the Pacific. In 1934 Congress provided for a withdrawal from bases in the American-ruled Philippines, and defences on the island base of Guam were neglected.

NAVAL BUILD-UP

Japan, by contrast, was building up naval strength. In 1934 it renounced the Washington and London pacts limiting its navy. The aim was to establish overwhelming naval superiority in the Pacific. Japan had been a world-class naval power since the turn of the century, thanks to an alliance with Britain, which began in 1902 and was renewed for ten years in 1911. The Japanese fleet which trounced the Russians in 1904-5 was mostly built in Britain, and its officers were British-trained. During the 1930s Japan itself built a succession of inventively designed, fast and well-armed ships. For example, its *Fubuki*-class destroyers were much admired by the Allies – who nicknamed them 'wolves of the sea' – for their speed and power during the Pacific war.

The Japanese were also quick to grasp the importance of naval air power. In 1922 they had commissioned the purpose-built aircraft carrier *Hosho*. By 1941 they possessed ten fleet carriers. The US Navy at the time had seven, with just three in the Pacific. Japan's Zero naval fighters were the world's best, and its 'Kate' torpedo bombers and 'Val' dive-bombers were also excellent aircraft.

In 1937 the navy ordered four enormous new battleships. They were built in total secrecy, and the first to be commissioned was the 70 000 tonne *Yamato* in December 1941. Its sister ship *Musashi* followed in August 1942. They were the largest battleships ever built, each armed with nine massive 460 mm (18.1 in) guns.

By the late 1930s, Japan was looking to further expansion to meet its needs for raw materials. The Philippines, Malaya, Indochina and the East Indies could provide them. These were under the control of the USA, Britain, France and the Netherlands – but if Japan could get hold of them it could become self-sufficient. The one cloud on its horizon was its diplomatic isolation – and that was removed in November 1936, when it signed the Anti-Comintern Pact with Nazi Germany. Significantly, the agreement was negotiated by the army, not the foreign ministry. It brought Japan into the same fold as the fascist Axis power

THE WAY OF THE WARRIOR

The values of a World War II Japanese soldier were essentially those of the medieval *samurai* warrior, enshrined in the *samurai* code of *bushido*, the 'way of the warrior': unquestioning fidelity and obedience to the leader, and the capacity to endure physical hardship. Official army manuals required 'absolute obedience to superiors', and willingness to fight to the death. To withdraw, surrender or be taken prisoner was forbidden. They despised Allied troops who had surrendered, and this led to fearful atrocities.

Army life demanded incredible physical toughness, and discipline was brutal. All this made Japanese soldiers fearsome infantrymen. They were superb, for example, in jungle fighting, where individual bravery, resource and skill are paramount. Late in the war, however, their commanders too often assumed that their fighting spirit could overcome a better-equipped enemy. It could not.

ARTS TO ARMS Aglow with war fervour, a painting shows students rushing to serve in the forces.

THE GOD EMPEROR

For most prewar Japanese, their emperor was a supremely remote, untouchable being, officially described in the constitution of 1889 as 'sacred and inviolable'. He was held to be descended directly from the sun-goddess Amaterasu, and in the state Shinto religion was revered as a 'living god'.

Prewar photographs of Emperor Hirohito (1901-89) were almost invariably formal – he was usually in uniform, often astride a white stallion. Photographers were not allowed within 45 m (50 yds). A genuine liberal, he was often blamed for not acting to stop Japan's mad rush to war. Though theoretically supreme, he had, in practice, limited powers. He appointed prime ministers, and cabinets were responsible to him – not the Diet (parliament) – as were the military. But his divine, priestly role kept him aloof from political and military decisions, and he rarely expressed an opinion to his ministers.

On some notable occasions, however, Hirohito did intervene – as when he quelled the attempted coup of *Kodo-ha* officers in 1936. And at the end of the war it was Hirohito who persuaded the government to surrender. His surrender broadcast on August 15, 1945, was the first time that most Japanese had heard his voice. On New Year's Day, 1946, he renounced divine status, telling his people that his relation with them did 'not depend upon mere legends and myths'. Informal photographs were published showing Hirohito and his family reading, swimming and engaged in other everyday occupations, as if to emphasise the changed times.

A GOD RIDES OUT Emperor Hirohito, 'living god', rides a horse called *Shirayuki* (Snow White) as he reviews troops outside his palace.

An Empire already at war

By 1937 the Japanese were firmly established in northern China; at home the military were all-powerful, and eager to sweep through China and beyond.

WORLD WAR II BEGAN, according to some historians, when a brief exchange of fire near Peking (Beijing) in July 1937 triggered off open war between China and Japan. During the night of July 7/8, Japanese troops on manoeuvres fired on Chinese soldiers guarding the vital Marco Polo (Lugou) Bridge over the Yonding river, only 15 km (9 miles) south-west of the city. The Chinese returned fire – and the Sino-Japanese War, which later merged into the wider Pacific War, broke out.

Since annexing Manchuria six years before, the Japanese had gradually gobbled up northern China, and by 1935 controlled all five provinces there. Their expansion had been made easier by a civil war between the *Kuomintang* (Chinese Nationalists) under Chiang Kai-shek and Communists led by Mao Tse-tung (Mao Zedong). By 1937, the Japanese military were spoiling for an outright invasion of China. However, China was now presenting a newly united front under Chiang. The Soviet leader Joseph Stalin had engineered a reconciliation between Nationalists and Reds, and promised Chiang US$50 million of aid, including fighter aircraft.

After the Marco Polo Bridge incident the Japanese War Minister, General Hajime Sugiyama, demanded more troops be sent to the area, and the more moderate prime minister, Prince Fumimaro Konoye, reluctantly gave way. Chiang had also sent troops to the region. Tension grew later in July when Chinese soldiers serving under Japanese officers in Japanese-occupied Tungchow (Tong Xian), near Peking, rose up and massacred their officers and over 200 Japanese and Korean civilians.

THE RAZOR'S EDGE

Hideki Tojo (1884-1948) was the son of a *samurai* and passionately devoted to the *bushido* code of honour. Nicknamed 'The Razor', he first won prominence as chief of the military police, then Chief of Staff of Japan's army in Manchuria. He was leader of the *Tosei-ha* ('Control Faction'), favouring expansion in China and south-east Asia and war against the USA and Britain.

Tojo became War Minister in Prince Konoye's 1940-1 cabinet and Premier in October 1941. Of all Japan's militarists, he was perhaps the most sincere advocate of a Greater East Asia partnership of free and independent nations. He had almost total charge of Japan's war machine during the war's first years. But when the tide began to turn from 1942 he came under increasing pressure to stand down. He resigned after the Mariana Islands fell in July 1944.

After Japan's surrender, Tojo bungled a suicide attempt, surviving to be tried and hanged as a war criminal.

Japan now loosed a full-scale invasion, storming Peking and the nearby port of Tientsin (Tianjin) in August, and moving south into Shantung (Shandong) province. Next they attacked Shanghai, where a Chinese army held out bravely for three months. In December, Chiang's capital, Nanking (Nanjing), fell. The Japanese unleashed their troops on the city in an orgy of destruction, murder, looting and rape. Around 200 000 Chinese were slaughtered and even Japan's Nazi allies were shocked.

By early 1938 the Japanese controlled China's coastline, major cities and most of its railways. Chiang was driven west, to set up a new capital at Chungking (Chongquing) in Szechwan (Sichuan) province. America and Europe were slow to react. In 1937 US President Franklin Roosevelt had warned of a spreading 'epidemic of world lawlessness'. But his speech contained no concrete proposals for dealing with Japan. Then, in December 1937, Japanese planes, in an excess of nationalist zeal, bombed and sank the US gunboat *Panay* in the Yangtze river (Chang Jiang). A British gunboat was also attacked. Apologies by Tokyo defused the situation, but the USA had been alerted: in 1938 Roosevelt began strengthening US defences in the Pacific – including the Philippines – and gave Chiang a loan.

At the same time, Soviet-Japanese territorial disputes were leading to clashes on the border of the Japanese puppet state of Manchukuo (Manchuria). The Russians got the worst of clashes in 1937-8, but in May 1939 a Japanese force attacked Nomonhan (Nomenkan) in Soviet-dominated Mongolia, and was driven back after nearly four months of fierce fighting by troops under Lt General Georgi Zhukov, later a hero of Russia's war against Hitler. By August the Japanese were encircled, losing about 18 000 dead.

STRONG WINE

But in July 1940 an even more aggressive Japanese government was formed. Prince Konoye returned as prime minister after a six-month gap, but real power lay with the war minister, the headstrong General Hideki Tojo. Emboldened by Allied reverses in Europe that summer, the Japanese began to reach beyond China. The US ambassador to Tokyo remarked that Nazi triumphs had 'gone to their heads like strong wine'. In September, with the acquiescence of the new Vichy government in France, they marched into French Indochina. Japan also sealed a growing bond with Italy and Germany by signing the Tripartite Pact, promising mutual military and economic aid. Roosevelt responded by banning oil and scrap-metal exports to Japan, and increasing financial aid to Chiang's China.

The Japanese now unfurled grandiose plans for a 'Greater East Asia Co-Prosperity Sphere', to include all colonised peoples of the region. 'Asia for the Asiatics', they called it, claiming that Japan wanted only to liberate east Asia from Western overlordship, and to develop a partnership working for peace and prosperity – a 'new order' in the continent.

However, Japanese motives were rather more self-interested. In June 1940, Tojo's predecessor, General Shunroku Hata, had said: 'We should not miss the present opportunity or we shall be blamed by posterity.' The opportunity was to end Japan's reliance on imported raw materials and food – from the USA, above all – by seizing Indochina's rice-paddies, the Dutch East Indies' oilfields and British Malaya's rubber plantations.

The year 1941 opened with an uneasy lull. In April the Japanese signed a non-aggression pact with the Soviet Union – an echo of the Nazi-Soviet pact of August 1939. But Hitler's invasion of the Soviet Union in June threw Japan's rulers

THWARTED REFORMER

Chiang Kai-shek (1887-1975) was one of a group of rivals to succeed Sun Yat-sen (Sun Zhong-shan) as leader of the *Kuomintang* (Chinese Nationalist Party) after Sun died in 1925. By 1928 Chiang ruled southern China, with his capital at Nanking (Nanjing).

Chiang had spent a brief spell in Moscow, but was no Marxist. Nor was he a democrat. He tried to unify his country through his 'New Life Movement', which mingled puritanism with teachings of the philosopher Confucius. He also tried to introduce social and economic reforms – but was hampered by discords within his own party, Communist insurgency and fractious local warlords.

From 1937 to 1949 Chiang was occupied with war – against the Japanese, then against China's Communists, led by Mao Tse-tung (Mao Zedong). By 1949 he had lost to Mao and retreated to the island of Formosa (Taiwan), returned by Japan to China after the war. He led a US-backed Nationalist government until he died.

During the war, the clumsy interference of his Westernised wife (with Chiang, below) soured Chiang's relations with Allied leaders. But she made a big hit with the American public and won support for the Nationalist cause.

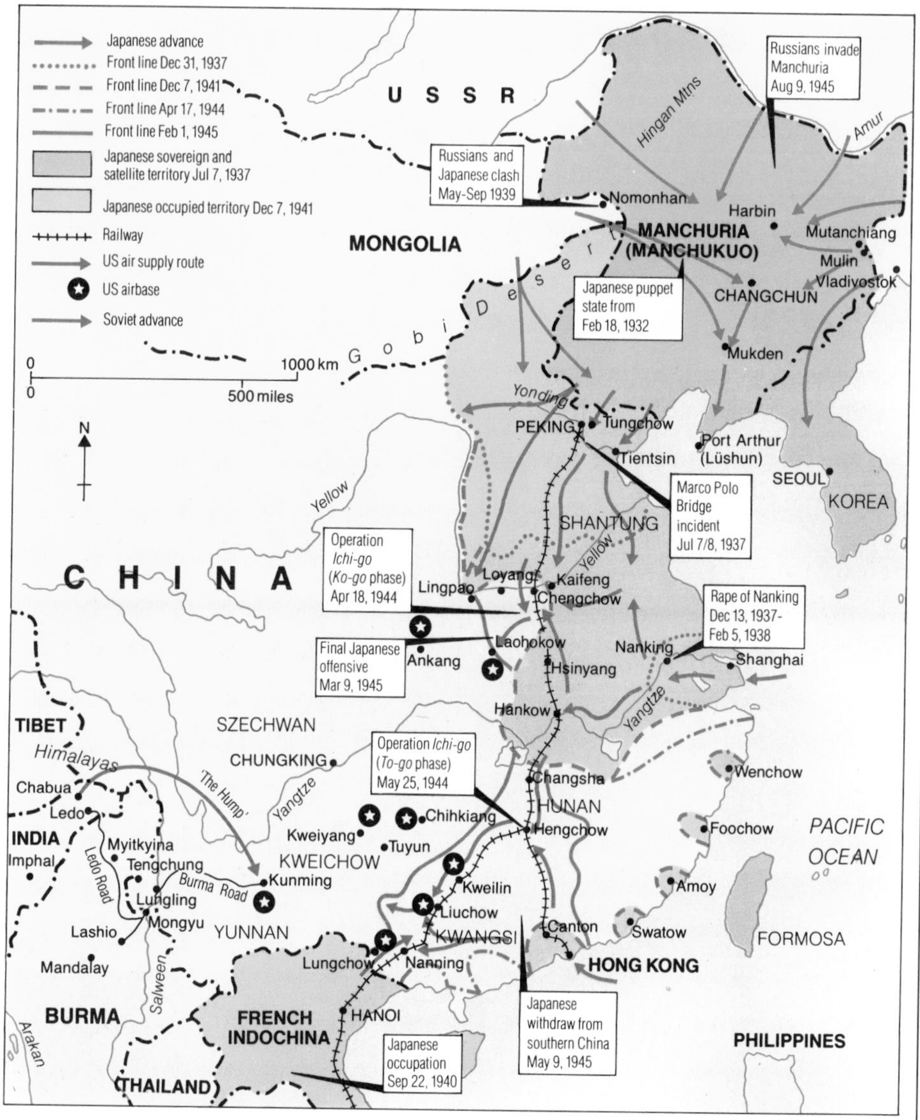

WAR IN THE EAST China was consumed by war from July 1937, when the Japanese invaded from their northern puppet state Manchukuo (Manchuria), taken over in 1932, until the Russian Army attacked in the dying days of World War II. In between, the Japanese mounted several major offensives against the US-backed Chinese.

into confusion – he had not told them. In the end they ignored the German-Soviet struggle and moved against Chiang and American and European-ruled territories in Asia.

JAPAN MAKES A MOVE

The first step Japan's rulers took was to complete their domination of Indochina by assuming a protectorate there in July 1941. Vichy was powerless to object – but Roosevelt suspended all financial and trading relations with Japan and froze Japanese assets in the USA. Britain and the Dutch government-in-exile followed suit. Cut off from oil, rubber and steel supplies, Japan was now on a collision course with the West.

In September a conference of Japanese ministers and armed service chiefs of staff, held in the Emperor's presence, decided that war against the United States was unavoidable, and preparations were stepped up. Talks continued in Washington, but when they failed Prince Konoye resigned and was replaced as prime minister by Tojo. On November 20 Tojo delivered an ultimatum to the US government: Japan would occupy no more territory in Asia if the US would cease to reinforce the Philippines; and Japanese forces would withdraw from southern Indochina if the US cut off its aid to Chiang and freed Japanese assets in America. In effect, Japan would remain free to subjugate China.

Not that Tojo expected Roosevelt to accept – while awaiting an answer, the Japanese fleet was grouping off the Kuril Islands, north of Japan. On November 26 six large aircraft carriers, two battleships, two heavy cruisers and 11 destroyers set course for Pearl Harbor in Hawaii.

USA CAUGHT UNAWARES?

At Roosevelt's first cabinet meeting in 1933, he warned that America might be forced into war with Japan. Three months later, US$300 million was allocated to building new warships. By the outbreak of the Pacific War in 1941, the USA was well prepared for action at sea.

Four new fleet carriers – *Yorktown, Enterprise, Wasp* and *Hornet* – had been built, making seven in all. Battleship strength was doubled to 17, and destroyers to 171; cruiser strength was tripled to 37. The fleet was well equipped with aircraft, and had specialist ships for landing troops under fire on enemy beaches.

However, the US Army and its air force lagged behind, largely due to a successful campaign by the isolationist America First Committee, which campaigned to keep the USA out of the looming war. Only when Hitler overran western Europe in 1940 did Congress vote for conscription. Even so, in 1941 the army had only 500 000 men and one armoured division.

THE PEOPLE'S PRESIDENT

Wealth and a landed background gave Franklin Delano Roosevelt (1882-1945) easy self-confidence. The East Coast patrician had President Theodore Roosevelt as a distant cousin.

In 1921 Roosevelt caught polio and was in a wheelchair until he died. In 1928 he was elected governor of New York. Four years later the Depression saw him swept into the White House with an innovative social and economic programme – the 'New Deal' – which put the USA on the road to recovery. He was elected for a record four successive terms as president.

An isolationist until Japan launched open warfare on China in 1937, he did all he could to prepare the United States for war, urging it to become the 'arsenal of democracy'. Once at war, Roosevelt established a warm relationship with Churchill that smoothed cooperation with Britain.

However, Roosevelt was a committed enemy of colonialism – including the British brand. He was also more conciliatory than Churchill to the Soviet Union. Where they disagreed, Roosevelt (representing the greater power) usually won. He died suddenly of a stroke on April 12, 1945 – 26 days before VE Day.

LEND-LEASE President Roosevelt signs the 1941 bill to supply arms to the Allies on easy terms.

11: TORA! TORA! TORA!

In a blitzkrieg that rivalled Hitler's, Japan gained control of a quarter of the globe.

Pearl Harbor: 'a date that will live in infamy'

Japan planned to destroy US might in the Pacific with one bold stroke. Its aircraft created havoc at Pearl Harbor – but two US aircraft carriers escaped.

END OF *ARIZONA* Clouds of smoke billow from *Arizona*. A bomb has hit its forward magazine, and the battleship has erupted in flames, leapt halfway out of the water, then broken in two and capsized, trapping some 1000 men.

DAWN WAS BREAKING over the US naval base of Pearl Harbor on the Hawaiian island of Oahu. From the bridge of the destroyer USS *Ward*, on patrol off the harbour entrance, Lieutenant William W. Outerbridge caught sight of a small dark submarine conning tower in the water off his starboard bow. It was moving at around 8 knots (15 km/h) along the channel leading to Pearl's main anchorage, in an area forbidden to American craft. Outerbridge ordered his main guns to open fire.

It was Sunday, December 7, 1941. At 6.45 am, a 4 in (100 mm) shell tore into the conning tower, and it sank from sight. Outerbridge reported the incident to his headquarters on shore. At the same time, 1600 km (1000 miles) to the north-east, torpedoes smashed into the hull of the American freighter *Cynthia Olsen*. Its radio operator tapped out a desperate message: an unidentified submarine was attacking his ship.

Across the International Date Line on Malaya's east coast it was already 2 am on Monday, December 8. Dug in on beaches just north of Kota Baharu, near the border with Thailand, British Indian troops peered through the dark and trained their rifles and machine guns on landing craft approaching from a convoy anchored off shore. As the craft ground onto the sand, they opened fire.

Simultaneously, in the little Thai port of Singora (Songkhla), 220 km (138 miles) north-west, strangely uniformed soldiers had appeared suddenly in the streets. Local police hesitated briefly as the strangers tried to communicate in broken Thai. Then, deciding the men were up to no good, they drew their pistols and shot them.

So began an extraordinary day. As the hours passed, Washington and London received reports of Japanese attacks over a massive front, from Hawaii right across the Pacific and Far East to the Gulf of Thailand. News of the surprise attack on Pearl Harbor reached Washington just before 2 pm, eastern seaboard time, on December 7. An hour later – just before 9 pm, British time – London learned of the Japanese landings in Malaya and Thailand. Within another two hours came reports that Singapore had been bombed – and later the news that Japanese troops were pushing into Hong Kong's New Territories. In Washington, dispatches continued to pour in. Airfields in the US-ruled Philippines had been bombed at least four times, and there were reports of landings. US bases on Guam, Wake and Midway islands also reported aerial attacks.

It soon became clear that losses were heavy. In just a few hours and without any declaration of war, the Japanese had destroyed more than 500 (out of a total of 1000) US and British aircraft in the Pacific and Far East, and had either sunk or badly damaged all eight of the US Pacific Fleet's battleships in Pearl Harbor. They had gained control of the skies and seas across a quarter of the earth's surface. In the next 20 weeks, they would extend their control from the borders of India to the central Pacific, from Alaska's shores to the seas washing Australia's northern coast.

YAMAMOTO'S BOLD PLAN

This bold and ruthless offensive was the brainchild of Admiral Isoruku Yamamoto, Commander in Chief of the Japanese Combined Fleet. When the Japanese first discussed striking out from territory already occupied in China and Indochina, most senior officers wanted to confine their attacks to Thailand and the territories of the European colonial powers. Yamamoto, swept along reluctantly by the war party, disagreed. He believed that the USA, with its awesome industrial capacity, was bound to join the war sooner or later – and Japan's only chance was to strike first.

What he proposed was one swift blow to destroy US power in the Pacific – to coincide with attacks on Thai, British and Dutch territories. In November 1940, 21 obsolete British Swordfish carrier-based torpedo bombers had sunk or damaged three Italian battleships at Taranto. Yamamoto had studied the British raid closely and proposed destroying the US Pacific Fleet at Pearl Harbor in the same way – but with 350 modern aircraft from six carriers. From intelligence reports, he knew that the US fleet often spent weekends anchored in Pearl Harbor – so that was when he would attack. Midget submarines would also be sent in.

After this, he calculated, American power would recover – but not before Japan had built a defensive rim of air and naval bases around the central and south-western Pacific. To break through this, the Americans would have to wage a long and exhausting campaign. Public opinion would eventually force President Franklin D. Roosevelt to negotiate a peace – leaving Japan with its gains from the British and Dutch empires.

Many Japanese officers – including Vice

GENDA: PEARL HARBOR PLANNER

When Minoru Genda (1904-) was chosen to draw up plans for the Japanese attack on Pearl Harbor, he already had a reputation for brilliant planning and staff work. He had served as assistant naval attaché to the Japanese embassy in London and had studied the Royal Navy's carrier attack on the Italian fleet at Taranto.

Along with Commander Mitsuo Fuchida, Genda threw himself enthusiastically into plotting the Pearl Harbor operation. He designed new torpedoes and bombs and constructed an elaborate deception stratagem. Afterwards, Fuchida commented: 'Genda wrote the script. My pilots and I produced it.' Genda went on to plan Midway, but was unable to take part in the battle due to illness. After the war he served in Japan's Self-Defence Force, commanding its air arm from 1959 to 1962.

Admiral Chuichi Nagumo, who would lead the Pearl Harbor raid – considered Yamamoto's plan downright reckless, but his persistence won the day and the plan was adopted. On November 26, 1941, Nagumo's *Kido Butai* (Carrier Striking Force) set sail from the Kuril Islands off north-eastern Japan. Nagumo spent the 12-day voyage to the attack's launching point north of Oahu in a fever of anxiety. 'If only I had been more firm and refused', he moaned, pacing the bridge of his flagship, the carrier *Akagi*. Storms and fogs pursued the fleet. They aided concealment – but increased the danger of collision so that complete radio silence was impossible.

Surprise was essential if the attack was to succeed, and the Japanese had been ingenious in ensuring it. To disguise the departure of Nagumo's fleet, for example, transmitters around the Inland Sea, between Japan's main island Honshu and Shikoku, conjured up a 'phantom fleet' by increasing the frequency of their signals.

At the same time, envoys in Washington were instructed to continue negotiations about a possible Japanese withdrawal from China until the very moment of the attack – 1.30 pm, Washington time (8 am, Hawaiian time), on December 7. Another ruse was to send the luxury liner *Tatsuta Maru* for a 12-day voyage to San Francisco. As newspapers speculated, hostilities were unlikely to start before the ship's return to Japan. However, *Tatsuta Maru* had secret instructions to turn about and make full speed for Yokohama at midnight just before the attack.

WARNINGS IGNORED

Nonetheless, several warnings of the attack reached Japan's enemies. US intelligence officers, for example, had noted the carriers' disappearance. In late November, the radio operator of a Honolulu-bound cruise liner, SS *Lurline*, and an intelligence officer in San Francisco started to detect weak low-frequency signals north-west of Hawaii. Could these be the Japanese carriers? A little later, Dutch Intelligence intercepted and decoded a message from Tokyo to the Japanese ambassador in Bangkok informing him that Malaya, the Philippines and Hawaii were about to be attacked. The Dutch warned the US authorities.

But this information never reached the higher levels of American command, getting lost instead in a bureaucratic maze. It never occurred to Roosevelt or Admiral Husband E. Kimmel, Commander in Chief of the Pacific Fleet, that Japan would attack Pearl Harbor, nearly 6400 km (4000 miles) from its main fleet bases. They expected the Japanese to strike British and Dutch possessions first – and possibly US bases in the Philippines. Kimmel sent out his two carriers, *Enterprise* and *Lexington*, with additional fighters for US airfields on Midway and Wake islands.

Aboard *Akagi*, news of the US carriers' departure (reported by Japanese spies in Hawaii) depressed Nagumo still further. A trap was being sprung, he feared – and his carrier force was sailing right into it. Commander Minoru Genda, in charge of the operation's detailed planning, shared his superior's anxiety. He had always regarded the carriers as the real target of the attack. If the carriers were missing, the entire operation became pointless. The two men watched with heavy hearts as the aircraft of the first strike, led by Lt Commander Mitsuo Fuchida, took off in the grey pre-dawn light.

Off Oahu, meanwhile, the US destroyer *Ward* was once more a hive of activity. Its sonar had just detected another submarine. It released five depth charges, and a huge black bubble erupted astern as the sub was hit. Lieutenant Outerbridge reported this new incident to his headquarters. By now, its staff should have realised that something was badly wrong. But nearly an hour passed before duty officer Commander Vincent Murphy phoned Kimmel with a garbled version of the morning's events. It was now 7.40 am.

Earlier, shortly after 7 am, the screen at an army radar station on Oahu's northernmost point had flashed with an unusually large blip. At first Privates Joseph Lockard and George Elliott

YAMAMOTO: DOOMED STRATEGIST

A rear admiral by the age of 44, Isoroku Yamamoto (1884-1943) was Japan's most lauded naval strategist. He opposed a war that he believed was bound to bring Japan into conflict with the USA – whose industrial might he had seen as a Harvard student and later as naval attaché in Washington. Nevertheless, when such a war seemed inevitable, he pressed for a swift knockout blow against the Americans. He was also a firm believer in the aircraft carrier, and during the 1930s, while head of his navy's technical branch, pushed for the construction of carriers and of the formidable new Zero fighter.

In 1939, he was appointed Commander in Chief of the Japanese Combined Fleet. When the Pearl Harbor raid failed to destroy the US carriers, Yamamoto planned the disastrous Midway operation. He went on to direct naval operations in the Solomons. But by March 1943, Yamamoto knew the war was lost. Deeply depressed, he went on a tour of forward bases in the Solomons to boost morale. US Intelligence knew of his plans and American fighters intercepted and shot down his aircraft (see box, p. 353).

HITTING BACK Americans take aim at the Japanese planes. Recovering quickly from the shock of the attack, men fired ack-ack and machine guns, rifles, even pistols. But this sputtering barrage did little to hurt the enemy.

suspected a malfunction, but a quick check showed all was in perfect working order. Elliott phoned duty officer Lieutenant Kermit Tyler, announcing the approach of a large formation of aircraft. It never occurred to Tyler that these might be hostile. There were two much more likely explanations: they could be B-17 Flying Fortress bombers due in from California that morning, or aircraft from *Enterprise*, expected around 8 am. 'Don't worry about it', he said. Thus the Americans lost their last chance of countering the Japanese.

HOMING IN

By now, Lt Commander Fuchida and his strike force, flying at 3000 m (9800 ft), were searching for a break in the carpet of thick cloud. Fuchida knew that they must be close to their target. They had been flying for $1\frac{1}{2}$ hours and were picking up the commercial radio stations from Oahu's chief city, Honolulu. But he was not sure of their exact location. Then, as if by miracle, the clouds parted; they were off the northern tip of Oahu. The planes flew on down the island's western coast.

At 7.40 am, Fuchida gave the signal to prepare for attack. Some aircraft wheeled inland to strike Oahu's airfields, while the rest prepared to attack Pearl Harbor. A little later, at Ewa air station, west of Pearl, duty officer Marine Captain Leonard Ashwell was scanning out to sea when he focused on a long line of torpedo bombers heading east. With a jolt, he recognised them as Japanese 'Kates'. As he ran to sound the alarm, Japanese Zero fighters roared down on Ewa.

At that very moment, Fuchida caught his first glimpse of Pearl Harbor, its waters shimmering in the early morning sun. Seven of the US Pacific Fleet's eight battleships were strung out along Ford Island's 'Battleship Row' (see diorama). They were *California, Maryland, Oklahoma, Tennessee, West Virginia, Arizona* and *Nevada*. Across the harbour *Pennsylvania*'s superstructure rose from a dry dock on the mainland.

Fuchida knew that success was certain. Not even a novice could miss these targets, and his crews were the most highly trained naval airmen in the world. Even as the attack began he sent the pre-arranged victory signal to Nagumo: '*Tora! Tora! Tora!*' ('Tiger! Tiger! Tiger!').

'THIS IS NO DRILL'

At his home on Makalapa Hill overlooking Pearl Harbor, Kimmel was still on the phone to Commander Murphy. He listened, dumbfounded, as Murphy broke off suddenly to relay a dispatch he had just received: 'The Japanese are attacking Pearl Harbor, and this is no drill.' Horrified, Kimmel dropped the phone and ran into his garden.

Below him, long lines of 'Kates', swooping down to less than 30 m (100 ft) to release their torpedoes, were causing enormous devastation. Within minutes, *California, Oklahoma, West Virginia, Arizona* and *Nevada* had all been hit – *West Virginia* at least six times. Then high-level 'Kates' roared over; this time *Maryland* and *Tennessee* were also struck. All along Battleship Row, men were jumping overboard and trying to swim ashore. By now, though, the harbour surface was coated with a thick layer of oil. It burst into flames, killing most of those in the water.

Kimmel sped downhill to his headquarters, where he and his staff leaned out of a window, watching helplessly. Suddenly, Kimmel was knocked off his feet by a spent bullet flying in through the window. He pocketed it and muttered, 'It would have been merciful had it killed me'. The admiral's army counterpart, Lt General Walter Short, had been caught equally unprepared. At 8 am, sitting in his quarters at Fort Shafter, 13 km (8 miles) inland, he heard the sound of aircraft engines and gunfire – but took no notice. He assumed it was yet another navy exercise. He rapidly lost his composure, however, when an officer burst in to announce that two nearby army barracks were under attack.

As the Japanese Zeros swooped down over the barracks, the pilots saw long queues outside the mess huts; it was breakfast time. Some Americans glanced upwards at the approaching aircraft, but none moved. Even when machine-gun fire started to cut large swathes through their lines, many remained in the open as if paralysed. Next, the Japanese turned on the nearby Wheeler Field USAAF fighter base. Soon the aircraft there – lined up close together on the runways – were all ablaze. There were similar scenes at Hickham Field and Kaneohe naval air station. The midget sub attack, however, had been a fiasco: only one out of five subs assigned to the operation made it into Pearl Harbor, and that was sunk.

PEACE TO WAR

For the Americans on Oahu, the transition from peace to war was shockingly sudden. One moment they were getting out of bed, putting on their clothes, eating breakfast and thinking of the usual routines of Sunday. The next, they were under savage attack. Once the reality sank in, however, they hurled themselves into activity. Fighter pilots raced for the few undamaged machines. Men ran to anti-aircraft guns and pumped shells skywards, though some defective shells failed to explode in the air and others dropped on Honolulu, killing and wounding civilians.

Meanwhile, the B-17s arriving from California and the aircraft from *Enterprise* – then not far to the south – had a harrowing reception. Several of *Enterprise*'s planes were shot down by Zeros. One, though, managed to send a message to the carrier, warning it to maintain radio silence and keep clear

FUCHIDA: PEARL HARBOR LEADER

Before Pearl Harbor, Mitsuo Fuchida (1902-76) had already clocked up more than 3000 hours of combat flying. He was one of Japan's most experienced naval aviators and was recommended by his friend Minoru Genda to lead the Pearl Harbor attack.

Fuchida went on to lead the attack of the *Kido Butai* (Carrier Striking Force) on Darwin, but at the time of Midway was in *Akagi*'s sick bay with appendicitis. Although in pain, he insisted on watching the attack get under way. Then, when American dive-bombers hit the ship, he shattered a leg leaping from the burning bridge. After a year's convalescence he took up a series of staff posts.

After the war Fuchida wrote extensively of his experiences, was converted to Christianity and became a Protestant minister. He frequently preached to Japanese immigrants in North America, and in 1966 became a US citizen.

A strike from the blue

The Japanese had to catch the enemy at Pearl Harbor by surprise. They succeeded. With the attack in full swing, many US soldiers, sailors and airmen could hardly believe what was happening.

1 Japanese 'Kate' torpedo bombers bear down on warships crowding Pearl Harbor – including seven battleships and over 100 heavy and light cruisers, destroyers and auxiliaries. Zero fighters (2) join in the fray.

3 Swarms of 'Kates' pound Ford Island's 'Battleship Row'. Smoke pours from *Nevada*, northernmost of the battleships. One torpedo has ripped a vast hole in its port bow. Minutes earlier, a Marine band on board was standing to attention, waiting to raise the colours at 8 am. Some bandsmen noticed aircraft diving at the other end of Ford Island and heard muffled explosions – but dismissed them as an unusually realistic exercise. Then, as they struck up 'The Star-Spangled Banner', a plane skimmed low over the harbour. It dropped a torpedo, then peeled off over *Nevada*, the rear gunner firing on the band, but only shredding the US flag. It was a 'Kate'. The band only ran for cover when the last note had sounded.

4 *Arizona* explodes like a fireworks display. It has been struck by torpedoes, then by a bomb from a high-level 'Kate'. At least six torpedoes have smashed into *West Virginia* (5); it sinks slowly to the harbour bottom. *Oklahoma* (6), hit several times, begins to keel over. *California* (7) is struck twice.

8 *Maryland* and *Tennessee* (9), protected from the torpedoes by *Oklahoma* and *West Virginia*, have been hit by bombs from high-level 'Kates'. Burning debris from *Arizona* also starts fires on *Tennessee*.

10 The eighth battleship *Pennsylvania* is in dry dock. It survives the first strike relatively unharmed, but in the second, at 8.40 am, becomes the focus of attack. Bomb after bomb screams down, but its luck holds: only one hits.

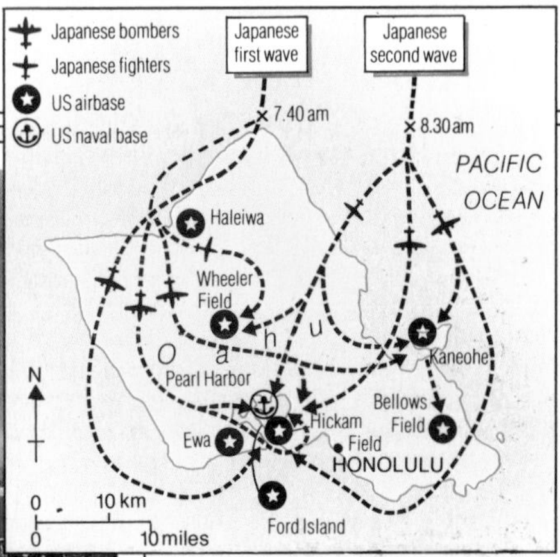

TARGET OAHU Sweeping in from the north, the Japanese struck Oahu's airfields as well as Pearl Harbor. Fires rage (left) as men clear up afterwards.

By the end of the attack, seven of the US Pacific Fleet's eight battleships are badly damaged, but only *Arizona* and *Oklahoma* will never sail again. Most shore-based navy and army aircraft have been destroyed, but other damage is remarkably slight. Shore installations have little or no damage; the cruiser and destroyer losses are unimportant; the submarines are unscathed. Above all, the aircraft carriers are untouched.

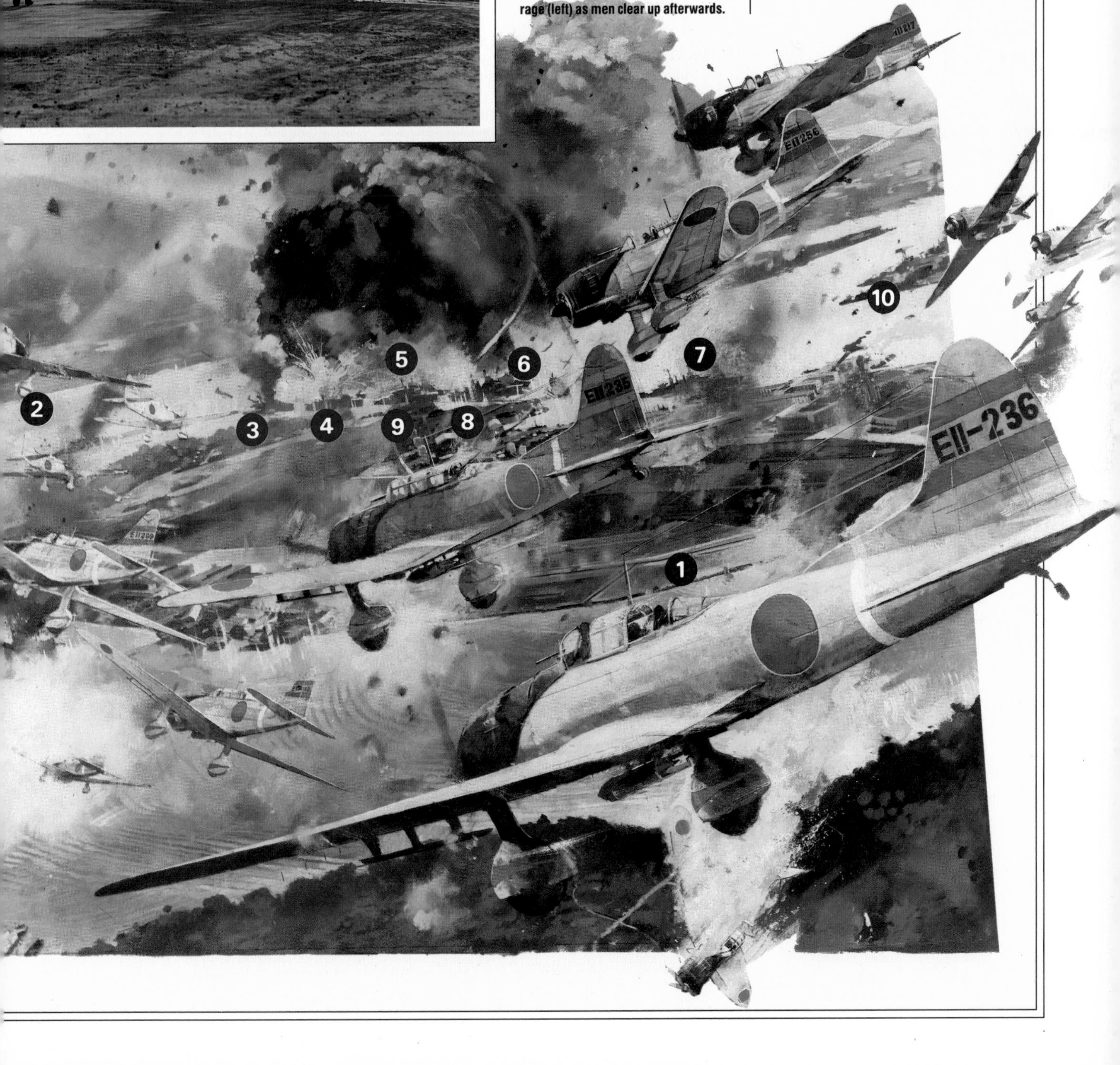

DEFENDERS DISMISSED

Despite more than 30 years' naval service, Husband Edward Kimmel (1882-1968) had little experience with carriers when he took command of the US Pacific Fleet on February 1, 1941. Washington warned him before Pearl Harbor that war was imminent, but he expected the Philippines to be hit first.

On December 17, only ten days after the assault, Kimmel was dismissed. The same fate befell Hawaii's army commander, Lt General Walter Campbell Short (1880-1949). Like Kimmel, Short never considered the possibility of an attack on Hawaii, and largely ignored reconnaissance and radar reports. Obsessed with the danger of sabotage by Hawaii's Japanese population, Short ordered his aircraft to park wing tip to wing tip in the centre of airfields, where they offered a perfect target for the Japanese planes.

In January 1942 Kimmel and Short faced a board of inquiry and were found guilty of dereliction of duty. A postwar Congressional investigation ruled that the men had merely made errors of judgment.

of Pearl. *Enterprise* sped off eastwards and lived to fight another day. The B-17s suffered worst from American ground fire as they tried to land.

At 8.40 am, a second wave of Japanese attackers crossed Oahu's eastern coast – 170 bombers and fighters. The Americans, now fully alert, gave them a warm reception. Lieutenant Fusati Iida, leading Zeros into a second attack on Kaneohe naval station, ran into a wall of fire. Badly hit, he radioed his flight to break off the action, then deliberately crashed his aircraft into a burning building – a harbinger of future *kamikaze* tactics.

The other aircraft converged on Pearl Harbor. USS *Nevada*, though damaged, had managed to get up steam and was heading slowly towards the open sea. Dive-bombers swarmed down and hit it five times. Next, they concentrated on *Pennsylvania*, still relatively undamaged. But smoke from burning ships and intense ground fire interfered with their aim. One bomb hit the destroyer *Shaw*, in dry dock nearby, and its forward magazine exploded. Thinking they had destroyed *Pennsylvania*, the Japanese turned on smaller ships. By 10 am, the raiders were all gone.

The Americans, however, fully expected them to return. By mid-afternoon Governor Joseph B. Poindexter had proclaimed martial law. Expecting an invasion, Short set up headquarters in the crater of an extinct volcano and prepared for a desperate defence. With reliable intelligence scarce, wild rumours began to spread – that the US carriers had been sunk, that the Japanese had bombed San Francisco and Los Angeles.

During the night of December 7/8, US forces suffered further losses – but these were self-inflicted. Five aircraft from *Enterprise* were shot down by trigger-happy gunners, and jumpy patrols fought pitched battles between themselves. They were not going to be caught napping twice. But the Japanese never returned. Fuchida's plane, the last to come back from the raid, landed on *Akagi* at 1 pm.

He reported immediately to the bridge, where a heated discussion was in progress. Genda wanted to send a further all-out strike. Pearl's dockyard installations and oil stores were still largely intact; the strike force had lost only 29 aircraft and the job should be finished. Nagumo was less buoyant. A further attack, he argued, would run into heavy ground fire, and the US carriers were still at large. He decided not to renew the attack.

When the news of the raid reached Tokyo, the Japanese people broke into jubilant celebration – ignorant that the chance of an even greater victory had been passed by. In the United States, shocked disbelief rapidly gave way to a mood of fury. Over 2400 people had died or were missing after the raid – the bulk of them sailors and shore-based navy personnel, but including 68 civilians. Another 1178 had been wounded.

The day that Uncle Sam went to war

One part of the Pearl Harbor operation went badly wrong for the Japanese. At 2.05 pm, Washington time, on December 7, Japan's chief envoys to the United States, Kichisaburo Nomura and Saburo Kurusu, arrived at the State Department in a state of breathless anxiety. Fifteen minutes later, they were ushered into the office of Secretary of State Cordell Hull.

Their reception was icy. Hull refused to shake Kurusu's outstretched hand. He snatched a document Nomura was holding, glanced at it briefly (he had already been given the text by State Department cryptographers) and threw it on his desk. The document was filled with 'infamous falsehoods and distortions,' he told them curtly, 'on a scale so huge that I never imagined until today that any government on this planet was capable of uttering them.' With a dismissive gesture he ordered out the hapless envoys – who did not know that Pearl Harbor had yet been attacked. 'Scoundrels and pissants!' he growled.

Ten days earlier, on November 27, the US government had sent Tokyo a note, demanding that it withdraw all troops from China and Indochina. Nomura's document contained Tokyo's rejection. According to Japanese plans, it should have been delivered to the Secretary of State at 1 pm, Washington time – 30 minutes before the Pearl Harbor raid was due to begin. But the envoys were delayed by problems in deciphering and typing out the message. When they met Hull, he already knew of the attack.

DISBELIEF AND FURY

Throughout the United States, people's reactions to the news were similar – stunned disbelief, followed by fury. That morning, most American newspapers had confidently proclaimed that the Japanese were fighting shy and that the prospect of war was remote. But even as Hull confronted Nomura and Kurusu, the first radio reports of the raid were being broadcast. One New York station interrupted coverage of a Giants-Dodgers football game to announce the news. Irate, unbelieving callers soon jammed its switchboard. As the casualty figures mounted on the news tickers in New York's Times Square, people in the crowds shouted angrily: 'We're going to get them for this – we're going to smash them to pulp.'

On the Pacific coast, there was panic as well as anger. One Los Angeles radio station announced that an invasion was on the way. Thousands of men armed with rifles and pistols turned up at the city's Hall of Justice in response. In San Francisco, Mayor Angelo T. Rossi declared a state of emergency. California Governor Calbert L. Olsen ordered out the National Guard.

FBI chief J. Edgar Hoover ordered the rounding up of all Japanese nationals resident in the USA. At Hollywood's baseball field, FBI agents arrived during a match between a Paramount studio team and a team of Japanese nationals living in California. Paramount was well ahead, though – and the agents let the game finish before arresting the Japanese. California's Nisei, Americans of Japanese descent, sent the White House telegrams denouncing Japan's actions. But they were later rounded up, under an order signed by President Roosevelt in February 1942.

UNITY BREAKS OUT

One of the most important results of the Japanese attack was the unity it brought between Americans. At dawn on December 7, the United States had been a nation bitterly divided. There was a minority who favoured entering the war (among them Roosevelt) and a majority who argued for neutrality (led by the America First Committee). By dusk it was united as never before.

Actions soon followed words. Labour leaders called off strikes and told union members to work around the clock if needs be. Thousands of Americans besieged recruiting offices. These had to draft in extra help and remained open night and day.

Shortly before 1 pm on Monday, December 8, the President addressed Congress and the Supreme Court, asking Congress to declare war on Japan. 'Yesterday, December 7, 1941 – a date that will live in infamy,' he began his speech, 'the United States of America was suddenly and deliberately attacked by naval and air forces of the Empire of Japan . . .' The speech was greeted with a thunder of clapping and cheers. He had spoken for all Americans.

Britain had declared war earlier the same day. Three days later Germany and Italy, honouring treaty obligations with Japan, declared war on the USA – now a fully fledged member of the Allies, an angry giant, committed to total war against the Axis. Nearly four years of hard fighting lay ahead, but with American industrial might committed, the issue was no longer in doubt.

Britain's shame: the fall of Malaya and Singapore

The rapid loss of Malaya and Singapore was one of the gravest humiliations ever suffered by the British Army. Although outnumbered three to one, Japan's 'Tiger' Yamashita bluffed 'Rabbit' Percival into surrender.

A MAN AND HIS BIKE Bicycles enabled the Japanese infantry to advance with a speed that astonished the British. This private holds a standard 6.5 mm Arisaka rifle.

THE FRIGHTENING CRUMP of exploding bombs brought a rude awakening to the British colony of Singapore at 4.15 am on Monday, December 8, 1941. One Englishwoman, long resident in the colony, grabbed the telephone and yelled down it at the police: 'There's an air raid going on!' Nearby, a bomb blast reduced a shop to rubble. 'Don't be alarmed,' came the soothing reply. 'It's only a practice.' 'Well, tell them they're overdoing it!'

There was to be a rude awakening in a wider sense for this trim, tightly controlled colony, domain of the memsahib and of empire builders in solar topis and knee-length shorts. The talk at tennis parties and in places like the bar of the Raffles Hotel was comforting: the Japanese had such weak eyes that they could neither fly straight nor shoot straight – and in any case, Singapore was a fortress and impregnable.

The complacency went so deep that when Singapore's radar first picked up alarming blips from the approaching Japanese bombers, no air-raid warning was sounded. Sir Shenton Thomas, Governor of the Straits Settlements (which included Singapore) thought sounding the sirens might cause the civilian population to panic. By the time he changed his mind, it was too late.

The Japanese pilots, when they arrived overhead, were amazed to find the city still brightly lit. Their well-aimed bombs destroyed several buildings and killed or injured around 200 civilians, most of them Chinese and Indian.

THE 'TIGER OF MALAYA'

The career of Tomoyuki Yamashita (1885-1946) was chequered. Involvement in the abortive 'Imperial Way' coup of 1936 earned him enemies in Tokyo, and relegation to Korea. But he had friends in the military hierarchy and soon re-emerged as a lieutenant general, serving with distinction in China. Despite brilliant success in Malaya, relegation once more followed – to Manchuria. Convinced that enemies, including Prime Minister Tojo, were plotting against him, the 'Tiger' had quarrelled with subordinates and superiors alike.

In 1944 he emerged again – to defend the Philippines. After a brave campaign, he gave himself up to the Americans. He was hanged for war crimes, despite evidence clearing him of the worst atrocities attributed to him.

BRITAIN DECLARES WAR ONCE AGAIN

'On the evening of December 7 His Majesty's Government . . . learned that Japanese forces, without previous warning . . . had attempted a landing on the coast of Malaya and bombed Singapore and Hong Kong. In view of these wanton acts of unprovoked aggression . . . His Majesty's Ambassador at Tokyo has been instructed to inform the Imperial Japanese Government . . . that a state of war exists between our two countries.' So Churchill informed the Japanese ambassador in London at 1 pm on December 8, 1941.

A month earlier Churchill had promised that 'should the United States be involved in war with Japan, a British declaration of war would follow within the hour'. In fact, Britain declared war several hours before the US Congress. At 3 pm Churchill broke the news to the House of Commons, then broadcast it to the nation that evening.

JAPANESE LANDINGS

At the same time, men of Japan's Twenty-Fifth Army under Lt General Tomoyuki Yamashita were coming ashore at three points on the Gulf of Thailand farther north – at Singora (Songkhla) and Pattani in Thailand itself (see map, p. 144) and near Kota Baharu in British-ruled Malaya. Crack Imperial Guards under Lt General Takuma Nishimura were simultaneously entering Thailand overland from Indochina.

The landings in Thailand met little resistance, but men coming ashore at Kota Baharu encountered high seas and fierce resistance from British Indian troops – yet they broke through by mid-morning. Yamashita sent a reconnaissance regiment under Lt Colonel Shizuo Saeki, with tanks and motorised infantry, to head south from Singora for the Malayan frontier town of Jitra. Other men followed on bicycles. They pedalled in long, chattering columns. The Japanese from Pattani struck south-west along mountain tracks.

The Pearl Harbor operation had been daring in the extreme; so was the Japanese plan for the conquest of Malaya and Singapore. Yamashita's orders gave him just 100 days in which to advance over 1000 km (620 miles) down the Malay peninsula and take Singapore. The capture of Singapore was crucial to Japanese ambitions in south-east Asia, for it controlled all regional lines of communication. Yamashita had just over 50 000 men to attack some 88 000.

The Japanese commander planned to make his main thrust down the peninsula's western side, along a wide plain with excellent road and rail systems. From the southern tip of Malaya, he would cross the narrow Johor Strait to land on Singapore island. Britain saw Singapore, the pride of its Far Eastern empire, as an impregnable fortress, but Yamashita knew otherwise. Its big guns pointed south, out to sea – and he would attack from the north.

BENNETT: CONTROVERSIAL COMMANDER

An irascible temper brought Henry Gordon ('Ginger') Bennett (1887-1962) into frequent conflict with other officers. Nonetheless, he was a brave commander, who had served ably in World War I and stayed in part-time soldiering in the Australian Militia afterwards, rising to major general. In September 1940, he was given command of 8th Division, Australian Imperial Force, and arrived in Malaya in February 1941. During the Japanese invasion he voiced scathing criticisms of British commanders, adding that, under attack, Indian troops 'scattered like schoolgirls'. His own successes, however, held back the Japanese for only 48 hours; he lacked the experience to handle a division-sized front in the jungle.

When Percival surrendered Singapore, Bennett and two of his officers decided to escape. But he had a chilly reception in Australia on the grounds that he should have stayed with his men. Bennett argued that Australia needed a general who had faced the Japanese in battle, but he was relegated to Inspector of Army Training. Australia's most controversial soldier was never given another fighting command.

DITHERING RESPONSE

Contrary to appearances, the Japanese had not caught the British by surprise. A full two days before they landed, the British Commander in Chief Far East, Air Chief Marshal Sir Robert Brooke-Popham, had been alerted at his head-

PERCIVAL – FATALLY INDECISIVE

A much decorated junior officer in World War I, Arthur Ernest Percival (1887-1966) rose rapidly to become General Officer Commanding Malaya in May 1941. Four years earlier he had prepared a report on the defence of Malaya in which he predicted almost exactly the eventual Japanese attack. He also prepared War Plan 'Matador', for a pre-emptive strike northwards into Thailand.

Percival's plans were perfect in theory, but in the event his indecisiveness proved fatal; frequent orders and counter-orders exhausted and confused his troops. He could never wrest control of the situation. By the end of the campaign, defeat was inevitable. But it could have been honourable had Percival considered Yamashita's problems in bringing up men and ammunition. A prisoner of war for 3½ years, he was freed in time to witness the Japanese surrender in September 1945.

quarters in Singapore to the approach of Japanese convoys. The army chief in Malaya, Lt General Arthur Percival, had duly ordered 11th Indian Division at Jitra to move north and stand by to defend possible landing areas, according to the prearranged 'Matador' plan. The Indians prepared enthusiastically to smash the invaders.

Then the British commanders dithered. At 8 am on December 8, staff at Percival's headquarters in Singapore phoned Brooke-Popham for permission to put 'Matador' into effect. The Commander in Chief waited for 1¾ hours – then decided to cancel 'Matador'. The enemy landings, he thought, were too strong for him to oppose. The Indians must return to defend Jitra. But by now, Percival – who had to give the withdrawal order – was away from his headquarters and did not return until 10.45 am. Extraordinarily, his staff made no effort to find him and pass on the news. Another hour had been wasted.

In the end, Percival merely sent the withdrawal orders to British headquarters in Kuala Lumpur, capital of the Federated Malay States. Staff there only managed to get them through, on overcrowded civilian telephone lines, at 1.30 pm. It was well into the evening before Maj General David Murray-Lyon, commanding the 11th Indian Division, could contact all his units and order them back. The episode demonstrated the weak-willed response shown time and again by British commanders in Malaya.

Things grew ever worse for the British. On December 10 they suffered two devastating blows: the sinking of the Royal Navy's *Prince of Wales* and *Repulse* (see box, p. 144), and the destruction of the huge Alor Star (Alur Setar) air base. 'In all the war I never received a more direct shock', Churchill wrote later of the loss of the two ships. Britain no longer had a navy or an air force to guard south-east Asia, and morale plummeted.

Then on December 12, Murray-Lyon, caught between Saeki attacking from the north and troops from Pattani cutting around behind him towards the west coast, was forced back from Jitra. Saeki, recently dressed down by his superiors for lacking 'offensive spirit', moved straight into Jitra, taking over 1000 prisoners – for the loss of just 100 Japanese killed and wounded.

The British were relentlessly forced south. On the night of December 17/18, the garrison and European population were evacuated from Penang island; the Japanese moved in the next night. The invaders pushed on, forced the British from a strong defensive position near Kampar, and entered Kuala Lumpur on January 10.

At the same time, the Japanese advancing from Kota Baharu had been struggling down the rugged, jungle-clad east coast with its many wide rivers. To the north, the Imperial Guards had swiftly passed through Thailand – which had little choice but to grant free passage and become a Japanese puppet – then turned south into Malaya.

SINGAPORE SHAKEUP

In Singapore, meanwhile, there had been a shake-up. Brooke-Popham had been sacked, and on January 7 General Sir Archibald Wavell, newly created Allied Supreme Commander in the Far East, had visited the island. He was disturbed by what he found. Substantial reinforcements were on their way, but until they arrived the Japanese advance had to be staved off. Percival and the Singapore authorities had refused (thinking it bad for civilian morale) to construct fortifications along the island's northern coast. Wavell ordered building to start at once.

Most officers were dispirited, but one exception was Maj General Henry Gordon ('Ginger') Bennett, commanding the Australian 8th Division. He and his men were full of fight and itching to get at the Japanese. They got their chance on January 14. Having placed explosives under a wooden bridge carrying one of the main west-coast roads near the town of Gemas, they were lying in wait in surrounding hills. At 4 pm they sighted their quarry – columns of Japanese cycling along four abreast and chatting loudly.

The Australians allowed the first 300 or so to cross the bridge, then struck. A huge explosion blew timber, bicycles and bodies skywards, while gunfire cut swathes through the packed columns. Those who escaped the massacre were driven south into the fire of other Australian units. Few survived. An elated Bennett informed war correspondents that the tide of battle had turned.

His optimism was short-lived. Even as he was speaking, Nishimura's Imperial Guards were launching an attack across the mouth of the Muar river, on the second main west-coast road. They cut through poorly trained Indian troops, then started to swing inland behind Gemas. Bennett, threatened with encirclement, sent two battalions to reinforce the Indians – but too late. Reinforcements and Indians alike were surrounded at Bakri – 4000 men against at least 12 000 Japanese.

But Lt Colonel Wright Anderson, commanding the trapped forces, was determined not to fall into Japanese hands. Between January 18 and 23, he and his men, wielding axes, hacked their way through flesh and timber, Japanese roadblock after roadblock, to rejoin British troops to the south-east. They kept busy an entire enemy division and allowed Bennett's 8th Division to withdraw in the direction of Singapore. This action won Anderson the VC.

A terrible fate befell those of his men – many badly wounded – who did fall into Japanese hands. Infuriated Imperial Guards tortured them for a whole day, then at dusk doused them with petrol and burned them alive. After that the Guards, anxious to redeem their honour, pushed south-east on the last leg to Singapore.

By January 28 Percival had given up all hope of holding southern Malaya. That day he ordered all his forces back to Singapore. The last men withdrew to the island three days later, blowing a gap behind them in the causeway across the Johor Strait. Yamashita had conquered Malaya in less than eight weeks, losing fewer than 2000 killed and 3000 wounded. Percival's losses so far were an estimated 4000 killed, 21 000 taken prisoner.

Yet Yamashita's mood as he faced Singapore was far from confident. He could muster only 30 000 soldiers, 300 tanks and 200 guns, many of them captured from the British. Ammunition was slow to arrive and much air support was being diverted to the Dutch East Indies.

Percival, by contrast, had been greatly reinforced. By February 5, he had 100 000 men – including 35 000 British and 15 000 Australian troops. He was short of aircraft and tanks, but had some 400 guns, including Singapore's massive 15 in (381 mm), 9.2 in (233 mm) and 6 in (152 mm) fortress weapons, originally facing out to sea but now trained north towards the mainland. He also had enough ammunition, fuel and other supplies to last three months. Little, though, had been done on the north-coast fortifications ordered by Wavell.

But the British commander fatally dissipated his strength. Uncertain where the Japanese would attack, he spread his forces all around the island's 115 km (70 mile) coastline. He left the north-west particularly vulnerable. Here, three under-strength Australian battalions under Bennett had to cover a flat stretch of mangrove swamp intersected by creeks. Wavell, who revisited Singapore on January 20, warned of this area's vulnerability and of the probability of an attack there – but Percival took no notice.

ASSAULT ON SINGAPORE

Wavell was right. On the night of February 8/9, Yamashita, in his first assault, unleashed the full force of 16 battalions against Bennett's attenuated three. Even so, the Australians gave the attackers a close-run battle. Firing at dark shapes approaching across the strait, they annihilated the first two Japanese assaults. The third wave, however, managed to land. Fierce hand-to-hand fighting followed, but by dawn the Australians had pulled back to a low ridge known as the Jurong Line. They had abandoned Singapore's western third to the Japanese.

That day (February 9) Percival reinforced the Jurong Line, while Yamashita consolidated his bridgehead. Then, at night, the Imperial Guards attempted a landing at Kranji – only to have their packed landing craft shot to pieces by more Australians. Japanese who made it ashore had to hide in mangrove swamps while bullets screamed overhead. Others left in the water were incinerated by sheets of blazing oil drifting from bombed fuel tanks at the Singapore naval base.

Then came a fatal misunderstanding. That day Percival gave Bennett a contingency plan: if the Japanese broke through, all troops would with-

'BANZAI' FOR VICTORY Japanese soldiers in Singapore rejoice in their triumph. There were similar scenes in Tokyo, where celebrations exceeded those for Pearl Harbor. For the British, by contrast, there was the bitterness of defeat. European women and children (inset) prepare to evacuate Singapore in the period before the Japanese onslaught. General Percival (top right) leads the way to surrender.

THE NAVY'S GREATEST SHOCK

Vice Admiral Sir Tom Phillips was running a terrible risk – and he knew it. It was late on December 8 and he was heading from Singapore up Malaya's east coast with Force 'Z', recently arrived in the Far East. It consisted of the brand-new battleship *Prince of Wales*, the older battlecruiser *Repulse* and four destroyers. The ships were making for the Japanese beach-heads, which Phillips planned to destroy from the sea if they could not be dealt with by land. He had no air cover, and relied on bad weather to protect him from enemy bombers.

On December 9, however, the cloud cover began to break and lookouts spotted Japanese reconnaissance planes. Phillips put about for base, but too late. Shortly after 10 the next morning, enemy planes attacked. Despite British manoeuvres, two torpedoes hit *Prince of Wales*, ripping a hole in its hull and damaging the rudder. It veered around in a drunken circle, out of control. The bombers turned on *Repulse*. Several torpedoes smashed into it, and shortly after midday it capsized and sank. The Japanese returned to *Prince of Wales* and soon it too was gone. Only the destroyers remained to pick up survivors. Nearly 3000 men, including Phillips, died. It was the worst British naval disaster of the war, and the first time aircraft on their own had sunk such large ships at sea.

draw to a defensive line just north of Singapore city. Bennett relayed the dispatch, in a garbled version, to his brigade commanders – who mistook it for an order to withdraw. Men who had just repelled the Imperial Guards pulled back, leaving the island's northern shore open to the enemy. Those on the Jurong Line also retreated.

Suddenly, all was a shambles. Japanese troops surged eastwards from the Jurong Line, capturing a huge British supply base at Bukit Timah and reservoirs that provided Singapore city's water. By February 12, the Japanese had taken four-fifths of the island and captured most British supplies. They fought well, but owed much to the sheer incompetence of British generalship. Singapore's much-vaunted fortress guns proved largely ineffective, because they were provided with armour-piercing shells, devastating against ships but not effective against infantry.

PANIC IN THE CITY

Life in the besieged city, meanwhile, was a nightmare. Fire raged in many areas. Precious water seeped through fractured mains. Bombs fell and shells exploded, while crowds of terrified civilians – Chinese, Malay, Indian and European – thronged debris-blocked streets. Drunken deserters looted indiscriminately. Large numbers of European women and children had already been evacuated in January. The last evacuation convoy left on February 12. Some men tried to force their way on at gunpoint. Others took their chances in assorted smaller vessels. About 1600 servicemen eventually escaped to India.

By the morning of February 15, the Japanese were just 4.5 km (3 miles) from the waterfront. At a conference of his senior commanders, Percival, disregarding injunctions from Churchill to fight to the death, decided on surrender. That afternoon he met Yamashita under a flag of truce.

Unknown to Percival, the Japanese commander was, in fact, in a dangerously weak position. His troops were outnumbered three to one and had only enough ammunition to last a few more hours. Unless Percival surrendered at once, he would have to withdraw temporarily to the Malayan mainland. Nonetheless, he ordered his men to keep firing, and threatened a renewed assault on Singapore that very night.

Percival, taken in by the bluff, capitulated unconditionally. His men had long irreverently nicknamed him 'Rabbit'; Yamashita's knew their general as 'Tiger'. The truth behind the names was very apparent that day. Never in the history of the British Army had such a large force laid down its arms to an enemy. Britain's power and prestige in the Far East, painfully built up over two centuries, had been wiped out in ten weeks. The next day, seemingly endless columns of prisoners were marched to Singapore's Changi jail.

'I realise how the fall of Singapore has affected you and the British people,' Roosevelt, also stinging from defeat, signalled Churchill, 'but no matter how serious our setbacks have been – and I do not for a moment underrate them – we must constantly look forward to the next moves that need to be made to hit the enemy.'

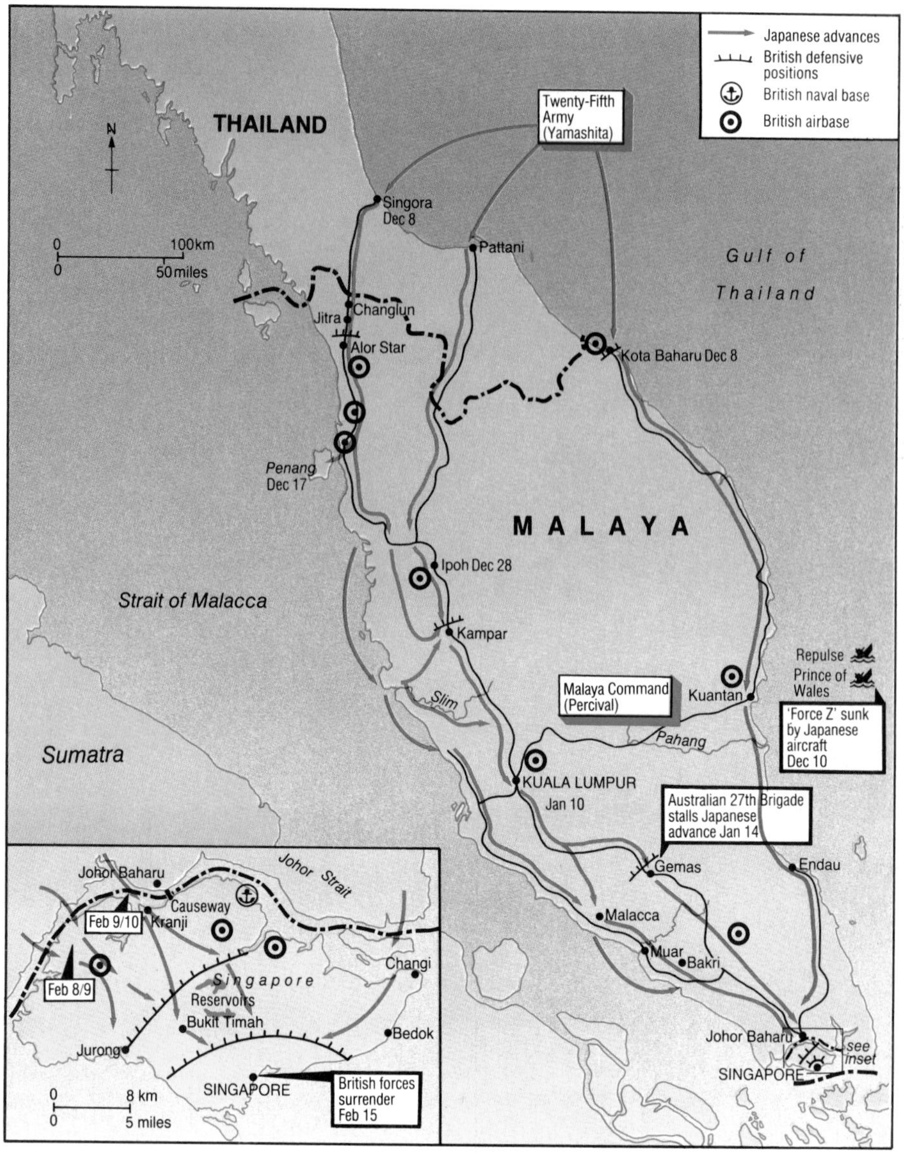

RAPID FALL The Japanese took just ten weeks to drive the British from the Malayan peninsula and take supposedly impregnable Singapore. The loss of HMS *Repulse* and *Prince of Wales* was another British humiliation.

AGGRESSIVE ADMIRAL 'TOM THUMB'

What Tom Spencer Vaughan Phillips (1888-1941) lacked in stature – he stood less than 1.62 m (5 ft 4 in) and was nicknamed 'Tom Thumb' – he made up in aggression and determination. He was a firm exponent of the 'big gun' school of naval warfare, believing that warships with efficient anti-aircraft gunners and room to manoeuvre had little to fear from the air. In October 1941 Phillips was placed in command of Force 'Z' and sent to the Far East to deter a Japanese attack. Here, while other British commanders dithered, he sprang into action, sailing without fighter cover to attack the Japanese beach-heads. Within 48 hours his warships were at the bottom of the Gulf of Thailand. Phillips chose to go down with them. The controversy of big guns versus aircraft had been settled.

The fall of Hong Kong: defeat with honour

After a deceptively easy start, the Japanese met in Hong Kong's Canadian, British and Indian defenders an enemy who made them fight for every inch.

TAKING THE SALUTE At last Hong Kong island has fallen, and General Sakai enters its streets in triumph. He had had a hard fight, for the British were determined that even if the Japanese won, they should not win easily.

LT GENERAL TAIKAISHI SAKAI was astonished at the speed with which he had conquered the mainland New Territories of Britain's colony of Hong Kong. At 7.30 am on December 8, 1941, troops of the Japanese Twenty-Third Army, under his command, had crossed the frontier from Japanese-occupied southern China. It was now December 13, and his men had reached the waterfront of the mainland city of Kowloon.

They had had to fight some tough actions, particularly against soldiers of the Royal Scots, on the fortified 'Gin Drinkers Line', across the New Territories' southern tip. But by now the British commander, Maj General Christopher Maltby, had withdrawn all his men across the harbour to Hong Kong island. The small RAF contingent had been destroyed on the first day.

NO SURRENDER

Elated at his easy victory, Sakai assumed that the British would surrender. He was wrong. On December 13, Hong Kong's governor, Sir Mark Young, rejected a surrender demand. Hong Kong island's mountainous terrain favoured the defenders, and Sakai realised he faced a hard fight.

He first decided to try a heavy bombardment of the city of Victoria, which lay invitingly exposed on the island's north-western shore. And for four days and nights Japanese shells and bombs rained down on the crowded streets, leaving heaps of mangled bodies. Factories, oil storage tanks and flimsy tenements went up in flames. Civilians crowded into tunnels in the granite hills behind, or sturdy buildings in the commercial districts.

On December 17, Sakai again demanded surrender – and was again refused. By now British and Indian troops were dug in along the north coast, together with units from the Hong Kong Volunteer Defence Corps, a force recruited from the colony's European community. Along the south coast Maltby had stationed newly arrived, partly trained Canadian troops, the Winnipeg Grenadiers and Royal Rifles of Canada. All told, he had 11 000 men, Sakai about 20 000.

On the night of December 18/19, men under Sakai's chief of staff, Colonel Ryosaburo Tanaka, landed undetected on Hong Kong's north-eastern corner, then moved west and by dawn were on the crest of Mt Butler, 3 km (2 miles) inland. Other Japanese landed nearer to Victoria, despite bloody hand-to-hand resistance from Indian troops. A further group landing near Victoria ran into heavy fire from the direction of a power station. Throughout the night and following morning the power station's defenders, mostly volunteers in their sixties and seventies, beat back the invaders. Then at 4 pm on December 19, their ammunition exhausted, the volunteers fixed their bayonets and charged the Japanese. Few volunteers survived.

FIERCE RETALIATION

Meanwhile, the Japanese had continued to pour across the harbour in convoys of junks and sampans, despite a dawn raid on the 19th by six British torpedo boats. Four of the boats were sunk or damaged, but not before they had inflicted heavy casualties. At the same time British and Punjabi troops, with Canadians from the south, launched attacks on Japanese positions throughout the north-east. Battles raged during the morning, but by noon most British attacks had been beaten back.

Only the Winnipeg Grenadiers on Mt Butler held on until the early afternoon, when the Japanese counterattacked in overwhelming numbers. Soon just one isolated Canadian position remained. In command here was Sergeant Major John Osborn. As the Japanese advanced, hurling grenades into his position, Osborn caught them and lobbed them back. But he missed one. It landed in the middle of the position. Osborn threw himself on it, taking the full blast to protect his men. He was awarded a posthumous VC.

Earlier that day, the Japanese had launched another attack on the Wong Nei Chong Gap – a deep valley, south-west of Mt Butler, with the island's main north-south road. In charge of the defence here was the Canadian Brigadier John Lawson. As the Japanese surged into the valley, he and his staff charged out of a bunker, guns blazing, and were immediately mown down. Other bunkers, defended by D Company of the Winnipeg Grenadiers, only fell three days later when the Japanese pushed field guns up to their walls and blasted them at point-blank range.

LAST STANDS

The Japanese were now pressing in on Victoria, and pushing southwards from Mt Butler, but the defenders never lost their fighting spirit. For four days from December 20, British troops repelled them from Leighton Hill, in Victoria's eastern suburbs, before withdrawing west to Mt Parish. Winnipeg Grenadiers held back more attackers on Mt Cameron. But by Christmas Day the defenders' situation was clearly desperate. They had been compressed into two widely separated areas, on the Stanley Peninsula in the south and around Victoria. The Japanese had captured all the island's reservoirs and Victoria was out of water. Sir Mark Young received another surrender ultimatum at 9 am on Christmas morning. Again he rejected it.

This was the last British gesture of defiance. At 2.30 pm the Japanese captured Mt Parish. Young and Maltby knew that the next battle would have to be fought in the capital's streets – where civilian casualties would be horrific. At 3.15 pm, Maltby ordered all units to surrender, though their last guns only fell silent early on December 26.

The Canadians alone had lost at least 300 dead and 500 wounded. Of the rest of Maltby's troops, at least 1300 died and 2300 were wounded. Thousands of civilians had also been killed or injured. But the Japanese had been made to suffer, too, with at least 1000 dead and 2000 wounded. 'The colony had fought a good fight,' Churchill wrote after the war. 'They had won indeed the lasting honour which is their due.'

'I shall return', vows MacArthur as the Philippines fall

The heroic last action of the 26th Cavalry Regiment and the defence of Bataan helped to restore American pride, rocked by early defeats. But they failed to prevent the Japanese conquest of the Philippines.

LOCAL HEROES A sergeant on watch with the Philippine Scouts stands by with shells for one of his gunners. The brave resistance of the Filipinos enraged the Japanese.

THE JAPANESE PILOTS could hardly believe their luck. Ten hours after the attack on Pearl Harbor, as they flew towards the main US air base in the Philippines, they expected the Americans to be waiting for them. Instead, when they arrived over their target – Clark Field, 80 km (50 miles) north-west of the Philippine capital Manila on the island of Luzon – they saw to their amazement row upon row of aircraft neatly lined up on the ground.

The Japanese planes – 108 bombers and 84 fighters – had taken off from Formosa (Taiwan), 400 km (250 miles) north of Luzon, at 10.30 am on December 8, 1941. Fog had delayed their scheduled takeoff, and they expected the Americans to be on full alert by the time they were due to arrive, 1½ hours later. Now fighters swooped down, guns blazing, while the bombers released their loads onto sitting targets. One by one the American planes exploded. Other airfields on Luzon suffered the same fate. The Japanese destroyed 105 of the 300 US aircraft on the island that morning and lost only seven of their own.

During the next two days they struck again. Tokyo had given General Masaharu Homma just 50 days to capture the Philippines, and the air strikes were the first step in his campaign. They were designed to wipe out the Philippines-based US Far East Air Force before his troops went ashore on Luzon.

On the American side, General Douglas MacArthur, Commander, US Army Forces Far East, had been warned at 3 am of a possible attack. His air force commander, Maj General Lewis Brereton, had urged a swift attack on Formosa. But MacArthur complacently disagreed. As a precaution, though, aircraft were ordered to patrol over central Luzon.

By mid-morning the danger of attack seemed to be receding and the patrols landed to refuel. At Clark Field, the aircrews retired to the mess hall, while ground crews began servicing the aircraft, ready to resume operations in the afternoon. When the Japanese arrived at midday, the American pilots were literally out to lunch.

BOLD APPROACH

The vast archipelago of more than 7000 islands was a former American possession, now a semi-independent 'commonwealth' with its own government under President Manuel Quezon, and promised full independence in 1946.

Homma's 57 000 men, who were to land on Luzon (see map), faced 140 000 army and air force men under MacArthur's command, but these were not as formidable as they seemed. At their core were 30 000 Americans and the excellent Philippine Scouts – American-officered Filipino troops, part of the US Army. But the rest of MacArthur's men were Filipino reservists, his pride and joy. For six years he had raised, officered and trained them, and his faith in them was absolute. MacArthur's chief of staff, Brig General Richard Sutherland, never dented his chief's faith in them by passing reports critical of the reservists onto the general's desk. But in the event they would prove far from reliable.

The most formidable of the opponents for the Japanese were Brereton's air force – including 35 Flying Fortresses and 70 modern Warhawk fighters – and the US Asiatic Fleet under Admiral Thomas Hart. Based at Cavite naval base, on the southern shore of Manila Bay, this fleet was small but its 27 operational submarines could easily overwhelm any invasion convoy. On December 10, however, Homma's bombers neutralised it in a massive two-hour raid on Cavite; Hart's entire torpedo stock went up. Once the submarines had used up the torpedoes they had on board, they would be useless. Then the islands could only be defended on land.

From long before the war, the Americans had had a carefully worked-out plan – War Plan 'Orange 3' – for the land defence of the Philippines. US forces would defend the Manila Bay area from the island forts at its mouth and the mountainous, jungle-clad Bataan Peninsula jutting down on its north-western side. They could hold out there for up to six months, barring seaward access to the capital's port until a relief force from the United States arrived.

To MacArthur, however, the plan smacked of defeatism. Instead of retreating to Bataan, he massed his men around the most likely invasion point – Lingayen Gulf on Luzon's west coast, from where the low-lying Central Plain led south to the capital. Hart's submarines armed with their remaining torpedoes patrolled the entrance, while Filipino troops under Maj General Jonathan Wainwright dug in around the shore.

IMAGINARY ENEMY

On December 10, 11 and 12, small Japanese forces landed at Aparri and Vigan in the north and Legaspi in the far south-east of Luzon. MacArthur recognised these as diversionary attacks, and refused to be drawn. Manila was also bombed on December 10. Then, on the night of December 12/13, a tremendous battle erupted in Lingayen Gulf. For hours defending forces blazed away, and the next day US headquarters proclaimed a great victory. But it soon emerged that the 'enemy' had been a reconnaissance motorboat.

The Americans failed markedly to recapture this heroic spirit when 85 Japanese army and naval transports, escorted by destroyers, really did enter Lingayen Gulf at dawn on December 22. Lt Commander Raymond Lamb, commanding the submarine USS *Stingray*, sighted the transports at point-blank range in the crosswires of his periscope – but then immediately dived and for 14 hours *Stingray* sat on the seabed while the Japanese vessels passed safely overhead. On Lamb's return to Manila, he was deprived of his command. Other submarine commanders claimed to have attacked the Japanese only to be driven back by depth charges. Hart was deeply depressed by the shameful performance.

Back at Lingayen, Homma's men fought their way through mountainous surf created by a nearby typhoon to land on the gulf's eastern side at Damortis. Several boats capsized and troops had to swim to shore without their equipment. Wainwright, scarcely believing his luck, ordered forward Filipino reservists under Brig General Clyde A. Selleck. The men were novices but Selleck felt confident that they could mow down a scattered and confused enemy. His confidence was misplaced. Battalion after battalion refused to advance and melted into the countryside, abandoning entire artillery batteries, which were

MACARTHUR – THE 'AMERICAN CAESAR'

Douglas MacArthur (1880-1964), one of World War II's most flamboyant and controversial figures, graduated top of the class of 1903 at West Point Military Academy. He served in the Philippines (where his father had been governor general), Panama and Mexico, before going to France in 1917. Twice wounded and much decorated there, he was promoted to major general in 1925 and became Army Chief of Staff by 1930. In this post, he clashed bitterly with admirals over US defence budgets.

In 1935 he was appointed military adviser to the Philippines, and in December 1941 commanded both the embryonic Filipino Army and US Army Forces in the Far East. The stubborn defence of the islands captured the public imagination. After he went to Australia in command of the South-West Pacific Area, he was soon at odds with Admiral Nimitz, Commander in Chief Pacific. MacArthur favoured recapturing the Philippines, Nimitz a thrust across the central Pacific. Finally, Roosevelt gave priority to both.

The Japanese surrender on August 15, 1945, took MacArthur by surprise. Worried that the US Navy would beat him to it, he flew into Atsugi air base near Tokyo on August 30 to take the formal surrender three days later. During 1945-51, when MacArthur was Supreme Commander for the Allied Powers (SCAP) in Japan, his rule was absolute but benevolent, accelerating Japan's reconstruction.

In 1950, at the age of 70, MacArthur was called to lead yet another campaign – in Korea. But the next year, after mixed success there, President Truman dismissed him amid dispute over whether to use atomic weapons. He returned to the US to a hero's welcome, but failed in a bid to be Republican presidential candidate in the 1952 election. Described by biographer William Manchester as the 'American Caesar', MacArthur saw himself as a man of destiny and became immodest to the point of egomania.

promptly seized by often weaponless Japanese.

MacArthur vented his rage on Selleck by reducing him to the rank of colonel, but the blame lay at his own door. His faith in the poorly trained Filipinos had been quite unwarranted. Now he had lost his chance to defeat the Japanese on the beaches. Later on December 22, Homma finally managed to land tanks and artillery at Lingayen and began moving south along the highway towards Manila. Wainwright, fearing a rout, rushed northwards his handful of regular Philippine Scouts, including the 26th Cavalry – one of the US Army's last horse-mounted regiments.

The 26th's 850 men were the last American unit to ride into battle on horseback. Dismounting before they reached Japanese positions on the main road from Damortis to the inland town of Rosario, they opened up with rifles and machine guns and stopped the enemy in their tracks for about two hours. They then vaulted into their saddles and galloped south to another enemy position. Again they halted the Japanese advance.

All day long they kept up a running battle, but at dusk in a sunken road north of Rosario, Japanese tanks caught up with them. As the tanks rolled forward, machine guns firing, riderless horses bolted into the night. Hundreds of men were mown down, hundreds more trampled by their mounts or crushed beneath the tracks of the enemy tanks. By the morning of December 23, the 26th had been reduced to 175 men.

TACTICAL RETREAT

On December 24, Wainwright urgently pressed MacArthur for permission to withdraw behind the Agno river, 80 km (50 miles) south of Lingayen. It was now clear that the Japanese could not be held, and MacArthur at last put Plan 'Orange 3' into effect. He was just in time. At dawn that day (Christmas Eve), more Japanese had landed at Lamon Bay, on Luzon's east coast, across the island's narrow centre from Manila. Though the country in between was mountainous and heavily forested, they pushed rapidly inland.

Over the next eight days and nights the road around the northern end of Manila Bay to Bataan was packed with convoys. MacArthur commandeered cars and buses to speed the flow. At the same time, Homma's men continued to push south from Lingayen through the Central Plain. They crossed the Agno river on Christmas Day. Early next morning, Hart left Manila for the Dutch East Indies; the bulk of his Asiatic Fleet had already withdrawn to help the defence of the Dutch islands. During that day MacArthur, his last troops withdrawn from Manila, declared the capital an open city. That night the lights of Manila, which had been regularly bombed since December 10, blazed once more, though the bombing continued for two more days.

The withdrawal of Wainwright's men from the north to Bataan was conducted with efficiency. Time and again Philippine Scouts turned and fought heroically against overwhelming odds to slow down the Japanese advance. Elsewhere major errors were made. Clark Field air base was evacuated in a hurry, and vast stocks of food and other supplies were left behind in the rush. MacArthur abandoned civilian food stocks.

HOMMA'S PLAN The 1800 km (1125 mile) archipelago of 7100 Philippine islands was vulnerable to invasion. But the direct route to the capital, Manila, past the island fortresses in Manila Bay, would be suicidal. Homma, the Japanese commander, decided to approach by land from several points and converge on Manila, grasping it in a giant vice.

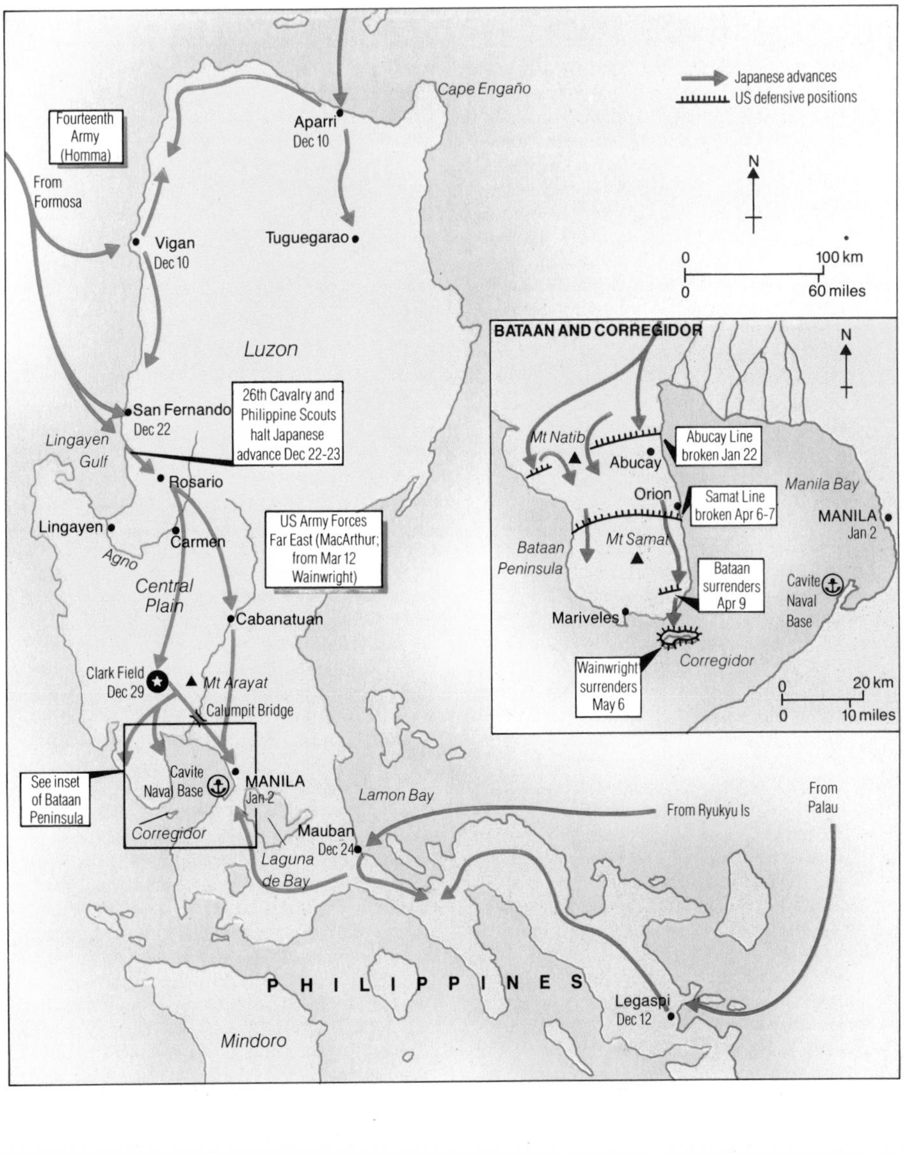

The 80 000 American and Filipino troops and 26 000 refugees in Bataan had ample ammunition, but little food and virtually no medical supplies.

Homma's men from Lingayen overran Clark Field on December 29 and entered the streets of Manila on January 2, 1942, linking up with those who landed at Lamon Bay. Their commander anticipated a prompt surrender, and so did the Japanese High Command. It ordered the Fourteenth Army's best 48th Division and a powerful air group south to the Dutch East Indies.

INTO BATAAN

The task of mopping up the Bataan Peninsula fell to 10 000 poorly trained, middle-aged Japanese reservists under Lt General Akiri Nara. They began their advance on January 10, marching down the coast road between Manila Bay and the forbidding peaks of Mt Natib.

The sugar-cane fields north of the town of Abucay and jungle covering the mountain slopes were ominously silent as the soldiers marched through, and the Japanese began to relax, slinging their rifles over their shoulders and chatting loudly. But their physical exhaustion coupled with relief at their good progress – they were only 32 km (20 miles) from Mariveles, the main US base at the southern tip of the peninsula – had blunted their alertness. Suddenly at 3.30 pm there was a thunderous eruption of shellfire. In an instant entire Japanese platoons were blown to pieces by exploding shells. Those Japanese who survived scrambled for cover. When, at midnight, they rallied and charged towards American guns, they became enmeshed as targets in barbed-wire entanglements and were soon cut to a bloody heap. By dawn, all surviving Japanese troops had been driven back.

The Japanese had blundered straight into the fortified Abucay Line, which ran from the eastern slopes of Mt Natib to Manila Bay. Dug in there were the US II Corps – three divisions backed by nearly 200 guns, under Maj General George Parker. News of the disaster threw Homma, now based at Fort Stotsenberg, next to Clark Field, into deep depression, darkened still further by reports from the western side of the peninsula, where more Japanese troops had been repulsed by Wainwright's I Corps. 'Orange 3' was taking effect at last, and American morale soared.

But Nara's patrols continued to search for a weak point in the American positions, and within two days found one. Parker and Wainwright, assuming that the jungles of Mt Natib were impenetrable, had not extended their defensive lines beyond its lower slopes. There was a 16 km (10 mile) gap in the centre which the Japanese exploited. While some of Nara's battalions continued frontal attacks, others hacked through the mountain's virgin jungle. On January 22, they burst out behind the Abucay Line. Taken by surprise, entire Filipino battalions panicked, dropped their weapons and fled south. Parker and Wainwright had to order a general retreat.

LAST STAND

It should have been a rout, but the Japanese, exhausted by their slog over Mt Natib, could not keep up with their enemy. The retreating Americans managed to form a new line along an old cobblestone road running east-west across the peninsula 20 km (12 miles) north of Mariveles. The slopes of Mt Samat, an extinct volcano in the centre of the line, gave a superb vantage point to US gunners, who mowed down repeated Japanese attacks. On February 8, Homma called a halt.

Later that day, the Japanese general outlined to his commanders the desperate nature of their position. Since January 9 they had lost 7000 men killed and wounded and 10 000 through disease; fewer than 3000 were ready for action. If the Americans discovered this weakness they might well break out of Bataan and be back in Manila within days. Fighting back his pride, Homma resolved to ask Tokyo for reinforcements. At that very point he received a telegram from Imperial Headquarters, expressing extreme displeasure at his lack of success. With tears pricking his eyes, Homma slumped on the table.

As Homma's star waned, MacArthur's rose. Throughout the Far East and Pacific, other Allied commands were surrendering – but Bataan held on. The American public, reeling from a succession of defeats, seized upon MacArthur and his troops as symbols of heroic resistance. From his headquarters in the island fortress of Corregidor the general issued dispatches referring to 'MacArthur's heroic resistance', 'MacArthur's victory' and so on. Ordinary Americans gave the commander credit for his troops' heroism.

Yet MacArthur had only once left Corregidor to visit his troops on Bataan. Their bitter mood is captured perfectly by one of the many battle-ballads they chanted, to the tune of the *Battle Hymn of the Republic*: 'Dug-out Doug MacArthur lies a-shaking on the Rock.' For the American and Filipino troops – and the 26 000 civilians – on the peninsula were feeling the consequences of his hasty and belated implementation of 'Orange 3'. Men subsisting on less than half normal combat rations foraged for food, sometimes behind Japanese lines. After widespread malnutrition came diseases such as dysentery, beriberi and malaria – just when quinine stocks ran out. In mid-March medical officers reported that 60 000 men were unfit for combat. Hunger and disease had accomplished what the Japanese could not.

But by then MacArthur had gone. On the night of March 11, acting on President Roosevelt's orders, the general and his entourage (including his wife and three-year-old son) boarded a flotilla of torpedo boats, slipped through the Japanese naval blockade around Luzon and landed on the still unoccupied island of Mindanao in the southern Philippines. From there they flew to Australia where MacArthur assured waiting journalists of his determination to recapture the Philippines: 'I shall return!' he declared.

By the beginning of April the balance of power on Bataan – where Wainwright was now in charge – had changed radically. Wainwright's 20 000

DEATH ON THE MARCH

On their arrival at Mariveles, at the southern tip of the Bataan Peninsula in 1942, the Japanese were amazed to find they had taken 76 000 prisoners. Their supply system could barely sustain their own men; the prisoners would have to be moved – most on a 105 km (65 mile) footslog to the railhead, then to Camp O'Donnell, a former US Army barracks near Clark Field air base.

Some of the captors deliberately set out to eliminate their prisoners. On April 11, several hundred Filipino officers and NCOs were tied up and killed by sword and bayonet. Killings continued when columns of Americans and Filipinos set out the same day for the railway. The Japanese guards beat them with rifle butts – and if they failed to get up, bayoneted them. Some groups of prisoners were deliberately run down by trucks. Day after day the columns staggered northwards – men with legs amputated hobbling on makeshift crutches; men crazed with malaria stumbling in erratic zigzags; men with amoebic dysentery having blood and faeces oozing down their legs. They were given no food, little water and little rest.

Japanese brutality became more systematic. Guards singled out members of the Philippine Scouts who, if they escaped, might lead local resistance. Many were shot, bayoneted or beheaded. A few were forced to dig their own graves, then buried alive. Yet in other columns the guards treated their charges well throughout.

At the railhead the prisoners were crammed into open trucks for the journey to Camp O'Donnell. Only about 54 000 reached the camp alive – and thousands more died of disease and malnutrition in the first few months of imprisonment.

SURRENDER FORGIVEN

A cavalryman who had served in World War I, Jonathan Mayhew Wainwright (1881-1953) took command of the Philippine Division in 1940, then, after MacArthur left for Australia in March 1942, he took over command of all US and Filipino forces in the Philippines.

Moral obligations to MacArthur made him fight on and denounce King's surrender of Bataan. When, a month later, he surrendered American forces throughout the islands, MacArthur was furious and refused to recommend him for the Medal of Honor. But when the two men met at the Tokyo surrender in 1945, MacArthur assured Wainwright – emaciated and broken in health from captivity in Manchuria – that all was forgiven. President Truman personally fastened the medal around Wainwright's neck on the general's return to the USA late in 1945.

FAILURE May 6, 1942: Wainwright orders all US forces throughout the Philippines to surrender.

INFANTRY DRESS Early on in the Pacific war, American soldiers wore a long-sleeved shirt and long trousers in khaki drill, with canvas leggings, brown ankle boots and webbing belt. The steel helmet was in the shallow British style. A 1902 Springfield rifle was common. Apart from the insignia (a colonel's eagle on the collar, left), officers and men wore the same uniform. It was too hot, uncomfortable and conspicuous – and was replaced later in 1942.

emaciated fighting men faced a Japanese army swollen to 50 000 by reinforcements. On April 3, the Japanese started shelling Mt Samat. It was now the dry season – little rain had fallen for over a month – and the cane fields that clad the lower slopes and hid the American positions ignited like a gigantic tinderbox.

Soon the mountainside was a mass of flames, and thousands of defenders suffocated or burned to death. The Japanese advanced through a grotesque and blackened landscape, past the charred remains of gunners lying by their still glowing weapons. Within three days they were over the mountains and on their way south. Fleeing Americans and Filipinos jammed the road to Mariveles. Wainwright, at his headquarters on Corregidor, forbade surrender, but his subordinate on Bataan, Maj General Edward King, knew the battle was over. On April 9 he ordered US forces on the peninsula to surrender; the Japanese occupied Mariveles and took thousands of prisoners (see box, *Death on the march*).

ISLAND FORTRESS

It took over a week to clear the last prisoners from the town. From the heights above, a vast battery of Japanese weapons – gigantic 240 mm ($9\frac{1}{2}$ in) mortars, the largest they possessed, and over 200 field guns and howitzers – were trained on Corregidor, only 3 km (2 miles) away in the mouth of Manila Bay. They bombarded the island for hours at a stretch. Corregidor, once lush and green, became a bleak moonscape. Wainwright still commanded 15 000 men there, but most were administrative troops, untrained for combat. The Malinta Tunnel complex, deep beneath the centre of the island, sheltered some 6000 of these plus Wainwright's headquarters and more than 1000 sick and wounded. Morale was low; only the few marines and soldiers who manned the beach defences and sheltered in bunkers and caves in Corregidor's cliffs remained cheerful.

Just before midnight on May 5, Japanese troops approached the narrow eastern end of the tadpole-shaped island. Driven by swift currents, they landed under a bright moon directly opposite an American strongpoint – two concealed 3 in (75 mm) guns. These fired straight into the crowded Japanese landing craft, blasting them out of the water. Other coast defence guns joined in and inflicted heavy casualties. Only a few hundred made land, but the senior surviving officer, Colonel Gempachi Sato, led them inland behind the US beach defences and fought through tenacious bands of Americans to the eastern entrance to the Malinta Tunnel. Thousands of Americans sheltered behind the tunnel's steel gates, but unlike the men at the shore they were little more than a frightened mob.

In mid-morning, with Japanese machine-gun bullets hammering against the gates, Wainwright radioed to President Roosevelt and MacArthur his intention to surrender Corregidor. At a meeting later that day, the exhausted American general – faced with the threat that the entire Corregidor garrison would be killed – agreed to the surrender of all US forces in the Philippines, even those well able to fight on in the still unconquered southern islands. At last something had gone right for Homma, but too late to save his career. Tokyo had already given effective control of the troops on the Philippines to Lt General Tomoyuki Yamashita, the victor of Singapore.

In the mountainous interior of several of the Philippine islands a few hundred American and Filipino troops defied the surrender order, slipped into the jungle and kept up a brave guerrilla resistance until MacArthur, as promised, returned nearly $2\frac{1}{2}$ years later.

HOMMA – AN INNOCENT EXECUTED?

Masaharu Homma (1887-1946) was an impressive figure. Almost 1.8 m (6 ft) tall and broadly built, he spoke perfect English. His admiration for British and Western values stemmed from his service as an observer with the British Army on the Western Front in 1918, and with the British Indian Army in 1922-5. In 1930 he was Japan's military attaché in London.

Homma disliked the extreme militaristic nationalism of 1930s Japan and its entry into the Axis pact. But military professionalism came before sentiment. After successful service in China from 1938, Homma was chosen in 1941 to command the Fourteenth Army's invasion of the Philippines. His lenient treatment of the Filipinos who fought with the US Army added fuel to Japanese criticism of a man already suspect for his Western leanings. In August 1942, Homma was relieved of his command and retired.

The Americans arrested him in September 1945 and tried him for war crimes. Evidence showed that Homma had done his best to prevent atrocities and had no part in the Bataan 'Death March'; in fact, he had disciplined the subordinates involved. Despite the impassioned pleas of his American defence lawyers – convinced of his sincerity and humanity – he was executed by firing squad on April 3, 1946.

JAPAN TRIUMPHANT One desolate colleague covers his face as Maj General King hears the surrender terms for Bataan. After six days of shellfire and burning of the cane fields, King surrendered the supposedly easy-to-defend peninsula on April 9, flouting the order of his superior, Wainwright. Posing proudly after the surrender, one of Homma's men (left) embodies the joy of victory.

Death in the Dutch East Indies

The Japanese set aside six months to conquer the oil-rich islands of the Dutch East Indies. They took them in two, despite many brave Allied actions.

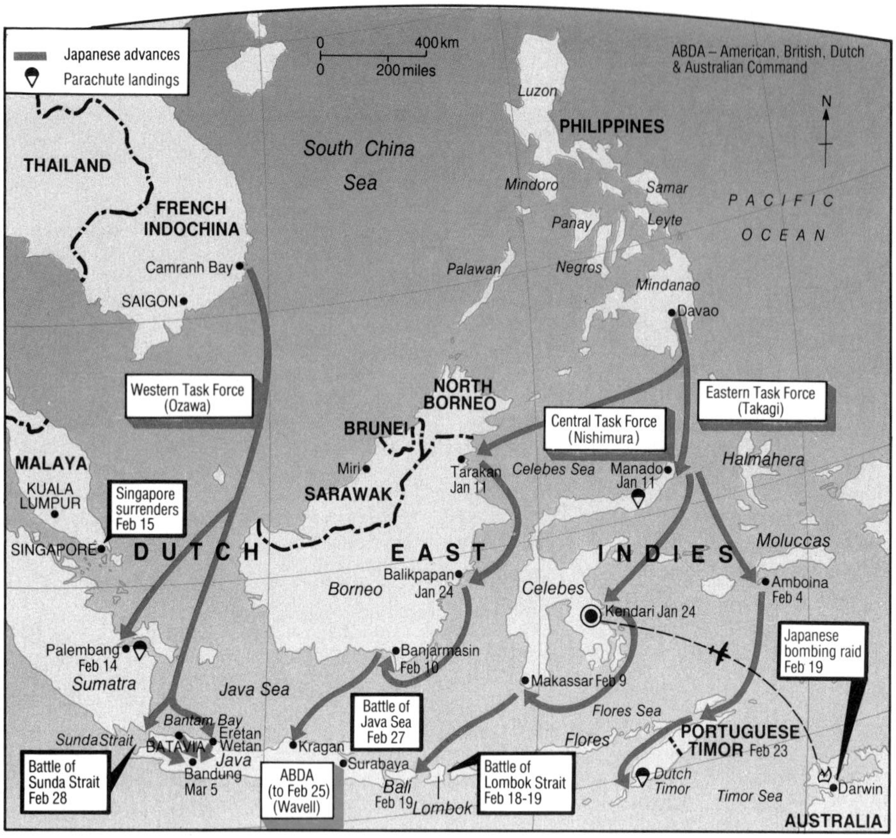

FROM THE BRIDGE of the Japanese light cruiser *Naka*, Rear Admiral Shoji Nishimura scanned the coastline of Tarakan island off Borneo in the Dutch East Indies (now Indonesia). Suddenly, a sheet of flame and clouds of smoke erupted from the island. Rather than let precious oil fields and refineries fall into enemy hands, the Dutch had set fire to them. It was the afternoon of January 10, 1942. That night Japanese soldiers and naval landing forces went ashore. To their relief, resistance was light – a little rifle fire. Then, just minutes after the attack began, Dutch and East Indian soldiers crawled out of the undergrowth, waving white flags. Within two days, the few pockets of troops that continued to resist had been mopped up.

The next morning, a little over 800 km (500 miles) farther east, 334 Japanese paratroops were dropped over an airfield near Manado on Celebes (Sulawesi). At first things went badly wrong for the paratroops. High winds scattered them and their weapon packs far and wide. Seeing Dutch defenders heading towards them, the Japanese prepared for the worst – until, to their surprise, they spotted white flags and raised hands. Resistance came to an end the next day. At this rate the conquest of the Dutch East Indies would be a walkover.

To capture this vast group of islands was one of the chief goals of the Japanese thrust into south-east Asia. The Dutch islands were rich in natural resources, particularly oil, and also formed part of the so-called Malay Barrier, stretching from the Malay Peninsula as far as northern Australia. Control of this would give the Japanese unhindered access to the Indian Ocean.

CLOSING IN ON JAVA

By early January 1942, successes in Malaya and the Philippines had enabled the Japanese to bring forward their assault on the Indies. They planned a three-pronged attack to close in on the most important island, Java. This had the bulk of the colony's population, its capital, Bandung, and its commercial centre, Batavia (now Jakarta).

Central and Eastern Forces were to move down the northern and eastern islands, cutting off Java from Australia, its chief supply source. They would then join forces and attack the island from the east. Nishimura and Rear Admiral Takeo Takagi led covering cruiser and destroyer forces. Once Singapore fell, Vice Admiral Jisaburo Ozawa's Western Force would sail from Indochina to attack Sumatra and western Java. The campaign's first moves were the taking of Tarakan by Central Force and Manado by Eastern.

The Indies' defences, meanwhile, had come under General Sir Archibald Wavell, newly appointed supreme commander of American, British, Dutch and Australian ('ABDA') forces in the Philippines, Burma, Malaya, the Indies and north-western Australia. At his headquarters near Bandung, he had tense confrontations with local Dutch commanders, Lt General Hein ter Poorten and Vice Admiral Conrad Helfrich. They begged for reinforcements for the islands north of Java, but Wavell refused to transfer large forces from Malaya and Singapore.

A detachment of 1100 Australians – 'Gull Force' – had already been sent to Amboina (Ambon) in the Molucca islands, and another – 'Sparrow Force' – to part-Dutch, part-Portuguese Timor. Ter Poorten would have to make do with these and the 100 000-strong *Koenig*

DOORMAN'S LAST STAND

Two long files of ships sailed on parallel courses across the Java Sea. On one side was the mixed Dutch, British, American and Australian fleet of Rear Admiral Karel Doorman; on the other, a Japanese fleet under Rear Admiral Takeo Takagi. The forces were roughly balanced in numbers – nine Allied destroyers and five cruisers, against 14 Japanese destroyers and four cruisers. But Doorman's fleet had no air support and had never seen action together.

It was February 27, 1942, and for an hour the fleets exchanged salvoes and darted torpedoes at one another. Then, at 5.14 pm, a 200 mm (8 in) Japanese shell smashed into the boiler of the British heavy cruiser *Exeter* – veteran of the River Plate. It exploded and the ship fell astern. A minute later, a torpedo hit the Dutch destroyer *Kortenar*, which exploded and jackknifed. Japanese destroyers closed in on *Exeter*, but it managed to escape, escorted back to Surabaya by the Dutch destroyer *Witte de With*. The destroyer HMS *Electra* now launched itself at the Japanese, scoring hits, but was itself hit, and at 5.25 it plunged beneath the waves. For an hour Doorman's ships weaved desperately to avoid Japanese shells, until at 6.30 Takagi suddenly broke off.

Doorman gave chase at high speed. It was a rash decision. Four old US destroyers were soon left far behind and had to return to Surabaya. At 9.30, the destroyer HMS *Jupiter* blundered into a Dutch minefield and exploded. Doorman told HMS *Encounter* to pick up survivors. His fleet was now down to four cruisers. At 11 pm, they sighted enemy warships and opened fire, unaware that they were being stalked by Takagi's cruisers *Nachi* and *Haguro*. At 11.20 torpedoes smashed into Doorman's flagship *De Ruyter* and *Java*. The Dutch ships burned furiously as Doorman ordered HMAS *Perth* and USS *Houston* to escape. Then *De Ruyter* was gone, taking Doorman with it.

INVADER'S SKY Japanese parachutes blossom in the night skies over Manado on Celebes at the beginning of the invasion. Later, smiling Javanese give Japanese troops a thumbs-up welcome; they saw the invaders as liberators.

Nederlands Indes Landmacht (KNIL – 'Royal Netherlands Indies Army'), a force recruited from Dutch settlers and native East Indians, all too likely to liaise with the invaders in the hope of avoiding internment if the Japanese won. With the Netherlands under Nazi occupation, no troops could arrive from home. Nor could ter Poorten hope for local support: anti-Dutch nationalist feeling was rising, particularly in Java.

DOWN THE ISLANDS

On January 24, the Japanese Central Force took Balikpapan and its oil fields on Borneo's east coast – in spite of losing four transports and an assault boat. These were sunk by American and Dutch forces in the first Allied naval success against the Japanese. Eastern Force took Kendari on Celebes the same day, thus winning the East Indies' largest airfield, then captured Amboina on February 4, after bitter fighting against 'Gull Force'. On February 9, they took Makassar on Celebes, and the next day Central Force took Banjarmasin on Borneo. From here eastern Java lay just 450 km (280 miles) across the Java Sea.

Action then switched to the west, where at dawn on February 14 – the day before Singapore finally fell – Japanese transports dropped 360 paratroops over an airfield (known as P1) at Palembang in southern Sumatra. Surprise was complete. RAF Aircraftsman Tom Jackson later recalled the sudden appearance of small white dots in the sky which 'grew and became parachutes'. Some unarmed British ground crew fled into the jungle. Others raced towards anti-aircraft guns which they trained on the paras. That night the battle was still raging, and paratroop attacks on nearby oil refineries had also been beaten off.

Early the next morning, the attack spread when an advance guard from the Japanese Western Force began to land at the mouth of the Musi river. They expected no trouble – but as dawn broke 60 Allied fighters and bombers swooped down. For once the Allies had outwitted the Japanese. Over the preceding months, they had constructed a well-camouflaged airfield, P2, in the jungle south-east of Palembang. The Allied planes sank a Japanese transport and scattered troops who had landed.

VULNERABLE

A determined leader could now easily have wiped out the Japanese. But Colonel Vogelensang, senior KNIL officer at Palembang, had only one thought – flight. By February 17 the Allies had evacuated Sumatra. Only the Sunda Strait now separated the Japanese from western Java.

In the east too the net was closing around Java. Troops landed unopposed on Bali on February 19, and the same day Japanese bombers devastated Darwin in northern Australia. On the night of February 19/20, a Japanese naval force sank a Dutch destroyer in the battle of Lombok Strait. Then Timor fell, despite brave resistance from 'Sparrow Force'. Its commander Lt Colonel William Leggatt surrendered on February 23, though the 2/2nd Independent Company – Australian commandos – kept up a guerrilla campaign until evacuated in December 1942.

Java's isolation was now complete; the end could only be days away. On February 25, Wavell wound up his headquarters and returned to India. 'I hate the idea of leaving these stout-hearted Dutchmen', he cabled Churchill. Ter Poorten was left with 25 000 KNIL troops, an unreliable Home Guard of 40 000, and some 10 000 Australians, Britons and Americans under the British Maj General H.D.W. Sitwell. Helfrich still had Allied naval forces at his disposal.

IMAMURA – ASIAN NATIONALIST

Overseas work as a military attaché left Hitoshi Imamura (1886-1968) convinced that, properly channelled, Asian nationalism could prove of great benefit to Japan. He had little chance to prove his ideas when serving with the Kwantung Army and in China, but he did so after he led Sixteenth Army in the conquest of the Dutch East Indies. Imamura established a liberal regime in the Indies, released Indonesian political prisoners and treated nationalist leaders such as Sukarno as equals in government. For a while, at least, he won the loyalty of Indonesians.

In November 1942, Imamura was posted to Rabaul, New Britain, as a full general in command of Eighth Area Army (Army Group), responsible for operations in the Solomons and New Guinea. By March 1944 he and his 100 000-strong New Britain garrison were encircled and remained blockaded until Japan's surrender. Afterwards, Imamura was put on trial for atrocities committed in the area under his command, but his defence lawyers proved that he was not in contact with any of the offending units. He was imprisoned until 1954, by which time passions had cooled and he was paroled.

JAVA LANDINGS

Java's defenders did not have long to wait. On February 26 a reconnaissance plane spotted an enemy invasion convoy, with powerful escort, north of the naval base of Surabaya. It was Central and Eastern Task Forces, now combined and preparing to land at Kragan. Next day an Allied fleet under the Dutch Rear Admiral Karel Doorman sallied forth. In the ensuing Battle of the Java Sea (see box), the Allies lost five ships sunk. Surviving ships fled to Surabaya, then set out for Australia and Ceylon (Sri Lanka).

By now Western Force's main part, bearing troops under Lt General Hitoshi Imamura, had also set out for Java from Indochina. On the evening of February 28, the convoy divided. One part headed for Eretan Wetan; the other, with Imamura himself, slipped into Bantam (Banten) Bay. Later that night, the men at Bantam began to disembark. For one Japanese officer it all seemed too easy. From the command ship *Akitsu Maru*, he watched troops rowing ashore and 'heaved a sigh of disappointment to think that this landing operation was to be made without firing a single rifle or gun, or without bloodshed'. Then suddenly 'there was the tremendous sound of guns'. Looking up, he saw two enemy 'battleships continuously firing their large guns'. Torpedoes exploded against four transports. Others were soon on fire. Men, including Imamura, had to leap into the water and swim ashore.

The 'battleships' were, in fact, the cruisers HMAS *Perth* and USS *Houston*, survivors of the Java Sea, which had blundered into the invasion force while making for the Sunda Strait in their flight to Australia. The chance seemed too good to miss. *Perth*'s Captain Hector Waller ordered an attack. But his two ships faced three enemy cruisers and ten destroyers. They sank the Japanese cruiser *Mikuma* and five destroyers, but were themselves soon pierced like colanders.

Shortly after midnight, *Perth* went down, taking with it Waller and 350 men. A little later, *Houston* too shuddered, and plunged beneath the waves. Only 368 of its 1000 men survived. Later that morning (March 1) the British cruiser *Exeter* and the destroyers USS *Pope* and HMS *Encounter* were sunk trying to escape through the Java Sea.

TRIUMPHAL PROGRESS

Perth and *Houston* had been pointless sacrifices. By dawn on March 1, Japanese troops had landed at three points on Java's long, vulnerable north coast – Eretan Wetan, Bantam and Kragan. Those landing at Kragan met little opposition and at once set out for Surabaya. Their advance became a triumphal progress, cheering Javanese lining the route, waving the long-banned red and white Indonesian nationalist flag.

Imamura's men in the west, meanwhile, headed for Batavia and Bandung in the mountains of the interior. The men from Eretan Wetan were stopped dead for 48 hours by 'Blackforce' – veteran Australian, British and American troops under the Australian Brigadier Robert Blackburn. But on March 4, as Imamura was beginning to despair of breaking through, 'Blackforce' was pulled back to Bandung. Batavia fell the next day. On March 8, ter Poorten announced the end of formal resistance. Bands of Australians and Britons attempted to carry on a guerrilla fight in the mountains, one led by South African-born Lt Colonel Laurens van der Post, later famous as a writer. But the locals were not with them, and one by one they were betrayed by the Javanese.

The mood of the Japanese at the surrender was euphoric. They were feted as liberators, girls hung garlands around their necks and crowds cheered. But Emperor Hirohito, more cautious than his war-thirsty ministers, was worried. 'The fruits of war,' he confided to a courtier, 'are tumbling into our mouth almost too quickly.'

UGLY BUT INDOMITABLE

Jisaburo Ozawa (1886-1966) was no beauty; his nickname was 'the Gargoyle'. But he was an intelligent and humane officer. Having covered the landings in Malaya, the Philippines, Borneo and Sumatra in 1941-2, he was given command of the Third Fleet, Japan's main carrier force, in November 1942.

In this post, he painfully rebuilt the Imperial Navy's air arm after shattering losses in the Solomons, and again after his defeat in the Philippine Sea – only to see his forces squandered once more at Leyte Gulf. In 1945, he prepared to meet an American invasion with *kamikaze* speedboats and human torpedoes.

Ozawa was a superb training officer and tactician. Pilots admired him for running high risks to rescue downed airmen. His plans for actions off the Palaus and in Leyte Gulf in 1944 were brilliantly, though vainly, conceived to try to counter US material supremacy with superior tactics.

To the edge of the Raj

The Japanese invasion of Burma was remorseless. British troops under Generals Harold Alexander and 'Uncle Bill' Slim fought gallantly, but by May 1942 they had let the enemy come within striking distance of India.

JAPANESE TROOPS pouring along dirt tracks through mountains and bamboo forests from Thailand (Siam) into the British colony of Burma on January 20, 1942, were pleasantly surprised. Tipped off by Burmese spies, their commander, Lt General Shojiro Iida, had expected a hard fight with British and Indian troops at Kawkareik, just across the border. Instead, the town fell almost without a struggle.

Iida's 18 000 men of the Japanese Fifteenth Army's 55th Division immediately pushed on west to Kyondo on the banks of the Gyaing river. Here, they came across scores of burned-out trucks and hundreds of rifles littering the ground, like tree branches after a storm – but no enemy.

Assuming (correctly) that the mere threat of a Japanese attack had put the British to flight, Iida dispatched a lightly armed advance force across the Gyaing towards the port of Moulmein. These men marched for five days and nights with little food, then on the morning of January 26 caught sight of a ridge, covered with Buddhist pagodas, their ornate pinnacles picked out in the morning sun. Beyond that, they knew, lay Moulmein – and just across the mouth of the Salween river was Martaban, from where road and railway lines ran around the head of the Gulf of Martaban to the Burmese capital, Rangoon.

On the British side, the commanding officer in Burma, Lt General Thomas Hutton, had long expected an invasion. At Burma's southernmost tip, Japanese troops had taken Victoria Point (now Kawthaung) and its important airfield as early as December 16, 1941. Since then Japanese bombers had attacked Rangoon from bases in Thailand and Indochina – though Allied fighters had struck back valiantly, inflicting heavy losses on the Japanese. On January 15, enemy troops from southern Thailand had started thrusting northwards up Burma's narrow southern tail from Victoria Point, taking more key airfields. Hutton also knew that Iida was building up forces in northern Thailand.

To face the enemy, Hutton had two divisions: 1st Burma and 17th Indian – nearly 50 000 soldiers. But many were of poor quality: the Indians were mostly ill-trained and inexperienced, and the Burmese – among whom nationalist, anti-British feeling was rife – were unreliable. Reinforcements were offered by the Chinese Nationalist leader, Generalissimo Chiang Kai-shek, whose chief supply route to the outside world lay through Burma. But Hutton's superior, General Sir Archibald Wavell, newly appointed Supreme Commander in south-east Asia, firmly rejected the offer. He suspected that Chiang simply wanted to seize the Shan-speaking provinces of eastern Burma, long claimed by the Chinese.

For air support, the British had just 17 RAF Buffalo fighters, later reinforced by two squadrons of Hurricanes and three of Blenheim bombers. A squadron of P-40 fighters, crewed by men of the American volunteer group the 'Flying Tigers', was also based in Burma.

Hutton's best chance of resisting the Japanese was to withdraw his troops behind the easily defensible Sittang river, north-east of Rangoon, where they could buy time for the arrival of reinforcements from the Middle East and India. Maj General John ('Jackie') Smyth, VC, 17th Indian Division's commander, whose men would bear the brunt of the defence, argued strongly for this strategy. But Burma's governor, Sir Reginald Dorman-Smith – backed by Wavell at his headquarters in far-off Java – was determined to defend the frontier. Withdrawal to the Sittang, he maintained, would dent British prestige and lead many Burmese to side with the invaders.

For the Japanese part, the main aim was to cut links between India and Singapore, to complete Chiang's isolation and to create a buffer against possible Allied counterattacks from India. As a bonus, they would capture Burma's oilfields.

PANIC-STRICKEN TROOPS

Events, when the invasion came, proved even worse than Smyth had feared. On January 20, his troops were making a planned withdrawal from Kawkareik when they heard distant gunfire. Immediate panic broke out. Pack mules stampeded through the streets and truck drivers tore down the road to Kyondo. Then they crossed the Gyaing, leaving trucks and weapons behind them, and fled on to Moulmein. Even senior British officers joined in the undignified scramble.

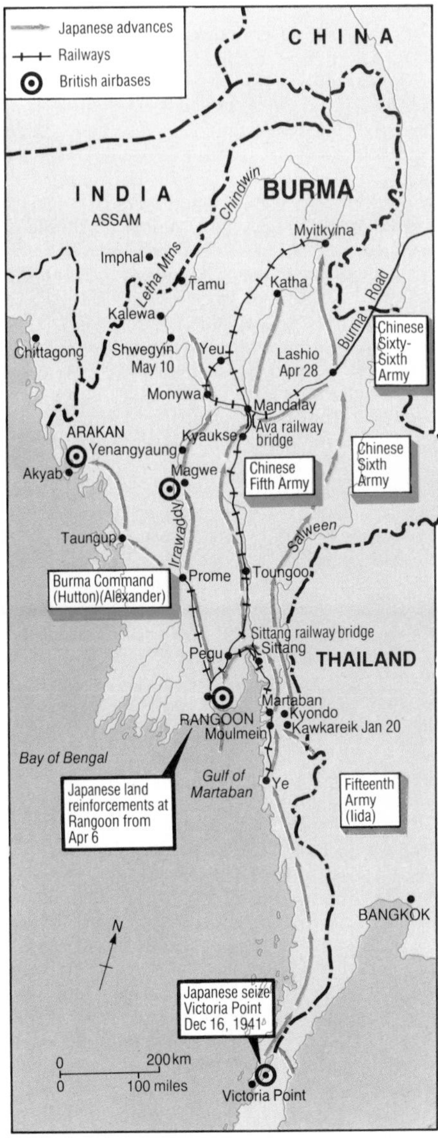

LONGEST RETREAT The British withdrawal through Burma was the longest in the history of Britain's army – 1600 km (1000 miles) from Moulmein to the Indian border.

In Moulmein the civilian population and part of the Burmese garrison also panicked and started streaming out of the city towards the ferry terminal on the Salween river, from where they crossed to Martaban. On January 22, Hutton, foreseeing already the possible fall of Rangoon, transferred three-quarters of his supplies from the capital to Burma's second city, Mandalay, 600 km (375 miles) north.

Iida's troops started to attack Moulmein on January 26, and four days later had broken through resistance from British artillery units. They soon set the wooden city ablaze. By the next morning the last British troops had withdrawn on ancient river steamers to Martaban.

Smyth now asked permission to withdraw to the Sittang, but instead his superiors ordered him to make his stand on the west bank of the shallow Bilin river. This was no obstacle to Iida's men – now reinforced by Lt General Shozu Sakurai's 33rd Infantry Division. By February 19, Smyth's line was crumbling, and permission came at last to

TWO COMMANDERS FALL

British forces in Burma needed an inspiring commander, but Wavell chose the remote Thomas Jacob Hutton (1890-1981). When Hutton ordered Rangoon to be evacuated, his superior was furious. He flew into Magwe airfield, upbraided Hutton in front of his officers and replaced him with Alexander. Hutton soon found his new position as second in command difficult and humiliating, asked to be relieved, and spent the rest of the war in a desk job.

John Smyth (1893-1983), by contrast, had a strong personality. A veteran of the Indian Army and World War I, he took part in the Dunkirk evacuation. Back in India in 1941, he was promoted major general and given command of 17th Division. His decision to order the Sittang bridge to be demolished was controversial and required enormous moral courage. Wavell did not appreciate this: Smyth was relieved of command, his military career finished. Undaunted, he carved out fresh careers as war correspondent, politician, playwright and author.

withdraw. With Sakurai's troops close behind, the British would have to make their way to the Sittang's sole crossing point on its wide, unfordable lower reaches – an iron railway bridge.

When the orders to withdraw were transmitted that night, Smyth's signallers failed to encode some of the messages, which were intercepted by the Japanese. They were a gift to Sakurai, who swiftly sent a regiment around Smyth's southern flank to try, if possible, to capture the Sittang bridge before the British.

Throughout February 20 and 21, trucks carrying Smyth's troops crawled bumper to bumper along narrow, pitted, dirt-track roads to the Sittang, while Japanese aircraft made repeated attacks. On the morning of the 21st the first trucks arrived at the bridge – but had to wait while engineers finished planking over its railway tracks. A truck also became entangled in the bridge girders, blocking it for a vital two hours. A massive tail-back built up, much of which Japanese bombers soon reduced to a mass of twisted wreckage.

That afternoon, mobs thronging the road sighted Allied aircraft in the skies to the north-west. They cheered loudly – until the planes dived, dropping bombs and firing guns. The attack lasted several hours. Someone had given the pilots the wrong bearings, and they discovered too late that they were attacking their own men. In the evening, trucks began to move across the river.

DEATH ON THE SITTANG

Meanwhile, the Japanese were drawing closer. They ran, sweat pouring off their faces, along jungle paths, carrying only rifles, water-bottles and the bare minimum of food. At 8.30 am on Sunday, February 22, they burst out of the jungle and charged into the milling British. Throughout the rest of the day and that night there was fierce fighting. Gurkha troops fixed bayonets and fought off mounting enemy attacks, while their comrades continued to crawl across the bridge. Shortly before dawn on Monday, Brigadier Noël Hugh-Jones, directing the evacuation, obtained Smyth's permission to demolish the bridge rather than let it fall intact into Japanese hands. At 5.30 am it collapsed in a huge explosion.

But three whole brigades had been left on the east bank. Hundreds tried to swim across the river, now widened to nearly 2 km (more than a mile) by an incoming tide. Many men were drowned, others shot by the Japanese or swept to their deaths in quicksand. At 2.30 pm, those left on the east bank surrendered. The 17th Indian Division had been reduced to under 3500, many unarmed. More than 5000 were either dead or taken prisoner. The remnants retreated to Pegu, south-west of the Sittang towards Rangoon.

The situation grew more and more bleak. On February 22, the Australian government refused to allow veteran troops returning from the Middle East to be diverted to Burma; now that Singapore had fallen, it wanted them to defend Australia. General Wavell had long insisted that Rangoon must be held at all costs, but without the Australian reinforcements this was no longer a practical alternative. Hutton ordered the evacuation of the city, but a furious Wavell countermanded the order on March 1. At the same time, he informed Hutton that Lt General Sir Harold Alexander would soon be arriving in Rangoon to take over Burma command. Hutton would stay on, but as Alexander's subordinate. Smyth too was finished by the chain of disasters. Exhausted and suffering from malaria, he applied for sick leave, but instead Wavell relieved him permanently of his command.

RETREAT FROM RANGOON

On March 3, the Japanese crossed the Sittang north of the ruined railway bridge by river craft. On the 5th, Alexander arrived in Rangoon. He quickly realised that retreat was the only sensible course of action – and managed to convince Wavell. At dawn on March 7, Alexander's men set out north up the Irrawaddy valley for Prome.

Their new commander had a reputation for luck – and events that followed confirmed this. Within an hour of leaving Rangoon, his men hit a Japanese roadblock across the highway and were unable to break through it. Meanwhile, Sakurai's forces – which would have annihilated the British in a head-on collision – were moving south towards Rangoon just a few kilometres to the west. Hoping to catch the bulk of the British in the city, Sakurai had decided to approach it by a side road parallel to the highway.

To his fury, the only signs of life when he entered Rangoon on March 8 were looters and lunatics released from an asylum. When the British tried the roadblock again the next morning, they found it abandoned.

Alexander's troops regrouped at Prome. Belated appeals to Chiang Kai-shek brought ill-equipped Chinese soldiers into Burma. Some 6500 men of the Chinese Fifth Army, led by the American Lt General Joseph ('Vinegar Joe') Stilwell, marched south to Toungoo, 240 km (150 miles) east of Prome. Stilwell had a low opinion of his Chinese troops, distrusted the British, but hated the Japanese even more.

Reinforced by sea with two further divisions and hundreds of aircraft, Iida now launched a two-pronged offensive up the Irrawaddy and Sittang valleys. In a series of attacks between March 20 and 27 on Magwe and Akyab (now Sittwe) airfields the Japanese crippled Allied air power. On March 30 the Chinese quit Toungoo after 11 days of fierce fighting, and on April 3 the British abandoned Prome. The same day, Mandalay was almost totally destroyed in a devastating air raid. By now Alexander had been joined by Lt General William Slim who took day-to-day charge of the British Empire troops, now renamed 'Burcorps', or Burma Corps. Appointing Slim was probably Wavell's wisest move in the whole campaign.

The Allied retreat through the dry lands of central Burma was slow and painful. The heat was intense, the men frequently lacked water and the local population was generally hostile. Panic could easily have set in, had it not been for 'Uncle Bill' Slim, as his troops came to call him, who moved among the men exuding an infectious confidence and offering words of encouragement.

Meanwhile, the Japanese had added a third prong to their offensive – towards Lashio and the Burma Road, which crossed the mountains into south-western China. From battle plans captured at Toungoo, Iida discovered that the Chinese had

LOAD BEARER A Japanese private humps a heavy tripod of the kind used for mortars. Transporting equipment was always a problem for the largely unmechanised Japanese Army, and soldiers often had to act as porters. This one wears a steel helmet over his field cap, and the cross-gartered puttees of Japanese other ranks.

IIDA: BURMA'S CONQUEROR – AND DEFENDER

A veteran of Siberia (1919) and China (1937), Shojiro Iida (1888-1980) was appointed commander of the Japanese Fifteenth Army in 1941. When, after his spectacular conquest of Burma, Imperial Japanese Headquarters pressed for an invasion of north-east India, it was Iida's opposition – on the grounds that British rule in India would collapse without an invasion – which halted the plans.

In Burma, Iida favoured local rather than Japanese interests: he established a civilian government under Ba Maw, purged the Japanese-trained Burmese National Army and dismissed its adviser, Colonel Keiji Suzuki. He had no time for Japanese 'carpetbaggers'. He had many enemies, and in April 1943 was relegated to the General Defence Command. Disgusted, he requested retirement in December 1944. But soon he was recalled to command the Thirtieth Army in Manchuria, where he kept his men fighting long after most other units had collapsed under the Russian attack in August 1945.

GUN HAULING A Japanese supply truck laboriously tugs a field gun across a wooden plank bridge in the Burmese jungle. Men stand and watch from the bank above. The gun is camouflaged with palm fronds and banana leaves.

left the route from Toungoo to Lashio virtually undefended. He realised that he could cut the Burma Road and complete the isolation of the Chinese Nationalists – long a Japanese goal – and dispatched a division north-eastwards in captured British trucks.

On April 16, Burcorps fought a savage battle around Yenangyaung, north of Prome, which contained Burma's precious oilfields. Troops under Maj General James Bruce Scott were almost trapped there, and in the rush to escape many wounded were left behind – to be butchered by the Japanese. By then the oil installations had been set on fire, on Slim's orders, rather than let them fall into enemy hands.

NOTHING TO DEFEND

On April 25, Alexander met Slim and Stilwell at Kyauske, near Mandalay, and announced that he intended to withdraw to India. With Mandalay destroyed and the Yenangyuang oilfields out of action, there was nothing left in Burma for the Allies to defend. The decision left Stilwell's Chinese, still south of Mandalay, unpleasantly in the lurch – for the impending fall of Lashio would make a retreat to their homeland almost impossible. Stilwell left the meeting with a bitter smile: once more the British had protected their own interests, with scant regard for those of others.

The campaign now entered its final stage. On April 29 the Japanese took Lashio, and two days later Burcorps' rearguard moved across the Irrawaddy on the Ava railway bridge, south-west of Mandalay. At midnight, they blew it up behind them. A race was now under way: long lines of locomotives pulled Burcorps east through Monywa on the Chindwin river, then north as far as Yeu. There they transferred to trucks, which bore them west over precarious mountain roads to Shwegyin, back on the Chindwin. Most then embarked on river vessels to be carried upstream to Kalewa; a rearguard had to trek overland.

From there, Burcorps began a 130 km (80 mile) slog up the Kabaw valley towards Tamu, on the Burmese-Indian border, losing hundreds to malaria and other tropical diseases. With the monsoon about to break, the men made it by the skin of their teeth. When the weather broke on May 12, most of Slim's troops had reached Tamu, from where they crossed the Letha mountains into India. Burcorps had left 13 000 dead, wounded and prisoners in Burma (the Japanese had lost 5000), but had survived as a fighting unit. The Chinese, meanwhile, had been retreating in even worse conditions towards Myitkyina, in the north-east. Many weeks later, small bands of Chinese survivors staggered across the border into China.

Stilwell, with a small American headquarters unit, had meanwhile trudged wearily through the monsoon across the mountains to Imphal in India. Still full of fight, he told astonished American reporters: 'I claim we got a hell of a beating. We got run out of Burma and it is as humiliating as hell. I think we ought to find out what caused it, go back and retake it.' 'Vinegar Joe' and one Englishman he had come to respect, 'Uncle Bill' Slim, went on to do just that.

HOLDING THE REAR British troops patrol the battered streets of Schwegyin. Here two British rearguard brigades beat off a sudden Japanese attack on May 10, before retreating along mountain tracks to rejoin their comrades.

Australia's gravest hour

'Australia is facing the gravest hour in her history', announced Prime Minister John Curtin after the raid on Pearl Harbor. As Japan's armies swept ever closer through the islands to its north, a nightmare that had haunted generations of Australians – invasion from Asia – seemed about to become reality.

A SUICIDE MISSION – that is what it was, and the men knew it, as they went out in eight obsolete training planes to intercept 103 Japanese fighters and bombers approaching Rabaul, the main Australian air base in the Bismarck Archipelago, north-east of New Guinea (see map, p. 356). Soon swarms of Zero fighters were closing in on the lumbering, single-engine RAAF Wirraways. One Wirraway had already crashed just after takeoff. Three were now shot down by the Japanese, and another two were seriously damaged in crash landings. Only two made it miraculously back to Rabaul, on the island of New Britain. The next day, January 21, 1942, Wing Commander J.M. Lerew, RAAF chief at Rabaul, radioed a laconic message to the High Command in Canberra: *'Nos morituri te salutamus'* ('We who are about to die salute you') – the words addressed to the emperor by gladiators entering the arenas of ancient Rome.

And death was indeed to be the fate of many of New Britain's Australian defenders. On the night of January 22/23, Maj General Tomitaro Horii's 5300-strong South Seas Force steamed into Rabaul harbour. The defenders, led by Lt Colonel John Scanlon, put up a brave fight, but eventually had to withdraw. Over the following days the Japanese overran the northern part of the island, capturing most of the Australians and brutally massacring 160 of them on February 4 at Tol Plantation, south of Rabaul. Most of the rest were to die in captivity.

But Lerew himself escaped. On the orders of

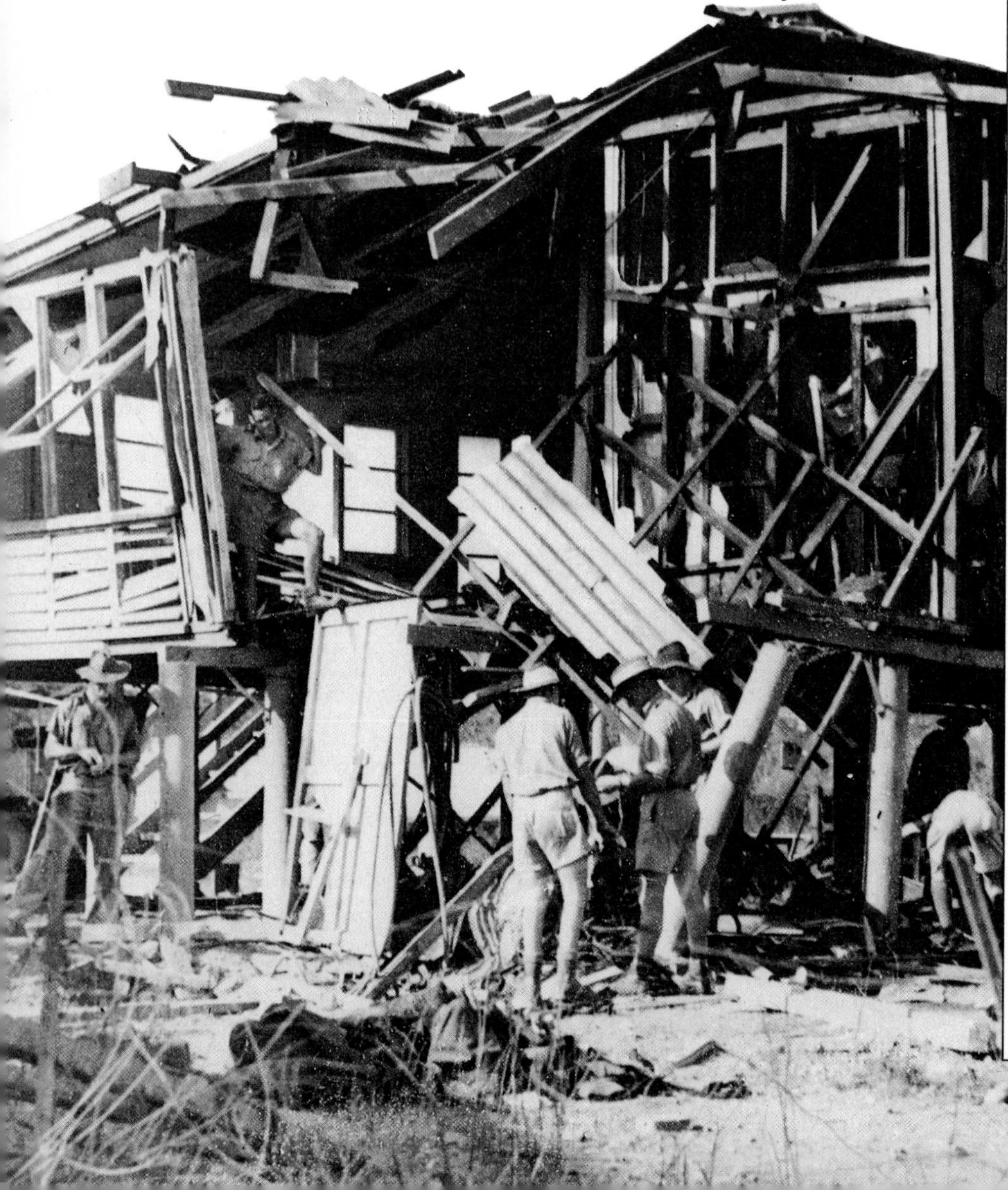

TARGET AUSTRALIA

War came to the Australian mainland like a bolt from the blue. A little before 10 am on February 19, 1942, 'wharfies' in the north Australian port of Darwin had just knocked off for a 'smoko' when 188 Japanese aircraft roared out of the skies to the north-west. During the night, four Japanese aircraft carriers from Vice Admiral Chuichi Nagumo's *Kido Butai* (Carrier Striking Force) had closed to within 320 km (200 miles) of Darwin, a key staging post in Allied supply routes to the East Indies.

For ten weeks, battles had raged in south-east Asia, to the north – but had seemed strangely remote to the wharfies of the North Australian Workers' Union. They had been holding Darwin paralysed for days at a time with wildcat strikes. As a result, Japanese planes found the harbour crammed with ships – many carrying vital supplies for Allied troops. A recent cyclone had added to the chaos in Darwin.

The attack lasted half an hour, devastating harbour installations and parts of the town, and sinking eight ships, including the US destroyer *Peary*. Thirteen more ships were damaged and a nearby airfield bombed. At noon 54 more planes flew in, this time from captured bases in the Dutch East Indies. They finished off the airfield, cratering runways and destroying hangars. Altogether, some 240 people, mostly ships' crews and civilians, were killed and over 300 injured.

The attacks created widespread panic in Darwin. Sure that an invasion would follow, militiamen and civilians alike grabbed any vehicle to hand – including a fully loaded night-soil truck – and fled southwards towards the settlement of Adelaide River, in what came to be known scathingly as the 'Adelaide River Stakes'. There was also widespread looting.

'There had never been greater loss of life in a single day in Australia,' wrote Douglas Lockwood, a journalist who was in Darwin that day, 'nor, in some respects, a day of greater ignominy.' To be fair, though, most anti-aircraft gunners and most men of the RAN ships in Darwin had stayed bravely at their posts during the raid.

Over the next 21 months, Darwin was bombed another 62 times, and other raids hit several more towns in the north. In June 1942, Japanese submarines shelled waterside suburbs of Sydney and Newcastle, and on May 31 three 25 m (80 ft) midget submarines penetrated Sydney Harbour, torpedoed a former ferry, but missed the cruiser USS *Chicago*. One of the subs blew itself up, one was depth-charged and the third disappeared. Three months earlier the result might have been more panic, but by now – three weeks after the Battle of the Coral Sea – Australia's nerve was much more robust.

AFTER THE RAID Troops clear wreckage left at Darwin by Japanese bombers in February 1942.

the Air Board in Canberra, he had evacuated Rabaul with the remainder of his force – the two surviving Wirraways and one Hudson bomber – just hours before the Japanese landed, pausing first to blow up the two airfields from which his planes had been operating.

'FREE OF ANY PANGS'

'Without any inhibitions of any kind I make it clear that Australia looks to America, free of any pangs as to our traditional links or kinship with the United Kingdom.' Thus had Labor Prime Minister John Curtin, only recently come to power, addressed his countrymen during the last days of 1941. Japan had erupted into the war less than three weeks earlier, and its startling expansion through south-east Asia had made Curtin and his government steadily more alarmed. For Australia was in no position to defend itself should it, too, come under attack. The Royal Australian Navy (RAN) consisted of just 12 cruisers and destroyers, and the RAAF had only 177 front-line aircraft – 101 of them Wirraway trainers pressed into combat service.

The army looked more impressive on paper, with 400 000 men, but many of its best troops – 100 000 men who had volunteered to serve overseas in the Australian Imperial Force (AIF) – were fighting in the Middle East. Militiamen, who composed the rest of the army, were conscripted only for the defence of Australia and its territories, and were still largely untrained and not yet fired with fighting spirit. The army was also short of equipment, including tanks.

In desperation, Curtin searched abroad for help to defend his country. Traditionally, Australia had looked to Britain. But Britain was also fighting for its life, and Churchill made it clear he could spare few troops for the Far East. Curtin then turned to the United States – but for the moment Roosevelt, himself reeling under a succession of humiliating defeats by the Japanese, was almost as powerless to help. In January 1942, at Churchill's suggestion, two of the three AIF divisions in the Middle East began to return to the Pacific theatre – though Curtin had to fight hard to stop Churchill diverting them to Burma and Java.

THE NET CLOSES

None of this could stop the Japanese advance. With the fall of Rabaul, Australian-ruled territory had for the first time been invaded, and further blows continued to fall. On February 3, Japanese aircraft bombed Port Moresby, chief base on the south coast of Australian-ruled eastern New Guinea and administrative centre for the whole territory. The garrison there – almost all conscripts – panicked when the first bombs fell and fled into the bush, only returning later to loot the town and drink the pubs dry. Many weeks passed before discipline was restored. Also on February 3, on the island of Amboina (Ambon) in the Dutch East Indies, Japanese troops overwhelmed the Australian 'Gullforce'.

Then Singapore fell on February 15, and the remnants of the AIF's 8th Division marched into captivity. 'The fall of Singapore opens the battle for Australia', warned Curtin. Sure enough, the Australian mainland came under attack for the first time on February 19, when Japanese aircraft bombed the northern port of Darwin (see box). Four days later, more AIF troops ('Sparrowforce') surrendered on the Dutch and Portuguese island of Timor.

On March 3, the Japanese again struck the mainland, bombing Broome in Western Australia and destroying 24 aircraft. Five days later, they crossed from Rabaul to New Guinea's north coast, taking Salamaua and the main town, Lae. In seven weeks' fighting in south-east Asia, Australia had lost nearly 30 000 men, killed or taken prisoner – a grievous blow to a country of some 7 million people.

By now it seemed to many Australians that invasion of the mainland was bound to follow, and in some areas – particularly in the north – panic set in. In the northern Queensland towns of Cairns and Townsville, houses sold for as little as £50 each (less than US$200) as their owners packed up and fled southwards. Even in cities such as Sydney, Brisbane and Newcastle, hysteria mounted and many people moved inland – buying places in the country if they could afford them, or going to stay with relatives.

At the same time, the Commander in Chief Home Forces, Maj General Sir Iven Mackay, was putting into effect defence plans that involved abandoning vast tracts of Australia to any invading force. With the bulk of his men in the country's 'living heart' – the corner south-east of a line from Brisbane to Adelaide – Mackay left only small garrisons outside this area. Their task was to withdraw before the enemy, destroying industrial plant and contaminating water supplies. Though criticised later, the plan was sensible given the forces at Mackay's disposal.

ENTER MACARTHUR

Australia lacked trained troops and equipment – but what it needed even more was a charismatic leader. The plodding Curtin, for all his virtues, was not such a man. On March 17, the country found the man it needed – an American. General Douglas MacArthur landed in Darwin that day from the Philippines. Roosevelt, his country now rapidly rebounding, had ordered MacArthur to Australia to take command of forces which would be assembled there for a counteroffensive in the south-west Pacific.

MacArthur transformed Australia's morale.

MONEY WHERE HIS MOUTH IS MacArthur, watched by Premier John Curtin, invests £1000 in Australian Liberty Loans. MacArthur transformed Australian morale, infusing courage into often panicky militiamen and civilians.

'We shall win or we shall die,' he told parliament in Canberra a week after his arrival, 'and to this end, I pledge you the full resources of all the mighty power of my country and all the blood of my countrymen . . . My faith in our ultimate victory is invincible, and I bring to you tonight the unbreakable spirit of the free man's military code in support of our just cause.' By the time he had finished speaking, many parliamentarians were on their feet cheering.

The next month MacArthur was confirmed as Allied Commander South-West Pacific Area. American reinforcements arrived, as well as more returning AIF troops, and these were, over a period, sent into the areas of Australia left undefended in Mackay's plan. On Anzac Day (April 25), MacArthur issued orders that no matter where the Japanese might land they were to be resisted and thrown back into the sea.

The Japanese High Command, meanwhile, had indeed been considering an invasion. The navy, in particular, was keen – but the army protested. To them, the war in China was all-important, and the generals refused to provide enough men to invade Australia. On March 4, the High Command reached a compromise: they would capture Port Moresby and push south-east through the Solomon Islands, New Caledonia, Fiji and Samoa, in order to cut Australia's shipping routes across the Pacific to the USA. Then they might consider an invasion of Australia itself. On March 31, they began the drive by invading Bougainville in the Solomons.

But, without knowing it, the Japanese had almost reached the limit of their spectacular expansion. The tide of war was about to turn. Attempts to capture Port Moresby would lead to their first major defeats – in the Coral Sea, then on New Guinea's Kokoda Trail.

12: TURNING THE PACIFIC TIDE

Spectacular naval battles and Japan's first land defeat led the Allies' slow Pacific comeback.

Revenge after Pearl Harbor

The United States soon bounced back after the surprise Japanese attack on its Pacific Fleet at Pearl Harbor in December 1941. While the Japanese Navy argued over its next move, the Americans cracked its operational code and Lt Colonel James Doolittle led a daring bombing raid on Tokyo.

PEARL HARBOR was meant to smash at a single blow America's resolution and its ability to retaliate. It failed on both counts. The Japanese sank or badly damaged seven antiquated American battleships, but since they were lost in harbour, many of their crews were saved and all but two of the ships salvaged. The raid also left most of Pearl Harbor's shore installations intact. Most important of all, the violation of US territory united the nation behind the declaration of war.

Moreover, the loss of the battleships forced the US Navy to use its aircraft carriers as the core of a more up-to-date Pacific fleet. The 1927 vintage *Lexington* and *Saratoga* and the much more modern *Enterprise* were out of Pearl Harbor during the raid and were untouched. In January 1942, they were joined by *Enterprise*'s sister-ship *Yorktown*, while the recently completed *Hornet* was ready to leave San Francisco at the beginning of April. The carriers were well fitted to take the offensive, for they carried large numbers of effective fighters and bombers.

AMERICA STRIKES BACK

On December 17, 1941, the highly capable Admiral Chester W. Nimitz replaced Admiral Husband E. Kimmel as CINCPAC (Commander in Chief of the US Pacific Fleet), when the latter was blamed for being caught unawares at Pearl Harbor. Nimitz decided to mount a series of raids on Japanese-held islands in the Pacific to harass the enemy, maintain the morale of his crews and give them valuable operational experience.

The first attempted raid – against Wake Island in January – had to be called off when an oiler was torpedoed. But on February 1 Vice Admiral William F. ('Bull') Halsey, with *Enterprise* and *Yorktown*, attacked Japanese bases in the Marshall and Gilbert Islands. Then in late February and early March he took the *Enterprise* group to hit Wake and Marcus – the latter just 1900 km (1180 miles) from Tokyo. These raids excited an American public crying out for success.

On March 10 over 100 planes from *Lexington* and *Yorktown*, positioned in the Coral Sea south of New Guinea, struck across the Owen Stanley mountains at Salamaua and Lae on New Guinea's north coast. Their targets were Japanese transport ships that had just brought invasion forces ashore. It was the biggest American strike yet, and some skilful flying was needed to make it. Many of the planes were too heavily laden with bombs or torpedoes to fly over the 4900 m (16 000 ft) mountains, and Commander William B. Ault had to lead them through a 2300 m (7500 ft) pass between the towering peaks of Mt Stanley and Mt Dawson. When they reached the north coast there was virtually no Japanese opposition in the air, and the escorting fighters joined the bombers in attacking the ships. They sank four Japanese ships and damaged five others, killing 130 Japanese.

It was the first time the Americans inflicted an important reverse on their foe, and it made impossible any immediate Japanese assault on Port Moresby – the main Allied base and capital of Australian-administered New Guinea.

A GREAT ALLROUNDER

'He had the capacity to organise both a fleet and a vast theatre, the tact to deal with sister services and Allied commands, the leadership to weld his own subordinates into a great fighting team, the courage to take necessary risks, and the wisdom to select, from a variety of intelligence and opinions, the correct strategy to defeat Japan.' So American historian Samuel Eliot Morison described Chester William Nimitz (1885-1966) – who, as Commander in Chief of the US Pacific Fleet (CINCPAC), led the Americans from humiliation after Pearl Harbor to a resounding victory over Japan four years later.

Nimitz, a Texan of German descent, was commissioned in the US Navy in 1907. After a shaky start (he grounded a destroyer), he rose to prominence in World War I as a submariner. In 1939, now an admiral, he was appointed head of the navy's Bureau of Navigation, a key administrative post in which he oversaw the service's rapid expansion in 1940-1.

Within weeks of Nimitz's appointment as CINCPAC, he had transformed his men's morale, infecting them with his own calm confidence in a final Allied victory. He also started to gather a team of gifted subordinates – such as the brilliant strategist Rear Admiral Forrest Sherman.

From April 1942, as Commander in Chief Central Pacific Area, he shared with General Douglas MacArthur responsibility for the conduct of the entire Pacific war. In December 1944 he was promoted to Fleet Admiral, the US Navy's highest rank, and in September 1945 was one of the Allied team that took the official Japanese surrender aboard the USS *Missouri*.

JAPAN'S OPTIONS

Meanwhile, as the Japanese Army scored success after success in Malaya, the Dutch East Indies (now Indonesia), the Philippines, Burma, New Guinea and neighbouring islands (pp. 141-57), senior officers of the Imperial Navy had been discussing their next move.

Naval planners put forward three options. One was for the Imperial Navy to concentrate on the Indian Ocean, where the British were building up their Eastern Fleet, based in Ceylon (now Sri Lanka). But Britain was not Japan's main enemy, and a strong thrust over such long distances was beyond even Japan's means. Most of its army was tied up fighting in China and south-east Asia, and its shipping almost fully occupied closer to home.

A second plan was to occupy north-eastern Australia, Fiji and Samoa. The aim would be to cut Australia off from the USA and so prevent the Americans from using Australia as a springboard for attacks on Japan's new empire from the south. The Japanese Army, however, felt unable to provide enough soldiers for this scheme, vetoing in particular any invasion of Australia.

The third plan was the brainchild of the Commander in Chief of the Japanese Combined Fleet, Admiral Isoroku Yamamoto. From the first he had recognised the gamble that Japan had taken by going to war with the United States. He was determined to crush American power in the Pacific while Japan had the upper hand. His idea was to draw the much weaker US fleet into the open sea with an attack on Midway island at the westernmost end of the Hawaiian chain. Here Japan's mighty forces would sink the US fleet in a single decisive battle. This plan prevailed – although elements of the other two were also used.

ATTACK ON COLOMBO

First came the operation against the British in the Indian Ocean. The objects of the modified plan were to neutralise the British Eastern Fleet, leaving the Japanese free to concentrate on US naval forces in the Pacific, and to remove any threat to the flank of the Japanese Army's thrust north through Burma.

The British fleet was not, in fact, as impressive as it seemed. It was large but weak. Four of its five battleships were slow, with weak armour and few anti-aircraft weapons. Even worse, its three aircraft carriers had no more than 90 aircraft between them – mostly slow (and by Japanese standards obsolete) Albacore and Swordfish biplanes – to take on 360 Japanese carrier aircraft, among the world's finest.

The main bases of Britain's Eastern Fleet were in Ceylon at Colombo and Trincomalee. Its commander, Admiral Sir James Somerville, also had a secret Indian Ocean base at Addu Atoll at the southernmost end of the Maldive Islands, some 970 km (600 miles) south-west of Ceylon.

In March, British Intelligence warned Somerville of an impending Japanese strike against Colombo, expected on or near April 1. In response, Somerville ordered his fleet to sea at the end of March, so that it could counterattack if an opportunity arose. In fact, the Japanese were not planning to hit Colombo until Easter Sunday, April 5 – hoping by attacking on a public holiday to repeat the surprise they had achieved at Pearl Harbor on Sunday December 7. Before then Somerville's ships were running low on fuel and water, and he had to return to Addu with most of them. The old aircraft carrier HMS *Hermes*, the cruisers *Cornwall* and *Dorsetshire* and the Australian destroyer *Vampire* went back to Colombo and Trincomalee.

On April 4 a British flying boat sighted the Japanese First Air Fleet 580 km (360 miles) south-east of Ceylon. Commanded by Vice Admiral Chiuchi Nagumo, the Japanese fleet had five modern aircraft carriers, four battleships and 14 other vessels. Somerville ordered *Cornwall* and *Dorsetshire* to leave Colombo and rejoin the rest of his fleet, sailing north-west from Addu.

Early on Easter Sunday nearly 130 Japanese planes attacked Colombo. They damaged the harbour and destroyed 25 British aircraft, but the only ships sunk were an armed merchant cruiser and an old destroyer. The main Japanese success came later after a float plane spotted *Cornwall* and *Dorsetshire* as they sped southwards to meet Somerville. A second wave of dive-bombers flew off and quickly sank the two British cruisers.

DANGER POINT

The loss of the two ships confirmed to Somerville that his fleet was no match for the Japanese by day and, after another vain attempt to find the enemy at night, he decided to withdraw westwards to safety. Earlier, the British First Sea Lord, Admiral of the Fleet Sir Dudley Pound, had counselled caution when facing the Japanese, and on April 7 London authorised Somerville to withdraw his weakest ships to East Africa. It also forbade the main fleet to use Ceylon as a base.

On April 9 the Japanese attacked Trincomalee, then shortly afterwards sank *Hermes*, HMAS *Vampire*, a corvette and two tankers which had fled the port. *Hermes* had been Britain's first purpose-built aircraft carrier – and now became its first to be sunk by another carrier's aircraft.

Meanwhile, a Japanese raiding force was seriously disrupting shipping off India's east coast. It was perhaps the British Empire's lowest point during the war. The Royal Navy could no longer protect India. Singapore had fallen to the Japanese Army in February, and Rangoon in March. The last British troops would shortly be driven from Burma. Churchill later called it 'the most dangerous moment'. It looked as if Ceylon might fall to the Japanese and, with India already restive, the core of the British Empire might quickly rot away. Luckily for Britain and its allies, though, the Japanese had already decided they could not exploit this strategic opportunity. Disappointed that they had not wiped out the whole Eastern Fleet, the Japanese ships turned back towards the Pacific.

The British, however, remained fearful of Japanese designs in the Indian Ocean. A particular fear was that the Vichy French government would turn over to the Japanese its colony of Madagascar off the East African coast. To nip this threat in the bud the British attacked the island in May (see box), eventually forcing the Vichy garrison to surrender in November.

MADAGASCAR – THE FIRST ALLIED INVASION

The Vichy French island of Madagascar, off Africa's east coast, had worried the Allies since late 1941. It stood near the route carrying British supplies to the Middle East and India, via the Cape of Good Hope, and oil in the opposite direction. German or, more likely, Japanese submarines could easily use it as a base to cut these supply lines. Churchill set in motion Operation 'Ironclad' to invade the island. 'Ironclad' was so secret that Free French leader General Charles de Gaulle was not told of it – to his fury – until the invasion had already begun.

In the early hours of May 5, 1942, 13 000 British Empire troops landed at two points on the western side of Madagascar's northern tip. Their job was to take the vast natural harbour of Diégo Suarez (now Antseranana) bay on the northern tip's eastern side.

They did so quite easily. Aircraft from the carriers *Illustrious* and *Indomitable* sank a French merchant cruiser and submarine in the harbour of Diégo Suarez town on the north side of its bay, and destroyed planes at a nearby airfield. By 4.30 pm 600 men from No 5 Commando had taken the town. The Vichy naval base of Antsirane, on the bay's southern side, was taken on the night of May 6/7. A stalemate west of the base had been broken after the destroyer HMS *Anthony* got into its harbour, braving French batteries, and deposited 50 marines on the dockside. Troops in the rest of the island, it was hoped, would soon surrender.

But Vichy Governor Armand Annet refused to give up so easily. At the same time, Japanese submarines began to cause havoc. On May 30 a midget sub got into Diégo Suarez harbour, sinking an oiler and damaging the battleship HMS *Ramillies*. In June and July, subs sank 34 Allied ships around Madagascar. They were operating with the help of auxiliary cruisers, but the British assumed that they were based in uncaptured parts of the island. The invasion had to be finished.

From September 10 to 29, 14 000 British, East and South African troops landed on the west and east coasts, while an overland advance was made from Diégo Suarez. The capital Tananarive (Antananarivo) fell on September 23. On November 5 Annet surrendered and on December 14 the Free French took charge. Madagascar had given the Allies their first experience of a large amphibious landing.

DOOLITTLE'S RAID

One nightmare of prewar Japanese military strategists had been the possibility of an attack by aircraft from US carriers on Japan's home islands; for this reason they even tried before the war to have aircraft carriers banned by international agreement. Their fears were fulfilled on April 18, 1942, when 16 US Army Air Force B-25 Mitchell medium bombers struck Tokyo, Yokohama, Kobe and Nagoya. They were commanded by Lt Colonel James Doolittle. Though normally land-based, Doolittle's 12 tonne bombers took off from the US aircraft carrier *Hornet* (p. 160).

The raid was supposed to take place at night, but in the early hours of April 18 *Hornet* and its companion carrier *Enterprise* stumbled into a Japanese picket-boat line, some 1125 km (700 miles) east of Japan. As a result, the attack had to be launched prematurely and in broad daylight in order to minimise the risks to the valuable carriers. Luckily for Doolittle and his fellows, they reached Tokyo and the other targets just after Japan's first air-raid drill. Japanese fighters let them approach the capital, assuming that these were their own aircraft taking part in the drill.

The American bombs did little damage, although incendiaries burned Tokyo's largest hospital to the ground. Some US planes flew directly over the Imperial Palace, but did not attack it; Doolittle knew from his experiences in London during the Blitz that any serious threat to the Emperor would only stiffen Japanese morale. The Japanese could not, at first, work out where the bombers had come from. President Roosevelt taunted them by announcing that the planes had taken off from Shangri-la.

For the B-25s to take off from an aircraft carrier had been a daring feat; for them to land on one was impossible. Instead they were due to fly on to land at Chinese bases still in the hands of the allied Nationalists. But none did. One reached a Soviet base at Vladivostok; the crew were interned. The others crashed when their planes ran out of fuel. Doolittle and 62 other US airmen parachuted to safety with friendly Chinese, four drowned and one was killed baling out. The Japanese captured eight airmen and executed three of them for 'inhuman acts'. Another died in a prison camp, but 71 of the 80 heroic fliers survived the war.

The effect of the Doolittle raid on Japanese public opinion was enormous. People were horrified, especially that the Emperor had been put at risk. One result was that Admiral Yamamoto's plan for a final showdown with the US Pacific Fleet was rapidly accepted by an Imperial Naval General Staff.

But Yamamoto did not know that his plans would soon be known to his enemies. For several months an American code-breaking team at Pearl Harbor had been leading Allied efforts to break the Imperial Navy's main operational code. By early April the team – code-named 'Hypo' – was able to read 15 per cent of the Japanese signals it picked up. Later that month they were decrypting 85 per cent of some messages. Although others continued to baffle them, US intelligence officers could divine Japanese intentions with remarkable accuracy. This gave the Americans an incalculable advantage in the crucial battles to come in the Pacific.

STRIKING JAPAN'S HEART A B-25 bomber takes off (above) from the carrier USS *Hornet* for the Doolittle raid. The normally land-based B-25s were much larger than carrier aircraft. Smoke rises from Tokyo (below) as the raiders hit their targets.

DAREDEVIL DOOLITTLE

Even before James H. ('Jimmy') Doolittle (1896-) led his raid on Japan, he had a reputation as a daring pilot. In the US Army Air Corps from World War I to 1930, then as an engineer and racing and publicity pilot, he won long-distance flying trophies and set records.

Back in the USAAF in 1940, his combination of daredevil skill and intelligence made him an obvious choice to lead the April 1942 raid. It earned him the Medal of Honor. He commanded the Twelfth Air Force in support of the 'Torch' landings in North Africa in 1942, then the Fifteenth in Italy and from early 1944 the Eighth in Britain.

The Coral Sea – a battle of errors

Neither Japanese nor Americans showed full mastery of naval air power when they met in the Coral Sea in May 1942. The battle – a milestone in naval warfare – was fought between ships and aircraft. Enemy ships never saw one another.

FIRST AIR FLEET – the formidable Japanese carrier force – was withdrawing from the Indian Ocean after its attack on the British Eastern Fleet around Ceylon, and was returning to the Pacific. That was the news given in April 1942 to Admiral Ernest King, US Chief of Naval Operations, by the eccentric American code-breaking genius Lt Commander Joseph Rochefort. He went on to report that, although the Japanese did not intend to invade Australia, as the Allies had feared, they were gathering forces for an operation to be launched from the Japanese base at Rabaul on the island of New Britain, to the north-east of New Guinea.

During April the Americans began to fit the intelligence jigsaw together. In the middle of the month they realised that a major offensive in the south-west Pacific was likely. Port Moresby, on New Guinea's south coast, was the obvious target, and by the end of the month US decoders had confirmed that this, as well as a secondary thrust in the Solomon Islands, was the Japanese plan. It was code-named 'Mo' (short for 'Moresby'). From there, the Japanese could dominate – if not actually invade – northern Australia.

For months, planners on Japan's Naval General Staff in Tokyo had been pushing for an attack on Australia, which they feared the Americans would use as a springboard for a counteroffensive in the south-west Pacific. At first they had proposed a full-scale invasion of Australia – but the army refused to provide the necessary troops. The so-called Australian School among the Japanese planners now intended simply to isolate Australia from the USA, first by seizing Port Moresby and establishing a seaplane base at the tiny island of Tulagi, in the Solomons, then by taking key points in New Caledonia, the New Hebrides and Fiji, farther south and east.

The Japanese always tended to divide their forces into numerous sub-groups – and those allocated to Operation 'Mo' were no exception. There were invasion forces for Port Moresby and Tulagi, protecting groups of varying strengths and the most formidable formation of all – a striking force, including six modern destroyers, two heavy cruisers and the large fleet carriers *Shokaku* and *Zuikaku*, carrying 123 aircraft. This force's task was to support both invasions and repel any American counterattacks.

Though the Port Moresby invasion force was to depart from Rabaul, other groups had to come from bases farther afield – *Shokaku* and *Zuikaku* from Truk in the Caroline Islands about 1600 km (1000 miles) north-east of New Guinea. Controlling the operation was Vice Admiral Shigeyoshi Inouye, from his flagship *Kashima* anchored at Rabaul. Under him Vice Admiral Takeo Takagi commanded the striking force, flying his flag on the cruiser *Myoko*.

RENDEZVOUS AT 'POINT BUTTERCUP'

The Rochefort report prompted the Americans to act quickly; the hunt was on. Even before *Shokaku* and *Zuikaku* had left Truk, the US Commander in Chief in the Pacific, Admiral Chester W. Nimitz, had ordered a makeshift but powerful three-part naval force to the Coral Sea.

In tactical command of the whole force was Rear Admiral Frank J. Fletcher on the carrier *Yorktown*, which was to lead Task Force 17. On May 1, this force linked up with Task Force 11, commanded by Rear Admiral Aubrey Fitch on the carrier *Lexington*, at 'Point Buttercup', south of the Solomon Islands. This was the best area for facing the expected two-prong attack. The two carriers, carrying 141 aircraft, were escorted by five cruisers and 11 destroyers, and later joined up with an Australian-US force of cruisers and destroyers under Rear Admiral John Crace, an Australian-born Royal Navy officer serving with the Australian Navy.

On May 3 the Japanese seized Tulagi without meeting any opposition, only to be struck the next day by aircraft from *Yorktown*. The American strike sank a destroyer and several minor Japanese ships, but cost the Americans the advantage of surprise, since the Japanese now knew that at least one US carrier was in the vicinity. Throughout May 5 and 6 Japanese and Americans sought each other out, but in vain – except for B-17 bombers based in Australia which found and unsuccessfully attacked *Shoho*.

ROUND ONE TO JAPAN

The two sides eventually made contact on May 7, but both suffered from errors and accidents. Just after 7.30 am a Japanese search plane spotted what it took to be an enemy carrier and cruiser south-west of Guadalcanal. Rear Admiral Tadaichi Hara – in immediate command of *Shokaku* and *Zuikaku* under Takagi – launched a full-scale attack with 51 bombers escorted by 18 Zero fighters. But the two ships were in fact the tanker USS *Neosho* and destroyer *Sims*. They were easy targets: *Sims* was sunk and *Neosho* so damaged by a second wave that it had to be scuttled later. More than 400 men died, including all but four of 158 *Neosho* crew members who panicked and took to the boats prematurely.

While the attack was under way, news reached Hara that the main US force had at last been spotted farther to the north-west – but all he could do was to wait anxiously for his aircraft to return. Luckily for him, the Americans had made a similar mistake. At 8.15 am a US reconnaissance

RULED BY CAUTION

Frank Jack Fletcher (1885-1973) was a brave leader and able staff officer, but his career as a senior commander was marred by bad luck and the wrong instincts and experience for carrier warfare. Carrier task forces needed more aggressive commanders for best results.

As a carrier task-force commander after Pearl Harbor – during which he was at sea in his flagship – the staff-trained Fletcher often gave undue priority to fuel and other supplies – at the expense of other considerations. Even so, he deserves credit for the victories in the Coral Sea and at Midway, though in both cases ably served by subordinates.

At Guadalcanal in August 1942, Fletcher pulled out his three aircraft carriers prematurely, allowing the Japanese to mount a damaging counterattack. His role in the Eastern Solomons later that month was also lack-lustre. He was wounded a week later when his flagship *Saratoga* was torpedoed. He spent the rest of the war in naval commands in the North Pacific.

LORD OF THE PACIFIC SKIES

Aubrey Wray Fitch (1883-1978) only started to fly at the age of 47, after long experience in the US Navy of traditional surface operations. But 'Jake' Fitch committed himself totally to his new specialisation. He went on to command the pioneer carrier *Langley* and eventually a carrier division.

After Pearl Harbor, he was passed over as the Pacific Fleet's senior carrier task-force commander in favour of Rear Admiral Fletcher – to the fury of his fellow aviators. Fletcher was, however, wise enough to delegate much of the tactical command to Fitch in the Coral Sea battle. Because of the loss of his flagship *Lexington* and because its successor *Saratoga* was not yet ready, Fitch missed the Battle of Midway.

In September 1942 he became the Pacific Fleet's overall air forces commander, in charge of the administration and training of all its aircraft and carriers, but was almost immediately transferred to the south-west Pacific as commander of all Allied air forces in that area. His land-based air forces supported the Solomons campaign so successfully that the back of Japanese naval air power was permanently broken. After this largely unsung success, Fitch was transferred to Washington to take overall responsibility for US naval aviation when it was at the peak of its size and importance.

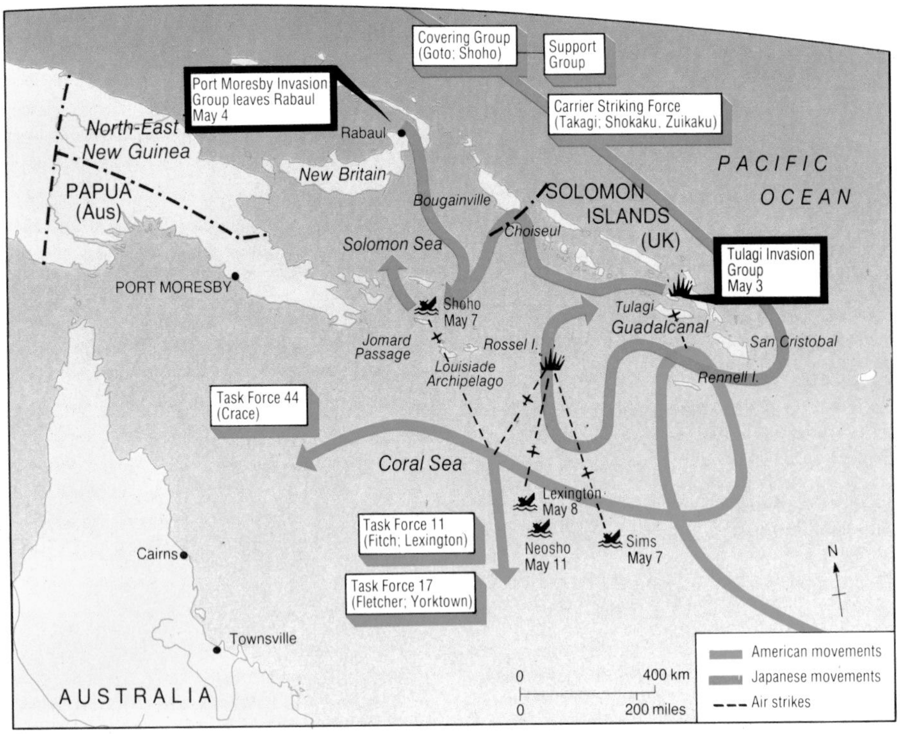

INVASION TURNED BACK Action started in the Coral Sea on May 4 with an American air attack on Tulagi. Then, on the 7th and 8th, planes on both sides launched heavy attacks. Losses were about even – but the Japanese had to abandon, for the moment, plans to seize Port Moresby.

plane reported sighting two Japanese carriers and four large cruisers just north of Misima island, 210 km (130 miles) to the east of New Guinea's easternmost tip. Admiral Fletcher on *Yorktown*, convinced that he had found the main Japanese force, launched a full-scale attack with 93 aircraft from both *Yorktown* and *Lexington*. In fact, the reconnaissance pilot had only spotted one of the support groups, consisting of two Japanese cruisers and two destroyers.

The day was saved for the Americans by the sharp eyes of Lt Commander Weldon L. Hamilton, commander of *Lexington*'s dive-bomber squadron. While on the way to attack the support group, Hamilton drifted off course to the east and spotted a much more important force – a covering group for the Port Moresby invasion force, commanded by Rear Admiral Arimoto Goto and including the light carrier *Shoho*. The American planes were redirected. At first the highly manoeuvrable Japanese carrier managed to dodge the American attacks, but *Shoho* was eventually overwhelmed and sunk (see box, *A short-lived quick-change act*). 'Scratch one flat-top!' signalled Lt Commander Robert E. Dixon of *Lexington*'s scout bomber squadron. 'Dixon to aircraft carrier, I repeat: Scratch one flat-top!'

Meanwhile, Fletcher had sent Crace's force against the Port Moresby invasion group – in what came to be called 'Crace's Chase'. The ships were attacked in the early afternoon of May 7 by land-based Japanese aircraft from Rabaul and later by US B-26s from Australia mistaking them for Japanese – but they evaded them all.

More bad luck struck the Japanese at dusk, after Takagi sent off a flight of 27 planes to find the American fleet carriers. Some of them found *Yorktown* – but mistook it for a Japanese carrier and tried to land. Ten were shot down and another 11 crashed later while trying to land on their own carriers after dark. That night, news of the loss of *Shoho* and of the presence of the US-Australian force off Port Moresby persuaded Inouye to delay the Port Moresby invasion. First he would deal with the US carrier fleet.

ENEMY FOUND

Early the next morning Fletcher and Takagi's main carrier forces finally located each other. After the loss of *Shoho* each side had two carriers. But the Americans had 118 operational aircraft, the Japanese only 95.

Shortly after 9 am the two sides' aircraft were in the air and a Japanese attack inflicted significant damage on both *Lexington* and *Yorktown*. *Yorktown* managed with clever manoeuvring to avoid the Japanese torpedoes, but bombs exploding in the water nearby badly damaged it below the water line. Another bomb went down through four decks, where it exploded, killing 37 men and wounding 33. *Lexington*, bigger and less manoeuvrable, was hit by two torpedoes as well as several bombs and was left listing to port.

Pilots from the two US carriers, meanwhile, were assaulting the Japanese carriers *Shokaku*

FIRST OF A NEW BREED

USS *Yorktown* was the first of a new breed of US aircraft carriers, its design incorporating the lessons of a decade in which the US Navy had solved better than anyone else the problems of operating the largest possible number of aircraft from a single ship. *Yorktown* was started in May 1934, partly to create jobs and beat the Depression. Completed in September 1937, the 20 000 tonne *Yorktown* was smaller and faster than some previous carriers, yet could operate a large and powerful air group. These factors provided its main defence. Further protection was given by armour plate on the hull up to 100 mm (4 in) thick and designed to withstand 6 in (150 mm) gunfire and 400 lb (180 kg) torpedo warheads. It was built as one of a pair with the USS *Enterprise*, and the design was considered successful enough to be repeated in *Hornet* (completed in 1941).

In the Coral Sea *Yorktown*'s air group consisted of 75 aircraft in four squadrons: 24 single-seat Grumman Wildcat fighters, 19 two-seat Douglas Dauntless dive-bombers, 19 Dauntless scout bombers and 13 three-seat Douglas Devastator torpedo bombers. It was Rear Admiral Frank Fletcher's flagship in the Coral Sea and at Midway, and was badly damaged in both battles. A Japanese submarine torpedoed it on June 6, two days after Midway. The carrier sank the next day.

and *Zuikaku*. *Zuikaku*, Hara's flagship, was hidden by a rain storm and the full weight of the American attack fell on its sister ship. The few defending Zero fighters on board *Shokaku* were able to force the first wave of American Devastators to launch their torpedoes too far away to make any hits. But the Dauntless dive-bombers that followed were more successful.

One Dauntless pilot, Lieutenant John James Powers, had vowed to sink an enemy carrier unaided. During the attack on *Shokaku*, he swooped daringly low to release his bomb a mere 90 m (300 ft) above the carrier's deck. In the resulting explosion Powers crashed to his death in the sea; he was awarded a posthumous Medal of Honor, the first ever given to an American pilot.

The explosion so damaged the carrier's flight deck that its aircraft could no longer take off. Two more American bombs, released at a more conventional height of about 460 m (1500 ft), did further damage, so that aircraft could not land on it either. *Shokaku* had to withdraw to Truk.

Zuikaku, meanwhile, could not carry the aircraft from both ships, and many Japanese planes had to be pushed over the side to make room for others to land. This added to the losses the Japanese had already suffered. Without air cover, Inouye had to call off Operation 'Mo' and withdraw the invasion force to Rabaul.

STRATEGIC SUCCESS

The Battle of the Coral Sea was thus a strategic success for the Americans, but it was marred by a serious and unexpected incident. About two hours after the last Japanese planes had retired, *Lexington* erupted in a huge explosion, set off by a spark from a generator accidentally left running. The fires were fed by petrol fuel and vapour from ruptured tanks, and the ship became an exploding inferno. It finally came to a halt at 4.30 pm on May 8 and was abandoned. The explosion of the ship's magazines and a torpedo fired by an American destroyer as a *coup de grâce* finally sent the 'Lady Lex' to the bottom that evening. An orderly evacuation saved 2735 of the crew, but 216 died.

In the Coral Sea, the Americans lost one carrier, a tanker and a destroyer, while the Japanese lost only *Shoho* and one destroyer. But only 564 US sailors and airmen died, and 66 aircraft were shot down, compared with Tokyo's losses of 1074 men and 77 aircraft. The battle turned back the

READY FOR ACTION
A US Navy pilot, wearing a 'Mae West' lifejacket over the lightweight jacket of his tropical battle kit, is ready for takeoff from his carrier. The first Medal of Honor (below) for a US pilot was given posthumously after the Coral Sea battle.

Japanese threat to Port Moresby – a great fillip to American morale just after the fall of Corregidor.

More significantly still, two of Japan's most modern carriers were put out of action for months to come – one through extensive damage, the other by losing many of its aircraft. Japan's admirals were already planning another battle where they hoped to cripple the US Pacific Fleet once and for all off Midway. The Japanese would sorely miss the damaged carriers when they fought – and lost – that showdown in June.

The Coral Sea had also been the first sea battle ever where two fleets had fought on the high seas without sighting one another and relying entirely upon aircraft to strike the enemy. The Americans would be quick to master the techniques of this new kind of naval warfare – and would use them to good effect at Midway, and in the Solomons, the Philippine Sea and Leyte Gulf.

A SHORT-LIVED QUICK-CHANGE ACT

The Japanese light carrier *Shoho* was built in 1934-9 as a submarine depot ship named *Tsurigisaki*. But, with another depot ship, it was designed to be easily turned into a carrier. At the time, the number of carriers in the Japanese Navy was limited by international treaty. In 1941-2 *Tsurigisaki* was duly transformed to become *Shoho* by fitting steam turbine engines, giving it a speed of 28 knots (52 km/h), and a flight deck.

Its career was short. When the air groups of *Lexington* and *Yorktown* attacked it in the Coral Sea, just over three months after its conversion, its own 21 operational aircraft – Zero fighters and 'Kate' bombers – were no match. And, to ensure speed and manoeuvrability, no protective armour had been fitted. After being hit by 13 bombs, seven torpedoes and a crashing dive-bomber, *Shoho* capsized and sank in ten minutes.

Showdown at Midway

By attacking Midway atoll, at the far western end of the Hawaiian chain, the Japanese hoped to lure the US Pacific Fleet into the open sea and destroy it. Instead, thanks to superb US intelligence and Japanese mistakes, the attack marked the end of Tokyo's supremacy in the Pacific Ocean.

ON WEDNESDAY, MAY 20, 1942, Allied listening stations around the Pacific picked up a lengthy radio signal, in code, from Admiral Isoruku Yamamoto to his fleet. The message, relayed to Pearl Harbor and deciphered there by the US Combat Intelligence Unit ('Hypo'), revealed that the Japanese Navy was about to mount a powerful attack on the tiny mid-Pacific atoll of Midway, with a diversionary attack on the Aleutians, far to the north. Soon, using other intercepted messages, 'Hypo' intelligence officers were able to add dates and times to the places: Dutch Harbor in the Aleutians would be hit on June 3, Midway the next day.

It was the culmination of a remarkable intelligence exercise. 'Hypo' had warned early in the year that a strike somewhere in the Hawaiian Islands was on the cards. On May 12, four days after the Battle of the Coral Sea, they discovered the Japanese code name of the target: 'AF'. But where was 'AF'? The evidence pointed to Midway – but it was not conclusive.

An officer at 'Hypo', Captain Jasper Holmes, then suggested a way to check. The US air base on Midway was ordered to send an uncoded radio signal that the island was having trouble with its water distillation plant. Soon afterwards the Japanese were signalling that 'AF' had water problems. The Americans now knew for certain where the Japanese blow would fall.

OVER-COMPLEX

Operation 'Mi' – the Midway strike – had all the hallmarks of Japanese planning. It was over-complex, made unjustified assumptions about how the enemy would react, and failed to concentrate force. Even so, it might well have worked had the Americans not discovered its secrets.

The very choice of Midway was flawed – one of Yamamoto's carrier captains called it 'an impossible and pointless operation'. But while the Japanese leaders, after a string of dazzling victories, were debating where they should strike next, their minds had been made up for them. Lt Colonel James Doolittle's raid on Tokyo with B-25 bombers, on April 18, had put the sacred person of the Emperor in danger. The mortified generals and admirals decided that every gap in Japan's defensive perimeter must be plugged – and Midway was such a gap.

Yamamoto believed that Operation 'Al', the attack on the Aleutians, would draw away part of the US fleet while the rest of his squadrons captured Midway, posing a serious threat to Pearl Harbor itself. His opposite number, Admiral Chester W. Nimitz, would then have to try to retake Midway. Waiting for him would be the powerful Japanese fleet, supported by land-based aircraft operating from the newly captured island. Yamamoto would spring the trap, and achieve what had eluded him at Pearl Harbor – the destruction of American naval power in the Pacific. With the western seaboard of the USA now at the mercy of the Japanese, President Roosevelt would have no alternative but to sue for peace – or so the argument ran.

HIGH STAKES

Yamamoto committed almost the entire Japanese fleet to his plan: some 160 warships, including eight aircraft carriers, and more than 400 carrier-based aircraft – compared with the three carriers, about 70 other warships and 233 carrier aircraft (plus another 115 planes stationed on Midway) at Nimitz's disposal. But Yamamoto separated his forces into five main groups, all too far apart to support or reinforce each other.

At the head of the procession was the First Carrier Striking Force under Vice Admiral Chuichi Nagumo, with four carriers – *Akagi, Kaga, Hiryu* and *Soryu* – and their 225 fighters and bombers. They were to give Midway a powerful preliminary bombardment before the 5000-strong invasion force landed from 12 transport vessels. Apart from its immediate escort, the invasion force was to be protected by two support groups, each 80-120 km (50-75 miles) away.

Over 950 km (600 miles) astern of Nagumo was the main Japanese battle fleet with seven battleships, led by Yamamoto's giant new flagship, the 70 000 tonne *Yamato*. These, Yamamoto planned, would finish off the US fleet after the carriers had inflicted the decisive damage.

Knowing that the odds were stacked heavily against him, Nimitz staked everything on his faith in aircraft carriers, with their ability to strike at long range. He decided that his much slower battleships would be a liability and ordered them to stay on the US west coast.

'CALCULATED RISK'

Nimitz divided his forces into two groups – Task Force 16 with the carriers USS *Hornet* and *Enterprise* and Task Force 17 with *Yorktown*. On May 28 Task Force 16 left Pearl Harbor under a new commander, Rear Admiral Raymond T. Spruance. Task Force 17 was delayed because *Yorktown* had only just returned from the Coral Sea so badly damaged that the Japanese believed it sunk. Miraculously, Pearl Harbor repair crews patched up the carrier in only 48 hours – such repairs normally took weeks – and *Yorktown* set sail under Coral Sea hero Rear Admiral Frank Fletcher on May 30.

Once at sea, Fletcher was to take tactical command of the US force. 'You will be governed by the principle of calculated risk', Nimitz commanded. The Americans were to engage only if they had a good chance of inflicting disproportionate damage on the Japanese. Warned by intelligence, they were in position well before 15 Japanese submarines established a cordon west of Hawaii to watch for the US fleet.

At 9 am on June 3, Ensign Jack Read, flying a Catalina flying boat based at Midway, spotted the Japanese invasion force steaming towards the atoll, some 750 km (470 miles) west of Midway. 'I believe we've hit the jackpot', he shouted to his co-pilot. But this was not the carrier force's main target, and Fletcher left it to bombers on Midway to attack that afternoon – to no effect.

The US carriers' main prey, Admiral Nagumo's Carrier Striking Force, was zigzagging through dense fog farther north, oblivious of its foe. It emerged from the bad weather into beautiful calm conditions in the early hours of the following morning, June 4. At 4.30 am Nagumo launched a strike of 108 planes at Midway, led by Lieutenant Joichi Tomonaga. They were spotted on Midway's radar, and its planes scrambled. The Japanese shot down many of the defenders and damaged the US base, but its bombers were safely out of the way and the airfield was still usable. Tomonaga signalled to Nagumo that a second attack was needed to knock it out.

FATAL DELAYS

This put Nagumo in a quandary. He knew neither where the US fleet was nor how many ships it had. But, as ordered by Yamamoto, he had held back his best aircrews, their planes armed with torpedoes and other anti-ship weapons, in case the US carriers arrived sooner than expected. Yet his search planes had spotted no enemy ships and he needed to finish the job at Midway. Just then Midway-based bombers started attacking his ships. They did no damage, but they made up Nagumo's mind for him – and changed the course of the battle. The Japanese commander ordered his second-wave torpedo bombers to be rearmed with bombs for another attack on Midway.

But at 7.28 am, 15 minutes after the torpedo bombers went below to be rearmed, one of Nagumo's search planes spotted ten US warships some 335 km (210 miles) north-east of the Japanese carriers. This plane had taken off half an hour late that morning, delayed when the launching catapult on the heavy cruiser *Tone* jammed. Had it taken off on time, it might well have spotted the US ships half an hour (*continued on p. 166*)

QUICK THINKER

Formidably high intelligence earned Raymond Ames Spruance (1886-1969) the nickname 'Electric Brain'. At the beginning of the war he was commanding cruisers in Rear Admiral William F. Halsey's carrier Task Force 16 in the Pacific, having previously served in battleships and as a land instructor. When Halsey had to go into hospital with a severe skin complaint before Midway, he nominated his able subordinate to take over his command.

Spruance was no airman, but he was a clever tactician and knew how to use experts – making him an even abler carrier commander than his often over-exuberant patron, 'Bull' Halsey. Spruance later became chief of staff to the Commander in Chief of the US Pacific Fleet, Admiral Chester Nimitz, and in August 1943 took over command of the US Fifth Fleet. He directed US operations in the Battle of the Philippine Sea in June 1944.

Destruction of a Japanese fleet

Lt Commander Wade McClusky scanned the sparkling blue Pacific north-east of Midway island – and made a quick decision. It was 9.25 am on June 4, 1942. He was leading 33 Dauntless dive-bombers from the carrier USS *Enterprise* in a hunt for the Japanese First Air Fleet. Where he expected to find the enemy there was nothing, and his planes would soon have to turn back for lack of fuel. But McClusky had a hunch: he wanted to continue his search a little farther west.

He decided to do so – and the gamble paid off. A little later, he spotted the wake of an enemy destroyer. Then he made another decision: to follow it. Just after 10 am, he found the Japanese carriers. Before 10.25, he and his men were swooping down to attack them.

But they were not the first Americans to find the enemy that morning. Only minutes earlier, the US fleet's Devastator torpedo bombers had also attacked. Most were shot down. But their sacrifice let McClusky's Dauntlesses come in unnoticed.

Indeed, McClusky – now joined by 17 more Dauntlesses from *Yorktown* – could not have arrived at a better moment. Nearly 100 planes crammed the decks of the Japanese carriers, ready for their own strike against the US carriers. All were loaded with explosives and high-octane petrol. Piles of bombs were loosely stacked on the hangar decks. The tiniest spark would turn them into floating infernos.

BRIEF REPRIEVE *Hiryu* zigzags nimbly to avoid bursting American bombs. It would finally be hit later on June 4.

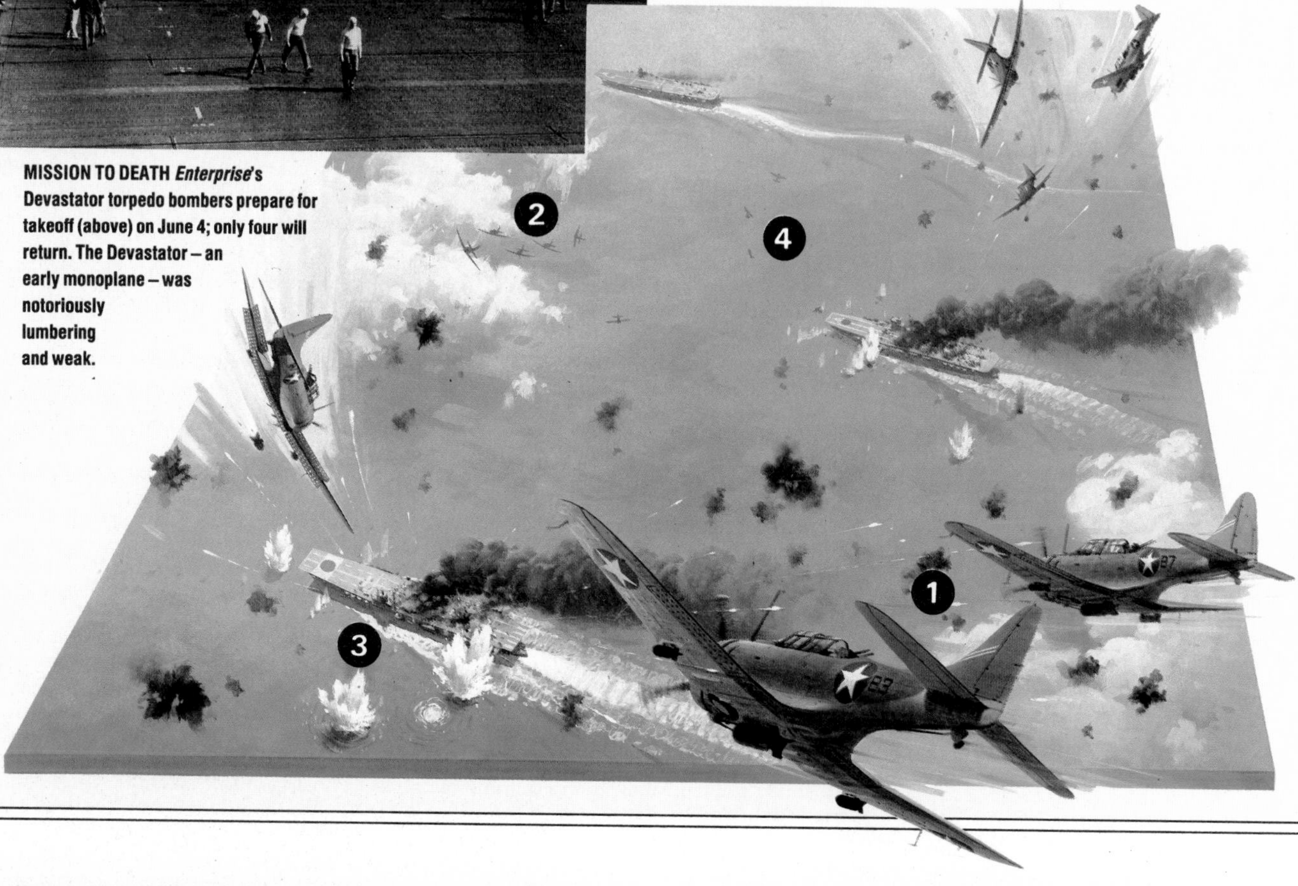

1 McClusky's Dauntlesses scream down at 520 km/h (325 mph). The first have already dropped their bombs.

2 Zero fighters appear – too late to beat off the attack. The Devastators have lured them down close to sea level.

3 *Akagi* is already ablaze, rocked repeatedly as burning planes and exploding bombs set each other off. A sailor was later to describe the damage: 'There was a huge hole in the flight deck just behind the amidships elevator. The elevator itself, twisted like molten glass, was drooping into the hangar. Deck plates reeled upwards in grotesque configurations. Planes stood tail up, belching livid flame and jet-black smoke.' *Akagi* is evacuated, but its hulk keeps afloat until the next morning, when a Japanese submarine sinks it.

4 *Kaga* (below) and *Soryu* (above) receive a similar mauling. They sink that evening, *Kaga* taking 800 men with it. A fourth carrier, *Hiryu*, escapes, hidden by a squall, but US bombers later catch up with it. Like *Akagi*, its wreck goes down the next morning.

MISSION TO DEATH *Enterprise*'s Devastator torpedo bombers prepare for takeoff (above) on June 4; only four will return. The Devastator – an early monoplane – was notoriously lumbering and weak.

DAUNTLESS IN ATTACK Two Douglas Dauntless dive-bombers scream down onto the Japanese fleet. Manoeuvrable, accurate and rugged, the Dauntless was a mainstay of US naval air power.

NORTHERN DIVERSION

The Japanese diversionary attack on the bleak and foggy Aleutian Islands began in the early hours of June 3. In the half-light of the near-Arctic summer night, 'Kate' torpedo bombers and Zero fighters from the carrier *Ryujo* attacked the US base at Dutch Harbor on Unalaska island. They damaged oil dumps, barracks, the hospital and a Russian Orthodox church. However, inexperienced pilots from *Junyo*, the other carrier with the 37 ship Japanese force under Vice Admiral Hoshiro Hosogaya, got lost.

The American defenders did little better. Their flying boats eventually spotted the Japanese, but they were too far away for the US ships or shore-based aircraft to make effective attacks. Nimitz, not deceived by the Japanese feint, had refused to divert large forces north. The Japanese made a final attack on Dutch Harbor on June 4, damaging fuel installations. Then their carriers were called off to reinforce the fleets fighting off Midway.

Two days later, Japanese troops occupied Attu and Kiska, the two westernmost islands of the chain, capturing little more than a weather station and two missionaries. It took four days for the Americans to discover that the Japanese were there. They retook the islands the following summer.

One significant prize did fall into American hands. A Zero fighter had had to make a forced landing in a bog. The pilot died, but his aircraft survived. The Americans later overhauled it, and used it to work out ways to counter the formidable Zeros.

earlier than it did and got the news back to Nagumo before he sent the torpedo bombers below. In this case, he would almost certainly have sent his aircraft against the approaching Americans. The course of the battle – and of the entire Pacific war – might have been very different.

As it was, Nagumo was in a quandary once more: should he turn his attention to the US ships or still concentrate on Midway? He halted the rearming, but had one more question – did the US force include aircraft carriers? Only at 8.20 am did the scout finally report: 'The enemy is accompanied by what appears to be a carrier.'

The news could not have reached Nagumo at a worse moment. Tomonaga's aircraft were just returning from Midway and had to land on the Japanese carriers. If he sent off his available bombers immediately they could only attack with bombs and not the more effective torpedoes. Moreover, his fighters needed refuelling, so the bombers would either have to attack unescorted or circle and wait for the fighters. Nagumo decided to clear the flight decks, rearm the bombers again with torpedoes, and prepare a proper attack on the American fleet.

The repeated delays proved fatal. Tomonaga's force did not finish landing until 9.18 am, and then the aircraft of the second wave had to be brought back up to the flight decks. Soon afterwards, the Japanese carriers were like floating bombs ready to go off at any moment. On their flight decks were jammed 36 highly explosive dive-bombers, 54 torpedo bombers and a dozen Zero fighters. On the hangar decks, bombs – just removed from the torpedo bombers – lay stacked where they had been left during the rearming. At at this moment bombers from the US carriers *Enterprise*, *Yorktown* and *Hornet* arrived.

FIRST ROUND TO NAGUMO

News that Catalinas from Midway had sighted the Japanese carrier fleet had reached Fletcher at 5.34 that morning. Fletcher sent Spruance with *Enterprise* and *Hornet* ahead to attack while he waited for his scout planes. On the advice of his chief of staff, Captain Miles Browning, Spruance started sending off his aircraft two hours earlier

JAPANESE HIT Puffs of black smoke blob the sky, where Admiral Fletcher's flagship, the carrier *Yorktown*, and its escort pump out anti-aircraft fire. Even so, one Japanese aircraft has got through and landed a bomb; others follow. (Inset) Damage-control crewmen totter along the sloping flight deck the next day. The Japanese attack reopened wounds from the Coral Sea (p. 163), and the carrier had to be abandoned. Yet it sank only after being torpedoed by a Japanese submarine on June 7.

than planned – just after 7 am – in an attempt to catch the Japanese just when they were busy landing aircraft from the attack on Midway. This was a crucial decision. It meant launching the US planes at dangerously long range, but the gamble paid off. In all, 152 aircraft were sent out. They made probably the most decisive single air strike in naval history – yet it got off to a bad start.

Nagumo had changed course when he decided to rearm his planes, and the first US bombers could not find their prey. The first ones that did – *Hornet*'s lumbering Devastator torpedo bombers – attacked without fighter support, and all 15 were shot down by Japanese Zeros. Devastators from *Enterprise* attacked shortly afterwards, followed by a squadron from *Yorktown*. All met a similar fate, with only four of *Enterprise*'s planes returning; two *Yorktown* aircraft survived the attack but

PROMISE THAT FAILED

Chuichi Nagumo (1887-1944) was floundering in command of Japan's First Air Fleet from summer 1941. Known until then for energy and intelligence, he had little feel for naval air warfare and had to rely heavily on his brilliant air operations officer, Commander Minoru Genda.

At Midway he sorely missed Genda, who was ill. Poor results in later battles off Guadalcanal lost him his command, and he was posted to Saipan. There he committed *hara-kiri* rather than surrender.

BATTERED, BRUISED The Japanese heavy cruiser *Mikuma* sinks beneath the waves on June 6, after a collision and two American strikes – one by a crashing bomber.

ditched in the sea on the way back to their carrier.

Nagumo was on the verge of a spectacular success. At 10.20 am he ordered his carriers to turn into the wind to launch their aircraft for the killer blow. Less than five minutes later, as the first plane was roaring down the deck of *Akagi*, a lookout shouted a warning: 50 US Dauntless dive-bombers were hurtling from the sky. And the Japanese carriers were like floating bombs themselves.

In what Nimitz later called 'the most important decision of the battle', the leader of the *Enterprise*'s dive-bombers had followed the wake of a destroyer hurrying to catch up with Nagumo's force. It led him to the Japanese carriers. Nagumo's deadly Zero fighters were all on the decks or down at sea level after their last dogfight, leaving the skies clear for the US bombers. The first few hits turned *Akagi*, *Kaga* and *Soryu* into exploding torches (see diorama, p. 165).

'The terrifying scream of the dive-bombers reached me first, followed by the crashing explosion of a direct hit', recalled a sailor from *Akagi*. 'There was a blinding flash and then a second explosion, much louder than the first.'

Within five minutes most of the dreaded Japanese First Air Fleet had been wiped out. The fourth carrier, *Hiryu*, was saved by a lucky squall and tried a desperate counterattack. Some of its aircraft got away and struck Fletcher's *Yorktown*. It had to be abandoned – and Fletcher had to hand over command to Spruance.

Later that day, however, Spruance turned his triumphant Dauntlesses on *Hiryu*. Again the Americans caught their prey with aircraft ranged on deck as the crew were eating their supper before another strike planned for twilight. Four bombs converted *Hiryu* into the same condition as the rest of Nagumo's force. *Soryu* and *Kaga* sank that evening. *Soryu*'s captain went down with his ship, calmly singing Japan's national anthem.

Early the following morning, June 5, *Hiryu* – burning like a torch – was abandoned by all who were able, except for its captain and the proud and aggressive Rear Admiral Tamon Yamaguchi, Nagumo's deputy. They tied themselves to the bridge and went down with the ship. *Akagi*, which had been turned into an inferno when one of the US bombs hit a torpedo store, went down shortly afterwards. Although it was abandoned helter-skelter, its officers still found time to obey their code: the portrait of the Emperor was removed from the doomed ship with reverence and ceremony. Four of Japan's finest carriers had gone and 332 aircraft. Well over 2000 highly skilled men had lost their lives.

Damage-control crews went aboard *Yorktown*, but it sank on June 7 after receiving a hit from a Japanese submarine. An escorting destroyer, *Hammann*, was sunk at the same time.

THE AFTERMATH

For the night of June 4/5 Yamamoto had planned a surface attack on the American carriers. Nagumo, now on the cruiser *Nagara*, was demoralised by his failure and contemplating suicide, so the job was given to Vice Admiral Nobutake Kondo's Second Fleet – the Midway invasion force support group. But by then it was too late; Spruance had retreated out of range. Yamamoto, knowing that he could not give Kondo's ships air cover, had to order a general withdrawal.

The epilogue to the battle was another Japanese fiasco. One of the withdrawing groups was thrown into appalling confusion by an American submarine on the night of June 4/5, and the cruiser *Mogami* rammed the cruiser ahead, *Mikuma*. US bombers attacked both ships and sank *Mikuma*. Badly damaged, *Mogami* amazingly limped back to the Japanese naval base at Truk.

The Battle of Midway was a significant moment in naval history. For the first time battleships fled before aircraft carriers. It was also a turning point in World War II. Japan had lost its main naval striking force and the US Pacific Fleet, far from being destroyed, had won a remarkable victory – despite the loss of a carrier, 137 aircraft and 307 men. By the time Japan rebuilt its carrier fleet in 1944, American industrial power was fully mobilised in all the unstoppable might that Yamamoto had so feared.

Battles at Australia's back door

After their reverse in the Battle of the Coral Sea, the Japanese made a second attempt to capture Port Moresby, the main Allied base in New Guinea. This time they approached overland on the rugged Kokoda Trail – but the result, after six gruelling months, was their first major land defeat of the war.

WAR CAME SUDDENLY to the remote northern coast of Papua – the south-eastern corner of the island of New Guinea – on July 22, 1942. On a sunny afternoon, the advance guard of the Japanese South Seas Detachment, a crack unit of jungle fighters, veterans of Guam and Rabaul, landed near the village of Buna and crossed the coastal swamps towards the jungle-clad slopes of the Owen Stanley mountains.

The handful of Australian missionaries, government officials and planters left in the area were taken completely by surprise and fled panic-stricken into the jungle. During the next few days the Japanese rounded them up, bayoneting some and ceremonially beheading others, one by one, on the beach at Buna.

The Japanese were aiming for Port Moresby on Papua's south coast. They planned to reach it via the Kokoda Trail, which wound 160 km (100 miles) south-westwards from Buna across eastern Papua's high mountainous spine, the Owen Stanley Range. Faulty aerial reconnaissance four months earlier had suggested to the Japanese that the trail was a substantial route that might even be widened to accommodate motor vehicles.

What they found was very different. When the landing force, accompanied by engineers, construction troops and hundreds of packhorses, had pushed inland 32 km (20 miles) they encountered their first obstacle – the wide and turbulent Kumusi river. After crossing the Kumusi on a foot suspension bridge (known in the local Pidgin language as Wairopi – 'Wire Rope' – bridge), they found that the trail dwindled to a muddy footpath. For 32 km more, the trail snaked around jungle-covered spurs, following river and creek valleys through the villages of Gorari and Oivi. Then it climbed an escarpment to the village of Kokoda, near which was the only airstrip between Buna and Port Moresby.

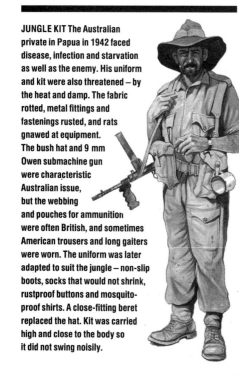

JUNGLE KIT The Australian private in Papua in 1942 faced disease, infection and starvation as well as the enemy. His uniform and kit were also threatened – by the heat and damp. The fabric rotted, metal fittings and fastenings rusted, and rats gnawed at equipment. The bush hat and 9 mm Owen submachine gun were characteristic Australian issue, but the webbing and pouches for ammunition were often British, and sometimes American trousers and long gaiters were worn. The uniform was later adapted to suit the jungle – non-slip boots, socks that would not shrink, rustproof buttons and mosquito-proof shirts. A close-fitting beret replaced the hat. Kit was carried high and close to the body so it did not swing noisily.

Thereafter the terrain became even more formidably difficult. Climbing near-vertical spurs or clinging to razor-back ridges, the trail rose through the villages of Isurava, Iora (Eora) Creek and Templeton's Crossing to the 2190 m (7185 ft) crest of the Owen Stanley Range. From there it descended and rose steeply again many times across valleys and ridges, and finally made a precipitous descent – the 'Golden Staircase' – to Uberi village. Just beyond this, at the junction known as Owers' Corner, it broadened into a road for the last 40 km (25 miles) to Port Moresby.

The advancing Japanese found that weather conditions, too, were much worse than expected. Dense cloud banks often reared to 12 000 m (40 000 ft) and the rain was incessant. Constantly wet, the soldiers' skin erupted in tropical ulcers, while many succumbed to malaria and bush typhus, a particularly virulent, usually fatal form of typhus endemic in Papua. Yet despite these difficulties, morale among the Japanese troops was good. Their commander, Maj General Tomitaro Horii, a portly bespectacled figure magnificently mounted on a white horse, never doubted that they would reach Port Moresby.

HORII TAKES A GAMBLE

Assessing the nature of the terrain near the beginning of the trail, Horii took a gamble. His men would travel light: they would carry weapons and ammunition, but little else. They would feed themselves from the 'gardens' of the islanders and from captured Australian supply dumps.

Horii based his judgment on the Japanese experience of war so far. In the preceding six months Japan had won a series of spectacular victories against demoralised enemies – and the first action on the Kokoda Trail suggested that the Papuan campaign would be similar. On the path to Wairopi, an Australian force ran away after the first shots were fired. Across the Kumusi, other Australian units were easily outflanked and forced to withdraw in disorder.

On July 29, the Japanese took Kokoda village in a night attack. The Australian defenders fought vigorously at first, but when their commander was felled by a bullet in the head, they quickly drew back. By the second week of August, the South Seas Detachment was just north of Isurava, 13 km (8 miles) beyond Kokoda. There they awaited reinforcements before the dash to Port Moresby.

Horii would have been less confident of victory had he known that his enemy in these first skirmishes was only a single company of the poorly trained Australian 39th Militia Battalion, young conscripts who at times had faced odds of 15 to 1. Under these circumstances the Australians had done surprisingly well. Like the Japanese, they were suffering acutely from the climate and from tropical diseases. Unlike the Japanese, they were ill-equipped and had no experience of jungle warfare.

While the Japanese waited, the 39th dug in at Isurava – and began to get the measure of their enemy. Their patrols became increasingly aggressive and they retook Kokoda – briefly. By the third week of August they too were expecting reinforcements – the 21st Australian Brigade, from the Middle East, and commanded by the imperturbable Brigadier Arnold Potts. He, however, faced immense problems in keeping his troops supplied as they advanced to Isurava. Attempts to airdrop supplies for them at Myola, 11 km (7 miles) south, delivered only a fraction of the rations required and the first reinforcements were not able to get through to the 39th until August 26. The very same day Horii, his force also by now reinforced, launched his attack from Isurava.

HEROISM AT ISURAVA

Horii expected an easy victory. Five thousand Japanese, supported by mortars and mountain guns, advanced upon 1700 Australians who had but one mortar and no artillery. But for the first time in the Pacific war the Japanese encountered, in the Australian reinforcements, troops who matched them in training, experience and morale.

The Australians regarded the defence of Port Moresby as vital to their own country's security, and throughout August 26, 27 and 28, Japanese attacks south of Isurava were bloodily repulsed. By the evening of the 28th, some of Horii's officers were beginning to despair. One confided to his diary: 'Our casualties are great . . . the outcome of the battle is very difficult to foresee.'

Early on August 29, Horii, infuriated by his reverses, threw the full weight of the South Seas Detachment into a massive onslaught against the Australians. Violent hand-to-hand fighting raged for the next 36 hours. One Australian corporal, Charles McCallum, a Tommy gun at his left shoulder and a Bren gun on his right hip, countered a Japanese attack single-handed, leaving a pile of 40 bodies around him. In another action, Private Bruce Kingsbury scattered a Japanese company who were forming up for an attack by charging, gun blazing, into their midst. But, despite individual acts of heroism, pressure of numbers forced the Australians back and during August 30 they had to abandon their increasingly precarious positions.

For the next two weeks, the Australians conducted a fighting withdrawal. Fever-ridden troops waded knee-deep in mud and slime through valleys, or crawled on hands and knees up precipitous slopes in pouring rain. Medical supplies were non-existent. Many wounded men, carried by exhausted but still loyal Papuan porters, were saved from gangrene only by the maggots that ate their putrid flesh.

Now outnumbered seven *(continued on p. 170)*

Victory on a muddy jungle trail

Port Moresby was the goal of the Japanese, but they landed on Papua's opposite shore, expecting an easy march over the mountains. They overlooked the difficult terrain and the problems of supply.

CHRISTMAS ANGEL Papuan 'fuzzy-wuzzy angel' Raphael Oembari (right) leads Private George Whittington to a first-aid post near Buna on December 25, 1942. The Australian was to die of his wounds a few days later.

1 The Japanese land at Buna on July 22, 1942, and cross the coastal plain. The Australians fall back without a fight over the plain and beyond Jumbora.

4 Just beyond Kokoda village the Japanese gain control of the airfield. They can now bring in planeloads of supplies for their troops.

NERVE OF STEEL A carnival spirit grew as Australian troops and Papuan carriers lurched across their makeshift bridge (above) over the swollen Kumusi.

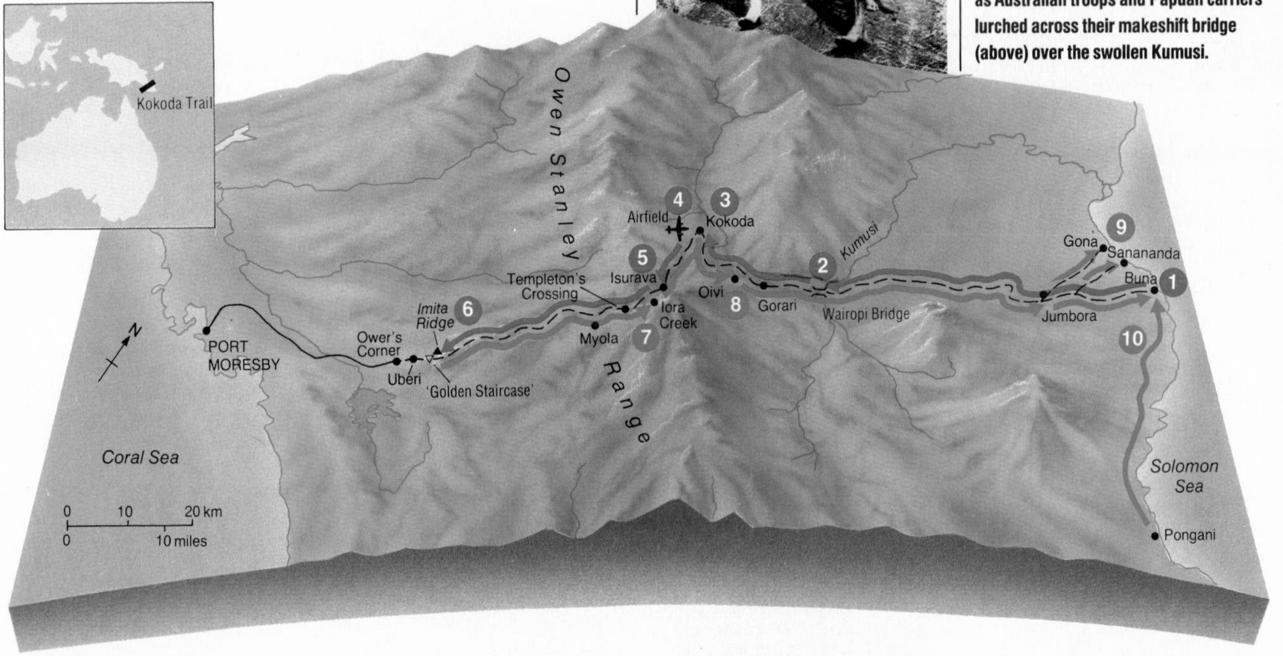

2 The inexperienced Australian conscripts cross the Kumusi at Wairopi but are outflanked and flee again in panic.

3 The Australians lose Kokoda village on July 29. Their commander, Lt Colonel W.T. Owen, is killed.

NATURAL ENEMIES The Japanese were only one of the enemies. The Australians (below) had to conquer sweltering heat, persistent rain, tearing hunger, sludge ankle deep and a slimy track that sometimes reared up impossible slopes, as at the 'Golden Staircase' (right).

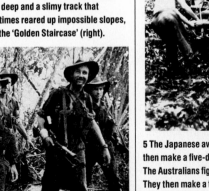

5 The Japanese await reinforcements then make a five-day attack on Isurava. The Australians fight fiercely but lose. They then make a fighting retreat through Templeton's Crossing. Outnumbered seven to one, they fall back beyond their supply dump at Myola.

6 The Australians' retreat ends at Imita Ridge on September 16.

7 The Japanese retreat while their rearguard holds Templeton's Crossing. Another delaying force at Iora Creek slows the Australian advance, but they retake the airfield on November 2. Now they can get supplies, and their advance quickens through Kokoda.

8 Strong Japanese resistance at Oivi on November 9-10 is bypassed. 600 Japanese are killed at Gorari. Many Japanese flee to Wairopi but the bridge is down. Their leader drowns there.

9 Others flee to defences on the coast. On December 9 they yield Gona. Nine days later Buna is attacked by Australian and American forces. It is overrun on January 2, 1943. The last Japanese resistance is crushed at Sananandá on January 22.

10 Americans advanced to join the Australians in the attack on Buna.

MILNE BAY DEFENDED

In the early hours of August 26, 1942, the men of the Australian 61st Militia Battalion were spread out in swampy jungle along the 32 km (20 mile) northern shore of Milne Bay, near the eastern tip of New Guinea. They scanned the skyline, for warnings had indicated that a Japanese naval convoy was bringing troops to attack Allied airfields near the bay.

When the Japanese attack came, however, it caught the 61st by surprise. Just after 1 am, in torrential rain, an Australian patrol dimly made out some dark figures emerging from the jungle. Thinking these were their countrymen, the men called out – and were answered with a hail of bullets. The heavily outnumbered Australians retreated, but were pursued through the mud until dawn.

The Japanese were part of a 1900-strong naval landing force given the task of seizing newly built airfields at the western end of Milne Bay. These were a threat to the Japanese base at Buna, and to a Japanese seaborne assault on Port Moresby that was planned to coincide with the land attack from the Kokoda Trail.

At dawn, as the Japanese unloaded supplies from beached landing craft, they realised that they had come ashore in the wrong place. The airfields lay 11 km (7 miles) east, down a muddy track.

Japanese intelligence had reported the airfields to be only lightly defended, but the intelligence was wrong. Within minutes of dawn, RAAF Kittyhawk fighters from the Milne Bay airfields roared out of the clouds, guns blazing, and soon made the Japanese beach-head a wreck of shattered landing craft and supplies. On the ground, there were nearly 7500 Australian soldiers and over 1000 US construction troops. The Australian commander, Maj General Cyril Clowes, had also been misinformed about the strength of his enemies; the retreating men of the 61st had greatly exaggerated the Japanese numbers. Fearing further Japanese landings, Clowes kept his force concentrated at the head of the bay and sent just one battalion, under Lt Colonel James Dobbs, to face the invaders on the northern shore.

The battle began, in driving rain, at 8 pm on August 27, when Japanese tanks attacked Dobbs' position 6 km (4 miles) east of Gili Gili. By midnight, the Japanese had broken through Dobbs' lines – and by dawn, they were close to their first objective, Airfield No 3. However, they were beaten back by fierce Australian fire. On the night of August 29/30, their reinforcements arrived – just 800 men. The following night, some 500 Japanese charged headlong onto the airstrip. The Australians mowed them down.

Over the next six days, the Australians pushed the Japanese relentlessly eastwards, in bloody hand-to-hand actions. Finally, on the night of September 5/6, the surviving Japanese were rescued by their navy. They left 700 dead behind.

to one, the Australians were unable to hold their supply dump at Myola. After contaminating as much of the food as possible, they continued southwards. The starving Japanese advance guard, gorging themselves on the rotting, flyblown supplies, rapidly contracted dysentery.

SIGHT OF THE SEA

On September 16, the Australian withdrawal ended at Imita Ridge, the last natural obstacle between the Japanese and the road to Port Moresby. By now, of the 1700 Australians who had fought at Isurava, only 300 remained. On the same day, Horii's troops, climbing to the crest of a ridge some 5 km (3 miles) north of the Australian position, had a first glimpse of the sea. Despite hunger, fever and dysentery, Japanese morale was sky-high. Victory seemed within grasp.

In fact, nothing could have been farther from the truth. Unknown to Horii, the Australians were receiving reinforcements, which would bring their numbers up to five veteran brigades, giving them numerical superiority over the Japanese for the first time. Moreover, having dragged two 25-pounder field guns up the Golden Staircase to the top of Imita Ridge, they at last had artillery to match that of the Japanese.

The threat to Horii's troops came not merely from the south. Plans were also being put into action to move the American 32nd Division by sea and air from training in Australia to Pongani on Papua's north coast, 48 km (30 miles) south-east of Buna. A gigantic trap was being prepared.

On the night of September 24, Horii sat in his tent in shocked disbelief. Japanese headquarters at Rabaul on New Britain, concerned about the Allied build-up and wanting to focus their effort at Guadalcanal, had ordered him to withdraw to the north. At first, Horii and his officers resolved to press on regardless – but an order from Tokyo, confirming the directive from Rabaul, forced their compliance.

On September 26, the Japanese began a carefully phased retreat. At Templeton's Crossing and Iora Creek, just north of the crest of the Owen Stanleys, Horii left strong rearguards to delay the Australian advance, while the rest of his men constructed major defences around Oivi and Gorari. By now, Horii's troops were dispirited. They had endured seemingly intolerable privations while there was a prospect of victory; now many began to drop from exhaustion and malnutrition. Others, driven by unbearable hunger, ate the flesh of dead Australian prisoners.

On October 14, the pursuing Australians, fighting the rearguard at Templeton's Crossing, stumbled upon the mutilated bodies of their countrymen. The horrific discovery gave them a new ferocity. In the fighting that followed, no quarter was asked, nor was any given. Though brave and resourceful, the Japanese had earned the Australians' hatred rather than their respect. After three days of bitter fighting, the Australians

WET WATCH Cramped on branches bridging the inescapable water, Australian troops are so close to the Japanese near Sananda that they can hear their voices.

forced the Japanese rearguard from Iora Creek on October 23.

On the previous day, 21st Brigade had been stunned, then angered, when Potts was relieved of command. Superiors who knew nothing of the appalling conditions on the trail saw the skilful withdrawal during September as a defeat. Brigadier S.H.W.C. Porter replaced Potts. On November 2 the Australians reoccupied Kokoda and its airstrip; now supplies could be airlifted to them, enabling them to quicken their advance. However, Horii, strongly dug in at Oivi and Gorari with some 1500 troops, intended to stop them – and at first he succeeded. On November 8, the Australians were stalled by fierce resistance before Oivi. But during the next two days they moved to the right of the Japanese and in a savage bayonet charge overran Gorari.

The surrounded Japanese fought desperately to escape. More than 600 were killed; several hundred more fled to the Kumusi where Horii, clambering onto a raft, overturned it and was drowned. (Wairopi bridge had by now been destroyed.) Others, weaponless and emaciated, staggered into Buna.

RECKONING AT BUNA

The Papuan campaign was about to enter its final phase. During Horii's retreat, the Japanese beach-head on Papua's northern coast had been transformed into a fortress. Some 7000 Japanese now occupied strongly constructed bunkers around Gona, Sanananda and Buna, their machine guns covering the flat swampy countryside around. Allied warplanes based in Port Moresby dominated the skies, however, and the Japanese defenders knew that they could not hope for reinforcements or supplies.

The Australian 7th Division advancing from the Kumusi, and the American 32nd from Pongani, did not know what to expect. In later battles, bunkers of the sort they now faced were smashed by heavy naval shells, their occupants suffocated by napalm or roasted by flamethrowers – but such weapons were not yet available. These had to be taken by infantry, backed by a few field guns and inaccurate air strikes. The initial attacks in the driving rains of late November were forced back. Australian and American troops failed to capture Sanananda, while at Buna the Americans, coming unexpectedly under Japanese machine-gun fire, panicked, threw down their weapons and ran. Only a renewed attack on Gona succeeded. It was made by the Australian 39th Battalion, rested after their ordeal on the Kokoda Trail and substantially reinforced. On December 9, they broke their way into the last Japanese bunkers at Gona – and discovered a charnel house. The defenders had fought to the last, from behind parapets built with the bodies of their own dead.

Nine days later Buna's defenders heard the ominous clank of tank tracks coming from the east. A few Australian light tanks and an infantry brigade had been brought in to help the Americans. They attacked relentlessly for the next 14 days, their tanks smashing holes in the Japanese bunkers through which the infantry hurled explosive charges. By January 2, 1943, Buna had been overrun. Most of the defenders were dead – though some escaped through the swamps. Now only Sanananda remained. The Australians opened the attack there on January 16, and six days later crushed the last resistance.

Six thousand Japanese lay dead in the beach-head bunkers, while inland another 6000 had been killed along the trail. Only 3000 survived, and 350 of these were prisoners; the South Seas Detachment had ceased to exist. But the Allied victory was expensive. The Australians lost over 2000 dead and 3500 wounded, while almost 30 000 had to be evacuated sick. The Americans too had suffered heavily, with over 900 dead, 1900 wounded and more than 8000 sick out of 14 600.

Yet the significance of the Papuan campaign cannot be measured solely in terms of losses. Until they set foot in Papua, the Japanese had never suffered a defeat on land. The battles on the Kokoda Trail and for the north Papuan beach-heads at last shattered – for both sides – the myth of their invincibility. The gallant survivors of 21st Brigade, however, received no thanks. At a parade in Papua on November 9, the Australian Commander in Chief, General Sir Thomas Blamey, spoke of troops running from the enemy like rabbits. They felt sure he meant them, though some say he meant the Japanese.

HUNTERS ON TRACK AND FOOT Australian-manned Stuart tanks (above) crisscross the lightly wooded ground near Buna to blast open well-hidden Japanese pillboxes. One of the infantrymen scouting on foot warns the tank crew about a pillbox close by before he and his colleagues take cover behind tree trunks to pick off the enemy as they rush out when their hideaway explodes into a fiery death trap.

FINAL STRETCH Keeping down in the coarse kunai grass of the coastal strip only 135 m (150 yds) from Gona, an Australian crew load their mortar, hoping to flush out nearby Japanese snipers.

PART THREE: THE PEOPLE'S WAR

AFTER THE FALL of France, the horrors and the heroism of war became part of the fabric of daily life. The bank clerk, the farm worker, the factory girl and the office fire-watcher were in the front line just as surely as the soldier. In the year after the Blitz started, more British civilians than fighting men died from enemy action.

The organisation of the home front became as important a part of the war effort as the raising of armies. Total war meant that people had to be fed, housed, trained, protected from air attack, supplied with gas masks and ration books. Morale had to be kept high through propaganda, and when life was at its grimmest, people needed something that would raise a smile.

In the occupied nations, some civilians joined the Resistance to 'set Europe ablaze'. The Nazis retaliated savagely, but reserved their greatest ferocity for their onslaught on the Jews: 6 million were murdered in Hitler's 'Final Solution'.

Another way in which civilians joined the battle was in the field of scientific warfare and espionage. Polish and British mathematicians broke the German 'Enigma' codes, and a stream of agents infiltrated enemy lands ●

(1) Official German photograph of Jews being rounded up in the Warsaw Ghetto. (2) Homeless victims of the Blitz in London's East End. (3) Precautions against gas.
(4) Australian women pack bananas for the war effort.
(5) London schoolboys collect pans to make planes.
(6) Fire-watcher's identity card.

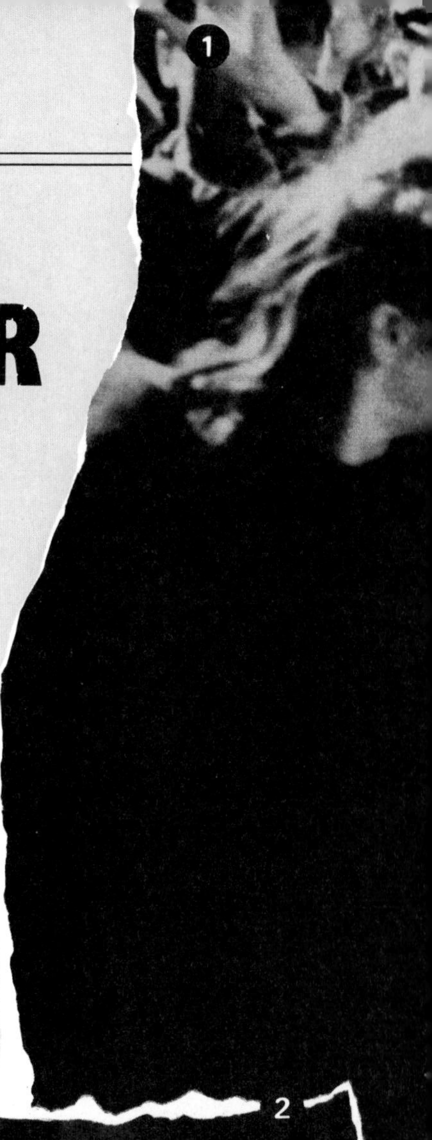

1

2

OFFICIAL
– day and night.
quickly.
Practise wearing it.
1. Hold your breath. Put on mask wherever you are. Close window.
BY VAPOUR GAS
BY LIQUID or BLISTER GAS
Dab, but don't rub the splash with handkerchief. Then destroy hand-
Rub No. 2 Ointment well into place.
(Buy a 6d. jar now from any chemist).
In emergency chemists supply Bleach Cream free.

3

6
BOROUGH OF WANDSW
Air Raid Precaut
This is to Certify th
M A. C. Fry.
of 24 Farlow
Putney.
is a member of a volu
fighting party which is re
the Wandsworth Borough
possesses the powers of
taking steps for extingui
for protecting property,
persons or property, fr
are conferred by the F
(Access to Premises) O
MUNICIPAL BUILDINGS,
WANDSWORTH, S.W.18
Date of Issue 27
No.
Signature of Bearer
"QUEENIE"
CHUCK IT IN 'ERE!
2000
ONE AER
5
ED BY THE MINISTRY OF HOME SECURITY
ATTACK
OUR GAS MASK
OUND
3. Put on gloves or keep hands in pockets. Take cover in nearest building.
you feel discomfort
First Aid Post
4
Take off at once any garment splashed with gas.
4
HANDLE CAREFULLY

Fighting from the home front

The 'total war' of 1939-45 was industrial as well as military. In the words of a popular song of 1942, 'it's the girl that makes the thing that holds the oil that oils the ring, that works the thingumebob that's going to win the war'.

BEHIND THE MEN who fought World War II, life in the fighting nations was organised to supply the arms and ammunition, the transport, clothing, fuel and food that were needed to keep the war machine running. The war spread far beyond the front line and for many countries became total war. The aim was to destroy the enemy utterly, and involved mobilising a country's entire work force and national resources. Inevitably, this meant that civilian populations became legitimate targets for the enemy, and civilian morale as important as morale in the front line.

Civilians knew they had a vital part to play in the struggle. Sometimes bombed and increasingly rationed, they knew that in fulfilling their production targets in the factories, they were sharing the burden of war. Churchill declared: 'The fronts are everywhere. The trenches are dug in the towns and streets . . . The front line runs through the factories. The workmen are soldiers with different weapons.'

In such a struggle the countries that organised efficiently the greatest manpower and industrial output had the advantage. After 1941 the Allies were stronger than their opponents in both these areas. The population of Germany (79 million), Japan (73 million) and Italy (45 million) was far less (even with the occupied nations added) than that of the USA (132 million), Britain (48 million) and the USSR (193 million). The Allies also controlled – through ownership, political rule or agreement – over two-thirds of the world's iron and steel industry, coal deposits and oil production. So long as they organised their populations and economies well and used their forces effectively, victory would be simply a matter of time.

RESHAPING THE ECONOMY

Britain started the war at a disadvantage. Whereas the Germans had begun to gear their economy to war well before 1939, the British had only just begun serious rearmament. But the outbreak of war and early setbacks brought great change. The British rallied behind Churchill's coalition government, formed in May 1940. They paid increased income tax (50 per cent in 1941) and bought National Savings Certificates to help pay for the war. Rationing and cuts in consumer production freed resources for war output and helped to spread the burden of shortages equally.

More than 20 million factory workers in Britain, Canada, Australia, New Zealand, Rhodesia and South Africa – a third of them women and mostly working at least 60 hours a week – built over 700 warships, thousands of merchant ships, 135 000 aircraft and more than 160 000 tanks and other armoured vehicles by 1945. In all, more than half Britain's wartime industrial production was devoted to arms.

In Britain's fields, farmers – helped by the 80 000 women of the Land Army – increased home food production. 'Boffins' – technical experts like Sir Henry Tizard, who directed the development of radar, and Frank Whittle, jet engine pioneer – made special contributions.

With a huge population and enormous natural resources, the USSR was well placed – at least on paper. But it was technically backward. Worst of all, at the start of its war with Germany, nearly half its industrial and agricultural production was immediately captured or destroyed by the enemy. This was a blow from which it never fully recovered: by 1945 Russian production of steel, coal and oil was still less than in 1940.

Only a country as big as the USSR could have survived such crippling losses and made a comeback. The Russian economic effort was extraordinary. In order to remove war production beyond the Germans' reach, entire factories – plant, workers and their families – were moved hundreds of kilometres eastwards, to and beyond the Urals. By the end of 1941 some 1500 factories had been moved, with 10 million people to work them. Homes and whole new towns were built.

Under the direction of the secret police chief, Lavrenti Beria, the Soviet home front was ruthlessly geared to the fight. The Russians had few consumer industries, but those that existed were cut drastically in favour of war production. Huge tax increases paid for the war, new oil and mineral sources were developed and factories concentrated on making arms. In 1942 Soviet tank production doubled and aircraft production tripled. By 1945 the USSR had produced as much weaponry as Germany, and outstripped it in tank and aircraft manufacture.

'ARSENAL OF DEMOCRACY'

Aid from the United States was the lifeblood of both the British and Russian war efforts. It began in earnest when Congress passed the Lend-Lease Act on March 11, 1941, and meant that American goods were sent to Allied (and sometimes neutral) countries without having to be paid for in full. It continued until after the final victory over Japan. Without Lend-Lease, Britain could not have afforded to fight after 1941, for its financial reserves were gone and its foreign trade paralysed.

The United States became, in Roosevelt's words, the 'arsenal of democracy' and between 1941 and 1945 built more than 250 000 aircraft, almost 90 000 tanks, 350 destroyers and 200 submarines, among other war products. It was the largest and strongest economy in the world – wealthy, technically advanced, and (an important advantage) far removed from the battle fronts, so that production could proceed unhampered by bombing. By 1944 the USA was devoting 40 per cent of its huge economy to war production, and producing 40 per cent of all the world's arms. Even with a world war on its hands, the American economy became so strong that it still managed to turn out consumer goods – despite some shortages – in ever greater quantities. American living standards improved over the course of the war, while they grew worse elsewhere.

AXIS: TOO LITTLE, TOO LATE

Despite the spectacular early victories of Germany and Japan, their war economies were not designed for a long test. Germany was the strongest Axis power, with well-developed industry, a skilled work force and large coal reserves. By 1939 it had large stockpiles of strategic materials such as oil, rubber and coal. In the first two years, Germany fought enemies who were less prepared, and Hitler's victories were so quick that there was no great strain on the economy. Germany also received huge amounts of material – oil, timber and iron ore – from the USSR under the 1939 Nazi-Soviet Pact.

After 1941, Germany plundered its occupied territories for raw materials, but even this could not make up for the strains of a long conflict. After the Battle of Stalingrad in 1942-3, things grew desperate; in February 1943 Propaganda Minister Josef Goebbels finally declared total war.

The German economy, under the direction of Armaments Minister (and former architect of the Nuremberg rallies) Albert Speer, began to achieve its full potential only in 1943 and 1944. Arms manufacture grew to account for 30 per cent of industrial output. In all, about 45 000 tanks and over 113 000 aircraft were built. But Nazi insistence on the role of women as 'housewives and mothers' ensured that the female work force grew by only about 250 000 – to 14.9 million – from 1939 to 1944. In the same period, the number of German men in industry fell from 25.4 million to 13.5 million, as they were called up into the armed forces. Hitler came to rely increasingly on labour from conquered lands abroad – 7.5 million men and women by September 1944.

Italy's economy was unfit even to fight a short war. When Mussolini entered the fray in June 1940 he expected a few quick victories; instead he became committed to costly campaigns in the Balkans and Africa. Italy lacked raw materials and had a mainly agricultural economy. Shortages and inflation began almost immediately. In 1942 mass strikes broke out among northern Italy's workers, who wanted 'peace and liberty'. Economic planning was almost non-existent, and arms production could not match demand.

Japan's economy, like Germany's and Italy's, could survive only short campaigns. But Japan had already been fighting China since 1937, and went to war in 1941 partly to seize raw materials, especially oil from the Dutch East Indies and iron ore, rubber and tin from the Asian mainland. After 1941, Japanese industry turned out 200 submarines and other warships and nearly 70 000 aircraft. The working population rose to over 33 million in 1944, and toiled an average of 11 hours a day. Industrial production was directed by the government, taxes were increased and the police enforced the 'labour draft'.

Yet Japan did not make the best use of its human resources – though women were enlisted with the slogan, 'Men to the front, women to the workplace'. But skilled workers were drafted into the army, depriving industry, and half the civilian work force was on the land, not in factories. By 1945, Japan's economy relied largely on women, Koreans, prisoners of war, the elderly, and children as young as ten.

But their effort was futile. In the end – when the stark alternatives were world domination or unconditional surrender, and all the combatants were straining to their utmost – what won the war was industrial muscle to back the fighting men. And that the Allies had in abundance.

Families see it through with a smile

Life on Britain's home front had its own duties, stresses and griefs – different from those of the fighting men but just as real: rationing, long days on vital war work, then long nights fire-watching – and waiting for the bombs to fall. Some of the Allies were farther from the fighting, but the war affected everyone.

DAILY LIFE in the first weeks of World War II was hardly distinguishable from peacetime for the great majority of civilians away from the front line – whether in Birmingham or Brisbane, Calgary or Cape Town. While the Commonwealth and Empire went to war in support of Britain, the British themselves – on the edge of explosive Europe – steeled themselves for the assault.

The authorities, expecting bombs to rain on the cities within hours of the outbreak of war, had made preparations during the previous year of crisis. Trench shelters were dug in city parks, brick and concrete shelters were built in the streets and gas masks issued. The masks were never needed – perhaps because Hitler feared retaliatory gas attacks when Germany had not enough rubber to provide masks for all its citizens. Elephantine silver barrage balloons began floating in British skies. Their cables prevented bombers from flying low enough to bomb accurately in cities – and stopped seaplanes landing on tempting stretches of inland water.

Every city dweller with a patch of garden was issued with an Anderson shelter, a cramped, corrugated-iron tunnel named after Sir John Anderson, Home Secretary of the day. Military conscription, the first in peacetime Britain, became law in May 1939 and the first conscripts were called up in July. Then, on the very eve of war, the government evacuated 1.5 million children and mothers with babies from the cities.

THE COMMON LOT

There were many British families whose menfolk were too old or too young for the forces, or did essential work in 'reserved occupations'. For them, unless the bombs started falling, war was mainly a matter of hours of tedious duty at the local ARP (Air Raid Precautions) station, fire-watching for incendiary bombs, occasional spells in the shelter or under the dining table when the siren sounded – and seeing Land Girls on the farms, buses with women drivers, and now and again a lorry-load of war prisoners going to work on building or civil engineering projects. But at the core of their lives was the universal wartime experience of those at home: rationing.

Britain did not at once introduce food rationing despite importing much of its needs – although ration books were issued in September 1939. The government, fearing unpopularity, misread the mood of the people, who welcomed the idea of its fair shares for all. A tentative start was made with bacon, sugar and butter in January 1940, meat followed in March, and in July tea was rationed to 2 oz (50 g) per person per week. Soon cooking fats, sweets, cheese, conserves, eggs (one each per week), clothes (in 1941) and most other things were controlled. Vegetables, many home-grown, supplemented the rations, and bread was not rationed until after the war.

Lord Woolton, the dedicated, high-profile Minister of Food, offered novelties such as whale meat, whose odd flavour could only be subdued by overnight soaking in vinegar, and such recipes as Woolton pie (potatoes, parsnips and herbs), carrot fudge, and sausage and sultana casserole. The wartime sausage became a national joke, the kindest description being 'breadcrumbs in battledress'. But Woolton also ensured that every British child got daily milk, cod-liver oil and orange juice to boost vitamin intake. He obtained dried eggs and dried milk from the USA, and set up British Restaurants in which workers, often far from home, could get an adequate meal at minimal cost. Everyone was a little hungry in wartime Britain, but no one starved.

Not only foods, but all life's small luxuries – cigarettes, spirits, beer, make-up, toys – were scarce or unobtainable. Queuing became the national pastime, salvage and improvisation the watchwords. People 'Dug for Victory' to raise vegetables, sacrificed iron railings to build ships and aluminium pots to make Spitfires, and unravelled old sweaters to knit socks and scarves for the troops.

PULLING TOGETHER

Similar shortages – though on a lesser scale – were felt in the Dominions. In Australia, tea, sugar and coffee were rationed. Travel and lighting were restricted to save oil and coal. Prices and rents were strictly controlled to prevent profiteering. The greatest cross Australians had to bear was the Minister for War Organisation of Industry, John Dedman, known as 'the man who killed Father Christmas' from his banning any mention of it in advertising during December 1942. He forbade the manufacture of any inessentials, among which

READY FOR THE WORST As war neared, city folk got their Anderson shelters to erect in their gardens. They tagged children with labels and sent them to the country by the trainload to escape the expected mayhem.

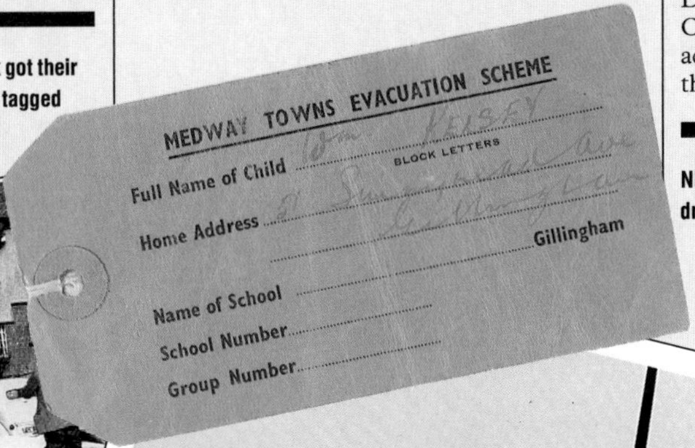
MEDWAY TOWNS EVACUATION SCHEME
Full Name of Child .... BLOCK LETTERS
Home Address ....
.... Gillingham
Name of School ....
School Number ....
Group Number ....

NEW POST Women readily took on the jobs of postmen, bus drivers, factory workers and other men now in the forces.

he included lawnmowers, pyjamas, toys, stripes on bull's-eyes and patterned socks. He introduced the single-breasted Victory suit, without waistcoat or turnups; women were advised to replace stockings with leg paint, while any form of frill or pleat on a dress was against the law.

New Zealand's rationing was similar to Australia's – and it unstintingly assigned its butter, cheese and meat to feed the United States' Pacific forces. South Africa, like everyone else, suffered a petrol shortage. To help conserve paper, it halved the size of postage stamps, but did not go so far as New Zealand, which issued large posters telling people to use both sides of every sheet of paper.

Canada, amazed by its own booming economy – stimulated by the rapid growth of industry to meet military needs – nevertheless imposed economies and poured its largesse not only into Britain but soon into Russia too. Its rationing was such that visiting British servicemen thought they were in paradise, but there were shortages, notably of liquor and car tyres. Canadian women were shown how to beat milk into butter to make it go farther, and the nation was urged to 'Use it Up, Wear it Out, Make it Do and Do Without'.

In Britain, official exhortations abounded: 'Go To It!' (Herbert Morrison, when Minister of Supply); 'Lend to Defend the Right to be Free' (National Savings); 'Is Your Journey Really Necessary?' (the railways); 'Stop! Wouldn't a Letter or a Postcard do?' (GPO telephones); 'Be Like Dad, Keep Mum!' (security); '*Your* Courage *Your* Cheerfulness *Your* Resolution WILL BRING US VICTORY' (HM Government – a slogan soon dropped because it suggested the 'upper classes' bossing the ordinary people). The cumulative message was: we're in it together.

Of course, some ignored the message. The British did not become a nation of self-denying patriots. The blackout and the Blitz provided new opportunities for thieves – though the penalties for looting from bombed houses were harsh. There were profits to be made on the black market by racketeers, soon to be called 'spivs'. But black marketeering was probably far less widespread than rumoured at the time – few could afford the prices – and certainly convictions for all crimes dropped: from 787 000 in 1939 to 467 000 in 1945. But the figures for divorce on grounds of adultery soared from 5000 in 1939 to 17 000 in 1945, reflecting hasty marriages and long separations.

CONSCRIPTS AND VOLUNTEERS

In May 1940, the month of the debacle of Dunkirk, the Emergency Powers Act in effect put most Britons under martial law; they could be directed anywhere to do anything to serve the common good. Thousands took up unlikely jobs. Debutantes became lathe operators, actors built aeroplanes, city secretaries brought the harvest home. But despite unlimited work hours, many people still gave voluntary service to Civil Defence, the Home Guard, the Women's Voluntary Service, the Auxiliary Fire Service or other bodies. From January 1941, fire-watching for incendiary bombs was a night-long compulsory rota duty at places of work. In December 1943, a most unpopular fate was forced on some by Ernest Bevin, Minister of Labour: the 'Bevin Boys' were drawn at random from each batch of new conscripts and sent to work in coal mines.

(*continued on p. 178*)

FAIR SHARES The weekly rations for a person in Britain (right) were stretched with unlimited bread, cereal, potatoes and whatever vegetables and fruit were available. Coupons for food and clothes were cut from the allowance books when goods were bought. To offset the austerity, favourite entertainers did their bit to raise morale – featherheaded Jane, whose clothing was always rationed, in the *Daily Mirror* cartoon strip, and George Formby with his dotty humour and songs in the Underground before the regulars settled down for yet another night of the Blitz.

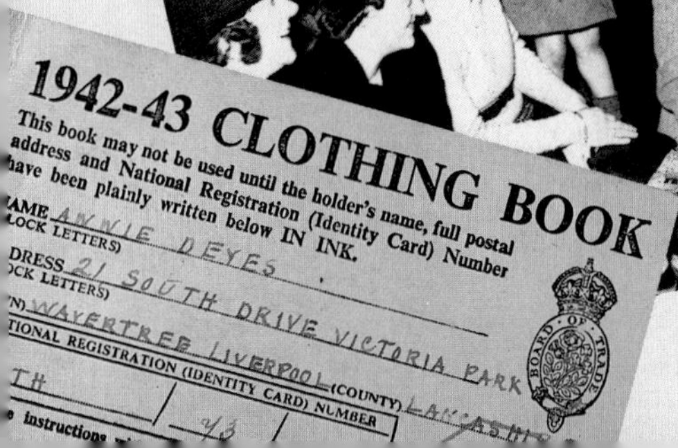
1942-43 CLOTHING BOOK
This book may not be used until the holder's name, full postal address and National Registration (Identity Card) Number have been plainly written below IN INK.
NAME (BLOCK LETTERS) ANNIE DEYES
ADDRESS (BLOCK LETTERS) 21 SOUTH DRIVE VICTORIA PARK
(TOWN) WAVERTREE LIVERPOOL (COUNTY) LANCASHIRE
NATIONAL REGISTRATION (IDENTITY CARD) NUMBER
Instructions

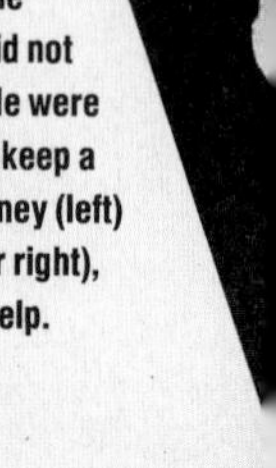

DO'S AND DON'TS The wartime shortages did not include advice. People were for ever being told to keep a tight rein on their money (left) and their tongues (far right), and where to go for help.

2d
KORKY THE CAT

ADDIE AND HERMY
THE NASTY NAZIS
JUMPING JIMINY

SECRET MISSIONS Youthful zest and the weekly defeats of nasty Nazis in *Dandy*, *Beano* and other comics could make a bold exploit of a gas-attack rehearsal.

The children's war

The adults did what they could to shield British children from the true terror of the war; childish optimism and love of excitement did the rest. Comics told the key facts of the war – that Musso the Wop ('he's a big-a-da-flop'), and weakling Adolf stood no chance against Pansy Potter the strong man's daughter. For many children war consisted of model Spitfires and Hurricanes, finds of shrapnel, coloured flags on a map. There was also much fun to be had in making rude noises by blowing into your slobbery, rubbery gas mask.

Losing your dad or your uncle was shattering, and almost everyone knew a family that had done so – but the impact only came later, for long separation had made these figures fictional. Reality lay in the dashes – when the siren went – to the school basement, to the smelly shelter or grimy coal cellar.

LEAVING HOME

Deep scars linger in many adults still from evacuation, that well-intentioned scheme. City children, bewildered and ill-prepared, were sent to faraway refuges. The ensuing culture shock hit both ways: hosts told of lousy heads, guttersnipe language and bed-wetting (no doubt from unhappiness and anxiety), and children suffered homesickness, boredom and terror of open spaces. So badly did things go that, when the raids did not come, two-thirds of the evacuees went home by Christmas 1939. Three later evacuation schemes ended in much the same way.

One Londoner recalls of his schooldays in the Blitz: 'We used to cycle to whatever school happened to be undamaged and open, skirting the ruins of the previous night's raids.

'One night the bombers came early, as my mother was getting blankets and provisions for our night's stay in the basement of the British Home Stores. We heard the drone of the engines and the fall of bombs. The guns opened up, and red-hot shrapnel pattered into the streets like iron rain. That night a bomb broke the water main outside the British Home Stores and water came pouring down the stairs, turning our cosy shelter into a deathtrap. When we got back home we discovered a bomb had removed a section of our block of flats as neatly as a dentist taking out a tooth.'

Rationing was a strain, relieved a little by the inventiveness of mothers, who concocted eggless, fatless cakes, wrought miracles with rabbit and fish, and relied on bread and marge or dripping to satisfy appetites. The diet was accepted as the norm by children who had few memories of prewar indulgence.

'Holidays at Home' were the high spots of the summer, with local fairs and shows replacing trips to beaches now covered with tank traps or mines. What did the seaside matter when a talent competition was going on in a marquee in the park? Above all you lived with the thrilling possibility of discovering a spy, and played out fantasies with false beards, codes and invisible inks. The grand dreams were fed by family trips to the pictures.

But the zenith of excitement was to come: the Victory celebrations, with flags, fireworks and street parties, the returning heroes – and the promise of a brave new world of unlimited sweets, oranges and bananas.

FEEDING THE FAMILIES Happy hours with neighbours on nearby allotments (below) boosted basic rations with vegetables. Land Girls (left) replaced called-up farmhands. They worked a 50 hour week, learning – and eating – on the job.

IF YOU ARE BOMBED OUT
and have no friends to go to
POLICE
ask a
POLICEMAN
or your WARDEN
where to find your
REST CENTRE
ISSUED BY THE MINISTRY OF HEALTH

You never know who's listening!
CARELESS TALK
COSTS LIVES

The worst plight faced the 2.5 million wives whose husbands were in the forces. Many lived on the poverty line. A mother of two whose husband was an ordinary serviceman struggled for most of the war to live on seven shillings (35p, or US$1.40) a week from her husband's service pay plus 25 shillings (£1.25, or US$5) a week government allowance. For a lucky few their husband's employer made up the income to its prewar level. Others did piecework at home or went out to work.

As in Britain, the economies of the Dominions were quickly put on a war footing, though mostly on a less severe basis. In Canada, the government directed labour and resources for home defence. The country also became a training centre for British airmen, and quiet Ottawa changed rapidly into the bustling control centre of a huge war effort. New Zealand instituted 'Manpower', the compulsory direction of labour and enrolment in civil defence of adults not in the forces. Australia, like Canada, directed labour and resources, especially to produce munitions. The country boomed and industry developed rapidly.

FACING THE BLITZ

For the most part, the Dominions lay outside the enemy's territorial ambition or strategic interest; even Australian fears of Japanese invasion were to prove groundless. True, Darwin and a few other places in northern Australia were bombed, and Japanese submarines shelled targets as far apart as New South Wales and British Columbia. But from the outset there was no doubt that the United Kingdom would be a prime Luftwaffe target.

When the bombing raids came, the horrors proved even worse than imagined. East Enders in the early days of the Blitz fled in thousands to the surrounding countryside – as well they might. They had no gardens in which to put Anderson shelters, and it was still forbidden then to use the Underground railway stations as shelters. All they had were the street shelters – brick shoe boxes to hold 20 people, whose concrete roofs tended to fall in when bombs exploded nearby.

The most successful shelter in such densely populated urban areas was designed at the instigation of a later Home Secretary, Herbert Morrison, and issued from spring 1941. The Morrison shelter was a low steel cage for use indoors; like the Anderson shelter it cost £7 (US$28) for the better-off but was free to others.

Many official preparations were wide of the mark. Millions of cardboard coffins were made to receive the legions of expected dead, but shelter for the bombed-out homeless was woefully inadequate. It consisted mostly of so-called Rest Centres – schools and church halls, in which shocked, exhausted people were meant to stay for only a night. Many had nowhere else to go, and stayed – some for weeks – in the centres, which became intolerably overcrowded.

Large numbers of East Enders made a home in such places as the Tilbury Shelter, an underground goods yard in Stepney, which accommodated 16 000 people in horribly insanitary conditions. Another 18 000 camped in Chislehurst Caves, a network of ancient tunnels in the chalk south-east of the capital. Other Londoners invaded the forbidden Underground stations. London Transport yielded as the Blitz stepped up, and supplied bunks, lavatories and some canteen facilities. The safety of the Underground was variable, for some stations were only a few metres beneath the street. Balham, for example, received a direct hit on the evening of October 15, 1940, and 64 people died.

As the weeks passed, people in London and elsewhere learned to live with the bombing, and even managed to extract a few wry jokes from it. A shop with shattered windows might bear the sign 'More open than usual', while a common lapel badge read: 'Don't tell me. I've got a bomb story too.' Children roamed the streets after raids, collecting shrapnel. After restless nights in a shelter, people still got to work next day, exhausted but glad of the normality it offered.

ON THE MOVE

A striking feature of wartime Britain was the large number of people on the move. A recurring image for many is of a train crammed with people, kitbags and cases, rattling endlessly through the night, blacked-out bulbs dimly illuminating tired faces. Servicemen and women were the majority, resigned at being shunted to yet another camp, while other faces registered the joy of going on leave. Among the civilians, there might be a doleful mother returning from a visit to her evacuated children, a skilled mechanic uprooted to work in a factory at the other end of the country, a conscientious objector off to unfamiliar work down a mine or on a farm, or a refugee released from internment on the Isle of Man to work for the BBC as a translator.

Never had Britain seen so many strangers – Italian and German prisoners of war working on the land or on public works (the same was true in Australia and Canada); volunteer West Indian firemen; but, above all, servicemen from every quarter of the globe. Intense Poles outdid even the stylish French in gallantry towards British women. Dutch, Norwegians, Danes and New Zealanders were 'just like us'. Canadians and Australians were critical of what they saw as a deferential society, but basically brothers.

GI IMPACT

The greatest dose of overseas culture was administered by some 1.5 million US servicemen who passed through Britain in 1942-5. Good-natured and eager to be loved, they showered

(*continued on p. 180*)

ALUMINIUM · DUMP
"STOP 'EM FRYING
KEEP 'EM FLYING
"STOP 'EM
FRYING
KEEP 'EM

ALL IN IT TOGETHER Countries of the Commonwealth were far from the early fighting front only in distance, not in spirit. Australian shoppers (left) had to eke out their coupons for rationed goods. South Africans (below left) handed in their pans for aircraft production. In Canada, volunteers made a memorable night of it (below) before they sailed for England.

A GIANT AWAKENED

Only six Americans – an Oregon pastor, his wife and four village children – were killed by enemy action in the continental United States when they investigated a Japanese balloon bomb. But had the enemy been on their doorstep, Americans could not have entered the war with greater dedication. The shock of Pearl Harbor saw to that.

Citizens grew vegetables in Victory Gardens on every spare plot of land, eagerly collected scrap paper, metal and fats and contributed US$135 billion to the cause in War Bonds. Comedian Jack Benny auctioned his fiddle and film pin-up Betty Grable her stockings to promote bond sales. Consumer shortages were scarcely noticeable by European standards, though certain commodities were rationed, due largely to the need for shipping space for the war effort. Among the controlled items were meat, sugar, coffee, butter, tyres and petrol.

Ironically, many Americans were better off than ever before as the nation swung into war production on an awesome scale. For the first time in more than a decade, there was full employment. There were other rewards too: by brilliant salesmanship, Coca-Cola became the official soft drink of the US forces and accompanied them to every theatre of the war, while Wrigley's convinced the government that every pack of emergency field rations should contain three sticks of gum. It even took over the packing of the rations.

As 16 million Americans went off to fight, 10 million others readily stepped into their jobs. But the war economy needed even more. One new Ford truck factory alone employed 42 000 people; a new labour reserve had to be tapped – women. Millions went to work as makers of bombs and aero engines, shipbuilders or railway workers. Rosie the Riveter and Wanda the Welder became new national images – though always exhorted to maintain their FQ (Femininity Quotient).

RIVETING TASK Women in a Chicago factory work on the wing section of a giant transport plane.

TROOPS' CHOICE Vera Lynn, voted the 'Forces' Sweetheart', reached them over the wireless and toured every battle front singing of love undimmed by parting and of golden tomorrows.

THE SOUNDS OF WAR

All the heartache and humour of wartime found memorable expression in the songs of the time, which reached a vast public through dance halls, sheet music, gramophone records, film musicals and, above all, the wireless.

The cocky *We're Gonna Hang Out the Washing on the Siegfried Line* was soon ousted by *We'll Meet Again*, *The White Cliffs of Dover*, and *Yours*. The clear, sweetly plaintive voice bringing many of them to every home belonged to Vera Lynn, who was equally popular in the Commonwealth, and, it was rumoured, the Wehrmacht. But the Germans provided the war's greatest and only universal hit-song, *Lili Marleen* (*Lilli Marlene* in English versions). It spread like wildfire from late 1941 on both sides of the front line and beyond – in numerous languages, in bawdy parodies and in versions more or less faithful to the original 1917 love poem.

Music was not the only attraction on the wireless. News readers Alvar Liddell, Stuart Hibberd, Bruce Belfrage and others became as well known as film stars. There was advice from Radio Doctor Charles Hill, and the *Brains Trust*, with its panel of pundits. There was the humour of *Happidrome*, Jack ('Mind my bike') Warner in *Garrison Theatre*, and *Hi Gang!* whose American stars Bebe Daniels, Ben Lyon and Vic Oliver won regard for opting to stay in London. *Much Binding in the Marsh* put Kenneth Horne and Richard Murdoch on a batty RAF station.

Towering over them all was *It's That Man Again!* – *ITMA* for short – starring Tommy Handley. Its quick-fire puns and host of weird characters were relished from cottage to castle. There was the char, Mrs Mopp ('Can I do yer now, sir?'); Colonel Chinstrap, who took any remark as an offer of a drink and replied, 'I don't mind if I do'; Funf, the inefficient German spy, and many more.

No sooner had the first American troops arrived than they were followed by the American Forces Network. Locals heard, with growing delight, such comedians as Bob Hope, Jack Benny, Jimmy Durante and Red Skelton, and revelled in the feast of swing music which made the bands of Glenn Miller, Tommy Dorsey and Benny Goodman as popular as the more sedate Jack Payne and Henry Hall.

upon the luxury-starved locals near their bases chocolate bars, cigarettes, tinned foods, ice cream, nylons, and, of course, chewing gum. The young men with easy, confident manners and the best-cut uniforms yet seen, captivated children – and many of their big sisters.

The GIs' lack of shyness in entering the grandest establishment – and their ability to pay for the privilege – caused resentment. They could dazzle local girls with outings far too dear for British suitors. Sixty thousand British GI brides confirmed the effectiveness of the American way. But while some Britons saw the Americans as fresh and outgoing, others regarded them as brash and conceited. They introduced new catchphrases, new fashions in looks, new styles in music and dancing. British girls were enchanted to receive their first lessons in jitterbugging.

It might seem that dancing was hardly a proper occupation at such a time, but it was only a brief relaxation. The girls in the hall might easily have come straight from a 12 hour shift in a munitions factory, some of the servicemen had just seen their friends killed, and others would shortly die themselves. Outside, the sirens still wailed in the dark streets and houses still crumbled and spilt across the pavement. This hour of forgetful gaiety apart, the dancers were in deadly earnest about the war – and not just for a simple victory over the Axis, but for a different, a better, a fairer world when that victory was accomplished.

One prejudice of the American visitors went down badly. White-black segregation was almost total in the US forces. Racial prejudice was by no means unknown among the British, but on this occasion – mindful of the efforts of coloured citizens of the British Empire on their behalf – they objected, especially when US authorities tried to put certain pubs out of bounds to black troops. The publicans retaliated by barring white troops. Savage battles ensued, mostly between Americans, and several were killed.

Extreme reactions to the arrival of US troops were not confined to the United Kingdom. When the GIs landed in Australia in December 1941, they were greeted as saviours. But the welcome swiftly turned sour. The GIs lavished candy, cigarettes, nylons and flowers on the Australian girls, attentions that raised the hackles of local men about to leave their wives and sweethearts for the Western Desert or New Guinea. A large number of brawls took place, especially in Brisbane, where on one occasion an Australian serviceman was shot dead by American military police and eight others were wounded. The widely held view of the GI presence in the UK – 'Overpaid, oversexed and over here' – awoke an echo in Australian hearts:

They saved us from the Japs, perhaps
But at the moment the place is too Yankful
For us to be sufficiently thankful.

UNFAMILIAR DESTINATIONS

Although their homeland was unscathed by enemy actions, Canadians felt more impact from the war than rationing and the separation from

HIGH LIFE GIs in Britain were paid well enough to live it up in their time off – and bowl over the local girls with a grand style of entertainment, perhaps taking them to London's West End for a night at the Rainbow Corner leave centre (right and below) off Leicester Square. There, international stars performed in the floor shows and couples danced to top-class bands.

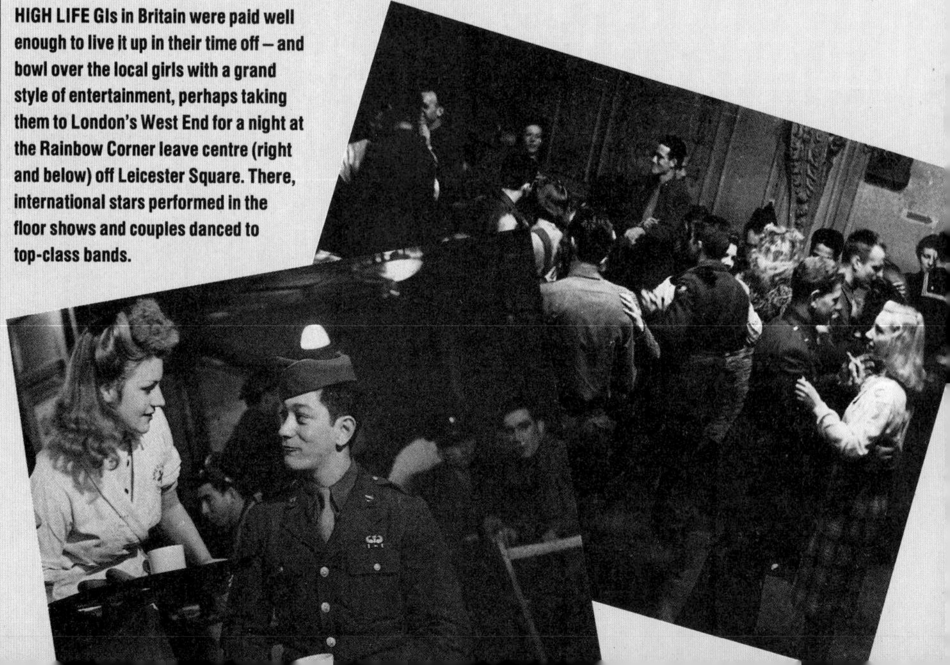

ENEMIES WITHIN

Not quite everybody was enthusiastic about Britain and the Dominions going to war. In Britain itself, the founder of the British Union of Fascists – former Labour party minister Sir Oswald Mosley – and 400 of his followers were interned under the 1940 Emergency Powers Act. To great public outcry, Mosley was released on health grounds in November 1943, but wisely kept his pro-Nazi and anti-Semitic views quiet.

In South Africa, opposition centred on the *Ossewa-Brandwag* ('Oxwagon Sentinels'), a society ostensibly devoted to the values of the Voortrekkers who in the 1830s trekked north away from British rule to found the Orange Free State. In fact the Ossewa-Brandwag – with its straight-arm salutes, *Stormjaers* (stormtroopers) and spread-eagle symbol – was virtually a Nazi organisation. It hoped a German victory would pave the way for an Afrikaner republic. Members resorted to sedition, sabotage and murder to aid their cause – and most (including the future State President B.J. Vorster) were eventually jailed or interned. But the great majority of South Africans of British descent were as fervent in the Allied cause as anyone in the Commonwealth and Empire.

their fighting men. Arrivals and departures were many and dramatic. The city of Halifax, for example, was one of the great crossroads of the wartime world. It was a coastal fortress, an air base, a Royal Canadian Navy training depot, a nerve centre of the Battle of the Atlantic, a dockyard where thousands of storm-damaged or battle-scarred Allied ships were patched up to fight again, and the closest major North American harbour to Britain.

Among the assorted arrivals on inbound convoys were Allied sailors and soldiers, evacuees from Britain, refugees, scientists and businessmen, German prisoners of war, survivors from torpedoed merchantmen, airmen on training courses under the auspices of the Empire Air Training Scheme. Other well-remembered venues of wartime comings and goings were Durban and the other ports of South Africa, whose citizens royally entertained the tens of thousands of servicemen who paused there on their way to Egypt or the Far East.

When it was all over and the journey back to civilian life was made, the fighting men, spruce in their demob suits, returned to homes impoverished by the war – materially in Britain, emotionally everywhere. In the reunited families, husbands and wives estranged by separation and different kinds of hardship, children shy and even resentful of the seeming usurper in the home, all had to turn from the excitement and purposefulness of war and refocus their efforts and hopes on the longed-for but humdrum tasks of an austere peace.

SOVIET HARDSHIPS Fans of generously sized grey *valenki* – felt boots that insulated Red Army feet in dry snow – spread over the workbench of a Soviet factory. Women were the producers, and not just of boots. As 20 million of their menfolk went to war – more than half of whom died – women replaced them at work, by order of the feared Lavrenti Beria. By 1945 there were more women than men in the Russian work force. Six million workers were uprooted when 1500 factories were moved east out of reach of the Germans. Most Soviet effort went into producing arms and equipment to supply the forces; goods for home consumption were a low priority. People could not leave their jobs, but had to work wherever they were sent – whether to factory, farm or construction site.

ENTERTAINMENT – OFFICIAL

Maintaining morale was a serious business in wartime, and the skills of many an entertainer were enlisted to help in the war effort. The British had ENSA (Entertainments National Services Association). The initials were also translated as 'Every Night Something Awful' – a little unkind considering its concert parties were stretched to entertain not only the forces, but in factories and air-raid shelters too. In fact, many top-class performances were put on at home and overseas, for example by the Hallé and other orchestras, Sybil Thorndike, George Formby, Anne Shelton and musical comedy star Dorothy Ward (right). The American United Services Organisation (USO) arranged for screen and stage idols to perform for the troops. Bob Hope (inset) and Marlene Dietrich were among the many who toured overseas bases and hospitals.

Life in Hitler's Reich

National expectations ran high with Hitler's stream of military successes, but the time of pride and plenty deteriorated into an age of misery and chaos.

NO CHEERING CROWDS saluted Adolf Hitler as he drove to a session of the Reichstag five hours after the lightning invasion of Poland had begun. The Berlin streets were virtually deserted that morning of September 1, 1939. Small groups of pedestrians gazed silently at the car bearing the Führer in his field-grey uniform. Germany's citizens greeted the news of war with a mixture of apprehension and bewilderment.

The impact of war was immediate along Germany's borders with Belgium, Luxembourg and France. That very night there was a mass evacuation of non-working civilians from frontier areas. Blackout was imposed throughout the Fatherland, and petrol rationing permitted fuel only for vehicles used 'in the national interest'. Food rationing began on September 25 and varied with the availability of items. Each German family reported to its local food office for colour-coded ration cards: blue for meat, yellow for dairy products, white for sugar, green for eggs, orange for bread, pink for cereals and purple for fruit. The weekly meat ration was 450 g (16 oz) per person, rather less than in Britain.

For a nation accustomed to the stringencies of the 1930s, this rationing was no great hardship. It allowed probably 40 per cent of the population more than they had in peacetime. The government gave the poor special cards, which guaranteed 22 million people certain quantities of margarine, butter fats, sausage, bacon and cheese at reduced prices. Farmers, designated 'self-suppliers', were exempt from rationing. Miners in the Ruhr, classed as 'extra-heavy workers', were allowed 2½ times the national average.

Inevitably, human nature triumphed over the patient efforts of bureaucrats. Hoarding – popularly known as *Hamstern* ('hamstering') – became a national obsession. Real coffee rapidly became one of the most prized items in the burgeoning black market when a nauseating substitute made from acorns, vaunted as *gesund, stärkend und schmackhaft* ('healthy, strength-giving and tasty'), was introduced.

On November 1, a clothes-rationing scheme was started, with cards being issued less than two weeks later. The 1940 allowance was 150 points, with 5 points taken for a pair of men's socks and 60 for a suit. Women gave 4 points for a pair of stockings (with two more pairs allowed at 8 points each), 16 for a bra and 35 for a summer coat. The needy could apply for supplementary chits.

National resolve soon replaced apprehension among the two major groups of the nation: active Nazi supporters and German patriots. And material benefits flowed from the conquered lands, particularly after 1940. The spoils included Norwegian furs, Dutch dairy produce and French silks and perfume. Rations were supplemented by foodstuffs and clothing sent home by soldiers in the occupied countries.

For most people, peacetime levels of consumption were maintained until 1941. Indeed, for the majority the normal pattern of work or school went on. Holiday-making, winter sports and women's beauty care continued at prewar levels. German war industry did little more than tick over while soldiers' wives lived in comfort on their state allowance, with supplements from the National Socialist People's Welfare programme set up for the needy. Not until 1941 was there any attempt to engage women in industry.

THE GOOD DAYS END

An early sign of the strain war would impose came in the bitter winter of 1939-40, when most of the railways' rolling stock was given over to the Wehrmacht – severely restricting supplies of domestic coal. In the winter of 1941-2, Germans experienced their first food crisis. Abundant crops of unrationed potatoes had bulked up their diet from the start of the war, but a lack of farm workers (called up for the attack on the Soviet Union) and freight cars (now used to supply the Eastern Front), combined with a cold snap, proved disastrous. Howard K. Smith, an American reporter based in Berlin, observed: 'People's faces are pale, unhealthily white as flour, except for red rings around their eyes . . . the un-uniformed millions get no vitamins and work in shops and factories 10-12 hours a day.'

The push eastwards appeared at first to be a massive re-run of the campaigns in the west. The law decreed that for the announcement of victories the radios in cafés, restaurants and other public places be turned up. Waiters stopped serving, customers paused in their eating as trumpets and drums heralded the latest triumph.

As the advance in Russia slowed, the public mood began to change. Large numbers of wounded appeared in German cities. When the casualty list grew, convalescents did not go home but were bundled off to distant nursing homes and recreation centres. Death notices in the newspapers were restricted to only a handful in each issue. A macabre ruling allowed grieving women to marry men killed in action – to give any unborn

LIFE GOES ON In 1941 a German soldier's ration card for a four-day leave yielded ample food supplies (right), and Berliners still enjoyed sitting and strolling in the boulevards. The harsh reality of war hit home only in 1943.

children a family name and provide the mothers with a war-widow's pension.

Shortages now began to bite. New clothing and footwear went entirely to the Wehrmacht. Children, air-raid victims and refugees from the east had first claim on the dwindling existing stocks. Improvisation became the order of the day. When cotton thread ran out, women darned their clothes with string dyed with shoe polish.

In June 1941, bread and meat rations were cut. In April 1942, fats were cut, potatoes were rationed and the daily diet deteriorated sharply. The film actress Hildegarde Knef, who grew up in wartime Berlin, remembered the staple diet as mainly weak ersatz coffee, margarine on rolls and 'powdered eggs diluted and stirred, scrambled and fried, tasting of glue'. In October 1942, rations were increased again, and troops coming home on leave were given 'Führer Parcels' containing tinned goods to take home to their families. Meat was cut once more in May 1943 – but then increased temporarily the following year, as herds of stock were driven into Germany from the occupied countries. A barter economy grew – and a vigorous black market. Forging passports, work-books, ration cards and other documents was a lucrative black-market business.

CITIES AND SOCIETY DISINTEGRATE

Anglo-American strategic bombing offensives brought the front line to Germany's cities in 1942. RAF 'area bombing' – beginning with Essen, Duisberg, Düsseldorf and Cologne – no longer had German war industry as its target but, in the phrase of the Bomber Command directive, the 'morale of the enemy civil population and in particular of the industrial workers'. For many of them, life in the early phase of the bombing became governed by the *Drahtfunk* ('cable radio'), a device attached to the family wireless set, which was kept switched on. The Drahtfunk's usual steady 'tock-tock' changed to a sharp 'ping-pong' whenever any enemy bombers approached. An announcer periodically gave the position, number and type of bombers and the expected target.

When Hamburg was crushed in the summer of 1943, 44 600 civilians and 800 servicemen were killed, and German leaders feared that the will to work on in armaments manufacture would crumble. Two-thirds of the city's 1.2 million population – most of the non-workers – were evacuated. Berlin also took a terrible hammering. About half of the German capital's 1.6 million dwellings were damaged; every third house was either completely destroyed or uninhabitable.

Hildegarde Knef remembered its distinctive 'smell of burning, and the sweet, fatty smell of the buried, not yet dug out'. And yet the city clung to a semblance of normality. Even with the Red Army at its gates in 1945, 12 000 policemen remained on duty, postmen delivered the mail, garbage was collected, the Berlin Philharmonic neared the end of its season, flower sellers plied their trade in the streets. Every morning about 600 000 Berliners negotiated the rubble-choked streets to man the 65 per cent of factories that were still working.

Nevertheless, the war distorted Berlin society. War casualties, the call-up of men and women and the evacuation of a million citizens cut the population by a third. Two out of three residents were female; the males were nearly all under 18 or over 60. The pattern was repeated across Germany. Gaps in vital services were filled by the Hitler Youth; 700 000 of them were messengers, telephone operators, hospital orderlies, firefighters and anti-aircraft gunners. When 16-year-old youths were called up on January 26, 1943, the League of German Girls filled their posts.

MOBILISING THE HOME FRONT

In 1943, Nazi leaders made a belated attempt to get the entire country behind the war effort. For 6 million workers were still producing consumer goods and 1.5 million women were maids and cooks. On February 18, 1943, after the defeat at Stalingrad, Propaganda Minister Josef Goebbels announced 'total war' measures in a speech at Berlin's sports stadium – measures that took five months to enforce, by which time they were too late. All men between 16 and 65 were registered for compulsory labour. Hitler Youths aged 10-15 were drafted to help farmers and collect rags. Criminals were put on war work. Factories had managed, even after a great publicity effort and offers of extra rations, to pull in only 900 000 women to help the war effort; most would have preferred office jobs, but these had already been filled by the wives of Nazi officials.

By September 1944, after the conscription of women was extended, Germany's 14.9 million women workers constituted over half the native labour force. Because of the shortage of men, 100 000 women were called up at the end of that summer to operate anti-aircraft batteries. At first they handled searchlights, detection instruments and communications, but within months some were firing the guns.

It was the millions of foreign workers – many of them little more than slaves (see box, p. 188) – who brought about the 230 per cent increase in war production between 1941 and 1944. They numbered over 7 million by 1944, including 5.3

THE EVACUEE EXPERIENCE

When more than a million Hamburg residents were moved out of their flattened city in 1943, many hosts and evacuees experienced the same lack of mutual understanding as Britons involved in their evacuation scheme. Like other evacuees from Germany's northern cities and the Ruhr and Rhineland, Hamburg citizens disturbed the even tenor of communities little touched by war.

In southern Germany they were often called '*Bombenpack Preussen*' ('a bunch of bombed-out Prussians'). City-dwellers failed to adapt to rural life. They were irked that farmers were exempt from rationing while their own supplies were meagre. 'They eat like kings and live like pigs', was a frequent complaint. Those evacuated to Poland found it unbearably primitive, while those sent to the Tyrol found the price of accommodation pushed up by profiteers.

Many evacuees yearned for the comradeship of life under the bombs, with all its hardships. Facing extreme adversity with dogged determination to cling to the vestiges of everyday life, they swarmed back home. By the winter of 1943 about half of Hamburg's evacuees had returned – to live in ruined houses or in garden sheds in the suburbs. One Hamburg woman, Anne-Lies Schmidt, recalled: 'Living conditions after the destruction were really extraordinary. The population became *Kumpels* ['mates']. We shared everything. One helped the other. Anyone could go alone into the streets and was not robbed or molested. I slept with the door on the ground floor open and nothing happened to me.' Factories reopened, commerce resumed and, within five months, industrial output had returned to 80 per cent of normal.

ABOUT-TURN The Nazi party believed a woman's place was in the home, but from 1941 some were taught new skills like welding (right) and put to work in industry. Young patriots (far right) were eager to read about military matters.

U-BOATS IN THE CAPITAL

When Berlin was declared *Judenrein* ('free of Jews') in 1944, some 4000 Jews in fact remained, leading a submerged life which earned them the nickname 'U-boats'. A few brave Gentiles were prepared to help them. In Berlin a group of two dozen with the code name 'Uncle Emil' ran a survival system for the 'U-boats'.

One of its members, Dr Tegel, was a master printer who could forge vital documents. A 'U-boat' was constantly on the move from cubbyholes to cellars and garden sheds. He was in perpetual fear of detection and represented an ever-present threat to his protectors. The chaos caused by Allied bombing enabled any 'U-boat' stopped and questioned to claim that he had been bombed-out – so long as his papers were in order and he did not look Jewish. Hunger was a constant companion as two or three 'U-boats' lived on one forged or donated ration card.

A few Jews passed as Gentiles. One, Hans Rosenthal – a popular entertainer after the war – found work as a gravedigger. On one occasion he had to dig a grave for two SS officers. He recalled: 'I told myself later that I was probably the only Jew in Germany who was burying Nazis.'

million civilian workers and 1.8 million prisoners of war. There were four groups: concentration camp *Aussenkommandos*; *Ostarbeiter* from the eastern territories; prisoners of war; and *Fremdarbeiter*, workers recruited from the occupied western countries. The foreign workers formed a separate society within the Reich – with its own camps, canteens and newspapers – with which German civilians had little contact.

FEW BRAVE DISSENTERS

War-weariness and cynicism increased among the Germans. In a country where listening to foreign radio broadcasts could be punished by death, they found an outlet in *Flusterwitze* ('whispered jokes') – 'Do you know that in the future teeth are going to be pulled through the nose. Why? Because nobody dares open his mouth.'

But on February 19, 1943, there was a remarkable outburst when 4000 students at Munich University howled down the *Gauleiter* (district governor) of Bavaria, Paul Giesler, during a speech calling the male students malingerers and asking female students for the 'annual testimonial' of a son for the Reich. Demonstrations and street riots followed.

The affair encouraged the *Weisse Rose* ('White Rose'), an underground resistance group which Hans Scholl, a Munich student, had formed in 1941. Scholl had been inspired by Professor Kurt Huber of Munich University and by the Roman Catholic Bishop of Münster, Cardinal Claus von Galen, who in the summer of 1941 preached against euthanasia of the mentally handicapped, the Gestapo, and Nazi treatment of occupied nations. The Nazis harried the Catholic Church, silenced the Catholic press, seized church property and imposed a punitive 'war-tax' on churches thoughout Germany. But within weeks of Galen's sermon, the euthanasia programme was ended.

Scholl's movement spread to a dozen cities, printed pamphlets calling attention to the fate of the Jews, and urged passive resistance and sabotage of war industry. Scholl, his sister Sophie and a colleague, Christoph Probst, were arrested a month after Giesler's speech for openly handing out leaflets. They were found guilty of treason and guillotined. Three other White Rose members were executed and 11 imprisoned.

The Church for the most part kept quiet about the plight of the Jews. But the Roman Catholic priest Bernard Lichtenberg of Berlin was put in a concentration camp for protesting in the pulpit against the anti-Jewish measures. Several public demonstrations were made: by women abusing SS guards who took Jews away, and by Gentile wives whose Jewish husbands had been deported from Berlin in March 1943. Otherwise, the disappearance of some 140 000 German Jews was marked by massive public indifference. Years of anti-Semitic propaganda ensured that the Jews were put out of sight and out of mind.

FINAL DISILLUSIONMENT

With the defeat at Stalingrad in 1942-3, the national expectation of victory had wavered. After D-Day the social fabric of Germany began to fall apart. The average daily diet fell below subsistence level. As the war neared its end, there was looting of food stores and of freight trains shot up by low-flying Allied fighters.

Refugees arriving from the east brought chilling tales of atrocities committed by the Red Army. Many Germans in the path of the Soviet advance carried poison to take rather than fall into Russian hands. To counter 'defeatism', the authorities applied greater terror. Roving SS squads exterminated *Volksschädlinge* ('enemies of the people') – such as the 17 Viennese post-office employees who were found to be pilfering chocolate from Wehrmacht parcels and were instantly shot in a nearby public square.

Incredibly, in the last months of the Third Reich, the great majority of the German people still placed their trust in Hitler, as if he were somehow detached from the wretchedness which the Nazis had brought on them and the rest of Europe. They regretted his death as they were confronted by the hardships of peace.

FACELESS GESTAPO CHIEF

The head of the Gestapo, or Secret State Police, Heinrich Müller (1900-48?), walked out of Hitler's beleaguered Berlin bunker on April 29, 1945, and vanished from the pages of history. Müller, a farmer's son touchy about his humble origins, made a career as an efficient, energetic Munich policeman. He worked first against the Nazis and – after Hitler's rise – with them.

When the German police and security services were merged in the Reich Security Office (RSHA) under Reinhard Heydrich on September 27, 1939, Müller was made an SS major general and head of Department IV – the Gestapo. He was responsible for crushing all internal opposition to the Nazi regime and, as the immediate superior of Adolf Eichmann, was directly involved in the Holocaust.

Though a key figure in the Nazi terror, Müller seems to have had left-wing political views, regarding high-ranking Nazis as decadent bourgeois. During the campaign against the vast communist spy network in Germany, the 'Red Orchestra', Müller apparently made contact with Soviet Intelligence. He is believed to have gone to Russia when he vanished and to have spent the rest of his life there.

SINISTER GATHERING As war breaks out in 1939, key Gestapo figures meet in Berlin: (left to right) Vienna Gestapo boss Huber, head of criminal investigations Nebe, SS supremo Himmler, Reich Security Chief Heydrich, and 'Gestapo Müller'.

Europe under the jackboot

High tide for the Nazi empire came in the summer of 1942. From the Channel Islands to the heart of Soviet Russia sprawled the German domain – a jigsaw of annexed and allied territories where the ultimate sanction was terror.

ROADS AND RAILWAYS were crowded in central France as some 10 million people scurried out of the way of Hitler's advancing armies in the late spring of 1940. Finding nowhere safe, the shocked inhabitants eventually went back home, where they found occupation already a fact of life. Nazi flags were flying from public buildings; roadblocks and curfews were in operation; buses were being used as troop transports; German soldiers were everywhere in the occupied zone.

Polly Peabody, an American nurse who had spent much of her life in France, wrote of a drive from Vichy to Paris in 1940: 'On the bridge at Moulin a grey-uniformed soldier inspected our papers, after which, in broken French, he directed us down the road we knew so well, thinking that we might not understand the large sign in the shape of an arrow, which read: "Nach Paris" ["To Paris"]. This was something I had never expected to see . . . I had a hard time fighting back the tears.'

This sense of helpless grief was not unique to France. Wherever the Germans struck in Europe, their lightning speed demoralised and paralysed the civilians. Nazi propaganda, streaming incessantly from radio and wall posters, warned that all resistance was futile.

The severity of Nazi repression, however, varied from country to country. Hitler's ambition was to make his Aryan master race supreme in Europe. He believed the Nordic people of Denmark and Norway to be Aryan kinfolk, so Nazi occupation there kept a relatively low profile. In occupied France, Belgium and elsewhere in western and southern Europe military control was stricter, while in eastern Europe the people were mere subject races. Poland, Russia and the Baltic states were places of terror, slavery and extermination where whole communities were wiped out to make *Lebensraum* ('living space') for the master race.

SEATS OF POWER

No native government was tolerated in the east. When Hitler invaded western Poland in 1939, a 'Government General' was set up under Hans Frank, a lawyer and Nazi party official who had sweeping powers. The eastern Polish, Russian and Baltic lands conquered in 1941 were put under the Nazi party head of foreign affairs, Alfred Rosenberg, who became Minister for the Occupied Eastern Territories.

Elsewhere, people could usually be found who were willing to work with the Germans. In France, the armistice of June 21, 1940, divided the country into occupied and unoccupied zones. The unoccupied zone in the south had its government in Vichy headed by Marshal Philippe Pétain, who respected the Germans' autocratic spirit and changed the French national motto of *Liberté, égalité, fraternité* ('Freedom, equality, brotherhood') to *Travail, famille, patrie* ('Work, family, country'). His prestige as France's greatest living soldier won his regime of collaboration the support of most French people in its early years. Pétain maintained some semblance of independence from the Germans – keeping control of the army, the fleet and the empire – but the charade was short-lived. From November 1942, when the Germans occupied the whole country, Pétain was a puppet head of state.

Real power in France – as in Greece, Yugoslavia and (after September 1943) Italy – lay with military authorities of the Reich. They decreed laws which the local military governor put into effect. In contrast, Norway and the Netherlands were put under civilian rule by Reich Commissioners who were directly responsible to Hitler. Denmark's initial status was unique: Christian X remained king and his government stayed in office, although they were not collaborators. The king, indeed, refused to acknowledge German salutes. In 1943 Hitler tired of this cold insolence and ordered tough repressive measures. The Danish cabinet refused to pass them and resigned. The Germans took direct control, whereupon the Danish Navy scuttled its fleet. The king was then confined as a virtual prisoner.

Wherever possible the Germans kept civil servants and local government bodies in place to manage the day-to-day running of the country. Germany's allies – Hungary, Romania, Bulgaria, Finland, Slovakia, part of Yugoslavia and (until September 1943) Italy – kept their own governments. But if any showed independence the German missions and consulates swiftly moved in. Even willing collaborators merely posed as rulers; they were never given real power. In Norway, for example, the former war minister, Vidkun Quisling, whose very name later meant traitor, proclaimed himself premier of a pro-German government in April 1940, but he had no authority. The legitimate government fled to London with King Haakon VII, and the real power was with the Germans' Reich Commissioner, Josef Terboven.

Much the same was true of Europe's small, noisy ultra-right-wing parties – such as the Rexists in Belgium and the Dutch Nazi party, the NSB. The Germans welcomed their political support and their files on likely opponents, but did not give them power. The occupied territories were, however, an invaluable recruiting ground for the Waffen-SS. More than 300 000 young Dutch, Flemings, Walloons, French, Norwegians and many others volunteered for what became, by the war's end, a multinational army.

Willingness to collaborate extended far beyond pro-Nazis – to profiteers, informers, ingratiating officials, and women with a natural desire for male company and such treats as cigarettes and liquor. Between those who eagerly aided the invaders and those who reluctantly cooperated, there were far more people than are now willing to admit it.

POLICING HITLER'S EUROPE

At the local level, the Germans always looked for cooperation from mayors, police chiefs and other functionaries. Although many of them were secretly loyal to their governments-in-exile and some had contact with Resistance workers, there were plenty of compliant officials repressing their countrymen. Some were prominent in right-wing security forces, organised as private armies. Especially loathed and feared in France was the *Milice*, or militia, of the enthusiastically pro-German Joseph Darnand. His force numbered some 45 000 men drawn largely from street thugs, gangsters and the dregs of French jails.

The Germans' control system was complex. The army was responsible for maintaining public order, and also under military control were the

POLAND'S TYRANT

A lawyer and politician, Hans Frank (1900-46) was head of the Nazi party's legal division and served in various ministerial posts in the 1930s. He became Governor General of Nazi-occupied Poland in 1939. Setting up his headquarters in Wawel Castle near Cracow, Frank ruthlessly commandeered food, supplies and labour for the Germans. Jews were herded off to extermination camps and Poland was made, in Frank's phrase, 'an intellectual desert'; he sent the entire teaching staff of Cracow University, for example, to internment or death.

Frank never had sole power, however; the SS had too strong a grip in Poland. Frank's authority had virtually gone by 1942, but he remained in office until January 1945 when he fled before the Red Army advance. He was picked up by the Allies in Bavaria and tried to commit suicide while awaiting trial for war crimes at Nuremberg. He had converted to Catholicism and admitted his guilt – of which his 42-volume journal gave hideous evidence. Frank was hanged in 1946.

HATCHET-MAN IN HOLLAND

An Austrian Nazi lawyer and politician, Arthur Seyss-Inquart (1892-1946) helped to pave the way for the *Anschluss* ('union') with Germany when, as chancellor, he invited the German Army into Austria on March 12, 1938. In October 1939 he was made deputy Governor General to Hans Frank in Poland, and in May 1940 was appointed Reich Commissioner for the Netherlands.

Seyss-Inquart was responsible only to Hitler. He assumed autocratic control, legislating by decree, and applied Nazi racial policies with great severity: of the Netherlands' 140 000 Jews, he deported 117 000 and confiscated their property without compensation. He put some 5 million Dutch citizens to work for the Germans and tried to make the whole country serve the needs of the German war effort. Seyss-Inquart was captured in May 1945, tried and found guilty at Nuremberg and executed in October 1946.

VOICES OF FREEDOM IN EXILE

The assortment of heads of state and governments who fled continental Europe as the Germans swept over it mostly settled in London. By 1941, Wilhelmina of the Netherlands, Haakon VII of Norway, George II of Greece, Peter II of Yugoslavia, the Grand Duchess Charlotte of Luxembourg and President Eduard Beneš of Czechoslovakia were there, together with premier Pierlot of Belgium, and Poland's General Wladyslaw Sikorski. General Charles de Gaulle, Free French leader, completed the band.

Some had left home in dramatic circumstances: when the Germans invaded Holland in May 1940, a paratroop company tried to seize Queen Wilhelmina. Her son-in-law, Prince Bernhard, exchanged gunfire with them in the gardens before the Royal Navy brought her out.

The exiles were welcomed in Britain, given accommodation and in some cases financial help. The BBC airwaves offered them the chance to speak hearteningly to their people – and to their secret agents.

Some exiles brought valued assets: Norway and the Netherlands had merchant fleets, for example. Many exiles relayed information from surviving parts of their intelligence systems. Most assembled units of their own fighting men, who made an immense contribution to the war effort. Exiled pilots from six nations fought in the Battle of Britain, for example, at a time when the RAF was in desperate need of experienced airmen, and the Free French and Poles at Cassino were indomitable.

Abwehr (Intelligence Service), *Geheime Feldpolizei* (Secret Field Police), which sometimes operated in plain clothes, and *Feldgendarmerie* (Corps of Military Police). Clashing with these military bodies were the Nazi police bodies, the Gestapo (*Geheime Staatspolizei*) and the Security Service (*Sicherheitsdienst* or SD).

Whipping, beating and worse tortures were often used by Gestapo and SD interrogators. Torture was endorsed by Hitler's notorious *Nacht und Nebel* ('Night and Fog') decree of December 1941, proclaiming that 'enemies of the Reich' might be interrogated by any method and executed without trial. Suspects simply disappeared into a miasma of darkness and dread.

Sadists devised many refinements in cruelty. At the fort of Breendonk, a Belgian *Auffanglager* or reception centre, victims under interrogation were suspended from a pulley-block and had to endure thumbscrews, head vices, electric needles or red-hot iron bars. If they still refused to give information, the maimed victims were fed to the dogs of the commandant, SS Major Schmitt.

Recalling this torture chamber with its odours of burned flesh and mildew, Soviet agent Leopold Trepper wrote that the SS guards were mostly Belgian or of other occupied nations. 'One greeted new arrivals with these words: "This is hell, and I am the devil!" He was not exaggerating.'

PARIS: LIFE GOES ON

Once the Germans took over a country, normal routines were quickly restored. In Paris, for example, shops and cafés reopened; horse-racing started again at Auteuil on October 12, 1940; and Maxim's restaurant opened its doors, becoming a favourite with Hermann Göring who entertained there sumptuously whenever he was in Paris.

At the Casino de Paris in 1942, Maurice Chevalier, epitome of Gallic charm, sang to packed houses of German officers and their French girlfriends. He did recognise the changed days in his songs – for example, *Symphonie des Semelles de Bois* ('Symphony of the Wooden Soles'). With an acute shortage of leather, French manufacturers were making 24 million pairs of wooden-soled shoes a year; their clattering on the cobbles was the authentic sound of the occupation. Chevalier was acquitted of collaboration after France was liberated, but symbolised all who seemed to smile and sing rather too cheerfully under the oppressor.

The surface glitter concealed real hardships, though, for most Parisians. The American nurse Polly Peabody saw German soldiers descending on the shops like 'a storm of locusts' at the beginning of the occupation, using special occupation marks which allowed them to buy at absurdly low prices. The food markets at Les Halles were stripped. Huge (*continued on p. 188*)

PAINFUL EVIDENCE Everyday objects were made nightmare instruments by the Gestapo, who inflicted this sadism in a Paris suburb. Breaking fellow creatures to wring out information was approved in the evil empire.

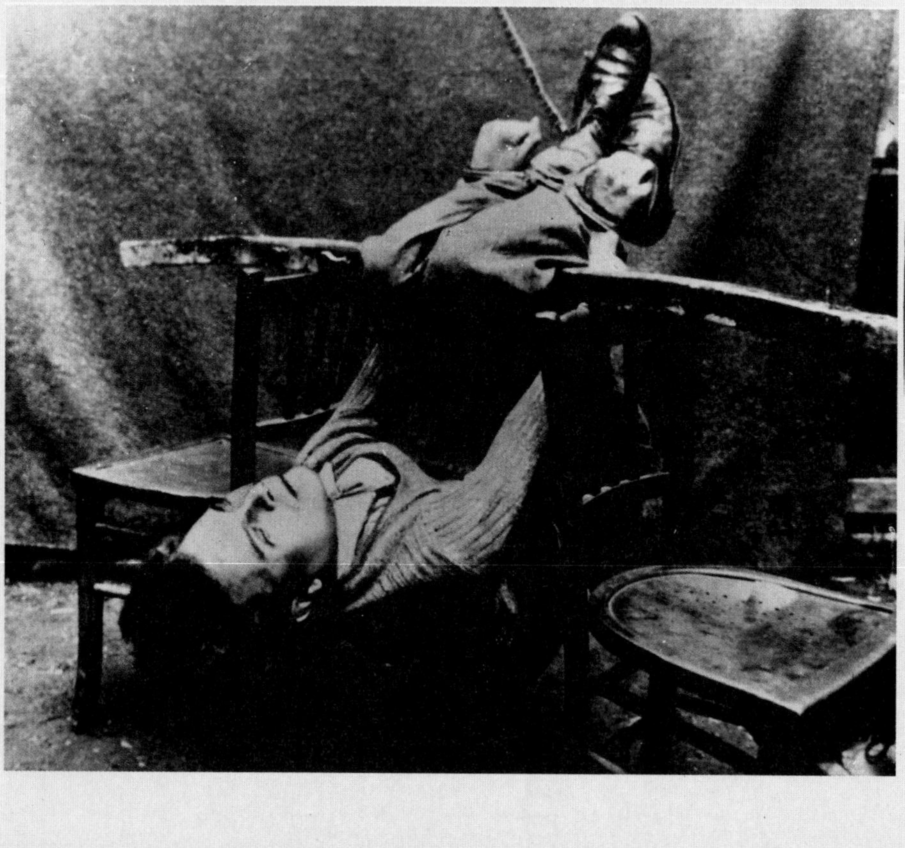

OASES OF NEUTRALITY

Foreseeing the outbreak of World War II, the Swiss declared in August 1939 that, at the first breach of their neutrality, they would destroy the Alpine tunnels. Without them the country was not worth a hard mountain campaign, so the Axis powers held off. Sweden, Spain, Portugal, Eire and the Vatican also managed to avoid occupation by foreign powers, although the war inevitably touched them. US and RAF planes accidentally bombed some Swiss towns, and German bombers making for Belfast damaged Dublin.

Maintaining neutrality was by no means easy. Sweden, sandwiched between occupied Norway and Germany's ally Finland, had to let Nazi war materials pass through on its railways, and continued to supply Germany with iron ore and sold ball-bearings to the highest bidder.

The neutrals were theatres of intrigue and espionage. German dissidents plotted via the Vatican to overthrow Hitler. Diplomatic circles in Turkey were rife with agents and double agents. Abwehr undercover men tried, but failed dismally, to use Eire as a springboard to penetrate England. Switzerland was the spy centre of the war: US spymaster Allen Dulles made Geneva the core of his OSS nets, and the Soviet Union's 'Lucy' spy-ring in Lucerne learned many German plans. In Portugal, Lisbon was a clearing house for intelligence – and for refugees.

Throughout the war, neutral nations were magnets for anyone on the run: workers avoiding labour service, Jewish refugees, escaped prisoners of war, fugitive agents and airmen shot down over occupied territory. Though Switzerland, Sweden and the Vatican offered aid to those who struggled over their borders and Portugal offered escape to Britain and Africa, Franco's pro-Axis Spain might hold them for months.

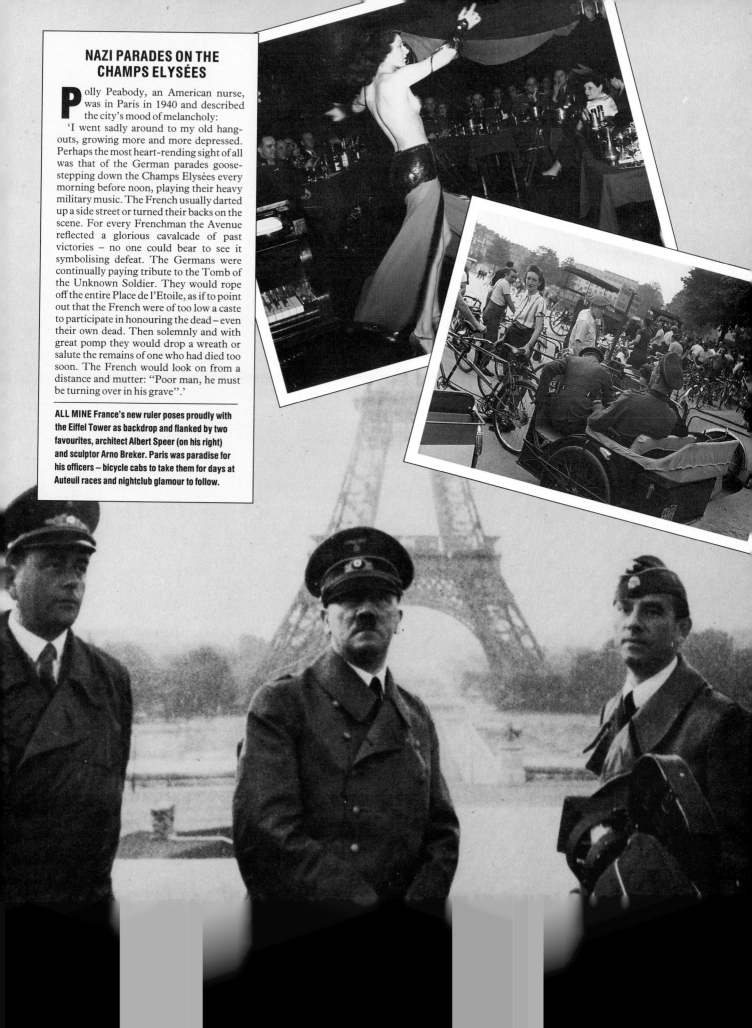

NAZI PARADES ON THE CHAMPS ELYSÉES

Polly Peabody, an American nurse, was in Paris in 1940 and described the city's mood of melancholy:

'I went sadly around to my old hangouts, growing more and more depressed. Perhaps the most heart-rending sight of all was that of the German parades goose-stepping down the Champs Elysées every morning before noon, playing their heavy military music. The French usually darted up a side street or turned their backs on the scene. For every Frenchman the Avenue reflected a glorious cavalcade of past victories – no one could bear to see it symbolising defeat. The Germans were continually paying tribute to the Tomb of the Unknown Soldier. They would rope off the entire Place de l'Etoile, as if to point out that the French were of too low a caste to participate in honouring the dead – even their own dead. Then solemnly and with great pomp they would drop a wreath or salute the remains of one who had died too soon. The French would look on from a distance and mutter: "Poor man, he must be turning over in his grave".'

ALL MINE France's new ruler poses proudly with the Eiffel Tower as backdrop and flanked by two favourites, architect Albert Speer (on his right) and sculptor Arno Breker. Paris was paradise for his officers – bicycle cabs to take them for days at Auteuil races and nightclub glamour to follow.

Slaves to a tyrant empire

EVERY MORNING, shaven-headed, tattooed and emaciated figures, clad in blue-striped pyjamas, were hustled out of Auschwitz concentration camp in south-east Poland and force-marched 7 km (4 miles) to the I.G. Farben rubber works which had been built to tap the camp's copious labour. Auschwitz inmates were just a fraction of the millions of men and women who reluctantly toiled for the Reich. Seven million were being used in German industry by 1944.

German manpower shortages became acute as many industrial workers died in Allied bombing raids and others were sent to man the Eastern Front. By September 1942, workers from occupied countries, concentration-camp inmates and prisoners of war were systematically put to work. The SS was paid 3-5 per cent of the value of the labour in the form of arms – but it did not take the initiative in offering prisoners: industrialists had to ask for them. The hundreds of firms using forced labour included arms manufacturers such as the giant Krupp company; the aircraft builders Messerschmitt, Heinkel and Junkers; electrical concerns such as Telefunken and Siemens; and motor makers Daimler-Benz and BMW (making armoured cars and aero engines).

The labourers' status affected their treatment. Krupp, for instance, treated skilled workers better than unskilled, giving them more food and better quarters. It was the same at other firms, but much depended on Nazi racial rankings. Forced labourers from France or Holland, for example, could expect better treatment than Russians or Poles, who were in turn treated better than Jews.

Even the camps for comparatively favoured Western workers were bare, insanitary barracks under armed guard and providing meagre rations. Nothing, though, equalled the plight of the concentration-camp slaves. At Auschwitz, for example, newcomers worked at the run unloading 45 kg (100 lb) cement bags from freight cars. Those who collapsed were kicked and beaten to make them work harder

FLAT OUT Soviet labourers, exhausted by 14 hour mine shifts, briefly stretch cramped limbs and gulp in clean air.

– or finish them off. Other pitiable inmates were sent to labour in mines, quarries and factories.

Under the ruthless routines, the lives of the half-starved, despairing, disposable victims were brief. At the I.G. Farben rubber works near Auschwitz, 30 000 people died. Among the despised Soviet prisoners of war, more than 3 million died through overwork, malnutrition or disease. Rudolf Höss, the commandant of Auschwitz, estimated that of forced labourers 'in severe working conditions – for instance in mines – every month one-fifth died or were, because of inability to work, sent back . . . to the camps . . . to be exterminated'.

lorries left Paris for Germany by night crammed with everything from paintings and rare furniture to silk stockings and perfume. One morning she saw German soldiers clustered around a gigantic military vehicle which she imagined full of weapons. 'But not at all. There, before my astonished eyes, was a pile of dainty parcels tied up with gaily coloured ribbons and labelled Chanel, Coty, Lanvin, etc, all ready and on their way to Germany.'

With petrol almost unobtainable, civilian cars were few and bicycles were at a premium, some fitted with sidecars to serve as taxis. Food and clothing were severely rationed. New foodstuffs such as peanut flour and soya beans did little to alleviate the general hunger, and with the onset of winter shortages increased. Coal and wood were almost impossible to obtain. Hygiene standards fell as soap became short – there were only scanty supplies of a hard grey soap that rotted the clothes it was supposed to wash. Children were afflicted with scabies, impetigo and other skin diseases.

Throughout France an uncontrollable black market flourished, supplied in particular by the peasants who became skilled at concealing food hoards from the Germans and selling them to townspeople at up to ten times the rationed prices.

Worse than the grim privations were the disquieting encroachments of Nazi power over daily lives. The 8 pm to 6 am curfew imposed when the Germans first arrived was varied often, to create an uncertain feeling of lawbreaking. Curfew-breakers were taken to the police station and could well end up punished in reprisal for Resistance attacks. Strikes and demonstrations were forbidden. Censorship was widespread. All movement was severely restricted, with train inspections and spot checks in the street. A walletful of papers was needed to go about routine business: identity card, travel pass, work permit, ration coupons, medical certificate. Even at home people were harassed by troops and police searching for enemies of the Reich.

As elsewhere, Jews fared worst. France had its own tradition of anti-Semitism, and the anti-Jewish campaign in Paris began in August 1941 when gangs of uniformed thugs stormed up and down the Champs Elysées breaking the windows of all Jewish-owned shops. The following year Jews were ordered to wear the yellow Star of David on their outer clothing. Mass deportations began on July 16, 1942, when German and French police herded 13 000 Jewish men, women and children into the Vélodrome d'Hiver, a sports stadium, before sending them to concentration camps.

Other 'undesirables', such as Resistance workers and communists, dreaded denunciation. Every Parisian's nightmare was of being taken to Gestapo headquarters in the Rue des Saussaies or to the SS headquarters in the Avenue Foch where SS General Karl Oberg presided.

THE PLUNDERGROUNDS

Throughout western Europe, occupied nations faced difficulties similar to those known in Paris. Malnutrition became so severe as the war dragged on that epidemics of tuberculosis, diphtheria and polio spread. Greece also was among the worst stricken countries: thousands died of starvation in Athens during the winter of 1941-2, and only the intervention of Red Cross workers taking in food prevented similar losses in succeeding winters.

Hitler cared little for the fate of subject peoples. All their food, raw materials, industrial plant and manpower were regarded as essential to the German war effort. Food was requisitioned in colossal volumes: occupied Europe yielded a total of some 25 million tonnes to Germany, hugely boosting the German civilian ration. (Only in Denmark did the population fare comparably – another example of Nazi favouritism to people they regarded as Aryan kinfolk.) Key businesses in western Europe were allowed to go on functioning so long as all or most of their output went to Germany. In the east, however, entire enterprises were uprooted and transported to the Reich. Industry was wholly geared to the needs of the German Army, and the only independent businesses permitted were those needed to maintain what Göring called 'the bare existence of the inhabitants at a low level'.

The greatest resource of occupied Europe was its workers, whom the Germans at first tried to cajole as volunteers to swell their own depleted work force. Advertisements extolled the benefits in pay and conditions of working in Germany, but those who went were quickly disillusioned by their treatment which, depending on their nationality, was generally much worse than that of German workers. The Nazis had to turn to forced recruitment (see panel). Many thousands of men took to the hills and forests to evade labour service. But many millions were taken to become tiny cogs in Hitler's war machine.

SWASTIKAS ON BRITISH SOIL

A corner of Britain suffered foreign occupation during World War II for the first time since 1066. In the Channel Islands, German troops crowded the pavements, Nazi films played in the cinemas, German currency circulated, and street names were Germanised.

The ordeal began once Germany's lightning thrust through France spilled over the north-west tip. Since the islands could not be saved, the British government offered to evacuate the people. Several thousand (including the entire population of Alderney) accepted, but 60 000 fell under the Nazi yoke when the Germans arrived on June 30, 1940.

Hitler saw the islands as the 'mailed fist' of his Atlantic Wall defences. As a result, gigantic quantities of steel, concrete and labour were poured in – but to no avail. During D-Day and after, the Allies completely bypassed the islands.

The occupiers generally behaved correctly, partly because their large garrison needed three-quarters of the people to maintain it. The islands' administration kept the running of affairs, though all laws had to be submitted to the German Commandant for approval, and offences against German military law were tried by German courts. People grew used to rationing and curfews. Anti-Jewish measures were taken and, on Hitler's personal insistence, 2000 UK-born islanders were deported to camps in Germany.

The islanders' own authorities advised passive cooperation, but some provocative incidents did occur: a rash of scrawled V signs appeared in July 1941, for example, after British radio appeals to put up 'V for Victory' signs in occupied Europe. But the Germans' main worry was preventing any islander from making off with plans of the islands' fortifications. For this reason all fishing vessels were strictly supervised.

After D-Day the islands were cut off from the French mainland, and both islanders and occupiers were in danger of starvation until the arrival of Red Cross food parcels in January 1945. Major Hans von Aufsess, German head of civil affairs on the islands, wrote in his diary of the troops' hunger: 'They are "kidnapping" and slaughtering cats and dogs everywhere. They made an application for permission to shoot seabirds, chiefly of course gulls, with carbines . . . Furniture is smashed and floorboards wrenched up for use as firewood. The first cases of soldiers dying of malnutrition have been reported from Guernsey . . . '

The Channel Islands were relieved on the day the war ended. The 27 000 German soldiers who were marooned there surrendered to British troops.

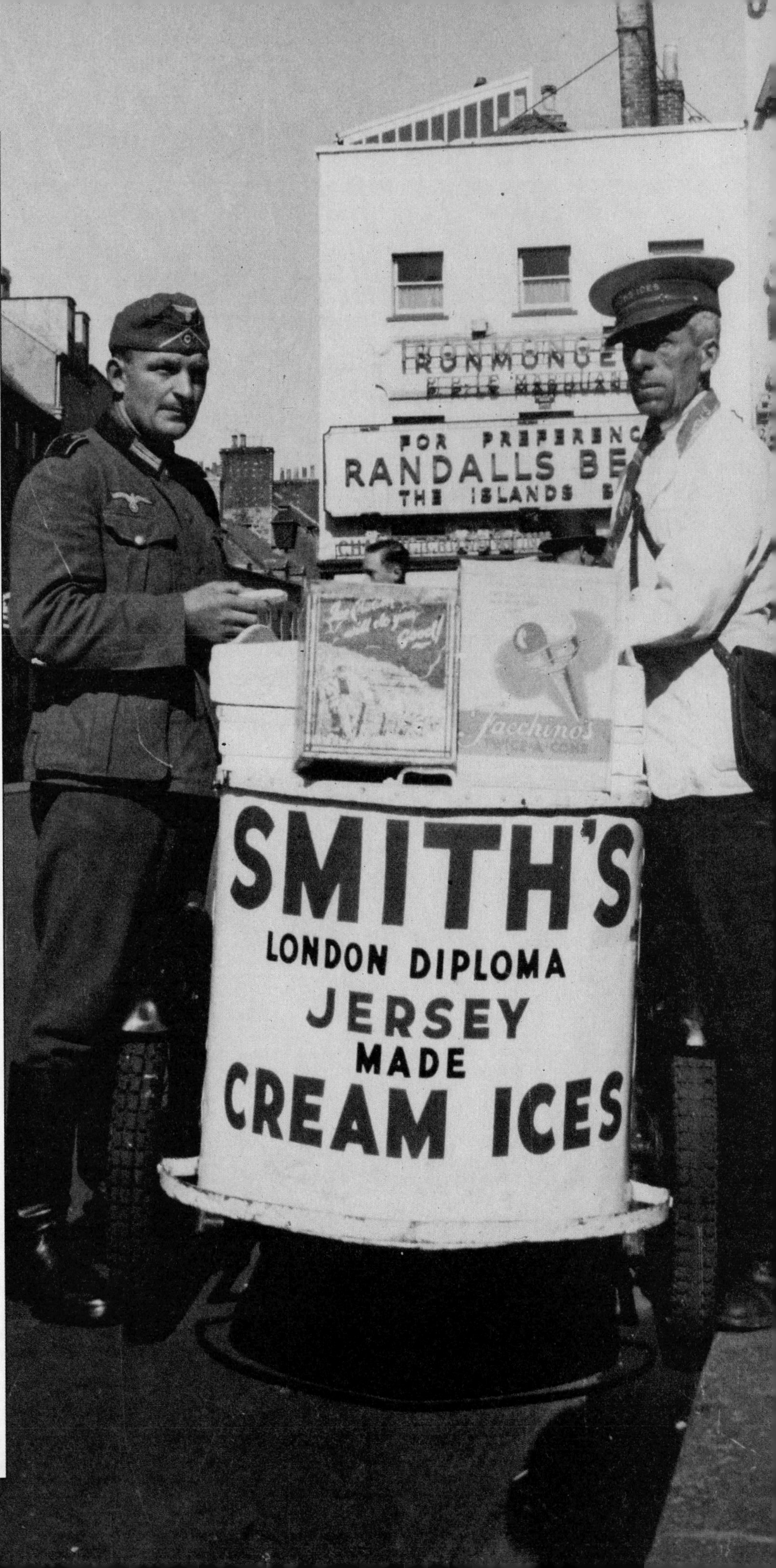

COOL RECEPTION **A German takes an ice cream from a stony-faced vendor in the Channel Islands, where edgy cooperation was the rule.**

The Holocaust: Hell on earth

The most tragic victims of the war were the millions of innocents murdered by the Nazis in the name of racial purity, or worked to death to supply the voracious German war machine. At Auschwitz, Belsen, Belzec, Chelmno, Dachau, Sobibor, Treblinka and many other camps, Hell was created on earth.

HEYDRICH – ARYAN IDEAL

Once a career naval officer, Reinhard Heydrich (1904-42) was cashiered in March 1931 for failing to marry his pregnant mistress. He saw in the Nazi party a means of avenging himself upon society and joined the SS, soon rising to become Himmler's deputy and head of the SD, its security arm. A blond, blue-eyed sportsman, musician and linguist, Heydrich was the ideal of Aryan manhood – though he may have had some Jewish blood. Even among the Nazis he was feared for his ruthlessness. In 1941 he became governor of the Czech part of Czechoslovakia. He was assassinated by British-trained Czech underground agents. In terrible revenge, the Germans killed almost every occupant of the village of Lidice.

SYSTEMATIC MURDER of all the Jews of Europe was the topic of a conference in a villa at Wannsee, a suburb of Berlin, on January 20, 1942. Among the participants were SS Lt General Reinhard Heydrich, Deputy Reich Protector of Bohemia-Moravia and head of the SD or Security Service; Heinrich Müller, head of the Gestapo; and Adolf Eichmann, head of the Jewish section of the Reich Security Office.

The phraseology of the speeches was delicate. 'The final solution of the Jewish question', 'resettlement', 'evacuation to the East', recur in the minutes of the conference, but there is no mention that the real work had already begun. At Chelmno (Kulmhof) Castle in Poland, thousands of Jews and Gypsies had been gassed during the previous six weeks, while in Russia, just behind the German front line, tens of thousands more had been executed by SS *Einsatzgruppen* – 'task forces' – recruited since June 1941 from the Waffen-SS (the fighting arm of the SS), the secret and civil police and the criminal prisons, aided by local police and militia.

Anti-Semitism was a major tenet of the Nazi creed, born out of a frantic search for a scapegoat on which to pin Germany's defeat in World War I, and based too upon the party's theories of Aryan racial purity. In his book *Mein Kampf (My Struggle)*, published 1925-6, Adolf Hitler made his aims plain, but German Jews, who had long been assimilated into the German nation and who had fought for their country in World War I, dismissed such stuff as the ravings of a lunatic.

After Hitler gained dictatorial powers in 1933, he began putting his anti-Jewish theories into practice. Jewish lawyers and later doctors were forbidden to practise; Jewish professors, teachers, civil servants, journalists, musicians and actors were expelled from their jobs. There were beatings and casual murders in the streets. The Nuremberg Laws of 1935 deprived Jews of German citizenship and forbade the marriage of Jews and non-Jews, and during the *Kristallnacht* of November 9/10, 1938, stormtroopers went on an orgy of window-smashing, assault, looting and synagogue-burning. Some Jews with money enough to buy freedom got out. Many stayed, mistakenly believing that the basic decency of German people would prevail.

Until the war, Hitler did not exert his full fury upon German Jews. There were too many foreign observers and, besides, he thought the problem might be solved in other ways – perhaps by forcing the Jews to go to Palestine or the United States, or by depositing them all in Madagascar.

The eastern expansion of the Nazi empire, first into Poland (in 1939), then into western Russia (in 1941), ended such woolly thinking. There, cut off from foreign eyes by hundreds of kilometres of occupied territory, lived about a third of all Europe's Jews – and among people just as anti-Semitic as the Germans. A few massacres, such as that of Babi Yar – when 33 000 Kiev Jews were machine-gunned and thrown into a ravine in September 1941 without a whisper escaping to the outside world – convinced the Nazis that here was the 'final solution' of the Jewish question.

DEATH SQUADS, DEATH CAMPS

As the Wehrmacht advanced eastwards, immediately behind it came the SS *Einsatzgruppen*, stirring up old hatreds and encouraging local mobs to carry out their own pogroms. Where the SS were in charge, groups of victims, a dozen or more at a time, were ordered to strip and were shot in trenches they had been forced to dig themselves. Later, some Jews were gassed in sealed vans by carbon monoxide pumped from the van's engine. By the end of 1941 a million or more had been killed by the SS, but it was not enough to satisfy the Nazi hierarchy. It was then realised that the concentration camps could fulfil the task.

These camps had been a feature of the Third Reich since its earliest days. The first, opened in 1933, were Oranienburg, north of Berlin, and Dachau, near Munich. Several others were built shortly after. They were originally prison/work camps for communists, trade-union leaders, Catholic priests, Jehovah's Witnesses, pacifists, homosexuals, tramps, petty criminals and anyone else who did not conform to the ideals of Nazi society. Each group was identified by a different coloured triangle sewn on the prison garb – yellow for Jews (later a yellow Star of David), pink for homosexuals and so on.

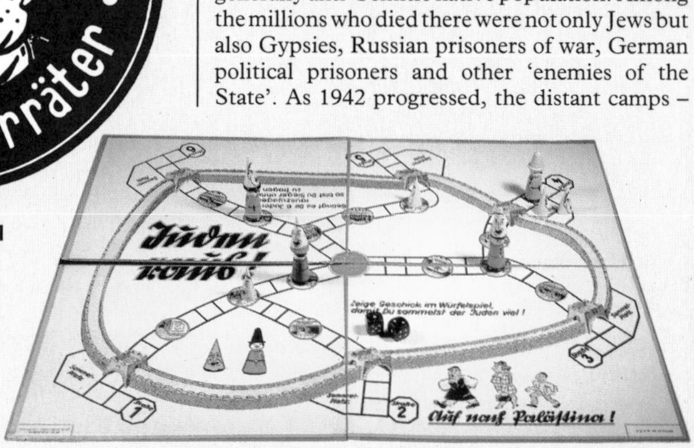

SATURATION CAMPAIGN With casual cruelty, Germans let anti-Semitism permeate every aspect of life. A beermat bears the message, 'If you buy from a Jew, you are a traitor'. A board game is called *Juden raus* ('Jews get out') – a group at exit 2 are 'off to Palestine'.

Work was hard, dull and often pointless, discipline harsh to the point of savagery, deaths in the camps frequent. But every German knew that such places existed and regarded them only as an unpleasant addition to the penal system.

In 1939, T-4 was born, totally unknown to most Germans. It was a euthanasia programme to rid the nation of mentally deficient or deformed children and adult lunatics. Probably about 72 000 were gassed, in chambers disguised as shower rooms, by carbon monoxide or by the lethal fumes from a form of cyanide known by its trade name of Zyklon-B.

From there, it was but a step to a new kind of concentration camp: the death camp, whose inmates were not expected to live more than 24 hours beyond arrival. Sobibor, Majdanek, Treblinka, Belzec and Birkenau (or Auschwitz II, the death camp adjoining the Auschwitz work camp) opened shortly after the Wannsee conference. SS boss Heinrich Himmler had ordered Rudolf Höss, commandant of Auschwitz, to prepare for the 'final solution' in August 1941. He said: 'The Führer has ordered that the Jewish question be solved once and for all . . . Every Jew that we can lay our hands on is to be destroyed . . . [or] the Jews will one day destroy the German people.'

Most death camps were in eastern Poland, far away from prying eyes and amid a thinly spread, generally anti-Semitic native population. Among the millions who died there were not only Jews but also Gypsies, Russian prisoners of war, German political prisoners and other 'enemies of the State'. As 1942 progressed, the distant camps –

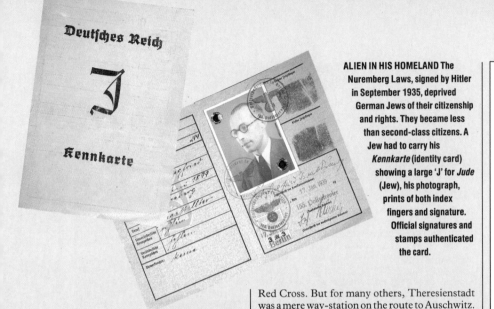

ALIEN IN HIS HOMELAND The Nuremberg Laws, signed by Hitler in September 1935, deprived German Jews of their citizenship and rights. They became less than second-class citizens. A Jew had to carry his *Kennkarte* (identity card) showing a large 'J' for *Jude* (Jew), his photograph, prints of both index fingers and signature. Official signatures and stamps authenticated the card.

then beyond the range of Allied bombers – became an almost unlimited source of cheap labour for the German war effort as inmates were worked to skeletons before being eliminated. The SS sold their services to factory owners, running the camps at a profit.

THE DEATH MACHINE

The Jews of Poland and the Balkans suffered the worst. They had already been crammed into ghettos by the Germans, and it was possible to round up the entire Jewish population of a city in one night and send it to the camps and oblivion. In the west, treatment varied greatly from nation to nation. Denmark refused to export its native Jews other than to neutral Sweden. Some 400 Danish Jews rounded up by the Germans were sent to Theresienstadt (Terezin) camp north of Prague, where their safety was monitored by the Danish Red Cross. But for many others, Theresienstadt was a mere way-station on the route to Auschwitz.

In Hungary and Italy, too, Admiral Horthy and Benito Mussolini refused to cooperate, and few Hungarian or Italian Jews were deported until late in the war, when the German Army took over. In the Netherlands, France, Belgium and other occupied countries, including parts of Poland, many people risked their lives to hide Jewish friends. But most Jews, segregated, humiliated and made conspicuous by the Stars of David they had to wear, quickly became demoralised.

Often, the Germans would appoint a *Judenrat*, a Jews' council, from the community's leaders and order it to select the fittest and most intelligent young men in the community for 'special and interesting work' in the east. The young men went off, believing that better prospects awaited them. They were never heard of again, except for one signed postcard to their families, and the Germans had got rid of the group most likely to resist.

Communities of only a few thousand would be rounded up in one go and crammed into trains – mere strings of cattle trucks in which many suffocated. Well-to-do Jews of western Europe often travelled in comfort in passenger trains, heading obliviously for the same fate.

At Auschwitz, many trains were greeted by the SS medical team, often including Dr Josef Mengele, nicknamed 'the Angel of Death' by survivors. The doctors hived off the able-bodied and those suitable for medical and surgical experiments. The remainder – the elderly or infirm, young children and their mothers, pregnant women – went straight to the gas chambers. At Chelmno, Sobibor or Treblinka, there was no selection. Everyone on board, bar the few needed to run the extermination process, would die.

The SS went to great lengths to prevent panic or resistance, sometimes with the brutality of dogs, whips and clubs, but often with false reassurance. The entrance to many camps was emblazoned *Arbeit macht frei* (roughly, 'Work brings freedom'). At one, the trains were greeted by notices which read 'First a wash, then breakfast, then work'; at another, a jovial SS man appealed to the crowd for 'Tailors, carpenters, shoemakers – plenty of work for you fellows here!' Before any further formalities, there was the mandatory 'showerbath' to delouse the prisoners after their long, crowded train journey. For the same reason, the women's hair was cut off by *Sonderkommandos* – work squads, mostly Jewish teenage boys. The prisoners were then herded into the 'showers', as many as 2000 to a room. The doors were barred and SS men poured Zyklon-B crystals through a trap in the roof; or, in some camps, carbon monoxide gas was pumped in.

The corpses were dragged out by the *Sonderkommandos*, searched for gold teeth and other valuables, and thrown into the crematoriums. The clothes and belongings were sold by the SS. Women's hair went to make slippers for U-boat crews, the gold to an SS account at the *Reichsbank*.

RESISTANCE AND RETRIBUTION

But why did the Jews not fight back? At the beginning they had nothing to fight with, no military skills or training, and the enemy was the SS: thoroughly trained, magnificently equipped, entirely ruthless. Those who wished to fight often hesitated for fear of bringing German wrath down on the most vulnerable. Most important, Nazi lies and secrecy ensured that, until late 1942 at least, no outsider knew what was going on in the camps.

It was realisation of the truth that led to the Warsaw Ghetto uprising. The ghetto had been walled by the Germans in 1940 and held some half-million Jews. The lucky ones lived a dozen or more to a room, the remainder in the streets. No

NAZI VICTIMS Two huddled little figures aged by lack of food and heartless persecution, deprived of their very childhood, are photographed in the Warsaw Ghetto for the archives kept by SS chief Heinrich Himmler.

MASTER OF NAZI HORRORS

The future *Reichsführer*-SS Heinrich Himmler (1900-45) had early careers as officer cadet, agricultural graduate and poultry farmer before he joined the Nazi party in 1923. Diligence earned him promotions. In 1929 he became head of the SS – Hitler's bodyguard – and soon raised membership from 300 to 50 000. By 1936, he was chief of all police, including the Gestapo. He was responsible for the death camps. He became Minister of the Interior in 1943, and his empire also included the *Waffen* (armed) SS. In the war's closing weeks, Himmler tried to open peace talks, and Hitler – bitter at the betrayal – ordered his arrest. When trying to pass a British checkpoint in May 1945, the fugitive was recognised and arrested; he bit a cyanide pill and was dead within a few moments.

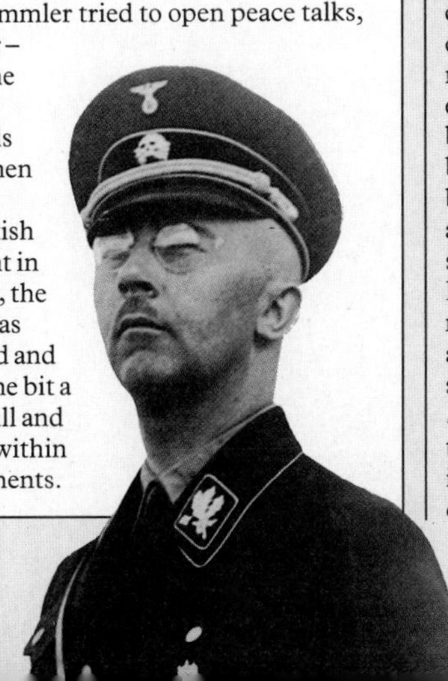

DEATH'S TECHNICIAN

Adolf Eichmann (1906-62) was charged with putting the 'Final Solution of the Jewish Problem' into effect. He was head of the Office of Jewish Resettlement and other organisations devoted to eliminating European Jewry. Though responsible for the deaths of millions, he took little active part. He devoted himself to streamlining the operation of the death camps, and to organising the transport of Jews across Europe. At the war's end he got away to Buenos Aires. In 1960, the Israelis found him, living under the name of Ricardo Klement. He was kidnapped, tried in Israel, hanged, and his ashes scattered on the sea outside Israeli waters.

DIARY OF A YOUNG JEWISH GIRL

'In spite of everything I still believe that people are really good at heart.' These words, written by a 14-year-old Jewish girl in her diary during the war, were finally translated into more than 30 languages and moved the world.

The girl was Anne Frank, and her diary – the record of two harrowing years spent hiding from the Nazis – was found by her father after the war. It was not the only writing his daughter had done during those two years. She was young and full of boundless optimism; she wrote tales of elves, bears and an elderly dwarf.

In 1933, her family had fled from Germany to Amsterdam. Under threat of deportation after the Germans occupied the Netherlands, the Franks went into hiding in the backroom office of a warehouse in July 1942. Neighbours kept them supplied with food until, in August 1944, an informer alerted the Gestapo and they were all sent off to concentration camps. Anne died of typhus in Belsen concentration camp in March 1945. Her father was the only member of the family to survive.

COMPASSIONATE HERO Oskar Schindler (1908-74), a German Catholic, risked his life to help and shelter Jews. In his kitchen utensil factory at Cracow he employed 1200 Jews he had obtained from the SS at the nearby Plaszow labour camp. Fed and protected by him, they survived – as did 300 women and children he rescued from Auschwitz and 100 Jews he found in a sealed train in 1945. Over 400 of the Jews he saved attended his funeral in Jerusalem.

contact was permitted with the outside, and little food was allowed in.

Then, in July 1942, deportations began, at the rate of 6000 and more a day. Most trains went no farther than the gas chambers of Treblinka. In mid-September, a young *Sonderkommando* named Abraham Krzepicki managed to escape from Treblinka and return to Warsaw, where he warned the *Judenrat*. Next day the underground ghetto newspaper blazed: 'Every Jew should know the fate of those resettled. The same fate awaits the remaining few left in Warsaw . . . We are all soldiers on a terrible front!'

Many resolved to fight, not for vain hope of survival, but for Jewish honour. In the next few months the 1200-strong Jewish army acquired pistols, 17 rifles, a couple of submachine guns and a few grenades. On April 19, 1943, the day the Wehrmacht and SS troops marched in for the final destruction of the ghetto, the Jews opened fire, wept for joy to see German blood on the ghetto streets, picked up German weapons and fought on. Incredibly, they held out until May 16, while the Germans bombed, shelled and burned the ghetto to rubble. About 70 Jewish fighters escaped through the sewers to join the Polish partisans; some 7000 non-combatants and combatants died among the ruins – and over 56 000 went to Treblinka or to labour camps.

THE TRAGEDY'S FINAL ACT

Only now did the outside world begin to wake up to what was going on in the camps. Some weak protests came from London, Washington and the Vatican. In the camps themselves, and the ghettos, the sacrifice of the Warsaw Jews brought new heart. At Sobibor the *Sonderkommandos*, led by a Russian-Jewish officer, rebelled, killed many of the guards with spades and axes, and ran for the woods. Out of 600 escapees, half survived to join the partisans.

Early in 1945, it became evident even to Himmler that Germany could not win the war. Determined that no prisoners should fall alive into Allied hands to tell their tale, he ordered that camps in danger of being overrun should be evacuated, their buildings burned and inmates made to disappear into thin air. The SS killed many and pushed most of the remainder onto the roads leading west. It was bitterly cold and the prisoners were ill-clad and emaciated. The guards forced them along at a cracking pace; anyone who lagged behind, who stumbled, who even turned his head was shot.

Of 10 000 marched out of the camps around Danzig, only a dozen survived. Hundreds of women from Ravensbruck, north of Berlin, died of cold and exhaustion, of the guards' brutality – and in Allied air-strikes along the way. But by far the greatest number, marching between the narrowing Allied lines, found themselves delivered in hundreds of thousands to the older concentration camps in the heart of Germany, such as Belsen and Dachau. There they died in thousands of starvation and typhus. Many of the SS fled. In the huts and on the bare ground, the dead and the living lay in heaps together.

And that was how the Allied troops found them in the spring of 1945. Battle-hardened Russians, Americans, Canadians and British, entering the camps, discovered a new dimension within themselves, in which horror, revulsion, pity, anger and sorrow were intermingled.

LAST TRAIN RIDE Fear haunts the faces peering through the barbed-wired slit in the rail truck. They dread what may come, though they have been promised a new life in a new place. But Auschwitz is the destination. As the arrivals stream along the platform (right), doctors part able-bodied men, who will be worked to death, from women, children and the frail. Those (far right), as they reach the camp, will strip for a 'shower' – of lethal Zyklon-B crystals.

Defiance in defeat

The will to oust the dictator persisted even under the harshest occupation regimes. The unquenchable human desire for freedom was affirmed by the thousands of trained and amateur Resistance workers who would not tamely knuckle under but instead risked – and all too often gave – their lives.

AT A HAIRPIN BEND on the outskirts of Prague, where cars had to slow down, a man stepped suddenly into the road, levelling a Sten gun at an open car carrying Reinhard Heydrich, the Nazi overlord in the Czech part of Czechoslovakia. The gun jammed, but a second assailant lobbed a grenade into the car. Metal and upholstery flew through the air and Heydrich was severely injured. He died in hospital a week later, on June 4, 1942.

The assassination, masterminded by Britain's Special Operations Executive (SOE), brought vengeance from Europe's Nazi oppressors. The Czech assassins, Jan Kubiš and Josef Gabčik, and a hundred other Resistance workers were shot as they sheltered in a Prague church. The nearby village of Lidice was destroyed in retribution. Every male inhabitant was killed in a leisurely ten-hour massacre. The women were sent to Ravensbruck concentration camp, and all but nine children – regarded as racially desirable – were deported to die later in the gas chambers. Similar revenge was taken on the smaller village of Ležaky, and virtually the whole Czech Underground was liquidated. Overall, some 5000 people died for Heydrich's assassination.

Throughout the conquered lands, one of the first responses to occupation was passive resistance. People performed any chores for the Germans incompetently. Amsterdam's bar and cafe customers left when Germans entered; Copenhagen youngsters wore red, white and blue knitted caps to honour the RAF. In Paris, young 'Zazous' displayed long hair, tight trousers and baggy jackets in mocking contradiction of German military style. They hung bicycle pumps around their waists, trooped noisily into restaurants and hung them on pegs next to the Germans' belts and holsters.

Such gestures embodied a spirit of defiance which deepened as the years passed. Passive resistance on a massive scale greeted Norway's puppet premier Vidkun Quisling when he tried in 1942 to force the country's 14 000 teachers into a collaborationist organisation. Some 12 000 refused, hundreds were arrested, and the schools closed until Quisling backed down.

'SET EUROPE ABLAZE!'

Despite the dangers, all the occupied countries had a handful of people from all walks of life ready to offer militant resistance as early as 1940. An early venture was to circulate pamphlets. Philippe de Vomécourt, a French pioneer of the Resistance, recalls: 'We gave hints, like "If you want to put a German car out of action, pour sugar into the petrol tank. Or [throw] three-headed nails . . . in front of the German cars".' These smudgy sheets were the forerunners of the underground newspapers – *Combat*, *Franc Tireur*, *Défense de la France* and *Libération* – which later nurtured and gave their names to many of the French Resistance groups.

Building arms stores, gathering intelligence, planning sabotage and escape lines were all vital tasks in subversion. In Britain, SOE was founded in July 1940 to assist all such activities and was ordered by Churchill to 'Set Europe ablaze'. Full of enthusiasm, but lacking experience, SOE's early history is one of bungled operations run from London's 64 Baker Street.

Many senior military men questioned the value of allotting the 'Baker Street Irregulars' much-needed RAF planes to drop civilians into occupied territory. The traditional secret intelligence service, MI6, resented SOE and feared that the work of its own spies would be jeopardised by SOE's high-profile sabotage exploits.

CODE NAME 'LOUISE'

Violette Szabo (1921-45) sold perfume in a Brixton store until her husband Etienne, a Free French soldier, was killed at El Alamein. Being bilingual, she was recruited by SOE in October 1942, given the code name 'Louise', and twice dropped into occupied France to help set up networks. On her second mission, in the Limoges area in June 1944, 'Louise' worked with a local Maquis leader to help coordinate sabotage operations at the time of D-Day.

While they were carrying plans to Resistance members, the SS Panzer Division 'Das Reich' identified their car and opened fire. In the fracas Violette twisted her ankle, but fired at the Germans while her companion got away. She was arrested, interrogated in Paris, then deported to Ravensbruck concentration camp where she was executed in January 1945. She was posthumously awarded the George Cross – the first British woman to receive it.

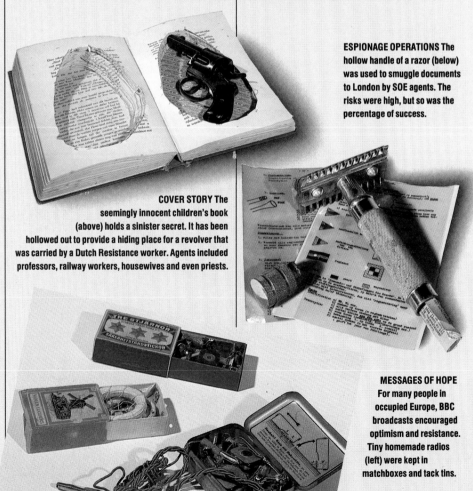

COVER STORY The seemingly innocent children's book (above) holds a sinister secret. It has been hollowed out to provide a hiding place for a revolver that was carried by a Dutch Resistance worker. Agents included professors, railway workers, housewives and even priests.

ESPIONAGE OPERATIONS The hollow handle of a razor (below) was used to smuggle documents to London by SOE agents. The risks were high, but so was the percentage of success.

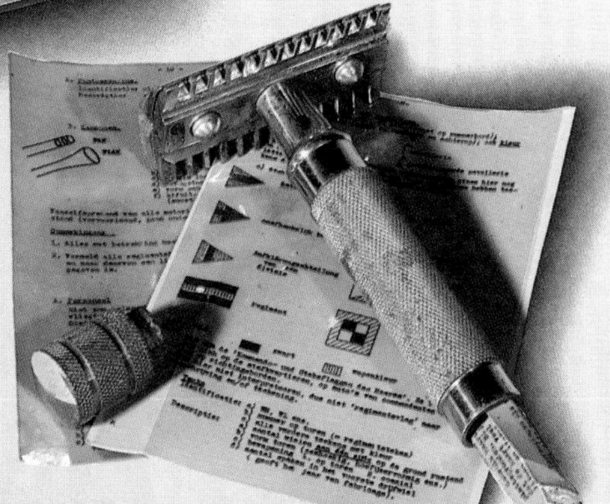

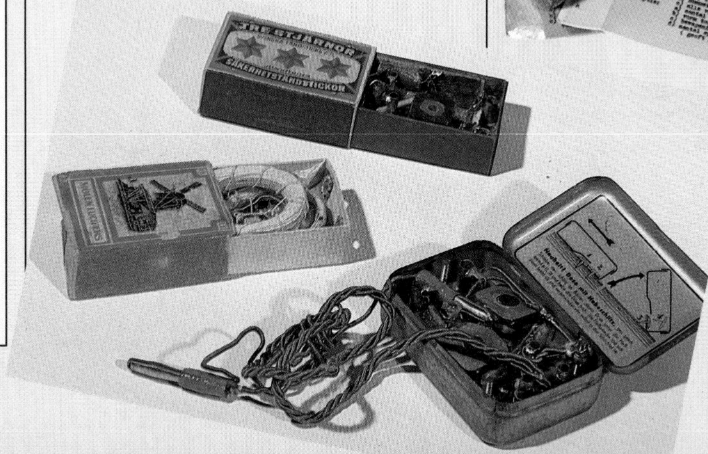

MESSAGES OF HOPE For many people in occupied Europe, BBC broadcasts encouraged optimism and resistance. Tiny homemade radios (left) were kept in matchboxes and tack tins.

Britain's Foreign Office had insisted that SOE's F (French) section work independently of General Charles de Gaulle, whom it did not altogether trust. Because of the fuss de Gaulle created when he found out, SOE had to form a second French section (RF) to work with the Gaullists.

Despite difficulties, SOE – led by Brigadier Colin Gubbins – installed a network of agents throughout Europe and the Middle East. Recruits like Yvonne Baseden, a 19-year-old bilingual WAAF member, received a dull official envelope from the Ministry of Pensions in Whitehall summoning them to an interview – and only there learned the true reason.

Willing recruits who passed a general aptitude test went for physical training at country houses, such as Lord Montagu's at Beaulieu in Hampshire. They were toughened up at a commando course at Arisaig on the west coast of Scotland. 'We stayed there for a month,' recalls SOE agent Harry Rée, 'learning about various explosives and how and when to use them. We'd pretend to blow up real tunnels or derail real trains steaming away to Fort William; and we'd go deerstalking or make for places miles away, on foot across the mountains, map-reading in the rain.'

The next stage was training in 'tailing' and shaking off tails, burglary, safebreaking, industrial sabotage, parachuting, hand-to-hand combat and silent killing. Wireless operators were given intensive courses. The Science Museum in London produced forged papers; workshops in the city tailored clothes to continental styles. After a mock Gestapo interrogation, the agents, versed in their false identities, were issued with cyanide capsules, known as L (for 'lethal') pills, for use in the event of capture.

Many agents parachuted into occupied Europe; others were put down on secret landing fields in black-painted Westland Lysanders, which needed only short takeoff and landing strips. Flights were on the few nights a month when the weather was clear and the moon bright enough for the pilots to see their way.

SECRET ARMIES

SOE was by no means the only organisation with agents in Europe. Several governments-in-exile maintained their own security services, while the Russian NKVD (State Security Service) and GRU (Military Intelligence) liaised with Communist networks and the Americans formed the Office of Strategic Services (OSS). When the Soviet Union entered the war in June 1941, thousands of Communists in occupied Europe joined the Resistance, providing disciplined groups skilled in underground work and prepared to risk reprisals. When the Germans imposed compulsory labour service in the western European occupied countries in 1942, many young men fled their homes to live like outlaws in makeshift camps in the forests. The French called them *Maquis* (a Corsican term for bush or scrub).

SOE and OSS made it their prime task to unite

JEAN MOULIN – THE UNIFIER

When Hitler's armies swept into France in 1940, Jean Moulin (1899-1943), Prefect of the Eure et Loire Department at Chartres, was tortured by the Germans for refusing to sign a document blaming certain atrocities on the wrong people. He tried to cut his own throat – and wore a scarf during secret missions to hide the identifying scars.

Moulin was released by the Germans and continued as Prefect until he was dismissed by the Vichy government in November 1940. Then he toured south-east France, linking Resistance groups in a movement called Combat. He also went to London via Lisbon to make contact with General Charles de Gaulle. In 1942 he was parachuted back into France where he spent some 18 months building contacts, and creating a nationwide body, the *Conseil National de la Résistance*, pledged to de Gaulle's cause. The CNR first met in May 1943 at the Rue du Four in Paris.

Moulin was arrested less than two months later at a doctor's house in a Lyons suburb. Though hideously tortured by the Gestapo he kept silent and was later put on a train bound for Germany, but it has never been established where or how he died. Ashes presumed to be Moulin's are buried at the Pantheon in Paris.

WEAPONS OF A SECRET WAR

An unusual arsenal of weapons and sabotage devices were developed for the clandestine work of SOE and the American OSS. There were explosive fountain pens and propelling pencils, explosive coal, and even an explosive 'cowpat' designed for laying on country roads. SOE made some 12 million pencil time fuses to use with plastic explosive. Another ploy was to supply factory workers in occupied territory with an abrasive grease which destroyed the very parts it was supposed to lubricate.

The guerrilla fighters' favourite weapon was the submachine gun, especially the Sten – lightweight, quickly assembled and easily taken apart to carry in a shopping bag. It had several drawbacks, however, for it was accurate only at close range, and was notoriously prone to jamming.

Other inconspicuous weapons included a bicycle pump concealing a single-action shotgun, and the Welrod silent pistol, designed at SOE's experimental section near Welwyn in Hertfordshire. It had a detachable 100 mm (4 in) butt and a 300 mm (12 in) barrel which could be hidden in a trouser leg. Welwyn also produced the Welman midget submarine to sabotage enemy shipping.

ELEMENT OF DISGUISE During a training session, a male SOE agent poses as a nanny for a mock ambush at a secret centre 'somewhere in Britain'.

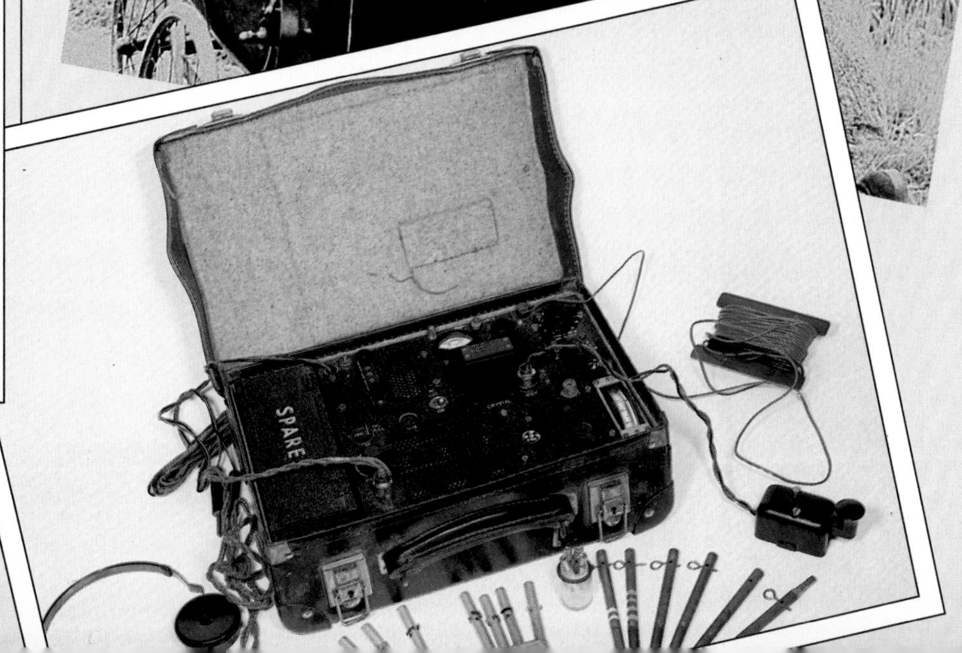

WEEKEND OF ACTION Hidden in a weekend suitcase is a transceiver for clandestine communications. The 'pencils' are really delayed-action detonators.

ESCAPE BY THE COMET LINE

Organising escape routes for crashed aircrew, prisoners of war, secret agents, Jews and other fugitives was a complex Resistance task. Couriers, guides and safe houses were needed as well as supplies of food, forged papers and civilian clothing. Dealings with strangers were inevitable, and any one of them could be an enemy plant or a traitor. One escape route, the 'Comet' line, took an astonishing 700 fugitives to freedom.

It was set up by a 24-year-old Belgian schoolmaster's daughter, Andrée de Jongh, known as 'Dédée'. She and a Basque guide called Florentino first conducted a British soldier and two young Belgians from Bayonne, in occupied France, over the Pyrenees into Spain in the summer of 1941, and presented them at the British consulate in Bilbao.

Dédée made 36 trips along the line from Brussels, through Paris and over the Pyrenees to Bilbao, from where the escapees reached Gibraltar. One of them, 20-year-old RAF pilot John Hoskins, later recalled: 'She was only a slip of a girl, but she had enormous strength and courage.' The de Jonghs and many of their contacts were betrayed and arrested. Dédée survived Ravensbruck concentration camp to become a nurse in Ethiopia.

such scattered forces and smuggle arms and supplies to them. The BBC broadcast coded messages about operations to Resistance groups on the foreign service. A host of cryptic announcements were made: 'Romeo embraces Juliet', 'Benedictine is a sweet liqueur', 'Cream cheese is rare', and so on.

The Allied strategy was to build up the secret armies in readiness for the invasion of western Europe, when they could be used to raise hell behind German lines with sabotage and armed assaults. In France Jean Moulin (see box), de Gaulle's secret coordinator, unified the various groups into the *Conseil National de la Résistance*. SOE's Wing Commander F.F.E. Yeo-Thomas – code-named 'the White Rabbit' – who assisted him, had to make an extra, sorting-out mission when Moulin was arrested in June 1943. Yeo-Thomas was betrayed and picked up by the Gestapo while waiting for his courier at the Passy Metro station in Paris. He had broken a cardinal security rule – never wait for an unpunctual contact. He was tortured and sent to Buchenwald concentration camp – but then escaped.

SOE committed many blunders while building up secret armies – none more catastrophic than in the Netherlands, where Major Hermann Giskes, a German intelligence officer, persuaded a captured SOE wireless operator, Hubert Lauwers, to transmit signals the Germans gave him. Lauwers did so but deliberately left out his security check (an agreed misspelling devised precisely for such an eventuality). Tragically, London ignored the omission every time and fulfilled requests to drop ever more agents into Holland where, the signals misleadingly said, the Dutch Resistance was achieving many successes.

The truth was that, between 1942 and 1943, 52 agents were delivered straight into German hands, along with vast quantities of arms and explosives. Eventually, however, two captured agents escaped to recount the calamity in England and the drops ceased. Giskes' last signal to SOE chiefs in London on All Fools' Day, 1944, mocked that if they came to the Continent, 'you will be received with the same care and result as those emissaries you sent us before. So long'.

Wireless operators, many of them women, were critically important to help agents to maintain contact with London, Moscow or elsewhere. One was the beautiful, luckless Indian princess Noor Inayat Khan, a descendant of the Sultans of Mysore, who was landed by Lysander in a field near Paris on June 16, 1943, at a time when Parisian Resistance groups were riddled with traitors. The betrayed princess gave nothing away under interrogation and died, shot in the neck, at Dachau concentration camp in September 1944.

Many drivers, couriers, safe-house keepers and organisers were women. Marie-Madeleine Fourcade, general secretary of a Paris publishing group, directed the 'Alliance' network with 3000 agents thoughout France. Violette Szabo (see box) was the first woman to win a George Cross. Odette Sansom, who sailed to France by felucca from Gibraltar in 1942, worked as a courier with Captain Peter Churchill's group in the south of France, and also won the GC.

The greater part of Resistance work was done by ordinary local people. René Duchez, a French housepainter and courier for the 'Century' network in Normandy, was redecorating the Caen office of a major in the Todt military construction organisation in 1942 when he noticed a large map on the desk. He anxiously hid it behind a mirror on the wall, and later gave it to 'Moreau' – Marcel Girard, regional head of the network – in a bar crowded with German soldiers.

Four hours later, behind locked doors at home in Paris, Girard discovered the map was a top-secret blueprint for the Germans' Atlantic Wall defences. Almost 2 m (6½ ft) long, the blueprint detailed the 200 km (125 mile) sector from Le Havre to Cherbourg, showing every bunker, flamethrower, munitions depot and observation post. Taken to England in a biscuit tin aboard a trawler, the map was London's first information on the Atlantic Wall and proved immensely valuable in preparing for D-Day.

Similar courage and resourcefulness was shown by the hundreds of Resistance workers who gave the Allies advance knowledge of the V-1 and V-2 missiles. Members of Polish Resistance even managed to capture and dismantle a V-2 that landed off-target in the Bug river. Their experts smuggled detailed scientific reports and photographs to London, and in July 1944 an RAF Dakota landed in a Polish field and collected 50 kg (110 lb) of vital components.

'PLASTIC'

Sabotage was a key activity of Resistance groups everywhere. Almost anyone could engage in it – by slashing the tyres of a German vehicle or throwing the proverbial spanner into machinery used in the war effort. Railway workers could switch the labels on sealed trucks so that a fighter airfield was left without vital aircraft parts.

Greater expertise was required for blowing up bridges and railways. SOE agents worked especially with plastic explosive, newly available in 1940, which could be moulded like putty and fixed to just about anything with adhesive tape. 'Plastic' was safe to handle, needing the detonation of a priming charge to set it off, and would even burn quietly in a grate. Jean-Claude, a saboteur in the Pyrenees, alarmed comrades by using it as a fuel. He told them: 'Sometimes I'm so cold that I have to do it to replace coal. It burns beautifully . . . '

In November 1942, 180 kg (400 lb) of plastic explosive from Cairo enabled British parachutists and Greek partisans to blow up the Gorgopotamos Bridge, on the Salonika-Athens railway which carried vital supplies for Rommel in North Africa, then retreating from El Alamein.

Another sabotage coup destroyed Germany's only supplies of heavy water, which the Allies

NAZI VENGEANCE An audacious French Resistance leader smiles at his executors as they take aim. Allied planners had to weigh their actions against the cost of reprisals.

feared would be used in research to produce an atomic bomb. After Commando and RAF raids badly damaged the only production plant at Vemork in Norway, the Germans tried to remove the last supplies of heavy water to the Fatherland. Knut Haukelid and a Norwegian Resistance team placed a time bomb in the bilges of the ferry carrying the drums over Lake Tinnsjø. Right on time, as the ferry crossed the deepest part of the lake on February 20, 1944, it was ripped asunder and plummeted to the bottom, taking with it Hitler's atomic ambitions.

EUROPE IN FERMENT

Towards the end of the occupation period the scale and effrontery of subversive activities increased, with widespread sabotage, guerrilla attacks, assassinations and abductions. In April 1944, for example, two SOE agents in Crete, Patrick Leigh Fermor and Stanley Moss, kitted out in German uniforms, waved red lights to halt the German divisional commander's car on a lonely road. They coshed the driver, kidnapped the general, Karl Kreipe, and drove him in his own car past 24 guard posts before making off into the mountains. The general was eventually smuggled to Cairo by submarine. The original plan had been to seize Kreipe's predecessor, the hated General Friedrich-Wilhelm Müller, but he was posted elsewhere just before the agents landed. The abduction went ahead, mainly for psychological effect, but severe reprisals against the local population inevitably followed.

Nazi repression in the occupied lands was so fierce by this stage of the war that it jeopardised all organised resistance in some areas. Gestapo sweeps multiplied, prisons were filled and Resistance leaders called for Allied help. RAF bombers attacked Amiens prison in France in February 1944 to try to free some Resistance leaders; in April a bombing raid destroyed the Dutch central population registry, obliterating records of Jews and others under threat. And in October 1944, Mosquito bombers made a low-level raid on the Gestapo offices at Aarhus, Denmark, destroying files and, by chance, killing 150 Nazi officers who were attending a conference.

In March the next year, however, a similar RAF raid against the Gestapo's six-floor Shellhouse building in Copenhagen resulted in tragedy. The first three Mosquitoes set the building on fire, Gestapo records were destroyed and several prisoners escaped. However, the fourth aircraft hit a pylon and crashed near a school. Following planes, misled by the smoke, dropped their bombs on the school and killed 86 Danish children.

Everywhere civilians paid a high price for resistance; it is reckoned that in France alone 150 000 men and women lost their lives in defying the German occupation. But their courage and self sacrifice wrote one of the noblest chapters in wartime history.

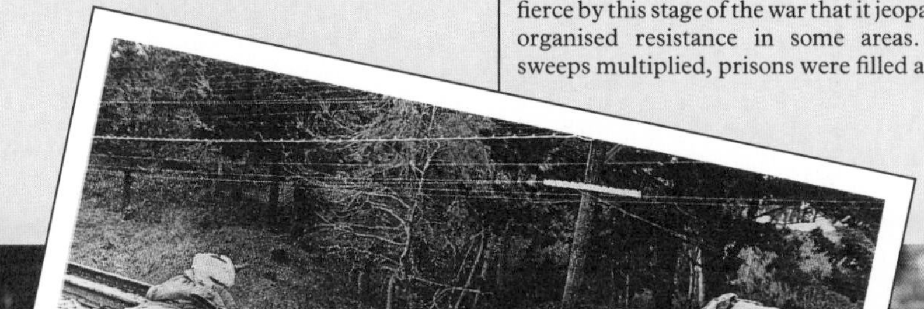

IRREGULAR WARS OF THE PARTISANS

'For the towns and villages burnt down, for the death of our women and children, for the torture, violence and humiliation wreaked on my people, I swear to take revenge . . . ' So ran the Soviet partisan army oath.

The wild terrain around the southern and eastern margins of Hitler's Europe was the battleground for the partisans, the unofficial military groups organised in occupied territories. In Russia, Yugoslavia, Greece, Albania and (after 1943) Italy, ragged armies of patriots waged guerrilla war against the hated German intruders.

But there were savage German reprisals for partisan coups. After a skirmish with Yugoslav partisans at Kraguvejac in October 1941, the Germans shot all male inhabitants over the age of 15 – 5000 men and boys died in one day of carnage. Some members of the German firing squads succumbed to nervous collapse.

Cold, damp, lice, scurvy and, above all, hunger and thirst were the common lot of partisans. Medical supplies were scant. They carried their wounded with them but occasionally they had to shoot them, lest they fall into German hands. Nevertheless, partisan disruption in Europe was incalculable. Yugoslavia's partisans under Tito virtually liberated their country. Soviet groups reckon to have wrecked 18 000 trains and killed, wounded or taken prisoner hundreds of thousands of German soldiers.

FOREST FIGHTERS Yugoslav partisans (left) tend their wounded after a bombing attack. In the occupied Crimea, Russian partisan fighters (inset) sabotage a railway line.

Prisoners of war

Barrack blocks, barbed wire, searchlights and sentry towers . . . the prison camp scene is familiar through war memoirs and escape stories. They were the holding powers' answer to the daunting problem of containing some 15 million war prisoners – many of whom saw restraint as a challenge to their ingenuity.

MASSIVE HAULS of men netted by the rapid strikes and encirclements of modern warfare gave their captors a huge task – for the men all needed feeding and housing. Virtually no thought had been given to this aspect of war. When the German blitzkrieg on Russia in 1941 produced some 2-3 million Red Army prisoners, getting to prison camps was the first nightmare.

Captain Pat Reid, inmate of Colditz Castle in Germany, has described (in his 1952 book) his shock at the condition of new Russian prisoners: 'Living skeletons, they dragged their fleshless feet along the ground in a decrepit slouch. These scarecrows were the survivors of a batch ten times their number which had started from the front. They were treated like animals, given no food and put out into the fields to find fodder amidst the grass and roots. Their trek into Germany took weeks. . . .'

Such hardship was far removed from the rules laid down in the Geneva Convention of 1929. Prisoners were to be adequately clothed, given food and quarters as good as their guards', permitted medical treatment and exercise, allowed their own belongings, able to practise their religion and to receive letters and gifts of food, clothes and books. Corporal punishment was not allowed, and the maximum penalty for breaking prison rules, even escaping, was 30 days' solitary confinement.

The International Red Cross administered the convention. However, it had no jurisdiction over German prisoners in Soviet hands or Russian prisoners in Germany. They endured some of the worst conditions imposed anywhere on captured servicemen. Moreover, Red Cross delegates won access only to a limited number of camps in Japan, Shanghai and Hong Kong, so there were many deviations from the convention.

All the combatant nations had agreed to the Geneva Convention except the USSR and Japan, but a 'get-out' clause allowed that 'operational necessity' might absolve signatories from following the Geneva rules to the letter. Meagre rations, scanty medical supplies and gimcrack huts were more or less inevitable amid the privations of wartime Europe. Dan Billany, a Yorkshire POW in an Italian camp, described the primitive cuisine in his book *The Cage*. Mud stoves were devised: 'It was just a matter of setting fire to a few twigs, and boiling the water for tea in a mess-tin or an old can. Most of the Red Cross food was eaten cold from the tins, or perhaps you took it into the dining hut and put it in the watery Italian soup we got for lunch and dinner.'

The most comfortable camps were in the USA: 124 000 Germans and 50 000 Italians travelled to them in upholstered railroad coaches, sustained by coffee and sandwiches. Many Italians captured in North Africa were sent to adequate camps in Australia, India and South Africa, while large numbers of Japanese POWs were held in New Zealand and Australia.

ENTERPRISE AND ENDURANCE

Even in well-run camps, the monotony and claustrophobia strained nerves. Britain's Captain John Mansell, captured in 1940, described in his diary kept at Thorn camp in Poland how senseless rage flared at the trifling mannerisms of roommates, such as the one 'who always hums to himself very quietly when he is reading or you are talking to him. The man who persistently strokes the long ends of his moustache with his tongue. The man who quietly spits out stray ends of tobacco from his cigarette, who eats abnormally slowly and endlessly chews a bit of nothing'.

To alleviate crushing boredom the Red Cross supplied books, games, musical instruments, sports equipment and more. POWs took study courses, improvised libraries and organised lectures on a host of subjects. The author Laurens van der Post, held in an atrocious Japanese camp in Java, gave Japanese language classes; lavatory paper was hoarded for notebooks. Improvised concerts and plays were put on

THE ESCAPER'S FRIEND

Maps hidden in playing cards and board games, compasses in collar studs, forged passes in chessboards, capsules of dye in toothpaste tubes and screwdrivers in handles of baseball bats – such items were smuggled to Allied prisoners of war in their personal mail. (Red Cross parcels were not used so as not to compromise the agency's neutrality.) The Allied escape and evasion services – British MI9 and US MIS-X – who sent the escape aids, also sent coded messages to POWs in letters.

One of the secret war's great eccentrics, MI9's Major Christopher Clayton Hutton – 'Clutty' to his friends – developed many hidden aids. One masterpiece was the all-purpose escaper's knife incorporating wire-cutters, lock-breaker and hacksaw blades. Aircrew flying over occupied territory routinely carried equipment produced by MI9 and MIS-X to help them to avoid capture if they were forced to land. They had rustle-free maps printed on silk, and tiny compasses in tunic buttons, pipes or fountain pens. Another Clutty gadget was the convertible, fleece-lined flying boot whose side pieces could be taken off to become two halves of a waistcoat, leaving a pair of lace-up 'civilian' shoes – with a flexible hacksaw blade inside one lace.

INTERNED AS ENEMY ALIENS

When Britain declared war on Germany, its 74 000 resident Germans and Austrians became enemy aliens – a grim irony, for most of them were refugees from Hitler's Reich. About 30 000 were rounded up – many to be released quickly, the others to live in camps in Britain or the Isle of Man, or to be deported to Canada and Australia.

The US government caused legal controversy in February 1942 when it put 110 000 West Coast residents of Japanese origin in detention camps. Despite the fact that 75 000 of them were Nisei – born in America and US citizens – most were kept in detention until the war ended.

Many hundreds of Allied women and children stranded in the Far East when the Japanese invaded in 1942 ended up in remote jungle camps, where they endured cruel hardship until the war was won.

ALL OFFICIAL False stamps, cut from lino, gave the authentic look to forged papers.

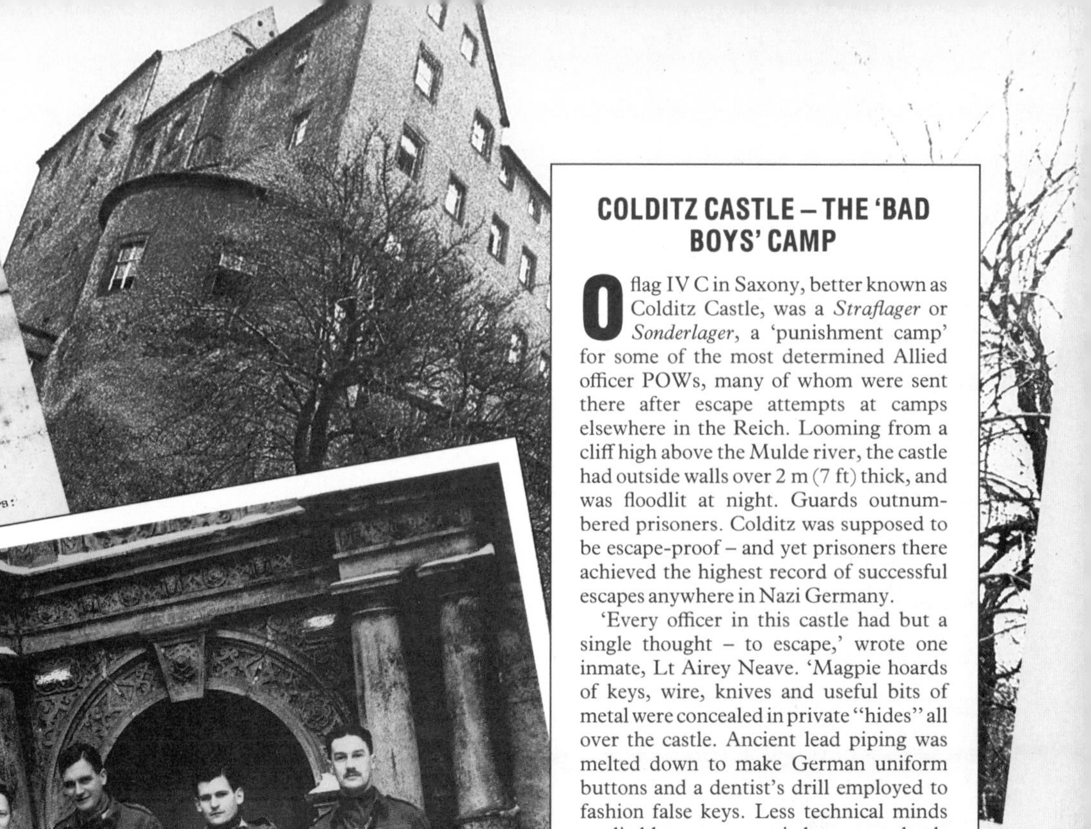

COLDITZ CASTLE – THE 'BAD BOYS' CAMP

Oflag IV C in Saxony, better known as Colditz Castle, was a *Straflager* or *Sonderlager*, a 'punishment camp' for some of the most determined Allied officer POWs, many of whom were sent there after escape attempts at camps elsewhere in the Reich. Looming from a cliff high above the Mulde river, the castle had outside walls over 2 m (7 ft) thick, and was floodlit at night. Guards outnumbered prisoners. Colditz was supposed to be escape-proof – and yet prisoners there achieved the highest record of successful escapes anywhere in Nazi Germany.

'Every officer in this castle had but a single thought – to escape,' wrote one inmate, Lt Airey Neave. 'Magpie hoards of keys, wire, knives and useful bits of metal were concealed in private "hides" all over the castle. Ancient lead piping was melted down to make German uniform buttons and a dentist's drill employed to fashion false keys. Less technical minds studied languages, copied maps, and collected stolen articles of civilian clothing.'

Pat Reid, another celebrated inmate, has written of the astonishing variety of methods by which POWs outwitted their captors. Six Dutch officers, for example, got out through a manhole cover in the exercise yard. Reid made his own dramatic escape in October 1942 by a sortie from the kitchens and a tortuous route over the rooftops. Peter Allan of the Cameron Highlanders was smuggled out in a straw prison mattress. RAF Flying Officer Dominic Bruce was got out in a metre square Red Cross packing case.

The most ambitious escape plan involved building a glider, with 10 m (33 ft) wingspan, in a walled-off area of an attic in the castle. The completed glider, though undiscovered by the Germans, never flew, for the war was ending by the scheduled time of escape. Nevertheless, an incredible 60 officers did escape from supposedly secure Colditz – of whom 20 scored successful 'home runs' to Allied or neutral territory.

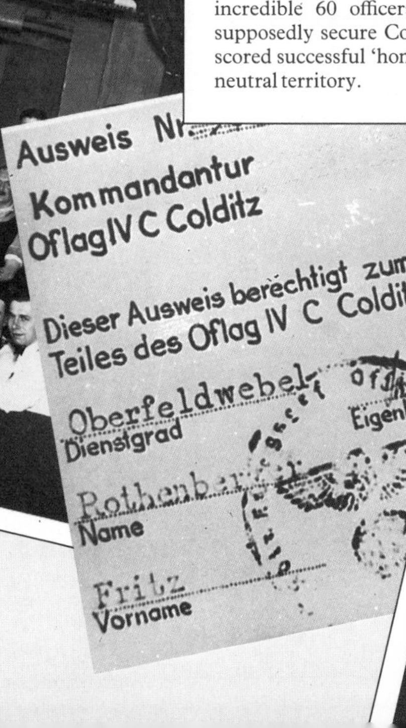

ESCAPE KITS The first British prisoners (above, centre) reached Colditz Castle (top) in November 1940. Escapers needed maps (hidden in cotton reels), forged papers such as the identity card made for Michael Sinclair (right) or the salesman's travel permit (top), perhaps a guard's disc (above left) and a concert to cover the moment of escape. The most ambitious scheme involved a glider (left centre), which was never used.

at every large camp. At Crewe Hall (Camp 191) in Britain, German POWs started a theatre with a rickety collection of old chests and costumes made from blackout material. But by the war's end, it was giving lavish productions of Shakespeare, song recitals of Beethoven, Mozart and Brahms, and its own exotic musical, *Der falsche Kalif*, with the Caliph and belly dancers dripping with superb tin-can 'jewellery'.

Some large camps devised secret distilleries to make a yeasty 'hooch' from currants or figs. Wireless receivers, put together from smuggled parts, picked up BBC news – invaluable in keeping up morale. Occasionally luxury items such as musical instruments turned up for sale in the canteen, which served as camp shop. Special German camp money (*Lagergeld*) might purchase, as Pat Reid recalled, 'the usual razor-blades, toothpaste, shaving soap, and occasionally some turnip jam or beetroots in vinegar'.

Work parties could offer a welcome change – on farms and in factories, for forestry, quarrying, roadwork and drainage schemes. The Geneva Convention forbidding dangerous or military work for prisoners was breached when Allied POWs worked down German mines and in munitions factories. Otherwise, working POWs of western Europe were generally treated as fairly as could be expected. Prisoners on the Eastern Front, however, were shamefully maltreated.

THE GREAT ESCAPERS

Among the half million German POWs held in Britain was Franz von Werra (1914-41), a fighter ace shot down over England in September 1940. He first escaped for three days in October. Then, on December 17, 1940, he escaped from imprisonment at Swanwick, Derbyshire, and made his way to Hucknall airfield. Posing as a Dutch pilot, he got into the cockpit of a Hurricane before an alert duty officer stopped him at gunpoint. Like all other German attempts to escape from Britain, Werra's had failed.

The prisoner was then packed off to Canada but jumped train, walked south for a day and a night and managed to cross the frozen St Lawrence into the still neutral United States in February 1941. Back in Germany, he was soon flying again. He died in October 1941 when his plane crashed off the Dutch coast.

Wounded and captured at Calais in 1940, Lieutenant Airey Neave (1916-79) escaped first from a German prison camp at Thorn in Poland. After recapture, he was sent to Colditz Castle. In January 1942 he walked out as a German *Oberleutnant*. His greatcoat was Dutch, fitted with epaulettes and insignia of silver-painted linoleum. Neave and Dutchman Tony Luteyn strode past the sentries in the driving snow. Luteyn boldly fobbed off a suspicious soldier who stared hard at him by angrily demanding a salute. Minutes later they were beyond the castle grounds. Posing as Dutch labourers, they made their way to Switzerland. Back in England, Neave became chief escape organiser at MI9. He was an MP when an IRA car bomb killed him.

Prisoners' right to exercise gave a chance to escape from Stalag Luft III at Sagan in Silesia. Among the makeshift gym apparatus was a vaulting horse under which, for several months, RAF Flt Lieutenants Oliver Philpot and Eric Williams, and Lieutenant Michael Codner of the Royal Artillery dug a 36 m (120 ft) tunnel under the perimeter fence as whooping vaulters covered the noise they made. The spoil was carried away with the horse after each session and the tunnel entrance disguised. On the night of October 29, 1943, the fugitives made off, wearing black-dyed woollen combinations, and carrying kitbags containing civilian clothing. All three reached the safety of the British legation in Stockholm.

ATROCITIES ABOUND

The fate of POWs held by the Japanese is notorious. Prisoners were worked to death on projects such as the Thai-Burma railway (see box). The death tolls were grim. About 22 000 Australians went into Japanese camps in 1942; nearly 8000 of them died. Of 50 000 British POWs of the Japanese, a quarter died.

Treatment by Japanese guards and their Sikh and Korean accomplices was savage. Laurens van der Post records how he was 'made to watch Japanese soldiers having bayonet practice on live prisoners of war tied between bamboo posts'. He witnessed numerous executions, for offences as trivial as 'not bowing with sufficient alacrity in the direction of the rising sun . . . I would never have thought . . . there could still have been so many different ways of killing people – from cutting off their heads with swords, bayoneting them . . . to strangling them and burying them alive'.

The worst cruelty was inflicted on Asian forced labourers. Len Baynes, a British POW at Chungkai camp on the Burma railway has described how in 1945 a group of Thais who had stolen blankets were 'held in the guardhouse all night, and every now and then we heard them scream; apparently they had been tortured by having hot water poured up their noses'.

Perhaps in Germany the sadists had been siphoned off by the SS and Gestapo. Certainly POW camp guards (unlike those in concentration camps) behaved relatively correctly – although there was always the risk of an escaper being shot 'while resisting arrest'. But unpleasant, brutal incidents might happen anywhere. In February 1943, 240 Japanese regular army POWs in a camp at Featherston in New Zealand objected to joining labour gangs. They threw stones and rushed the guards, who opened fire with machine guns, killing 48 prisoners and wounding 74 more.

DEATH BY THE RIVER KWAI

A nightmare for some 61 000 British, Dutch, American and Australian POWs in Asia began in 1942 when the Japanese government ordered the hurried construction of a 415 km (258 mile) railway to improve communications in its new empire. The prisoners, along with Tamil, Chinese, Malay and Burmese workers lured by false promises of easy money, were to build it from Ban Pong in Thailand to Thanbyuzayat in Burma. The route ran through mountains and jungle, much of it beside the Kwai Noi river.

The Burma railway was completed in October 1943, but large numbers of POWs were still needed to maintain it and repair the damage done by Allied air raids, which were an extra hazard for the workers. Brutality by the guards was routine. The famished workers were expendable slaves toiling from dawn to dusk in torrid heat or driving monsoon. Boots disintegrated, clothes turned to shreds. Men slept on communal bamboo platforms and in the latrines had to wade through excrement.

Untreated malaria, beriberi, cholera and dysentery caused extra suffering. Huge tropical ulcers ate so deeply into legs that bones were exposed and rotted; maggots fed on the victims' bone marrow. More than 16 000 Allied POWs and at least 80-100 000 Asian labourers died on the 'Death Railway' – one for each 4 m (13 ft) of track. Many were buried where they fell beside the railway, only a short section of which remains in use.

ESCAPE!

The urge for freedom dominated many POWs' lives, and most camps in Europe, at least, had escape committees to coordinate efforts. But not

DESPERATE Given neither food nor water by their German captors, Russian soldiers taken on the Eastern Front ate what they could find in the fields and licked drops of water that condensed on wrecked guns.

PRISONERS AT CHANGI

When Singapore fell to the Imperial Japanese Army in February 1942 over 50 000 Allied POWs were jailed in the barracks and bungalows of Changi military cantonment in the east of Singapore island. (Interned civilians went to nearby Changi Prison.) Since there was nowhere for prisoners to escape to, the Japanese let them look after themselves. 'Looking back, these were the good times,' records Australian George Aspinall, a keen photographer who took secret pictures of life at the camp.

A turn for the worse came when the Japanese front-line troops were replaced by occupation forces who included Sikhs of the rebel Indian National Army and Koreans. On March 31, 1942, POW David Nelson recorded in his diary: 'We have had face-slapping incidents and cases of brutality; I have seen prisoners beaten to the ground with rifle butts.' Even so, by the standards of the work camps Changi was reasonably well run, and the following year Nelson reported that physical 'persuasion' was banned.

Ill health and malnutrition were the problems. So many healthy POWs were removed for work parties elsewhere that there were not enough fit prisoners to run the place. Supplies also became scarce. The inmates survived for some time on a meagre rice ration eked out with tapioca, sweet potatoes and dried fish. Things were desperate by 1945, when seaweed seemed to be the only food. By August, when the atomic bombs ended the war, Changi's inmates were hanging on at below subsistence level.

THE SURVIVORS Even Changi's large barrack blocks could not house all the Allied POWs. Many had makeshift shelters in the courtyard. By the end, when food was scarce and only the sick and injured had not been sent to slave and die on building projects, the men's bodies were skeletal but their eyes were bright – for they had lived and would get back home.

all prisoners dreamed of escape. Many chose to endure, took the chance to read and study, and limited their protests to 'goonbaiting' – annoying the guards. In the Far East, escape attempts were particularly rare; a white fugitive was conspicuous among the Asian population, and in any case reprisals were horrific. Prisoners were sometimes grouped in tens and if one tried to escape the other nine would be executed.

Allied authorities were particularly keen to recover highly trained aircrew (held by the Germans in camps designated *Stalag Luft*) and officers (in *Oflag* camps) – and the Germans knew it. These camps were more secure than the ordinary *Stalag* camps for other ranks.

At Stalag Luft III in Sagan, Silesia, in 1944, the escape committee planned a mass break-out through 'Harry', a tunnel 120 m (400 ft) long. It was lit by tapping the camp wiring, had rails to bring out trolleys of earth, and was ventilated with pipes of dried milk tins and bellows made from two kitbags. In the end 79 inmates passed through the tunnel when the 'Great Escape' was made on March 24, 1944. Three were seized near the exit, three got back to England, and the others were recaptured. Fifty of them were shot without trial, apparently on Hitler's personal order.

Generally break-outs were by small groups, as in the 'Wooden horse' escape (see box). Such groups could receive maximum assistance in the form of forged papers, civilian clothing, maps, money and rations. In Britain a secret service called MI9 was set up in 1939 to foster escape and evasion attempts, and the United States formed a similar body, MIS-X (see box, p. 198).

Axis POWs showed less enthusiasm for escaping, perhaps because the fortunes of war were turning against their homelands after 1942. Still, attempts were made. At Cowra in New South Wales 1000 Japanese POWs attempted a mass break-out in August 1944. Of these, 234 died fighting their guards – and the 378 who got through the wire were all picked up in a few days.

The most astonishing bids for freedom relied on improvisation and sheer nerve. In July 1941, when Lieutenant Mairesse Lebrun, a French cavalry officer held in Colditz Castle, was doing leapfrog during exercises in the park outside the main castle walls, he suddenly ran at a friend's cupped hands and sailed over the 2.7 m (9 ft) fence. He dodged bullets from the sentries, scaled another wall, got free and reached Switzerland.

Altogether, some 23 000 Allied servicemen escaped enemy hands during the war. (About 10 000 went in mass break-outs when Italy signed an armistice in September 1943.) Although this figure represents only a tiny fraction of the millions held by Germany, Italy and Japan, their courage and ingenuity kept the flickering image of freedom alight in the minds of the rest.

In thrall to the Rising Sun

An early welcome for the self-styled bringers of freedom to south-east Asia withered as the Japanese made plain their contempt for the occupied nations.

SEVEN DAYS RESHAPED ASIA as the Japanese took Singapore on February 15, 1942, after just a week of fighting. The symbol of British supremacy in south-east Asia had fallen, and soon Japan would rule from the Bay of Bengal to the Solomon Sea. Many of its 150 million new subjects rejoiced, for Japan at least professed the goal of Asian freedom from colonial rulers – 'Asia for the Asians' – whereas, according to Mohan Singh, first leader of the anticolonialist Indian National Army, 'the British had not given even an empty promise to grant us complete freedom after the war'.

The unexpected speed and size of their victories caught the Japanese out. They were short of trained administrators, so staffed most of the new colonial governments with local people and put rebel nationalist leaders in charge: Aung San and Ba Maw in Burma, Achmed Sukarno in the Dutch East Indies (Indonesia), Jorge Vargas and José Laurel in the Philippines. Most south-east Asians did not feel they were being treacherous collaborators. They were at last serving their own nation's interests rather than those of the European empires.

Some Japanese leaders on the spot, such as Colonel Keiji Suzuki in Burma (who helped create Aung San's Burmese National Army, or BNA), sincerely believed in Japan's liberating mission, but others did not share this aim.

TRUE COLOURS SHOW

Fear and hostility soon replaced good will. 'The Japanese behaved like animals whose language we could not understand. By comparison, the Englishman's sins were soon forgotten', said S.C. Goho, president of the Indian Association of Singapore. The Chinese in Singapore were early victims of brutality as Operation 'Clean-Up' screened thousands for 'anti-Nippon elements' and executed those who failed the interrogations. Anyone with tattoo marks was also executed because in Japan a tattoo meant membership of a criminal or secret society. The Japanese later admitted killing 5000 Chinese in Singapore.

Japanese behaviour was unnervingly unpredictable. Cynthia Koek, a 20 year English resident whose husband was a member of the Legislative Council, later recounted that the Japanese officers who visited her home soon after Singapore fell were courteous, drank tea, listened to records, then left. They warned that replacement forces might be less tolerant: 'As we go out to other campaigns, the troops who come in will come increasingly from the lower classes until you get down to the peasants . . . they will hate you because you are white, and they will do everything they can to insult you and they will beat you.'

That very afternoon different Japanese burst into the Koeks' home, pointing rifles at them and shouting menaces: 'We will kill you. Our sword, see. This side dreadfully sharp. Poong, ping! Head come off.' Cynthia Koek said coolly: 'Good. Head come off very quickly. No hurt. Come off slowly, very bad.' The disconcerted Japanese then pointed to her one leg as though he suddenly understood everything: 'Ah, you got one leg. You very brave woman.' She shook her head. 'I'm not brave at all, but I'm not frightened.'

With this the man sat down, demanded tea, and an hour later, after listening to a recording of Beethoven's Fifth Symphony, he and his companions left. The Koeks had learned, as some others did, that standing up to the Japanese could win their respect and be a lifesaver.

It quickly became clear that European imperialism was only to be replaced by Japanese imperialism. Tokyo time, Japanese occupation money and the Japanese calendar came into use. Only the Japanese flag could be displayed. Singapore was renamed *Shonan* or *Syonan* – 'Light of the South'. American music and films were prohibited, and children had to learn Japanese. Western languages were supposedly banned, but in fact English often had to be used.

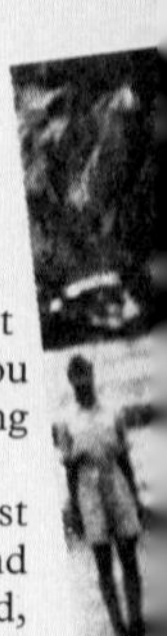

WINNER TAKES ALL Rice became a scarce and costly commodity in south-east Asia. Armed soldiers kept a close watch on Filipino women as they planted new shoots in the paddy fields. The Japanese took most of the crop, paying for it with their virtually worthless new money.

VIEWS DIFFER Criticism of the new rulers soon appeared on hoardings on Panay (above) in the Philippines when the island was occupied in April 1942 – to Japanese troops' anger. Back home, flag-waving Tokyo students (right) staged delighted parades at the news of Singapore's fall.

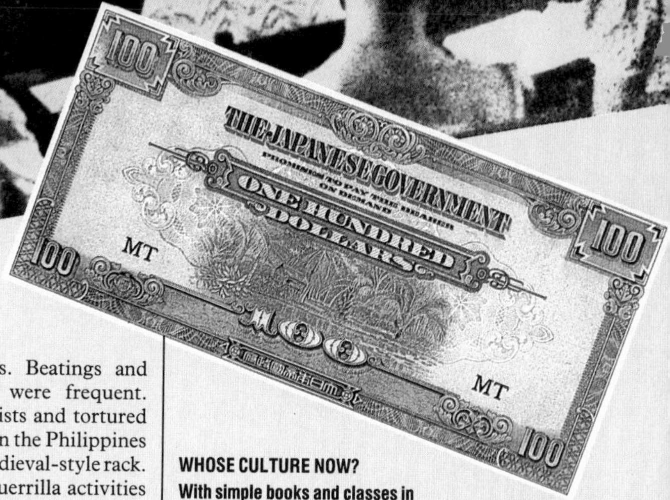

'Superior' Japanese modes of thought and behaviour were promoted. Lessons in Japanese customs appeared in newspapers. Bowing was expected. All public meetings began with a collective bow towards Tokyo and the Emperor; people were slapped for not doing so or not bowing properly to Japanese officers. All non-approved political parties and public assemblies were banned, newspapers censored and listening to overseas radio broadcasts forbidden. Everyone had to carry an identity card and get a special pass to travel. In some places armbands denoted how trusted people were.

Personal and painful humiliation was inflicted by the *Kempeitai* (military police), who became dreaded for their ruthlessness. Beatings and jabbing with bamboo spears were frequent. Victims were hung by their wrists and tortured with electricity and chemicals. In the Philippines they were even stretched on a medieval-style rack. Serious offences ranged from guerrilla activities and sabotage to dealing in foreign currency and listening to a short-wave radio.

In 1943 Japan declared Burma and the Philippines independent in an effort to stem revolt as military successes dwindled. But the independence was sham. Burma's Defence Minister Aung San declared at the first anniversary ceremony: 'Our independence exists only on paper and the peoples have yet to enjoy its benefits.'

WHOSE CULTURE NOW?
With simple books and classes in Japanese, the issue of new money, and strict rules of behaviour, the conquerors imposed their culture. In many nationalist leaders, though, the fall of colonial powers lit hopes of independence. Next door to Japan's domain, Subhas Chandra Bose (top left) raised the Indian National Army to fight with Japan against Britain, and in 1943 formed a government recognised by the Japanese.

FEEDING THE WAR

It became obvious that the Japanese proclamation of a 'Greater East Asia Co-Prosperity Sphere' in practice meant 'Asia for the Japanese'. The area's rich natural resources, especially oil, were fed into the Japanese war effort while the local populations suffered shortages or prices beyond their means. Great Japanese commercial combines, such as Mitsui and Mitsubishi, monopolised business and trade. Black markets pushed the price of foodstuffs skyhigh. A 60 kg (132 lb) sack of rice, for example, rose from five Singapore dollars in 1941 to 5000 in 1945 – if one could be found. As the American stranglehold on Japanese shipping tightened, rice imports shrank and it disappeared even from the black market.

Cities were hardest hit. The Japanese had to open public feeding centres in Manila in May 1944. In northern Indochina (northern Vietnam) – where Vichy French administrators collaborated with the Japanese – the great famine of 1944-5 claimed the lives of 400 000 people according to the French, 2 million according to the Vietnamese. Malnutrition, tuberculosis, pneumonia, malaria and dysentery increased. The few medical supplies went to the Japanese Army. Life in the countryside was less tense on the surface, but the occupation made its impact. The Japanese encouraged farmers to grow food crops and cotton, but requisitioned a large part of the harvest. Tapioca and maize replaced the expensive rice as the staple in the local diet.

Forced labour was the greatest hardship. Men of 16-40 and single women of 16-25 were rounded up in the Dutch East Indies, Malaya and Burma, and sent anywhere to work. The worst destination was the notorious Thai-Burma railway, where thousands died. People left in the villages faced greater impoverishment since the most able-bodied were no longer there to do the work.

UNEXPECTED BENEFITS

By 1945, the occupied nations' unrest burst into revolts. Blitar in Java saw the first stirrings. It was the stronghold of the Indonesian Communist party, home of many nationalist leaders, including Sukarno, and a base for Peta (the Japanese-trained independence army). Peta soldiers fired mortars at the town's Sakura Hotel, where Japanese officers were quartered, at 3 am on February 14, 1945, and the Kempeitai headquarters was machine-gunned; both buildings were in fact empty. The instigator was Suprijadi, a quiet, young man given to meditating and fasting, who was a Peta platoon commander. A mixture of force and promises of no retaliation ended the revolt. Suprijadi was never caught, and never reappeared.

In Burma the revolt spread much farther, involving nearly the entire BNA. Many skirmishes occurred between Japanese and Burmese. Bo Ba Htut, a BNA commander at Mandalay, declared war on Japan on March 8, 1945, and he and his men joined the advancing Allies. On May 30 the British recognised the BNA as the Patriotic Burmese Forces, and began negotiations with Aung San and other leaders over independence.

The status of the nations throughout south-east Asia changed irrevocably because of the Japanese occupation. The image of an invulnerable West was destroyed. One returning British official observed: 'The old unquestioning confidence had gone – on both sides.'

The Japanese had not only unleashed powerful nationalist sentiments but had given administrative and military training. In Java, for example, they ran a tough officer-training programme for selected youths. Knowledge of military science and techniques was not the aim although there was some guerrilla training. The youngsters mainly learned endurance, persistence, confidence and self-reliance. Many high-ranking generals in the postwar Indonesian Army emerged from this training; General Suharto, later President of Indonesia, was one. Another was General P.H. Djatikusumo, who afterwards said they learned from the Japanese 'how to create an army from scratch and lead it. We learned how to fight at company level, how to recruit soldiers, and how to devote yourself to your country'.

With Japan's collapse, both white and non-white invincibility had been exposed as myth. The peoples of south-east Asia were left with the resolve never again to submit to foreign rule and with the means to carry out that resolve.

Back home in Japan, high hopes fade

It was the deep, slightly uneven voice of Captain Hiraide who gave most Japanese their first news of 'a death-defying air raid upon the American fleet' at Pearl Harbor, in a radio broadcast on the cold winter's morning of December 8, 1941 (December 7 in the USA). Ecstatic approval greeted the news, and even when the United States formally declared war euphoria was only slightly tinged by fear. Mutsuo Saito, then at high school, remembers those first months of Japan's incredible military victories. He recorded each conquest with a small rising-sun flag on a wall map and each enemy vessel sunk with a little crossed-out picture of a warship.

Public morale remained high even though the government had tightened censorship and imposed regulations on every facet of daily life. Neighbourhood associations involved everyone in communal activities – distribution of rations, sale of war bonds, farewell parties for new recruits and, later on, air-raid drills. People were eager to undertake volunteer work, and women took over the jobs left vacant by men going to the front.

The successes ended at the Battle of Midway in June 1942 – although confidence was given a bad jolt by the Doolittle air raid on Tokyo two months earlier. The Japanese people were not told of the defeat at Midway, but Mutsuo noted something odd about reports of the battle: 'It was the first time that the loss of a Japanese warship had been officially announced.' With the prospect of a longer war, austerity increased.

As the struggle for Guadalcanal began in November 1942, students who had pursued life untroubled except for a few hours' military training each week, were sent off for a week-long military training camp, which then became a regular feature of their life. In mid-1943 their normal student life ended. They joined all those still at home in compulsory factory or farm work. When they reached the age of 20, they could no longer defer military service. Mutsuo was one of 25 000 students who attended a huge farewell rally in Meiji Garden Stadium in Tokyo in October 1943 before they went into the services. They wore their black school uniforms and carried wooden rifles, all that the grim military and economic situation allowed. A crowd of 70 000 gathered in the rain to see them off.

By late 1944, the daytime crowds in Tokyo streets wore ragged clothing, faded kimonos. There were few vehicles since fuel was scarce, and many luxury stores ran out of stock and closed. By night the city lay dark and quiet; blackouts were in force for fear of the 'B-san' (B-29) raids which began in November.

Rationing – especially in Tokyo and other big cities – became stricter even than in Japan's overseas empire, as the government prepared for prolonged resistance. Everything except vegetables was cut down. One person's rice ration was 225 g (8 oz) a day, half the normal consumption. Fish was restricted to 85 g (3 oz) twice a week. Soap was rationed, but the government could not even provide the allowed quantity.

Rice became virtually unobtainable by 1945 and people ate pumpkin instead. Every scrap of ground was cultivated, even the land alongside railway tracks and in the stadium built for the aborted 1940 Olympic Games. Restaurants and geisha houses shut down, travel was restricted to save fuel, and air-raid drills were held more frequently.

On a gusty night in March, low-flying B-san brought a new horror to Tokyo – 2000 tonnes of incendiary bombs. The big circles of fire turned into firestorms, leaping across streets and open spaces and killing as many as 200 000 people. Hundreds of thousands of survivors fled into the countryside, where they took up the daily struggle against starvation. All the future promised was a ferocious war of attrition with invading American forces.

Such savage fighting was taking place on Iwo Jima and then on Okinawa, but Tokyo was spared this horror by the Emperor's surrender on August 15 (August 14 in Europe and the USA). As Europeans had done in May, Mutsuo Saito thrilled to the first sign of peace: 'Along every street stretched great lines of light. I just stood and stared . . . I had never realised that electric lights could be so beautiful.'

BIG SEND-OFF Ceremonial rallies marked the end of college days and the start of military life.

The Persuaders

Wars are fought with ideas as well as bullets; for people's minds as well as for territorial gain. In this kind of war the line between truth and propaganda often becomes blurred whether the motive is to subjugate or to inspire.

SWAYING MEN'S MINDS was a skill in which nobody outdid Adolf Hitler and his brilliant but flawed Minister of Propaganda, Dr Josef Goebbels. In his political testament *Mein Kampf* (*My Struggle*; 1925-6), Hitler made plain propaganda's purpose for him: 'Its task is not to make an objective study of the truth. Its task is to serve our right, always and unflinchingly.' He certainly did not flinch from constructing his own versions of history to assist his rise to power during the next ten years.

A most potent myth was that the German Army was not defeated on the field of battle in World War I, but was betrayed by Communists, liberals, Jews and agitators on the home front. Allied to this was a myth of Goebbels' making: that Hitler himself was a strategic genius whose demonic energy embodied the will of the German people – a man who would restore Germany to its rightful status, easily outmanoeuvring the flabby western democracies which had lost the will to fight. 'My object,' Goebbels wrote in *Der Angriff* ('The Attack'), the Nazi newspaper he founded in Berlin, 'is to arouse outbursts of fury, to get men on the march, to organise hatred and suspicion – all with ice-cold calculation.'

The Reichstag fire in February 1933 was a godsend to the Nazis. It gave an excuse to bring in emergency decrees that helped make Germany a totalitarian state. Among them were severe penalties for any editor publishing news likely to endanger public order, and rights of surveillance over publications, letters, telegrams and telephone calls. With a docile Press, Nazi propagandists could mould public opinion more easily.

But Goebbels did not have things all his own way. There was bitter jealousy between him and Foreign Minister Joachim von Ribbentrop, who had set up a rival propaganda organisation. Hitler also had his own personal press officer, Otto Dietrich, appointed Reich press chief in 1938. However, Dietrich made a series of propaganda blunders, the biggest being his confident announcement in October 1941 that the Russians were defeated. Another was to order special newspaper editions in 1942 to announce prematurely the fall of Stalingrad. Such raising and subsequent let-down of hopes, Goebbels knew, could quickly sap morale.

Morale, however, remained high, for during the early years of the war there was an abundance of success for the Nazi propaganda machine to work on. Huge maps were displayed in public squares, on which civilians could follow the advance of the panzers deep into eastern Europe. The German weekly newsreel used daredevil cameramen to bring the feats of German arms to cinema screens. Goebbels took a great interest in the newsreel and, to increase its impact, he insisted on a five-minute pause after it finished, before the main feature film started.

Goebbels' ministry organised heart-lifting talks and rallies in all 42 of the Nazi party districts, and speakers were given advice not just about their topics but also about platform style. Pacing back and forth, playing for applause and raising the voice to a scream were all frowned upon; one Führer, it seemed, was enough.

Hitler fell victim to his own 'managed' news system. He expected 'inferior' Slavs to crumble when he invaded Russia in June 1941. He refused to believe figures of Soviet tank production, and neglected to provide his soldiers with proper winter clothing since he expected a summer walkover.

How would the propaganda machine work when the tide turned? Curiously, as life grew harsher for the Germans, Goebbels' popularity grew. He, not Hitler, visited bomb-blasted cities and talked to the survivors. He won an enthusiastic response as he hammered away at the theme of 'no capitulation' – his riposte to the Allied demand for unconditional surrender.

With the defeat at Stalingrad, Goebbels created a new myth. 'The heroic struggle of Stalingrad will become the greatest epic of German history', he told the Press – and followed up with a new slogan: 'Hard times, hard work, hard hearts!' Barely two weeks later at Berlin's Sportpalast he made the speech of his life. The German people, he said, were demanding an end to 'kid glove methods'. When he asked 'Do you want Total War?', 15 000 zealots screamed the required '*Ja!*' and Goebbels exhorted 'Now, nation arise! Let the storm break loose!' The machine would manage the nation's mind still.

Even as late as 1944 Goebbels was able to turn Allied policies into goads to stiffen German resolve. The Morgenthau Plan for postwar Germany, proposed by President Roosevelt's Secretary of the Treasury Henry Morgenthau, was grist to his mill. He used its intention to dismantle Germany's heavy industry and turn the country into a 'potato patch' to whip up ever fiercer resistance.

THE BRITISH WAY

Manipulating the news was not an admissible notion in Britain. The very word 'propaganda' seemed hardly respectable, so on the eve of war the government set up a Ministry of Information.

In a typically British compromise, censorship was both real and voluntary. Editors were free, inside Britain, to print what they liked – but they risked penalties for printing what could help the enemy. 'D' notices – so called because they were issued under the Defence Regulations – gave guidance on what was unsafe to publish. The armed services maintained their own censorship – mainly on servicemen's letters home.

The Press was generally keen to present a positive picture of how things were going. The papers played their part in converting the disaster of Dunkirk into a legend of an invincible nation refusing to contemplate defeat. 'Bloody marvellous!' proclaimed the headline in the *Daily Mirror* over its leading article on the flotilla of little ships that helped to bring home the troops stranded on the beaches.

Government and Press were sometimes at odds. The Communist *Daily Worker* was banned in January 1941, while the Nazi-Soviet pact still held good, and the ban remained in force for a year after the Russians became allies of Britain. The *Daily Mirror*, itself full of zeal for the war effort, fell foul of the government through its robust attacks on slackness in high places. Churchill attributed to the *Mirror* 'a spirit of hatred and malice towards the government'.

Matters came to a head in March 1942, when the paper published a Philip Zec cartoon showing the survivor of a U-boat attack with the caption: 'The price of petrol has been increased by one penny – Official.' The point of the cartoon was to make people think twice before they used petrol, but another interpretation was that oil companies were being allowed to make fat profits for which brave seamen risked their lives. The Home

POSITIVE IMAGES Germany's 'house magazine' for the army, *Die Wehrmacht*, gave the men a rosy view of the war. *Signal*, also army-produced but under Ministry of Propaganda control, skilfully presented German excellence to occupied Europe and the neutrals. It was published fortnightly in 20 languages. At its peak it sold almost 3 million.

Secretary, Herbert Morrison, threatened to shut the *Mirror* down.

The threat recognised the power of newspapers – albeit passed through the coarse filter of government regulations – to shape national attitudes and spirit. The power was shared by radio. In theory, the BBC was answerable to the Ministry of Information, but in practice its high reputation for reliability meant it was left alone. A minor revolution was that the BBC's anonymous announcers suddenly acquired names. 'Here is the news – and this is Alvar Liddell reading it' was an announcement the Germans might fake, but there was no faking the familiar voice.

Great initial success was achieved by the Allied 'V for Victory' campaign, which was partly derived from Churchill's two-fingered sign. The head of the BBC's Belgian Service, Victor de Laveleye, suggested that anti-Nazis should display the letter V wherever possible, because it stood for the French word *victoire* and the Flemish and Dutch *vrijheid* ('freedom'). The campaign was spread across Europe by the BBC's Douglas Ritchie, whose radio name was Colonel Britton, and it soon took new forms. The dot-dot-dot-dash rhythm of V in Morse code – played on a muffled kettledrum as a BBC call sign – echoes the rhythm of the opening bars of Beethoven's Fifth Symphony which introduced programmes to the occupied countries. To many, those few notes – 'fate knocking on the door' – expressed the solemn and relentless determination of the Allies.

Goebbels managed to neutralise the campaign to some extent by adopting it himself, putting huge Vs (for *Viktoria*) on the Eiffel Tower and other public buildings in occupied Europe, with the slogan 'Germany wins on all fronts'.

Broadcasts from Britain to occupied Europe often gave practical tips on how to feign illnesses to avoid being sent to German labour camps. Its encouragement to workers to commit minor acts of sabotage made the Dutch government-in-exile protest to the Foreign Office about some of

TOKYO ROSE, THE GIs' FRIEND

Homesick GIs in the Pacific during 1943 and 1944 could tune in to *Zero Hour*, a 15 minute radio show of news, music and sweet voices – from Tokyo. And the dreamiest, silkiest voice of all belonged to Iva Ikuko Toguri (1916-), who became known as Tokyo Rose. Her style was that of a flirtatious disc jockey, but her intention was to sap the men's fighting spirit and induce war-weariness. 'Hello, you fighting orphans in the Pacific. How's tricks?' she would say, and insidiously suggest to the 'poor forgotten soldiers' that her music was not nearly as sweet as the music their wives were making with factory workers back home.

Her American accent was authentic, for she was a Nisei – an American-born Japanese. Stranded in Japan while visiting at the outbreak of war, she got a job as a secretary. Then, as an alternative to being sent to work in a munitions factory, she became an announcer with the Japanese Broadcasting Corporation, NHK. She was arrested in September 1945 – by which time she was Mrs d'Aquino – but was released in August 1946. She was tracked down in 1949 by a reporter for the GI magazine *Stars and Stripes* and then charged with treason.

Tokyo Rose was jailed for ten years and was fined US$10 000. At the Reformatory for Women at Alderson, West Virginia, she became an enthusiastic gardener and was known as a fervent patriot, always standing rigidly to attention for the American anthem. After six years she was released, and President Ford pardoned her in January 1977.

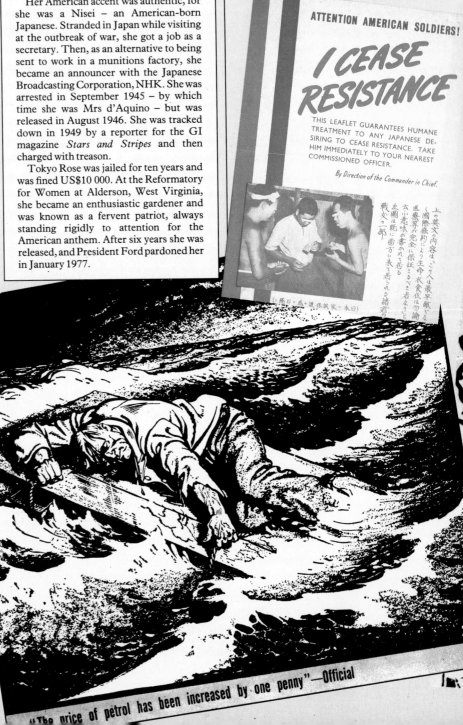

Saturday. June 1. 1940

Daily Mirror

Geraldine House, Fetter-lane, E.C.4. Holborn 4321. 42-48, Hardman-street, Deansgate, Manchester, 3. Blackfriars 2185-6-7-8-9.

BLOODY MARVELLOUS!

FOR days past thousands upon thousands of our brave men of the B.E.F. have been pouring through a port somewhere in England, battle-worn, but, thank God, safe and cheerful in spite of weariness.

We may hope that already at least half of that gallant force has been withdrawn from the trap planned for them by Nazi ruthlessness.

Throughout this operation—always one of the most dangerous and difficult in the art of war—the Navy has toiled night and day, without sleep for scores of naval officers and men. They persist. The work of rescue neve[r] pauses. "The Navy," says one observe[r] "is doing forty-eight hours work every twenty-four hours."

Praise in words is a poor thing for this huge and heroic effort. But praise we must offer for all engaged, and for the brilliant leadership in the field that shows us we have found a great soldier in our hour of need.

Praise, then, for him and for them! "A bloody marvellous show," says a high officer.

How, with such men, can we yield to the great enemy of us all ... doubt! Give men such

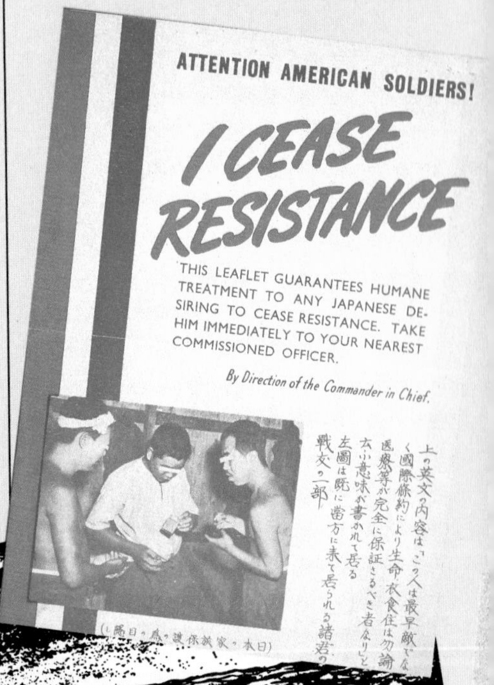

ATTENTION AMERICAN SOLDIERS!
I CEASE RESISTANCE
THIS LEAFLET GUARANTEES HUMANE TREATMENT TO ANY JAPANESE DESIRING TO CEASE RESISTANCE. TAKE HIM IMMEDIATELY TO YOUR NEAREST COMMISSIONED OFFICER.
By Direction of the Commander in Chief.
上の英文の内容は「この人は最早敵でなく國際條約により生命.衣食住は勿論醫療等が完全に保証さるべき者なり」と云ふ意味が書かれて居る
左圖は既に當方に來て居られる諸君の戰友の一部

"The price of petrol has been increased by one penny"—Official

WISHFUL THINKING Forced withdrawal became a kind of victory in the *Mirror*'s leader (above). The paper claimed its cartoon (right) was saying that petrol should be used sparingly because men died to deliver it. It misfired: oil companies thought it criticised them. The USA hoped its leaflets (above right) would persuade Japanese soldiers to surrender – a vain hope, for they believed it was an ineradicable disgrace to give up.

'PLUM' DISGRACED

The biggest mistake ever made by P.G. Wodehouse (1881-1975), 'Plum' to his friends, was to behave like his own silly-ass character Bertie Wooster – and with no Jeeves to save him.

Wodehouse was rounded up at his Le Touquet villa, south of Boulogne, during the collapse of France, and interned at Tost in Upper Silesia. After his release he gave five radio talks about camp life – partly to thank all the neutral American fans who had written urging his release, and partly to demonstrate the cheerful spirit of the British in adversity. Describing life in his 'Upper Silesian loony bin' as 'quite an agreeable experience', Wodehouse said: 'The old dodderers like myself lived the life of Riley.' His tone was flippant, and he clearly saw the camp officials as incurably funny foreigners. But they had long ceased to be so.

The devastating reaction to these talks in Britain was summed up by William Connor, the 'Cassandra' columnist of the *Daily Mirror*, who saw clearly that the broadcasts were a propaganda triumph for the Nazis. 'No doubt Goebbels thinks he's being particularly smooth in using Wodehouse,' said Cassandra on a radio programme. 'But even if he sings with the tongues of angels this clubfoot from hell will fool none of us.'

After the war, Wodehouse settled in the United States and rarely visited Britain. It was not until 1975, when passing time had made the broadcasts seem innocuous, that the New Year Honours List signalled that he was forgiven by the award of a knighthood – two months before his death.

Colonel Britton's broadcasts, for the Germans exacted savage reprisals on civilians.

Often the most effective propaganda was spread by word of mouth. The British rumour factory (run by a section within Special Operations Executive and later called the Political Warfare Executive) planted stories in neutral capitals where they would quickly reach the enemy. One of the most effective, spread in 1940 when Britain expected invasion, was that scientists had found a way to set the sea on fire. The rumour was given impetus when a number of German soldiers, hideously burned in an incendiary raid on Calais, were sent to hospitals near Paris and Berlin.

There were rumours, too, about Hitler's mental stability. Tales of him in a rage, foaming at the mouth and chewing the carpet, made him a figure of fun; such a ridiculous figure could never subjugate the British Empire.

AMERICA CATCHES UP

The United States, which was catapulted into war with its forces, intelligence outfits and propaganda services all unprepared, had by the war's end one of the most effective propaganda operations of all. Milton Eisenhower, brother of the army commander and future president, persuaded the government to set up OWI – the Office of War Information – in June 1942.

OWI was headed by Elmer Davis, a popular radio commentator; and Milton Eisenhower became associate director. The poet Archibald MacLeish and the playwright Robert Sherwood were among its 'idealist' *(continued on p. 211)*

LORD HAW HAW: TREACHERY OVER THE AIRWAVES

The most notorious traitor of them all was Lord Haw Haw, broadcaster of Nazi propaganda in English from Hamburg. The nickname was inspired by *Daily Express* columnist Jonah Barrington, who wrote in September 1939 of a German radio announcer: 'He speaks English of the haw haw, dammit-get-out-of-my-way variety.' Barrington may have heard Wolf Mittler, a German broadcaster with an English mother. More probably he heard Norman Baillie-Stewart (1909-66), who was cashiered from the Seaforth Highlanders and imprisoned in 1933 for selling official secrets to Germany. After his release in 1937 he moved to Austria and applied for German citizenship. He became a radio announcer and was on the air in September 1939.

William Joyce (1906-46), who became Haw Haw, began regular work on German radio in September 1939. The title fitted him well, for he was a man with a sneer in his voice. His call sign 'Jairmany calling, Jairmany calling' introduced his programme of views on the news, to which Britain turned for comic relief in the days of the Phoney War.

Joyce, son of an Irish-born naturalised American, was taken to Ireland when he was three and later moved to England. While studying in London he discovered a taste for right-wing politics and a gift for oratory. He became propaganda chief of Oswald Mosley's British Union of Fascists, and in order to go to the Nuremberg Rally in 1933, he got a British passport. On the application form he falsely gave Galway as his place of birth.

It was a lie that was to hang Joyce, for it refuted his plea at his Old Bailey treason trial in 1945 that he was an American national but a naturalised German since 1940. He did not deny being Lord Haw Haw – a title Baillie-Stewart insisted was his. He too was tried after the war, but not for treason since he was no longer a British citizen. He was jailed for five years.

OFFICIAL VIEWS Soviet citizens got all their – suitably doctored – news of the war from official reports in the papers or broadcasts over public loudspeakers (left). A typical Japanese cartoon (far left) showed the British crushing Asian workers, enslaving their women and selling off the treasures of the East.

THE MOVIES GO TO WAR

'The problems of three little people don't mean a heap of beans in this crazy world. Someday, you'll understand that . . . Here's lookin' at you, kid.' With those words, Humphrey Bogart rounded off Casablanca, *parted from Ingrid Bergman and went off with Claude Rains to join the Free French. Hollywood had gone to war.*

GOING TO THE PICTURES was one of the chief pleasures of the 1930s. The cinema shaped people's dreams, their morals, thoughts, speech and knowledge of the outside world. As war approached, governments were eager to use such an influential form of mass communication to promote national spirit, and movie-makers had a rich source of thrilling and heart-wringing stories, true or fictional.

Hollywood was swift to make plain where its sympathies lay even before America was at war. In the vanguard was the 'March of Time' documentary series of 20-minute films – produced monthly from 1935 – many of which attacked American isolationism. Other issues in the series, such as *Inside Nazi Germany* (1938) and *The Ramparts we Watch* (1940), prepared Americans for the coming conflict.

The film capital was personally alive to the dangers. Many of its moguls and talents were from Europe's oppressed; many indeed were Jews. Warner Brothers' representative in Germany – a Jew named Joe Kaufman – had been kicked to death by Nazi thugs in Berlin in 1937. In Warners' documentary-style thriller, *Confessions of a Nazi Spy* (1939), FBI agent Edward G. Robinson hunted for a spy hiding in the ranks of the pro-Nazi League of German-Americans; many German-Americans were furious. Joel McCrea also battled with German spies in Alfred Hitchcock's first American film, *Foreign Correspondent* (1940). This had a closing line meant for all Americans: 'Don't let the lights go out all over Europe.' In the same year, Mervyn LeRoy's *Escape* publicised the existence of concentration camps.

DELIVERING THE MESSAGE

The film industries of Britain and the Empire were quick to turn their talents to the war effort. Film stock was rationed, since it used nitrocellulose which was needed for explosives, but still many excellent films were made. Alexander Korda's semi-documentary *The Lion Has Wings* (1939), Britain's first war-film effort, tried to convince cinemagoers that the country was prepared for war.

For a time, the British government closed the picture palaces through fear of air raids, but it soon reopened them to dispense morale-boosting entertainment – and propaganda. In every programme the feature film was preceded by shorts about air-raid precautions, National Savings, careless talk, or saving fuel or food, plus the heavily censored newsreel.

Among the documentaries, *Target for Tonight* followed the preparation and execution of a bombing raid, while *Fires Were Started* portrayed 24 hours in a fire station during the London Blitz. *The Way Ahead* followed the story of a platoon of conscripts from call-up to gallant destruction, and *Western Approaches* was an 'I was there' account of the Atlantic convoys.

Across the Atlantic, Canadians at war needed something more than the American product which had long filled Canadian screens. In 1939 the government established a National Film Board directed by British film-maker John Grierson, who produced two fine documentary series, 'Canada Carries On' and 'World in Action'.

War themes spilled over into the fictional films. Britain's *Millions Like Us* focused on a group of women armaments workers, and *San Demetrio, London* was based upon a true incident (p. 65) in which merchant seamen sailed their stricken tanker back to Britain. *In Which We Serve* was based on the exploits of Lord Mountbatten's HMS *Kelly*.

Charles Chauvel, doyen of Australian film-makers, produced several major features, notably *Forty Thousand Horsemen* and *The Rats of Tobruk*. Both celebrated the fighting qualities of the Australian 'Digger'.

Hollywood's most acclaimed war fiction was the Academy Award winning *Mrs Miniver* (1942), the Hollywood portrayal of an 'everyday' British family – headed by Greer Garson and Walter Pidgeon. Mrs Miniver

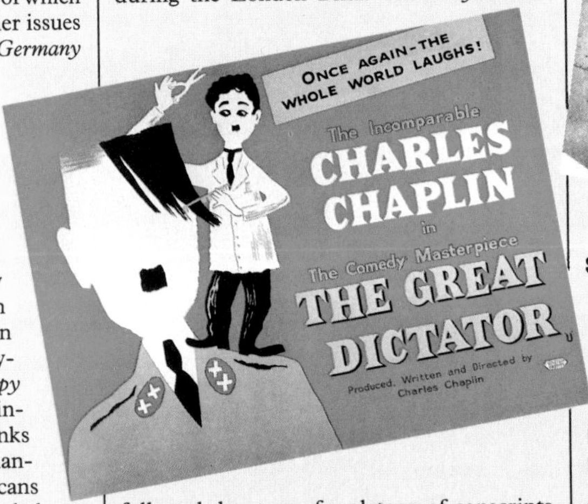

STARS' WARS Screen image and reality merged as idols joined the war effort. Clark Gable served in the USAAF with the bold ease that charmed film fans and fed their fantasies. Chaplin's familiar tramp easily translated into the humble Jewish barber in *The Great Dictator*. As the double of the tyrant Adenoid Hynkel – a parody of Hitler – the barber is mistaken for him at a rally and speaks against all oppressors.

HEROES ALL Wartime films presented picturegoers with models of how to behave under stress. Typical were the bittersweet romance of *Casablanca* and Britain's drama-documentary *In Which We Serve* (left), both made in 1942. The destroyer captain (played by Noël Coward) and his crew epitomise quiet courage and dogged recognition of duty as they see action and are sunk in the Mediterranean. Even the hard-boiled Casablanca bar-owner (played by Humphrey Bogart) sacrifices his hope of happiness to save the Resistance leader whose wife he loves.

JUD SÜSS
FERDINAND MARIAN · KRISTINA SÖDERBAUM
HEINRICH GEORGE · WERNER KRAUSS
EUGEN KLÖPFER · ALBERT FLORATH · MALTE
JAEGER · THEODOR LOOS · HILDE VON STOLZ
ELSE ELSTER · WALTER WERNER · JACOB TIEDTKE

PROMOTING NAZISM Leni Riefenstahl's *Triumph of the Will* (left), official record of the 1934 Nuremberg rally, created a hypnotic sense of order and purpose with its marching ranks and rapt spectators. *Jew Süss* showed tax collector Süss Oppenheimer taking over Württemberg before the people hang him and drive out all Jews.

epitomised calmly and graciously doing one's bit – sending her husband off to Dunkirk in his cabin cruiser and capturing a German airman single-handed. Winston Churchill thought the film's value to the war effort 'exceeded that of a flotilla of battleships'.

Apart from portraying Britain at war, Hollywood made a few warlike films set in the USA – such as *Dive Bomber*, in which Errol Flynn tested new aeroplanes.

Another group of films that often used the war as a background were comedies. In Britain the films of Will Hay (*The Goose Steps Out*), the Crazy Gang (*Gasbags*), Tommy Trinder (*Sailors Three*), George Formby (*Get Cracking*), and Arthur Askey and Richard Murdoch (*The Ghost Train*) helped to lighten the dark years. Hollywood, too, extracted much humour from the situation, as in Bob Hope's *Caught in the Draft* and Abbot and Costello's first starring movie, *Buck Privates*.

After Pearl Harbor, service life no longer seemed so amusing to Americans. Studios vied to reflect the new war. The results were *Wake Island*, *Bataan* and *Guadalcanal Diary* – tales of US bravery against overwhelming Japanese hordes. Among the best war films were the realistic *Story of GI Joe*, based on the dispatches of war correspondent Ernie Pyle, and *The Best Years of Our Lives*, which looked at the problems of returning veterans.

In those days, everyone went to war: Donald Duck in *Der Führer's Face*, Lassie in *Son of Lassie*, Tarzan in *Tarzan Triumphs* and even Sherlock Holmes fought the Germans. Outside the USA, rage greeted tales of

American success (by Humphrey Bogart) against the Afrika Korps in *Sahara* and Errol Flynn winning the war in *Objective Burma* – exciting films but ignoring the fact that British and Empire troops were the heroes.

President Roosevelt encouraged Hollywood to instruct the nation on the conduct of the war, courage of the fighting services, view of the enemy (basically OK but with nasty leaders), the Allies (partners rather than dependants), greater output from the Home Front (women should work and be faithful).

Not all films of the period were about the war. Servicemen and women on leave, tired factory workers, and families anxious about loved ones serving overseas wanted escapist relief. Many memorable film comedies come from the early 1940s – *Arsenic and Old Lace*, a number of the Crosby-Hope-Lamour 'Road' films – as well as battalions of musicals. Some, like *Yankee Doodle Dandy*, touched lightly on the war, but plenty did not. There was *Rhapsody in Blue*, for example, such Betty Grable vehicles as *Springtime in the Rockies* and Judy Garland in *Meet Me in St Louis*.

Off screen, the stars and studios made other contributions to the war effort. Many actors enlisted. The Walt Disney Studios made animated training films and designed symbols and badges for fighting units, ships and aircraft. They also made *Victory through Air Power* (1943), a brilliant history of aviation and study of its supremacy in war.

At official request, Veronica Lake sliced off her tresses to encourage factory girls to part with their own locks (which could be lethal near machinery). Bette Davis and John Garfield founded Hollywood Canteen, where servicemen could dance with their idols. Out of it grew the United Services Organisation, or USO, which sent stars to entertain the troops.

CAMERAS AT THE FRONT

Almost everywhere that Australian fighting men went, there also went the news cameraman Damien Parer – to Palestine, the Western Desert, Tobruk, Greece, New Guinea. His *Kokoda Front Line* was a brilliant portrayal of the miseries and fears of the Kokoda Trail (p. 168). In New Guinea, too, he filmed *Attack on Salamaua*, complete with footage of air strikes, ambushes, supply columns, the wounded – all seen with sympathy and admiration for the men involved. Later he went with the US marines on their island-hopping battles in the Pacific. He was killed in action on Peleliu island in 1944.

A number of Hollywood's top directors took their trade to distant battlefields, where they made documentaries and training films for the services. With the US Navy in the Pacific, John Ford made *Battle of Midway*. Frank Capra abandoned comedies to make the 'Why We Fight' series, including *Battle of Britain* and *Battle of Russia*.

John Huston's documentaries were among the most thoughtful of the period. His *Battle for San Pietro*, made during the Italian campaign, highlighted the magnificence and futility of war – and ran into trouble with the military, who thought it too anti-war. Another Huston film, *Let There Be Light*, showed shell-shocked soldiers undergoing psychiatric treatment, and it too was deemed unsuitable for public showing at the time.

ON FOREIGN SCREENS

The European dictatorships were even swifter to see the cinema's potential as a mass persuader. In Germany, Leni Riefenstahl's *Triumph of the Will* was followed by *Olympiad* (1936) which celebrated 'Aryan' strength-through-joy values.

Fictional films too helped to get the party's policies across – for example, by hitting at Jews in *The Rothschilds, The Wandering Jew* and the 1940 remake of *Jew Süss*. Other targets were the communists and the British.

Stukas typified German war features – monotonous displays of firepower. Japan's war films were on similar lines – *Suicide Troops of the Watchtower* and *General Kato's Falcon Fighters* were typical products.

Fine Russian wartime documentaries – *The Defeat of the German Armies Outside Moscow, The Siege of Leningrad*, and *Stalingrad* – were made by cameramen working at the front. Soviet feature films tended to indict German atrocities or extol working and dying for Russia. Hardest worked of Russian actors were Stalin's doubles, who appeared urging on Bolsheviks in *Unforgettable Year, 1919* or inspiring generals in *The Great Turning Point*.

As the oldest Fascist nation, Italy practically invented the grand parade documentary. Mussolini fostered the Italian film industry, but censored it so heavily that little more than frothy comedies got through. He was deposed before Roberto Rossellini made the powerful *Rome, Open City* and *Paisa*.

When France was invaded, many top French directors and stars were working in Hollywood. Nevertheless, the French film industry continued to thrive and made more than 300 features during the occupation, most of them escapist. A few subtly gave the message that French hearts and France itself could not be destroyed. The Continental Film Company, financed by the German propaganda ministry, made many films in France. The head of the ministry, Josef Goebbels, knew the persuasive power of film.

Indeed, many of the films made during the war – whether archives of heroism and horror at the front, idealised stories to inspire nations, or incidental glimpses of what life was like then – still have power to move, appal, delight and, perhaps, persuade.

ENEMY FANTASIES **Noisy battles with wooden stereotype heroes and interchangeable plots came from Japan's wartime cinema. *Story of Tank Commander Nishizumi* (left) was typical. Only the blandest of films reached the screen in Mussolini's Italy. Roberto Rossellini's *Man of the Cross* (below) sent an Italian priest to the Russian front. German films often derided the British: in *Uncle Kruger* (right) a drunken Queen Victoria entertains the Boer leader.**

staff, concerned not just with victory, but with the kind of world current policies were moulding, while Eisenhower was strictly practical, telling Davis: 'I must insist that our job is to promote an understanding of policy, not to make policy.'

They were all concerned to present America to the world with a strong positive emphasis. Typical was a booklet called *Small Town, USA*, based on the folk of Alexandria, Indiana. It simply described how the hard-working, decent population of 4081 went about their daily business. As Sherwood said: 'The truth, coming from America, with unmistakable American sincerity, is by far the most effective form of propaganda.' Getting at the truth was far from easy, however. Although the first Amendment to the US Constitution guarantees freedom of the Press, the forces were at first niggardly with information. Only accredited reporters were allowed in war zones, and to be accredited they had to agree to submit copy to the censors.

General Douglas MacArthur was one war leader with a keen idea of the value of keeping the public informed. He was a past master at projecting an image, and made sure that the photographers were there to take his picture at key moments, such as his return to the Philippines in 1944. General Dwight D. Eisenhower, too, set tremendous store by properly organised public relations.

At times the US Press censored itself. When Lt General George Patton slapped a shell-shocked soldier in hospital in Sicily and called him a 'yellow bastard', the war reporters who knew of the incident agreed not to report it. They were reluctant to knock a hero off his pedestal, and it was three months before the story broke.

In the Pacific theatre, American propaganda scored some notable successes. For Japanese soldiers, the supreme dishonour was to be taken prisoner. It took psychological understanding of a high order to persuade them to surrender – yet on Okinawa some 10 000 did so. The Americans avoided the shameful word 'surrender' and instead appealed to the Japanese sense of duty – the duty to live and help to rebuild their country.

As the Americans began preparing for the assault on mainland Japan, B-29 bombers dropped 90 million leaflets over Japan, and a spate of broadcasts reinforced their message that unconditional surrender did not mean dishonourable enslavement for the people of Japan. It meant simply that Japan's armed forces had to choose between 'a wasteful, unclean death' and peace with honour.

Whether the campaign was convincing is not known, for choice was overtaken a few days later by Emperor Hirohito's announcement, after the atomic bombs were dropped on Hiroshima and Nagasaki, that the war was over.

STALIN'S U-TURN

Inside the USSR, censorship was total. The majority of private radios had to be handed over to the military. People got their news about the war from official sources, among them loudspeakers in public places. Promoting the right attitudes was a simple matter of official communiqués and ruthless actions. Public opinion was inseparable from the leader's opinion – and swerved radically to keep step with it.

As long as the Nazi-Soviet pact held, Stalin defended Germany's motives. Just a week before the German invasion of the USSR, he issued a communiqué through the news agency Tass, saying: 'Rumours about Germany's intention to break the pact and to attack the USSR are devoid of all foundation.' Once the Soviet forces were reeling under the German onslaught, Stalin diverted criticism by finding a scapegoat. He declared General Dmitri Pavlov, Commander of the Soviet West Front (Army Group), guilty of treason and had him shot, along with several other high-ranking officers.

Stalin then set about building his own legend as a supreme strategist. Even as the Red Army fell back and back, his scorched-earth tactics thwarted the Germans militarily and boosted the Russians psychologically by refusing to give anything away to the enemy. In one of the biggest propaganda U-turns of the war, Stalin dropped the orthodox Marxist-Leninist view of war as a class struggle and revived the old concept of Mother Russia. Atheist though he was, he even appealed for sacrifices to defend the soil of 'Holy Russia' as German troops reached the very suburbs of Moscow.

SUNSET FOR JAPAN

On the day Japan attacked the American fleet at Pearl Harbor, a politely worded message was broadcast to the Japanese nation: 'All the people of Japan, please gather around the radio. We expect you to wholeheartedly trust the government's announcements over the radio, because the government will take all the responsibility and will give you the complete truth.' The politeness, the authoritarian attitude and the diminishing of individuality were deeply ingrained. Japan had the strictest censorship among the World War II combatants. An Information Committee set up in 1936 banned just about any news that could embarrass the government, impair the Emperor's dignity, disturb public order, or impugn the honour of the government or forces.

The first few months of the war gave the news agency Domei and the Japanese Broadcasting Corporation NHK a string of dazzling victories to announce. NHK's victory announcements were heralded by a specially written march. It was easy then to substantiate one of the main themes of Japanese propaganda – that its armies were liberators, ending the domination of the white races in Asia. When the Japanese entered Manila, the locals said 'The angels have come' – according to NHK. The troops were establishing a 'co-prosperity sphere' in 'Greater East Asia'.

The inhuman treatment of prisoners of war which so shocked the world was converted by Imperial Headquarters into reports that: 'More than 200 000 war prisoners are being accorded the best possible treatment by virtue of *bushido* generosity.' Atrocities were unmentionable – and so was defeat. The strategic defeat in the Battle of the Coral Sea was hailed by the Japanese as 'a signal victory . . . America is reduced to a fourth class naval power'.

The final task of Japanese wartime propaganda was to persuade a nation which had never been conquered to accept the unthinkable. The danger of fanatical last stands was averted by the same ingrained obedience that had sustained the war effort. Studiously avoiding such inflammatory words as 'defeat' and 'surrender', Emperor Hirohito declared the decision over the radio with exquisite tact: '. . . the war situation has not necessarily improved and the general trends of the world are not to Japan's advantage.' The war that had begun with a polite radio announcement ended with an equally polite circumlocution.

THEY SAW IT HAPPEN

War correspondents on both sides had a double task: to report the truth and to keep up morale. The two were not always compatible.

On the Allied side, there were many newsmen – Chester Wilmot, Quentin Reynolds, Wynford Vaughan-Thomas, William L. Shirer, Ben Robertson, William L. White, and others – whose reports brilliantly combined telling the facts with fostering national spirit. Reporters such as Ed Murrow and Richard Dimbleby on the radio and Ernie Pyle in the newspapers brought the sights, sounds and very feel of war into millions of homes.

Murrow was head of Columbia Broadcasting System (CBS) in Europe. When he reported from London on the Blitz, the tension in his deep, gravelly voice could be heard through his matter-of-fact, monotone delivery. Murrow's honesty was renowned. Of Dunkirk he said: 'There is a tendency . . . to call the withdrawal a victory and there will be disagreement on that point.' On a bombing raid over Berlin he said: 'Men die in the sky while others are roasted alive in their cellars.' Murrow's zeal for truth led him in the 1950s to speak out boldly against the Communist-obsessed witch hunt of Senator Joseph McCarthy.

Dimbleby, the BBC's first war correspondent, had an equal gift for painting memorably sharp pictures. Going ashore with the infantry on D-Day, he reported seeing: 'Three German soldiers running like mad across the main road to fling themselves into cover. And, near the battle area – much nearer the battle area than they – a solitary peasant harrowing his field, up and down behind the horses, looking nowhere but before him.'

When the Allies uncovered the horrors of the concentration camps, Dimbleby described the scene with humanity and dignity. Of Belsen he said: 'Some of the poor starved creatures whose bodies were there looked so utterly unreal and inhuman that I could have imagined that they had never lived at all. They were like polished skeletons.' Dimbleby after the war became the presenter of BBC television's *Panorama* and commentator on state occasions. He died, as did Murrow, in 1965.

There was no postwar career for Ernie Pyle, whose wartime reports were syndicated in some 300 newspapers in the United States. Pyle was the GI's friend, recording every detail of the infantryman's slog through North Africa, Sicily, Italy, France and the Pacific. 'I love the infantry because they are the underdogs,' he wrote. 'They are the mud-rain-frost-and-wind boys . . . in the end they are the guys that wars can't be won without.' The infantry loved him in return. Different units clamoured for him to be assigned to them. Pyle, who won a Pulitzer prize for his coverage of the war, fell victim to a Japanese sniper on the tiny island of Ie Jima, off Okinawa, in April 1945.

The undercover war of spies and spytraps

Spying has been called 'the second oldest profession', for in both war and peace nations have sought each other's secrets. Britain had a vast spy network, but in November 1939 a disastrous blunder left it shattered and discredited.

THE BAIT was as tempting as could be imagined for British Intelligence chiefs – a meeting with a German general plotting a coup against Hitler. The war was only two months old, but if the coup were to succeed there would be immediate peace talks. The rendezvous was to be at 4 pm at the Café Backus, only a few steps from the customs post on the border between the neutral Netherlands and Germany, near the town of Venlo. Two British agents, Major Richard Stevens and Captain Sigismund Payne Best, drove there from The Hague with Lieutenant Dirk Klop, a Dutch Army intelligence officer.

As they arrived and their German contact, a Captain Schaemmel, signalled to them from the café verandah, another car screeched to a halt in front of theirs. Men standing on its running boards fired submachine guns. Klop was gunned down and died later that day. The two Britons were bundled handcuffed into the car, which roared over the border into Germany.

'Schaemmel' was in fact an SS major, Walter Schellenberg, who had duped Stevens and Best with stories of an anti-Nazi plot, hoping to learn the names of Germans involved in a real plot against Hitler. Unfortunately for the two agents, on November 8, 1939 – the eve of the Venlo meeting – Hitler had narrowly escaped death when he left a Munich beer hall only minutes before a bomb went off, killing seven Nazis and injuring 63 more. In a great rage, he blamed the British secret services and Schellenberg was ordered to abduct Stevens and Best.

The two were kept apart and subjected to rigorous questioning – though never tortured. They revealed a mass of detailed information, which included the identities of fellow agents and the structure of Britain's Secret Intelligence Service (SIS). Repatriated and debriefed after the war, both admitted having been quite open with their captors, but no action against them was taken. Stevens died in 1965, Best in 1978.

The Venlo Incident, as it came to be called, generated rumours that Britain was trying to negotiate a separate peace behind French backs – which created an atmosphere in which contact with German anti-Nazis became taboo, denying help to men genuinely plotting against Hitler. It also hardened suspicions long held in the British armed forces that SIS was manned by bungling incompetents.

To be fair, the head of SIS, Colonel Stewart Menzies, had smelt a rat when reports of the German general's supposed defection reached his desk. Nothing in the story tied in with other approaches by anti-Nazi groups which had reached Menzies through the Vatican. Stevens and Best were warned not to agree to a meeting near the German border, but did so anyway.

Menzies had just become 'C' – official code name for the chief of SIS. He had been deputy to Admiral Sir Hugh Sinclair, who headed the service for 14 years until he died just five days before the Venlo disaster. The new 'C' inherited a shambles. When Hitler marched into Austria in 1938 the SIS chief in Vienna was quickly arrested. The German occupation of Czechoslovakia destroyed a network based in Prague. Many agents elsewhere – such as Stevens and Best – were known to German Security.

Most of these networks were based in British embassies, where the agents were ostensibly chief passport officers – often retired naval officers glad of a tax-free income abroad. Few were skilled spies. They had little access to worthwhile information and they were easily identified by an enemy – who could identify 'our man' simply by going to an embassy and asking for a visa.

MI5, MI6 AND 'Z'

The British intelligence service was formally established in July 1909 to discover what potential enemies were up to, so robbing them of a potent weapon: surprise. A second role was to provide the armed forces with that same weapon by duping enemies about British intentions. There were separate home and foreign sections. MI5 – standing for Military Intelligence Department 5, but officially called the Security Service – covered Britain and its empire. MI6, officially SIS, covered everywhere else – though apart from stations in New York, Istanbul and Buenos Aires, its activities were in fact confined to Europe.

In 1936, Sinclair set up a third force under a former MI5 agent, Lt Colonel Claude Dansey, code-named 'Z'. Its agents, spread through Europe, worked for wine shippers, art dealers, tourist companies and similar commercial organisations with widespread connections – even a film company was involved. At The Hague, for example, Best – a monocled, flamboyant businessman given to wearing conspicuous 'spats' – was one of Dansey's Z-men; Stevens, passport officer at the British legation, was SIS head of station. Stevens did not know that Best was an agent until Best was instructed to report to him on September 4, 1939 – the day after Britain declared war and the two networks were merged, to prevent duplication of effort.

As a result of the Venlo affair the 'Z' network – and the Hague station – had to be closed down. With Hitler's occupation of most of Europe, SIS networks had to be shut down until the service had virtually no agents left on the Continent.

SURVIVING SOURCES

Britain was, however, left with other intelligence gatherers, a number of them operating outside the main networks. For example, some senior embassy staff in neutral countries had long-established contacts with influential locals, and diplomatic dinner parties encouraged indiscretions among guests. The armed forces also had their own agents. Military attachés reported back to Military Intelligence titbits picked up from political meetings and organisations, other attachés, social contacts and local newspapers. The Naval Intelligence Division, under Rear Admiral John Godfrey, had officers reporting from Royal Navy bases abroad, and had observers on most naval and merchant ships in 'areas of interest'. The RAF had its Air Intelligence Branch (AIB), led by Wing Commander Fred Winterbotham. He introduced special high-flying Spitfire and later Mosquito photographic planes which provided accurate knowledge of enemy ground and sea movements.

Prisoners of war were another intelligence source. Offers of better treatment – and listening devices or informers planted in shared cells – produced information on enemy strength, locations and movements. Such ploys were not always needed; German naval officers captured during the fall of France and aircrew brought down in the Battle of Britain, for example, arrogantly blurted out many details of technology that they believed would destroy Britain's defences.

In neutral and even occupied countries, refugees, informers and pro-Allied sympathisers were keen to pass on secrets – but SIS always suspected volunteered information. One gem that it viewed as a plant was the Oslo Report, ten pages of technical details on a range of German projects including pilotless aircraft, radar and a new bomb fuse. The report – with a bomb fuse – arrived at the British legation in Oslo on November 3, 1939, with a note signed 'a well-wishing German scientist'. It was passed on to London. Dr R.V. Jones of Air Intelligence read the data, had the fuse tested and decided that the information was genuine. SIS chiefs discounted it, but later events – including the V-1 flying bombs and the German guidance beams used during the Blitz – proved it to have been authentic.

Some information continued to come from remnants of the prewar networks. For example,

A MAN CALLED 'C'

Stewart Menzies (1890-1968), wartime head of SIS, was from a rich Scottish whisky family. He was no scholar, but at Eton he was Master of Beagles and president of Pop, the elite club and debating society. He won the DSO and MC with the Life Guards in World War I and was badly gassed. Posted to General Headquarters to recover, he was put into Intelligence, where his flair led him into SIS. His tough, rather aloof, objective approach to the work surprised those familiar with his affluent lifestyle.

He became head of the military section and, after a year deputising for his gravely ill chief Admiral Sir Hugh Sinclair, succeeded him as 'C' – head of SIS – in November 1939. He rebuilt the demoralised service after the Venlo Incident, promoted the role of the code and cipher-breakers at Bletchley Park, and ended the war a major general with a knighthood and a US Legion of Merit. He retired in 1951 to Wiltshire, and was over 70 when a hunting fall started a decline in his robust health.

TWO STAR GENERALS

The greatest performance actor Clifton James (1897-1987) ever gave was as General Montgomery, in May 1944, when he was a lieutenant in the Army Pay Corps. He flew in Churchill's aircraft to a reception in Gibraltar, and after a showy farewell flew on to tour North Africa. At each stop he called the troops around him in true Monty style and signed his 'autograph', perfected after much practice.

Monty lookalike James was recruited by British Intelligence after the *News Chronicle* pictured him doing a stage impersonation of the general at London's Comedy Theatre. Further coached in Monty's brusque speaking style, his salute, walk and quirks of dress, James became part of an elaborate web of deception woven to cloak the imminent Allied invasion of Europe. If Britain's battlefield leader was seen in North Africa, the Germans would surely not suspect he was actually preparing for the Normandy landings.

the Stockholm legation kept up a flow of reports on German shipping in the Baltic and along the Norwegian coast. Once France had fallen, Lisbon was the last fully operational SIS station in Europe. The head of station from spring 1941, Commander Philip Johns, trained informants among the local British colony and among Portuguese business families who had trading connections with Britain. He also collected reports from the innumerable refugees who found sanctuary in Portugal. Johns and his successor, Cecil Gledhill, compiled files on 1900 known German agents and 350 more suspects.

Prime sources of information for SIS were spy networks left in place by the governments and others in exile in London. The Czechs had an agent in Prague, 'A-54', who sent a wealth of information on German Intelligence, the Wehrmacht and the Luftwaffe. He even gave prior warning of the German invasion of Poland. He was Paul Thümmel, a senior officer in the *Abwehr* (German Military Intelligence), and a disenchanted Nazi. He was eventually caught by the Gestapo and imprisoned for three years before being shot.

The exiled Poles had radio contacts with agents in Poland and still had a network in occupied Paris. The Danes gained accurate information from their homeland, but the Dutch were not so willing to cooperate – apart from the Venlo disaster, they lost other agents through British lapses. The French and Belgians, too, had rival intelligence set-ups jealously guarding their status against one another and against a feared British takeover. For SIS controlled their radio traffic with agents and thus gained a mass of intelligence out of reach of its own efforts.

RESISTANCE LINK-UP

In July 1940, a completely new undercover organisation was set up – Special Operations Executive (SOE). Less defensive than SIS, its task was to undertake unconventional warfare and propaganda projects in occupied Europe. Sabotage was its chief weapon. It used local Resistance workers as well as sending in agents. At its largest it numbered about 13 000.

SIS chiefs did not approve of what they saw as rivals in the field, and insisted on controlling all communications with SOE agents. These men and women, though carefully selected, trained and equipped, faced stiff odds. They often found themselves parachuting into groups of waiting Germans, and a high proportion were captured. Perhaps one-quarter or one-third of them were killed – many after torture. Rumour had it that an SIS traitor – perhaps Dansey – betrayed them.

THE 'SNOW' MEN

MI5 had much success in its counterespionage role. It had networks in all the countries for which it was responsible, and though Canada and India virtually ran their own security services, MI5 officers liaised closely with them. In Britain MI5 had before the war compiled lists of foreign residents and foreign-born people who had taken British nationality. When the war started, 10 000 Germans and Austrians were interned, and thousands more were rounded up the following year. Many German spies were among them.

The flood of refugees into Britain from occupied countries between September 1939 and June 1940 overstretched MI5's capacity to filter out and track possible agents, but once Britain was isolated, the few who came were easily screened. Clandestine landings by boat or parachute were watched for by an army of observers recruited to do their bit for the war effort.

MI5 had the services of 'Snow' – supposedly the Germans' top spy in Britain. He was Arthur Owens, an electrical engineer born in Wales, brought up in Canada, and a frequent prewar business traveller to Germany, where he posed as an ardent Welsh Nationalist. He offered to serve the Abwehr in 1937, then contacted the British authorities. The day after Britain declared war, Owens was rounded up among Nazi sympathisers and put in Wandsworth Prison. But MI5 installed a radio for him and he transmitted to Germany information supplied by MI5. Later he was sent to meetings he arranged in Holland and Hamburg, where he handed over vetted plans of British equipment, factories and bases.

Back in Britain, Owens began collecting a network of German agents – who were actually double agents controlled by MI5. He also found safe houses and forgers who could prepare false papers for incoming spies – also under MI5 control – so MI5 knew where and when to watch for them. Often there was a secret dash to reach newly landed agents before the local police got to them, to avoid any publicity. First to arrive were Wulf Schmidt and Jorgen Björnson, a Danish Nazi. They parachuted in near Salisbury in September 1940. Björnson hurt his ankle and was picked up; Schmidt was interrogated and 'turned' by MI5. He became agent 'Tate', sending misinformation to Germany throughout the war – services for which he won the Iron Cross!

As other double agents joined the network, the Twenty Committee (written in Roman numerals, XX, to imply the double-cross nature of the work) was set up under Major John Masterman – later Professor Sir John – to concoct a mixture of false and genuine information for the Germans. About 120 German agents were turned by MI5, though not all were used.

However, problems arose when Germany instructed these double agents to commit acts of sabotage. To preserve credibility, some had to be carried out convincingly. 'Zigzag', for example – a known safe-blower named Eddie Chapman – was told to sabotage the de Havilland aircraft factory at Hatfield. On January 29, 1943, he blew up a carefully chosen part of the factory – which German planes were allowed to photograph.

INCREDIBLE 'LUCY'

Every day in his Lucerne flat, Rudolf Rössler (1897-1958) tuned in a radio transmitter/receiver given to him in 1939 by two friends he had made when serving in the German Army in World War I. Strong liberal views cemented the friendship between them and eight others, and they all remained close during the 1920s and 30s. Rössler edited an Augsburg newspaper, then a Berlin magazine, until his anti-Nazi publications made it wiser for him to leave for Switzerland in 1933.

By 1939, his friends – anti-Nazi career officers – held high rank in the Luftwaffe and Wehrmacht. They sent a stream of information to Rössler, who at first gave it to Major Hans Hausaman of Swiss Intelligence. But Hausaman did not always pass it on to the Allies – and when he did, they were incredulous. In March 1940, the Danes and Norwegians ignored his warning of Hitler's invasion; in May, the Allies were surrounded in France even though Rössler had told of the plan to bypass the Maginot Line through the Sedan Gap.

In December that year, when Rössler was forewarned of Operation 'Barbarossa', he contacted a Swiss communist friend, Christian Schneider, and soon became linchpin of a Soviet spy ring. Rössler, code-named 'Lucy', gave other reports to another Swiss comrade, Xaver Schnieper, who passed them to Sandor Rado, Russian spymaster in Switzerland. Alexander Foote, an English communist living in Lausanne, became the group's radio operator. Throughout the German campaign against the Soviet Union, 'Lucy' revealed their battle plans, troop strength and positions, enabling the Russians to counter their moves. The Swiss, well aware of his activities, held him in protective custody for five months in 1944, but he was at no risk anyway – the Germans never discovered his identity.

THE GERMAN SIDE

Germany's *Abwehr* (literally, 'Defence') was set up in 1921 for counterespionage. It had departments for each of the armed forces, which also ran their own intelligence sections – as did the Foreign Ministry and the foreign trade section of the Economics Ministry. Later came the Nazi political intelligence organisations – the *Schutzstaffel* (SS, meaning 'Defence Echelon') and *Geheime Staatspolizei* (Gestapo, 'Secret State Police'), as well as the *Sicherheitsdienst* (SD, the Security Service).

When the Germans invaded Poland, Abwehr agents went with the leading troops to seize Polish Intelligence officers and documents. In France the following year, the Abwehr was again with the front-line units. Crates of seized papers and a mass of information went back to Germany from the occupied countries. But, despite the apparent speed and efficiency of the system, the Abwehr was not really effective. Its agents were poorly trained and, as in Britain's SIS, its cells often centred on travel firms, trading companies or scientific or diplomatic missions – all high on any enemy suspect list as spy nests.

Again like the British, the Germans were better at foiling foreign spy networks than at spying. They captured and turned many Allied agents who then fed back false information. But they failed to crack the biggest Allied secret of the war – the codebreaking and deciphering of German signals (see *The 'Ultra' secret war*, p. 216).

All but a few of the Abwehr spies who landed in Britain and Ireland – usually by parachute or submarine – were caught. Many were turned. Luftwaffe Captain Hermann Görtz, for example, was parachuted into Ireland in full uniform, wearing World War I medals, on May 5, 1940. He was briefed to convert anti-British sentiment in neutral Eire into a promise to let the German Army invade England from Ireland. The trouble was, he dropped into *Northern* Ireland. His radio was crushed and his jackboots and breeches distinctive – even after discarding his uniform tunic. He walked 110 km (70 miles) to Eire, going without food because he did not know that his Irish money could be used north of the border. He reached a Dublin safe house utterly exhausted, to find that it belonged to an SIS double agent.

Görtz escaped and stayed free for 19 months, but failed to win any IRA support. Indeed, the IRA was in the habit of trading in alien spies to swell its own funds. In November 1941, Görtz

TRAGEDY OF CANARIS

'Damned brave and damned unlucky' – that was the verdict of Stewart Menzies on his opposite number, Wilhelm Franz Canaris (1887-1945), head of German Military Intelligence. This small, congenial, humorous son of a well-to-do family joined the Kaiser's navy in 1905. His ship *Dresden* was scuttled in the South Atlantic after the Falklands naval battle in World War I, and he was interned in Chile. Disguised first as a Chilean peasant, then a half-English widower, and using his fluent foreign languages, he made his way home. For a time he was an intelligence officer in Madrid, but ended the war in command of a submarine that sank 18 Allied vessels.

On January 1, 1935, Canaris became head of the Abwehr – a mistake for Germany, for despite being a fervent patriot he was by 1936 firmly anti-Nazi. He sheltered dissidents and also encouraged negotiations through the Vatican to ward off war. Numerous Abwehr failures and defections made his position increasingly precarious. Finally, in February 1944, one of his agents, Erich Vermehren, defected to the British in Turkey, taking with him his wife Elisabeth and the Abwehr code book. Canaris was sacked and the Abwehr dismantled.

After the Hitler bomb plot of July that year, Canaris was among the thousands of anti-Nazis arrested by the Gestapo. Naked, with several teeth knocked out and his nose broken by his torturers, he died after hanging for 30 minutes in an iron collar at Flossenburg concentration camp in Bavaria, on April 9, 1945.

FATAL FAILURES

Of the German spies put on trial in Britain during World War II, 16 were sentenced to death. Among them was Josef Jakobs, who parachuted in on January 31, 1941. He broke a leg on landing and lay all night in a field until his shouts and shots were heard. He was the only one of the 16 executed by firing squad – on August 14, 1941, at the Tower of London. The others were hanged at Pentonville or Wandsworth prisons.

First of these were Jose Rudolf Waldberg – a German of French extraction – and Carl Meier, a Dutchman. They arrived in a fishing boat near Dungeness, Kent, on September 3, 1940. Meier tried to buy drinks at the Rising Sun in Lydd at 9.30 am – out of licensing hours. He was told to return later and was arrested when he did. Waldberg was seen next day near the beach where they had left food and a radio. Both were hanged on December 10.

'Vera Erikson', 'Francois de Deeker' and 'Werner Walti' landed in a flying boat off Buckie, in north-east Scotland, on September 30, 1940, and went ashore in a dinghy. The first two walked to Portgordon station. They claimed to be refugees. The stationmaster called the police. 'Deeker' had a pistol, a coding device, a radio – and some German sausage.

'Walti' was arrested at Waverley station, Edinburgh, when he returned for a water-stained case that an alert station worker had noticed. The men were hanged on August 6, 1941. 'Erikson' was interned. Rumour says she worked for British Intelligence, then lived on the Isle of Wight.

SPY CHIEF Admiral Canaris was the anti-Nazi head of Germany's *Abwehr* (Military Intelligence) – but a hard-working one, flying often to see his agents. His dogs were company for nights at HQ as well as on walks.

was arrested and imprisoned. Released after the war, he settled in Ireland but was rounded up in 1947 and handed to the British for repatriation to Germany. Fearing the worst, poor Görtz committed suicide by taking a cyanide capsule.

In Britain, captured German spies who were not turned were tried. Most were imprisoned; 16 were executed (see box, *Fatal failures*).

TRANSATLANTIC VENTURES

Britain was only one area of interest to the Abwehr, a worldwide organisation with sympathisers – the 'Fifth Column' – in many countries. Fifth Columnists were numerous among German expatriates in Latin America. They wore stormtrooper uniform and carried the Nazi flag on ceremonial occasions. Certain totalitarian governments condoned and even encouraged these activities. Axis agents operated radio stations, reported British ship movements and sent their men north into the United States.

In June 1940, President Roosevelt ordered J. Edgar Hoover, director of the Federal Bureau of Investigation (FBI), to deal with non-military intelligence activities in the Western Hemisphere. Hoover had men organised and moving south within a month. Working alongside British agents and local anti-Nazis, they brought off a number of coups. In Brazil, for example, they exposed a German spy ring centred on the Rio de Janeiro radio station CEL, which had sent information to Berlin. In January 1942, Brazil severed relations with the Axis, and its police, acting on FBI information, broke up six spy rings and sent 86 Axis spies to prison. On August 22, Brazil declared war on Germany and Italy.

Hitler expected much support from powerful German immigrant communities and isolationists in the United States, but Pearl Harbor outraged American patriots – including German Americans. Moreover, FBI men had penetrated Nazi support groups such as the German-American 'Bund' (Brotherhood), and rapidly picked up agents who had got in before America entered the war. Many of them were turned.

The Abwehr tried landing teams of saboteurs – most of whom had grown up as German Americans – by submarine. They formed two four-man teams under Edward Kerling and George Dasch (who had returned to Germany in 1939 only days before he was due to become a US citizen). When Dasch's team landed in fog on Long Island in June 1942, a coastguard surprised them on the beach. They bribed him and got away, but he reported seeing them. Dasch was already wavering and a couple of days later he confessed to the FBI. All eight were caught. Dasch and another were jailed, the rest executed.

The catalogue of Abwehr failures came largely from the lack of commitment at the top. Admiral Wilhelm Canaris, its chief executive from 1935, was a patriot but a committed anti-Nazi, who gathered other anti-Nazis as his closest colleagues. Brigadier Hans Oster, his chief of staff, was at the very heart of the *Schwarze Kapelle* ('Black Orchestra'), a group of dissidents who plotted Hitler's downfall. It was the Abwehr that fell first – in 1944, after the latest of many defections. SS boss Heinrich Himmler took charge of all intelligence.

ENTER 'WILD BILL'

The United States had virtually no non-military intelligence service apart from Hoover's special group – though the FBI zealously guarded US internal security. Roosevelt filled the gap in 1942 when he appointed Colonel William ('Wild Bill') J. Donovan to set up the Office of Strategic Services (OSS).

Donovan, a World War I hero and millionaire lawyer, had many international contacts. He had supplied Britain's SIS with astute assessments and forecasts of Italy's role in Ethiopia in the 1930s, and among his contacts was William Stephenson, Britain's intelligence chief in America. Stephenson provided Donovan with the professional know-how to set up OSS, which became an information-gathering and sabotage organisation. The new agency was welcomed and aided by SIS, Menzies hoping to gain some influence over its operations in Europe.

But OSS soon outgrew any foreign help. Its teams swarmed over Europe and North Africa. By the end of the war Allen Dulles, its chief in Switzerland, was running a powerful network which had relations with anti-Hitler Germans and with serving officers hoping to make the best possible deal when the inevitable defeat arrived. OSS was closed after the war, but resurrected during the 'cold war' as the Central Intelligence Agency (CIA). Dulles later became its chief.

THE 'CICERO' AFFAIR

Cornelia Kapp, secretary to Ludwig Moyzisch, Nazi party security chief in Ankara, Turkey, shook the British Intelligence station there on April 6, 1944, with a startling tale: her boss had a spy inside the British embassy. She knew only his code name – 'Cicero'. Kapp wanted to join her lover, an American agent, in the United States, and used her information to 'buy' her entry.

Investigators found that documents had been leaked from the office of Sir Hughe Knatchbull-Hugessen, the Ambassador. Only then was the recent disappearance of Sir Hughe's Albanian valet recognised as the getaway of a spy.

The valet, Elyesa Bazna (below), had stolen Sir Hughe's keys to make copies. Then, while Sir Hughe slept, 'Cicero' would open his safe and dispatch box and photograph the contents. For six months, 'Cicero' supplied the Germans with a priceless stream of information, including records of the Tehran summit conference which planned the invasion of Europe. Luckily the Germans thought the information was a plant. They paid 'Cicero' with forged money. He was jailed for passing counterfeit notes and died in poverty.

Kapp was allowed into the USA, but was interned there for the rest of the war.

REPORTING TO MOSCOW

The Soviet Union started the war with a great asset: worldwide devotees of Communism who rallied to Russia's aid when the Germans invaded. The *Rote Kapelle* ('Red Orchestra') was one such group inside the Reich. Led by Harro Schulze-Boysen, an Air Ministry intelligence officer, and Arvid Harnack, an idealist at the Economics Ministry, it fed intelligence to the Russians until, in 1942, the Gestapo traced one of its transmitters. The Orchestra's members were seized and died hanging from meat hooks.

Richard Sorge, a German communist, was Far East correspondent of the newspaper *Frankfurter Zeitung*. He became press attaché at the German embassy in Tokyo and made many friends in the city. The Ambassador, Lt General Eugen Ott, spoke freely to him about the strength and plans of Germany's Army. For eight years before and during the war, Sorge and his radio operator, Max Clausen, sent a stream of high-grade information to the Soviet Union.

In May and June 1941, he warned of an imminent German invasion. His warnings were ignored – but proved correct. In September, he reported that Japan would not attack the Russians – enabling them to move armies from the east to face the Germans. Sorge ran out of luck later that year, when one of his agents was rounded up in a purge of communists and broken by the Japanese interrogators. Sorge himself was arrested and, after many interrogations, sentenced to death. He was hanged in November 1944.

The Russians did not acknowledge Sorge for many years, but now he is a hero in the Soviet Union. Other Russian agents were acknowledged even later, or never at all. There are claims that Russian agents kept both Allied and Axis spies well supplied with each other's secrets in order to create conflict and so weaken the Western powers in the face of Stalin's plans for postwar expansion. Abwehr sources claimed after the war that their agent Arthur Owens – they never knew he was a double agent – was given high-grade information by a Russian posing as an ex-RAF officer and Welsh dissident, who was known to the Germans as 'Mr Brown'.

Admiral Canaris was suspicious of Brown, who seemed able to travel freely from Britain, and who even agreed to a prompted suggestion from Owens that he should meet Abwehr officers in Hamburg. After questioning, Brown was booked to return to London through Lisbon. Canaris had his agents watching at Lisbon airport. When Brown returned with Owens to London, he reported that the Germans had questioned him and he had told the truth. Owens' life as a spy ended and the ring of agents – perhaps enemy agents – who used him as a contact was finished.

Certainly while Stewart Menzies was being honoured for the rebuilt espionage empire that was the fruit of his efforts, the fruit was already being eaten away by maggots – Kim Philby, Guy Burgess, Anthony Blunt, Donald Maclean and others whose real loyalty was to Moscow.

The 'Ultra' secret war

Away from the heat and din of battle, both sides fought a war of the airwaves, as each strove to decipher the other's secret radio signals. The Allies won hands-down – by an inspired combination of courage, persistence and genius.

THE ATTACHÉ CASE brought by two cross-Channel passengers alighting from the boat train in London was rather bulky, but otherwise unremarkable. Waiting at Victoria Station to meet the visitors from Paris on August 16, 1939, was a man in a dinner jacket, sporting – as a courtesy – the red ribbon of the *Légion d'Honneur*. Greetings were exchanged and the case was handed over. Inside it was an ultra-secret device that would play a crucial part in saving Britain from defeat and in the Allies' final victory.

The travellers were Captain Gustave Bertrand, head of the code and cipher department of French Intelligence, and Commander Wilfred Dunderdale of British Intelligence in Paris, who was acting as diplomatic courier. Welcoming them was Colonel Stewart Menzies, deputy chief of Britain's Secret Intelligence Service (SIS). He now held in his grasp a replica of Germany's top-secret *Schlüsselmaschine E* ('Cipher Machine E'), or 'Enigma', which could produce messages in ciphers so baffling that some of the world's finest brains could not crack them.

The machine was born of an idea patented in 1919 by a Dutchman, Hugo Koch. He never made the machine but a German engineer, Dr Arthur Scherbius, bought the patent, made some improvements, and by 1923 a Berlin company was marketing his cipher machine under the name Enigma as a business device for keeping commercial messages secret. Scherbius demonstrated it at the International Postal Union congress in 1923. Cipher experts of the German Navy bought an Enigma in 1923 and began to develop it for secret military purposes, but commercial models were on sale until at least 1929.

Enigma resembled a cross between a portable typewriter and a small cash register. It had adjustable rotors for enciphering (coding) the letters typed by the operator into an almost infinite variety of different letters, or the reverse – deciphering a coded message produced on a similar machine (see feature, *The ins and outs of Enigma*, p. 219). It ran on batteries and was ideal for the blitzkrieg tactics Germany's military were developing, which called for quick communication between highly mobile forward positions and headquarters that could not be reached by telephone. Only radio could do the job – but radio was open to enemy ears. To keep messages secret, an unbreakable cipher was needed.

Enigma seemed ideal, for it robbed cryptanalysts of their main break-in point to conventional codes – letter frequency. All languages have 'favourite' letters. In a simple cipher of English, for example, the most frequently used letter will represent E, the next most frequent A, and so on. Enigma had no such pattern and produced coded messages with no apparent pattern at all. From 1926 to 1935 it became standard equipment for all Germany's armed services and intelligence departments. Virtually every unit used it, and at least 100 000 were made during the war.

FIRST ON THE TRAIL

Poland and France, alarmed by Germany's increasing militarism, were swift to tackle the baffling new ciphers emerging from that country. The Poles had a first-class cipher bureau – *Biuro Szyfrów* – where the stars of the German section, BS-4, were Marian Rejewski, Jerzy Rózycki and Henryk Zygalski, brilliant mathematicians head-hunted while studying at Poznan University in a German-speaking region. In 1932 they started work on the ciphers, which they correctly deduced as coming from an Enigma machine similar to one they had seen in photographs.

Using purely mathematical analysis of the intercepts, with marathon trial-and-error sessions and flashes of intuition, they worked out the wiring pattern of the machine in 4½ months. Later in 1932, a mass of information given to them by Bertrand confirmed their deductions. Bertrand's source was Hans-Thilo Schmidt, code-named *Asché* (from the German for 'ashes'), who worked in Berlin for the German army cipher department. He handed over photographs of hundreds of documents before he was transferred to other work in 1933. Among them were details of non-machine ciphers, operating instructions for Enigma, tables of Enigma enciphering settings – known as 'keys' – and a plain text message with its Enigma version.

The Poles designed an Enigma copy and over two years they built 15 such machines. The main breakthrough came at the end of 1932. Ironically, they first began regularly to crack German Army signals in mid-January 1933, just two weeks before Hitler came to power. From then until September 1938 they regularly worked out German Enigma keys, but then the Germans modified their machines, making the task much more difficult. To continue, the Poles needed more equipment than they could produce.

At Bertrand's suggestion, Polish, French and British cryptanalysts met in Paris in January 1939, but all hung back from revealing how much they knew. They met again in late July at BS-4's concrete bunkers in a forest near Warsaw. Menzies attended the second meeting – where the British group was thunderstruck at the Poles' achievements. It was agreed that the Poles would concentrate on the mathematical approach, the British on the practical side and the French on non-machine ciphers – which were still widely used. The Poles gave details of the perforated sheets and electro-mechanical scanners ('bombes') they had devised for testing possible keys, and promised to send two Enigma copies to Paris. The attaché case brought to Britain by Bertrand contained one of them.

The agreement came none too soon. The German invasion of Poland two weeks after Bertrand's trip to London forced BS-4 to destroy its work and clear out. Some of the cryptanalysts continued their work in France – even in hiding in Vichy France after the German invasion – until forced to flee again. In 1943, Rejewski and Zygalski reached Britain; Rózycki died on board a ship sunk in the Mediterranean in 1942. Others were captured, interrogated and killed. None ever revealed that Enigma had been cracked.

OVER TO BLETCHLEY

Within days of receiving the Polish gifts and information, Britain's cryptanalysts were at work. Knowing how the Enigma machine worked was not enough – the key had to be discovered. The Enigma key was changed three times a day during the war – and had to be worked out anew each time. And no attempt could be made until at least 60 messages in the same key had been intercepted.

A section of 'Y Service' – the vast wireless interception service – and volunteer radio 'hams' operated the secret network of listening posts that gave the Enigma cryptanalysts their raw material. Successive shifts of service and civilian listeners strained to catch the faint Morse signals on special, sensitive American receivers, and took down tediously meaningless groups of letters with absolute accuracy. The messages went by landline or dispatch rider to Bletchley Park, a country house 80 km (50 miles) north-west of London – the centre from August 1939 of the Government Code and Cypher School (GC&CS), soon to be renamed Government Communications Headquarters (GCHQ).

Commander Alastair Denniston was its head and a civilian, Alfred Dillwyn Knox, was chief of cipher breaking. New versions of the Polish key-scanning 'bombes' were made and operators recruited to set them up to check possible decipherments. Brilliant mathematicians were called in to work out the constantly changing keys being used by the Germans; decipherers came to

ULTRA-SECRET GUARDIAN

As a teenager Frederick Winterbotham (1897-) travelled widely in Europe – becoming fluent in French – then worked as a labourer in Australia and as a lumberjack in Canada. While in the Royal Flying Corps in World War I, he was captured and spent his time perfecting fluent German. After repatriation, he used his back pay studying law at Oxford.

Winterbotham was made head of Air Intelligence Branch in 1929, and built up a network of agents in Germany. But from 1933, Nazism made it increasingly dangerous for them to continue. Winterbotham went to Germany himself, professing to admire Hitler. He made friends with Nazi leaders, picking up valuable information over the years until his purpose was discovered in 1938.

Winterbotham then organised aerial spying. He had an aircraft adapted to pass warm air from the cabin over the lens of a mounted camera. This kept the lens clear of condensation up to 9000 m (30 000 ft), allowing the plane to spy from a safe height. The flights gathered extensive knowledge of Luftwaffe strength. Later, as Chief of the Air Department of SIS, Winterbotham devised and controlled the strict and foolproof distribution system that kept 'Ultra' flowing, by way of the Special Liaison Units, to Allied field commanders.

process messages, translators to turn them into English and a department to evaluate and distribute the information. Eventually about 10 000 people worked at Bletchley Park, in a hotchpotch of hastily built 'huts' furnished with trestle tables and folding chairs. Secrecy was strict. None of Bletchley's workers knew what people outside their own section were up to.

PASSING ON THE SECRETS

Information from deciphered Enigma signals ranged from routine situation reports, requests for supplies and mobilisation orders to complete battle plans – and reports from the field back to Berlin. The British gave this most secret – ultra-secret – information the code name 'Ultra'. The problem that now arose was how to prevent the Germans from realising that their radio traffic was being read. At first 'Ultra' was passed onto Allied commanders as coming from SIS spies – but their standing was so low among the armed forces that their information was distrusted.

Group Captain Fred Winterbotham of Air Intelligence set up a network of Special Liaison Units (SLUs) to pass relevant 'Ultra' to commanders it concerned. Only the three chiefs of staff, the three services' directors of intelligence, and the chiefs of Fighter Command and Home Forces received all 'Ultra' as a matter of course. The most important information also went to Churchill. Commanders in the field got 'Ultra' only when it concerned them, direct from their SLU officer – who then immediately destroyed the signal. Nobody was allowed to mention 'Ultra' or raise any suspicion that it was the reason for decisions or actions; sometimes reconnaissance flights or other ruses were used to provide a credible source for information.

The United States shared fully in 'Ultra' from the start of 1942 and Americans worked at Bletchley Park, but the Russians were never allowed to share in it – though they were sometimes given 'Ultra'-based information. The public did not learn of it until 1974, when Winterbotham was allowed to publish a book.

The Germans never realised that their messages were being read – yet they had a clue. On September 11, 1942, the Royal Navy motor gun boat *MGB 335* was captured with documents and charts detailing German convoy movements and mine-free channels. The information could only have come from deciphered Enigma signals, but the Germans never caught on.

Field commanders each had an SLU. Some wanted them constantly on hand, while others snubbed them. Ironically, the existence of 'Ultra' information sometimes proved disastrous for commanders. Generals Sir Archibald Wavell and Sir Claude Auchinleck were in their time both sacked by Churchill after defeats in North Africa, for not acting forcefully on 'Ultra' material they had been given. Montgomery's acclaimed successes in the desert were based on his sounder evaluation of 'Ultra' information. During the Battle of Britain, many of Air Chief Marshal Sir Hugh Dowding's decisions for Fighter Command, based on 'Ultra', were criticised by less well-informed officers – but he could not defend himself without revealing his source.

In other campaigns, 'Ultra' told the Allies where the German forces were weakest – for example, during the landings in Sicily and Italy. However, the codebreakers' supreme contribution was to 'Overlord' – the Normandy landings – and the subsequent breakout, where time and many lives were saved by Allied foreknowledge of German positions.

One of several notable failures when 'Ultra' was ignored was the airborne landing at Arnhem in 1944, which went ahead despite reports that two panzer divisions were refitting in the area – with tragic results. In February 1942, the German warships *Scharnhorst*, *Gneisenau* and *Prinz Eugen* were allowed to break out of Brest harbour despite 'Ultra' warnings of the German Navy's plans.

SIGNAL FAILURES

In Germany, the High Command, the Foreign Office and the SS had separate and rival codebreaking organisations. They relied on linguists rather than mathematicians, even though the ciphers they tackled were problems of permutation theory rather than linguistic analysis. For Britain also had a cipher machine, called the

SOMETHING FISHY

The highest-grade German communications did not go by Enigma but by *Geheimschreiber* ('Secret Writer'), known to the Allies as 'Fish'. It had ten rotors in two sets of five. One set converted the message into Murray telegraph code – similar to Morse code, but with five-element combinations of 'on' or 'off' switch positions, represented as 1 or 0. The other set of rotors produced its own random string of 1s and 0s. 'Fish' automatically added the two together (two 1s or two 0s gave a 0, one of each gave a 1) and transmitted the result to a receiving machine set to the same key. This reversed the process and turned the string of 100101100110 and the like, into the original message.

To deal with 'Fish', the British designed 'Colossus', a huge primitive electronic computer. Cambridge mathematics professor Max Newman and a Post Office engineer, Dr Thomas Flowers, were its chief begetters, and it started deciphering at Bletchley in December 1943. 'Colossus' scanned the message over and over with a photoelectric reader at 5000 characters a second, automatically subtracting every possible permutation of 1s and 0s to try to recover the Murray code. A cryptanalyst scrutinised the printout until he saw a gradual build-up of recurring letters and letter-groups. This meant the cipher was being solved and had reached the point where the message was readable.

CRUCIAL STEPS Captain Gustave Bertrand and Major Gwido Langer, heads of the French and Polish cipher bureaux, stand on the top step behind some of their joint team at the Château de Vignolles north of Paris, where the Poles fled as their homeland fell. Using wiring plans worked out by Langer's team in 1932, the AVA Radio Manufacturing Company in Warsaw (right) had made 15 copies of Enigma. One copy gave vital aid to Britain's codebreakers.

TypeX – which, ironically, was also based on the early commercial Enigma. Used with tables that enciphered the signals further – and without the Germans' careless procedures – TypeX proved so secure that the Germans gave up trying to read it in 1941. However, they had considerable success in breaking non-machine ciphers.

The Royal Navy, convinced that its own system was sound, stuck for several years to old-fashioned book ciphers that had been broken by the Germans before the war – with disastrous consequences for the convoys. In 1942, the Germans were reading about 2000 convoy signals a month. A tragic situation developed where convoys were ordered to change course to avoid U-boats pinpointed by 'Ultra'. The Germans then deciphered the convoy orders and gave their U-boats new courses. It was November 1943 before the navy adopted a secure cipher machine produced by the US Navy for Allied convoys.

PACIFIC 'MAGIC'

American cryptanalysts achieved a major success in breaking 'Purple', a Japanese machine cipher first used in March 1939. The Japanese made only 25 of the complex electronic 'Type B' machines that produced 'Purple', which was used for passing highest-grade government information between important overseas embassies. Japan's earlier 'Type A' machine, code-named 'Red', was broken by the Americans in 1935 when Colonel William Friedman became head of a new US codebreaking team. After a burglary of the Japanese naval attaché's office in Washington, Friedman produced a copy of the Type A, which was based on an early Enigma model given to Japan by Germany.

Type B was very different. It had no rotors but a plugboard and a huge assortment of electronic stepping switches resembling a telephone exchange. Friedman and his team took almost two years to fathom it, using mathematics, guesswork, intuitive reasoning, and two deciphered messages – the messages breakable because of predictable formal phrases. The effort gave Friedman a nervous breakdown. The Americans built four Type B copies; one was sent to Britain.

Information from 'Red' and 'Purple' – distributed among the Allies under the code name 'Magic' – gave the Americans crucial information before the 1942 Battle of Midway. And it enabled them to intercept and shoot down Admiral Isoroku Yamamoto's aircraft in April 1943.

TRAGIC GENIUS

Alan Turing (1912-54), son of an Indian Civil Service official, was one of the Cambridge mathematics dons recruited into wartime codebreaking. In 1936 he had described a theoretical 'universal computing machine'. Building on the work of Polish mathematicians, Turing played a major role at Bletchley Park in the design of the 'Bronze Goddesses', which worked out Enigma keys.

Unhappily, Turing's struggle to suppress his homosexuality made his personal life a misery – his turmoil was already apparent when he met other cryptanalysts in Paris in 1939. The Pole Marian Rejewski remembered him speaking intensely of the autumn crocuses on the dinner table being a powerful poison. In 1954, Turing poisoned himself with cyanide.

MESSAGE RECEIVED? Signals typed on an Enigma keyboard were enciphered for Morse transmission. It also deciphered received messages. The Germans thought it unbreakable – the number of possible cipher combinations totalled five followed by 103 zeros – and they overlooked (or dismissed as boasting) a telltale 1941 newspaper report (left) the British censor missed.

THE DAILY MIRROR

Friday,

New 'Leave Japan' Warning by U.S.

American citizens yesterday received a third notice urging them to withdraw from Japan "in yours and the best national interests."

The U.S. Consulate distributed copies of the notification following instructions from Washington.

The Consulate-General in Shanghai sent a similar notice to American women, children and non-essential men, urging them to leave.

It was learned reliably that the reiteration of the advice to withdraw was not intended as an indication that Washington foresees a worsening of relations, but that the U.S. Government is desirous of minimising the number of Americans in Japan in order to facilitate diplomatic conversations about their disposition in the event of any rupture.—Associated Press.

SPIES TAP NAZI CODE

BY A SPECIAL CORRESPONDENT

BRITAIN'S radio spies are at work every night. During the day they work in factories, shops and offices. Colleagues wonder why they never go to cinemas or dances.

But questions are parried with a smile—and silence. Their job isn't one to be talked about.

Home from work, a quick meal, and the hush-hush men unlock the door of a room usually at the top of the house. There, until the small hours, they sit, head-phones on ears, taking down the Morse code messages which fill the air.

To the layman these would be just a meaningless jumble of letters.

But in the hands of code experts they might produce a message of vital importance to our Intelligence Service.

No pay is given to the men who tap the air for these messages.

A network of them covers the country.

Their Reward

They are drawn from the radio enthusiasts who operated their own short-wave transmitters before the war.

"We are glad to serve the country in this way," one of them told me.

"A letter of thanks from headquarters telling us that we have been able to supply some useful information is all the reward we ask.

"Naturally we have no idea of the codes used by German or other agents.

"But it is a great thrill to feel you might be getting down a message which, decoded, might prove of supreme importance."

U.S. TO 'FREEZE' FOREIGN FUNDS

PRESIDENT ROOSEVELT intends to issue an order "freezing" all foreign funds in the United States as soon as Congress passes the Lend-and-Lease Bill, according to reliable information received in Washington.

The actual executive orders to make this possible have already been prepared, it is added.

Friendly nations such as Britain, China, Greece and the Latin-American countries would be issued with general licences making it possible for them to withdraw funds from the United States at will.

The control of all these foreign funds may be vested in a new department of the Treasury, which would be manned by experts.—British United Press.

ANOTHER MAN MADE ATTACK

—Says Seaman

A MAN accused of assaulting the wife of an air gunner who is posted as missing was remanded yesterday after his advocate had stated that the defence would be an alibi.

NAME FASCISTS IN KEY JOBS

To eliminate danger to the State in case of invasion, will you send to the heads of departments a list of people in key positions who were in the British Union of Fascists when war began?

The ins and outs of Enigma

A WEHRMACHT Enigma machine had three rotors or drums on a shaft. Each carried an alphabet around the outside. Inside each was electrical wiring that connected the position for each letter on one side to that for a different letter on the other – transposing B to S, say. Each of the rotors made a different set of transpositions. When the operator pressed a key like a typewriter key, electric current flowed through the three rotors in turn, each of which transposed the letter. The signal was then 'reflected' back through the rotors, which transposed it three more times. It was transposed once more at the plugboard – an array of lettered sockets (below the keyboard) with 13 cables available for numerous possible cross-connections. The current finally lit up a lettered porthole on the lampboard.

A second operator noted the letters as they lit up. The message was divided into groups of five letters and transmitted in Morse code. The machine was wired in such a way that it could decode as well as encode: if the sender typed A and R lit up, then A lit up when the receiver typed R.

Each time a key was pressed, the first rotor moved round by one letter. As a result, the letter transposition was quite different. When that rotor reached a certain point, the second rotor moved round a place, so that the transpositions were changed between the second and third rotors. When the first rotor reached the turnover point again, the second clicked round by another place, and so on. When the second rotor had completed its cycle, the third came into play. No fewer than 17 576 letters could be typed before the rotors returned to their original positions – but that was enough to discern a pattern, so long as there were enough messages using the same key.

ADDED COMPLICATIONS

From December 15, 1938, two extra rotors were issued for each machine, giving the operator a choice of three from the five he now had. Instead of six possible orders for putting the rotors on their axle, there were now 60 and the job of the codebreakers was made much more difficult. German Navy Enigma machines used four rotors instead of three – and these were chosen from a total of eight – making the possibilities almost limitless. (The capture in May 1941 of a German Navy Enigma with its full set of rotors from the sinking U-boat *U-110* south of Greenland made it easier for the codebreakers to handle that problem.)

It was not enough to capture a machine in order to decipher the enemy's signals. The 'keys' had to be discovered too: the choice and order of the rotors on the shaft, the position of movable rings on each rotor (which could click to any of 26 positions) and the plugboard connections. This combination of settings applied only to a particular signals network at a particular time, and was called the 'daily' key – although it was changed every eight hours at the height of the war. Daily keys were issued monthly to cipher clerks as printed tables.

With his machine set to the daily key, the operator chose three letters at random (say GLF) and turned the rotors until these letters showed at the small windows over the rotors. Then he transmitted, not in cipher, his call sign and these letters at the beginning of a message. Next he chose three other letters at random (say BMP) as the message key and tapped them twice as the first six enciphered letters of the message – which might come out XOLAVJ. The receiver set his machine to the daily key and with the unciphered key GLF at the rotor windows. He typed the first six letters of the coded message, XOLAVJ. BMPBMP lit up, and he reset the rotors to show BMP at the windows before recovering the rest of the message.

MATHEMATICS AND MIND-READING

The repeating of the message key – a safeguard against mistakes in transmission – was what gave the Polish mathematicians their way into Enigma. They knew from *Asché*'s information that the first and fourth ciphers represented the same letter, the second and fifth both represented another, as did the third and sixth. By analysing the first six ciphers of 60 to 80 messages from the same source on the same day, the Poles made various connections: how often the fourth ciphers of one message matched the first of another, or the first and fourth ciphers of one message were the same, and so on. They worked out cycles and chains of letters from the connections and then used theories of permutation and probability to build equations. Finally, tentative solutions to the equations emerged and these were tried out on the message.

Marian Rejewski permutated every possible rotor position and pinpointed some characteristic patterns. He drew up an index of characteristics, called a cyclometer; messages were checked against it to give the best starting points for decipherment. Then similar information was put on sheets devised by Henryk Zygalski. They looked like graph paper with the alphabet running twice along the top and twice down the side, and represented all possible relative positions of the rotors. Holes were made where characteristic patterns occurred. When enough message keys had been analysed to spot their characteristics, the sheets were laid over one another on a light table and moved in certain ways (over 700) to test and reject possibilities. When the light shone through only one set of perforations, a possible key had been found and was tried on a message.

BOMBES AND GODDESSES

In May 1940, the Germans stopped the repeat and the enciphering of the message key. All the comparisons it had offered ended and electro-mechanical 'bombes' were the only way in. They checked at speed whether certain encipherments were possible – but the mathematicians still had to draw up a 'menu' of likely encipherments, and operators had to set a bombe to test them. It clicked through the possibilities and stopped when it had pinpointed a probable key to try out.

It was late 1940 before British bombes – nicknamed 'Bronze Goddesses' – were ready. From May until then, mathematicians relied on the operators' bad habits in choosing message keys. They might repeat the same letter – AAA, perhaps – or use three consecutive letters of the alphabet, or three that fell next to one another horizontally or diagonally on the keyboard. Guesswork might also hit on the opening phrase or the signature of a message.

SECRETIVE TYPE When one of Enigma's keys was tapped, electric current flowed to light a lamp at a lettered porthole behind the keys. On the way the current was repeatedly routed from one letter to another by passing and returning through three large toothed rotors and by cables below the keys.

PART FOUR

A CRESCENDO of guns ushered in the dramatic Third Act of the war: the guns that blazed at El Alamein and, through the fearsome winter of 1942-3, at Stalingrad.

With these two resounding Allied successes the war reached a turning point. Although the path that lay ahead had many steep and treacherous sections, the Allies knew that it was the path to final victory.

To bring that day nearer, British and American bombers pounded Germany from the air. Brave sailors ran the gauntlet of U-boat packs in the Atlantic. On the Eastern Front, the Red Army trounced the once-invincible panzers at Kursk, the greatest tank battle in history, and went on to give Hitler a harsh lesson in blitzkrieg tactics. The Afrika Korps was driven out of North Africa, Italy was invaded and Mussolini deposed.

Then, in June 1944, Allied troops stormed ashore on the beaches of Normandy. Hitler now faced what he feared most: war on two fronts.

As defeatism spread through the German High Command, a plot to assassinate Hitler came within an ace of success. But the German Army fought on stubbornly. Their attack through the Ardennes, to fight the Battle of the Bulge, was a last desperate gamble.

With its failure, the avengers closed in on a Reich which Hitler had promised would last a thousand years ●

THE TIDE TURNS

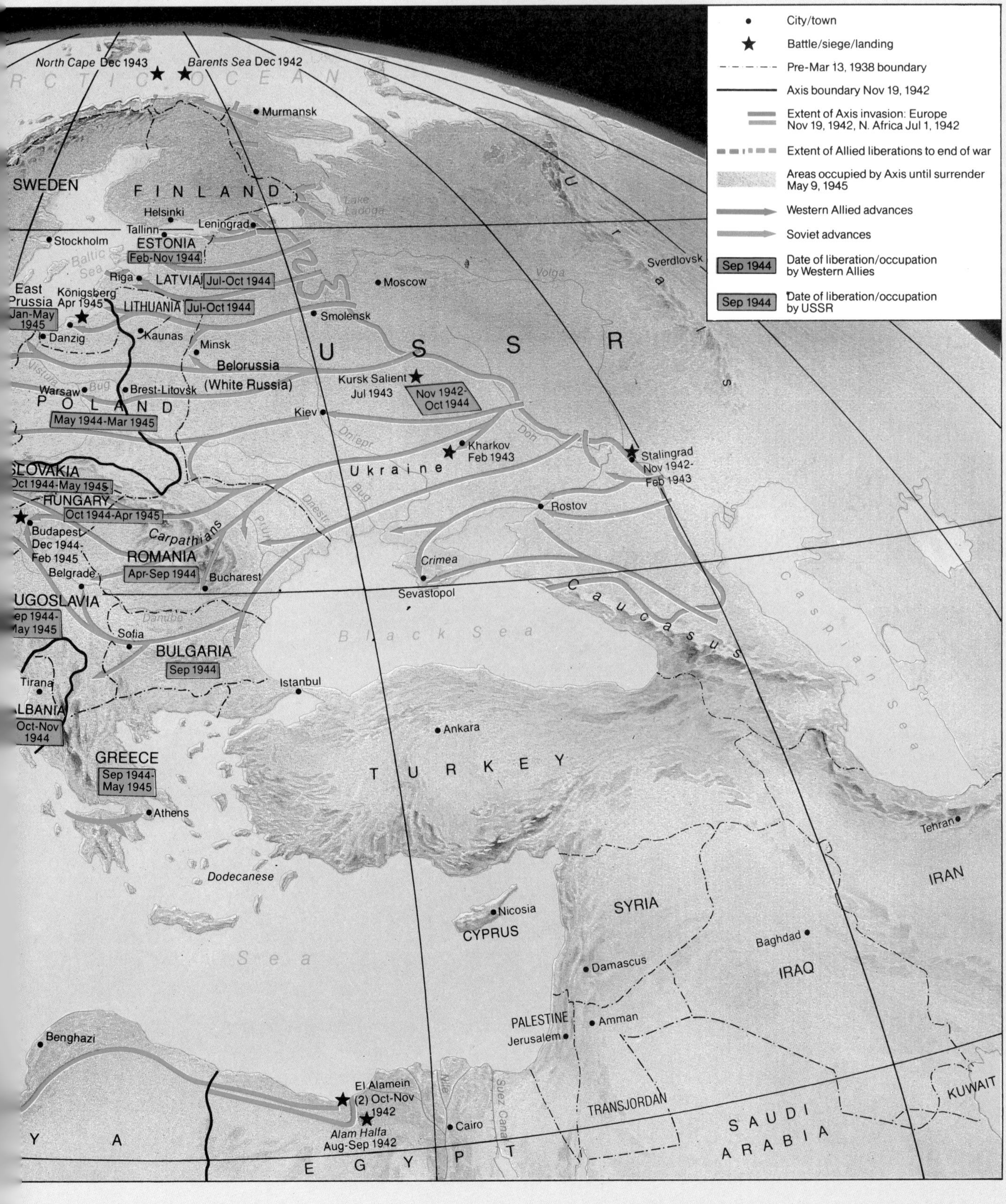
City/town
Battle/siege/landing
Pre-Mar 13, 1938 boundary
Axis boundary Nov 19, 1942
Extent of Axis invasion: Europe Nov 19, 1942, N. Africa Jul 1, 1942
Extent of Allied liberations to end of war
Areas occupied by Axis until surrender May 9, 1945
Western Allied advances
Soviet advances
Sep 1944 Date of liberation/occupation by Western Allies
Sep 1944 Date of liberation/occupation by USSR
North Cape Dec 1943
Barents Sea Dec 1942
Murmansk
SWEDEN
FINLAND
Helsinki
Leningrad
Tallinn
Stockholm
ESTONIA
Feb-Nov 1944
Baltic Sea
Riga
LATVIA Jul-Oct 1944
Moscow
East Prussia Jan-May 1945
Königsberg Apr 1945
LITHUANIA Jul-Oct 1944
Smolensk
Kaunas
Danzig
Minsk
Belorussia (White Russia)
USSR
Kursk Salient Jul 1943
Nov 1942-Oct 1944
Warsaw
Brest-Litovsk
POLAND
May 1944-Mar 1945
Kiev
Kharkov Feb 1943
Stalingrad Nov 1942-Feb 1943
Ukraine
Sverdlovsk
Volga
Urals
SLOVAKIA Oct 1944-May 1945
HUNGARY Oct 1944-Apr 1945
Budapest Dec 1944-Feb 1945
Carpathians
Rostov
ROMANIA Apr-Sep 1944
Belgrade
Bucharest
Crimea
Sevastopol
Caucasus
Caspian Sea
YUGOSLAVIA Sep 1944-May 1945
Sofia
BULGARIA Sep 1944
Black Sea
Istanbul
Tirana
ALBANIA Oct-Nov 1944
Ankara
TURKEY
GREECE Sep 1944-May 1945
Athens
Tehran
Dodecanese
IRAN
Nicosia
CYPRUS
SYRIA
Baghdad
IRAQ
Damascus
PALESTINE
Amman
Jerusalem
Benghazi
El Alamein (2) Oct-Nov 1942
Alam Halfa Aug-Sep 1942
Cairo
TRANSJORDAN
SAUDI ARABIA
KUWAIT
EGYPT

13: OUT OF AFRICA

After all the dashing to and fro, a great British victory sent Rommel running. Then landings in the west cleared the way for Axis troops to be finally driven from the African continent.

Montgomery's first victory

With Tobruk in German hands and Rommel still looking dangerous, Auchinleck was replaced as Middle East chief by Alexander. With him came a new Eighth Army commander – a man who would prove more than a match for the Desert Fox.

NIGHT TURNED INTO DAY as Desert Air Force bombers circled over pinned-down units of the Afrika Korps, dropping a non-stop cascade of flares. Diving low, more bombers released their loads of high explosives onto the plainly visible men and tanks. 'All movement was instantly stopped by the low-flying attacks,' said Field Marshal Erwin Rommel, the Axis commander in North Africa. 'Soon many of our vehicles were alight and burning furiously.'

Casualties were heavy and the air and artillery onslaughts relentless. Both were continued in daylight the next day – August 31, 1942 – when swarms of fighter-bombers screamed down on troops and vehicles mercilessly exposed in the barren scrubland of the assembly areas, and caught in British-laid minefields to the west of Alam Halfa ridge, some 25 km (15 miles) south-east of El Alamein. Flying rock splinters were as lethal as the bombs themselves. Seven of Rommel's key staff officers were killed.

MONTY TAKES THE STAGE

The ridge of Alam Halfa ran east-west for about 12 km (7 miles), and had been deliberately chosen as a killing ground by the British Eighth Army's new commander, Lt General Bernard Montgomery. He thought Rommel would attack from the south-west in an attempted encirclement, and Alam Halfa lay on Rommel's expected route to the sea. 'Monty', as his troops soon nicknamed him, had been on a short list of officers for the job of Eighth Army commander when Prime Minister Winston Churchill flew to Egypt at the beginning of August that year. 'The following issues had to be settled in Cairo,' the premier wrote later. 'Had General Auchinleck or his staff lost the confidence of the Desert Army?'

The short answer was 'yes – they had', and Churchill's main adviser, Sir Alan Brooke, Chief of the Imperial General Staff, felt that Auchinleck, despite his success in blocking the Axis advance at El Alamein in July, lacked the ruthlessness to finish Rommel off. This view was not shared by the enemy. Lt General Fritz Bayerlein, Rommel's chief of staff at the time, wrote: 'If Auchinleck had not been . . . the best Allied general in North Africa . . . Rommel would have finished the Eighth Army off.' Nevertheless, Auchinleck was replaced as Commander in Chief Middle East by General Sir Harold Alexander, a hero of Dunkirk. Command of Eighth Army went to the aggressive Montgomery only after Churchill's first choice, Lt General William 'Strafer' Gott, was killed on August 7, while flying to assume command. His plane was attacked by German fighters and crash-landed. One fighter came in low to strafe survivors – and killed 'Strafer' Gott.

Monty quickly sized up his troops as mainly 'civilians in uniform' and not professional soldiers. Even so, he considered them to be 'truly magnificent material' who had suffered from poor leadership, indiscipline and 'bellyaching'. 'In the Eighth Army, orders had generally been queried by subordinates right down the line,' he wrote later. 'Each thought he knew better than his superiors and often it needed firm action to get things done. I was determined to stop that state of affairs at once. Orders no longer formed "the basis for discussion", but for action.'

His orders from Churchill were typically blunt: 'Destroy the German-Italian Army commanded by Field Marshal Rommel.' Monty was informed by decoded German signals and other intelligence sources that his opponent was about to make a final, all-out attempt to break the British defensive line – which ran south from El Alamein – and capture the port of Alexandria and the Nile Delta, then Cairo and the Suez Canal.

Rommel had received reinforcements – the 164th Infantry Division and four brigades of paratroops under Brigadier Bernhard Ramcke. But three out of every four ships bringing Rommel's supplies were being sunk by the Royal Navy and Malta-based RAF planes, and the Germans were desperately short of ammunition and fuel. Unless the situation changed, or the panzers managed to capture Allied supply dumps, their resources would be spent within days.

Rommel had been guaranteed 6000 tonnes of fuel – 1000 tonnes of which would be immediately air-lifted – by Field Marshal Albert Kesselring, Commander in Chief South, who was his overall commander in the North African campaign. 'The whole battle depends on it', Rommel had told Kesselring on August 27, three days before launching the attack.

Meanwhile, Montgomery deployed the recently arrived 44th Infantry Division at Alam Halfa – 20 km (12 miles) behind his front line –

SMOKE OF BATTLE Men of the Royal Sussex Regiment advance past a burning enemy tank at Alam Halfa. Men like these were described by Montgomery as 'magnificent material' in need of better leadership.

BOMBS AWAY! An RAF Martin Baltimore light bomber sends its load crashing among Axis vehicles in a dispersal area. Fierce air raids and artillery fire wreaked havoc among Rommel's forces in the Alam Halfa battle.

together with 400 tanks in dug-in positions and a screen of 6-pounder anti-tank guns. He vowed there would be no more retreating, but did not mind the enemy penetrating his defences – as long as they were entering a trap. To help get the Germans where he wanted them, Montgomery let them capture a specially prepared map which showed that the going was good south of the ridge – where the sand was actually extremely soft. The map was left in a blown-up scout car near the German lines.

Montgomery knew what to expect from Rommel, and the plan left him by Auchinleck catered for a re-run of the Gazala battle in May and June. While German infantry made diversionary attacks against the northern part of the British line, Rommel would lead his armour (15th and 21st Panzer Divisions, 90th Light and Italian XX Corps) in a wide sweep inland, aiming to turn the less well defended southern end of the defences and cut off the British from the rear. In doing so, he would run into Montgomery's trap.

MIDNIGHT MOVE

The main Allied line consisted of an extensive complex of minefields, behind which lay a series of strung-out boxes, or strongholds, manned by Australian, Indian, New Zealand and South African infantry. Covering Alam Halfa itself were the tanks of the 7th and 10th Armoured Divisions, part of XIII Corps, commanded by Lt General Brian Horrocks, who had served under Montgomery in England.

Rommel – sick with jaundice at the time – started his attack shortly after midnight on August 30/31. Motorised troops closed in on the southern bastions of the ridge, skirting their own minefield only to find themselves in the middle of the vigorously defended belt of British mines. Soon the blast of exploding mines mingled with the screams of injured and dying men. Maj General Georg von Bismarck, commander of the 21st Panzer Division, was killed outright. General Walther Nehring, in command of the Afrika Korps, was badly wounded in an air attack.

Rommel believed that air power was the key to victory in North Africa, so nagging doubts began to assail him as the RAF launched their non-stop series of attacks only hours after his first advance. On the ground, his armour had run into a steel wall of three armoured brigades, and the very soft going slowed the assault force. Rommel estimated that ten British shells answered every one fired by the Germans. The element of surprise, on which his plan rested, had failed.

While Rommel came close to despair, Montgomery remained relaxed and confident. He was asleep when the battle began, and when his chief of staff, Brigadier Francis de Guingand, woke him with news of progress, he replied, 'Excellent, couldn't be better', and went back to sleep. To add to Rommel's difficulties, he was attacked on August 31 by a new and equally dispiriting foe – sandstorms, which further hindered the Afrika Korps tanks and vehicles. After the storms, British air and ground attacks were resumed with even greater ferocity.

For the next two days, Rommel tried to close on the British positions, but his men wilted under such firepower. Meanwhile, Kesselring had failed to deliver the promised – and desperately needed – petrol supplies. By the evening of September 2, Rommel had only enough petrol for his vehicles to travel about 100 km (60 miles).

He had no alternative but to end the battle, and that night he ordered a retirement by stages to a line at Bab el Qattara, about 32 km (20 miles) to the west. His assault force had been blasted by around 1300 tonnes of bombs and some 2900 Axis troops were dead, wounded or missing. They had lost about 50 tanks and 400 lorries, plus 55 anti-tank and field guns. Allied losses were about 1750 killed, wounded or missing; 67 tanks and 15 anti-tank guns were destroyed.

Judging Rommel's forces close to defeat, Monty acted: 'I ordered a thrust southwards from the New Zealand Division area to close the gap through which they had entered our positions,' he wrote later. 'The enemy reaction was immediate and violent; they began to pull back quickly to the area of our minefield through which they had originally come. We left them there and I called off the battle.'

The Axis withdrawal was not completed until the morning of September 6. One of Rommel's staff officers, Lt Colonel F.W. von Mellenthin, later described the battle as 'the turning point of the desert war . . . first in a long series of defeats on every front which foreshadowed the defeat of Germany'. For Montgomery it was a great personal and military triumph. Within days of taking over he had beaten Rommel in a vital battle and put new heart into his Eighth Army.

AN ARISTOCRAT AT WAR

Handsome, debonair and always immaculate, Harold Alexander (1891-1969) served in World War I as an Irish Guards officer – winning the MC and DSO – and rose to be Supreme Allied Commander in the Mediterranean in World War II. 'Alex', son of a Northern Irish peer, hid his toughness beneath an aristocratic charm, modesty and reserve.

In 1940, when commanding the 1st Infantry Division, he supervised the last British evacuation from Dunkirk. He then took over Southern Command from December 1940, when invasion still threatened, to February 1942. After a spell as commander in chief in Burma, Alexander succeeded Auchinleck as Middle East commander in August 1942. Later, as Mediterranean supremo, he directed the Italian campaign and received the German surrender in Italy on April 29, 1945. Created a viscount after the war, he was Governor General of Canada from 1946 to 1952, when he was made Earl Alexander of Tunis, and was Churchill's Defence Minister until 1954.

ALEX Bearer of a famous conqueror's name, this cool and immaculate leader was rated a 'lucky general' by his men.

Winning the desert air war

Monty and the Desert Air Force commander Coningham fought Rommel as a close-knit team, while Rommel fought with his Luftwaffe chief. And that made all the difference.

IN SPITE OF differences in tactics and temperament, General Bernard Montgomery and Field Marshal Erwin Rommel agreed on one major aspect of the war in the desert: that it would be won by the side with superior air power. Montgomery and the Desert Air Force (under Air Vice Marshal Arthur Coningham) formed what he called 'one fighting machine'. Rommel was less fortunate.

In February 1941, Rommel recorded that the fighters and bombers of the Luftwaffe's *X Fliegerkorps* (X Flying Corps) had held up the British desert forces at the Libyan coastal town of El Agheila. By April, however, he felt that the airmen – based in Sardinia and Sicily, with detachments in North Africa – were not providing enough support to protect his own supply convoys from Sicily, which were being crippled by Malta-based RAF planes.

Rommel's overall commander in the North African campaign, with control of all German forces including the Luftwaffe, was Field Marshal Albert Kesselring, Commander in Chief South. His Stuka dive-bombers, which were based at El Adem near Tobruk, were probably most effective during the long siege of the port, when they repeatedly blasted the Allied garrison.

In June 1942, however, he and Rommel clashed over the assault on the Free French fort of Bir Hacheim in Libya. Kesselring complained that his planes were overused, with losses unacceptably high. Later that summer the RAF concentrated its Douglas Boston and Vickers Wellington bombers on communication lines from the ports of Bardia, Mersa Matruh and Tobruk. 'They were shooting up our transport columns and sinking one barge and coastal vessel after another,' Rommel wrote. 'No ship lying in the harbours was safe.'

Montgomery arrived in North Africa that August, and triumphed at Alam Halfa. 'Army and Air Force worked on one plan,' he wrote later. They were 'closely knitted together, and the two headquarters were side by side.' In just under a week, 1300 tonnes of high explosives pounded the enemy positions, and Rommel recorded that the air attacks had pinned down his army and 'paralysed' his tanks and trucks.

A few weeks later, the RAF played an even deadlier part in the second battle of El Alamein, when its Curtis Kittyhawk fighter-bombers attacked airfields and shot up scores of tanks and supply trucks. In addition, non-stop night attacks against the Axis forces were followed by hourly raids made by groups of 18-20 aircraft. By the beginning of November, Rommel – who felt he had been 'deserted' by the Luftwaffe at El Alamein – had lost all faith in Kesselring. 'He thinks of everything from the standpoint of the Luftwaffe', Rommel complained bitterly. But Montgomery – with the backing of planes based in Cyrenaica – was planning the RAF's role during Rommel's retreat through El Agheila and Tripoli to Tunis.

In January 1943, with Tripoli back in British hands, Coningham was chosen by Air Chief Marshal Sir Arthur Tedder, Commander in Chief Middle East Air Force, to head the First Allied (North African) Tactical Air Force in the Tunisian campaign. By then, 'Tedder's Carpet' – a method of pattern bombing designed to soften up defences before the army attacked – had been perfected.

The carpet was laid to devastating effect by Coningham's successor, Air Vice Marshal Harry Broadhurst, who organised a deadly daylight blitz on Tunis on March 26. Some 200 Kittyhawks and special Hawker Hurricane tank-buster fighters, escorted by Spitfires, took part.

Montgomery recorded that 'anything that appeared or moved was shot to pieces,' and went on: 'Brilliant and brave work by the pilots completely stunned the enemy; our attack burst through the resistance, and the battle was won.'

BACK FROM THE RAID Desert Air Force crewmen, safely returned from a night attack on German-held Tunis, clamber out of their aircraft.

AN ACE NAMED MARMADUKE

Fighter pilot Marmaduke T. St John ('Pat') Pattle (1914-41) shot down an estimated 60 enemy planes over North Africa and Greece in less than a year, winning the DFC and Bar. He joined the RAF in England in 1936, after being rejected by the air force in his native South Africa for lack of flying ability. When World War II started, he was a flight commander with No 80 Fighter Squadron in the Middle East. He made most of his 'kills' over the Western Desert, flying obsolete Gloster Gladiator biplanes against faster Italian Fiats and Reggianes.

Sent to Greece late in 1940, he switched to Hurricanes, was promoted squadron leader of 33 Squadron, and soon added German planes to his tally. On April 20, 1941, while aiding another pilot over Eleusis Bay near Athens, he was attacked from behind by two German fighters and crashed in flames into the sea.

KNIGHT OF THE DESERT SKIES

Film-star good looks made Luftwaffe fighter ace Hans-Joachim Marseille (1920-42) the idol of wartime German cinema audiences. A brilliant, reckless flier, he made 158 'kills'. Posted to Libya in 1941, his Messerschmitt Me109 with its distinctive yellow propeller spinner soon became the scourge of the RAF in North Africa.

Marseille's particular skill was the difficult art of deflection shooting – firing ahead of an enemy aircraft to hit it. He destroyed 17 Allied planes during the battle of Alam Halfa alone. However, on September 30, 1942, while returning to base, his engine caught fire. As thick black smoke filled the cockpit, he baled out. But he hit the tailplane and plunged down into the desert, his parachute unopened.

MAGAZINE HERO Marseille prepares for battle.

Victory at El Alamein

At Alam Halfa, Montgomery had out-fought and out-thought Rommel. Now, at the second Battle of Alamein, Monty was ready to send the Germans running.

A FULL, SILVER MOON hovered close to the desert horizon. The only sounds were the haunting cries of night birds. Suddenly – at 9.40 pm on October 23, 1942 – the peace was shattered by the eruption of 1000 heavy guns and the rumble of hundreds of tanks grinding over the sand. The earth trembled under the bombardment, blinding flashes lit the sky, and the ear-splitting thunder of the guns was heard as far as Alexandria, about 100 km (60 miles) away.

Sappers moved gingerly through 8 km (5 mile) deep German minefields, clearing paths for infantry and tanks, marking the way with white tape. As abruptly as it had started, the bombardment ended at 9.55 pm. Lt General Bernard Montgomery, commanding the British Eighth Army, wrote afterwards: 'Absolute silence followed, a breathless silence.' Then searchlight beams flashed skywards. At precisely 10 pm, the beams crossed – and the British guns unleashed a second, even fiercer bombardment, at a rate of 1000 shells a minute. Allied infantry advanced at a steady 75 strides a minute towards the Panzerarmee Afrika.

After months of planning by both Montgomery and the Axis commander, Field Marshal Erwin Rommel, battle had finally been joined at El Alamein – a head-on trial of strength in which an overwhelming Allied force had to blast a way through strong, complex defences in great depth, held by a brave and resourceful enemy. For there was no way around them (see map, p. 229).

They stretched south from the coast just west of El Alamein to the eastern reaches of the Qattara Depression, deep in the desert and impassable to tanks. To hold them, Rommel had 50 000 German and 54 000 Italian troops, almost 500 tanks, more than 1300 guns (but only 86 of the deadly 88 mm variety) and 350 serviceable aircraft. Against him, Montgomery could field 195 000 men, more than 1000 tanks (including 422 powerful Shermans and Lee-Grants), over 2300 guns and 530 serviceable planes – in fact, the Allies had complete air superiority.

Rommel had shielded his whole line with a dense minefield (see feature, p. 226). In the north, on Miteirya Ridge, were the German 164th Light Division and Italians of the Trento Division backed by tanks of the German 15th Panzer and Italian Littorio Divisions; in the centre, Ruweisat Ridge and Bab el Qattara were held by the Italian Bologna and Brescia Divisions; from here south to Qaret el Himeimat stood the Italian Folgore and Pavia Divisions, backed by tanks of the 21st Panzer and Italian Ariete Divisions.

MONTGOMERY'S PLAN

Montgomery had been under great pressure from Churchill to launch the attack. Operation 'Torch – the Allied landings in French North Africa – was due early in November; a decisive desert victory beforehand would perhaps encourage the Vichy French to support the Allies and would discourage Spain from allowing German reinforcements for North Africa through its territory. But Montgomery refused to move until he considered his army thoroughly trained and equipped. Meanwhile, he had the advantage of knowing his enemy's intentions – British codebreakers had allowed him to read Rommel's signals, which detailed his needs and shortages. They even told Monty when Rommel had to be invalided home with jaundice and high blood pressure in September, and that his replacement was Lt General Georg Stumme, from the Russian Front and inexperienced in desert warfare.

Montgomery's plan was ready on October 6, and he promised Churchill certain victory. The Highlanders, Australians, Indians, South Africans, New Zealanders and two armoured brigades of Maj General Oliver Leese's XXX Corps would make the main assault in the north; Maj General Brian Horrocks' XIII Corps – the renowned 7th Armoured Division, two infantry divisions plus Free French and Greek brigades – would stage massive diversionary attacks in the south. The 1st, 8th and 10th Armoured Divisions – Maj General Herbert Lumsden's X Corps – would be ranged behind Leese's men, to follow them through and smash the Axis armour. All would be preceded by intense artillery and aerial bombardment.

In October, Allied bombers from Egypt and Malta began systematically bombing Axis supply bases in southern Italy and behind enemy lines in Cyrenaica (eastern Libya). Naval forces attacked Axis convoys in the Mediterranean. As a result, almost half the German supplies never reached the men at the front. Finally, in the days immediately before the battle, Monty led the enemy to believe that his main attack would come in the south, rather than the north. He had a dummy army base built in the southern sector, complete with fake lorries, *(continued on p. 229)*

MONTY – THE SOLDIERS' GENERAL

A photograph of Rommel and a quotation from Shakespeare's *Henry V* – 'O God of battles! steel my soldiers' hearts' – hung in the caravan of Lt General Bernard Law Montgomery (1887-1976) throughout the desert war. They were a constant reminder of the man he called 'the field marshal' – the man he was determined to conquer. They also added to his public image – as did his multi-badged Australian slouch hat and black beret bearing the Royal Tank Regiment badge and his general's badge. 'That beret,' he once remarked, 'is worth two divisions!' It made him instantly recognisable to his men – whose well-being always ranked high with him. He always made sure that his orders – and the reasons for them – were made clear to them. They affectionately nicknamed him 'Monty'.

This Anglo-Irish son of a clergyman had been in the carnage of World War I. It left him forever careful of his men's lives. In World War II he commanded the 3rd Division in France, then the Eighth Army in Egypt. Victory at El Alamein made him the first British general to beat a German commander in a major World War II battle. He commanded the British land forces in Sicily and Italy, then the Allied land forces in the D-Day landings before leading 21st Army Group in France, the Low Countries and Germany until the end of the war. In May 1945, he accepted the German surrender at Lüneburg Heath.

Critics, who occasionally included both Churchill and General Eisenhower, Supreme Commander in Europe, felt that he sometimes erred too much on the side of caution – and was unwilling to heed advice from his superiors. Promoted field marshal in 1944, he was created Viscount Montgomery of Alamein in 1946.

MIGHTY EIGHTY-EIGHT **Designed in 1933 as an anti-aircraft gun that could hurl heavy flak more than 14 km (9 miles) high, the German 88 mm gun proved a fearsome weapon in the desert war, where it was fixed in strongpoints and tanks or towed behind armoured trucks. It unleashed 20 high-velocity rounds a minute, and not only against Allied bombers. With an effective horizontal range of over 10 km (6 miles), its devastating fire could put any tank out of action.**

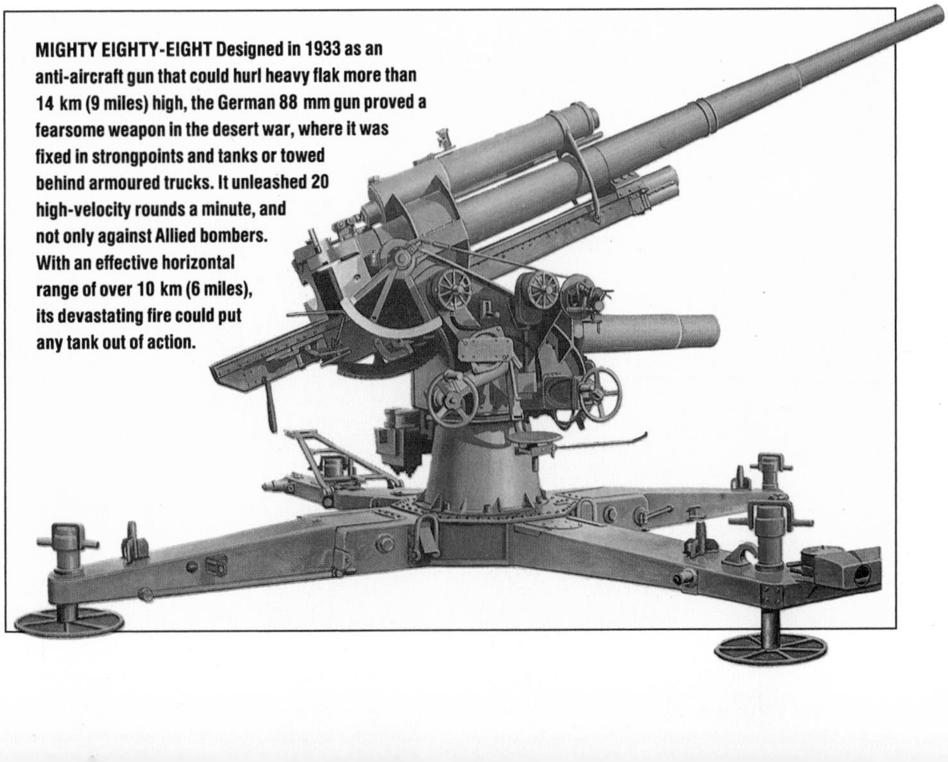

DEATH IN THE DEVIL'S GARDENS

Rommel's engineers laid a maze of mines, bombs, booby-traps and barbed wire at El Alamein. The Allied troops had to cross these 'Devil's Gardens'.

IN THE SUMMER of 1942, Rommel's engineers worked on a deadly defensive system against the Eighth Army assault they knew would come. They laid a dense series of minefields along the entire 60 km (40 mile) length of their line, from the coast to the Qattara Depression, and called them 'the Devil's Gardens'. The minefields' complexity – up to 8 km (5 miles) deep in places – took the Eighth Army by surprise, despite its intensive training in dealing with mines.

The Germans had incorporated captured British minefields into its system, bringing the total number of mines to almost half a million. Many were linked by tripwires or formed booby-traps. Among them were captured artillery shells and 115 kg (250 lb) Luftwaffe bombs, some to be detonated electrically from concealed German 'battle outposts'. Various types of mine were used, notably the infamous 'S-mine' which, when trodden on, leapt into the air and exploded at waist height, cutting down anyone nearby with a hail of shrapnel. Another was the Tellermine, which needed 115 kg pressure to detonate its 5.5 kg (12 lb) of TNT. Infantry could walk over it but trucks and armour following behind would be blown up. It had also a device which made it explode should anyone try to lift it.

Sometimes mines were laid at random, but with a clear path through, cunningly plotted to lead the enemy into more heavily mined 'killing grounds'. Fortunately, two Polish officers stationed in Scotland had devised an electrical mine-detector. Shaped like an upright vacuum cleaner, it was swept across the ground in front of the operator as he moved slowly forward – leaving him extremely vulnerable to enemy fire – and sending a high-pitched whine through his earphones when it passed over any metallic

DESERT THUNDER Just one of a thousand Allied guns roars into action to open the second Battle of El Alamein. After ferocious resistance, Rommel is on the run, and (right) British infantry with bayonets fixed take prisoner a survivor in a knocked-out German tank.

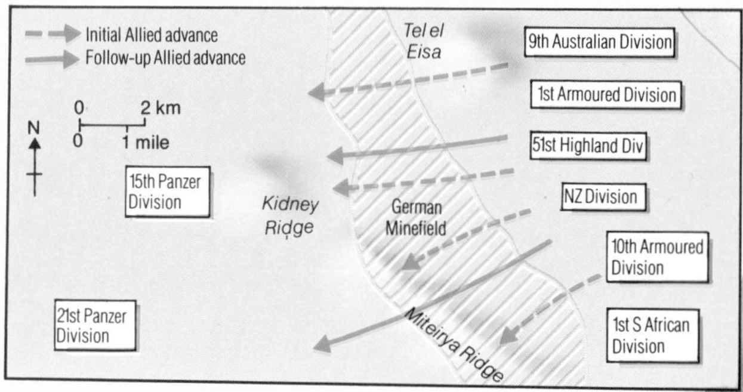

NO ALTERNATIVE The Devil's Gardens stretched south 60 km (40 miles) from the sea to the impassable Qattara Depression. There was no way around them – sappers had to clear a path through for the infantry and tanks, who then had to face three formidably defended ridges: Miteirya, Kidney and Ruweisat.

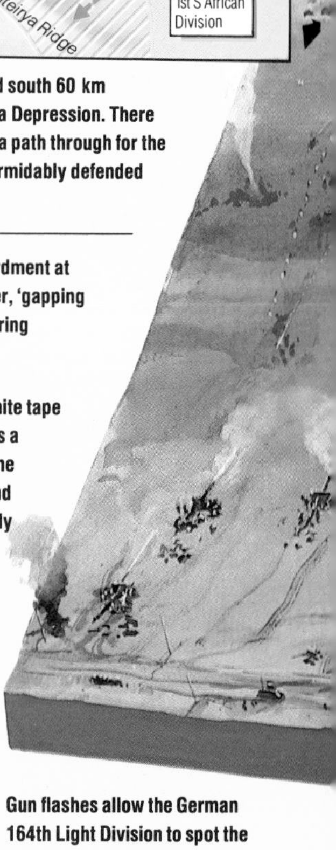

1 The British guns begin their opening bombardment at 9.40 pm on October 23, 1942. Under its cover, 'gapping parties' of sappers start the perilous task of clearing pathways through the dense minefields.

2 The sappers mark cleared pathways with white tape and illuminate them with hooded lanterns. As a second, even greater barrage begins at 10 pm, the 51st Highland, 1st South African and New Zealand Divisions advance along them towards the heavily defended Miteirya Ridge.

3 The Highlanders advance so fast that they run into their own barrage and are hit by both British and German shells. But with pipes skirling, they storm the ridge with bayonet and grenade.

4 The rapid infantry advance also causes the tanks to fall behind. Knocked-out vehicles blocking the cleared pathways further delay the armour, which becomes entangled with infantry following up the initial attack amid dust and smoke.

5 Gun flashes allow the German 164th Light Division to spot the oncoming infantry against the night sky, and their machine guns take a heavy toll; artillery begins to batter snarled-up British tanks.

VICTOR AS PROMISED Monty's scheme for Alamein was meticulously planned, and the men were thoroughly trained. He refused to hasten the attack but assured Churchill he would win – and kept his word.

ON THE COVER Rommel – shown on a German magazine cover in May 1942 – spent much of that summer cultivating the Devil's Gardens. He returned to the desert from sick leave two days after the battle started.

object underground. Five hundred were available at Alamein. In addition, there were 'Barons' – obsolete Matilda tanks fitted with rotating flails of thick chain mounted on forward-projecting arms, which detonated any mines in their path.

Under heavy fire on open ground, 'gapping parties' of about 15 sappers with a heavily sandbagged truck or a Baron cleared lanes through the minefields, marking them with white tape and hooded lanterns for the infantry and tanks that followed on. 'The sappers had done wonders', said Monty when the battle was won. Even so, the Devil's Gardens claimed many lives in the maelstrom that was Alamein.

8 The 1st South African Division, misled by faulty intelligence about the strength of the Germans facing it, is stopped in its tracks and has to fight off a fierce counterattack before it can move forward again.

9 Apart from 500 000 mines, the Devil's Gardens are laced with hundreds of kilometres of thickly coiled barbed wire. Behind it, in concealed positions, Germans wait to trigger buried, electrically detonated bombs.

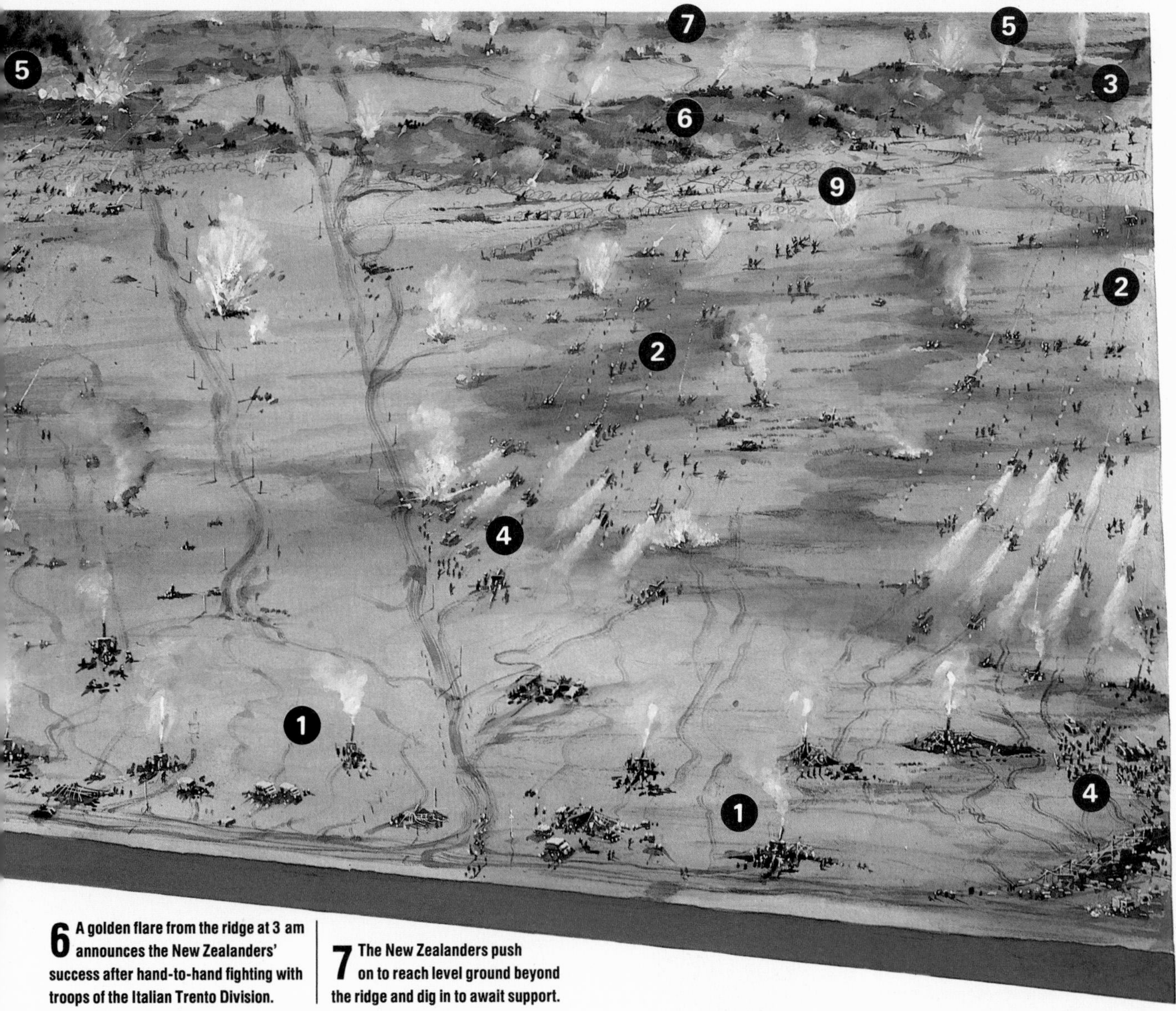

6 A golden flare from the ridge at 3 am announces the New Zealanders' success after hand-to-hand fighting with troops of the Italian Trento Division.

7 The New Zealanders push on to reach level ground beyond the ridge and dig in to await support.

SCENES FROM A BATTLEFIELD

The thousand-gun artillery bombardment that preceded the Allied attack at El Alamein 'stunned even our own troops, and the ground vibrated under our feet just like the skin of kettledrums'. Major H. Gillam, of the 9th Australian Division, was recalling his feelings as the Aussies, along with Highlanders of the 51st Division, New Zealanders and South Africans approached Miteirya Ridge.

The infantry walked steadily forward into a dense pall of smoke drifting back from the barrage ahead. Every three minutes the barrage jumped forward 90 m (100 yds) and the infantry moved up behind it. Leading the Highlanders were their pipers playing *The Road to the Isles*; 19-year-old Piper Duncan McIntyre was soon wounded twice as the defenders retaliated, but continued playing. A third wound felled him for good.

Choking dust and oily smoke blanketed the battlefield: dust from tank tracks, sand-trapped lorries, exploding shells and mortar bombs; smoke from blazing Allied vehicles and knocked-out armour. It clogged the mouths and noses of sappers working to lift mines and booby-traps.

In the south, near the Qattara Depression, intelligence officer George Greenfield was with the 2nd Battalion The Buffs (East Kents). He wrote later: 'My worst memory was coming across a smashed Bren-gun carrier . . . and finding the body of one of my friends in it. An 88 mm shell had blasted through the front bulkhead, through the driver, through the officer behind him and out through the steel plate at the back . . . you could look right along the neat series of holes . . .'

AT THE SHARP END With eyes smarting from dust raised by artillery and churning tanks (right), Allied infantrymen advanced through the maze of German defences (see map). They held bayonets ready (top) – and used them, as they picked their way among fallen soldiers, battered armoured cars and strongpoints where enemies lurked. Once safe, they could take pity on a wounded German.

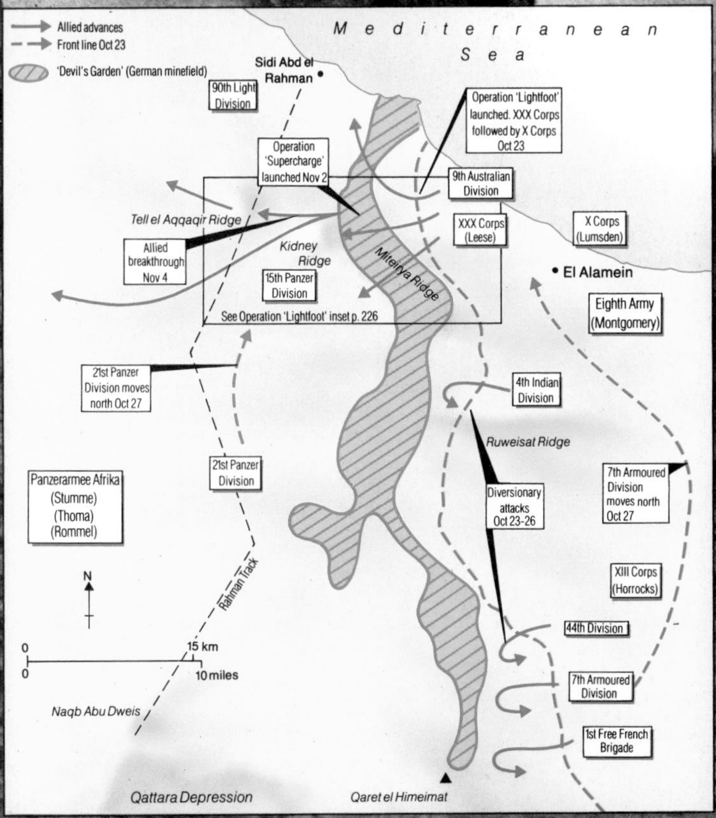

tanks, guns, ammunition dumps, reservoirs – even cardboard soldiers wearing tin hats. He also had a dummy pipeline laid and 8 km (5 miles) of false railway track (from petrol cans). Meanwhile, Monty's real base was built secretly in the north, and cunningly camouflaged. Work was completed on October 21.

It had taken months of energy-sapping toil under desert conditions, in which the men lived on dry biscuits and bully beef, endured dysentery, 'bathed' in their shaving mugs, fried eggs on the scorching metal tops of their vehicles, dealt with the odd scorpion and snake, and were plagued by sandstorms – which, said the Arabs, could drive a man mad in five days. The order to attack, when it finally came, was almost a relief.

STUMME DISAPPEARS

At first, the offensive – code-named Operation 'Lightfoot' – went mostly according to plan. The New Zealand Division carried out a 'crumbling' operation in which the enemy lines were penetrated and broken up. By dawn the Germans had lost long stretches of Miteirya Ridge, often to savage bayonet charges. But not everything was going the Allies' way. Despite all the sappers' efforts, the Axis minefield was causing chaos and delays. The bulk of the British armour was hopelessly entangled with its supporting infantry in a massive traffic jam. Sappers worked tirelessly, trying to clear new paths in the choking smoke and dust. Meanwhile, the German 88s and other anti-tank guns picked off sitting-duck targets.

However, the Germans had suffered a serious blow. Early on October 24, Stumme set out to view the situation at first-hand. As his staff car reached the front, it ran into a hail of fire and a colonel riding with Stumme was killed outright. The corporal driver swerved the car violently and Stumme either jumped or fell out. The corporal failed to notice what had happened and returned to base without his commander. Days later, Stumme – who had high blood pressure – was found dead in the desert from a heart attack.

Meanwhile, Montgomery had become concerned about the plight of the 10th Armoured Division, which had failed to get through the minefield to take up its planned open defensive position. He did some 'prodding', as he termed it, and the position was achieved. Then, in the early hours of Sunday, October 25, he learnt that the same division was suffering heavy casualties on Miteirya Ridge. 'A certain infirmity of purpose appeared in the mind of X Corps commander,' Montgomery wrote, 'and he was beginning to think that my plan was not on.'

A conference was hastily convened in Monty's caravan at 2.30 am between him and Lumsden, with Leese present. Monty made it clear that the battle would continue as ordered and that he, and he alone, was in charge. 'Some people are not always feeling their best at 2.30 am,' he wrote afterwards. 'I have often thought that if I had weakened at that moment we might have lost the battle.' He was now 24 hours behind schedule. He had estimated that the 'dogfight', as he called it, would last for 10-12 days, to coincide with the 'Torch' landings. He would not 'mess about'.

ROMMEL RETURNS

In Germany, it was becoming obvious to Hitler that, without Rommel, the North African campaign was doomed. Since the 'disappearance' of Stumme, the Panzerarmee Afrika had been led by a battle-scarred veteran, Maj General Wilhelm

Ritter von Thoma, and despite his fighting prowess, he was no Desert Fox. So Rommel flew back to El Alamein to discover a situation grimmer than he had feared. 'Units of the 15th Panzer Division had counterattacked several times on the 24th and 25th October,' he recorded later, 'but had suffered frightful losses in the terrible British artillery fire and nonstop RAF bombing attacks. By the evening of the 25th, only 31 of their 119 tanks remained serviceable.'

During the night of October 26, relays of bombers continued the attack, and at 2 am heavy artillery began a savage barrage. 'Soon it was impossible to distinguish between gunfire and exploding shells,' wrote Rommel, 'and the sky grew bright with the glare of muzzle-flashes and shell-bursts.' The Desert Air Force was sending up 800 bomber sorties and 2500 sorties by fighter-bombers each day.

Fighting now became centred around the Allied-held Kidney Ridge, to the north-west of Miteirya – named by the troops from its shape on their contour maps. The 21st Panzer Division had been moved north, and with the 15th made five determined efforts to regain the ridge on October 27. Four times they were flung back with heavy casualties. Then, as they regrouped for a last, all-out assault, the RAF launched another devastating bombing strike. For over two hours wave after wave of bombers dropped high explosives, concentrating on an area measuring just 5 by 3 km (3 by 2 miles).

The panzers tried again to take the ridge the following day, with similar results. A frustrated Rommel commented later: 'Rivers of blood were poured out over miserable strips of land which, in normal times, not even the poorest Arab would have bothered his head about.'

However, Montgomery was planning a new and even fiercer offensive, code-named 'Supercharge'. Intelligence had informed him of the 21st Panzers' move north, so he halted the diversionary attacks in the south and moved the 7th Armoured Division northwards. Leaving the Australians to fight a bruising, drawn-out battle in the far north towards Tell el Eisa and the coast road – which bought the Allies valuable time – he would renew the attack in the Kidney Ridge area.

VICTORY OR DEATH

'Supercharge' began at 1 am on November 2 with a three-hour Allied bombardment and waves of night bombers. Under cover of the artillery fire, advancing infantry cleared a way through German minefields, and the 7th Battalion Argyll and Sutherland Highlanders captured a vital enemy field headquarters on the Rahman Track, an Axis supply line running south-west from the coast into the desert.

Simultaneously, 220 tanks and armoured cars of the 1st Armoured Division battered through the Axis lines intent on capturing Tel el Aqqaqir Ridge, which guarded the Rahman Track behind Miteirya. But progress was held up by mines and dogged German resistance, and when dawn broke, the tanks were in full view of German anti-tank guns. Fighting continued for most of the day – and at the end of it 200 British tanks had been wrecked. However, Leese's XXX Corps had driven a path 3.6 km (over 2 miles) into the enemy lines, and along it poured the 9th Armoured Brigade and the 7th and 10th Armoured Divisions, with New Zealand infantrymen in support. They fought clear of the German lines north of Kidney Ridge and out into the desert.

Rommel was steeling himself to retreat when, soon after lunch on November 3, he received orders from Hitler to stand fast. 'Yield not a metre of ground and throw every gun and every man into the battle,' commanded the Führer . . . 'Your enemy, despite his superiority, must also be at the end of his strength . . . As to your troops, you can show them no other road than that to victory or death.' That night a stunned Rommel wrote to his wife, Lu: 'I lie open-eyed, racking my brains for a way out of this plight for my poor troops . . . The dead are lucky, it's all over for them.'

Next morning, after an hour's artillery bombardment, Montgomery resumed his offensive. The Afrika Korps' armour – under Thoma since Rommel's return – beat off the Allied attacks which were supported by about 200 tanks. Then, late that day, Hitler changed his orders and Rommel was able to begin a general retreat. However, Thoma had already withdrawn the Afrika Korps – 'I cannot tolerate this order from Hitler,' he had declared – and, setting his tank on fire, awaited capture. That evening, while Thoma dined with Monty at British headquarters, Rommel and his remaining infantry and motorised forces headed west.

During the battle the Allies had killed or captured 50 000 men – almost half the Axis army – including the cream of the Afrika Korps, and had knocked out all but about 35 panzers and 20 Italian tanks. Monty put his losses at just over 13 500, with about 600 tanks knocked out, of which 350 were repairable. Back home in London, a jubilant Churchill ordered Britain's church bells to be sounded on Sunday, November 15, for the first time since 1940 – when they were silenced, to be rung only as warning of invasion.

ROMMEL ESCAPES

Meanwhile, by November 4, Rommel and his army had retreated 100 km (60 miles) west along the coast road to Fuka, then pushed on a further 100 km to Mersa Matruh. It was rough going. As lorries crammed with troops, German and Italian tanks, and staff cars full of stunned and shaken officers choked the road, they were strafed by wave after wave of Allied fighters. 'There was wild confusion,' Rommel admitted later. And in eager pursuit came the British armour and the New Zealanders.

The confusion lasted two more days, during which the 21st Panzer Division, battered to a standstill by ferocious air attacks, destroyed its few remaining tanks and struggled on westwards in lorries. For a time it seemed that the entire Axis forces would be destroyed or captured, but Monty's pursuit was cautious. He did not want to be lured into any rash moves through what he considered to be needless haste, and he would not allow his armour to range ahead.

His eventual outflanking moves to get around and behind Rommel came just in time to be frustrated by bad weather. On November 6 torrential rain turned the whole coastal region into a morass of yellow mud. Lorry-borne infantry and supply columns got bogged down; the tanks were reduced to crawling pace; the strafing fighters were grounded.

Rommel, however, slogged on another 125 km (80 miles) to Sidi Barrani. By this time he had only ten tanks, but he fought a series of brilliant rearguard actions, blowing bridges and culverts, and laying cleverly concealed minefields. They slowed the Allied pursuit, but Monty seemed not unduly worried and pressed on, announcing that his next objective was Tripoli, capital of Libya. Rommel hastened ever westwards. Gutted and abandoned, Tobruk, of bitter memory, fell to the British on November 13. Benghazi was taken five days later after only token resistance – the fifth time the city had changed hands in the desert war.

THE FÜHRER RAGES

On that very afternoon of November 18, Rommel, summoned peremptorily to Hitler's headquarters at Rastenburg in East Prussia, was being accused by the Führer of disobedience, disloyalty, treachery and cowardice. In a great rage, Hitler demanded that the field marshal should hold a major bridgehead at Mersa el Brega, on the coast about 190 km (120 miles) south-west of Benghazi. Rommel, by now doubtful of Hitler's sanity, returned to Libya and settled his men in for a battle at El Agheila, a few kilometres west of Mersa el Brega.

No airborne supplies had arrived, and nine out of the ten ships sent to Tripoli to supply him were sunk. The tenth turned out not to be carrying any petrol – vital for Rommel's tanks and lorries. He formed his defensive line – of infantry and artillery, with his few remaining tanks as a mobile reserve – between El Agheila and desert salt marshes about 25 km (15 miles) inland. But he knew he could not win.

The Allied pursuit reached El Agheila on November 24, but it was not until December 12 that the 7th Armoured Division made a cautious frontal attack on Rommel's line, while an armoured column of the New Zealand Division swung south, then north-west, in an attempt to reach the coast behind the Germans. Rommel ordered a withdrawal, and his men, split into small groups, burst out through the New Zealanders, who did not have the strength to stop them. Even so, there was fierce fighting, which climaxed on December 16, when the panzers were badly mauled by the New Zealanders and battered from the air. Rommel still managed to pull back to his next defensive line at Buerat, over 320 km (200 miles) west.

The Eighth Army reached Sirte, about 80 km (50 miles) east of Buerat, on Christmas Day. The men feasted on turkey, plum pudding and beer while they paused to regroup. Their supply lines now stretched back 1300 km (800 miles) to Alexandria. At Buerat, Monty repeated his El Agheila outflanking move, and though Rommel managed to get out of the trap again, there was to be no letup in the pursuit before Tripoli.

The Germans tried to make another stand in the Djebel Nefusa hills, south-east of Tripoli. From there, given time, a strong line could have been forged between Homs, on the coast, and Tarhuna 50 km (30 miles) inland. However, Rommel sent a strong force southwards, anticipating another Montgomery outflanking move. Monty outgeneralled him by switching his main attack to the coast. The 51st Highland Division and 22nd Armoured Brigade stove in the German defences and took Homs. They were now only 90 km (55 miles) from Tripoli.

At dawn on January 23, 1943, troops of the 7th Armoured, 51st Highland and 2nd New Zealand Divisions entered Tripoli, piped in by a Gordon Highlander. They found that Rommel had gone and had destroyed the port installations. It was three months to the day since the break-out at El Alamein, 2250 km (1400 miles) to the east. Ahead lay the hard road into Tunisia, to meet Allied troops fighting east from the 'Torch' landings.

Torch to North Africa

Only four days after their victory at El Alamein, the Allies struck the blow that would squeeze Axis forces right out of North Africa – a massive operation to put British and American forces ashore in Morocco and Algeria.

LEND A SHOULDER THERE! American soldiers heave a gun off one of the 'Torch' landing beaches in November 1942. Their comrades stand in groups and watch.

THE LARGEST amphibious invasion force the world had yet known assembled off the North African coast late on November 7, 1942. More than 500 ships, ranging from converted cargo vessels to once-luxurious passenger liners, had been pressed into service to carry around 107 000 men and thousands of tonnes of weapons and supplies, and land them on the beaches of Morocco and Algeria. Many of the ships had sailed direct from the United States, others from Britain. Code-named Operation 'Torch' and with US Lt General Dwight D. Eisenhower in overall command, the invasion was mounted to occupy Vichy-French North Africa, then attack Axis forces from the west while the Eighth Army advanced from the east. The aim was to squeeze them out of North Africa.

It was the first major Anglo-American operation of the war, with three-quarters of the force American and the rest British. Most of the men – especially the Americans – were new to combat. Moreover, no one knew who would be the first enemy they encountered, for the shores were controlled by Vichy French forces whose sympathies were uncertain. The British element in the landing force was to maintain a low profile to avoid further antagonising the French after the Royal Navy's attack on the Vichy French fleet at Mers El Kébir, near Oran, in 1940. Only later would British reinforcements join the Americans.

Would the invaders be greeted with flowers and garlands for a liberating army, or with shells and bullets for a foe? Shortly after 1 am on November 8, under a new moon, the darkened fleet disgorged its landing craft. As the first wave hit one of the many landing beaches, shipboard loudspeakers blared across the water in French: 'Don't shoot. We are your friends. We are Americans.' The message was drowned by gunfire, and the sea erupted. The French were resisting.

THE BEST LAID PLANS

For months before the landings, the Allies had known that the French might resist. The Vichy government had been formed to rule that part of France not occupied by the Germans. It was generally anti-British, but retained diplomatic relations with the USA. Robert D. Murphy, an American with French friends in high places, was US Diplomatic Agent in North Africa, and to him Roosevelt secretly assigned the task of sounding out the French attitude to an American landing.

Murphy's main hopes lay with two men – Admiral Jean François Darlan, vice-premier to Marshal Philippe Pétain, and General Henri Giraud. Giraud, a hero of both world wars, had fled to unoccupied France after escaping from German captivity, and was known to be no lover of the puppet regime. Darlan, however, had sworn allegiance to the Vichy government and was Commander in Chief of its forces. But he had indicated to Murphy that his men in North Africa would probably turn against the Germans if supported by a large force of American troops.

Less than three weeks before the landings were due to begin, Murphy arranged a meeting in Algeria between French and American officers. In a top-secret operation, US Maj General Mark Clark – Eisenhower's deputy – and three other officers were ferried ashore in canvas canoes from the British submarine HMS *Seraph* to a lonely villa on the coast west of Algiers. There they met French officers led by Maj General Charles Mast, deputy commander of the French forces in Algeria – and strongly pro-American.

The meeting, on October 22, achieved little. The French required details of the invasion – especially the British role – but Clark dared not reveal Allied plans, or that part of the invasion fleet was already on its way. And, after a narrow escape when French police raided the villa, he was almost drowned getting back to *Seraph*.

Murphy made a final desperate attempt to persuade the French not to resist. In the early hours of November 8 he called on General Alphonse Juin, commanding French forces in Algeria, and pleaded with him to order his men to lay down their arms. Juin refused, pointing out that any such order would be countermanded by Darlan, but he agreed to telephone Darlan, who was in Algiers. Darlan's reaction was one of anger and indecision – the invasion had come too early and seemed to him too small. In any case he could not break his oath of allegiance to Pétain.

Three forces made up the invasion fleet: the Western Task Force of 25 000 men, commanded by Maj General George S. Patton, would land at three points near Casablanca in Morocco; Maj

GIRAUD – DE GAULLE'S RIVAL

When the Germans overran the French Ninth Army headquarters at Sedan in 1940, they captured Lt General Henri Giraud (1879-1949), who had just taken over command. He was held prisoner in Germany for two years before escaping to Vichy France, where he worked secretly for his country's re-entry into the war on the Allied side.

The Allies had him smuggled out of southern France by submarine two days before the 'Torch' landings, hoping to negotiate through him a bloodless invasion. Instead they had to deal with Admiral Darlan. When Darlan was assassinated, Giraud replaced him as High Commissioner in French North Africa.

Giraud and General Charles de Gaulle became bitter rivals for leadership of the Free French forces, but Allied pressure made them joint Presidents of the Committee of National Liberation. By October 1943, de Gaulle had manoeuvred Giraud into resigning, and from that time he faded from the scene.

General Lloyd Fredendall commanded the Central Task Force of 39 000 men heading for two beaches east and west of Oran in Algeria; while the Eastern Task Force, under Maj General Charles M. Ryder, was made up of 23 000 British and 20 000 American troops destined for three beaches near Algiers itself. The Morocco landings would ensure that the Germans could not send men to North Africa through Spain, and from the three major ports the Allies could strike east into Tunisia and seize Tunis and the fortified port of Bizerta. But the unexpected ferocity of the French almost ruined the plan.

SETBACK AT ALGIERS

Algiers was the first objective to fall, but not without a setback. Just before dawn the British destroyers *Malcolm* and *Broke* made a direct assault on the port to put 600 Americans ashore. As the warships neared the harbour entrance, searchlights stabbed the darkness and artillery above the bay opened fire on them. *Malcolm* was crippled and had to retire. *Broke* rammed the harbour booms and managed to land 250 men on a jetty. But after seizing a power station and an oil installation they were overcome by the French and briefly held as prisoners. *Broke* came under heavy gunfire and sank.

The beach landings nearby were more successful. Fort de Sidi Ferruch gave no resistance and the airfields at Maison Blanche and Blida were quickly overcome. But a coastal battery at Cap Matifou had to be dive-bombed and shelled by warships before surrendering. Tanks and armoured cars sped towards Algiers, and by mid-afternoon were outside the city. General Juin, with Darlan's approval, surrendered.

The Central Task Force fared worse. Two ex-American coastguard cutters, HMS *Walney* and *Hartland*, carrying 600 men, were met by blistering fire as they tried to enter Oran harbour. Shore batteries rained salvo after salvo onto the ships; destroyers and submarines in port opened up at point-blank range. Within minutes both had been hammered to pieces. *Walney*, ablaze from stem to stern, rolled over and sank; *Hartland* drifted helplessly and later blew up. More than 300 men died and the rest were taken prisoner.

South of Oran, troops failed to take airfields at La Senia and Tafaraoui when bad weather held back paratroop reinforcements. Meanwhile, the main force landing on beaches west of Oran met stiff opposition from the French, under Maj General Robert Boissau. American armour and infantry had to fight all the way, and it was more than 48 hours before they finally reached Oran and forced the city to surrender, on November 10.

BATTLESHIPS DUEL

At Casablanca Patton got the hottest reception of all. The port harboured a powerful naval contingent, including the 35 000 tonne battleship *Jean Bart* which, though still under construction, was able to use four 380 mm (15 in) guns. As dawn came it had a duel with the US battleship *Massachusetts* standing about 20 km (12 miles) offshore. Eight hits from *Massachusetts* and repeated bomber attacks knocked out *Jean Bart*.

However, at the height of the battle seven French destroyers, eight submarines and the cruiser *Primauguet* stole out of the port under a smokescreen, to attack the main landing force at nearby Fedala. But as soon as they emerged from their smokescreen they came under fire from the US cruiser *Augusta* and other warships. Patton was in *Augusta*, and wrote in his diary that the American ships were 'all firing and going like hell in big zigzags and curves'. The French force was annihilated.

Meanwhile, Patton's men had made it to the beaches, but there, as he discovered to his horror, confusion reigned. Lack of experience of such a large amphibious operation had led to a major foul-up. Vehicles that should have been moving materials inland were still on board the ships – so were the engineers who should have laid firm pathways out of the soft sand. Landing craft were waiting to be unloaded; men cowered in foxholes as French planes strafed the beach. An angry Patton went ashore and strode among his men, swearing and bellowing orders and giving a hefty boot to any man who ducked for cover.

On November 10, Eisenhower signalled to Patton: 'The only tough nut left is in your hands. Crack it open quickly.' Patton saw only one way to obey his chief's orders – an air and naval bombardment of the city at dawn next day. But only minutes before the attack was due to begin the Allied bombers were recalled and the warships told to stand down. Back in Algiers, Darlan had finally agreed to a ceasefire, and an armistice was signed – on the anniversary of the armistice that ended World War I. The German reaction was immediately to march into Vichy France. On November 27, the French fleet in Toulon scuttled itself to avoid falling into Hitler's hands. The Italians occupied Corsica.

IKE – A MAN FOR ALL SEASONS

Dwight David Eisenhower (1890-1969) was selected in June 1942 to head US forces in Europe. Five months later he commanded the 'Torch' landings in North Africa – and just over a year after that he was named Allied Supreme Commander for the invasion of north-west Europe. It was a meteoric rise for a man who had never before exercised command in battle.

'Ike', as he was affectionately known throughout his multinational command, was among an elite group of colonels chosen for advancement by General George Marshall, US Army Chief of Staff. Born in Texas, he went to West Point military academy, and when war broke out was chief of Washington's war planning division. When he was given overall command of the 'Torch' invasion, he had to coordinate the efforts of subordinates who in many cases were vastly more experienced. He created a joint command headquarters and an integrated staff, with a British and an American officer for each job. This worked brilliantly. He dealt with such prima donnas as Patton and Montgomery with tact and skill.

In war he acquired a political ability which led him to the White House. His Presidency covered two terms – from 1953 to 1961 – and he was extremely popular.

THE CHIEF Eisenhower did not pretend to be a fighting general, but his handling of fighters was superb.

THE VICHY ADMIRAL

After the fall of France, Admiral Jean François Darlan (1881-1942), Commander in Chief of the French Navy, promised Churchill that his ships would not fall into Nazi hands. Then, as navy minister in Marshal Philippe Pétain's Vichy government, he sent most of them to North Africa, where they were destroyed by the British fleet in July 1940. He never trusted the British again.

After the 'Torch' landings, Darlan – then High Commissioner in French North Africa and head of Vichy's armed forces – agreed to a ceasefire on condition that he should become head of liberated France's government. The British, who had de Gaulle earmarked for the job, reluctantly complied. But on Christmas Eve 1942, Darlan was shot dead by a young Gaullist fanatic, Bonnier de la Chapelle.

FRENCH FURY An anti-aircraft gunner on a French warship in action against the Allies. The strength of Vichy resistance to the North African landings was a surprise.

The rocky road to Tunis

A handshake on a Tunisian plain between a British sergeant and an American private meant that two Allied armies had linked up – and that nemesis was approaching for Rommel's once invincible Panzerarmee Afrika.

PARAS ON PATROL Crack German paratroops pick their way through rocky Tunisian terrain on a reconnaissance patrol. Groups like this were frequently guided by Arab scouts with specialised knowledge of a region.

SHEETING RAIN drenched the Coldstream Guards as they struggled knee-deep in mud up the lower slopes of 'Longstop Hill', a 250 m (800 ft) twin-peaked obstruction on the road to Tunis from the west. They clawed their way to rockier, firmer ground above . . . where the Germans were waiting. In the pitch darkness bayonets flashed and rifle butts crunched flesh and bone as British and Germans grappled in hand-to-hand combat. In the end the Germans were forced into retreat and the 2nd Battalion Coldstream Guards dug in.

Dawn brought American infantry to relieve the British, and during the day they managed to make some ground towards the second, rearmost peak. But the Germans clung on – then put in a surprise counterattack that knocked the Americans back down the hill. In the late afternoon, the Coldstreams began slogging their way up Longstop again, but by now mud and rain had made the going almost impossible. Trapped in mire and pinned down by mortar and artillery shells, the Guards settled in for a hard night on the hillside.

It was Christmas Eve, 1942. On Christmas Day, the Germans attacked again and by noon more than 500 men had died or were wounded – and the Guards were ordered to withdraw.

The Coldstreams were at the sharp end of Lt General Kenneth Anderson's First Army, driving eastwards from the 'Torch' invasion beaches in Algeria and Morocco as Hitler poured men and guns into Tunisia following the sudden capitulation of the Vichy French in North Africa on November 11 (see map, p. 236). Recognising the new threat this posed to the southern flank of the Axis, the Germans had immediately occupied Vichy France, bringing the whole country directly under Nazi domination. French commanders in North Africa now had no doubts as to whose side they should be on, and the Allies gained an extra 200 000 fighting men.

However, the Luftwaffe controlled the air above the short sea routes from Sicily to Tunis and Bizerta, and across this 'bridge' came troops, artillery and squadrons of Axis dive-bombers and fighters. A swift thrust into Tunisia was essential, and the task fell to the force which had landed at Algiers and had been renamed the British First Army, under its new commander, Lt General Anderson.

On the evening of November 10, Anderson's troops – 10 000 Americans and 23 000 British, including two Commando units – left Algiers by land, sea and air, and within days had captured the eastern Algerian ports of Bougie, Djidjelli, Philippeville and Bone. By November 16 they were in Tunisia and had reached Souk el Arba, 130 km (80 miles) from Tunis. However, Anderson was unhappy about the length of his supply lines. The narrow-gauge coastal railway was old and totally inadequate for carrying tanks; moreover, the terrain ahead looked hostile.

Fortunately, Lt General Walther Nehring, the Axis commander in Tunis, was busy strengthening Tunis and Bizerta, and Anderson could press on against little opposition. But by December 2 Anderson was aware that his supplies were now desperately thin, and his troops vulnerable to air attacks from fighter-bombers and dive-bombers massed on the Tunis and Bizerta airfields. His superiors agreed to a temporary halt. On the enemy side, the lacklustre Nehring was replaced on December 9 by General Jurgen von Arnim, a veteran of the Russian front, as commander of the Axis forces in Tunisia.

First Army's breather ended on December 22. Anxious to move ahead, Allied commander Lt

A WINTER'S TALE

When the British First Army's advance into Tunisia ground to a halt in December 1942, the weather became a foe as implacable as the Axis army. Violent storms lashed the hills, torrential rains flooded the roads, and the ground became a quagmire that could suck the boots from a man's feet. Tanks floundered, their tracks churning great furrows, and aircraft stood embedded in clay on landing strips. Mules had to be used to bring up rations, and any man who could handle these temperamental beasts was much sought after.

During those winter months British newspapers reported a 'lull' in the fighting, but there was no lull for the infantry. Nightly they went out on patrols, returning the next morning looking like clay figures. Most of the day would be spent scraping mud from clothes and equipment and cleaning weapons. Then they went out on patrol again.

There was no lull for the Germans either, and their incessant artillery barrages added to the misery of the bogged-down British. In their exposed positions – it was impossible to dig trenches – the troops were at the mercy of shellfire, and half the casualties of the entire Tunisian campaign were suffered during the winter months. It was reminiscent of the worst trench warfare on the Western Front in World War I.

OPERATION MUDLARK Paratroop Sergeant Frank Tucker cleans the Tunisian mud from his boots.

General Dwight D. Eisenhower ordered a thrust at Tunis by the British 6th Armoured Division, whose left flank would be covered by troops occupying the hills above the Medjerda river valley. One hill was particularly important – whoever held it could command the entire valley stretching for 40 km (25 miles) to Tunis. This was 'Longstop Hill', and the Allies' failure to break through the valley was a serious setback. But Eisenhower, realising the impossibility of making headway in the appalling conditions, postponed the offensive, deciding to spend the rest of the winter building up reinforcements and supplies. For the men in the front line, it meant weeks of misery and discomfort (see box, p. 233).

On January 14, 1943, Churchill and Roosevelt met in Casablanca (see box, p. 237). Despite the follow-through from 'Torch' not going to plan, they were optimistic. In the east, Rommel was still on the run from Montgomery's Eighth Army, and a new push from the west in spring would surely spell the end for the Axis forces. The next step was to be the invasion of Sicily and then Italy. Eisenhower would concentrate on preparations for this move. General Sir Harold Alexander would command a newly constituted 18th Army Group in Tunisia, combining the British First and Eighth Armies and the US II Corps.

ROMMEL'S RESENTMENT

By late January, the Eighth Army was close to the Tunisian border. Rommel's Panzerarmee Afrika (the Afrika Korps and Italian forces) was pushed into Tunisia, linking up with Arnim's Fifth Panzer Army. The two men were not the best of friends – Rommel resented being technically subordinate to Arnim, and also the far superior resources that were allocated to Arnim's forces. Their relationship worsened when Arnim's first move on Rommel's arrival in Tunisia was to detach the 21st Panzer Division from the Afrika Korps for an attack on Allied positions in the west. However, the Desert Fox soon recognised the opportunity of a concerted attack – even at the risk of leaving his rear thinly defended against Montgomery. He would attack the Allies to his west before the Eighth Army could catch up.

In western Tunisia, the Allies had formed a front along a barren mountain range called the Eastern Dorsal, which runs north-south for almost 320 km (200 miles), from Pont du Fahs to Gafsa, and is split by narrow passes. The British V Corps held the northern sector, the centre was manned by the French XIX Corps and the southern end by the US II Corps.

Poorly led by Maj General Lloyd R. Fredendall, the Americans were vulnerable. On February 14, howling Stuka dive-bombers plastered the village of Sidi Bou Zid, at the western end of Faid Pass, while the tanks of the 10th Panzer Division – including newly arrived Panzer VIs, or Tigers, with powerful 88 mm guns – poured through the pass under cover of a sandstorm. In an encircling movement, the 21st Panzer Division broke through the mountains to the south. By mid-morning two groups totalling 2500 Americans in the hills were surrounded, and by evening the Germans held Sidi Bou Zid.

Next day, Fredendall counterattacked in a desperate bid to rescue his marooned men. Led by Colonel James Alger, a battalion of US 1st Armored Division tanks roared across the plain towards Sidi Bou Zid. The Germans waited until the Americans were almost upon them, then an artillery barrage ripped into the first wave of tanks. Stukas appeared overhead as if from nowhere; and too late, Alger saw German tanks approaching on each side. The Americans were annihilated, losing 46 tanks, 15 officers and 298 men. Alger was captured. The men still marooned in the hills tried to fight their way out. Only 300 made it; the rest were killed or captured.

Now the remaining Americans were in full flight, heading for the Western Dorsal mountains, 80 km (50 miles) away. There a stand had to be made, for one vital way through the mountains, the Kasserine Pass, led to a large Allied supply base at Tebessa, about 65 km (40 miles) west. Weary and near panic, and with Fredendall totally at odds with Maj General Orlando Ward, commanding the 1st Armored, there seemed little hope of the Americans stopping the panzers.

KASSERINE ROUT

Rivalry now flared between Rommel and Arnim. Rommel wanted to press on quickly after the Americans, while Arnim argued that supplies were too low to support such a move. In the end Field Marshal Albert Kesselring, Commander in Chief South – to whom both men were answerable – flew in from Rome and supported Rommel, putting him in command of Army Group Africa.

RETURN TO THE HILL Grim-faced British infantrymen, with stretcher-bearers, move into position in the Longstop Hill area in April 1943. They were to avenge a defeat suffered on the hill at Christmas 1942. But again casualties were heavy.

THE FOX'S RIVAL

The rivalry between Jurgen von Arnim (1889-1971) and Erwin Rommel was bitter and enduring. But while Rommel is best remembered as the architect of the Afrika Korps' early successes, it was Arnim who made the Allies' final triumph no easy victory. He was a soldier of the old Prussian school, complete with polished jackboots and monocle. He distinguished himself in Russia leading panzer formations, and was wounded in June 1941. In December 1942 Hitler sent him to Tunisia to command the Fifth Panzer Army, and when Rommel returned to Germany in March 1943, Arnim was given command of Army Group Africa. As Hitler ordered, he fought to the last bullet before surrendering to the Allies.

WE'VE GOT IT! Men of the East Yorkshire Regiment enjoy their triumph after capturing a German pillbox in the Mareth Line. (Top) American soldiers rest beside their anti-tank gun. In the background is shellfire from the Kasserine Pass.

On February 19, panzers commanded by Brig General Karl Bülowius stormed into the Kasserine Pass, which at its narrowest point is only 1.4 km (less than a mile) wide. The Americans stopped them with artillery and anti-tank guns.

Bülowius was told to step up his attack, and on February 20 the Americans were on the receiving end of the most ferocious assault they had encountered so far. Rockets from German six-barrelled launchers called *Nebelwerfers* (literally 'fog throwers', but nicknamed 'Moaning Minnies' by the British) screamed into the pass, and behind a fearsome artillery barrage Axis troops poured through the gap. The Americans fell back in disarray and 11 British tanks, sent in as reinforcements from the 2nd Lothian and Border Horse, were lost.

BAZOOKA MAN This soldier is typical of the US troops who fought at the Kasserine Pass. He is armed with a bazooka, a portable rocket launcher developed during the war and named after a comic instrument. The mesh shield on the front protected the firer from rocket gases.

Now the way was clear for Rommel to thrust into Algeria, via Tebessa and Thala, 50 km (30 miles) to the north-east. But he expected an Allied counterattack, and chose instead to consolidate his position. His hesitancy cost him dear. When no counterattack came he resumed the advance next day, but now British and American reinforcements had poured in – the Americans to defend the road to Tebessa, and the British to hold the road to Thala. The American defence held, but the 10th Panzers, under Maj General Fritz von Broich, pushed the British all the way back to Thala. There they dug in and overnight were joined by the American 9th Division's artillery, which had raced more than 1000 km (600 miles) from Oran in four days. On the morning of February 22 the American guns stopped Broich's panzers in their tracks.

The expected Allied thrust never came, but Rommel had already decided that the flow of Allied reinforcements was too great to counter, and next day he quietly pulled his troops out of Kasserine Pass. It was 24 hours before the Allies realised he had gone. The American II Corps had lost 300 dead, 3000 wounded and 3000 missing, mostly captured.

ROMMEL'S LAST THROW

Now Rommel turned to face his old adversaries, Montgomery and the Eighth Army. His main defence was to be the Mareth Line, a formidable barrier of tank traps, pillboxes and concrete bunkers some 130 km (80 miles) west of the frontier. Rommel proposed to attack the British at the town of Medenine, south-east of the line, but air reconnaissance and decoded German mes-

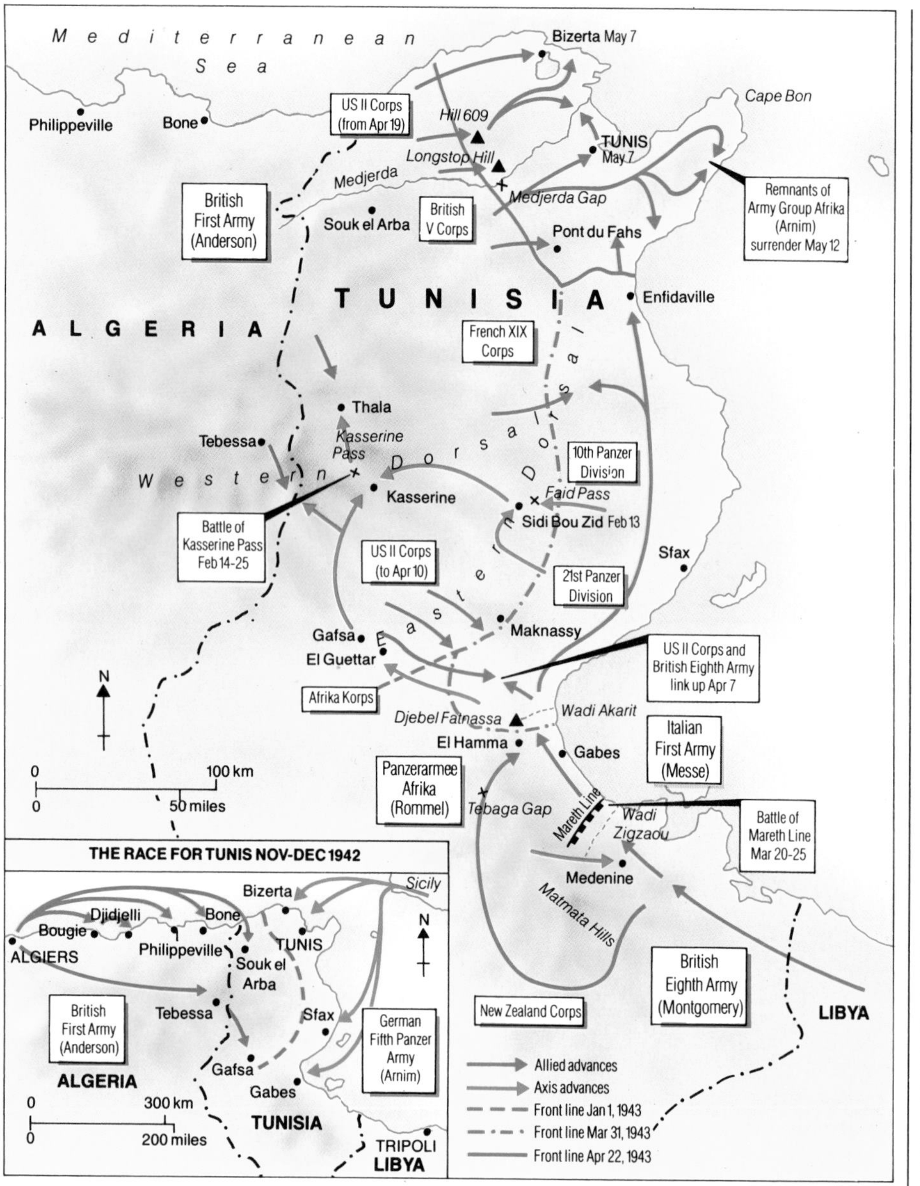

THE WAY OUT Mountains, rocks, mud and desert all played their part in the fortunes of the Tunisian campaign. After the Eighth Army's entry into Tunis, the Germans were chased up the Cape Bon peninsula – and right out of Africa.

sages forewarned Monty, who even knew the date of Rommel's assault: March 6.

Pausing in their advance, the 51st Highland and 7th Armoured Divisions set up a superbly camouflaged line of six-pounder anti-tank guns. They waited until the panzers were within 365 m (400 yds) before opening fire. Armour-piercing shells turned the tanks into flaming funeral pyres. Three panzer divisions – the 10th, 15th and 21st – were badly mauled, losing 52 tanks and suffering nearly 700 casualties. Monty commented that Rommel had 'made a balls of it'.

Three days after Medenine, Rommel flew to Berlin and pleaded with Hitler to withdraw from North Africa. The Führer's reaction was predictable – Rommel, still sick with jaundice, was sent on leave and never returned to Tunisia. Arnim took Rommel's place as commander of Army Group Africa, and at the same time the Americans replaced Fredendall with Maj General George S. Patton, who had shown his spirit in the Casablanca landings.

Patton took over on March 6 and set about whipping II Corps into shape. He restored discipline, and confidence was further boosted by the arrival of new Sherman tanks with 75 mm guns – a match for Panzer IVs. Even so it was not enough. Before assaulting the Mareth Line, Alexander asked Patton to probe the enemy's western flank through the mountain passes at El Guettar and Maknassy, at the southern end of the Eastern Dorsal. For three weeks Patton tried in vain to hammer a way through – but the Axis strongholds had been beefed up by panzer divisions taken from the Mareth Line. He had, however, succeeded in weakening the opposition facing Montgomery.

MONTY'S LEFT HOOK

That opposition was put to the test on the night of March 20/21, but not before Monty had set in motion an ambitious outflanking move. In the second week of March, the 25 000-strong 2nd New Zealand Division, under Maj General Bernard Freyberg, set out on a huge swing south-west and then north-west, to get behind the Mareth Line. It entailed an arduous cross-desert journey of 320 km (200 miles) along the western side of the Matmata Hills – a route pioneered by the Long Range Desert Group. Then, as the rest of the Eighth Army made a frontal assault on the line, the New Zealanders would drive through the Tebaga Gap and into the El Hamma valley to attack El Hamma, near the coast 50 km (30 miles) behind the line.

The frontal assault was made on the night of the 20th, but heavy rain had turned the Wadi Zigzaou, which ran in front of the Mareth Line, into a moat. Tanks and infantry floundered in thick mud, and by morning only a small force of the 151st Brigade had made a bridgehead on the far bank. That afternoon the 15th Panzer Division counterattacked, and, with only a handful of obsolete Valentine tanks to support them, the British infantry stood no chance.

Seeing the hopelessness of the situation, Montgomery switched tactics to go for the knockout with what he called his 'left hook' and sent the British 1st Armoured Division after the New Zealanders. But now the 15th Panzers were rushing from Wadi Zigzaou to the aid of the Italian Young Fascists Division, back in the El Hamma valley. The stony hills and little side valleys gave excellent cover for the panzers and anti-tank guns, so the RAF was called in to bomb and strafe the area before Freyberg's infantry attacked. At 3 pm on March 26, waves of Kittyhawk and Spitfire fighters roared along the valley, blasting anything that moved. Under their cover the New Zealanders advanced.

That night they paused to let the 1st Armoured tanks through, but progress was slow in the rough, rock-strewn and bomb-cratered terrain, and by morning the Germans had a screen of 88 mm guns across the exit from the valley. They held off the British tanks for two days but, even so, Monty's left hook was threatening the rear of the Mareth Line. So, in a sandstorm, its defenders fell back 65 km (40 miles) to Wadi Akarit.

The wadi (riverbed) ran 30 km (20 miles) inland from the coast north of Gabes to the Shott el Fedjadj salt marshes. Among the hills nearby was the 275 m (900 ft) Djebel Fatnassa, a formidable strongpoint commanding the wadi.

SUNSHINE IN SHADOW

Kenneth Anderson (1891-1959), who commanded the First Army in the advance on Tunisia, was a dour, unsmiling Scot, sardonically nicknamed 'Sunshine' by his troops. Montgomery said he was unfit to command an army, and Alexander called him 'a good plain cook'. Yet his army – which consisted of British and American infantry new to combat, and a sprinkling of ill-armed Frenchmen – advanced more than 640 km (400 miles) in six weeks, until hostile terrain and atrocious weather halted them. Whatever his failings in the field, Anderson was a highly competent organiser, and his rapid movement of reserves and reinforcements to counter the Germans played a vital part in defending the Kasserine Pass.

After the Tunisian campaign, Anderson returned to England and was given a training command.

Montgomery gave the task of eliminating it to Gurkhas of the 4th Indian Infantry Division. At midnight on April 6, the men from Nepal swarmed up the hill and fell upon the Italian positions. With kukris (long, curved knives) drawn, they charged and silenced the enemy machine guns. The main attack could begin.

A few hours later an artillery barrage – likened by the Italian commander, General Giovanni Messe, to 'an apocalyptic hurricane of steel and fire' – thundered down on Wadi Akarit. Then the 50th Infantry Division and the 51st Highland Division attacked in darkness and overran the Italian Spezia and Trieste Divisions.

But behind the captured Italian lines a spirited defence by the 15th Panzer Division halted the British. However, Messe signalled to Arnim that he could not hold out much longer. Arnim agreed and ordered the Italians to pull back. At the same time he withdrew his own forces from El Hamma and El Guettar. Now the Axis forces were in full retreat towards Tunis and Bizerta, and as the Eighth Army drove north, the US II Corps moved in from the west.

THE LINK-UP

On April 7, on a plain south-west of Sfax, two men met and shook hands. 'This is certainly a pleasant surprise,' said Sergeant William Brown, on patrol with the British 12th Lancers. 'Well, it's good to see somebody besides a Nazi', replied Private Perry Searcy of the US II Corps. The two Allied armies had linked up.

Arnim, despite a severe shortage of supplies, prepared for a last-ditch stand in the north-west corner of Tunisia. Along a 200 km (125 mile) front – from about 40 km (25 miles) west of Bizerta to Enfidaville – the Germans and Italians dug in. They were aided by a chain of mountains which included Longstop Hill, of bitter memory to the Allies, and Hill 609, so-called because French maps showed its elevation as 609 m (1998 ft). On April 22, the British First Army bombarded Longstop with heavy artillery. But the defenders lay low in deep dugouts, only emerging at night to repel two battalions of the 36th Infantry Brigade. The next day the 8th Battalion Argyll and Sutherland Highlanders met the same murderous fire. Urged on by Major John Anderson, they stormed to the summit despite heavy casualties.

To the north, the US II Corps took Hill 609 with a clever ploy by Maj General Omar Bradley, who had replaced Patton, now involved in planning the Sicily invasion. After unsuccessful infantry assaults, Bradley tried tanks – highly unorthodox against a hill position. But his 17 Shermans lumbered up the lower slopes and blasted the German strongpoints with their 75 mm guns. The infantry followed up and by the end of the day Hill 609 was theirs.

SINK, BURN, DESTROY

Arnim was now down to about 175 000 men. He had barely enough petrol for his 130 tanks and 400 aircraft; and ammunition for his 400 field guns would last three days, used sparingly. Against him were ranged about 380 000 men, 1200 tanks, 1500 guns and 3000 aircraft. Behind the beleaguered Axis army, Admiral Sir Andrew Cunningham's Mediterranean naval forces sat ready to strike at any mass evacuation attempt, with Axis air forces incapable of striking back. An Order of the Day from Cunningham on May 6 read: 'Sink, Burn, Destroy – let nothing pass.'

On May 6 a concentrated air attack and an artillery barrage by 600 guns hammered the Axis front. The 4th Indian and 7th Armoured Divisions – transferred from the Eighth to the First Army – were at the centre of the action. Gurkhas overcame the Germans occupying the heights above the Merjerda Gap, and the door to Tunis was open for the 7th Armoured.

But all along the rest of the front, German and Italian defenders fought stubbornly against tremendous odds. In the north, the Americans pushed their way towards Bizerta, while in the south-east, men of the Eighth Army were making slow but sure progress in the difficult terrain around Enfidaville.

The end came suddenly. The Americans, only 25 km (15 miles) from Bizerta, found the road clear and drove in on the afternoon of May 7 – just as the Eighth Army entered Tunis, led by armoured cars of the 11th Hussars. In both cities there was only token resistance from a few bewildered Germans left behind. Arnim and the remnants of his army had fled, east and north, up the Cape Bon peninsula. Here, on Hitler's orders, they were to 'fight to the last bullet'.

Pursued by the British 6th Armoured Division, the German general turned at bay as the remaining tanks of the 10th Panzer Division ran out of fuel. On May 12 they fired a last defiant salvo, and Arnim surrendered. In the hills around Enfidaville the remnants of the Afrika Korps, under Lt General Hans Cramer, had also fought on bravely. But that same day Cramer sent a signal to the German High Command: 'Munitions expended, weapons and war equipment destroyed . . . The Afrika Korps has fought to a standstill as ordered. The German Afrika Korps must rise again. *Heia Safari* [the Korps' Swahili war cry, meaning "tally-ho"].'

Maj General Graf von Sponek, commanding the formidable 90th Light Division, asked to surrender to his old adversaries, the equally formidable New Zealanders.

At 2.15 pm next day General Alexander signalled to Churchill: 'Sir, it is my duty to report that the Tunisian Campaign is over. All enemy resistance has ceased. We are the masters of the North African shores.'

FLAWED LEADER

Maj General Lloyd R. Fredendall (1883-1963) was the first American commander to be sacked in the Western theatre of World War II. A quarrelsome man, he did not get on well with the other Allied commanders – and he was incompetent.

When Eisenhower inspected the sector covering Kasserine, under Fredendall's command, he was horrified to find thinly scattered troops in no position to counter a strong attack. And Fredendall had set up headquarters in a remote ravine some 130 km (80 miles) to the rear. His downfall came after his inept defence of Sidi Bou Zid, just after Eisenhower's inspection. Maj General Ernest Harmon, commanding the US 2nd Armored Division, told Eisenhower: 'This is Rommel and tank warfare at its latest – way above poor Fredendall's head.' Fredendall was sent home to a training command.

AIRLIFT TO DISASTER

In the final days of the Tunisian campaign, some Axis troops managed to requisition small boats and head for Sicily. Most fell victims to warships and aircraft, and only about 700 made the crossing. The Luftwaffe also tried to airlift the fleeing troops, using their huge Messerschmitt Me323 Gigant transport planes – six-engined aircraft developed from the Me321 glider and bristling with armaments. They could carry a company of infantry or a 20 tonne load; but with a top speed of less than 320 km/h (200 mph) they were cumbersome and vulnerable to fighters. On April 22, 20 of these mammoths were dispatched from Sicily, and by flying almost at sea level hoped to avoid detection. But RAF Beaufighters were waiting for them, and 16 were shot down.

CONFERENCE OF THE CONQUERORS

Before the Tunisian campaign was much advanced, Winston Churchill and Franklin D. Roosevelt met at Casablanca on January 14, 1943, to discuss the next moves after victory in North Africa – and indeed for final victory.

Also present were the Chiefs of Staff, including Generals Alexander, Eisenhower, Marshall and Giraud, Admiral Lord Louis Mountbatten, and eventually General de Gaulle. De Gaulle had flatly refused to attend until Churchill pointed out that his position as head of the Free French movement would have to be reviewed if he did not cooperate. At first he would not even meet Giraud, but the two men finally shook hands for the benefit of photographers.

While the Chiefs of Staff thrashed out plans for defeating the Axis, Churchill and Roosevelt agreed on the terms of that victory – unconditional surrender.

SHAKY RELATIONSHIP A cool Casablanca handshake between Giraud and de Gaulle.

14: RED ARMY TURNS THE TIDE

As the Russians' strength grew, Germany's forces paid dearly for Hitler's overconfidence.

Stalingrad – death of an army

Stalingrad became a symbol of the titanic struggle between Hitler and Stalin. Over a million people died in a battle that became a byword for close-combat ferocity. For Germany, it was the first great disaster of the war.

AS DAWN BROKE over the plains of southern Russia on August 23, 1942, the tanks of the 16th Panzer Division – having crossed the Don river – rumbled towards Stalingrad, only 60 km (35 miles) to the east. The men – spearhead of General Friedrich von Paulus's Sixth Army – were in good spirits. They had already punched a hole in the Soviet defences, and were now riding easily over flat, open lands baked hard by the summer sun. Above them roared squadrons of Junkers Ju88 bombers and Ju87 Stuka dive-bombers, fresh from raids that had already begun the devastation of Stalingrad.

Ahead, the city was in flames, smoke from burning oil tanks and thousands of workers' wooden homes veiling the morning sun. Very soon, the city would fall – of that the German commanders were confident.

Certainly the previous two months had gone well. Originally, in his massive Operation *Blau* ('Blue') offensive towards the Caucasus, Hitler had given Stalingrad scant consideration. Reorganising his southern armies into two groups on July 13, he ordered one – Army Group B under General Maximilian von Weichs – to hold the northern flank, while the other – Army Group A, under Field Marshal Wilhelm List – advanced in the south. But the apparent success of *Blau* changed his strategy. Russian troops had withdrawn to avoid unnecessary losses in battle, and Hitler, scoffing at reports of a huge Russian build-up to the east, ordered his southern force to seize the entire Caucasus.

Weichs, meanwhile, was to shell and bomb Stalingrad, to prevent a build-up of Soviet forces. So confident was the Führer that the city would be an easy target that on July 13 he transferred Fourth Panzer Army to help out in the south – only to change his mind on the 29th, when its help proved unnecessary. This delay fatally weakened the assault on Stalingrad, when Hitler chose the city itself as an objective on July 23.

An important rail and river transport centre on the west bank of the great Volga river, Stalingrad was to be taken through a three-stage assault by two armies. First, Paulus's Sixth Army would slice through the north of the city. Then Fourth Panzer Army under General Hermann Hoth would strike from the south. Finally, the mass of Paulus's army would sweep in to push any remaining Russian defenders into the Volga.

LITTLE KATES Truck-mounted Soviet 'Katyusha' rocket launchers let off a salvo near Stalingrad. The rockets, with 3 kg (6.5 lb) warheads, had a range of up to 5.5 km ($3\frac{1}{2}$ miles). Larger ones had 18 kg (40 lb) warheads.

In fact, Stalingrad, with its 500 000 population, was not at all the easy target that Hitler imagined. It was well positioned for defence, was a great manufacturing centre (particularly for arms), and had a special emotional significance for Stalin. Straggling for 32 km (20 miles) along the precipitous western banks of the Volga, Stalingrad produced a quarter of the Red Army's tanks and other vehicles. In the north stood a bulwark of grim concrete industrial sites: the Tractor Factory (now turning out tanks), the Barricades arms plant, the Red October steel works, and the Lazur chemical plant. All would soon be fortresses.

Farther south, beyond the 100 m (330 ft) high Mamayev Kurgan (a burial mound), lay the city centre – squat, ugly stores and government buildings, and two railway stations. Through this area the 60 m (200 ft) deep gorge of the Tsaritsa river ran down to the Volga. Ferries connected the city to the railway on the Volga's eastern bank. While the ferries ran (there was no bridge), supplies would continue to arrive from the east. And unless the Germans could cross the Volga, Russian guns on the eastern bank would be free to batter German lines.

STALIN'S SPECIAL CITY

Finally, Stalingrad was Stalin's city. He had been in command of the place – then named Tsaritsyn – for four vital months during the civil war of 1919-21, following the Revolution. He had renamed it in his own honour in 1928. (The city was renamed Volgograd in 1961, after Stalin's excesses were condemned.) When Russian resistance to the German advance collapsed in the summer of 1942, he ordered that Stalingrad was to be the USSR's southern bastion, the final fortress from which there would be no retreat.

Every citizen had been mobilised to build up three lines of field defences around the city. Men and boys in non-essential jobs were drafted into the infantry irrespective of age, status or health – among them 7000 teenagers not yet of military age. Husbands were snatched from their families; others never returned from factory or shop; yet more were last seen by distraught wives or mothers marching out, still in civilian clothes. Young women were conscripted for nursing and signals work. To stop the Red Army retreating eastwards, Stalin's order '*Ni shagu nazad!*' ('Not a step backwards!') was transmuted into a slogan – 'There is no land beyond the Volga'.

But Hitler had ordered the city's capture. He, too, would soon see Stalingrad as the embodiment of his ambitions, the supreme test of German will. On that first day – August 23 – it seemed that Hitler was about to get the victory he had demanded. As night fell, German tanks rumbled through the northern suburb of Rynok and emerged onto the cliffs above the Volga.

That night, secure behind their barricade of tanks, the Germans watched the apparent death-throes of the city. Six hundred planes of VIII Air Corps kept up their bombardment, further destroying the central area, including the waterworks and telephone exchange. Thousands of

CHUIKOV – RUTHLESS BUT BRILLIANT

A rapid rise during the post-Revolutionary civil war saw Vasily Chuikov (1900-82) – a peasant's son – progress from Red Army recruit in 1919 to regimental commander two years later. He later studied Far Eastern affairs, and spent 11 years as military adviser to Chinese Nationalist leader Chiang Kai-shek. But he achieved wider fame when he took over command of Sixty-Second Army in Stalingrad in September 1942.

When Chuikov arrived, the Sixty-Second was retreating in panic. His volatile, abrasive personality proved ideal for the task he faced. Using brutal methods, but also sharing the privations of the front line, he forced his soldiers to become expert street fighters, turning his army into an anvil against which advancing Russian forces could hammer Germany's Sixth Army into surrender.

After leading the Sixty-Second – now renamed Eighth Guards Army – across the Ukraine and Poland into Germany, Chuikov found himself the first Russian general to enter Berlin. It was through him that the Germans requested a cease-fire on April 30, 1945. After the war, Chuikov was for a time Commander in Chief of Soviet forces in Germany.

non-combatants – mainly women with children and the elderly – crowded onto the ferries to flee east, easy victims for the howling Stukas. By the end of that night, 40 000 inhabitants were dead.

Victory, however, was far from assured. Hoth's panzers were now under strength and exhausted. They were hemmed in by the ravines that crisscrossed the whole area, and it took them several days to extricate themselves. Only on the last day of August did Hoth manage to break through the outer Russian defences and advance 32 km (20 miles) towards the heart of the city.

At that moment, the Germans might have won, had Paulus thrown his infantry forward as planned between the two armoured thrusts. He could not. The advance had left large Russian forces untouched to the north. Concerned about possible attacks to his side and rear, Paulus delayed for almost two weeks. Only on September 13 did he begin the attack that was supposed to finish off Stalingrad.

THE RED ARMY RESPONDS

By then, the Russians had begun to recover. The remnants of Sixty-Second and Sixty-Fourth Armies had had time to regroup, moving back to Stalingrad from the surrounding countryside. On August 27, Stalin had appointed General Georgi Zhukov, hero of the previous winter's defence of Moscow, as Deputy Supreme Commander, and from then on Zhukov coordinated the defence of Stalingrad. A long-term strategy emerged: Stalingrad would become bait for a huge military trap. The city would be kept alive – just, with the least possible reinforcement – while reserves gathered to the north and the south-east. Then the trap would be sprung.

Within the battered city itself, the burden of defence fell upon Sixty-Second Army's new commander, General Vasili Chuikov. While his immediate boss General Andrei Yeremenko, commander of the South-East Front (Army Group), supervised operations from across the river – along with his political counterpart, the future Soviet leader Nikita Khrushchev – Chuikov had to turn a shattered force into experienced and committed fighters. He was just the man for the job. On the day of his arrival – September 12, just one day before Paulus's infantry attack – he told Yeremenko: 'We shall hold the city, or die there!'

Scanning Stalingrad from his first headquarters on Mamayev Kurgan, he found himself facing near-disaster. He had just 55 000 haggard men. One tank brigade, once 80-strong, had been reduced to a single vehicle. Against him, 100 000 Germans and 500 tanks were assembled in the Stalingrad area.

FIGHTING FOR PILES OF RUBBLE

At first, the power of the German heavyweight assault forced the Russians back. Swastika flags marked the forward German positions and Stukas dive-bombed ahead of them. On September 13, three of Paulus's infantry divisions and four of Hoth's panzer divisions drove in from the west and south, bringing the total German strength flung against the Stalingrad area to 200 000 men. Their aim was to take the heart of the city and seize the ferry crossing points.

For three days, they fought across the city centre behind the Stuka barrage, leaving the Gorki Theatre and the huge Univermag department store empty, scarred ruins, lined with bodies decaying in the heat. Mamayev Kurgan changed hands several times. Only the arrival by ferry of 10 000 Russian troops of the elite 13th Guards Division saved the city from collapse. On September 16, the Russians retook Mamayev Kurgan and brought the German advance to a messy halt. However, the Germans still managed to seize the main ferry landing.

Now the Germans found themselves engaged in brutal street-to-street, house-to-house, room-to-room fighting. The only way to clear buildings was to invade them, and either burn them out or capture them room by room. But both sides rapidly adapted to the conditions. They used groups of a dozen or so men – *Kampfgruppen*, the Germans called them – teams of specialists armed with machine guns, submachine guns and grenades. The Russians developed the concept of 'killing zones' – houses and ruins that had been heavily mined, through which only the Russians knew their way. They wrapped their feet in cloth to deaden noise and carried shovels with sharpened edges to double as weapons in hand-to-hand combat.

For the Germans, used to space, movement and supporting tanks, Stalingrad became a nightmare. 'We would spend the whole day clearing a street from end to end,' wrote one officer, 'But at dawn the Russians would start firing from their old positions at the far end . . . They had knocked holes between the garrets and attics, and during the night would run back like rats in the rafters.'

Often, a downstairs room would be seized by German infantry, while immediately above lurked a Red Army unit. The stairs would be a no-man's-land across which both sides would pour men, grenades, machine-gun bursts and sheets of fire from flamethrowers. Of one fire-fight – for a grain elevator – a Russian soldier wrote: 'We sensed and heard the enemy soldiers' breath and footsteps, but we could not see them in the smoke. We fired at sound.'

The ruins provided perfect cover for snipers. The Russians set up a snipers' training school in the Lazur chemical works. It was run by Vasili Zaitsev, a deer-hunter from the Urals who was a formidable shot: in one ten-day period, he killed 40 Germans. Determined to eradicate this menace, the Germans flew in their own expert, SS Colonel Heinz Thorwald, head of the sniper training centre in Zossen, near Berlin. For three days, the two stalked each other. Then Zaitsev spotted a piece of sheet metal that would provide ideal cover. Waiting until the sun was behind him, Zaitsev induced a colleague to raise his helmet and see if he could draw the German's fire. There was a shot, and Zaitsev's man screamed as if hit. Thorwald raised his head to check, and Zaitsev shot him between the eyes. (Zaitsev eventually killed 242 Germans – according to Russian accounts – before being blinded by a land mine.)

By the end of September, the commanders on both sides were near breaking point. Chuikov, unaware of Zhukov's secret long-term plans, had developed a severe nervous eczema on his hands. He had lost 80 000 dead and wounded, and there seemed no end in sight. Paulus, his left eye beginning to twitch with a tic of tension, was in despair. The Russian defenders seemed to be growing in strength, and despite his capture of the main ferry landing, Stalingrad held out, supplied by dozens of boats and rafts that slipped over from the east, covered by a flotilla of gunboats.

Russian reinforcements arriving faced a terrifying prospect. From the far river bank, Stalingrad seemed enveloped in fire. One observer reported: 'There were times when these

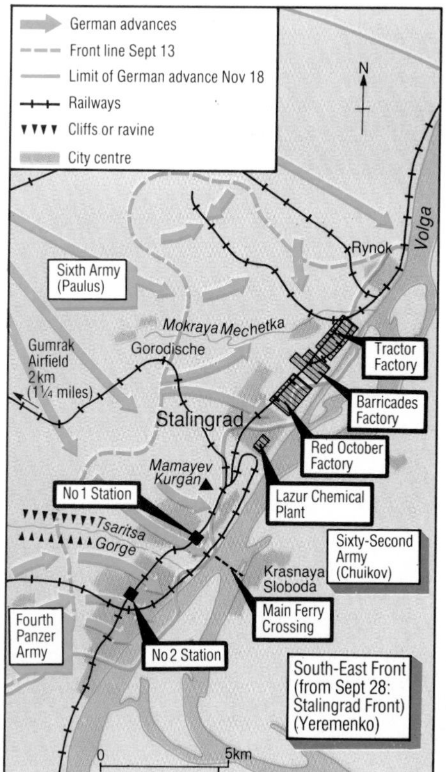

CITY THAT FAILED TO FALL The Germans managed to capture 90 per cent of Stalingrad, but the remaining 10 per cent allowed the Russians to launch their counteroffensive.

reinforcements were really pathetic. They would stand there on the shore shivering with cold and fear, 5 or 10 out of 20 already killed by German shells. But the peculiar thing was that those who reached the front line very quickly became hardened soldiers. Real frontniks.' Soon winter would come, the Volga would freeze, and the Russians would be free to send in even more troops over the ice. Paulus could only assure Hitler that just one more push would win the day.

'FINAL' OFFENSIVE

On October 4, Paulus's 'final' offensive opened with an assault on the three remaining Soviet strongpoints – the Tractor Factory, the Barricades arms plant and the Red October steel works. One German officer recorded 'tanks clambering over mountains of debris and scrap, crunching through chaotically destroyed workshops, firing at point-blank range into rubble-filled streets and narrow factory courtyards'. In the Tractor Factory, workers would finish fitting out a tank and drive it straight into battle, while others would drop tools and seize arms, joining women and teenagers to repel the enemy.

In ten days, half the Red October plant and most of the Barricades complex had fallen. By early November, the Germans had reduced the Russian-held area to two tiny enclaves, one 13 km (8 miles) long and 1.5 km (1 mile) deep, the other an even smaller outpost in the far north.

But these were all that Zhukov needed. The two months of Stalingrad's agony had bought him time enough to build his reserves. Altogether, the Volga Flotilla made over 35 000 runs into Stalingrad and 122 000 men landed on the west bank. Meanwhile, another 27 infantry divisions and 19 armoured brigades had arrived in the area for training, travelling by night in small groups in order not to attract the attention of German spotter planes. By mid-November more than a million men, some 13 500 heavy guns, 900 tanks and 1100 aircraft were in position. The Germans, in contrast, had little prospect of reinforcement.

In the city, the horror continued, captured in the words of a German officer: 'Ask any soldier what half an hour of hand-to-hand struggle means in such a fight,' he wrote. 'And imagine Stalingrad, 80 days and 80 nights of hand-to-hand struggles . . . The street is no longer measured in metres but in corpses . . . and when night arrives, one of those scorching, howling, bleeding nights, the dogs plunge into the Volga and swim desperately for the other bank . . . Animals flee this hell . . . only man endures.'

But not for much longer. Early on November 19, the weary men in the ruins woke to the distant boom of heavy guns from the north-west. The Russian counteroffensive had begun.

STALIN STRIKES BACK

For some time, it had been clear to Germans on the spot that Stalingrad had become a trap, and not just for Sixth Army. Weich's Army Group B as a whole, holding a 480 km (300 mile) front north and south of Stalingrad, was in no shape to withstand a large-scale assault. With mostly German forces locked in Stalingrad, the rest of the front was held in part by poorly equipped allies – Romanians, Hungarians and Italians.

Despite Russian secrecy, Paulus in Stalingrad had long known of the Russian build-up. Deserters had told their German interrogators of it. But the Germans had no means of knowing the full scale of the operation, let alone the scale of Stalin's longer-term plans. He aimed to destroy not just Sixth Army, not just all of Army Group B; he planned to shatter the whole of Germany's forces in the southern Soviet Union in one huge operation from the Don river to the Black Sea.

The counteroffensive, code-named 'Uranus', was to open in three stages. First, Fifth Tank and Twenty-First Armies would strike south-eastwards from positions already established on the Don north-west of Stalingrad; then, from the south of the city, the Fifty-Seventh and Fifty-First armies would drive north-west. When the two Russian forces met, the German Sixth Army, including part of Fourth Panzer Army, in Stalingrad would be clasped in the arms of a great pincer. Meanwhile, a second pincer movement

STALINGRAD HORROR

From the few first-hand German accounts from troop level of the Stalingrad fighting there emerges a picture of utter horror: 'It is hard, often impossible, to distinguish between night and day, for vast clouds of smoke blot out the light. We live a semi-troglodyte existence in ground which shudders without pause from shellfire and amid a noise which stuns the senses. The darkness is often broken by the flames of the rocket projectiles – the Katyushas, which the Ivans have learned to mass in whole regiments so as to saturate selected areas of the battlefield. The rocket flames have scarcely died before the missiles in hundreds and in thousands crash around us. They aim at no specific target, nor can our gunners . . . distinguish between the Ivans and ourselves, for our positions are too intermingled to permit accuracy. Russian rockets kill Red Army men. Our artillery buries us during our bombardments. Stalingrad stinks of the corrupting dead, of fire, of destruction, and the sour smell of hopelessness.'

INTO THE BREACH Winter-clad Soviet troops dodge through ruined buildings in the open steppe around Stalingrad. Russian armies attacking south of the city from November 20 rounded up 10 000 prisoners and pushed 50 km (30 miles) into German-held territory in two days.

farther out would make sure that no reinforcements could reach the besieged garrison.

The night of November 18/19 was bitter, with flurries of snow falling through freezing fog. Besides the bone-chilling cold, the Romanians guarding the German front line 160 km (100 miles) north-west of Stalingrad had other causes for concern. Not only had they heard rumours of the Russian build-up, but their old 37 mm (1.5 in) anti-tank guns were obsolete. Moreover, the German 22nd Panzer Division's tanks had been idle for over two months through lack of fuel, and when ordered to support the Romanian front line just before the Russian assault, many of the tank drivers could not start their engines. One reason was that mice – attracted by the straw and reeds protecting the tanks – had gnawed through electrical insulation, causing short circuits.

DEATH BY SLOW STRANGULATION **The aim of Operation 'Uranus' was to trap Paulus's Sixth Army in a vast Russian pincer, and then batter and storm it into surrender. By the beginning of February 1943, the plan had succeeded.**

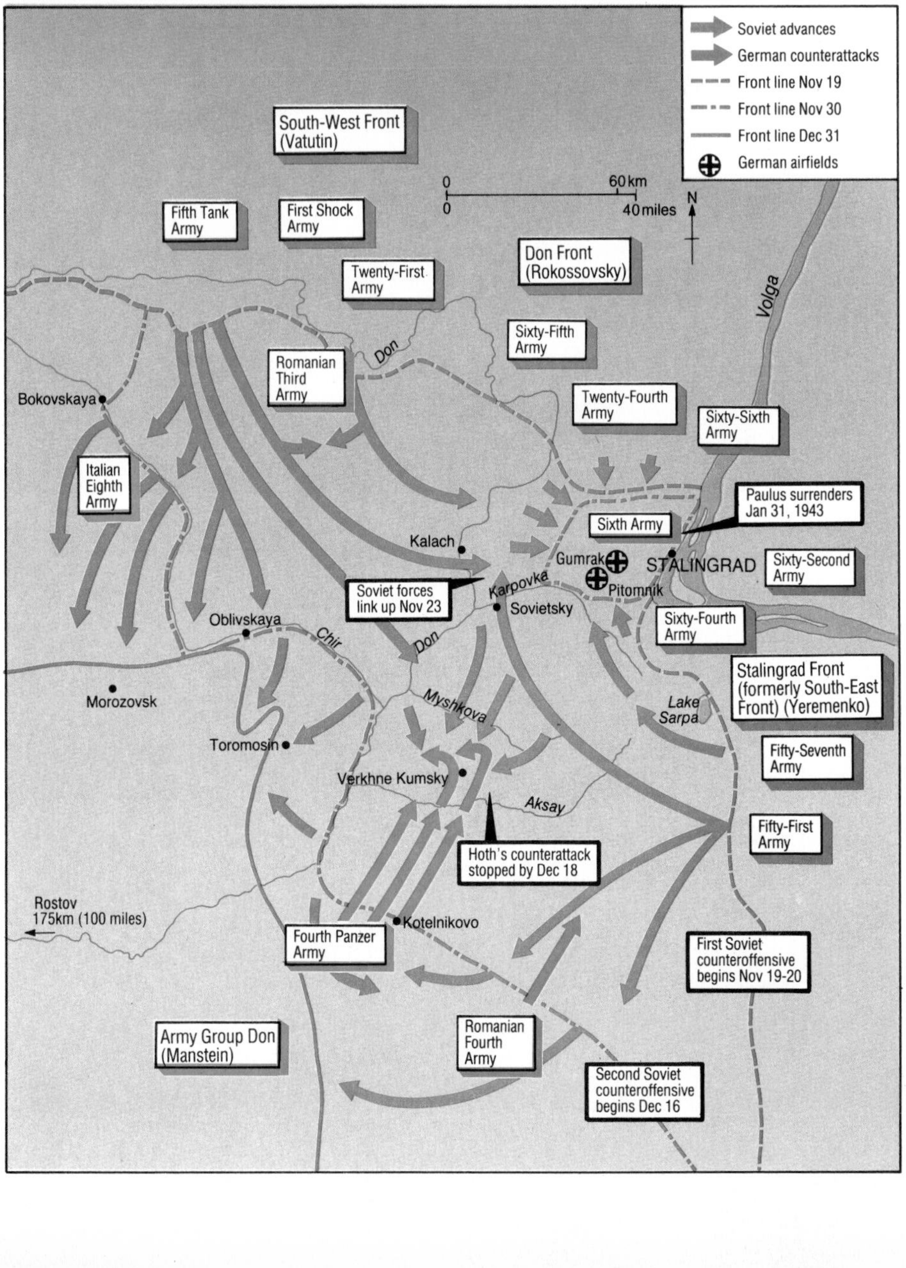

At dawn on the 19th the Romanians' worst fears were realised: 3500 Russian guns opened up on them, in salvos that buried hundreds alive in their collapsing bunkers. Within two hours, the survivors were overwhelmed by Russian infantry in white winter camouflage overalls, padding out of the snow and fog, ghostly figures accompanied by the dreaded T-34 tanks. Many Romanians fled, leaving a gaping 80 km (50 mile) hole in the Axis lines. The next day, the Russian armies south of Stalingrad launched their attack, with equally devastating effect.

CLOSING THE PINCERS

Both Soviet forces were now racing towards one vital point: a bridge over the Don at Kalach, 65 km (40 miles) west of Stalingrad. First to approach it were units from the northern forces – XXVI Tank Corps. The commander, Maj General A.G. Rodin, knew that the bridge would be wired for demolition, so he ordered a detachment to approach it behind five captured German tanks. Early on November 22, the column roared out of the pre-dawn darkness, lights blazing. A bemused German platoon waved the tanks on. Before they knew what was happening, 60 Russians leaped from accompanying trucks, seized the bridge and made the charges safe.

Next day, at the village of Sovietsky, 50 km (30 miles) south-east of Kalach, the commanders of the leading units of the South-West and Stalingrad Fronts met and embraced each other with three formal kisses on the cheek. To the east, now trapped inside the arms of the Russian pincer, were 250 000 Germans and Romanians.

DISASTER LOOMS

In his headquarters at the Gumrak railway station 10 km (6 miles) from the centre of Stalingrad, Paulus realised the terrible truth. 'Army heading for disaster,' he signalled Hitler. 'It is essential to withdraw all our divisions from Stalingrad.' His assessment was fully supported by his superior, Weichs. Both men expected Hitler to agree.

The Führer was indeed shaken by the news of the Russian assault – until Göring announced grandly that his Luftwaffe would save the Sixth Army. His words evoked a glorious vision: Sixth Army holding its position, fed and armed by air, the wounded being safely evacuated to the Fatherland, tying down the Russian hordes, until relief arrived and the city fell. On November 24, to the horror of Paulus and Weichs, Hitler signalled: 'I will do everything in my power to supply it [Sixth Army] adequately, and to disengage it when the time is convenient.'

Even as the airlift got under way, however, it was obvious to those on the spot that Hitler's plans were mere fantasy. To supply Sixth Army with its immediate daily requirements – 120 tonnes of fuel and 250 tonnes of ammunition – would take 165 flights each day by Ju52 transport planes. Later,

PAULUS – LOYAL TO A FAULT

Friedrich von Paulus (1890-1957) was the archetypal German staff officer: meticulous, respectful, loyal. It was a fearful irony that he was destined to lead 200 000 men to death or captivity in Stalingrad, be castigated by Hitler as a coward, and turn against his Führer.

Emerging as a captain from World War I, Paulus rose gradually through the ranks of the Wehrmacht. As a panzer general in 1939, he showed enough ability for General Franz Halder, Chief of Staff, to appoint him his deputy. When Hitler decided on war with Russia, Paulus was one of those responsible for planning the campaign. In 1941, he became commander of Sixth Army and played a leading part in the German summer offensive in 1942 which ended at Stalingrad.

There, in the cruel winter of 1942-3, his code of honour prevented his disobeying Hitler and ordering the break-out that might have saved some of his troops. When finally Paulus surrendered, Hitler accused him of being a 'characterless weakling' for preferring captivity to suicide.

As a prisoner, Paulus turned against the Nazis, organising military opposition and broadcasting pleas to his former colleagues to defect. He remained in Russia until 1953, before returning to live in East Germany, where he acted as an adviser to the East German Army.

OUT AND INTO THE NIGHT Two German airmen, silhouetted against the beam of a searchlight, approach their Stuka dive-bomber. Stuka attacks played a key part in initial German successes at Stalingrad, but by late September the Red Air Force was getting the upper hand.

the German troops would need food as well – another 75 plane-loads daily. The airlift would take almost all the transport planes the Luftwaffe possessed – and hundreds were already allocated to North Africa. The only airfields were at Gumrak and at Pitomnik, 24 km (15 miles) from central Stalingrad. If they fell, air supply would be impossible.

In practice, the airlift was a disaster from the start. By the end of September the Red Air Force had begun to get the upper hand and now its air raids regularly prevented takeoff. Losses in the air were high. On November 29 and 30, for example, 38 Ju52s took off, but only 12 landed; the rest failed to find the target airfields. On many days, fog stopped all flights. Even on the best days, no more than 140 tonnes of supplies got through.

Those who bore the brunt of the failure were the wounded. The administration buildings at Gumrak were lined with stretchers, which were carried out every day to the runways to await evacuation. At night, after another fruitless day of waiting in the cold, they were carried back inside again. One attempt to ease their plight by using two giant Ju290 transports, which could carry 10 tonnes of cargo each, ended in disaster. On January 10, 1943, one of the planes, loaded with wounded, took off at such a steep angle that the injured men slid to the back, causing the aircraft to stall and crash. The other was shot down.

FINAL FAILURE

If the Luftwaffe could not save the day, perhaps a new commander could. Paulus's Sixth Army, the shattered Romanian armies and Hoth's Fourth Panzer Army – split between the Stalingrad garrison and the southern front line facing the Soviet ring – were all combined into a new unit, Army Group Don, under the command of Field Marshal Erich von Manstein, who had masterminded the conquest of France in 1940 and the capture of Sevastopol earlier in 1942.

Manstein's orders were to 'bring the enemy attacks to a standstill and recapture the positions previously occupied by us'. All he could really hope to do was mitigate disaster. His plan, code-named *Wintersturm* ('Winter Storm'), was to send units of Hoth's panzers to carve a corridor through the newly established Russian lines and provide Paulus, trapped in an enclave 50 by 32 km (30 by 20 miles), with a chance to break out.

On December 12, Hoth began his advance towards Stalingrad, 130 km (80 miles) away. He swept forward over halfway, but then, near the village of Verkhne-Kumsky, a Russian mechanised corps held up his tanks long enough for reinforcements, rushed in along a local railway line, to form a defensive shield along the Myshkova river. There Hoth stuck, just 50 km (30 miles) from the besieged German garrison.

Now was Paulus's chance to break out, but he chose not to take it. His losses would have been frightful, and he would not move without Hitler's order. He shared his troops' belief that they could hold out for as long as they were fed. 'After the winter,' he wrote hopefully to his wife, 'there is another May to follow.'

Not for Paulus, though. Manstein had asked Hitler's permission to authorise the break-out, but Hitler did not even deign to give him a reply. Already the Russians were tightening their grip. On December 16, they had counterattacked on the upper Don, sweeping aside the Italian Eighth Army and wheeling south to threaten Manstein's rear. He could wait no longer. On December 23, he ordered Hoth to withdraw, leaving the men in Stalingrad to their fate.

HAVOC ALL AROUND The men of a Soviet gun crew lie in wait at a railway intersection near Stalingrad. In the background, smoke rises from the ruined city.

In Stalingrad itself, conditions became steadily more horrific. On Christmas Day 1942 alone, 1280 Germans died of frostbite, dysentery, typhus and starvation. Paulus sanctioned the slaughter of 400 draught horses for food; when they were gone, he set a minimum daily ration of 50 g (2 oz) of bread and a bowl of soup. The troops were a picture of dejection, with pinched features and hollow eyes – yet determined to fight on.

Back in Germany, the conditions were either ignored or denied. Hitler's liaison officer reported the collapse by radio after visiting the icy foxholes, crowded hospitals and lice-infested bunkers. He described seeing a man whose numb, frostbitten feet had been partly eaten by rats as he slept. Göring dismissed the report out of hand as Russian propaganda. The enemy must have 'captured the transmitter', he argued, and was sending these 'defeatist messages'. Hitler agreed. Besides, he added, Sixth Army was doing a useful job tying down Russian troops that would otherwise be used in the battle for Rostov, then in progress to the south-west.

When the propaganda minister, Josef Goebbels, laid on his Christmas broadcasts, supposedly relaying celebrations from the farthest reaches of the Third Reich, he announced: 'And now – from Stalingrad!' To the embittered surprise of soldiers in the beleaguered city, a cheery song followed to assure Germans everywhere that all was well on the Eastern Front.

The Russians holding out in their two tiny pockets along the cliffs of the Volga showed no signs of collapse. On the contrary: on December 31, the Volga locked solid with ice floes, and the first supply trucks began to ease across with food and ammunition. There was even a New Year's Eve party, with actors, musicians and ballerinas driven over to entertain the Russian troops.

RUSSIAN VICTORY

With the end in sight, and a need to send troops elsewhere, the Russians offered Paulus the chance to surrender on January 8. They pointed out the bleak prospects persuasively – 'the encircled troops . . . are suffering hunger, sickness and cold. The severe Russian winter is only beginning; hard frosts, cold winds and blizzards are still to come, and your soldiers have not been provided with winter uniforms . . . You have no real possibilities of breaking the ring of encirclement. Your situation is hopeless.' In return for giving up themselves and their arms, they were offered food, medical aid and the right to keep uniforms, medals (swords in the case of officers) and to return home after the war. Paulus rejected the terms out of hand. Two days later, Russian forces moved in for the kill.

Steadily, day by day, the German enclave shrank back towards Paulus's airfield headquarters at Gumrak. As the runway became clogged with wrecks and scarred with shell-craters, the last planes lifted off. Along with the wounded, the planes carried final letters from the dying Sixth Army. 'We're quite alone, without any help from outside,' wrote one man. 'Hitler has left us in the lurch.' Another wrote to his wife: 'Do not stay single for long. Forget me if you can, but never forget what we endured here.'

When a Luftwaffe liaison officer told Paulus that there would be no more landings, Paulus knew all hope had gone. His face twitching with the tic that had now become uncontrollable, he shouted at the man in helpless rage: 'The army is doomed! It's four days since they have had anything to eat! The last horses have been eaten! . . . Why on earth did the Luftwaffe ever promise to keep us supplied?'

When Paulus abandoned Gumrak, he was faced with a grim decision. What was to be the fate of the thousands of wounded lying day and night on the ground in the open, waiting for planes that would never come? There was only one answer, brutal but inevitable. They would be left for the Red Army. The doctors and stretcher-bearers were ordered out, to help the wounded in those parts of the city the Germans still held. When the Russian tanks rumbled in towards the administration buildings, they drove straight over the wounded, possibly not even seeing them.

Still Hitler would not accept what was happening – even when told that German troops were reduced to eating the frozen brains of their dead horses. 'My Führer,' an aide arriving from Stalingrad told him, 'permit me to state that the troops in Stalingrad can no longer be ordered to fight to the last round, because they are no longer physically capable of fighting, and because they do not have a last round.'

Hitler, looking at him in surprise, dismissed him offhandedly – 'Man recovers very quickly,' he said, then radioed Stalingrad: 'Surrender is forbidden. Sixth Army will hold their positions to the last man and the last round and by their heroic endurance will make an unforgettable contribution to the salvation of the Western world.'

But by this time in Stalingrad, endurance and heroism no longer counted. Dead bodies lay everywhere, while 20 000 men, starving and frostbitten, their weapons lost or abandoned, roamed the streets without a base or command. Senior German officers, their formations destroyed in the fighting, took up rifles and fought as infantrymen. Another 20 000 – the wounded who had never reached the airfields – were camping out in the icy ruins. Russian guns, tanks and infantry harried them from east and west. In one grisly incident, a three-storey building housing hundreds of wounded in south Stalingrad was struck by a shell and began to burn. Most of the wounded perished in the flames and smoke.

The end came in a strange and macabre way. On January 30, Hitler made Paulus a field marshal. His motives were transparent: never had a German field marshal surrendered. Clearly, in Hitler's estimation, Paulus now had only two possible courses: to fight to the death or commit suicide. He did neither. The next day, a Russian tank lieutenant entered Paulus's newly established headquarters in the ruined Univermag store. Paulus stepped out. He surrendered to the Soviet commander of the Sixty-Fourth Army. Two days later German troops holding out in northern Stalingrad followed suit.

The cost had been fearful for both sides. Virtually the entire city lay in ruins. The Luftwaffe had lost nearly 500 aircraft trying to supply the garrison, and about six months' production from German war factories had been wasted. Here and on other parts of the Stalingrad front 300 000 Germans had died, along with 450 000 of their allies. The Russians had lost 750 000, including many civilians. For the Germans, the suffering was not yet over. About 108 000 men were taken prisoner, shuffling to almost certain death in prisoner-of-war camps. Only 5000 would ever see Germany again.

Manstein's fighting retreat

The Soviet triumph at Stalingrad was a first step in Stalin's dream of sweeping German forces out of the south. Only a few weeks of winter were left for action before spring turned the battlegrounds into a quagmire. At first, the Red Army was dramatically successful, but the Germans were not beaten yet.

ANNIHILATION of the German Sixth Army at Stalingrad in January 1943 did more than release some 200 000 Russian troops to help the southern assault against the Germans; it infused new life into the exhausted Red Army. Every one of the 707 000 Russians who survived Stalingrad received a medal, and over 100 were awarded the country's highest honour: Hero of the Soviet Union.

Officers, too, were honoured. Gone, suddenly, was the harsh Revolutionary egalitarianism that was so destructive of morale. Now the army demanded respect for its officers. Their men had to salute them, and they were given gold and silver braided epaulettes to mark their new status. Red Army units received new banners, marking the occasion with grand rituals – bands playing, embraces, oaths of allegiance.

Alexander Werth, correspondent of the London *Sunday Times*, sensed the new spirit when he visited the Stalingrad area: 'Horses, horses and still more horses blowing steam and with ice around their nostrils were wading through the deep snow, pulling guns and gun-carriages and large covered wagons; and hundreds of lorries with their headlights full on . . . Thousands of soldiers were marching, or rather walking in large irregular crowds, to the west through this cold, deadly night. But they were cheerful and strangely happy, and they kept shouting about Stalingrad and the job they had done . . . They knew the direction was the right one. In their felt boots and padded jackets, and fur caps with the earflaps hanging down, carrying submachine guns, with watering eyes and hoar-frost on their lips, they were going west. How much better it felt than going east!'

There was good reason for the revival of spirits. As the besieged German garrison in Stalingrad was squeezed to capitulation in the winter of 1942-3, the Russians were driving west along an 800 km (500 mile) front in two great thrusts: towards the great industrial city of Kharkov and the Ukraine in the north and through the Caucasus towards the Black Sea in the south. They were aiming to reclaim both the Caucasus and much of the Ukraine, driving the Germans back to the Dniepr river before the spring thaw turned the ground to slush.

Far to the south, the German Army Group A, which had advanced so rapidly over the forested hills of the Caucasus the previous summer, was unable to move against hundreds of kilometres of earthworks thrown up by local civilians conscripted as labourers. Now the Germans, commanded by General Ewald von Kleist, faced a three-pronged assault. The Russians attacked westward from Stalingrad and from either side of the Caucasus, aiming to isolate Kleist as they had already isolated Paulus in Stalingrad. If the three thrusts succeeded, Kleist would be in a hopeless position, some 500 km (300 miles) from his main base, Rostov at the mouth of the Don river. Moreover, his armies, needed back in the Ukraine, would be trapped and destroyed. Hitler was unwilling to sanction any retreat and almost left it too late. Only on December 28 did Kleist receive the order to save his forces.

His retreat was a miracle of organisation. Within a month, his five armies – 250 000 men – pulled back out of the Caucasus into the Taman Peninsula on the north coast of the Black Sea opposite the Crimea, while the Red Army spearheads closed in behind them across the snow-covered, empty wastes. The Russian intent was to trap them there and seal them in by taking Rostov. The German and Russian front-line soldiers fought for villages, houses, barns – any place to shelter from the extreme cold.

The German troops to the east of Rostov fought a delaying battle against three Russian armies, meeting every Red thrust with a counterattack, but the overwhelming weight of the Soviet forces drove them slowly back, until by the second week of February 1943 Soviet troops had battled their way to the eastern outskirts of Rostov. The battle for the city was short. For the German commanders it was less important to hold bricks and mortar than to pull back and regroup ready for the counterthrust that was already being planned. The Germans gave up Rostov with as little struggle as had the Red Army during the previous summer. It fell, ruined and with only the German rearguard left, on February 14.

DRIVE TO KHARKOV

In the Ukraine, too, the Russians advanced fast. Starting in mid-December, General Filip Golikov sent five armies – including 900 tanks – surging towards the cities of Kursk and Kharkov. Kursk fell on February 8, creating a base for a further offensive in the spring.

But the major objective of the Russian counteroffensive was Kharkov, the Soviet Union's fourth largest city and already the focus of fierce battles in the spring of 1942. This huge industrial centre had been in German hands for over a year. Once it had had a population of almost a million; now two-thirds of its people had vanished – 230 000 deported by the Germans as slaves, killed by hunger, cold and starvation, or simply murdered. The rest had fled, leaving the survivors to eke out a meagre existence supplying the German forces of occupation. It was little more than a ghost town, but its recapture would set a seal on the Russian winter offensive.

Hitler ordered the city to be held whatever the cost. The task of defence fell on II SS Panzer Corps under Lt General Paul Hausser. This tough old warrior saw at once that he had a hopeless task, for the Soviet forces outnumbered the Germans seven to one and seemed intent on recapturing Kharkov. Hausser's corps consisted of three Waffen-SS divisions – 'Leibstandarte' (originally Hitler's bodyguard), 'Das Reich' and *Totenkopf* ('Death's Head') – and he had no intention of sacrificing them needlessly. 'City burning,' he cabled. 'Systematic withdrawal increasingly improbable each day . . . Request renewed Führer decision.' Back came a blank refusal: 'Panzer Corps will hold to the last man.'

Hausser, accepting that his action could well lead to his own execution, simply ignored the order. On February 15, he pulled out through the remaining narrow corridor between the encircling Russian armies, leaving Kharkov to the exuberant and astonished Russians.

Stalin was delighted. 'The mass expulsion of the enemy from the Soviet Union has begun,' he proclaimed, and shortly afterwards named himself Marshal of the Soviet Union. *Red Star*, the Soviet army newspaper, crowed: 'Now it is we, and not the Germans, who are going to plan the future of the war.'

MOBILE DEFENCE

Not for a while, though. The Russians had reckoned without the genius and persistence of Hausser's superior and commander of Army Group South, Field Marshal Erich von Manstein. Manstein favoured a strategy of mobile defence that allowed for tactical retreats. Such an approach was anathema to Hitler, but he had been so shocked by the failure of his stand-fast strategy at Stalingrad that he had grudgingly sanctioned Manstein's withdrawal westwards. Now Manstein planned to use his mobility to retake Kharkov – if he could get Hitler's support.

That would not be easy. Two days after Kharkov fell, Hitler, appalled at Hausser's disobedience, flew to see Manstein at his headquarters at Zaporozhye, 260 km (160 miles) south of Kharkov. The Führer intended to fire Manstein and order an immediate assault on Kharkov.

Manstein held his ground. The Russians were overextended, he explained; they were 320 km (200 miles) or more from their supply bases. The German troops, however, were close to bases established over a year before. Hausser's SS Panzer Corps was intact, and General Hermann Hoth's Fourth Panzer Army had recovered well after its failure to relieve the Stalingrad garrison. Now was the time to strike at the Russians out in the open, before the ground unfroze. Then, and only then, could Kharkov be retaken and held. His plan would turn the tables on the Russians, drawing them into the same kind of trap that defeated the Germans at Stalingrad.

Hitler consented. On February 19, Hausser, still retreating some 100 km (60 miles) south-west of Kharkov, was ordered to about-face near Krasnograd. When he did so, the pursuing Russian Sixth Army ran slap into him. Reinforced by Hoth's tanks and supported by the Luftwaffe, he attacked. The aim was to turn back the right flank of the Russian South-West Front and then strike at Voronezh Front. The Russian advance would be deflected towards Kursk, into the path of Second Panzer Army which was driving south.

The Germans caught the Russians at their weakest, exhausted by battles and long foot marches and short of food thanks to over-

DISMAL CITY Kharkov falls yet again under the Nazi heel in March 1943. Liberated by the Red Army on February 15, 1943, German panzers rolled back down its once-elegant, lime and poplar-lined boulevards exactly a month later.

extended supply lines. In a week of vicious small-scale actions, the Germans killed 23 000 Russians, took another 9000 prisoner, and captured or destroyed 615 tanks. Only a shortage of German infantry to follow up the attack allowed the surviving Russians to retreat north-east across the Donets river.

On March 15, German tanks rolled back into Kharkov – the third time the city had fallen in 18 months. The Germans just had time to take Belgorod, 70 km (45 miles) to the north, before the spreading thaw brought operations to a sticky halt, leaving the Russian high command contemplating with apprehension a German summer offensive. The planned German pincer movement had failed to cut off the Russians around Kursk; instead they held a large blunt salient projecting west between the two German forces. Almost certainly, Stalin thought, German attention would focus on this Russian-held bubble.

Stalin was right; on March 13, two days before his troops retook Kharkov, Hitler issued a directive setting out his plans for the summer. He planned to hit the Red Army so hard that it could not fight back that summer – or, he hoped, the following winter either. The first step would be to eliminate the Kursk salient. As the Russians feverishly built up their defences in the area, the scene was set for the mightiest clash yet between the two great armies.

ON TO KHARKOV Soviet troops in hot pursuit of retiring Germans stumble through the ruins of a village near Kharkov. Manstein's tactics of mobile defence were soon to halt the Red Army's triumphant advance after Stalingrad.

HAUSSER – SS CHIEF WHO DEFIED THE FÜHRER

Concern for the welfare of his men earned Paul Hausser (1880-1972) the nickname 'Papa'. He had already retired from the Reichswehr when in 1932 – aged 52 – he was chosen by Heinrich Himmler to set up an SS military academy. In 1936, he became Inspector General of the SS *Verfügungstruppen* ('General Service Troops'), the forerunners of the Waffen-SS. He was one of the few regular army officers to transfer successfully to the SS.

At the start of World War II he formed the SS division 'Das Reich'. He served in France and the Eastern Front, where a piece of Russian shrapnel took out his right eye. His disobedience of Hitler's order to hold Kharkov in February 1943 was partly redeemed in the Führer's eyes when he retook the city in March. Even so, Hitler delayed four months before including him among the Kharkov medal winners.

In 1944-5, Hausser rose to command the Seventh Army in Normandy and Army Group G in southern Germany.

Kursk – the greatest tank battle ever fought

The real turning point of the war in Europe, according to many historians, was the Battle of Kursk. More than 6000 tanks clashed there, and the Russians for the first time checked a German blitzkrieg. By the end of the two-week battle Germany had lost the initiative – never to regain it.

THE PRE-DAWN SKIES of south-western Russia erupted in a fury of flame and thunder. It was 2.20 am on Monday, July 5, 1943, and the massed German armies were preparing to attack a dangerous Russian salient, or bulge, 255 km (160 miles) across, that jutted fist-like into their front line. It extended from north of Kharkov to Orel, around the industrial city of Kursk. But it was not a German barrage that first thundered through the rain of the summer night. The Red Army, warned by spies of an imminent German attack, had let loose their artillery first.

The sheet of light burned from one side of the sky to the other. Flashes from heavy artillery sited well behind the Russian front line created a distant flickering white light. Nearer guns produced a yellowish flare, while closest at hand multi-barrelled Katyusha launchers fired rockets, their flight marked by a trail of red flame. Tens of thousands of rockets, screaming nerve-tearingly as they flew, crashed down hour after hour upon the German soldiers. The barrage reached its crescendo at dawn.

The Red Army's Chief of Staff, Marshal Georgi Zhukov, was known throughout the army as a hard man. But even he felt sorry for those at the receiving end of the barrage. 'Around us,' he wrote later, 'everything was in motion . . . We both felt and heard the hurricane of fire, and imagined . . . the frightening picture on the enemy side. The enemy soldiers hiding in holes, pressed to the earth to escape from the furious hail of bombs and shells.'

A BITTER CHOICE

In the spring of 1943 the German Army on the Eastern Front had faced a bitter choice – between inaction, which would surrender the initiative to the Soviets, and further offensive operations with forces badly weakened by the Russian offensives of the previous winter.

In the end, politics decided the issue. Germany could not be seen to falter; it must remain on the attack. In an operation code-named *Zitadelle* ('Citadel'), Hitler and his generals chose to attack the deep salient in the region of Kursk that had been left by Field Marshal Erich von Manstein's 'mobile defence' of the previous winter.

Hitler promised his generals the most up-to-date equipment and vast numbers of men for *Zitadelle*. In the event production difficulties held up deliveries of a new tank, the Panzer V (or Panther) – but reinforcements poured in. By the end of June, the German Army Groups Centre and South had almost a million men available for the operation. In support were 10 000 artillery guns, 2700 armoured fighting vehicles and two Luftwaffe air fleets with more than 1800 operational combat aircraft.

The Germans planned to destroy the salient with an overwhelming blitzkrieg-style pincer operation. The Ninth Army under General Walther Model would attack from the north, while General Hermann Hoth's Fourth Panzer Army would strike the southern side of the salient. The two armies would meet east of Kursk, cutting off all Russian forces to the west of them.

Uncharacteristically, Hitler had misgivings about *Zitadelle*, admitting that his stomach turned over at the mere thought of it. Indeed, a shortage of armour made him postpone the operation three times – in April, May and June – giving the Russians a vital opportunity to prepare their defences. Nor were Hitler's soldiers under any illusions. One who survived the ordeal – SS Lance Corporal Günther Borchers of the 'Adolf Hitler' Division – recorded his thoughts in his diary: 'I am in a flamethrowing team, and we are to lead the Company attack. This is a real suicide mission. We have to get within 30 metres of the Russians before we open fire. It's time to write out the last Will and Testament.'

The German plans, meanwhile, were no secret

DIGGING FOR VICTORY Red Army soldiers dig trenches in the Kursk salient in 1943. By the time the Germans began their onslaught on July 5, the Russians had completed a staggering 6000 km (3750 miles) of trenches, with 9333 command and observation posts and more than 48 000 artillery and mortar positions.

THE FORWARD SLOG In a battle-devastated landscape near Kursk, a German Tiger tank (below) swivels its turret to blast a Soviet T-34. By contrast, SS soldiers sitting in front of a Tiger elsewhere on the front (far left) present a distinctly pastoral picture. SS panzer grenadiers inspect captured trenches (left) and a collapsing village dwelling. Though furious and skilful, the German advance never picked up momentum, thanks to deep Soviet defences. By the end of the first day, Model's men in the north had advanced little more than 6.5 km (4 miles). In the south, Hoth's units covered only 32 km (20 miles) in four days.

to *Stavka*, the Soviet Supreme High Command. Inside Hitler's Supreme Command, a group of senior Wehrmacht officers had for some time been feeding military secrets to Rudolph Rössler, a member of the 'Lucy' spy ring operating from Switzerland – who in turn passed them on through his contacts to the Russians.

To meet the attack, Zhukov proposed an aggressive defence. He would force the Germans to make the first move against his carefully prepared positions – then, once they were worn down, Soviet counteroffensives would follow.

Aware that the war on the Eastern Front had reached a critical stage and that the battle in the Kursk salient must be won, Zhukov committed 40 per cent of the Red Army's entire infantry and armoured divisions to defend it. Central Front (Army Group) under General Konstantin Rokossovsky would defend its northern side, while Voronezh Front under General Nikolai Vatutin would defend the south. Together the two fronts had more than 1.3 million men, 20 000 field guns and 3500 tanks; they were supported by more than 2650 aircraft. In reserve was a newly formed Steppe Front under General Ivan Koniev, with over 500 000 men.

The countryside over which the battle would be fought was lightly wooded and rolling, crossed by several rivers and deep ravines, most of which ran east-west – thus forming natural obstacles against the planned German assaults. But these natural defences were not enough for Zhukov. Starting in April the Russians built successive belts of trenches protected by barbed wire and minefields (see box). More than half a million mines were laid in the first trench system alone – amounting to two mines for each German soldier who would take part in the first assault. Artillery was massed in the open country between the trench systems. The work was completed by late June.

WAR TO THE DEATH

On July 2 'Lucy' warned Stavka that the German attack was imminent. Stavka passed the message on to the commanders in the field, and early on July 5 Zhukov let rip his long-prepared pre-emptive artillery barrage. Rokossovsky's guns opened up first, and were followed a few hours

UNAFRAID TO DIFFER

Nobody cowed Walther Model (1891-1945). Staring through his monocle, he once interrupted Hitler curtly: 'Who commands Ninth Army, my Führer, you or I?' He rose to prominence on the Eastern Front and stayed there until 1944. But in August 1944 – now a field marshal – he became Supreme Commander West. There, he warned Hitler that his plans were unrealistic. On September 5, 1944, Model was replaced as Supreme Commander by Gerd von Rundstedt, but he kept command of Army Group B. Trapped in the Ruhr in April 1945, he committed suicide.

MASTERS OF THE SKY Smoke rises from a column of German trucks struck by Soviet aircraft. The Red Air Force soon gained air superiority over the Kursk battlefield.

BLITZKRIEG THAT FAILED

At Kursk, for the first time, the Russians successfully withstood a German *Blitzkrieg* ('lightning war'). Marshal Zhukov did so by using battle techniques of earlier wars – trench systems and massed artillery.

With a perimeter stretching some 575 km (360 miles), the Kursk salient could not possibly be defended with infantry and tanks alone. Instead, Zhukov later wrote: 'I proposed to wear down the enemy in defence operations, knock out his tanks and then bring in fresh reserves, launch a general offensive and finish off his main grouping.' The Germans must not be allowed to penetrate far, in case they gathered momentum to move on, blitzkrieg-style, and destroy Soviet positions.

Zhukov first packed the salient with two entire Red Army fronts, then he constructed field defences. By late June, these crisscrossed the whole salient. Each system had a triple trench line with barbed wire and mines front and rear. Countless mines were laid along the perimeter – seven for every 2 m (7 ft) of front.

A main principle of blitzkrieg is to bypass strong defences. Zhukov created areas which seemed easy to take but were, in fact, strongly defended. German tanks taking the bait ended up in minefields, facing massed anti-tank guns. Where an assault looked like breaking through, mobile mine-laying teams went into action. Two-thirds of German tanks destroyed in the battle were the victims of mines. Others fell prey to the Red Army's superb 76.2 mm (3 in) anti-tank gun.

After Kursk, blitzkrieg would never again in World War II win a campaign.

later by Vatutin's in the south. So important did Rokossovsky judge the psychological impact of the initial barrage that he used up more than half his stock of shells in that one night.

But the Germans did not take long to respond. Starting at 3.30 am, rain-soaked soldiers of Model's Ninth Army in the north began to climb out of the shell-battered holes in which they had crouched all night. *Zitadelle* had opened. Behind the infantry came tanks, while covering them overhead screamed Stuka dive-bombers. German artillery, having recovered from the Soviet bombardment, let loose its own massive barrage, which consumed in a few hours more shells than the Germans had used in both the Polish and French blitzkrieg campaigns taken together.

The German foot soldiers fought their way across the minefields and through the barbed wire to the first Russian trench lines. Using hand grenades and machine pistols, they had to take each trench and dugout individually. Sometimes they had to fight hand-to-hand using rifles and bayonets or entrenching tools to cleave their enemies' skulls. Already it was proving an exceptionally bloody and ferocious struggle.

The fury of Model's assault shook Stavka – though the bravery of the Russian infantry succeeded in holding it at first. Then two Red Army divisions crumbled under German panzer attacks. Fearing a breakthrough, Rokossovsky ordered massive air strikes. These enabled his infantry, backed by brigades of anti-tank guns, to block the German thrust. During the first day Model's men, for all their courage and determination, advanced little more than 6.5 km (4 miles).

In the south meanwhile, Hoth's men had faced similar conditions. The few new Panther tanks that had reached the German armies in time for the battle proved unreliable. Before they even got to the battlefield many fell out with mechanical defects – or burst into flames when their engines overheated. The farthest advance made by any of Hoth's troops on the first day was 12 km (7½ miles). Moreover, some 65 km (40 miles) of the 225 km (140 miles) that still separated the northern and southern prongs of the German pincers were covered with the same kind of obstacles and defended by the same calibre of men who had fought so furiously during the first day of the battle. It was a fearful prospect.

Both German generals remarked on the skill of the Red Army commanders – and regimental officers reported the improved abilities of the Russian rank and file. Intensive Russian training in the preceding months was paying off. The Red Air Force was equally impressive. German progress remained painfully slow.

GERMAN HOPES DASHED

On July 11, however, it seemed briefly that the situation might improve for the Germans. Hoth, unable to make any way northwards, had switched his thrust east towards the village of Prokhorovka. His advance was spearheaded by the crack SS 'Adolf Hitler' and *Totenkopf* ('Death's-head') Divisions of panzer grenadiers. Under Stuka cover they captured their first objectives – two hills on the road to Prokhorovka. The history of the 'Adolf Hitler' Division records that the attack went smoothly, 'almost as if on manoeuvres', and there was a general feeling that the Russian opposition was beginning to weaken.

But the next day came a battle that flew clean in the face of German tactical doctrine – that, in a blitzkrieg offensive, the purpose of panzers is to exploit an enemy weakness, not to fight tank versus tank. In the war's largest tank battle, near Prokhorovka, Lt General Pavel Rotmistrov's Fifth Guards Tank Army, from Steppe Front, dashed German hopes of a decisive breakthrough in a close-range confrontation (see diorama).

By the end of July 12 most of the German troops were in despair. Their hard-earned expertise was proving near useless in the chaos of close-range battles. Their dismay was matched at Hitler's headquarters, where news had come through of Allied landings in Sicily two days before. Closer at hand, the Russians had on July 12 launched a massive counteroffensive around Orel, just north of the Kursk salient. Hitler had been expecting a counterattack, but this came much sooner than anticipated and quickly gathered momentum. He had no choice but to switch three divisions from Model's Ninth Army to Orel.

On July 13 Hitler decided to break off the battle around Kursk – despite assurances from Manstein, in command of the southern sector, that it could still be won in the south. Only limited operations were continued to cover the withdrawal of the remains of Fourth Panzer Army. The battle was lost – and the fault was Hitler's, for it was his delays that had allowed the Russians to prepare their defences and train their men.

The collapse of *Zitadelle* marked the turning point of World War II. The operation may not have been, as Soviet writers later claimed, 'the swan song of the German panzer arm'. Nor did the Russian victory at Kursk break completely the offensive power of the German war machine – but it did wrest the strategic initiative from the Germans. After Kursk the German Army became an anvil upon which the Red Army's hammer-blows fell with increasing weight and power until the end of the war.

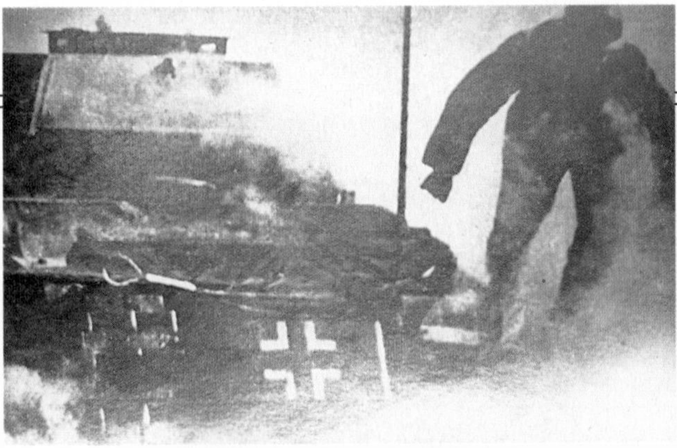

QUICK ESCAPE A German soldier leaps nimbly from his blazing tank. Hundreds of panzers were lost during *Zitadelle*. Many were destroyed by Russian anti-tank guns – probably the best in the world – others by mines or explosive charges attached by foot soldiers.

Death ride at Prokhorovka

The Germans looked likely to break through on the Kursk front on July 11. Hoth's Fourth Panzer Army had fought its way through several Russian trench systems and was heading for the village of Prokhorovka. Rotmistrov, of the Soviet Fifth Guards Tank Army, was given abrupt orders to stop Hoth.

Rotmistrov sent out reconnaissance patrols before dawn on July 12. His first tanks met Hoth's crack SS 'Adolf Hitler' panzer grenadier division at 4 am – and were destroyed. Two hours later, SS troops flung back a regiment of Soviet T-34 tanks. But the main clash came just outside Prokhorovka. The Germans were crushed in what came to be called the 'Death Ride of the Fourth Panzer Army'.

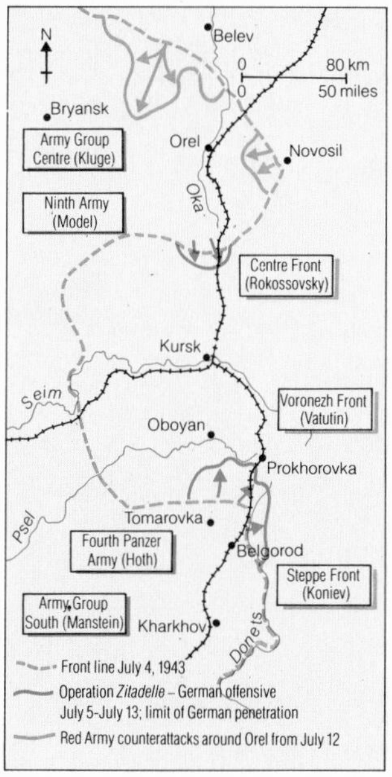

1 Outranged by the German tanks, the Soviet T-34s attack at close quarters. Soon the battlefield is one vast, confused tangle. The enemy 'were all around us', an SS panzer NCO remembered later. 'They were above us and in between us. We fought individual battles and when we were knocked out, we carried on the fight on foot, attacking the T-34s with satchel charges, blowing off their tracks, or using hollow charge grenades to smash their stern plates.'

2 A thick choking fog develops in parts of the battlefield where sandy soil flung into the air mingles with the smoke of burning tanks. In the chaos, many tanks collide. Others search for supply and fuel columns, then return directly to the fray. The crews have no time for rest or refreshment.

3 Hitler's unreliable new Panther tanks are easily knocked out by the more manoeuvrable Soviet T-34s.

4 Even the sturdy German Tigers suffer heavily. By the end of the day, Hoth has lost more than 350 tanks and assault guns, as well as 10 000 men. Russian losses are probably as high. But Hoth's threatened breakthrough has been effectively blocked.

DANGEROUS BULGE The Kursk salient protruded fist-like into the German lines. Hitler planned to destroy it with a blitzkrieg-style pincer, but reckoned without the deep Soviet defences.

Drive to the Dniepr

The tide of war turned against the Germans after Kursk. In July 1943, the Russians began their first summer offensive, with massive superiority in men and weapons. The German Army had no alternative but to begin an agonising withdrawal back towards the heartland of the Third Reich.

LIKE THE CHESS MASTERS they were, the Russians were thinking several moves ahead of their crushing victory over the German armour at Kursk even before the battle began. Once the Russian bulge into German-held territory seemed secure, they planned to straighten the front line by attacking towards the Desna river past Orel in the north and retaking Kharkov in the south.

Then the Red Army, on a straight front 950 km (600 miles) long, would roll the Germans back to the Dniepr river. Once again, the Ukraine – with its huge agricultural and industrial wealth – would be under Russian control, and the way open towards the heart of the Reich.

The Russians knew that their position was a strong one. With 2.6 million men and 2400 tanks, they far outnumbered the Germans' 1 million men and 2000 tanks. Moreover, the Russians could still call on massive reinforcements – total forces of 5.5 million, with another half-million in reserve, together with 10 000 tanks, now being turned out at the rate of 2000 a month. Copious American aid too was arriving.

The Russians knew from their spies that there would be no reinforcements for the Germans. Troops in western Europe – facing imminent Allied invasion – could not be spared, and the Eastern Front armies had no reserves.

RUSSIAN ASSAULT

On July 12, with the tank battle at Prokhorovka, south of Kursk, still at its height, Russian forces around Orel exploded westwards. They advanced through fields of shoulder-high steppe grass grown up on lands devastated by the German invasion in 1941. For a month, the Russians slogged slowly forward towards the city of Orel. When on August 5 they finally entered it, they found the city empty. The Germans had retreated west. The guerrilla tactics of Russian partisan forces – complete with ack-ack regiments – played a vital part behind German lines.

In the south, the Germans were in even worse trouble. General Nikolai Vatutin, commander of the Voronezh Front, prepared the ground for his advance by disguising his intentions. Fake wireless messages flashed between fictitious Red Army units. Dummy guns and tanks scurried back and forth. Following advances across the Mius and Donets rivers in mid-July, Vatutin opened his main assault towards Belgorod on August 3. Linking up with General Ivan Koniev's Steppe Front armies, which advanced from east of the Kursk salient, Vatutin surged forward, taking the city in just two days. At last the Russians had learned to use massed tanks in speedy pushes to outpace the enemy infantry. They were turning blitzkrieg tactics against the army that had first perfected them.

That night, on Stalin's orders, Moscow shook to the boom of twelve 124-gun salvos celebrating the victory. 'Eternal glory to the heroes who fell in the struggle for freedom for our country!' Stalin concluded his order. 'Death to the German invaders!' Those words were to become familiar to Russians – Stalin used them whenever he announced a Russian victory: more than 300 times in all before the war's end.

PRESS ON!

As the Russians drove swiftly on towards the great city of Kharkov, south of Belgorod, the brilliant Field Marshal Erich von Manstein, commander of Army Group South, switched tank units back and forth, using them like fire-fighters to control random conflagrations. But it was useless.

For their part, the Russians had overcome earlier supply problems. Roads and railways were built, civilians forcibly enlisted as supply and munitions carriers. 'Tell them to press on!' ordered Vatutin to com-

GREAT PATRIOTIC RESISTANCE Soviet partisan machine gunners (below), working behind the German lines in the Kiev forests, prepare to lay an ambush on a highway west of Kiev. Nothing daunted by appalling head wounds, a Red Army commissar (political officer; left) urges on his men. The Russian High Command coordinated partisan attacks on roads, railways, factories and airfields with operations by Red Army units.

manders concerned about isolating themselves ahead of their infantry. 'The deeper we thrust, the less chance the Fascists have of forming a stable front.' Manstein saw that he would have to pull back. But Hitler refused, driving Manstein into a frenzy. 'If the Führer thinks he has at hand a C-in-C or an Army Group with nerves stronger than ours . . . I am ready to hand over my responsibilities. But whilst these are still mine, I reserve the right to use my brains!' Hitler was adamant, insisting: 'Kharkov must be held at all costs!'

Within a week, Russian tanks threatened the city from three directions. For a few days, they were halted by the Germans' last desperate attempts to obey Hitler's orders. In one assault, from the north-west, General Pavel Rotmistrov's Fifth Guards Tank Army launched three head-on attacks on General Erhard Raus's II Corps, forming the city's main defence. Each time the Russians attacked, they were driven back, leaving blazing T-34s behind them – some 300 in all.

The defence was to no avail. Hitler at last gave way, and on August 22 Manstein ordered Raus to leave Kharkov. The next day, the city fell to the Red Army after the fourth battle it had endured since October 1941.

'SCORCHED EARTH'

To the north-west of Rostov, General Fedor Tolbukhin's South Front was hammering at the German Sixth Army, a replacement for the one that had been destroyed in Stalingrad. A breakthrough there would give the Russians a clear run through the southern Ukraine as far as the Dniepr. Manstein requested either help or permission to withdraw. 'Don't do anything,' Hitler cabled. 'I am coming myself.' But in the end he had to authorise withdrawal to the Dniepr.

The retreat was chaotic. Hitler's delays meant there had been no time to prepare roads, river crossings, demolition charges, or minefields. Manstein had to get 750 000 men – plus refugees and prisoners – across six bridges, then turn them to defend over 650 km (400 miles) of the river. Supposedly, the Dniepr would be part of a great defensive bastion, the East Wall. In fact, construction had barely begun; it was a mirage.

An operation – code-named *Verbrannte Erde* ('Scorched Earth') – to 'sterilise' the rich farmlands and coalfields between the Donets and Dniepr rivers was rather easier to carry out. Its object was to deprive the advancing Russians of anything they could use. In their retreat, the Germans took with them 350 000 head of cattle and 270 000 tonnes of grain, destroying another 13 000 cattle and almost a million tonnes of grain. Factories, power plants, railways and bridges fell to their explosives. The Germans uprooted railway tracks and even destroyed the massive hydroelectric dam on the Dniepr at Zaporozhye, which provided electricity for the whole Ukraine.

TOE-HOLDS ACROSS THE DNIEPR

Meanwhile, the Russians scrambled to outflank the retreating Germans. The result was almost a dead heat, the first Red Army units arriving on the east bank of the Dniepr opposite Kanev on September 21, as the Germans blew the last bridge and settled down on the west bank.

That night, a small band of Russian troops rowed with muffled oars across the river at Bukrin, just north of Kanev. Others soon followed, on crude rafts made of oil drums or bits of timber, forming two dozen small bridgeheads across the river by the end of September. For a while it proved impossible to strengthen them. An attempt to parachute in 7000 reinforcements to Bukrin was a disaster; only 2300 survived.

Then, early in October, the Fifth Guards Tank Army reached the Dniepr near Zaporozhye and found two large abandoned German barges. They repaired them, and overnight on October 5/6 ferried 60 tanks across. Two weeks later, the Russians managed to reinforce another bridgehead at Lyutezh, 32 km (20 miles) north of Kiev, by building a pontoon bridge. On November 4, tanks of the Third Guards Tank Army broke out of Lyutezh, headlights blazing, sirens howling, and soldiers riding on their flanks firing wildly. And two days later the Red Army took Kiev.

Farther north and south, Soviet forces were equally successful. In the southern Ukraine, they advanced unopposed in the closing weeks of 1943 to the mouth of the Dniepr, trapping the entire German Seventeenth Army of more than 65 000 men in the Crimean peninsula. Some 1000 km (600 miles) farther north, the Red Army recaptured Smolensk, key to road and rail links westward from Moscow, on September 25.

By the end of 1943, along a front stretching from the Black Sea to the latitude of Moscow, the Russians had advanced over 320 km (200 miles) – almost halfway to the 1939 border between the Third Reich and the Soviet Union.

EVER WESTWARD Soviet armies drove the Germans steadily back to the Dniepr in 1943. They retook Kharkov in August, Smolensk in September and Kiev in November. By the year's end, they had reached the mouth of the river.

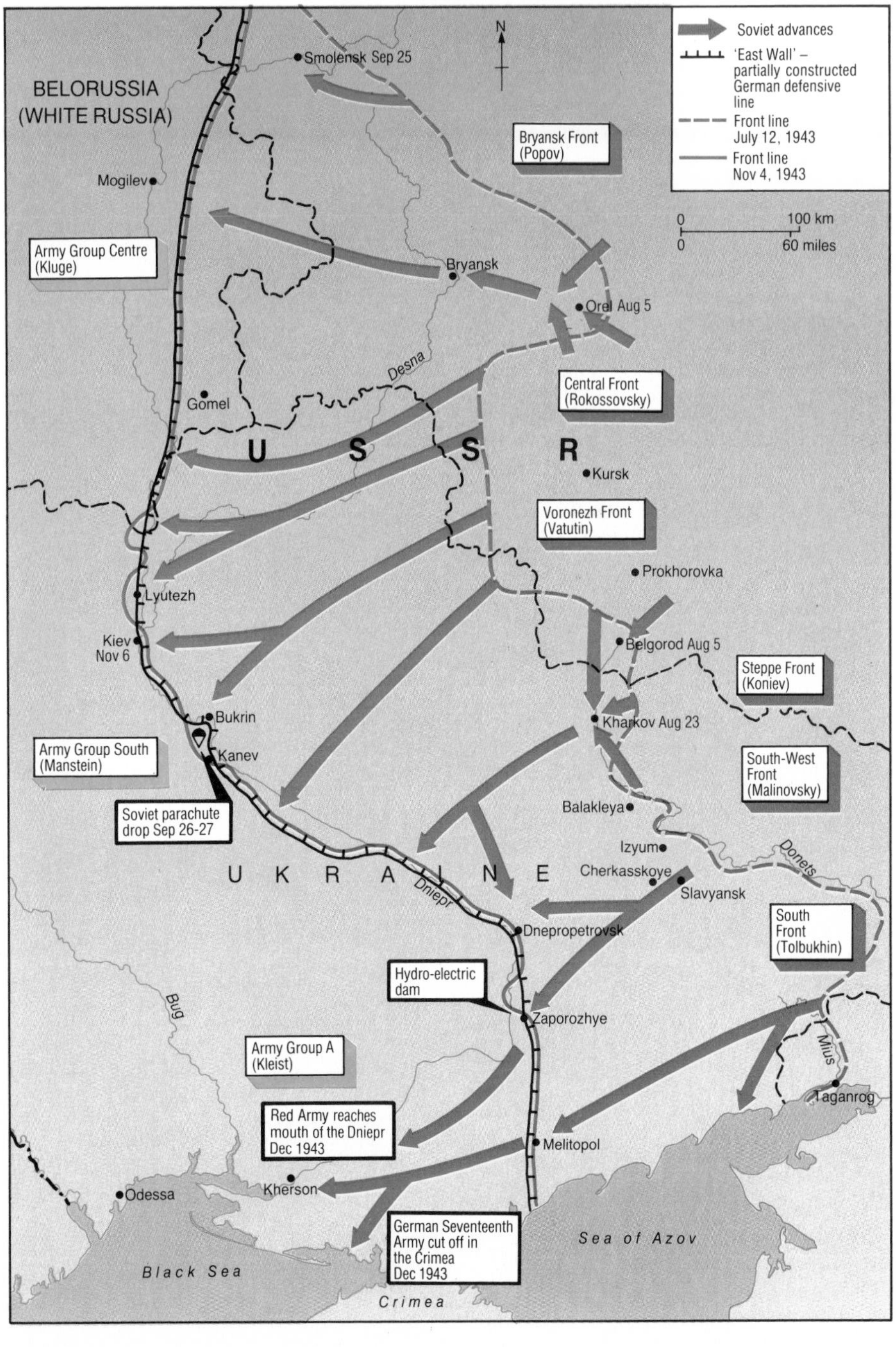

15: VICTORY AT SEA

Germany gradually lost the Battle of the Atlantic both on the surface and under the waves.

Battle of the Barents Sea

When the British Home Fleet finally confronted the Germans in the Arctic, the Kriegsmarine's heavyweights were put to flight – and Hitler flew into a rage. The Nelson touch won a British destroyer captain the VC.

A VIOLENT GALE – not unexpected in the Arctic Ocean at the end of December – blew convoy JW51B, bound for Murmansk, well off course to the south as it pushed through the Barents Sea north of Norway. It seemed to be heading straight into the arms of the German Navy's Norwegian-based Northern Battle Group. In fact the Germans were going to get more than they bargained for.

After the disaster of convoy PQ17 and the heavy losses of PQ18, there was a lull in Russian convoy activities while much of the Allied naval forces in the Atlantic covered Operation 'Torch', the North African invasion. Convoys were resumed in December 1942, coded JW outward bound, RA homeward. On December 22, JW51B sailed for Russia with a powerful escort of six destroyers, two corvettes, a minesweeper and two armed trawlers, under the command of Captain Robert Sherbrooke in the destroyer HMS *Onslow*. It was also shadowed by a covering force of two British cruisers – *Sheffield* and *Jamaica* – and two destroyers, under Rear Admiral Robert Burnett.

Though depleted by the absence of the pocket battleship *Admiral Scheer* and the battleship *Tirpitz* – both being overhauled – the Northern Battle Group still had the heavy cruiser *Admiral Hipper* and the pocket battleship *Lützow* based in Altenfjord. These, along with an escort of six destroyers, should have been more than a match for the convoy escort and its covering force. Certainly Vice Admiral Oskar Kummetz, commander of the group, seemed to think so, and split his force to make a two-pronged attack during the twilight hours of New Year's Eve.

Sherbrooke and his ships were, however, well drilled in convoy defence, and although *Hipper* sank the minesweeper *Bramble*, Sherbrooke's tactics of laying smoke screens and threatening torpedo attacks kept the Germans at a distance.

HEROISM ON THE BRIDGE

Then Burnett's covering force appeared. The German destroyer *Friedrich Eckholdt* mistook *Sheffield* and *Jamaica* for German cruisers, but was quickly enlightened by a hail of shells from the cruisers' 6 in (152 mm) guns. Kummetz, in *Hipper*, did his best to draw off the escorts. He had already damaged the oldest destroyer, *Achates*, which later sank, and repeatedly hit Sherbrooke's lead destroyer, *Onslow*, with 203 mm (8 in) shells. Sherbrooke was severely wounded in the head by a flying splinter, losing an eye.

Nobody around on *Onslow*'s bridge noticed that he had been hit, as he continued to give orders in his normal voice. Two more shells hit *Onslow*'s foredeck, knocking out both guns there. Sherbrooke ordered a turn to starboard to lessen the effect of wind fanning the flames, laid a smoke screen, handed over command to another destroyer and headed back to the convoy. Only then would he have his wound treated.

Hipper itself was badly damaged, hit by shells from both *Sheffield* and *Jamaica*. *Lützow* turned away, fearing that the cruisers were lead ships of the British Home Fleet. Both big ships and the five remaining German destroyers beat a hasty retreat to Altenfjord. Sherbrooke, the man with the Nelson touch, was awarded the Victoria Cross for his part in what became known as the Battle of the Barents Sea.

THE FÜHRER'S RAGE

Hitler was incensed – especially as the first news of the defeat had come from Reuters news agency. His wrath fell first upon Vice Admiral Theodor Krancke, the navy's representative at armed forces headquarters. The delay in informing him of the defeat, he ranted, was an unheard of piece of impudence typical of a *Kriegsmarine* (German Navy) that had never been anything but a breeding ground of revolution. The High Seas Fleet was idle and useless, he said – content to sit around in port. Then the Führer dropped his bombshell: the surface fleet would be abolished and the men and materials put to better use.

Grand Admiral Erich Raeder, Kriegsmarine Commander in Chief, was forced to endure a 90 minute monologue from Hitler on his navy's failings. He tendered his resignation and was replaced by Admiral Karl Dönitz, the commander of the U-boats, who was also a devoted Nazi. Dönitz actually managed to talk Hitler out of decommissioning all the Kriegsmarine's big ships, pointing out that the Northern Battle Group tied down forces that might well make the difference between victory and defeat in the U-boat war. Nevertheless, Hitler had work stopped on the 27 000 tonne carrier *Graf Zeppelin* and on several carrier-conversion projects.

LURKING MENACE The German heavy cruiser *Admiral Hipper* lies at anchor in Altenfjord, Norway. It was part of the force sent packing by the British in the Barents Sea.

The Atlantic wolf packs meet their match

March 1943 saw the Battle of the Atlantic reach its climax, when U-boat wolf packs sank 21 Allied ships in a convoy attack lasting five days. But new countermeasures and new technology would drive them from the ocean.

WHERE NEXT? That was the poser facing the commander of Hitler's U-boat fleet, Admiral Karl Dönitz, when his submarines were driven from the US eastern seaboard in mid-1942. But he now decided to exploit fully a flaw in the otherwise massively protected Atlantic convoy routes: south of Greenland there was an 'air gap', where patrolling aircraft could not protect shipping. Allied sailors called it 'Torpedo Junction'.

In the early spring of 1943, up to 240 U-boats were operational and Atlantic wolf packs were on the prowl again in force, patrolling both sides of the gap in wait for convoys entering from east or west. However, ferocious storms made their task impossible until the beginning of March, when ill luck put two convoys in the gap at the same time. Three wolf packs of 18, 11 and eight U-boats were ready and waiting.

The two convoys had set out eastbound within three days of each other, the slow SC122 from New York on March 5 and the faster Halifax (Nova Scotia) convoy HX229 on March 8. Both were large yet relatively lightly protected – SC122 had 50 ships escorted by two destroyers, one frigate, five corvettes, an armed trawler and a rescue ship; HX229 had 40 ships escorted by only four destroyers and two corvettes. The escort leaders were equipped with HF-DF, or 'Huff-Duff' – high-frequency radio direction finding gear, which should have allowed them to home in on U-boat signals – but they lacked ships to send off in pursuit of contacts.

HX229 was spotted by a lone U-boat returning to its base, and a pack of eight more moved in on March 16. Heavy seas shielded the U-boat from the convoy escorts' radar. The Germans also had a new weapon, the *Federapparat* ('clockwork') torpedo, or FAT, which, fired at long range, could weave among the lines of ships with a good chance of hitting one. That night, eight ships were sunk, three by the new torpedoes. At the same time the largest pack of 18 U-boats was closing in on SC122. Better defended, it held off the initial attack, but *U-338* later evaded the escorts and sank four ships with five torpedoes.

Just before 9 am next day, a long-range RAF Liberator bomber appeared from Aldergrove in Northern Ireland. This, and a second which arrived that afternoon, forced the U-boats to dive. However, the daring captain of *U-338*, Lt Commander Manfred Kinzel, made an underwater attack which sank another ship. When the second Liberator went home, it left the U-boats again in command in the gathering darkness. SC122 lost two more ships. Meanwhile, HX229 was still over 220 km (140 miles) behind SC122 – just beyond range of air cover – and the attack on it continued during the day, with the loss of two more ships.

So the slaughter went on, with both convoys in disarray. Then, on March 18, HX229 came within range of air cover, and the tide began to turn against the Germans. Circling aircraft prevented U-boats from attacking, and only *U-221* had any success, sinking two ships. Early on the 19th another ship was sunk, but later that morning one U-boat was, in its turn, sunk by a Sunderland flying boat. Two more were heavily depth-charged and damaged by escort vessels. Finally, on March 20, the U-boats withdrew, with a score of 21 ships sunk.

During the whole of March, 120 Allied ships were sunk, and the U-boats seemed to be winning again. As the British Admiralty put it, 'the Germans never came so near to disrupting communication between the New World and the Old'. In Germany, Dönitz was well pleased.

U-BOAT MASTERMIND

Admiral Karl Dönitz (1891-1980) led the German Navy's U-boat force throughout the war, and the entire Kriegsmarine from the beginning of 1943, when he replaced Grand Admiral Erich Raeder. Dönitz commanded a U-boat in World War I, and was captured by the British when his boat was sunk in October 1918. He helped keep German submarine expertise alive between the wars and took command of the U-boat service in 1935.

A convinced Nazi, Dönitz enjoyed the total trust of Hitler, especially after the 1944 bomb plot involving army officers. So close was he to Hitler that he was designated Führer after Hitler's suicide in 1945. His 'reign' lasted less than a month – on May 23 he was arrested by the British. Tried for war crimes and found guilty, he was jailed for ten years – a light sentence for the man who persuaded Hitler to unleash unrestricted U-boat warfare.

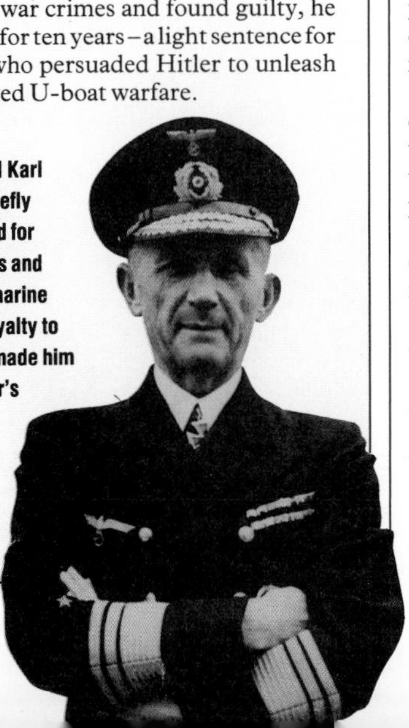

LOYAL NAZI Karl Dönitz is chiefly remembered for ruthlessness and skill in submarine warfare. Loyalty to the Führer made him briefly Hitler's successor.

FLYING PORCUPINE

The Germans called the Short Sunderland the 'Flying Porcupine': the Mark III version bristled with machine guns – in its final development it had no fewer than 18. The plane was developed from a prewar passenger flying boat, and gave RAF Coastal Command its first long-distance capability, with the tremendous range of 4700 km (nearly 3000 miles) and a top speed of 330 km/h (205 mph). It first went into service in 1938, and the Mark V version was still in service in 1959.

The Sunderland could carry a 900 kg (2000 lb) bomb load, though the antisubmarine bombs originally carried tended to explode on hitting the water, peppering aircraft making low-level attacks with shrapnel as they pulled away. Its main role became finding and harrying U-boats in cooperation with surface vessels. Later it was equipped with search radar and depth charges, and became a scourge of the U-boats. Almost 750 Sunderlands were built, many serving also with the Australian, Canadian and New Zealand air forces.

NEW SHIPS, NEW WEAPONS

Two vital factors turned the tide, however: the air gap was closed, and decoded German signals were used to concentrate limited resources where they were most needed. By April 1943, RAF Coastal Command had supplemented its Sunderland and Catalina flying boats with 30 very long range or VLR Liberators, increased to 50 in May. They flew from Northern Ireland, Iceland and Newfoundland, reaching all sections of the convoy routes. These aircraft also carried a deadly new weapon, the 'Mark 24 Mine' – not a mine at all but a homing torpedo (see box, p. 255).

Odds against the U-boats were shortened further in April by the introduction to the Atlantic of three new escort aircraft carriers and later new merchant aircraft carriers, or MACs – grain ships and tankers with short flight decks carrying three or four Fairey Swordfish biplanes.

Another weapon used with increased effectiveness – though it had been around since 1942 – was 'Hedgehog', which launched a barrage of 24 bombs in an oval pattern ahead of the escort ship. As a result, it no longer mattered that the escort's asdic beam lost contact when a U-boat was directly underneath.

The escort carriers, each of which carried about 20 fighters and antisubmarine planes, were soon in action as centrepieces of 'support groups' operated by Admiral Sir Max Horton, commanding Western Approaches from Liverpool. He now had just enough groups of convoy escort ships to assign some to act as 'firemen' – speeding to aid the close escorts wherever intelligence

showed their convoys to be in greatest danger. The support groups could then harry the attacking U-boats to death in head-on battles while the close escort continued with the convoy – which had effectively acted as 'bait' to draw the enemy.

TURNING POINT

On April 21-22, convoy ONS5 sailed west from Britain. Its close escort was the experienced Commander Peter Gretton's group – two destroyers, a frigate, four corvettes and two rescue trawlers. It also had the services of two support groups – Captain James A. McCoy's team of five destroyers and, under Commander Godfrey Brewer, three frigates, a sloop and a former US Coast Guard cutter. Brewer's force joined the convoy later from Newfoundland. However, the merchantmen were slow, the seas mountainous on the deliberately chosen northern route, and sometimes the convoy was barely making way. And waiting for them off Newfoundland were three wolf packs – more than 30 U-boats.

The first U-boat was spotted on April 28 and driven off by Gretton's ships. Next day an American freighter was sunk and the day after that another U-boat was held off by two corvettes equipped with HF-DF. The bad weather was also hampering the U-boats, but on May 1 conditions became so impossible that the convoy began to break up. Gretton managed to round up most of the stragglers and plugged on westwards, accompanied by McCoy's destroyers. But now the destroyers – including Gretton's own ship, HMS *Duncan* – began to run short of fuel. Brewer was called out from St John's, Newfoundland, to replace them, and sailed on May 4.

That day Dönitz regrouped his wolf packs, now 42 boats strong. Early in the evening, a flying boat sank one of them, but at nightfall they attacked. Six got through and sank seven ships – but suffered serious damage in return from Gretton's and McCoy's remaining escorts. As May 5 dawned, Allied listening posts picked up, and the codebreakers deciphered, signals from U-boat headquarters urging its captains to further action – and *U-192* was promptly sunk by HMS *Pink*, a corvette guarding some stragglers astern of the convoy. By early evening 11 U-boats were within striking distance of the main convoy, and sank three merchantmen in 30 minutes. But as darkness came three more U-boats were sunk.

Brewer, speeding towards the battle, chafed at missing the action. His radio was alive with reports from the convoy escorts ahead, he wrote later. One ship radioed, 'U-boat has exploded on the surface astern'. Another reported, 'Have rammed U-boat'. A third said, 'Have detected U-boat on the surface . . . U-boat has dived . . . am attacking with depth charges'. By 4 am Brewer's group was in the thick of the action. The sloop *Pelican* picked *U-438* out of the mist on radar, caught it on the surface and depth-charged it to destruction as it crash-dived. And soon the frigate *Spey* surprised *U-634* on the surface and shelled it, then depth-charged it as it dived.

In all, the British sank six U-boats, badly damaged five and also damaged another 12; two more were lost in collisions. The U-boats had sunk a dozen merchantmen – poor reward for such a concentration of force, and such heavy losses.

Max Horton reported triumphantly that the ONS5 victory marked 'the end of a period of large-scale attacks by U-boats'. He added: 'It may well be that the heavy casualties inflicted on the enemy have greatly affected his morale and will prove to have been a turning point in the Battle of the Atlantic.' He was right. The remaining May convoys enjoyed better weather and more air cover from Liberators and escort carriers. During the month 43 U-boats were lost and Dönitz called his wolf packs home to lick their wounds and seek less lethal hunting grounds.

THE SECRET TORPEDO

The so-called 'Mark 24 Mine', the world's first lightweight anti-submarine homing torpedo, was one of the most effective weapons of the war. Just over 2 m (7 ft) long, it weighed only about 310 kg (680 lb), including a 42 kg (92 lb) warhead, and had a range of over 3600 m (4000 yds). It homed in on the U-boat's propeller noise, and the Germans never knew what had hit them.

Developed in the USA in great secrecy – hence the misleading name – it was first produced late in 1942. By April 1943, production models were being delivered to Allied air-sea patrol squadrons and were immediately successful. In July the American escort carrier USS *Santee* used them to sink three U-boats with a clever new ploy: one of its Grumman Avenger aircraft scared them into diving, then a second Avenger planted a Mark 24 in the disturbed water.

Mark 24s continued to sink U-boats until the war ended; 346 were dropped (mostly by the British), 68 U-boats were sunk and 33 damaged.

PROTECTOR ON PATROL A Liberator drones protectively above an Atlantic convoy. This long-range patrol aircraft became a threat to U-boats in the gap where Allied ships had previously lacked air cover. (Top inset) An exploding depth charge throws up a massive geyser as the US Coast Guard cutter *Spencer* attacks *U-175* in April 1943. The U-boat went down with seven men. Some of the 41 Germans rescued are seen (bottom inset) on board *Spencer*.

SPINES OF WAR Clusters of bombs are the spines of this 'Hedgehog', a very effective weapon against the U-boats. The contact-fused bombs were fired about 180 m (200 yds) ahead of an escort vessel to fall in an oval pattern around a U-boat, reducing its chances of taking avoiding action.

Epic of the four-man X-craft

In one of the war's most daring exploits, six British midget submarines went for Hitler's three most powerful ships in a Norwegian fiord.

BRIGHT SUN made Lieutenant Donald Cameron screw up his eyes as he raised and swivelled the periscope of midget submarine *X-6*. Then, against the dazzling morning light reflected from the water of Kaafjord, in northern Norway, he made out a long, dark shape: *Tirpitz*!

Almost immediately there was a bang, a flash – and clouds of choking smoke filled the control room. The electric motor that raised the periscope had short-circuited and was in flames. After a rapid dive to 18 m (60 ft), Cameron and his crew of three doused the blaze with fire extinguishers. But water was leaking through the periscope. The tiny, cramped submarine was already in trouble with a flooded side charge – one of the two explosive devices attached to it on either side – and began listing heavily.

Surveying his tense, red-eyed men, Cameron wondered if it was time to scuttle *X-6* and try to get ashore and escape overland to Sweden. *Tirpitz*'s anti-torpedo net still had to be negotiated, and *X-6* was leaving a trail of bubbles on the surface – they were bound to be spotted. But they had come a long, hard way for a crack at Hitler's most powerful battleship. Cameron put it to his men: should they go on?

INGENIOUS

Six midget submarines had set out from Scotland 11 days before, on September 11, 1943, to penetrate the lair of the German Navy's Northern Battle Group. Anchored in a Norwegian fiord, they were a constant threat to Allied convoys to Russia. The midget subs, called X-craft, were towed across the North Sea to within range by larger submarines, then taken over by four-man attack crews.

Ingeniously designed, X-craft were only 16 m (52 ft) long, and conditions for the crew were extremely cramped. They displaced around 30 tonnes, could make 6-8 knots (11-15 km/h) submerged and had a 1900 km (1200 mile) range; they could dive to 90 m (300 ft). The two side charges, weighing about 2 tonnes apiece, could be detached and planted under an enemy ship.

Three X-craft were to attack *Tirpitz*, two the lighter battleship *Scharnhorst* and one the pocket battleship *Lützow*. However, two were lost while on tow and a third malfunctioned. That left only *X-6*, Lieutenant Henty Henty-Creer's *X-5* and Lieutenant Godfrey Place's *X-7* – all those that were targeted on *Tirpitz*.

CHARGES LAID

In *X-6*, as the smoke slowly dispersed, Sub-Lieutenant John Lorimer answered Cameron: 'Let's see what she's worth, Skipper!' The periscope was wiped clean and could be worked by hand. *X-6* struggled forward and bumped into the anti-torpedo net. Cameron took it up to periscope depth – and spotted a harbour craft heading through a 'gate' opened in the net. He quickly followed, *X-6* bumping along the shallow bottom.

Once through he dived for deeper water, then up for a quick look to locate *Tirpitz*, then down again, heading for the battleship's stern. Suddenly, with a shattering crash, *X-6* struck a rock, bounced upwards and broke surface – first 180 m (200 yds) from its huge quarry, then only 75 m (80 yds) away.

It quickly dived again, but the second time it had been seen. When, after snagging an underwater obstruction, *X-6* came up for a third time just under the battleship's port bow, *Tirpitz*'s sailors opened fire. Bullets rattled off the hull and grenades exploded. Quickly Cameron dived again and moved under *Tirpitz* to plant his charges below its forward gun turrets. That done, he ordered secret documents to be destroyed, surfaced, set *X-6* to scuttle itself and calmly surrendered to a motor launch lowered from *Tirpitz*. The time was 7.25 am.

Then came interrogation on board *Tirpitz*, enlivened by the knowledge that beneath the ship lay at least 4 tonnes of explosive – 12, if the other two X-craft had been successful – timed to detonate in minutes. The explosion might well trigger the ship's ammunition magazines, destroying *Tirpitz* and everyone in it.

The British said nothing while the Germans, guessing that mines had been laid, tried to shift the great ship by pulling on its mooring cables. Then Place's *X-7* was sighted. It was 7.40 am.

X-7 WINS THROUGH

Place, after a heart-stopping brush with a mine cable, had spent an hour entangled in the anti-torpedo net. In struggling free, *X-7* bobbed to the surface about 25 m (30 yds) from the battleship. Place promptly dived again, banging against *Tirpitz*, and released one charge under its forward turret and the second about midships. *X-7*'s compass had failed and air pressure was low, but Place tried to escape – and tangled with the nets again.

That was when, at 8.12 am, the charges exploded, Cameron's triggering Place's and possibly also Henty-Creer's – if, as seems likely, he got through successfully. The huge battleship rose bodily from the water and crashed back listing heavily to port, a large hole blown in its hull. Its rear gun turret was torn loose, the steering gear and engines were seriously damaged, and the lighting, radio and damage-control systems were wrecked. But Cameron and his men were only shaken, and casualties were slight among *Tirpitz*'s crew – one man killed and about 40 wounded.

X-7 was blown clear of the netting and so damaged that it could only 'porpoise' along the surface, shot at every time it appeared. Place got it alongside a moored gunnery target and leapt onto it – just as *X-7* sank. Sub-Lieutenant Robert Aitken surfaced 2½ hours later, using *X-7*'s escape apparatus after his frantic efforts to save the other two crew members failed. *X-5*'s fate is a mystery, though it is probable that Henty-Creer laid his charges under *Tirpitz*. Just before 8.45 his sub broke surface beyond the torpedo nets and was hit by *Tirpitz*'s guns. It submerged and German hydrophones picked up sounds indicating that Henty-Creer and his crew were trying to repair damage. But *X-5* was never seen again, probably sunk by depth charges from the destroyer *Z-29* and German patrol boats.

Both Cameron and Place, who were held as prisoners of war until the war's end, were awarded VCs. *Tirpitz* took six months to repair, *Lützow* was sent to safer waters and, of Hitler's capital ships, only *Scharnhorst* remained operational in Arctic waters – soon to confront the Royal Navy at sea.

MIGHTY MIDGET The diminutive X-craft were a deadly threat to ships in shallow water with their 'mining effect' charges.

Down go two heavyweights

When *Scharnhorst* was lured to confront the Royal Navy's Home Fleet, it was a fight to the finish. Then the RAF destroyed its bigger sister *Tirpitz*.

THE ARCTIC WATERS off northern Norway were engulfed in darkness at 4.48 pm on Boxing Day, 1943, when star shells fired by the British battleship *Duke of York* lit the far horizon. Silhouetted against its flickering glow was the black, unmistakable outline of the small German battleship (or battlecruiser) *Scharnhorst*. An officer on the nearby cruiser HMS *Jamaica* wrote later: 'She stood out clearly, as if removed bodily from her page in *Jane's Fighting Ships*.'

Duke of York's radar had picked up the German ship at a range of almost 40 km (25 miles). On board the British ship was Admiral Sir Bruce Fraser, commanding the Royal Navy's Home Fleet. He was a happy man, for it was in anticipation of this encounter that he had sailed at the same time as the Russian convoy escorts, hoping that *Scharnhorst* would leave the Northern Battle Group's lair in Norway's Altenfjord to attack the merchantmen. The lure of convoy JW55B brought *Scharnhorst* out late on Christmas Day – and the German radio signal ordering it to sea was intercepted and deciphered by British codebreakers, who passed it to Fraser.

Waiting for *Scharnhorst* – commanded by Admiral Erich Bey – were not only *Duke of York*, *Jamaica* and four destroyers, but the convoy's covering force, the cruisers *Sheffield*, *Belfast* and *Norfolk*, under the command of Rear Admiral Robert Burnett. When Burnett's cruisers came upon the German ship on Boxing Day morning, a shell from *Norfolk*'s 8 in (203 mm) guns knocked out its forward radar. *Scharnhorst* turned and made off, but Burnett caught up with it again. Now *Scharnhorst* fought back and knocked out *Norfolk*'s main radar with 280 mm (11 in) shells. A near-miss raked *Sheffield* with steel splinters. Bey broke away again and went in search of the convoy. He never found it, and decided to give up and go home.

However, the British ships had not given up, and pursued *Scharnhorst* relentlessly until Fraser sighted it bathed in star-shell light. 'There she was, guns still fore and aft,' he wrote exultantly afterwards. 'It was terrific – I can still see that illumination now.' As the range closed to 12 000 m (about $7\frac{1}{2}$ miles), *Duke of York* and *Jamaica* opened fire at 4.49 pm. Three 14 in (355 mm) shells from *Duke of York* hit *Scharnhorst*, one knocking out the foremost turret. Fraser moved in, *Duke of York*'s big guns belching fire and smoke as they fired broadside after broadside at the fleeing battleship.

BUTTONS AND BRAID Dressed for winter duty, a *Scharnhorst* petty officer wears the *Kriegsmarine's* (German Navy's) standard gilt-buttoned 'pea jacket' – probably named after a thick cloth called *pij* in Dutch – with the ribbon of the Iron Cross Second Class. Collar and sleeve badges indicate his rank of coxswain, and the collar is edged with gilt wire braid. His cap is the standard *Schiffen* – the navy's normal working wear for those below officer rank.

It was like a slogging match between two heavyweight boxers, both with a knockout punch but both capable of taking punishment. *Scharnhorst*'s shells were having little effect on the heavily armoured *Duke of York*, but the British battleship was not inflicting much damage either. Gradually, *Scharnhorst*'s speed lengthened the

DISTINGUISHED DUKE

HMS *Duke of York* was the last British capital ship to sink another in a surface engagement, and its survival against *Scharnhorst* owed much to its thick belt of armour plate – 374 mm (14.7 in) at its stoutest – and a deck up to 150 mm (6 in) thick. Despite its great weight – a displacement of more than 45 000 tonnes when fully loaded – its four turbine engines drove it at 28 knots (52 km/h). *Duke of York* was just over 227 m (745 ft) long with a beam of 31 m (103 ft).

Ten 14 in (355 mm) guns made up the main armament, in two quadruple turrets and one twin. The gun installations were complex and prone to jamming. Secondary armament at the time of *Scharnhorst*'s sinking consisted of sixteen 5.25 in (130 mm) guns, six eight-barrelled pom-poms and twenty-eight 20 mm Oerlikon quick-firing cannon. The ship's radar and fire control systems were the most comprehensive of any British warship. *Duke of York* was scrapped in 1957, 16 years after its launching.

CHILLING CHASE The snow-bedecked *Duke of York* pursues *Scharnhorst*. The *Duke*'s gun crew (inset) pose on deck with its big guns.

range – but this was its undoing, for now British shells were shrieking down at steeper angles, and could penetrate its armour better.

At about 6.20 pm a 14 in shell smashed into *Scharnhorst*'s starboard boiler room, putting it out of action. Heroic work by the ship's engineers got it going again, but Fraser's destroyers had had time to catch up. They moved in with torpedoes, hitting *Scharnhorst* four times. Now Fraser and Burnett opened fire again; *Jamaica*, *Belfast* and the destroyers loosed off more torpedoes. *Scharnhorst* was raked from stem to stern as the missiles struck. At 7.45 pm it sank by the bows, with all but 36 of its 1968 officers and men. British losses were 18 killed and 16 wounded. The action became known as the Battle of North Cape, after Norway's northernmost promontory.

TALLBOYS SINK *TIRPITZ*

Meanwhile, strenuous efforts had been made to dispose of the last German leviathan – the mighty, 51 000 tonne battleship *Tirpitz*. It was disabled but not destroyed in a brilliantly daring raid by British midget submarines in September 1943. In March 1944, word came from the codebreakers that German repairers had been busy, and *Tirpitz* would be ready for full-speed sea trials on April 3. Admiral Fraser decided on a major carrier-borne strike, to hit *Tirpitz* in Kaafjord – the upper end of Altenfjord – before it was ready for sea. The aircraft, from the fleet carriers *Victorious* and *Furious*, reinforced by the escort carriers *Emperor*, *Searcher*, *Pursuer* and *Fencer*, struck *Tirpitz* as it was raising steam.

The Germans were caught completely by surprise. Fighters roared in, raking the decks with fire, while Fairey Barracudas rained down armour-piercing bombs. *Tirpitz* was hit or near-missed 16 times – but from too low a level for the bombs to penetrate its armour. They killed 122 of its crew and wounded 316, but the battleship was disabled for only three months.

Heavier bombs were clearly needed, but *Tirpitz* – still in Kaafjord – was beyond the normal range of RAF heavy bombers. The solution was to send two Lancaster squadrons to operate from Yagodnik in northern Russia. On September 15, 27 Lancasters of Nos 9 and 617 (Dambuster) Squadrons took off, most carrying 12 000 lb (5400 kg) 'Tallboy' bombs. They flew into a smoke screen that completely hid *Tirpitz*, but a lucky strike that blasted the battleship's foredeck left it unseaworthy again. The Kriegsmarine Commander in Chief, Admiral Karl Dönitz, ordered it to Haakøy island, near Tromsø, to act as a floating fortress against any Allied invasion of Norway – but now it was within range of bombers based at Lossiemouth in Scotland. The Lancasters were sent there.

They were fitted with long-range fuel tanks and more powerful engines, and were stripped of armour to lighten them. Bad visibility hampered their first attempt, on October 29, although one bomb caused damage. The bombers' appearance alerted the Germans, who moved a fighter force into a nearby airfield. At 3 am on November 12, the Lancasters set off again. In spite of perfect weather, no fighters appeared.

VICTOR OF NORTH CAPE

Lord Fraser of North Cape (1888-1981) took his title from the battle that sank *Scharnhorst*. As Cadet Bruce Austin Fraser, he joined the navy in 1902. During World War I he was a gunnery officer. His first command was the cruiser HMS *Effingham*, and in 1933 he became Director of Naval Ordnance, planning gunnery for new battleships. After commanding the aircraft carrier *Glorious*, Fraser was promoted rear admiral and became chief of staff to First Sea Lord Sir Dudley Pound.

In 1939 he was made Third Sea Lord and had charge of building warships. He took command of the Home Fleet in 1943 and later led the Far East Fleet. A thinking man who inspired confidence, Fraser was First Sea Lord from 1948 to 1952.

As the bombers flew in at 4600 m (15 000 ft) they found *Tirpitz* clearly outlined against the shimmering sea. Just as a last, desperate smoke screen closed over it, the first 'Tallboys' struck. Flames, smoke and flying debris erupted from the stricken ship and it heeled over as water roared into a gaping hole torn in its side. Minutes later the magazine exploded, and *Tirpitz* slowly capsized. Out of nearly 1000 men trapped in the hull, 87 were rescued. So ended the last threat of surface warships to the Allies in the west.

HIT-MEN HUDDLE Fleet Air Arm crews are briefed (left) for an attack on Germany's giant battleship *Tirpitz* in April 1944. The bomber was always the weapon it had most cause to fear. A stack of RAF bombs (below) include 5.4 tonne 'Tallboys' – the type that finally sank the great ship.

THE SILENT THREAT

Tirpitz – pride of Hitler's navy after the loss of *Bismarck* in May 1941 – did more harm to the Allies by its very existence than by any naval action. Before the fateful action of November 12, 1944, it fired its main guns in conflict only once – in a minor bombardment of Spitsbergen.

Tirpitz was the largest battleship built in Europe up to that time, with a battle load displacement of 50 954 tonnes and an overall length of 254 m (832 ft). Its main armament was eight 380 mm (15 in) guns and twelve 150 mm (5.9 in) low-angle guns. For anti-aircraft protection, it mounted sixteen 105 mm (4.1 in), sixteen 37 mm and sixteen (later increased to a massive 78) 20 mm guns. Eight 533 mm (21 in) torpedo tubes were fitted after the ship was completed in July 1941, when it became clear that its main role would be as a sea raider against commercial shipping rather than as a front-line fighter against other capital ships.

Had *Tirpitz* gone into action against Allied warships it would have proved a formidable foe – as did its sister-ship *Bismarck*. Yet ironically it suffered the same flaw as *Bismarck*'s victim HMS *Hood* – inadequately armoured decks. This made the ship vulnerable to air attack, as its final action proved.

Last throw for the U-boats

After the disasters of spring 1943, Dönitz tried to break back into the Atlantic by sending his U-boats into the Bay of Biscay, armed with homing torpedoes and better radar. But the Allies managed to stay one step ahead.

GOING DOWN Stern-first, a U-boat rapidly sinks after direct depth-charge and machine-gun hits from a Coastal Command Sunderland flying boat crewed by RAAF men.

THE HUNTING PACKS in the Atlantic in the summer of 1943 were no longer made up of German U-boats, but of Allied aircraft – and the once-dreaded sea wolves were their prey. Admiral Karl Dönitz, Kriegsmarine commander, sent his U-boats to a new hunting ground – the Bay of Biscay. Their targets would be convoys from North America to the Mediterranean, but the submarines had themselves to sail in convoys for protection from aircraft.

The U-boats now had improved radar search equipment, and a new acoustic torpedo which, like the Allied 'Mk 24 Mine', homed in on the sound of a ship's propellers. The subs were to dive at night to avoid radar detection, and stay on the surface by day and fight it out with aircraft. They were heavily armed against air attack – *U-441* was even fitted out as an 'aircraft trap', armed with two quadruple 20 mm and one 37 mm gun, and hoped to lure aircraft within range. But on July 12, *U-441* attracted a flight of heavily armed Bristol Beaufighters, which demolished its superstructure and killed many of its gun crews. The 'air trap' idea was quickly abandoned.

On July 30, a British B-24 Liberator patrol plane spotted two 'milch cow' tanker submarines – *U-461* and *U-462* – with *U-504* in attendance. The Liberator called up an aircraft pack consisting of an American Liberator, two Halifax bombers, two Sunderland flying boats and a Catalina flying boat. One Halifax was damaged by gunfire from the subs, but the other dropped depth charges and brought *U-462* to a halt; and as the Liberators drew the fire of *U-461*, a Sunderland blew it in two with seven depth charges. The Catalina then called up a surface group of sloops, which finished off *U-462* and sank *U-504*.

BACK TO THE PACK

In September the U-boats returned to wolf-pack tactics in their old hunting grounds, planning to use their acoustic torpedoes to sink Allied convoy escorts. On the 19th, convoys ON202 and ONS18 were intercepted by 19 U-boats south-east of Iceland. The two convoys closed up, and a support group was sent to augment the already strong escort. The big convoy, now 66 ships guarded by 20 escorts, met the U-boats head on. Three escorts and six merchant ships were sunk, but the Germans lost two U-boats, with two more badly damaged. One of the boats, *U-338*, was sunk by a homing torpedo dropped from a Liberator. This was a poor result for the U-boats, and things got worse in October – 23 boats were sunk while attacking convoys. In one attack, on convoy SC143, three U-boats were sunk for the loss of one merchantman and one escort ship.

U-boats now had to submerge for longer periods, and rely on aircraft such as the Focke-Wulf Fw200 Condor to find their targets. In November the Luftwaffe sent four-engine Junkers Ju290s to help the Condors, and also Blohm and Voss six-engine flying boats. But they were no match for fighters from the escort carriers. As the year ended, Dönitz recommended his commanders to fire blind at greater depth, which wasted torpedoes and led to poor morale among crews.

As 1944 came there were enough carriers – purpose-built and converted merchantmen – as well as land-based patrol aircraft, to give full air cover to every convoy. U-boats had now to stay submerged for as long as possible, and act singly instead of in packs. Still their losses to convoy escorts grew – 9 in January; 12 in February; 12 in March; 11 in April and 6 in May. The Germans introduced the snorkel air-breathing system, with which U-boats could use their diesel engines under water, giving them some protection against air attack. But they were still vulnerable to escort ships, and the first boat with a snorkel, *U-264*, was sunk by an escort.

In June the U-boats went to attack the D-Day invasion ships in the Channel, but lost 11 boats for only six Allied ships sunk. And as the Allies overran France, Dönitz lost his Bay of Biscay U-boat bases. The convoy escorts could now manage without the support groups, which turned to sub-hunting, aided by radio intelligence, improved asdic and new weapons like 'Squid' (see box).

And so the Battle of the Atlantic drew to an end. U-boats sank 2603 merchant ships and 175 Allied warships in the Atlantic over the duration, but lost 784 boats out of 1162 built. And out of the 40 900 men of the U-boat service, nearly 26 000 died and over 5000 were taken prisoner. The sailors manning the Allied convoys – civilians called upon to keep Britain and the Allied war effort supplied – also paid a heavy price: 30 000 of them were killed.

THE SQUID STRIKES

'Squid' was a triple mortar, which fired depth charges in a triangular pattern ahead of the escort ship – much like 'Hedgehog' but coupled with advanced asdic equipment which gave the precise depth of a submarine. This allowed the bombs to be fused to explode at the same depth as their quarry. They were fitted to 'Castle' Class corvettes in September 1943 and to 'Loch' Class frigates in April 1944. HMS *Loch Killin* made the first 'Squid' kill when, with the sloop HMS *Starling*, it sank *U-333* in the English Channel on July 31, 1944.

TOO LITTLE, TOO LATE

The Germans worked on a number of advanced U-boat designs in the closing stages of the war, the most successful of which was the Type XXI. It had a large battery capacity and could move even faster submerged than on the surface. Though 121 were commissioned they were too late to turn the tide. The first operational boat, commanded by Captain Adalbert Schnee, a well-known ace, went on patrol just a week before the war ended. Using his high underwater speed, Schnee managed to evade a convoy escort group, but sank no ships before being ordered by Dönitz to surrender. A similar but much smaller boat, the Type XXIII, carried only two torpedoes. From February 1945, XXIIIs carried out eight operational patrols along the British east coast, sinking six ships at no loss to themselves.

16: STRIKING THE REICH'S HEART

British and US air chiefs differed on methods but agreed that bombing could win the war.

Germans destroy the myth of the invincible bomber

Daylight raids over Germany without fighter escorts proved largely suicidal and, initially, night bombing made little impact on the enemy's war effort. By the end of 1941 the outlook for RAF Bomber Command appeared bleak.

UNDER CLEAR SKIES, 24 Wellington bombers of No 3 Group, RAF Bomber Command, took off from airfields in East Anglia at 9.30 am on December 18, 1939, and began a slow, heavily laden climb to rendezvous over the Norfolk coast. At 4300 m (14 000 ft), the Wellingtons levelled off and set course for their target: the German naval base at Wilhelmshaven on the North Sea coast. The air was crystal clear and bitterly cold.

An hour or so out across the North Sea, two aircraft fell out through engine trouble and returned to base. The remaining 22 closed up into defensive formations. Gunners stamped their feet and swung turrets on lubricants made sluggish by the cold. Some 50 km (30 miles) off the German coast, the group was picked up by German *Freya* radar on the island of Wangerooge, but the sighting was dismissed as a flock of seagulls; no one believed that the RAF would attack in such ridiculously clear conditions.

When the bombers crossed the coast, they were greeted by black puffballs of flak – anti-aircraft ground fire – exploding harmlessly below. Soon the defenders were watching with horror, then astonishment, as Wellingtons with open bomb bays roared over docked warships without dropping a single bomb. Flight commanders had strict orders to avoid civilian casualties, and found that housing crowded too close to the docks. However, some German ships were bombed near the naval base. This was where belatedly scrambled German fighters – single-engine Messerschmitt Me109s and twin-engine Me110s – fell upon the British. Attacking from the side – an angle not covered by the bombers' guns – they chopped the Wellingtons down. Two German fighters fell; only ten Wellingtons got home.

BOMBING FOR VICTORY

Casualties apart, these and similar losses in the early months of conflict were a grievous blow to senior British officers who, between the wars, had fought for a bomber force with a defensive armament that would outmatch any fighter opposition and carry destruction into the heart of the enemy's territory. There, they believed, such a force would wreak havoc on industries, communications, military installations and other vital resources through accurate daylight bombing.

The British politician Stanley Baldwin said in 1932: 'The bomber will always get through!' Pundits pointed to the panic caused by the Zeppelin airships and Gotha bombers that had attacked London between 1915 and 1918, and by the Allied bombers that had attacked Germany extensively in 1918. As the size and range of bombers increased, the argument ran, a bombed and fear-crazed enemy population would compel its government to sue for peace before its ground forces had even seen action. Britain's former Chief of Air Staff, Sir Hugh (later Lord) Trenchard, had said: 'It is not . . . necessary for an air force, in order to defeat the enemy nation, to defeat its armed forces first.'

The other side of the coin was the prospect of German bombing of Britain. Official Whitehall forecasts, made in 1937, of likely casualties – 150 000 in the first week – proved wildly pessimistic. Nobody had an air fleet capable of dropping such death-dealing loads. The most the warring nations possessed in 1939 were single and twin-engine bombers, the largest of which, like Britain's Armstrong-Whitworth Whitley, could carry no more than 3200 kg (7000 lb) of bombs.

The RAF entered the war with 17 operational squadrons of Vickers Wellingtons, obsolescent Whitleys and Handley Page Hampdens, six of Bristol Blenheims and ten of single-engine Fairy Battles. The notion that they would leap the enemy's front line and swiftly ruin its entire economy was soon shattered. Wilhelmshaven and later raids showed that for bombers to fly by day unescorted into Germany was little short of suicidal. On the other hand, night flights to bombard the Reich with anti-Nazi propaganda leaflets met little or no opposition. By spring 1940, Bomber Command had decided that there was more future in night operations than in day.

AREA BOMBING BEGINS

On May 10, 1940, the Germans unleashed their blitzkrieg upon the Low Countries and Britain's new prime minister, Winston Churchill, at once insisted on more widespread bombing of Germany. On the night of May 11/12 an attack was mounted on the Mönchengladbach railway junction on the west bank of the Rhine. Four nights later, 93 British bombers struck at oil plants and blast furnaces at Duisburg and at other targets in the Ruhr, and between May 29 and June 5, 350 further sorties were carried out.

For a while, after the fall of France in June, priority was given to the bombing of Dutch, Belgian and northern French ports, where troop-carrying barges were being assembled for the invasion of England. But, on the night of August 25/26, 1940, British bombers raided Berlin for the first time in a tit-for-tat operation ordered by Churchill following the bombing of London, Birmingham, Bristol and Liverpool by the Luftwaffe the previous night. Out of 103 attacking aircraft, about half reached Berlin. Damage was negligible, but it made nonsense of Göring's promise that Berlin would never be touched; the Nazis riposted angrily by blitzing London's docks.

News of the Berlin raid heartened the British, whose newspapers reported widespread devastation in the city. In the last months of 1940 and the first half of 1941, further stories of shattered oil installations and U-boat docks led the British to believe that whatever else was happening the bombers at least were winning. The stories gained in credibility as the four-engine Stirlings and Halifaxes came into service.

However, air-reconnaissance photographs of the Gelsenkirchen oil refineries taken after a

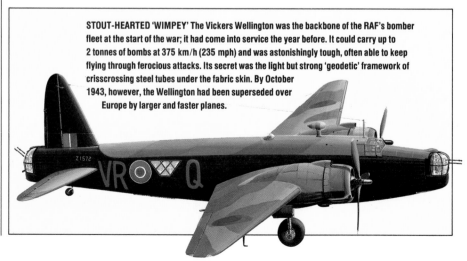

STOUT-HEARTED 'WIMPEY' The Vickers Wellington was the backbone of the RAF's bomber fleet at the start of the war; it had come into service the year before. It could carry up to 2 tonnes of bombs at 375 km/h (235 mph) and was astonishingly tough, often able to keep flying through ferocious attacks. Its secret was the light but strong 'geodetic' framework of crisscrossing steel tubes under the fabric skin. By October 1943, however, the Wellington had been superseded over Europe by larger and faster planes.

heavy RAF raid in December 1940 revealed remarkably little damage, and similar observations were made at other targets. In July 1941, David Butt, a senior civil servant, was ordered by the Cabinet Office to make an in-depth study of the previous few weeks' bombing results.

He discovered the sad truth that only one in three attacking aircraft dropped its bombs within 8 km (5 miles) of its aiming point; for targets in the heavily defended and smoke-shrouded Ruhr, the figure was one in ten. Having studied the Butt Report, the Air Ministry concluded that night attacks on specific targets were beyond the abilities of aircraft and crews, at that time. On St Valentine's Day, February 14, 1942, Bomber Command was directed to concentrate on 'dislocating the German transportation system' and 'destroying the morale of the civil population and, in particular, of the industrial workers'. Area bombing – the Germans came to call it 'terror bombing' – had arrived with a vengeance.

DODGING THE DEFENCES

A new era was also starting in the battle between bombers and defenders. In July 1940, Brigadier Josef Kammhuber had been appointed to command Germany's night fighters. Through the following winter he established a belt of searchlights and sound detectors down the coasts of north Germany and the Low Countries. Night fighters – mostly converted Me110s and Junkers Ju88s – patrolled assigned sectors, poised to strike at enemy planes picked up by the searchlights. Deadlier still were the Ju88 intruder planes that roared low over the North Sea, to hit British bombers when they were most vulnerable – at takeoff or landing on airfields in eastern England. Fortunately for the RAF, Hitler ordered an end to intruder raids in October 1941 – he wanted people to see enemy bombers destroyed over Germany.

The relief was short-lived. By early 1942, the Kammhuber line of defence had become much more sophisticated: a series of overlapping night-fighter zones were each served by a *Freya* early warning radar that could give the course and position of approaching bombers up to 160 km (100 miles) away. As a fighter assigned to the box nearest to his airfield took off, the approaching bomber was picked up by a shorter-range *Würzburg* radar. A second *Würzburg* tracked the night fighter, which the controller would guide by radio to a point some 3 km (2 miles) from the bomber. From there, the fighter could use its *Lichtenstein* airborne radar. Often, the bomber crew knew nothing until cannon shells tore their world apart. This *Himmelbett* ('four-poster bed') defence system was honed to ferocious efficiency.

Bombers that survived went on to face the increasing accuracy of searchlight and flak defences. If they still survived, fighter ambushes waited for them on the way home. Bomber Command was partly to blame for the rising

BEFORE AND AFTER British bomber crewmen don their flying kit before a raid on Berlin in 1940. But many failed to return from raids. In a German photograph (inset), Luftwaffe officers interrogate a shot-down RAF crewman.

casualty rate. Aircraft were still being dispatched singly to their targets, whenever their crews chose within a timespan of two to three hours. Staggering the bombing times was meant to prolong the misery of the victims, but it only created ideal conditions for the waiting fighters.

It had to be faced. The defences were gaining the upper hand, bombing results were poor and the RAF's aircraft losses were mounting: in four months, Bomber Command had lost the equivalent of its entire original front-line strength. Professor Pat Blackett, an Admiralty adviser, pointed out in February 1942 that British bombers had been killing German civilians at roughly the rate that German defences were killing expensively trained British aircrew.

Such opinions filtered down even to aircrews who had begun to wonder what their friends had died for – a fate that, tonight or tomorrow, might well overtake themselves. In this second month of 1942, Bomber Command's fortunes had reached their lowest ebb. New leadership was needed. It arrived in the stocky, aggressive figure of Air Marshal Arthur 'Bomber' Harris.

German cities die by night

The effectiveness of night bombing was put to the test when Arthur Harris took over RAF Bomber Command early in 1942. Despite heavy casualties on both sides, it gave Britain some spectacular and much-needed successes. But it did not win the war, as 'Bomber' Harris kept vainly assuring Churchill it would.

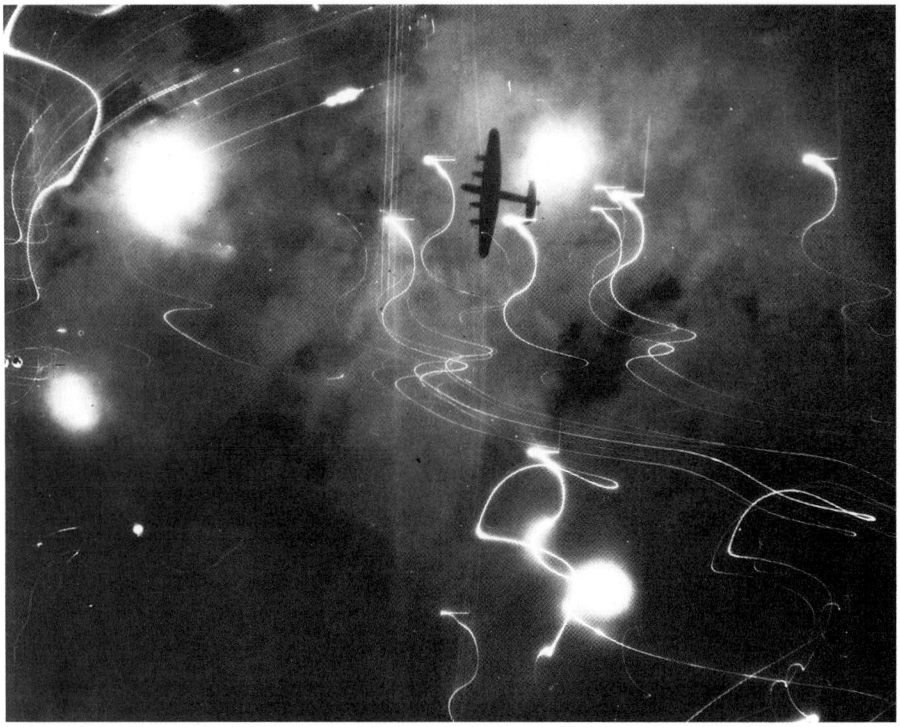

NIGHT RAIDER'S SKY Bursting German shells and flak leave weird trails of light. A Lancaster's silhouette stands out.

ONE PILOT MUTTERED into his intercom, again and again, 'Oh God, those poor bastards', as he swung his aircraft away from the blazing inferno that was Hamburg. He and the other Bomber Command aircrews were looking at a horrific firestorm, in which fire, building up to well over 800°C (1500°F), sucked in all the surrounding air, creating 240 km/h (150 mph) hurricanes of flame.

They were also witnessing the death of at least 44 000 people, almost all of them civilians. There was nothing to be seen below but a single, pulsating, crimson glow, in the midst of which 4000 lb (1.8 tonne) 'cookies' – heavy blast-bombs – made golden sunbursts. Bombing Hamburg on the night of July 27/28, 1943, was like 'stoking a furnace', and crews gazed at their handiwork with a mixture of awe, fascination and pity.

BEEFING UP BOMBER COMMAND

Little more than a year before, Bomber Command had reached a low point, with losses cripplingly heavy and crews under mounting strain. Then, on February 22, 1942, only eight days after the Air Ministry issued its St Valentine's Day area bombing directive, Air Marshal Arthur Harris was appointed its Commander in Chief. He was a man in accord with the policy expressed in this directive – that the only way to crush a modern, industrialised enemy was to destroy its industries and cities from the air, causing its civilian population to panic and demand peace, and its armies to collapse.

An essentially private man, 'Bomber' Harris scarcely left the Valhalla of Bomber Command Headquarters at High Wycombe between 1942 and 1945, and rarely visited a front-line station. But he backed his crews to the hilt, demanding over and again production priorities in heavy aircraft, and more and more scientific research into new gadgetry that would enable them to hit their targets harder and increase their chances of survival.

The crews themselves made Bomber Command the most international of all Allied forces. Throughout the war, about 70 per cent of the men were British; the next largest group were Canadians, followed by Australians and New Zealanders. There were also many Rhodesians, South Africans, Americans (before their country entered the war), and volunteers from neutral Ireland, as well as Free French, Poles and Norwegians. The odds that a crew would complete its first 'tour' – usually of 25, later 30, operations – intact were at no time any better than even; in 1942, the first year of Harris's command, only three crews out of every ten would on average survive to their tour's end.

REAL CURTAIN-RAISER

Harris started with three fairly undramatic night attacks on the Ruhr industrial city of Essen in early March, before launching his real curtain-raiser, the destruction of Lübeck on March 28/29. Lübeck was a target of moderate importance, but was lightly defended. Its Old Town consisted largely of highly inflammable medieval wooden buildings – 'more like a firelighter than a human habitation', said Harris – and, being on the coast, it could easily be found by RAF navigators.

The attack was led by ten Wellingtons equipped with 'Gee' – a new radio-navigational aid – to light up the target with flares, followed by other bombers carrying incendiaries to mark it with fire; behind them came the main force of 234 bombers, of which 191 reached the target, many armed with 4000 lb (1815 kg) high-explosive bombs and more incendiaries. Lübeck blazed, as did Rostock, selected for a four-night attack a month later. Blitz-scarred Britain received the news with grim satisfaction. German propaganda chief Josef Goebbels described the damage as 'devastating'.

More was to come. At the end of May, British headlines proclaimed '1000 bombers hit Cologne!' Harris had scraped together 1047 aircraft, the largest air fleet ever assembled, and crews later spoke of a city ablaze from end to end, incendiaries sparkling white against whirlpools of cherry flame. Silhouetted by the glare, the twin towers of the cathedral could be seen clearly from the attacking aircraft. In 90 minutes, 2500 fires were

BOMBER CHIEF

Arthur Travers Harris (1892-1984), like many who were junior officers in World War I (he served in South-West Africa), was determined that the horrific wastage of the trenches would never happen again. His alternative was the heavy bomber.

It fell to Harris – appointed Commander in Chief of RAF Bomber Command on February 22, 1942 – to put into effect the Air Ministry's area bombing directive, issued eight days earlier. This meant sending large fleets of heavy bombers to very large targets – whole cities, for example – that they could not miss, even by night. He supported the policy and strongly resisted the switching of bombers from German cities to targets in France in the build-up to D-Day in 1944.

His single-mindedness led the press to dub him 'Bomber'; his friends called him 'Bert' and his crews, with rueful affection, 'Butch' – short for 'Butcher'. After the war he stoutly maintained that area bombing – which the Germans called 'terror bombing' – had been the right course. His outspokenness did not endear him to senior officers and politicians, who shared his responsibility for bombing strategy, yet were anxious to distance themselves from what became a controversial issue. It may have cost Harris a peerage; however, he became Marshal of the RAF in 1945 and a baronet in 1951.

INTERROGATION A bomber crew is debriefed after taking part in one of the raids on Berlin in November 1943. Meticulous analyses of bomber crews' reports and photographic reconnaissance led gradually to improved accuracy.

started, some 3330 buildings destroyed and 469 people killed. Forty-one aircraft failed to return.

The Cologne raid – and less successful 1000-bomber raids on Essen and Bremen that quickly followed – seized the imagination of the British public and government alike. Perhaps Bomber Command really could win the war, and while it was given an opportunity at least to try, the navy would have to reduce its demands for aircraft, and the army its desperate requests for more arms. Having won the RAF top priority in factory production, Harris settled down to pound Germany into submission.

BOMBER MEN

His warriors were like none other in the history of arms. By 1942, every aircrew member was at least a sergeant. Promotion, if you were talented and lived long enough, was swift – one Australian sergeant pilot became a squadron leader in eight months. Then there was extra flight pay and the hero-worship of your countrymen and women. Leave was reasonably plentiful, and food rations – orange juice, real eggs, and steaks – were on a scale that civilians could only dream about.

Tools and techniques to complete the task in hand were the best that could be devised. In early 1942, the four-engine Avro Lancaster was coming into service, fitted with the Mark XIV bombsight that was supposed to be almost psychic in its accuracy. New electronic aids to accurate navigation, such as 'Gee', 'Oboe' and 'H2S', were being developed or coming into service (see box). And by pushing a carefully timed aircraft stream through a single night-fighter zone of the German Kammhuber defensive line, Bomber Command hoped to overwhelm the German shield.

The sharp end of all this care and attention was operations against the enemy, known to the crews simply as 'ops'. There might be four or five in a week, or fewer in a whole month, depending on the decisions of High Wycombe and vagaries of weather. Each new raid brought the same heightening of tension, gnawing anxiety and near-certain knowledge that one crew at least from your airfield would not be returning.

By late summer 1942, the US Eighth Army Air Force was flying daylight missions from England to attack precision targets, and Harris joined in with some of his precious Lancasters. Brave, low-level day strikes proved at best inconclusive and at worst disastrous, as a raid on Augsburg, near Munich, back in April had amply proved. On that raid – an attempt by Harris to prove that his Lancasters could defend themselves in a daylight operation – only five bombers returned, all damaged, out of 12 that set off. Only 12 bombs exploded on the target.

There were no more 1000-bomber raids for a while in the face of demands from Training

PRECISION TARGETING 'Gee', the RAF's first radio navigational aid, worked on a grid system. In the next, 'Oboe' (below), a Kent tracker station code-named 'Mouse' emitted a radar pulse that kept the bomber on an arc at a constant distance to take it over the target. A pulse from a station ('Cat') in Norfolk indicated when to release the bombs. 'H2S' radar (right), carried in the aircraft, gave a map-like picture of the landscape beneath.

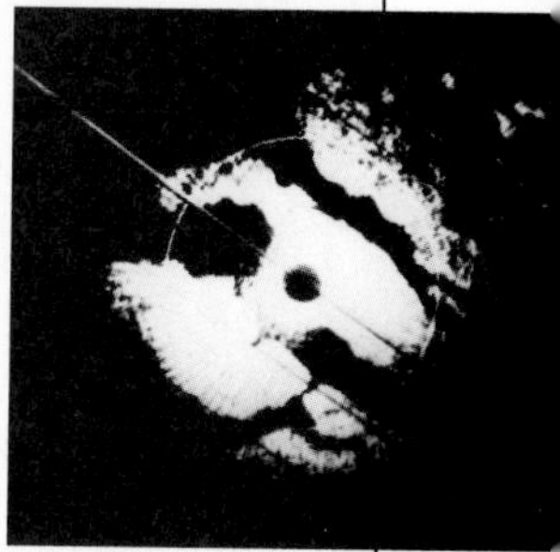

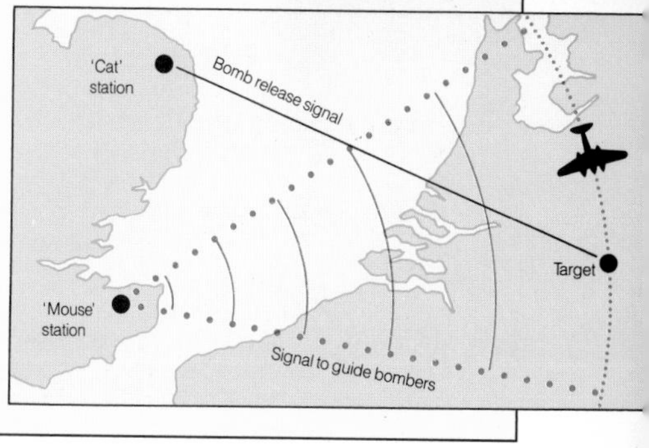

JOURNEY INTO NIGHT

The traditional 'breakfast' of bacon and eggs started the night of an 'op'. Next for flight crews came the briefings, to learn amid nervous jokes and laughter their target – maybe the 'Big City' (Berlin) or 'Happy Valley' (the Ruhr). Then to the locker rooms, where men left personal possessions and collected parachutes, flying-kit, and 'illegal' mascots such as mementos from girlfriends. They were taken to their planes by airwomen drivers. A last cigarette, then the crew climbed aboard. In a Lancaster, the pilot, flight engineer and bomb-aimer sat just ahead of the navigator and wireless operator. Far down the fuselage sat the lonely mid-upper and tail gunners.

One by one, the four great Rolls-Royce Merlin engines were started up, and the bomber began the long trundle to the main runway, there to await the takeoff signal – a single green flash from an Aldis lamp. 'You've got your green, Skipper.' 'Thanks, gunner. Everyone OK? Well, here we go' – and 30-odd tonnes of aeroplane, bombs, fuel and crew would roar down the flarepath and into the night.

KILLING TIME Bomber crewmen lounge in the station restroom, reading idly, or listening to the wireless, to pass the uneasy hours before an 'op'.

Command and other parts of the RAF. But throughout the remainder of 1942 and into the winter of 1942-3, hardly a night passed, weather permitting, without bombers penetrating deep into Germany and even as far as Turin, in northern Italy. The attacks varied in strength from half a dozen aircraft to air fleets up to 300 strong, with results that ranged from massive damage to simply depriving the enemy of sleep. In addition, raids were mounted on October 17 on the French arms factory at Le Creusot, and on December 6 on the Philips factory at Eindhoven in the Netherlands. Both were precision daylight raids of great daring and carried out at treetop height to minimise French and Dutch casualties.

A significant development at this period, however, was the evolution of a target-finding force highly trained in the new navigational aids. Its task was to guide the main bomber stream to the target and help it to bomb with much greater accuracy. Harris called it the Pathfinder Force.

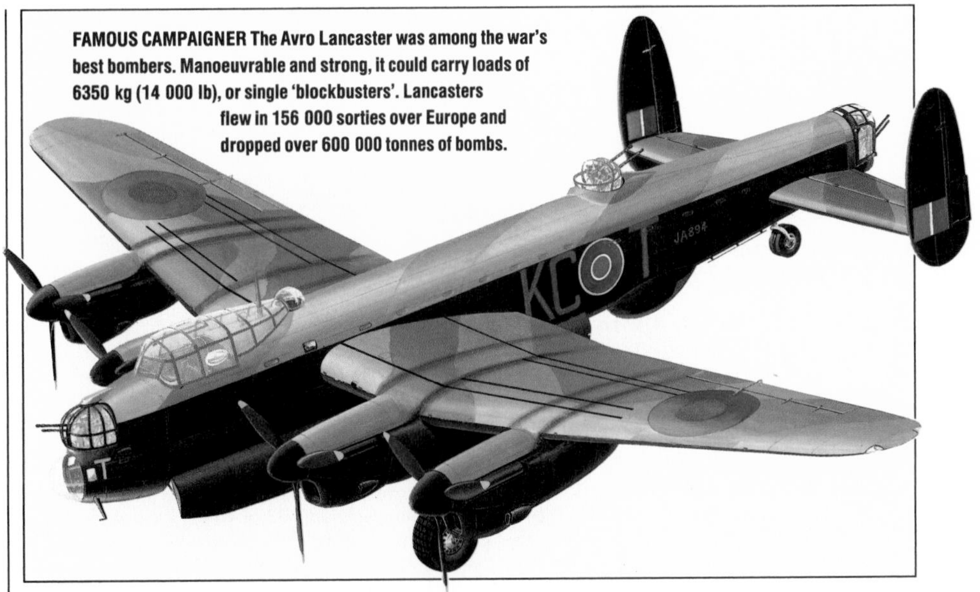

FAMOUS CAMPAIGNER The Avro Lancaster was among the war's best bombers. Manoeuvrable and strong, it could carry loads of 6350 kg (14 000 lb), or single 'blockbusters'. Lancasters flew in 156 000 sorties over Europe and dropped over 600 000 tonnes of bombs.

HITTING GERMAN INDUSTRY

On the night of March 5/6, 1943, the bombing war reached a new dimension when Harris launched a series of attacks that became known as the Battle of the Ruhr. Eight fast pathfinder Mosquitoes equipped with 'Oboe' dropped yellow flares along the approach to Essen and then marked the target – the Krupp industrial complex – with glowing red indicators. Twenty-two pathfinder heavy bombers reinforced the yellow approach markers and dropped green target indicators on the preliminary red ones. The main force followed with mixed high-explosive and incendiary loads, dropping 1070 tonnes in 38 minutes. Krupp's was badly damaged, 65 hectares (160 acres) of the city were totally destroyed and 30 000 people made homeless. In four further attacks stretched over four months, a total of 1552 aircraft dropped more than 4000 tonnes of bombs.

The battle lasted until July and neighbouring industrial towns also suffered; and, to keep the defences dispersed, cities in other parts of Germany were also attacked. Of this period, Sergeant Don Charlwood, an Australian navigator, wrote: 'I would try to tell myself then that this was a city, a place inhabited by beings such as ourselves, a place with the familiar sights of civilisation. But the thought would carry little conviction. A German city was always this, this hellish picture of flame, gunfire and searchlights, an unreal picture because we could not hear it or feel its breath. Sometimes, when the smoke rolled back and we saw streets and buildings, I felt startled. Perhaps if we had seen the white, upturned faces of people, as over England we sometimes did, our hearts would have rebelled . . .'

RAF losses too were grievous. Out of 18 506 sorties flown in 43 major attacks between March and July 1943, 872 bombers failed to return. Among them were nearly half the aircraft dispatched on the 'Dambuster' operation, the most spectacular raid of the Ruhr battle (see box).

'GOMORRAH' TODAY

In July 1943 the bombers turned on Hamburg, which they devastated in a series of attacks named with terrible aptness Operation 'Gomorrah'. It was the first combined offensive by the British and American air forces, the USAAF bombing by day and the RAF by night. It was also the first operation in which a device code-named 'Window' was used. Thousands of strips of aluminium foil 265 mm (10½ in) long – half the wavelength of the German radar – were dropped when the German defences were reached. The effect was spectacular. As the strips drifted earthwards the radar screens of night fighters and flak defences were swamped with 'snowstorms'. The British 'H2S' radar, working on a much shorter wavelength, was immune.

CHESHIRE – ACE PATHFINDER

Claiming only to be 'an average pilot blessed with luck', Geoffrey Leonard Cheshire (1917-) was a major contributor to the later phase of the bombing of Germany in 1944-5, through his skill as a pilot and leader of men.

Early in the war, 'Chesh' flew Whitleys and then Halifaxes, rising to command 76 Squadron. In April 1943, at the age of 26, he was promoted temporary group captain, but reverted to wing commander when offered command of 617 (Dambuster) Squadron, by then a specialist precision bombing and marking unit. Flying Mosquitoes, he pioneered new marking techniques that led the way to more accurate bombing patterns.

In July 1944, Cheshire left 617 Squadron with a VC, DFC, and two bars to his DSO. He spent some time in staff jobs before being official British witness to the atomic bombing of Nagasaki in August 1945. After the war, he and his wife Sue Ryder devoted themselves to organisations providing homes for the disabled.

The destruction of Hamburg began in the early hours of July 25 with a heavy RAF raid. When day came, the American B-17 Flying Fortresses flew in, and did so again on the 26th. At 1 am on July 28 the RAF returned, and the people of Hamburg were about to endure the horrors, unexpected by either side, of a firestorm (see box). In the words of Nazi propaganda chief Josef Goebbels, the result was 'a catastrophe . . . which staggers the imagination'. On the night of the 29th, Bomber Command returned yet again, but this time casualties were relatively few; more than a million people had fled the city.

The Luftwaffe too was learning. Abandoning the radar zones of the Kammhuber line, they sent in the *Wilden Säue* – 'wild boars' – free-ranging, single-engine fighters that picked out the bombers against the searchlights and fires of the burning city. Among 'sprog' (inexperienced) British crews, slow in reacting to fighter attacks, casualties were particularly high. Later, *Wilden Säue* gave way to the more sophisticated *Zahme Sau* ('tame boar') tactic – night fighters directed onto bombers by radio operators, who were briefed by ground observer stations. The final approach was made using the fighter's own radar.

The RAF's final attack on Hamburg, on August 3, was less effective. The attackers flew into a ferocious electrical storm that alone downed at least four bombers. Those that got through bombed more or less blind, then played hide and seek with night fighters through canyons and ravines of dense cloud. Operation 'Gomorrah' was over. In disrupting the life of a great enemy city, it was the most successful use of area bombing so far. Whether it shortened the war remains debatable.

TARGET PEENEMÜNDE

Of more immediate concern to the British was the successful bombing of a German experimental station at Peenemünde, on a lonely Baltic shore. A sharp-eyed WAAF photo-interpreter, Flt Officer Constance Babington-Smith, had spotted something odd in a reconnaissance photograph. Further reconnaissance and some notable espionage eventually confirmed that Peenemünde was producing Hitler's long-rumoured secret weapons, the V-1 'flying bomb' and V-2 rocket.

Harris did not wait for final confirmation; on

THE DAMBUSTERS RAID

'In the early hours of this morning a force of Lancasters . . . attacked with mines the dams of the Möhne and Sorpe reservoirs. The Eder dam . . . was also attacked.' Thus the BBC announced what would become Bomber Command's most renowned exploit.

The main contingent, nine Lancasters of Wing Commander Guy Gibson's 617 Squadron, took off from RAF Scampton, Lincolnshire, just after 8.30 pm on May 16, 1943. Each carried one of Barnes Wallis's 'bouncing bombs' – a kind of gigantic depth charge that would skip across the water to hit the dam wall and sink 9 m (30 ft) before exploding. It had to be dropped precisely 18 m (60 ft) above the water and 388 m (425 yds) from the dam. Each Lancaster was fitted with angled lights on its nose and rear fuselage, whose beams would meet on the water when the plane was at the correct height. Bomb-aimers used various makeshift techniques to judge the distance.

The Möhne dam was hit first. One aircraft was lost on the outward flight, but the others attacked individually. The fourth made a perfect hit, then the fifth pilot placed his missile to the left. The dam crumbled impressively. A gigantic torrent – 100 million cubic metres of water – poured through the gap, passing on to devastate a huge area.

Five Lancasters, three still carrying their bombs, flew on to the Eder. Two bombs failed to rupture the masonry, but the final one struck. Damage from the resulting tidal wave extended over a radius of almost 400 km (250 miles).

Separate raids with conventional bombs also hit the Sorpe dam, whose concrete-and-earth structure made it impervious to bouncing bombs, and the Ennepe dam. But they failed to cause a decisive breach. Altogether during the raids eight Lancasters, and their highly skilled crews, were lost. Though the damage was spectacular, its strategic effect was relatively minor. Breaching the Sorpe would have damaged the Ruhr much more seriously.

617 SQUADRON Guy Gibson leads his crew (below) aboard one of the Dambuster Lancasters. His highly trained squadron was specially assembled for the raid. Water pours through the breached Möhne dam (left) after the raid.

August 17, 1943, he sent in 597 aircraft, led by a famous pathfinder, Group Captain J.H. Searby. Within the bomber stream were Mosquitoes that flew on to Berlin as a diversion, dropping 'Window' to lure off fighters, while the heavies turned away for Peenemünde. Forty aircraft were lost on the return journey, but the V-1 station was badly damaged and many scientists killed, slowing production by three months or more.

ON TO BERLIN

In autumn 1943, Harris, now an air chief marshal with a knighthood, suggested to Churchill that a joint RAF-USAAF effort could 'wreck Berlin from end to end . . . [and though the cost would be] 400-500 bombers, it will cost Germany the war'. Churchill was keen but the Americans declined, partly because of their heavy losses in late summer, but also because area bombing was still contrary to USAAF policy in Europe.

Harris decided to go it alone, and on November 18 launched the first of 16 major attacks on the German capital. Crews soon learned to fear Berlin's defences. As one pilot recalled, 'from afar [Berlin] was peaceful, silent and harmless with moonbeams shimmering on its many lakes', then it would suddenly erupt into a volcano of gun flashes and shrapnel.

At the receiving end, Goebbels, who was also Gauleiter (governor) of Berlin, wrote: 'The air is filled with smoke and smell of fires. The Wilhelmplatz and the Wilhelmstrasse present a gruesome picture . . . Gradually we are learning to accustom ourselves again to a primitive standard of living. In the morning in Göringstrasse [his home] there is no heat, no light, no water. One can neither shave nor wash.'

As was customary, Bomber Command attempted to disperse enemy defences by switching targets. On March 30, 1944, 795 bombers were sent to Nuremberg, deep in southern Germany, on the RAF's most disastrous single action. Afterwards, there were dark mutterings about careless talk and spies, but the causes of the debacle were simple: mistakes and bad luck.

For a start, crews found themselves bathed in bright moonlight rather than the predicted cloud. Furthermore, atmospheric conditions caused the bombers to leave telltale white vapour trails that could be seen from far away. Finally, it happened that the stream's course ran exactly between two night-fighter beacons. Before they crossed the Rhine the crews began to see the pale red night-fighter flares they hated; they flew between them as though between the lamps of a brightly lit avenue, where every dark 'side street' concealed a skilled gunman. Planes began to fall, trailing flame, or vanished in a great explosion of light.

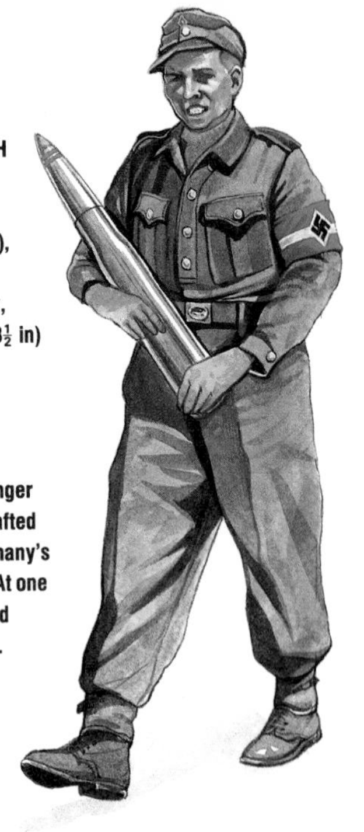

MOBILISING YOUTH A young German *Luftwaffenhelfer* (Luftwaffe Auxiliary), helping to man an anti-aircraft battery, carries an 88 mm ($3\frac{1}{2}$ in) shell. As the Allied bomber offensive intensified, and the Reich's manpower dwindled, ever younger auxiliaries were drafted in to help man Germany's ack-ack defences. At one stage boys of 14 and younger were used.

The principal instrument of destruction was a newish German invention, code-named *Schräge Musik* (literally, 'slanting music' – or jazz): simply a pair of 20 or 30 mm cannon pointing diagonally upwards from behind the pilot's seat in a twin-engine night fighter. They were fired from a 'blind spot' position beneath the enemy bomber. The invention was said to have been the brainchild of a pilot who came out of cloud immediately below a stream of Lancasters and remained there petrified, until he realised that the bombers were totally blind on the underside. Other aircraft fell to normal night fighters and flak. Altogether, 95 bombers were shot down that night and 59 were seriously damaged – a total loss rate of 19 per cent, including the damaged aircraft. Nuremberg was badly damaged, but its spirit was unbroken and its war production barely affected.

Between November 1943 and March 1944, Bomber Command lost 1047 aircraft, with another 1682 badly damaged. Although area bombing would continue almost to the end of the war in Europe, it was becoming clear that it was not a means of winning that war. Despite all the effort, final victory would be gained by invasion and land battles. Harris would soon have part of his command diverted to ensure the success of that invasion.

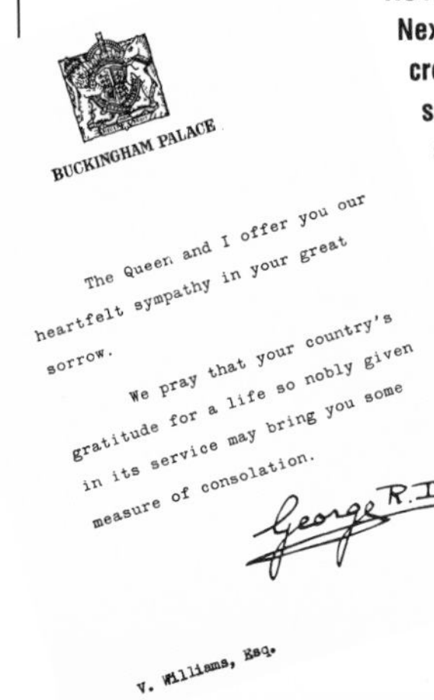
BUCKINGHAM PALACE

The Queen and I offer you our heartfelt sympathy in your great sorrow.

We pray that your country's gratitude for a life so nobly given in its service may bring you some measure of consolation.

George R.I.

V. Williams, Esq.

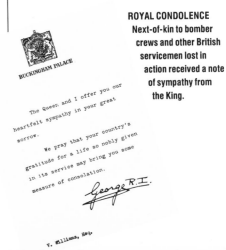

ROYAL CONDOLENCE Next-of-kin to bomber crews and other British servicemen lost in action received a note of sympathy from the King.

HELL COMES TO HAMBURG

It all started a little after 12.30 am on July 25, 1943, when Hamburg's air-raid alerts sounded, followed later by local radio warnings that large numbers of enemy aircraft were approaching. The city's 1.5 million citizens rushed into air-raid shelters and basements; gun and searchlight crews prepared for battle. But suddenly every radar set seemed to go mad, their green screens a mass of meaningless 'snow'. No one realised the cause: the foil strips the RAF called 'Window'. Searchlights groped across the sky; ack-ack guns fired blindly.

By the time the all-clear went, soon after 3 am, Hamburg was a ruin. At 9 am eight major fires still raged unchecked. Only in the early afternoon could people begin to take stock. Docks, factories, shops, public buildings and innumerable private dwellings had been hit; the famous zoo had been destroyed. About 1500 people were dead, and thousands injured. And Hamburg's ordeal was not yet over. Later that day, and again the next, American B-17 Flying Fortresses flew in, then the RAF returned on the night of July 27/28.

Now began even greater horrors. Falling close together, the British bombs set off several small fires in an area of about 10 km^2 (4 sq miles). Within minutes fires were uniting, fanned by a light wind. Hot air rose above the conflagrations, sucking in surrounding air that fed and united more fires. These dragged in yet more air in currents that built up to hurricane force and roared through the streets.

Children and old people were sucked from pavements and flung into the flames. Others, licked by tongues of heat, died instantly, reduced to half their bodily size. Those in shelters suffered even more heavily: they died in thousands from heat, suffocation or carbon-monoxide poisoning, most of them long after the RAF had gone home. The bombing lasted about an hour, the firestorm about four.

CITY IN RUINS Hamburg citizens walk through the devastation of their once proud and beautiful city.

Daylight raids cost US dear

The Yanks had come, and with them the heavily armed B-17 Flying Fortress and the Norden bombsight that could 'drop a bomb into a pickle barrel from 20 000 ft'. But, like the night-flying RAF, the daytime fliers of the United States Army Air Force had some bitter lessons to learn.

TO AMERICAN AIRMEN the sky over Europe was a horizontal clock face, with 12 o'clock straight ahead and 6 o'clock dead astern. Hence Lt Colonel Beirne Lay's introduction to his report of the battle on the way in to bomb Regensburg on August 17, 1943: 'Swinging their yellow noses around in a wide U-turn, the 12-ship squadron of Me109s came in from 12 to 2 o'clock in pairs and in fours, and the main event was on. A shining silver object sailed past over our right wing. I recognised it as a main exit door. Seconds later a dark object came hurtling through the formation, barely missing several props. It was a man, clasping his knees to his head, revolving like a diver in a triple somersault. I didn't see his 'chute open.

'A B-17 turned gradually out of the formation . . . in a split second [it] disappeared in a brilliant explosion, from which the only remains were four small balls of fire, the fuel tanks, quickly consumed as they fell . . . I watched a B-17 turn slowly out to the right with its cockpit a mass of flames. The co-pilot crawled out of his window . . . reached back for his 'chute, buckled it on, let go and was whisked back into the horizontal stabiliser. His 'chute didn't open . . . The fighters queued up like a breadline and let us have it . . .'

MODEST BEGINNINGS

By the time of the Regensburg operation, the US Eighth Air Force had a battle-scarred history. Eighteen months earlier, in February 1942, Brig General Ira C. Eaker had arrived in England to pave the way for the mighty air armada that would, the Americans were convinced, bring Germany to its knees. Already the method had been settled. Unlike the British, who bombed at night, they would use their force as a rapier to make daylight precision attacks by close-flying formations of self-defending bombers upon key industries and military targets. After a slow start, the British-based heavy bomber force gradually grew in the summer of 1942. Ground crews were shipped over from the USA, while the bombers were flown in by the men who would fly them in action. Dozens of airfields were hastily constructed, mainly in the area of East Anglia that lies between The Wash and Cambridge.

On August 17, 1942, a dozen B-17s took off for the first all-American mission, with Eaker himself riding in a plane called 'Yankee Doodle'. The target was the marshalling yards at Rouen, in northern France. All returned safely, some bearing a few flak scars. Bomber Command chief Arthur Harris wired congratulations to Eaker: 'Yankee Doodle certainly went to town, and can stick another well-deserved feather in his hat.'

The British press lauded 'the remarkable success of the new Flying Fortress' and cheered the B-24 Liberator bombers too, when they went to war in October. Between August 17 and December 31, 1942, American heavy bombers flew 1547 sorties, many of them against the concrete-roofed U-boat pens in occupied France. The average American loss rate per raid at this period was only 2 per cent, half that of the RAF. But no American bomber had yet flown to Germany, beyond the range of friendly fighter cover.

In January 1943, a directive issued at the Casablanca Conference defined the chief war aim of Allied bombing commanders as 'the progressive destruction and dislocation of the German military, industrial and economic system and the undermining of the morale of the German people to a point where their capacity for armed resistance is fatally weakened'.

FACING THE FIGHTERS

Prodded by this, 91 B-17s and B-24s were sent against the naval base at Wilhelmshaven on January 27. From this first German target, beyond fighter protection, only three bombers failed to return, a fairly encouraging result. But by February the German defences began to find the measure of the 'invincible' Fortresses and Liberators. That month, 22 bombers were shot down, each crewed by ten highly trained specialists.

As spring advanced, losses escalated; out of 115 aircraft attacking Bremen on April 17, 16 were lost and 44 seriously damaged. On June 13, 22 out of 60 B-17s went down in a single raid on Kiel, a grim curtain-raiser to 'Blitz Week' in July – which included the Eighth's part in Operation 'Gomorrah' against Hamburg – that cost over 100 aircraft lost or damaged and the equivalent of 90 crews killed, wounded or taken prisoner.

The principal cause of the losses was the limited range of the Allied fighters then available. Taking off from English airfields, they could escort the bombers only to and from the borders of Germany. It was with foreboding that the bomber men watched the 'Little Friends' – code-name for Allied fighters – depart, for as they left, gnat-like swarms of Messerschmitts and Focke-Wulfs rose ahead to make their attacks from head-on. This took iron nerve and great skill, but the Luftwaffe had soon learned that the American bombers, lightly armed forward, were most vulnerable to this kind of tactic. One bombardier recalled: 'They came in from 10, 12, 2 o'clock, guns winking, then just feet away, would break below, some of the hot-shots actually doing a roll as they went. You could feel the shells hitting the ship, but you were holding formation, and apart from a quick burst from the forward guns, there wasn't a damn thing you could do about it.'

Combat in a B-17 was always a nerve-stretching, physically exhausting business. From below, the rigid formations, each plane trailing dramatic white plumes of condensation from the engines, seemed serene and invincible. In fact, these contrails were a pilot's nightmare, advertising his presence from scores of kilometres away.

Behind the flight deck stretched a vibrating green metal tunnel draped with cables and ammunition belts, filled with deafening noise. Those who could endure real claustrophobia volunteered for the 'ball-turret', under the belly of the bomber. In this plexiglass bubble, the gunner curled foetus-like, plied his trade and hoped that in an emergency, his friends would remember to open the hatch above him. This was because there was no room for a parachute in the turret – he had to reach up into the fuselage for it.

Escape was not easy for anyone. In a compartment beneath the flight deck in a B-17 there is a tiny hatch through which, if the plane were badly hit, five men encumbered by flying suits and parachutes were meant to squeeze. But if the plane went into a spin, no one would get out at all; centrifugal force simply pinned the crew to the walls. By mid-1943, it was apparent to any crew member that his chances of completing a tour of 25 missions were little better than one in three.

Not only the crews, but the Allied High Command were becoming seriously alarmed. The Luftwaffe's determination and skill were biting hard. If the fighters gained the upper hand,

LEADING FROM THE FRONT

Ira C. Eaker (1896-1987) was a brilliant pilot and a firm believer in the ability of the heavy bomber to win wars. Daylight precision bombing was the method he advocated, and the heavily armed B-17 Flying Fortress the tool he chose. To demonstrate his faith, on August 17, 1942, at the age of 46, he flew in one of his 12 Flying Fortresses to bomb the marshalling yards at Rouen – the first all-American bombing attack made by the USAAF in western Europe. He pressed the case of daylight precision bombing at the Casablanca Conference in January 1942, when 'Bomber' Harris pressed equally hard for area bombing by night. It was agreed that both forms of attack should continue, giving rise to the 'round-the-clock' Combined Bomber Offensive.

Eaker was promoted lieutenant general in 1943, and in the following year was made commander of Allied air forces in the Mediterranean. Flying from bases in Italy, his new command continued the offensive against Germany and played a major part in the Italian campaign, including the bombing of the monastery of Monte Cassino, and supported the invasion of southern France.

TARGET PLOESTI **Dense black smoke pours from a burning Ploesti refinery (right) during the American raid of August 1943; a shaft of light strikes one US B-24 Liberator. The crew of 'Wash's Tub', a B-24 that returned safely, pose (below) on the tarmac. Of 178 B-24s that set out, 46 went down, eight took refuge in Turkey, 58 were badly damaged.**

then the policy of destroying German industry could not be carried out. Worse, as Hitler had discovered in 1940, without command of the air there was no chance of mounting a cross-Channel invasion. In June 1943, the Combined Chiefs of Staff issued a directive code-named 'Pointblank'. Henceforward, the US Eighth would concentrate on destroying German fighter power – through bombing aircraft factories and associated targets; the RAF would continue to concentrate on 'the general disorganisation of German industry'.

DIVIDED THEY FELL

An early 'Pointblank' mission was flown against Romanian oil refineries at Ploesti, on August 1. It was carried out by the Eighth's sister force, the Ninth USAAF, from Benghazi in North Africa, and involved a 4350 km (2700 mile) round trip across the Balkans. The plan was for 178 B-24 Liberators to attack at low level and knock out Ploesti. In the event bad weather, murderous flak and swarms of enemy fighters caused a fiasco; 310 US crewmen were killed and 114 became prisoners of war. Little damage was done to Ploesti and its output was soon back to normal.

In England, Eaker prepared for a double assault – the biggest American sky battle so far – on the Messerschmitt aircraft assembly works at Regensburg and the vital ball-bearing factories in Schweinfurt. Two overwhelmingly large task forces would go out together on August 17. A surprise move was to send the Regensburg planes on to land in North Africa while the Schweinfurters returned to England, hoping to divide the defenders into two weakened forces chasing off in opposite directions.

The plan began to go wrong at the outset, when low cloud put the Schweinfurt force's takeoff back by $3\frac{1}{2}$ hours. Two separate raids on the same target were thus created. Because they failed to coincide, neither raid diverted German fighters from the other. The Regensburg force lost 24 bombers and took over 11 hours to reach Africa, losing two more aircraft on the way. The Schweinfurt planes finally managed to get off the ground in late morning and, just after 1 pm, 216 B-17s in two task forces crossed the enemy coast. At the limit of their range, the protecting RAF Spitfires and American P-47 Thunderbolts had to turn back near Aachen. At once a formidable array of German fighters rose up to harass the bombers. Twenty-one Fortresses were shot down before reaching the target, one fell to flak over Schweinfurt, and another three were lost to fighters as the squadrons turned for home.

Of 230 Fortresses sent against Schweinfurt, 36 went down. In addition to the 24 lost on August 17, the Regensburg task force left 60 badly damaged aircraft in North Africa and lost another three on the return flight to England. The Germans had lost only 25 fighters and, although reconnaissance pictures seemed to show a devastated Schweinfurt, in fact the bombs had done little more than strip the roofs off the workshops, leaving the heavy machinery relatively unscathed. Within four weeks they were back in full production.

LONG-RANGE SUPPORT

Other operations at that period were hardly more successful. However, the men flying 93 B-17s bound for Frankfurt on October 4 were considerably cheered by an escort of Thunderbolt fighters. These were fitted with extra fuel tanks beneath the fuselage to increase their range. The 'drop-tanks' slowed the fighters up, and resulted in instant incineration if hit, but they could be jettisoned before going into action. The Germans soon learned to attack P-47s just as they crossed the coast, forcing their pilots to drop the tanks and thus reducing their range to near to what it had been before.

Undaunted, the Eighth decided to visit Schweinfurt again on October 14. This time, the plan involved three task forces of B-17s and B-24s, each flying separate routes, and each covered by an escort of twin-engine P-38 Lightning fighters equipped with drop-tanks sweeping ahead. But the P-38s were not operational in time; once again the bombers would have to go it alone. The crews learned of their destination with deep gloom. At one briefing, the commanding officer

SKY MARKSMAN **The waist gunner of a B-17 grips his Browning 0.5 in (12.7 mm) machine gun. His parachute lies at his feet, attached to his clothing by webbing so that he can find it in a hurry. He wears a fleece-lined leather flying suit, and large leather overboots. Earphones in his flying helmet keep him in touch with the rest of the crew.**

tried to raise his audience's spirits with a pep talk: 'It's a tough job, but I know you can do it. Good luck, good hunting and good bombing.' A doleful gunner added from the rear: 'And goodbye!'

Because of poor weather, the Liberators were badly scattered, and could not be sent against Schweinfurt. Not until midday did 291 B-17s in two task forces set out over the North Sea. The Luftwaffe homed in as soon as the Americans crossed the Dutch coast and again the fiercest fighting took place south of Aachen as the 'Little Friends' departed. A new and highly unnerving form of attack was the rocket-carrier. 'Suddenly the German fighter seemed to disappear behind four bright flares,' recalled one airman. 'The rockets were on their way. Then he came in close to use the 20 mm cannon.'

The battle on the way home was even tougher than the one to the target. No sooner was Schweinfurt left behind than some 200 single and twin-engine German fighters flung themselves on the bombers and harried them on their homeward journey. Fifty-eight Fortresses fell victim to German fighters and two to flak; another five crashed after crossing the English coast.

These losses finally convinced even its most ardent advocates that there was no such thing as a

TOGGING UP American bomber crewmen tug on overboots and pull flying suits over their uniforms. They needed every scrap of clothing to protect them from freezing gales that blew in through open waist-gun positions.

THE FORTRESS IN BATTLE

Tough, heavily armed and capable of absorbing a tremendous amount of punishment, the Boeing B-17 Flying Fortress was the most famous American heavy bomber of World War II. It was born out of the strategists' plea for an aircraft that could carry destruction deep into enemy territory and fight its way out again, independent of friendly escort cover. Gathered into an 18-aircraft formation, devised by Colonel (later General) Curtis LeMay, in which the planes were concentrated into three boxes to give mutual covering fire, the Fortress was indeed a formidable foe.

It had two faults, however. The bomb load was only about half that of a Lancaster, and by late 1942 German fighter pilots discovered that the B-17 was extremely vulnerable to a head-on approach, where few of its guns could be brought to bear. To counter both faults, at the beginning of 1943 LeMay advocated the combat wing, in which three 18-aircraft formations were united into three close-knit groups, high, centre and low. A pilot-controlled 'chin turret', just under the aircraft's nose, was also introduced.

As the combat wing approached the target the senior bombardier, in the leading aircraft, took over control of the plane. When the target was correctly aligned in his bombsight, he released with his bombs a smoke marker, on which the other 53 planes released their bombs. LeMay argued that, whatever the B-17's shortcomings in load, it made up for in concentration and accuracy. For defence a combat wing of 54 Fortresses could bring a total of 702 heavy machine guns to bear.

Yet still American losses mounted. Worst of all for the bombers were the head-on attacks. With iron nerve and skill, old Luftwaffe hands would come tearing in, hold their fire until the B-17 filled the whole of their gunsight, then give a one or two-second burst of cannon fire, before rolling over and down through the edge of the formation. That short burst was usually sufficient, smashing through the nose of the B-17, perhaps killing the pilot then tearing down the fuselage.

successful self-defending bomber. Bomber leaders clamoured for some new and wondrous long-range fighter that would solve their dilemma. In fact, it already existed – the North American P-51 Mustang, which had been around for a while but was considered underpowered. However, fitted with a Rolls-Royce Merlin engine instead of its American Allison it grew mighty indeed. In Washington, General Henry 'Hap' Arnold, Commanding General of the US Army Air Forces, ordered the new P-51D version into immediate large-scale production; using an American-built version of the Merlin, it had a range of up to 3680 km (2300 miles) and a top speed of 703 km/h (437 mph).

Awaiting its arrival, the Eighth was forced to reduce its efforts. The Reich gained a respite, at least from daylight bombing, during the winter of 1943-4. Then, on the last day of February 1944, England-based bombers, protected by older fighters plus Mustangs, were joined over Germany by Fifteenth Air Force heavies flying from Italy. Together, by the end of March, the two commands were dispatching a combined force of 1000 bombers a day into enemy territory. To the bomber theorists, American and British alike, it seemed that victory through air power alone was now a distinct possibility. But the picture changed: Supreme Allied Headquarters decreed that both the Eighth and RAF Bomber Command should now direct their attentions largely on communications, and military installations in Northern France, as part of the run up to D-Day.

Together to the end

As part of the great plan for the invasion of Europe, RAF Bomber Command and the US Eighth Air Force combined to strike day and night at the enemy, but where to strike – and where to draw the line – caused sharp discord.

AS SPRING CAME to Europe in 1944, British and American airmen alike sought to erase the grim memories of the late winter months, when losses mounted and the chance of completing a 'tour' of 30 operations seemed ever more remote. Germany's arms factories were still humming with activity. Its workers, far from being cowed by heavy civilian casualties, seemed to be spurred by the bombing to work even harder for victory.

But there were signs that the tide was about to turn. Mustang fighters were now escorting the daylight bombers all the way to distant targets and back, and were destroying ever-increasing numbers of their opponents. Especially damaging was their killing of experienced Luftwaffe pilots, who were forced to defend vital targets against impossible odds.

On April 14, 1944, General Dwight D. Eisenhower, in charge of the invasion of Europe, officially took overall command of both Bomber Command and the American Eighth Air Force to coordinate their roles with those of other arms in the build-up to the invasion of France. It was clear to him what those roles should be: to support the ground forces and in particular to destroy French railway and other communication systems so as to hamper German forces after D-Day – the so-called 'Transportation Plan'.

Churchill and his Bomber Command chief, Air Chief Marshal Sir Arthur Harris, both disagreed – as did Lt General Carl Spaatz, newly commanding US Strategic Air Forces in Europe. Spaatz saw his Mustangs axing down German fighters to carve avenues through which his Flying Fortresses and Liberators could fly on daylight precision raids. These would destroy oil plants, cutting off Germany's fuel and thus destroying its *ability* to fight. Harris was equally certain that night-time pounding of German industrial centres and civilian workers would destroy the *will* to fight. The two envisaged slotting together their different styles of raid to mount a ferocious round-the-clock assault that would demolish all German resistance.

Eisenhower got his way by making a direct appeal to Roosevelt and General George Marshall, chairman of the Joint Chiefs of Staff Committee in Washington: either the Transportation Plan was put into effect, or 'Overlord', the Allied invasion plan, was doomed. Their answer was predictable: the invasion had absolute priority, and from about April 1 the RAF and USAAF began to switch their targets.

As a result, by June 1944, less than 10 per cent of British bombs dropped were being aimed at Germany. The heavies flew instead to northern France and Belgium, bombing marshalling yards at Le Mans, Trappes, Courtrai, and many other places. On the night of June 5/6, several squadrons were briefed to attack German batteries on the French coast. Crews were warned particularly to keep course and not to jettison bombs in the Channel. On their way back from the targets at dawn, they saw why – spread beneath them lay the vast panoply of the D-Day invasion fleet.

BOMBING BEGINS TO HURT

Before starting on the Transportation Plan, Spaatz had obtained permission from Washington for a number of full-scale raids against German oil installations – the 'Oil Plan'. Their purpose was to force the German fighters into combat and to destroy as many of them as possible before D-Day, while also reducing the Luftwaffe's stocks of aviation fuel. On May 12 he sent 886 bombers and 735 long-range fighters to bomb oil installations around Leipzig. The Americans lost 46 planes, but claimed 56 German fighters. Further attacks were made on May 28 and 29.

The German Armaments Minister, Albert Speer, wrote later: 'Until then we had managed to produce approximately as many weapons as the armed forces needed, in spite of their considerable losses. But with the attack . . . upon several fuel plants in central and eastern Germany, a new era in the war began. It meant the end of German armaments production.'

The major part of Spaatz's effort after D-Day was devoted to ground support and to destroying V-weapon sites. Even so, by using only about 15 per cent of his force, he cut German petroleum production from 940 000 tonnes in March to virtually nothing by the autumn. A respite came with the bitter winter of 1944-5, which limited flying and allowed the Germans to build up enough oil stocks to open the Battle of the Ardennes. But it was not enough. The Germans did their best to protect their oil, cramming the whole Leipzig area with anti-aircraft batteries. But however many bombers they shot down, more took their place.

Harris turned his attention back to the cities in September 1944, until Supreme Headquarters extended the Transportation Plan to Germany. The Reich's communications presented tougher targets, but the means to hit them were already at hand – a 10 tonne 'earthquake' bomb, code-named 'Grand Slam' and designed by Barnes Wallis, who had earlier created the dambusting 'bouncing bomb'.

Wallis meant 'Grand Slam' to be dropped from 12 000 m (40 000 ft) to penetrate 30 m (100 ft) or more into the ground before exploding. The resulting underground shock wave, like an earthquake, would bring down the sturdiest of structures. However, no aircraft was yet capable of carrying such a weight to such a height. Even so, a scaled-down 6 tonne version, code-named 'Tallboy', was used with spectacular effect on railway tunnels, U-boat pens and the battleship *Tirpitz*. On March 14, 1945, 'Grand Slam' was given its first trial on the Bielefeld Viaduct on the Hamm-Hanover railway. Dropped from only half the designed height and aided by a few 'Tallboys', it reduced the great arch to rubble.

CLIMAX OF AREA BOMBING

Skills evolved and polished in the Transportation Plan helped Bomber Command when it returned to bombing German cities. For example, aircraft approached targets from several angles and released their bombs at different set timings

A MAN AND HIS BOMBS

Barnes Neville Wallis (1887-1979) was a brilliant, innovative British aeronautical engineer whose early training was in marine engineering. He was an early designer of airships, including *R100*, which used his 'geodetic' framework of lightweight, crisscrossing rods. He later used such a framework in the Wellington bomber.

But Wallis is best known for the 'bouncing bombs' used in the 1943 dams raid. His 6 tonne 'Tallboy' and 10 tonne 'Grand Slam' bombs – the most powerful in the world until the advent of the atomic bomb – were used with devastating effect on such previously unreachable targets as railway tunnels and concrete-roofed U-boat docks. After the war he was a pioneer of the swing-wing concept for supersonic aircraft. When Wallis died, in his 92nd year, he was working on designs for an airliner that would fly halfway round the world in only four hours.

TOOEY AT THE TOP

Carl Spaatz (1891-1974) – nicknamed 'Tooey' – commanded a US Army Air Corps squadron in France in World War I, and early in World War II was an official observer with the RAF. He returned to England in 1942 as commander of the Eighth Air Force.

Spaatz went to the Mediterranean to organise air support for the 'Torch' landings, and stayed there until returning to England in January 1944 as commander of US Strategic Air Forces in Europe to work closely with the RAF in the combined bomber offensive on Germany. Under protest, he diverted to give support to the D-Day landings.

In 1945, Spaatz went to the Pacific to direct air operations against Japan, including the atomic bombing of Hiroshima and Nagasaki. He became Chief of Staff of the new independent United States Air Force a year before he retired in 1948.

BETWEEN RAIDS The men who meted out death from the skies, making light of danger with mascots like Lady Luck (top), had to live with tension and fatigue. Papers, pets and pin-ups kept these foes at bay – until the next raid.

beyond the markers – a technique called 'overshoot' – thus spreading the destruction even wider. The ancient city of Darmstadt, attacked on September 11, 1944, suffered terribly in this way. The bombs, dropped from seven different angles, opened what Darmstadters later termed a *Todesfacher* ('death fan') of fire from the central markers to engulf a large part of the city. The same methods destroyed three-quarters of Bremerhaven a week later and Brunswick and many other targets in October.

These and many more attacks through the winter of 1944-5 were mere curtain-raisers to the climax – Operation 'Thunderclap', designed to destroy German morale with a series of cataclysmic raids upon cities. The force and techniques needed for such missions became available only in mid-February 1945 – by when it was clear that Germany was doomed. But Churchill and Roosevelt, bound for the Yalta Conference, wanted to give Stalin some concrete evidence of Western support for his offensives in the east. They asked their air chiefs for action against east German cities.

Dresden, the seventh largest city in Germany, was just one name on the target list. According to a briefing note, 'it is the largest unbombed built-up area the enemy has . . . With refugees pouring westward (to escape the Russians) and troops to be rested, roofs are at a premium'. A raid on Dresden would also 'show the Russians when they arrive what Bomber Command can do'.

The Dresden raid saw the culmination of the RAF's 'master bomber' technique – a refinement of earlier 'pathfinder' methods. Marker flares were dropped by the master bomber flying low in a fast twin-engine Mosquito. Back-up Mosquitoes followed and then came high-flying pathfinder Lancasters followed by the main force. During the whole raid the master bomber patrolled over the target – braving enemy flak and RAF bombs – to order corrections and, if necessary, further markers. In this way Bomber Command's accuracy became greater even than that of the daylight-flying Americans.

The master bomber placed his markers on Dresden at about 9 pm on February 13, and 786 RAF planes dropped 2690 tonnes of bombs from relatively low altitudes – for there was no opposition. Soon the city was an inferno visible to aircrew 320 km (200 miles) away. With daylight came the Americans to stoke the blaze still higher – as they did again on the 15th – but the target was already a towering vortex of devouring flame. Nobody knows how many people died there, because of the uncounted refugees; estimates vary between 25 000 and 200 000.

When the extent of the cataclysm became known, there were uneasy murmurings among the Allied High Command. Had someone gone too far? Spaatz re-stated the USAAF's policy of bombing only specific industrial or military targets; civilian deaths were inevitable when bombing, say, railway junctions, but they were not part of the policy. Even Churchill began to wonder if RAF policy ought to be reviewed, but Harris was adamant: 'I do not personally regard the whole of the remaining cities of Germany as worth the bones of one British Grenadier.'

In the end, did strategic bombing work? In the sense of the prewar dream that the bomber could win wars all by itself, it did not – except, arguably, in the case of the atomic bombing of Japan. In the early war years the bombers showed that war could be carried to the heart of the all-conquering Third Reich. Despite the horrors, bombing failed to break German morale and, until the last months of the war, did not decisively affect German industrial production. Its greatest contribution was probably to pave the way for the armies, by depriving the enemy of oil and destroying fighters, communications and heavy guns – all precision rather than area targets.

JOINT VENTURE The US P-51D Mustang fighter had a British Rolls-Royce designed engine. Extra under-wing fuel tanks put eastern Germany within range, and a bubble canopy improved visibility.

THE FIRST JET

The Messerschmitt Me262 might have changed the course of the air war in Europe if its development had not been delayed. Hitler was so impressed when he watched the 870 km/h (540 mph) twin-jet fighter put through its paces on November 26, 1943, that he ordered it into immediate production – as a fighter-bomber. The result was confusion and delay as numerous variants – all-weather fighters, reconnaissance planes, ground-attack models and fighter-bombers, as well as day fighters – were produced. Some 1430 Me262s were built, but only a quarter of these went into action, beginning in April 1944. The fighters were heavily armed with cannon, and highly effective against Allied bombers – but they were too few and too late.

The Me262 had been under development since 1938 and – together with the accident-prone rocket-propelled Me163 'Komet' – was by far the fastest aircraft in 1944-5. It was considerably faster than the first British jet fighter, the Gloster Meteor, but the two never met in combat. Meteors did not fly over Germany until the very last weeks of the war, when shortages of fuel and skilled pilots and Allied air superiority kept most Me262s grounded.

17: SLOW MARCH THROUGH ITALY

Success in Sicily tempted the Allies ever farther north into Italy, but it proved to be a hard grind.

Two ways to Messina

Allied rivalry and Sicilian rapture accompanied the first venture onto Axis home territory. It began with the biggest amphibious invasion in history.

SICK AND SWEATING, crammed in the airless holds of ships that reared and plunged in huge seas, the troops – British, Canadian and American – longed to set foot on land. But they could not feel too easy about that, for when they stepped ashore it would be on the enemy's land. Operation 'Husky' was under way.

Sicily was the destination. The troops were to be the first Allied forces to venture onto Axis home ground. Now malign fate had blown up a gale on the carefully chosen night – and had waited until the leading vessels were only 12 hours from the beaches, much too late to get word to the huge fleet to turn back.

They were a town afloat, filling the sea behind as far as the eye could see: 2500 ships and landing craft, carrying 181 000 men of US Lt General George S. Patton's Seventh Army and British General Sir Bernard Montgomery's Eighth – a total of seven divisions. They had 14 000 vehicles, 600 tanks, 1800 guns, ammunition, food, stoves, soap, cigarettes and matches, and for the Americans throwaway shaving gear and packets of gum.

The gigantic force approaching Sicily's southern and south-eastern shore on July 9, 1943, was no half-hearted affair, but it was a compromise and only its immediate aims were decided. As victory in North Africa had neared, the Allied chiefs disagreed on their next move. The British wanted to keep up activity in the Mediterranean, nibbling away at the edge of Axis territory. The Americans argued fiercely for concentrating everything on the main goal of a landing in France as the most direct route to Germany. Britain was adamant that the Allies could not gather enough forces to strike across the Channel in 1943.

In the end, Churchill and Roosevelt, meeting at the Casablanca Conference in January 1943, compromised on the invasion of Sicily, whose mountainous triangle sat across the Mediter-

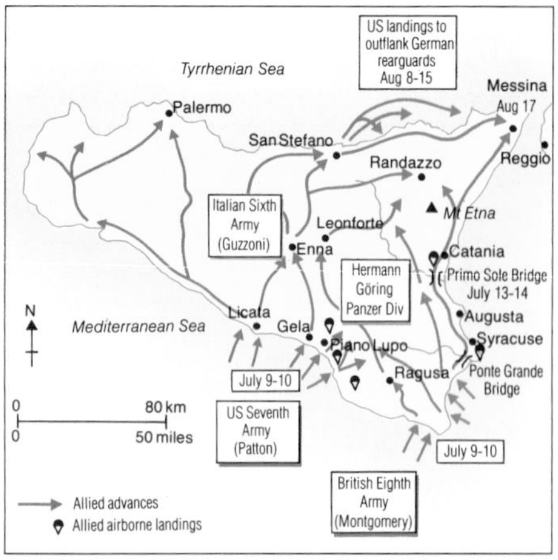

ON ENEMY SOIL Montgomery insisted the whole invasion made for south-east Sicily, within Allied fighter cover. Then he headed north, with the Americans covering to the west.

FRIEND OR FOE? Wine, handshakes and smiles all round marked the swift British drive off the beaches, through the olive groves and beyond Syracuse on July 10, 1943.

ranean shipping lanes; once it, as well as North Africa, was in Allied hands, the supply routes to India and the Far East, and to the Soviet Union by way of the Suez Canal and Iran, would be safe. Churchill also hoped that the fall of Sicily might knock Italy out of the war – a prestigious victory for the Allies. The Americans insisted, however, that the invasion should not be allowed to draw men or equipment from the build-up for eventual landings in northern France.

The night of July 9/10 was agreed for the assault because the moon would rise early and aid the first – airborne – landings, but go down before the beach landings, at 2.45 am. But Patton and Montgomery disagreed about where to land.

Montgomery turned down plans for one army to land near Catania on the east coast and the other near Palermo on the north. The whole island, with 315 000 Italian soldiers and 50 000 Germans to defend it (plus another 40 000 Germans as fighting progressed), would separate the two forces. He insisted that they land on a 135 km (85 mile) stretch of coast from Syracuse to Licata. This was within range of Allied fighters from Malta, Gozo and North Africa. Six British battleships would give powerful support.

OPENING GAMBITS

While the troopships, escorts and landing craft needed for the operation were being mustered from the Middle East, North Africa, Britain and the United States, air bombardments pulverised the outlying Italian islands of Pantelleria (where there were airstrips and underground hangars) and Lampedusa.

British Naval Intelligence provided 'Husky' with one of the most brilliant decoy plots of the war. A corpse, given the false identity of a Royal Marines officer and later famous as 'the man who never was', was washed ashore on the coast of Spain in May. His briefcase, fastened to his wrist, was full of false papers which quickly reached German Military Intelligence. They 'revealed' that the Allies would make a feint attack on Sicily as a cover for their real target of Sardinia, which would be the springboard for invading northern Italy and the Balkans.

Decoded German signals confirmed that most of the enemy were duped – though Field Marshal Albert Kesselring, the German Commander in Chief South – was not convinced. The Allies also knew how many enemy troops there were in Sicily and which were the vital points to take in order to block their movements.

Much less successful was the airborne operation before the beach landings. Troops were to drop just before midnight and take bridges, airfields and high ground from which the enemy could see and attack the advancing Allies. The 1200 British airborne troops were towed from North Africa in 144 gliders during the gale. The formations broke up and miscalculated the distance. Nearly 70 of the gliders were released too early and came down into the sea, where more than 200 men were drowned. Men who landed on Sicily were nowhere near the Ponte Grande, their target just south of Syracuse. Only 73 men reached this bridge, and 65 of them were killed or wounded during the night's fighting to control it.

The 2781 American paratroops in their 226 C-47s were also plagued by the weather. The inexperienced pilots and navigators had seen only daylight photographs of the landing area. Blown off course and peering at the night-time landscape, they could recognise nothing. The paratroops were scattered throughout Sicily. The 200 who landed near Piano Lupo, above the planned landing beach, came under heavy fire.

LANDFALL Troops decanted from the ships at night in a welter of landing craft, including the new amphibious trucks – DUKWs – which made their debut in Italy. By dawn, men, tanks, guns, transport and stores crowded the beaches.

TOEHOLD ON THE BEACHES

The Allied amphibious forces had much better luck. Shortly before midnight, the winds miraculously dropped. The troopships took up positions marked for them by submarines, and the men came ashore unopposed.

The Americans had the same good fortune at Licata, where Italian troops made off without a fight. But at Gela the Italians were stiffened by the German 'Hermann Göring' Division, which attacked with giant 56 tonne Tiger tanks. The battleships, which Patton had deemed unnecessary, now stopped the Tigers dead.

The next day the tanks attacked again – 60 monsters pushing the Americans back to within 2 km (1¼ miles) of the sea. The naval guns could not fire without hitting the Americans. Unloading was stopped by repeated Italian and German bomber attacks, but finally the Americans landed an artillery battalion which gradually pushed the panzers back. Then a naval bombardment forced the German tanks to withdraw.

Even so, Patton played safe and called for 2000 extra men, paratroops from North Africa. They arrived over Gela on the night of July 11/12, after a day of attacks on the US ships by enemy bombers. The ships' gunners thought they were facing another attack and fired with all they had at the low-flying planes. Not until one of them crashed near the US destroyer *Beatty* did the navy men realise they were firing on their own reinforcements; 229 paratroops were killed or wounded.

BUDDIES The Americans, hailed by Sicilians as friends, gave out candy and cigarettes and received wine, fruit and other food. Relations with the locals were warm because many of the Americans came of Italian stock.

CHALK AND CHEESE Patton, hot-headed and ever ready to seize unexpected chances, was riled at playing a supporting role to Monty (left), whom he thought insufferably pleased with himself, too careless about his men's appearance and attitude, too inflexibly cautious about his battle plans.

FOOTSLOGGING ADVANCE

The ground forces had survived the most dangerous period – the landing – and within two days were established on a third of Sicily's coast. Montgomery and his Eighth Army had moved swiftly away from the landing areas and by the evening of July 10 were established in Syracuse. To the south of the town they had been able to march safely across the Ponte Grande, held all night by the survivors of the glider disaster.

On July 13, commandos were dispatched ahead of the main advance to secure vital bridges on the road to Catania. They suffered 153 casualties at the Ponte dei Malati Bridge, but 12 hours later advancing troops of the Eighth Army were able to take the bridge intact. The same night the British 1st Parachute Brigade from Tunisia gained a precarious hold on the Prima Sole Bridge over the Simeto river, just south of Catania.

For the confident Eighth Army the 160 km (100 mile) advance up the east coast from Syracuse to Messina was a painful transition from Africa's motorised war to vertical, footslogging terrain. The few roads, frequently demolished or mined, zigzagged steeply up crumbly cliffs, vulnerable to ambushes. Off the roads it was impossible to use vehicles and everything had to be manhandled. At Augusta, barely 25 km (16 miles) north of Syracuse, Montgomery's advance stalled. He could not break into the plain around Catania, farther up the coast, which German troops were holding grimly to deny its airfields to the Allies.

For once Montgomery made an on-the-spot change of plan and sent part of his force – the Canadian 1st Division – on a long westward loop through the centre of the island and around Mount Etna to bypass the enemy. At daybreak on July 13 they were fighting for Highway 124 at Vizzini – to the dismay of the Americans, who had the same objective, as laid down in their orders. When the American units were ordered to stay clear to the west, Patton was goaded beyond his extremely limited patience. He flew to Tunis to protest to General Sir Harold Alexander, the overall commander. Alexander, unaware of the Americans' deep resentment and amazed by Patton's tense demands, readily agreed that the role of guardian to Montgomery could be changed. Patton's men could make their own positive drive north-westwards to seize Palermo.

RACE TO THE TOWN HALL

Now the initiative swung to the Americans, who were in more open country. Patton made for Palermo with impressive speed. There was little resistance. Sergeant Ross Carter of the 504th Parachute Regiment later wrote: 'War had never been as good as this before. Cheering crowds greeted us in the towns. Peasants brought food and drink when we stopped. Barbers shaved us for a cigarette. Many girls could fall in love for a chocolate bar.' Italian soldiers surrendered in droves at the first opportunity. The Germans were already drawing away into the island's north-east corner near the mainland, aiming to delay the Allies at a series of defensive lines.

Montgomery's 'left hook' around Etna was not proving much faster than the coast route. The Canadians' chief enemies were choking dust, the suffocating heat, thirst, fleas, malaria – and the terrain. German demolition work on the roads added to the difficulties, so that the tanks and artillery could rarely keep up with the infantry.

At every small hilltop town of close-packed houses, the Germans put up a stout – and delaying – defence. It was impossible to use the road to approach Assoro, perched on top of a cliff in the middle of the island, because it wound up a spur exposed to the enemy. Major Lord Tweedsmuir led his Canadian troops to the east where, at dusk, they started struggling up the 300 m (1000 ft) sheer sides of gullies, tiptoeing along ledges fearful of giving the game away by sending a rock clattering into the valley. At dawn they surprised the sleepy Germans and occupied the crest – but they had to perch on it under heavy fire for another day before the Germans left the village.

While Montgomery's men were trying to beat their way up the east coast and around the foothills of Etna, Patton was making a two-pronged drive along the north coast, determined to get to Messina first. The Seventh Army had to fight hard at every little township along the road running through mountains about 32 km (20 miles) inland. But once they had dislodged the German defenders, the Sicilians greeted them as friends. Along the coast road, Patton bypassed tail-end attacks by the retreating enemy by making small seaborne loops.

At 10.15 am on August 17, he reached the steps of the town hall in Messina, beating Montgomery by two hours. It had taken the Allies 38 days and 31 158 casualties to reach Messina, and by that time the German forces had escaped. As early as July 27, Kesselring had issued orders for the evacuation of Sicily. He saw the actions that cost the Allies so dear simply as delaying measures, while the bulk of his own troops and some 62 000 Italians were ferried across the 5 km (3 mile) Strait of Messina to the mainland. For once, Hitler in his East Prussian headquarters agreed and did not order the ground to be held 'at all cost'. Taking their weapons and heavy equipment with them, the Axis troops crossed the water round the clock between August 3 and 17, under a protective Luftwaffe umbrella. The Allies never expected such a well-organised evacuation, and made little attempt to interfere.

For Patton it was a hollow victory. He was in deep trouble for striking two hospitalised GIs. He accused them of cowardice because they had no visible wounds – malaria and shell shock not being improved by dressings. The press eventually leaked the story. Eisenhower, knowing Patton's great gifts as a soldier and a leader, fended off the worst of the public outcry, but Patton spent a year in the shadows before returning to command the US Third Army in Normandy.

Fall of the Fascists

After fate caught up with Mussolini, he was saved by a daring rescue . . . but only for a time.

A HANDSHAKE from the courteous King Victor Emmanuel dismissed Benito Mussolini at the door of the Villa Savoia in Rome after an early evening audience on July 25, 1943. As Mussolini walked sadly to his limousine, military police armed with submachine guns hustled him into an ambulance, and off to Podgora Barracks.

Italy's Fascist dictator for 21 years had gone to tell the King of the vote of no confidence passed on him the previous night by the Fascist Grand Council. Meeting for the first time since 1939, the council voted to return supreme power to the King. Mussolini had expected the King to let him deal with the crisis, but Victor Emmanuel had already agreed with Marshal Pietro Badoglio, a former lukewarm supporter of *Il Duce*, that Mussolini was to be stripped of his power.

Badoglio formed a new government without one Fascist member, and started negotiating with the Allies. The Italians wanted to surrender and change sides, but the Allies were loath to fight alongside such recent enemies.

Eventually, on September 3, the Italians had to agree to an unconditional surrender – with Victor Emmanuel remaining as a constitutional monarch – but it was not to be announced until September 8, when the Allied invasion of Italy would be too far advanced for the Germans to respond effectively. The American 82nd Airborne Division was to parachute into Rome to bolster the Italians, but in the event the Italian garrisons were not ready. The Germans moved troops into Rome – and other key cities – so quickly that the parachute drop was called off. Italy found itself occupied by opposing armies.

The Germans immediately set up a military administration. The King, Badoglio and his government escaped aboard a corvette to Allied territory in the south. The Italian fleet escaped under attack to internment in Malta. Mussolini was in secret captivity, guarded by the King's loyal men.

Italian soldiers discarded their uniforms, hid their weapons and melted away. In the north, however, many were rounded up by Field Marshal Erwin Rommel, German commander there since August 17, and sent to forced labour camps. South of Rome, Field Marshal Albert Kesselring disarmed the Italians and let them go home. Some 600 000 Italian troops in Axis-held Crete, Greece and other parts of the Balkans had the choice of fighting alongside German units or working as forced labour in the Fatherland. Few chose to fight.

Hitler asked the Italians to hand over his friend and admirer Mussolini, whom he intended to restore to power. When they did not cooperate, Hitler entrusted the task of finding him to SS Captain Otto Skorzeny.

RESCUE FOR *IL DUCE*

His jailers moved Mussolini half a dozen times to foil rescuers. But security was lax; an intercepted radio message put Skorzeny on his trail. He was traced to the Albergo Rifugio, a mountain-top ski hotel almost 2000 m (6500 ft) up at Gran Sasso in the Abruzzi Mountains north-east of Rome; it could be reached only by a funicular railway. On September 12, Luftwaffe paratroops seized the station at the foot of the funicular while gliders carrying Skorzeny and some 90 men crash-landed beside the hotel. The few Italian guards and armed police were stunned. Skorzeny's men stormed the hotel and freed Mussolini without a shot being fired.

The 1.93 m (6 ft 4 in) tall Skorzeny and the now haggard Mussolini crammed into a light aircraft. The grossly overloaded plane lurched off the mountain top and plunged giddily towards the valley floor before the pilot regained control and flew it to a Luftwaffe airfield. Mussolini was taken to Hitler's headquarters at Rastenburg in East Prussia.

Mussolini ended his grand dreams as so-called ruler of the Italian Social Republic based at Salò beside Lake Garda – a state that only Germany, its satellites and Japan recognised. He remained there as a mere puppet of Hitler until April 1945, when he tried to join the Nazis in a last stand in the Alps and was captured – for the last time – and shot by Communist partisans.

SNATCH EXPERT

An early member of the Nazi party in his native Austria, Otto 'Scarface' Skorzeny (1908-75) became a fanatical devotee of Hitler. He was in the prewar SS, then served in the Waffen SS in France in 1940 and on the Eastern Front until he was wounded.

Sent to security headquarters in Berlin, he set up a commando unit for undercover work. The rescue of Mussolini made him Hitler's chief trouble-shooter. His next major task, in October 1944, was to stop the Hungarian dictator, Admiral Horthy, concluding an armistice with the Russians. Skorzeny kidnapped Horthy's son, the chief negotiator, and bundled him off to Berlin. Skorzeny's men then took over the Budapest citadel and forced Horthy to step down; Hungarian Nazis replaced him.

During the Ardennes offensive, Skorzeny and some of his unit dressed as Americans and infiltrated Allied lines. They also spread tales that a 'hit team' was after Eisenhower (see box, *The Greif Commandos*, p. 328).

Acquitted of war crimes, Skorzeny became a businessman in Spain.

LEADER AT LARGE His jubilant men cluster around Otto Skorzeny (above; centre) after their rescue of Mussolini (on Skorzeny's left) from a mountain-top hotel north-east of Rome. His captors, King Victor Emmanuel III's men, were taken unawares. Without a shot fired, *Il Duce* was flown via Vienna and Munich to meet his friend Hitler (left) who had demanded the rescue. Hitler aimed to save face by making Mussolini titular head of a tiny Fascist state.

The 'five-day' Naples romp that became a month-long slog

Keeping German troops out of France and Russia was the only goal the Allies agreed on as they fought ridge by ridge up the obstacle course of Italy's spine.

LIGHT-HEADED GLEE seized the men on board the troopships carrying US General Mark Clark's Fifth Army on Operation 'Avalanche' towards Salerno. They cheered, capered, sang, blessed their good fortune and looked forward to waltzing unopposed over the creamy crescent of sand, through the market gardens, the walnut and olive groves on the plain beyond, and north to Naples beyond the encircling mountains. Italy had surrendered; the men had heard it over the ships' radios and it was useless for their senior officers to try to quell the high spirits. But the Germans would soon do so.

As darkness closed in that Wednesday evening of September 8, 1943, the 450 ships carrying 69 000 men and 20 000 vehicles approached land with doused lights and took up position in the Gulf of Salerno. Parties of men scrambled down nets into landing craft which moved away to join the other craft circling 7 km (4 miles) offshore. Tanks, guns and ammunition followed closely. At 3.30 am the invaders would begin landing.

ALLIES AT ODDS

As the campaign in Sicily ended, the British and Americans continued to debate at length whether to continue the Mediterranean campaign or to concentrate on the planned invasion of France. The Allies agreed finally to keep as many German troops as possible tied down away from Normandy and the Russian front and, if possible, to squeeze Italy out of the war. But the Normandy landings were to have first claim on all resources.

When Mussolini fell on July 25, the Allies' plans for landings on the Italian mainland became bolder. Instead of a prudent hop across the Strait of Messina onto Italy's toe, why not hit the kneecap? Salerno, the farthest point Allied fighters could cover, became the goal. Its port would give entry for supplies, Allied planes could operate from the nearby Montecorvino airfield, and a road ran north to Naples (see map, p. 282).

But Salerno was not ideal. There were few exits off the beaches and the routes through the hills behind led through narrow passes which an enemy could easily control. Worst of all was the corridor of the Sele river which, once clear of the hills, would cleave the invading forces into two separate bodies. Until the Allies took Battipaglia and Eboli on the left of the corridor and Altavilla and Hill 424 on its right, they would be vulnerable to German sallies down the corridor. Battipaglia had to be an early objective, as it was an important road and rail centre through which the Germans could reinforce the Salerno plain.

Nevertheless, Clark expected to land safely on September 9 and be in Naples five days later. His Fifth Army, recently formed in North Africa, consisted of X Corps, mostly British, under Lt General Richard McCreery, and the US VI Corps under Maj General Ernest Dawley. McCreery would invade north of the Sele corridor while Dawley struck on the southern side of it.

On September 3 General Sir Bernard Montgomery, leading Operation 'Baytown', went ahead of the main invasion, launching his Eighth Army across the Straits of Messina to clear the Germans out of Calabria and advance north quickly to join Clark. Even though decoded messages revealed that the Germans were withdrawing, the cautious Montgomery laid on a bombardment by four British battleships, British and American planes and batteries of artillery lined up wheel to wheel along the shore of Sicily, before his men set foot unscathed on the beaches at Reggio. The only casualties were a few luckless civilians and a shell-shocked puma that had escaped from Reggio Zoo. The Germans had departed, demolishing bridges, mining the narrow mountain roads and blocking the tunnels.

A rather makeshift support landing, Operation 'Slapstick', was put together after the Italians surrendered. On the day of the Salerno landings, the British 1st Airborne Division made a seaborne landing at Taranto and Brindisi to advance up the east coast and take the air bases at Foggia.

Field Marshal Albert Kesselring, the German commander in southern Italy, believed the Allies would land north of Naples and moved his eight divisions accordingly. Only General Heinrich von Vietinghoff's division was left near Salerno. The Germans tracked the invasion fleet from North Africa, and when it anchored off Salerno Vietinghoff's men spread out above the beaches, set up their guns and lay in wait.

INTO ACTION

The first of the invaders to land, at 3.10 am, were Lt Colonel William Darby's three battalions of US Rangers. Almost unopposed, they landed at Maiori; by dawn they were in the 1200 m (4000 ft) Chiunzi Pass, ideally placed to spot and attack any German troop or supply moves.

The British had insisted on a heavy naval bombardment before landing. They came ashore against light enemy fire, established themselves on the beach and took control of Salerno's port, but could not take the Montecorvino airfield, nor make headway up the Sele corridor.

The US VI Corps had the worst time. Clark had rejected any naval or air cover, hoping vainly to surprise the enemy. As the first wave of his landing craft grated on the dark, silent beaches a strident voice came over a loudspeaker. It called, in English: 'Come on in and give up. We have you covered.' Flares flooded the shore with brilliant light and guns blared at point-blank range. The men who had approached so blithely were now prone, crawling and wriggling among barbed wire and enemy fire desperately seeking a protective dune. Bullets whined past their ducked heads and grenades plummeted onto them. The craft carrying their weapons and ammunition exploded.

While the Americans were still struggling towards the plain, Vietinghoff's panzers surged forward belching fire. With rifles, bazookas, machine guns, grenades and knives, the invaders held off the Germans. By late afternoon, the Germans began to fall back, some equipment and supplies were ashore and VI Corps even attempted a few tentative pushes inland.

Thursday ended with a precarious Allied hold on the beach, but there the small success ended. During Friday and Saturday, the thunderous noise, intense fear, constant crouching and scuttling seemed as if it would never end. The men were exhausted, able to snatch only fitful naps beside their guns. There were no safe rear areas on the beaches. Try as they might, neither the British nor the Americans could find a way into the hills. The enemy blew apart anything that moved in daylight. On the night of September 9/10, the British 167th Infantry Brigade took Battipaglia, only to lose it next day.

Kesselring became convinced he could push the invaders into the sea. He rushed reinforcements south-east from Naples and west from Bari to join Vietinghoff. He even called men from Calabria to hurry north, leaving few to hinder Montgomery. While the reinforcements were on their way, the Luftwaffe bombed the Allied fleet, sinking four transport ships and seven landing craft and damaging many more vessels – and not just with fighters and bombers. Remote-

LUCKY LOSER

As Commander in Chief of all Axis forces in the Mediterranean, Albert Kesselring (1885-1960) directed the skilful German retreat through Sicily and the length of Italy, greatly hindering the Allied advance there in 1943-4. It was his third military career.

Kesselring was a soldier by training, and stayed in the Reichswehr after serving as an artillery officer in World War I. In 1933, he was transferred to help the infant Luftwaffe as an administrative colonel and became its Chief of Staff in 1936. But the following year, the ambitious State Secretary for Air, Erhard Milch, dismissed him after a quarrel – a rare setback for the able and affable Kesselring.

He soon found favour again with Luftwaffe chief Hermann Göring, and was put in command of *Luftflotte* (Air Fleet) 1, which bombed Poland's capital and the Low Countries in 1939 and 1940. Then he commanded Luftflotte 2, main striking force in the Battle of Britain. His pilots called their tall, happy-go-lucky chief 'Smiling Albert'. He favoured bombing British cities – the critical diversion from RAF airfields that enabled Britain to hang on; stories persist that he flew on the Coventry and other Blitz raids.

His squadrons moved to the Eastern Front, then to Italy, from where they bombed Malta. In December 1941, Kesselring became Commander in Chief South – once again an army commander. Weeks before the end, in March 1945, Hitler appointed him Commander in Chief West.

The death sentence passed on him by a British court martial for war crimes in Italy was commuted to life imprisonment. In 1952, poor health brought his release.

UP AND AWAY After ten days of lethal German attacks, the panzers pulled back under artillery and naval gunfire, and American GIs could safely stand upright on their exposed Salerno beach. Fresh troops arrived to join the push into the surrounding hills.

controlled glide-bombs swooped down on their targets at 880 km/h (550 mph). The cruiser HMS *Uganda* was badly damaged when a glide-bomb hurtled through its seven steel decks.

There was no time, or spare shipping, to bring Clark more men from Sicily or North Africa, and Montgomery, his only possible help, had halted almost 200 km (125 miles) away, having run out of materials for bridging the demolished route.

CRISIS

Kesselring began driving forward on Sunday, September 12, leaving the more experienced British to their own devices while he concentrated on VI Corps. Then Clark made a blunder. He closed the gap with the British across the Sele corridor but put in too few men to hold it and ordered an over-eager advance on Altavilla. The Americans took it but had to take it again and again for the Germans kept pouring down the corridor and reclaiming it.

Black Monday was the worst day. The Germans again rolled down the corridor, and kept rolling until they were within 3 km (2 miles) of the beach. Cooks, clerks, bandsmen – all who could move – were given a gun and thrust into the US line. Roads, trees and fields were blown to smithereens as the makeshift infantry and regular artillery fired at the looming tanks. The ships offshore unleashed thousand of shells. Even so, it was late afternoon before the panzers drew back.

As darkness closed in the guns fell silent, and Clark pulled back to a shorter defence line, just a couple of kilometres from the sea. He drew up plans for a total retreat from Italy. The next day, however, the new line held, fired more than 10 000 rounds and put 30 panzers out of action.

The Germans came again with Wednesday's dawn. Now Vietinghoff made an inexplicable blunder: instead of hammering again at the Americans, he attacked the British north of the Sele corridor, who had overwhelming firepower. At each panzer advance, the British battalions stood firm, and salvoes from their warships offshore aided them. Late in the afternoon Vietinghoff called off his troops.

Other strongholds in the mountains changed hands many times in bloody hand-to-hand fighting. It was near Altavilla, on Hill 424, that paratroop Sergeant Ross Carter, who had found war so easy in Sicily was a member of a unit detailed to take an enemy observation post. He wrote later: 'Darkness was falling as we began to climb the foothills, shells screaming over us . . . each explosion covering us with dirt and rocks. I'd never known real terror until that moment . . . Cadavers of men from previous attacks lay scattered all over the hill. It was a horrible experience for us to see these countless dead men, many of them purpled and blackened by the intense heat.'

Finally the crisis passed and the Germans moved northwards – not beaten, merely carrying out a retreat that had always been intended, and still dictating the pace of the Allied advance. New faces appeared as reinforcements arrived, and at last the exits from the beaches were crammed with equipment. On September 18, the British and US forces linked up solidly across the rear of the Sele corridor and were ready to move north. Two days later Montgomery made contact with the Fifth Army 32 km (20 miles) east of Eboli.

There were many more days of bitter fighting before the Allies broke free of the hills around Salerno, and it was not until October 5 that their tanks trundled into Naples to a rapturous welcome from the local people. By then 12 000 men of the Fifth Army had been killed, wounded or taken prisoner. Dawley had been sacked after the near catastrophe in the Sele corrider and replaced by Maj General John P. Lucas.

Naples lay in ruins after German demolition and Allied bombing, but within a week, with local help, the wreckage was cleared. Supplies and men poured in through Naples and Salerno. By October 10, the Allies had landed 200 000 men, 35 000 vehicles and 15 000 tonnes of supplies on the west coast. In the east the Eighth Army took the Foggia airfields by October 1. Southern Italy was now safely in Allied control.

OBSTACLE COURSE

Kesselring's men were pulling back to the line of the Volturno and Biferno rivers and Clark's men followed without delay. Facing only token German resistance, they reached the Volturno in early October. In the east, Montgomery pushed on from the Foggia airfields and crossed the Biferno river on October 3. The Allies were not satisfied; the Luftwaffe could still reach Naples and Foggia. The Allies wanted Rome 160 km (100 miles) farther north – for the psychological victory it represented and for its airfields.

The Germans decided to fight hard before they ceded Rome – and the countryside favoured the defenders. Italy is divided not only by the mountainous backbone, but also by rugged ribs that run off to each side. Apart from the narrow coastal strips, the journey north is a switchback of ridges and valleys. The few roads are open to attack from the hills and off the roads vehicles are useless. It is footslogging country. Kesselring was going to defend along the ribs. The defences were being strengthened at the Gustav Line to

CLARK – AMBITIOUS CHARMER

Born into an army family and a graduate of West Point, Mark Clark (1896-1984) had a few weeks of combat experience in World War I. After 1940, the rise of the gangling, immensely likable Clark was meteoric. He was a corps commander by 1942 and then became Deputy Commander in Chief (under his close friend Eisenhower) for the North African 'Torch' landings. While overseeing US training for them, he made a secret visit from England by submarine to Algeria to try to win French aid.

Clark wanted command and action: Eisenhower gave him the Fifth Army for the Salerno landings. His greatest triumph was taking Rome. He managed his motley army of 16 nationalities with firm charm and flair. In November 1944, Clark became commander of 15th Army Group. He accepted the unconditional German surrender in Italy in May 1945. He was later UN Commander in Chief in Korea.

MUTINY AT SALERNO

An urgent order arrived at Number 155 Transit Camp at Tripoli in North Africa at the height of the battle for Salerno, when Mark Clark was desperate for men. Fifteen hundred men had to go at once. Three cruisers rushed them over. The 51st Highland and 50th Northumbrian were keen to go to the rescue of their fellows, but when they arrived, a mere handful went straight into action – with unfamiliar regiments from the Midlands, Hampshire, the Home Counties and the Guards. The rest kicked their heels for four days, then were sent to the same alien regiments.

Some 700 men refused. Lt General McCreery, leading the British force, admitted that an error had been made and promised they would return to their own regiments once Salerno was safe; 192 still refused. They were charged with mutiny, which was punishable by death. All were found guilty. Three sergeants were to be shot and the rest were given penal servitude – ten years for corporals, seven years for the others. The sentences were suspended when the men agreed to return to fight – with new units.

STEP LIVELY **It's ration time, and the crates unloaded from a NAAFI van mean bulging pockets and smiling faces. They even refresh the weariest parts, enabling the sore feet to celebrate with a little jig.**

the north. In October Hitler gave him two infantry divisions from Rommel's armies in northern Italy. He made Kesselring Commander in Chief of all German forces in Italy, and sent Rommel to France.

Clark and Montgomery badly needed men, bulldozers and Bailey bridges. Instead, they were to lose men. Seven divisions were going to Britain in November, along with aircraft and shipping. Some French, Moroccan and Algerian troops would come over from North Africa. Kesselring had gained 40 000 men when the Germans evacuated Corsica and Sardinia two months after Mussolini's fall (and spared the Allies in southern Italy any threat from these strategic positions).

The Volturno was already swollen by the start of the winter rains, which usually came in November but were a month early in 1943. The river rushed west between steep banks. The US VI Corps under Lucas was aiming for two areas of high ground. Lucas hid his artillery and kept it quiet for a few days before the crossing.

The infantry marched to the river bank as lorries brought up the loads of life jackets, ropes, rubber boats and floating pontoons. Just before 2 am on October 13, the advance battalion swam across with guide ropes under cover of gunfire and smoke shells. They fixed the ropes for boat loads and rafts of men to cling to as they made their way over, covered from both banks by the hidden artillery and the advance battalion. By midday they had gained the high ground and by the following day, VI Corps was established on a 7 km (4 mile) strip beyond the Volturno. The engineers built three bridges on which artillery, supplies and heavy armour moved over in support.

Nearer the coast, where the British X Corps under McCreery was supposed to cross, the Volturno was 90 m (300 ft) wide. The only four roads were exposed on raised causeways, and the olive groves and farm buildings between them hid pockets of German soldiers. There was no hope of getting safely across. Eventually, three infantry battalions were ferried across the river mouth. The 17 tanks they took on landing craft were put out of action by mines or mud, but the infantry pushed forward 7 km (4 miles) and made a safe area on the far side of the river, where they were joined by three more battalions on October 15. The right flank of McCreery's men finally had to use one of VI Corps' bridges to get across.

GRINDING TO A HALT

The next targets were the bare, stony heights that reared up on either side of Highway 6, guarding its entry into the Liri Valley that led to Rome. Only along the sector nearest the coast did they make progress. Here X Corps penetrated defended positions known as the Barbara Line and got to the Gustav Line at the Garigliano river.

Farther inland both the British and American corps were picking their way in scattered bands up and along the numerous stony steeps that were mined, booby-trapped and dotted with well-armed Germans sitting in holes blasted into the rock. Exhausted, frozen, cut off from neighbouring bands by icy streams, running out of food and ammunition, keeping in touch by carrier pigeon, the men were advancing little more than 1.5 km (1 mile) a day. They had to cling to crevices, crouch on ledges or build a wall of small rocks as shelter against lethal rock splinters that shot out from shell and mortar hits. The sleet and thick mist made conditions even worse. On November 15, Clark ordered a two-week halt to rest and build up supplies before an assault on the heights.

On the eastern side of Italy's spine, Montgomery's Eighth Army fared no better. After crossing the Biferno, they had to delay until late October to gather supplies. All available shipping on the east coast was bringing materials to make the Foggia airfields operational. Also the lie of the land, the incessant rain and the strong German defences at the Trigno river and, behind that, at the Sangro made it hard going.

Seas of mud and minefields slowed troops and tanks. Makeshift tracks were made by throwing bundles of branches onto the mud and spreading steel matting over them. By the last week of

KEEPING OPEN HOUSE **Camping in the remnants of their home (top), a Naples family begin repairs. The battle has moved on to Ortona where a Canadian tank (above) prowls to flush out any lurking enemy from the ruined houses.**

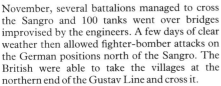

November, several battalions managed to cross the Sangro and 100 tanks went over bridges improvised by the engineers. A few days of clear weather then allowed fighter-bomber attacks on the German positions north of the Sangro. The British were able to take the villages at the northern end of the Gustav Line and cross it.

On Italy's mountainous central spine, Montgomery's 1st Canadian Division had made the Germans retreat from one village to another until they were right back at the Gustav Line. Montgomery's division on the coast stalled at the Moro river, where Orsogna and Ortona were particularly strongly defended. At Ortona, Canadian troops devised clever ways of advancing. Where heaps of rubble from blown-up buildings were piled into road blocks, they used artillery to blow the tops off the piles and the tanks seesawed over them. To avoid the German snipers who shot at any movement in the streets, the Canadians worked their way along indoors by 'mouse-holing' – dynamiting holes through from one building to the next. By the end of December, the weariness and casualties among his men made Montgomery call a halt. Leese then took over Eighth Army and Montgomery left for England to prepare for the Normandy landings.

AGAINST THE GUSTAV LINE

After their two weeks of rest, Clark's Fifth Army resumed their attacks on the mountains south of Highway 6. In the fine weather of December 1, 900 bombing runs and artillery fire softened up the defences of Monte Camino – but it took three attempts to seize it. Monte la Defensa was taken after a joint Canadian-US special force, experts in climbing, scaled 300 m (1000 ft) to surprise the Germans. Monte Maggiore was gained with comparative ease. The Allies still had to take Monte Lungo – and Monte Sammucro on the northern side – to control the highway.

The attempts to take Monte Sammucro had been going on since before the November rest. Sergeant Ross Carter, the paratrooper, was again in the assault force. 'We piled into trucks and drove through the rain . . . to the foot of the biggest mountain we had yet seen. Dozens of 105 mm howitzers and 155 mm Long Toms and

QUIET PERSUADER

A career soldier from Eton and Sandhurst, Richard McCreery (1898-1967) was an expert on armoured warfare. During World War II he was Chief of Staff to Sir Claude Auchinleck (who, after many disagreements, sacked him), then to General Alexander, Commander in Chief Middle East. Just days before the Sicily invasion, Alexander brought McCreery from London, where he was involved in planning the Normandy landings, to command X Corps; its first leader, Lt General Brian Horrocks, had been injured in a German air attack.

The quiet, unassuming McCreery was admired by his officers and could inspire his men. He took great pains with people, trained his men well and was frequently seen at the front line during the Italian campaign. He commanded Eighth Army from autumn 1944. After the war he commanded the British occupation forces in Austria.

Disaster in the Dodecanese

A necklace of islands, the Dodecanese, guards the route past the Turkish coast into the Aegean. Winston Churchill believed that if the Allies occupied the Italian-held islands – especially Karpathos (Scarpanto), Kos, Leros, nearby Rhodes and Samos, with their airfields and harbours – Turkey might join the Allies and allow supplies to pass through the Dardanelles to the USSR. And if the islands and Turkey joined the Allies, the Balkan states might then switch sides and draw off German resources.

The Americans were against such sideshows, but since the Aegean came under Britain's General Sir Henry Maitland Wilson, Commander in Chief Middle East, the United States could not veto the scheme.

CHANCE COMES

When the Italians were negotiating an armistice with the Allies, it seemed likely that the Italian garrisons on the islands would obey their king and surrender to the Allies, not to the Germans. Major Earl Jellicoe and two companions parachuted into Rhodes on September 9, 1943, to sound out the Italians. But they landed scattered and off target. When Italian patrols found them, the interpreter, Major Dolbey, had a broken leg and Jellicoe had for security reasons eaten a letter written by Wilson to the Italian garrison commandant, Admiral Campioni. Jellicoe, his signaller and Dolbey – on a stretcher – had inconclusive talks with a nervous Campioni.

When the Italian surrender was announced the Germans moved fast. On Rhodes, 7000 of their troops seized control; Jellicoe was lucky to get away before Campioni surrendered to the Germans.

Despite this failure, the British now attempted to take the remaining islands. A scratch force from Malta was loaded onto sailing boats and motor launches, and on September 15 the Italian garrisons on Kos, Leros and Samos each received a battalion of British reinforcements; a few troops also landed on Kalimnos (Calino), Kastellorizon (Castelrosso) and Simi.

NO AIR COVER

Kos was the first to suffer sustained bombardments from Luftwaffe fighters, bombers and dive-bombers. What the defenders needed was air cover but the Americans, who opposed the venture, would not provide it. All they got was a squadron of RAF Spitfires and some patrols by Beaufighters. On October 3, a German parachute unit landed on the airstrip while other troops landed on the beaches. The 900 British soldiers along with 2500 Italians were taken prisoner.

The British High Command next increased the garrison on Leros. A few American fighters were sent over from Italy for just four days and the balance briefly swung in favour of the Allies, as the planes attacked German convoys bringing in more forces.

When the fighters were withdrawn, the skies over Leros were left free for the Stukas. A month of savage dive-bomber onslaughts left nowhere to take cover on an island no more than 16 km (10 miles) long and 5 km (3 miles) wide.

On the morning of November 12, the Germans landed men at three places and split the defenders while the Luftwaffe put their guns out of action. In the early evening of November 16, the British surrendered. Some 3200 British troops and 5350 Italians went into captivity. Fewer than 250 of them escaped in small boats sent by the Royal Navy. The navy also took off more than 1000 men from the other islands – now abandoned to the Germans – but many others were lost as the misguided shoestring operation ended.

other breeds of howitzers were all around, firing day and night. A man had to be stone-deaf to get any sleep. Germans were hidden in the grottoes, caves, camouflaged pillboxes, foxholes and behind rocks. Big artillery sat leashed like giant dogs awaiting a signal to tear us to death . . . we would die in heaps on that hideous pile . . . Along the path lay bloodstained bandages, belts, mangled boots, abandoned stretchers and helmets with holes in them . . . We were gripped in a mind-numbing fear.'

Especially strongly held – by Hitler's specific order – was San Pietro, one of the villages on the looming mountain. His order reflected his displeasure that his men were falling back from village to village without his say-so. For ten days his order was obeyed while the village was blown apart by Allied tanks. On December 17 the Germans pulled out and the Americans moved into a silent wasteland of rubble. Sergeant Carter was by then on the summit of Monte Sammucro – and there spent the most miserable Christmas Day of his life. 'For 17 days we had existed on the peak in freezing weather, constant rain, icy winds and inconceivable danger. In all that time we had never washed our hands or shaved, and had managed to get our boots off three times. Lice were eating the hide off our bodies and desperation was eating out our hearts.'

So 1943 ended with the Allies at a standstill in Italy. They had reached the focal point of the Gustav Line, where, guarding the route to Rome, stood the monstrous fortress of Monte Cassino.

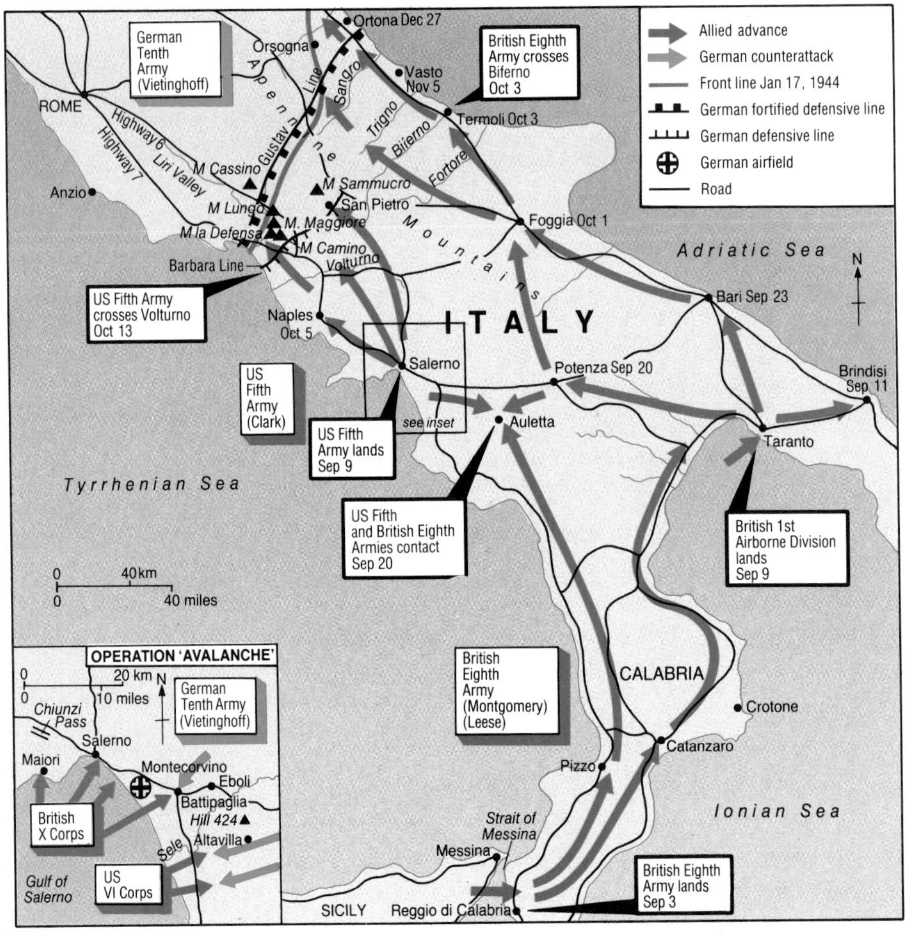

TRIDENT TO PIERCE ITALY Three invasion points were chosen for the Italian mainland: Reggio to clear Italy's toe, Taranto to strike for Foggia's airfields, and Salerno within reach of a major target – the port of Naples.

The maelstrom of Monte Cassino

German-held Monte Cassino dominated the route to Rome and posed a major obstacle to the advancing Allied armies. But after bombs reduced the monastery to ruins and crack German troops dug in, it was well-nigh impregnable.

ANY INVADER marching on Rome from the south of Italy has first to get past a tremendous hump of rock called Monte Cassino. Towering to 516 m (1693 ft) above the town of Cassino, crowned by a medieval monastery and backed by fearsome mountains, it dominates the town and the entrance to the valley of the Liri river. This was the obstacle, some 120 km (75 miles) south-east of Rome, that lay in the path of the footsloggers and armour of the British Eighth and US Fifth Armies during the miserable winter of 1943-4.

In time of war, the monastery's spectacular setting has been its tragedy. It was founded by St Benedict, on the site of a Roman temple to Apollo, in AD 529, and only 40 years later it was sacked by the Lombards. It fell to the Saracens in 883 and to the Normans in 1030. In 1799 it was taken yet again, by the brilliant young revolutionary general Napoleon Bonaparte. Four times destroyed and four times rebuilt, Monte Cassino now faced its fifth and sternest test.

Contrary to Allied belief at the time, the monastery complex was neither fortified nor occupied by troops, but not out of respect for its architectural importance or its priceless library: Lt General Fridolin von Senger und Etterlin, commander of XIV Panzer Corps responsible for the Cassino section of the Germans' Gustav defensive line, deemed it too obvious a target. His cunningly camouflaged defences were farther down the hill and on neighbouring ridges.

The Allied armies in Italy contained a mixed bag of nationalities. As well as British and Americans, there were Canadians, New Zealanders, South Africans, Poles, the US 'Nisei' battalion of Japanese descent, muleteers from Cyprus, Gurkhas and Rajputanas from India, the French Expeditionary Corps of Algerians and Moroccans – the Goumiers – led by French officers, and a combined US-Canadian special force known as the Devil's Brigade. To minimise the problems of fighting with such a cosmopolitan force, the American-equipped divisions were grouped together, as were the British-equipped. That made it easier to set up supply lines, particularly for ammunition.

FRONTAL ATTACK

The Battle of Monte Cassino was, in reality, four separate battles. The first began on January 17, 1944, when Lt General Mark Clark, commander of the Fifth Army, planned a traditional frontal assault, to be followed a few days later by landings behind the Gustav Line at the fishing village of Anzio (see feature, p. 284). On the main front, the Americans were in the centre of the line with the French to their right and the British to their left. General Alphonse Juin's French Expeditionary Corps made some progress to the north of Cassino; at one stage they kept two-thirds of the Germans engaged, but their losses were heavy.

Blizzards raged through the mountains, exhausting the men and hindering the supply of food to them. One of their officers, General René Chambe, wrote in his diary: 'Battalions cling to the hillsides . . . Everywhere, the enemy is counterattacking furiously . . . Men fall asleep under shellfire, in the midst of mines and bullets. They are killed almost before they realise it. Only wounds make them wake up.'

Near the coast, the British X Corps crossed the Garigliano river and established a bridgehead 3 km (2 miles) deep, but fought themselves to a standstill. In the centre of the front line, the Americans were taking a savage mauling. The 36th (Texas) Division failed disastrously in a first attempt to cross the Rapido river on January 20. Tapes marking areas cleared of German mines were obliterated by the bombardment, and the Texans wandered into clumps of evil anti-personnel mines that would blow a man's foot off or leap in the air and disembowel him.

A few days later, the 34th Infantry Division were more successful farther north, but it took their engineers five days to move the tanks through the churning mud. The Americans edged through freezing rain and driving snow to work their way up Monte Calvario – Point 593 on military maps – and along a connecting ridge towards Monte Cassino. Only a quarter of the 34th got within a few hundred metres of the monastery – and they had to pull back.

The first battle ended in deadlock on February 11 with 4145 British dead, and 10 230 Americans. At Anzio the Allies were trapped on the beaches.

THE SECOND BATTLE

Clark grudgingly accepted reinforcements from his superior, General Sir Harold Alexander, commander of 15th Army Group. The burden of the assault now passed to the New Zealand Corps, led by Lt General Sir Bernard Freyberg, VC, and made up of New Zealand, Indian and British divisions. They were to cross the Rapido river just north of Cassino. At the same time the French corps would attack Monte Belvedere to the north and pass behind Monte Cassino to reach the Liri valley. The Germans brought up crack paratroop reinforcements. (*continued on p. 286*)

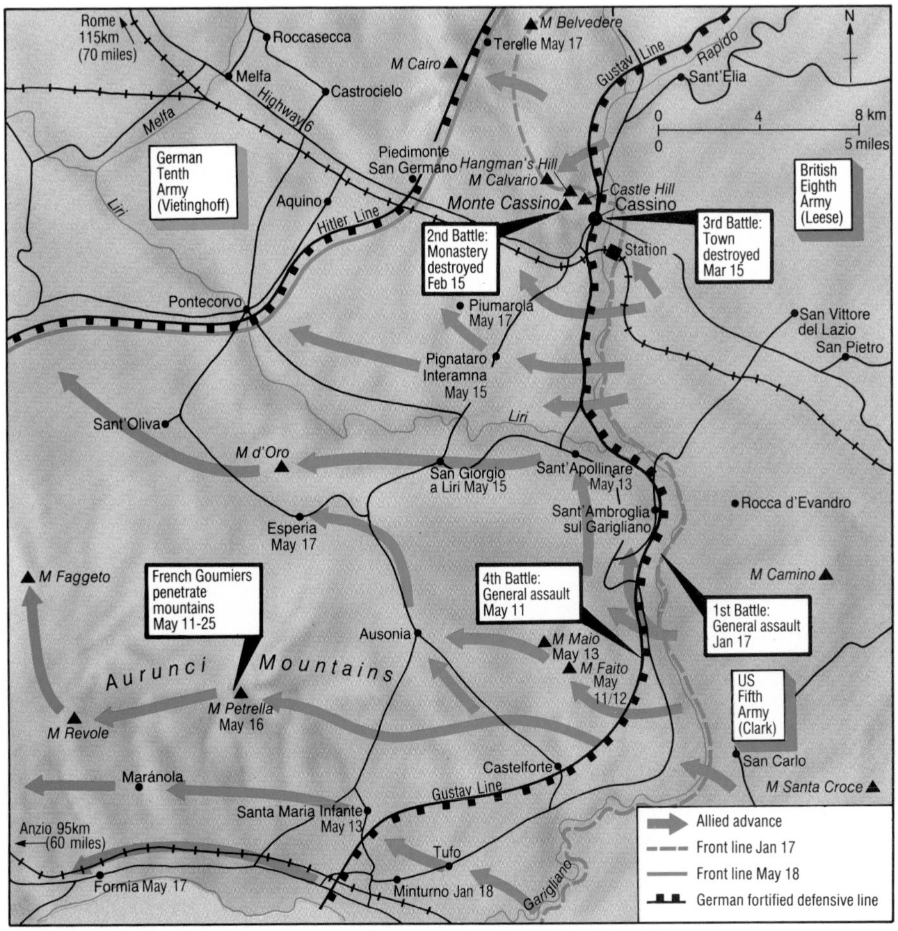

OPENING THE DOOR TO ROME **Cassino was the linchpin of the Gustav Line which crossed Italy's mountainous waist. The Allies had to take it to reach the Liri valley, the only easy way to Rome. The attempt to bypass it, using Anzio as a back door, proved a far from easy alternative.**

STRANDED AT ANZIO

With the Allies held at Cassino, Churchill saw a quick way to break the deadlock – a landing on beaches north of the Gustav Line and a swift dash to Rome. But it became a four-month nightmare.

A FIVE-MINUTE BARRAGE of rocket fire descended upon the little Italian seaside resort of Anzio at 2 am on January 22, 1944. Offshore, the watchers on warships and transports waited anxiously for the returning fire. None came. There was no sign of movement on the shore. It was as if Anzio were a ghost town.

Nervously a fleet of landing craft headed for the shore. Something, it seemed, was not right. Anzio was occupied by the Germans; surely this must be a trap. The landing craft ground ashore and disgorged their troops, and still no resistance came. Soon they discovered why: Anzio was indeed a ghost town. Its entire civilian population had been evacuated and the Germans had abandoned it. The landings had taken the Germans completely by surprise.

Operation 'Shingle', as the Anzio landing was called, had been the dream of Winston Churchill, but to men like Lt General Mark Clark, US Fifth Army commander, with memories of the Salerno landings still rankling, it was more a nightmare. British Intelligence had assured him that there would be little opposition, but Clark was not convinced. Even less keen was US Maj General John P. Lucas, commander of the Anglo-American forces in VI Corps, which was to make the landing at Anzio. Like Clark, Lucas was sure that the Germans would counterattack swiftly, as they had done at Salerno, and he planned to wait until his initial force of 40 000 men had been reinforced with 60 000 more, plus plentiful supplies, trucks and ammunition, before advancing.

This was not at all what Churchill and General Sir Harold Alexander, commander of the Allied 15th Army Group, had in mind. A swift thrust from the beaches to the Alban Hills, south-east of Rome, would cut Highways 6 and 7 – the main German supply routes for the western end of the Gustav Line, where the Allied advance was stuck in front of the formidably defended Monte Cassino. They expected that the Germans, threatened from the rear, would withdraw from the line, allowing the Allied troops to break through and quickly link up with Lucas's force.

HE WHO HESITATES

By late afternoon on January 22, most of Lucas's assault force had landed – the British 1st Infantry Division, under Maj General Ronald Penney, plus two Commando battalions and the 46th Royal Tank Regiment, north of the port; the US 3rd Infantry Division, a tank battalion, a parachute infantry battalion and three battalions of US Rangers at the port and to the south. The road

MOVING OUT AT LAST It was late May before the Allies got beyond the soggy, mosquito-infested, reclaimed marshes and took over the ruins of Cisterna on the highway that led to Rome.

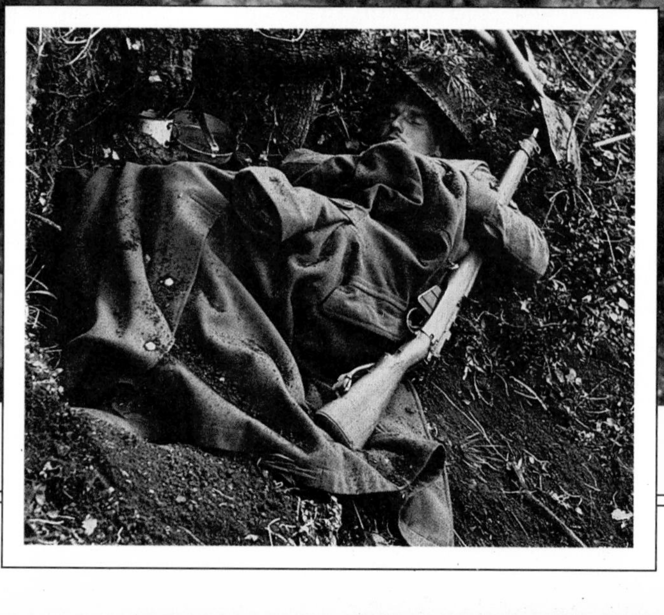

SOUR DREAMS Soup and dry socks arrived each night and soldiers slept in foxholes dug in a smelly drainage dyke.

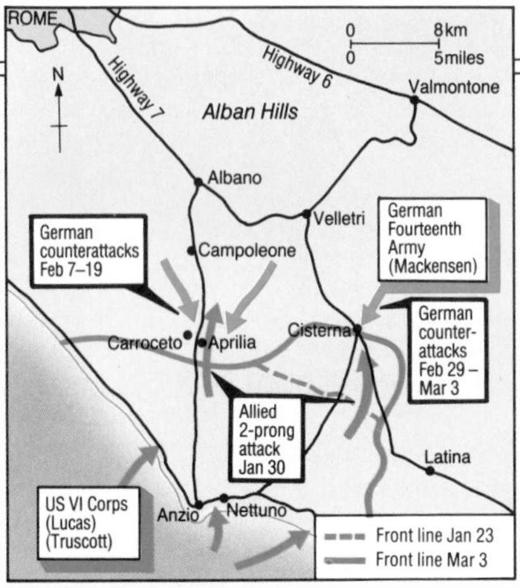

WHY ANZIO? Within Allied air cover from Naples, Anzio was well placed for attacking supply roads to the Gustav Line farther east, and the rear of the line itself.

to Rome lay open and a bold commander would have taken it. Lucas stayed put. Churchill's comment said everything: 'I had hoped we were hurling a wild cat onto the shore, but all we got was a stranded whale.'

German reaction to the landings was immediate. By daylight on the 22nd, Field Marshal Albert Kesselring, Commander in Chief of German forces in Italy, had local garrison troops and guns guarding Highway 7, and divisions were on their way from France, Yugoslavia, Germany and northern Italy. Two days later there were 40 000 Germans in the beach-head area, under the command of General Eberhard von Mackensen. They were supported by tanks and artillery including 'Anzio Annie', a 280 mm (11 in) calibre railway gun capable of hurling 255 kg (560 lb) shells almost 65 km (40 miles). With the threatened Allied invasion of north-western Europe very much in his mind, Hitler was determined to put the Allies off the idea of beach landings for a long time to come.

Lucas at last decided to send out patrols to test the German strength on the roads to Cisterna and Campoleone on January 25. At Carroceto British troops came up against panzer grenadiers concealed in the newly built farming community of Aprilia, nicknamed 'the Factory' by the British. They took it after fierce fighting, and held it next day after a German counterattack. On the Cisterna road the Americans ran up against the 'Hermann Göring' Division, firmly established in every farmhouse, barn and shed. Meanwhile, artillery – 'Anzio Annie' in particular – and the Luftwaffe bombarded the beach-head.

At last, on January 30, Lucas made a decisive move – a two-pronged attack on Cisterna and Campoleone. The attack on Cisterna was carried out by US Rangers in an incredibly daring but ultimately disastrous manoeuvre. They crept by night along an irrigation channel, sometimes passing within a few metres of sentries patrolling the banks, then emerged to make the final dash in the open. But their approach had not gone undetected, and they ran into an ambush. A deadly crossfire cut them down, and when daylight came German tanks emerged to gun down the survivors in the ditches. Only six men out of 767 got back to the beach-head.

DEATH AT CAMPOLEONE

The British fared little better at Campoleone. The Scots and Irish Guards suffered heavy casualties along the road, and in the final assault on the town (which the British captured after four days) the 2nd Battalion Sherwood Foresters was almost wiped out. American Maj General Ernest Harmon, commander of the US 1st Armored Division, was to write of Campoleone: 'I have never seen so many dead men in one place. They lay so close I had to step with care.'

GRIM MESSAGE You've been here three months, sneered German leaflets dropped at Anzio, and you are still on the beach-head, now paved with Allied skulls.

In February, driving rain and sleet added to the misery of the men pinned down at Anzio, and on the 3rd a merciless artillery barrage pounded the narrow salient held by the Allies. On the 7th, Mackensen counterattacked with everything he had, but the next day German artillery pulverised the Factory and by the 9th it was in German hands again.

Metre by metre the Allies were driven back in some of the bloodiest fighting of the war, and casualties mounted on both sides. Morale among the beleaguered men slumped, while their commanders squabbled.

At dawn on February 16, Mackensen sent in six divisions against British-manned defences on the Anzio-Carroceto road. The ground attack was led by the Lehr Infantry Regiment, a demonstration unit of hand-picked troops. But they were fighters in theory only, and under heavy fire turned and ran. Yet the Germans punched a wedge 3 km (2 miles) wide and 1.6 km (1 mile) deep in the Allied lines.

Lucas signalled to Clark, now busily engaged at Monte Cassino, for air support – and on the 17th it came: wave after wave of bombers. But still the Germans moved on. One final push would drive the Allies into the sea. Allied artillery – 432 guns, and broadsides from two cruisers – added to the carnage. It was more than the Germans could take, and by the 19th their attack had lost momentum. They began to withdraw.

On February 22 Clark relieved Lucas of his command – ironically, just as the commander was getting the upper hand. Throughout the whole battle Lucas had rarely moved from his headquarters in a wine-cellar at Nettuno, just east of the village of Anzio, and had come in for increasing criticism – especially from the British – for his 'negative' attitude. His replacement was US Maj General Lucien K. Truscott Jr, a far more aggressive leader respected by the British and Americans alike.

A week later Mackensen attacked again – this time near Cisterna – but Truscott's artillery was ready, and B-24 Liberators and B-17 Flying Fortresses joined in, pounding Cisterna and the nearby towns and villages. Kesselring ordered Mackensen to halt the attack. Deadlock had been reached.

BREAKOUT

The stalemate continued through spring. By day, all was quiet apart from occasional flurries of mortar or sniper fire. By night, the men repaired trenches, moved up supplies and patrolled the muddy terrain between the Allied and German positions.

Then, on May 13, the breakthrough was made at Cassino. Five days later, the Allies began to advance towards Rome. Kesselring was forced to withdraw a division from Anzio, and on May 23 Truscott, strengthened by the US 36th Division, moved forward across the shell and bomb-cratered landscape towards Cisterna and Campoleone. The dead, missing and wounded included 10 775 Americans, 10 168 British, and 10 306 Germans.

Freyberg, a hero of World War I, wanted to launch the attack with a massive bombardment of the monastery. Clark demurred. It was one of Europe's great treasure houses and German assurances that it was unoccupied seemed to be confirmed by the total absence of fire from it. But Freyberg's 2nd Division contained many of New Zealand's young men; he felt all the treasures in Cassino were not worth the life of one of them. He eventually won the support of Alexander.

The Allies gave ample warning for the buildings to be cleared. Most of the monks, and the priceless art treasures, had been evacuated by the Germans the previous October; only the abbot and five monks remained. They fled from prayers on the morning of February 15, when a relentless air strike by B-26 Marauders, B-25 Mitchells and B-17 Flying Fortresses dropped 450 tonnes of high explosive and incendiary bombs.

The Germans were dug in far down the slope – but not for long. Standing, the monastery had been vulnerable to attack, but now – reduced to huge craters, piles of masonry and deep, indestructible cellars – it presented an opportunity too good to miss. The Germans turned the ruins into a fortress that was to prove virtually impregnable. Merciless crossfire from the new stronghold easily repelled an attack mounted by the Gurkhas – small, tough mountain fighters from Nepal.

Cassino could not be taken and held as long as the shell-torn peak of Monte Calvario remained in German hands. The peak was to be captured and lost many times – but never more ironically than on the raw night of February 16, when a battalion of the Royal Sussex Regiment stormed it. Fierce opposition from the German paratroops holding it was weakening, but just as the British reached the top, someone on the German side fired three green flares – the Royal Sussex withdrawal signal. Bewildered, they fell back down the hill. It was then the turn of the Rajputanas, but they were pinned down just below the summit.

It fell to the New Zealand Corps to try to take Cassino town, but they fared no better. Late on the night of the 17th they captured the railway station. As dawn broke the next day, tanks and Maori infantry crossed the Rapido river behind a thick smoke screen but were flung back by a lurking detachment of German panzers. After three days of mounting casualties, Freyberg brought the second battle to a halt.

THE THIRD BATTLE

Sheets of rain were falling as New Zealand and Indian divisions prepared for the third big push. The men at Anzio had now been forced back to the last sliver of their beach-head, and it was vital to draw the Germans to Cassino or break through there. The slightest movement of Allied troops attracted sniper and shellfire from the German paratroops, who seemed to be everywhere in and around Cassino town. The preparations took three weeks; this time tanks were to support the infantry entering the town. On March 15, over 1000 tonnes of bombs and 195 000 shells destroyed it; not one building remained intact.

The New Zealanders advanced into the ruins through incessant rain, often having to bridge flooded craters. The fighting – against tenacious paratroops who had miraculously survived the bombardment – was ferocious. The New Zealand Corps lost 2106 of its men – New Zealanders, Indians and British among them. Maj General Howard Kippenberger, commander of the New Zealand 2nd Division, had one of his feet blown off by a mine hidden among the rubble; his other was so badly injured that it had to be amputated.

Again the bombardment hindered rather than helped the Allies. Major Rudolf Böhmler, commanding a German paratroop battalion and the monastery garrison, later wrote: 'The towering piles of rubble, the torn and debris-strewn streets, the innumerable deep bomb craters made it quite impossible for the New Zealand 4th Armoured Brigade to penetrate into the town and support the infantry.' The New Zealanders again captured the railway station but got no farther.

Above Cassino town, a combined force of the Essex Regiment, New Zealanders, Rajputana Rifles and Gurkhas were often locked in ferocious hand-to-hand combat with the enemy as they succeeded in winning some neighbouring peaks, such as Castle Hill and the ominously dubbed Hangman's Hill. But still the Allies got no closer to Monte Cassino itself. On March 23, Freyberg called off the attack; it was another stalemate.

SURPRISE FORCE The break through the Gustav Line was made by Goumiers of the French Expeditionary Corps. The Goumiers, trained in their native Atlas Mountains in Morocco, were sure-footed enough even in comparatively flimsy sandals to climb the precipitous Aurunci Mountains south of Monte Cassino, which the Germans thought could not be scaled. A Goumier (right) combines his familiar uniform with a selection of Allied-issue items. He wears US combat uniform under his *djellabah*, whose colours proclaim his tribe. The favourite rifle was a 1913 US Springfield and the helmet French.

BREAKTHROUGH

Alexander decided that the only chance of success was to crush the Gustav Line by sheer weight of numbers – a three-to-one superiority in artillery, armour and aircraft – once the weather improved. In a wily deception plan, radios crackled with messages moving fictitious Allied units. Field Marshal Albert Kesselring, German Commander in Chief in Italy, was led to expect a new Allied amphibious landing behind his line and moved men from the mountains to the coast.

Meanwhile, Alexander amassed about 14 divisions, including many fresh troops previously earmarked for landings in the south of France, now postponed, and most of Eighth Army moved from the Adriatic sector. They were positioned along a 32 km (20 mile) front stretching from the mountains north of Cassino to the sea. For every kilometre (1100 yds) there were more than 50 Allied guns, 60 tanks and 90 bombers. Facing them were 14 weary, depleted German divisions, with many wounded and short of ammunition.

It was just after 11 pm on May 11 when the

SAPPING MORALE German propaganda leaflets showered on the Allied troops stuck at Cassino warned of certain death waiting to devour them in Italy's ravening mountains. Other morale-hitters scoffed that wives in Britain had found GIs to replace husbands serving overseas.

CASSINO
The mountains and valleys of "Sunny Italy" WANT TO SEE YOU...
The Cassino débacle

BURIED AT CASSINO

The man who led the final assault on Monte Cassino, Wladyslaw Anders (1892-1970), has his grave beside his men who fell in the battle. He began his distinguished military career as a dragoon in the Tsar's army early in World War I – and then fought against the Reds in the Polish-Soviet war of 1919-20. In September 1939 he led his cavalry brigade against Hitler's panzers, then was captured fighting the Red Army and jailed in Moscow for nearly two years. When the Germans invaded the USSR, Anders was released to form a Polish division, and commanded II Polish Corps in 1943-5. Exiled from postwar Poland, he lived among fellow-exiles in London.

STORMING THE TOWN With smoke pots misting the air to cover their advance, New Zealand infantry (above) clear a house of German troops – but in vain; the enemy has simply slipped away to yet another strongpoint.

CRITICAL TARGET The decision to bomb the hilltop abbey (right) was uneasy – for the treasure house symbolised the culture and values the Allies were fighting to preserve.

READY TO STRIKE With racks of grenades to hand and a self-propelled gun ready, the Germans wait to pick off Allied infantry advancing on foot over the rubble that has blocked their tanks. Ruined houses hide nests of snipers.

entire Allied front opened fire. The valley burst into flame. Palls of dust and smoke were riven by flying steel and splintered rock. The pounding guns made the whole mountain tremble. Then the Allied infantry divisions advanced. But it was the subtle advance of Juin's North African Goumiers that made the significant breakthrough. Just 45 minutes after the bombardment began, they began moving up the ravines and crags of the Aurunci Mountains, south of Cassino.

No general on either side – except Juin – had ever imagined that such terrain, towering up to 1533 m (5030 ft), was passable by troops. With 4000 mules to carry their supplies the 9000 Goumiers climbed the heights, surprising and overwhelming one key position after another. In three days, they were through the mountains and swinging right to enter the Liri valley behind the Germans and threaten their escape route.

The Gustav Line was broken. Kesselring brought over a division from Anzio to bolster the flagging Tenth Army, but by May 17 he had no choice but to order a fighting withdrawal. If the British, who had crossed the Rapido river just south of Cassino, had not been halted at Pontecorvo on the Liri, Kesselring's retreat might indeed have been cut off.

The assault of Monte Cassino itself had been assigned to the 50 000 men of II Polish Corps – fanatical fighters against the Germans who had seized their homeland – led by Lt General Wladyslaw Anders. In the grey early hours of May 12, they had launched their attack. It was a frantic struggle up exposed mountain slopes, against resolute and stubborn defenders dug into solid shelters. The Poles clambered up as close as they dared to their own bursting shells – their only chance of cover. For five days this continued.

On the morning of the 18th, the Poles noticed that a deathly quiet had fallen over the monastery ruins. A scouting party of Lancers approached cautiously, only to discover a huddle of German wounded, too ill to be moved, their sunken haunted eyes reflecting their defeat, pain and exhaustion. Otherwise the place was deserted.

The Lancers fashioned a makeshift regimental pennant from a Red Cross flag and a blue handkerchief, and planted it in the ruins. Monte Cassino was taken at last – after five months of horrifying carnage. The casualties on all sides were estimated at around 45 000, thousands of them never brought out from the rubble.

As the German Tenth Army began to pull back from the Gustav Line all along its south-western half, Eighth Army pursued them up the Liri valley. The Americans, who had breached the line near the coast, were advancing to meet their colleagues who had at last broken out of the Anzio beach-head. The forces linked up on May 26 and were ordered to head off the fleeing Germans at Valmontone, east of the Alban Hills. But another prize beckoned Clark: Rome.

Through Rome to oblivion

For the Allied Fifth and Eighth Armies, the glory that was Rome was eclipsed in two days. Their campaign became a side show, but a long-running one.

ECSTATIC ITALIANS poured into the streets of Rome as the Allies arrived on the evening of June 4, 1944. Lt General Mark Clark had won the prize for his US Fifth Army – and had changed his superiors' orders to do it. The VI Corps had been speeding north at last, away from Anzio and towards the Valmontone gap to trap the Germans retreating from Cassino before they reached the Alban Hills. Suddenly Clark issued new orders. His officers were appalled but obeyed. Only one division continued to Valmontone; the others made for Rome.

Clark did not share the view of General Sir Harold Alexander, commander of 15th Army Group, that the Germans could be cut off; Clark figured that they would simply move farther east. He also feared attacks from the Alban Hills as he passed their southern edge. But most of all he wanted the glory of taking Rome for himself and his Fifth Army. He knew from decoded German signals that the Germans were pulling out; he suspected Alexander's plan would let the British Eighth Army liberate Rome. As it was, the Eighth passed by east of Rome, and the bulk of the German Tenth Army escaped north to fight again.

Meanwhile, VI Corps had found a gap in the German defences in the Alban Hills. Near Velletri the Americans slipped silently through the gap on the night of May 30, slitting the throats of the sentries they came upon. By morning they had breached the last obstacle before Rome, and two days later Field Marshal Albert Kesselring, German commander in Italy, pulled out. The Allies gained the psychological victory they wanted before invading France. Rome was free.

The Romans had a special reason to celebrate. The name Kesselring had been reviled and feared since, on March 23, 1944, 335 hostages were shot in caves outside the city, in reprisal for the killing of some 35 SS men in a bomb attack.

As the Americans moved in, Vera Cacciatore watched them from her home in Piazza di Spagna. After a few tanks, 'the soldiers came marching in the moonlight. They were silent, very tired, marching almost like robots. The people came out of the houses to cheer them but they only smiled, waved and kept on going.

'One company of them disappeared, then another, but finally an order was given and hundreds of soldiers came to a halt. The civilians crowded around them, patting them on the back, kissing them. The soldiers asked for something to drink, water or wine, and when they had drunk they slumped down on the stones and fell asleep. They slept on the street, on the sidewalks, on the Spanish Steps . . . Next morning the air, the smell of Rome had changed. Before, Rome had always smelled of cooking, wine, dried fish, garlic. Now suddenly it was Chesterfields.'

The soldiers' rest – and their glory – in Rome was brief. On June 6 the Allies landed in Normandy, and Italy became yesterday's news. The troops there became a forgotten army, heading once more for the harsh mountains. They gave vent to their bitterness in their own campaign song, fitted to the tune of *Lilli Marlene:*

We're the D-Day Dodgers out in Italy,
Always drinking vino, always on the spree.
Eighth Army skivers and their tanks,
We live in Rome, among the Yanks,
For we're the D-Day Dodgers, in sunny Italy.

Looking round the mountains in the mud
and rain,
There are lots of little crosses, some which
bear no name.
Blood, tears, sweat and toil are gone.
The boys beneath them slumber on.
These are your D-Day Dodgers,
who'll stay in Italy.

ON TO THE GOTHIC LINE

Germans fleeing north from Rome demolished roads and bridges behind them. While the pursuing Allies patched the damage and their heavy and medium bombers did their best to hinder the German retreat, Allied forces regrouped to advance in line. Clark's Fifth Army – including a British as well as American corps – followed the west coastal plain and the valley of the Tiber, while General Sir Oliver Leese's Eighth Army (which had strong Polish and Canadian contingents) pushed up the Adriatic coast and through the hills of Umbria in the centre.

In the 12 days after Rome fell, they advanced 145 km (90 miles), but then Kesselring ordered his rearguard to hinder the Allies while his main defensive position at the Gothic Line – right across northern Italy – was finished. In the next three weeks the Allies advanced only 70 km (45 miles). By early August they reached the Arno river, having liberated Perugia, Ancona, Siena and Livorno (Leghorn). There was to be no fighting in historic Florence, Kesselring decreed, but bridges were blown or blocked to impede the Allies, who entered the outskirts on August 4; the Germans were cleared out by the 21st.

Kesselring was well pleased with his skilful retreat, which allowed work to continue on the Gothic Line until autumn was close. The line had been started just before the Germans pulled out of Sicily, and zigzagged 320 km (200 miles) across Italy, beginning just south of La Spezia and running through the Apennines before following the Foglia valley to reach the Adriatic at Pesaro. Just behind it ran Highway 9, the main road from Milan through Bologna to Rimini, allowing supplies and troops to be moved.

The Fifth and Eighth Armies' orders were to break through this formidable obstacle and cross the Po valley to the southern rim of the Alps. Churchill, already fearful of the Soviet Union

ROMAN HOLIDAY Spreading through the air of the Italian capital was more than the aroma of American cigarettes. Relief, gratitude, above all an elated sense of liberty radiated from the Romans who fêted the weary US troops.

becoming a threat to the postwar world, glimpsed a chance to get into Yugoslavia, Austria – even Hungary, Czechoslovakia and Germany – before the Russians. Roosevelt and the Chiefs of Staff insisted that the planned landings in the south of France on August 15 should have priority as support for the Normandy invasion, and they took seven divisions from Italy to bolster them.

Hitler was so worried about Allied progress north that even during the fighting in Normandy he moved seven divisions into Italy from Denmark, the Netherlands, Hungary and the USSR.

RACE AGAINST WINTER

Alexander – who had a clear idea from decoded messages of the strength and position of his enemy – altered his plans as his armies shrank. He devised a double bluff. At 11 pm on August 25, the first move was made on the Adriatic coast and surprised the Germans. As they fell back, Eighth Army troops crossed the Metauro river south of Pesaro and bridged it for others to follow. The Germans withdrew into the Gothic Line.

Then came the second bluff. Men of the Fifth Army made an ostentatious push 200 km (160 miles) to the west and got across the Arno; they took Pisa on September 2 and within a few days were at the Gothic Line. The Germans, thinking the east coast move was a feint, rushed men west. Finally, Alexander's real offensive came on September 12. Over the past 15 days, eight divisions of Eighth Army, with support corps and 80 000 vehicles, had secretly moved east across the Apennines. They attacked along a 50 km (30 mile) front, breached the Gothic Line, took the key position of San Fortunato and entered Rimini.

'I have the terrible feeling that the whole thing is beginning to slide', Kesselring noted in his diary when Rimini fell. The Allies' hopes of reaching the Po valley soared, but then faded with the summer days. Torrential rain began to fall in late September, turning streams into rushing torrents that surged over the plain – which became more of an obstacle than the mountains.

Impetus now passed to Clark's Fifth Army, which had continued pushing north of Florence and by September 16 had reached the Futa and Giogo passes leading through the Apennines towards the Po valley. Clark took the minor, twisting road through the Giogo. Amid minefields, barbed wire and fire from pillboxes, a 200-strong assault group took two days to work their way to the 880 m (1900 ft) summit of the pass. Only 50 survived the climb. Once across the pass, Clark's men suffered more than 2700 casualties to take the surrounding peaks.

GOTHIC DEFENCES Anti-tank ditches (above left), barbed-wire barriers and minefields made a 16 km (10 mile) deep obstacle belt of Kesselring's major defensive line across Italy. The line had 30 tank turrets with 88 mm ($3\frac{1}{2}$ in) guns on steel and concrete bases, 2376 machine-gun nests, 479 artillery positions, 100 steel shelters and long trenches and tunnels for infantry, as at Futa (above).

Clark then swung north-east towards Imola on Highway 9, but Kesselring brought troops from the east coast to block the way. If the Allies cut the highway, he would lose everything to the east. In the high passes, the sheets of rain turned to sleet and snow as winter approached. Late in October Clark had to halt, only 16 km (10 miles) short of the Po valley. In a drier spell before Christmas, Eighth Army, now commanded by Lt General Sir Richard McCreery, probed a little farther and reached Ravenna before winter finally closed in. But that was as far as the Allies reached in 1944.

Once the Joint Chiefs of Staff learned that there would be no more action in Italy for several months, they whittled away further at Fifth and Eighth Armies to bolster the efforts in north-west Europe and Greece. The stalwarts left behind settled down for another cruel winter.

18: ASSAULT ON FORTRESS EUROPE

From small beginnings in commando raids, the momentum grew to the climax of D-Day.

The commandos strike back

'Britain will fight on,' Churchill proclaimed in June 1940, as the last dazed survivors returned from Dunkirk. 'We shall go back.' And back went Britain's special forces – newly formed commando and paratroop units – to launch daring raids up and down Hitler's long European coastline.

DAWN BROKE crisp and clear over the Lofoten Islands, off Nazi-occupied Norway's north-western coast. It was 4 am on March 4, 1941 – and bitterly cold. On board two former cross-Channel ferries were 500 British commandos, 52 Royal Engineers and 52 Norwegian volunteers – all bound for a surprise raid on the Lofotens.

As the slow Arctic dawn turned to full daylight, the men piled into lowered landing craft which started chugging shorewards. Behind them lurked five sleek, grey British destroyers and beneath the waves prowled the submarine *Sunfish*. Cautiously, expecting an ambush at any moment, the raiders approached the quays of four small island fishing ports – Stamsund, Henningsvaer, Svolvaer and Brettesnes. But instead of armed Germans, they were met by crowds of cheering locals who helped them ashore.

The raid proved a walkover. The islands were virtually undefended and as morning advanced a series of explosions and billowing black clouds of smoke showed that the British sappers had accomplished their principal objective – the demolition of factories producing cod and herring oil, used to make glycerine for explosives and vitamin A and D pills for German troops. The raiders also destroyed fuel stores and captured 225 prisoners – mostly German merchant seamen and a few Norwegian collaborators. When they re-embarked just after midday, they also took 315 recruits for Free Norwegian forces in Britain.

'HUNTER CLASS' TROOPS

The Lofoten raid was, in the words of the Royal Navy's official historian, 'the genesis of the great combined operations of the later years of the war'. In a memorandum to his Chiefs of Staff in June 1940, Churchill had called for 'enterprises' to be prepared with 'specially trained troops of the hunter class who can develop a reign of terror down the enemy coast'. Later he asked for a 'corps of at least 5000 parachute troops' to be formed, to emulate recent German successes, such as at Fort Eben Emael in Belgium.

The paras would later have great successes, but the surface raiding forces were the first to be formed and within weeks were in action. Late on June 23, 1940, six RAF air-sea rescue launches carried 120 men to the coast of France between Boulogne and Le Touquet. They stayed ashore for only a few hours, achieving little of military value, but news of their exploit, at a time when Britain's chances of survival looked slim, did much to boost morale.

Volunteers for the Special Service Brigade, as the new force was called, were not difficult to find. They came from units throughout Britain – despite opposition from commanding officers loath to lose their best men to a 'private army'. 'It is the greatest job in the army,' remarked an enthusiastic early volunteer, Captain Geoffrey Appleyard, 'no red tape, no paper work . . . just pure operations.'

The men were formed into 500-strong units known as 'Commandos', after the Boer guerrilla units of the South African War (1899-1902). They were to combine guerrilla-like resource and independence with the discipline of professional soldiers. On July 17, a World War I naval hero, Admiral of the Fleet Sir Roger Keyes, was appointed to command them as Director of Combined Operations. Excitement mounted.

But enthusiasm was not enough. Despite Churchill's backing, opposition from sceptical senior officers and Chiefs of Staff grew and a frustrated Keyes found plans for operations blocked – as were attempts to obtain equipment. Matters were not helped by the abject failure of a second raid, against Guernsey on the night of July 14/15. The raiders brought back no prisoners and left behind three of their men.

MOUNTBATTEN IN CHARGE

Next year, however, things improved. The Lofoten Islands raid in March was followed on August 18 by another successful raid against the Norwegian Arctic island of Spitsbergen – carried out by Canadian and Free Norwegian troops with British commando support. They captured a German wireless crew and destroyed coal stores.

Then, in October, the elderly Keyes was replaced by the energetic Lord Louis Mountbatten, later promoted to vice admiral, with the title of Chief of Combined Operations. A new raid was planned, against the Norwegian island of Vaagso (Våsøy) to show Hitler that no part of occupied Europe's vast coastline was safe from attack, and to oblige him to divert troops to defend it all.

The force set sail on Christmas Eve, 1941 – 576 commandos under Brigadier Charles Haydon on two assault ships, escorted by the light cruiser HMS *Kenya* and four destroyers. A few minutes before 9 am on December 27, *Kenya* opened fire on the small island of Maalo (Måløy), which lies in the Ulvesund, between Vaagso and the mainland, off the village of South Vaagso. Overhead, RAF Hampden bombers dropped smoke bombs. Men of No 3 Commando landed on the island, led ashore by Major 'Mad Jack' Churchill playing the bagpipes and wearing a Highland claymore broadsword. They took the German defenders by surprise and soon had Maalo in their control.

Across the Ulvesund in South Vaagso itself, their comrades had a tougher fight. Here, the battle went on all morning, with, according to one troop commander, Captain Peter Young, 'determined men in ones and twos . . . stumbling and slithering through snow-covered backyards to burst open the doors of cold, featureless buildings' held by the Germans. Nevertheless, by

ROYAL HERO As Chief of Combined Operations, the King's cousin, Lord Louis Mountbatten (1900-79), was an inspired choice. He had boundless energy and proved well able to argue the value of commandos. Mountbatten had started the war commanding the Fifth Destroyer Flotilla in the North Sea and Mediterranean, where his daring won wide popular renown. At Combined Operations he played a key part in D-Day planning, until sent to south-east Asia in 1943 as Supreme Allied Commander. There, he was energetic in visiting troops and did much to raise morale. After the war, he became last Viceroy of India (1947-8), First Sea Lord (1955-9) and Chief of Defence Staff (1959-65). He was killed by an Irish terrorist bomb. Wealth and royal connections no doubt helped his career, but he was also a skilled seaman and a born leader of men.

2.45 pm, the commandos were able to reboard their ships with over 100 prisoners. The raiders had lost 20 killed and 57 wounded, but had done enough to silence their critics in Britain.

RAID ON ST NAZAIRE

Encouraged by these successes, Mountbatten went on to plan two more Combined Operations raids. The first – in February 1942 – was to capture a German radar set at Bruneval, near Le Havre (see box, p. 294). Its success proved the worth of the newly formed Parachute Brigade.

The second was the most ambitious commando operation so far. Its target was a dry dock at St Nazaire, near the mouth of the Loire river in southern Brittany. It was the only dry dock close to the Atlantic big enough to take the German battleship *Tirpitz*, then in Norway but likely to break out at any time. If the dock were destroyed, *Tirpitz* would have to stay in Norway or return to Germany, rather than risk battle damage that could not be repaired.

The plan of attack was worked out by Royal Navy Captain John Hughes-Hallett. He proposed sending a destroyer, packed with explosives, to ram the outer gate of the dock and flood it. At the same time, commandos would go ashore to destroy vital port installations.

The destroyer chosen was HMS *Campbeltown*, an old US warship transferred to Britain in 1940. Early in the afternoon of March 26, 1942, *Campbeltown*, disguised as a German warship, sailed from Falmouth harbour. Accompanying it were 16 motor launches, a motor gunboat, a torpedo boat and an escort of two destroyers. On board the launches and *Campbeltown* were 257 commandos under Lt Colonel Charles Newman. At 10.30 pm on March 27 they entered the Loire. During a diversionary RAF bombing raid, the flotilla managed to get within 3 km (2 miles) of its objective without incident.

Then, when *Campbeltown* had less than 1.6 km (1 mile) to go, the Germans woke up to the menace. 'Within minutes, the waters of the Loire were ablaze with light and flame,' remembered Lieutenant Stuart Chant, on board *Campbeltown*. Heavy fire swept the destroyer's decks but its captain, Lt Commander Stephen Beattie, took the wheel and, increasing speed to 20 knots (37 km/h), placed the ship against the dry dock's outer gate. Commandos were soon clambering down rope ladders onto the dock. Success seemed assured.

The men in the smaller craft were faring less well, however. Shore guns had rapidly destroyed nine launches, tipping their occupants into the water. But some commandos from *Campbeltown* did make it ashore to carry out their missions, destroying guns and harbour installations. In the raid's most daring feat, Lieutenant Chant and four sergeants broke into the dock's main pumping station and raced down 12 m (40 ft) of stairs to plant explosives among the pumps. Once the fuses had been set, they had 90 seconds to escape. 'We took 60 seconds to climb the stairs, the longest minute I can ever remember,' recalled Chant.

KILTED RAIDER An army commando from the Liverpool Scottish Regiment proudly wears the regimental kilt for the St Nazaire raid. He has his commando knife strapped to his sock, and commando toggle rope around his waist. This could be used for many purposes – to hold onto when sliding down another rope, for example, or, if several were tied together, to make a rope bridge. He carries a Smatchett knife and Thompson submachine gun.

By now the river was strewn with burning wreckage and there was little hope of escape by sea. Most of the raiders were rounded up or killed before dawn. Of 611 commandos and sailors who had set out, 397 failed to return to Falmouth. But their sacrifice – recognised by the award of five VCs – was not in vain. On March 28, at 11.30 am, *Campbeltown* exploded, killing more than 380 Germans and destroying the dry dock. The St Nazaire operation had been a considerable, if expensive, success. (continued on p. 294)

FIRE AND SNOW Flames leap from a burning fish oil factory on Vaagso island during the raid of December 1941. Two British soldiers kneel on a snow-covered jetty, keeping watch for German snipers or a possible counterattack.

FIASCO AT DIEPPE

The Anglo-Canadian surprise raid on Dieppe in August 1942 was a costly disaster. But Admiral Lord Mountbatten was to comment: 'For every soldier who died at Dieppe, ten were saved on D-Day.'

GREY LANDING CRAFT, packed with men of No 3 Commando, moved through the darkness towards the coast of France. Suddenly a star-shell bathed them in a weird light. It was 3.47 am on August 19, 1942, and one arm of Operation 'Jubilee' – a joint Canadian and British amphibious attack on the port of Dieppe – had blundered into a small German merchant convoy with armed escort.

For several minutes the sound of gunfire echoed through the pre-dawn mist, as two British gunboats battled with the Germans. They sank the two German escorts, but during the fighting the British landing craft became hopelessly scattered. Some were sunk; most others limped back to England. By 4.50 am, only seven out of 23 craft bearing No 3 Commando were still heading for France.

LAYING PLANS

The Dieppe raid – initially code-named 'Rutter' – had been conceived six months earlier, in the euphoria following the successful attack on St Nazaire. Churchill and senior Allied commanders wanted to seize a port in occupied France for about 12 hours, capture enemy documents and prisoners, and test German readiness for an Allied invasion. They also wanted to help to take some pressure off the struggling Soviet Union.

Vice Admiral Lord Louis Mountbatten, Chief of Combined Operations, was put in charge, and troops came from the Canadian 2nd Division, under Maj General John Hamilton Roberts. The instigator of the St Nazaire raid, Royal Navy Captain John Hughes-Hallett, chose Dieppe as the target. 'Let's take the old peacetime route,' he said. 'Newhaven to Dieppe and back.'

But 'Rutter' never took place; scheduled for early July, it was cancelled when the weather worsened. Then, a month later – after everyone involved had been told that Dieppe was the target – it was revived as 'Jubilee'.

The attack was to have five prongs. The central one would be against Dieppe itself; Canadian infantry would go in first, followed by tanks. But before this, enemy strongpoints on the high cliffs on either side had to be dealt with. A landing to the east would secure one headland overlooking Dieppe's harbour. Another would take a headland to the west, before pushing inland to capture a German headquarters. On the flanks, the British Nos 3 and 4 Commandos were to destroy enemy gun batteries, code-named 'Goebbels' (in the east) and 'Hess' (west). Altogether, Roberts had just over 6100 men – including 50 commando-style US Rangers.

LOST SURPRISE

The attack was dogged by disaster from the start. Surprise, essential to success, was lost in the entanglement with the German convoy. Six of the remaining landing craft carrying No 3 Commando reached a beach in front of the village of Petit Berneval – half an hour late, at 5.20 am, in daylight. As Sergeant Wally Dugdale observed: 'You could see the Germans through binoculars, watching us come in.' Machine-gun fire swept the narrow beach. Although most of the 120 men reached the clifftop, casualties were high and landing craft were destroyed. By 10.20, the Germans, now reinforced, had rounded up the survivors.

The only bright spot in No 3 Commando's part of the assault was 2 km (1½ miles) farther west, where the single remaining landing craft, carrying 20 commandos under Major Peter Young, beached. They scrambled painfully up the cliff over coils of German barbed wire, fired on 'Goebbels' battery, then withdrew. By noon, Young was back in Newhaven, his group intact.

To the west of Dieppe, meanwhile, the 250 men of Lt Colonel Lord Lovat's No 4 Commando had achieved against 'Hess' battery one of the few successes of the day. The men were divided into two groups – one under Major Derek Mills-Roberts to land just east of 'Hess', the rest under Lovat to go ashore to the west. They arrived on time at 4.50 am. Mills-Roberts' group scrambled up a narrow gully to the clifftop and were soon on their way towards 'Hess', while Lovat took his men in a wide arc to approach the battery from the rear.

At 6.28 am, RAF Spitfires roared down to strafe the target and two minutes later the commandos charged, bayonets fixed. Within minutes, the battery had been seized and the guns destroyed. The commandos then returned to the beaches and headed back for England, having lost 45 men.

BATTLING AT PUYS

Elsewhere, disasters piled up. Just after 5 am, men of the Royal Regiment of Canada began landing on a steep pebble beach, backed by cliffs and overlooked by the village of Puys, east of Dieppe. This became a slaughterhouse as German soldiers poured a devastating fire into the landing vessels. Men 'plunged into about two feet [0.6 m] of water and machine-gun bullets laced into them,' according to war correspondent Ross Munro. 'Bodies piled up on the ramp [of the landing craft]. Some staggered to the beach and fell.' One group was trapped beneath cliffs at the beach's western end by fire from the top. At 8.30, the shattered survivors surrendered; 211 had been killed. The eastern headland overlooking Dieppe harbour was still in German hands.

West of Dieppe, the South Saskatchewan Regiment, followed by the Queen's Own Cameron Highlanders of Canada, landed in front of Pourville village. They made better progress – but they had landed on the wrong side of the Scie river from their target, Dieppe harbour's western headland. When they tried to cross the river, murderous machine-gun fire stopped them. By 10 am, it was clear that they would get no farther and the order to evacuate was given. Only 341 men managed to get off; 144 were killed and 541 captured.

With both headlands still in German hands, the main assault on Dieppe was almost bound to fail. But Roberts, offshore in the destroyer HMS *Calpe*, knew next to nothing of what was happening. Thick smoke screens blocked his view and radio contact with his units was poor. At 5.10 am, as planned, he sent in the main assault force – the Royal Hamilton Light Infantry and the Essex Scottish (Canadians despite their name). Before they landed, destroyers offshore and Hurricane fighters from bases in England let rip a ten-minute preliminary bombardment.

The troops got ashore with surprisingly few losses. They soon reached the sea wall, beyond which lay a broad grassy esplanade backed by hotels. Then the Germans opened up from the headlands and from blockhouses among the hotels. On the left, the Essex Scottish were mown down in droves. On the right, the Hamiltons came under terrifying fire from Dieppe's Casino, which stood forward from the hotels, overlooking the beach. George Ryall, a naval signaller with the Hamiltons, remembered crawling up the beach under 'mortar fire so heavy that stones were being thrown up over my head, legs and back'.

TANKS ASHORE

At 5.35 am, tanks started to go ashore – Churchills manned by the 14th Canadian Tank Battalion. The Germans, now fully alert, loosed everything they had against them. Nonetheless, 27 out of 29 Churchills landed safely and 15 made it to the esplanade – but no farther. The Germans had built concrete barriers across all streets into the town.

Bottled up on the esplanade, the Churchills, in the words of Trooper Dick Clark, just went 'round in bloody circles, using up our ammo, using up our gas, being shelled, rolling over people'. Some Hamiltons, meanwhile, had managed to break into the lower floors of the Casino – though they never managed to flush the Germans from the top floor. Other parties got into the town, but were soon driven back.

At 7 am Roberts, still hopelessly out of touch, received an isolated message that men had penetrated beyond the beach. It seemed encouraging and he decided to commit his reserves. First in were the French-Canadian Fusiliers Mont-Royal – who were massacred. Few even reached the beach. The second reserve formation – Royal Marines – were saved from a similar fate by their commanding officer, Lt Colonel Joseph Phillips. As he emerged from the smoke screen and took in the shambles before him, he knew that an attack was hopeless. He managed to wave back his men before he was killed by a German bullet.

By 9.50, Roberts began to realise, from the reports of returning marines and radio messages, the scale of the disaster. At 10.50 he decided to withdraw. Under heavy fire, landing craft picked up nearly 300 survivors, but had to withdraw as losses mounted, leaving over 900 of Canada's finest troops to surrender, and over 500 dead. In all, the few hours of hell at Dieppe had cost 1027 dead and 2340 captured. The RAF, battling overhead, had lost 53 men killed. But the Allies learned lessons – above all, that it was near impossible to seize head-on a well-defended seaport. That contributed vitally to the success of the D-Day landings just under two years later.

BEACH OF DEATH Canadian soldiers stagger forward onto Dieppe beach in war artist Charles Comfort's painting of the raid. Tanks rumble ashore, and shells explode. The white hulk of the Casino stands up proud.

VICTORY SWIG The fighting over at Dieppe, a German light field-gun crew slake a well-earned thirst. Smoke pours from a beached British landing craft in the background.

MIXED FORTUNES

Not all the raids that followed St Nazaire were equally successful, and some were even more costly – notably the fiasco at Dieppe in August 1942 (see feature, p. 292). Even so, Hitler was sufficiently stung to order the 'slaughter' of all commandos, whether or not armed or in uniform. Most later raids were on a smaller scale.

Just after 10 pm on December 7, 1942, ten Royal Marine commandos under Major 'Blondie' Hasler paddled five canoes, or 'cockles', away from the submarine HMS *Tuna* off the French coast and into the Gironde estuary. Their target: the inland port of Bordeaux, where they were to attach limpet mines to German merchantmen. Only four reached Bordeaux. In four days of paddling by night and hiding by day, two men drowned after their canoe capsized; four more who capsized got safely ashore, but were later captured and shot. The survivors attached the bombs – which damaged five ships – but two of them were also taken and shot. Of the 'Cockleshell Heroes', only Hasler and his crewman, Marine William Sparks, escaped into neutral Spain.

At the same time, raids were mounted against a plant at Vemork in southern Norway producing heavy water; the Allies feared that German scientists were using this in atomic weapon experiments. A raid by glider-borne saboteurs in November 1942 failed miserably. But an attack on the night of February 27/28 fared better: six Norwegians, parachuted in several days earlier, approached the plant on skis, broke in and planted bombs that destroyed key parts. Nine months later the plant, now repaired, was bombed by the Allies; remaining heavy water was destroyed by Norwegian Resistance men while it was being transferred to Germany.

Meanwhile, operations had also continued against the Channel Islands. Between September 1942 and December 1943, commandos and a special Small-Scale Raiding Force mounted six raids. Each resulted in reprisals on the islands from the Germans – including deportations to France. But later raids, and similar operations on the French coast, provided useful information on German coastal defences. This had become the preoccupation and priority of Combined Operations Headquarters – now under Brigadier Robert Laycock after Mountbatten's transfer to the Far East – as the date for the invasion of France approached. It was all part of the preparation for the most elaborate amphibious landing of them all – D-Day for Operation 'Overlord'.

TARGET: GERMAN RADAR

The night of February 27/28, 1942, was still and cold. Just after midnight, 120 men of the British 2nd Parachute Battalion, under Major John Frost, were dropped over the French coastal village of Bruneval, north of Le Havre. With them were a party of Royal Engineers led by Lieutenant Dennis Vernon and an RAF radar specialist, Flt Sergeant Charles Cox. Their mission was to capture intact a German *Würzburg* precision radar set. Its dish aerial had been located three months earlier in the grounds of an isolated clifftop chateau during a low-level Spitfire reconnaissance mission.

The operation was an outstanding success. Once on the ground, Frost with one group of men crept across snow-covered fields towards the chateau. Vernon, with another group, headed for the radar. When Frost's men had reached and surrounded the chateau, he blew a whistle. 'Immediately,' he recalled later, 'explosions, yells and the sound of automatic fire came from the proximity of the radar set.' Inside the chateau they found only one German.

At the radar set 20 m (65 ft) away, Vernon's men worked furiously. Vernon took flashlight photographs, which attracted a hail of bullets from a nearby farmhouse. One raider attacked the aerial with a hacksaw. Cox traced its cable back to the transmitter and dismantled as much as he could. Other men made sketches and ripped off manufacturers' labels.

After only ten minutes, Frost ordered the men back to a nearby beach, from where, after a brief – but alarming – delay, landing craft returned them to England.

NIGHT ATTACK Moonlight floods down in war artist Richard Eurich's depiction of the Bruneval raid.

Gearing up for D-Day

With Hitler's legions spreading terror and destruction in the Soviet Union, Stalin was desperate for the Allies to open a Second Front. But the invasion of western Europe called for months of preparation, a massive build-up of men and supplies – and the inspiring leadership of an Eisenhower.

IN THE SPRING OF 1942, with Allied forces on the defensive or in retreat from the Western Desert to the Pacific, a little-known 'backroom brass hat' in Washington came to a conclusion: 'We've got to go to Europe and fight. We've got to quit wasting resources all over the world.' His name was Dwight D. Eisenhower, then a major general and head of the US Army's Operations and Planning Department.

Ever since Hitler had launched his invasion of the Soviet Union on June 22, 1941, Britain had been under pressure to open a 'second front' in Europe. 'It seems to me,' a desperately embattled Stalin wrote to Churchill on July 18, 1941, 'that the military situation of the Soviet Union as well as of Great Britain would be considerably improved if there could be established a front against Hitler in the west.'

When the United States entered the war in December 1941, it too pressed for a prompt invasion of Europe, preferably before the end of 1942. General George C. Marshall, the US Army Chief of Staff, desperately needed action in Europe to justify the Allies' 'Germany first' policy and to silence the US Navy, which wanted to give priority to the Pacific war. From 1942, in an operation code-named 'Bolero', he began a massive build-up of US troops in Britain to be used in an invasion.

A TIME AND PLACE

But Churchill had a more realistic idea of the difficulties in mounting such an operation – made all the more glaring by the disastrous raid on Dieppe – and refused to be rushed. This created considerable strains in the Anglo-American alliance. Nonetheless, at the Casablanca conference of January 1943, the Americans agreed that the invasion – code-named 'Overlord' – should not be loosed before May 1, 1944. Two months after the conference, the British Lt General Frederick Morgan was appointed Chief of Staff to the Supreme Allied Commander (COSSAC) – even though no Supreme Commander had yet been chosen – to put together preliminary plans for 'Overlord'.

At their London headquarters in Norfolk House, St James's Square, Morgan and his staff had to tackle some of the war's knottiest problems. First and most important, they had to choose the landing area. To help them to make this decision they had access to a wealth of information about the enemy coastline.

Throughout 1942, the RAF had been taking high-altitude photographs of enemy-occupied coasts opposite Britain, and in early 1943 more detailed information was supplied by low-level Spitfire sweeps of selected regions. At the same time, French Resistance agents began to provide detailed intelligence about German defences, while a special team based at Oxford University – the Inter-Services Topographical Unit under Royal Marine Colonel Sam Bassett – scoured other sources of information.

These included appealing to the public, through the BBC, for holiday snaps and postcards of 'any part of the world'. The response was overwhelming. After only 24 hours, Bassett had 'a frantic phone call from the BBC to say that Broadcasting House had been snowed under with letters. Thirty thousand had arrived by the morning post'. Over 10 million pictures were eventually collected and 50 American servicewomen had to be flown specially from the USA to sort them out.

Using impressively accurate and detailed maps, compiled by Bassett's team, Morgan was able to narrow the choice of landing area. This had to be within easy fighter range of Britain, which ruled out Norway, the Netherlands and Bay of Biscay, and left only northern France or Belgium.

The most obvious place was the Pas-de-Calais, only 35 km (22 miles) across the Channel from Dover. But it was clear that the Germans too had come to this conclusion and were defending the area heavily (see box, *The other side of the water*). Morgan then looked west, zeroing in on the Normandy coast between Le Havre and the Cotentin Peninsula, which leads north to the port of Cherbourg.

This was within fighter range and was less well defended than the Pas-de-Calais, while Cherbourg, if captured early on, would provide an invaluable port for bringing in supplies. In June 1943, Combined Operations Headquarters accepted Morgan's choice, despite the misgivings of those who thought it too far from the invasion's eventual objective, Germany.

The invasion area had been chosen – but some checks were still necessary. To make sure, for example, that the sand on the selected beaches was hard enough to bear the weight of heavy vehicles, particularly tanks, men from a special unit of swimmers and canoeists – the Combined Operations Pilotage Parties (COPPs) – spent many cold, uncomfortable and dangerous nights in late 1943 and early 1944 going ashore in Normandy in order to bring back samples of sand for analysis. At the same time, teams were solving other problems, such as how to bring in supplies without immediately capturing an enemy port and how to deal with enemy beach obstacles (see box, *Portable ports and funny tanks*).

SUPREME COMMAND

All these developments were well in hand when, on December 7, 1943, a Supreme Allied Commander was at last appointed. Because the Americans would be contributing most men and equipment to the invasion, Churchill and Roosevelt had agreed that the Supreme Commander should be an American. After some hesitation, Roosevelt plumped for Eisenhower,

PORTABLE PORTS AND FUNNY TANKS

'If we can't capture a port we must take one with us', said British naval planner Commodore John Hughes-Hallett. Once the first men were ashore, some kind of port would be needed to bring in supplies. Hughes-Hallett proposed making prefabricated harbours (later code-named 'Mulberries'), which could be towed across the Channel after the invading force and slotted together.

According to his plans, a breakwater and outer sea wall would be constructed some 3 km (2 miles) offshore, using sunken blockships and vast caissons – hollow, floating concrete blocks, which could be flooded to sink them. This would create an area of calm water, within which special floating roadways ('Whales'), made with articulated steel sections, would lead to piers onshore. Ships anchored at the Whales would disgorge trucks full of supplies. It was decided to build two 'Mulberries' – one off the US landing beaches, the other off the Anglo-Canadian. By May 1944, over 200 caissons were ready. To ensure fuel supplies, an aluminium alloy 'pipeline under the ocean' ('PLUTO') was to be laid between the Isle of Wight and a terminal in Normandy.

A new tank formation, the 79th Armoured Division, was raised to give close support to assault infantry. Its veteran commander, Maj General Percy Hobart, developed special tanks which became known as 'Funnies'. The workhorse of these, the Sherman Duplex-Drive (DD), had propellers and a canvas skirt to keep it afloat when it was launched offshore. Another was a flamethrowing tank, the Churchill Crocodile.

BOBBIN One of the armoured 'Funnies' developed for the invasion forces was a tank with a bobbin-like device for laying down matting as a track across soft sand.

MINE-BEATER The 'Crab' was a Sherman tank with flails at the front for setting off mines.

The other side of the water

The Germans waited while the Allies prepared for 'Overlord'. They knew that an invasion had to come – there was no other way for the Allies to achieve victory – but they did not know where or when.

As early as December 1941, the Führer had ordered plans 'for the construction of a new West-Wall to assure protection of the Arctic, North Sea and Atlantic coasts'. Work began on the Atlantic Wall in 1942, and by early 1944 blockhouses and gun emplacements dotted the coastline of occupied Europe from the tip of Norway to the western end of France's border with Spain. Mines and obstacles covered the beaches.

The defences from the Dutch-German border to the Loire river were particularly formidable. This was the sector of Army Group B, commanded from January 1944 by Field Marshal Erwin Rommel. He planned to lay a belt of mines, nearly 1000 m (over half a mile) deep, all along the coast, backed by a deeper 8 km (5 mile) belt farther inland; it would need 200 million mines. Rommel boasted that the beaches would be a 'zone of death'.

But the Atlantic Wall was still far from complete in mid-1944, and many doubted its value. 'The Wall is a myth,' asserted Rommel's superior, Field Marshal Gerd von Rundstedt, Commander in Chief West. 'Nothing in front of it, nothing behind – a mere showpiece.'

The coastal front was also too long. Rundstedt lacked the resources to defend every beach and port, yet neither could he ignore any – for the Allied attack might fall at any point. The result was that no single area was adequately defended.

To make matters worse, Hitler kept moving divisions from the west to reinforce the Eastern Front, until Rundstedt's forces were largely made up of the over-age, the unfit and recruits from prisoner-of-war camps.

Among the few effective troops were the six divisions of Lt General Geyr von Schweppenburg's Panzer Group West. He and Rundstedt wanted them held in reserve near Paris, able to counterattack 'when the enemy is deeply committed'. Rommel argued that this would be too late; the only way to defeat the Allies was on the beaches. In the end Hitler ordered four divisions to stay near Paris, to be released only on his orders. It was an unsatisfactory compromise bound to delay any counterattack.

MENACING MONSTER A giant camouflaged German gun points towards the Channel.

But as low-flying reconnaissance Spitfires spotted the build-up of Rommel's beach defences in early 1944, the Allies began to worry. They had little need. The Germans, denied aerial reconnaissance of most of southern England by Allied air supremacy and blinded by deception measures (see box, *The fake invaders*) were as ignorant as ever of the time or place of the invasion.

who had planned the 'Torch' landings in North Africa and was now a full general in command of Allied forces in the Mediterranean.

At Supreme Headquarters Allied Expeditionary Force (SHAEF), based at Bushy Park in London's western suburbs, Eisenhower gathered a group of brilliant commanders. Air Chief Marshal Sir Arthur Tedder was the Deputy Supreme Commander, continuing a relationship that had worked well in the Mediterranean. Air Chief Marshal Sir Trafford Leigh-Mallory was given command of Allied air forces and Admiral Sir Bertram Ramsay of sea forces for the invasion. General Sir Bernard Montgomery was to command the assault troops, and Lt General Omar Bradley and Lt General Miles Dempsey were named commanders of the main invasion forces – the US First and British Second Armies. Eisenhower's long-standing chief of staff, Maj General Walter Bedell Smith, remained in that post, with Morgan as his deputy.

Almost immediately controversies arose. Morgan's plan envisaged an invasion force of three divisions, with airborne support on the flanks; Eisenhower and Montgomery insisted on increasing this to five, still with airborne support. This created transport problems, for 1000 extra landing craft would be needed and these were in short supply. Only with extreme reluctance did US Chiefs of Staff – suspicious that Churchill would transfer the extra craft to Mediterranean operations dear to his heart – release more vessels, though not the full 1000.

An even greater controversy (which nearly led the normally even-tempered Eisenhower to resign) broke out when the Supreme Commander demanded unrestricted use of British and American heavy bombers to 'soften up' roads, bridges, railway lines and German defences in northern France. It was vital to wreck lines of communication throughout the region, in order to prevent the Germans from rushing reinforcements to the invasion area when the attack was launched.

But both British and US 'bomber barons', Air Chief Marshal Sir Arthur Harris and Lt General Carl Spaatz, bristled at this proposal. Harris reckoned that his Lancasters and Halifaxes could win the war without the need for land campaigns. Spaatz wanted to concentrate his bombers on oil targets. Only intervention by Roosevelt and Churchill brought them into line. The bombing of targets related to the invasion eventually started on April 1, 1944.

THE FAKE INVADERS

Strange things were happening in south-east England in early 1944. At Dover, the shore sprouted elaborate but phoney jetties, oil storage tanks, pipelines and anti-aircraft guns – designed by the eminent architect Basil Spence. Fake landing craft and planes appeared.

It was all part of Operation 'Fortitude', an Allied campaign to simulate a build-up of forces opposite Calais, while disguising the real concentration opposite Normandy. The First US Army Group was created, largely of fictitious units, and the air buzzed with its signals. The Germans were deceived, and the build-up continued in the Pas-de-Calais.

A NEARLY SINKING ISLAND

By then Britain was crammed with men and equipment. Since 1942, Marshall had dispatched a staggering 950 000 US troops to Britain, as well as vast amounts of supplies. Whole sweeps of the south were covered from horizon to horizon with row upon uniform row of tanks, armoured cars and aircraft. Farmers' fields in Kent were crowded with howitzers. Half-cylindrical steel containers sheltering piles of ammunition lined the grassy shoulders of country roads. Depots were piled high with everything from boxes of dried eggs to drums of motor oil, brooms to prefabricated Nissen huts. A current joke went that only the thousands of barrage balloons bobbing in Britain's skies kept it from sinking beneath the waves.

At the same time, amphibious training exercises began, with troops making mock assaults on parts of the coast that resembled the projected landing areas. South of Dartmouth, eight small villages were evacuated and land requisitioned to create the Slapton Sands Assault Training Area.

None of the exercises was a great success and some were costly. On the night of April 27/28, convoy T4, consisting of a corvette and nine tank-landing ships out on an exercise, was attacked west of Portland Bill by seven German E-boats out of Cherbourg. The night sky exploded as torpedoes and gunfire ripped into the poorly

BEDELL SMITH: MAN WHO MANAGED THE WAR

'The general manager of the war' was how Eisenhower described Walter Bedell Smith (1895-1961). Known to his contemporaries as 'Beadle' or 'Beetle', Smith was an exceptionally able staff officer. Yet after service in France in 1917-18, he was still only a major when, in 1939, General George Marshall gave him a staff job in Washington. Then Smith began to shine, and by 1942 he was secretary to the Combined Chiefs and a brigadier general. Eisenhower, given command of the invasion of north-west Africa, insisted on taking Smith as his chief of staff. Their partnership lasted for the rest of the war.

Smith's grasp of detail was invaluable, but he was humourless, abrupt to subordinates and often difficult to work with.

protected convoy. Two landing ships were sunk and one badly damaged, killing 639 US servicemen. Alarmingly, ten officers with special knowledge of the 'Overlord' plan were found to be missing. Not until all ten bodies had been recovered could the Allies breathe freely again. What happened to the bodies of the other men remains shrouded in controversy. Many claim that they were secretly buried in mass graves near Slapton Sands.

SECURITY NIGHTMARES

'If the enemy obtains as much as forty-eight hours' warning of the location of the assault area, the chances of success are small,' Morgan had warned, 'and any longer warning spells certain defeat.' Strict security surrounded the preparations but, even so, there were several scares. In April 1944, a package burst open in Chicago's central post office to reveal documents marked 'Overlord'. In a moment of distraction, a US sergeant at SHAEF had addressed the package to his sister. Later the same month, a US general told fellow officers at a cocktail party that the invasion would take place before June 15. On another occasion, a British colonel informed friends that he was preparing to go to Normandy. Both officers were relieved of their commands.

Then a series of crossword clues and answers in *The Daily Telegraph* began to alarm the British counter-intelligence agency, MI5. On May 2, the clue to 17 across was 'One of the US'; the answer was 'Utah'. The answer to 3 down ('Red Indian on the Missouri') was 'Omaha'. These were the code names of the American landing beaches in Normandy. In May 27's puzzle, the answer to 11 across ('But some big-wig like this has stolen some of it at times') was 'Overlord'. Was vital information being passed to the enemy? MI5 interrogated the compiler, a 54-year-old teacher from Leatherhead in Surrey called Leonard Dawe, but decided that it was just a bizarre coincidence.

As the invasion approached, all troops were forbidden any contact with the world outside their camps. Their vast encampments in southern England – the American ones in Devon and Dorset opposite the planned US landing area; the British and Canadian ones farther east in Hampshire and Sussex – were surrounded with barbed wire and armed guards. Men were not allowed to send letters or bid farewell to their girlfriends or families. No visitors were allowed in. Civilians who accidentally wandered into restricted areas were detained. Their families were told that they were well – but would be unable to return home for some time.

Eisenhower, meanwhile, had been tireless in visiting his troops. He wanted, if possible, to visit every single unit involved in the invasion. 'It pays big dividends in terms of morale,' he said, 'and morale is supreme on the battlefield.' On May 15, 1944, he conducted a full-scale briefing of his senior commanders in front of King George VI and Churchill at St Paul's School in west London. US Rear Admiral Morton L. Deyo recalled it being said that the Supreme Commander's smile was worth 20 divisions. 'That day it was worth more. He spoke for ten minutes. Before the warmth of his quiet confidence the mists of doubt dissolved. When he had finished, the tension had gone. Not often has one man been called upon to accept so great a burden of responsibility. But here was one at peace with his soul.' The date for the assault – 'D-Day' – was set at June 5.

RAMSAY: RETIRED BUT NOT FORGOTTEN

When World War II broke out, Bertram Ramsay (1883-1945) was a vice admiral on the Royal Navy's retired list and his career seemed over. Yet he was to prove one of the ablest naval staff officers of the war.

Ramsay served in destroyers in World War I, before qualifying as a staff officer. By 1935, he was Chief of Staff to the Atlantic Fleet, but he retired at 55. In September 1939, however, he was called back and put in command of Dover, where he organised the evacuation from Dunkirk. He was given an immediate knighthood as a result. In 1942 he planned naval operations in the Mediterranean and in October 1943 was put in charge of naval forces, including transport, for 'Overlord'. He died in a plane crash in January 1945.

TEDDER: APOSTLE OF AIR-GROUND COOPERATION

One of the most important military lessons of World War II was the need for close coordination between air and ground forces. Few commanders really recognised this and, of those few, Arthur Tedder (1890-1967) stands out.

He joined the Royal Flying Corps in 1916, and flew bombing and photo-reconnaissance missions over the Western Front. He transferred to the new RAF in 1918, and by 1939 was Director-General of Research and Development in the Air Ministry. Two years later he was posted to the Middle East, first as Deputy Commander and then Commander in Chief of Allied Air Forces. His appointment in 1943 as Commander in Chief Mediterranean Air Command brought him close to Eisenhower, who in January 1944 made him Deputy Supreme Commander for 'Overlord'. Ike described him as 'one of the few great military leaders of our time'.

ON THE MOVE In what could almost be a Liberation scene, American troops passing through the East End of London on their way to the Normandy beaches (top) are greeted by women eager to give them drinks, food and cigarettes. But the job is still to be done on the other side of the Channel. (Below) British troops on the way to France take a light-hearted look at the booklet they were given as a guide.

D-Day – the greatest assault

'OK, let's go.' With these words General Eisenhower set rolling the D-Day assault on Normandy. Some 5000 ships and 150 000 men were launched across the English Channel as the Allies returned, at last, to north-western Europe.

NO ONE EXCHANGED A WORD. The men's faces were set and tense. It was cold, but sweat stood out on their brows. Many were grey with seasickness. Each was sunk deep in his own world of memory, fear and anticipation. 'As we moved in toward the land in the gray early light,' wrote the American novelist Ernest Hemingway, who accompanied the men in a US landing craft heading towards the beach code-named 'Omaha', 'the 36 ft [11 m] coffin-shaped steel boat took solid green sheets of water that fell on the helmeted heads of the troops packed shoulder to shoulder in the stiff, awkward, uncomfortable, lonely companionship of men going to battle.' Salt stains crusted men's clothes and equipment. Vomit sloshed around their feet.

Overhead, hundreds of Allied bombers and fighters droned towards targets in northern France, then back to England. The men in the landing craft could hear the regular crump of exploding bombs and the rattle of fighter cannon fire. From behind them came the thunder of naval guns, as 207 Allied warships – ranging from battleships to corvettes – unleashed salvo after salvo of a devastating bombardment.

As they drew near the shore, men began to break dazedly into life. Officers in the leading craft fired smoke signals. The naval guns stopped and there were a few moments of relative silence. Then, at 6.31 am British time, just a minute behind schedule, the first ten craft off 'Utah' beach, west of 'Omaha', lowered their ramps and 300 American soldiers leapt waist-deep into the cold sea. It was D-Day – June 6, 1944 – and the seaborne part ('Neptune') of Operation 'Overlord', the invasion of Normandy, had begun.

HARD DECISION

The order to start the invasion had not been an easy one for Supreme Allied Commander General Dwight D. Eisenhower to make. D-Day was originally set for June 5. But on June 1 the weather, until then warm and sunny, broke. Rain poured; visibility was poor and in the Channel seas were heavy. At 4.15 am on June 4, Eisenhower met his senior commanders in the oak-panelled library of Southwick House, outside Portsmouth, where he had established his headquarters in the run-up to D-Day. If the assault was to be made on the 5th, he had to give the word now, to allow the invasion fleet time to gather and cross the Channel. With heavy hearts, the commanders agreed to order a 24 hour delay. Warships already under way had to be recalled and soldiers, packed into landing craft, faced another uncomfortable day and night of waiting.

At 9.30 that evening, Eisenhower called another meeting of his commanders. Rain lashed down outside and the prospect looked bleak. But the meteorologist, RAF Group Captain James Stagg, offered a glimmer of hope. Reports from weather ships suggested that a brief period of clearer weather would begin early on June 6.

Ike was on his own: the final decision lay in his hands. As the meeting fell silent, he paused, then consulted his colleagues. His deputy, Air Chief Marshal Sir Arthur Tedder, and the air forces commander were unenthusiastic: effective air support needed good visibility. But both navy and army chiefs were in favour of ordering the assault. 'I would say – go', was Montgomery's opinion.

Eisenhower's chief of staff, Maj General Walter Bedell Smith – struck, he recorded later, by 'the loneliness and isolation' of his boss – watched him weigh the pros and cons. At last, after a long, heart-stopping silence, the Supreme Commander spoke: 'I am quite positive we must give the order . . . I don't like it, but there it is.' A final

BURROWING IN THE SAND Troops on 'Sword' beach keep their heads down as they gather for a dash inland.

DECEPTION

To catch the Germans by surprise and create the utmost confusion were essential to the success of D-Day. For months, the Allies had done their best to make the Germans expect a major assault against the Pas-de-Calais. On D-Day they carried the deception to its limits.

As the real invasion fleet steamed for Normandy, naval launches headed across the Channel towards Calais and Boulogne. Each towed balloons with special reflectors that produced radar echoes similar to those of large troop ships. Overhead, Lancaster bombers dropped streams of 'window' – strips of aluminium foil which also created false radar images. Dummy parachutists dropped early on June 6 at points along the French coast added to the confusion.

The deception worked. German radar operators reported vast air and sea fleets approaching the Pas-de-Calais. Even after discovering this error, German commanders remained convinced until early July that the Normandy landings were a feint, and expected the real blow around Calais.

meeting was called for 4 am the next day, June 5. The weather reports then were still favourable and Eisenhower committed the Allies to an assault the following day. 'OK, let's go', he said.

INTO THE BLUSTERY CHANNEL

Almost immediately, from ports along the south coast of England, a vast armada – some 5000 ships, from battleships to gunboats, from troop transports to tank landing craft – started to put out into the blustery Channel. 'The first files to move out looked pathetically small against the great stretch of sea,' remembered tank commander David Holbrook, watching infantry landing craft leave Gosport in Hampshire. 'Each small vessel flew its own [barrage] balloon and the open holds were covered with nets, knotted with coloured hessian, green, yellow and brown . . . More and more came on behind, towing their comic little silver fish above, like an uncanny water carnival . . . Nothing could stop the immense movement of "Overlord" now.'

On the transports, meanwhile, men were given final orders. The assault area was a 100 km (60 mile) stretch of the Normandy coast west of Le Havre (see panorama, p. 300). Lt General Omar Bradley's US First Army would attack beaches in the west, while Anglo-Canadian troops of the British Second Army under Lt General Miles Dempsey would land on the beaches farther east.

At nightfall on the 5th, airborne troops began to prepare for their part. The sea armada was by now well on its way across the Channel. Chaplains held services on the tarmac of scattered airfields, and men filed into their transport aircraft and gliders. In the next morning's early hours, before the seaborne assault began, they were to seize bridges and coastal batteries along the flanks of the invasion area – again, British and Canadians on the east flank, Americans on the west. With the seaborne troops, they were to carve out a beach-head strong enough to withstand enemy counterattacks, while supplies were built up.

On the German side, meanwhile, nothing was suspected. Field Marshal Erwin Rommel, commanding Army Group B and responsible for the defence of the north French coast, was in Germany. June 6 was his wife Lucie-Maria's birthday, and he planned to spend it with her. Many senior officers of General Friedrich Dollmann's Seventh Army in Normandy were absent from their headquarters. *(continued on p. 302)*

A DAY AT THE BEACH

'Overlord' was astonishingly complex, involving numerous parachute and glider landings as well as assaults on five separate beaches.

As midnight approached on the night of June 5/6, the German Seventh Army in Normandy was oblivious of what was heading for it. Rommel was in Germany. Many senior commanders were at Rennes, in Brittany, for a war game. It was an appalling night. Gusts of wind blew heavy clouds across the sky and there were constant showers of rain. No one expected much enemy activity in weather like this. The Germans would be caught totally off guard when the Allied invasion began at 12.16 am, British time.

1 Private Helmut Römer is on night sentry duty at Bénouville (later 'Pegasus') Bridge over the Caen Canal. Suddenly, an aircraft swoops out of the sky to the north. It is a British Airspeed Horsa glider and is followed by two more. As Römer dives for safety into a trench, British soldiers leap from the gliders. Within minutes, they have taken the bridge. Other airborne troops take a bridge over the Orne river. D-Day seems to be starting well for the Allies.

2 It is 1.15 am. US para John Steele has landed on the church steeple of Ste-Mère-Église. He dangles, feigning death, for two hours before being cut down and taken prisoner. He is lucky. Some of his fellows fall into trees in the square below. He hears screams as the Germans pick them off. Although badly scattered, US paras come together and take Ste-Mère-Église at 4.30 am.

3 Some US paras land – and drown – in flooded areas around the Douves river. In the previous months, Rommel has had likely airborne dropping zones flooded, or planted with mine-tipped poles – 'Rommel's Asparagus'.

4 A dangerous German shore battery at Merville overlooks 'Sword' beach. According to Allied intelligence, there is another at Pointe-du-Hoc (5). Lt Colonel Terence Otway's British paras overcome severe difficulties to destroy the Merville battery by 5 am. Just after 7 am, Lt Colonel James E. Rudder's US Rangers land at Pointe-du-Hoc. After fierce fighting they reach the clifftop – to discover that no battery exists.

6 The first troops to land in force are from Maj General Lawton ('Lightnin' Joe') Collins' US VII Corps at 'Utah'. They come ashore too far south – but this proves a blessing. The beach here is weakly defended. By 8, the Americans have seized causeways across flooded areas behind 'Utah'. By nightfall, they have linked up with pockets of airborne troops inland and have 23 000 men ashore – at the cost of 200 casualties. 'The landing just wasn't a big deal after all', comments Private Roy Mann later.

7 The massed warships of the Allied navies have gathered offshore during the night. At 5.30 they begin a massive bombardment. Overhead, wave after wave of Spitfires, Thunderbolts, Marauders, Flying Fortresses – a total of 9000 aircraft – add to the maelstrom.

8 At 'Omaha' the invasion nearly comes unstuck. The beach is a defender's dream – high cliffs, few routes inland – and the Germans mow down men of Maj General Leonard T. Gerow's US V Corps. But the Americans begin to break out of the beach by 9 am. By nightfall, at the cost of 3000 casualties, they have a 3 km (2 mile) deep beach-head.

9 'Gold', 'Juno' (10) and 'Sword' (11) are assigned to the British and Canadians. The 50th (Northumberland) Infantry Division comes ashore at 'Gold' at 7.25 am. The men meet heavy opposition around Le Hamel but soon break through elsewhere. By nightfall, 25 000 have landed, taken Arromanches and are on the outskirts of Bayeux. But there is a worrying gap between them and 'Omaha'.

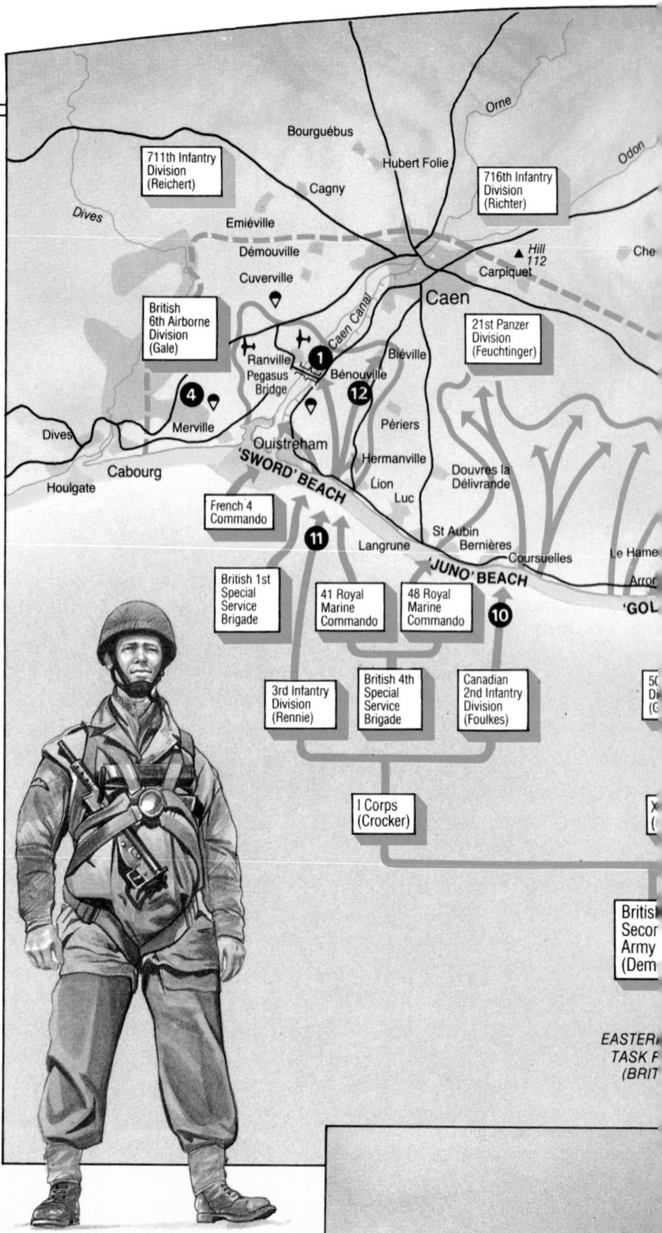

ARMED AND PREPARED This British para is ready for the landings. He wears a green oversmock and has a Sten gun tucked into his parachute harness.

10 'Juno' is the Canadian beach. The sea is rough and the first attack comes in ten minutes late at 7.35 am. German resistance is fierce. But the Canadians are determined fighters and soon break through. By nightfall, they are approaching Caen's outskirts.

11 The assault on 'Sword' is easier than expected. Resistance is patchy, and by 1.30 pm commandos under Lord Lovat have linked up with paras at the Caen Canal bridge. Free French commandos have cleared Ouistreham, and Hermanville has been seized. But there is another dangerous gap between 'Sword' and 'Juno'.

BLEAK BEACH SCENE Any shelter will do for Americans landing under deadly enemy fire on 'Omaha' (above). They hide behind 'tetraheda', steel beach obstacles laid by the Germans to rip the bottom out of landing craft. Among troops landing on 'Juno' beach to the east would have been this well-laden Canadian Bren gunner (right) from the Royal Winnipeg Rifles.

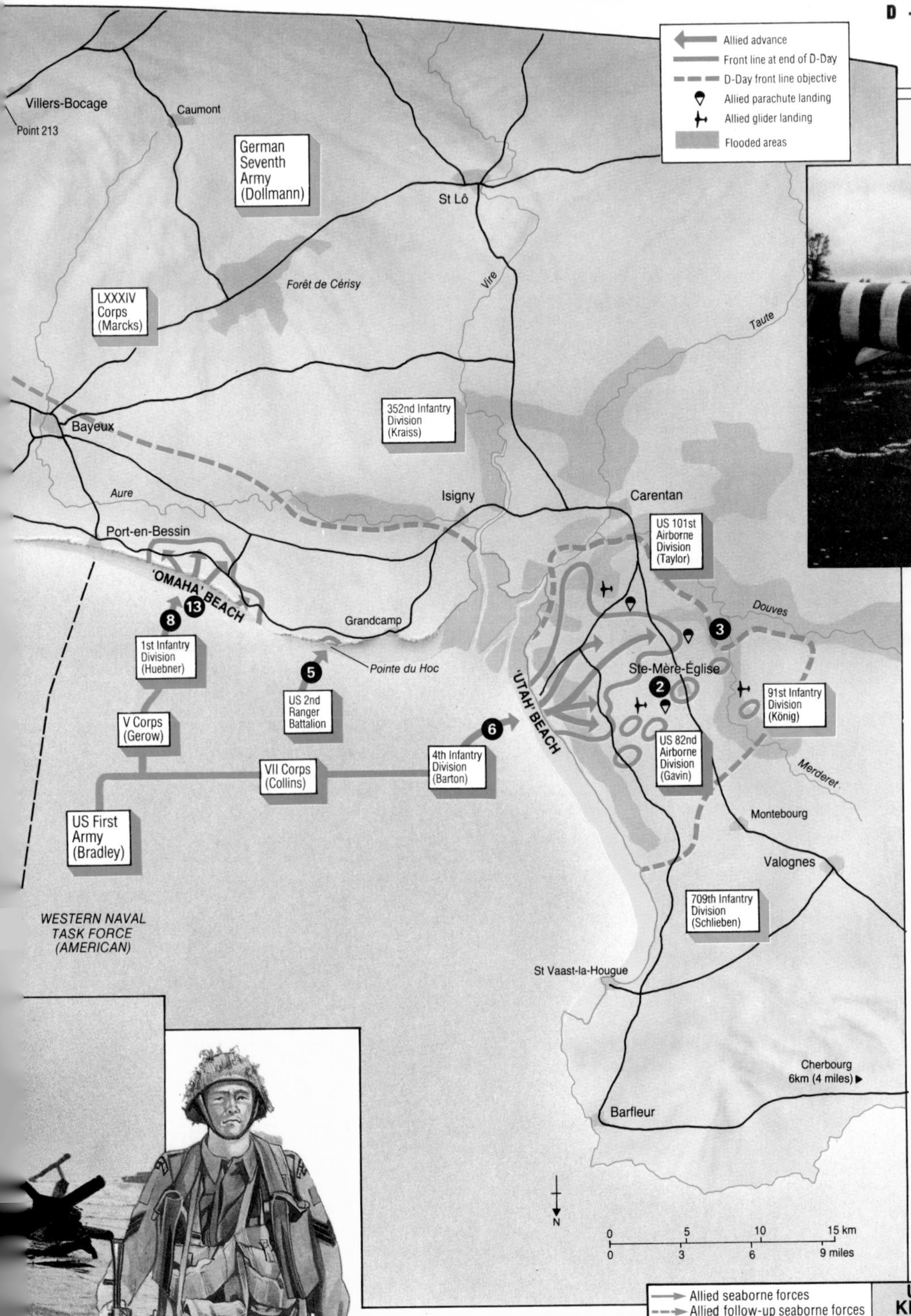

DEATH'S SOMERSAULT American gilderborne troops lie dead among the daisies of a Normandy meadow. Their crashed Airspeed Horsa (behind) has flipped right over on impact.

12 By mid-afternoon men of the King's Shropshire Light Infantry and Staffordshire Yeomanry are on their way from 'Sword' to Caen – chief Anglo-Canadian objective for D-Day. At 4 pm, they meet part of 21st Panzer Division south of Biéville. The panzers charge, but the British force them to swing east towards the Périers ridge. There, the Germans meet more British and lose 13 panzers. They withdraw to Caen but the British fail to pursue them. Managing to keep the Allies out of Caen is one of the few German successes of the day.

13 Off Arromanches is the site for the British prefabricated harbour, or 'Mulberry'. The US 'Mulberry' is to be built off 'Omaha' beach.

As night falls on D-Day, the Allies can congratulate themselves on a remarkable achievement. In less than ideal weather, they have landed over 150 000 troops by sea and air. Nor have the costs been excessively high: the death toll is later put at 2500.

DESTINATION NORMANDY Allied ships from as far as Wales and East Anglia gathered for the amphibious 'Neptune' landings. Operation 'Fortitude' deceived the Germans into expecting an attack around Calais.

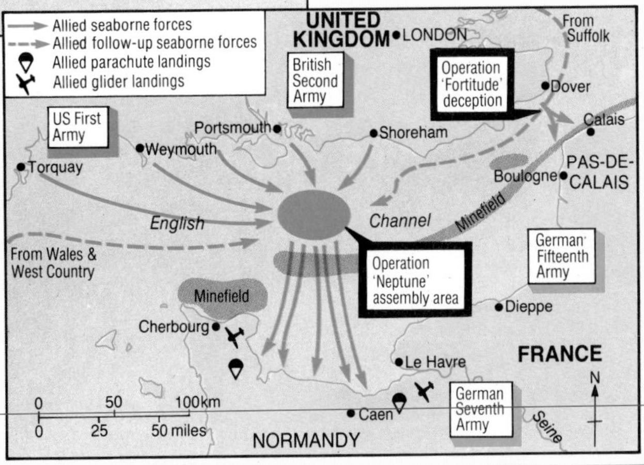

SABOTAGE

Two lines by the poet Paul Verlaine mobilised the French Resistance for its key sabotage role in the Normandy landings. On June 1, the BBC's French Service broadcast, among a jumble of nonsensical phrases, the line: *Les sanglots longs des violons de l'automne* ('The long sobbing of the violins of autumn'). This was a prearranged signal to put the Resistance on the alert.

Then, on June 5, came the signal for action: the poem's second line - *Blessent mon coeur d'une langueur monotone* ('Wound my heart with a monotonous languor'). That night Resistance cells carried out nearly 1000 attacks throughout France. Railway lines were blown up, telephone wires cut and ambushes laid. Telephone workers removed key circuits and railwaymen diverted troop trains.

Nor were the French alone. In Denmark, for example, a general strike prevented the movement of reinforcements.

OUT OF THE NIGHT SKY

Then, at 12.16 am British time, the invasion began. (All times given here are British. French and German time was one hour behind.) At that moment, three gliders, carrying D Company, 2nd Oxfordshire and Buckinghamshire Light Infantry, commanded by Major John Howard, loomed out of the night sky west of the Caen Canal. Their landing was rough, but uncannily accurate. Less than 20 m (22 yds) from the leading Horsa glider was Howard's objective – the canal bridge later christened 'Pegasus Bridge'.

British troops, faces blackened and led by Lieutenant Den Brotheridge, leapt out of the gliders and made for the bridge. German soldiers on sentry duty were taken completely by surprise. One managed to loose off a few rounds of machine-gun fire, which killed Brotheridge, but the sentry was himself killed by a grenade. Within three minutes the bridge was in British hands and engineers were hastily disconnecting demolition charges. Farther east, a similar attack on a bridge over the Orne river was equally successful, even though one of three gliders failed to arrive.

Elsewhere on the two flanks, things ran less smoothly. Inexperienced transport pilots, buffeted by high winds and turning and twisting to avoid anti-aircraft flak, dropped men as far as 55 km (35 miles) wide of their targets. In the American sector, many paras jumped to prompt and horrific ends. US Corporal Louis Merlano, picking himself up off a beach on the eastern side of the Cotentin Peninsula, heard terrified screams coming out of the darkness. At that moment, he learned later, 11 of his comrades were flailing helplessly in the cold waters of the Channel, dragged down by their heavy equipment.

Order was, nonetheless, restored and targets were captured. In the east, British troops took Ranville – the first village of occupied France to be liberated – and a parachute battalion assaulted a powerful coastal battery at Merville. The paras, with luminous skulls and crossbones stencilled on their smocks, were badly scattered and only 150 out of 635 made it to the rendezvous point south-east of the battery. Even so, they managed to capture and destroy the guns. In the west, small groups of US paras, signalling to each other with toy metal 'crickets' (one click to be answered by two), came together and took the village of Ste-Mère-Église at 4.30 am.

By then gliders were beginning to deliver a second wave of airborne troops in both sectors, with much-needed anti-tank guns and extra ammunition. The flanks of the assault area had been secured, at least in part. Allied bombers, meanwhile, had been busy since midnight, seeking out and destroying batteries and bridges along the coast, dropping over 5000 tonnes of bombs.

THE REAL INVASION

'General!' exclaimed Dollmann's chief of staff, Maj General Max Pemsel, down the telephone to his boss, 'I believe this is the real invasion.' It was a little after 1.15 am and reports had just come in of parachute drops east of the Orne estuary.

But with so many commanders absent, the German response was slow and uncoordinated. In Paris, Field Marshal Gerd von Rundstedt, Commander in Chief West, was little disturbed by the news. This could not, he believed, be a major operation. The Germans were further confounded by Allied deception operations (see box). Only at 6 am did Rundstedt finally agree to place all coastal units in Normandy on full alert. No one had yet contacted Rommel.

By then, the Allied invasion fleet had already gathered off Normandy and troops were transferring from transports to smaller landing craft. In the convoy of landing craft destined for 'Utah' beach, however, things had gone awry. As the craft jostled for position, hidden from the shore by cloud and a smoke screen, patrol craft *PC 1176* – responsible for shepherding them to the right point – hit a mine and disintegrated. The other craft headed on, but, without realising it, drifted in an offshore current. The men scrambled ashore nearly 2 km (1¼ miles) too far south.

Commanding the first troops to land on 'Utah' was Brig General Theodore Roosevelt Jr – son of former President 'Teddy' Roosevelt and cousin of the current President. He was 57, small, with an arthritic shoulder and used a walking stick. He was also full of fight. He had pleaded with Bradley to be allowed to go ashore with the first wave – 'to steady the boys', he put it – and was the only general to do so. He quickly realised that the new beach was weakly defended and ordered follow-up troops to land there. The assault proved remarkably simple. German resistance crumbled and the attackers were soon pushing inland. Roosevelt died of a heart attack six days later and is buried at Ste-Mère-Église. He won a posthumous Medal of Honor for his D-Day role.

BLOOD AT 'OMAHA'

The American assault on 'Omaha' beach met much tougher resistance. There, the Germans had established formidable defences. From concrete strongpoints inland, at least eight large-calibre guns, 35 anti-tank guns and 85 machine guns were trained on the beaches and – unknown to the Allies – the 352nd Infantry Division, veterans from the Eastern Front, had recently moved into the area. The preliminary bombardment had left the German positions largely intact.

The Americans bound for 'Omaha' hit trouble from the start. As landing craft assembled in heavy seas up to 18 km (11 miles) offshore, ten sank. In others men had to bail furiously with their helmets to keep afloat. Amphibious 'DD' tanks were launched too far out to sea, and 21 out of 29 plummeted straight to the bottom. Units became hopelessly entangled as offshore currents dragged craft away from their objectives.

Just before 7 am the surviving vessels approached the beach, nearly half an hour late. Inside, men heard a continuous pinging as bullets rained against the craft's sides. Then the ramps

dropped. Machine-gun fire ripped through the American ranks, felling several men on the spot. Others jumped into deep water and drowned, weighed down by their equipment. Those who made it across the open shingle were pinned down against a sea wall.

With no special obstacle-clearing tanks – the Americans had scorned to use the 'Funnies' developed by the British – the attackers were in a deadly stalemate. Landing craft brought in more men, equipment, bulldozers, jeeps and other vehicles, which piled up uselessly on the beaches. 'The first, second, third, fourth and fifth waves lay where they had fallen,' remembered Hemingway, 'looking like so many heavily laden bundles.' By 8 am General Bradley, monitoring events from the cruiser USS *Augusta*, was seriously contemplating calling off the 'Omaha' assault.

About this time, however, a few small groups of US infantry at last started to break inland. 'Two kinds of people are staying on this beach,' Colonel George A. Taylor shouted to his men, 'the dead and those who are going to die – now let's get the hell out of here.' By 9 am, some groups had reached the top of the bluff. Half an hour later, men were opening a route inland.

At the same time, Maj General Clarence R. Huebner, in charge of the assault troops, took decisive action. On board his command ship, he received a message that too many vehicles were clogging up the beach. Combat troops were needed instead. Huebner immediately sent in a reserve regiment with amphibious tanks, and called in the navy. At great risk, destroyers came close into shore to pound enemy strongpoints.

The tide of battle began to turn. Men started to push inland more freely and follow-up waves were able to land. By nightfall, the Americans had 33 000 troops ashore at 'Bloody Omaha'.

To the west of 'Omaha', 226 commando-style US Rangers had also had a tough day. Early that morning they had assaulted a battery believed – wrongly, it turned out – to be on the 30 m (100 ft) Pointe du Hoc headland. They were to remain stranded there until June 8, by when fewer than 90 men were still on their feet.

ANGLO-CANADIAN ASSAULTS

In the Anglo-Canadian sector, meanwhile, the first sign of activity had been almost imperceptible. At 4.45 am, two midget submarines – *X20* and *X23* – slid silently to the surface of the Channel, 1.6 km (1 mile) offshore and 32 km (20 miles) apart, at the outer limits of the assault area. Their job was to guide in the invasion craft with radar and sonar signals. Forty-five minutes later, the naval bombardment began. It started 20 minutes earlier than off the American sector and lasted over an hour longer, until 7.20 am.

At 7.05, groups of frogmen swam in to clear paths through underwater obstacles. But by 7.25, with the first landing craft approaching, their work was still unfinished. One frogman, Private Peter Jones, watched helplessly as a vessel, caught in heavy swell off 'Gold' beach, collided with a mine-tipped steel tripod. It 'shot up into the air as though lifted by a water spout,' he remembered. 'At the top of the spout bodies and parts of bodies spread like drops of water.'

The run in for the British and Canadian craft had been shorter than for the Americans and they arrived in better order. But they too met fierce resistance. On 'Juno' beach, landing craft, tanks and bulldozers were soon ablaze, their metalwork twisting weirdly in the heat.

But the terrain in the easterly sector was less favourable to the defenders than at 'Omaha'; there were no commanding cliffs and routes inland were plentiful. The British 'Funnies' also proved their worth. Amphibious DDs were often in action before the landing craft had lowered their ramps. Flail tanks blazed trails through minefields, and mortar-firing Churchills blasted holes in sea walls. Troops were soon pouring off the beaches. At 'Sword', commandos under Lord Lovat were led inland by their commander's personal piper.

WAITING PANZERS

On the German side, meanwhile, all was still confusion. On the outskirts of Caen, Lt General Edgar Feuchtinger, commanding the sole panzer division in Normandy, the 21st – veterans of North Africa – had been alert and waiting for orders since 2 am. But none came.

At 5.30 am he finally decided to take matters into his own hands and sent his tanks against the enemy airborne forces on the Orne river. Then at 9 am, orders arrived – to mount a counterattack against 'Sword' beach. Laboriously, Feuchtinger had to recall his tanks, move them through Caen, then north towards 'Sword'. This took the rest of the morning and much of the afternoon.

Only slowly were the Germans beginning to realise the extent of the invasion – for bombing and sabotage by the French Resistance (see box) had wrought havoc with their communications. Around 9.30 am, Rommel in Germany was at last informed of the landings. Suddenly it seemed to dawn on him what was happening. 'How stupid of me!' he murmured as he put down the telephone. He cancelled a scheduled meeting with Hitler – to beg the Führer for more men and equipment to defend the Channel coast – and immediately prepared to return to France.

At the German High Command, however, staff officers persisted in believing that the main attack would come in the Pas-de-Calais. Throughout the morning they refused to release panzer reserves held near Paris. Nor did they tell Hitler of the landings until he awoke at noon. He seemed as little upset as they. 'The news couldn't be better,' he commented. 'As long as they were in Britain we couldn't get at them. Now we have them where we can destroy them.' Only at 4 pm did the reserves receive orders to move north.

By then, a contingent of about 40 panzers from the 21st, under Colonel Hermann von Oppeln-Bronikowski, had at last made contact with the British north of Caen. 'The future of Germany may very well rest on your shoulders,' a senior commander informed Oppeln prophetically. 'If you don't push the British back, we've lost the war.' But after two encounters with their enemy, Oppeln's panzers had to withdraw to Caen.

By the time darkness fell on June 6, the Allies had achieved many of their objectives. They had secured all five landing beaches and were already stockpiling supplies. The Germans had been caught completely by surprise. But there were worrying gaps between some of the beach-heads, and 'Omaha' was vulnerable to counterattack. Moreover, Caen, one of the major objectives of the day, had not been taken. It would remain a thorn in the Allied side for over a month. The Allies had made a 'break-in', but the battle for Normandy was only just beginning.

BIKES ASHORE Canadians disembark at 'Juno'. Order has been established, but earlier the fighting was tough. One company lost half its strength – 65 men – in a single dash across 90 m (100 yds) of another part of the beach.

19: FREEDOM FOR FRANCE

After a bruising struggle in Normandy, Hitler's armies on the Western Front were put to flight.

Havoc in the hedgerows

The Allies were desperate to break out of their D-Day beach-heads. But among Normandy's narrow lanes and tangled, high-banked hedgerows – the *bocage* – lay deathtraps for men and tanks alike. It was touch-and-go for many days.

A LONE TIGER TANK of I SS Panzer Corps rolled out of woods north-east of Villers-Bocage, a village south of Bayeux in Normandy. It was just before 8.30 am on June 13, 1944 – a week after D-Day. The tank commander, SS Lieutenant Michael Wittmann, and his four crewmen could scarcely believe their eyes. To their right, the road out of the small village, rising to high ground marked Point 213 on Allied maps, was packed with British vehicles: Sherman Firefly, Stuart and Cromwell tanks, Bren-gun carriers and half-tracks. Khaki-clad soldiers were standing around smoking or brewing tea. Wittmann's gunner muttered: 'They're acting as if they'd won the war already.' Wittmann replied: 'We're going to prove them wrong.'

Leaving three more Tigers and a Panzer Mark IV to keep watch, Wittmann moved along a sunken lane into Villers-Bocage. There he found four Cromwells in the main street. Wittmann's Tiger opened fire and all four were quickly ablaze. Rejoining his company, the commander ordered an attack on the column near Point 213. The Tigers – using their 88 mm guns against the tanks and machine guns against the infantry – had a field day. In less than five minutes, a further 23 British tanks – outgunned by the heavily armoured Germans – had been destroyed. The carriers and half-tracks were engulfed in flames and nearly 100 men of the 4th County of London Yeomanry and the Rifle Brigade had been killed or captured.

A tank ace of the Eastern front, where he had knocked out no fewer than 119 Russian tanks, Wittmann was promoted captain and awarded Swords to his Knight's Cross. On August 8 he was killed when his tank was blown apart.

BOCAGE NIGHTMARE

The engagement at Villers-Bocage marked the end of a British attempt to bypass the key town of Caen, some 16 km (10 miles) inland from the Anglo-Canadian landing beaches (see panorama, p. 300). Caen should have been seized on D-Day itself, June 6, enabling Allied land-force commander General Sir Bernard Montgomery to push south and east out of the beach-head area. But German reinforcements arrived and vicious fighting continued as stalemate set in.

Panzer attacks against the British 6th Airborne Division east of the Orne river, which flows through the centre of Caen, were barely held off. To the west of the town, casualties mounted among British and Canadian infantry struggling through the *bocage* – a treacherous network of narrow sunken lanes, impenetrable hedgerows and small fields – which seemed to bristle with German tanks, machine guns and *Nebelwerfer* multi-barrelled mortars.

IN THE BOCAGE British troops from O'Connor's VIII Corps fire on German positions during Operation 'Epsom'. The *bocage* is a maze of such sunken lanes and hedgerows.

The nightmare nature of *bocage* fighting was summed up later by the historian of the US 314th Infantry Regiment, which fought over similar terrain: '. . . you become so dulled by fatigue that the names of the killed and wounded they checked off each night, the names of men who had been your best friends, might have come out of a telephone book for all you knew. All the old values were gone, and if there was a world beyond this tangle of hedgerows, you never expected to see it.'

RIGHT HOOK AT CAEN

A few kilometres west of the Orne, US troops from 'Omaha' beach had seemed to be making progress in the Aure river valley, through a gap in German defences. Montgomery ordered his highly experienced 7th Armoured Division (the 'Desert Rats'– veterans of El Alamein and other North African battles) to make a right hook south down the same valley in an attempt to get past Caen on June 12. The 4th County of London Yeomanry formed the spearhead that appeared behind German lines at Villers-Bocage – and Wittmann's action effectively halted the advance. It gave 2nd Panzer Division time to plug the gap.

Montgomery had to think again. His next plan was to advance some 60 000 men and 600 tanks of Lt General Sir Richard O'Connor's VIII Corps into the Odon river valley, just south-west of Caen. But as the tanks and infantry rolled through the valley's rich farmland, the weather broke (see box, *The channel storm*) and a continuous downpour turned the ground to mud. Even so, VIII Corps was in position near Carpiquet by June 25. Operation 'Epsom', Monty's major bid to take Caen itself, was to start next day.

Describing the Allied bombardment that preceded 'Epsom', a soldier of the 11th Battalion Royal Scots Fusiliers recalled: 'Looking back behind me, the sky was lit with flash after flash, increasing rapidly in tempo until the skyline was outlined almost in one continuous glow.' But it was not enough to subdue the enemy defences, manned by units of three panzer divisions – 12th SS, 21st and Panzer Lehr. Teeming rain severely limited air support, and the 15th Scottish Infantry Division fought desperately around Cheux, west of Carpiquet.

Allied casualties mounted as they pushed eastwards. SS Captain Hans Siegel – the commander of an SS panzer company – described later how he knocked out numerous enemy tanks in wooded country near Cheux, only to have his own tank destroyed: 'Shell after shell left the barrel of our gun, each one a hit. We fired so fast that the ventilators could hardly cope with the fuming gases . . . Abruptly, the ground in front of us appeared to explode – a tank shell fired from the right flank . . . The lone enemy tank . . . was 365 m [400 yds] away . . . Before we could even swing the gun around to bear, he hit us. Flames blew up around us and escape hatches flew open.

'Through the left hatch, the gunner bailed out, his clothes flaming; through the right hatch went the gun-loader. I could not get out through the turret hatch, so tried to follow the loader; and at the same moment, the radio operator had the same idea. Nothing for it but to go back into the flames . . . With my eyes tight-shut against the fire, and with my last effort, I pushed the radio operator bodily through the hatch and tumbled after him. And then I found myself in mid-air, hanging down the side of the tank, with machine-gun fire rattling against the plating . . . I had forgotten to unplug the wireless lead which was fastened round my neck . . . But after a desperate struggle I got free, fell to the ground, and rolled out of the line of fire.' Siegel, his face and hands burnt, was awarded the Knight's Cross.

O'Connor unleashed his armour, only to see it badly hit by hidden anti-tank guns. The first day of 'Epsom' ended in a sea of mud less than 7 km (4 miles) from the British start-line. After a panzer counterattack had been beaten off the following day, better progress was made. By early morning on June 28 spearheads of 11th Armoured Division had crossed the Odon river and taken high ground – designated Hill 112 on Allied maps – south of Carpiquet airfield.

Lt General Sir Miles Dempsey, in command

MINNY MOANS German soldiers fire one of the ***Nebelwerfer*** mortars, dubbed 'Moaning Minnies' by the Allies.

THE SERGEANT'S RHINO

A major problem for Allied tanks was that their lightly armoured bottoms were vulnerable to German fire as they attempted to crash through the deep-banked hedgerows of the *bocage*. The US First Army commander, Lt General Omar Bradley, explained: '. . . our Shermans bellied up over the tops of those mounds instead of crashing through them. There they exposed their soft undersides to the enemy while their own guns pointed helplessly toward the sky.'

The problem was eventually solved by an American farm boy, Sergeant Curtis G. Culin Jr, who welded a set of pointed steel plates to the front of his tank and cut his way through the hedges with guns blazing. By July, three out of every five tanks involved in action in the *bocage* had been fitted with these 'horns' and were known as 'Rhinos'. Culin was awarded the US Legion of Merit medal for his invention.

THE CHANNEL STORM

Late on June 18, 12 days after D-Day, the weather began to deteriorate, heralding a Channel storm which was to last five days. In reality the wind never exceeded Force 6 – a 'strong breeze' of up to 27 knots (50 km/h) – but it seriously delayed the Allied build-up in Normandy. Amid crashing seas, ships of all sizes sought shelter inside the partially completed 'Mulberry' harbours.

But off the American beaches the breakwater virtually collapsed as blockships settled in the sand and caissons (floats) broke up. Its British equivalent off Arromanches was more resilient. Even so, some 800 ships were stranded or destroyed. During the storm the Americans landed only 6000 men and 1000 vehicles, compared to 19 000 and 3000 between June 15 and 18. The build-up was put back by a week. Moreover, Allied planes could not fly close-support missions, allowing the Germans to redeploy their forces.

of the British Second Army, had been made aware through decoded signals that German reinforcements were on the way. Afraid that O'Connor's tanks would be cut off, he ordered them withdrawn across the river on June 30. By then, VIII Corps had suffered more than 4000 casualties – mostly in 15th Scottish Infantry Division. As II SS Panzer Corps arrived, 'Epsom' was called off. With Caen still in German hands, the British and Canadians were stalled.

TARGET CHERBOURG

Both Hitler and Field Marshal Erwin Rommel, commanding Army Group B in France, believed that the Allied invasion could not succeed without the capture of the key port of Cherbourg, on the north coast of the Cotentin peninsula, to land supplies. 'Even if the worst comes to the worst, it is your duty to defend the last bunker and leave to the enemy not a harbour but a field of ruins', declared the Führer to Maj General Karl-Wilhelm von Schleiben, commander of the 16 000-strong garrison there. The task of taking it fell to Lt General Omar Bradley's US First Army.

Although the fighting was no less intense, the situation in the American sector was marginally better than that around Caen. By the end of D-Day, the American beach-head consisted of a number of scattered groups – on 'Omaha' and 'Utah' beaches, and in isolated pockets of troops inland. Their first priority was to link up, to create a solid line. Maj General Leonard T. Gerow's V Corps started by smashing out of 'Bloody Omaha'. By June 7, leading units of his 1st Infantry Division – known as the 'Big Red One', from their shoulder patches, a red figure '1' on a green shield – had seized crossings on the Aure river. By the following day, they had linked up with the British XXX Corps from neighbouring 'Gold' beach, to the east. In the west, meanwhile, US Rangers isolated at Pointe du Hoc had been relieved and contact made with the 101st Airborne Division on the Vire river. 'Omaha' and 'Utah' were joined up four days later.

But 'Utah' had problems, for although the initial landing by Maj General J. Lawton ('Lightnin' Joe') Collins' VII Corps had been relatively easy, early attempts to break out and strike west – to cut off the peninsula across its base – proved difficult. As in the drive to Caen, the Germans took full advantage of the *bocage*, described by Bradley as the 'damndest country I've seen'.

Despite linking with 82nd Airborne Division at Ste-Mère-Église, the American infantry – lacking tank support because of the difficult terrain – made little progress. By June 13 they had still not secured bridgeheads over the Merderet river, which had been D-Day objectives. However, three days later, Collins' crack 9th Infantry Division, along with the battle-hardened 82nd Airborne, had thrust in short, violent bursts of fighting across the Merderet and the Douve beyond it. On June 18 they reached Barneville on the west coast, effectively cutting off the northern half of the peninsula – and Cherbourg.

SURROUNDED

With poor weather disrupting the flow of supplies across the beaches, taking Cherbourg was now vitally important. Collins quickly turned VII Corps northwards, and by June 21 all three divisions were on the outskirts of the port. Schleiben was surrounded. He ignored Collins' surrender terms, so more than 1000 Allied aircraft strafed and bombed the port for 80 minutes on June 22 before the infantry went in. Although stunned, the defenders' positions in blockhouses and concrete pillboxes were strong. American historian Russell F. Weigley described 'infantry advancing under artillery cover to within 300 or 400 m [330-440 yds] of these emplacements, machine guns and anti-tank guns firing into the embrasures while demolition squads worked around to the rear doors, the demolition teams finally blowing up the doors and thrusting . . . grenades inside'.

Slowly the steel ring around the port tightened and the Germans finally cracked on June 25, after further bombardment by three US battleships, four cruisers and a host of destroyers. Schleiben was taken prisoner the following day, but the last breakwater fortress did not surrender until June 29, and troops on Cap de la Hague – the north-west tip – held out until the 30th.

However, a shock awaited the victors: the Germans, true to the Führer's orders, had comprehensively destroyed the harbour, laying mines, sinking blockships and demolishing all facilities. Colonel Alvin G. Viney, who supervised the reopening in early August, described it as 'the most complete, intensive and best-planned demolition in history'. The Americans had captured 40 000 prisoners in the northern Cotentin at a cost of 1800 dead and about 15 000 other casualties. Now they had to break out to the south. Their problems were just beginning.

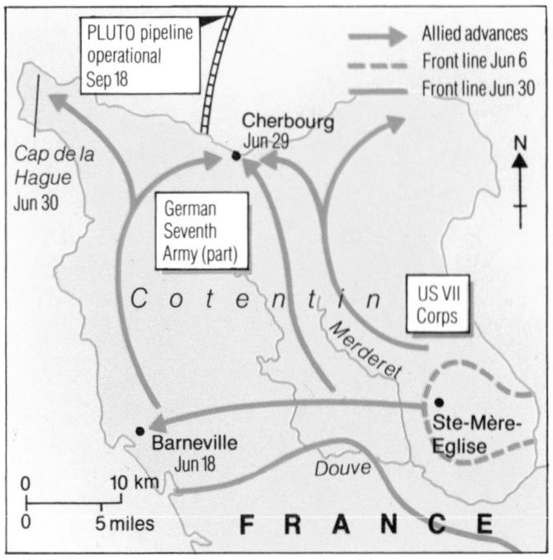

CUTTING COTENTIN The Americans cut across the Cotentin peninsula to Barneville, then north to Cherbourg. The underwater 'PLUTO' pipeline was soon brought ashore.

IN THE NAME OF THE REICH

Two days after D-Day the 2nd SS Panzer Division 'Das Reich' – 15 000 men aboard 1400 vehicles, including 209 tanks and assault guns – left Montauban, near Toulouse in southern France. Directed to clear a route north, they were soon involved in a series of clashes with the French Resistance, intent on delaying the movement of German reinforcements towards Normandy. It took 'Das Reich' over two weeks to make a journey that should have taken only three days – but the costs to the French were high.

At first, Resistance attacks were easily swept aside, but as the panzers approached Tulle, in the Limousin region, more organised opposition emerged. Tulle itself had been seized by the Resistance on June 7/8, and 139 German soldiers killed. The SS, outraged that they had been 'diverted . . to deal with this nonsense', retook the town and exacted a terrible revenge. On June 9 they seized 120 civilians and hanged 99 from lampposts and balconies; the other 21 escaped only because the Germans ran out of rope.

But even this atrocity was overshadowed by events farther north, around Limoges. On June 9, the commander of one of the 'Das Reich' battalions, SS Major Helmut Kampfe, was captured and later killed by the Resistance, triggering a widespread search of surrounding villages. One of these – Oradour-sur-Glane – suffered the attention of 120 panzer grenadiers under SS Major Otto Dickmann. The men of Oradour were herded into barns and shot. Women and children were killed in the church and the village put to the torch. A total of 642 people died on June 10. The village was never rebuilt; its ruins still stand in mute testimony.

Dickmann was killed in Normandy on June 30. At war crimes trials of 21 of his men, two NCOs were sentenced to death (later commuted) and the rest were either jailed or acquitted.

NORMANDY GENERALS

Missouri-born Omar Nelson Bradley (1893-1981) was in the same West Point Military Academy class as Eisenhower. Quiet, calm and bespectacled, Bradley had an impressive command of tactics, and was chosen by Ike to supervise the US D-Day landings. He had made his mark commanding II Corps in North Africa, taking Bizerta in May 1943. He also led II Corps into Sicily. After D-Day he took command of the US 12th Army Group, kept his head during the German Ardennes offensive and took his troops across the Rhine. Undistinguished in appearance and somewhat reserved, 'Brad' still managed to inspire the confidence of both his superiors and the men serving under him. Newspapers dubbed him 'the GIs' general'.

Tall, slim and impeccably dressed, Miles Dempsey (1896-1969) was regarded by his contemporaries as an outstanding commander. He led the British Second Army from Normandy to the Elbe, yet was overshadowed by his more publicity-conscious boss, Montgomery. In 1940 he had shown his potential by taking over 13th Infantry Brigade during the difficult retreat to Dunkirk. After helping to rebuild the army in England, he went to North Africa in December 1942 to command XIII Corps under Montgomery. Later he led his corps in Sicily before spearheading the invasion of Italy. His success in north-west Europe – around Caen, in the advance to Brussels, through southern Holland and, eventually, onto the North German plain – was rewarded with two knighthoods. He retired in 1947.

Caen – crucible of victory

The 55 000 people of Caen shook in their cellars or fled outright as the Allies battered their town to rubble and the Germans fought on in every ruin and bomb crater. The nightmare went on and on . . .

OUT OF HELL For these nuns, at last, there is escape from the noise and terror that were part of their lives in ravaged Caen. They are evacuated, with RAF men helping – but memories of the people they tended haunt them still.

A SEEMINGLY ENDLESS STREAM of 467 British and Canadian aircraft came in from the north, the low rumble of their engines filling the air. The sky erupted with German flak, but nothing could stop the aerial armada. For weeks, the historic town of Caen had been hammered by Allied bombardment. But on the night of July 7, 1944, it was reduced almost to rubble by one of the heaviest air attacks of the entire Normandy campaign.

A nun tending civilian refugees in the Hôpital du Bon Sauveur said: 'They say that 5000 are dead. I know that many hundreds are still buried in the debris, still alive . . . The piteous cries of those we could not reach will haunt us.' Miraculously, the 1000-year-old Abbaye-aux-Hommes church was unscathed – housing 2000 other refugees who had lived there for weeks. Women had given birth at the foot of its sanctuary; wounded had been treated above William the Conqueror's tomb.

General Sir Bernard Montgomery, commanding the Allied land forces in Normandy, had called for the massive air attack as a prelude to his last desperate effort to capture Caen by frontal assault – Operation 'Charnwood', scheduled for July 8.

According to the invasion plan, Caen should have been taken on D-Day itself – but a panzer division got in the way. So began the murderous struggle for this key area. Until Montgomery could break out past it, the Anglo-Canadian beach-head would be jammed with men and supplies, unable to move and vulnerable to counterattacks. Moreover, Monty had not yet captured any airfields – on July 3 the Canadians had failed to take one at Carpiquet, 7 km ($4\frac{1}{2}$ miles) west of Caen – and he was under pressure from London to win through into more open terrain.

Churchill was worried that a stalemate would set in, 'similar to that of World War I or . . . Anzio'. Heavy casualties meant also that infantry reserves were dwindling, and since the first of Hitler's V-1 flying bombs had already struck London, capturing the launch sites east of the beach-head had to be given priority.

'Charnwood' was meant to solve such problems, but it did not. The Germans quickly took advantage of Caen's destruction by manning defensive positions within the ruins. British troops found progress hampered by giant craters and hills of rubble. With casualties mounting, the attack was called off after 48 hours. Only half the town, north of the Orne river, had been taken; the enemy still held Carpiquet and the Colombelles steelworks, to the north-east. Meanwhile, an attack by 43rd (Wessex) Division to recapture Hill 112 (see box, p. 308), to the south-west, led to bitter fighting with little territorial gain.

Carpiquet had, in fact, been held by only 150 teenagers of the 12th SS Panzer Division – 100 on the airfield and 50 in the village. Yet Canadians of the Royal Winnipeg Rifles, with tank and flame-thrower support, took the village only with great difficulty on July 4. It was found to have well-built underground blockhouses, connected by passages. By the end of the day 117 Canadians were dead and 260 wounded.

NORMANDY SLAUGHTERHOUSE

Montgomery's strategy – 'to jab at the Germans from both flanks until their defences cracked' – was not working. 'The Normandy slaughterhouse was swallowing up the infantry', remarked a British officer. An alternative was to shift emphasis to the American sector. They had greater manpower reserves, and as the battles around Caen developed it became apparent that German armour was mostly concentrated in the east, leaving Lt General Omar Bradley's forces in the west under less pressure. By July 10 a new breakout strategy had begun to emerge: the British and Canadians would slog it out in the east, tying down German forces, while Bradley built up for an advance south of St Lô in the west.

But while tying down the Germans, Monty still had to avoid costly infantry assaults like 'Charnwood'. London had warned that, at the current loss-rate, replacements would run out by the end of July. And the Caen experience had revealed drawbacks in aerial bombardment.

There were disagreements about the purpose of the next breakout attempt, Operation 'Goodwood'. The Americans – and Montgomery's own chief planner, Brigadier Charles Richardson – hoped that the Second Army's tanks, outnumbering the panzers four to one, would break out from a bridgehead east of the Orne river and strike south towards Falaise, open country and the road to Paris. Monty had more modest ambitions for 'Goodwood'. He saw it simply as way of eliminating the obstacle of Caen and keeping the panzers away from the Americans, who would then be poised to make the major breakout. The American attack – Operation 'Cobra', south of St Lô – would start on July 25.

EAR TO THE GROUND

'Goodwood', set for July 17, involved all four British and Canadian corps in Normandy. Three armoured divisions – the Guards, 7th and 11th – of Lt General Sir Richard O'Connor's VIII Corps would strike out of the Orne bridgehead to take the high ground of Bourguébus Ridge, about 6 km (4 miles) to the south-west.

Delays in troop positioning put back the start of 'Goodwood' by a day, but hopes ran high. It began with an air, naval and artillery bombardment to blast a path for 750 tanks. However, Germans on the Colombelles steelworks' high towers saw the preparations, confirming earlier Wehrmacht intelligence warnings of 'a major operation'. SS General Josef 'Sepp' Dietrich, of I SS Panzer Corps, used a trick picked up on the Russian Front to verify the reports, putting an ear to the ground, Red Indian style, to detect the rumble of the oncoming British tanks.

Unfortunately for Monty, a lull in intelligence from codebreaking left him unaware of German preparations. And their defences south of Caen were formidable – four belts of natural and man-made obstacles, with tanks in reserve. The stone-built villages of the open, rolling agricultural land were dominated by ridges concealing 88 mm flak/anti-tank guns; and the villages themselves were defended. Farther south, I SS Panzer Corps' 80 Panthers and Tigers waited out of artillery range. To make matters worse, the Orne bridgehead had only six narrow river crossings for nearly 8000 vehicles, and an uncleared British minefield also restricted them.

However, the massive preliminary air bombardment – begun at 5.30 am on July 18 – had a devastating effect on the Germans. Lieutenant Freiherr von Rosen, whose Tiger tank company was in orchards near the village of Emiéville, east of Caen, described it as 'like hell'. He went on: 'I am still astonished that I ever survived . . . It was next to impossible to see anything as so much dirt had been stirred up by the explosions . . . impossible to hear anything because of the unceasing crashing of explosions . . . so nerve-shattering that we could not even think . . . [By the end] 50 men of the company were dead, two soldiers had committed suicide . . . another had to be sent to a mental hospital for observation . . .'

An artillery bombardment followed, and 11th Armoured Division tanks advanced at 7.30 am. Bypassing the villages of Cuverville and Demouville, just east of Caen, they ignored dazed and demoralised pockets of Germans. But the narrow Orne bridgehead slowed down follow-up units, and by 11 am a massive traffic jam was delaying the Guards and 7th Armoured Divisions. Furthermore, some Germans were still fighting. In Cagny, a village north-east of Bourguébus, for example, four 88 mm guns – ordered into action at pistol-point by a panzer officer – suddenly opened fire, knocking out 16 British tanks within minutes. The attack began to lose momentum.

Then, as O'Connor struggled to free more tanks from the Orne bottleneck early in the afternoon, Dietrich sent his panzer reserve to the Bourguébus area. Catching the British trying to take the ridge from the north through the village of Hubert Folie, the Panthers sent Sherman after Sherman up in flames. The attack ground to a halt and by the end of the day VIII Corps had lost nearly 200 tanks. Although infantry attacks had finally cleared southern Caen, 'Goodwood' had failed to produce the expansion intended.

Fighting continued until July 20, when heavy rain prevented further movement. A decisive Allied breakthrough seemed no nearer, and yet another corner of Normandy had become a killing ground. One observer described it as 'a scene of utter desolation . . . Trees were uprooted, roads were impassable. There were bodies in half, crumpled men . . . The place stank'.

TAKING HILL 112

A massive artillery bombardment followed by squadrons of rocket-firing Typhoon fighter-bombers failed to dislodge the German defenders as lead battalions of the 43rd (Wessex) Infantry Division neared Hill 112, south-west of Caen, on July 10, 1944. The crest of the hill gave a panoramic view of the whole Caen battlefield, and the attack on it – code-named Operation 'Jupiter' – was no easy matter.

The spearhead advance by men of the Duke of Cornwall's Light Infantry ran into an SS heavy panzer battalion equipped with Tigers. The infantry were virtually wiped out. One survivor, Lance Corporal Gordon Mucklow, recalled: 'All hell let loose, red-hot bullets were sizzling in the earth inches from our helmets.' Other battalions followed, but within six hours over 2000 men had been lost for no appreciable gain. As artillery shells roared onto the hill, the Tigers held on – and did so for more than two weeks, blocking a natural route towards more open country around Falaise. Hill 112, a bloody quagmire, fell on July 31, when Typhoons caught the Tigers in the open.

GHOST TOWN Smoke spirals up from shattered houses. A few towers stand sentinel over the wreckage. Caen, subjected to weeks of bombardment and fierce ground fighting, has fallen – the heart knocked out of it.

Buzz bombs and rockets

Just as the Allies thought the war was almost won, Hitler sent a nasty surprise: two Vergeltungswaffen – *'Reprisal Weapons' – the V-1 and V-2.*

A THROBBING BUZZ, 'like a Model T Ford going up a hill', heralded the arrival of the first of Hitler's long-rumoured secret weapons in the skies over south-east England on the unseasonably cold early morning of June 13, 1944 – just a week after D-Day. The noise came from the simple but ingenious pulse-jet engine that powered the V-1 pilotless flying bomb. But the most frightening characteristic of the 'buzz bombs' or 'doodlebugs', as they were soon nicknamed, was that the engine noise would sooner or later abruptly stop. Then the projectile would go into a dive and, about 15 seconds later, its 850 kg (1875 lb) warhead would explode.

Mrs Phyl Bowring, a Sussex housewife, was one of the first people to experience a doodlebug explosion, at 4.20 am on that first Tuesday morning. She recalled 'the uncanny silence when the engine cut out and then the ear-shattering explosion'. Soon millions of fellow Britons realised that, if the engine cut out after it had passed overhead, they were safe. If not, those 15 seconds of silence might be their last. The tense wait invoked memories of the worst horrors of the Blitz – quite deliberately so, for the German intention was to create terror rather than to destroy precise military targets.

The plan, formulated by Field Marshal Erhard Milch in 1943, was to launch up to 500 V-1s a day. The people of London, he believed, 'will never endure it . . . It will be the end of any real life in the city'. But air reconnaissance and reports from Resistance agents enabled the RAF to bomb the launch sites in northern France from April 1944, which delayed the campaign's start. Then, when the doodlebugs appeared, anti-aircraft gunners and fighter pilots soon worked out ways of dealing with them.

Ack-ack guns were concentrated along the south coast. Controlled by radar and firing shells carrying proximity fuses (so that they exploded near their targets), the guns shot down an impressive 1859 V-1s between June 1944 and March 1945. In addition, the Hawker Tempest V and Spitfire IX fighters – and later, the Gloster Meteor jet – had the speed to intercept and down buzz bombs with cannon fire. They had to fire at only about 180 m (200 yds) to be sure of a hit. Wing Commander Roland Beamont, a Tempest pilot, described it: 'You were travelling at 400 mph [650 km/h] or more and you'd have no time to avoid the explosion . . . You'd go through the centre of the fireball.'

Some pilots placed their wingtip under that of the buzz bomb, then gently raised it. This upset the V-1's gyroscopic guidance system, sending it out of control to crash in an unpopulated area. The RAF downed 1771 V-1s in all. As the Allied armies advanced, the Germans built new launch sites in the Netherlands and also managed to launch V-1s from Heinkel He111 bombers. Altogether, some 10 500 were launched, including 2448 that hit Antwerp, Belgium, after it was liberated in autumn 1944.

Of 6725 buzz bombs that reached England, 2420 fell on London. Over 6000 people were killed and nearly 18 000 badly injured; damage was severe and widespread. The indiscriminate attacks played on people's nerves – they sheltered once more in London Underground stations as in the Blitz, and children were again evacuated to the country.

ENTER THE V-2

Meanwhile, V-2 rockets, which carried a 1 tonne warhead 320-350 km (200-220 miles), began to fall – with no warning at all. The V-2 was the lethal achievement of a brilliant team led by Dr Wernher von Braun at Peenemünde, on the Baltic coast. The first V-2 to hit England fell on Chiswick, in west London, on September 8, 1944, killing three people and badly injuring another ten. It had been launched only minutes before from The Hague, in Holland. Accuracy was impossible, but London was a huge target for this terror weapon.

The Allies already knew of the V-2 through intelligence and photo-reconnaissance reports, but it was kept secret. The blasts were attributed to gas explosions, which the British government did not deny, fearing panic. It was not until November that Churchill revealed the truth. The V-2 assault reached a climax in February 1945, when 232 hit southern England. Altogether, 1115 fell, 517 of them in the London area. The last two exploded on March 27, 1945. In all, they killed 2754 people and seriously injured about 6500.

The only real defence against the V-2s was to destroy the trains and lorries transporting them and their fuel. They could be launched from almost any piece of level ground, and sites were switched constantly to avoid detection. Peenemünde was attacked repeatedly, but the main assembly plant, turning out 900 V-2s a month underground in the Harz mountains near Nordhausen, in eastern Germany, was never bombed. Indeed, 100 or so V-2s were found intact there by US troops in 1945 and spirited away to America – along with von Braun and his scientists.

V-3 AND V-4

Two other German terror weapons, V-3 and V-4, never got into action. The V-3 was a huge gun that would send missiles 160 km (100 miles) at speeds of 5400 km/h (3350 mph). The V-4 was a kind of piloted V-1 for *kamikaze*-style attacks. By the time it was developed late in 1944, there was not enough fuel to train SS volunteers to fly it.

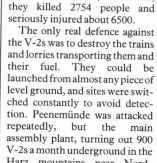

DEADLY DOODLEBUG The V-1 (or Fieseler Fi103) was only 8 m (26 ft 3 in) long, with a wingspan of 5.7 m (18 ft 9 in). The pulse-jet engine, mounted above the fuselage, drew air in at the front. Petrol burned in a series of explosions, producing a jet of flaming exhaust gas from the tailpipe and the characteristic staccato throbbing noise. The V-1 was launched from fixed ramps and was guided by a gyroscopic automatic pilot. The fuel was cut off automatically at a predetermined range.

ROCKET BOMB The V-2 (or A4 to the Germans) was 14 m (46 ft) long and 1.65 m (5 ft 5 in) in diameter, weighing over 12 tonnes. The rocket motor ran on alcohol and liquid oxygen; hydrogen peroxide powered the turbine fuel pumps. Its speed reached 5750 km/h (3600 mph) and its trajectory 30 000 m (100 000 ft). It was launched from a platform towed by a truck.

Normandy breakout

The stalemate in Normandy was finally broken when British and Canadians took on Hitler's panzers while the Americans smashed their way south and west in Operation 'Cobra'. Then Bradley unleashed 'Blood and Guts' Patton, and squeezed 100 000 Germans into a fiery furnace at Falaise.

AS CHERBOURG FELL in late June 1944, Lt General Omar N. Bradley, commanding the US First Army, regrouped his forces. He was aiming to keep going as far south as Avranches on the west coast – the gateway to Brittany. 'We want to smash right on through', he said. Afterwards, Lt General George S. Patton's newly deployed US Third Army would be unleashed to seize a number of Breton ports – St Malo, Brest and Lorient – which were essential as supply bases. However, the need to clear pockets of Germans south of Cherbourg delayed Bradley's attack until July 3.

He favoured a 'broad-front' advance, initially to a line running from Coutances through St Lô to Caumont, involving all three American corps then in the Cotentin peninsula. Unfortunately, they were poorly placed amid some of the worst terrain imaginable: a network of hedgerows and sunken lanes – the *bocage* – interspersed with flooded marshland, which the Germans turned into a nightmare of defensive positions.

First to attack was Maj General Troy H. Middleton's US VIII Corps, driving towards the village of La Haye-du-Puits, near the west coast south of Cherbourg. But progress was painfully slow. By July 7, after four days of heavy fighting, Middleton's three divisions had advanced less than 6 km (4 miles). Back east, near Carentan, Maj General 'Lightnin Joe' Collins' VII Corps fared no better. Meanwhile, Maj General Charles H. Corlett's XIX Corps, heading for St Lô, soon became bogged down. On July 14, Bradley halted the attacks. In 12 days, the Americans had suffered nearly 10 000 casualties for less than 11 km (7 miles) of ground gained.

One reason for the failure was that the intended route to Avranches – through St Lô and Coutances – was predictable, and the Germans had prepared their defences. On July 10, after meeting General Sir Bernard Montgomery, in command of the Allied land forces, Bradley suggested a new plan – code-named 'Cobra' – which he hoped would trap the main enemy force, Maj General Dietrich von Choltitz's LXXXIV Corps, against the coast. Collins would lead, striking south-west towards Coutances from the road between St Lô and Périers. Middleton would surge south from the La Haye-du-Puits area, squeezing the Germans into a pocket. Bombers would first blast a path forward for Collins, then concentrate on Germans trapped in the pocket.

However, before 'Cobra' could begin, Bradley's forces first had to secure the road from Périers to St Lô. During the night of July 15/16, Collins renewed his attacks, aided by XIX Corps and Maj General Leonard T. Gerow's V Corps around St Lô. After more heavy fighting, the town was captured on July 18. But after 18 days the American casualties were more than 40 000, and replacements little more than raw recruits, only 21 weeks in the army. On the scheduled eve of 'Cobra' – July 23 – Collins had still not reached Coutances and the weather was worsening.

GERMAN COMMAND CHAOS

Yet the Americans had some advantages – though they did not know it. Despite the failure of Operation 'Goodwood' (p. 307), the British and Canadians were tying down ever more German forces around Caen, to the east. By late July, 14 enemy divisions – including six panzer divisions – were engaged, leaving the Americans facing a

'CLEVER' KLUGE

'I am no pessimist. But in my view, the situation could not be grimmer.' That was the judgment of Hans Günther von Kluge (1882-1944), less than two weeks after he replaced Rundstedt as Commander in Chief West on July 1, 1944.

Between 1939 and 1941 'clever Hans' (a play on the German *kluge Hans*) commanded the Fourth Army in Poland, France (for which he was promoted field marshal) and Russia. In December 1941, he took over command of Army Group Centre on the Eastern Front. He was an able general but showed little personality – except when he challenged fellow general Heinz Guderian to a pistol duel and asked Hitler to be his second; the Führer suggested that the two men sort out their disagreements.

On August 15, 1944, during the Falaise onslaught, Kluge lost contact with his headquarters for several hours. Hitler, convinced that he had been negotiating with the Allies, ordered him to be relieved and to return to Berlin. On the way, Kluge committed suicide.

CROMWELLS ON THE MOVE Canadian Cromwell tanks rumble across the Normandy countryside. The fast and agile British-built Cromwell first saw action after D-Day.

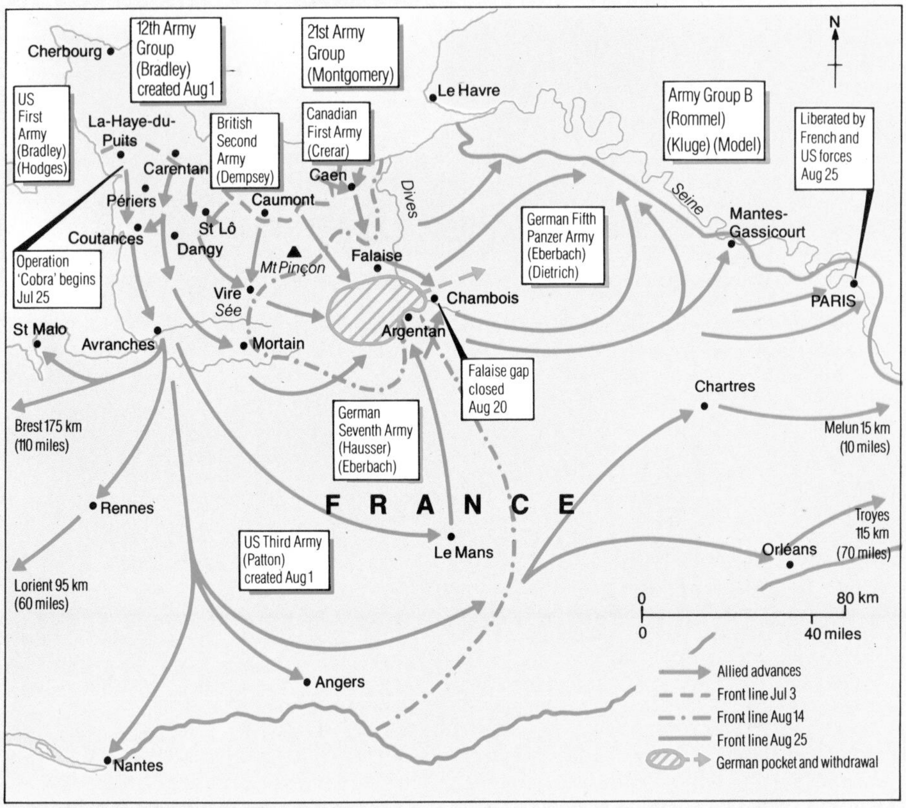

FROM COTENTIN TO PARIS in just a month from July 26, 1944, Allied forces swept from Normandy into Brittany and across northern France to the Seine and Paris.

miscellany of understrength infantry units backed by only two panzer formations. And the German command chain was in chaos.

On July 1, Field Marshal Gerd von Rundstedt – accused by Hitler of 'defeatism' – had resigned as Commander in Chief West, to be replaced by Field Marshal Hans Günther von Kluge, an Eastern Front veteran with little experience of fighting the Western Allies. Sixteen days later Field Marshal Erwin Rommel, commanding Army Group B, was injured when his car crashed while being strafed by a British fighter-bomber. Finally, on July 20, came the bomb attempt on Hitler's life, after which the Führer totally distrusted his army commanders and refused them any flexibility of control on the battlefield. When Rommel was later implicated in the plot he took the option of suicide, depriving Germany of one of its ablest generals.

THE CANNY CANADIAN

Montgomery had considerable faith in the level-headed, no-nonsense Henry ('Harry') Duncan Graham Crerar (1888-1965). In July 1940, Crerar had been sent by the Canadian government to London as Chief of the Canadian General Staff; his job was planning training programmes for 100 000 Canadian troops. But, eager for up-front action, he later resigned this desk job and soon became commander of I Canadian Corps in Sicily. Two years later he took over First Canadian Army, which also included Polish, Czech, Belgian, Dutch, British and American units.

DISASTROUS START

Even so, 'Cobra' had a disastrous start. Scheduled for July 24, it was delayed because of bad weather. After three days of pouring rain, Bradley eyed the leaden sky on July 23 and growled laconically: 'Dammit, I'm going to have to court-martial the chaplain if we have many more days like this.' He postponed the attack for 24 hours.

Unfortunately the decision to postpone was made after Allied bombers had taken off from England. Although most were recalled, about 350 dropped their bombs through heavy cloud. Some bombs fell short, killing 25 American soldiers; and the same thing happened again when the operation was revived. Altogether, 111 Americans were killed, including Lt General Lesley J. McNair, commander of Army Land Forces and the highest-ranking American to die in the north-west Europe campaign.

Not surprisingly, the ground assault on July 25 did not go well, for the Americans were shocked and somewhat demoralised. Bradley said later that as reports of the bombing and of tough fighting against still-determined Germans filtered into his headquarters, dejection 'settled over us like a wet fog'. Yet another costly failure

seemed on the cards. But Bradley was wrong. The Germans had been battered by more than 5000 tonnes of high explosives and napalm. Maj General Fritz Bayerlein, commanding the Panzer Lehr Division, recorded: 'By noon nothing was visible but dust and smoke. My front lines looked like the face of the moon and at least 70 per cent of my troops were out of action – dead, wounded, crazed or numbed . . .'

The German defenders, denied reinforcements from the east – where Kluge was convinced the breakout would take place – could put up only token resistance. When Collins decided – against all calculable odds – to commit his tanks to the battle on July 26, they smashed through the facade of enemy defences and took off. Driving southwest from the St Lô to Périers road, the Shermans of the US 2nd and 3rd Armored Divisions finally left the *bocage* and marshlands behind them, and approached Coutances through more open country late the next day.

PATTON IN ACTION

Middleton's corps set out again on July 26, but were halted by well-prepared defences. Then, as Collins' armour raced for Coutances, the Germans melted away, trying to avoid being crushed against the coast. But now Middleton's men ran into deep minefields, so on July 27 Eisenhower authorised Patton to take command – VIII Corps would become part of Patton's Third Army once it went into action in Normandy.

Patton ordered the US 4th Armored Division to ignore the mines and push hard for Coutances. The town fell on July 28, as Collins' tanks came speeding in from the north-east. As they raced through the village of Dangy, they passed a house in which Bayerlein was holding a conference. He fled through the back door.

The Americans had got what they wanted – a mobile war in open country – and Allied morale and determination soared. The pocket around Coutances was closed. The Germans lost more than 100 tanks and 250 other vehicles, although many men managed to escape on foot. On July 30, three bridges over the Sée river at Avranches were taken intact. The gateway to Brittany was open, and the Americans could push for St Malo and the other ports. Said Patton: 'Brad had really pulled a great show, and should get credit for it.'

Middleton's corps poured through the 'Avranches gap' and as one armoured division raced south for Rennes, another forged west along the coast towards St Malo and Brest. Middleton's men drove 65 km (40 miles) on August 1. But Bradley – made overall commander of US 12th Army Group, including the US First and Third Armies on August 1 – began worrying about the significance of the gains. So did Patton. The main German forces were not even in the Brittany peninsula and, although the Allies desperately needed the ports, they would obviously be defended to the last. Patton noted in his diary: 'We are in the biggest battle I have ever fought and it is going fine except at one town [St Malo] we have failed to take . . . I am going there in a minute to kick someone's ass.' However, St Malo did not fall until August 16, and Brest held out until September 18. Both Lorient and St Nazaire were still in German hands when the war ended.

Bradley realised that Patton was in danger of becoming bogged down and on August 3 ordered him to leave a minimum force in Brittany and drive eastwards from Rennes. The new plan was to push through the 'Orléans gap' to the banks of the Seine east of Paris, outflanking German forces slogging it out with the British and Canadians from Caumont to Caen. The Germans would then have little choice but to retreat across the lower Seine or risk being encircled.

'CAUTION OVERBOARD'

The Anglo-Canadian forces were already contributing to this strategy. On July 30, Lt General Sir Miles Dempsey's Second Army had attacked between Caumont and the Anglo-American boundary, about 16 km (10 miles) west, using the 15th Scottish Infantry Division to break open a gap through which tanks could pour southwards towards the town of Vire. As soon as he had

'OLD BLOOD AND GUTS'

One of the war's most flamboyant Allied commanders, George Smith Patton Jr (1885-1945) cultivated his image, practising his 'war face' before a mirror, wearing pearl-handled pistols, and ensuring that his men's exploits won wide publicity. In the process, he alienated other generals – notably Montgomery.

A tank corps staff officer in World War I, he went on to study armoured warfare, training his men to 'catch the enemy by the nose and then kick him in the pants'. He pushed his soldiers hard, believing that 'sweat saves blood'. In World War II, he fought in Tunisia, then led Seventh Army into Sicily. It was there that he slapped shell-shocked soldiers, accusing them of cowardice – an act that almost cost him his career. But 'Old Blood and Guts' was too good a general to ignore, and after D-Day he led the US Third Army brilliantly. After Brittany, he took Paris, then swept across eastern France to Lorraine. In March 1945 he crossed the Rhine, sending his tanks in a breathtaking advance as far as Czechoslovakia. He died after a car crash in Germany in December 1945.

HOUSE TO HOUSE American infantrymen take aim at German sniper positions in St Malo. The Germans defended the Breton ports with skill and astonishing determination.

accepted Bradley's new plan, Montgomery ordered Dempsey 'to throw all caution overboard and . . . step on the gas for Vire'.

But the operation rapidly assumed a familiar pattern. Among the *bocage*, German ambushes were frequent and the advance soon stalled. By August 6, high ground at Mont Pinçon had been seized by the 43rd (Wessex) Infantry Division, but at enormous cost: a battalion of the Wiltshire Regiment was cut from 800 to 60 men in less than two days. The advance was called off.

But now the Allies got some unexpected help from Hitler. Reacting to the American breakout, on August 2 he ordered 'all available panzer units, regardless of their present commitment . . . to be taken from the other parts of the Normandy front . . . and sent into a concerted attack' at Mortain, east of Avranches. His intention was to close the bottleneck, isolating Patton's forces to the south of Avranches from the Normandy beach-heads. Kluge was thunderstruck. Diverting his panzers from defensive tasks elsewhere would put the whole front in jeopardy. But Hitler was adamant, and on the night of August 6/7 the newly created XLVII Panzer Corps – about 100 tanks under General Hans von Funck – struck from Mortain into the American flank.

Bradley, alerted by decoded German signals late on August 6, refused to give way, convinced that the attack was a last desperate gamble by the enemy. American infantry, holding high ground east of Avranches, stood firm and as Funck became more deeply enmeshed in the fighting, Patton seized the chance to strike eastwards. His infantry entered Le Mans on August 8, and over the following three days his tanks liberated Nantes and Angers before advancing towards the Seine through Chartres and Orléans. They encountered little opposition.

'MAD CHARGE'

The Allied commanders saw the potential of their situation, and on August 8 Eisenhower and Bradley devised an encirclement strategy that might not only force the Germans to withdraw but, with luck, could wipe them out. Units of Patton's Third Army – including Maj General Jacques Philippe Leclerc's French 2nd Armoured Division – would turn north from Le Mans towards Argentan, to link up with Anglo-Canadian forces attacking south from Caen and Falaise, creating a huge pocket within which the enemy would be trapped. As Bradley said later: 'It was an opportunity that comes to a commander not more than once in a century.'

Patton diverted Maj General Wade Haislip's XV Corps north from Le Mans. On August 12 the first Americans entered Argentan, with strict orders to go no farther. But an attack southwards from Caen by Lt General Harry Crerar's newly activated Canadian First Army on August 7 failed to link up. It began well enough. Two columns of tanks, with infantry in new armoured personnel carriers called 'Kangaroos', advanced down both sides of the Caen-Falaise road protected by air strikes. But the advance soon stalled as the 4th Canadian and 1st Polish Armoured Divisions stopped to deal with every centre of resistance. By August 9 the attack had ground to a halt, less than halfway to Falaise.

Five days later, the Canadians and Poles tried again, in a 'mad charge' of 250 tanks. A French Canadian tank commander, Sergeant Leo Gariepy, recalled: 'There seemed to be tanks as far as the eye could see and behind them, our "little friends" in their Kangaroos. At precisely 1200 hours [on August 14], the "Mad Charge" began . . . It was a beautiful sunny day and this great column of armour moved through fields of waving grain like eerie avenging centaurs straight from hell . . . Speed, nothing but speed, and on we went, crashing through obstacles at 20 to 25 mph [32-40 km/h].'

It worked. The charge took the Canadians and Poles to the outskirts of Falaise, which fell on August 16. But still a gap of about 25 km (15 miles) lay between the Canadians and Americans. The pocket was not closed. Patton grew angry, threatening to ignore orders and 'drive the British into the sea for another Dunkirk'. But Bradley – in a controversial decision – stopped him, arguing that it would lead to an uncontrolled clash between Allied forces. He preferred 'a solid shoulder at Argentan to a broken neck at Falaise'.

The gap allowed many Germans to escape. By midnight on August 20, when the Falaise pocket was finally snapped shut, about 40 000 men had run a gauntlet of artillery shells and Allied troops and fled eastwards across the Dives river. The Poles and Canadians had linked up with the Americans at Chambois the previous day.

'CONCENTRATED HELL'

But all was not lost – inside the pocket, reduced to about 10 km by 11 km (6 by 7 miles) by the evening of August 19, thousands more Germans were still packed, blocking the narrow lanes with vehicles and under intense artillery and air attack. Squadrons of rocket-firing Typhoons and P-47 Thunderbolts pounded the area. It was 'a case of banging concentrated hell into an area packed with terrified Jerries', said a gunner officer later.

On the receiving end was Sergeant Major Hans Erich Braun of 2nd Panzer Division. For him it was a case of 'forward through hell, but also towards the enemy, past the dead and the wounded', he recalled later. 'We had been tempered, like the steel plating of our tanks . . . We were alive, but inside dead, numbed by watching the horrible scenes which rolled past on both sides . . . Anyone dying on top of those rolling steel coffins was just pitched overboard so that a living man could take his place.

'The never-ending detonations – soldiers waving to us, begging for help – the dead, their faces screwed up still in agony – huddled everywhere in trenches and shelters, the officers and men who had lost their nerve – burning vehicles from which piercing screams could be heard . . . [men] driven crazy, crying, shouting, swearing, laughing hysterically – and the horses, some still harnessed to the shafts . . . screaming terribly, trying to escape the slaughter on the stumps of their hind legs. But also there were civilians . . . still clinging to [their belongings] even in death . . .'

Burning villages, flaming vehicles and blinding gunfire turned night into day in the hellish Falaise pocket. 'It was literally possible to walk for hundreds of yards . . . stepping on nothing but dead and decaying flesh', said Eisenhower, after visiting the area. About 10 000 Germans died there and around 50 000 prisoners were taken. Of 50 German active divisions in June, only ten remained. The Normandy battle was over at last.

US TANKMAN An American tank crewman wears the fibre helmet and zip-up field jacket issued to US armoured vehicle crews. A radio headset dangles around his neck. Insignia on his left sleeve indicate his rank – corporal – and unit – 3rd Armored Division, which served in Patton's Third Army in northern France.

KNOCKING OUT A PANTHER

The village square of St Lambert, north-west Chambois, was dominated by a single German Panther tank on August 14, 1944. It knocked out the leading Sherman of the 14 tanks of Major David Currie's South Alberta Regiment. The next moment, two RAF Typhoons mistakenly hit Currie's command tank with rockets. Wisely, Currie decided to withdraw for the night to the end of the village.

Next morning, a patrol led by Lieutenant G.G. Armour stalked and rushed the Panther. Armour had just climbed on top of it, grenade in hand, when its commander suddenly emerged. They fought hand to hand until an infantryman shot the German. Another crew member who stuck up his head was also shot. Then Armour leapt back aboard – and lobbed a grenade down the open turret hatch. The village square was won.

YOUTH GUNNER A gunner of the 12th SS Panzer Division *Hitler Jugend* ('Hitler Youth') stands in aggressive stance, holding his MP-40 machine pistol. The division, raised in 1943, was drawn from the Hitler Youth movement; the first recruits' average age was 17. It played a key role in keeping open the Falaise pocket until August 20.

On the Riviera

Churchill didn't like it and it was two months late – but Operation 'Dragoon', the invasion of southern France, proved a runaway success.

IN A PEP-TALK to his men before parachuting into the French Riviera, Lt Colonel William P. Yarborough told them: 'Troopers, you have been chosen to spearhead the invasion that may break the Krauts' back. You know . . . where you are going. We are going to hold there 'til hell freezes over or we are all relieved, whichever comes first.'

The objective of the US 509th Parachute Infantry Battalion on that August day in 1944 was the small town of Le Muy, straddling one of the few roads through a high ridge just inland, 40 km (25 miles) west of Cannes. Its capture would open routes to Grenoble and west to Avignon.

The invasion, code-named 'Dragoon', had been planned a year before as 'Anvil' to coincide with the Normandy landings in June. The Americans were enthusiastic, arguing that German forces would be caught between converging attacks. The British, especially Churchill, opposed it vigorously, preferring to advance up Italy towards Germany. Finally he gave in but insisted the new code name (changed for extra security) should show that he had been 'dragooned' into it.

When a shortage of landing ships caused a postponement until after D-Day, the British view looked like prevailing. But the Americans – by now dominating the Western Alliance – insisted. They took three experienced infantry divisions from Italy in June and formed an Anglo-American 1st Provisional Airborne Division – including Yarborough's men – from units in the Mediterranean. Meanwhile, Free French forces under General Jean de Lattre de Tassigny were set to exploit the initial landings.

DOWN THROUGH FOG

Air attacks on German coastal defences, manned by Lt General Friedrich Wiese's under-strength Nineteenth Army, began on August 6. Meanwhile an invasion fleet of 880 ships assembled at Naples. At 4.18 am on August 15, paras began dropping through fog near Le Muy and commandos assaulted Port Cros and Levant islands, covering the left flank of the invasion beaches. The three American infantry divisions, protected by air and naval bombardment, stormed ashore at 8 am on beaches from Cannes to St Tropez. They met little resistance. Aided by local Resistance units, they had linked up with the paras around Le Muy by nightfall.

Now French forces poured through the beaches, heading west for the ports of Toulon and Marseilles. Spurred by the thought of liberating their homeland, they raced ahead, outstripping naval support, and by August 28 both ports were in Allied hands and the Germans were retreating northwards up the Rhône valley.

Lt General Alexander M. Patch, commanding the US Seventh Army, decided to trap them by moving units to their north, around Montélimar. As the US 3rd and 45th Infantry Divisions drove westwards from the beaches, the 36th moved through the mountains towards Grenoble. They took the town of Gap on August 20, and then cut across country towards Montélimar. But they did not have enough strength to close the trap, which was held open by units of 11th Panzer Division. Wiese's Nineteenth Army fled north through the opening towards Lyons.

Simultaneously, the paras pushed eastwards from Le Muy towards the Italian frontier, taking Nice on August 30. Patch then tried a second trap, sending the 36th from Grenoble (liberated on August 24) to cut roads to the east of Lyons. Again he was frustrated. The Germans, joined by troops retreating from south-western France, pulled back to the defendable Belfort Gap – a pass between the Vosges and Jura mountains – early in September.

With Lt General George Patton's Third Army approaching the same area from the Seine, much had been achieved. Southern France had been liberated by mid-September at a cost of some 13 000 Allied casualties. More than 79 000 German prisoners and much of their heavy equipment had been captured. The Allied armies in northern and southern France were about to link up, creating a solid line along the German frontier. Despite Churchill's original misgivings, 'Dragoon' ended as a significant strategic victory.

SWORDSMAN GENERAL

As a World War I cavalry officer, Jean Joseph Marie Gabriel de Lattre de Tassigny (1889-1952) was badly wounded in a mounted sword duel with a German *Uhlan* (lancer) in 1914. A tough and determined professional soldier, he was jailed for ten years in 1942 for speaking against the enlarging of the German-occupied zone of France. The following year he escaped to England.

He was given command of Free French forces in North Africa and headed the First Army in the south of France. In 1944-5 he directed winter operations in Alsace and eventually led his troops into southern Germany and Austria. He later commanded French forces in Indochina and was made a posthumous Marshal of France.

GOALS ACHIEVED **Despite thick dawn fog, gliders found the landing zones around Le Muy and units of paras hurried to link up with the other forces. On August 28, Free French tanks rumbled through newly liberated Avignon (inset).**

Wine, women and bullets as Paris is freed

A German general defied Hitler to save Paris, then the capital went wild as a French general led the Allies in and snipers' bullets danced around de Gaulle.

TERROR AND TRIUMPH Parisians welcoming Allied tanks run for cover as German snipers fire from nearby buildings. (Left) Members of the Communist-led FFI, in a Citroen, join a liberation drive down the crowded Champs Elysées.

IN SINGLE FILE, each man holding onto the man in front, American soldiers inched across the remains of a partially destroyed dam. Beneath them, through the inky blackness of a rain-sodden night, they could hear the river, but no sudden burst of gunfire shattered the night to disrupt their advance. By dawn on August 20, Lt General George S. Patton could announce that he was across the Seine at Mantes-Gassicourt, less than 50 km (30 miles) north-west of Paris.

The city was in a frenzy, anticipating immediate liberation after four years of German occupation. The day before, French police had occupied the Prefecture 'in the name of the Republic', and Communist-led French Forces of the Interior (FFI) had seized public buildings. Even so, the new commander of 'Fortress Paris', Maj General Dietrich von Choltitz, hesitated to carry out Hitler's order to leave the city 'a field of ruins'. As night fell on August 19, he agreed to a ceasefire, hastily arranged by the Swedish Consul, Raoul Nordling. An uneasy calm descended.

General Charles de Gaulle, leader of the Free French, saw the FFI uprising as a Communist bid to seize political power. He called for an immediate Allied drive to the capital. On August 20 he met Eisenhower, who offered no encouragement. The Allied Supreme Commander was wary of committing troops to costly street fighting amid historic buildings. Ike preferred to bypass Paris, forcing the Germans to pull out.

In desperation, de Gaulle ordered Maj General Jacques Philippe Leclerc, commander of the French 2nd Armoured Division, to detach his men from Lt General Omar Bradley's US 12th Army Group and conduct his own, independent advance. Later that same day, a small French force of 17 tanks and ten armoured cars moved quietly out of orchards in Normandy. By then, the FFI's Paris leader, 'Colonel Rol' – real name Henri Tanguy – had given new life to the uprising, issuing a general order '*Aux barricades!*' As more than 400 barricades, built from stones, sandbags, household goods and vehicles, sprang up throughout the city, the streets echoed to the crack of rifle fire and crump of shells.

Realising that a bloodbath might be the result, Eisenhower said resignedly to Bradley: 'Well, what the hell, Brad. I guess we'll have to go in.' Releasing the French 2nd Armoured to follow its unofficial spearhead, he put the US 4th Infantry Division into the race late on August 22.

The advance was by no means easy. It rained incessantly and the Germans put up stiff opposition. But Leclerc's men, eager to liberate the capital and worried that the Germans might destroy vast areas along with the civilian inhabitants, searched tirelessly for a crack in the defences. At last, at 10.30 pm on August 24, Captain Raymond Dronne, leading three Sherman tanks, made the breakthrough. By midnight, surrounded by ecstatic Parisians, he was parked in front of the Hôtel de Ville (town hall).

WAVE OF EMOTION

The next day was one of utter confusion. Some Allied units were simply swept into Paris, according to American Major Frank Burk, on 'a physical wave of human emotion' through 'fifteen solid miles of cheering, deliriously happy people waiting to shake your hand, to kiss you, to shower you with food and wine'. Others found themselves in nasty skirmishes with diehard German troops, holed up in the Palais du Luxembourg, the Quai d'Orsay and other treasured historic sites.

As Hitler kept up the frenzied demand 'Is Paris burning?', French troops were closing in on the German headquarters in the Hôtel Meurice. At 2.30 pm on August 25, Choltitz surrendered. Although scattered fighting was to continue for another 24 hours, Paris threw itself into a celebration orgy, ably exploited by de Gaulle. On August 26, he led a victory march through cheering crowds down the Champs Elysées to Notre Dame cathedral, unflinching as occasional bullets whined past him, fired by German snipers. By his personal intervention in the liberation of Paris, he ensured that the Communists were denied power.

By then, more than 20 000 German troops had been captured, and as other German survivors of 'Fortress Paris' pulled back, the Allies consolidated crossings of the Seine. The route seemed clear all the way to the German frontier.

WARRIOR PATRIOT

In May 1940, French infantry Captain Jacques Philippe de Hautecloque (1902-47) was ordered to surrender to the advancing Germans. Instead he deserted and joined those still fighting. Wounded and captured, he escaped and, taking the name Leclerc to protect his family, joined de Gaulle in England.

Sent to French Equatorial Africa, Leclerc raised a force of Free French. He worked with the British Long Range Desert Group, and in February 1941 led an epic 900 km (570 mile) march to take Kufra, a vital group of five oases in the central Libyan desert. His force joined Montgomery's Eighth Army in Tunisia. Fittingly, this great French patriot – now a major general – received the formal surrender of Paris in August 1944. He died in an air crash and was posthumously created a Marshal of France.

20: ROUGH ROAD TO THE RHINE

After ten weeks of bitter fighting in the hedgerows of Normandy, the German armies on the Western Front were broken and the end of the war seemed in sight. But now a quarrel broke out among the Allied commanders about how best to achieve complete and swift victory.

PARIS WAS FREE, the Seine had been crossed and the approaches to Germany seemed clear. There was, in Winston Churchill's words, 'a feeling of elation, of expectancy and almost bewilderment'; the war would soon be over.

General Eisenhower had good reason to feel optimistic as, on September 1, 1944, he took over direct command of the Allied armies in Western Europe. On the left, advancing parallel to the coast, was the Anglo-Canadian 21st Army Group, led by Sir Bernard Montgomery, newly promoted to field marshal and fizzing with confidence. His spearhead tank units were racing through Belgium: Brussels was to be liberated by the Guards Armoured Division on September 4, and the desperately needed port of Antwerp captured by the 11th Armoured Division the following day, its docks in working order.

To Monty's right, lead units of the US First Army, under Lt General Courtney H. Hodges, were already across the Seine. They were poised to enter Germany itself in the wooded and hilly Ardennes – the very region used by the panzers, coming the other way, to deliver their killer blow in the blitzkrieg that had led to the fall of France in 1940. To the south of the First Army, the swashbuckling Lt General George S. Patton and the tanks of the US Third Army were approaching the fortress city of Metz, gateway to the province of Lorraine. The two US armies formed Lt General Omar Bradley's 12th Army Group.

Heading north along the Rhône valley was Lt General Jacob M. Devers' 6th Army Group; by mid-September he would have linked up with Patton and turned east to face the forbidding Vosges mountains, completing an Allied line running unbroken from the Channel to the Swiss frontier. Even the German Commander in Chief, Field Marshal Gerd von Rundstedt – though not Hitler – was resigned to defeat in the west.

SUPPLY PROBLEMS

But Allied momentum was already slowing down. The rapid advance from Normandy had placed enormous strain on the movement of supplies, nearly all of which were still having to be brought ashore across the invasion beaches. Many of the Channel ports – Le Havre, Dieppe, Calais and Dunkirk – were too small to cater for the supply needs of 47 Allied divisions – around 2 million men – or were still in enemy hands. Even Antwerp, lying 90 km (56 miles) inland from the North Sea, could not be used so long as the Germans held on to the Scheldt estuary, covering its seaward approaches.

By early September, the supply line from the Normandy beaches had been stretched to over 480 km (300 miles) and, despite valiant efforts to move petrol, food, ammunition and spare parts forward by road along the 'Red Ball Express', both Hodges and Patton were running out of fuel. Some enemy stockpiles were captured, and Patton's men, if they had to, were prepared to 'liberate' supplies destined for other Allied armies. But vehicles soon ground to a halt, leaving American units far short of their next major objective – the Rhine.

Montgomery's 21st Army Group, moving on the 'inside track' along shorter lines of communication, was marginally better off. But by the middle of the month even it was feeling the pinch, particularly when all 1400 British lorries had to be withdrawn simultaneously with gearbox failure – wrong parts had been fitted.

Other problems loomed, including the weather. As autumn and winter approached, roads would soon turn from dust to mud – conditions which would be made worse by the constant movement of heavy tracked vehicles. This would affect the Germans as much as the Allies, but they had less need to maintain mobility as they fell back towards the static defences of the *Westwall*, or 'Siegfried Line' on the borders of the Reich. In addition, as the Allied advance slowed, the Germans began to recover. They transferred units from other fronts to face the threat from the west, increased tank production and created fresh divisions – the *Volksgrenadiers* – from unwanted U-boat and Luftwaffe crews.

By mid-September, despite the losses in Normandy, sufficient forces had been found to plug the gap. To the German commanders, it was known as 'the Miracle of the West'.

THE COMMANDERS CLASH

Against this background, the last thing the Allies needed was a bitter dispute between their leaders about strategy – but that was exactly what they got. Montgomery thought he saw a chance to end the war quickly: a swift strike into the industrial heartland of the Ruhr would destroy the enemy's fighting capability. This decisive blow would require up to 40 divisions. The British and Canadian troops would need reinforcements from the US First Army and would have first call on all available supplies.

As this would force Patton to halt his advance, neither he nor his fellow Americans gave the plan any support. They preferred a 'broad front' strategy of advancing in unison, at least as far as the Rhine. Eisenhower, at first unsympathetic, finally came round to Montgomery's view and on September 10 ordered him to prepare his assault. Patton was furious. 'To hell with Monty,' he exploded in his diary. 'I must get so involved in my own operations that they can't stop me.'

Whether Patton liked it or not, Montgomery was determined to go ahead. But his plan had a built-in risk: it depended on the Allies seizing a number of vital river and canal crossings . . . including a bridge over the Rhine at a Dutch town called Arnhem.

THE RED BALL EXPRESS

The decision to advance beyond the Seine in late August 1944 brought Allied planners a logistic nightmare. With the French railway system wrecked and transport aircraft unable to deliver more than a trickle of supplies, the only way to maintain the spearhead units in their pursuit of the enemy was by road. Between August 25 and September 6, over 6000 trucks were used to deliver 81 614 tonnes of supplies in the US sector alone.

Dubbed the 'Red Ball Express' from a US railroad term for fast freight, the trucks picked up supplies at St Lô, close to the Normandy beaches, before travelling on a one-way loop highway to Chartres (for First Army) or Dreux (for Third Army) and back again.

The drivers competed to see who could finish the journey in the shortest time, ignoring all rules of the road; as one British soldier put it, the only way to escape oncoming US trucks was to 'not only get off the road but climb a tree'. But the price was high. Not only did the trucks use 1 137 000 litres (250 000 gallons) of petrol a day just to keep moving, but the wear and tear on men and vehicles was considerable. By early September, despite the efforts of the Red Ball drivers, both American armies had run short of essential supplies.

FRONT RUNNER Trucks raced day and night for 81 days around the 1120 km (700 mile) circuit. The drivers, mainly black privates in the US Transport Corps, had to push the vehicles beyond their limits. Mechanics worked around the clock.

Disaster at Arnhem

Operation 'Market Garden' was perhaps the boldest Allied failure of the war. It might easily have shortened the fighting by months, but instead Arnhem is remembered as a tragedy. It was the site of the 'bridge too far' that stretched Allied capabilities to breaking point.

MAJOR 'BOY' WILSON, commander of the 21st Independent Parachute Company, floated down onto a calm and seemingly empty panorama of patchwork fields and isolated houses. 'Everything looked so peaceful. Not a sign of fighting or war. Not a glimpse of the enemy.' The time was 1.15 pm on Sunday, September 17, 1944; the place, west of the Dutch town of Arnhem. Operation 'Market Garden' was under way. As Wilson's men hurriedly laid out landing markers in time for the main body of paratroop transports and over 300 gliders that were soon to follow, it was obvious that the German forces stationed in the area had been taken by surprise.

This had its drawbacks. As soon as word of the landing spread, enthusiastic Dutch civilians milled onto the landing zones, many of them in their best Sunday clothes and clutching bottles of wine for their 'liberators'; their arrival delayed the next British move. Major Freddie Gough's 1st Parachute Reconnaissance Squadron should have been on the move immediately, rushing to seize vital bridges across the Neder Rijn (Lower Rhine) river in Arnhem town. But by the time the men had sorted themselves out – and realised that most of their precious jeeps had failed to arrive – vital time had been lost.

It was only the first of a catalogue of errors and misfortunes that turned a brilliant, potentially war-winning plan into a disaster.

HITLER'S BACK DOOR

Field Marshal Sir Bernard Montgomery, whose idea it was to mount 'Market Garden', was a commander renowned for his caution, but in late summer 1944 he came up with a breathtakingly bold and simple idea. His forces would bypass Hitler's defensive Siegfried Line and assault Germany by the 'back door', through the Netherlands. Airborne troops, in the largest operation of its kind ever mounted, were to seize the main bridges crossing the southern Dutch waterways. Then a corridor 100 km (60 miles) long would be established from the bridges back to the advanced units of Montgomery's 21st Army Group in northern Belgium. These could then advance swiftly through the corridor, into the industrial

BACK DOOR TO BERLIN The plan was simple: do not tackle the Siegfried Line but skirt its northern end, then aim for Berlin. Only a narrow corridor was needed but it had to include the bridges at Eindhoven, Nijmegen and Arnhem. The first two were won, but at Arnhem the paras were trapped.

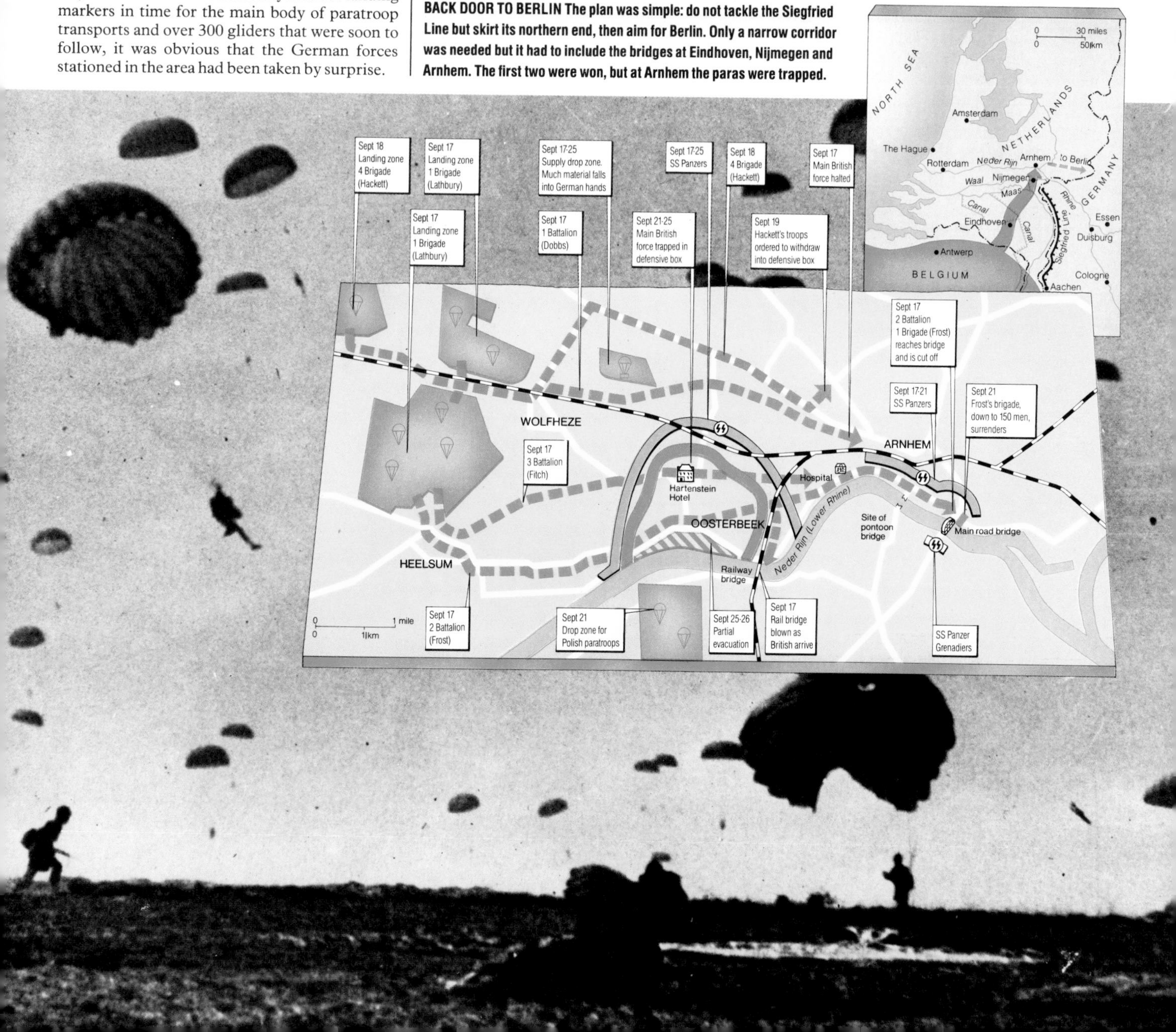

GUARDING THE APPROACH **Crouching among the trees, men of Major Gough's 1st Parachute Reconnaissance Squadron cover the route from Wolfheze towards Arnhem. Trained on the railway crossing is a Piat anti-tank gun weighing 15.7 kg (34 lb) with a range of 105 m (350 ft). This substantial weapon was a mixed blessing since most of the squadron's jeeps failed to arrive and the men had to go on foot the 13 km (8 miles) to Arnhem.**

SUPPLY DROP

BBC war correspondent Stanley Maxted, a Canadian, recorded an eye-witness account of a supply drop at Arnhem on September 20, 1944:

“Just a few minutes ago the fighter cover showed up and right behind them came those lovely supply planes which you can hear up above us now. Yesterday and this morning our supplies came and were dropped in the wrong place. The enemy got them, but now these planes have come over and they've dropped them right dead over us.

Everybody is cheering and clapping, and they just can't give vent to their feelings . . . All those bundles and parachuted packages and ammunition are coming down here all around us, through the trees, bouncing on the ground. The men are running out to get them, and you have no idea what this means to us to see this ammunition and this food coming down where the men can get it. They're such fighters, if they can get the stuff to fight with.”

Ruhr and on to Berlin. With one bold stroke the war might be over by Christmas.

Two US airborne divisions – the 101st and the 82nd – were assigned to capture the bridges across the Wilhelmina Canal north of Eindhoven, the Maas and Waal rivers at Grave and Nijmegen, and the Maas-Waal Canal lying between them. The British 1st Airborne Division, commanded by Maj General Robert Urquhart, was to capture the three most northerly bridges – road, rail and pontoon – at Arnhem.

As soon as these were all in Allied hands, XXX Corps – part of Lt General Sir Miles Dempsey's British Second Army – would advance northwards from the Belgian border to link the landing zones used by the airborne divisions.

CATALOGUE OF FLAWS

Urquhart was told of the operation on September 10 and given just six days to prepare. Problems arose straight away. There were not enough transport aircraft to put all Urquhart's men – nearly 10 000 of them – on the ground at the same time; three separate ‘lifts’ would have to be organised, all on different days. As a result his forces could not be concentrated for maximum effectiveness – a crucial defect.

In addition, the RAF thought – mistakenly – that Arnhem was heavily defended by anti-

At the bridge

Rumbling and growling onto the Arnhem road bridge come 22 German vehicles – half-tracks, armoured cars and lorries of infantrymen making what speed they can among the smoking wrecks of their earlier attempts. It is about 9.30 am on Monday, September 18. Frost's 500 men must face the onslaught alone again. Their own venture onto the bridge in the night was swiftly repelled by Captain Paul Grabner's column of tanks from the 9th Panzer Division. Despite intelligence warnings that the panzers were near Arnhem refitting after the pounding they took in Normandy, the push for the bridge at Arnhem went ahead.

Frost's group cannot contact the rest of the division as their radios fail. They expect to hold on until help comes, but before Tuesday dawns, they will be low on ammunition, food and medical supplies for the many wounded.

Seventy-two savage hours from now, only about 50 men will be fit enough to try to escape; most of them, like Frost, will be captured.

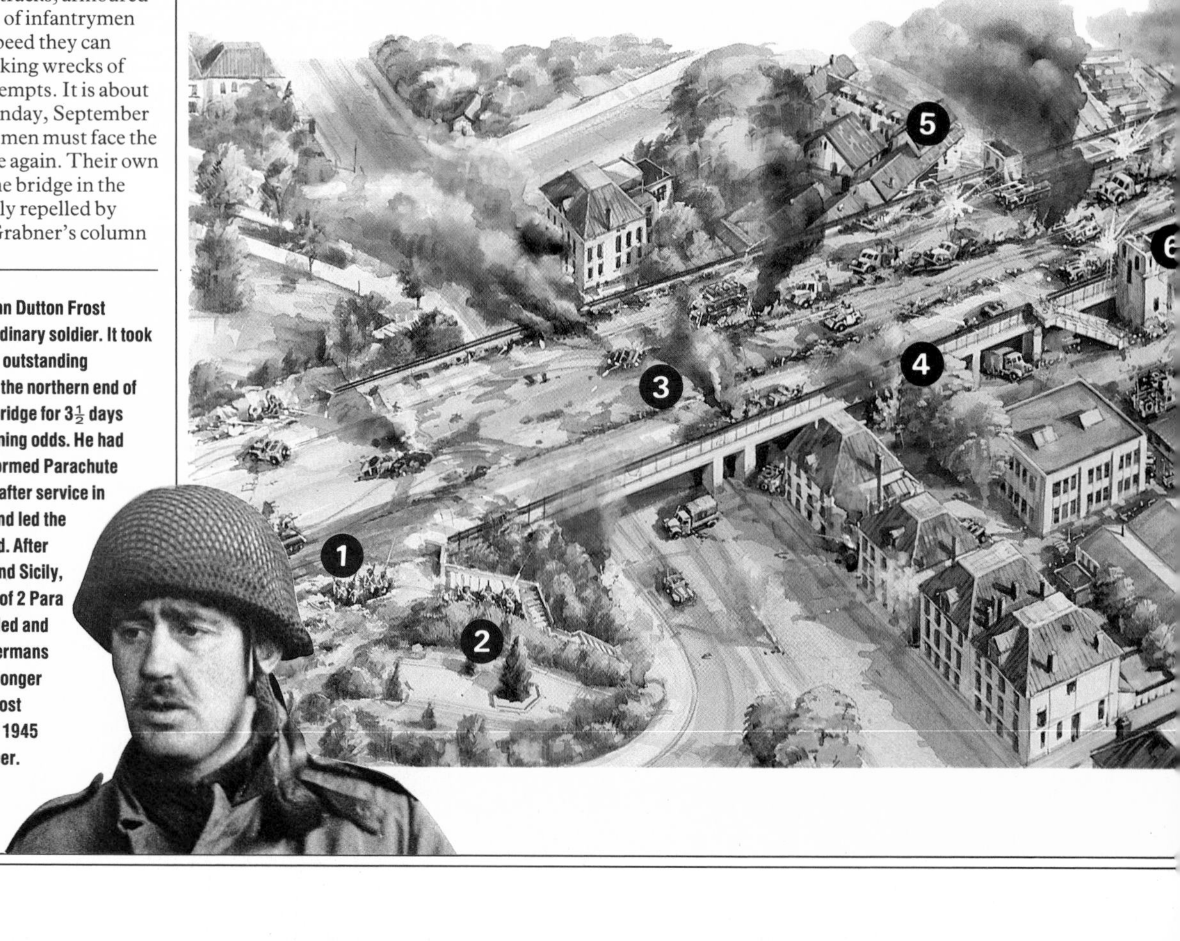

BRIDGE HERO **John Dutton Frost (1912-) was no ordinary soldier. It took sheer bravery and outstanding leadership to hold the northern end of the Arnhem road bridge for $3\frac{1}{2}$ days against overwhelming odds. He had joined the newly formed Parachute Regiment in 1941 after service in Britain and Iraq, and led the 1942 Bruneval raid. After action in Tunisia and Sicily, he took command of 2 Para at Arnhem. Wounded and captured by the Germans when he could no longer hold the bridge, Frost was repatriated in 1945 to resume his career.**

aircraft guns, so it was reluctant to fly close to the town. It persuaded Urquhart to agree to landing zones well to the west, so that the airborne troops would have to march 13 km (8 miles) before reaching the three bridges across the Neder Rijn. That was the second big flaw.

It was vital to capture the bridges quickly, but the small force being landed on the first day could be sure of success only if the town was not strongly defended. Early in September, however, General Willi Bittrich's II SS Panzer Corps, of two armoured divisions, had moved into the area to regroup following their retreat across France. The Allies knew of this from decoded German signals, and the Dutch Resistance confirmed it. They also knew that the commander of the German Army Group B, Field Marshal Walther Model, had his headquarters in the Hartenstein Hotel at Oosterbeek, on Arnhem's outskirts. But the intelligence was all ignored.

By September 16, the plan had been finalised. In the first lift, paratroops and glider-borne forces were to land to the north of Heelsum during the early afternoon of the following day. One brigade, under Brigadier Philip Hicks, was to hold the landing zones, while Brigadier Gerald Lathbury's three battalions of paras struck east on three separate routes to seize the Arnhem bridges.

Twenty-four hours later, Brigadier John Hackett's 4th Airborne Brigade would land nearby and push towards Arnhem's northern outskirts, to block the approaches from that direction. Finally, Maj General Stanislaw Sosabowski's 1st Polish Parachute Brigade were to land south of the river to act as a link with XXX Corps driving up the land corridor. The whole operation was to take two or three days at most.

SLOW GETAWAY

The delays at the first landing zone meant that it was 2.45 pm on the 17th before Lathbury managed to dispatch the first of his battalions, and gradually others followed. The 2nd Parachute Battalion, commanded by Lt Colonel John Frost, had the key task, following a southerly route to the east of Heelsum along the river towards the bridge sites. They were slowed down first by welcoming Dutch civilians and then by German snipers in houses along the route. By 4 pm, as the battalion reached Oosterbeek, the snipers brought them to a complete standstill. They were unsure what to do next.

Frost split his force, sending C Company to seize the railway bridge and A Company, shielded by B Company, to race for the main road bridge; the Germans had already blown up the nearby pontoon. As C Company reached the railway bridge a German machine gun opened fire from

URQUHART – A GENERAL DOOMED TO FAIL

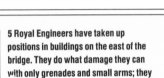

The man most surprised by the decision to appoint Robert Elliot Urquhart (1901-88) to command the British 1st Airborne Division in 1944 was undoubtedly 'Roy' Urquhart himself, since he had no experience of airborne warfare. But Urquhart was chosen as a man 'hot from battle' in southern Italy.

Urquhart was unlucky to be pinned down for nearly 36 hours in an attic at Arnhem, out of contact with his division and unable to coordinate their operations. Despite Arnhem, he held senior army posts until 1955.

1 Frost's men are ready to lob grenades and blanket the road with fire from anti-tank guns, machine guns and rifles.

2 Trenches and pits cut in the embankment protect more of Frost's paratroops.

3 The leading German vehicles reach the ramp road at the northern end of the bridge before the hail of fire stops them.

4 Two German half-tracks swerve as mines explode on the bridge. They crash through the parapet in flames.

5 Royal Engineers have taken up positions in buildings on the east of the bridge. They do what damage they can with only grenades and small arms; they have no anti-tank guns.

6 Paratroops venture out from cover onto the bridge parapet to get better shots at the Germans.

7 Firing from paratroops in the buildings on the west side of the ramp road brings return fire from Germans crossing the bridge.

8 Wrecked vehicles from earlier forays make an obstacle course for the Germans, who have to swerve around them, slowing down their dash across the bridge.

9 Already, on the second morning, wounded are beginning to fill the buildings that are at a safer distance from the bridge.

NEARING THE TARGET Explosions echo back and forth, and Arnhem's shops and the apartments above crumble as shells smash them open. Crashing masonry, billowing dust and the shimmering heat from blazing buildings screen enemy snipers who flit from one vantage point to another as the British troops try to force their way to the bridge.

the south bank of the river. Obscured by a smoke screen, the leading platoon started to cross the bridge, but then there was an enormous explosion and the section in front of them collapsed into the river. Meanwhile, members of B Company became involved in vicious street fighting with German defenders. Only A Company, accompanied by Frost and some sappers, made any progress, advancing along unfamiliar streets towards the road bridge.

They sighted it at 8 pm, looming above them in the gathering gloom of an autumn evening, hours later than planned. Moving cautiously, they occupied buildings overlooking the northern approaches. German machine-gun fire prevented them going any farther, so they dug in, waiting for reinforcements.

But these never arrived. The rest of Lathbury's brigade had already run into strong opposition from panzers, which had moved into Arnhem as soon as the battle began. When Urquhart and Lathbury in their command jeep drove forward to investigate the holdup, they suddenly found themselves cut off in confused fighting and narrowly escaped capture by hiding in one of the houses.

With a German tank crew sitting just below their window they were forced to stay in the attic for nearly 36 hours, isolated from their command staff at the Hartenstein Hotel. (Model had hurriedly vacated his headquarters there as soon as he heard of the British landings – which he at first thought were aimed at kidnapping him.)

A SHAMBLES

Hicks now took command, ordering two companies of glider-borne troops to leave the landing zone near Wolfheze, due to be used by Hackett's brigade the next day, September 18. German troops, who already knew the British plan from documents found in a crashed glider, crept into the landing zone; as Hackett's men arrived, they opened fire. Aircraft were shot down and soldiers picked off as they dangled helplessly beneath their parachutes. To cap it all, heather covering the zone caught fire, filling the area with smoke. It was, as one of the paras commented, 'a bit of a shambles'.

Hackett was furious. After a blazing row with Hicks, he gathered his men together and headed towards his objectives to the north of Arnhem. On the way, he too ran into strong panzer opposition. By the end of the second day, no one seemed to be making much progress.

This was particularly worrying for Frost, completely isolated at the Arnhem road bridge and still awaiting reinforcements to enable him to capture it. Although a few more men had managed to join him, increasing his force to about 500, he had faced 24 hours of increasingly bitter fighting. Two attempts by his men to capture the southern end of the bridge had been beaten back by the panzers. At the same time, German troops trying to reach the northern end of the bridge on foot and by lorry had been repulsed and their vehicles set on fire.

But by mid-morning on the 18th, as Bittrich took proper control of his forces (Model played little part), more organised assaults using armoured cars and half-tracks had taken the place of the early, poorly coordinated German attacks. Cannon and machine-gun fire raked Frost's positions, while tanks and self-propelled guns shelled them from the south bank. The paras hung on, firing on the Germans from the ruins of shattered buildings, but with each passing hour their stocks of food, water and ammunition diminished while German strength increased. Frost's men desperately needed reinforcement and relief.

Urquhart finally reappeared at the Hartenstein early on September 19. By then there was little he could do to regain control of a chaotic battle, now spread out in and around Arnhem. Coordination between his scattered units was poor – trees and tall buildings disrupted radio communications – and high winds, cloud and rain limited air support, so that the division seemed to be fighting in a vacuum.

Indeed, a breakdown in ground-to-air contact had already resulted in wasted resupply drops; the Dakota pilots of RAF Transport Command had braved intense anti-aircraft fire to deposit supply canisters on preselected drop zones which were still in enemy hands. The only piece of good news was that XXX Corps had linked up with US airborne units at Nijmegen, only 16 km (10 miles) from Arnhem.

STRANDED AT THE BRIDGE

With all this in mind, Urquhart decided to draw in his units to create a defensive perimeter around the Hartenstein Hotel, which was about 5 km (3 miles) west of the Arnhem bridge. As a preliminary, he ordered Hackett to withdraw and turn south, into the town itself.

It was a disastrous move; as one para remarked, 'You can't just get up and rush away from the enemy in daylight . . . You just can't bloody well do it.' As the paras pulled back, the Germans stayed on their heels, pouring artillery and mortar fire onto Hackett's men as they struggled to cross the railway line at Wolfheze. By nightfall, the brigade had virtually ceased to exist, with isolated groups of men fighting for their lives against overwhelming German forces. Hackett himself was taken prisoner, severely injured; after surgery in a field hospital, he was eventually to escape with the South African doctor who saved his life, helped by Dutch Resistance workers.

The collapse of the protective forces on his northern flank left Frost in a hopeless situation at the bridge, without any chance of relief or support. While his men repelled repeated infantry assaults throughout September 20, German Tiger tanks were now able to fire on their positions at will, destroying the buildings they occupied. 'Wherever you looked you could see daylight,' one of the men recalled. 'Splattered everywhere was blood; it lay in pools in the rooms, it covered the smocks of the defenders and ran in small rivulets down the stairs . . . The only clean things were the weapons.'

The situation could not last. By dawn on the 21st, there were only about 150 defenders left,

FIGHTING AT THE BRIDGE

Private James Sims of 2nd Battalion, The Parachute Regiment, described the situation at Arnhem road bridge on September 19, 1944:

"The Germans withdrew a short distance and began to mortar and shell our positions systematically . . . The very air seemed to wail and sigh with the number of projectiles passing through it. The enemy had also brought up some self-propelled artillery, heavy stuff, and against this we were virtually helpless. One by one the houses held by the paratroopers were set alight. There was nothing to fight the fires with, even if we had been able to. The airborne soldiers kept on firing from the blazing buildings even with the roof fallen in; then they moved to the second floor, then to the first, and finally to the basement. Only when this was alight did they evacuate the building and take over another. As each hour passed we were driven into a smaller and smaller area. Casualties began to mount rapidly. Our food and water were practically gone, but worst of all the ammunition was running short . . ."

SOUTH TO SAFETY Oosterbeek, where the British withdrew into a defensive horseshoe, was pounded by the Germans for four days before the British were forced to retreat on September 25. Only 2163 made it through the littered alleys and shells of houses to safety south of the river.

AMERICANS DROP IN

While Urquhart's men struggled for the bridges at Arnhem, two US airborne divisions – the 82nd and 101st – fought farther south, opening the way for the ground thrust.

Maj General Maxwell Taylor's 101st Airborne – the 'Screaming Eagles' – had the task of capturing bridges across the Wilhelmina Canal at Zon and the town of Eindhoven. The landing on September 17 was flawless, but the Germans blew up the Zon bridge before they could seize it. Nevertheless, the 101st had liberated Eindhoven when the British XXX Corps, together with Canadian engineers, arrived at 7 pm on September 18.

This enabled the British and Canadians to race north through Zon and Veghel, searching for contact with Brig General James M. Gavin's 82nd Airborne Division – the 'All Americans'. These had been ordered to seize the Groesbeek ridge east of the main road, as well as bridges across the Maas at Grave, the Waal at Nijmegen and the Maas-Waal Canal in between.

At first all went well; they had captured intact the Grave bridge and one of the four across the canal by dusk on the 17th, but the advance into Nijmegen was blocked. It was not until just after 7 pm on the 20th – by which time XXX Corps had linked up – that they captured the Nijmegen bridge. By then, the Germans had effectively blocked the road north to Arnhem, and it took another two days to break through.

END OF AN EPIC Exhausted survivors of the ten-day bid to take the bridge at Arnhem are rounded up at gunpoint by the Germans. They trudge over the cobbles to imprisonment after a grim defence, often under heavy fire and finally trapped with little food and less sleep in sodden foxholes. It is a tragic reversal of their fêted arrival as liberators. Now 1200 of their colleagues are dead, killed in the fighting or drowned as they tried to escape.

most of the buildings had been reduced to rubble and the stocks of ammunition had just about run out. Three Bren-gun carriers had tried to break through to them with supplies and ammunition, but two had been destroyed and the other forced to turn back. Reports of XXX Corps' arrival at Nijmegen offered a faint chance of relief, but this soon disappeared when 10th SS Panzer Division, occupying strong positions around Elst, to the south of the river, prevented further progress. At 9 am on September 21, Frost surrendered.

CRUMBLING PERIMETER

This was not an ideal moment for the Polish paratroops to arrive. Delayed by fog on the airfields of England, they landed to the south of the Neder Rijn at 5.15 pm on September 21, too late to affect the battle at the bridge. Even if they had arrived earlier, they had no way of crossing the river until lead units of XXX Corps reached them with amphibious vehicles. They tried to cross into the perimeter still held by Urquhart's men on the night of September 24/25, but this ended in disaster.

By then, the British defensive position around the Hartenstein Hotel had been under attack for nearly four days and the perimeter had begun to crumble as Urquhart's men, denied proper food or sleep since September 17, gradually weakened. Summoning up reserves of courage, they hung on – 'fed up but flipping stubborn' according to one of the men – but Montgomery had to face the fact that the Arnhem attack had failed. On September 25, he authorised Urquhart to withdraw south of the river.

That night, as Canadian and British engineers worked feverishly to provide the necessary boats, the Hartenstein Hotel was abandoned. The nightmare was still not over; the Germans, aware of what was happening, bombarded likely crossing points with heavy artillery and machine-gun fire, destroying boats and inflicting yet more casualties. To add to the discomfort, it rained incessantly. By September 27, a full ten days after the initial drop, only 2163 out of the original force of nearly 10 000 had made it to safety; with 1200 dead and 6642 captured, wounded or missing, 1st Airborne Division had been effectively wiped out. It was the end of an epic yet fruitless battle.

WHAT IF ARNHEM HAD SUCCEEDED?

'Market Garden' was a gamble; if it worked it would have shortened the war in Europe. With the Dutch bridges in Allied hands, the way would be open to the North German Plain. The British Second Army could have outflanked the Siegfried Line – which ended at Kleve, some 40 km (25 miles) south of Arnhem – and crossed into Germany, only 30 km (20 miles) away.

Montgomery could have thrust north-east towards the Ruhr before the winter. And, if that region had fallen, the soldiers' cry of 'end the war in '44' might have become a reality. A route would have been cleared to Berlin, which could have fallen to the Western Allies rather than the Soviets. However, Montgomery was expecting too much of his troops; Arnhem was, indeed, 'a bridge too far'.

Autumn of attrition

After the painful reverse of Arnhem, seven Allied armies pressed on towards Germany in incessant rain. But Arnhem had provided a foretaste of the bitter struggles to come as the Germans fought for every metre of ground with their backs to the Rhine. The Fatherland itself was under threat.

AUTUMN 1944 was one of the wettest and most miserable on record in north-western Europe. There was misery too for the soldiers who during the bitter and bloody summer months had fought their way from the beaches of Normandy. Their hopes for a quick end to the war were vanishing in the smoke and murderous confusion of Arnhem. Montgomery's bold strategy of seizing a string of vital bridges to cross the Rhine and strike at the Ruhr, the industrial heart of Germany, was clearly not going to work. The Allies needed an alternative plan, and at his new headquarters in Versailles the Supreme Commander Eisenhower eagerly fell back on the original 'broad front' strategy favoured by the American generals. This meant that the Allies would attack in four areas.

Antwerp, one of Europe's greatest ports, had been liberated on September 4, but it lies inland and could not be opened to supply convoys while the Scheldt estuary remained in enemy hands. The job of clearing it fell to the British and Canadians of Montgomery's 21st Army Group. Once they succeeded, the Allies would have a solid base for future attacks on the Ruhr. To Montgomery's south, Lt General Omar Bradley's 12th Army Group was allotted two objectives: the US First Army was to clear up the area around Aachen and the US Third Army, led by Lt General George Patton, was to advance towards the Saarland industrial region, and then towards the Rhine. Still farther south, 6th Army Group under Lt General Jacob Devers would penetrate the Vosges mountains, aiming to take Strasbourg.

But the Allied advances when they began were severely hampered by the weather. Rain fell in endless torrents and turned the ground to glutinous mud. At the same time, German defences hardened and, as Allied troops forced their way towards (or in some cases across) the frontiers of the Reich, they encountered a combination of natural and man-made obstacles.

Open farmland easily crossed by tanks gave way to dark impenetrable forests and high commanding hills. German defences were strong and the German soldier, fighting for his Fatherland, was a disciplined and formidable opponent. Allied casualties mounted, not just from enemy action but also increasingly from trench foot, influenza and physical exhaustion. The heady advances of late August gave way to a hard slog.

SECURING ANTWERP

In the north, the first priority for Montgomery, still smarting from the debacle at Arnhem, was the Scheldt estuary, defended by remnants of the German Fifteenth Army. These occupied flooded positions on the islands of Walcheren and South Beveland to the north of the estuary and an area around Breskens to the south.

Units of Lt General Harold Crerar's First Canadian Army were given responsibility for clearing the area, and they found the going hard. They had occupied the 'Breskens Pocket' by October 21, but South Beveland and Walcheren proved much tougher. On October 31, Allied commandos (including French and Dutch as well as British troops), backed by guns of the Royal Navy, landed on Walcheren from the sea. But not until November 8 did they capture the coastal batteries there, with amphibious craft taking commandos into the centre of the town of Middelburg to root out the last pockets of enemy resistance. The first Allied convoy reached Antwerp on November 28.

Meanwhile, Lt General Sir Miles Dempsey's Second Army, working in close cooperation with American units, had faced fierce opposition in the low-lying Peel Marshes to the north of Maastricht; it did not fully occupy the area until December 3. By then, the rain had turned to snow. Montgomery was forced to halt further operations until the spring.

FOREST NIGHTMARE

Aachen, where Charlemagne had been crowned Holy Roman Emperor in AD 800, would be the first German city to fall into Allied hands – once, that is, Lt General Courtney Hodges' First Army had captured it. The attack began on October 2 in poor weather. Only on the 21st, after bitter house-to-house fighting had left it in ruins, did the last defenders surrender the ancient city.

Hodges' men now advanced north-eastwards up the 'Stolberg Corridor', a narrow strip of open country with industrial suburbs on their left and the nightmare of the Hürtgen Forest on their right (see box, *In the witches' lair*). They made little headway. The static defences of the Siegfried Line were the backbone of an elaborate defensive system, based on villages, farmhouses and woods.

Exhausted GIs, trudging through knee-deep mud in seemingly ceaseless rain, encountered the very best Germany could throw at them – diehard SS men manning cleverly protected machine guns, mortars and artillery ranged on key road junctions, and formidably armed Tiger tanks positioned to make best use of the terrain. One

WATERY PROGRESS British troops clamber across flooded fields around Nijmegen. In Aachen, German artillerymen rush to their positions to fight off US soldiers under General Hodges. The advancing Allies met toughened German resistance in late 1944. Villages and towns had been fortified against them with daunting arrays of anti-tank ditches, minefields and blockhouses. Rivers and dykes had been flooded to try to force the Allies to stick to roads swept by German artillery, mortar and machine-gun fire.

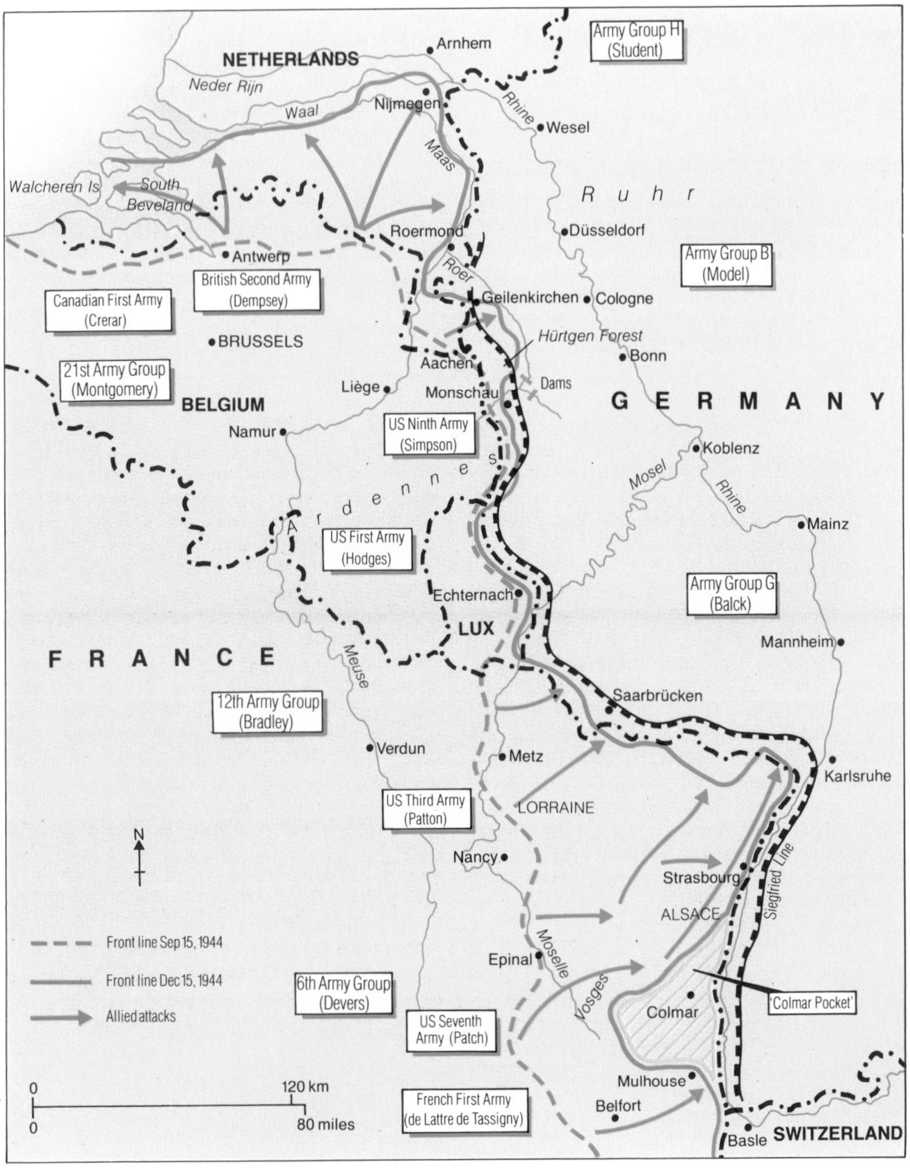

BROAD FRONT Montgomery's plans for a 'single thrust' through the Low Countries into Germany were abandoned in autumn 1944 in favour of an advance on a 'broad front', stretching from the North Sea to the Swiss frontier.

IN THE WITCHES' LAIR

An eerie, haunting region fit for a witches' lair' – that was the description given by one American historian to the dark evergreens of the Hürtgen Forest in 1944. The forest, covering some 80 km^2 (31 sq miles) to the south-east of Aachen, was packed with mines, barbed wire and pillboxes.

Between September and December 1944, four US infantry divisions were sent into the forest. All suffered appalling casualties. In late September, men of the 9th Division, later reinforced by the 28th, tried to seize the crossroads at Schmidt, in the south-east. By November 4, the two divisions had suffered nearly 10 000 casualties and their progress could be measured in metres.

A second attack took place on November 16, using the 4th and 8th Divisions, with armoured support. Despite vicious weather, they reached the forest's north-eastern fringes by December 1, but their casualties were also high: over 8000 men killed, wounded or missing, plus 4000 evacuated with trench foot or exhaustion.

answer might have been Allied air power, but the weather kept aircraft grounded for long periods. Even when the skies cleared and vast armadas of bombers were used, the bombs merely churned the ground to even deeper mud.

In late September a third US army – Lt General William H. Simpson's Ninth – was thrown into the fray. It was initially sent to the Ardennes, south of Hodges, but on October 9 Simpson – 'tall, lean, egg-bald, restrained and modest' – assumed responsibility for the area from Aachen north to Roermond. In November, he committed his untried units against a dangerous enemy salient projecting westwards around the German border town of Geilenkirchen.

They succeeded in pinching out the salient, but the fighting was hard. Few buildings remained intact by the time they entered Geilenkirchen itself. 'Holes had been punched in roofs and walls for firing ports', recalled the men of Rifle Company K in an after-the-battle report. 'By knocking holes between cellar walls, the defenders had created block-long tunnels to connect strongpoints. Household goods – clothing, books, cookware, furniture, children's toys – spilled through gaps in the walls. Alleyways and streets were blocked with jumbled piles of bricks, roof tiles, charred beams, electric cable and telephone wires. Mud churned up by bombs and artillery seemed to cover everything. Fires smouldered, and the stench of wet-burned wood and dead horses clung to the city.'

THE GAP OPENS

It took until early December for Simpson and Hodges to break through the Siegfried Line, only to face a new major obstacle – the Roer (Rur) river with its seven dams which, if breached, threatened to flood the entire region. Even more worryingly, a dangerous gap had developed between them and Patton's Third Army to the south. The Ardennes sector was protected by only a single under-strength American corps.

Patton, meanwhile, had advanced from the Moselle to the Saar (Sarre) river in poor weather and against stubborn enemy defences. An attack on Metz in early September had ground to a halt beneath the guns of the French-built Maginot Line which were now facing west.

'I hope that in the final settlement of the war, you insist that the Germans retain Lorraine,' wrote a frustrated Patton to US Secretary of War Henry L. Stimson, 'because I can imagine no greater burden than to be the owner of this nasty country where it rains every day and where the whole wealth of the people consists in assorted manure piles.' Metz did not fall until November 25, after which Patton turned north-east. As the Germans rallied and winter closed in, his men faced yet more obstacles on the Saar, well short of their stated objective of the Rhine.

Only in the south was any real progress made. Devers' 6th Army Group, comprising General Jean de Lattre de Tassigny's First French and Maj General Alexander M. Patch's US Seventh Armies, attacked into the Vosges mountains on November 16, aiming for the strategic 'Belfort Gap' between the Vosges and the Jura. French armoured units raced through the Gap on November 20, taking the Germans by surprise, and reached the upper reaches of the Rhine north of Basle later the same day. To their north, French and American troops achieved a similar break-through a few days later, seizing the 'Saverne Gap' and taking Strasbourg.

But the gains were not held firmly. De Lattre's army had effectively shot its bolt, losing casualties it could not easily replace, and a German salient – the 'Colmar Pocket' – had been left between Strasbourg and Belfort. As Eisenhower ordered Devers to turn north along the Rhine's west bank to protect Patton's right flank, there was a risk of an enemy counterattack out of Colmar.

By early December 1944, therefore, the Allies had made some progress but were by no means secure. Most ominously, the Ardennes were only thinly held. Unbeknown to the Allies, Hitler had noted the fact: a new storm was about to break.

The Ardennes – Hitler's last great gamble

With Allied armies poised to invade the German homeland from the west, Hitler became convinced that his only hope of saving the Third Reich was to concentrate all his reserves on a last desperate gamble. Hit hard enough, he thought, the Western Allies might still be prepared to make peace.

TO THE 83 000 American soldiers spread so thinly over the Ardennes section of General Dwight D. Eisenhower's 1600 km (1000 mile) front line in the early winter of 1944, it was a place where nothing much happened. Occasionally, infantry patrolling these eerily quiet, snow-clad wooded hills and valleys of eastern Belgium, Luxembourg and nearby areas of Germany came across a few Wehrmacht troops and there would sometimes be an exchange of fire. But all the action, and the main concentrations of German forces, seemed to be elsewhere.

The illusion was shattered at 5.30 am precisely on Saturday, December 16, when secretly massed German artillery opened up with a sudden, ear-splitting roar. To the German soldiers who were waiting in the pre-dawn cold to advance, it was 'an earth-shaking inferno'. To the GIs on the receiving end it was a stunning, terrifying surprise. To the German High Command it was simply confirmation that Operation *Wacht am Rhein* ('Watch on the Rhine') had begun on time.

The German plan, dreamt up by Hitler three months before, was ambitious. Once the hour-long bombardment lifted, infantry would advance along a 96 km (60 mile) front between Monschau, 25 km (16 miles) south-east of Aachen, and Echternach in Luxembourg, probing American defences and opening the way for a two-wave tank assault. The first wave would move through the woods and hills of the Ardennes to seize bridges across the Meuse river between Liège and Namur. The second would then pass through to take the port of Antwerp, cutting off the Anglo-Canadian 21st Army Group and the left wing of the US 12th Army Group.

Hitler was confident that strains in the Western alliance would prevent them launching a coordinated counterattack; the Anglo-Canadians, he argued, would probably evacuate the southern Netherlands in a 'new Dunkirk' and the Americans, isolated and unsupported, would turn away from Europe to concentrate on the war against Japan. He could then turn his full strength against the Red Army in the east.

THE HIDDEN ARMY

Preparations for the assaults were conducted in the utmost secrecy – and successfully fooled Allied Intelligence. Although reports of German activity in front of the Ardennes were received, it suited Allied commanders to believe that the Germans were concentrating reserve formations in case the Americans made a sudden breakthrough there. No one contemplated the possibility of counterattack against existing Allied positions. As late as December 9, Eisenhower was confidently informed that the enemy 'could not stage a major offensive operation'. And despite the evidence of 1940, when a surprise German attack through the Ardennes had staggered the world, the Allies still believed the region to be 'impassable' to tanks.

This mixture of complacency and disbelief allowed the Germans to concentrate 25 divisions – ten of them armoured – by December 15. On the German right was SS General Josef 'Sepp' Dietrich's Sixth Panzer Army; after breaking through the Allied front, this would aim for the Meuse south of Liège and then make the main attack towards Antwerp. In the centre, General Hasso von Manteuffel's Fifth Panzer Army was ready to attack towards St Vith, Clairvaux and Wiltz, protecting Dietrich's left flank. On the left, General Erich Brandenberger's Seventh Army was preparing an infantry assault between Wiltz and Echternach. A further two divisions and two brigades were in reserve, making a grand total of 275 000 men, 1900 heavy artillery pieces and 950 armoured vehicles.

Facing this formidable force were just six divisions of the US First Army under Lt General Courtney Hodges, fielding no more than 83 000 men, 394 artillery pieces and 420 armoured vehicles between them. The 2nd and 99th Infantry Divisions, part of Maj General Leonard Gerow's V Corps, were concentrated in the north. But the rest, belonging to Maj General Troy H. Middleton's VIII Corps, were strung out in exposed positions along the German border. It was a flimsy defence.

CREATING THE BULGE

As the dawn artillery bombardment ended, German soldiers moved forward through the early morning fog, seeking lines of least resistance for the panzers to exploit. To one GI facing Dietrich's troops, it 'seemed like they were coming right at us and . . . ignoring everyone else'. There was panic, confusion and disorganised retreat in some parts of the line. But not everywhere. In small villages and isolated farmhouses, in the frozen foxholes and along icy forest tracks, pockets of Americans held firm, denying to the Germans the one thing they needed to ensure success – an early breakthrough to the Meuse.

In the north, where Dietrich committed his infantry to seize the high ground of the Elsenborn ridge and the more open terrain beyond, there was further frustration. A parachute assault behind American lines, scheduled for early on December 16, had to be postponed when trucks carrying the men to their aircraft ran out of fuel. When it did take place, 24 hours late, high winds scattered the force and destroyed its impact. Not that this mattered, for by then Dietrich's infantry were

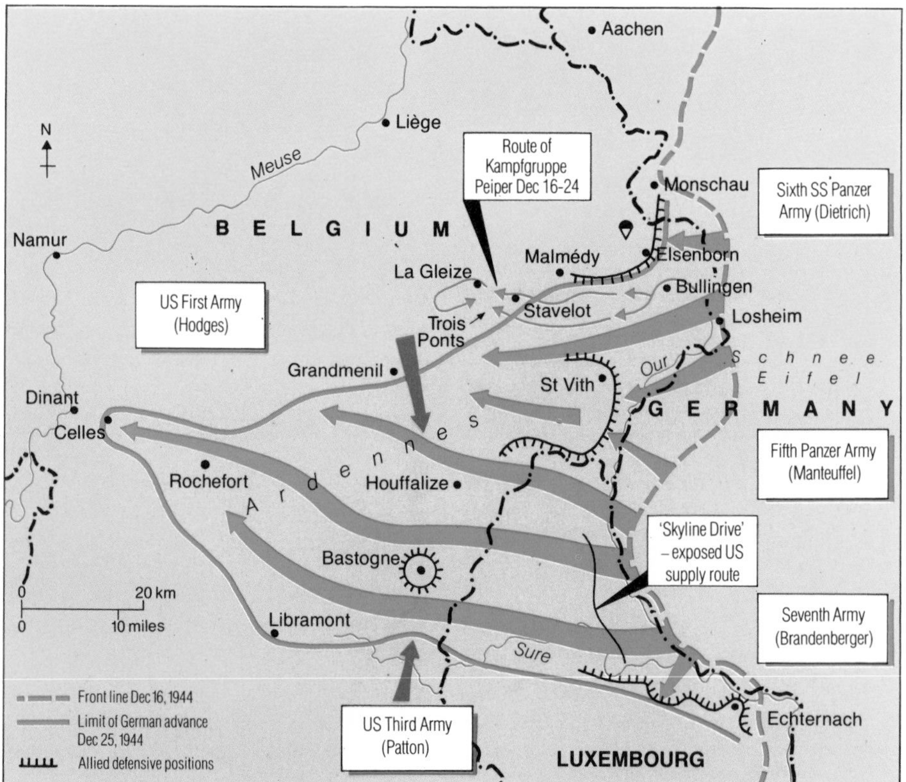

THE BULGE By Christmas Day 1944, the Germans had punched an 80 km (50 mile) dent in the Allied lines, creating a salient that became known as the 'Bulge'. With St Vith taken and Bastogne besieged it seemed that Hitler's gamble might pay off. But Celles was as far as they got.

RIDING HIGH German paratroops hitch a ride along the road between St Vith and Malmédy on a King Tiger tank of 1st SS Panzer Division. These 69 tonne monsters, also known as Tiger IIs, had sloping armour up to 180 mm (7 in) thick, making them almost invulnerable, and a powerful 88 mm ($3\frac{1}{2}$ in) gun. But they used a lot of fuel and were liable to break down.

WAR SPOILS German soldiers pass a blazing American half-track (above), while others inspect captured jeeps and guns in a farmyard (right). In the first days of the Ardennes campaign the Germans struck hard at the weakly held Allied lines, taking the Americans by surprise and forcing them to retreat. Just over a week later the German attack was held and then reversed – but it took until the end of January to squeeze out the 'Bulge'.

MANTEUFFEL – HITLER'S TROUBLE-SHOOTER

Hasso-Eccard von Manteuffel (1897-1985) first came to Hitler's attention in 1941 when, as a colonel, he led a panzer grenadier regiment that penetrated the suburbs of Moscow.

After Moscow, the Führer began to use this diminutive man – only 1.58 m (5 ft 2 in) tall – as a 'fire brigade' officer, sending him wherever dynamic leadership was needed. He commanded the elite Grossdeutschland Division, the Fifth Panzer Army, then Third Panzer Army with which he fought in the final battles around Berlin before surrendering to the British. He faced no war crimes charges and was a member of the West German *Bundestag* (National Assembly) in 1953-7.

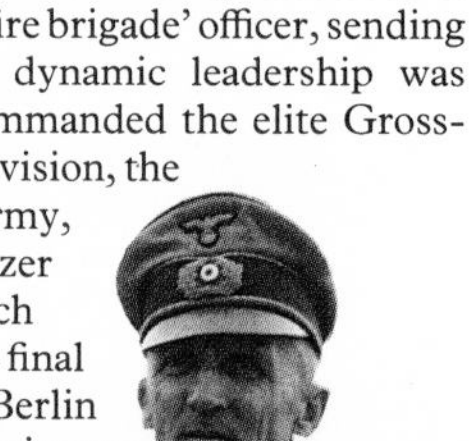

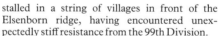

stalled in a string of villages in front of the Elsenborn ridge, having encountered unexpectedly stiff resistance from the 99th Division.

Dietrich responded by shifting the 12th SS Panzer Division south, in the hope of finding an easier target. There, attacked by units from both panzer armies on the 16th, the US 14th Cavalry Group, overextended and poorly supported, had failed to hold the 8 km (5 mile) 'Losheim Gap' – a natural avenue of German advance. This allowed German infantry to move around behind the Schnee Eifel – a salient of small villages and forest-covered hills – from the north, outflanking the inexperienced 106th Division, kept busy countering assaults by Manteuffel's infantry.

To the south, Manteuffel's Fifth Panzer Army was making further gains. His panzers crossed temporary bridges over the Our river late on the 16th, then rumbled forward to support infantry units attacking US troops strung out in isolated outposts along 'Skyline Drive', a supply road running parallel to the front line. Despite desperate fighting, the Americans could not prevent a breakthrough which left the road to Bastogne – a vital road centre – exposed.

German attacks farther south, by Brandenberger's Seventh Army, enjoyed less success against the tanks of the 9th Armored and experienced riflemen of the 4th Infantry Divisions; here the Americans held their ground.

By the end of the first 48 hours, therefore, the future pattern of the battle was becoming clearer: thwarted in both north and south, the Germans were already being channelled into a salient – the 'Bulge' – which denied them the shortest and most obvious route to the Meuse. Even so, enemy penetrations through the Losheim Gap, around the Schnee Eifel and towards Bastogne, left little room for Allied complacency.

THROUGH THE GAP

The situation was most threatening for the Allies in the Losheim Gap. There Dietrich, hoping to exploit a route along the Amblève valley towards the Meuse, concentrated his tank assault. His spearhead was *Kampfgruppe* (Task Force) Peiper – 110 tanks and 4000 men from the elite 1st SS Panzer Division 'Leibstandarte Adolf Hitler'.

SS Colonel Jochen Peiper, a ruthless 29-year-old veteran of the Eastern Front, was a proven tank commander, but he ran into problems from the start. Because of the need for secrecy, he had been unable to conduct a preliminary reconnaissance. He had to advance, in the depths of winter, along roads that he described as fit 'not for tanks but for bicycles' and with precarious supply lines. Surprise was his only asset.

Peiper approached the battle area early on December 16, expecting the infantry to have cleared the way. But an unrepaired railway bridge, creating a huge traffic jam, and dogged American resistance threw him hopelessly behind schedule. That night, when his panzers should have been racing for the Meuse, they were stuck

A COLD WAR Against a desolate, wintry landscape, men of the US 26th Infantry Regiment take to the road (far left) to meet a German attack at Butenbach on December 17. Many of the Germans were veterans of the Russian Front, and were more acclimatised to fighting in wintry conditions than the Americans. On the road between Malmédy and St Vith an amphibious vehicle of Kampfgruppe Peiper stops while its crew checks a signpost (above). But for one of their comrades the fighting is over - a young panzer grenadier of the Waffen-SS, captured by soldiers of the US 82nd Airborne Division while on patrol near Malmédy, is brought in (left) at the point of a Tommy gun.

in Lanzerath, a few kilometres from his start line.

There was better news for Peiper the next day: the 14th Cavalry Group had fallen back. But once more he was held up – first by a temporary shortage of fuel, then when he was forced to make a detour for fear of becoming bogged down along the direct cross-country route towards the Meuse. Finally, Peiper skirted Malmédy – where at about 2 pm occurred one of the worst atrocities of the north-west Europe campaign (see box) – and achieved his breakthrough. Nothing now seemed to stand between him and the Meuse.

He was stopped not by massively superior forces, but by small groups of American combat engineers. As Peiper approached Stavelot – a small village containing a vital bridge across the Amblève – late on the 17th, a force of only 13 men from Company C, 291st Combat Engineer Battalion, disabled his leading Panther with a lucky bazooka shot, effectively blocking the road. By now it was pitch dark and Peiper, unsure of the scale of the American defence, delayed his assault on Stavelot until the following morning.

In the event, he captured the village with ease, but the delay had allowed men of another engineer company to attach demolition charges to three bridges across the Amblève and Salm rivers at Trois Ponts, a few kilometres farther west. As Kampfgruppe Peiper approached Trois Ponts a few hours later, the bridges were blown, forcing Peiper to move north onto minor roads to search for alternative crossing points. His King Tiger tanks were once again running short of fuel and, despite the discovery of an intact bridge at Cheneux just beyond the village of La Gleize, the advance was halted when a sudden break in the weather allowed Allied fighter-bombers to attack. They destroyed only one Tiger, but this blocked the bridge long enough for US engineers to destroy the only other bridge Peiper could use.

For six days Peiper fought for survival as the Americans concentrated their forces against him. Units of the US 30th Infantry Division, moving south from Ninth Army on Eisenhower's orders, recaptured Stavelot on December 21, while yet more of what Peiper called 'the damned engineers' destroyed bridges to the west. Cut off, surrounded and short of supplies, the remains of Peiper's task force formed a defensive ring around La Gleize. But their destruction was only a matter of time. By Christmas Eve, Peiper had no choice but to order his men to escape as best they could; fewer than 800 out of the original 4000 succeeded.

BATTLE FOR ST VITH

By then, the Americans had also fought a holding action farther south, around the road junction of St Vith. With their 106th Division outflanked and virtually surrounded on the Schnee Eifel, two of its three infantry regiments surrendered on December 19. St Vith would have fallen quickly had not the 7th Armored Division, ordered down from the US Ninth Army, arrived late on the 17th. Their tanks, supported by engineers and an

THE MALMEDY MASSACRE

Shortly after 1.30 pm on December 17, vehicles belonging to an American artillery observation battalion reached the Baugnez crossroads, just outside Malmédy. As they turned towards Ligneuville they came under heavy fire. Leading tanks of Kampfgruppe Peiper suddenly appeared from the east.

The Americans were unprotected by tanks or heavy weapons, and quickly surrendered. As Peiper's panzers swept on, about 150 men were herded into a nearby field. At about 2 pm a single pistol shot rang out, followed by machine-gun fire as German soldiers, left behind to guard the prisoners, cut them down in cold blood. Soon 85 GIs lay dead.

The survivors, wounded and shocked, stumbled into Malmédy that night. News of the massacre was given wide publicity, and helped to stiffen American resolve. After the war, surviving members of the Kampfgruppe – including Peiper – were put on trial and sentenced to death, though the sentences were later commuted. Paroled in 1956, Peiper was killed (some say by former members of the French Resistance) in a house fire 20 years later.

artillery battalion, hastily manned roadblocks to the east of the town; these became the cornerstones of what was eventually a 'horseshoe' defence, with the open end facing west.

At first the Germans seemed intent on bypassing St Vith to north and south, but all this changed on December 20. Hitler reluctantly accepted Dietrich's failure in the far north (where, after heavy fighting, the US 2nd and 99th Divisions had pulled back to create a solid defensive line on the Elsenborn ridge) and decided to concentrate the main effort on his more successful Fifth Panzer Army. This made the capture of St Vith and its vital road network essential.

December 20 was also a day of decision for the Allies. Eisenhower, aware of the problems posed for Lt General Omar Bradley now that his 12th Army Group was split by the German attack, turned to the British Field Marshal Sir Bernard Montgomery and gave him command of the northern sector of the Bulge. Montgomery's first move was to strengthen the northern shoulder defences by ordering south the US 82nd Airborne Division – veterans of Nijmegen (p. 321) – to forge a link between St Vith and Werbomont, west of Trois Ponts. But this could not save St Vith. By December 21 it was under heavy attack and on the 23rd it fell.

It was a Pyrrhic victory, for the need to concentrate on capturing St Vith had delayed the Germans long enough to allow Montgomery to strengthen further the northern shoulder, positioning fresh troops to protect the approaches to the Meuse. By Christmas Day the most westerly panzer advances, just a few kilometres short of the Meuse at Dinant, had been contained. The Bulge was rapidly beginning to resemble the jaws of a trap from which the Germans were now most anxious to remove the 'tooth' of Bastogne.

DIETRICH – 'CUNNING, ENERGETIC AND BRUTAL'

Hitler described Josef 'Sepp' Dietrich (1892-1966) as 'simultaneously cunning, energetic and brutal' – characteristics that made him an ideal lieutenant for the Führer.

Dietrich, a Munich policeman, joined the Nazi party in 1928. In 1933 he created a special SS bodyguard – the Leibstandarte Adolf Hitler – to protect the Führer and other Nazi leaders, and he took an active part in the 'Night of the Long Knives' in 1934 (p. 18). By the outbreak of war his group had been transformed into an elite military unit, becoming a full division in 1941. Dietrich led it in France in 1940, on the Eastern Front in 1941-3 and in Normandy in 1944.

He was put in charge of Sixth Panzer Army for the Battle of the Ardennes and commanded it – despite his failure to break through to the Meuse – until the end of the war, fighting in Hungary and Austria. He was one of only 27 men to be awarded Diamonds to his Knight's Cross. After the war he was tried for war crimes – mainly connected with the massacre at Malmédy (p. 327), although he took no active part in it – and received a life sentence. He was paroled in 1955, but rearrested by West German officials and spent another 18 months in prison for his part in the 'Night of the Long Knives'.

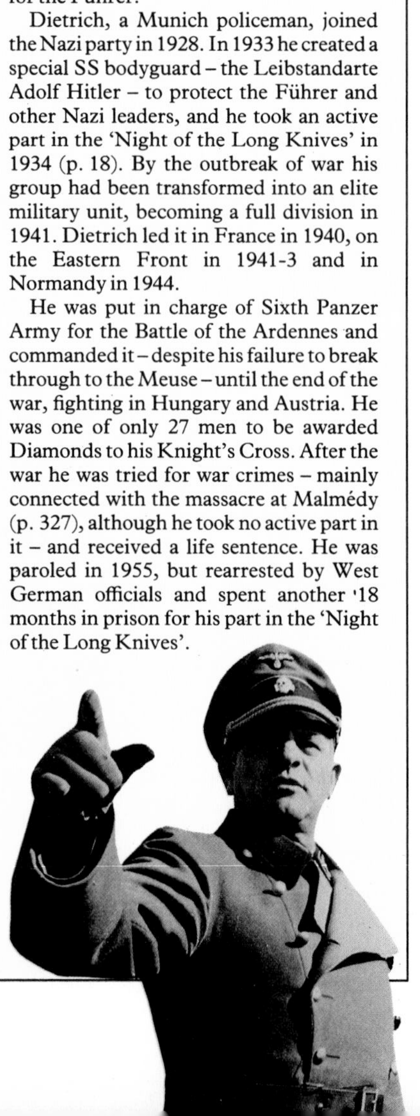

BASTOGNE BESIEGED

The market town of Bastogne, situated on a level plateau surrounded by wooded hills, was central to the outcome of the Battle of the Bulge. If the Germans had captured it, as planned, they would have gained access to an important road network. By defending the town, the Americans prevented a build-up of German momentum in the south.

At first, Manteuffel's forces did well; by December 17, the eastern approaches to Bastogne had been exposed by the destruction of the 110th Infantry Regiment on 'Skyline Drive'. But the Americans were quick to appreciate the danger. Maj General Middleton, with his corps headquarters in Bastogne, sent tanks from his mobile reserve to halt the Germans. They did not last long, being overwhelmed by German advance units within 24 hours, but their sacrifice did prevent an early breakthrough into the town.

This gave Middleton time to bolster his defences, using reinforcements rushed to him on Eisenhower's orders. A tank unit diverted from General George S. Patton's US Third Army in the south arrived late on December 18; Middleton immediately divided the tanks into three teams and sent them to protect Noville (to the north), Longvilly (to the north-east) and Wardin (to the east). They were joined by men of the 101st Airborne Division under Brig General Anthony C. McAuliffe. Although all three teams were eventually forced back in bitter fighting, by December 19 an arc of defence was beginning to take shape around Bastogne.

Eisenhower was convinced that the key to victory in the Bulge was to hold the northern and southern shoulders, out of which the Americans could mount destructive counterattacks, and for this he recognised the importance of holding Bastogne and its road network. On December 20, he ordered Patton to suspend operations against German forces in the Saarland and strike up through the flank of the German advance to reinforce Bastogne. Patton obliged with impressive speed. He would have preferred to continue his own offensive but, as he said, he would still be fighting the Germans.

Manteuffel's panzers, meanwhile, were thrusting north and south of Bastogne, and on December 22 German infantry arrived in strength; their first move was to offer surrender terms. McAuliffe's reply – 'Nuts!' (see box) – reflected a growing confidence among the 14 500 Americans. The previous day a break in the weather, heralding snow, had allowed Allied aircraft to fly in much-needed supplies. Even so, when the German attack began, the defensive ring around Bastogne was gradually squeezed in; by Christmas Eve, the 'hole in the doughnut' was only 25 km (16 miles) in circumference.

THE GREIF COMMANDOS

It was Hitler's own idea to use English-speaking German soldiers, dressed as GIs and familiar with American slang, to spread confusion and carry out raids behind American lines in the Ardennes. For a short time it worked. The so-called *Greif* ('Griffin', but also meaning 'grasp') Commandos were led by SS Lt Colonel Otto Skorzeny, famous for his daring rescue of Mussolini in 1943, and were attached to Dietrich's Sixth Panzer Army.

Four groups of reconnaissance commandos and two of demolition commandos – each consisting of three or four men in a captured American jeep – were sent out during the first few days of the German offensive in December. Although they succeeded in carrying out few acts of sabotage, their presence fuelled American confusion, leading to the spread of wild, unsubstantiated rumours and situations bordering on farce.

For a time, the aim of the commandos was thought to be the capture or assassination of General Eisenhower, who became a virtual prisoner in his headquarters at Versailles. Many genuine US jeeps and staff cars (including General Bradley's) were delayed through roadside 'interrogations' by wary GIs. These involved 'trick' questions – ranging from the name of President Roosevelt's dog to the capital of Illinois – which, it was felt, only 'real' Americans could answer. Not all could.

The American solution to the Greif Commandos problem was simple and effective. Any Germans captured wearing US uniforms were shot as spies – and no more turned up after about December 20.

SWIFT END A Greif commando faces execution.

The Germans mounted an even more ferocious attack on Christmas Day, concentrating on Hemroulle to the west, defended by men of the 502nd Parachute Infantry Regiment. The fighting was bitter and close. At one point, when the American commander asked over his field telephone where the Germans were, the answer came: 'If you look out of your window now, you'll

WHAT IF BASTOGNE HAD FALLEN?

The successful defence of Bastogne by men of the 101st Airborne Division in December 1944 was a key to American recovery in the Ardennes. If the town, with its many roads leading off in all directions, had been captured during the first few days of the offensive, German forces would have been free to attack the St Vith defenders from the rear and to reach the Meuse virtually unopposed.

As it was, the 2nd Panzer Division, skirting Bastogne to the north, came close to the Meuse. But it lacked the support of units which had been diverted to capture the town and to deal with Patton's counterattack which raised the siege on December 26. Like a rock in the centre of a raging stream, Bastogne reduced the momentum of the German assault. If it had fallen, the initial German thrust would have been deeper and the Allied recovery made far more difficult.

'NUTS!'

'We are parlementaires,' German Lieutenant Hellmuth Henke shouted out, in English. It was 11.30 am on December 22, 1944, and Henke was one of four Germans approaching, under a flag of truce, the lines of the beleaguered US garrison at Bastogne. As he was motioned forward, a rumour spread among the Americans that the Germans were about to surrender.

In fact, Henke carried a typed message from his commanding officer demanding the surrender of the Americans in Bastogne. He was led blindfold to a company command post and the message passed up the line to the acting commander of the 101st Airborne Division, Brig General Anthony C. McAuliffe. His initial response was 'Aw, Nuts!' and when he came to compile a written reply he could think of nothing more appropriate: 'To the German Commander: NUTS! The American Commander.'

BADGE OF HONOUR McAuliffe receives the Distinguished Service Cross from General Patton.

be looking right down the muzzle of an 88.' But the paras held on, destroying a total of seven tanks with little more than bazookas and 'a maelstrom of fire'. The German attack ground to a halt.

Meanwhile, Patton's men – from the 4th Armored and two infantry divisions – had been working hard to break through to Bastogne. Despite an initial advance of 11 km (7 miles), heavy fighting developed as soon as they reached the German flank, and by December 23 Patton seemed in danger of stalling. When the same happened the next day, he hastily reorganised his units. Catching the Germans by surprise, he took Remonville the next day. By dusk on Boxing Day his troops had linked up with McAuliffe's men.

Not only was Bastogne saved, but Patton's armour had driven a great gap through the line of the enemy advance in the southern Ardennes. Panzer formations already to the west of Bastogne were threatened with isolation. It was a turning point in the battle.

SQUEEZING THE BULGE

Bradley called December 26 the 'high-water mark' of the German offensive. It was an apt description, for although tough fighting still lay ahead, the Americans had successfully absorbed the shock. As if to confirm this, Hitler the same day authorised some panzer units caught to the west of Patton's corridor to withdraw.

But the Führer had not abandoned his dream. He suspected that all was not well in the Allied camp and believed their efforts were uncoordinated. If only Patton's corridor to Bastogne could be eliminated, he thought, an advance to the Meuse and beyond was still possible. A fresh crisis did indeed arise in the Allied command.

On December 30, Montgomery wrote an extraordinary letter to Eisenhower, reviving his demand for a 'single thrust' towards the Ruhr. He even went so far as virtually to name himself as its commander. Eisenhower, sick of the controversy, threatened to refer the whole matter to the Joint Chiefs of Staff in Washington. They were likely to back the Supreme Commander, and it began to look as if Montgomery would have to resign. Only enormous diplomatic efforts behind the scenes managed to smooth over the affair. Then on January 7, the disagreement blew up again when Montgomery, in a rather tactless statement to the press, implied that he had 'saved the day' for the Americans by taking over command of the northern sector of the Bulge.

All this wrangling coincided with continued fighting in the Ardennes, as Eisenhower prepared his forces for simultaneous attacks from north and south, to link at Houffalize, 16 km (10 miles) north of Bastogne, and 'squeeze out' the Bulge. Montgomery, still dealing with the remnants of panzer units close to Dinant, at the tip of the German advance, could not be expected to mount his northern assault until early January. So the emphasis shifted to the south, where Patton's corridor to Bastogne needed strengthening.

Once he received reinforcements, Patton attacked to the west and east, aiming to broaden the corridor, on December 30. But he had little success, and the heavy fighting was made worse by appalling snowstorms and bone-chilling wind.

The stalemate was broken by a number of seemingly unconnected events elsewhere. Just before midnight on New Year's Eve, the Germans opened a new offensive, Operation *Nordwind*, much farther south in the Vosges mountains (see box); although this caused Allied concern, it used enemy forces which might otherwise have been committed to the Ardennes. A few hours later, the Luftwaffe launched a massive attack against Allied airfields in Belgium and the southern Netherlands. It destroyed nearly 300 Allied aircraft, but the Allies shot down 215 of the attackers (and the Germans themselves shot down another 85 of their own), crippling Hitler's air arm for good. Finally, on January 12, 1945, after an appeal from Churchill, the Red Army opened an offensive on the Vistula river, which forced Hitler to divert troops from the Western Front to meet the threat.

All this meant that when Montgomery began his attack towards Houffalize on January 3, the balance was already tilting in favour of the Allies. Conditions were poor – deep snow and icy roads delayed the advance – but by the 7th, American tanks had taken Baraque de Fraiture on the Liège-Bastogne road. Two days later, Patton launched a renewed attack northwards from Bastogne and Echternach with nearly 100 000 men. On January 15 the two pincers met at Houffalize. Mopping up was to take until the end of the month, but by then German forces had been largely destroyed and the Bulge squeezed out.

The Ardennes battle cost the Americans over 75 000 casualties (8497 killed, 46 000 wounded and 21 000 missing or captured), but in the process the cream of Hitler's forces had been mauled. German losses were almost 120 000 (12 652 killed, 57 000 wounded and 50 000 captured). In early 1945 these were irreplaceable.

OPERATION NORDWIND

The German offensive in Alsace, which Hitler hoped would catch the Allied armies off-balance, opened an hour before midnight on New Year's Eve, 1944. Forces belonging to General Johannes Blaskowitz's Army Group G – a total of ten divisions – attacked General Jacob Devers' 6th Army Group. Code-named Operation *Nordwind* ('North Wind'), the plan was for elements of the German First Army to attack southwards around the town of Bitche while units of Nineteenth Army broke out northwards from the Colmar Pocket (p. 323) to link up. The aims were to trap seven Allied divisions along the Rhine and to recapture the city of Strasbourg.

Although the fighting was hard, in bitter cold and snow, the offensive stood little chance of success. Warned by intelligence gleaned from prisoners of war, Eisenhower authorised Devers to pull back to absorb the punch and, by January 3, 1945, the initial thrusts around Bitche had been blunted. The situation was more dangerous in Strasbourg, which the French insisted on defending, but by January 20 the enemy had been contained, enabling General de Lattre to squeeze out the Colmar Pocket – a process completed by February 10.

Despite nearly 16 000 casualties the Allies were the victors. The Germans in Alsace lost 25 000 men they could not replace, valuable reserves had been denied to the Ardennes and the way was now clear for Allied attacks into the Saarland.

21: 'THE YEAR OF TEN VICTORIES'

For the Russians, 1944 was the year in which they gave Germany and its allies a taste of the fire and sword that the Nazis themselves had inflicted on so many weaker opponents. The relief of Leningrad was just the first triumph in the Soviet Union's 'Year of Ten Victories'.

JOSEPH STALIN, surveying the world from his Kremlin headquarters overlooking Red Square, could look forward to the New Year of 1944 with a certain amount of grim optimism. The previous year had seen two mighty body-blows dealt to the German invaders: by February their Sixth Army had been battered into surrender at Stalingrad, and in July, Hitler's desperate gamble with his armoured reserves at Kursk had ended in disaster as the Red Army's massive counteroffensive swept them aside. By the autumn of 1943, Russian forces had come within striking distance of their prewar frontier.

Only the western Ukraine, the Baltic coast and the Soviet republic of Belorussia (White Russia), bordering on Poland, remained under German control. It seemed just a matter of time before the Red Army liberated these territories – and then erupted into central Europe, heading for Hitler's Reich itself.

Berlin's view of the situation was not much different. The heady days of 1941, when the Wehrmacht had almost succeeded in destroying the Russian enemy in a ten-week campaign, were long over. There were to be no more shattering blitzkriegs like those of 1942, when the advancing German soldier could say with confidence: '*Russland ist kaputt*' ('Russia is shattered').

On November 3, 1943, Hitler had issued Directive 51, ordering almost all fresh men and equipment to the west, rather than to the Eastern Front, to face the threat of invasion from England. By the end of the year the Russians greatly outnumbered Axis forces on the Eastern Front. Some 6.5 million men, including about half a million in the Red Air Force and Navy, were massed against Germany's 4.3 million men in the east, including various allies.

The Red Army also had more equipment – they could field 5600 tanks against a total of 2300 German armoured fighting vehicles, and had some 90 000 field guns and 8800 aircraft against German figures of 54 000 and 3000. On the other hand, the German Panzer V, or Panther, and even the improved version of the Panzer IV, could hold their own against Russian T-34 tanks. In addition, German war production had improved markedly since 1942 under the leadership of Armaments Minister Albert Speer. Nor had the German generals lost any of their tactical brilliance, or the German troops their remarkable fighting skills.

LENINGRAD RELIEVED

In September 1943, General Leonid Govorov had been given an awesome task – to plan and launch a massive offensive that would drive the Nazis from the gates of Leningrad. The people of Russia's second city had been besieged since September 8, 1941, and only the most precarious of supply lines kept the city alive.

CHAMPION TANK Red Army men advance in their T-34 medium tanks – among the best of its type in any of the warring armies and widely used even after 1945.

General Georg Lindemann's Eighteenth Army, holding the northernmost sector of the Eastern Front, was to be the main target of the Russian attack. The plan was to lay siege to the besiegers, striking simultaneous blows against Eighteenth Army from the north, north-east and east. In the north, two armies from Govorov's Leningrad Front (Army Group) would nip out a German salient that projected to the Baltic coast near the town of Krasnoye Selo, 20 km (12 miles) south-west of Leningrad. Forty-Second Army would attack from the Pulkovo Heights south of the city, while the veteran Second Shock Army would break out of a Russian bridgehead on the

Baltic coast around Oranienbaum (now Lomonosov), beyond Krasnoye Selo to the west.

At the same time, Eighth and Fifty-Fourth Armies, from General Kiril Meretskov's Volkhov Front, would strike the Germans in the north-east; while Fifty-Ninth Army, also part of Volkhov Front, was to smash German forces around Novgorod, on Lake Ilmen, 160 km (100 miles) south of Leningrad. The German Sixteenth Army, south of the Eighteenth, would be kept busy with thrusts by General Markian Popov's 2nd Baltic Front.

For the blows against Eighteenth Army, the Russians fielded overwhelming forces – about 375 000 men against the Germans' estimated total of 168 000. The Germans were in no way prepared for such an onslaught. Poor intelligence had led them to expect only a limited push, on a date that they were never able to discover.

To make things worse for them, Hitler vetoed a sensible plan proposed by Field Marshal Georg von Küchler, commanding Army Group North, to pull back to the 'Panther Line'. This ran south along the Narva river (which flows into the Baltic south-west of Leningrad), then down the east banks of Lakes Peipus (Chudskoye) and Pskov, and through the towns of Pskov and Ostrov farther south. The Führer refused point-blank to abandon territory without a fight.

The Russians, meanwhile, had a ticklish time getting Second Shock Army secretly into the Oranienbaum bridgehead. Night after night during November 1943, the Soviet Baltic Fleet used every vessel it could lay hold of – barges, steamers, small coastal craft – to carry the men along the coast and into the bridgehead. Then in the pre-dawn hours, there would be frantic activity as all signs of the transports and extra men and equipment were hidden from the encircling Germans. Surprise was essential.

A CITY FREED At last the siege of Leningrad is over, and survivors read in the newspaper about the ending of the blockade. There were celebrations, but inhabitants were shocked by the scars the Germans had left on their beautiful city. And there were some 900 000 dead.

HAIL OF SHELLS

The Russians managed to achieve it. At 9.35 am on January 14, 1944, a thunderous, 65 minute artillery barrage opened up around Oranienbaum, pouring a devastating 100 000 shells on the Germans. Then Second Shock Army's assault troops stormed out of the bridgehead and ripped into the startled III SS Panzer Corps.

At 9.20 am the next day, another barrage opened up from the Pulkovo Heights. In just under 1¾ hours, 3000 Soviet guns fired over 200 000 shells. Then Forty-Second Army streamed out against the Germans. They made good progress until they ran into the artillery reserve of a German corps. A devastating hail of shells blew men and vehicles to pieces and slowed the advance. But the following morning the Russian troops continued to push forward and by the evening of January 17 had penetrated German defensive lines by up to 8 km (5 miles).

Back in the Oranienbaum area, men of the 10th Luftwaffe Division – former Luftwaffe ground crew who no longer had aircraft to service and were now assigned to III Panzer Corps – fought back furiously against Second Shock Army, but were hard pressed to stop the battle-hardened Russians. Küchler was also assailed by simultaneous blows in the Novgorod area and from the north-east. Nonetheless, he was convinced that the offensives lacked depth and was confident that the superior skill of the Germans and their central position would enable him to check the attacks.

By January 17, however, Küchler's confidence was crumbling in the face of sweeping Russian successes. Eighteenth Army's sole reserve formation, 61st Infantry Division, had been plunged into the battle in the north, yet the arms of the Soviet pincer movement drew ever closer around the Krasnoye Selo salient. On the north-eastern flank, XXVI Corps was fighting for its life against the encircling troops of the Russian Eighth and Fifty-Fourth Armies.

Taking his courage in his hands, the field marshal asked Hitler to be allowed to fall back south-west to a position on the Leningrad-Moscow highway. As usual, the Führer refused, but the steady Soviet advance forced Küchler to disobey the orders from Berlin.

It was almost the finish for Army Group North. In Novgorod, 28th Division was surrounded by an attacking Russian force with seven times its manpower – five battalions against eight Soviet divisions. Desperately, the defenders broke out of the city on the night of January 19. They were repeatedly attacked by Soviet aircraft and ran a gauntlet of artillery, machine-gun and tank fire. The city, one of Russia's oldest and most beautiful, was severely damaged by the bombing and shelling, its outskirts carpeted with the refuse of war – cartridge and shell cases, wrecked vehicles, empty ration cans and, everywhere, twisted, maimed and blackened corpses, dusted with powdery snow.

Küchler knew by now that his army group was near collapse. He told the German High Command that only a swift withdrawal to the Panther Line would save even a proportion of his force. He was promptly sacked.

ORDEAL OVER

Küchler was replaced by the tank expert Field Marshal Walther Model. But the time was long past when reshuffling generals could save the situation. On January 26, Govorov's men cleared the last enemy troops from the Leningrad-Moscow railway. Supplies could now flow freely into Leningrad; the siege was broken. The next day, the Soviet authorities formally announced that the city's 890 day ordeal was over. The 600 000 survivors – most of them half-starved, emaciated and unbearably weary – emerged from the rubble to sing and dance in celebration.

But even in their hour of joy, they had to recoil from some of the terrible sights that met their eyes. The retreating Germans had vandalised buildings which had so far escaped damage, including the magnificent 18th-century Catherine Palace, in the southern suburb of Pushkin. Also in Pushkin, sickened soldiers had to cut down the corpses of four Russians left hanging from hooks embedded in a tree. They were among an estimated 900 000 Leningrad citizens who died during the siege. (The official death toll was 600 000, but some estimates put the figure at 1.5 million, including servicemen.)

Nor did the Soviet offensive stop with Leningrad's relief. Even as this was happening, troops from Leningrad Front continued to push the enemy ever westward, despite tough German resistance. On February 1, men from Second Shock Army captured Kingisepp on the Luga river, and others reached the Narva river. On February 12, men from both Leningrad and Volkhov Fronts took the town of Luga, 135 km (85 miles) south of Leningrad. On February 15, Model decided to pull Eighteenth Army back to the Panther Line, where he was later joined by Army Group North's Sixteenth Army, driven back by Popov's 2nd Baltic Front.

Leningrad was just the first of the Red Army's Ten Victories of 1944. Those that followed were at Korsun (February-March), in the Crimea (April), Finland (June), Belorussia (also June), western Ukraine (July-August), Moldavia and Romania (August), Estonia and Latvia (September), Hungary, Czechoslovakia and Yugoslavia (October), and Petsamo, where the Germans were driven back into northern Norway.

Russian ring of steel at Korsun

It was a frantic battle against mud, as well as the enemy, as 60 000 trapped Germans tried to blast their way out of an ever-tightening ring of Russian forces.

THROUGH MUD AND SNOW Men work on a tipped truck. Other trucks queue up behind horse-drawn carts taken from local peasants. Moving from one place to another was a nightmare for the beleaguered Germans in the Ukraine.

DUG IN west of the Dniepr river in the Ukraine, troops of the German Army Group South faced the New Year of 1944 with mounting anxiety. They were defending a line that bulged alarmingly deep into Russian-held territory – a bulge that could be nipped off by the rampaging Red Army, to leave them encircled.

In the last days of 1943, they had faced the first Russian moves. On Christmas Eve and Boxing Day, General Nikolai Vatutin's 1st Ukrainian Front (Army Group) had launched attacks west and south-west of Kiev. On December 27 the German commander, Field Marshal Erich von Manstein, had proposed pulling his men back. Hitler refused permission: the line must be held to the death, he ordered. But the town of Korosten fell on December 29, Zhitomir two days later.

Then on January 5, General Ivan Koniev's 2nd Ukrainian Front launched an attack in the Kirovograd area and took the city. Holding a smaller bulge around the nearby town of Korsun were the German Eighth and First Panzer Armies. Knowing that his troops faced annihilation, Manstein flew to Hitler's headquarters in East Prussia, to put his case again in person. The Führer fixed him with a manic glare and again refused. 'That gaze told me how he had contrived to dominate so many', Manstein wrote later. He returned gloomily to the front.

SOVIET BLITZKRIEG

The ground shook on January 24, as a thunderous Russian bombardment pounded German positions south of the Korsun bulge. Stunned and deafened defenders were then hit by Koniev's Fourth Guards and Fifty-Third Armies, and the following day by the veteran Fifth Tank Army. The Germans broke, and the 50 km/h (30 mph) Russian T-34 tanks rumbled forward. The outnumbered panzers counterattacked but had little hope of halting the Red Army's blitzkrieg.

On January 26, 1st Ukrainian Front struck a devastating blow to First Panzer Army from the north of the Korsun bulge. The armour and infantry of Vatutin's Sixth Tank Army followed hard on the heels of a 'hurricane' bombardment, and a flying wedge of 50 tanks spearheaded a rapid advance in classic blitzkrieg style. By January 28 they had joined with Koniev's 2nd Ukrainian Front, advancing from the south. The Germans around Korsun were encircled.

Inside this 32 km (20 mile) wide pocket – called 'Little Stalingrad' by the Russians, who employed here tactics similar to those used at Stalingrad itself a year earlier – about 60 000 troops were trapped. They included the 5th SS *Wiking* (Viking) Panzer Division.

Manstein planned a desperate rescue operation to free the trapped men. A task force under Lt General Hans Hube began on February 4 to smash its way into the pocket. The reinforced XLVII Panzer Corps attacked the south-eastern face, while III Panzer Corps struck at the west. But this was no lightning dash. An early thaw forced the Germans to battle against mud as well as fierce Russian opposition. Tracked vehicles, tanks and assault guns found the going difficult. Supplies had to be moved by horse-drawn sledge.

At last, on February 11, III Panzer Corps managed to batter a hole in the outer Russian defences and pushed on to Lysyanka. Battle conditions were reminiscent of World War I – gruelling duels of attrition, slogged out in thick slime. And the Russian ring of steel around Korsun still closed in remorselessly. The Luftwaffe tried to drop supplies by air, but the weather, the Red Air Force and Russian ack-ack guns took a fearful toll of the slow Junkers Ju52 transport planes – 44 were lost in five days.

On the night of February 16/17, in a snowstorm, the German commander in the pocket, General Wilhelm Stemmermann, attempted a break-out. Armed with knives, a number of his men crept out and cut the throats of Soviet sentries. German vehicles followed and struck out towards Lysyanka, hoping to join III Panzer Corps.

But it was a disaster. Just as, in the morning's bleak first light, the Germans thought that they had reached safety, Soviet tanks bore down on them. As Leon Degrelle, among Belgian SS troops serving with the Germans, recalled later: 'In this frantic race vehicles were overturned, throwing wounded in confusion to the ground. A wave of Soviet tanks . . . advanced through the carts, breaking them . . . like boxes of matches, crushing the wounded and the dying horses.' Cossack horsemen hunted down Germans who escaped. With a cheerful disregard for international convention, they lopped off the hands of those who approached, arms up in surrender.

German sources claim that 30 000 escaped; Soviet histories – prone to exaggeration – say there were 72 000 German casualties. The truth probably lies somewhere in between. But there was no disputing that a gaping hole had been made in the German Army Group South's defences. On February 29, the Russians themselves suffered a loss when Vatutin was mortally wounded in an ambush by Ukrainian nationalist guerrillas, engaged in a desperate war on two fronts against both the hated Russian Reds and the Germans.

THROUGH THE MUD

Manstein now tried to stabilise his front line, shuffling his forces to the left to cover what he believed would be the direction of the next Russian attack. Common sense reasoned that the Red Army would need time, after a battle on the scale of Korsun, to draw breath, regroup and allow the ground to dry and harden. So the Germans were stunned when, on March 4, Russian guns began to pound their positions again, and tanks from 1st Ukrainian Front, now commanded by Marshal Georgi Zhukov, surged forward through a sea of mud. The broad tracks of Russian T-34 tanks and Lend-Lease Studebaker trucks made the Red Army extremely mobile in contrast to the German horse transport.

The overall Russian plan was to hit the Germans with three fronts, attacking one after another in quick succession. Koniev's 2nd Ukrainian Front joined the offensive on March 5, Marshal Rodion Malinovsky's 3rd on March 6. By March 10, Zhukov's and Koniev's fronts were threatening to capture the First Panzer Army. Koniev's had raced south and west past the Germans' exposed right flank, heading for Romania. On March 23, Zhukov took Chortkov and severed a railway which served as First Panzer Army's main supply line. By March 28, Hube, now commanding the panzers, had been encircled in the area of Proskurov and Zhmerinka.

Still the Red Army advanced, with fighters and bombers ranging forward of its tanks, infantry and artillery. The Luftwaffe – short of planes and fuel – was finding it increasingly difficult to resist. Meanwhile, Hube was preparing to smash a way

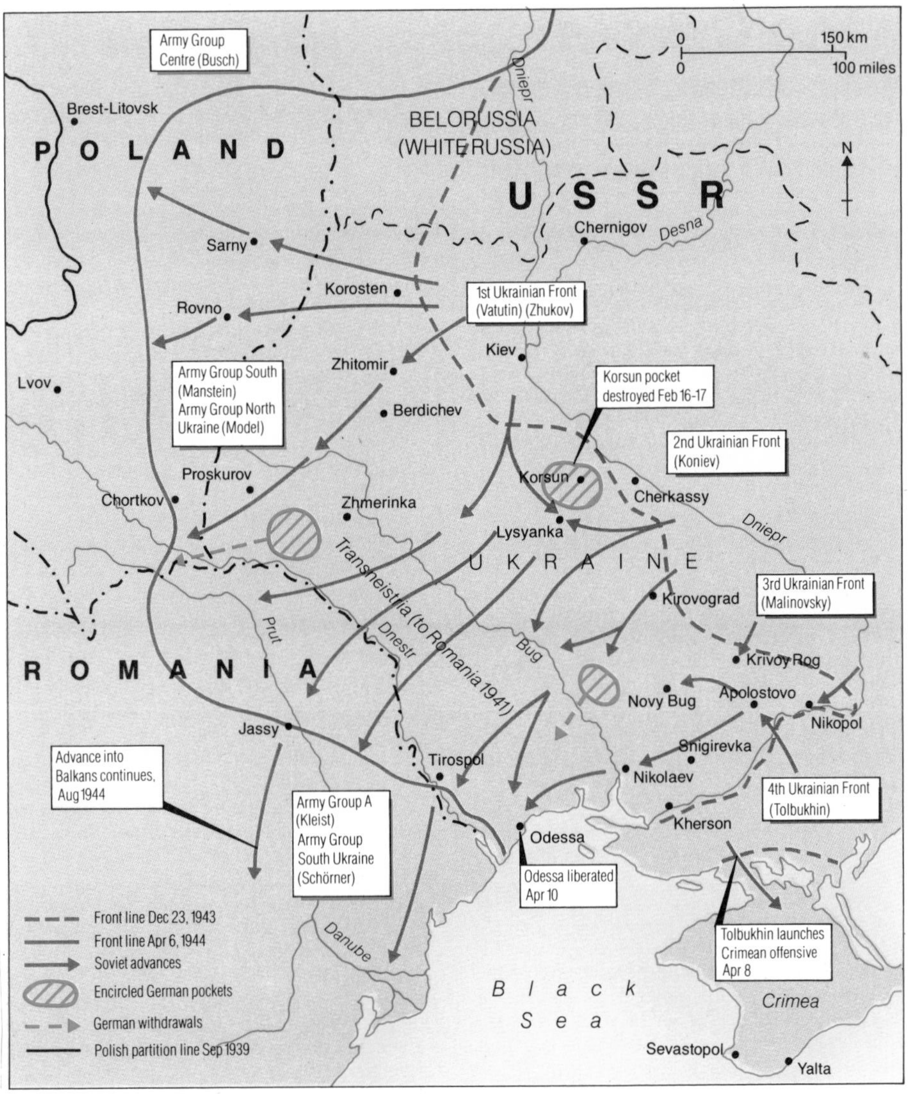

DRIVING BACK THE GERMANS The Soviet offensive in the Ukraine opened at Christmas 1943. By the following April, Stalin's armies had freed the region and were plunging into Poland and across the Dnestr river into Romania.

out of the new pocket, but before orders for the break-out could be issued, Manstein flew to see Hitler again. The field marshal wanted him to suspend Führer Order No 11 of March 8, which laid down that encircled formations should form 'fortresses' where they were, to slow the Russian advance. This time, after enduring a stream of insults, Manstein got his way and II Panzer Corps was called from France to aid the break-out.

Hube struck on March 30 – and managed to take the Russians by surprise. He moved west, rather than by the direct, southern route, where the main Russian forces were waiting. The Germans broke through a thin Russian cordon and joined relief forces of Fourth Panzer Army. By April 10 it was clear that First Panzer Army had escaped. Even so, Hitler sacked Manstein, who was replaced by Field Marshal Walther Model; Army Group South was renamed Army Group North Ukraine. Manstein had stated an unpalatable truth all too plainly. In the same sweep, Field Marshal Ewald von Kleist of Army Group A was replaced by General Ferdinand Schörner; Army Group A was now called Army Group South Ukraine.

Correspondent Alexander Werth noted the songs of disillusioned German soldiers: 'It is all over, it is all gone; three years in Russia and can't understand anything.'

INTO ROMANIA

Farther south, Malinovsky's 3rd Ukrainian Front was carving its way into Romania. Germany's Balkan ally had been enlarged by the addition of 'Transneistria' – a gift from Hitler.

Malinovsky and General Feodor Tolbukhin's 4th Ukrainian Front had started the year's offensive on January 10 and 12. During February, Malinovsky's troops liberated Apostolovo, an important rail junction, and Krivoy Rog; Tolbukhin's took Nikopol. Then on March 6, Malinovsky struck out towards Odessa – while Tolbukhin prepared for an April offensive in the Crimea. In three days of fierce fighting, tanks of Malinovsky's Eighth Guards Army smashed 8 km (5 miles) into the positions of Lt General Karl Hollidt's Sixth Army. Once through the crust of his defences, two Russian guards corps were able to race forward 40 km (25 miles) to Novyy Bug.

Hitler raged in vain that his armies should fight where they stood. His soldiers fought with their usual skill and courage – a favourite way of knocking out T-34 tanks was to hide in a shell hole, then leap out to clamp a magnetic mine on their steel sides. But by March 11 the Red Army blitzkrieg had already reached the Bug river.

That day Hollidt hurled his panzers into a desperate but doomed counterattack at Novyy Bug. His Sixth Army escaped destruction only because Malinovsky had unwisely divided his men at Nikolaev. Hollidt smashed his way out to the west, and by March 21 had established a defensive line of sorts on the Bug. But he too was sacked when Hitler lost confidence in him. General Maximilian de Angelis took over the Sixth.

Advancing Russians had similarly pushed back German forces farther north and on March 28, with Hitler's reluctant consent, the Germans began to fall back from the Bug river. On April 2, the Red Army again surprised the Germans by attacking in appalling conditions – a blizzard. The German defenders opposite General Vasili Chuikov's elite Eighth Guards Army and Forty-Sixth Army were thunderstruck to see T-34s looming out of the snow.

By April 6, the Russians had broken through to the Dnestr river, cutting communications with Odessa. Sixth Army fled to the opposite west bank, harassed by the Red Air Force. In near panic they left trucks and armoured vehicles abandoned and wagons strewn by the roadsides.

Four days later Odessa was liberated, and Russian forces were rumbling through Romania proper. Sensing the chance of seducing Romania from the Axis alliance, Russia made reassuring noises about its good intentions. Romanian leaders hastened to secret talks in Moscow.

AN ATTACKING GENERAL

Ivan Koniev (1897-1973) was perhaps Zhukov's main rival for the title of the greatest Red Army commander of World War II. Born a peasant, Koniev was an NCO in the Tsar's army in World War I. He joined the Communist party during the Revolution and fought both as a guerrilla leader and as a political commissar in the civil war that followed it. In 1926 he graduated from the Frunze Military Academy, and at the outbreak of war with Germany was commanding the Transcaucasian Military District. Pitched into the battle of Moscow as commander of the Kalinin Front in September 1941, he played a major role in checking the German advance.

Koniev was an aggressive, attacking general and his greatest triumphs came in the Soviet offensives of 1943-4. His 'blitzkrieg through the mud' following Korsun showed clearly his willingness to take risks and use unorthodox methods to deceive and surprise the enemy.

In January 1945, Koniev moved into Poland and by April had joined with Zhukov's 1st Belorussian Front in surrounding Berlin. When Koniev's men reached the Elbe they became the first Russian troops to make contact with American forces advancing from the west, at Torgau. In 1946 Koniev was appointed commander-in-chief of Soviet ground forces and nine years later became commander of all Warsaw Pact forces.

To the death in the Crimea

When Hitler ordered his Seventeenth Army to hold Sevastopol at all costs, he was virtually sentencing them to death. The Red Army meted out a bloody execution.

THE CRIMEAN PENINSULA was steeped in blood. In 1942, the Russian garrison and Black Sea Fleet had held out for an epic 250 days against the Germans. Then, in April 1944, the Russians returned to wreak vengeance – smashing an Axis force of about 122 000 in 35 days, and needing just five more days to take the fortress city of Sevastopol.

In November 1943, General Feodor Tolbukhin's 4th Ukrainian Front (Army Group) had landed on the north coast of the Crimea and hung on to bridgeheads on the Perekop isthmus and the salt lakes and marshes of Sivash, despite counterattacks by the German Seventeenth Army, marooned on the peninsula. General Andrei Yeremenko's Independent Coastal Army had landed near Kerch, in the extreme east.

Faced by overwhelming numbers, with few tanks and doubting the reliability of Romanian troops in his army, the German commander, General Erwin Jaenicke, wanted to evacuate the peninsula by sea. His superiors, Field Marshal Ewald von Kleist and General Kurt Zeitzler, supported him, but Hitler could see only the blow to German prestige resulting from the loss of the Crimea – plus its effect on Romanian morale. *Festung Sewastopol* ('Fortress Sevastopol') would be held at all costs, he decreed. By April, Jaenicke had been reinforced by sea, bringing his strength up to about 76 000 Germans and 46 000 Romanians, with over 200 tanks and assault guns.

On April 8, Russian artillery rained destruction on the Perekop Line, across the narrow strip of land at the neck of the peninsula. Then Tolbukhin unleashed Second Guards and Fifty-First Armies. A day later the 10th Romanian Division, ranged opposite Fifty-First Army's bridgehead, gave way. Outflanked, the defenders abandoned the Perekop position and made their way as best they could back to the Gneisenau Line, covering Sevastopol itself. Also on April 9, Yeremenko broke out of his bridgehead and took Kerch. From here he headed for Sevastopol.

Morale in the Red Army was high – as, for a time, it was in the German Seventeenth Army, whose men were firmly convinced that their navy and the Luftwaffe would get them out if necessary. But on April 24, Hitler repeated his order: 'Defend to the last man.' Jaenicke protested against this virtual death sentence on his army – and was sacked, to be replaced on April 27 by General Karl Allmendinger. With sinking hearts, the defenders crouched behind barricades around Sevastopol – the Gneisenau Line had been penetrated on April 13-14 – and awaited the inevitable.

Facing them were three armies – about half a million men, with nearly 600 tanks. The Red Air Force ruled the skies, and by the first week in May, only 12 German planes were left out of 150. Preceded by a hail of bombs and shells, Second Guards Army attacked in the north on May 5, scaling the heavily defended Mackenzie Heights. Two days later, Fifty-First and Independent Coastal Armies attacked Sapun Heights, a key position south of Sevastopol, from Balaklava, where the British Light Brigade had made its hopeless charge against Russian guns 90 years earlier. Fifty-First Army attacked from the east, while Yeremenko struck from the south.

The heights were taken on May 8 and held against German counterattacks. The next day, Sevastopol itself fell, after bitter street fighting. About 30 000 desperate defenders struggled down to the beaches of Cape Kherson, which projects west into the Black Sea just south of Sevastopol, and hoped to be rescued by sea – for Hitler had finally given permission to evacuate.

That night, around 1000 men were picked up from the beaches, but Russian guns sank two ships. Soviet land-based guns, warships, gunboats and aircraft put an end to further rescue attempts. Planes of the Red Air Force reduced the beaches to a shambles. Tanks smashed into the defences.

Germans and Romanians surrendered in droves. However, about 750 SS troops obeyed the Führer's original orders and literally fought to the death. Altogether an estimated 31 700 Germans and 25 800 Romanians died or went missing in the Crimea. Another 37 000 Germans and 5000 Romanians are believed to have died in air strikes and in naval actions against Axis shipping there.

THE STALKERS Grim-faced and eager for revenge, men of a Soviet landing force advance to take the enemy from behind on the Crimean Peninsula. (Bottom) Another coastal raiding party – of Red Army Marines – storms a hill.

FIGHTING MARSHAL

Feodor Tolbukhin (1894-1949) was a captain in the Tsar's army in World War I and a Bolshevik staff officer in the Russian Civil War. In 1941 he was successively chief of staff of the Transcaucasian, Caucasian and Crimean Fronts, and in 1942-3 was an army commander at Stalingrad. His distinguished performance brought him promotion to command Southern Front.

It is his success in the Crimea in May 1944 for which Tolbukhin is best remembered. Later, in August and September, he trapped 200 000 German troops in Jassy (Iasi) and Kishinev in Moldavia; for this he was promoted marshal. Uniting with Marshal Tito's Yugoslav Communist partisans, he was instrumental in liberating Belgrade in October 1944. He then helped drive the Germans from Hungary. He became commander of the Soviet Union's Southern Group of Forces in July 1947.

A bomb for the Führer

'I am immortal', declared Hitler, after a bomb failed to kill him at two metres' range. Five thousand people were executed in retribution.

BY JUNE 1944 all hope of Germany winning the war was lost. Hitler seemed unable or unwilling to grasp this, obvious though it was to his generals. Any suggestion of peace negotiations was met by the Führer with fits of rage. Many generals and some prominent civilians were prepared to see Hitler killed if Germany could be saved. Among them were General Ludwig Beck, a prewar Chief of the Army General Staff, Maj General Baron Henning von Tresckow, chief of staff in Army Group Centre on the Eastern Front, Lt General Friedrich Olbricht, head of the Supply Section of the Reserve Army, and Carl Gördeler, a one-time mayor of Leipzig and former member of Hitler's government.

Attempts had been made on the Führer's life before 1944. In March 1943, Tresckow and a friend, Captain Fabian von Schlabrendorff, had tried to kill him using a delayed-action bomb hidden in a parcel containing brandy bottles. The bomb failed to go off. Luckily for the plotters it was not discovered. On another occasion, Colonel von Gersdorff volunteered to stuff his greatcoat pockets with time-bombs and jump on Hitler just as they were about to go off, killing himself and the dictator at the same time. But Gersdorff could not gain close enough access to Hitler.

The person who came closest to killing the Führer was Colonel Count Claus Schenk von Stauffenberg, a brilliant officer of 37 who had lost his right arm, his right eye and two fingers of his left hand with the Afrika Korps in Tunisia. Hitler recognised his qualities, and on promotion to full colonel Stauffenberg became Chief of Staff to General Friedrich Fromm, commander of the Reserve Army. This post gave him personal contact with the Führer. Stauffenberg came from an old Catholic family and, although patriotic, abhorred the Nazi regime. He told his wife: 'I feel I must do something now to save Germany.' He, Gördeler, Beck, Olbricht and other anti-Nazis worked out a plan – Operation 'Valkyrie' – to destroy Hitler and install a government which would seek peace with the Western Allies.

On the morning of July 20, Stauffenberg and his young aide, Lieutenant Werner von Häften, flew to the Führer's *Wolfsschanze* ('Wolf's Lair') headquarters at Rastenburg, deep in East Prussia (now Ketrzyn in northern Poland). Each carried a briefcase containing a 1 kg (2 lb) bomb fitted with a time fuse. On arrival, Stauffenberg learned that the conference he had been called to had been brought forward by an hour or so because Mussolini was due to visit Rastenburg that afternoon. This meant that he could get the job over sooner than he had thought. But there was a drawback: the underground bunker in which he proposed to plant his bomb was being strengthened, and a flimsy wooden hut was being used as the operations room. There, with windows open against the heat, the bomb would not be nearly so effective as in the confined bunker.

Stauffenberg ordered his pilot to be ready for takeoff at immediate notice, and left Häften with the staff car, ready for a quick getaway. Inside the hut Hitler, Field Marshal Wilhelm Keitel and 23 other officers were studying maps on a large oak table. Stauffenberg placed the briefcase against the table support, about 2 m (6 ft) from Hitler. The fuse had been set, and mumbling an excuse about making a phone call to Berlin, Stauffenberg left the hut. Behind him, another officer, Colonel Heinz Brandt, moved closer to the Führer. He kicked against the briefcase, picked it up and moved it – away from Hitler.

Meanwhile, Stauffenberg was strolling towards the waiting staff car. As he reached it at 12.42 pm, the bomb exploded. Smoke and flames rose from the shattered hut and screams rang out. Stauffenberg, convinced that Hitler was dead, flew back to Berlin with Häften.

LAIR OF DESTINY Days before the bomb blast, Adolf Hitler is greeted at the 'Wolf's Lair'. Stauffenberg is on the left, Keitel on the right. (Right) Benito Mussolini views the bomb damage.

But Hitler was very much alive – though injured. Moving the briefcase and the flimsiness of the hut had combined to reduce the effect of the bomb blast. A stenographer died instantly. Luftwaffe Chief of Staff General Günter Karten, the Chief of Army Personnel, Maj General Rudolf Schmundt, and Colonel Brandt were all mortally wounded. But Hitler limped away from the scene, supported by Keitel. The Führer was cut and bruised and had perforated ear drums. But he told his doctor: 'I am invulnerable, I am immortal.'

At the Berlin War Ministry, Stauffenberg, Häften, Olbricht and his chief of staff, Colonel Mertz von Quirnheim, were arrested, summarily court-martialled and shot. They were the lucky ones. On Hitler's orders the next eight conspirators arrested were hanged by piano-wire nooses from meathooks. Their agonising deaths were filmed for Hitler's entertainment.

The purges went on for months, horrific 'show trials' being staged by so-called People's Courts presided over by the notorious Judge Roland Freisler. Altogether about 5000 people were executed. Among them was the remarkable Protestant pastor and theologian Dietrich Bonhöffer, in prison since April 1943 for his anti-Nazi activities; he also had been involved in the conspiracy. Another victim was Admiral Wilhelm Canaris, former head of the Military Intelligence Department, the Abwehr. His department had been used as a cover for the conspiracy.

Many others involved with the plot, including Beck, committed suicide. Tresckow did so by walking into Russian gunfire on the Eastern Front. And in October Field Marshal Erwin Rommel took the poison offered him by the Gestapo as an alternative to being court-martialled. Rommel had known of the plot, but had not been involved in it.

The Red Army's superblitz

Three years to the day after Hitler launched his invasion of the Soviet Union, more than a million Russian troops began their own vast offensive. Soon the Germans were reeling, as blow followed blow in history's greatest blitzkrieg.

WHILE THE STRUGGLE in Normandy in the days after D-Day absorbed Hitler and the Western Allies, the Red Army was gathering itself for a gargantuan attack on the Eastern Front. An estimated 1.2 million troops in 166 divisions, with over 4000 tanks and self-propelled guns, were supported by 6000 Red Air Force planes. The German armies, which had earlier stunned the world with their blitzkriegs, were about to be given a demonstration of power beyond their wildest imaginings. They never recovered.

The Russians waited until June 22, 1944 – third anniversary, as it happened, of 'Barbarossa' and just over two weeks after D-Day – to launch their offensive. Stalin code-named it 'Bagration', after a Russian general who had fought in the 1812 war against Napoleon. Planning began in April, and the objective was Belorussia (White Russia), the heavily forested Soviet republic bordering on Poland. Here, defending German forces held a gigantic bulge into Russian-held territory, concentrated around four key points – Vitebsk, Orsha, Mogilev and Bobruysk (see map, p. 338). The Russians planned to smash these defences, to clear the way for a general westward advance.

General Ivan Bagramyan's 1st Baltic Front (Army Group) was to attack north of Vitebsk, and hold back any attempt at interference by the German Army Group North. Its left was to assault the city, aided by elements of General Ivan Chernyakhovsky's 3rd Belorussian Front; these would encircle Vitebsk from the south, linking up with 1st Baltic to the west. The rest of 3rd Belorussian would head through Orsha for Minsk, the republic's capital.

Lt General M.V. Zakharov's 2nd Belorussian Front would overrun Mogilev, then also attack Minsk. Meanwhile, Marshal Konstantin Rokossovsky's 1st Belorussian Front would surround Bobruysk, then join the others in wiping out German forces around Minsk. The next Soviet objective would be Poland's capital, Warsaw.

HITLER WRONG AGAIN

German intelligence reports warned General Ernst von Busch, commander of Army Group Centre, of the Russian build-up in his sector. But Hitler believed that the attack there would only be secondary. He thought that the Romanian oilfields to the south would be the major Soviet objective – and sent 48 infantry and three panzer and panzer grenadier divisions down there. This left Busch's forces dangerously stretched: he had only 38 infantry and two panzer divisions – some 500 000 men – to cover his vast 1050 km (650 mile) front.

The Russian blitz opened, at 5 am on June 22, with a massive bombardment by Bagramyan's 1st Baltic Front, followed at 7 by Chernyakhovsky's 3rd Belorussian. Chernyakhovsky alone had 178 guns per kilometre (285 per mile) of front line, supported by 166 Red Air Force sorties. Any German foolhardy enough to emerge from cover while the Russians launched these assaults would have seen countless T-34 tanks rumbling in, followed by hordes of Soviet infantry. Behind them came the grim silhouettes of SU-22 assault guns. General Georg-Hans Reinhardt's Third Panzer Army, facing 1st Baltic on the Dvina river, north of Vitebsk, was soon fighting for its life.

The Russians were using new tactics. No longer did they attack on a broad front with heavy artillery support all along the line. Instead, they concentrated the infantry in tight groups, which were supported by equally concentrated fire from heavy weapons.

By June 23 the speed and strength of the Russian advance, the overwhelming numbers of its tanks and men, had swept Third Panzer aside, despite brave German counterattacks. Reinhardt's LIII Corps, holding Vitebsk, was being encircled by Bagramyan's and Chernyakhovsky's Fronts. Reinhardt asked for permission to fall back. Busch, backed by Hitler, refused. Then, on June 24, Hitler relented – but by then it was too late. Vitebsk fell on June 27. About 20 000 Germans were killed and 10 000 taken prisoner.

PROGRESS IN THE SOUTH

Meanwhile, farther south, another succession of sledgehammer blows was falling on the hapless Germans. On June 27, Chernyakhovsky's armies put in a mighty left hook that took Orsha. Zakharov's 2nd Belorussian Front, to their south, had created a sizable bridgehead across the Dniepr and was ready to attack Mogilev. Farther south still, the tough veterans of Lt General Nikolaus von Vormann's Ninth Army put up a tremendous resistance. For a few days, they even managed to slow down the advance of Marshal Rokossovsky's 1st Belorussian Front, north-east of Bobruysk. But now Rokossovsky was on the move again – and picking up speed. Lead units of his IX Tank Corps linked up on June 27 with the Soviet Sixty-Fifth Army, pushing up from the south, and Bobruysk was encircled. Six of Vormann's divisions – about 40 000 men – were trapped. Hitler refused to let them break out.

Things were now desperate for the Germans. Even Busch had begun to realise it, but the Führer would not budge. On June 28, he instructed Army Group Centre to hold a line running from Polotsk

STALIN ON D-DAY

On the evening of June 6, 1944, Russian listeners heard Moscow Radio announce a great event: Allied troops were landing in Normandy. The news was received with genuine enthusiasm by most Russians, some of whom joined British and US officials celebrating in a Moscow restaurant that evening. Stalin was more cautious. 'History will record this action as an achievement of the highest order', he announced – but only published the tribute on June 14, when assured of the landings' success. Soviet leaders also stressed that it was the Red Army's successes that had made D-Day possible. To them, the Eastern Front was the war's key theatre. They played down the importance of the Western Front – for which they had repeatedly been calling since 1941.

ONE MAN AGAINST A SOVIET TANK

OVERWHELMING RUSSIAN superiority in armour during 1944 forced German troops to rely heavily on such portable anti-tank weapons as hollow-charge grenades. One panzer grenadier left this dramatic account of an anti-tank action:

"The first group of T-34s crashed through the undergrowth. My trench was almost in the front line . . . All that I had learned in the training school came flooding back and gave me confidence, but I must admit that I was frightened . . . we were ordered to attack just as the tanks entered the thicket.

My T-34 was now so close that I was in a blind spot and not in any immediate danger . . . The grenade had a safety cap which had to be unscrewed to reach the rip-cord. My fingers were trembling as I unscrewed the cap, felt the loop of the cord tighten in the crook of my first finger and, holding the grenade in my right hand, climbed out of the trench . . .

The T-34 was now only a few metres away on my right . . . Crouching low, I started towards the monster, pulled the detonating cord and prepared to fix the charge. I now had nine seconds before the grenade exploded and then I noticed, to my horror, that the outside of the tank was covered in concrete like our *Zimmerrit* [anti-magnetic] paste. My bomb could not stick on such a surface. It had to be flat and metal.

Worse was yet to come. The tank suddenly spun on its right track, turned so that it pointed straight at me, and moved forward as if to run over me.

I flung myself backwards and fell straight into a partly dug slit trench . . . As the tank rolled over me there was a sudden and total blackness. Luckily, the tracks passed on either side of me, but so close that the shallow earth walls of the trench began to collapse. As the belly of the monster passed over me, I reached up instinctively as if to push it away and, certainly without any conscious thought, stuck the charge on the smooth, unpasted metal. The three magnets held the bomb in position and barely had the tank passed over me than there was a loud explosion. Smoke poured out, then with a tremendous roar the vehicle burst into flames and blew up. I was alive and the Russians were dead . . ."

'THOSE MONSTERS'

Although Russian soldiers were undoubtedly guilty of outrages – murder, rape and arson frequently marked their path westwards – the Germans seemed particularly inhuman. The extermination of Jews continued to the end – in Klooga, Estonia, for example, the war correspondent Alexander Werth saw the charred remains of some 2000 Jews recently shot and burned on bonfires.

One Russian soldier recalled a bitter day when his regiment surrounded some Germans near Parichi, a village south of Bobruysk: 'The enemy put up a desperate resistance, but we pushed them into a pocket and went at them with our *Katyushas* [rockets]. That was when a farm woman came running to our forward line. Tears streaming down her face, she said: "Sons, come and see what those monsters have done!" We went.

'In the village, by a house that had served the Nazis as a field hospital, she showed us a pit that had been covered over by soil. That soil still breathed . . . We shovelled it away and the sight of what was beneath filled us with horror. The pit was full of the bodies of little boys and girls between ten and 12 years. We learned that the Nazi butchers had used them to give blood transfusions to their wounded officers and then had thrown them in the pit. I sincerely wish that no one ever feels what we did at that moment.'

CRY OF THE BEREAVED Russian villagers grieve over their menfolk, massacred by the Germans.

in the north to the Berezina river in the south, below Bobruysk; it took little account of the actual situation in Belorussia. That same evening, Busch, for all his blind faithfulness to Hitler, was removed and replaced by the veteran Field Marshal Walther Model.

The situation Model inherited was bleak. The Germans were being harried by increasingly powerful bands of partisans – who had put almost all Belorussian railways out of action, paralysing the Wehrmacht supply network before the Russian onslaught had even begun. Then, in the five days before June 28, the Russians had advanced 150 km (95 miles), destroyed 13 German divisions and inflicted 200 000 casualties.

Now, on June 28 itself, Zakharov's troops took Mogilev, and Rokossovsky's tanks and Red air strikes began battering the Bobruysk pocket. Marshal Georgi Zhukov, of the Soviet Supreme Command, described the scene: 'Hundreds of bombers flew sortie after sortie . . . Fires broke out on the battlefield. Dozens of vehicles and tanks were in flames; fuel and lubricant dumps, too. The whole battlefield was brightly lit up . . . This entirely hideous "choir" was augmented by artillery shelling from Forty-Eighth Army. Half-crazed German soldiers were running in all directions; those who did not want to give themselves up died on the spot.'

About 6000 Germans survived to be taken prisoner when Bobruysk fell on June 29. By then, Rokossovsky's tanks were already racing towards Minsk. Always one step ahead of their enemy, the Russians planned to destroy the German Fourth Army east of Minsk. Troops of 2nd Belorussian Front, pushing westwards from Mogilev, would pin down the retreating Germans while fast-moving armoured forces from 1st and 3rd Belorussian Fronts worked around their flanks to create a giant 'bag' to trap them.

The armour made good progress – but the going was not always easy. On June 30, a Russian tank force reached Borisov, on the west bank of the Berezina. Only one tank managed to cross the river into the town before the Germans blew up

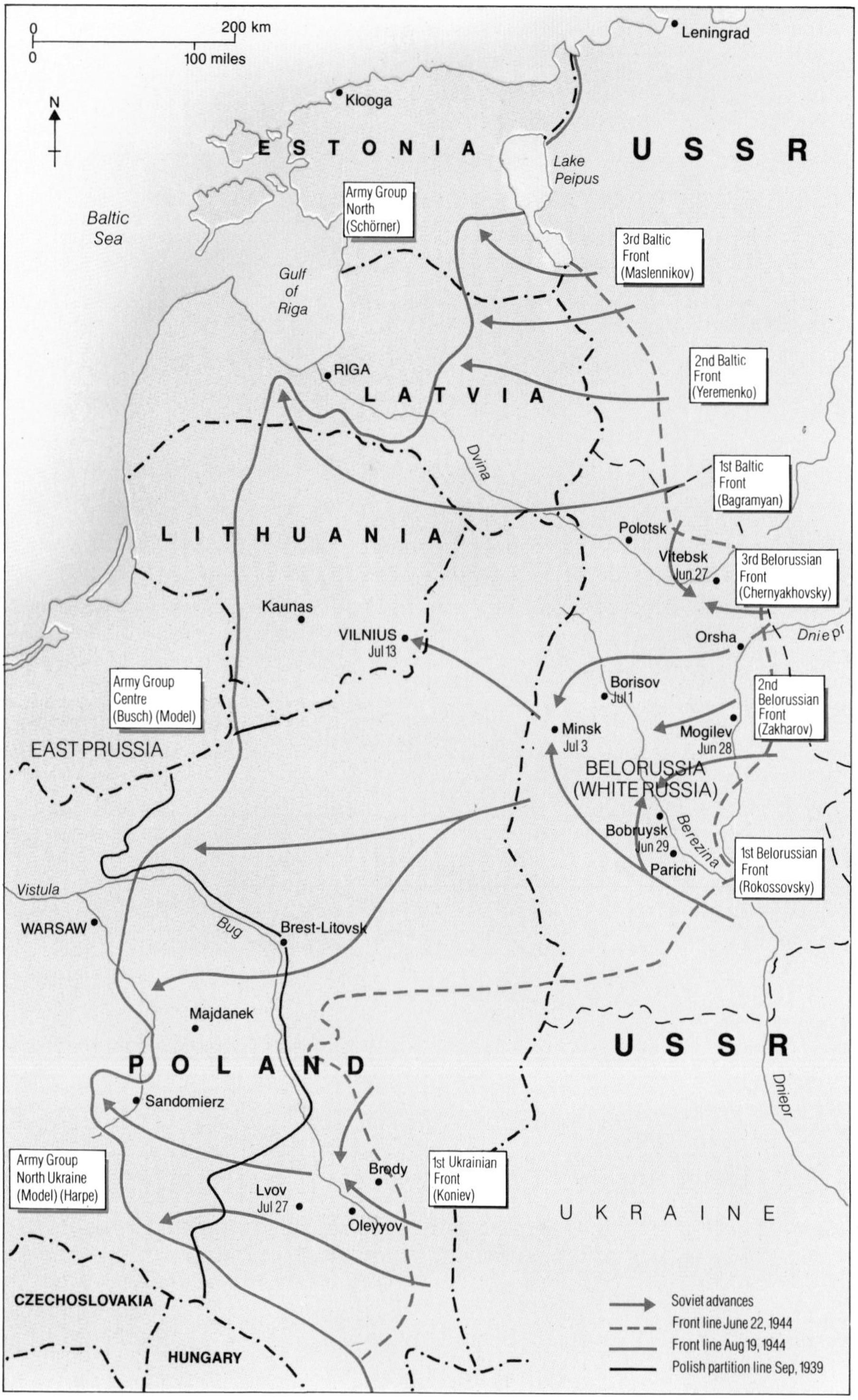

PUSHED BACK AND BACK 'Bagration' opened in June 1944. By August, despite brave German resistance, the Red Army had reached the Vistula, East Prussia and the Gulf of Riga.

the bridge, leaving the tank isolated. The crew held out valiantly for 16 hours, and managed to destroy a German headquarters before they were overwhelmed by sheer numbers.

Borisov fell on July 1 and Minsk two days later – reduced to ruins in fierce fighting. Over 100 000 Germans were now stranded on the east bank of the Berezina. The Soviet drive west took priority, but three armies were diverted to annihilate the surrounded Germans. Fourth Army's XII Corps, under Lt General Friedrich Muller, surrendered on July 8. About 35 000 men of Ninth Army were also captured in the 'Minsk Pocket'.

Russians, meanwhile, were streaming through the 400 km (250 mile) gap now torn open, and were soon pushing into the Baltic states. Chernyakhovsky's troops took the Lithuanian city of Vilnius (Vilna) on July 13, smashing the battered remnants of Third Panzer Army. By July 31, nearly six weeks after the offensive began, the Russians had reached the Gulf of Riga, cutting off Army Group North. True, they were beginning to outrun supply lines, and had to slow down, but Belorussia was won – the fifth great success in the Red Army's Year of Ten Victories.

TAKING WESTERN UKRAINE

The German Army Group North Ukraine, holding the area south of Army Group Centre, was made up of 31 German divisions with some Hungarian and Ukrainian SS formations. They expected an onslaught – and they got one, as the Red Army swept to the sixth of the year's great victories, in the Western Ukraine. Marshal Ivan Koniev's 1st Ukrainian Front struck in the region east of Lvov (Lemburg) on July 13. The Soviet attack was not preceded by the usual bombardment and was relatively ineffective – until the next day, when the baritone chorus of Red Army artillery at last opened up.

But the Germans were brave and fought back with their customary skill. In a counterattack on July 14, 1st Panzer Division, from Fourth Panzer Army, smashed into the Russian flank at Oleyyov, east of Lvov, and stopped its advance dead. The 8th Panzer Division was not so lucky, and was caught on the move by the Red Air Force. One German recalled: 'Long columns of tanks and lorries went up in flames and all hopes of a counterattack disappeared.'

The Germans were forced steadily back. By July 18, Fourth Panzer Army was back on the Bug river, near the 1939 frontier between German and Russian-occupied Poland, from which 'Barbarossa' had been launched. And Soviet tanks had cut off XIII Corps at Brody.

Maj General Friederich von Mellenthin, 8th Panzer Division's temporary commander, witnessed a desperate bid by XIII Corps to smash its way out of the Brody death trap: 'Thousands of men formed up in the night in a solid mass and, to the accompaniment of thunderous "hurrahs" threw themselves at the enemy. The impact of a great block of desperate men, determined to do or die, smashed through the Russian line . . . But all guns and heavy weapons had to be abandoned and a huge gap opened in the front.' Barely 5000 men, out of 30 000, reached the German lines.

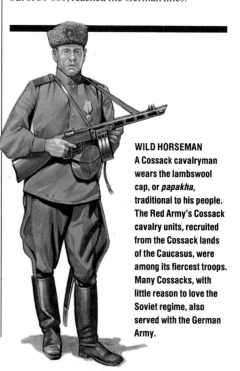

WILD HORSEMAN
A Cossack cavalryman wears the lambswool cap, or *papakha*, traditional to his people. The Red Army's Cossack cavalry units, recruited from the Cossack lands of the Caucasus, were among its fiercest troops. Many Cossacks, with little reason to love the Soviet regime, also served with the German Army.

THREE GENERALS

Ivan Danilovich Chernyakhovsky (1906-45) was one of the youngest top-ranking Soviet commanders of the war. The son of a Ukrainian railway worker, he joined the Red Army in 1924. He gained experience as a divisional commander in 1941, then after a brief spell with the XVIII Tank Corps, took command of Sixtieth Army in July 1942. He led it in the great tank battle at Kursk a year later.

Chernyakhovsky's performance so impressed his superiors that he was promoted to full general and given command of 3rd Belorussian Front in April 1944 for the Belorussian offensive. He was just 38. He liberated Vilnius (Vilna) in Lithuania, and by the end of the year was battering his way into East Prussia, where in February 1945 he met an untimely death when hit by shell fragments. He had twice been made a Hero of the Soviet Union.

Chernyakhovsky's opponent at Vitebsk, Georg-Hans Reinhardt (1887-1963), commanded XLI Panzer Corps in the 1940 campaign in western Europe and the same formation in 'Barbarossa' in 1941. His corps was the armoured spearhead of Fourth Panzer Army, and in September 1941 made the farthest penetration of any German formation towards Leningrad. The next month he was appointed to command Third Panzer Group (later renamed Third Panzer Army) in Army Group Centre's advance on Moscow.

He spent the next two years leading Third Panzer, and after the 1944 disaster in Belorussia he was promoted to command Army Group Centre as full general. However, he failed to halt the Soviet advance into East Prussia and was sacked in January 1945. Reinhardt was a competent panzer commander, promoted too late to demonstrate his skill in the offensive.

The commander of Army Group Centre during Operation 'Bagration', Ernst von Busch (1885-1945), was a career soldier and World War I veteran. He became a dedicated Nazi after Hitler took power in 1933. Five years later he was commanding VIII Corps, and fought in Poland in 1939 and in the west the following spring. Busch was awarded the Knight's Cross, and as a further mark of Hitler's favour was selected to spearhead the proposed invasion of England at the head of Sixteenth Army. Instead, he took part in the attack on Russia in 1941. He was appointed to command Army Group Centre in October 1943.

During the fighting for Belorussia in June 1944, Busch's insistence on carrying out Hitler's orders to the letter contributed to Army Group Centre's poor performance – and he was sacked for his pains. However, in March 1945 he was brought back as Commander in Chief North West, directing German forces in Denmark, Schleswig-Holstein and the northern Netherlands. Captured by the British in 1945, Busch died in a prison camp.

Lvov fell on July 27 and, scarcely pausing, the Russians drove ever westward.

Meanwhile on July 18, Rokossovsky's 1st Belorussian Front had resumed its drive into Poland. German hopes in this sector rested in a stout defence of Brest-Litovsk (now Brest) on the Bug – a key position. If Fourth Panzer Army could hold on there, they might even comply with Hitler's demands for a counterattack.

HOPES STRUCK DOWN

Their optimism was soon shattered. Russian spearheads began pushing north and south of the stronghold, and by July 25 had passed it and reached the Vistula river. The day before, the Russians had entered Majdenek death camp, west of Lublin. This had already been evacuated by the Germans, but Soviet troops stumbled in horror on the charred remains of bodies, and the gas chambers and crematoria. It was one of the first such camps to be freed.

Then, with ferries and pontoon bridges – sturdy enough to take the heaviest tanks – Rokossovsky's and Koniev's troops crossed the Vistula and established a bridgehead at Sandomierz, 180 km (110 miles) south of Warsaw. Despite a German counterattack, Rokossovsky's men were soon within 13 km (8 miles) of the Polish capital, where the tragedy of the 'Uprising' was about to unfold (see feature, p. 340).

Elsewhere, the flight of Army Group Centre allowed the Red Army to attack the flank of Army Group North in Estonia. Here, General Ferdinand Schörner could field only 33 battered divisions against 133 Soviet ones. Despite a skilful defensive battle, Schörner was by October trapped, with his back to the icy waters of the Baltic. Army Group North stayed marooned there until the war ended, though Schörner himself was transferred to Army Group Centre in January 1945. The taking of Estonia and neighbouring Latvia to the south was the eighth of the Russians' ten victories.

Operation 'Bagration' and the follow-up offensives to north and south added up to the most staggeringly successful operation of the war. One German general, Siegfried von Westphal, wrote: 'On the Eastern Front, during the summer and autumn of 1944, the German armies suffered the greatest disaster of their history, which even surpassed the catastrophe of Stalingrad.'

'NIGHT WITCHES' AND OTHER AIRFOLK

By 1944 the Red Air Force had made a remarkable comeback. In 1941 it had seemed near annihilation; it lost 7500 aircraft and thousands of airmen in the first three months alone of 'Barbarossa'. But now the tables were turned: the Russians had some 8500 operational front-line planes against the Germans' 2000. Factories in the east of the Soviet Union were churning out sturdy machines, such as the Ilyushin Il-2 Stormovik, and the Russians had received hundreds of US and British aircraft under Lend-Lease.

The Red Air Force had also tapped the skills of some remarkable fliers – its three all-women regiments, for example, including the so-called 'Night Witches' of the 588th (later 46th Guards) Night Bomber Regiment. These regiments first saw action in 1942, and in September that year Valerya Khomyakova became the first woman in the history of air warfare to shoot down an enemy plane, a German Junkers Ju88 bomber. A remarkable male flier was Ivan Kozhedub (1920-) – with 62 'kills', top Red Air Force ace. Over Kursk he shot down two Stukas and two Messerschmitt Me109 fighters in one day. Later in Romania in 1944 he shot down eight German aircraft in seven days. The top-scoring woman ace was Lydia Litvak, killed in action in 1943, with 12 kills.

But the Russians had no monopoly on valour. The German Erich Hartmann (1922-) was the war's highest-scoring fighter ace of either side. He was active over Kursk and Belorussia, and continued his victories to the end. On May 9, 1945 – after VE Day but before the surrender on the Eastern Front came into effect – he shot down his last Russian over Brno in Czechoslovakia. The Germans credited Hartmann with 352 victories; official British and US sources gave him 263 – still a remarkable record.

WOMAN PILOT The Red Air Force's all-women regiments served over Stalingrad, Kursk and throughout the Soviet westward advance.

ACES, FEMALE AND MALE Top Russian woman ace Lydia Litvak (above, on left) studies the map before an 'op'. Her male counterpart was Ivan Kozhedub (right).

The horror of Warsaw

With the Red Army only 13 km (8 miles) away, Warsaw's Underground rose against the Nazis.

THE RADIO messages were electrifying: 'People of Warsaw, to arms! Attack the Germans! Help the Red Army . . . show the way.' The first call, broadcast in Polish from Moscow, came on July 29, 1944: 'The hour of action has struck . . . By fighting in the streets of Warsaw we shall bring nearer the moment of ultimate liberation . . .'

Few of the Polish AK (*Armija Krajowa*, or Home Army) had any illusion about their task. Although they numbered some 40 000 men, armed mainly with captured German weapons, plus 210 000 unarmed helpers, they had nothing to repel the heavy armour of the Luftwaffe Hermann Göring Division, supported later by the 19th Panzer Division. However, they hoped to seize and hold key areas until the Russians arrived. Maj General Tadeusz Bor-Komorowski, the AK's leader, was in touch with the Polish government-in-exile in London and had its approval for the venture.

EXPLOSIVE ATTACK

At 5 pm on a hot August 1, the rising exploded. With the advantage of surprise, the Poles seized three-fifths of the city in four days. Even as they were striking the first blows, however, the Germans threw in elements of three new armoured divisions against the Russians outside Warsaw and Marshal Konstantin Rokossovsky's 1st Belorussian Front was driven back about 100 km (60 miles).

German reinforcements also began to pour into the embattled city under the command of SS Lt General Erich von dem Bach-Zelewski, an expert in crushing – and slaughtering – partisan groups. His forces included the 4000 murderous thugs of the Dirlewanger penal brigade and 6000 Russian defectors and prisoners of war in the Kaminski brigade. They enthusiastically obeyed Himmler's order of August 1 to 'destroy tens of thousands'. Nevertheless, at the end of the first week, the Poles still held the Old Town and two other areas, one north of it, the other to the south.

The main German drive, against the Old Town, steadily herded the AK into a shrinking territory. The 100 000 citizens of the area huddled in their cellars. Colonel Karol Wachnowski, the AK district commander, wrote gloomily in his diary on August 29: 'No food, little water, bad sanitary conditions, dysentery . . . little sign of speedy help.' The Polish men, women and children – some as young as ten – fought with a courage born of desperation. Even the disabled joined in. One unit leader, Janusz Zawodny, later wrote that 'an armed platoon of deaf mutes defended their own building'.

The young girls who carried messages and orders crawled for miles inside slimy sewers to avoid snipers' bullets. Often they emerged with torn clothes and infected wounds from coils of barbed wire planted by the Germans. With the numbers of wounded soaring, Polish doctors had to operate anywhere handy – often by flashlight or candlelight and without anaesthetics or even disinfectants.

Buildings changed hands again and again. Eventually the combatants were fighting for debris. On September 24, the 2500 insurgents left alive in the Old Town withdrew through the sewers to the northern sector of the city. The fighting in the other areas followed the same pattern: the Poles fought heroically but were pushed back street by street, house by house.

An underground newspaper put out in Warsaw reported: 'We . . . caught sight of the existence of Hell in Zeromski Park and the forts. Collections of the most diverse social groups are living there in desperate conditions. Hunger is written all over their miserable grey faces. Many have had nothing in their mouths apart from water for several days. The lamentable state of the children cries out for help.'

Rape and murder accompanied the relentless German advance. In areas the Germans cleared, Polish males were shot. The German commander Bach-Zelewski himself saw 'wild masses of policemen and soldiers . . . shooting civilians. I saw the heap of dead bodies splashed with gasoline and set afire.' Civilians – even the wounded – were used as living barricades in front of tanks. Doctors and nurses in captured hospitals were shot on the spot. Any wounded left behind when the Poles retreated were doused with petrol and burned. Although Bach-Zelewski forbade such behaviour, his sadistic troops continued it.

From their positions to the south and east, the Russians could clearly see Warsaw's burning buildings and pall of smoke. Too late, on September 10, they began to advance on Warsaw's suburbs. Had they deliberately hung back, hoping to see the AK crushed? After all, the AK – whom Stalin called 'power-seeking criminals' – were loyal to the government-in-exile founded by Wladyslaw Sikorski, while Stalin planned to have a pro-Soviet group in power in postwar Poland. He even denied some British aircraft the right to refuel at Soviet bases after dropping supplies to the AK.

On the other hand, the Red Army had outrun its supply system and had to gather strength before assaulting the tough German defences around Warsaw. Rokossovsky himself said later that the timing of the uprising 'would have made sense only if we were already on the point of entering Warsaw. That point had not been reached . . . We could not have got Warsaw before the middle of August.' Any blame for the tragedy would seem to attach more to Stalin – for encouraging a premature uprising – than to the Russian army commanders on the ground.

SURRENDER WITH HONOUR

Finally, on October 2, with the Russians unable to break through, the Poles capitulated. Some 200 000 civilians and 15 000 AK members had died. There were 10 000 dead among the 26 000 German casualties. The Germans surprisingly granted the Polish insurgents prisoner-of-war status.

More than 15 000 of them, including 2000 women and 550 children, were marched off to prison camps. As they went, thousands upon thousands of Warsaw's bloody, emaciated, starving population wept. Some rushed to embrace the soldiers, some knelt as they passed. As they joined in singing their national anthem, it was evident that Poland's heart beat still.

A CITY LAID WASTE German troops prepare to fire 380 mm (15 in) rockets, which arch (far right) over the desolation of Warsaw's streets.

Dirty work in the Balkans

As the Red Army burst into the Balkans in 1944, Axis allies began switching sides. Guerrilla leaders scuffled viciously over who would take control when the war ended, while the Powers used them as pawns in a greater political game.

DICTATORS were fashionable in the Balkans in 1940-1. In Romania, Ion Antonescu had seized power from King Carol, forcing him to abdicate in favour of his son, Prince Michael; Prince Paul of Yugoslavia had taken over the dictatorship set up by his brother; and in Bulgaria a tsarist monarchy held sway, under King Boris. Hungary, too, was ruled by a pro-German leader, the self-styled regent, Admiral Miklós Horthy, while Albania had been overrun by Fascist Italy in 1939. Greece was ruled by the dictator General Ioannis Metaxas.

Hitler therefore had every reason to believe that a German 'alliance' (in fact, more like an occupation) would be welcomed in these countries. And in many it was, to begin with – though Yugoslavia and Greece dared to resist. But when the Russians began to pour across their frontiers in 1944 there were rapid and violent changes of heart – dictators deposed monarchs, monarchs deposed dictators, and partisans fought rival groups of partisans.

At the same time, Stalin and Churchill, meeting in Moscow, agreed to carve up the Balkans into spheres of influence: Romania and Bulgaria would fall predominantly into the Russian sphere; Hungary and Yugoslavia were supposed to come equally into British and Soviet spheres, but ultimately fell under Communist control; Greece was to be left mostly to the British.

ROMANIAN ROULETTE

The Germans entered Romania in October 1940. It was an uneasy alliance, for although Antonescu was loyal to his German masters, other politicians and some Romanian army commanders were secret Russian sympathisers. It was not until the Russians made their determined westward thrust, however, that Romanian disenchantment with their alliance began to show. On August 20, 1944, Soviet shock troops of the 2nd and 3rd Ukrainian Fronts (Army Groups) attacked the Romanian Third and Fourth Armies, which lay at Tiraspol and Jassy (Iasi) on either flank of the German Sixth Army, on the Russian-Romanian border. The Romanians put up little resistance.

Events then took a rapid turn. On August 23, King Michael arrested Antonescu and announced that he would accept Allied armistice terms. Hitler promptly demanded the King's arrest and the reinstatement of Antonescu or another pro-German leader. General Johannes Friessner, commander of the German Army Group South Ukraine, sent 6000 troops to support German forces already in Bucharest. But the Romanian army put up a fierce defence and the Germans were halted. Hitler ordered the Luftwaffe to bomb the royal palace and government buildings. King Michael retaliated by declaring war on his country's erstwhile ally on August 26.

Now the Russian drive in north-eastern Romania began to gain impetus. At Jassy, 2nd and 3rd Ukrainian Fronts had surrounded the German Sixth Army, which suffered enormous casualties – by August 29 about 200 000 Germans were dead, missing, wounded or prisoner. With the Sixth Army decimated, the German Eighth Army was in retreat into the northern passes of the wild and rugged Carpathian mountains. On August 31 the Russians entered Bucharest.

Meanwhile, King Michael, having restored political rights and freed prisoners, sent peace emissaries to meet Allied representatives at Cairo. They were sent on to Moscow, where they signed an armistice with 2nd Ukrainian Front's commander, Marshal Rodion Malinovsky, on September 12. The British and American ambassadors were present – but took no part in the proceedings. Romania became a Soviet satellite. Michael abdicated in 1947.

> ### SLOVAK UPRISING
>
> In August 1944, an armed uprising flared in Slovakia, the eastern part of prewar Czechoslovakia that had become a nominally independent German satellite state. The anti-German rebels consisted of Soviet-led partisans and troops from the Slovak state's army, acting under orders from Moscow, local leadership and the Czechoslovak government-in-exile in London.
>
> From late 1943, resistance leaders had been planning an uprising, and since June 1944 partisans had been active in the mountains of central Slovakia. Then in August, Hitler, angered by the partisans' successes, ordered German troops into Slovakia. On the 29th, rebel Slovak officers gave the signal for a military revolt, while resistance leaders broadcast a call to arms.
>
> The rising was premature. Only in central Slovakia did the rebels win control of large amounts of territory, holding back the Germans. Meanwhile, on September 8 and 14, troops of the Soviet 1st and 4th Ukrainian Fronts started an offensive in the Carpathians along Slovakia's northern borders. The fighting was tough, but on October 6 Soviet and Czechoslovak troops fighting with the Red Army managed to take the key Dukla Pass. It seemed that the Red Army might be able to link up with the Slovak rebels.
>
> These hopes were dashed on October 18, when seven German divisions advanced into Slovakia, brutally burning villages, shooting villagers and deporting thousands to concentration camps. By the end of October, 'Free Slovakia' was free no more; the rebels, who had sustained some 100 000 casualties, fled to the mountains to keep up a guerrilla war. The Russians continued an exhausting advance through the Carpathians until late November.

SKULDUGGERY IN BULGARIA

Bulgaria too would become a Russian satellite. Although King Boris had declared war on Britain and the USA in December 1941, Bulgaria was never officially at war with the Soviet Union. However, Boris died in August 1943 – rather mysteriously, after a stormy visit to Hitler; it was rumoured that he had been poisoned. A regency council then took power on behalf of the new King Simon II, still a child. The council – Boris's brother Prince Cyril, Professor Bogdan Filor and General Nikola Michov – announced Bulgaria's withdrawal from the war on August 26, 1944.

But Stalin refused to accept this declaration, and on September 5 declared war on Bulgaria. He wanted to make sure that the Soviet Union 'liberated' it, and that peace negotiations took place in Moscow, with Britain and America excluded. Three days later, men from Marshal Feodor Tolbukhin's 3rd Ukrainian Front crossed into Bulgaria; they met no resistance. That same day, Bulgaria declared war on Germany. It made no difference: as had happened in Romania, the armistice was signed in Moscow, on October 28, watched by Field Marshal Sir Henry Maitland Wilson, representing the Western Allies, who took no part. Stalin's armies had won the seventh of their ten victories of 1944.

A new Communist government was set up in Bucharest, which embarked upon a reign of terror, imprisoning and shooting about 40 000 pro-Germans and other adversaries – including the three regents.

HUNGARY GETS THE MESSAGE

While Romania and Bulgaria fell easily to the Russians, the Soviet advance through Hungary was slow. An attempt by Admiral Horthy to defect to the Russian side in early October was quickly foiled by the Germans. They first tried to put pressure on him by kidnapping his son, Nikolaus (Mussolini's rescuer, Otto Skorzeny, carried out this deed). They then imprisoned the 76-year-old admiral and replaced him with Ferenc Szalasi, a fanatical fascist. At a meeting with Hitler, Szalasi agreed that Budapest, the Hungarian capital, must be held 'at any price'.

Meanwhile, on October 5, men from Malinovsky's 2nd Ukrainian Front had lunged across the border from Romania into Hungary. They pushed back the Hungarian defenders, but met stiff resistance from the Germans. On October 10 a fierce tank battle raged on the flat plain north of the ancient city of Debrecen, when III Panzer and XXIX Corps encircled the Russian I Tank and II Guards Cavalry Corps. This limited success could not be sustained but the Germans made the Red Army fight every bit of the way.

After a series of furious clashes on the plain, General Issa Pliev's Cavalry Mechanised Group took Nyiregyhaza, north of Debrecen, only to be driven out again. On October 30, Malinovsky's troops entered the city once more. Now the Russian-occupied part of Hungary decided to back the winner, and set up a Provisional National Assembly in early December. In a stirring address to the Hungarian people, its chairman, Debrecen's mayor, Dr Vasary, urged: 'Turn your arms against the German oppressors and help the Red Army . . . for the good of a Free and Democratic Hungary.' A coalition government was led by General Bela Miklos and included three communists. Meanwhile, Szalasi was still trying to hold to his agreement with Hitler.

On October 29, Lt General I.T. Shlemin's

Forty-Sixth Army started a swift drive towards Budapest. By November 4, IV Guards Mechanised Corps had reached the southern and eastern suburbs of the capital, but were then held by German armour. A second assault lasted for 16 days, and still the Russians failed to take Budapest. Though now cut off, the city did not fall until February 13, 1945. By then, on Russian estimates, the Germans and Hungarians had lost 50 000 killed and 13 000 taken prisoner.

TURMOIL IN YUGOSLAVIA

When the Germans invaded Yugoslavia in 1941, a leading communist named Josip Broz was living in the suburbs of Zagreb. Broz, known as 'Comrade Tito', immediately set about organising partisan resistance. Now began a long, bloody and confused guerrilla war in which Serbs fought Serbs – not to mention Yugoslavia's numerous other national groups, such as the Slovenes and Croatians – as well as the invaders. At the same time, two men struggled to impose their conflicting ideologies on postwar Yugoslavia.

From mountain strongholds, Tito's National Liberation Army harried the Germans at every opportunity, blowing up railways, cutting telegraph wires and ambushing troops. To begin with these were mere pinpricks, but in June 1941 the partisans attacked Italian occupation forces and drove them almost into the Adriatic Sea. The Germans had a full-scale revolt on their hands.

Meanwhile, a former army colonel named Draza Mihailovic had formed a group of guerrillas known as the Chetniks. Tito and Mihailovic met at Ravna Gora in September 1941, but at once it was apparent that there could be no agreement between them. Tito was determined to turn Yugoslavia into a Communist state, whereas Mihailovic was an ardent royalist.

They met again in October, by which time the Allies had started to take an interest in their guerrilla activities, which prompted the landing from a submarine off the Adriatic coast of Captain 'Bill' Hudson of the British Special Operations Executive (SOE). Hudson's instructions were to contact Mihailovic. At the second meeting, at which Mihailovic refused to let Tito meet Hudson, negotiations broke down, and fighting began between the Chetniks and Tito's partisans.

The Allies, however, continued to support Mihailovic, sending him supplies – though, unknown to them, he was also accepting arms from the Germans and taking part in major offensives against Tito's partisans. Tito, meanwhile, was organising and recruiting an efficient fighting army, and by the end of 1942 had built up a force of 150 000 men. During the next year they withstood five major Axis offensives, but Tito hung on grimly, hoping for Russian help.

The Allies had little knowledge of Tito's activities. But by the end of 1942 messages from British liaison officers with the Chetniks made it clear that Mihailovic was double-crossing them. In May 1943, Allied liaison officers were parachuted into Tito's headquarters in Croatia, arriving in time for the Axis' fifth and most determined offensive, by German, Italian and Bulgarian forces as well as Chetniks. Greatly outnumbered, the partisans found themselves trapped in the mountains of Montenegro, but in ten days of fighting in June three partisan divisions broke through the Sutjeska Gorge and Tito's army had survived – though with the loss of 8000 men and women. When the Italians quit the war in September, Tito seized the Dalmatian coast, along with huge stores of Italian arms.

In the same month, Brigadier Fitzroy Maclean was parachuted into Yugoslavia as Churchill's personal envoy to Tito. After a favourable report from Maclean (later joined in Yugoslavia by Churchill's son, Randolph), the British began to throw their support behind the partisans, and by mid-1944 Tito had liberated large areas of southern Yugoslavia. In September, he met Stalin in Moscow, and on October 20, after a week-long siege, Tito's forces with men from Tolbukhin's 3rd Ukrainian Front liberated Belgrade. The Russians claimed it as their ninth victory of the year (though it was as much Tito's victory as theirs); the eighth victory had been in Estonia and Latvia. Mihailovic was tried and executed in 1946 by Tito's postwar government.

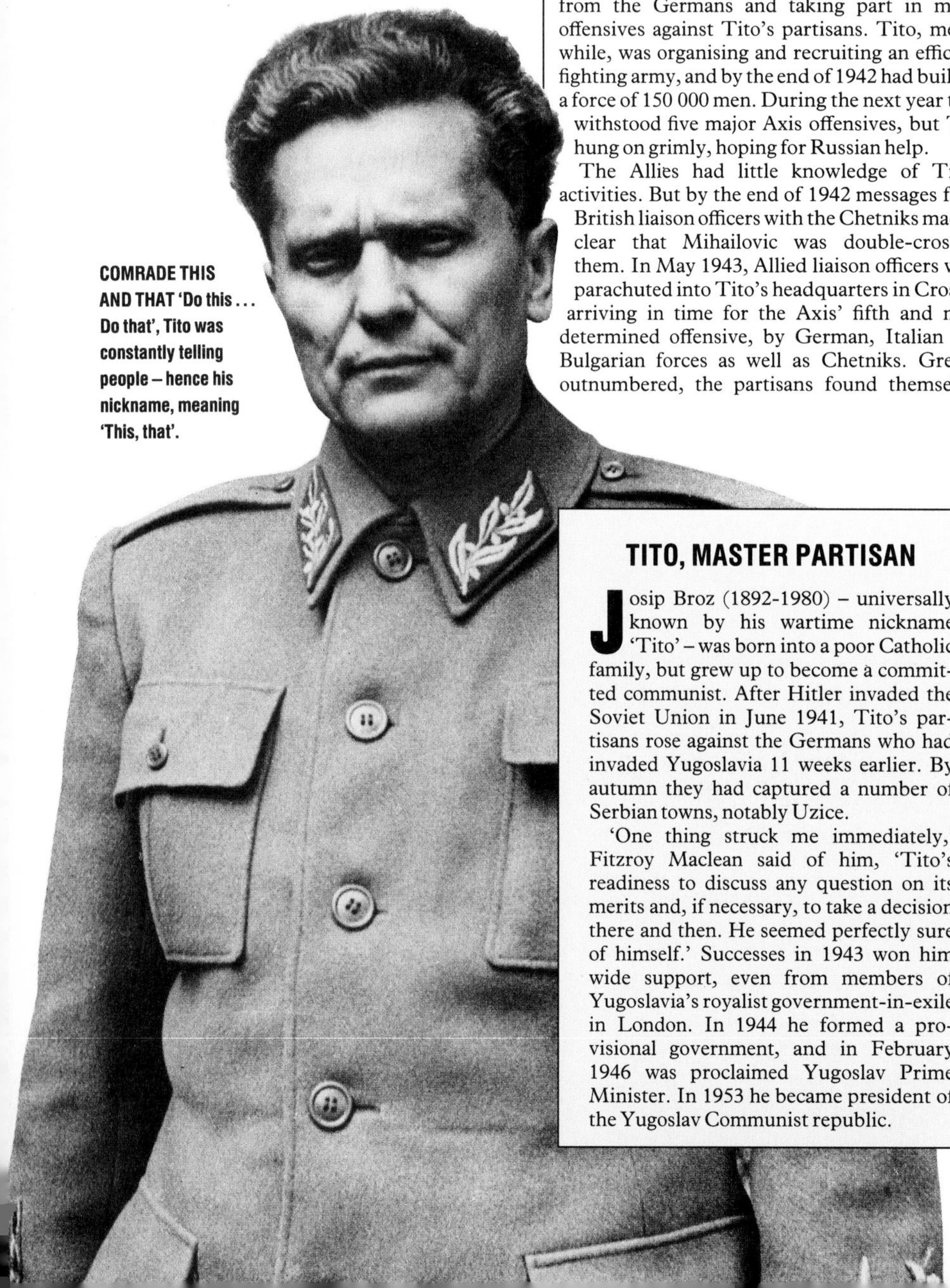

COMRADE THIS AND THAT 'Do this . . . Do that', Tito was constantly telling people – hence his nickname, meaning 'This, that'.

TITO, MASTER PARTISAN

Josip Broz (1892-1980) – universally known by his wartime nickname 'Tito' – was born into a poor Catholic family, but grew up to become a committed communist. After Hitler invaded the Soviet Union in June 1941, Tito's partisans rose against the Germans who had invaded Yugoslavia 11 weeks earlier. By autumn they had captured a number of Serbian towns, notably Uzice.

'One thing struck me immediately,' Fitzroy Maclean said of him, 'Tito's readiness to discuss any question on its merits and, if necessary, to take a decision there and then. He seemed perfectly sure of himself.' Successes in 1943 won him wide support, even from members of Yugoslavia's royalist government-in-exile in London. In 1944 he formed a provisional government, and in February 1946 was proclaimed Yugoslav Prime Minister. In 1953 he became president of the Yugoslav Communist republic.

GOINGS-ON IN GREECE

In Greece and Albania in the autumn of 1944 the Germans suddenly found themselves in danger of being cut off from the Reich. General Alexander Löhr received orders to start pulling out his Army Group E immediately after Romania's surrender and Bulgaria's declaration of war on Germany. He managed it, though a third of the 60 000 men garrisoning the Aegean islands – including Crete – were left behind, cut off until the war ended.

Löhr's progress north was eased considerably by a secret pact reached with the communist guerrillas of ELAS, the Greek National People's Liberation Army: they agreed not to hinder Löhr's retreat in return for heavy arms and equipment. This they used, in what developed into a full-scale civil war, against partisans loyal to King George II of the Hellenes, whose government returned to Athens from exile in England in October. British troops escorting them became embroiled in December in bloody street fighting in Athens against ELAS forces.

Meanwhile, there had been more trouble for the retreating Germans in Albania, where a guerrilla force led by the Albanian communist Enver Hoxha swooped down on them from mountain strongholds. In November, Hoxha's guerrillas mauled Löhr's XXI Mountain Corps.

In Yugoslavia, Löhr fought his way past the partisans and the west-thrusting Russian armies to meet General Maximilian de Angelis's Second Panzer Army at Sarajevo in mid-November. The remainder of Army Group E gradually caught up – hampered by such annoyances as the bombing of the bridge over the Drina river at Visegrad, which caused a 135 km (85 mile) traffic jam.

As 1945 dawned, momentous events in northern Europe had consigned this area of the Balkans to a minor role, and the Germans were left holding a line stretching roughly along the Danube from the Hungarian border to Vukovar, in northern Yugoslavia, then south along the Drina; this line changed little until the war ended. British troops, however, were still closely involved in events in Greece, where fighting continued in the streets of Athens until a pact was signed on January 11; in six weeks the British had suffered over 2000 casualties in the Greek capital. A non-communist regime was set up, but Greece – indeed, most of the Balkans – would remain in a state of turmoil for some time to come.

THE ARTFUL ALBANIAN

The Moscow-trained general secretary of the Albanian Communist party, Enver Hoxha (1908-85), was the exceptionally tough and vigorous initiator of the National Liberation Movement (LNC). Hoxha, a former schoolteacher, raised a fighting force of some 13 000 men, which included non-communists. A rival, anti-communist National Front movement also emerged, however, and sometimes collaborated with the Germans who occupied the country after Benito Mussolini's fall in 1943.

In his memoirs, *The Artful Albanian*, he was sardonic about British aid; sometimes, he said, it consisted of weapons without enough ammunition, or boots for only one foot. When the Germans withdrew in October 1944, Hoxha formed a provisional government, liquidated his anti-communist opponents, and in January 1946 became head of the Albanian Communist republic.

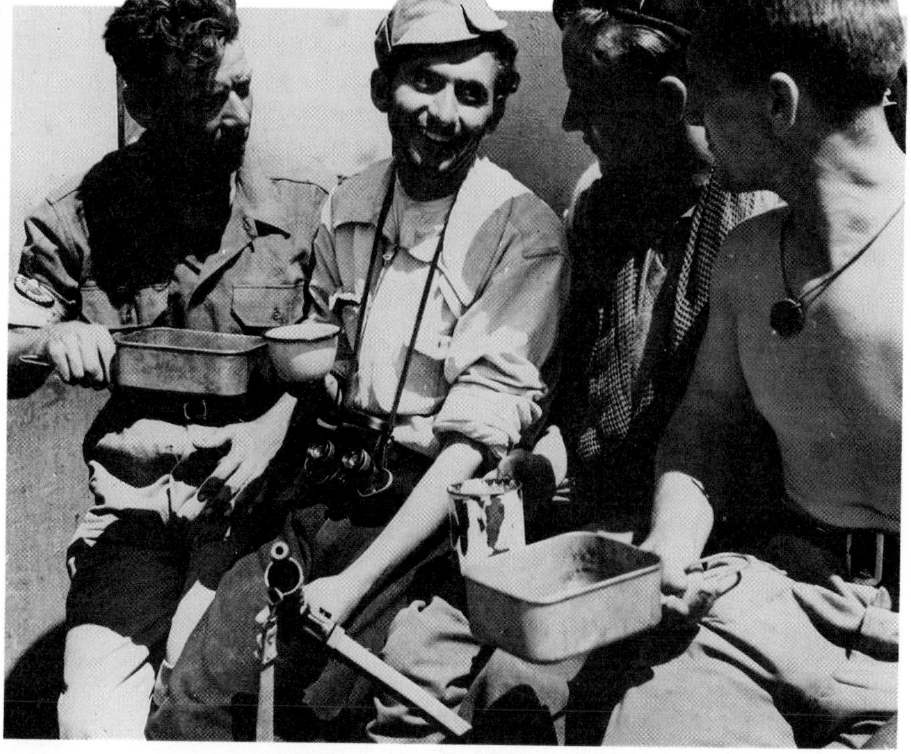

ALLIED TEA CEREMONY An Albanian partisan officer takes tea with British commandos. Britain aided both Albania's partisan groups, but favoured Hoxha's as more effective.

Soviet stalemate 'victory' in Finland

A DEEP RUMBLE, as of an approaching storm, woke the citizens of Helsinki on June 9, 1944. It was the thunder of Russian guns – not at the gates of the Finnish capital but on the front line between Soviet and Finnish forces, about 270 km (170 miles) away on the Karelian Isthmus. Such was the ferocity of the Red Army's assault. For almost every 1.6 km (1 mile) along the south-western end of this front the Russians had ranged 600 to 800 guns. They remembered the Finnish Army's courage and tenacity during the Winter War of 1939-40 and its counterattack, with German help, in 1941. This time they were taking no chances.

The Russian victory at Leningrad early in 1944 had cut off Finland from its key ally – the German Army Group North in the Baltic States – and in March the Finns had sent a secret peace delegation to Moscow. But the Russian terms were harsh – demanding, for example, the surrender of the nickel-rich Petsamo region in the far north and reparations payments of US$600 million in goods.

The terms were rejected by the Finnish parliament, and the Russians prepared an offensive. The Karelian Front (Army Group), under Marshal Kyril Meretskov, was massed along the long frontier stretching north to the Barents Sea, and Marshal Leonid Govorov's Leningrad Front was to attack in the Karelian Isthmus towards Viipuri (now Vyborg). In all, the Russians had about 450 000 men, 800 tanks and 2000 aircraft. The Finns had some 268 000 front-line troops, 110 tanks and nearly 250 aircraft. In northern Finland, guarding Petsamo, were elements of the German Twentieth *Gebirgsarmee* (Mountain Army).

Despite the massive pre-assault bombardment, the initial Russian assault was valiantly repelled all along the line. However, by June 10, Soviet T-34 tanks had battered through at Valkcasaari, north-east of Leningrad, and Finnish Commander in Chief Field Marshal Carl von Mannerheim was forced to order a retreat to the Finns' second – and main – line of resistance: the VT Line, from Vammelsu in the west to south of Taipale. He hoped to delay the Russians while his armoured division prepared a counterattack.

A savage battle followed on June 13-15 as the Finns fought ferociously to hold the line, but on the west coast of the isthmus the Russians used a battering ram of a division and a brigade of tanks to crash through a Finnish weak point. The Russian armour raced through towards Viipuri. Despite furious counterattacks on June 15, the Finns were forced to draw back to their final, VKT Line, which stretched from Viipuri to Kuparsaari, then east along the Vuoksi river to Taipale.

Action now switched north. On June 20 at Maselskaya, to the north of Lake Onega, the Soviet Thirty-Second Army broke through the Finnish II Corps. Next day Seventh Army attacked between Lakes Ladoga and Onega, but the Finns pulled back to yet another obstacle – the U Line, arcing inland from Ladoga's eastern shore. There, they halted.

On the Karelian Isthmus, meanwhile, Russian progress was still slow. Although on June 20 they had occupied Viipuri, abandoned the day before by the Finns, they were unable to punch through decisively. The tough Finns – adept at taking advantage of rugged terrain – fought with a courage born of despair. By July 17 the Russians had curtailed their fruitless attacks. The following month, Mannerheim became Finland's president after the more pro-German President Rysto Ryti was forced to resign. He resumed talks with Moscow and, by September 19, the Finns had withdrawn from the war.

The Russians counted this as the fourth of 1944's ten victories, but it was more of a stalemate. The Finns took pride in the fact that their war ended with some of their troops east of the 1940 frontier. They had to give up Petsamo and territory (including Viipuri) won in 1941, and had to pay reparations worth US$300 million. But they escaped the fate of becoming a Soviet satellite.

The Finns may have stopped fighting, but in Lappland the German XIX Mountain Corps – from Twentieth Gebirgsarmee – was still dug in. On October 7, Meretskov sent forces north. Two days later Soviet naval infantry landed from the Barents Sea. The Germans fell back to Petsamo, but the rapid advance of the Red Army drove them out by October 15. The last German stand was at Kirkenes in Norway. The Red Navy launched a daring, hazardous landing, while Russian infantry marched through snow and ice to crack the tough German position from the landward side. Kirkenes fell on October 25. The Russians had won their last victory of 1944. Now they could concentrate on the Reich itself.

PART FIVE

FROM THE MOMENT it failed to achieve a total and crushing victory at Pearl Harbor, defeat was inevitable for Japan. But turning inevitability into reality was to take a heavy toll in human lives, for the Japanese were tenacious fighters.

Men faced death on the beaches of palm-fringed islands and in steaming jungles; in the vastness of the Pacific Ocean and in the skies above; on muddy trails and in prison camps.

General MacArthur, when he left the Philippines, had vowed: 'I shall return.' He did so, in a spectacular campaign of island-hopping, at Leyte in October 1944. The second prong of the American attack worked its way across the Pacific by way of bloody battles like those for Tarawa, the Marshall Islands and Saipan.

In China, Chiang Kai-shek fought on under the promptings of 'Vinegar Joe' Stilwell. And in Burma the 'forgotten' Fourteenth Army, under General Sir William Slim, beat the Japanese at their own game of jungle fighting.

On land, at sea and in the air the Japanese were driven to the last desperate resort of a nation staring defeat in the face – suicide attacks. But *banzai* charges and *kamikaze* raids could not stave off the Allied advance.

As Act Four of the global drama closed, the sun was going down rapidly for the Empire of Japan ●

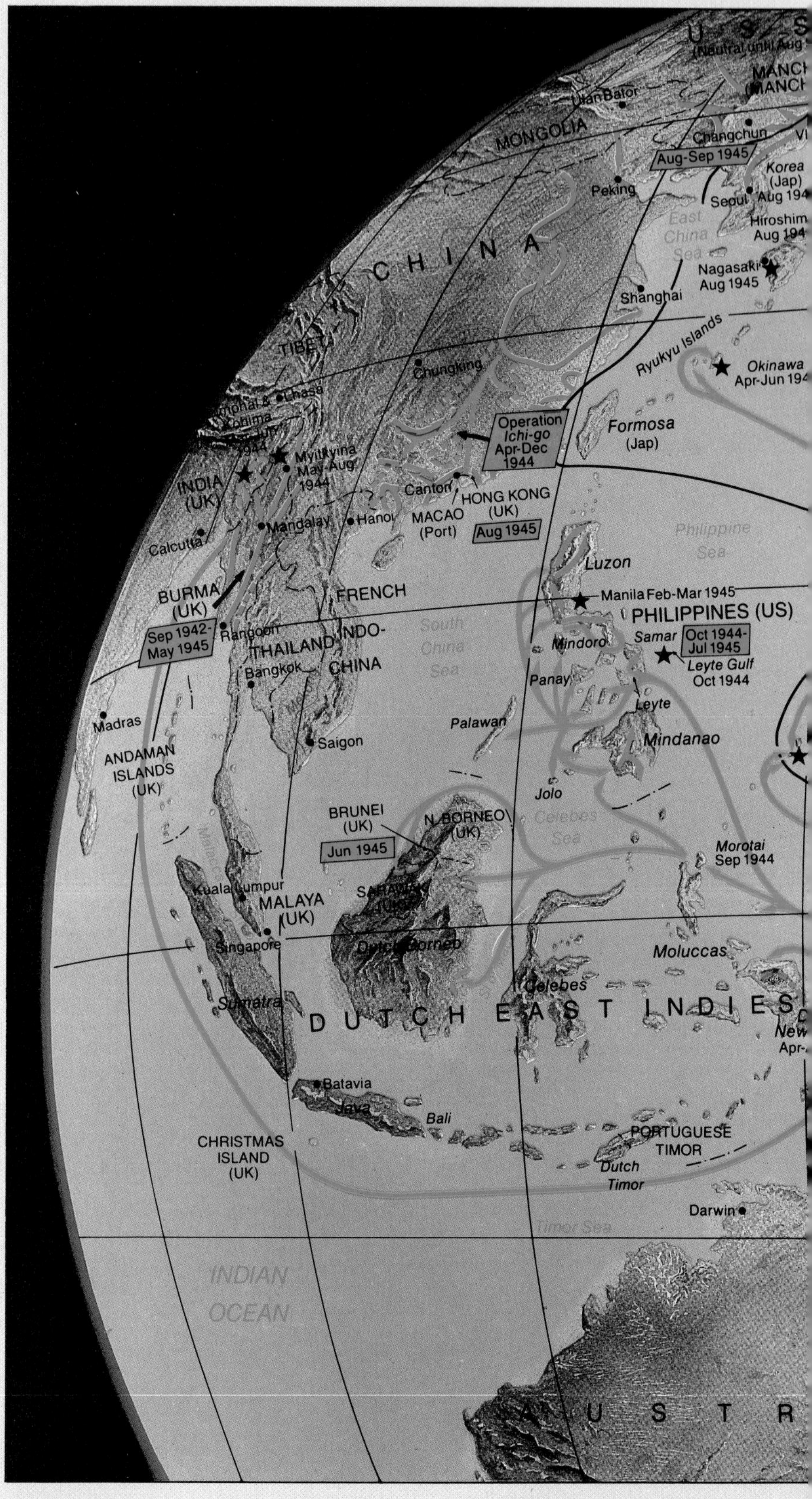

SUN SETS IN THE EAST

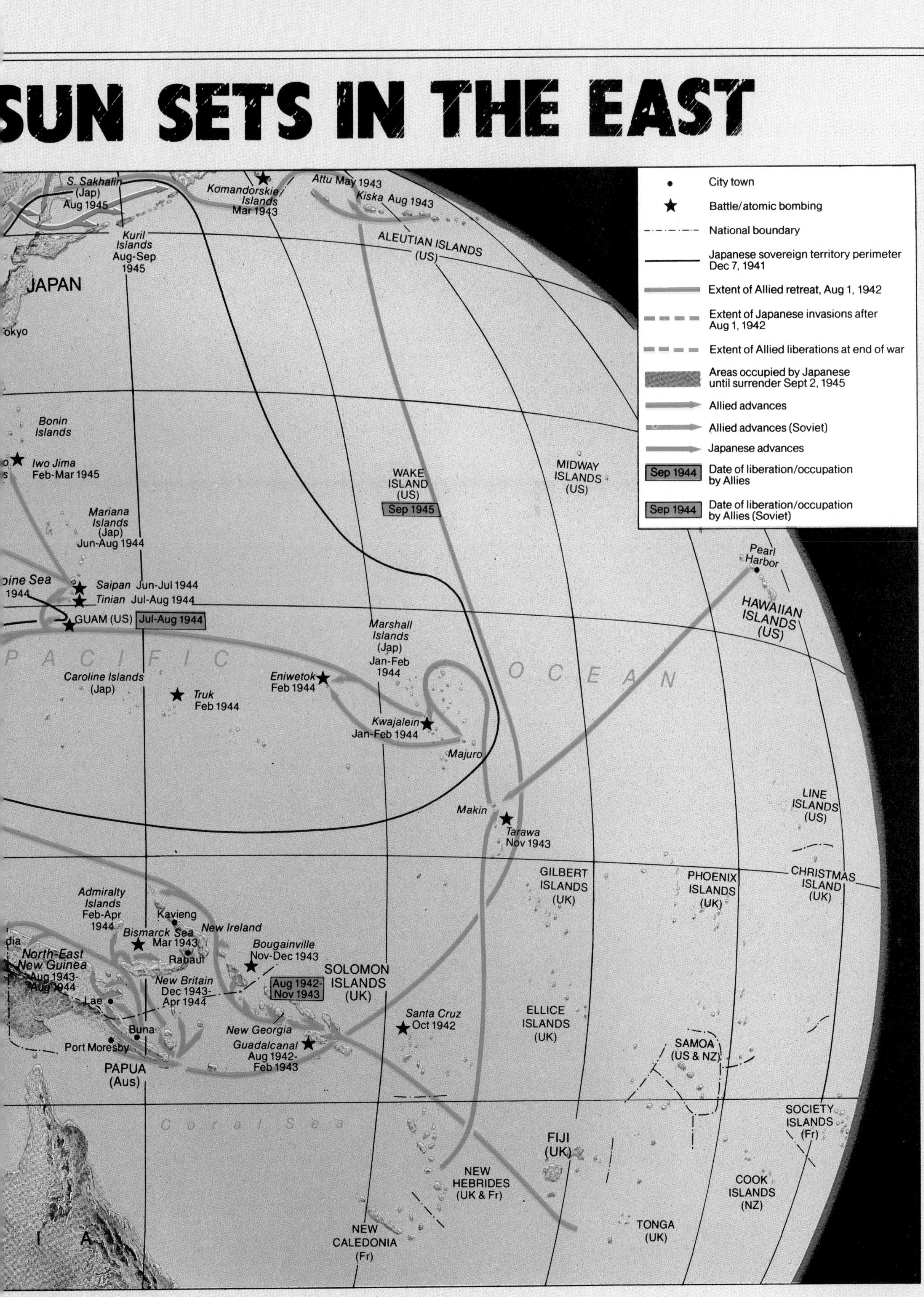
City town
Battle/atomic bombing
National boundary
Japanese sovereign territory perimeter Dec 7, 1941
Extent of Allied retreat, Aug 1, 1942
Extent of Japanese invasions after Aug 1, 1942
Extent of Allied liberations at end of war
Areas occupied by Japanese until surrender Sept 2, 1945
Allied advances
Allied advances (Soviet)
Japanese advances
Sep 1944 Date of liberation/occupation by Allies
Sep 1944 Date of liberation/occupation by Allies (Soviet)
S. Sakhalin (Jap) Aug 1945
Komandorskie Islands Mar 1943
Attu May 1943
Kiska Aug 1943
ALEUTIAN ISLANDS (US)
Kuril Islands Aug-Sep 1945
JAPAN
okyo
Bonin Islands
Iwo Jima Feb-Mar 1945
WAKE ISLAND (US)
Sep 1945
MIDWAY ISLANDS (US)
Mariana Islands (Jap) Jun-Aug 1944
Saipan Jun-Jul 1944
Tinian Jul-Aug 1944
GUAM (US)
Jul-Aug 1944
Pearl Harbor
HAWAIIAN ISLANDS (US)
Marshall Islands (Jap) Jan-Feb 1944
P A C I F I C
O C E A N
Caroline Islands (Jap)
Truk Feb 1944
Eniwetok Feb 1944
Kwajalein Jan-Feb 1944
Majuro
Makin
Tarawa Nov 1943
LINE ISLANDS (US)
GILBERT ISLANDS (UK)
PHOENIX ISLANDS (UK)
CHRISTMAS ISLAND (UK)
Admiralty Islands Feb-Apr 1944
Kavieng
New Ireland
Bismarck Sea Mar 1943
Rabaul
Bougainville Nov-Dec 1943
North-East New Guinea Aug 1943-Aug 1944
New Britain Dec 1943-Apr 1944
Aug 1942-Nov 1943
SOLOMON ISLANDS (UK)
Lae
Buna
Port Moresby
Santa Cruz Oct 1942
New Georgia
Guadalcanal Aug 1942-Feb 1943
ELLICE ISLANDS (UK)
SAMOA (US & NZ)
PAPUA (Aus)
C o r a l S e a
SOCIETY ISLANDS (Fr)
FIJI (UK)
NEW HEBRIDES (UK & Fr)
COOK ISLANDS (NZ)
NEW CALEDONIA (Fr)
TONGA (UK)

22: THE ALLIES' PACIFIC COMEBACK

After the US Navy's decisive victory at Midway the Allies began the hard job of recapturing the Pacific islands seized by the Japanese during the first six months of 1942.

Guadalcanal – a name written in blood

It began with the relatively easy capture of an airfield, but it turned into a six-month nightmare at sea and in the festering jungle as the Japanese poured reinforcements into Guadalcanal aboard the 'Tokyo Express'.

AS DAWN BROKE in the south-west Pacific on August 7, 1942, the sound of distant gunfire had Martin Clemens reaching for his binoculars. From his mountain hideout on Guadalcanal in the Solomon Islands he saw what he later called 'a fleet majestical' – the transport ships, cruisers, destroyers and aircraft carriers of the Allied South Pacific Amphibious Force.

Clemens was a member of a unique organisation known as the Coastwatchers – a group of Australian and British traders, colonial officers and planters who had been working in the Solomons when the Japanese invaded, and had stayed behind in hiding to report on Japanese movements. They had been equipped with radio transmitters, and it was Clemens who in May told the Allies that the Japanese were building an airfield on Guadalcanal. If completed it would give them air supremacy in the area and threaten the sea routes between the USA and Australia.

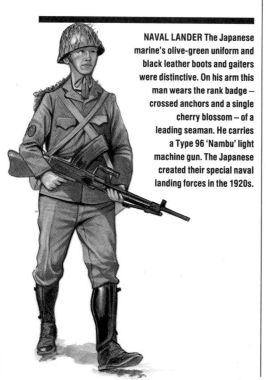

NAVAL LANDER **The Japanese marine's olive-green uniform and black leather boots and gaiters were distinctive. On his arm this man wears the rank badge – crossed anchors and a single cherry blossom – of a leading seaman. He carries a Type 96 'Nambu' light machine gun. The Japanese created their special naval landing forces in the 1920s.**

As the men of the 1st US Marine Division waded ashore from their landing craft that tropical dawn, a naval and air bombardment pounded the Japanese defending the airfield. Taken completely by surprise, they fled into the jungle, and by late afternoon on August 8 the airfield was in American hands. It was the Americans' first land victory over the Japanese. They were relieved at the lack of resistance – but their relief was to be short-lived.

ABANDONED TO THEIR FATE

It was in any case not shared by their commander, Maj General Alexander A. Vandegrift. The news of the Japanese airfield had prompted Admiral Ernest J. King, Chief of Naval Operations in Washington, into hasty action, and Vandegrift had been given the task of taking the island with barely two months to prepare. His 18 700-strong force consisted largely of new recruits with no combat experience, and even the hard core of seasoned marines were new to jungle warfare. Furthermore, his naval escort had little or no experience of an amphibious operation.

Vandegrift counted himself extremely lucky that the Japanese offered little resistance, for the landing, near the mouth of the Tenaru river, a few kilometres from the airstrip (see map, p. 350), was a shambles. Supplies were dumped on the beach in hopelessly mixed-up piles and men wandered around waiting for orders.

Simultaneous landings on Tulagi, Tanambogo and Gavutu – three islets 35 km (22 miles) to the north – had met strong opposition. On Tulagi the 1st Raider Battalion, under Lt Colonel Merritt ('Red Mike') Edson, were counterattacked with mortars and grenade throwers four times before they took the islet, and on Gavutu and Tanambogo only devastating gunfire from US warships eventually blasted the defenders from their caves.

Rear Admiral Richmond Kelly Turner, the task force commander, shared Vandegrift's concern, as did the red-bearded Rear Admiral Victor Crutchley, VC, the Royal Navy commander of the joint American/Australian covering force of eight cruisers and 16 destroyers.

Then came an alarming message from Vice Admiral Frank Fletcher, commanding the supporting US carrier force: his fighter strength had been reduced from 99 to 78 in dogfights and he was going to withdraw his force, which included the carriers *Saratoga*, *Wasp* and *Enterprise*. It was a controversial decision, and almost certainly unnecessary. Fletcher feared his carriers would be too exposed to air attack, but his own fighter force was still impressive. In view of Fletcher's decision, Turner also resolved to pull out. The withdrawals left an angry Vandegrift and some 10 000 marines on Guadalcanal on their own.

DUEL IN THE NIGHT

The Japanese did not take long to respond to the Allied landings. By mid-afternoon on August 7, a force of seven cruisers and a destroyer, commanded by Vice Admiral Gunichi Mikawa in the cruiser *Chokai*, was speeding towards Guadalcanal. Though heavily outnumbered, Mikawa was supremely confident – and with good reason. His force had developed the skills of night fighting to a high degree, and every ship was armed with the deadly 'Long Lance' torpedoes. Propelled by liquid oxygen, these torpedoes carried a 450 kg (1000 lb) warhead and could travel at 36 knots (65 km/h) over a distance of 40 km (25 miles) – or even faster over a shorter range.

Meanwhile, Crutchley had split his force into three groups to patrol the approaches to Savo, with the destroyers *Blue* and *Ralph Talbot* stationed west and north of Savo as pickets. Just before 1 am on August 9, the highly trained lookouts on *Chokai* spotted the destroyers 10 km

JUNGLE CAMOUFLAGE **An American marine wears a one-piece camouflage suit. He carries a Browning Automatic Rifle and, on his back, a camouflage poncho. This invaluable item could give protection when marching through rain, or serve as a tent. Camouflage reached new levels of sophistication in World War II.**

BRILLIANCE UNREWARDED

Raizo Tanaka (1892-1969) became a legend in the Japanese Navy as the 'conductor' of the 'Tokyo Express' during the fighting for Guadalcanal. He started his career as a torpedo specialist and by 1941 was a rear admiral commanding the 2nd Destroyer Squadron in the Dutch East Indies. He and his destroyers then took part in the battles of the Coral Sea and Midway before being ordered to Rabaul in the summer of 1942.

For six months, Tanaka's destroyers and transports kept supplies and reinforcements running to the beleaguered Japanese on Guadalcanal and fought the Americans hard. As losses mounted, he became openly critical of his superiors, particularly their inability to coordinate air and surface operations. Infuriated by his criticisms, they posted him to a staff job back in Japan. Although Tanaka was eventually promoted vice admiral, he was never given another active command.

(6 miles) away, patrolling their lonely course. They were several kilometres apart, and the Japanese slipped audaciously between them, in search of larger prey. Just after 1.30 am Mikawa's force sighted the dim silhouettes of the cruisers HMAS *Canberra* and USS *Chicago*, part of Captain Howard D. Bode's patrol group, south of Savo. Unlike their Japanese counterparts, the Allied lookouts were tired, and Bode was sound asleep in his bunk on board *Chicago*.

Minutes later Japanese torpedoes and shells were speeding towards their victims. *Canberra* was soon ablaze, and a torpedo blew in *Chicago*'s bows. The damage was not crippling, and the befuddled Bode turned westward in search of the Japanese. But by now they were well to the north-east and swinging in a wide arc to attack the northern patrol group.

On board the US cruisers *Vincennes*, *Quincy* and *Astoria* their captains had heard the sound of gunfire to the south-west, and were still trying to find out what was going on when Mikawa's searchlights floodlit the American vessels and he unleashed a deadly onslaught of 200 mm (8 in) shells and torpedoes. Captain Toshikazu Ohmae, Mikawa's aide, later recalled: 'Every torpedo and round of gunfire seemed to be hitting a mark. Enemy ships seemed to be sinking on every hand.'

Within minutes all three American ships were on fire and sinking. The Japanese raced on, gave *Ralph Talbot* a mauling as they went, and disappeared into the night. The Battle of Savo Island had been a humiliating disaster for the Americans and Australians, and the aftermath was bitter. A virulent press campaign in the USA attacked Crutchley, who had been with the landing force at the time of the action. Bode – who held himself responsible – later shot himself.

SLAUGHTER AT ILU RIVER

On Guadalcanal, sapped by the heat and humidity and preyed on by the buzzing, scurrying, stinging insect life of the jungle, the marines dug in. On the 20th, 19 Wildcat fighters and 12 Dauntless dive-bombers flew into the airfield, christened Henderson Field after a hero of Midway. Now the beleaguered marines had a fighting chance. They were aided, too, by Martin Clemens and his men,who spied on the Japanese in the east of the island. On August 19, a former Solomon Islands policeman, Jacob Vouza, was captured by the Japanese, bayoneted and left for dead. But he managed to crawl back to the beach-head with the news that an attack was coming from the east.

Vouza had stumbled across a battalion led by Colonel Kiyono Ichiki, an arrogant and head-strong officer with nothing but contempt for the Americans. Although he knew he was heavily outnumbered, Ichiki was convinced that his small force of 815 men could destroy the marines. At 1.30 am on August 21, the Japanese burst from a coconut plantation in a bayonet charge at the mouth of the Ilu river, just west of the Tenaru. The marines were waiting.

A hail of bullets cut down the first wave and the Japanese hit the ground. Ichiki rallied his men and they charged again, only to be blasted by 37 mm ($1\frac{1}{2}$ in) canister shots (like huge shotgun blasts). The Japanese fled back to the shelter of the plantation. At dawn the marines surrounded them and unleashed another terrifying hail of shells. An aerial bombardment came from planes based at Henderson Field. But still the Japanese refused to give in. Finally, Stuart tanks rolled in, their steel tracks crushing the living, the dead and the dying. 'The rear of the tanks,' Vandegrift recorded, 'looked like meatgrinders.'

Ichiki and some of his men escaped, but were later cornered. The defiant Ichiki burnt his regimental flag and then committed *hara-kiri*. Some wounded Japanese booby-trapped themselves. They would wait until Americans came to help them and then blow themselves and their helpers to pieces with a hand grenade. At the end of the day 800 Japanese were dead, and 35 Americans.

MURDER ON THE TOKYO EXPRESS

Colonel Ichiki's battalion had been landed on Guadalcanal by ships under the command of Rear Admiral Raizo Tanaka on the first of a succession of runs that the Americans dubbed the 'Tokyo Express'. Tanaka planned another run, this time as part of a massive trap for the American fleet devised by none other than Admiral Isoroku Yamamoto, the man who masterminded Pearl Harbor. A powerful fleet of battleships, cruisers, destroyers and the aircraft carriers *Zuikaku* and *Shokaku* would sail as escort. But ahead of the main force would be a 'sacrificial goat' – the light carrier *Ryujo* and three escorts. Yamamoto planned to lure the American fleet north, where the larger armada would annihilate them, clearing the way for Tanaka to land fresh troops on Guadalcanal.

But by now Fletcher's task force had recovered its full complement of planes and was patrolling east of the Solomons. On August 24, dive-bombers from his carriers *Enterprise* and *Saratoga* swooped down on *Ryujo*. A clutch of 1000 lb (450 kg) bombs and a single torpedo blasted it, and it sank at 3.50 pm. Vice Admiral Nobutake Kondo, commanding the main Japanese force, immediately sent his dive-bombers to attack the American carriers. But Fletcher had not left them defenceless. The Japanese arrived to find 50 Wildcats airborne and waiting for them.

The fighters tore into the attackers, while anti-aircraft fire from the carriers dealt with any that managed to break through. One flight of 'Val' dive-bombers eluded the defenders and dropped three bombs on *Enterprise*, badly damaging its flight deck, but the carrier was able to recover its aircraft and steam to safety. *Saratoga* escaped unscathed, and by dusk the Battle of the Eastern Solomons was over.

Tanaka and his 'Tokyo Express', however, sailed on for Guadalcanal. Wildly exaggerated reports by the Japanese fliers had put the score at three US carriers sunk, so Tanaka was confident that he could continue unmolested. He was in for a shock. As dawn broke on August 25, dive-bombers from Henderson Field screamed down out of the rising sun, scoring a direct hit on his flagship, the light cruiser *Jintsu*, and the transport vessel *Kinryu Maru*. Tanaka beat a hasty retreat in the damaged *Jintsu*. *Kinryu Maru* and a destroyer were later sunk by American bombers. On August 31, the Japanese took revenge when a submarine torpedoed and badly damaged *Saratoga*. Fletcher was wounded in the attack.

Back at his base in Rabaul, on the island of New Britain, Tanaka decided that the daylight runs to land troops on Guadalcanal were suicidal, so long as American bombers could operate from Henderson Field. They continued at night, however, and by September 12, a total of 5200 Japanese troops were ashore.

BAD DAY AT BLOODY RIDGE

Meanwhile, Vandegrift brought Edson's battalion from Tulagi to Guadalcanal and positioned them on a ridge about 1.6 km (1 mile) south-west of Henderson Field, ready for the next Japanese attack. He did not have to wait long. At 9 pm on September 12 a cruiser and three destroyers began shelling the ridge, and 20 minutes later 2000 Japanese swarmed out of the jungle.

The Americans, dug in at the base of the ridge, met them with concentrated fire, then fell back to the higher ground. They spent the next day

HERO OF GUADALCANAL

Alexander Archer Vandegrift (1887-1973) embarked on the Guadalcanal operation with deep misgivings, for his 1st Marine Division was only partly trained. However, he was used to outlandish and sometimes dangerous assignments. After joining the US Marine Corps in 1909, Vandegrift had served in Nicaragua, Panama, Mexico, Haiti and China. He took command of the 1st Marine Division in March 1942.

When he arrived in Guadalcanal in early August, his men's lack of experience forced him to adopt a largely defensive strategy. He knew that control of Henderson Field was the key to the island and that the Japanese would exhaust themselves attacking it. His dogged defence of the beach-head turned Vandegrift into a national hero. MacArthur, clearly peeved at the resultant publicity, said to him as he left for a period of leave in America: 'Vandegrift, what are you going back to the States for? To become president?'

In March 1943, Vandegrift was promoted to command I Marine Amphibious Corps in the South Pacific, where he masterminded the taking of Bougainville. Soon afterwards he was promoted Commandant of the Marine Corps, a post he held until his retirement in 1947.

furiously digging in and laying barbed-wire entanglements. At 6.30 pm the Japanese came again, yelling: 'Marine, you die!' Their sheer weight of numbers overwhelmed Edson's right flank. Some surged along the American line, others made for the airfield. Three who burst into Vandegrift's command bunker were gunned down by the commander's clerks.

Throughout the night the battle raged. Some of the Americans ran, but were rallied by Edson. 'The only thing the Japs have got that you don't is guts', Edson yelled at two running men. He radioed for artillery fire – 'closer, closer' – until it held like a wall between his men and the Japanese.

Dawn revealed a field of carnage. More than 600 Japanese lay where they had fallen along what the marines were already calling 'Bloody Ridge', and 500 more had been wounded or were missing. The Americans, too, had suffered heavy losses – 260 killed or wounded – but had held on.

Yet there was to be no respite. Night after night the 'Tokyo Express' brought in fresh supplies and troops, while warships hurled shells, screaming like express trains, at the marines in their dugouts. Vandegrift desperately needed reinforcements. On September 15 a convoy had brought 4000 men of the 7th Marine Regiment, with a covering force that included the carrier *Wasp* and the battleship *North Carolina*. The troops and equipment landed safely, but during their return to the island of Espiritu Santo in the New Hebrides (now Vanuatu) *Wasp* was hit by three submarine torpedoes. The crew had to be evacuated and the carrier sunk. *North Carolina* was also damaged and a destroyer sunk.

On October 9, Lt General Harukichi Hyakutake, commander of Japan's Seventeenth Army, landed on Guadalcanal along with the bulk of the 2nd Division, a squadron of medium tanks and at least one 150 mm (6 in) howitzer – which the marines christened 'Pistol Pete'.

At the same time, more US reinforcements were dispatched – this time the 164th Infantry Regiment of the Americal Division on board two transport ships, protected by the aircraft carrier *Hornet*, the battleship *Washington*, five cruisers and five destroyers. Their commander, Rear Admiral Norman Scott, had a dual purpose: in addition to protecting the transports he hoped to derail the 'Tokyo Express', and had trained his crews in night fighting. His chance came on the night of October 11/12.

HEAT OF THE NIGHT

That afternoon, planes from *Hornet* had spotted a Japanese cruiser and destroyer force heading towards Guadalcanal. Scott waited for them off Cape Esperance, just west of Savo island, but whether trained or not in night fighting, his men were still not practised in night recognition. Just before midnight the cruiser *Helena*'s radar picked up a blip. Was it the enemy force or other ships in Scott's convoy? *Helena* tracked the contact for ten minutes before informing Scott, who decided to wait until he was sure. But by now *Helena*'s captain was sure, and he opened fire, without permission, at a range of 4.5 km (2.8 miles).

The Japanese, showing an unusual lack of alertness, were caught totally by surprise. Shells rained down on the cruiser *Aoba*, followed seconds later by salvos from the other American warships. The cruiser *Furutaka* was set ablaze and later sank. The destroyer *Fubuki* also sank. Meanwhile the Japanese cruiser *Kinugasa* and destroyer *Hatsuyuki* had turned away, and in doing so came across the destroyer USS *Duncan*.

The Americans now paid a heavy price. In the confusion, some of their destroyers were fired on by their own cruisers. *Duncan*, hit by American shells, was set ablaze and had to be abandoned. In an attempt to identify a target the light cruiser USS *Boise* switched on a searchlight, giving the Japanese a perfect aiming point. *Aoba* – still in action despite its pounding – and *Kinugasa* raked it with gunfire, and it was saved from being sunk only when the cruiser *Salt Lake City* took on the two Japanese ships, allowing *Boise* to limp away. Shortly after midnight, Scott called off the battle.

The Americans hailed the Battle of Cape Esperance as a victory, but while the battle raged the 'Tokyo Express' had safely landed its troops and artillery on Guadalcanal.

BAPTISM OF FIRE

The US reinforcements escorted by Scott landed on October 13, and the Japanese gave them a more than warm welcome. That night the battleships *Kongo* and *Haruna*, cruising off Lunga Point, opened fire with their 355 mm (14 in) guns. The ground heaved as 918 shells rained down on the beach-head and airfield in just two hours. The soldiers and marines clawed deeper into the mud to avoid the rain of death. Nevertheless, 41 were killed, and by dawn hundreds more were wandering about, dazed and shell-shocked. Henderson Field resembled a moonscape, and half its aircraft were destroyed. The following two nights, Japanese cruisers poured in another 2000 shells.

Vandegrift knew that his exhausted and fever-ridden men could not hold out much longer without naval help, and he radioed an urgent message to Admiral Chester W. Nimitz, Commander in Chief Pacific. Nimitz ordered a shakeup at the top: the dynamic Vice Admiral William 'Bull' Halsey was made Commander in Chief South Pacific, and the wounded Fletcher was replaced by Rear Admiral Thomas Kinkaid.

Yamamoto, meanwhile, was not wasting time. With Henderson Field out of action and the Americans surely demoralised, he planned another offensive. He would make a two-pronged attack from the west and south on Henderson, followed by a carrier attack on the American fleet.

Hyakutake's main land offensive, planned to start at dusk on October 23, was held up in the near-impenetrable jungle, and Hyakutake called off the attack for 24 hours. But Maj General Tadishi Sumiyoshi, commanding the secondary western force, failed to receive the message, and at the appointed hour his tanks and infantry advanced across a sandbar at the mouth of the Matanikau river. The concentrated fire of nine US artillery batteries annihilated them.

Hyakutake shrugged off this setback, and sent in his main force the following night. Led by Lt General Masai Maruyama, the men crept through the jungle in driving rain and into a sector held by the 1st Battalion, 7th Marines. By the light of flares they charged towards the airfield. One group, under Colonel Tosharini Shoji, broke through and crossed a flat, grassy space – and Shoji radioed that Henderson Field had been

UP RIVER, AND DOWN Lush foliage overhangs the Tenaru river on Guadalcanal. A party of US marines wading upstream take a breather. With them are native guides. (Inset) On another river, two boats meet, one heading upstream with supplies, the other down with wounded.

taken. It was not in fact the airfield – but only one man stood between the Japanese and their goal.

Sergeant John Basilone, manning a Browning machine gun, held his ground as the Japanese swarmed towards him. Bodies piled up around him as he gunned down Shoji's men, now only steps away from the airfield they were never to reach. Basilone survived, and his valour earned him the Medal of Honor. Hours later men of the Americal Division hacked their way back to join in the battle, and by dawn Maruyama had withdrawn, leaving 1500 dead behind.

Hyakutake's giant howitzer 'Pistol Pete' went into action the next day – dubbed by the marines 'Dugout Sunday' – and Japanese aircraft roared down in seven separate attacks. At dusk Maruyama's men charged again, and again were cut down. By dawn on the 26th he had had enough and withdrew into the jungle. The Japanese had sacrificed a total of 3500 men.

THE BATTLE OF SANTA CRUZ

Meanwhile, Vice Admiral Kondo had sent his carrier fleet sailing south to do battle with the newly appointed Kinkaid. On the morning of October 26 the two fleets were 400 km (250 miles) apart, near the Santa Cruz Islands, a group some 600 km (375 miles) east of Guadalcanal. It was to be a carrier battle, and after reconnaissance planes from both sides had located their targets, 67 Japanese planes from *Shokaku*, *Zuikaku* and *Zuiho* were winging south, while 73 bombers and fighters from *Enterprise* and *Hornet* sped north.

Incredibly, the two strike forces passed within sight of each other, and only a handful of Japanese fighters peeled off to engage in a dogfight with the American planes. The rest roared on. Soon after 9 am the Americans were over the Japanese fleet. While Wildcats fought off attacks by Zeros, Dauntless dive-bombers zoomed down to score direct hits on *Shokaku*'s flight deck. More bombers, from *Wasp*, hit and damaged *Zuiho*.

Ten minutes later it was the turn of the Japanese. Wildcats from *Hornet* tore into them, but several got through and *Hornet* was hit by torpedoes and bombs – plus two Japanese suicide planes. A second wave made for *Enterprise* and, although anti-aircraft fire and Wildcats downed most of them, two bombs landed on the carrier's flight deck. A third wave damaged the battleship *South Dakota* and the cruiser *San Juan*. *Enterprise* was still able to take on its aircraft, and Kinkaid decided to call it a day. After still more Japanese attacks, the blazing *Hornet* had to be abandoned, and was sunk next day by Japanese destroyers.

GUNFIGHT OFF GUADALCANAL

Within two weeks Yamamoto was ready to try again. He positioned Kondo's fleet 240 km (150 miles) north of Guadalcanal, dispatched a 17-ship task force under Vice Admiral Hiroake Abe to shell Henderson Field into oblivion, and a third fleet under Rear Admiral Tanaka was to land reinforcements at Tassafaronga Point, just north-west of the American beach-head.

On November 11, Rear Admiral Scott's cruiser and destroyer force had returned to the Solomons. On the night of November 12/13, Abe's fleet collided head-on with the Americans in Ironbottom Sound (so named by the Americans back in August, because of the number of ships sunk there), south-east of Savo island. What followed was one of the bloodiest engagements in naval history. The 37 000 tonne battleship *Hiei*'s 355 mm (14 in) guns demolished the bridge of Scott's flagship *Atlanta*, killing the admiral and most of his officers. Minutes later the battleship *Kirishima* savaged the cruiser *San Francisco*, killing Rear Admiral Daniel Callaghan.

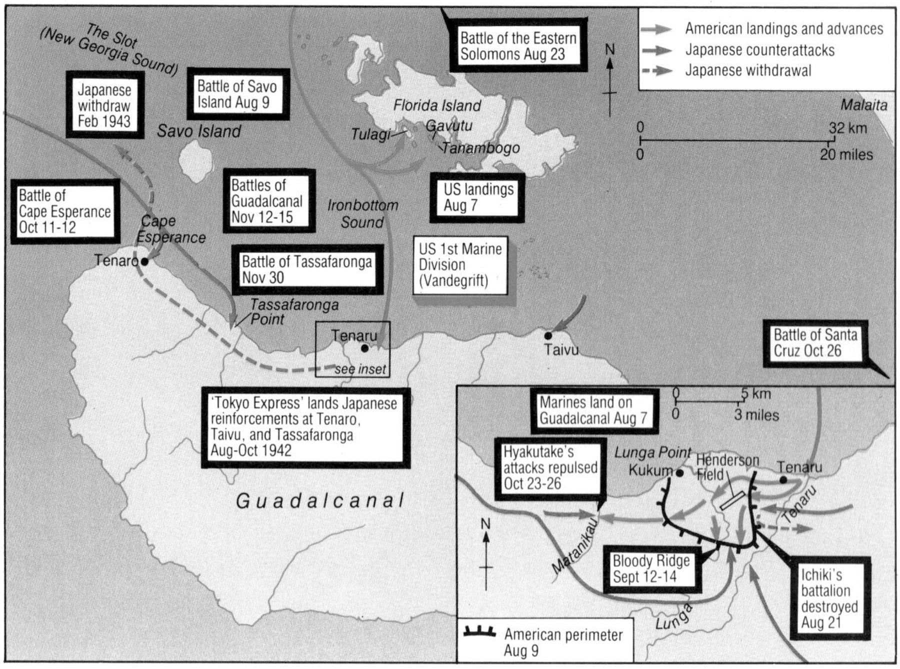

HALF A YEAR TO VICTORY American marines landed on Guadalcanal, near the mouth of the Tenaru river, on August 7, 1942. Only in February 1943, many bloody land and sea actions later, did Japanese resistance end.

Then eight American destroyers closed on *Hiei*. Four were blown out of the water, but the rest got so close that *Hiei*'s main guns could not be brought to bear. Hit more than 50 times, the battleship limped away. Two of Abe's cruisers were also on fire and sinking, and *Kirishima*, damaged by a 200 mm (8 in) shell, withdrew. The Japanese later scuttled the crippled *Hiei* – the first Japanese battleship to go down in the war.

At dusk on November 14, the second Japanese force under Kondo headed eastwards through the Solomon Sea for an attack on Henderson Field. They were headed off by the battleships *Washington* and *South Dakota* and four destroyers, under Rear Admiral Willis A. Lee. Japanese torpedoes and gunfire sank two of Lee's destroyers and a third had to be scuttled. Kondo's *Kirishima* put *South Dakota* out of action. Eagerly moving in for the kill, Kondo failed to notice that *Washington* had closed to within 7.5 km (4½ miles). A devastating broadside from the American battleship set *Kirishima* ablaze and it began to list. Its captain ordered the crew to abandon ship and scuttled it. Kondo, in the cruiser *Atago*, put about and fled.

Meanwhile, Kinkaid's fleet, including the still damaged *Enterprise*, was heading north, and came across Tanaka's convoy. US aircraft sank seven transports. When the remaining four grounded at Tassafaronga next morning, they were pulverised by dive-bombers from Henderson and artillery. All three elements of Yamamoto's plan had failed.

VICTORY AT LAST

The cost to the Americans of the naval battle off Guadalcanal was high – two cruisers and six destroyers sunk and many more damaged. But the Japanese had suffered far worse: apart from two battleships, two cruisers, three destroyers and 11 transports sunk, they had landed only a demoralised fragment of their 38th Division. Further attempts to land troops and supplies were savaged by the US Navy – though the Americans suffered one setback on the night of November 30/December 1.

That night eight heavily laden destroyers of Tanaka's 'express' ran into a US force of five cruisers and seven destroyers off Tassafaronga. Tanaka brilliantly escaped what should have been a massacre by bringing his ships round to face the Americans and unleashing a devastating salvo of torpedoes. Four US cruisers were damaged. One of them, *Northampton*, later sank. Even so, the 'express' was unable to deliver its cargo of men and materials to Guadalcanal, and generally by now American control of the waters of the Solomon Islands was total. By the end of the year starving and diseased Japanese soldiers roamed Guadalcanal, looting native villages. The islanders exacted terrible revenge, and Japanese heads decorated the native longhouses for years.

Vandegrift's exhausted marines were replaced by US Army formations under Maj General Alexander M. Patch, and steadily Patch's men pushed the Japanese back to Cape Esperance and the sea. Japanese aircraft from Rabaul scored successes on January 29 and 30, 1943, when they attacked US cruisers and destroyers escorting a convoy for Guadalcanal. During battles with planes from US carriers and the island, they sank the American cruiser *Chicago* with an aerial torpedo. But this one setback could not reverse the American advance. Between February 1 and 7, the Japanese evacuated 13 000 men, leaving 25 000 dead behind. Two days later, Patch sent Halsey a message: 'The Tokyo Express no longer has a terminal on Guadalcanal.'

The Americans had lost 1592 marines and soldiers killed and another 4300 wounded. The turning point of the Pacific war had been reached and passed. For the Americans, Guadalcanal was the first rung on the 'Solomons Ladder'. For Japan it was now to be an uphill struggle to prevent the Allies reaching the homeland itself.

The Cartwheel rolls

After the slog for Guadalcanal, the Allies decided to mount two great thrusts towards Japan. In an operation code-named 'Cartwheel', they began the arduous task of cutting off Tokyo from its new south-east Asian empire.

IT WAS 6.40 AM on June 30, 1943. Rear Admiral Richmond Kelly Turner, on the bridge of the US Navy transport ship *McCawley*, trained his binoculars on the shore of Rendova island and swore violently. He smelt of alcohol, but no one would reprimand him for that – even in the 'dry' US Navy – for Turner with a few drinks on board was a better commander than many others stone-cold sober. Besides, Turner was witnessing a scene to shake any commander's nerves.

Troops of the US 43rd Infantry Division were wading ashore and milling around on the beach in confused mobs, while landing craft continued to dump supplies in chaotic mounds. Then, to cap it all, sporadic sniper fire from the tiny Japanese garrison hit some of the incoming landing craft. As Turner watched, their jumpy machine-gunners opened up indiscriminately on the beach, sending their own men diving for cover.

The admiral sprang into action. For most of that morning he rapped out orders over the radio, using language that startled the officers of the 43rd. Gradually a semblance of order was imposed on the disorganised GIs and they moved inland. Huge 155 mm (6.1 in) howitzers were dragged into position among the palm trees. The following afternoon, the guns were lobbing shells onto the giant Japanese air base at Munda, 16 km (10 miles) away on the island of New Georgia. The Americans were poised for their assault on the perimeter of the Japanese empire.

THE HARD STUFF

Richmond Kelly Turner (1885-1961) was an extraordinary commander: his loud-mouthed, hard-drinking, tough-guy image disguised a cool, razor-sharp brain. His bouts of explosive rage frightened his subordinates as much as he frightened the Japanese, who called him 'the Alligator' – once he bit into something he never let go, they said.

Turner had, in fact, undergone a remarkable sea change. Until August 1942 he had been admired as a brilliant, hard-working, quiet and abstemious staff officer in Washington. Then Admiral Ernest King, Chief of Naval Operations, chose him to conduct the amphibious assault on Guadalcanal. Once at sea, Turner suddenly became an aggresive fighting sailor with a salty tongue that could make a marine blush. From Guadalcanal he went on to conduct the Solomons offensive and led V Amphibious Force through the central Pacific campaigns to Iwo Jima.

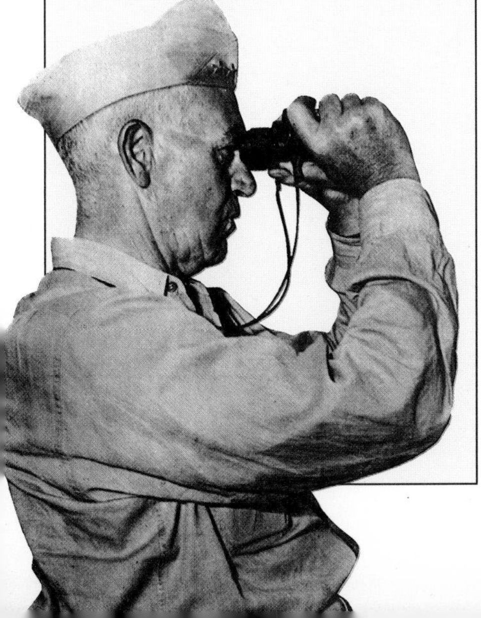

TWIN THRUSTS

After the epic victory on Guadalcanal, Admiral Ernest King, US Chief of Naval Operations, had persuaded the Joint Chiefs of Staff that new operations should aim to throw Japan onto the defensive. The question was where they should be launched and which should have priority.

There were two alternative routes – one through the south-west Pacific towards the Philippines, the other across the central Pacific towards Formosa (Taiwan). General Douglas MacArthur, commanding the south-west Pacific forces, argued for the first course. This route would, he believed, cut the Japanese off from their gains – particularly the oil-rich East Indies (Indonesia) and the rubber of Malaya – more quickly than the central Pacific strategy. Admiral Chester W. Nimitz, commanding the US Pacific Fleet, argued that America's growing naval strength, organised into carrier task forces, would be better used in the open Pacific than in the narrow waters around New Guinea. Nimitz also wanted to restrict MacArthur's role and keep naval forces out of his hands.

Meanwhile, that naval strength was being rapidly increased. By October 1943 there would be seven battleships, seven heavy and three light carriers, eight cruisers and 34 destroyers in the US central Pacific fleet alone, with more vessels arriving daily. And V Amphibious Force, a specialist assault fleet to be commanded by Kelly Turner, was being formed. In the south-west Pacific, a fleet of 200 landing and support ships was being built up under Rear Admiral Daniel Barbey, to form VII Amphibious Force.

Four new *Essex*-class carriers, capable of 33 knots (61 km/h), would each carry 100 aircraft. Superior new planes such as the Grumman Hellcat fighter and Avenger torpedo bomber, the Curtiss Helldiver dive-bomber and the superb Chance-Vought Corsair fighter were coming into service – and, thanks to more intensive training, US pilots were improving rapidly. By late 1943, Lt General George C. Kenney's Fifth Air Force would have about 1000 planes – including new P-38 Lightning fighters and B-25 Mitchell bombers – flying from Papuan airfields.

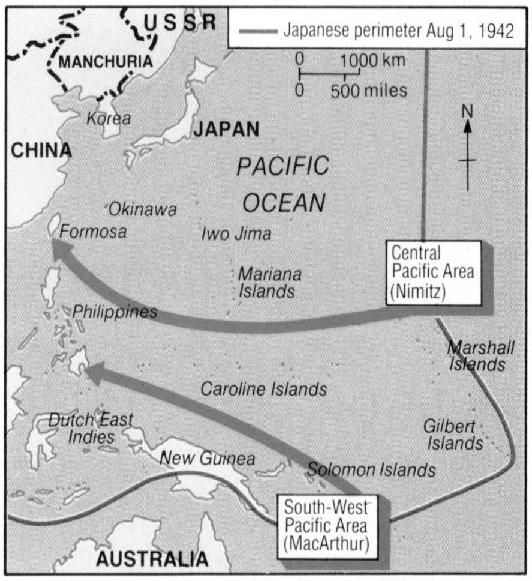

DOUBLE ATTACK The Allied strategy, agreed on March 28, 1943, was that MacArthur should push up through the south-west Pacific islands north of Australia, while Nimitz hopped from island to island across the central Pacific.

But even American resources were to be stretched by the Joint Chiefs' final decision, taken in late March 1943, to launch twin thrusts, by MacArthur's forces in the south-west and by Nimitz's fleet in the central Pacific. Later they would converge on Formosa and Japan.

DEATH IN THE BISMARCK SEA

Meanwhile, the Japanese were still determined to hold New Guinea and neighbouring islands. In January 1943, 3000 of them had left their base near Salamaua, on the north coast of eastern New Guinea (see map, p. 356), to close on 'Kanga Force', the 400-strong garrison of the small Australian base of Wau, in the mountains 50 km (30 miles) to the south-west.

The Australian commander, Brigadier Murray Moten, knew the situation was desperate. For days, heavy cloud banks over the surrounding peaks had made airlifts of vital reinforcements impossible. At 4 am on January 29 – when the enemy had got within 275 m (300 yds) of the Wau airstrip – the rain eased, and two hours later sunlight pierced the dismal cloud cover. At 9.15 a Dakota transport plane squelched down. Even before it had stopped moving, 20 men leapt out, weapons blazing at the surrounding jungle, to create a zone of relative safety for another 59 planes carrying over 800 reinforcements. 'Kanga Force' was saved. By the end of February, the Japanese had been pushed back to their original position, leaving 1200 dead for the loss of fewer than 200 Australians.

But Admiral Isoroku Yamamoto, commanding the Japanese Combined Fleet, was still determined to hold his bases at Salamaua and nearby Lae. On February 28, eight destroyers and eight transports carrying 6000 troops slipped out of the main Japanese base at Rabaul, on the neighbouring island of New Britain, and headed along the coast and through the Bismarck Sea to Lae.

Next day, the convoy was spotted by an RAAF Liberator. Despite an initial raid by Flying Fortresses which blew up two transports laden with explosives, the convoy stayed on course. They were about to turn west around the Huon Peninsula for the final run to Lae when, on the morning of March 3, 84 American bombers and

fighters, accompanied by 13 RAAF Beaufighters, swept in mast-high out of the morning sun.

Four destroyers and the remaining transports sank, leaving hundreds of men floating and clinging to wreckage. More and more Allied aircraft – 330 in all – now zoomed in to machine-gun the hapless survivors. That night, the grisly work continued, to stop any remaining Japanese swimming to shore. American torpedo boats swept in, searchlights piercing the darkness and machine guns chattering. About 3000 died in what the Japanese called the Bismarck Sea Massacre. Only 850 ever reached Lae, where they too soon perished. After that, Yamamoto had little hope of reinforcing his New Guinea force.

Yet he did not give up. He transferred squadrons from carriers based at Truk, in the Caroline Islands, to Rabaul; and in the first half of April he ordered air strikes against Guadalcanal island and Oro Bay, Port Moresby and Milne Bay in Papua. They had little effect and over a third of the 370 aircraft involved were lost. To raise the

ALL ASHORE The landing craft *Little Chic* crunches onto the beach (left) and New Zealanders, in their distinctive lemon-squeezer hats, pour onto Vella Lavella island, the last major target before Bougainville.

KEEP IT MOVING! American troops unload ammunition on Rendova island after order has been restored. The Allies brilliantly solved the problem of keeping their Pacific forces supplied.

morale of his pilots, Yamamoto decided to visit his forward bases. On April 18, as his plane flew over Bougainville island, 16 P-38 Lightning fighters roared out of the blue and sent the admiral to a fiery death (see box, *Target Yamamoto*).

TWO WAYS TO RABAUL

Yamamoto's fate seemed to symbolise Japan's plummeting fortunes and the Allies' increasing confidence. During late April and early May 1943, MacArthur and his number two, US Third Fleet commander Admiral William ('Bull') Halsey, worked out a complex plan – Operation 'Cartwheel' – for the advance northwards. In June, MacArthur would sweep west along the north coast of New Guinea and then north-east into New Britain. At the same time, Halsey would go island-hopping north-westwards from Guadalcanal along the Solomons chain. Then, in October, after Halsey had taken the large Japanese base of Munda on New Georgia, both arms would converge on Rabaul, where Japanese Eighth Area Army (Army Group) commander General Hitoshi Imamura had his headquarters.

Within six days of Kelly Turner's Rendova landing, which initiated Halsey's thrust, a force of ten Japanese destroyers carrying 2600 troops sped east from heavily garrisoned Kolombangara island across Kula Gulf to reinforce New Georgia. Unknown to them, an American force under Rear Admiral Walden Ainsworth was cruising in the gulf. In a fierce night-time clash, two Japanese destroyers were lost for the cruiser USS *Helena*. Only 850 Japanese ever reached New Georgia. A week later the light cruiser *Jintsu* and five destroyers made a dash across the gulf. Again Ainsworth intercepted, sinking *Jintsu* with all hands for the loss of one destroyer.

On land, too, fighting was heavy. Two days after the Rendova landings, the 43rd Division's 169th and 172nd Regiments slipped ashore on New Georgia at Zanana Beach, only 10 km (6 miles) from the Munda air base, and spent four days building a bridgehead unmolested by General Noboru Sasaki's 2500 defenders. Then, on July 6, Sasaki struck – and the Americans fell back in panic. A week later both regiments, despite support by artillery and air strikes, had advanced only 1100 m (1200 yds). Reinforcements arrived on July 14, but under enemy fire the infantry ran for cover, leaving newly arrived Marine Corps tanks with no option but to follow.

Sasaki, sensing that one major attack might overrun the Americans, sent troops forward. This time they were not so lucky. They ran into some small detachments of equally determined marines – the tank crews. In one position, two marines manning a machine gun held up an entire Japanese company all night. The marines were found next morning, one dead and one dying, surrounded by piles of dead Japanese.

The disastrous 169th Regiment was withdrawn, reinforcements were landed and a new commander, Maj General Oscar Griswold, was appointed. On July 25, Griswold saturated Sasaki's positions with bombs and shells. Then tanks and bulldozers rolled forward, with infantry carrying flamethrowers. In the first day they scorched the first 450 m (500 yds) of jungle into a moonscape. For ten more days they advanced until, on August 4, Griswold's tanks rolled onto Munda airfield. It was undefended. The survivors had already retreated north, where over the next few weeks they were hunted down and killed.

After one more Japanese failure to land men on

TARGET YAMAMOTO

A top-secret cable reached Major John W. Mitchell, commanding No 339 Fighter Squadron on Guadalcanal, at 5 pm on April 17, 1943. It came direct from Navy Secretary Frank Knox in Washington, and it told Mitchell that Naval Intelligence had decoded the next day's itinerary for Admiral Isoroku Yamamoto (above), Commander in Chief of the Japanese Combined Fleet.

The admiral and his staff would be flying from Rabaul to Bougainville in two 'Betty' bombers escorted by six Zero fighters, and would land at Kahili airfield at 9.45 am. Knox ordered that Mitchell's P-38 Lightning fighters 'must at all costs reach and destroy Yamamoto and his staff'.

Bougainville was 900 km (500 miles) away to the north-west – beyond the P-38s' range. But Knox had already organised fuel drop-tanks to be flown in from New Guinea. These arrived at Henderson Field at 9 pm in torrential rain. Mitchell and his pilots spent the night preparing their planes. Haggard and unshaven, 16 pilots took off at 7.20 am.

They raced just above wave height for $2\frac{1}{4}$ hours, sighted the island at 9.35 am and were busy gaining height to look for Yamamoto's flight when one pilot broke radio silence to announce briefly: 'Eleven o'clock.' There, sure enough, above and slightly left, was the target. The pilots ditched their drop-tanks and climbed to intercept. Lieutenant Thomas G. Lanphier Jr had just got one 'Betty' in his sights when three Zeros came at him. He turned to meet them, fired a burst, then saw the 'Betty' below at treetop level. Diving at 640 km/h (400 mph), he fired a long burst into it. One wing and engine burst into flames and the bomber fell into the trees and exploded.

Lanphier had got Yamamoto, though the Americans could not be sure until Lieutenant Rex Barber downed the second 'Betty' – the admiral had to be in one of them. All but one P-38 – shot down by the Zeros – made it back to Henderson for a very quiet celebration. The coup was kept top secret so that the Japanese would not realise that their code had been broken.

COURAGE OF THE COASTWATCHERS

On February 21, 1943, an assault group of the US 43rd Infantry Division stormed ashore on Banika island, in the Russell group, 65 km (40 miles) west of Guadalcanal. They were met not by charging Japanese, but by two bearded Australians. Lieutenants A. Campbell and Andy Andresen offered the Americans tea and said there was no need to hurry – the Japanese had long gone.

The Australians were members of the Coastwatching Service, a secret organisation set up in the south-west Pacific in 1919 and expanded in 1941. Never more than 50 strong at any one time, they were planters, traders, government officials – men who knew their area well and volunteered to stay behind if the Japanese came, hiding out to report enemy movements by radio. They were given ranks in the Royal Australian Navy Reserve. Most also organised local intelligence networks among trusted Melanesians. They formed an observation screen from Aitape, near the border with Dutch New Guinea, to the New Hebrides (Vanuatu).

The Americans first came to appreciate their value in May 1942, when Coastwatchers warned of Japanese progress in building an airfield on Guadalcanal. Then, on August 7, two Coastwatchers on Bougainville, Lieutenants Paul Mason and Jack Read, warned that a major Japanese air attack was on its way to hit the US beach-head at Guadalcanal. Their warning gave Rear Admiral Frank Fletcher two hours to prepare a fighter welcome for them. 'Bull' Halsey said: 'The Coastwatchers saved Guadalcanal and Guadalcanal saved the Pacific.'

The Coastwatchers paid a high price for their success. Japanese patrols using bloodhounds scoured the islands and offered large rewards for information. Altogether 36 Coastwatchers were killed. The price paid by loyal Melanesians was even higher. No wonder US Navy Captain C.M. White described the Coastwatchers as 'the bravest men I have ever known'.

LOYAL AND BRAVE Coastwatcher Martin Clemens stands with six of his Melanesian helpers.

THE SINKING OF PT 109

The light was dying when a flotilla of American motor torpedo (PT) boats slipped away from Rendova island in the Solomons on August 1, 1943. They moved into Blackett Strait, looking for Japanese convoys running reinforcements to Kolombangara island. Just before midnight they sighted four destroyers approaching from the north. The PT boats launched torpedoes – and all missed. The boats scattered, three of the destroyers raced on, but the fourth, *Amagiri*, turned to sniff out its assailants.

The night was by now pitch black and at 1.15 am, *PT 109*, commanded by Lieutenant John F. Kennedy, crossed *Amagiri*'s course and was cut in half. Two of Kennedy's crew of 14 died instantly. The rest were left clinging to the still-floating bow section of *PT 109*. They drifted through the night and into the next day. At midday the bow section turned turtle.

Kennedy decided that they had to swim to the nearest island. Lashing pieces of wreckage into a raft for the injured, and after hours of swimming and pushing the raft, the 12 survivors flopped ashore on bizarrely named Plum Pudding island. Next day and the day after, Kennedy, a powerful swimmer, swam out to look for passing PT boats – but in vain. By August 5 they had eaten all their food. They all took to the sea again and swam 2.5 km (1½ miles) to Olosana island. Kennedy and another man then swam on to Naru island. They found a canoe, tried to paddle the 50 km (30 miles) back to Rendova, but had to give up. Now they could only wait and hope. Unknown to them, help was at hand.

An Australian Coastwatcher on Kolombangara, Lieutenant Reginald Evans, had spotted them in the sea on August 2 and sent his Melanesian scouts looking for survivors. They found the Americans on August 6 and paddled Kennedy back to Kolombangara hidden under palm fronds. Rendova was contacted by radio and a PT boat was sent to recover Kennedy. He then picked up his crew from Olosana.

Exhausted, Kennedy could not even recall Evans' name when he came to write his report, and only discovered it in 1961 – when he was President of the USA.

PT HERO The sun-bronzed Lieutenant John F. Kennedy sits at the wheel of *PT 109*.

New Georgia – on August 6 three of their destroyers were sunk in Vella Gulf – there was no further attempt to reinforce the central Solomons.

It was clear to Imamura that Halsey would next strike at Kolombangara. He awaited the attack eagerly, for he had 12 000 crack troops well entrenched there. But Halsey had other ideas, and sailed on by – to Vella Lavella, 16 km (10 miles) farther west. He was lucky. In the assault, many tank landing ships hit an uncharted reef, causing an immense jam of vessels that made an easy target. But the garrison on Vella Lavella made no response: it was only 900 strong.

The GIs did not know this. They dug in and stayed put for a month, until the 3rd New Zealand Division arrived on September 18, itching for action. After several small, vicious engagements in torrential rain which left 300 Japanese and 32 New Zealanders dead, fighting on the island ended on October 6, when 600 surviving Japanese were evacuated. They too had a narrow escape. Shortly before 11 pm three American destroyers, *Selfridge*, *Chevalier* and *O'Bannion*, closed in on the evacuation convoy. Japanese destroyers unleashed torpedoes that sank *Chevalier* and badly damaged the other two vessels, allowing the troops to be ferried away to safety. But torpedoes and shells from the stricken ships hit the Japanese destroyer *Yugumo* and ripped it apart.

DOUBLE BLUFF

Next on Halsey's hit list was Bougainville. Here he faced a formidable foe, Maj General Harukichi Hyakutake's Seventeenth Army: 65 000 men supported by 450 aircraft. But Halsey planned to fool the Japanese again with a double bluff.

His elaborate plan began to unfold in the grey pre-dawn of October 27, when 3rd New Zealand Division's 8th Brigade headed into Blanche Harbour on the southern coast of Mono island. They took it after a bitter but swift assault. On the same morning, Lt Colonel Victor H. Krulak's 2nd Battalion of parachute marines landed on Choiseul island. For six days, Krulak's men roamed the jungle. The Japanese, convinced this was a major invasion, moved large forces towards Krulak's beach-head – only to find that his force had been spirited away by the US Navy.

The diversions worked brilliantly. Hyakutake, now convinced that Halsey was preparing to land on the eastern tip of Bougainville, concentrated his forces there. On November 1, men of the 3rd Marine Division began pouring ashore at the reef-studded, surf-battered Empress Augusta Bay, 80 km (50 miles) from the Japanese. Hyakutake was astounded. His commanders had assured him that a landing there was impossible, especially as the bay was backed by swamps.

He hit back with all he had, by land, sea and air. Troops set off overland. Sixty Zero fighters took off – only to be met by New Zealand and US planes which downed 31 Zeros for the loss of four aircraft. And that night, a Japanese task force of three heavy cruisers, a light cruiser and six destroyers swept into Empress Augusta Bay. It was met by Rear Admiral Stanton ('Tip') Merrill's four new light cruisers and eight destroyers, which rapidly sank two Japanese ships. In the darkness, the Japanese force dissolved into chaos, four ships colliding before they could withdraw.

The Americans did more damage on November 5, when carrier-based planes zoomed down on Rabaul harbour to hit newly arrived naval reinforcements. Six Japanese cruisers were badly damaged. The following day four Japanese destroyers raced down Bougainville's coast and landed infantry in small boats just west of the American beach-head. But pounding surf capsized many boats and the survivors made easy targets – 400 were killed, the rest fled into the jungle. Meanwhile, the marines were pushing inland through the swamps, and by November 17 the Americans held an area 10 km (6 miles) long and 5 km (3 miles) wide. Engineers had partially drained it, and an airstrip was half built.

At last Hyakutake understood Halsey's strategy and determined to crush the beach-head. He sent in a major attack on November 18. Unfortunately for the Japanese, a patrol led by Lieutenant Slim J. Cubik slipped around their right flank and occupied a hill behind them, 5.5 km (3½ miles) inland. Reinforced over the next few days, Cubik's Hill, as it came to be called, dominated the Japanese lines of communication. In increasing desperation, waves of Japanese surged up it until, on November 26, after more than 1200 had been killed, Hyakutake called off the attack. The Americans were on Bougainville to stay, and Rabaul was within bombing range.

FIGHTING BULL

William Frederick Halsey (1882-1959) was a destroyer expert in the early 1930s, but was attracted by the new technology of air power. In 1935, at the age of 52, he qualified as a pilot. When war broke out he was commanding the US Pacific Fleet's air forces. His aggressive early counterstrikes – such as the daring Doolittle raid – led the Press to dub him 'Bull'. Illness kept him from Midway, but he was given tactical command in the south Pacific in 1943, specifically to add more belligerence to the leadership. He once told subordinates that their job was to 'kill Japs, kill more Japs'.

But he sometimes ran dangerous risks – notably in the 1944 Battle of Leyte Gulf. In December 1944, his eagerness to keep attacking the Japanese exposed his ships to a typhoon in which three destroyers sank, with nearly 800 men. A court of inquiry blamed Halsey for 'errors of judgement'. Nevertheless, he alternated with Admiral Raymond Spruance in command of the central Pacific fleet (called the Third Fleet when Halsey led it and the Fifth under Spruance) from 1943 to 1945.

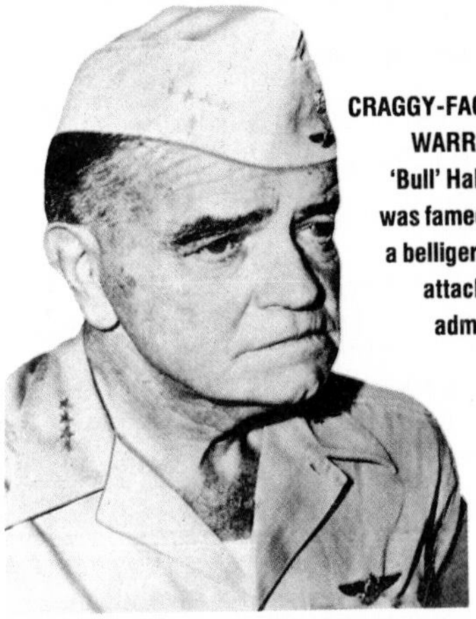

CRAGGY-FACED WARRIOR 'Bull' Halsey was famed as a belligerent, attacking admiral.

Jungle trail to seal off Rabaul

The Allied troops forming the western prong of Operation 'Cartwheel' faced formidable terrain, gruelling conditions, and fanatical Japanese resistance.

THE PIMPLE was a poisonous little spot – a 450 m (1500 ft) jungle-clad hill in eastern New Guinea, held by fanatical Japanese troops. Australians trying to take it had to move with infinite caution – and not just because of the Japanese. At one point, Corporal D. Smith pushed his way a few steps off the trail to look for stretcher-bearers – and within moments was simply swallowed in the dense jungle. It took him three weeks to find his battalion again.

And the Pimple – as the Diggers nicknamed the hill – was only the first of many obstacles facing Maj General Stanley Savige's Australian 3rd Division. It was trying to fight its way over a whole series of hills and ridges from its base at Wau to the north coast near Japanese-held Salamaua, to link up with American forces due to land in late June 1943. They were all part of General Douglas MacArthur's plan to secure the north coast of eastern New Guinea before the two prongs of Operation 'Cartwheel' closed on the Japanese regional headquarters at Rabaul on the island of New Britain (see map, p. 356).

The distance from Wau to Salamaua was just 55 km (35 miles), and the Aussies, setting off on April 24, had two months to cover it. But in the buckled, rain-sodden terrain, against determined defenders, it seemed to them like ten times that distance. On May 7 a company of the veteran 2/7th Battalion was forced back after losing 12 dead and 25 wounded on the Pimple. This set a pattern for the next six weeks – seesawing attacks and counterattacks for hills and ridges. During May and June, however, Australian patrols worked around the Japanese left flank until, on the night of June 29, they reached Nassau Bay, to the south-east of Salamaua. They were just in time.

Shortly after midnight, landing craft carrying Colonel Archibald MacKechnie's landing force of US infantry and engineer units came plunging through mountainous surf and crash-landed onto the beach. Dawn revealed 21 hulks twisted by the breakers. Miraculously, none of the engineers had been drowned – though 18 died the following night when jumpy Americans blazed away at strange jungle sounds while the veteran Australians went to ground.

Gradually, order was brought to the beach-head. A week later, MacKechnie's men, now reinforced, were in action on the Australians' right flank, and the Aussies were ready for a full-scale assault on the Japanese 51st Division and its headquarters at Mubo, 25 km (15 miles) up the Bitou river valley from Salamaua.

TAKING SALAMAUA AND LAE

At 9.30 am on July 7, 120 B-24 Liberator and B-25 Mitchell bombers swept over the Japanese positions, enveloping the entire valley in thick black smoke broken by sheets of flame. After six days, the Australians had almost encircled the Japanese, who pulled back to the last ridge lines before Salamaua. There, over the next month, the Australians joined with the Americans to create a pincer movement. Salamaua seemed about to fall.

But that was not the Allied intention. In mid-August, the fresh Australian 5th Division, under Maj General Edward Milford, relieved the exhausted 3rd – with orders to keep up pressure on Salamaua. However, this was a ploy to draw in Japanese reinforcements from their port and base at Lae, 40 km (25 miles) north – and Lae, not Salamaua, would become the main Australian target. At 6.30 am on September 4, four battalions of the Australian 9th Division, veterans of Tobruk and El Alamein, charged ashore 25 km (15 miles) east of Lae. They were expecting a hard fight, but by mid-morning, after scarcely firing a shot, the Australians knew there were virtually no Japanese in the area. The plan had worked: almost all the defenders had gone to Salamaua.

Next morning, the Japanese commander at Lae, Lt General Hidemitsu Nakano, got another shock. An outpost at Nadzab, 35 km (20 miles) up the Markham river, reported streams of Allied transports dropping thousands of paratroops. Then communications ceased. In all, some 3000 Americans and 31 Australians dropped that day. By nightfall, they had cleared a base for Dakota transport planes to land a brigade of the Australian 7th Division. Three days later, they were pushing down the Markham towards Lae.

Nakano made the only decision possible. He pulled the beleaguered Salamaua garrison back to Lae – where he faced another hard decision. Three Australian divisions were closing in on him. If he stayed and fought, he would lose the rest of his force. He had to make a break for it – and got lucky. Torrential rain stopped air supplies and blocked the route of the Australian 9th Division. On September 11, when the first of Nakano's sodden columns trudged north out of Lae, into the rugged Finisterre mountains, the jaws of the Australian pincer were still 11 km (7 miles) apart. Nakano lost 2000 men in bloody rearguard clashes, but 6000 survived to fight another day, leaving Lae and Salamaua in Allied hands.

VICTORY AT FINSCHHAFEN

On September 22, 9th Division struck again, this time 100 km (60 miles) east of Lae at the small town of Finschhafen, on the tip of the Huon Peninsula. American Intelligence had promised the assault force – three battalions of Brigadier Victor Windeyer's 20th Brigade – that between 350 and 1800 Japanese held Finschhafen.

American Intelligence, it transpired, had got it wrong. In fact, the Huon Peninsula was held by 13 000 men under Lt General Shigiru Katagiri. When the Australians landed there had been 6000 Japanese in Finschhafen, but they had fled – the only time in World War II that the Japanese ran from a smaller Allied force. Now Katagiri planned revenge. With Windeyer's battalions spread along 15 km (10 miles) of the coast, he concentrated most of his men around Sattelberg, a 1040 m (3400 ft) peak, and prepared to push the Diggers into the sea.

First he launched an amphibious assault. At 2.55 am on October 17, Private Nathan Van Noy and Corporal Stephen Popa, American engineers working on the Australian beach-head, were woken by shouts and gunfire. Less than 100 m out to sea, heading straight for them, was a flotilla of Japanese barges. The Americans leaped behind a Browning machine gun and, as the leading barges lowered their ramps, fired directly into them. Enough Japanese survived to shower them with

PARAS AWAY! A screen of smoke rises from the jungle as US paratroops float down into New Guinea's Markham valley. The paras are to join in the attack on Lae.

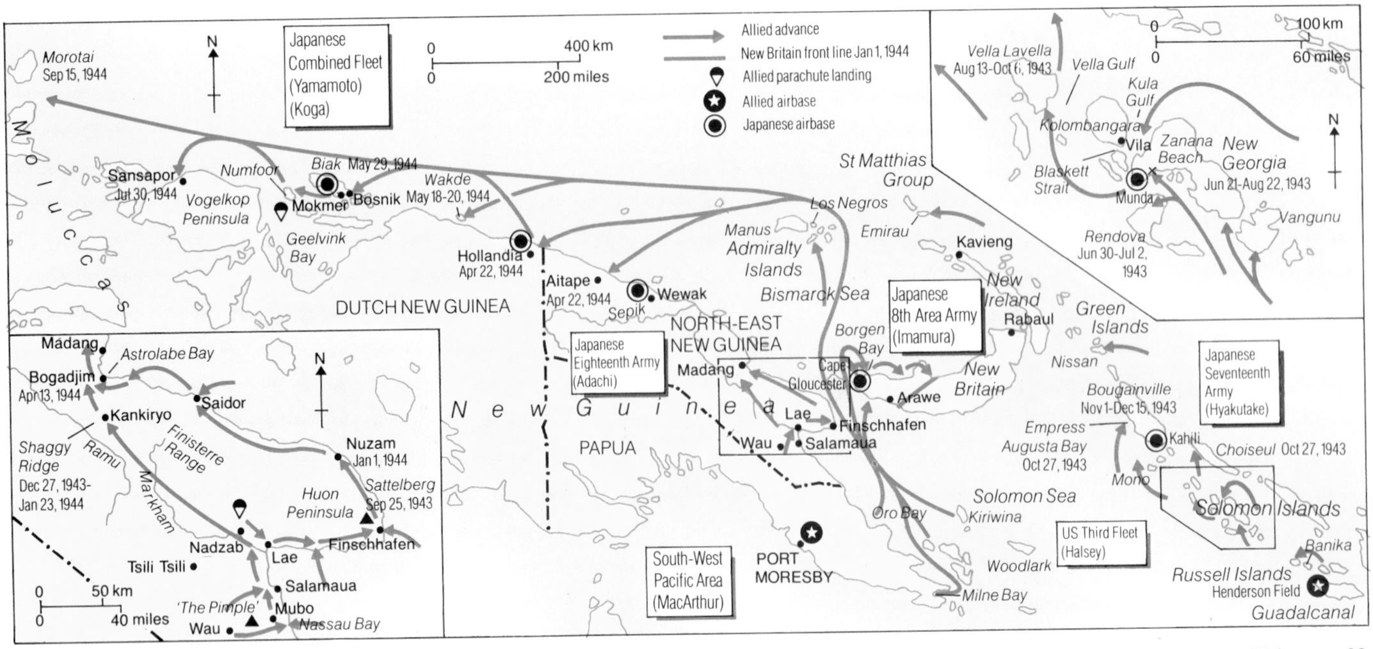

TARGET MOROTAI 'Cartwheel' was unleashed in June 1943: MacArthur moved west through northern New Guinea; Halsey hopped his way up the Solomons. They isolated Rabaul, then pushed on along New Guinea's coast.

grenades, and both were badly wounded. Van Noy, one leg shattered and the other blown off, kept firing until more grenades silenced him.

The sacrifice was not in vain. Australian anti-aircraft gunners had been given time to level their 40 mm (1.6 in) Bofors gun and sweep the beach with fire. It was soon over. The Australians found Van Noy dead and Popa unconscious, surrounded by 30 dead Japanese. Van Noy was awarded a posthumous Medal of Honor.

Inland later that morning, the men of 2/3rd Pioneer Battalion were attacked by waves of Japanese. The Australians fell back into a circle atop a nearby hill. The main Japanese assault flowed past below, driving towards the sea – and almost made it. Only the 2/28th Battalion stood in their way, but as each day passed the Australians grew stronger. Lt General Sir Leslie Morshead, North Africa veteran and new commander of Australian forces in New Guinea, soon had more men and supplies moving towards Finschhafen.

On October 23, the Japanese made their final assault. Like all the others, it was bloodily repulsed. The reinforced 9th Division went on the offensive towards Sattelberg and on November 19, fougasse – the prototype of napalm – was used for the first time. It burned only briefly but badly shook the Japanese defenders. Six days later, Sattelberg fell and Katagiri, with only 5000 of his original 13 000 men still alive, retreated westwards. The last obstacle to an assault on New Britain was removed – at the cost of 283 Australians dead and over 10 000 wounded.

SEALING OFF RABAUL

With the island of Bougainville, 800 km (500 miles) east, also secure, the two arms of 'Cartwheel' were closing in on New Britain. In Rabaul, the Japanese area commander, Lt General Hitoshi Imamura, knew the Allies would land soon. But where? His garrison of more than 100 000 was strong, but could hardly cover all the island's 1600 km (1000 mile) coastline. At best they could defend the main bases – in particular Rabaul. But the Allies now had no intention of taking Rabaul. The Joint Chiefs of Staff had decided to modify the original aim of 'Cartwheel' and seal off Rabaul rather than assault it.

Imamura's subordinate in western New Britain, Maj General Iwao Matsuda, was sure the enemy would first land on Cape Gloucester, the north-western tip of the island, to try to seize its air base. There were a number of places where the Americans could land, but there was one place he was sure they would not land: Borgen Bay, fringed with swamp and quicksand, 16 km (10 miles) east of the cape.

That was precisely where the Americans did strike. On December 26, a regiment of the US 1st Marine Division splashed ashore unopposed, and waded through black mud up to their waists to high ground about 800 m (900 yds) inland, aiming to attack the airfield from the rear. Matsuda rushed in men to dig protective bunkers, but too late. The marines, supported by tanks, landed on the bay's drier western side and pulverised the hastily built defences. At dawn on December 29, the tanks rolled across the airfield, scattering defenders. Next day, mobs of screaming Japanese launched suicidal *banzai* charges against the entrenched Americans, to be scythed down by machine guns, mortars and artillery.

At the other end of the island, Imamura was ready behind the formidable bunkers and 'killing grounds' that surrounded Rabaul. Through January 1944, the Americans built their own defence line clear across the island. If Imamura wanted a fight, he would have to come to them.

Next, the outlying islands had to be neutralised. On February 15, men of the 3rd New Zealand Division stormed ashore on Nissan island, largest of the Green Islands, 225 km (140 miles) east of Rabaul. Imamura lost 12 of his 32 remaining aircraft in its defence. The small Japanese garrison of 70 was cornered on a cliff and wiped out. Within a month, Allied planes were flying from a new runway on Nissan.

The Admiralty group, 600 km (375 miles) north-west of Rabaul, were next to fall. The US 1st Cavalry Division stormed ashore on the outlying island of Los Negros on February 29. Three nights later, the surviving defenders – more than 1000 men – charged the American perimeter in a screaming mass, only to be obliterated by artillery. A few days later, cavalrymen crossed to the main Admiralty island of Manus, overwhelming fanatical but uncoordinated resistance to end a campaign that cost 326 American lives – and ten times that number of Japanese deaths.

Allied bases now guarded Rabaul to the west, south and east. Only the north remained clear. On March 20 that corridor too was closed, when the US 4th Marine Division took Emirau in the St Matthias group, 400 km (250 miles) north. Imamura and his men were out of the war without a fight, and the Allies could move on unhampered.

ACE OF AMERICAN ACES

Richard I. Bong (1920-45) was the highest-scoring US fighter pilot of World War II. Most of his victories were in the south-west Pacific, flying Lockheed P-38 Lightnings. By April 1944, he had downed 27 Japanese planes and passed the US record set by Captain Eddie Rickenbacker in World War I. He was promoted major and ordered home, in case his loss in combat affected morale.

Bong would have none of this, however, and was soon back in the combat zone. By mid-December 1944, when he shot down his final victims, his score stood at an unsurpassed 40. Returned finally to America for a non-combat job, he died testing a new jet fighter on August 6, 1945, the day of the Hiroshima atomic bombing.

SMILING ACE Bong's feats in the Pacific skies won him the Medal of Honor.

Coast route to Morotai

A grim slog for possession of a razorback ridge and an air strike that swept the Japanese from the skies prepared the way for a massive, final lunge for victory in New Guinea, opening up the route to the Philippines.

TURKEY, PLUM PUDDING and the screech of incoming shells were served up on Christmas Day, 1943, to the Australians below Shaggy Ridge, in the mountainous interior of eastern New Guinea. To many of them, it seemed a short-odds bet that this would be the last Christmas dinner they would eat. They had just received orders to capture the 1500 m (5000 ft) ridge, which was heavily defended by hundreds of determined and well dug in Japanese.

After the Japanese base at Lae on the north coast had fallen in September, the Australian 7th Division managed to push 200 km (120 miles) west up the Markham and Ramu river valleys, between mountains running parallel to the coast (see map, p. 356). In early October they swung north, aiming to fight their way across the near-impenetrable Finisterre mountains to the coast, to cut off Japanese retreating from the Huon Peninsula. The Finisterres' sheer-walled heights made the crossing extremely difficult – except where the range dipped into a saddle near Kankiryo village. A 5 km (3 mile) hog's back protruded south from the saddle like the outworks of a fortress. The Australian Diggers, whose advance had been stalled on its slopes for two months, called it Shaggy Ridge.

The Japanese had burnt fire lanes through its covering of rough kunai grass and studded the steep slopes with heavily bunkered positions. On December 27, the Australian assault swung into action. At 8.02 am RAAF Boomerang fighters roared up the Ramu valley and strafed the ridge. Three minutes later Kittyhawk fighter-bombers swooped down, dive-bombing bunkers. At 8.55, as the last Kittyhawks climbed away, a massive Australian artillery bombardment rained down 3368 shells in two hours. Maj General George A. Vasey, the 7th's commander, circled above the ridge in a light plane to get a better view.

At 9.01, as explosions pockmarked the ridge, Lieutenant Charles Geyton and his platoon, carrying long bamboo ladders, scrambled up the slopes towards a sheer cliff wall. It was like scaling a medieval castle. As they clambered from ledge to ledge the Japanese above dropped grenades onto them, but covering fire forced the Japanese in turn to keep their heads down. At 9.46, Corporal Mike Hall's section reached the southern rim of the ridge, and dashed along the crest to seize a knoll from which they had a clear view along the ridge. Far to the north, beyond the saddle, they could see the gleaming blue waters of Astrolabe Bay.

Through the afternoon and the following day they pushed cautiously forward from knoll to knoll, knocking out Japanese bunkers with grenade attacks. By evening on December 28 they controlled about 900 m (1000 yds) of Shaggy Ridge, but the attack had bogged down. Australian and Japanese positions were only 75 m (80 yds) apart and for the next three weeks they stayed that way, the Aussies always seeking a new advantage: attacking from different directions, seizing knolls, charging with fixed bayonets, calling in air strikes. Eventually two Australian battalions were only 800 m (900 yds) apart, squeezing the Japanese into an ever-diminishing area. At midday on January 23, 1944, the Diggers linked up. The battle had cost them 43 killed and 150 wounded. The Japanese had lost at least 500.

Meanwhile, the Australian 9th Division had been slogging west through the streams, rivers and trackless swamps of New Guinea's north coast in pursuit of the remnants of Lt General Shigiru Katagiri's 20th Division, who were retreating from Finschhafen on the Huon Peninsula. Bush typhus and dengue fever claimed far more casualties than the frequent skirmishes with Japanese rearguards. The advance was spearheaded by local Papuan troops, who managed to kill about 15 enemy stragglers each day, but by January 1, 1944, the advance had only reached Nuzam, a village 65 km (40 miles) along the coast from Finschhafen.

Hopes of trapping the Japanese were boosted next day by the landing of the US 126th Regimental Combat Team 160 km (100 miles) farther west at the village of Saidor. But these hopes were soon dashed after the 126th merely dug a tight defensive perimeter and allowed Katagiri's exhausted columns to march around them. On February 10, when the Australians trudged into Saidor, they did not mince words.

One chance remained to trap the Japanese – if the Australians now controlling the Kankiryo saddle could reach the coast at Astrolabe Bay. It was only 25 km (15 miles) to the north – but that was 25 km of jungle-clad ridges and ravines. The exhausted 7th Division was relieved by the 11th's untried militia troops, who advanced cautiously. By the time they entered the now deserted Japanese base at Bogadjim on April 13, many of Katagiri's men had reached the estuary of the Sepik river, 200 km (125 miles) farther north-west, and were ferried another 100 km (60 miles) to the relative safety of Wewak.

LIGHTNING STRIKE

In his headquarters at Wewak, Lt General Hatazo Adachi, Japanese commander in New Guinea, was convinced that the Australians would push on along the north coast. He had moved his reserves from Hollandia (now Jayapura), in Dutch New Guinea, into the Wewak area, and had nearly 50 000 men ready to meet the Australians on the western banks of the broad Sepik. He also had more than 600 aircraft on airfields around Wewak.

Apparent confirmation that Wewak was the Allies' next objective came on March 11, when hundreds of fighters and bombers of Lt General George C. Kenney's US Fifth Air Force, based near Lae, swept down onto the Wewak airfields. The attacks continued for five days, then the Japanese pulled their surviving planes back to Hollandia – beyond the range of Kenney's escort fighters, they thought. They did not know that Kenney now had new long-range P-38 Lightnings.

AMPHIBIOUS MASTER

Robert Lawrence Eichelberger (1886-1961) became the south-west Pacific's supreme expert in amphibious assaults. Superintendent of the West Point Military Academy when the USA entered the war, he was put in command of I Corps, which was to assist the Australians in the reconquest of Papua in 1942-3. After retraining American troops exhausted and demoralised by the Papuan operation, he commanded US Army forces in the New Britain and Hollandia campaigns of 1944. His experience, drive and flexibility stood him in good stead, and in 1945, during the Philippines campaign, he led his forces in the series of complex landings in the central and southern islands. He went on to spearhead the occupation of Japan, where he worked until his retirement in 1948.

On March 30, Liberator bombers roared over Hollandia and Japanese fighters took off, expecting rich pickings. Within minutes Kenney's Lightnings had downed them all. After another attack next day, 520 of the Japanese planes had been destroyed and 2000 ground crew were dead. The survivors withdrew to Manado on Celebes (Sulawesi), 1800 km (1120 miles) away in the East Indies. The skies over northern New Guinea had virtually been cleared of Japanese aircraft.

OPERATION 'RECKLESS'

During April 21, Japanese patrols reported Australians advancing on the outskirts of Madang, the abandoned Japanese base just north of Bogadjim. The Allied thrust seemed to be from the direction Adachi had predicted, and his forces were prepared. But at that moment General Douglas MacArthur, Allied commander in the south-west Pacific, was 320 km (200 miles) north-west of Wewak on board the cruiser USS *Nashville*, in the midst of a 217-ship convoy about to launch Operation 'Reckless'.

At 6 am on April 22 most of the 12 000 Japanese in Hollandia – mainly middle-aged reservists and supply troops – were eating breakfast or still asleep when thousands of shells suddenly screamed in and explosions shook the earth. The horizon to the north was a blaze of pulsating light from which rockets in thousands arched through the sky. Panic spread, and within minutes thousands of Japanese were running south.

By 7 am hundreds of landing craft were surging shoreward through the waters of Hollandia's magnificent harbour, Humboldt Bay. The first of MacArthur's 80 000-strong invasion force to wade ashore had little to do. An endless trail of abandoned rifles, ammunition and uniforms showed the scale of the Japanese panic. Within weeks the Americans had hunted down the fugitives. Despite the Japanese 'no surrender' ethic, 611 gave themselves up. Another 3300 were killed for the loss of about 150 American lives; the remainder either died in the jungle or escaped.

On the same morning (April 22), the American 163rd Regimental Combat Team had landed at Aitape, halfway between Wewak and Hollandia. Here too the Japanese garrison was taken by surprise. For the loss of two dead, the Americans killed 625 Japanese and took 27 prisoners. The other 348 fled east towards Wewak. Adachi and his 50 000 men were now completely isolated – either by Allied land and naval forces or by impenetrable jungle mountains.

Within days of landing, American engineers began transforming Hollandia from a small town into America's largest base in the south-west Pacific, with extensive docks and airfields. Lt General Robert Eichelberger, tactical commander of 'Reckless', wrote: 'Where once I had seen only a few native villages and an expanse of primeval forest, a city of 140 000 men took occupancy.' This would become the launching pad for the reconquest of the rest of New Guinea, and the eventual return to the Philippines.

COAST-HOPPING

It was obvious to MacArthur that the remaining Japanese forces along the north coast of western New Guinea must be very weak. He now ordered Rear Admiral Daniel Barbey's VII Amphibious Force to hop along the coast to Morotai in the Molucca islands, seizing suitable airstrip sites on the way. Barbey's first target was the tiny offshore coral islet of Wakde, 200 km (125 miles) west of Hollandia. At dawn on May 18 the first assault wave went in, anticipating an easy victory. But the 759 Japanese defenders all fought to the death. It took the Americans another two days and 140 casualties to take Wakde.

Nine days later the 162nd and 168th Regiments went ashore on the southern side of the forbiddingly steep Biak island, 320 km (200 miles) west of Wakde. Their landing was unopposed and they established a beach-head at Bosnik village, then advanced 14 km (9 miles) west along the narrow coastal shelf towards Mokmer, where the cliff wall swung inland, creating a deep valley. Here the Japanese had built three airstrips.

By mid-morning on May 29 the Americans were moving into Mokmer and crossing the easternmost airstrip. Then all hell broke loose. Japanese guns concealed in deep cliff-side caves loosed devastating salvos, inflicting heavy casualties. Frantically the Americans dug in, the intense crossfire preventing any attempt at withdrawal. Biak's garrison commander, Colonel Naoyuki Kuzume, had used the airfields as enticing bait in a gigantic trap, concealing nearly all his 11 000 men in the surrounding cliffs.

The only way to secure the airfields was to exterminate the Japanese positions one by one. That took over ten weeks, and involved one of the very few tank battles of the Pacific war. Kuzume killed 400 Americans and wounded 2000 more – though he lost 4700 of his own men. The remaining Japanese escaped across Geelvink Bay at night to the Vogelkop Peninsula, New Guinea's western extremity. But MacArthur's forces were now so powerful that a tactical reverse could no longer disrupt his timetable, and his men were already pushing farther west.

September 13, 1944, was symbolic for MacArthur and all those who served under him. Shortly before midday a task force of 100 ships carrying 40 000 troops crossed the Equator: the forces of South-West Pacific Area were carrying their offensive into the Northern Hemisphere. They reached their objective, Morotai island, halfway between New Guinea and the Philippines, on September 15. The 250-strong Japanese garrison offered only sporadic resistance, and at 10.15 am MacArthur stepped ashore. It was just 17 months since the decision to begin Operation 'Cartwheel'. Standing on the beach, he gazed north-west towards the Philippines, now only 620 km (400 miles) distant. 'They are waiting for me there,' he said. 'It has been a long time.'

'A WASTED EFFORT?'

As US forces got ready to land on Luzon in the Philippines in January 1945, four Australian divisions were fighting the 160 000 Japanese holding out on Bougainville and New Britain, and at Wewak on New Guinea. The Australians were heavily outnumbered and had little air and naval support, but by August they had killed 21 000 (while 20 000 more Japanese died of starvation and disease) for the loss of 1100 Diggers.

The campaign was a great success, but did nothing to hasten Japan's surrender. Many Australians shared the sentiments expressed in the *Melbourne Herald* headline of August 22, 1945: 'WAS OUR WAR IN ISLANDS A WASTED EFFORT?'

A year earlier, the isolated Japanese were proving more than a match for the six US divisions detailed to contain them. When MacArthur ordered the Australians to take over the job, their commander, General Sir Thomas Blamey, reckoned that six brigades would be enough, freeing the rest of his men to help in the Philippines. MacArthur overruled him, partly perhaps to avoid embarrassment and partly to keep the Philippines an all-American affair. So Blamey decided to fight rather than just contain the Japanese.

MOUNTAIN MEN Bivouacked precariously on the edge of a precipice in New Guinea's Ramu valley (top), Australian Diggers clean their rifles, sit and rest. In the Finisterre mountains (above), men slip and slide their way up a seemingly endless ladder of mud.

23: A TRIP THROUGH THE ISLANDS

Seizing the Gilbert Islands would be the first step in America's island-hopping advance across the central Pacific. Instead of the easy start they expected, it became a cruel baptism of fire.

BULLETS PINGED 'like hailstones off a tin roof' from Marine Private N.M. Baird's caterpillar-tracked amphibious landing vehicle – 'amtrac' or 'tractor'. It was churning across the blue lagoon of Tarawa Atoll towards the beach of a tiny, palm-fringed island on November 20, 1943. 'Two shells hit the water 20 yards [18 m] off the port side and sent up regular geysers,' Baird recalled later. 'I swept the beach [with a machine gun] just to keep the bastards down as much as possible. Can't figure out how I didn't get it in the head or something.

'We were 100 yards [90 m] in now and . . . they were knocking boats out right and left. A tractor'd get hit, stop and burst into flames, with men jumping out like torches . . . Bullets ricocheted off the coral and up under the tractor. It must've been one of those bullets that got the driver . . . The lieutenant jumped in and pulled the driver out, and drove himself till he got hit.'

Private Baird – an Oneida Indian – was describing his unit's landing at Betio, a coral jewel reduced to a flaming, dust-shrouded shambles by carrier-borne bombers and the concentrated firepower of three battleships, four heavy cruisers, five escort carriers and 21 destroyers of the US Fifth Fleet. In just 2½ hours, between dawn and 9 am, over 3000 tonnes of bombs and shells had pulverised the 3 km (2 mile) length of the island to 'soften it up' and make it easier for Maj General Julian Smith's 2nd Marine Division to storm ashore.

PACIFIC PROBLEM SOLVER **High-speed civil engineering miracles were the speciality of the US Navy's Construction Battalions (CBs) – generally known as the Seabees. Laying pipelines for fuel, burying power cables, bulldozing tracks in impossible country and building airstrips or floating docks within days were among their many jobs, all essential for taking over the Pacific islands. Some Seabees wore one-piece green overalls (left), but they were often kitted out with a mixture of items from any service. A two-piece outfit let them strip off the top for work, as many would have done in their prewar jobs in the building trade. The pith helmet doubled as sun hat and protective hard hat.**

The first three waves of landing craft and amphibious vehicles got ashore unscathed, but follow-up waves met a storm of machine-gun, artillery and mortar fire from suicidally brave Japanese defenders, emerging from a complex warren of more than 500 concrete bunkers and other strongpoints concealed within the palms that had somehow survived the bombardment.

The Japanese had buried seven tanks hull-deep, and the triangular lagoon was covered by 14 heavy coastal guns – including four captured from the British in Singapore – and 25 lighter field guns which easily had sufficient range on such a small island. The beaches were strewn with barbed-wire and log barricades. Offshore, concrete obstacles and coconut-log fences were positioned to channel incoming vessels into lanes swept by fire. In addition, jagged reefs around the island forced the Americans to disembark from some of their landing craft up to 650 m (700 yds) off the beaches to wade and scramble for the shore.

'ABSOLUTE DEFENCE'

Betio was a fair example of what awaited all too many US troops in their great island-hopping drive across the Pacific. For the Japanese were bent on defending their gains no matter what the sacrifice. Their own lightning Pacific expansion had ground to a halt after the fierce naval battles of 1942 and the bitter conflicts in New Guinea and the Solomons.

In September 1943, Tokyo ordered a 'zone of absolute defence' to be established, stretching from Burma and Malaya in the south-west, through the Dutch East Indies to New Guinea, the Caroline and Marshall Islands and northwards to the Kuril Islands. Any territory outside this zone would be held to the last man, to buy time to prepare the defences within it. American landings were to be destroyed on the beaches by heavy fire and counterattacks before beach-heads could be expanded.

In November 1943, the US Joint Chiefs of Staff finally decided, after numerous discussions since May, that those landings would take place along two main axes (see map, p.351). General Douglas MacArthur would push through the islands of the south-west Pacific towards the Philippines. Admiral Chester W. Nimitz's forces would at the same time take on the islands and atolls of the central Pacific, aiming for Formosa (Taiwan). Eventually the two forces would combine to assault Japan itself.

First on the central Pacific hit list were the tiny Gilbert Islands atolls of Tarawa and Makin, which lie about halfway between Hawaii and Australia. The operation – code-named 'Galvanic' – would see the debut of what was to become Nimitz's standard operational command team for the atoll war: Vice Admiral Raymond A. Spruance in overall command, Rear Admiral Richmond Kelly Turner commanding the landing forces, and Maj General Holland M. ('Howling Mad') Smith commanding the marines.

SAD SIDESHOW IN THE ALEUTIANS

In a diversionary attack during the Battle of Midway in June 1942, the Japanese had captured Attu and Kiska, islands in the Aleutian chain strung out between Alaska and Siberia. The US Joint Chiefs of Staff were determined to get them back.

For the raw US 7th Infantry Division who stormed ashore on Attu on May 11, 1943, the struggle was bitter and bloody. Preliminary bombing and a naval bombardment by three battleships had not wiped out Japanese defences. The Americans came under heavy fire from the 2500-strong garrison commanded by Colonel Yasuyo Yamakaze.

The Americans, having their first taste of combat, were poorly clad for the Arctic conditions. As the ferocious fighting went on, about 1500 became ill from the cold. But Yamakaze was running out of supplies and ammunition. His men made desperate suicidal charges, fighting viciously and breaking through the American lines – only to be cut down. Finally, on May 31, all Japanese resistance was crushed. Except for 28 prisoners, the entire Japanese garrison had been killed in the charges or had committed suicide. A thousand US troops had died.

After the tragic cost of retaking Attu, Kiska was reclaimed in an embarrassing farce. It was August when 29 000 US and 5200 Canadian troops assaulted the craggy, windswept island, only to find it empty. More than 6000 Japanese had left undetected weeks before – weeks during which the island had been bombarded by American planes and warships, and photographed by reconnaissance aircraft.

PAINFUL RETURN A wounded US soldier is taken for help on bleak Attu, where 1000 Americans died.

LESSONS OF TARAWA

The very reason for the US Marines' existence – assault landings on defended beaches – was sorely tested on Tarawa. But valuable lessons were learned and applied in later operations. The first and most obvious was the need for overwhelming strength to crush the Japanese – and to have men to spare for diversionary and supporting attacks. Better reconnaissance and intelligence were needed, including underwater exploration and demolition of beach defences by frogmen. The navy had to provide heavier and longer pre-assault bombardment, with long-range plunging fire using armour-piercing shells to destroy the well-built Japanese bunkers. Where possible, small islets within artillery range of the main target should be taken, to provide bases for supporting fire.

The chain of command needed to be made clearer, with better radio communications from command level down to individual units – which needed waterproof radios. Amtracs were needed for *all* assault troops, and landing craft converted into gunboats were required to get close to the beaches and give supporting fire. The marines had to have more flamethrowers and more automatic weapons such as the Garand rifle and Browning automatic rifle, backed up by M4 Sherman medium tanks to replace the light M2s. Last but not least, the transport of supplies over the vast ocean had to be improved.

BEACH-HEAD With enemy fire raking Tarawa's lagoon and the palm-fringed shores around it, US marines had to slide on their stomachs to reach the trees, and destroy the dugouts and bunkers (inset) that hid the Japanese gunners.

Tarawa and Makin, it was felt, would provide valuable practice in amphibious landing techniques and air bases from which to attack the Marshall Islands, farther west. The veteran 2nd Marine Division, recovering in New Zealand from the bitter fighting on Guadalcanal, would have an easy task – the taking of Tarawa – after its previous ordeal.

FIGHT TO THE DEATH

Rear Admiral Keiji Shibasaki, charged with defending the Gilberts (today the nation of Kiribati), thought otherwise. He had transformed Betio, one of the small islands ringing Tarawa atoll, into a formidable fortress. His Korean construction workers were not keen to die for the Japanese Empire, but the 4200 Japanese among the garrison of 4836 had sworn to fight to the death – as Private Baird and his comrades were shattered to discover.

'About 30 yards [27 m] offshore a shell struck the boat,' he wrote later. 'The concussion felt like a big fist – Joe Louis maybe – had smacked me right in the face . . . Guys were sprawled all over the place. I looked across at my buddy, who was only 5 ft [1.5 m] from me. He was on his back and his face was all bloody and he was holding his hand over his face and mumbling . . . Our boat was stopped and they were laying lead to us like holy hell. Everybody seemed to be stunned, so I yelled Let's get the hell out of here . . . I grabbed my carbine and an ammunition box and stepped over a couple of fellas lying there and put my hand on the side so's to roll over into the water. I didn't want to put my head up. The bullets were pouring at us like a sheet of rain . . . Only about a dozen out of the 25 went over the side with me and only about four of us ever got evacuated.'

Lieutenant William D. ('Hawk') Hawkins, a 29-year-old Texan, had earlier led a 34-man scout-sniper platoon in an attack on a pier in the central part of the island. He was hit by shrapnel, but seemed oblivious to it. The next day, while mopping up Japanese machine-gun posts single handed, he was shot in the shoulder. He continued fighting until he took a bullet in the upper chest and died later that day. He received a posthumous Medal of Honor, along with three other men of 2nd Marine Division who fought and died gallantly in the assault on Betio.

During the landings, one Japanese gun crew several times accurately fired a shell into landing craft as their ramps opened – killing the troops on board before they could disembark. The emplacement was finally wiped out by destroyer fire from the lagoon. Heavily laden marines splashing down on the offshore reefs from other craft found themselves in deep water and drowned, dragged down by their kit.

GAINING THE ADVANTAGE

At 6.15 am on the second day, war correspondent Robert Sherrod watched Major L.C. Hays Jr's 1st Battalion 8th Marine Regiment landing on Betio's central beach. They immediately came under fire and within minutes Sherrod counted at least 100 lying dead on the beach. An hour later there were 200, including those in the shallows, but over half of the battalion's 800 men got ashore safely. They were enough to help those already there to start reversing the desperate situation.

By the morning of November 23, the Americans had wiped out the three main pockets of Japanese defenders on the island – using grenades, explosive charges, tank fire and flamethrowers. Shibasaki died in his bunker when the Americans sealed it off, then poured petrol into the ventilators and lit it. Maj General Smith declared Betio secure, although it took a few more days to kill or round up the few remaining defenders. Only one Japanese subaltern, 16 Japanese soldiers and 129 Korean labourers remained alive. The Americans lost more than 1000 dead and more than 2000 wounded. The American public was shocked to receive news and pictures of what was proportionally one of the most costly battles in US history.

TAKING MAKIN

Makin atoll, the other main objective in the Gilberts, turned out to be less heavily defended. Lieutenant Seizo Ishikawa, garrison commander, had around 800 men, roughly a third of them naval infantry and the rest labourers. Its defences were largely concentrated in a central belt of the narrow, T-shaped island of Butaritari, which lies at the southern tip of the coral atoll. They consisted of underground dugouts, pillboxes, anti-tank ditches and three 80 mm (3 in) guns.

But although the commander of the Makin assault, Maj General Ralph C. Smith, had almost 6500 men and superior equipment to the Japanese, his men were raw and inexperienced. His plan was for two battalions to storm ashore at the western end of the island, establish a beach-head, then drive north-eastwards to the main Japanese positions. The regiment's remaining battalion would attack the northern end.

After a bombardment by battleships, destroyers, cruisers and carrier strike planes, Smith's first two battalions surged ashore on Butaritari half an hour before the marines hit the Betio beaches. Luckily, the Japanese did not resist in the western landing area; the American troops would have been easy targets wading waist-deep across a treacherous, boulder-strewn reef pitted by potholes. But at 10.41 am Smith's third battalion splashed ashore and soon found themselves in the centre of Japanese defences, fighting grimly at such close quarters that neither offshore guns nor air strikes could help. Even so, each landing force secured a firm foothold.

Next day, tanks, infantry and engineers toting flamethrowers and explosive charges began systematically attacking and destroying enemy positions on Butaritari. But the inexperienced men often reacted nervously to Japanese snipers and harassing tactics, diving for cover and spraying the area indiscriminately with bullets.

By evening on November 21, the Americans had destroyed most of the main Japanese positions, and the next day a battalion fought eastwards through dense brush concealing trenches and bunkers. Small groups of Japanese counterattacked repeatedly, but by morning on the 23rd, the only tasks that remained were brief mopping-up operations. The infantry had won their first battle, with some 60 men killed and about 150 wounded. Only one Japanese sailor and 104 Korean labourers surrendered – all the remainder of Butaritari's defenders were dead. As the morning ended, Ralph Smith was able to radio a two-word message to Rear Admiral Turner that signalled the end of the Gilberts offensive. It read simply: 'Makin taken.'

However, the Japanese had the last word: on November 23 their submarine *I-175* torpedoed the escort carrier *Liscombe Bay* offshore. The ship's store of aerial bombs exploded and it went down with 644 crewmen.

Powering through the Marshalls

Lessons learned at tragic cost on Tarawa were applied with devastating effect as the Americans struck at the mid-Pacific Marshall Islands. And when their carriers had finished with Truk, there was no need for a landing.

THE WHOLE ISLAND 'looked like it had been picked up to 20 000 ft and then dropped', commented Maj General Holland M. ('Howling Mad') Smith. It was 9.30 am on February 1, 1944, and he was observing from a warship off the banana-shaped coral island of Kwajalein. This tiny dot in the central Pacific, only 4 km (2½ miles) long and part of the atoll of the same name, had been all but pulverised by a three-day bombardment from US battleships, cruisers, destroyers, carrier strike aircraft – even B-24 Liberator heavy bombers.

Now, at 9.30 am and after a further three hours of concentrated hell from two battleships only 1400 m (1500 yds) from the beach, Maj General Charles Corlett's US 7th Infantry Division was surging shorewards in its landing craft and amphibious vehicles. Rocket-firing gunboats and artillery on nearby islets seized earlier laid a continuous barrage ahead of them; carrier planes strafed anything that moved onshore. It was an overwhelming display of force – and it worked.

After their grim time in the Aleutians, the 7th had drilled hard, and the landings went like one of their exercises. The hard lessons of Tarawa, in the Gilbert Islands, had been well learned: the Americans were determined there would be no repeat of that shambles when they planned their assault on Kwajalein and the other Marshall Islands. More men, more training, more fire-power and better equipment were needed – and were provided.

The objective in seizing the Marshalls – Japanese territory since World War I – was to neutralise and isolate the massive Japanese naval base at Truk, farther west in the Caroline Islands, and to win bases for the next leap, against the Mariana Islands, to the north-west. Admiral Chester W. Nimitz, in charge of central Pacific operations, proposed bypassing the strongly defended atolls of Wotje, Maloelap, Mili and Jaluit, in the eastern Marshalls, and thrusting straight for the main enemy stronghold in the central Marshalls, Kwajalein atoll.

Vice Admiral Raymond A. Spruance (Fifth Fleet), Rear Admiral Richmond Kelly Turner (who would command the Kwajalein assault) and Holland Smith (V Amphibious Corps) all disagreed strongly, arguing that even if Kwajalein was taken it would be vulnerable to air attack from the bypassed islands, which should be taken first. But Nimitz, pointing to General MacArthur's example in the south-west Pacific, refused to budge. When Turner and Spruance still argued, he offered to 'find someone else' to do the job. Turner and Spruance backed down, but Nimitz did accept Spruance's suggestion that Majuro, another atoll between Maloelap and Mili, should be taken to provide a good fleet base and airfield.

Nimitz's hunch paid off. The Japanese expected just what his subordinates had advocated – an atoll-by-atoll advance towards Kwajalein. Admiral Mineichi Koga, charged with defending the Marshalls, had left Kwajalein less heavily defended than the easterly islands, counting on them to slow the advance and inflict heavy losses before the Americans even reached Kwajalein.

APOCALYPSE NOW

To prepare the way ahead, Task Force 58, led by the redoubtable Rear Admiral Marc A. Mitscher, pounded the Marshalls in December and January. Mitscher had 12 carriers – six heavy and six light – with over 700 planes and supported by eight fast battleships and numerous escorts. In late January the bombardment was stepped up to apocalyptic proportions, and when the troops went ashore not one of the 150 Japanese aircraft in the Marshalls could take off to oppose them. The bypassed islands were isolated and impotent, and their garrisons could only sit out the conflict.

Kwajalein, the world's largest atoll, has a huge 125 km (78 mile) long lagoon ringed by coral reefs and small islands. The main islands are the causeway-linked Roi and Namur in the north and Kwajalein island, 80 km (50 miles) to the south.

By the evening of February 1, Corlett had six battalions ashore on densely wooded Kwajalein island, with tanks in support. Struggling inland through thick undergrowth, the infantrymen began to meet fierce resistance from the 5000-strong garrison under Rear Admiral Monzo Akiyama. Using techniques learned in Tarawa and perfected in training, the Americans burned and blasted underground bunkers and camouflaged strongpoints with flamethrowers and large explosive charges. It took them four days to subdue Akiyama's men, who finally ran

into the jaws of death in fruitless *banzai* charges that pushed the total Japanese dead up to 4938. Only 174 prisoners were taken. The 7th Infantry Division lost 173 dead and 793 wounded.

'CLOSE-IN CONOLLY'

Leading a task group at Roi-Namur, Rear Admiral Richard A. Conolly earned the nickname 'Close-in Conolly', urging his battleships and cruisers to 'move in really close' – as, indeed, Kelly Turner had done at Kwajalein island. Conolly's ships got within 1800 m (2000 yds) of the beaches and gave them the full treatment. Artillery he had landed on islets seized nearby added to the holocaust. Just before noon on February 1, troops of the 4th Marine Division began landing on Roi through rough surf, while others landed on Namur.

SMOKING RUINS Naval and air bombardments, explosives and flamethrowers (below) reduced Namur island to a wilderness of rubble before it was secure and the US flag flew (left). Similar treatment demolished Eniwetok. (Bottom) Afterwards, marines relax with mugs of coffee.

The surf at Roi pounded over a rugged coral reef, and several landing craft were damaged in collisions or ran onto the reef's jagged teeth. Others sank as they tried to struggle back to their parent vessels. But the marines met little resistance and suffered few losses on the beaches. They pushed on across the open island – much of it given over to airfield runways and taxiing strips – knocking out already battered defence positions. By 6 pm, they had reached the north coast. Their commander, Maj General Harry Schmidt, declared the island secured, though mopping-up operations continued into the following day.

Namur, however, was thickly wooded, and the intensive bombardment had reduced the dense vegetation – along with bunkers and pillboxes – to a dangerous confusion of cover for the remaining defenders and isolated snipers. Every cluster of fallen palm foliage was a potential hideaway for lone, armed survivors. But tanks were able to batter their way through the jumble of debris. Japanese resistance was fierce but uncoordinated, and the American forces were gaining ground when a horrific accident stopped them in their tracks. A demolition team lobbed a large explosive charge into a blockhouse and detonated a cache of torpedo warheads stored inside. The massive explosion hurled great chunks of concrete and tree trunks in all directions, killing about 20 marines and wounding 100.

That night, survivors had to fight off counter-attacks, but by noon on February 2, only scattered remnants of the defenders remained. Namur was declared secure by 2.18 pm. Again, the Japanese had fought and died like *samurai*. Of the 3563-strong Roi-Namur garrison, only 91 survived to be taken prisoner, including 40 Koreans. General Schmidt lost 195 killed and 545 wounded.

ON TO ENIWETOK

The rapid success of the Kwajalein assault allowed Nimitz to bring forward his next operation, an attack on Eniwetok, a far-flung Marshalls atoll about 550 km (350 miles) away to the north-west that was to become famous after the war as a nuclear weapons test site. He had scheduled the assault for May 1, but his forces included 8000 reserves who had not been needed at Kwajalein, so he immediately sent them to take Eniwetok – a cluster of small islands and reefs around a 40 km (25 mile) diameter lagoon.

On February 17, Rear Admiral Harry Hill put the first units ashore on several of the atoll's smaller islands. On the 18th, Colonel John Walker's 22nd Marine Regiment assaulted and captured Engebi island, which had the atoll's only airfield. Engebi had been given the usual pounding by Spruance's carrier planes and by land-based bombers – so much so that one Japanese defender said it was 'no wonder that some soldiers have gone out of their minds'.

The 22nd Marines joined the 106th Infantry Regiment in taking the atoll's other main island, also called Eniwetok, by February 21. It was riddled with camouflaged and tunnel-linked foxholes and trenches – a potentially lethal labyrinth amid dense undergrowth and palm-shaded, wooded areas. But, as at Kwajalein, the Japanese were smashed to a standstill. Of the 2741 defenders on the island of Eniwetok atoll, 2677 were killed and 64 were captured. The Americans lost 258 dead and 568 wounded.

Even so, fighting against the suicidally determined Japanese was ferocious. A marine wrote later: 'That night was unbelievably terrible. There were many of them left and they all had one fanatical notion, and that was to take one of us with them. We dug in with orders to kill anything that moved. I kept watch in a foxhole with my sergeant and we both stayed awake all night with a knife in one hand and a grenade in the other. They crept in among us, and every bush and rock took on sinister proportions. They got some of us, but in the morning they lay about, some with their riddled bodies actually inside our foxholes. Never have I been so glad to see the sun.'

KNOCKING OUT TRUK

Even as Hill's troops were subduing Eniwetok, Mitscher's fast carrier Task Force 58 was taking on Truk – Japan's biggest stronghold in the Pacific, generally considered impregnable. Secure within a 60 km (40 mile) diameter lagoon dotted with rocky, volcanic islands was the main Japanese Combined Fleet anchorage, thought to be immune to attack by surface ships. Four airstrips held nearly 400 planes at the ready.

Mitscher cut it down to size in two days on February 17 and 18, sending in waves of fighters to bomb and strafe the airstrips, destroying two-thirds of the Japanese planes on the ground and hacking down any that rose to fight. Waves of dive-bombers, torpedo bombers and yet more fighters now swarmed in on the ships at anchor, sinking 12 naval vessels and 17 merchantmen. Mitscher lost about 30 planes, and one carrier – USS *Intrepid* – was slightly damaged.

Spruance, who had sailed with the task force, cruised around the islands with the battleships *New Jersey* and *Iowa*, two cruisers and four destroyers. He found a Japanese light cruiser and destroyer trying to escape and sank them, too. It had been a devastating demonstration of carrier operations by Mitscher, perhaps the greatest exponent of the art. There was now no need to mount a potentially costly invasion of Truk – what was left of its garrison was marooned there, helpless and impotent as the war moved on to the next big battleground – the Marianas.

Japan loses its last chance in the 'Marianas Turkey Shoot'

If America's island-hopping advance across the Pacific was to be halted, Japan had to hold on to the Mariana Islands. The result was the Battle of the Philippine Sea, the biggest carrier battle of the war, with so many Japanese aircraft shot down that US pilots dubbed it 'the Great Marianas Turkey Shoot'.

THE AMERICAN TASK FORCE heading for the Marianas in June 1944 was a daunting prospect for the Japanese. While, half a world away, another huge fleet was crossing the English Channel to land Allied troops in Normandy, Admiral Raymond Spruance, commander of the US Fifth Fleet, assembled the largest naval force ever seen in the Pacific Ocean. It consisted of four carrier groups and one battle group, in which there were seven fleet and eight light fleet carriers with a total of 902 aircraft, plus seven battleships, 21 cruisers and 69 destroyers. This enormously powerful armada was known simply as Task Force 58, or TF58, and was under the command of Vice Admiral Marc Mitscher.

The job of TF58 was to cover and support the amphibious assault on the most important Japanese strongholds in the Marianas – Saipan, Tinian and Guam. The Japanese, though, could be expected to throw everything into defending the islands, for they had twofold strategic value. First, American planes based in the Marianas would be within bombing distance of the Japanese mainland; and secondly, the islands lay across the Allied invasion route to the Japanese-held Philippines.

One problem facing the Japanese commanders was knowing exactly when and where the attack would fall. They had a 3200 km (2000 mile) ocean perimeter to defend, bulging eastwards from northern New Guinea to the Marianas. All they knew for certain was that the battle, when it came, would be decisive.

In fact, the first blow was struck by the Americans on June 11, when aircraft from TF58 bombed the airfields of Saipan, Tinian and Guam. US battleships followed on June 13 and 14, and at dawn on the 15th, by heavily shelling Saipan prior to the first troop landings on June 15 (p. 368). Meanwhile, American carrier-borne aircraft bombed Iwo Jima and Chichi Jima, in the Bonin and Volcano islands farther north, and Rota and again Guam in the Marianas. In all, they destroyed 150 Japanese planes – one-third of the total based on the central Pacific islands.

By the evening of the 15th, with 20 000 American troops ashore on Saipan, Japanese Combined Fleet commander Admiral Soemu Toyoda knew where his decisive battle was to take place. He ordered the First Mobile Fleet under Vice Admiral Jisaburo Ozawa to sail from its anchorage at Tawitawi, in the south-western Philippines, into the Philippine Sea to position itself for the planned showdown, code-named Operation *A-Go*.

There, 24 hours later, it was joined by a naval attack division under Vice Admiral Matome Ugaki, which had steamed hurriedly up from the Moluccas. This contained the giant battleships *Yamato* and *Musashi*, but Ozawa knew only too well that his now substantially strengthened forces were still no match for the Americans. He had five fleet and four light fleet carriers with 473 aircraft, five battleships, 11 heavy cruisers, two light cruisers and 28 destroyers.

The odds against him on paper, both in ships and aircraft, were more than two to one. But in reality they were worse than that. The American task force was a seasoned fighting machine, which had already battled its way across thousands of kilometres of the Pacific, taking first the Gilbert Islands, then the Marshalls, in its stride. It had better aircraft and better trained and more experienced pilots. The terrible losses inflicted on the Japanese during the Solomon Islands campaign and at Rabaul on New Britain in November 1943 were now about to be felt.

All this Ozawa knew as, just after midnight on June 18, he relayed a message from the Emperor to all his ships: 'This operation has immense bearing on the fate of the Empire.' This was no more than the truth, for while Japanese victory might stem the Allied advance for a period, defeat would spell undoubted doom.

SWIFT-MOVING TACTICIAN

The softly spoken, unflappable Marc Mitscher (1887-1947) was the US Navy's most skilled air warfare expert of the war. Graduating from the Naval Academy at Annapolis in 1910, he was one of the first naval officers to specialise in aviation, and in 1916 became the navy's 33rd qualified pilot.

He started World War II commanding the carrier *Hornet* – from which, in April 1942, Colonel James Doolittle launched his raid on Japan (p. 159). Then in April 1943 – by now a rear admiral – Mitscher took control of Allied air forces in the Solomons.

But it was in 1944 that he came into his own, when in January he assumed command of the Fast Carrier Task Force 58. He moulded TF58 into a formidable and supremely mobile strike weapon, which fatally battered Japan's naval air forces in the Pacific. He was three times awarded the Distinguished Service Medal and was promoted full admiral after the war in 1946.

MANOEUVRING FOR ADVANTAGE

Ozawa hoped with a quick first blow to reduce the odds stacked against him. With luck, he might even destroy the main body of the US Fifth Fleet. But the Americans had 43 submarines operating in the western Pacific, some patrolling the exit from the San Bernardino Strait into the Philippine Sea. As Ozawa's First Mobile Fleet passed through the strait, its approach was reported to Spruance.

TF58 was immediately reorganised for battle, gathering to the north-west of Guam. Spruance ordered the formation of a battle line of seven fast battleships, four cruisers and 13 destroyers and stationed it between his carrier groups and the enemy. His plan was to deal the Japanese a devastating blow: 'Our air will first knock out enemy carriers, then will attack enemy battleships and cruisers to slow down or disable them. Battle line will destroy enemy fleet either by fleet action if the enemy elects to fight or by sinking slowed or crippled ships if enemy retreats. Action against the retreating enemy must be pushed vigorously by all hands to ensure complete destruction of his fleet.' However, his prime task of protecting the Marianas landings meant that he would not be able to pursue the Japanese very far, and this was to change Spruance's stance from an offensive to a defensive one and ultimately to limit the scale of American victory in the Philippine Sea.

Ozawa had decided on two main tactics which, together, might defeat the Americans. The first was to dispatch a decoy force – Force 'C', of three light carriers, protected by battleships and heavy cruisers – some 200 km (125 miles) ahead of his main fleet. He hoped that the decoy would lure away and destroy Spruance's aircraft while planes from his main formation – Forces 'A' and 'B', with five fleet carriers and one light fleet carrier – swooped down and smashed Spruance's task force, which he hoped would now be left with much-diminished air cover.

His second tactic was to keep his main forces outside the range of a counterattack. His aircraft, including the Zero fighter and Nakajima 'Jill' torpedo bomber, were generally inferior to the American planes – above all, the US Grumman Hellcat fighter (see box, p. 366) – except in one respect: Ozawa's planes had a greater range. They could also fly on to Japanese-held Guam or Rota after an attack to refuel and rearm before returning to their carriers.

THE TURKEY SHOOT

Ozawa decided against risking an air strike in the late afternoon of June 18, and under cover of darkness that night his fleet took up battle formation. The next morning, before dawn, the first Japanese aircraft took off to try to locate the Americans. In the early morning light of a cloudless day they established contact and

RIPPED FROM THE SKY A Japanese dive-bomber, shot down off Saipan, plunges seaward, trailing clouds of smoke. In the foreground, a US Grumman Avenger torpedo bomber sits, wings folded, on the deck of the carrier *Kitkun Bay*. The American invasion of Saipan drew Admiral Toyoda's fleet into the Philippine Sea – and to crushing defeat.

reported back. Ozawa gave orders for the first attack, by aircraft from the decoy force, to be launched.

What Ozawa and the Japanese High Command still did not know was that the Americans had broken the Japanese naval codes. As the first Japanese aircraft set off at 8.25 am on June 19, Spruance already knew how the Japanese intended to fight the battle and had 450 fighters ready to meet the attack. Out of 69 aircraft in the first attack, 45 were shot down. The second strike, launched at 8.56 am from Ozawa's main force, fared even worse: out of 127 aircraft dispatched only 29 returned. The Japanese launched two further strikes at 10 am and 11 am, but they fared no better than the earlier ones.

In all that morning, 373 Japanese aircraft took off, but only 130 survived. Total American losses were 18 fighters and 12 bombers. The total result of Ozawa's four strikes on TF58 was slight damage to the carrier *Bunker Hill* and the battleships *Indiana* and *South Dakota*. For the jubilant Hellcat pilots, it had been 'as easy as shooting turkeys'. Japanese planes that had managed to escape the Hellcats were in many cases caught by the massive anti-aircraft crossfire of the task-force ships.

This was not the end of Ozawa's problems that morning. In the course of launching its aircraft for the second attack, his flagship *Taiho* – the Imperial Navy's newest and biggest carrier – was hit by a torpedo from the US submarine *Albacore*; it might well have received a second hit but for a suicidal act in the true tradition of *samurai* bravery by pilot Sakio Komatsu. Seeing the second torpedo streaking towards *Taiho*, he dived his 'Jill' torpedo bomber straight into it. The torpedo that struck *Taiho* jammed the forward elevator and severed fuel lines, but otherwise left the ship intact. It maintained speed and continued flying operations. Inside, however, fumes from the damaged fuel lines began to gather – and these would spell the ship's doom.

Having launched his four strike missions, Ozawa turned his fleet away to the north-west, intending to refuel next day and resume the battle on June 21 after he had recovered his aircraft from Guam and Rota. At this stage he was unaware of the losses he had sustained, and had been badly misled by numerous reports – that day and earlier – from Guam that spoke of major American losses and continuing Japanese operations from airfields in the Marianas.

Then he suffered two further disasters. First, at 12.20 pm, *Shokaku* was hit by three torpedoes fired by the US submarine *Cavalla*. The veteran carrier was engulfed in flames that could not be extinguished, while nothing could block the torrent of seawater flowing in through the great hole torn in its side. *Shokaku* settled slowly by the bows, the end coming at 3 pm when fires finally ignited a magazine; the ship disintegrated.

Then, 32 minutes later, Ozawa's flagship *Taiho* suffered a massive explosion that was deflected outwards and downwards by the ship's armoured deck. No further bomb or torpedo had hit it, but a damage-control officer, worried by the build-up of fuel fumes, had given the order to ventilate the ship. This only spread the fumes and a small spark was sufficient to set off the explosion. The carrier settled immediately and sank an hour later. Ozawa transferred first to the destroyer *Wakatsuki* and then to the heavy cruiser *Haguro*.

JAPANESE AT BAY

It was not until the next day, June 20, after he had boarded the carrier *Zuikaku*, that Ozawa realised, for the first time, the extent of the previous day's losses. To add to that black news, Ozawa discovered that during his enforced confinement aboard *Haguro* his fleet had become disorganised and no attempt had been made to start refuelling, because no one took responsibility. None of this lessened his determination to continue the battle. He immediately set about restoring order so that the fight could resume on June 21, as planned. But in the meantime the American task force had succeeded in locating the Japanese fleet.

All day American reconnaissance aircraft had been searching for Ozawa. Having dealt a deadly blow at his air power, Spruance was determined to destroy Ozawa's ships. Had he located them earlier, he would have probably done so. But, despite perfect weather conditions, it was not until late in the afternoon, at 3.38 pm, that one of his Avengers found Ozawa and reported him to be 440 km (275 miles) north-west of TF58.

Although the Japanese were at the extreme edge of the American aircraft's range, Vice Admiral Mitscher, commander of the four fast carrier groups, immediately ordered a two-wave attack. Turning his carriers into the wind, he launched 240 fighters, dive-bombers and torpedo bombers inside an hour. There was no attempt to take up formation; the distance to be flown left no time for such fuel-consuming niceties. Then, 30 minutes after setting out, the American pilots were told of a correction that put Ozawa 100 km (60 miles) farther away. Not surprisingly, the fighter radio circuits, usually overloaded with chatter, went very quiet. The correction forced Mitscher to abandon any thought of a second attack.

The American pilots found Ozawa at 6.25 pm with the sun low over the western horizon. Having eavesdropped on the enemy wavelengths, the Japanese knew they were about to be attacked and had stepped up their speed to 24 knots (44 km/h) in a vain effort to get out of range. In the process their oilers were left behind and the formations steered divergent courses. Force 'C', which had acted as decoy in the battle of the previous day, was ordered to operate as rearguard and break up the full impact of the incoming attack. But it did not have any chance to take up station before the

THE PLANE THAT TURNED A BATTLE INTO A TURKEY SHOOT

It was the Grumman F6F fighter aircraft, known as the Hellcat, that destroyed any chance Vice Admiral Ozawa might have had of smashing the giant US naval task force in the Philippine Sea. Its appearance aboard US carriers in 1943 heralded the end of Japanese naval air superiority which had started in 1936 with the introduction of one of the classic warplanes of history, the Mitsubishi A6M, known – and feared – as the Zero.

The Hellcat was fitted with two 20 mm cannon to match the Zero and four wing-mounted machine guns, compared with the Japanese fighter's two. But what gave the Hellcat its total dominance in the air was its engine – at 2000 hp more than twice as powerful as the Zero's, and giving the aircraft great speed and manoeuvrability. During two years of wartime service with the US Navy, Hellcats shot down 4947 enemy aircraft in operations from carriers and another 209 from shore-based units – nearly 75 per cent of all the US Navy's wartime air combat 'kills'.

American planes came streaking down on them.

The first targets for the incoming pilots were the Japanese carriers. Aircraft from *Hornet*, *Yorktown* and *Bataan* attacked Ozawa's Force 'A'. His flagship *Zuikaku* was so badly damaged that it seemed certain to be abandoned; however, the fires were finally extinguished and it eventually returned to Kure in Japan under its own power. Aircraft from *Bunker Hill*, *Monterey* and *Cabot* set about Force 'C'. The carrier *Chiyoda* was hit so severely that they switched their attention to the battleship *Haruna* and heavy cruiser *Maya*. Meanwhile, aircraft from *Wasp* went after the oilers, damaging two so severely that they were scuttled.

But it was the Japanese Force 'B' that took the brunt of the American attack, with hits on all three of its carriers. *Ryuho* was hit by a single bomb, but escaped serious damage. *Junyo* was hit amidships by two bombs but remained in action. *Hiyo*, however, was brought to a halt by two torpedoes from *Belleau Wood*'s Avengers and was then hit by dive-bombers from *Enterprise*. By the time the attack had ended it was sinking – the only Japanese warship sunk by air attack in the course of the battle.

The Japanese fought back ferociously. Flak was heavy and the pilots of the Japanese combat air patrol were skilled and determined, but they were simply brushed aside by sheer weight of numbers. Only 17 American aircraft were lost in the day's fighting compared with 80 Japanese. But the day was not yet over for the American pilots – the search-and-destroy mission against Ozawa had taken them beyond their range. Night was falling and they now had the task of finding their way back to their home carriers, knowing that there was little or no chance that they would make it.

CRASH LANDINGS

In all, 82 aircraft were lost on the return journey, most of them coming down in the sea as they ran out of fuel, others written off in crash landings. Although Mitscher ordered the task-force carriers to switch on their lights in order to guide the aircraft to safety, the carrier decks became scenes of carnage as pilot after pilot crash-landed, in a desperate attempt to touch down before running out of fuel. As a result, at least 13 aircraft-carrier decks were closed between 8.15 and 11.05 pm because wreckage was obstructing them. The worst incident happened on *Lexington* when five aircraft were destroyed in a multiple crash.

A returning Helldiver pilot who crash-landed on *Lexington* told the ship's surgeon, Dr Neal Baxter: 'We caught a hell of a burst over the Jap fleet – thermite, I guess it was. It ripped this hole in my port wing, and the edges turned red-hot and started to eat away. I kept watching it melt. I was hit in the back, here. I didn't know how bad it was, but I could feel the blood running down my back. This hole in the wing got larger and larger, and she fell off on that side and we started to spin. I figured I'd better make a water landing before the whole wing was eaten away, but pretty soon I saw the edges weren't red anymore, so I decided to try to make it home. We got back, but I don't know how. I found this carrier, but the landing circle was jammed. I didn't have but a handful of gas left and no lights. I couldn't have made it around again. I knew I couldn't. I pushed my way into the circle. I saw the wave-off [the signal not to land] but I couldn't make myself take it, I just couldn't . . . I wish to God I had, now. I'd give anything – those men I killed [on the carrier's deck] . . .'

HELLCAT RESCUE An American flight-deck crewman leaps heroically onto a burning Hellcat fighter to try to rescue the pilot. Weary pilots often misjudged landings – and the men who made it back to their carriers after the foray of June 20 caused particular havoc. A number of men died, and planes had to be pushed overboard to clear decks.

THE LONG FLIGHT HOME

Vice Admiral Mitscher, commander of the four American carrier groups in the battle for the Marianas, knew when he sent his aircraft off to attack the Japanese fleet on the afternoon of June 20 that they would be flying to the limits of – and probably beyond – their range. He made every effort to shorten that distance by steaming at full speed towards the Japanese fleet. But he knew that, inevitably, most of his pilots would be flying back in total darkness, with little or no fuel to spare, and with no means of finding their carriers.

Despite the risk of advertising the task force's position to prowling Japanese submarines, he decided that to save his pilots he must switch on the landing lights on board his carriers. There is no doubt that his decision saved many of his pilots from coming down in the sea. Most of those who did – mainly the crews of the torpedo planes and dive-bombers who had run out of fuel before they could reach their ships – were rescued; 101 air crew were picked up that night and a further 59 during the following day.

One pilot, later recalling that flight back in total darkness, remembered how the radio chatter between pilots gradually subsided into silence as first one and then another announced to his colleagues that he had run out of fuel and would be ditching his plane in the sea.

'I've got ten minutes of gas left, Joe. Think I'll put her down in the water now. So long, Joe!'

'This is 46. Where am I please? Somebody tell me where I am!'

'Can't make it, fellows! I'm going in. Look for me tomorrow if you get a chance, will you?'

After the rescue, James Fahey, a seaman on board the cruiser *Montpelier*, wrote in his diary: 'It was a great decision to make [to switch the carrier lights on] and everyone thought the world of Admiral Mitscher for doing this.'

Even after the American strike, Ozawa tried to continue the battle and ordered Force 'C' eastward in order to force a night action. Direct orders from Tokyo, however, ended this effort. Ozawa set course for Okinawa with the result that TF58 could not re-establish contact with his fleet on the 21st and 22nd. It thereafter had to content itself with attacks on Pagan, in the northern Marianas, on the 23rd and the Bonin Islands on the 24th. With the destruction of about 60 Japanese aircraft on the island of Iwo Jima, the Battle of the Philippine Sea was over.

Thus ended one of the most one-sided battles in naval history. The Imperial Navy had a carrier force second only to that of the United States, but in a two-day battle it neither sank nor badly damaged a single American warship and lost 426 aircraft and seaplanes in the process. At the end of the battle Ozawa retained just 35 operational aircraft. He offered his resignation but this was refused. The Americans' losses over the same two days were 130 aircraft, and their successes were not limited to operations against Ozawa's fleet: some 200 Japanese aircraft were destroyed on the islands of the Bonins and Marianas before, during and after the fleet action.

The American victory was overwhelming. It paved the way for the advance into the western Pacific and destroyed the Japanese Combined Fleet as an effective force. Never again was it able to reconstitute its carrier air groups and put to sea a properly balanced naval task force. The American victory ensured the fall of the Marianas, from whose airfields Japan itself could be attacked by B-29 Superfortresses.

'Hell is on us', was the famous comment of Japan's Foreign Minister, Mamoru Shigemitsu, after the battle, and indeed it was; the Battle of the Philippine Sea ended Japan's last hope of escaping defeat. But meanwhile Ozawa's fleet was still afloat. The Americans, in spite of all their efforts, had not achieved the complete naval victory they were seeking. That was still to come, four months later, in the waters of Leyte Gulf.

Suicide in the Marianas

'Whether we attack or . . . stay where we are, there is only death.' So said the Japanese general at Saipan. A mighty US fleet had descended on the Mariana Islands – from whose airfields heavy bombers could strike at Japan itself.

SEIZING SAIPAN and the other key Mariana islands of Guam and Tinian would break the inner ring of Japan's Pacific defensive perimeter. The US Navy could establish advance bases there, and the islands' airfields would put American heavy bomber squadrons within range of the Japanese home islands.

To Lt General Yoshitsugu Saito, commanding the 32 000 men defending Saipan, the idea was unthinkable. But he stood no chance against the forces hurled at the island, and on July 6, 1944, after 21 days of fierce combat, Saito told his men: 'Whether we attack or whether we stay where we are, there is only death. However, in death there is life. We must utilise this opportunity to exalt true Japanese manhood. I will advance with those who remain to deliver still another blow to the American Devils and leave my bones on Saipan as a bulwark of the Pacific.'

Next day about 3000 Japanese – including some already wounded – staged a last-ditch, futile *banzai* charge against the US 27th Infantry Division. By sheer weight of numbers and driven on by suicidal determination, they cut through the American lines, killing and wounding scores. But finally they ran into the point-blank fire of the marines' 105 mm (4.1 in) howitzers – and their straggling remnants were finished off by staff officers, bakers, cooks and typists who stood firm at a command post in the north of the island.

MOUNTAINS AND CAVES

The Americans began with Saipan because it had a ready-made air base within 2400 km (1500 miles) of Japan – and could cut off the enemy airfields on Guam, farther to the south-west, before the assault on that island. The Marianas had been under regular air attack since February, and from June 13 the big guns of Vice Admiral Raymond A. Spruance's Fifth Fleet, now more than 530 ships strong, began stepping up the bombardment. But, though constant pounding from above and offshore left many Japanese coastal emplacements wrecked, many other strongpoints, which were more carefully camouflaged, remained unscathed.

Newly promoted Lt General Holland M. ('Howling Mad') Smith, commanding the amphibious landing force, had few illusions about what awaited his men on reef-bound, mountainous Saipan. Grimly surveying it as his command ship USS *Rocky Mount* approached, Smith declared: 'We have learnt how to pulverise atolls, but now we are up against mountains and caves where the Japs can dig in. A week from today there will be a lot of dead marines.'

Under cover of the onslaught, two teams of American frogmen – each with 16 officers and 80 men – explored Saipan's coast. Four were killed but the rest, with five wounded, got out under a smokescreen laid by the destroyer *Wadleigh* and the battleship *Tennessee*. They reported that there were no mines or other obstacles, and gave advice on tides, currents, channels and depths.

The cloudless dawn of June 15 was shattered as hundreds of planes from Vice Admiral Marc A. Mitscher's escort carriers and gunfire from warships battered the landing beaches. Within 20 minutes, 8000 men of 2nd and 4th Marine Divisions had been put ashore by 700 amphibious vehicles on eight beaches along Saipan's south-west coast. They met a fierce reception, and by nightfall they had suffered 2000 casualties. But another 18 000 were put ashore – enough to fight off counterattacks, helped during the night by the light of star shells from the ships. By dawn on June 17, hundreds of Japanese lay dead and 31 of their tanks had been knocked out.

Now Holland Smith put ashore reserve infantrymen, who fought eastwards to the opposite coast, taking the vital Aslito airfield on the way. Within seven days the southern end of the island had been overcome. Offshore, meanwhile, Mitscher's planes fatally crippled Japanese naval air power in the Battle of the Philippine Sea.

A gruelling northward drive then began on Saipan, the terrain growing more rugged as the Americans came up against the formidable 465 m (1525 ft) Mount Tapotcheu, in the centre, and the craggy reaches of the Kagman Peninsula to the east. Japanese lurked in ravines, crevasses and natural caves of coral and limestone, but after ten days' dogged fighting the Americans were on the summit of Tapotcheu – the vital vantage point. By July 1, the operation was entering its final phase. The debris-strewn town of Garapan, near Mutcho Point on the west coast, and the docks and nearby seaplane base at Tanapag were next to fall.

FINAL HORROR

Five days later, after Saito's final *banzai* charge, the remaining defenders and about 8000 civilians had been pushed back into Marpi Point at the island's northern extremity. The civilians – mostly Japanese settlers – had been told by Saito that they would be tortured and killed by the Americans, and so fell victim to the final horror of the entire operation. Clutching their children or hurling them ahead, the terrified islanders leapt from the towering cliffs of Morubi Bluff to the rocks and pounding surf below. The surviving troops, who encouraged them, either followed them or blew themselves up with grenades.

Some 16 000 prisoners were taken on Saipan – most of them Japanese civilians, and fewer than 2000 troops. Almost 3500 Americans were lost and more than 13 000 were wounded. Saito did leave his bones there: he ate a last meal of tinned crab and *sake*, then committed *hara-kiri* before being shot through the head by his adjutant.

INTO GUAM

Guam, the next island to be invaded, lies 240 km (150 miles) south-west of Saipan. It had been an American possession for more than 40 years before World War II, but its liberation was not merely a matter of honour: it would provide more air bases within range of Japan, and its western bays offered protected anchorages.

After prolonged naval bombardment, concentrating upon Apra Harbor, the Piti Navy Yard, the Orote Peninsula and the island's capital Agana – all on the west coast – marines and infantry landed on either side of Orote. There were 5500 Japanese naval personnel, commanded by Captain Yutaka Sugimoto, on the peninsula, where there was an airfield and an old marine barracks. In the mountainous, southern jungle terrain, and in the dense undergrowth of the north, around 13 000 army troops under Lt General Takeshi Takashina were holed up in caves, on cliffs and in hilltop redoubts.

The first wave of Maj General Allen H. Turnage's 3rd Marine Division landed on a crescent beach west of Agana at 8.29 am on July 21. Under a hail of mortar fire from rugged hills inland, the marines forged through dry rice paddies and won a wide beach-head – paid for with 105 dead, 56 missing and 536 wounded.

South of the Orote Peninsula, around Agat, 350 men of Brig General Lemuel C. Shepherd's 1st Provisional Marine Brigade were lost or wounded and 24 amphibious vehicles were put out of action. But by dusk the brigade was on the slopes of Mount Alifan, knocking out mortar positions and four enemy tanks with bazookas and their own Shermans. Japanese infantrymen counterattacked with grenades and demolition charges, and fought hand-to-hand with bayonets. But star shells summoned from warships helped the marines to see their foes – and by morning on July 22 they could count 600 dead Japanese.

'WAKE UP AND DIE!'

With Alifan secured, Shepherd thrust northwards for the Orote Peninsula, coping with defenders who used mortars, mines, tanks, artillery and automatic fire to fight delaying actions in the difficult, swampy terrain. Meanwhile, in the thick undergrowth to the north of Shepherd's brigade, men of the 3rd Marine Division were struggling up a series of ever-steepening ridges towards the Tenjo-Alutom-Chachao heights east of the Orote Peninsula. Others pushed along the Apra Harbor shore,

STUBBORN SAITO

Lt General Yoshitsugu Saito (1890-1944) commanded the Japanese 43rd Infantry Division, which was transferred from China to Saipan only weeks before the American invasion. On the way it lost much of its equipment to American submarines.

In the absence of Lt General Hideyoshi Obata – away on an inspection tour – Saito found himself in charge of the garrison on Saipan, an island he did not know. Caught by surprise, he attempted to follow standard Japanese tactics of defeating the American forces on the beaches. When that failed, he conducted a stubborn defence which he felt might have stood a chance had it not been for overwhelming American naval gunfire. Wounded by a shell, Saito committed ritual suicide on July 6, outside his command centre. Aides burned his body but the Americans gave his ashes a military funeral.

WARRIORS' END Victory or death was the only honourable end to a battle for Japanese soldiers. On Saipan, thousands of them found honour in suicidal charges on the beaches (left), others in a leap from the high cliffs. Their commander chose the ritual sword (above) and killed himself with it.

RISKY STEPS Amtracs – tracked landing craft – trundled onto Saipan's beaches to within strides of the protective dunes. Some 26 000 US marines took those few strides; 2000 were hit.

WORSE THAN DEATH Heads bowed in shame, prisoners of war on Guam face the ultimate disgrace for a Japanese fighting man – to be taken alive. While 1250 were captured there, more than 17 000 died or disappeared.

SUCCESSOR TO TOJO

The capture of bases within range of Japan, along with news of the naval disaster in the Philippine Sea, spelt doom for Japan – and forced the resignation of the arch-hawk Prime Minister Hideki Tojo on July 18, 1944. A growing peace faction was not, however, strong enough to secure the premiership. Instead, to placate the army, the post went to another right-winger, the retired Lt General Kuniaki Koiso (1880-1950).

But the peace faction did manage to get a sympathiser, Admiral Mitsumasa Yonai, appointed Navy Minister and virtual vice-premier. The new government was to carry on the war as best it could, but would look for an honourable settlement.

Its head, Koiso, was a political general, experienced in counterespionage rather than combat, and a hard-line nationalist. A Tokyo staff officer in the 1920s, he had links with right-wing political and terrorist groups, and as chief of the Military Affairs Bureau in 1931 was involved in a coup that failed, but he kept his post. He was deeply involved in engineering the Manchurian incident of October 1931, and was Vice Minister of War before becoming chief of staff of the Kwantung Army in China, then Governor of Korea in 1942-4. Koiso was premier until March 1945. Tried as a war criminal, he was sentenced to life imprisonment at the Tokyo war-crimes trial and died in prison.

capturing the Piti Naval Yard and tiny Cabras island as they went.

Then on the night of July 25/26, Takashina launched a seven-battalion all-out counterattack from the mountains south of Asan Point, just west of Agana. In a torrential downpour, marines in waterlogged foxholes fought wave after wave of Japanese troops screaming in English: 'Wake up Americans and die!' The whole beach-head erupted in fierce, close combat – even wounded men in the marines' hospital had to defend themselves. By noon next day, as the skies cleared, around 3200 Japanese lay dead in the area. But Turnage's division had suffered 600 casualties, some 200 of them killed or missing.

Shepherd's brigade, too, faced a futile counterattack. In a steady tropical downpour, the Japanese wielded broken bottles, baseball bats and pitchforks, and charged screaming at the marine positions. Artillery and mortar fire quickly cut them down, and by morning hundreds of Japanese lay dead, some in foxholes alongside marines they had killed.

Despite their losses, the Japanese still had plenty of tanks and artillery, and in the jungles of the north desperate pockets held out against Turnage's tiring 3rd Division. Guam's northern coast was not in US hands until August 10. Among the 1744 American dead and 5970 wounded were victims of their own fleet's shelling and bombing. Only 1250 Japanese prisoners were taken among the 19 000 Japanese accounted for. Small groups of Japanese remained at large in Guam's jungles after the war ended – two surrendered as late as 1967 and another in 1972.

TINIAN DEFENDERS FOOLED

Tinian, largely cliff-girt but otherwise rather flat, and separated from Saipan by only 5 km (3 miles) of sea, was assaulted on July 24. Apart from the gentle, flat coastline off Tinian town (now called San Jose), on the west coast, the only other convenient landing places were two tiny inward-curving beaches – designated 'White 1' and 'White 2' – at the island's north-western end.

Off Tinian town, transports assembled to bring Maj General Thomas E. Watson's 2nd Marine Division to stage a decoy landing in the morning. Frogmen had already reported 'White 1' and '2' beaches – where the real attack would fall – free of mines and obstacles. The Japanese garrison commander, Colonel Keishi Ogata, duly concentrated most of his men, almost 9000 of them, on the beaches by Tinian town, and the sight of the marines scrambling into landing craft drew artillery fire from guns hidden in caves behind the town. Two ships were damaged, more than 60 lives lost and some 140 men wounded. However, Watson's men were not due to land until the following day.

Meanwhile, in the north, assault troops of Maj General Clifton B. Cates' 4th Marine Division swept ashore under cover of a ferocious bombardment from massed US artillery across the channel on Saipan, and showers of napalm bombs from aircraft – the first use of napalm. There was brief, vicious opposition from two blockhouses, but by nightfall over 15 000 Americans were ashore at a cost of 15 killed and 225 wounded.

In darkness at 2 am on July 25, 600 howling Japanese naval troops charged the left side of the beach-head, but were beaten off. Half-an-hour later another 200 hacked their way deep into the beach-head before they were stopped. Another hour later, star shells lit up five tanks rumbling in from the right. The marines' artillery and bazookas blew them to pieces. Japanese infantry following the tanks fought fiercely until dawn, by which time 1250 of them lay dead.

When Watson's marines finally went ashore on the morning of July 25 at the 'White' beaches, they quickly cleared Ushi Point, the northern tip of Tinian, then drove down the east coast. South of them, the 4th Division surged to the heights of Mounts Maga and Lasso, destroying defensive positions with tanks, flamethrowers and explosive charges. Mitscher's ships reduced Tinian town to rubble and, within a week, almost the whole island was in American hands.

Ogata had pulled back his dwindling forces to the craggy heights at the south-east end of the island, where they prepared for their final stand. While warships and bombers rained 700 tonnes of explosives upon the area, marines scrambling up the heights were peppered with machine-gun and rifle fire from the shadows of caves and fissures. Fierce hand-to-hand fighting took place, and just before dawn came a futile *banzai* charge by more than 600 Japanese. But the marines stood firm. In the north 200 more Japanese put in a last-ditch attack. A Sherman tank and a platoon of marines wiped them out.

Despite Japanese officers' urging, Tinian's 9000 or so remaining Japanese civilians declined to hurl themselves from cliffs. Ogata had lost virtually his whole garrison. Nearly 400 Americans were dead and some 1800 wounded, out of a landing force of 40 000. Holland Smith later described the Tinian offensive as 'the perfect amphibious operation in the Pacific War'.

'Hell is on us', said a senior Tokyo naval adviser. He was right – though he did not realise to what extent. American engineers were soon building four runways on Tinian, transforming it into an 'unsinkable aircraft carrier'. A year later they became the launching base for the atomic raids that forced Japan's surrender.

Palaus – a pointless sacrifice?

The Americans lost nearly 2000 men taking the Palau Islands in the south-west Pacific, in a bloody confrontation as bitter as that on Tarawa ten months earlier. It was not at all as planned – and arguably not even necessary.

EXPLOSIONS among the ragged coral outcrops sent razor-sharp slivers of steel and stone scything in all directions among the Americans on 'Bloody Nose Ridge'. Gritting their teeth, getting their heads down and bleakly counting the dead and wounded, they soldiered on amid grenades and mortar bombs. Despite overwhelming odds in their favour, taking tiny Peleliu in the Palau Islands was proving an unexpectedly deadly and dangerous operation.

Fifteen days of desperate fighting followed the American landings there before the island was finally declared secure on September 30, 1944. Even then, mopping up the last scattered groups of Japanese went on until December. By then the grim tally of American casualties in the Palaus totalled 1950 killed and 8515 wounded – most of them on Peleliu. It was a casualty rate on the unacceptable scale of Tarawa, in the Gilberts, and when it was published many Americans questioned the military need for the Palau operation.

CHANGING PRIORITIES

Back in July, President Roosevelt had met Admiral Chester W. Nimitz, commanding central Pacific operations, and General Douglas MacArthur, in command in the south-west Pacific. MacArthur advocated his cherished dream of returning to Luzon and liberating the Philippines. Nimitz wanted to bypass Luzon and strike straight at Formosa (Taiwan) or even Japan itself. The President backed MacArthur to the extent of approving landings in the Philippines, but reserved judgment on what should follow. Nimitz in turn insisted that he should first secure the Palaus – lying 1300 km (800 miles) south-west of Guam, in the Caroline Islands – to provide staging areas for the Philippines assault.

In September came news that carrier raids by task forces of Admiral William ('Bull') Halsey's US Third Fleet had revealed the Philippines to be poorly defended. Within hours, Roosevelt, Churchill and their staffs – attending the 'Octagon' summit conference in Quebec – approved an immediate invasion of the central Philippines. Unfortunately the Allied leaders' decision came too late to affect the Palau operation.

FAULTY INTELLIGENCE

After the American successes in the Marshalls and Marianas, Nimitz's planners saw the Palaus as a quick and easy task for Maj General Roy S. Geiger's III Amphibious Corps, consisting of one US Army and one Marine Corps division; Halsey was operational commander. On September 6, all four groups of Vice Admiral Marc A. Mitscher's Task Force 58 – including 16 carriers, with Halsey himself on the battleship *New Jersey* – began bombarding Peleliu and other islands in the group. But on September 15, when the first of Geiger's 24 300 marines landed on Peleliu, they got a hot reception.

Faulty intelligence had led the Americans to underestimate the opposition on the island – only 9 km (5½ miles) long but with an airfield that made it the primary objective. Maj General William H. Rupertus had told the regimental leaders of his 1st Marine Division that this operation would be 'a quickie'. But when his men landed on the south-west shore, near the airfield, they discovered that the preliminary bombardments had not been very effective. Many beach defences remained intact and Japanese artillery knocked out numerous amphibious vehicles as they ploughed shorewards. Tank attacks smashed through the marines' lines before being halted.

However, Colonel Kunio Nakagawa, defending Peleliu, had no intention of expending his 10 500-strong garrison in trying to smash the Americans on the beaches. The Japanese fell back to well-fortified lines of caves and concreted emplacements on ridges and high ground north of the airfield, and stepped up their resistance as the attackers slogged their way inland.

The forward push on Peleliu became a monotonous grind as the marines, reinforced on September 23 by units of the 81st Infantry Division, struggled to ferret out the Japanese from coral fortresses on the central Umurbrogol ridge – soon nicknamed 'Bloody Nose Ridge' by the Americans – using flamethrowers, grenades and explosive charges. At one of the largest caves they ran into more than 1000 defenders. There was vicious hand-to-hand fighting before the remaining Japanese were finally burned out by new, long-range flamethrowers mounted on tracked landing vehicles. A marine recalled: 'The terrain was abominable. Sharp coral cut our shoes and clothing. The island had been mined for phosphate, so there were many tunnels.'

The Americans soon ran short of drinking water on the stark, humid island. 'By the fourth day,' one man said, 'there were as many casualties from heat prostration as from wounds.'

EASIER ON ANGAUR

By comparison, the 81st Division faced lighter resistance when they stormed the beaches on the north-east coast of Angaur, 10 km (6 miles) south-west of Peleliu, on September 17. Like Nakagawa, Major Ushio Goto, the garrison commander, did not commit all of his 1600 troops to a counterattack against the landings – but he had been distracted by a decoy landing in the west.

Finally he pulled back to a network of pillboxes and bunkers hewn from Angaur's ragged coral terrain, then concentrated on a series of night counterattacks, which the Americans fought off. The southern part of Angaur was firmly under US control by September 21. But although Geiger was able to switch the 321st Regimental Combat Team to help the hard-pressed marines on Peleliu two days later, Angaur was not completely overcome until October 21.

Possession of the Palaus, along with Ulithi farther north-east, gave Nimitz's fleet excellent anchorage – 'our secret weapon', he called it – from which to operate during 1945. But a high price had been paid on both sides. Of the 13 600 Japanese who died in the struggle, about 10 500 fell on Peleliu. Only 400 prisoners were taken – mostly Koreans and Okinawans.

PRECIOUS DRAUGHT A wounded US marine gets a drink of water from a comrade during the fighting on the island of Peleliu. The troops ran short of drinking water and the extreme heat caused many casualties. As the campaign went on the weather changed to heavy rain and gales.

24: RETURN TO THE PHILIPPINES

Fleeing the Philippines in 1942, MacArthur had pledged: 'I shall return.' Two and a half years later he did so, with drama and flamboyance. But it took a hard campaign – including more than 60 amphibious landings and the world's greatest sea battle – to secure the islands.

A PROMISE KEPT General MacArthur (second from left) wades ashore on Leyte with Philippines President Osmena (on his right) after their landing craft has grounded just off the beach. Troops landed two hours earlier.

ABOUT NOON on October 20, 1944, General Douglas MacArthur put on a crisp new uniform, stepped into a landing craft from USS *Nashville*, picked up the Philippine president-in-exile Sergio Osmena from another ship, and headed for the palm-fringed 'Red' beach on the east coast of Leyte island, which his men had invaded at 10 am. He waded ashore, then, for nearly an hour, wandered about 'to get the feel of the fighting'. As the action swirled away into the jungle, a Signal Corps soldier arrived with a transmitter. At 2 pm, MacArthur took the microphone and broadcast a brief oration.

'People of the Philippines, I have returned!' he said, his voice trembling with emotion. 'Rally to me! . . . For your homes and hearths, strike! In the name of your sacred dead, strike! . . . Let no heart be faint. Let every arm be steeled. The guidance of Divine God points the way. Follow in his name to the Holy Grail of righteous victory!'

Five weeks earlier, on September 13, pilots of the US Third Fleet had raided Japanese air and naval bases in the central and southern Philippines. They were preparing the way for the invasion of the Palau Islands, 800 km (500 miles) to the east, and were expecting strong opposition. To their astonishment, there was very little. They destroyed 478 Japanese planes, most of them on the ground, and sunk 59 ships. It was 'unbelievable and fantastic', reported the Third Fleet's commander, Vice Admiral William Halsey; the area was 'wide open' for assault.

His words settled a long-standing debate. By the summer of 1944, Japan was stricken. Two massive prongs were thrusting towards the heart of its empire – one under MacArthur driving through the south-western Pacific islands and along the north coast of New Guinea, the other under Admiral Chester W. Nimitz advancing through the central Pacific. Success raised an urgent question: how best to reach Japan?

MacArthur was emotionally committed to the liberation of all his beloved Philippines. It made sound military sense, and besides – as he told the US Joint Chiefs of Staff – 'we have a great national obligation' to the loyal Filipinos. But Japan was not within bombing range of the Philippines. The Joint Chiefs, Admiral Ernest King, Chief of Naval Operations, and Nimitz wanted to hop from the southern Philippines straight to Formosa (Taiwan), 1600 km (1000 miles) farther to the north, and thence to the Chinese mainland. From there, American planes could bomb Japan into submission.

In July, Nimitz and MacArthur argued their views to President Roosevelt, who flew to Pearl Harbor for the occasion. Roosevelt listened – and made no decision. Only one thing was certain: the southern Philippine islands would have to be taken first. Plans were made to seize Mindanao in November and Leyte in December.

Then came Halsey's raid. The invasion should begin at once, he said, and the Joint Chiefs rapidly agreed. MacArthur was told that he could invade the central island of Leyte two months ahead of schedule. That in its turn settled subsequent strategy. It would be quicker and safer to take the northern Philippines – in particular the main island of Luzon, with the capital Manila. The Formosa strategy was abandoned and Nimitz's central Pacific thrust diverted north to Iwo Jima and Okinawa. MacArthur was on his way back.

FALTERING PLANS

But Halsey's assessment, and thus the whole US strategy, was based on a misapprehension. Japan was still far stronger than Halsey dreamed.

Imperial General Headquarters had a comprehensive scheme called *Sho* ('Victory'), which embodied separate defensive plans for each of four zones. No commander could commit his forces until authorised (hence the lack of opposition to Halsey's raid). The plan for the Philippines – *Sho-1* – would go into effect only when the Americans invaded Luzon. There, the Japanese would build impregnable defences inland, away from the vulnerable beach-heads. Other Philippine islands would have to fend for themselves.

As Allied forces approached, the Japanese became convinced that the Philippines would be the scene of the decisive battle. More airfields were built; reinforcements arrived. A mighty fleet would oppose the invasion. General Tomoyuki Yamashita, the conqueror of Singapore, was appointed to command the area's 224 000 men. He assumed command in Manila on October 9.

As it happened, even before the invasion, Japanese strategy became fatally confused as much by their own blundering as by American actions. Halsey's carrier-borne air raids did great damage – the inexperienced Japanese pilots were no match for the Americans – but when, on October 12, Japanese torpedo bombers attacked Halsey's carrier fleet, damaging two cruisers, the pilots claimed that they had sunk 11 carriers, two battleships and three cruisers – half Halsey's major ships. Astonishingly, they were believed. Celebrating a great victory, Japanese newspapers even crowed about a 'Second Pearl Harbor'.

As a result, Yamashita's strategy for the defence of Luzon seemed to have been overtaken by events. His superior, Field Marshal Hisaichi Terauchi, ordered him to start *Sho-1* where the Americans were landing: at Leyte Gulf.

Leyte Gulf – the world's greatest sea battle

The decisive naval action of the Pacific War was a massive three-day battle fought between the world's greatest navies across an area the size of France. Partly by luck, the Americans destroyed Japanese naval power for good.

THE US SUBMARINES *Darter* and *Dace* lay surfaced in the narrow waters of Palawan Passage, between the Philippine island of Palawan and northern Borneo. It was a routine patrol on which nothing much had happened since they had sunk two Japanese freighters and damaged two more on October 12. But now, in the early hours of October 23, 1944, Lt Commander David H. McClintock of *Darter* was alerted by blips on his radar screen showing ships at a range of about 28 km (17½ miles), moving north-eastwards up the passage.

McClintock immediately warned *Dace*'s Lt Commander Bladen D. Clagget by megaphone; Clagget yelled back a laconic, 'Let's go get them!' The two subs, still on the surface, sped to the attack. As they drew near and caught their first glimpse of their target, the captains could hardly believe their good fortune. In the brightening dawn two columns of cruisers, destroyers and battleships stood out against the cloud-streaked skyline, like ducks in a shooting gallery.

Dace signalled details of the sighting to Pearl Harbor as the subs closed in. *Darter* was the first to score. Six torpedoes hissed from its bow tubes at a range of 900 m (1000 yds), and four caught the cruiser *Atago* full amidships. McClintock swung the sub around and fired four more from the stern tubes at the cruiser *Takao*; two found their mark and the cruiser turned away, badly crippled, to struggle back home. *Atago* was not so lucky; ablaze from stem to stern, it sank within 25 minutes. Now it was *Dace*'s turn: it put four torpedoes into the cruiser *Maya*, which blew up and sank almost immediately.

What McClintock and Clagget did not know was that their victims were members of Vice Admiral Takeo Kurita's First Striking Force, part of a mighty Japanese fleet that was sailing to attack the American fleet giving protective cover to the Leyte landings. But now the Americans knew they were coming.

SET PIECE FOR A BULLFIGHT

For the seizure of Leyte, the Americans brought together Admiral William F. Halsey's Third and Vice Admiral Thomas C. Kinkaid's Seventh Fleets – some 800 ships in all. There had never been a bigger naval force, yet it had two weaknesses at its heart. Neither Halsey nor Kinkaid was given overall command, and Halsey had a potential conflict of interest that was to prove very nearly catastrophic. His 98 large combat vessels and 1000 aircraft were supposed to provide most of the protection for General Douglas MacArthur's landings. Yet Halsey was answerable not to MacArthur but to Admiral Chester Nimitz, in Hawaii – who had given Halsey instructions to destroy the Japanese fleet if he should get the chance. Halsey could not simultaneously protect MacArthur and pursue Japanese ships.

Japan's naval plans for *Sho-1* – the code-name for the defence of the Philippines – were in outline simple enough: keep the Philippines, sink the American invasion fleet, save Japan from invasion. The details, however, were complex, and there was certainly nothing easy about putting them into practice.

For this, the greatest of set-piece sea battles, the Imperial fleet would be divided into three forces containing 63 major combat vessels: a decoy force of almost empty carriers to lure away the pride of Halsey's Third Fleet, and two arms to create a pincer movement in which the battleships and heavy cruisers would destroy the remaining American ships and the landing forces. Like the Americans, the Japanese had no overall commander at sea: Admiral Soemu Toyoda, commander of the Combined Fleet, would control the action from his Tokyo headquarters.

The decoy fleet would consist of four carriers, escorted by two hybrid battleship-carriers and 11 cruisers and destroyers. They would approach Luzon from the north-east, apparently threatening any US landing on Leyte. There would be few planes to defend them. Their commander, Vice Admiral Jisaburo Ozawa – vanquished Japanese commander during the Battle of the Philippine Sea four months earlier – was ready to sacrifice his entire force, if that was what it took to lure Halsey northwards. 'We expected complete destruction', he recalled later. He had, he thought, a good chance of success. Halsey was known as 'Bull' because of his tendency to charge at tempting targets, and Ozawa intended to make himself as tempting as possible.

The more powerful of the two 'pincer' arms would be Kurita's 32-ship force that tangled with *Darter* and *Dace*. Among his five battleships were the 70 000 tonne monsters *Yamato* and *Musashi* – the world's largest – with huge 460 mm (18.1 in) guns and 410 mm (16.1 in) thick plating. Kurita, who boasted of the fleet's 'suicide spirit', would drive from Borneo straight through the central Philippines, via the Sibuyan Sea, and then swing south through the San Bernardino Strait between Luzon and Samar islands to hit the American fleet in Leyte Gulf.

At the same time, Vice Admiral Shoji Nishimura's Southern Force, with seven warships, would also depart from Borneo, and would enter Leyte Gulf through Surigao Strait between Leyte island and the northern tip of Mindanao. Behind him as a reserve would be Vice Admiral Kiyohide Shima, approaching southwards from Japan, via the Formosa (Taiwan) Strait, with seven cruisers and destroyers.

The decision to proceed with this plan was difficult – 'as difficult as swallowing molten iron', according to Toyoda. But it had to be faced. If the Americans took the Philippines, they would cut off the Japanese Navy wherever it was. If isolated south of the Philippines, the fleet would be denied supplies from Japan; if trapped to the north, it would have no oil from the East Indies. For Japan, it was all or nothing.

KURITA: TOO CAUTIOUS TO WIN

After commanding the Close Support Force at the Battle of Midway in June 1942, Vice Admiral Takeo Kurita (1889-1977) was put in command of the powerful Centre Force during the Battle of Leyte Gulf two years later. Delayed by his encounter with two US submarines, he then lost his giant battleship *Musashi*. Though shaken, he signalled Admiral Toyoda in Tokyo that he would 'break into Leyte Gulf and fight to the last man'. After all, Japan's survival depended on holding the Philippines and 'would it not be shameful to have the fleet remaining intact while our nation perishes?' In the subsequent running fight with Rear Admiral Clifton Sprague's 'Taffy 3' force of escorting mini-carriers, which he wrongly believed to be the main US task force, Kurita's second giant battleship, *Yamato*, was hounded from the action.

Despite his promises, Kurita never displayed the suicide spirit. Rather than risk his scattered vessels further, he withdrew when only 70 km (45 miles) from threatening the American ships carrying the invasion force in Leyte Gulf. His withdrawal allowed the Americans to win the battle and recapture Leyte.

DISASTERS ON BOTH SIDES

Almost at once, things began to go wrong. Kurita had been in *Atago* when *Darter* sank it, and the admiral had taken an unwelcome dip in the South China Sea before being rescued by the destroyer

TROPICAL KIT Japan had the most recently formed navy among the great powers in World War II. The wartime uniforms were little changed from the original late 19th-century styles, which followed closely the style of US uniforms of the period. Navy blue was the standard colour, but in summer and in tropical waters the navy wore white. Over his cotton trousers, a lieutenant (right) wore a loose cotton tunic with stand-up collar. His badge of rank was shown on the shoulder straps – three cherry blossoms between stripes for the lieutenant. The peaked cap had a white cover and the shoes were white leather. A short dagger was worn with ordinary working uniform; it hung under the tunic.

Kishinami. Even more significantly, the warning from *Darter* of Kurita's approach had fully alerted Halsey. Next day, search planes spotted the other two forces, and Halsey ordered an air attack on Kurita which lasted for several hours.

First, though, the Americans were faced with a disaster. At dawn on October 24, some 200 Japanese planes from Luzon attacked carriers patrolling east of the island. The group's Hellcats shot down almost half the attackers – one pilot, Commander David McCampbell, accounted for nine planes – and the crews were elated. But at 9.38 am a lone Japanese dive-bomber swooped down and dropped a 250 kg (550 lb) bomb on the carrier *Princeton*. It went straight through the flight-deck, exploding deep in the bowels of the ship, setting off a chain reaction of exploding torpedoes and burning petrol.

Other ships came alongside to help and take off survivors. The fire seemed almost under control when it reached the reserve magazine. A monumental explosion tore *Princeton*'s stern apart; the doomed ship was scuttled later that day. The blast also damaged the nearby light cruiser *Birmingham*, wreaking terrible carnage; chunks of metal tore across the deck, killing 220 men and wounding another 420. An officer described the scene as medical staff gave what aid they could to 'men with legs off, with arms off, with gaping wounds in their sides, with the tops of their heads furrowed with fragments'.

The Japanese had suffered far worse at the hands of Halsey's fighters and bombers, however. In five great waves, 259 American planes swarmed over Kurita's battleships and cruisers, with their thickets of anti-aircraft guns. Kurita's flagship *Yamato* was hit, and the great *Musashi* shuddered as four torpedoes struck its port side, causing serious flooding and slowing its progress. As *Musashi*'s plight became obvious, the American pilots concentrated on it and it began to fall still farther behind.

Musashi had a secret weapon: its nine 460 mm guns could fire special exploding shells, with time-delay fuses that sprayed the sky with 6000 steel pellets. Yet even these, when *Musashi*'s commander, Rear Admiral Inoguchi Toshihira, finally used them, failed to deter the attacking Helldivers, with their armour-piercing bombs, and the Avengers with their torpedoes. And the blast effects of the huge guns killed or injured many of the battleship's ack-ack gunners.

Finally, at 2.45 pm, a bomb struck *Musashi*'s bridge, seriously wounding Toshihira. Nine torpedoes had by now slammed into the battleship; 11 others followed. More and more sections had to be flooded to try to control its list. Slowly the behemoth died, wallowing in a circle, bows slipping beneath the waves until the executive officer shouted, 'All crew abandon ship!' It rolled over to port, with Toshihira standing grimly on the bridge; pointed its stern to the sky, with several men still clinging to it; and plunged underwater. It took 1023 men – almost half its crew – with it.

There was no help for Kurita. A message from Toyoda, safe in Tokyo, warning Kurita to 'be alert' for enemy submarines did nothing for his 'suicide spirit'. Prudently, he decided to avoid further risk by turning westwards, away from the narrow San Bernardino Strait, to wait until Halsey's aircraft took Ozawa's bait. This would also make it seem that the main Japanese surface force was retiring – and so help the decoy plan.

A VAIN PURSUIT

Halsey had indeed taken the Japanese bait. He knew that there had to be more to the Japanese assault than Kurita. In particular, he knew that there had to be more carriers, the decisive offensive weapon in modern naval warfare.

That afternoon, he spotted what he was looking for: Ozawa's four carriers off the north-east tip of Luzon. It was, he said, 'the last piece in the puzzle'. Unaware that the carrier force was a decoy with few planes, and certain that Kurita had decided against advancing, 'Bull' Halsey set off in pursuit of Ozawa's red rag. The only acknowledgment he made to the threat posed by Kurita was to warn four of his six battleships, and some of his cruisers and destroyers, to be ready to form a special group – designated Task Force 34 – which would turn back if necessary. His messages were picked up by Kinkaid, who believed that Task Force 34 would very soon be formed.

The result of Halsey's action, and Kincaid's misunderstanding, could have been catastrophic, for now San Bernardino Strait was unguarded, and no one knew it. And, as the fall of night and the diversion of Halsey's aircraft made the going safer, Kurita was on his way through, exactly as he had planned. Soon MacArthur's land forces, almost unprotected, would come into his sights.

BLOCKING THE SOUTHERN ROUTE

To the south, overnight on October 24/25, Nishimura's force was weaving into Surigao Strait. Waiting for him, however, were six vintage American battleships, backed by eight cruisers,

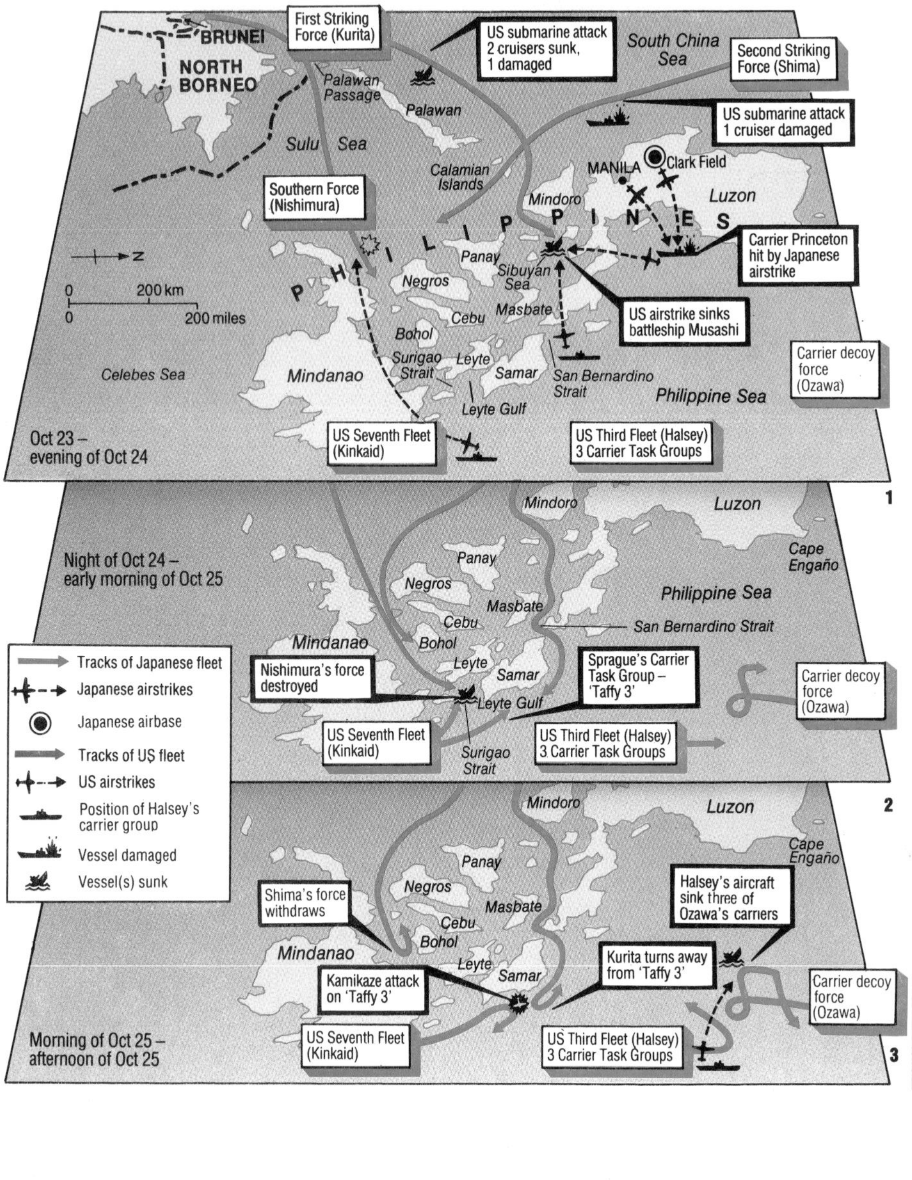

LOSS OF FACE AND FLEET FOR JAPAN
1 The northern arm (Kurita's) of the Japanese First Strike Force is attacked by US submarines, but rounds Mindoro before aircraft from carriers patrolling Luzon's east coast halt it. The southern arm (Nishimura's) is hit by aircraft from Kincaid's Seventh Fleet, there with Halsey's Third Fleet to help retake Leyte. Japan's Second Strike Force (Shima) heads south to support Nishimura. Halsey spots a Japanese decoy force (Ozawa) approaching from the north.
2 Ozawa turns north, luring Halsey with him. Kurita races through San Bernardino Strait, aiming to round Samar and threaten Leyte Gulf. Nishimura, passing through Surigao Strait, is destroyed by Oldendorf's battleships from Seventh Fleet; his back-up, Shima, turns tail.
3 Kurita speeds towards Leyte Gulf but sights US ships, thinks they are Halsey's and engages them. They are only Sprague's 'Taffy 3' – a group of makeshift mini-carriers to help cover the Leyte landings – but they hold off Kurita. Halsey turns back but Kurita withdraws.

28 destroyers and 39 PT (motor torpedo) boats, all under Rear Admiral Jesse B. Oldendorf.

Oldendorf found himself in a wonderful position. With the PT boats able to reconnoitre rapidly and send him accurate information, he blocked the strait and delivered a mass of broadsides at Nishimura's single-column force. In 18 minutes, over 4000 shells arched across 15 km (9 miles) of darkness into Nishimura's hapless vessels. Hit also by torpedoes from the destroyers, all but one of them were crippled or sunk. Among them was Nishimura's flagship, the battleship *Yamashiro*, which took the admiral down with it.

Behind Nishimura came his supposed colleague in the southern thrust, Shima. Shima could have been of considerable help to Nishimura, but the two men were approaching from different angles – and, in any case, they loathed each other. Shima, a political intriguer, had gained seniority over the old sea dog Nishimura, who stolidly refused to communicate with Shima. All that awaited Shima as he entered Surigao Strait were the burning hulks of his dead rival's ships. He stayed just long enough – a mere five minutes – for his cruiser *Nachi* to collide with a burning cruiser of Nishimura's force, *Mogami*. Then he retreated back to safety, unable to contribute anything to the battle. The southern prong of the Japanese naval pincer existed no more.

GALLANTRY OF 'TAFFY 3'

At daybreak on October 25, Kurita emerged unopposed from San Bernardino Strait, and raced southwards towards Leyte Gulf along the east coast of Samar island. Suddenly, his officers sighted five American carriers. He assumed they were Halsey's fast carriers, and ordered an immediate attack. Pell-mell, in increasing disorder, his ships set off in pursuit. In fact the American ships were nothing more than modified merchant ships with short flight decks, assigned to provide air cover for the Leyte landings. These 'baby flat-tops', as they were disparagingly called, formed one of three groups code-named 'Taffy'. This one – 'Taffy 3' – was no match for Kurita's massive force.

LANDING AID Coming back to his base on an aircraft carrier, a US pilot would be looking out for the signaller guiding him in. With the khaki cotton trousers and shirt of his service dress the signaller wore a pullover and often a helmet, both in conspicuous yellow. The helmet helped to muffle the constant roar of engines. The signaller displayed two colourful, eye-catching 'bats' with outstretched arms. The position in which he held the bats indicated to the pilot how he was approaching the flat carrier deck – for example, if he was making a level approach and, if not, which wing was dipping. Sometimes the signaller stood in front of a dark screen so as to be easier to pick out.

There then followed an extraordinary running battle. When the commander of 'Taffy 3', Rear Admiral Clifton Sprague, spotted the pagoda-shaped masts of Kurita's fleet, he launched every plane, threw out smoke screens, and radioed for help. Salvos began to drop around the American mini-carriers, sending up fountains of coloured dyes that helped the Japanese gunners adjust their aim. It seemed to Sprague that none of his command could survive another five minutes. Closer and closer the shells fell, until suddenly fate intervened: 'Taffy 3' ran into a rain squall.

By the time the clouds cleared, the Japanese had lost their aim, and Sprague's planes were doing their work. For the next three hours, as Kinkaid frantically called for Halsey to come and attack the real target, Sprague dodged Kurita. His planes flew sortie after sortie, using up their bombs, then their torpedoes, then depth charges, and finally making dry runs to keep the Japanese ships off balance. So effective were these tactics that Kurita continued to believe that he was engaging a far larger force.

The destroyer *Johnston* was hit by three 356 mm (14 in) shells – an officer said it was 'like a puppy being smacked by a truck' – and went down with 189 men. The destroyer *Hoel* was sunk after a brave but futile torpedo run. The carrier *Gambier Bay* and a little destroyer escort, *Samuel B. Roberts*, also sank. Then, after 2 hours and 23 minutes of battle, just when it seemed that Kurita was ready to pounce on Sprague's surviving ships, the Japanese turned away.

'THE WORLD WONDERS'

Why? The answer lay with equally astonishing events far to the north, off Luzon's north-eastern tip, Cape Engaño, where Halsey had been in hot pursuit of Ozawa all through the night.

Halsey had been surprised by the urgent requests to help Sprague, which he did not consider to be his prime task. He was looking forward to battle. His planes had already wreaked considerable damage, fatally wounding Ozawa's flagship, the carrier *Zuikaku*. Ozawa 'would be under our guns before noon', Halsey wrote later. 'I rubbed my hands at the prospect of blasting the cripples that our planes were setting up for us.'

Around 10 am he had his mind changed for him by the arrival of a remarkable radiogram. It was from his commander, Admiral Nimitz. 'WHERE IS RPT WHERE IS TASK FORCE 34 RR THE WORLD WONDERS.' The apparent sarcasm – the repetition of the question, and especially the sardonic final words – infuriated Halsey. Nimitz intended a mild prod, but no insult. The repetition, added by a signaller, was standard procedure for important words, and 'the world wonders' was an unfortunate choice of cryptographic padding designed to bemuse the Japanese if they intercepted the message – and should have been stripped from the signal by Halsey's decoders. But it did the trick. Halsey took the request as an order, and in his words, 'I turned my back on the opportunity I had dreamed of since my days as a cadet'. He swung south.

He left behind him a few of his ships to do yet more damage to Ozawa's fleet. Ozawa had expected as much. In receiving such blows he was doing no less than his duty. He thus became the only Japanese commander to execute his assignment successfully. When *Zuikaku* finally succumbed to a 200-plane raid and began to roll over, Ozawa prepared to go down with it. He was saved by his officers, who dragged him to safety.

It was at this point that Kurita – convinced that he was in the midst of Third Fleet, which would soon swarm around and destroy him – decided to break off action with 'Taffy 3' and regroup his scattered ships. From intercepted messages between Third and Seventh Fleets, many transmitted uncoded, he knew that Halsey was to his north, and at first he intended to take on Third Fleet. But when he got to San Bernardino Strait, still without meeting Halsey, he felt that 'fuel shortages' compelled him to enter it and retreat: that, at least, is how he rationalised his decision to withdraw. The battle was now as good as over.

Sprague was dumbfounded at the sight of the Japanese turning away northwards: 'I expected to be swimming by this time', he wrote later. 'It took a whole series of reports from circling planes to convince me. I could not get the fact into my battle-numbed brain.' He had done more than simply survive. He had held his own against a fleet many times his superior, and in doing so had kept Kurita's attention away from the Leyte beachheads. His success was due, he wrote later, not simply to the tactics he had adopted but also 'to the definite partiality of Almighty God'.

Equally astonishing had been Kurita's premature withdrawal. Halsey had committed the biggest and fastest US battleships to a useless pursuit in which he had not fired a single shot. In doing so he had unwittingly imperilled the whole assault on Leyte. Kurita's decision to pull back cancelled out Halsey's error.

It was not entirely the end – later that day, Sprague's ships were astonished by their first experience of *kamikaze* attacks (see feature, p. 376) – but the Japanese were broken. The Americans had lost one light carrier and five other vessels, together with some 3000 men. Japan had lost four carriers, three battleships, 19 cruisers and destroyers, and about 10 000 men. The US not only controlled the Philippine Sea, they had knocked the Japanese Navy out of the war. And MacArthur and his men were safe ashore, already on the way to taking control of Leyte island.

KINKAID: COOLNESS AND CONFIDENCE

Thomas Kinkaid (1888-1972) came to prominence as commander of an attack group during the Battle of the Coral Sea in May 1942. In November of the same year, he inflicted huge losses on Japanese aircraft in the Battle of Santa Cruz in the Solomons.

After a year spent building up US forces in the Aleutian Islands, he took command of the Seventh Fleet, the naval force supporting General MacArthur's South-West Pacific Command, and was largely responsible for the defeat of Vice Admiral Shoji Nishimura's Southern Force during the Battle of Leyte Gulf.

Though the division of command with Admiral William Halsey could have proved catastrophic, Kinkaid avoided potential problems by the effective use of his venturesome and persistent subordinates, Rear Admirals Clifton Sprague and Jesse B. Oldendorf. Kinkaid was made a full admiral in 1945.

Kamikazes: warriors of the 'Divine Wind'

On October 17, 1944, Vice Admiral Takijiro Onishi, newly appointed commander of Japan's First Air Fleet in Manila, arrived to find an almost useless force. He had fewer than 100 outclassed aircraft with which to support Kurita's First Striking Force in the coming Battle of Leyte Gulf. He needed a radical new weapon to use against his enemy.

Two days later, he shocked his staff with an extraordinary plan. It was known that bomber pilots who crashed their planes into ships often did more damage than a whole squadron intent on survival. Onishi proposed to make such tactics official. Only human missiles could guarantee spot-on bombing through the vulnerable flight decks of the American aircraft carriers.

The advantages of suicide attacks were obvious. They could be performed accurately by inexperienced pilots in any kind of aircraft. They were hard to stop, for the incoming attacker had to be completely destroyed, not simply damaged, by anti-aircraft fire. Moroever, the heroism of the pilots would do much to bolster morale throughout the Japanese armed forces.

Onishi assembled his 23 non-commissioned pilots, stressed their country's dire need and asked for volunteers to form a Special Attack Corps. All 23 volunteered, forming a unit named *Shimpu*. A second suicide corps was formed shortly afterwards and given the name *Kamikaze*. Both names mean 'Divine Wind', after a typhoon that destroyed a Mongol invasion fleet in 1281. The term *kamikaze* came to be applied by the Allies to all suicide pilots.

EARLY PREY Explosions rip apart the US escort carrier *St Lo* in Philippine waters in October 1944. It was one of the *kamikazes'* first victims.

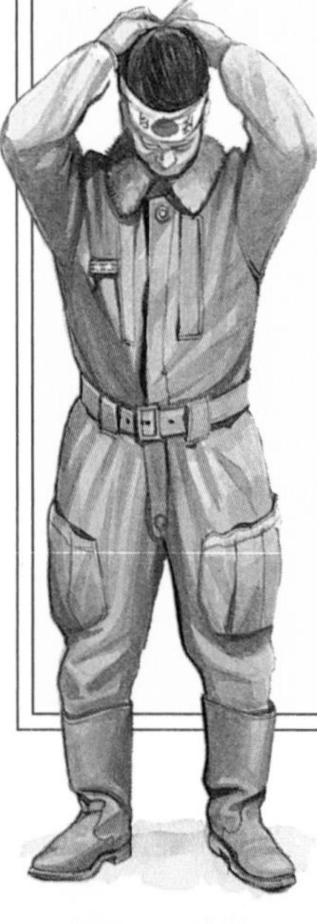

PREPARING TO DIE A *kamikaze* pilot ties his *hachimaki* – the white headcloth, often decorated with the rising sun, copied from the *samurai* warriors of old. The pilot wears a standard lined winter flying suit, with two stars to indicate his rank – Private 1st Class.

'ALREADY GODS'

The fervour of the *kamikazes* was intense. Some were inspired by *bushido* military traditions of self-sacrifice. Others, certain they would die anyway, welcomed a chance to die gloriously in a worthy if hopeless cause.

Like the *samurai* warriors they emulated, they were each given *hachimaki*, a folded white cloth to tie around the head, originally intended to keep the warrior's eyes clear of hair and sweat. And like the *samurai* they displayed a calm that befitted acceptance of a certain and righteous death. Treated like heroes, assured of national honour, they spent their time reading, writing and studying. Onishi was proud of them: 'You are already gods without earthly desires', he told them.

Before departure the young pilots gave their belongings to friends and wrote final letters, enclosing relics like fingernail clippings and locks of hair. 'Please congratulate me,' wrote 23-year-old Isao Matsuo. 'I have been given a splendid opportunity to die. This is my last day . . . I shall fall like a blossom from a radiant cherry tree . . . May our death be as sudden and clean as the shattering of crystal.'

Then came the final briefing, with calm talk about tactics – 'more like a discussion of a good fishing place than an analysis of a rendezvous with death', as one commander put it. They flew off with a few mementos beside them: photographs of loved ones or a flag. They sought to preserve their studied calm to the end, observing 'The First Order of the *kamikazes*: Do not be in too much of a hurry to die. If you cannot find your target, turn back; next time you may find a more favourable opportunity. Choose a death that creates a maximum result.'

The suicidal attacks had a hypnotic fascination for American seamen. One American officer who had to face them wrote later: 'We watched each plunging *kamikaze* with the detached horror of one witnessing a terrible spectacle rather than as the intended victim . . . And dominating it all was a strange mixture of respect and pity.'

There seemed to be no shortage of *kamikaze* volunteers. No fewer than 1465 navy and army aircraft were expended, for example, in ten massed *kamikaze* attacks around Okinawa between April 6 and June 22, 1945. They came near to crippling the Allied Pacific Fleet: the *kamikazes* sank 11 ships and damaged 102.

THE 'DIVINE WIND' BLOWS One suicide plane has already smashed into this American fleet carrier (below), ripping a massive hole in its wooden flight deck. Two more *kamikazes* follow. On deck, desperate firefighters man the hoses, while ack-ack guns fire rapid rounds hoping to down the attacking aircraft before they hit. Men push an undamaged Avenger torpedo-bomber out of the line of fire. In the background, another carrier is under attack, while a destroyer darts through the waves seeking to help the vulnerable giants. (Right) Six stern-faced members of a *kamikaze* corps, holding their ritual *samurai* swords, pose for a group photograph before such an attack. Having chosen to die for the defence of their country, *kamikazes* were fêted like young gods.

Leyte island – a muddy, bloody first base

Taking Leyte was to have been a swift operation, but Japanese resistance soon proved tougher than expected. The weather was hellish, the terrain a nightmare. It took a gruelling three months before the Americans were ready to move on.

SOFT GOING Members of the 1st Cavalry Division (above) cross Leyte's swampy coastal plain on the first day. The rain began before daylight faded, and 890 mm (35 in) fell over the next month, slowing the conquest of the island and hindering plans to make it a key air base. Engineers trying to build landing strips and roads (above left) battled with deep mud, and one in four planes landing at Tacloban ended up as wrecks, embedded in soft spots.

THE PROUD CONQUEROR of Malaya and Singapore, Lt General Tomoyuki Yamashita, made a great blunder when he planned the Japanese defence of the Philippines. He expected the main blow to fall on the northern island of Luzon, but instead General MacArthur struck at Leyte, in the centre of the island group. By nightfall on October 20, the day of the attack, the US Sixth Army, under Lt General Walter Krueger, was well dug in around Leyte's capital, Tacloban, and around Dulag to the south. There had been little opposition on the beaches, for the Japanese followed their new tactics of retreating inland to escape the pre-invasion bombardment. Then they hoped to lure the Americans to destruction in front of well-prepared defences.

Yamashita moved swiftly once he was ordered to shift the focus of his defence strategy from Luzon. He told his officers on October 22: 'The Japanese will fight the decisive battle of the Philippines on Leyte.' And he began reinforcing the 21 500 troops already on the island. He would eventually have an army of 65 000 men there – far fewer than the US Sixth Army's 180 000, but still a significant force. So confident were the Japanese of victory that at one stage they seriously discussed overrunning Tacloban, seizing MacArthur, who had his headquarters there, and demanding the surrender of the entire US Army.

MacArthur had other plans. His first aim was to secure Leyte Valley, a broad plain where he could build the bases from which American planes could strike at the Japanese from the Philippines to China. But high winds and monsoon rain soaked ground, men and supplies. One engineer described Tacloban airstrip as 'a thin slice of coral or metal laid upon a jelly mould'.

Frequent raids by the 2500 planes of the Japanese Fourth Air Army did severe damage to the Tacloban base. The carriers of the US Seventh and Third Fleets could not give MacArthur control of the air. Many of their planes needed repairs after the Leyte Gulf action, and others were needed elsewhere. Even when planes flew, they were often baulked by the thick clouds that shielded both the central mountains and Ormoc, the Japanese headquarters and supply port on the west coast, where the local commander, Lt General Sosaku Suzuki, directed the island's defence.

SLOG FOR BREAKNECK RIDGE

After securing his east coast beach-heads, MacArthur's main target was the northern coastal town of Carigara. Both sides needed it, for it controlled the road to Ormoc. Krueger's men got to Carigara first, and the Japanese settled into the hills to the south-west. When the Americans marched in on November 2, they were astonished to find the streets empty.

The real battle would be for the rugged country blocking the way south to Ormoc. Two regiments of the US 24th Infantry Division bore the brunt of the formidable task. The Japanese 1st Division controlled 5 km (3 miles) of road that snaked over steep ridges, angular spurs and rocky knolls, giving them ideal vantage points. The whole tortuous maze of foxholes and firing pits was named 'Breakneck Ridge' by the Americans.

The assault on Breakneck took three grim weeks. The Americans had an advantage in fire-power; the Japanese knew the terrain. The result was a bloody, muddy, rain-sodden hand-to-hand fight between mud-encrusted men. By the second week of November, units of the 24th Division had dragged themselves near the central crest. Engineers crawled forward in front of the tanks, probing for mines, constantly alert for lone Japanese who would leap from their foxholes with machine guns and grenades. By November 16 they reached the crest, and the battle for Breakneck was over. It had cost the Americans some 700 lives. They had killed more than 6000 Japanese and advanced just 3 km (2 miles).

A DARING, HOPELESS SCHEME

Yamashita was now convinced that the commitment to Leyte was leading to disaster, but the defence continued by order of his superior, Field Marshal Hisaichi Terauchi. Yamashita ordered up two more convoys to ship in supplies, and requested air cover from the Fourth Air Army commander, Lt General Kyoji Tominaga. By

now, some 1000 Japanese reinforcement aircraft had arrived in Manila, mainly from Indochina, but American air power had grown at the same time. Tominaga and Yamashita devised a plan which would, they fondly hoped, annihilate American air power on the island completely.

The plan, Operation *Wa*, involved a sequence of heavy bombings, night-time crash-landings of troops, paratroop assaults and infantry attacks, all leading to the destruction of American air installations. Their first target was the huge American base at Burauen, in the southern part of Leyte Valley, which had three airfields.

Wa got off to a disastrous start. When three transports delivering raiders by crash-landings roared in over Burauen at 2.45 am on November 27, one plane was shot down and the other two came down too far away for the troops to do any damage. The next day, American planes were grounded by rain. The absence of raids convinced Yamashita and Tominaga that the initial landings had been successful. They pushed on with the infantry and paratroop operations.

The battle-weary infantry – 2000 men under Maj General Shiro Makino – were to cross the mountains and attack soon after the paratroops. The 1400 paratroops were superbly fit and well-equipped – their gear even included musical instruments such as harmonicas, bugles, whistles and flutes for jungle communication at night. The infantry were already on their way when the paratroop drop was postponed because of bad weather. The news, however, did not get through to Makino. As a result, when he attacked the first airfield, Buri, at dawn on December 6, he did so without support. He captured half the field before the Americans knew what was happening, then was forced back into trenches along one side.

That night, transport aircraft carrying the first wave of 360 paratroops arrived over Burauen. The Americans forced the pilots off course with anti-aircraft fire. Only 60 paratroops managed to land safely and make contact with Makino. The rest drifted down on a neighbouring American field, San Pablo, which held mainly non-combat headquarters personnel. The Japanese created bedlam, hurling grenades into the tents, bayoneting survivors, sounding their musical instruments to keep in contact with each other, and setting fire to planes and ammunition dumps.

As dawn came, they realised that they were on the wrong airfield, and set off for Buri, 3 km (2 miles) away. They linked up with the beleaguered Makino, and by mid-morning the Japanese had seized the whole strip. By now, though, the Americans were mustering tanks, heavy mortars and artillery. The Japanese had no real chance. Their reserves of infantry were trapped in the mountains and bad weather prevented more para-drops. After three days, the survivors fled.

Ironically, the whole operation had been unnecessary. The Americans had already stopped work at Burauen because of the muddy soil. Moreover, *Wa* had removed Japanese from Ormoc, where they were now most needed.

THE FINAL OFFENSIVE

In Ormoc, some 2000 Japanese were awaiting Yamashita's first convoy, with its 5000 reinforcements. At the same time, Krueger put into action a daring plan to capture Ormoc by amphibious assault, intending to stop Japanese reinforcements and split Japanese forces inland.

Both operations coincided on December 7. Fifty-six American P-47 fighters attacked the Japanese convoy, sinking most of the ships. The American invasion fleet lost two destroyers to *kamikazes*, but downed about two-thirds of the Japanese planes, and landed its troops – of the 77th Division – almost unopposed near Ormoc.

Almost at once, the weight of American armour began to tell. On December 10, when Ormoc in the words of one American officer was 'a blazing inferno of bursting white phosphorus shells, burning houses and exploding ammunition dumps', the Japanese pulled out towards the mountains. The next day, the 77th linked up with troops from the north. Other units had already cut across the island below Suzuki's retreating troops. By Christmas the remaining Japanese were bottled up in the mountainous hinterland, without any hope of reinforcement.

The survivors, however, were ready to fight on to the death. One soldier wrote home: 'I am writing this letter to you by dim candle-light. Our air force has not arrived. General Yamashita has not arrived. Hundreds of pale soldiers of Japan are awaiting a glorious end, and nothing else.'

Though it took months to mop up – indeed, isolated groups of Japanese survived until the end of the war – the Americans held Leyte's coasts and airstrips, and they were ready to move on.

SUPREME TACTICIAN

Arriving from his native Prussia, Walter Krueger (1881-1967) joined the US Army and served in the Spanish-American War of 1898 and in World War I. He was on the War Department general staff before taking command of the Southern Defense Command at the outbreak of World War II. He took command of the US Sixth Army in early 1943 and led it through New Guinea and other south-west Pacific actions, chiefly the reconquest of the Philippines.

Under his leadership, Sixth Army fought in every sort of condition – coastlands, swamps, jungles, plains and mountains. The taking of Manila made Krueger one of the war's most widely experienced commanders. He proved strong enough to resist MacArthur when necessary, yet shrewd enough to avoid the publicity that MacArthur craved.

PACIFIC VETERAN Krueger, one of MacArthur's principal ground commanders, had the tactical skill and experience to withstand General MacArthur's demands for haste in the Philippines.

Through kamikaze swarms, jungle and fire to free Manila

In the fight for Luzon, almost 200 000 Japanese died for the loss of 8000 Americans. But the victory was bought at an appalling cost to the Filipinos – frightened civilians trapped between two armies fighting to the death.

MINDORO, a craggy and malaria-ridden island to the south-west of Luzon, is an inhospitable place at the best of times. Nevertheless, to General Douglas MacArthur it offered the chance to build the solid runways not possible on Leyte's swampy terrain. And such air bases, MacArthur felt, were vital to provide cover for the core plan of his entire Philippines campaign: the capture of Luzon and the capital Manila.

On December 12, 1944, the Western Visayan Task Force, commanded by Brig General William C. Dunckel, sailed from Leyte with combat troops of the US Sixth Army and airfield engineers, including a Royal Australian Air Force works squadron. Almost immediately they were hit by a *kamikaze* attack. Flying low and dodging around islands to avoid radar detection, the first plane smashed into the superstructure of the light cruiser *Nashville*, killing 137 men and wounding nearly 200, including Dunckel who suffered painful burns. (*Nashville* was designated MacArthur's flagship, but the general was not on board.) Another *kamikaze* assault a few hours later damaged the destroyer *Haraden*, killing 15 and wounding 25.

Both ships limped back to Leyte, but the task force stayed on course. Carrier-based Hellcats fended off further attacks, shooting down some 30 Japanese aircraft before they came within striking distance of the Mindoro-bound convoy. As the task force drove towards the Mindoro shore the landing craft loosed a deadly barrage of rockets to soften up the defenders.

GATE TO LUZON

Once ashore the Americans met little resistance from the 1000 Japanese, and a week later two new airstrips were in use. 'I was at last ready for Luzon,' MacArthur wrote later. 'Mindoro was the gate.' He now had the 200 000 men of Lt General Walter Krueger's Sixth Army, transported and shielded by Vice Admiral Thomas Kinkaid's Seventh Fleet, with air cover provided by Admiral William Halsey's Third Fleet and Lt General George Kenney's Far East Air Forces, firmly based in Leyte and Mindoro.

There was only one good place to invade Luzon: on the sweeping, palm-fringed beaches of Lingayen Gulf – as the Japanese well knew from their own invasion three years before. The Japanese could not hope to prevent the Americans from landing. On paper, their force looked formidable: 275 000 men of Fourteenth Area Army commanded by the experienced Lt General Tomoyuki Yamashita. But in fact Yamashita had no chance, and he knew it. After Leyte Gulf the Japanese had virtually no navy left. He could expect no supplies or reinforcements. And he had fewer than 200 planes. His one hope was to confine the Americans to the Central Plain with a delaying action fought from the surrounding mountains. In this way he might be able to prevent the Americans from making the island a staging area for an attack on Japan itself.

To this end, he divided his forces into three groups: Shobu – 150 000 men holding the rugged northern mountains; Shimbu – 80 000 men to defend the hills east and south of Manila, and the dams and reservoirs that supplied the city's water; and Kembu – 30 000 men west of the Central Plain to dominate Clark Field. He had no intention of trying to hold Manila itself. Not that the city was entirely abandoned. There remained 17 000 naval troops under the obdurate Rear Admiral Sanji Iwabuchi (not under Yamashita's direct command), who would hold out to the last. His attitude was to have horrendous consequences for Americans, Japanese and Filipinos.

RUNNING A GAUNTLET OF KAMIKAZES

The spearhead of the American invasion fleet – battleships, cruisers, carriers and destroyers under Rear Admiral Jesse Oldendorf – set out on January 2, 1945. Despite strong air support, the six-day journey from Leyte was an ordeal by fire at the hands of the *kamikazes*. One so damaged the escort carrier *Ommaney Bay* that it had to be sunk. As the force passed Manila Bay, *kamikazes* damaged another nine American and Australian

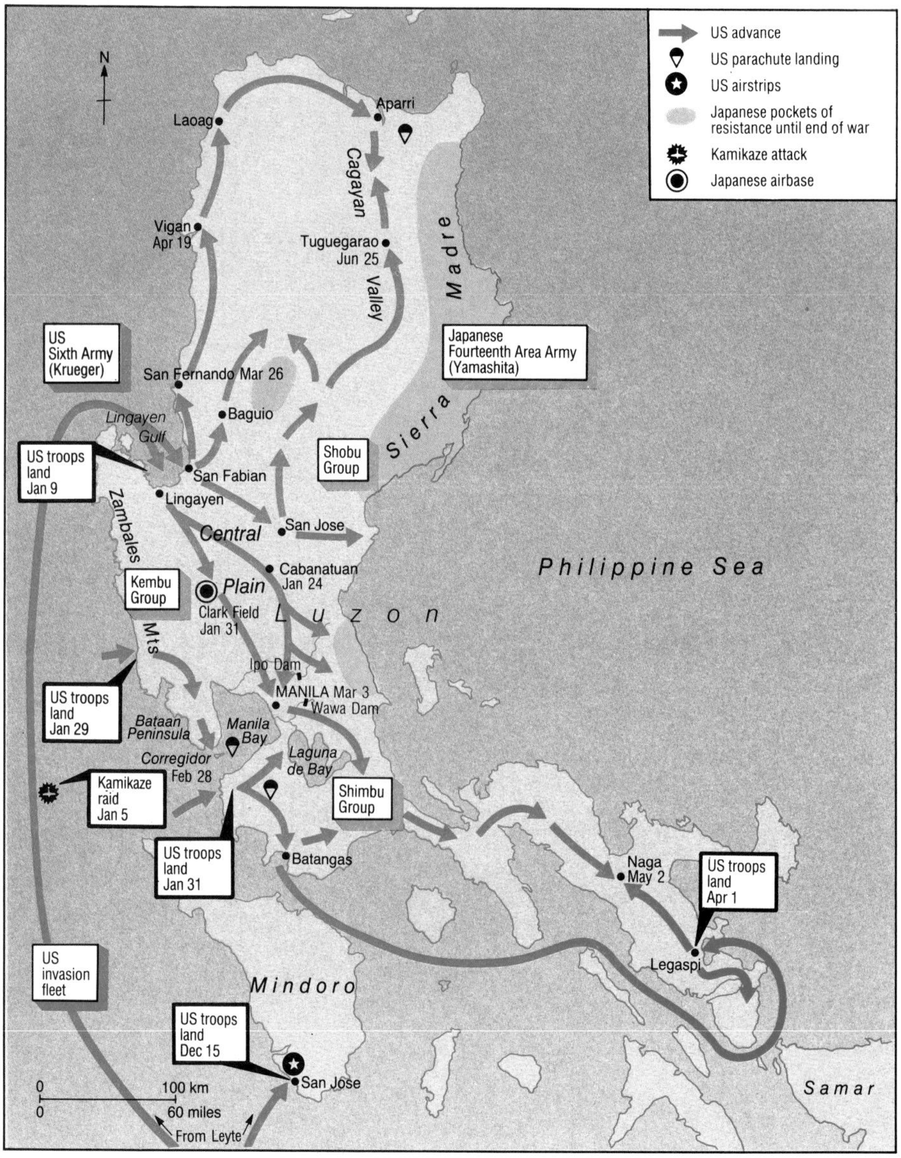

ENTRY POINT Lingayen Gulf was the way in to recapture Luzon. It bit into the Central Plain which gave a clear run south to the huge Clark Field air base, the capital Manila and the magnificent anchorage of Manila Bay.

vessels. One escort carrier, *Savo Island*, escaped a hit by blinding the pilot with a searchlight.

In Lingayen Gulf itself, a devastating raid sank a minesweeper and damaged a dozen other vessels, including two battleships. One victim was Lt General Herbert Lumsden, Churchill's personal liaison officer with MacArthur. He was killed with 28 others when a flaming *kamikaze* crashed into the bridge of the battleship *New Mexico*. But by now the Japanese were running out of both aircraft and pilots. Admiral Halsey's planes had battered the Formosa and Luzon airfields so heavily that almost all the surviving Japanese planes were withdrawn.

Luckily so, for behind Oldendorf's ships there came a 65 km (40 mile) long convoy – almost 1000 ships carrying the Sixth Army. They surged ashore without opposition. Among the few Japanese around were four frightened soldiers who were caught trying to escape from the town of San Fabian disguised as women. By nightfall, the exhilarated Americans had a beach-head 32 km (20 miles) wide and up to 6 km (4 miles) deep.

On his arrival at the beach MacArthur repeated the dramatic walk through the shallows that had won him so much publicity on Leyte. A large crowd of Filipinos cheered him up the beach.

SOUTH TO MANILA

The drive to Manila involved two thrusts. Maj General Oscar Griswold's XIV Corps had the task of advancing on the city. But first, Maj General Innis Swift's I Corps had to secure the left flank against counterattack from Yamashita's Shobu group, now dug in along the Caraballo Mountains overlooking the plain.

It was slow work, for the soldiers had to crawl metre by metre to seize territory crisscrossed by fields of fire. Many of the strongpoints were tanks turned into pillboxes, and surrounded by nests of riflemen. It took almost a month to isolate Yamashita in his mountain fastness in the north-east, an advance that included a dramatic rescue by Filipino guerrillas and American rangers of some 400 inmates from a prison camp at Cabanatuan, deep behind enemy lines.

Griswold, meanwhile, had an easy time of it, for a while at least. The two divisions of XIV Corps marched south towards Manila almost unopposed, feted by cheering Filipinos with feasts of chicken, bananas, coconuts and rice. MacArthur, dashing from one sector to another, urged more speed. He needed to seize Clark Field, 80 km (50 miles) from Manila. Equally important, he was eager to free a prison camp housed in the former university of Santo Tomas in Manila before the inmates were starved or killed in reprisals.

But Griswold could not move fast. On January 23, he came up against Yamashita's Kembu group – the 30 000 men defending Clark Field and the nearby Zambales Mountains. On January 31, a direct assault on the air base itself forced the Japanese back into their mountain defences. In late January, as part of MacArthur's plan to close in on Manila from all sides, two more US units landed – Maj General Charles Hall's XI Corps north of Manila Bay, and Maj General Joseph Swing's 11th Airborne Division to the south.

MacArthur had become increasingly concerned about the 3700 prisoners in Santo Tomas. 'Go to Manila,' he urged 1st Cavalry Division's commander, Maj General Verne D. Mudge. 'Go around the Nips, bounce off the Nips, but go to Manila. Free the internees at Santo Tomas!'

Mudge at once formed two flying columns, each of 700 men and a tank company. They aimed to travel light and fast. With Marine Corps planes scouting the way ahead, the trucks and tanks roared off along back roads, skirting any Japanese forces. At last, one final hurdle remained – the gorge of Novaliches, 8 km (5 miles) from Manila, spanned by a stone bridge. The Japanese had prepared the bridge for demolition; its destruction would hold up Mudge's columns for at least a day. When the first trucks roared up to the bridge, the Japanese defenders lit the fuses and fled. Without hesitation, cavalrymen leapt onto the bridge and cut the fuses with seconds to spare.

Meanwhile, Marine Corps planes had been buzzing Santo Tomas. One of them dropped a message tied to a pair of goggles. 'Roll out the barrel,' it read, to the delight of the inmates. 'Santa Claus is coming.' The first flying column arrived on Saturday, February 3. Guided by guerrillas, the tanks raced to the camp. The inmates heard the din of battle, then a welcome bellow outside: 'Where the hell's the front gate?' followed by a crash as a 1st Cavalry tank came smashing through. After a tense day negotiating the release of some hostages (see box), mail, medical supplies and food poured in. Though it would take many months to repatriate the hostages, at least they now had hopes of surviving.

MacArthur himself arrived on the 7th, greeting old friends from before the war by name. He wrote later: 'I cannot recall, even in a life filled with emotional scenes, a more moving spectacle than my first visit to the Santo Tomas camp . . . When I arrived, the pitiful, half-starved inmates broke out in excited yells . . . It was a wonderful and never-to-be-forgotten moment – to be a life-saver, not a life-taker.'

A CITY CRUCIFIED

Now, with Manila apparently theirs for the taking, the Americans came up against the redoubtable Iwabuchi. As a naval commander, he did not answer to Yamashita. Determined to keep the port out of American hands, he refused to follow Yamashita's troops to the hills, and ordered his men to fight to the death.

Iwabuchi had turned central Manila into a fortress, defended by barbed wire, machine-gun nests in sandbagged houses, and naval guns dug into strategic street corners. He now ordered all bridges to be blown up, along with the water and power supplies. The explosions set much of the city ablaze, hampering the American advance.

Although MacArthur announced that the complete destruction of the Japanese was imminent, Iwabuchi proved a far tougher nut than anyone had dreamed possible. The fighting became a

CAMP COIFFURE At the former university of Santo Tomas, internees and prisoners of war share improvised hair-washing facilities at an old bath propped on scrap timber. They were crowded into rooms and squalid shanties.

TENSION IN SANTO TOMAS

Soon after breaking into crowded Santo Tomas prison camp, US soldiers heard cries for help from the former university's Education Building. Some 220 internees were being held hostage by 65 Japanese, under the camp commander Lt Colonel Toshio Hayashi.

Lt Colonel Charles Brady was sent in to negotiate. Nervously twirling his waxed moustache, he faced Hayashi, who was equally nervous and kept drawing and replacing his pistols. Throughout the day, with a Canadian missionary interpreting, the two men negotiated a surrender that the Japanese could accept without too much loss of face.

Finally the Japanese gave up hostages, grenades and machine guns but kept their personal arms. The Japanese were taken near their own lines and released. Terrified of being shot, they sprinted to safety.

COST OF FREEDOM After hurling artillery fire for six relentless days at Intramuros, the old centre of Manila, the Americans rammed tanks through the walls (inset). Then infantrymen picked their way among the slithering debris, searching for lurking Japanese – and for Filipino survivors.

vicious house-to-house, often room-to-room slog. Machine guns chattered from fortified buildings, and the air was filled with the smoke and dust from American tank and howitzer bombardment. It was only by reducing buildings to rubble that the Japanese guns could be silenced. By the 12th the Americans were nearing the old inner city of Intramuros, with its stone walls up to 12 m (40 ft) thick and 7.5 m (25 ft) high.

Everywhere the battle raged, the hapless Filipinos suffered. Hundreds were caught in the crossfire. Many were shot by the retreating Japanese. Thousands more died when the Americans decided that the only way to get the Japanese out, even from civilian areas, was to open up with artillery. When 7000 Filipinos took refuge in the General Hospital, they found themselves in a deathtrap. The Japanese made it a fortress, and the Americans shelled it.

With the city already in chaos the Japanese holed up in Intramuros, taking some 4000 Filipinos with them as hostages. Griswold pleaded for their release. 'Your situation is hopeless – your defeat inevitable,' he told the Japanese, urging their surrender. 'In the event that you do not accept my offer, I exhort you that true to the spirit of the Bushido and the Code of the Samurai you permit all civilians to evacuate Intramuros.' There was no response.

Shelling began on February 17, and for the next six days the ancient fortress shook to a massive bombardment – 130 artillery pieces delivered 8000 shells, with howitzers firing point-blank to blast holes in the walls. On February 23 the Americans stormed in. Hundreds of Japanese had died in the bombardment, but the survivors fought on from tunnels and dungeons. Each strongpoint had to be taken in grisly fashion with grenades and flamethrowers. There was one brief respite when some 3000 women and children were released – most of the Filipino men had been shot – but after two days the last resistance succumbed. A thousand Japanese had died for the loss of 25 Americans.

By March 3, after a month of fighting, Manila was finally liberated. It had been a brutal and costly business. The Americans had lost 1000 dead and 5500 wounded, while only 4500 of Iwabuchi's 17 000 men had survived. But the main sufferers were the local people. The capital lay in ruins, and 100 000 innocent Filipinos lay dead – six civilians for every fighting man killed. 'Manila was a charnel house,' wrote a local journalist, Carlos Romulo. 'Wherever I went I felt like a ghost in a dead city.'

SECURING MANILA BAY

During the battle, the Americans had already begun clearing the surrounding areas. XI Corps had swept easily down the Bataan Peninsula, to the west of Manila Bay – for the Japanese had no intention of being trapped there as the Americans had been in 1942. Of greater significance were the islands and forts that dominated the sea approaches to the bay. The greatest of these sturdy outposts was Corregidor (see box).

But dogged Japanese held out in four other forts. All were slowly cleared with flamethrowers and burning oil. After Corregidor, Fort Drum (El Fraile) was the most formidable – a tiny islet entirely encased by a concrete blockhouse 105 m (350 ft) long by 45 m (150 ft) wide. On April 13, GIs climbed onto it, pumped in 13 500 litres (3000 gallons) of oil, and ignited it with a 270 kg (600 lb) charge of TNT. When the burning oil reached the fort's magazine, it exploded like a huge bomb, obliterating the 70 Japanese inside.

After that, there was nothing to slow the work of clearing the harbour of its litter of sunken ships. Within two months, 90 000 tonnes of supplies were arriving every week. 'It was the end of a 4000 mile [6400 km] journey,' MacArthur wrote later. 'It had been a long, hard journey, but in some ways the last five miles [8 km] was the hardest.'

LONG SLOG TO VICTORY

Even so, the battle of Luzon was still far from over. While MacArthur was now free to turn his attention to securing the other Philippine islands, Yamashita still had 172 000 troops at large. Manila itself was within range of Japanese guns, and the dams and reservoirs containing the city's water supplies were still in Japanese hands.

The most immediate problem was posed by the Shimbu group, in the southern end of the Sierra Madre mountains. This force had cut off 30 per cent of Manila's water supply. To crush them would not be easy. For one thing, MacArthur had now transferred a large force from Sixth Army to Eighth Army in the southern Philippines, leaving Krueger short of manpower. For another, Krueger's offensive was marred by two major intelligence errors. He believed that the Japanese numbered only 20 000; and he did not know that his first target, the Wawa Dam, no longer supplied water to Manila.

The Japanese had had months to prepare their mountain defences, which included formidable warrens of interconnecting tunnels. The men could fire from the mouth of one tunnel, retreat to safety, and emerge again from another. The only effective tactic was for the Americans to deliver a continuous artillery barrage and then sneak up to throw in grenades while the defenders were still taking cover. The GIs could then seal the tunnel mouths with explosives and release a burning charge into the chamber, asphyxiating the Japanese inside.

Progress was excruciatingly slow. Then, after two months, Krueger discovered that his attack on the Wawa Dam had no purpose at all, and he switched his attention to the Ipo, 20 km (12 miles) to the north. On May 17, after two massive raids in which hundreds of fighter-bombers dropped over 450 000 litres (100 000 gallons) of napalm on the approaches to the dam, a joint attack by Americans and Filipino guerrillas captured it intact. The Wawa fell on the 28th.

In the west, the remaining 25 000 soldiers of Kembu group were no longer much of a threat, though mopping up the sick and starving refugee troops would take months. In the south, an isolated pocket of the Shimbu group was hounded down the southern tail of Luzon island.

There remained the greatest obstacle of all: the 110 000 or more remaining troops of Yamashita's Shobu group in the island's north. Yamashita, from his headquarters in the traditional Philippine summer capital of Baguio, had prepared well, digging into the Philippines' steepest mountains. It was a perfect position, protected by overgrown gorges and rocky ravines, intersected only by a few twisting, easily defended roads, and backing the fertile Cagayan Valley that provided the troops with food.

With just 70 000 men of his own, Krueger did not have enough troops to advance fast. In the agonising ridge-by-ridge struggle, every man needed several litres of water a day to combat the heat, and a single ridge could take battle-weary troops all day to climb. The entrenched Japanese, often living like animals in their foxholes, would sometimes spray petrol over the tall grass and start fires that sent choking black smoke over the American lines. So close was the fighting that many Japanese had arms blown off after trying to catch and throw back grenades.

But by mid-April Yamashita was nearing his end. With guerrillas harassing his supply lines, his troops were down to a handful of rice a day. He pulled out of Baguio, escaping into the mountains to the north. There, with his troops reduced to 65 000 men, Yamashita contested every metre of ground, keeping four American divisions tied down until the end of the war.

These last remnants of the Imperial Army thus in part succeeded in obeying the orders of their Emperor to hold the Philippines. Yamashita surrendered only when his country did, on September 2, 1945, his indomitable spirit still strong. But he refused to conform to *samurai* tradition, saying: 'If I kill myself, someone else will have to take the blame.'

RETAKING CORREGIDOR

The fortified island of Corregidor, dominating the mouth of Manila Bay, seemed virtually impregnable. Its narrow beaches were mined, and the tunnels that networked the rocky spine had been crammed with supplies and ammunition. It was defended by 5000 Japanese determined to fight to the death. Nevertheless, the Americans were resolved to reclaim MacArthur's former headquarters, surrendered in May 1942.

On February 16, paratroops of the 503rd Parachute Infantry Regiment landed on the island's western plateau. Some surprised the rock's commander, Captain Akira Itagaki, in his observation post; he had been expecting an amphibious assault. The Americans attacked, killing Itagaki, and took over much of the high ground before a 4500-strong force completed the seizure of the island above ground. But that was just a start. For the next two weeks the Americans blew up tunnel-mouths by day, and the Japanese dug out and counterattacked at night. On February 21, the Japanese beneath Malinta Hill planned to break out of their trap with a small-scale explosion. It went terribly wrong: the hill blew up in an uncontrolled inferno. An avalanche of rock careered down the slope and tongues of flame licked out of tunnel-mouths and fissures. Some 600 surviving Japanese fled to tunnels farther east.

For five more days, the Americans pressed after them. Then the defenders detonated another vast explosion, which shook the whole island. It marked the end of Japanese resistance. Only 19 survived to be taken prisoner.

Ordeal on Mindanao – clearing the southern Philippines

MacArthur was determined to free every Philippine island. The campaign to do so saw a mass of intricately planned invasions – and one on Mindanao that was as gruelling as anything the GIs undertook in the whole Pacific war.

EVERY FILIPINO had to be liberated: that was the task General Douglas MacArthur had set himself. In February 1945, even before the capital Manila was taken, he was planning to complete his mission by freeing every island bypassed in the drive north. He gave the job to the US Eighth Army under Lt General Robert Eichelberger, a battle-hardened and engaging man, popular with the public but wise enough to avoid the limelight beloved by his superior. ('I would rather have you slip a rattlesnake in my pocket than to have you give me any publicity', he told the War Department's public relations bureau.) Reinforced with just over two divisions from Sixth Army, Eichelberger planned one of the most complex series of amphibious operations ever – 52 landings in the course of the next four months.

The assaults developed a regular pattern: an amphibious assault with little opposition from the Japanese who were holed up in the mountainous, jungle-clad interior; a pursuit; a few skirmishes; and a withdrawal, allowing Filipino guerrillas to mop up. Only in a few islands was the going tough – in some cases so tough that MacArthur has since been criticised for undertaking operations that had no strategic justification.

The first task was to retake the islands controlling the Visayan passages south of Luzon to ensure a safe and more direct journey for shipping from Leyte. The assaults, which began on February 19, went well, with no serious resistance from any of the small islands.

Next it was the turn of Palawan, a long, rugged spine of an island off to the south-west, and a good base for later operations in the Dutch East Indies. When the Americans landed on February 28 the Japanese had already left the port, Puerto Princesa, but they found something else: the remains of 150 American prisoners who had been doused with petrol and burned alive when their captors saw ships bound for Mindoro the previous December. Nine men had escaped, and only three lived to tell what happened.

There followed a series of landings to take the Sulu Archipelago, which stretches like a line of steppingstones towards Borneo (see box), and to liberate the four major islands of the Visayan Group: Panay, Negros, Cebu and Bohol. These islands, spanning the central Philippines, were already neutralised by American-held territory to the north and south, but their people could not be left in enemy hands.

Most of Panay had long been in the control of Filipino guerrillas, who met the Americans with a guard of honour lined up smartly on the beach. The remaining Japanese were simply left to wither away in their mountain hide-outs until the end of the war. Bohol held only 330 Japanese, who offered no threat to the invaders. Cebu was tougher. The 14 500-strong Japanese garrison had mined the beaches, and put up stiff resistance. It took three weeks and cost 410 American lives before the island was finally secured on April 18.

Negros posed a problem. Between the landing beaches and the island's capital, Bacolod, was a gorge spanned by a 200 m (650 ft) steel bridge, already mined for demolition. The Americans launched a pre-invasion amphibious raid to take it. After creeping forward through the darkness, the 63 men drove off the defending Japanese, but were themselves pinned down by fire before they could remove the charges. A Japanese soldier rushed forward to the detonator, but was shot dead before he could push down the plunger. The other defenders fled. The Americans seized the whole span, and the invasion went forward as planned on March 29.

MINDANAO: THE FINAL ASSAULT

Now, in mid-April, came the biggest and bloodiest of the campaign's actions – the battle for the most southerly major island, Mindanao, some 95 000 km^2 (37 000 sq miles) of flat swampy coastlands and mountainous inland rain forest. Its interior, largely in the hands of some 24 000 guerrillas, was almost trackless: it had only two roads, leading north-south and east-west.

In fact, the US invasion had already started a month earlier with the invasion of the Zamboanga Peninsula, jutting westward from the main part of the island. But the peninsula was connected to the island only by an impassably rugged isthmus. The rest of the island, and the 43 000 men left of Japan's Thirty-Fifth Army, had to be taken in a separate operation. There were two main targets, the major one being the port of Davao in the south-east, where the Japanese had developed large commercial interests before the war. Some 13 000 Japanese civilians lived there, and it was well defended by the 100th Division. The second target was the Japanese 30th Division on the northern coast around Macajalar Bay.

Eichelberger decided on a landing at Illana Bay, on the west coast. There, an airstrip at Malabang would provide protection for an advance over the 175 km (110 miles) of wilderness to Davao. As it happened, guerrillas captured the airstrip in advance of the invasion and on April 17 units of Maj General Franklin Sibert's X Corps swarmed ashore 27 km (17 miles) south, at Parang. There was little opposition. Moreover, the Japanese in the area had no radio contact with Davao. In Parang, a US lieutenant came across several dead or injured carrier pigeons each carrying the same message: 'The Americans are here.' But no message had got through to Davao and the Japanese there did not even know that the Americans had landed for five days.

The 24th Division now struck out eastwards. It

BAREFOOT FIGHTERS

When the Americans invaded Mindanao, they were wary of the warlike Moro Muslims who controlled the interior. As it turned out, most of the Moros were now loyal to the local guerrilla commander, Colonel Wendell Fertig. He had offered 20 centavos (10 US cents) and a bullet for every pair of Japanese ears they brought in, thus recruiting a rag-tag army of some 33 000 guerrillas (above) that had been fighting the Japanese non-stop for three years.

Thousands of Filipinos formerly under American command had melted into the jungle, with their arms and ammunition, when the Japanese invaded in 1942. Every major island had several guerrilla groups; Luzon had a dozen. After initial clashes caused by religious and political rivalries, order was restored, based on nationalism and faith in the United States' promises of independence. While Mindanao began as a patchwork of rivalries, Fertig built up enough of a power base in the north-west to run a whole province around the town of Misamis. Slowly the small bands of guerillas joined forces, and news of them reached Australia and the USA.

MacArthur asked the guerrillas to provide him with intelligence. As his trust in them grew, he began to supply them with arms and radios to add to their machetes and poisoned arrows. The jungles and mountains gave them ideal sanctuaries, and the shores of 7000 islands offered countless hideaways.

Eventually, the guerrillas had more than 150 coast-watching stations keeping their eyes on the Japanese. Inland, they rescued crashed US airmen and searched downed Japanese planes for intelligence, which they passed to the Americans.

When the US invasion began they were eager for action, destroying bridges, blowing up supply dumps and cutting Japanese communications in advance of the main invasion, then reinforcing the regular troops. Without doubt the guerrillas saved many thousands of American lives.

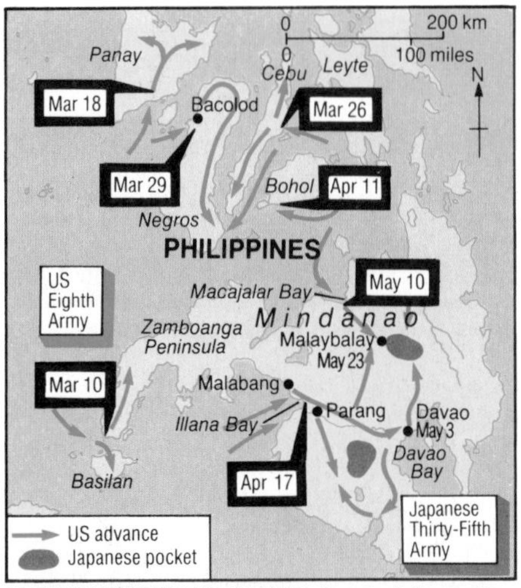

MISSION MINDANAO The US Eighth Army took the smaller nearby islands before concentrating on Mindanao. From the landing at Illana Bay, there was an overland slog to the port of Davao. More US troops landed at Macajalar Bay.

turned out to be the most gruelling march of the Pacific war. The monsoon was due and the weather extremely hot and humid. Much of the road was nothing more than a trail. While some men struggled slowly through the jungle, occasionally flushing out small groups of Japanese, others made their way by boat up the Mindanao river. After five days, when they were almost halfway across the island, the GIs seized a vital road junction, giving them control of roads leading both north and east. The Japanese forces on the island were divided.

Sibert could not afford to dawdle. He divided his forces, now reinforced by the arrival of the 31st Division. The faulty Japanese communications helped him: only now did they hear of the American invasion. But the local commander, Lt General Jiro Harada, was sure that the main American thrust would come by sea in Davao Bay, and he did nothing about the landward force.

The 24th headed east on foot, building up the road as they went. Skirmishing with small Japanese units, plagued by insects, drained by the heat, they found that the Japanese had put their store of bombs to good use. Hundreds had been implanted in the highway, wired up so that Japanese in nearby foxholes could set them off with a jerk of the hand. They also rigged up a few bombs to drop from trees. When one exploded in front of a squad of GIs, an eyewitness recorded that 'nothing was left of the squad except a blackish smear on the tree trunks'.

On April 26, the advance patrols reached the coast. In Davao, Harada at last realised what was happening and abandoned the town, retreating to fortifications in the hills. All the 13 000 Japanese civilians went with him. The Americans rebuilt a blown-up bridge with a makeshift span of logs and ropes, and entered Davao unopposed on May 3. The monsoon still had not broken.

STRUGGLE TO MACAJALAR

Meanwhile, the 31st Division had begun to force its way north up the Sayre Highway, to clear the Japanese 30th Division from Macajalar. A Japanese force, heading south to meet them, was scattered after a vicious skirmish. But the greatest obstacle was the road itself. For 15 muddy kilometres (about 10 miles), its decaying surface collapsed under the weight of a single truck. In the first 40 km (25 miles) there were 70 bridges, all down. Many had to be rebuilt under Japanese sniper fire. Sometimes, howitzers or trucks had to be swung over cables stretched between trees.

The Japanese fought a savage rearguard action all the way, for their commander, Lt General Gyosaku Morozumi, wanted time to regroup in the mountains to the east, along with his artillery. On May 10, another landing at Macajalar Bay spoiled his plans. Morozumi abandoned his artillery and took to the hills, where his force would be no further threat. The two American forces met near the town of Malaybalay on May 23, but took weeks to gain control of the region.

HARADA'S LAST STAND

Back in the Davao hinterland, Harada was still far from beaten. His 40 km (25 mile) defence line, with its well emplaced artillery, was only a few kilometres inland. Moreover, the positions were right up against abandoned fields of abaca (Manila hemp). As combat reporter Jan Valtin wrote, the plants made 'a welter of green so dense that a strong man must fight with the whole weight of his body for each foot of progress. No breeze ever reached the gloomy expanse of green, and more men – American and Japanese – fell prostrate from the overpowering heat than from bullets.'

Even on more open ground the Japanese were cleverly concealed in pillboxes built into the contours of the ground so that the minute firing slits were invisible until they spat bullets. Slowly the Americans cut their way forward, destroying each position with grenades and flamethrowers, digging in at night behind wire and booby-traps.

Not until June 10 did Harada's resistance finally die, and only on June 30 could Eichelberger tell MacArthur that Mindanao was secure. In their heroic but futile defence, the Japanese had lost 13 000 men. Another 22 000 surrendered and some 8000 were never accounted for. The Americans had lost 820 men, victims of a largely thankless grind – 'Hard weeks,' Eichelberger said testily, 'for the GIs who had no newspapers to tell them that everything was in hand.'

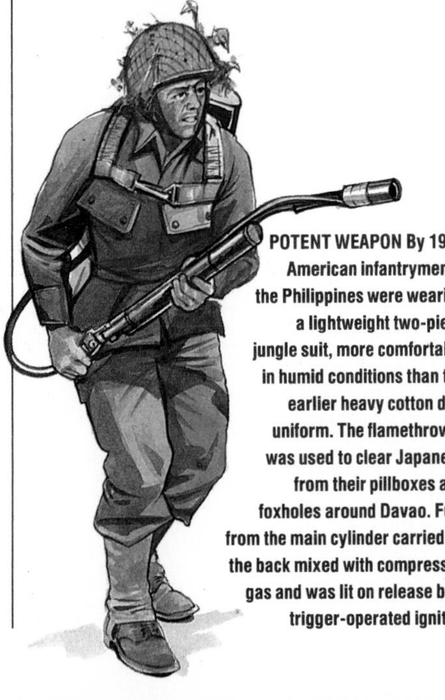

POTENT WEAPON By 1945 American infantrymen in the Philippines were wearing a lightweight two-piece jungle suit, more comfortable in humid conditions than the earlier heavy cotton drill uniform. The flamethrower was used to clear Japanese from their pillboxes and foxholes around Davao. Fuel from the main cylinder carried on the back mixed with compressed gas and was lit on release by a trigger-operated igniter.

BORNEO: AN EASY TARGET, A CONTROVERSIAL CAMPAIGN

Part of MacArthur's plan for the liberation of the southern Philippines involved the retaking of Borneo, the British and Dutch possession that had supplied the Japanese with 40 per cent of their fuel oil since they seized it in 1942. Although its 31 000-strong garrison was now isolated, MacArthur argued that Borneo could make a good Royal Navy base and taking it could occupy the Australian 7th and 9th Infantry Divisions, languishing in northern Queensland since mid-1944. There were further plans for a campaign in the rest of the Dutch East Indies (now Indonesia).

From the first, there was resistance from the British and Australians themselves, who could not see the point of risking lives for such a limited objective. As usual, though, MacArthur had his way. He planned three Borneo landings at Tarakan island off the east coast, at Brunei Bay in the north, and at Balikpapan in the south-east – each preceded by massive bombardments. Balikpapan, for example, was battered by 3000 tonnes of bombs and 38 000 shells from the US Seventh Fleet. The British and Australians thought that this amount of softening up went far beyond what was necessary.

The Australians landed at Tarakan on May 1, intending to seize the oil wells and the airfield. The 2100 defenders had retreated inland. Australian engineers cleared mines and booby-traps and laid pontoons across the muddy beaches. Then Australian infantrymen fought off the Japanese. In the end, 225 Australians died, but the oil fields and airfield were too badly damaged to be of use.

The messy operation had heightened the controversy among the Allies. The Americans accused the Australians of lack of skill, and the Australians blamed the Americans for poor landing equipment.

On June 10, the Australian 9th Division poured ashore in Brunei Bay. The bombardment had cleared the whole shoreline and there was not a single Australian casualty. Inland, they went on to seize two oil fields at Seria and Miri. But 37 of the wells had been set on fire by the Japanese, and it took the Australians three months before they were able to control the plumes of flame and smoke.

The final target, Balikpapan, had been largely flattened by the bombardment before 21 000 Australians landed. Shells and bombs had destroyed storage tanks, sending flaming sheets of oil into the Japanese entrenchments. There were only ten dazed or wounded defenders on the beach, along with 460 bodies lying in wrecked pillboxes and trenches. By nightfall another 117 Japanese from a 4000-strong force were killed, and the battered survivors took refuge in the inland hills. Before they were routed, 1800 of them and 229 Australians lay dead.

25: THE FORGOTTEN WARS

In the jungles, mountains and plains of Burma and China, men waged a tough, lonely war.

Arakan: a bitter lesson learnt

British troops were in no shape to hit back at the Japanese in 1942. An attack down Burma's Arakan coast taught a painful but valuable lesson.

THE GOING was fiendishly difficult as the 14th Indian Division slogged south through the jungles, malarial swamps and leech-infested creeks of Arakan's Mayu Peninsula. Their goal: the island airfields of Akyab (now Sittwe), from which the Japanese could bomb Calcutta and Chittagong, across the Bay of Bengal. Torrential rain – 330 mm (13 in) fell in one day – added to the 14th's misery and made progress even slower. Much too slow, as it turned out.

However, there was little Japanese resistance until the 1st Royal Inniskilling Fusiliers came up against them dug in at Donbaik, a desolate spot only 16 km (10 miles) from the tip of the peninsula. The Inniskillings sent a company into the attack. Murderous fire drove them back. Then the whole battalion attacked – and failed again, swept by fire from the deep earth-and-log bunkers ahead of them, from concealed foxholes behind them (which they had been allowed to pass), and from Japanese hidden in the bamboo jungle escarpment on their left. The Inniskillings lost 100 dead and wounded.

It was early January 1943, over three months since the division had set out from Chittagong, only 260 km (160 miles) north. The Japanese, well outnumbered with only two brigades in Arakan, used those months to fall back, choose their own killing grounds and bring in reinforcements. In a gap of a few hundred metres between sea and jungle at Donbaik, they stopped the 14th in its tracks with in-depth defences of interlinked bunkers. On the east side of the peninsula, across the Mayu Range of hills, another line of bunkers stopped the 10th Lancashire Fusiliers' drive on Rathedaung. Maj General William Lloyd, commanding the division, pressed on with frontal attacks, bringing up some tanks and the fresh 6th Infantry Brigade. Still he failed to break through.

Lt General Takeshi Koga's 55th Division had moved up from the Prome-Toungoo area, about 240 km (150 miles) south-east of Akyab, crossing the 1700 m (5600 ft) Arakan Yoma mountain range to reach the coast at Taungup, then Akyab itself. Ordering the troops in the Donbaik and Rathedaung bunkers to hold out at all costs, Koga sent columns swinging north-east and then west, crossing jungle ridges thought impassable by Lloyd, to hit the British both from behind and from their left flank. On April 5, the Japanese overran 6th Infantry Brigade headquarters. By May 14, the 14th Division was back where it had started from eight months earlier.

JUNGLE BATTLEGROUND Steep ridges and thick undergrowth were as much a hindrance to movement in Burma as enemy positions. One solution was small-scale air-supplied operations such as those of the Chindits. Another was the construction of all-weather roads.

PROUD TO BE IN THE FORGOTTEN ARMY

The first problem faced by Slim and Mountbatten in 1943 was to persuade the newly created Fourteenth Army to put the sorry history of the recent past behind them, and to convince them that they were capable of beating the Japanese at their own game.

Neither man tried to hide the difficulties; what they sought to do was to give Allied troops a renewed sense of confidence and purpose. This could not be done by talking. It was clear that to face and overcome such a formidable enemy the troops needed better training and commanders at all levels who could inspire confidence. The third element was to introduce aggressive jungle patrolling.

In this way Slim demonstrated that neither the jungle nor the Japanese were to be feared. Operations no longer stopped with the onset of the monsoon and, if units were cut off by Japanese infiltration, they would continue to operate supplied by air.

An important subsidiary role was played by two journalists from London: Mountbatten's press adviser, Charles Eade of the *Sunday Dispatch*, who organised the forces' programme on All India Radio, and Frank Owen of the *Evening Standard*, who started the forces' own newspaper, *SEAC*, in January 1944. Soon it became a matter of pride to belong to the 'Forgotten Army'.

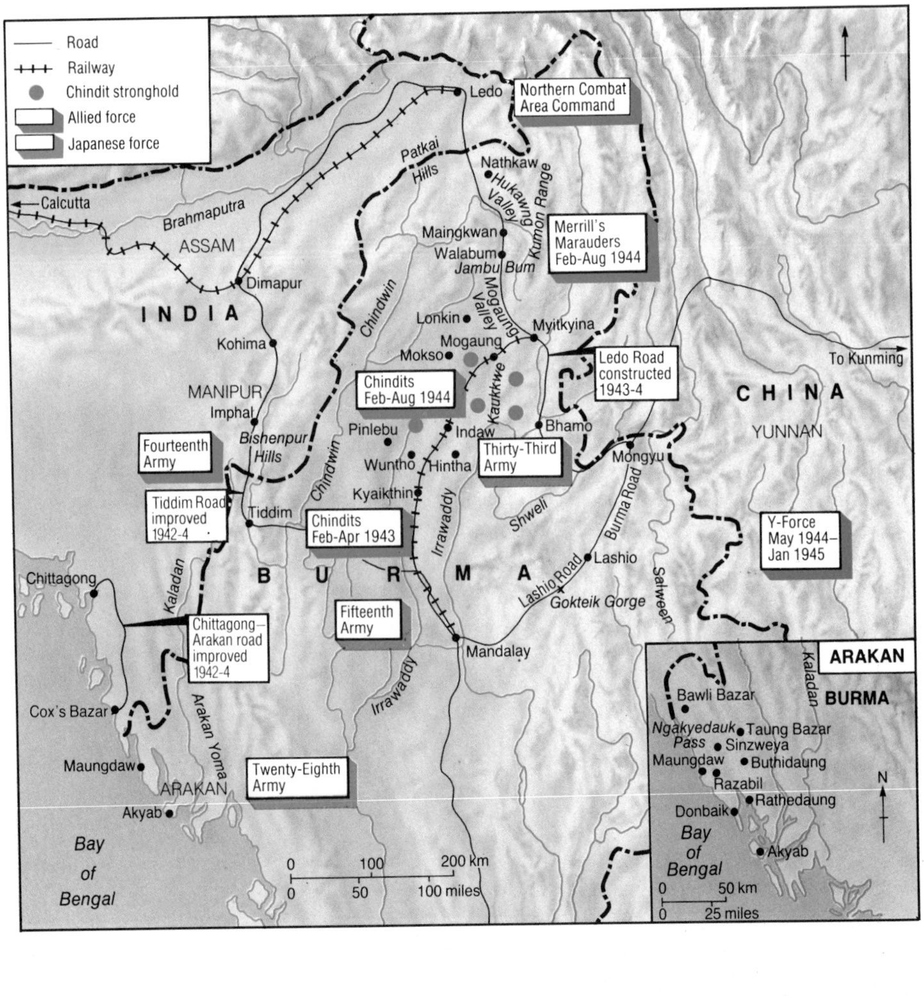

THE INVISIBLE ENEMY

For every Allied soldier wounded in the struggle for Burma in 1943, 120 fell sick. The annual malaria rate alone that year was a staggering 84 per cent of total manpower.

One weapon in the health war was science. Mepacrine tablets revolutionised the battle against malaria, liquid dimethyl phthalate proved an effective mosquito repellent, the hitherto little known DDT a powerful insecticide, and sulpha drugs important for the treatment of dysentery. Strict health discipline was a second weapon. Slim made officers supervise the twice-daily dosage of mepacrine. Shorts were prohibited and shirt sleeves had to be rolled down at dusk.

A third weapon was the establishment of Malaria Forward Treatment Units (MFTUs), always within 24 hours' travelling time of the front line, so that men could return to the fighting within weeks rather than the months it had taken previously when they had to be evacuated to India. By 1945 there were only six men sick for every one wounded and the annual malaria rate was down to 13 per cent.

PRESSURE FOR ACTION

The whole operation had looked overambitious from the outset. It was planned originally simply as a diversion, to draw off the two Japanese battalions defending Akyab, while the British 29th Independent Brigade made a seaborne assault on the island, using landing craft and supported by the 6th Infantry Brigade, with a strengthened RAF overhead. In the event, the 29th never materialised (it had been sent to recuperate in Durban, South Africa, from operations in Madagascar); and the RAF's planes were outmatched by the Japanese.

However, General Sir Archibald Wavell, Commander in Chief India, was under pressure from Churchill for some kind of action, and he decided to go ahead with the overland part of the operation. To add to his problems, forceful demands for independence were coming from India, and some 57 British and Indian battalions were needed to quell 'demonstrations' in the eastern provinces alone. There was no question of reinforcements from Britain – men and resources would still have to come from the Indian Army, for Burma was the lowest-rated theatre of war in the Allied order of priorities.

It was a situation depressingly familiar to the browned-off men of the 'Forgotten Army', as Burma campaigners had taken to calling themselves. Bundled unceremoniously out of the country in 1942 by an enemy who displayed alarming mastery of jungle warfare, they remained embittered, distrustful of their commanders and thoroughly demoralised.

The Akyab operation, albeit a failure, forced a change of leadership. On the day 6th Brigade headquarters was overrun, Lt General Noel Irwin, commanding the Eastern Army, gave overall command of the Arakan front to Lt General William ('Uncle Bill') Slim, the man destined to turn the tide in Burma. Lloyd was sacked, to be replaced eventually by Maj General Cyril Lomax. But Slim had few immediate options. The 14th Division troops, sick and exhausted by months of jungle fighting, were about to be encircled. Slim persuaded Irwin that a strategic withdrawal was needed. The British had suffered 5057 casualties against 1775 Japanese. Morale had sunk to a new low.

NEW COMMAND

Now came a massive shakeup at the top. Within weeks, Wavell was made Viceroy of India and General Sir Claude Auchinleck became Commander in Chief India. General Sir George Giffard took over the Eastern Army from Irwin.

The Indian Army was reorganised and retrained. There was a more realistic appraisal of the problems of operating in the difficult terrain and weather conditions, where monsoons swamped the Arakan coast and swept away roads in the neighbouring Indian province of Assam. With what Slim called 'an injection of ginger', the supply of ammunition and stores to the Assam front was improved. By autumn 1943 work had started on four new all-weather roads in northern Bengal and Assam – from Chittagong into northern Arakan, from Dimapur via Kohima to Imphal, from Imphal to Tiddim, and from Ledo to the Chinese frontier.

Meanwhile, the 'Quadrant' Conference of the Allied Combined Chiefs of Staff, held in Quebec, Canada, set off an even bigger top-level reorganisation. A new South-East Asia Command (SEAC) was created, covering the entire theatre from Ceylon (now Sri Lanka) to Thailand. Vice Admiral Lord Louis Mountbatten was given command, with the American Lt General Joseph ('Vinegar Joe') Stilwell as his deputy. Eastern Army was abolished, Giffard headed a new 11th Army Group, and under him Slim was put in command of a new Fourteenth Army in Burma. Air Chief Marshal Sir Richard Peirse commanded SEAC air forces and Admiral Sir James Somerville the Eastern Fleet. Furthermore, stories about Brigadier Orde Wingate's daring Chindit operations behind Japanese lines were filtering back. Morale took an upturn.

The Japanese, facing ever-stiffening opposition in the Pacific, halted on the borders of Assam believing themselves secure.

UPHILL FIGHT **Advancing against an enemy that seemed to be almost uncannily skilled in jungle warfare, men of the Indian Army's Frontier Force Rifles push towards Taungup on the Arakan coast.**

THE SOLDIERS' SOLDIER

'Success did not inflate him, nor misfortune depress him.' That was the verdict of Auchinleck on William Joseph Slim (1891-1970), commander of Fourteenth (Burma) Army, who did so much to put heart back into Allied forces in south-east Asia and convince them that they could beat the Japanese.

By the time Slim was given command of the Burma Army he had had his fair share of both success and misfortune. In World War I he had served as a young officer at Gallipoli, and in Mesopotamia he had been wounded twice, winning the MC. He later served with the Gurkhas, and by 1940 had commanded Indian Army formations in Eritrea, Iraq, Syria and Persia (Iran). Then in March 1942 he took charge of Burcorps (Burma Corps). The task he faced was not a happy one: to cover the long retreat from Rangoon to India before the monsoon broke.

Later, in charge of the newly created Fourteenth Army from October 1943, he was to fight his way back, with the benefit of air cover and relying on air supply to provision his troops. He reached and occupied Rangoon in May 1945. In the course of this offensive the morale of the army he commanded was transformed. He established a wonderful rapport with soldiers of all races, who called him 'Uncle Bill'.

Slim was knighted by Wavell on the field of Imphal in 1944, and went on to become Commander in Chief of all Allied land forces in south-east Asia (1945-6), Chief of the Imperial General Staff (1948-52), a field marshal (in 1949), Governor General of Australia (1953-60) and a viscount (in 1960).

Chindits – lions of the jungle

Brigadier Orde Wingate believed that a small force of fast-moving guerrilla troops, operating behind enemy lines and supplied by air, could seriously hamper Japanese operations in Burma. His 3000 men were called the Chindits – from the Burmese word *chinthé*, a mythical lion.

EMERGING from the bamboo jungle in moonlight, the Chindit officer edged silently towards a village hut, grenade in hand. Outside it, four men squatted talking around a fire. Politely, in Burmese, he asked the name of the village. When they looked up, he realised that they were Japanese. And he was only a few paces from them.

Resisting, as he said later, a curious instinct to apologise for interrupting them, he pulled the safety pin from the grenade, tossed it into the fire, and ran. It had only a four-second fuse and it exploded as the Japanese sat frozen with fright and surprise, killing them all.

The officer was Major Bernard Fergusson, leading one of seven Chindit columns on a desperate venture far inside enemy-held Burma in February 1943. He told his story in a book, *Beyond the Chindwin*, written while recuperating in India a year – and many further actions – later.

Killing Japanese, spreading alarm and destruction, surprising and demoralising the enemy – Fergusson's bonfire was, on a small scale, a model of the entire Chindit operation.

Brigadier Wingate's force, officially the 77th Indian Infantry Brigade, was created early in 1943. General Sir Archibald Wavell, Commander in Chief India, had noted the success of Wingate's 'long-range penetration group' tactics in the Middle East and Ethiopia, and wanted to use them in Burma. The brigade was made up of British, Gurkha and Burmese troops, and the staff of the former Bush Warfare School near Mandalay. Wavell intended their first jungle expedition to coincide with larger-scale operations involving Chinese forces in northern Burma. However, these plans were cancelled, leaving Wingate's guerrillas all keyed up for action but with nowhere to go.

Wingate then proposed an independent raid far behind enemy lines, with supplies dropped from the air. The jungle fighting experience would be invaluable, he argued, and the action would prevent his men going off the boil. Wavell agreed.

Wingate split his force into several columns, each of about 400-500 men and accompanied by RAF radio operators. On February 13 they crossed the Chindwin river – just over the Burma-India border – south-east of Imphal (see map, p. 386). Their tasks: to attack Japanese outposts, cut railway lines and blow up bridges.

Two columns led by Lt Colonel Leigh Alexander went south to attack the Mandalay-Myitkyina railway at Kyaikthin, some 200 km (125 miles) north of Mandalay, in early March. Wingate and the other five columns would hit the same railway line between Wuntho and Indaw, farther to the north.

BONFIRE PARTY

The attacks took the Japanese by surprise, but they recovered quickly and began closing in. Many small but ferocious actions were fought. The one Fergusson described was at Hintha, about 65 km (40 miles) south of Indaw. After throwing his grenade he ran into Lieutenant Philippe Stibbé. Fergusson's account goes on: 'I told him to get in at once with the bayonet and capture that end of the village. As I spoke a man ran past me in the direction of the fire: I shot him in the side with my pistol . . .'

As Stibbé and his men reached the fire, machine guns opened up and they had to go to ground – 'though not before they had spotted several men

THE ERRATIC GENIUS

Erratic, abrasive and unpredictable Charles Orde Wingate (1903-44) certainly was. Was he also a genius? Views are still deeply divided. For some his achievements were magnified out of all proportion by the press. For Bernard Fergusson, who served with him in the first Chindit campaign, he was 'a military genius of a grandeur and stature seen not more than once or twice in a century' – though he was more critical of later operations (p. 393). The son of Plymouth Brethren parents and, though not Jewish, an ardent Zionist, Wingate first attracted the attention of his superiors in 1937-8 by organising Jewish 'special night squads' to tackle trouble-making Arab armed bands in Palestine. Wavell then appointed him to lead 'Gideon Force' in Ethiopia in 1940. Success there led only to a minor staff post; depressed and suffering from malaria, he tried to kill himself by cutting his throat in a Cairo hotel. 'You know,' he remarked to his doctor afterwards, 'I am not the only great soldier who has tried to commit suicide. There was Napoleon, for instance.' He died, by now a major general, when his aircraft crashed into the Assam jungle near Imphal.

THE WAY OF A CHINDIT

Spending day after day in dense, hot, wet jungle, life as a Chindit was like fighting a war submerged in a green sea. 'Sometimes the going was frightful, sometimes it was very bad, and occasionally it was just bad.' That was how Sergeant Tony Aubrey, who was on Wingate's first expedition, summed it up.

Every Chindit had his own pet hate about jungle life in Burma – the torrential rain, the constant marching in sodden clothes, the oozing black mud, the fearsome red ants with their vicious sting, the leeches, the huge spiders. But the biggest curse was probably the dense thickets of prickly bamboo, whose leaves and stalks cut both clothes and flesh to ribbons. Many Chindits wore beards, because it was easier than carrying a shaving kit, also because a beard was the best possible camouflage for the face and – even more vital – kept out mosquitoes and ticks.

The day's march would start just before dawn and was divided into one-hour stages. Each soldier carried a pack weighing about 27 kg (60 lb), while pack mules carried supplies. Rations were slender – less than 1 kg (about 2 lb) per day. They consisted of biscuits, cheese, nuts and raisins, dates, tea, sugar, milk and chocolate. These were sometimes supplemented by rice, bananas and other fruit from friendly villagers. Some supplies were dropped by air, but this became more difficult when the columns dispersed. How the Chindits were supplied was initially a mystery to the Japanese.

JUNGLE-HARDENED WARRIORS Chindits stride along a jungle trail (top), carrying a wounded comrade. He is lucky; many wounded were left behind. (Above) No 3 Column's Major Calvert gives orders amid rubble in the Burmese town of Mogaung.

running out of the house'. Fergusson called to ask if Stibbé could go on. He replied: 'I don't think I can – it's pretty hot. I'm afraid I've been hit myself.' Fergusson returned and found him wounded in the shoulder. As they spoke, more Japanese charged in from a jungle track, flinging grenades. One landed near Fergusson, who threw himself down but was hit in the hip by a splinter. Stibbé was wounded again.

At that moment they heard a series of loud bangs: Corporal Peter Dorans, in a ditch, had rolled half a dozen grenades among the Japanese. Wrote Fergusson: 'Where I had seen them dimly in the moonlight and shadows, there was now a heap of writhing bodies into which Peter was emptying his rifle.'

However, things were not going so well for two other columns: No 2 in the south and No 4 in the north were forced to disperse and make their perilous way back as best they could. Fergusson's No 5 Column and Major Michael ('Mad Mike') Calvert's No 3 Column pressed on, crossing the Irrawaddy river with orders to blow up the Gokteik Gorge viaduct, which carried the Lashio road about 100 km (60 miles) north of Mandalay. Wingate and the rest of his force followed.

Now the columns had to cross a triangular area between the Irrawaddy and Shweli rivers. To their dismay, they found it to be open, waterless country, bisected by roads and tracks along which Japanese tanks and armoured cars patrolled. For guerrilla operations, it was hopeless.

BACK TO INDIA

On March 25, with his remaining men weak from hunger, exhaustion and disease, Wingate ordered them to try to get back to India in small independent groups. Wounded had to be abandoned. Stibbé was one of them. He later described his first night alone in the jungle: 'As it grew dark I heard a lot of rustling in the leaves near where I lay, and to my horror, I saw several large spiders about the size of my hand, crawling towards me. No doubt they were attracted by the smell of blood. It was a beastly sensation lying there unable to move while these loathsome creatures crawled nearer.' Lieutenant Ian MacHorton later recalled watching No 2 Column move off without him: 'At the moment when I gave up straining my ears for any last faint sound of my vanished comrades, my utter loneliness engulfed me.'

Wingate got back to India on April 29. Fergusson, Calvert and Dorans also made it. Stibbé was captured but survived. Of the original 3000, 2182 returned; over 800 were lost, killed, wounded or captured – many as they recrossed the Chindwin, where Japanese patrols awaited them. Only 600 were ever fit enough to fight again.

Was their sacrifice worth while? In material terms, little was achieved: some railway lines were cut and a few hundred Japanese were killed. But in terms of morale, their achievements were incalculable: in one blow they had destroyed the myth of Japanese invincibility. Battered, starving and disease-ridden they might be, but they had taken on the Japanese man for man in his own backyard, beaten him and returned to tell the tale.

The tale ran like a flame through the dispirited armies in India and blazed in headlines around the world. Heroes were sorely needed and Wingate was a hero. He was summoned by Churchill to the Quebec conference of Allied leaders in August and won approval for an expanded Chindit force and a more ambitious expedition in cooperation with the Chinese.

Keeping China in the game

Tying down large Japanese forces in China could divert them from India and the Pacific. But Chiang Kai-shek did not see the Japanese as his chief enemy.

THE JAPANESE had virtually eaten China, but they could not digest it. By mid-1942 they had overrun that vast country's most important areas, but did not have the manpower to control all that they had won – the coastal plains of the north and centre, the great valleys of the Yellow (Huang He) and Yangtze (Chang Jiang) rivers, and the main ports of the north (see map, p. 135). Most of the occupied area was controlled by compliant locals recruited by the Japanese, gangs of stragglers from defeated Kuomintang (Chinese Nationalist) armies and local warlords. Even so, 620 000 Japanese troops were on duty in China.

Anxious that this large Japanese force should not be freed to invade India or fight in the Pacific, America sought to keep it heavily engaged in China by supplying the Nationalist Generalissimo Chiang Kai-shek with a constant flow of money, arms, equipment – and military advice. The advice came, initially, from Maj General Joseph W. ('Vinegar Joe') Stilwell, appointed by Washington in January 1942 to head a military mission and act as Chiang's chief of staff.

CHIANG'S OBSESSION

The Japanese had driven Chiang and his followers deep into the mountainous west of China, where he had set up headquarters in Chungking (Chongqing). Although his best divisions had been destroyed by the Japanese in 1937-9, Chiang, contrary to Japanese expectations, had rejected all peace feelers. But his armies were disorganised, badly trained and ill equipped. The Japanese had taken all China's arsenals and industrial centres and, by 1942, had cut the Burma Road link to India, which could have carried vital supplies to Chiang. Furthermore, Nationalist army tactics were of the 'stand and defend' variety. Chiang's men had no capacity – or inclination – to set about reconquering their homeland.

But their greatest handicap of all was Chiang's obsession with defeating his own Communist countrymen – the Reds. He knew the Allies would, in the end, defeat Japan, and therefore saw the Reds as the greater threat. 'The Japanese are lice on the body of China,' he said, 'but Communism is a disease of the heart.' He was convinced that the Reds and Russians were plotting to seize power when the war ended, and was bent on saving his armies to fight them.

The Communists, led by Mao Tse-tung (Mao Zedong) did little to allay Chiang's fears. They, too, avoided confronting the Japanese head-on. Most of their efforts were devoted to setting up guerrilla bases behind the Japanese lines, from which they could later overthrow Chiang's Nationalist Government, and to struggling with Chiang's men for political control in the villages of occupied China. Gradually, through superior organisation, the Reds gained the upper hand.

Stilwell, overcoming Chiang's reluctance to risk his troops, persuaded him that Chinese forces could reconquer northern and western Burma, enabling a new road link into India to be built, along which supplies could come. The fighting would be undertaken by 30 Chinese divisions from Yunnan (reorganised and retrained by American advisers there), plus a new Chinese Army in India formed from survivors of the fall of Burma and fresh troops flown over from China. At the same time a British force would advance from India into Arakan and on into southern and central Burma. Work on the new road began at Ledo in Assam in December 1942. It was to run south to join the old Burma Road (see box, *The Triumph of 'Stilwell's Folly'*, p. 403).

FIRST BOMBS ON JAPAN

Meanwhile, on April 18, 1942, the unthinkable happened in Japan: bombs fell on Tokyo. It was the morale-shaking event that the Japanese High Command secretly dreaded – and the blow had come from an unexpected quarter. As the Japanese saw it, the threat of air attack on their homeland lay in western China, where Chennault's 'Flying Tigers' had been operating since December 1941. Where Chennault's fighter planes could go, bombers could follow.

In fact the attack was made by bombers operating from the American carrier *Hornet*. It was led by Lt Colonel James Doolittle, who had planned to land on Nationalist-held airfields on the Chinese mainland just north of Formosa (Taiwan). They did not, but the Japanese saw the danger and sent seven divisions to strike into the area. Brushing aside Nationalist resistance, they destroyed the airfields.

Soon afterwards Tokyo suspended active operations in China and withdrew men to provide reinforcements for the Pacific theatre. Even so, over half a million Japanese troops were still in China in 1945. Despite Chiang Kai-shek's reluctance, the Allied strategy had worked.

FLYING 'THE HUMP'

When the Japanese cut the Burma Road in April 1942, China's overland supply route disappeared. The only way its armies could be supplied was by air. The US Tenth Air Force quickly established a base at Chabua, in Assam, and one of the most spectacular airlifts of the war began – flying over the flank of the Himalayas or, as the pilots called it, flying 'the Hump'. Some of the mountains were over 6000 m (20 000 ft) high, but they were not the only obstacle. Japanese fighters patrolled from northern Burma, so the route had to avoid them – over south-eastern Tibet into western Yunnan, landing at Kunming.

Air supplies to China increased from 3700 tonnes in all of 1942 to nearly 35 000 tonnes in the month of October 1944. Measured against China's total needs, these amounts were small – but vital. They enabled the successors to the 'Flying Tigers', Chennault's US China Air Task Force and later his US Fourteenth Air Force, to extend their operations over Chinese air space, making Japan's hold on China all the more difficult to maintain.

THE 'FLYING TIGERS' This group of about 90 American pilots, released or retired from the US Army, Navy and Marines before the war, fought as mercenaries for China in the Sino-Japanese War. They earned US$600 a month plus a US$500 bonus for every Japanese plane they shot down. Their leader, once an obscure, retired US Army Air Corps captain, was Colonel Claire Lee Chennault (1890-1958). He drilled his men endlessly and devised the brilliant tactics that enabled the obsolescent Curtiss P-40B fighters – despite poor manoeuvrability, limited range and inadequate gunsights – to destroy nearly 300 Japanese aircraft between December 20, 1941, and July 4, 1942, when they became part of the US China Air Task Force. American ground crews (right) serviced the planes, which had vicious looking sharks' teeth painted on them (below).

Arakan avenged

The Allies' second thrust into the Arakan region of Burma happened to coincide with a ferocious Japanese offensive. It ended with the Japanese out-fought and out-thought; their myth of invincibility was finally destroyed.

COOKS, MULE HANDLERS, clerks and an assortment of orderly room men crouched anxiously behind a high bank above a dried-up riverbed, or *nullah*. The Japanese were making savage night attacks on the 7th Indian Division's 'Admin Box' – its large administration and supply base in the Arakan region of Burma – and all hands were in the makeshift defence line. Ears straining, Regimental Sergeant Major Jim Maloney of the West Yorkshire Regiment suddenly heard faint footsteps – then saw in the bright moonlight a party of Japanese moving up along the *nullah*.

Whispered instructions told his men not to fire until ordered. The Japanese, some 100 of them, came trudging on, completely unaware. Maloney waited until they were in plain view below, then . . . 'Stand fast the 14th of Foot!' he bellowed, using the regiment's old name. 'Fire!'

The West Yorkshires let go with everything they had – rifles, machine guns and grenades – killing many of the enemy immediately. Others died as they struggled up the steep opposite bank. The Japanese lost 60 men, but columns continued to appear along the *nullah* for several days afterwards, suffering losses so severe that the West Yorkshires named the spot 'Blood Nullah'. The Japanese, it transpired, had decided to use the *nullah* as a rendezvous point and stuck to the fixed plan despite the consequences.

The action took place early in February 1944, and was typical of the confused fighting that broke out when the second British thrust into Arakan ran into a serious problem. Coinciding with their thrust, the Japanese had launched an offensive – a prelude to their major assault into Assam.

PLANS AWRY

Allied plans for operations in Burma had already been cut back because of needs in Europe. The cuts meant that opening land links with China and increasing air supplies from Burma to China would have to wait. This in turn gave the Chinese leader Chiang Kai-shek an excuse to renege on his promise to attack into north-east Burma from Yunnan province.

South-East Asia Command (SEAC) nevertheless decided on an advance into Arakan. Three Chinese divisions, under American Lt General Joseph ('Vinegar Joe') Stilwell and supported by the Chindits, would take the key Japanese stronghold and airfield of Myitkyina in northern Burma. At the same time, in Arakan, the three Fourteenth Army divisions comprising XV Corps would make a three-pronged advance (see map, p. 386).

While the 5th Indian Division fought its way down the western side of the Mayu hills to take Maungdaw and nearby Razabil, the 7th Indian Division would attack down the eastern side of the range to take Buthidaung. The 81st West African Division would guard against Japanese 'hooks' from their left by pushing south down the Kaladan river valley, farther east. The 5th and 7th Divisions would be connected by a supply road built over the east-to-west Ngakyedauk Pass, in the Mayu hills near Sinzweya, about 13 km (8 miles) north of the Tunnels Road between Maungdaw and Buthidaung. Supplied through Maungdaw, they could then advance south on Akyab (now Sittwe) and its island airfields.

It was all murderously difficult terrain – a mixture of razor-sharp, jungle-clad ridges, leech-infested creeks and streams, malarial swamps and open paddy fields. The Ngakyedauk Pass – soon 'Okeydoke Pass' to the British troops – rose and fell 300 m (1000 ft) within 5 km (3 miles).

EERIE ADVANCE

Operations got under way in the closing days of 1943, and the 2nd West Yorkshires – part of Maj General Harold Briggs' 5th Indian Division – met little resistance in their advance on Maungdaw. C Company under Major John Roche came under some heavy but inaccurate mortar fire, then crossed open paddy fields unopposed in brilliant moonlight to enter the silent town – devastated in previous fighting – on the night of January 8/9, 1944. It was eerie, heart-stopping stuff, and Roche wrote feelingly about it later:

'When the expected volley failed to materialise, the men crept stealthily forward until some noise brought them to a standstill. The grotesque shadows cast by the moon played fantastic tricks, and many a man lunged with his bayonet at a grinning Japanese face only to find that it was no more than a small bush, or a bundle of straw caught in the barbed wire.'

The enemy had fled Maungdaw – but Razabil was altogether different. The Japanese had turned it into an almost indestructible fortress, tunnelling bunkers, storerooms and living quarters 9 m (30 ft) underground to create a 'keep' which the British ruefully dubbed 'the Tortoise'. The West Yorkshires were among many who failed to break in. Roche's company alone suffered 20 killed and 20 wounded extricating itself, as the defenders made ferocious counterattacks. Even a full-scale assault mounted on January 26, with artillery, Lee-Grant tanks of the 25th Dragoons and a hammering from bombers, failed. Lt General Philip Christison, commanding XV Corps, opted to switch his main attack to the 7th Division's front. Razabil held out until March 12.

MESSERVY'S BOX

To aid Maj General Frank Messervy's 7th Indian Division, Christison sent 9th Brigade from Briggs' Division east over the Okeydoke Pass. Included were three companies of the West Yorkshires, most of the 25th Dragoons and their tanks, and a regiment of medium artillery. They reached Messervy's Admin Box at Sinzweya in the first days of February. The Box was a cup-shaped area of about 1 km^2 (just under $\frac{1}{2}$ square mile), made up of dried paddy fields, wooded hillocks and streams, bounded by high, jungle-clad hills. In it were about 8000 assorted troops maintained by air-dropped supplies.

Messervy had set up his own headquarters about 6 km (4 miles) north-east of Sinzweya. All seemed set for the attack towards Buthidaung, to start on February 8. Instead, Messervy's force found itself fighting for its life; the Japanese had struck first, with their usual ferocity.

HA-GO IS GO

Lt General Tadashi Hanaya, commanding the Japanese army in Arakan, had planned a bold and ambitious counteroffensive, code-named *Ha-go* ('Operation Z'), designed to smash into Messervy's left flank and annihilate both the 7th and 5th Indian Divisions, opening the way north. This in turn would draw Allied reserves down into Arakan at the very time when a large Japanese force was due to strike at Imphal, the major SEAC forward base.

Hanaya launched *Ha-go* on February 4. A column of his 55th Division, under Maj General Shozo Sakurai, slipped north on the east side of the Kalapanzin river, heading for the Taung Bazar river crossing. From Taung, a battalion headed by Colonel Masao Kubo marched over the precipitous Mayu Range, attempting to cut 5th Division's supply road. A third – and the most formidable – column, 5000 strong and led by the aggressive Colonel S. Tanahashi, struck south-west from Taung to hit Messervy's Admin Box from behind and cut Okeydoke Pass, aiming to trap all 5th Division troops east of the Mayu hills.

Ha-go caused tremendous disruption, and many bitter actions were fought, with heavy losses on both sides. But Hanaya had too few men (7000 against two divisions) and was over-confident, anticipating another British rout and relying on captured food and transport to sustain his men. Also he lacked air power: 65 of his 100 planes were destroyed in 13 days, the new 'Tojo' fighters outmatched by the RAF Spitfires.

Amazingly, Kubo's troops fought their way to the coast, and even cut the road before being annihilated to a man. Tanahashi overran Messervy's headquarters (the general escaped), cut the Okeydoke Pass and came desperately close to taking the Admin Box.

On the night of February 7/8, a Japanese raiding

ENTER THE SPITFIRES!

The bomber assault on Razabil early in 1944 had been made possible by a dramatic reversal of air supremacy in Burma. Japanese pilots had spent the previous months attacking airfields in Assam, shooting down Allied supply planes, strafing shipping and even bombing Calcutta and Chittagong. Outdated British Hurricanes had lost heavily trying to stop them. Then, on the last day of 1943, newly arrived RAF Spitfires destroyed 13 Japanese bombers and fighters. They easily outperformed enemy Zero and 'Oscar' fighters and a fortnight later, British and Indian troops around Maungdaw had their spirits lifted as they saw 16 Japanese planes shot down. It spelt the end of Japanese air supremacy in the area. The Allies were able to protect their 80 or more transport aircraft whose role in dropping supplies was crucial.

SLOW TRAIN By taking Buthidaung, the Allies controlled the only all-weather road in Arakan. Supplies could be taken east on it through the two tunnels under the Mayu hills.

CLAWING BACK Allied tanks blaze away near the top of Okeydoke (Ngakyedauk) Pass to root out concealed Japanese who had breached the Allied supply route over the ridge and threatened to cut off all the troops east of the Mayu hills.

party crept in along a ravine and fell upon the medical unit's main dressing station. When the enraged West Yorkshires drove them out in the morning, they found that more than 50 patients and staff had been butchered. It was the next night that Maloney's massacre at Blood Nullah took place. The items of loot and British rations found on the dead Japanese were proof that these were the men who had committed the atrocity at the dressing station.

On February 24, XV Corps' 123rd Brigade reopened Okeydoke Pass from the west and relieved the beleaguered Box. General Briggs, riding in on a tank, brought bottles of Scotch whisky as presents for the garrison. The 26th Indian Division was almost through from the north. Hanaya called off *Ha-go* the same day. Denied swift success, his columns had run out of supplies and were rapidly running out of men. In the battle for the Box and the pass they had lost about 5600, against XV Corps' losses of 3506. Buthidaung fell to the British on March 11 – the day before Razabil. It was virtually all over in Arakan, but for the victorious 5th and 7th Indian Divisions, another struggle lay ahead at Imphal.

Chindits, Marauders – and Vinegar Joe

Three highly individual Allied forces fought to take Myitkyina – Stilwell's Chinese, Wingate's Chindits and Merrill's Marauders. They were tested almost to destruction, and on a black day for the Chindits Wingate's plane crashed.

FOR 'VINEGAR JOE' – American Lt General Joseph W. Stilwell – the advance on Myitkyina was a headache before it began. The town was the key Japanese stronghold and air base in northern Burma, and it lay square on the middle of the route planned for the Ledo Road (see map, p. 386). Stilwell was committed to pushing through this road to carry supplies from India to Chiang Kai-shek's army in western China. In the British view, Myitkyina was not crucial to defeating the Japanese in Burma, but Stilwell saw it as a target of major importance.

In late February 1943 his road-builders got stuck on the India-Burma border through a shortage of engineers and equipment. And in early March the Japanese 18th Division seized the whole Hukawng Valley north-west of Myitkyina and struck up towards the head of the road. Stilwell had to send in part of his Chinese 38th Division, which stopped them at Nathkaw village, about 80 km (50 miles) south of the road's starting point at Ledo (now Likhapani).

The Japanese pulled back and for months there was a stalemate. Then, in October, the 38th Division began probing down the rugged Refugee Trail once again. New drafts of American engineers pushed the road along behind them. There was little resistance, and optimism grew. But on November 3, the Japanese 18th Division sprang a surprise counterattack. Three Chinese battalions were cut off and surrounded.

Suddenly, Stilwell arrived at the Hukawng Valley in person, having flown from Delhi. Wearing his battered campaign hat and carrying a carbine, he moved among the 38th Division's front-line men, ignoring snipers' bullets, cajoling, bullying and praising the Chinese into aggressive action. As December ended, the 38th broke through to two of the besieged battalions and the Chinese 22nd Division relieved the third.

But as soon as Stilwell left the area, there was stalemate again. He returned late in February 1944 with a new card – an American independent infantry unit soon to earn renown as 'Merrill's Marauders' after their leader, Brig General Frank D. Merrill. They were hardened Pacific war veterans and, though only 3000 strong, made an instant impact. In a series of actions during March, the Chinese battled down the Hukawng Valley defeating Lt General Shinchi Tanaka's 18th Division at Maingkwan, Walawbum and Jambu Bum, while the Marauders thrust in flanking actions deep behind the enemy lines.

Elated, Stilwell headed for Myitkyina with the Marauders and part of the Chinese 30th Division – about 7000 men. They struck east from the Mogaung Valley, crossed the 1800 m (6000 ft) Kumon mountains by trails known only to their Kachin guides, then moved down the Irrawaddy Valley and seized Myitkyina airfield on May 17. However, Myitkyina town was not to fall as easily, and events elsewhere were threatening the air supplies which kept Stilwell going. The Japanese had struck into the Manipur district of Assam and were besieging Imphal and Kohima.

CHINDITS HIT TROUBLE

Thanks to the success of Orde Wingate's first Chindit expedition his stock stood high with Churchill. He had been promoted to major general and the Chindits were six brigades (23 000 men) strong when he was briefed to support Stilwell's drive on Myitkyina. He also had a 'private air force', for he was allocated the use of the USAAF No 1 Air Commando – 25 transport planes, 12 medium bombers, 30 fighter-bombers, 100 light planes and 225 gliders under Colonel Philip C. Cochran. His orders were to draw off enemy forces, prevent reinforcements reaching them and create havoc behind the Japanese 18th Division south-west of Myitkyina.

Wingate decided to send three brigades south to establish a series of air-supplied permanent 'strongholds'. Brigadier Bernard Fergusson would lead his 16th Brigade of 3900 men on a tough, six-week march of nearly 400 km (250 miles) due south from Ledo, to set up a stronghold code-named 'Aberdeen'. From there he would attack the key communications centre of Indaw some 80 km (50 miles) farther south. The 77th and 111th Brigades would be flown by glider to make 'Broadway' stronghold, 80 km east of 'Aberdeen', and strongholds at 'Piccadilly' and 'Chowringhee' still farther south.

Fergusson set out on February 5, 1944. Simply reaching the Chindwin river – not even their halfway point – proved an appalling, 23 day struggle. He wrote later: 'The rain was torrential

A DASH OF VINEGAR

'Vinegar Joe' they called Joseph W. Stilwell (1883-1946), and the nickname was apt. During his career as Chief of Staff to the Chinese leader Chiang Kai-shek from March 1942, and as deputy to Vice Admiral Lord Louis Mountbatten – Supreme Allied Commander South-East Asia from August 1943 – the tetchy, quick-tempered Stilwell managed to quarrel with almost everybody. Most importantly, he fell out with Chiang. A brilliant commander in the field, he was an old China hand, fluent in the language. Angry at the corruption and incompetence he found in Chiang's regime, he demanded that those responsible be purged and that Chiang should stop fighting the Communists and join with Mao to fight the Japanese.

Chiang had no intention of complying, and requested Stilwell's recall – to which Roosevelt finally agreed in October 1944. As a belated gesture, Chiang renamed the completed Ledo Road the 'Stilwell Road'.

SWEET AND SOUR 'Vinegar Joe' in a rare good mood during a tour of the Chinese front line.

WHAT DID THE CHINDITS ACHIEVE?

The heavy losses of the first Chindit expedition (p. 388) left Wingate's immediate superiors unenthusiastic about further forays. Churchill, however, was deeply impressed by Wingate's daring, innovative ideas and charismatic personality, and by the propaganda value and morale-boosting effect of the operation on the shattered veterans of the Burma rout. His approval brought Wingate promotion and a greatly enlarged force.

Just as impressed were the Japanese, who had thought the jungle-clad ridges and mountains of northern Burma to be impenetrable and a natural barrier to the invasion of India. The Chindits having proved them wrong, they decided to mount the offensive into Assam that ended at Imphal and Kohima (p. 396).

By now, Wingate's second, larger-scale incursion was under way – and again in trouble. His decision to set up fortified strongholds, instead of remaining mobile, invited attacks by the Japanese. But as a result many Japanese units were destroyed and others were prevented from reinforcing those in Assam.

After Wingate's death, Stilwell badly misused the exhausted Chindits as assault troops at Mogaung, but the survivors made significant contributions to the eventual capture of Myitkyina. However, there was criticism that the expedition tied up vital resources of manpower and aircraft for little gain and more fearful losses.

Perhaps the final word on Wingate should rest with a Japanese officer who wrote in his diary: 'Wingate . . . planted himself centre stage and conducted on all fronts with his baton, which he called the Chindits. He reduced the Japanese power to wage war on the four Burma fronts and so fatally affected the balance.'

JUNGLE SHARPSHOOTER A Chinese marksman serving with Stilwell trains his sights on a jungle trail, alert for Japanese snipers who may have penetrated the lines.

AMERICAN PATROL A platoon of Merrill's Marauders cross the Chindwin river to strike at the Japanese behind their lines during Stilwell's Hukawng Valley offensive.

and almost continuous; the gradients were often one in two . . . Many mule loads had to be carried by hand up steep slopes, and the path had to be rebuilt two or three times.'

On March 5, half an hour before the 77th Brigade of Michael ('Mad Mike') Calvert was due to begin the glider flight, last-minute aerial photos revealed that the landing area at 'Piccadilly' was covered with felled trees. The whole brigade made for 'Broadway', with each Dakota towplane pulling two gliders – much against the pilots' advice. Only 35 out 61 gliders reached 'Broadway'. Some broke their tow ropes as the Dakotas, engines overheating, struggled over the high mountains. Others missed the target zone. Gliders and Dakotas crashed over a wide area, killing or injuring many of their occupants.

Those that reached 'Broadway' landed unopposed. The next night 55 gliders towed singly landed safely. By March 11, the 77th and half Brigadier William ('Joe') Lentaigne's 111th had arrived and Fergusson was nearing 'Aberdeen'. Two days later, Wingate had 9000 men in position. Calvert's troops soon established another stronghold, code-named 'White City', astride the Mandalay-Myitkyina railway, about 32 km (20 miles) south-east of 'Aberdeen'.

WINGATE KILLED

Wingate was pressing Fergusson to take Indaw quickly, on the night of March 24/25, despite the men's exhaustion after 50 days on the march. On March 24 Wingate paid them a flying visit to see how the plan was progressing. It was the 26th when Fergusson's troops eventually attacked Indaw with great persistence and gallantry – only to be beaten back by the well-prepared defenders.

After four days, Fergusson had to abandon Wingate's plan and pull back. But by this time Wingate was dead. On the evening of the very day he had visited Fergusson, his American B-25 Mitchell bomber crashed into the westward slopes of the Bishenpur Hills south-west of Imphal. Lentaigne, promoted major general, became commander of the Chindits on March 27. That same day, the Japanese attacked 'Broadway', and were driven back only after three days' heavy fighting. On the night of April 6/7 they attacked 'White City' with an artillery bombardment and three infantry battalions.

Lt General Masakuzu Kawabe, commanding the Japanese Burma Area Army, had taken two weeks to react to the glider landings. However, by April 4 he had sent the 24th Independent Mixed Brigade (six battalions) and the 4th Infantry Regiment (four battalions) under Maj General Yoshihide Hayashi into the Indaw area. Another two battalions were sent to attack 'Broadway' and other Chindit guerrillas blocking the Bhamo-Myitkyina road.

When Hayashi began his ten-day assault on 'White City', there were ten British, Gurkha and West African battalions from a mixture of brigades well dug in behind wire there, with artillery, mortars, machine guns – and limitless ammunition available by airdrop. On the 11th day, Calvert counterattacked with four battalions, getting behind the Japanese and hitting them from the rear, to pin them against the stronghold's wire. Hayashi himself died in a last fanatical *banzai* charge, and altogether the Japanese lost 700 out of their 6600 men trying to take 'White City'. The remnants of the Japanese forces escaped south beyond Indaw. Kawabe then diverted Lt General K. Takeda's 53rd Division to help Tanaka's hard-pressed 18th Division.

UNDER STILWELL'S COMMAND

Meanwhile, the monsoon clouds were building, hampering air-supply operations, so Lentaigne decided to evacuate 'White City' and 'Broadway', which were booby-trapped and abandoned. Fergusson's totally exhausted men were flown out to India. Calvert and Lt Colonel John Masters (who had taken over the 111th Brigade when Lentaigne was promoted) moved their brigades north, the whole Chindit force coming under Stilwell's command on May 16.

Masters was ordered to set up a stronghold and airstrip code-named 'Blackpool', to block the railway valley about 32 km (20 miles) south-east of Mogaung. He had barely begun work when the whole Japanese 53rd Division (having rushed through empty 'Broadway' and 'White City') came up the valley and hit him. Aided by accurate air strikes against the Japanese, the 111th held out for five days. On May 25, almost out of food and ammunition, Masters withdrew through rain and mud, taking with him 100 wounded. Two days later they reached safety at Mokso, 40 km (25 miles) west.

Calvert was next ordered to take Mogaung – by now strongly defended by one of Takeda's regiments. The 77th was down to 2000 men, owing to casualties, disease and reinforcing other

THE SUPPLY WAR

Extraordinary feats of engineering, organisation and sheer endurance sustained the Allied forces in Burma and China. Air transport was the key. It was almost suicidally dangerous in the period of the airlift over 'the Hump', when Japan ruled the Burma skies. It became a sophisticated, large-scale operation as British and American fighters gained the upper hand in 1943-4.

Fighting men on the ground could be supported on demand by pinpoint accurate airdrops and air strikes, enabling them to operate even when cut off by the Japanese. The Chindit forays deep into enemy territory were possible only with airdrops. Between 1943 and 1945 Allied planes in Burma airlifted 650 000 tonnes of supplies, flew in 315 000 men and flew out 110 000 sick and wounded.

The port facilities of Calcutta and Chittagong were entirely rebuilt and enlarged, and the fuel supply into Burma was improved by laying a new pipeline from Bombay to connect at Bhusawal, 440 km (275 miles) to the north-east, with the railway running to Allahabad and east through Assam. By October 1944, the railway was carrying 4400 tonnes of supplies a day, against its prewar capacity of 600 tonnes. The Ledo Road (later named Stilwell Road) was a major triumph for American engineers, built under incredibly arduous conditions.

brigades. Attacking in lashing monsoon rain, without tank or artillery support, they fought for three weeks and suffered 1000 casualties (plus many more from sickness) before managing to capture the town on June 26 with help from Stilwell's Chinese.

By now the whole remaining Chindit force was exhausted; on July 11 a doctor reported that almost every officer and man in the 77th and 111th was worn out. Other brigades were in little better shape. Average weight loss was 19 kg (42 lb) and all had suffered or were suffering from malaria.

Stilwell rejected all requests that they be withdrawn until Mountbatten told him: 'If they are not soon relieved, we may both be faced with the . . . accusation of keeping men in battle who are unable to defend themselves.' Even then Vinegar Joe took the remaining fit men of the 111th, only a company strong, and put them on garrison duties. The rest began flying out to India; by August 27 all had left. The second Chindit operation was over. In all they had lost 5000 killed, wounded or missing, 3800 of them after Wingate's death, when Stilwell ruthlessly used the lightly armed Chindits as assault troops against heavily defended positions – a role for which they were neither trained nor intended.

MARAUDERS' ORDEAL

Vinegar Joe was equally ruthless with his American guerrillas – Merrill's Marauders. By the time Myitkyina airfield had been taken, they were, like the Chindits, exhausted and sick; Merrill himself had suffered a debilitating heart attack in one of their earlier hectic actions and they were down to less than 1500 of their original 3000 men. Moreover, they thought they were going home, having been promised that they would fight in Burma for only three months. Instead, Stilwell threw them at Myitkyina on May 17 in an attack which rapidly became a fiasco.

Unknown to Stilwell and his American local commander, Brig General Haydon L. Boatner, the Japanese still had supply lines from Bhamo, and by early June had strengthened the Myitkyina garrison to 3500 men; however, Boatner had three Chinese divisions and the Marauders – outnumbering the Japanese by about ten to one. Despite this, the Marauders' initial attacks were driven back. Artillery was thrown in to help – and still the attacks were repulsed. And the Marauders' morale suddenly collapsed. They had been jungle fighting and marching since March and they could do no more. Men were falling asleep firing their weapons and hardly one could walk normally for fatigue and skin diseases.

The Japanese held out in Myitkyina through a rain-soaked, mud-clogged, summer-long siege. But when Allied forces had gradually cut off all Japanese supply lines, the town finally fell on August 3. The Ledo Road builders and 'Hump' supply planes moved in immediately. But the cost had been high on both sides: about 3000 Japanese died. The Allies lost 1244 killed and 4140 wounded; 188 Chinese and 980 Americans were evacuated sick, including 570 Marauders.

Imphal and Kohima – the jungle Stalingrad

Cocky, irascible Lt General Renya Mutaguchi reckoned that his Fifteenth Army would overrun the main Allied forward base at Imphal, in north-east India, within a month . . . and then the doorway to the jewel of the British Empire would stand open to the Japanese troops. Mutaguchi was disastrously wrong.

THE JAPANESE SAW IT as a fight to the death. One British officer likened it to a game: 'It was the nearest thing to a snowball fight that could be imagined. The air became thick with grenades, both theirs and ours, and we were all scurrying about, trying to avoid them as they burst.' Major Mike Lowry, of the 1st Battalion The Queen's Own Royal (West Surrey) Regiment was describing his company's attack on a Japanese hilltop bunker outside Kohima, to the north of Imphal. But, like all the numerous actions in what was one of World War II's epic battles, it was far from being a game. A Japanese order of the day, issued at the climax of the struggle, was chillingly to the point: 'You will fight to the death,' the troops were told. 'When you are killed you will fight on with your spirit.'

GATEWAY TO INDIA

Imphal was the chief town of the isolated Indian border district (now state) of Manipur, and lay only 60 km (38 miles) west of the Burmese border. It was a colourful sprawl of houses, bazaars and gilded temples, set about the Maharajah's palace, and with the bungalows of the European community on the outskirts. It stood at the centre of the 1800 km^2 (700 sq mile) Imphal Plain, vividly green with rice paddies during the May-October monsoon season, dun and sunbaked for the rest of the year, and surrounded by high, densely jungle-clad peaks.

One narrow road linked Imphal with the outside world; it wandered 210 km (130 miles) through the mountains, traversing the saddle ridge of Kohima – where the Deputy Commissioner's bungalow stood – before continuing to the railhead at Dimapur. Two other tracks, little more than bridlepaths, also gave access, linking villages and crossing torrents by rope-and-plank bridges. One ran west to the lowland town of Silchar, 115 km (70 miles) away; the other meandered south-east to the Burmese border and beyond, to the 450 m (500 yd) wide unbridged Chindwin river.

Even late in 1941, the war seemed a long way off to the people of Imphal. Then, starting in January 1942, there came pouring along little-used mountain tracks hundreds of thousands of refugees – Indians, Anglo-Indians, Anglo-Burmese and Europeans – closely followed by the defeated Burma Corps, tattered, emaciated, dispirited, but still bearing arms and ready to fight the Japanese who, they imagined, were close behind. But the Japanese had overstretched their supply lines and halted to regroup at the Chindwin. This, for the next 18 months, became virtually the boundary between the British and Japanese forces.

Far from accepting defeat, however, Lt General William Slim, commanding Burcorps (Burma Corps), was already resolved to retake Burma, and used the lull in fighting to make Imphal his springboard for the task. Thousands of labourers were recruited to improve roads enough to be used not only by trucks but also by tanks. Airfields, hospitals, workshops and other facilities were built and great dumps of food, fuel and ammunition were stockpiled.

In charge of the build-up was Lt General Geoffrey Scoones, who was also responsible for the 320 km (200 mile) wide Assam Front, which he held with three divisions. One of these, the 17th Indian Division, in the jungle-clad hills to the south, had occasional savage brushes with the Japanese 33rd Division, old adversaries from the Burma retreat.

The Japanese high command was well aware of Slim's preparations but, deeply committed elsewhere, it was not until July 1943 that it gave outline approval for an operation, *U-go* ('Operation C') – the taking of Imphal, which could open a way to India itself. Lt General Renya Mutaguchi, commander of Fifteenth Army, began making plans. Little impressed by the performance of British and Indian troops so far, he reckoned that three divisions would be enough to do the job. Lt General Mazakuza Kawabe, commanding the Japanese armies in Burma, finally approved Mutaguchi's plan in January 1944, with a start date in the first week of March. But he stipulated that *U-go* should be coordinated with *Ha-go*, an attack on the XV Indian Corps in Arakan, timed for a month earlier and designed to draw off Slim's reserves.

With a maximum of ostentation, *Ha-go* was mounted on February 4, but Slim was not deceived. Though Mutaguchi's build-up for the assault on Imphal was being carried out with the utmost secrecy, RAF reconnaissance planes had already spotted telltale signs – roads being built and bridges repaired behind the Japanese lines. British patrols across the Chindwin were bringing back evidence, taken from captured sentries and the like, of fresh Japanese units in the area.

U-GO LAUNCHED

On the night of March 7/8 Mutaguchi – 'aided by the gods and inspired by the Emperor', and employing an ingenious bridge of boats that were swung out on the current across the Chindwin – began moving 100 000 men, with armour and artillery, over the river. He knew that Imphal must be taken quickly; once committed, his troops could depend on no more than the three or four weeks' supplies they could carry with them. And there was also the coming May monsoon to consider: jungle warfare would then become well-nigh impossible.

Straightaway he sent two columns of his 33rd Division into the hills south of Imphal, hoping to cut off their old enemy, the 17th Indian Division, from the town and then annihilate it. So swift was the thrust that he almost succeeded – and would have done so had Scoones not sent two brigades of precious reserves into the fray. Even so, it took the 17th three weeks and 1200 casualties to extricate itself in a fighting retreat to the Imphal Plain.

Parallel with this attack, Mutaguchi launched another two-pronged assault upon the 20th Indian Division (which like all Indian Army divisions was one-third British), dug in on the hills above Palel, a vital all-weather airfield south-east of Imphal. Here the only tank battles of the campaign took place. Both sides fought like tigers, but the heavy Lee-Grant tanks and the infantry together managed to hold the Japanese on the Shenam Saddle, the last ridge before the Imphal Plain.

Despite these successes, Slim was disturbed by the speed of the Japanese attack, especially when

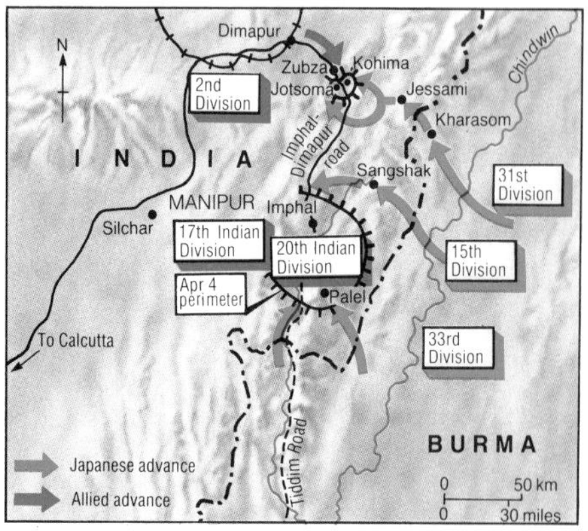

BRITISH BESIEGED The Japanese planned to take the communication centres of Imphal and Kohima and end the build-up being prepared to retake Burma. The British, rapidly penned in, depended on supplies through Imphal's airfields and on help coming to Kohima from the north-west.

Kohima, about 100 km (60 miles) to the north, was isolated on March 29 by a Japanese thrust that cut across the Imphal-Kohima road – and a brigade sent to relieve it was cut off in turn. Imphal was effectively besieged, even though the Silchar track remained open.

What made the fighting so desperate was that both sides had to win. The Japanese Fifteenth Army was doomed if it could not capture supplies at Imphal – and the whole future of Nippon in Asia hung in the balance. The British knew that if they did not halt the Japanese here, the way into India lay open – and a not inconsiderable section of the populace there might be only too ready to welcome the new conquerors.

Vice Admiral Lord Louis Mountbatten, overall Allied commander in south-east Asia, reacted with his usual decisiveness. He organised an enormous airlift of RAF and USAAF transport planes to fly two divisions – the victorious 5th and 7th Indian – from Arakan north to Imphal. Some of these troops had to break off fighting in Arakan one afternoon, load their equipment onto aircraft and go into action again next morning without having the slightest idea where they were. The last of these reinforcements arrived on March 29, the day the Japanese cut the road to Kohima.

FIVE VCs

The steep jungles about Imphal, during the next 86 days, were the scene of some of the most desperate fighting of the war. There were the grand set pieces, such as that of the 50th Indian Parachute Brigade which fought a deliberate, bloody, delaying battle at Sangshak on March 21-26 before cutting its way out through the encircling Japanese. But much of it was a matter of platoon against platoon, even section against section, bumping into one another by chance in the tangled bewilderment of the forest.

Sergeant Hanson Victor Turner of the 1st West Yorkshire Regiment personally repelled five Japanese attacks with showers of hand grenades before he was killed; *Jemadar* (Lieutenant) Abdul Hafiz of the 3/9 Jat Regiment, though mortally wounded and armed only with a Bren gun, forced a company of Japanese into headlong flight. Both men were awarded the Victoria Cross; three more were to be won in the vicious little battles among the trees.

The Japanese troops fought heroically – and often suicidally – to gain ground gradually blasted clear of cover by artillery and the RAF. Their corpses lay everywhere, so many in one place that Gurkha defenders plugged their nostrils with cotton wool to try to cut out the stench.

In the end, however, it was not the courage of either side that counted, but simple logistics – the air shuttle that kept the British supplied with food, ammunition, petrol, reinforcements, even cigarettes, while Japanese reserves of everything dwindled daily. While the fighting continued, the RAF and USAAF flew 18 824 tonnes of supplies and 12 561 reinforcements into Imphal, and evacuated 13 000 casualties, as well as 43 000 non-combatants before the siege began.

INDIAN SUMMER Boulders and trees made slippery handholds for Allied troops fording the monsoon-swollen torrents that cut the muddy tracks. The troops drove the Japanese south from Kohima and freed the road to Imphal.

CRISIS AT KOHIMA

While the Imphal battle raged, an equally dangerous situation was developing at Kohima. During the night of March 15/16, Lt General Kotoku Sato's 31st Division crossed the Chindwin at Homalin and made a beeline for the strategically important little settlement garrisoned by no more than a few spare platoons from the Assam Rifles and other regiments.

Slim later admitted that he badly misjudged the Kohima situation; he quite reasonably assumed that the principal Japanese target was the vital railhead at Dimapur, farther to the north-west, and dispatched the 161st Indian Infantry Brigade – the only largish body of troops available – to cover it. Nevertheless, Colonel Hugh Richards, late of the Chindits, was appointed commander at Kohima, and companies of the Assam Regiment were ordered to make strongpoints at Kharasom and Jessami, on the track between the Chindwin and Kohima. Should the Japanese come that way, the troops were to hold out 'to the last man and the last round'.

On March 30, the Japanese did come. Captain Peter Steyn of the Assams wrote later: 'The inexperienced sepoys fought like veterans; red-hot machine-gun barrels were ripped off, regardless of burns suffered in the process.' But by the following night it was clear that the Assams would be overwhelmed. At Kharasom, Captain 'Jock' Young, unaware that the 'last man, last round' order had now been rescinded, told his men to fall back upon Kohima, while he remained fighting a lonely battle until he was killed.

MANPOWERED CROSSING Improvisation got 100 000 Japanese troops across the wide Chindwin river with its strong currents. Some hauled themselves across on rafts, using a rope an advance party had fixed.

Troops of the 2nd British Division, and of other units of the British XXXIII Corps hastily scrambled from Delhi, arrived at Dimapur. Their commander, Lt General Montagu Stopford, at once released the three battalions and a battery of mountain artillery that made up 161st Indian Infantry Brigade to help out at Kohima. Two battalions and the artillery dug in at Jotsoma, a hill village 3 km (2 miles) along the road to the west of the ridge; the third battalion, the 4th Royal West Kents, entered Kohima itself. Richards sent them to fortify a rise on the edge of town which he called Garrison Hill. Other bumps and hillocks within the defensive ring were also fortified and given names – Jail Hill, Gun Spur, Treasury Hill and so on – or simply initials, such as GPT Ridge.

Richards had done all he could, but was only too aware that even with the remnants of the Assam Regiment companies fallen back from Kharasom and Jessami, his command amounted to perhaps 1500 men, while the advancing Japanese were said to number 12 000. He could only hope that the British 2nd Division at Dimapur would send a relief force before he was overwhelmed.

SURROUNDED

The Japanese arrived at Kohima in the early hours of April 5, and took over Naga village. The next day they sprang attacks on Jail Hill, DIS and FSD, and eventually took them, but lost many men in the fighting – especially junior officers and NCOs, always to the fore in any Japanese action. The British position was grave: Kohima was now surrounded, as was the 161st Indian Brigade's position at Jotsoma. Worse, the road was blocked to both north and south, below Dimapur and above Imphal, making relief ever more difficult.

Even so on April 11 Stopford felt confident enough to send the 5th British Infantry Brigade down the road from Dimapur to attempt a rescue. It hit the first Japanese roadblock at Zubza, and was at first repulsed, but on the 14th, by sheer weight of artillery and armour, it smashed its way through to relieve Jotsoma the following day. The next task was to relieve Kohima itself, but the towering, jungle-clad saddle presented a daunting face, and the commanding officer decided to wait for reinforcements arriving on the 18th.

The delay almost proved fatal for the defenders, for on the night of the 17th Sato ordered the fiercest attack yet upon Garrison Hill. Heavy shelling was followed by victory-or-death charges that ended in savage hand-to-hand combat, illuminated by blazing buildings. The Japanese overran a number of strongpoints, including the important Kuki Piquet and FSD, but the main line held.

Daylight, however, revealed a tragic picture of trenches overflowing with Indian and British dead, and Richards knew that defeat was only hours away. But dragging reserves of strength from somewhere, the garrison managed to hold on until April 20 when, in truly epic fashion, troops of the Royal Berkshires broke through almost at the moment when resistance was at an end. The sadly depleted Assams and the West Kents, followed by their gallant commander, walked down the hill to waiting trucks and were transported out of the Kohima story – which was, in fact, only just beginning.

SATO'S SIGNAL

Though Garrison Hill was safe for the moment, much of the Kohima massif was now held by the Japanese, well dug in and blocking the way to Imphal. With the monsoon imminent, Slim urged Stopford of XXXIII Corps, and Stopford urged Maj General John Grover of 2nd British Infantry Division, to get a move on. The urgency was backed by a remarkable piece of intelligence that fell into British hands.

A signal was found on the body of a Japanese sergeant major, ordering Sato to send a third of his troops to support Mutaguchi at Imphal. Slim demanded increased pressure on the Kohima front to prevent Sato from complying and to rob Mutaguchi of Sato's support.

While yet another Japanese assault raged on the slopes of Garrison Hill, repulsed by troops of the Royal Berkshires and Durhams, the remainder of 5th Brigade made a left hook around Kohima involving a single-file climb over the precipitous Merema Ridge. They set out on April 22/23 and simultaneously 4th Brigade, led by Royal Norfolks, was dispatched on a right hook through the trackless jungle on the slopes of Mt Pulebadze, towering 900 m (3000 ft) above Kohima. The local Naga people warned the British that if the rains came both these routes would become totally impassable, but Grover thought the risk worth taking and pressed on.

On April 27 the monsoon broke, and the miseries and terrors of the battlefield were multiplied a hundredfold. The world dissolved into mud and water, the rain sheeted down and disease – especially malaria and dysentery – seemed to rise out of the ground. Despite appalling difficulties, 4th and 5th Brigades continued inching through the glutinous forest mud.

The 5th emerged to take Naga village on high ground to the north on May 3/4, but could make no further progress. The 4th stormed the crest of GPT Ridge. Between May 4 and 7, 6th British Infantry Brigade – Royal Berkshires, Durham Light Infantry and the Royal Welch Fusiliers – together with the newly arrived 33rd Indian Infantry Brigade, which consisted of Punjabis, Gurkhas and the Queen's Royal West Surreys, attempted to take the strongpoints in the centre, but were pinned down by fire from the bunkers dug into the reverse slopes of GPT Ridge. The Royal Norfolks were ordered to clear them, and charged them head on. But the combined fire from the bunkers proved too intense, despite the gallantry of Captain John Randle, who blocked one of the gun ports with his own mortally wounded body, earning a posthumous VC.

INCREDIBLE INFANTRY

For days the battle of Kohima raged on, the British and Indians gaining here and there a few metres of muddy, shell-torn slope. The Japanese made them pay in blood for every tiny advance, but despite this implacable resistance, the Japanese position was growing hourly more perilous as meagre stocks of food and ammunition dwindled. When Mutaguchi's long-promised supplies failed to appear, Sato grew steadily more critical of his commanding officer. He knew perfectly well that supplies depended on taking Imphal, and his constant inquiries as to when that event would occur did not endear him to Mutaguchi. But, starving and diseased, the Japanese infantry held on, impervious, it seemed, to tanks, artillery, air strikes and flamethrowers.

The breakthrough began on May 11 with an attack by the Punjabis and the Queen's on Jail Hill. It was backed by Lee-Grant tanks, but mostly it was hand-to-hand stuff, including Major Lowry's 'snowball fight' with grenades. Gradually, the other strongpoints in the centre fell as the Japanese fought until the last man died. Finally, by dint of hauling a tank up the mountainside, the last two central strongpoints – the Deputy Commissioner's bungalow and its tennis court – were taken (see feature, *Battle of the tennis court*, p. 399).

There remained only Church Knoll, Hunter's Hill, Aradura Spur and other strongpoints to the north and south, which on May 27 were treated to an obliterating air strike. Then the Punjabis went

INDIA'S DEFENDERS
More than two-thirds of the troops fighting the Japanese at Imphal and Kohima were Indian. The Punjab was normally the main source of India's army, but in the war half came from other provinces. Traditionally a Punjabi Sikh (right) was a soldier. The Indian Army wore standard British shorts with a pullover over a khaki or collarless grey shirt. The *puggree* (turban) varied in shape, showing the man's caste and religion. More than 40 000 Indian Army men died in Burma.

A LATTER-DAY SAMURAI

A hectoring, impatient bully, totally devoted to the craft of war, Renya Mutaguchi (1888-1966) was a throwback to the heroic days of the samurai warriors. Like them, too, he had gentler virtues: his sabre left aside, he was a passionate rose grower.

In 1938, he was appointed Chief of Staff to the Japanese Fourth Army in China and later commanded the 18th Division in the conquest of Malaya and Singapore. This experience led him, not surprisingly, to a poor opinion of the British as opponents. So, when given command of Fifteenth Army in March 1943, he advocated a major offensive into Assam, promising a walk-over. But by the time he attacked he was in a different war, with the Allies having advantages in weapons and equipment perhaps beyond his belief. At any rate, his refusal to face the real problems doomed his offensive almost from the beginning.

Impatient equally of argument and failure, he ended up sacking his three divisional commanders, but was himself removed from active duty in August 1944. He was placed on reserve in December and soon after joined the staff of the Military Academy. He kept up a public vendetta against Lt General Kotoku Sato who, he felt, had caused his downfall by retiring from Kohima against orders.

in, only to be thrown back by resistance as fierce and determined as ever. But Sato had had enough. At the end of May, he signalled Mutaguchi, angrily repeating his demand for supplies and warning of his intention to pull out. Mutaguchi riposted: 'Retreat, and I'll court-martial you.' Thoroughly disgusted, Sato answered: 'Do as you please; I'll bring you down with me.' On the 31st, Sato dispatched a last bitter signal to the effect that 'Cadets know more about tactics than the staff of Fifteenth Army'. Then he closed down his radio station and ordered what was left of the 31st Division to fall back to Imphal.

They were harried all the way, but given the opportunity the skeletal, ragged battalions still somehow found the strength to turn and rend their pursuers. Outside Imphal, Mutaguchi continued to berate Sato, but it was obvious even to him that Fifteenth Army was no longer capable of fighting a major battle. On July 8, he ordered a general retreat, and his starving columns began the terrible march back to the Chindwin.

A Japanese war correspondent, Shizuo Maruyama, described the gruelling retreat: 'We had no ammunition, no food, no clothes, no guns . . . the men were barefoot and ragged and threw away everything except canes to help them walk . . . all they had to keep them going was grass and water . . . At Kohima we were starved and then crushed.'

Imphal was saved and Slim had his springboard for the reconquest of Burma, having inflicted over 60 000 casualties (including 13 376 dead) on the Japanese. The price was 17 587 British and Indian troops killed, wounded or missing. Many of the dead lie at Kohima below a monument that bears the sombre epitaph: 'When you go home, tell them of us, and say: For your tomorrow, we gave our today.'

Battle of the tennis court

One of the most vicious episodes of the Kohima campaign was the battle that took place around the British Deputy Commissioner's bungalow and its tennis court in the middle of May 1944. The bungalow and other hilltop strongpoints on the central Kohima Ridge had been overrun by the Japanese on the night of April 9 and promptly fortified by them; the terraced hillsides were particularly well suited to the construction of bunkers and weapon pits. By May 12, the British had retaken all the surrounding strongpoints, but the Japanese were still holding on grimly to the bungalow and tennis court.

Rooting them out became the unenviable task of the 2nd Battalion Dorsetshire Regiment. From positions often no more than a few metres away, they poured fire upon the Japanese without much visible effect – while the enemy, well dug in, could pick off any Dorset rifleman who moved. The trouble was that the terraces below the position were far too steep to allow tanks up to support the infantry.

However, the Royal Engineers bulldozed a path up the rear of the spur behind the bungalow, and with tremendous effort a Lee-Grant tank was winched up to the crest. On the following morning, May 13, it pushed itself over the edge, skittered down the slope and came to rest in the tennis court with its tracks smack on the still-visible baseline. At point-blank range, the gunner opened fire, pumping shell after shell into the gun slits of the Japanese bunkers.

The surviving enemy soldiers scrambled out of the back and tumbled down the hill, where the vengeful Dorsets were waiting for them.

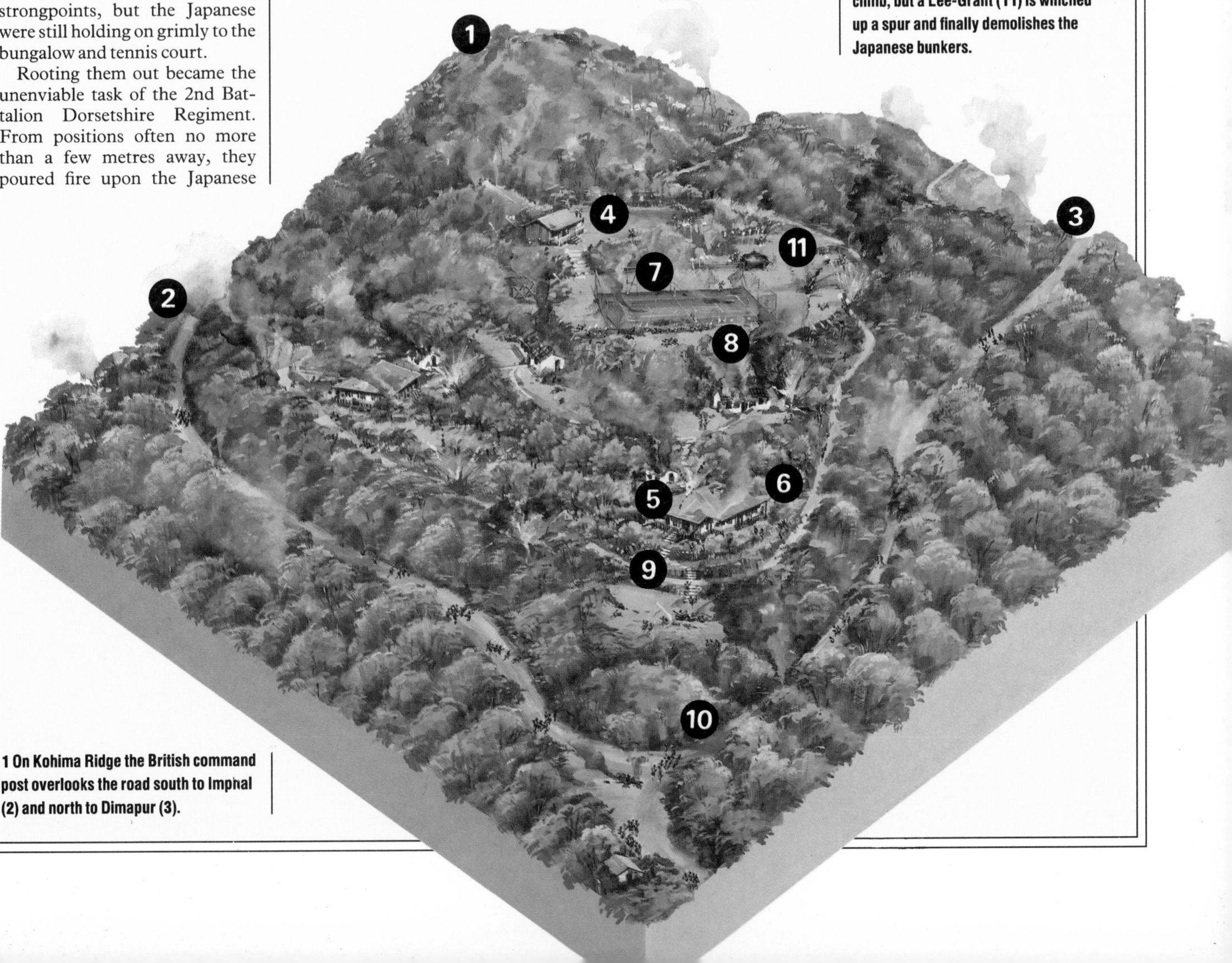

4 British troops occupy the tennis pavilion, the mound behind it and the area in front above the court.

5 The Deputy Commissioner's bungalow is still held by the Japanese.

6 Shells from Indian batteries to the north pepper the terraces.

7 The tennis court, along with the bungalow, remains in Japanese hands after the British have retaken all the surrounding strongpoints.

8 Japanese dug in at the court blast any British attempts to advance. They also occupy the terraced ground (9) below the bungalow.

10 The slope is too steep for tanks to climb, but a Lee-Grant (11) is winched up a spur and finally demolishes the Japanese bunkers.

1 On Kohima Ridge the British command post overlooks the road south to Imphal (2) and north to Dimapur (3).

The road to Rangoon

After the stirring victories in Arakan and at Imphal and Kohima the British Fourteenth Army's tail was well and truly up. When Mountbatten ordered Slim to prepare for the total reconquest of Burma, 'Uncle Bill' set to with a vengeance.

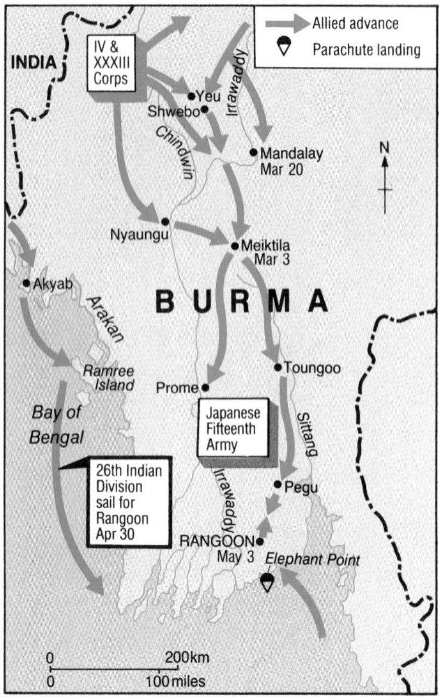

HARD RIDE TO VICTORY Fanatical Japanese resistance met Slim's troops all along the road to Mandalay, Rangoon and victory in Burma. But they did it. By August 4, 1945, the entire country was back in British hands.

A JAPANESE SOLDIER sat in a hole in the ground, a 115 kg (250 lb) aerial bomb clasped tightly between his knees and a stone in his hands, ready to strike the detonator when a tank passed over him. He was one of many that Gurkha troops stumbled across as they fought their way south through Burma in 1945. The author John Masters, then an officer with the advancing army, wrote later: 'The Japanese seemed doped, for they made no attempt to defend themselves or strike the bomb when our men looked down on them. They only peered up, seemed to say to themselves, "A man! I'm waiting for a tank", and again bow their heads, in which position they were shot.'

After Imphal the few battered remnants of Lt General Renya Mutaguchi's Fifteenth Army were saved from total destruction only by the onset of the monsoon, as they were hounded back to the banks of the Chindwin river. But the rains that had saved the Japanese also delayed the British Fourteenth Army, which did not reach the Chindwin until November 24, 1944. But then Royal Engineers flung a 352 m (1154 ft) Bailey bridge – a record span at that time – across the torrent in less than 48 hours. The chase was on again.

But having crossed the Chindwin, the army's commander, Lt General Sir William Slim – knighted on the field of Imphal – found that the demands of other campaigns had diverted much of his air support and there were no roads fit to carry an army. The most he could now hope to field were two tank brigades and four infantry divisions. His plan was to catch the Japanese in the sort of trap he had laid for them at Imphal – this time in the open Shwebo Plain, 80 km (50 miles) north-west of Mandalay.

Although he now faced a new opponent, Lt General Hyotaro Kimura (Lt General Mazakuza Kawabe had been sacked as commander of Japanese forces in Burma after the defeats at Imphal and Kohima), Slim imagined that he would react in much the same way as his predecessor, and fight his pursuers on the plain. But Kimura was a wilier bird than Kawabe, and pulled back across the Irrawaddy. This tremendous river, with cliffs towering as high as those of Dover in some places, was a fearful obstacle.

BLUFF AT MANDALAY

What followed was perhaps the supreme example of Slim's generalship. He had to cross the river, and his only hope lay in fooling the Japanese about his actual crossing point. This he did by switching the main thrust of his attack, sending XXXIII Corps to establish phoney bridgeheads opposite Mandalay. The real crossing, however, would be made by IV Corps at Nyaungu, over 160 km (100 miles) farther downstream. The bluff worked, in that it drew most of the Japanese forces to Mandalay – but there were still plenty left at Nyaungu, where the river was an awesome 2.5 km (1½ miles) wide.

At dead of night on February 13/14, 1945, Gurkhas carried assault boats down to the shore, sinking knee-deep in the sand under the weight. The crossing was to be made by the South Lancashires, who quietly embarked. But the boats' engine noise alerted the enemy, who poured a terrible fire into the approaching craft.

As light grew, the Gurkhas and a company of tanks returned fire against the cliffs opposite and, under cover of this, a couple of Indian battalions crammed into the remaining assault boats and chugged across to support the few Lancashires who had made it. With fixed bayonets, they winkled out the defenders, many of whom, they found, were members of the anticolonial Indian National Army.

With its bridgehead secured, IV Corps poured across the Irrawaddy and into the burning, dusty central Burma plain. Next objective was Meiktila, nerve centre for all Japanese road, rail and air communications in Burma; if it was captured, the Japanese would have to pull back from Mandalay. And they fought for it like tigers. Even with backing from tanks, the British and Indian infantry were forced to hack, burn and blast their way into every strongpoint and every fortified cellar, bayoneting the defenders. It was here, too, that the Gurkhas found those bomb-hugging Japanese crouched in holes.

Meiktila finally fell on March 3, and three days later British troops entered Mandalay, although the elderly Fort Dufferin held out until the 21st, when its walls were blown open in a low-level strike by B-25 Mitchell bombers.

Slim was now poised for a sweep into southern Burma, though his supply problems were made worse by the removal of still more aircraft, this time to help stem the Japanese *Ichi-go* offensive in China. However, with another monsoon only a month or so away, he had to secure Rangoon before the weather broke. Accordingly, XXXIII Corps were dispatched on a feint down the Irrawaddy valley, while once again IV Corps made the real attack, on foot and in trucks down the line of the Toungoo-Pegu railway farther east.

It was a terrible risk – IV Corps would be operating within a dangerous strip nearly 480 km (300 miles) long and only 3 km (under 2 miles) wide thrusting into the heart of enemy territory. But swiftness won the day. At Toungoo on April 23, a Japanese military policeman was still busily directing traffic when he was squashed by the first British tanks coming round the corner.

ON TO RANGOON

Still concerned about the imminent monsoon, Slim now dusted off a previously shelved plan, Operation 'Dracula' – the taking of Rangoon by amphibious and airborne forces – to back up IV Corps. As the first stage of 'Dracula', Lt General Sir Philip Christison's XV Corps had attacked in the Arakan in December 1944. They seized the port of Akyab on January 4 and Ramree Island, with its vital airfields, on January 21.

Now, with the plan revived, 50th Indian Parachute Brigade were flown on May 2 through turbulence and storm to drop on to Elephant Point, south of the city. It was using a steam hammer to crack a walnut, for there were only 37 defenders, and the paratroops' main casualties were caused by a B-24 Liberator dropping its bombs short. Meantime, with formidable navy backing, 26th Indian Division was landed on both sides of the Rangoon river.

SLIM'S WILY OPPONENT

There was nothing in the previous career of Hyotaro Kimura (1888-1948) to suggest that, as commander of the Burma Area Army he would prove to be such an outstanding tactician. Trained as an artilleryman, he had spent most of his career in staff appointments. He was Vice-Minister of War in 1941-3, and had an administrative job in Tokyo when he was suddenly dispatched to Burma to save Japan's honour.

The odds were very much against him, facing forces that he knew were much stronger in every way. Within a fortnight of his arrival, however, he had totally recast Kawabe's plans for the conduct of the campaign. While he failed to retrieve the situation for Japan in Burma, his flexibility and grasp of strategy made him a formidable opponent for Slim in the last stages. He was tried, and hanged, for war crimes – including responsibility for atrocities on the Burma-Thai railway.

As it turned out, the fall of Toungoo and Pegu had convinced Kimura that Rangoon could not be defended and he had already pulled out. An RAF plane spotted messages painted by prisoners of war on the roofs of Rangoon Gaol: 'JAPS GONE BRITISH HERE. EXTRACT DIGIT.' The British and Indians marched into the city on May 3 to the cheers of the populace.

COMMAND PROBLEMS

The taking of Rangoon promised Slim all the supplies he needed, but he was not out of the wood yet. Kimura was determined to make a stand east of the Sittang river, near the Burmese-Thai border, and still he had over 600 000 men.

However, just as Slim was dividing his forces for the anticipated attack on Malaya and Singapore, the British government suddenly announced that any soldier who, by June 1945, had served more than three years and four months in the Far East theatre could apply for repatriation. The queues were not slow in forming! By pleading that he needed them, Slim managed to hang on to some key men who might have gone; and many other servicemen volunteered to stay.

At the same time, a curious incident occurred back at high command in Delhi. On the day Rangoon fell, Lt General Sir Oliver Leese, Commander in Chief Allied Land Forces, South-East Asia, told Slim – who naturally expected to lead his Fourteenth Army into Malaya – that he would instead be appointed to Twelfth Army, for mopping-up operations in Burma. Slim took this to mean that high authority had lost confidence in him, and he applied to Lord Louis Mountbatten, head of South-East Asia Command (SEAC), to be allowed to retire from the service.

Horrified, Mountbatten rescinded the order and sacked Leese instead; Slim – one of World War II's outstanding commanders – was appointed to replace him. In the event, though, the defeat of Japan made an invasion of Malaya unnecessary. The last battles in Burma were conducted by Lt General Sir Montagu Stopford.

TO THE BITTER END

The ground by the Sittang river that Kimura had chosen for his last stand was flat and featureless. Now the monsoon had come, reducing the area to a wilderness of mud and water, paddy and coarse grass, leeches, mosquitoes, rats – and Japanese. Here, split down into companies, platoons and even sections, British and Indian infantry, knee-deep and often waist-deep in water, fought a thousand tiny, bitter battles.

In one such, Rifleman Manbir Ale, of the 4/8th Gurkhas, was unable to lie down to fire his Bren gun because of the mud, so he stood up and, firing from the hip, covered his section attack on a Japanese machine-gun position. An officer, Denis Shiel-Small, wrote: 'His right hand and lower arm were at once smashed by bullets from the bunker. Nevertheless, this gallant soldier, supporting his gun on his shattered arm, carried on firing until he fell, mortally wounded.'

The Japanese fought with equal bravery, but the result was inevitable. John Masters wrote: 'The machine guns got them, the Brens and rifles got them, the tanks got them, the guns got them. They drowned by hundreds . . . and their corpses floated in the fields and among the reeds. In July 1945, we of the Fourteenth Army killed and captured 11 500 Japanese for the loss of 96 killed.' On August 4, the shooting died away, for there was no one left to kill.

PATROLLING THE PAGODA Two British tommies on patrol pick their way through rubble in northern Burma. Behind them rises the splendour of the Bahe Pagoda. It is all a far cry from the green valleys of their native South Wales.

FIERY FIGHTING ON THE IRRAWADDY Men of the British XXXIII Corps cross an open space near the Irrawaddy. Flames from a burning building leap up behind. The corps was making its diversionary attack across the river opposite Mandalay.

A close-run thing in China

China was almost lost to a huge Japanese offensive which struck into its heart in April 1944. The American Fourteenth Air Force, on which Chiang Kai-shek relied, proved no substitute for an efficient Chinese army on the ground.

WHICH WAY TO SAFETY? Crammed into trains at Kueilin (Guilin) in south China, even bridging the buffers and perching on the roof with treasured bundles, Chinese flee the Japanese horde. A few raise smiles; most are grim.

OPERATION *ICHI-GO*, the greatest Japanese offensive in China for years, was not inspired by any move of the largely ramshackle armies of Generalissimo Chiang Kai-shek. Rather, it was provoked by US submarine successes against Japanese shipping bringing supplies to the troops and by the raids of the US Fourteenth Air Force. Flying from bases in south-western China, the Americans were playing havoc with Japanese supply lines. Even more alarming to Tokyo was intelligence that the huge new B-29 Superfortresses were coming to these bases, from which they could reach the Japanese homeland.

Supply lines could be assured by gaining control of the main north-south railway in China and by taking the US-held airfields. If the operation succeeded, there might be other bonuses. There was a chance that a crushing defeat might bring down Chiang and his Kuomintang (Nationalist) government.

Chiang and his army did not impress the Japanese. Despite the urgings of Chiang's American adviser, Lt General Joseph ('Vinegar Joe') Stilwell, most Chinese divisions were as poorly trained and equipped as ever. Chiang preferred to listen instead to the charismatic commander of the Fourteenth Air Force, former 'Flying Tiger' Maj General Claire Chennault, who persuaded him that air power alone could annihilate any Japanese offensive.

The first phase of *Ichi-go* ('Operation No 1') was called *Ko-go*, and was to clear the Peking-Hankow (Beijing-Wuhan) section of the railway (see map, p. 135). The second phase, *To-go*, was to clear the Hankow to Canton (Guangzhou) section and the spur running from Hengchow (Hengyang) into French Indochina (now Vietnam). The Japanese could then thrust north-west towards the main Chinese force around Chungking (Chongqing) and knock out the airfields.

JAPANESE BLITZKRIEG

Ko-go began in mid-April 1944 with 150 000 Japanese, supported by aircraft, pushing towards Chengchow (Zengzhou), some approaching from the east along the Yellow (Huang He) river, others coming up the railway from the south. Chengchow fell on April 22. From there they pressed west and took Loyang (Luoyang) in May and Lingpao (Lingbao) in June. By now the Japanese were dangerously strung out and the mountainous country was difficult for their tanks, but they had help from locals who felt little loyalty to a government that could not solve the recurrent famines. From late April, the Japanese were also pushing down the railway from Chengchow and north up it from Hsinyang (Xinyang). By mid-June a 300 000-strong Chinese army was reduced to a fleeing rabble and the Japanese held the railway from Peking to Hankow.

To-go began at the end of May, when 200 000 Japanese moved south from the Hankow area on a 240 km (150 mile) front towards Changsha. Here, the Chinese began to show that they too could fight. The Japanese Eleventh Army reached the city on June 5 and had to fight a two-week battle to take it. The Chinese fought fiercely again at Hengchow, the junction where the railway branched off for Indochina. The siege of the city began on June 23. When it fell on August 8, the Japanese had suffered 20 000 casualties and were almost out of supplies. The Chinese had lost 15 000 of the 16 275 defenders.

The Japanese were now ready for the more ambitious stage of *To-go*. In late August they put together the Sixth Area Army (Army Group) of 350 000 soldiers plus three air regiments. They fought the epic battle of Kwangsi-Kweichow (Guangxi-Guizhou) over four provinces. They advanced on Liuchow (Liuzhou), coming south-west down the railway from Hengchow and west from Canton. It was the middle of the south China rainy season – unusually long that year – which reduced the air attacks on them but hampered their tanks. Kweilin (Guilin), Liuchow and Nanning with their airfields were in Japanese hands by November. A force moved north-west up the railway from Liuchow to its terminus and beyond, to Tuyun (Duyun), heading for the US air base at Kweiyang (Guiyang).

Chiang Kai-shek's capital Chungking itself was now under threat. If this too fell, China would be out of the war, releasing hundreds of thousands of

'Y-FORCE' COMES GOOD

There was an irony in Stilwell's victory at Myitkyina in 1944, achieved by five divisions of Chinese troops with help from 'Merrill's Marauders' and the Chindits. Stilwell had demonstrated in Burma what Chiang Kai-shek had prevented him proving in China: that Chinese troops, properly trained and equipped, could match – and beat – the Japanese. Yet just over the border, in China's Yunnan province, was 'Y-Force' – 30 Chinese divisions, admittedly badly prepared, which had yet to play any part in the north Burma campaign.

Chiang was persuaded to agree to a 'Y-Force' offensive. It began in May 1944, just before the monsoon season, when 12 divisions crossed the Salween river (Nu Jiang to the Chinese) towards Burma. Immediately in front of them lay the Japanese 56th Division and the towns of Tengyueh (Tengchung) and Lungling, held for two years by the enemy.

However, they lacked the aggression shown by Stilwell's men, and their offensive soon bogged down between the two towns, in the face of a strong Japanese counterattack. Then the Japanese launched their China offensive, Operation *Ichi-go*, and the pressure on 'Y-Force' suddenly eased. Tengyueh was captured in September, and Lungling in October. Finally, at Mongyu, close to the Chinese border in northern Burma, 'Y-Force' linked up with Stilwell's successor, Sutton, on January 2, 1945.

WHAT WAS CHINA'S CONTRIBUTION?

American commitment to China continued despite Chiang Kai-shek's failure to act. It diverted precious war supplies from other fronts – from Burma, for example, where American aircraft were withdrawn because of the need to support China. Had the planes remained in Burma they would have helped enormously in completing the destruction of the Japanese armies there.

Similarly, Stilwell's efforts in north Burma, especially building the Ledo Road (see box, *The Triumph of 'Stilwell's Folly'*), were essentially diversions to help Chiang; the real battle for Burma took place elsewhere. By the time the Chinese were becoming a serious threat to the Japanese the war had already moved on to the Japanese homeland.

But China did manage to occupy a million Japanese soldiers for most of the war – soldiers who might have been used to more devastating effect elsewhere. And the fact is that nobody foresaw the tremendous success of the American drive across the Pacific. Until that was far advanced, it was automatically assumed that operations from China would be vital in the final defeat of Japan.

CHINESE IDEAL Only lucky privates in Chiang's army had the quilted winter uniform (left). Although US-trained by the 1940s, their stick grenades slung around the neck are relics of earlier German aid. (Above) Wedemeyer, who made great efforts to improve the Chinese Army, inspects a graduation parade of Chinese officers.

Japanese soldiers to fight in Burma or the Pacific. Panic reigned in Chungking, with Chiang and his staff 'impotent and confounded', according to Chiang's new American adviser, Maj General Albert Wedemeyer, who had replaced Stilwell in October 1944.

Fortunately for the Allies, from then on the attackers' momentum slowed, although a column of troops did come up the railway from Indochina to link with the Japanese forces at Lungchow (Longzhou) in December. The Imperial forces had achieved their objective and controlled the railway from Peking into Indochina – briefly. They were thinly spread, short of supplies and facing reinforced and more resolute Chinese.

New Chinese conscripts had arrived on foot, in trucks and in US transport planes. They were not the most robust troops, to be sure. Indeed, Chiang Kai-shek wept when he visited one batch and saw their condition and their appalling barracks. He ordered the officer in charge to be put to death. Nevertheless, numbers told, the Japanese were stopped and China was still in the war. But it was a close-run thing; the Japanese had inflicted an estimated 700 000 casualties upon the Kuomintang, and they still held the original objectives of *Ichi-go* – the railways and airfields.

CHIANG REORGANISES

Chiang Kai-shek emerged from the *Ichi-go* nightmare with no option but to agree to what Stilwell had pressed him to do for years – stop relying on the USAAF to fight the Japanese for him and rebuild his army. Finally persuaded by Wedemeyer in November 1944, Chiang agreed to the re-equipping and training of 39 divisions. Corrupt officers who deprived the men of rations, pay and adequate clothing had to go.

However, on September 29, a month before Wedemeyer took over, the Japanese had launched still another offensive in southern China, to seize the Canton-Hengchow railway and other strategic points in south Hunan. It was a repetition of previous encounters, with the poorly equipped Chinese swiftly overwhelmed. But this was to be the last Japanese success in China. From December the Chinese were pecking away at their forward positions, and in the following spring they won back many of the towns lost in the Kwangsi-Kweichow battle.

The triumphant American progress across the Pacific now raised the possibility of an Allied landing on the China coast. Tokyo therefore ordered forces to withdraw to positions on the coasts. But before pulling out of the interior, the Japanese mounted two farewell operations.

In March 1945 the Imperial forces drove westwards inland, between the Yellow and Yangtze (Chang Jiang) rivers, in an attempt to seize the American air bases of Laohokow (Guanghua) and Ankang. They captured Laohokow, but a fierce and unexpected Chinese counterattack stopped any further advance. At the end of April the Japanese swung their attack south onto the American air base at Chihkiang (Zhijiang). Here too they were intercepted by determined Chinese opposition and forced into bloody retreat. It was the first serious defeat for Japanese arms in China for years.

On May 9, Tokyo ordered the evacuation of south China. Apart from the danger of Allied landings on the coast, a new threat would soon emerge – a belated declaration of war against Japan by the Soviet Union, followed by a Russian invasion of Manchuria.

THE TRIUMPH OF 'STILWELL'S FOLLY'

Work on the road which quickly became known as 'Stilwell's Folly' began in December 1942. Chiang Kai-shek reckoned it would take no more than five months to build a road from Ledo, in eastern Assam, over the 2750 m (9000 ft) Patkai Hills, then through the Hukawng Valley to Mogaung, Myitkyina and Bhamo, to join the old Burma Road to Kunming in China. US Army engineers thought it would take over two years – and they were proved right.

The astonishing thing was that the road was completed at all, since it crossed ridge after ridge of jungle-clad mountains and deep river valleys, all awash for part of the year with monsoon rains. Some 50 000 Americans with 30 000 more Chinese and Indians shared the work, as well as the leeches, mosquitoes and many other hazards of jungle living – including the Japanese. For each 1.5 km (1 mile) of road, 13 culverts had to be built to carry away the heavy rains – as much as 360 mm (14 in) in 24 hours at the height of the monsoon in July. During good weather, construction of single-track roadway proceeded at just over 1 km ($\frac{3}{4}$ mile) a day.

The British felt the road was simply not worth the expenditure in men, resources and unremitting effort, since it could never carry the weight of supplies China needed. In their view the answer to the China blockade was an all-out offensive to drive the Japanese out of Burma. Stilwell also had to face the fact that lorries using the road would consume a tonne of fuel to deliver each tonne of cargo to China. The Americans, anxious to keep Chiang happy, found the solution in a fuel pipeline which finally snaked all the 2900 km (1800 miles) from Calcutta to Kunming.

By the time the first convoy rolled along the Ledo Road in January 1945 (above), Stilwell had been removed as Chiang's adviser, at the Generalissimo's request. But although Chiang had so often rejected Stilwell's advice, in the end he showed his gratitude for one thing – and he suggested a new name for it: the Stilwell Road.

PART SIX: VICTORY AND AFTERMATH

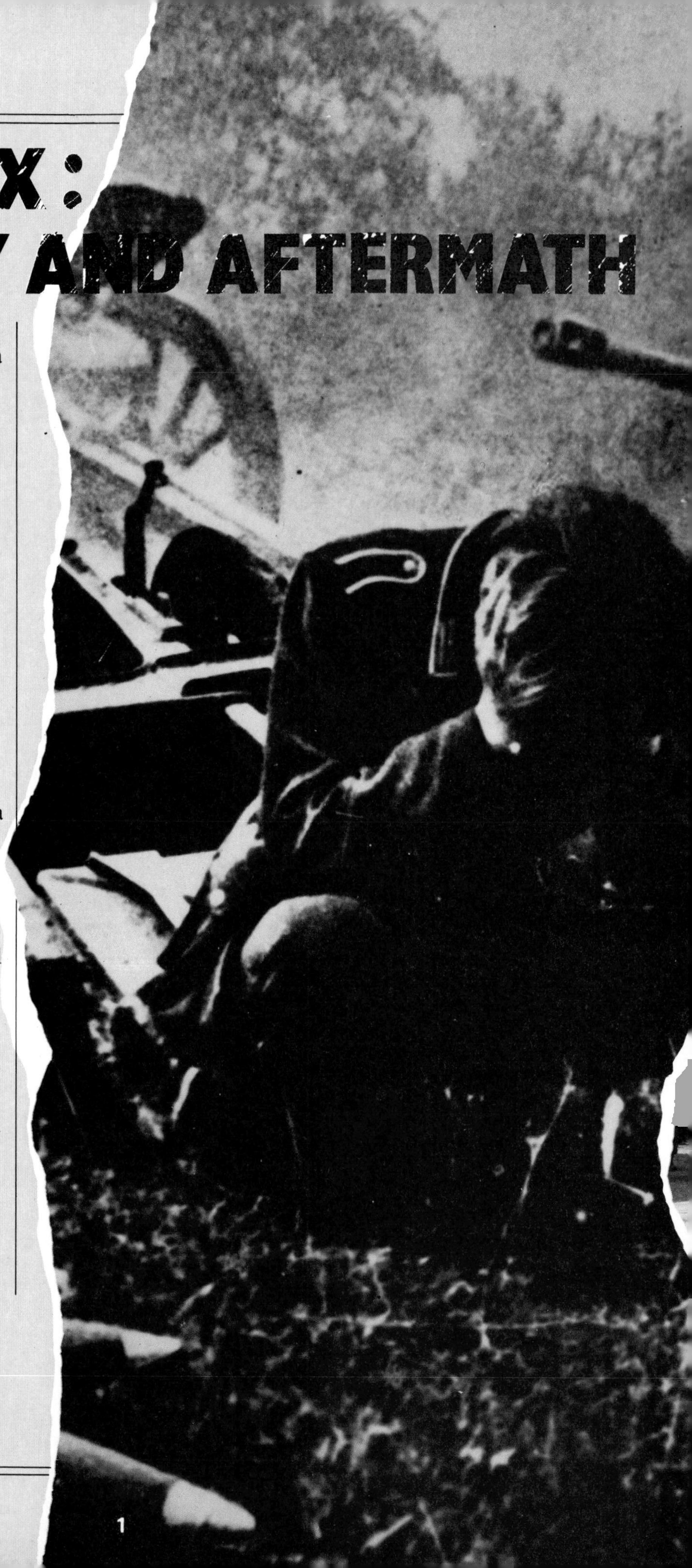

THE FINAL ACT of the most tremendous drama the world has ever seen opened on January 12, 1945, when the Red Army crossed the Vistula to take Warsaw and drive into Germany.

In the west, the Americans and British pushed deep into the Reich. From his bunker in Berlin, a shattered and ailing Führer directed imaginary armies until even he realised it was over, and killed himself. His body was soaked in petrol and burned – a fitting end for the man who had plunged the world into flames.

Across on the other side of the world, the Japanese were suffering their own punishment by inferno. Iwo Jima and Okinawa fell after fanatical resistance, as Tokyo and other cities suffered the horrors of firestorm raids. Still worse was to come, when atomic bombs fell on Hiroshima and Nagasaki. Japan surrendered, and the war was over.

Now came the epilogue, and the trials of war criminals. It was a portent for the future that the Marshall Plan, which put Europe back on its feet, was funded with American money. For the war had seen the emergence of the two superpowers. The seeds were sown for the Cold War ●

(1) For one young German, on the Eastern Front, the war is over. (2) April 1945: tanks of the US Ninth Army roll into a devastated town in the Ruhr. (3) The once-thriving industrial city of Hamamatsu, Japan, after a fire-raid.

3
2

26: END OF THE THIRD REICH

After the defeat in the Ardennes and a crushing year in the east, Nazism's nemesis loomed.

Red Army rolls into Germany

January 1945 saw Stalin's huge armies launch out from the Vistula river on a massive front. By March the Soviet steamroller was poised on the banks of the Oder, just 56 km (35 miles) from the outskirts of Berlin.

THE GREATEST OFFENSIVE of World War II opened in fog, snow and thick cloud in the early hours of January 12, 1945, at Baranów on the Vistula, about 200 km (125 miles) south of Warsaw. Well before dawn German troops opposing a substantial Russian bridgehead on the west bank were woken by heavy Soviet artillery fire. In the next few hours Russian shelling of unbelievable ferocity all but annihilated the Germans' artillery positions.

At 10.30 am the infantry, followed by tanks, of the Soviet 1st Ukrainian Front under Marshal Ivan Koniev moved in on the German lines. Massively outnumbered, with just one tank for every seven Russian tanks at the centre of the attack, the Germans were no match for their assailants. As darkness fell the Russians had penetrated 20 km (12 miles) behind the German lines and were still moving relentlessly forward.

EARLY OFFENSIVE

For six months, the Russians had remained tantalisingly static on the east bank of the Vistula, while their armies in south-eastern Europe drove the Germans from the Balkans, forcing Romania and Bulgaria to change sides and join the Allies.

Now their offensive across the Vistula began over a week earlier than planned. On January 6, in the thick of the Battle of the Ardennes, Winston Churchill had sent Stalin a telegram requesting urgent help: 'The battle in the West is very heavy . . . I shall be grateful if . . . we can count on a major Russian offensive on the Vistula front, or elsewhere, during January.'

'In view of our Allies' position on the Western Front,' the Soviet leader replied, 'GHQ of the Supreme Command have decided to complete preparations at a rapid rate and, regardless of weather, to launch large-scale offensive operations along the entire Central Front not later than the second half of January. Rest assured we shall do all in our power to support the valiant forces of our Allies.' He was as good as his word.

Koniev's opening attack at the Baranów bridgehead on January 12 caught the German Army Group A under General Josef Harpe completely by surprise. Harpe's men were unable to stop the Russians, who in five days crossed the Warta and pushed out 160 km (100 miles) from Baranów on a 255 km (160 mile) front.

The German Army Group Centre under General Georg-Hans Reinhardt to the north was initially more successful. On January 14 Zhukov's 1st Belorussian Front (Army Group) launched an attack near Warsaw, followed by Rokossovsky's 2nd Belorussian Front just to the north. For two days the Germans held on – thanks largely to poor visibility which stopped the Red Air Force giving their ground troops effective air support. But when the weather cleared, the Russians brought in their Stormovik fighter-bombers to attack the German positions, and Reinhardt was driven north-east into East Prussia.

Meanwhile, Harpe had lost Warsaw after only five days of fighting. His garrison in the city had been almost completely surrounded by troops under Zhukov's command, later joined by the Soviet-sponsored First Polish Army. It was forced to withdraw on the evening of January 17.

The fall of Warsaw cost Harpe his command. Hitler replaced him with an ardent Nazi, General Ferdinand Schörner. But not even Schörner could hold out against attacks to the south from both Zhukov's and Koniev's forces. Army Group A was pushed rapidly back and by January 31 Zhukov's leading troops had reached the Oder at Zehden (now Cedynia), just 70 km (40 miles) north-east of Berlin. During the next weeks the

SOVIET SWEEP FOR VICTORY The massed Soviet armies on the Vistula outnumbered the Germans four to one. Polish, Czechoslovak, Romanian and Bulgarian divisions swelled their number. Now their multi-pronged attack was ready, one thrust to aim north for the Baltic, the others to lunge across to the Oder before converging on Berlin.

LOSSES AVENGED Uncaring, Russian soldiers pass by the German dead as Red Army tanks roll inexorably westwards through Mülhausen – and other East Prussian towns. They knew what the Germans had done to their land and people. German civilians fled before them, but German soldiers were forbidden to retreat. For them, death was inevitable.

rest of Zkukov's armies closed up to the Oder south of Zehden and began preparing to cross the river for the last lap to Berlin. A sizable German pocket left behind at Poznan fell on February 23.

Panic, meanwhile, gripped the populations of eastern Germany. As the Russian soldiers had moved westwards, liberating their own country, they had seen the devastation wrought by the invading Germans in 1941-2. Destroyed villages and the corpses of peasants gave them a thirst for revenge. Now horrific tales of Russian rape, murder and pillage travelled west ahead of them.

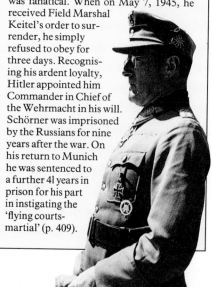

In driving snow and the bitter sub-zero temperatures that afflicted most of Europe in the first months of 1945, millions of Germans left their homes in the east to seek refuge in the heart of the Reich. By mid-February almost two-thirds of the population of East Prussia had fled. As the Red Army surrounded them, many left by sea in hopelessly overcrowded ships. Between October 1944 and May 1945 the Germans lost 24 ships to Soviet submarines in the Baltic, including the liners *Wilhelm Gustloff* and *Steuben*. *Wilhelm Gustloff* set sail from Gdynia on January 30 with some 8000 passengers, mostly refugees from the Russians. It was torpedoed that night and after a terrible panic only 964 were saved.

HUNGARIAN DIVERSION

The Russian advance was aided by a fatal decision made by Hitler in mid-January. His acting Army Chief of Staff, General Heinz Guderian, urged him to concentrate all his forces, including those withdrawn from the west after the failure in the Ardennes, to defend the Oder. But the Führer had another idea: an attack in Hungary.

In late 1944, Marshal Rodion Malinovsky and his 2nd Ukrainian Front had driven the Germans out of most of eastern Hungary. But more troops of the German Sixth Army still held out in the capital, Budapest. At the beginning of January Hitler sent an SS panzer corps to relieve the Budapest garrison – but they failed. He now proposed sending in Sixth Panzer Army, to be withdrawn from the Ardennes, under his faithful former SS bodyguard 'Sepp' Dietrich.

On February 13, just as the first of Dietrich's men reached Budapest, the city finally fell to the Russians. They drove the Germans back to a line to the west, running from the Danube to the Drava river through Lake Balaton.

Hitler now became obsessed with the defence of the Hungarian oilfields, south-west of Budapest near Lake Balaton. He ordered Dietrich and Lt General Hermann Balck, who had taken over command of Sixth Army, to counterattack the Russians in the Balaton area and establish a secure defensive barrier east of the oilfields. The two armies were part of Army Group South under the overall command of General Otto Wöhler.

This offensive, code-named *Frühlingserwachen* ('Spring Awakening') was launched on March 6. It was the last German offensive of the war – and was doomed to failure. The Germans faced a massive Russian superiority of men and equipment. Moreover the ground that they assumed would still be frozen was not; the German attack soon became bogged down in mud. The Russians counterattacked and Dietrich was forced to withdraw, without Hitler's authorisation. He had to leave behind most of his heavy equipment and took with him a bare 50 tanks.

Hitler, enraged, ordered Dietrich's Waffen-SS officers to be stripped *(continued on p. 409)*

FAITHFUL TO THE LAST

One of the last German officers Hitler promoted to the rank of field marshal, on April 5, 1945, was Ferdinand Schörner (1892-1973). Son of a police official, Schörner was a World War I hero with the Pour le Mérite and was an early Nazi convert.

In World War II he served in and later commanded the Mountain Corps and fought in the Balkans, Crete and on the Eastern Front in 1940-2. He later commanded all German troops in Norway, and in 1943 went to the Eastern Front to command XL Panzer Corps. In March 1944 he was promoted to command Army Group South Ukraine, and later Army Group North on the Baltic coast and Army Group Centre in Czechoslovakia.

Schörner's devotion to the Nazi cause was fanatical. When on May 7, 1945, he received Field Marshal Keitel's order to surrender, he simply refused to obey for three days. Recognising his ardent loyalty, Hitler appointed him Commander in Chief of the Wehrmacht in his will. Schörner was imprisoned by the Russians for nine years after the war. On his return to Munich he was sentenced to a further 41 years in prison for his part in instigating the 'flying courts-martial' (p. 409).

MOBILISING THE REICH'S LAST RESOURCES

Thanks largely to the devoted efforts of Hitler's brilliant Armaments Minister Albert Speer – as well as the extensive use of slave labour – Germany's production of arms and vital war supplies increased steadily until as late as September 1944. But from then, output began to fall dramatically. The chief damage was created not by Allied air attacks on factories – many of them by now scattered about the countryside – but by the disruption of transport as Allied bombers intensified their attacks against oil depots and the road and railway networks. As the Germans were forced back to their own borders, they also lost the sources of many vital raw materials, such as oil from Romania.

In August 1944, in a desperate effort to fill the ranks of Germany's depleted labour force, Josef Goebbels ordered total mobilisation. The working week was increased to 60 hours, and theatres and many restaurants were closed. But the effort came too late.

To make matters worse, Hitler was demanding more men for the army to try to make good the shattering losses of the last two years; a million men were killed in the west alone in 1944. One result was a proclamation in October 1944 calling up all remaining able-bodied men aged between 16 and 60 to join a home guard force, the *Volkssturm* ('People's Guard').

As the Allies drew in on German territory in early 1945, it was this under-trained, ill-equipped force that bore the burden of much of the final fighting. In fact, many members were over 60 and others were boys as young as 11 or 12.

Many of the youngsters were in the Hitler Youth and had known nothing but Hitler's rule during their short lives. Their fanaticism rivalled that of the most hardened SS men. The Allied troops fighting against these youths were tempted to treat them like naughty schoolboys – but a rifle or submachine gun was just as lethal in their hands as in those of a fully grown man.

HITLER'S HOME GUARD **Under-trained and badly equipped Volkssturm members formed the Reich's last defence. Lucky ones would have a rifle, machine gun or *Panzerfaust* – a one-shot anti-tank grenade launcher (right). Schoolboy recruits from the Hitler Youth (main picture) watch keenly as they are instructed in how to use the weapon.**

THE SOLDIERS WHO FOUGHT TO THE LAST

As the Allied armies closed in on Germany from east and west in early 1945, few German soldiers harboured any illusions that Hitler's Reich could still win the war. In the west many were content to surrender after no more than a token display of resistance, but other elements, particularly the fanatical Waffen-SS units, were prepared to fight on to the bitter end. On the Eastern Front, German resistance was even more determined.

'Even the last soldier was now aware that the war was lost,' recalled one German officer who fought against the Russians at Küstrin on the Oder in March 1945. 'He was aiming to survive, and the only sense he could see was to protect the front in the east to save as many refugees [escaping the Russians] as possible. He felt bitter to have to fight on German soil for the first time this century and he could not foresee any alternative but to stay with his unit and to stick to his oath of allegiance. He realised that the attempt of July 20, 1944, against Hitler had failed and, despite the obvious facts, he was hoping for a political solution for ending the war, not knowing however which kind of solution. Last but not least the demand for unconditional surrender left in the light of self-respect no alternative but to continue the hopeless fighting.'

Another factor that kept the Germans fighting on all fronts was the 'flying courts-martial'. Hitler would brook no withdrawals, however sound the reasons for making them. Any officer suspected of making an unauthorised withdrawal and any soldier found separated from his unit was tried by a travelling military court. If found guilty the defendant was summarily shot or hanged.

At the same time, serveral strategically important towns, such as Königsberg (now Kaliningrad) in East Prussia and Breslau (Wroclaw) in eastern Germany, were designated fortresses. Any commanding officer who surrendered one of these was liable to suffer a similar fate – trial by flying court-martial. When the commander of the Königsberg garrison, General Otto Lasch, faced with overwhelming odds, surrendered the town to the Russians on April 10, Hitler sentenced him to death in his absence. The Führer also ordered the SS to take Lasch's family as hostages. Happily, his family survived until Germany's surrender; Lasch himself was wounded and captured by the Russians.

Most German civilians, meanwhile, had long ceased to believe the Nazi leaders' strident promises that new 'miracle weapons' would dramatically reverse the tide of defeat. Fearing both the approach of the dreaded Bolsheviks and jail or death for criticising the Nazis, they greeted the Western Allies with complete apathy as they drove through the Reich's battered towns and villages; the Soviet troops they fled in terror.

of their decorations and the men under them of their treasured divisional armbands. He ordered SS chief Heinrich Himmler to the front to ensure that his orders were carried out. Even Himmler bridled at this. 'I would have to drive to the Plattensee [Lake Balaton] to take the crosses off the dead,' he remonstrated. 'A German SS man cannot give more than his life to you, my Führer.'

Hitler was adamant – and his vindictiveness added to the growing disillusion of Dietrich and many of his officers. Nor did it have any effect; the oilfields fell to the Russians on April 2.

DEFEAT ON THE ODER

Meanwhile, the absence of Dietrich's army in Hungary had been sorely felt on the Oder. In mid-February Koniev seized several bridgeheads over the southern part of the river despite desperate resistance from Schörner's Army Group Centre. By the end of the month, his men had reached a 100 km (60 mile) stretch of the Neisse river south from the Oder-Neisse junction, just 105 km (65 miles) south-east of Berlin. The Germans kept a solitary toehold on the Oder's east bank at Küstrin (now Kostrzyn), astride the direct route west to Berlin. During March Koniev drove most German troops out of Silesia, in southern Poland, leaving only a few pockets – including one at Breslau which held out until May 6.

In late January Hitler had created a new Army Group Vistula to defend the region of Pomerania on the Baltic coast north-east of Berlin. Its commander, despite his negligible military experience, was Himmler – an indication of Hitler's almost insane distrust of his generals at this stage of the war. During February men from both Zhukov's and Rokossovsky's fronts drove Army Group Vistula out of Pomerania.

Meanwhile, in East Prussia the remnants of Reinhardt's forces were caught by encircling Soviet armies under Rokossovsky, General Ivan Bagramyan and General Ivan Chernyakhovsky (who died in the fighting). Reinhardt was now completely cut off from the rest of Germany. By the end of March, the Russians had taken the ports of Gdynia and Danzig (Gdansk) and the remaining German troops held only two small pockets on the Gulf of Danzig, which did not fall until the final German surrender in May.

RETREAT FROM HUNGARY

Back in Hungary, Wöhler's Army Group South was in danger of being outflanked to the north as Malinovsky thrust towards Bratislava on the Danube in southern Czechoslovakia. At the same time, Marshal Feodor Tolbukhin's 3rd Ukrainian Front was pushing Wöhler back towards Austria. On April 6 Hitler replaced Wöhler with General Lothar Rendulic – but he had no option but to continue the withdrawal.

The Führer now gave Dietrich and the Sixth Panzer Army a new, well-nigh impossible task: to defend Vienna. Dietrich was under no illusions. 'We call ourselves Sixth Panzer Army,' he remarked, 'because we have only six tanks left.'

He had little time to prepare the defence of the city, for by April 6 the Russians were on its outskirts. Malinovsky and Tolbukhin then combined their forces and encircled the city; by April 10 they had reached its centre. Much of Vienna was now in flames. Austrian deserters and escaped slave labourers added to the confusion by shooting at the German troops. Dietrich, in danger of being cut off, withdrew west behind the Traisen river. He held out for two weeks, while the Russians switched their main attack northwards to the Czechoslovak town of Brno, which fell on April 26. Dietrich surrendered to the US 36th Infantry Division on May 9.

In Berlin, Hitler and his inner circle, living in the unreal atmosphere of the vast underground Führerbunker, had turned to astrology. Hitler's study was dominated by a portrait of his hero, the Prussian King Frederick the Great. He and Goebbels were now expecting a miracle similar to the death of Tsarina Elizabeth of Russia, which saved Frederick from defeat towards the end of the Seven Years' War (1756-63). When, on April 12, US President Roosevelt died of a stroke, their hopes seemed confirmed.

Hearing the news the next day, Goebbels telephoned Hitler in high excitement: 'My Führer, I congratulate you! Roosevelt is dead. It is written in the stars that the second half of April will be the turning point for us. This is Friday, April 13. It is the turning point.'

They were sadly deluded. Three days later the Red Army crossed the Oder for the final thrust to Berlin. The Western Allies were also racing across Germany, and on April 25 American and Soviet troops met at Torgau on the Elbe. Nazi Germany was split in two across its middle.

HITLER'S PLAN FOR A TWILIGHT OF THE GODS

'If the war is lost, the German nation will also perish,' Hitler informed his Armaments Minister, Albert Speer, in March 1945. 'There is no need to take into consideration the basic requirements of the people . . . Those who will remain after the battle are those who are inferior; for the good will have fallen.'

With his Reich dissolving around him, the Führer mistrusted his generals, and believed the German people had failed him. His defeat, though, could be turned into an epic – a Wagnerian twilight of the gods. Speer was brave enough to protest that there was a duty to maintain 'a basis of existence for the nation to the last'.

But Hitler paid no heed. On March 19 he issued an order commanding the destruction of anything that might be of use to the enemy – military installations, bridges, industrial plant, energy sources, railway wagons and engines, ships, waterways, even food stores. *Gauleiters* (Nazi party district leaders), military commanders and some specially appointed 'commissars for defence' were to ensure that his order was carried out. Four days later Hitler's secretary Martin Bormann issued another grim order: the whole population, including foreign slave workers and prisoners of war, was to be moved from the outlying parts of the country to the centre – with no thought for their needs.

Horrified, Speer went secretly to Field Marshal Walther Model, military commander of Germany's industrial heart, and persuaded him to ignore Hitler's decrees. He then returned to Berlin and convinced Hitler that they were impossible to carry out. Hitler modified, though he did not rescind, the decrees – but Speer made sure that none of them was carried out.

Across the Rhine

Early in 1945 a gigantic vice began to close on the Third Reich. As the Russians bore down from the east, the Western Allies, after their temporary setback in the Ardennes, were approaching the Rhine – the last major natural obstacle between them and Germany's heartland.

TEETH OF DEATH General William H. Simpson (1888-1980), commander of the US Ninth Army, shows Field Marshal Montgomery the 'dragon's-teeth' tank traps of the Siegfried Line. Simpson, a Texan, first saw action in 1916 against the Mexican revolutionary leader Pancho Villa, then in France in 1918. Eisenhower brought him to Europe in September 1944. Simpson's Ninth Army liberated Brest, then was transferred to the Ardennes. His concern to visit all his men earned him the nickname 'Doughboy General', from the slang term for a US infantryman.

A LANKY US SERGEANT, Alex Drabik, sprinted across the Ludendorff Bridge in the little town of Remagen, south of Bonn, and at 3.55 pm on March 7, 1945, became the first Allied soldier to reach the east bank of the Rhine. He covered the smoke-shrouded span of more than 300 m (330 yds) by ducking and weaving from girder to girder to avoid the machine-gun fire being sprayed from two towers on the German-held side of the bridge and the shellfire from guns pounding on the nearby river bank. But he achieved fame by mistake. He made his lone dash under the impression that his platoon leader, Sergeant Joe DeLisio, was ahead of him. In fact, DeLisio and other men of the US First Army followed Drabik to establish the first east-bank bridgehead.

The unexpected triumph at Remagen was a great psychological fillip for the Allies, but when General Omar Bradley, commander of 12th Army Group, gleefully reported the news to the headquarters of the Supreme Allied Commander, US General Dwight D. Eisenhower, one of Eisenhower's senior aides, replied: 'Sure, you've got a bridge, Brad, but it's in the wrong place. It just doesn't fit the plan.' Bradley retorted angrily: 'What in hell do you want us to do, pull back and blow it up?' Eisenhower, though, later called its capture 'one of my happy moments of the war'.

Since the beginning of the year, the Allies' overriding aim had been to reach and then cross the Rhine – western Europe's greatest river, which rises in Switzerland and flows 1320 km (825 miles) to the North Sea. Flanked for much of its length by cliffs or high hills, swift flowing and 500 m (550 yds) or more wide in many places, it presented a formidable barrier (see map, p. 415).

Following the D-Day landings in Normandy in June 1944, the Allied armies had driven the Germans out of most of France, Belgium, Luxembourg and the southern part of the Netherlands. They had made a costly attempt to cross the Lower Rhine at Arnhem in Operation 'Market Garden' and failed. But by the time they launched their 1945 New Year offensive they had penetrated German territory and established a line along the Maas, Waal and Roer rivers, then south to the west bank of the Rhine just north of Strasbourg – not a practicable crossing point because of the steep cliffs on both sides.

The offensive was due to be launched in January, but was put back some four weeks by the Battle of the Ardennes. According to Eisenhower's plans, the main thrust of the attack would be made in the north. British Field Marshal Sir Bernard Montgomery's 21st Army Group, whose combined British, Canadian and US troops on the Maas and Roer rivers were closest to the Rhine, would aim for the river between Emmerich and Düsseldorf. Theirs would be the first and most important crossing.

Farther south, Bradley would advance with 12th Army Group through the Eifel, a region of moors and forests, to the stretch of the river between Cologne and Koblenz. There they would make a second crossing – just in case Montgomery's failed to split the German forces. German resistance on the east bank was expected to be fierce. A double crossing fitted well with the Allies' next main objective – to encircle and gain control of Germany's industrial heartland, the Ruhr valley. Farther south, US Lt General Jacob Devers' 6th Army Group was given the task of driving the Germans out of the Saarland and moving on to the Rhine at Mannheim.

During January it would have been logical for the Germans to withdraw across the Rhine to conserve their forces. But Hitler wanted to hold on to the river for as long as possible. It was a useful supply route and many Germans considered it an insurmountable psychological barrier against the Allies. Moreover, the fortified Siegfried Line down Germany's western frontier and the Roer and Maas rivers made good defences. The Führer ordered his troops to resist to the last.

BRITISH RESERVATIONS

The British – particularly Montgomery – were at first unhappy with Eisenhower's plan since they did not believe that the Allies had the resources for more than one thrust across the Rhine. Montgomery even threatened to resign, but Eisenhower eventually convinced him that the 'broad front' strategy should stay in place.

Montgomery's plans for his part of the initial offensive had two parts – code-named 'Veritable' and 'Grenade'. Operation 'Veritable' was assigned to the Canadian First Army under Lt General Henry Crerar, based around Nijmegen in the eastern Netherlands. They would strike south-east down a narrow corridor between the Maas and Rhine rivers, through the Reichswald (a dense forest, where visibility was often only a few metres), to reach the Rhine south of Emmerich. Also under Crerar's command was Lt General Brian Horrocks' British XXX Corps. Meanwhile, in Operation 'Grenade', the US Ninth Army under General William H. Simpson would sweep north-east from the Roer towards Düsseldorf and link up with the Canadians opposite Wesel, where Montgomery planned later to cross the Rhine.

First, however, an awkward German salient projecting into the Allied lines just north of Simpson's army had to be cleared. The so-called 'Roermond Triangle' was a patch of wooded countryside crisscrossed by waterways around the Dutch town of Roermond. The operation to clear it – 'Blackcock'– was assigned to the British XII Corps under Lt General Neil Ritchie.

Until mid-January the weather around Roermond was bitterly cold, the ground frozen hard and covered with snow. But on the eve of 'Blackcock', warmer weather brought a sudden thaw and fog, forcing a 12 hour postponement. When the attack began on January 16 it made slow progress. The Germans, now fighting close to their own frontier, resisted fiercely and it took ten days to complete the operation.

CLOSING ON THE RHINE

Operation 'Veritable' began at 5 am on February 8 with a massive artillery bombardment from more than 1000 guns, firing at a single German

division along an 11 km (7 mile) front. At 10.30 am Horrocks' corps went into the attack and made rapid progress. By the end of the day they had captured 1300 German prisoners. However, many of the troops opposing them during the first day came from among the poorest units of the German Army – including the so-called 'Stomach Battalion' of sick soldiers. Hardened paratroops of the First Parachute Army under General Alfred Schlemm were quickly brought forward.

At the same time the continuing thaw had caused widespread flooding. The mud and dense evergreens of the Reichswald slowed down the Allied advance. The Germans had also fortified several of the villages of the region. Nonetheless, by February 16 the Allies had cleared the forest and the little town of Kleve and were on the Rhine opposite Emmerich. By February 21 they were in Kalkar and Goch and had closed up to the Rhine as far south as Xanten. Operation 'Veritable' was accomplished.

General Simpson's Operation 'Grenade' was originally due to begin the day after 'Veritable' on February 10. That day, however, the Germans released the water from behind a series of dams on the Roer and flooded the country across which the

BRIDGE THAT WOULD NOT DIE The Ludendorff Bridge at Remagen was an unexpected prize for the Americans, and for ten days it resisted German air and V-2 attacks trying to destroy it. Troops poured across, until it could take no more and collapsed. (Inset) Medics attend an injured man among the fallen girders. More than 100 engineers were on the bridge when it fell; 28 died. By then, pontoon bridges had gone up nearby and troops continued to cross.

Americans were due to advance. General Courtney Hodges with the US First Army – part of Bradley's 12th Army Group – had been sent forward to capture the dams, but arrived too late.

Simpson had to wait until February 23 before the operation could begin. Once started, however, he met little resistance, for 'Veritable' was tying down the bulk of the German reserves to the north. The US Ninth Army's tanks quickly negotiated the remains of the floods and moved onto drier ground beyond the Roer. They seized Mönchengladbach on March 1, then divided. Some headed north-east to link up with the Canadians; the rest headed east and the next day reached the banks of the Rhine near Düsseldorf.

THE UNSUNG LEADER

Bradley's two chief commanders in 12th Army Group made an interesting contrast – George S. Patton, bombastic and publicity-seeking, and Courtney H. Hodges (1887-1966), quiet, reserved and the least famous of the great American commanders of the war.

Hodges rose through the ranks to become chief of the US infantry at his country's entry into the war. Before and during the Normandy landings he served as Bradley's deputy commander in the US First Army, then on August 1, 1944, assumed full command. In the last months of 1944 he liberated Luxembourg and southern Belgium, and his cool command of events during the Battle of the Ardennes played a major part in the German defeat there. In 1945 his men seized the Remagen bridge over the Rhine and in April linked up with Soviet troops on the Elbe.

Back in the north, British and Canadian troops of Crerar's army were now advancing south-east. They took Geldern on March 4, then headed east towards Wesel. By now the German First Parachute Army had been squeezed between Simpson's men from the south and Crerar's from the north into the wooded hills of the Hochwald, a formidable defensive position opposite Wesel. They were forced out on March 2 after three days' desperate fighting, though an obstinate pocket of German troops held out until March 10.

Meanwhile, in the south, Hodges' US First Army and General George S. Patton's US Third Army (constituting 12th Army Group) had been attacking German positions along the Siegfried Line. With the launching of 'Grenade' in late February, and the consequent shifting of German forces to the north, they were able to break through and were soon racing for the Rhine from Cologne south to Koblenz.

Farther south again, the US Seventh Army and French First Army of Devers' 6th Army Group had driven the pocket of German troops around Colmar back across the Rhine and were clearing remaining German forces from the Saarland. All was now set for the final Allied thrust in the west, called Operation 'Undertone'.

REMAGEN DRAMA

As Hitler's armies were pushed back beyond the river, the Führer issued strict orders. Bridges were to be kept open for as long as possible and none prepared for demolition until the enemy was within 20 km (12 miles). But neither must they fall intact into enemy hands. Morale, meanwhile, plummeted. One German general, Friedrich Kochling, observed: 'The willingness to fight has given way to resignation and apathy on the part of the command as well as the completely worn-out troops.'

On March 7, men of the US First Army reached the Rhine at Cologne. Here, the retreating Germans had demolished all bridges. But it was on the same day, 45 km (28 miles) farther south at Remagen, that a company of GIs made, almost by accident, the first crossing. Just after noon, 2nd Lieutenant Emmet Burrows reached the top of a gorge at Remagen and was astonished to see below an intact railway bridge. Hastily overcoming minor German resistance on the west bank, 1st Lieutenant Karl Timmermann, Burrows' company commander, dashed for the bridge, which was named after the World War I General Ludendorff. As he and his men were approaching, there was an explosion. It was 3.17 pm. A German engineer had detonated charges on the eastern ramp to the bridge, making a small crater. The Americans pressed on, supported by heavy shelling of German positions on the east bank.

Meanwhile, on the German side, engineers struggled desperately to detonate further charges. Suddenly, at 3.50, there was another explosion. The bridge rose in the air, then settled again. The charges had only partly damaged it. Timmermann's men, led by Sergeant Drabik, charged onto the structure and across, cutting

ON THE MOVE Through the rubble-lined streets of Speicher (top), trucks carry troops of the 385th Infantry Regiment, 76th Division, US Third Army. (Below) Pontoon bridges quickly replaced those destroyed by the retreating Germans. This one carries tanks and jeeps of the US Third Army across a wide stretch of the Rhine south of Koblenz.

FIRST-AID HEROES The men who carried a first-aid kit into battle instead of a Tommy gun were always in the thick of the action, alongside their fighting comrades. Here an American medic attends to an injured parachutist of the US 17th Airborne Division during the landings near Wesel.

everything that might be a demolition cable. The unbelievable had happened: the Americans had captured a bridge over the Rhine – a full two weeks before the main crossing under Montgomery was due to begin, on March 23.

In his characteristically methodical way, Montgomery had begun planning for his crossing as early as October 1944. During the winter he had assembled 250 000 tonnes of material and supplies and 59 000 British and US engineers. It was vital that the crossing should be successful and that there were sufficient troops to exploit it. By March 10, 1945, Montgomery's men had closed up to the Rhine opposite Wesel.

For the Americans in the south, matters were less cut and dried. A number of suitable crossing points were identified, but none led to worthwhile objectives on the other bank. In the end, planners decided that Patton's Third Army should make the second crossing between Koblenz and Mainz. However, when the Remagen bridge was taken, Patton was still fighting some way west of the river. An immediate thrust from Remagen would have been dangerously exposed while Patton and Montgomery were still unready to cross. For the time being, therefore, Eisenhower ordered Hodges simply to consolidate, then slowly expand his bridgehead.

THE FÜHRER'S FURY

The Americans' capture of the bridge was the last straw for Hitler: in a fury he sacked his Commander in Chief on the Western Front, the 70-year-old Field Marshal Gerd von Rundstedt, replacing him with Field Marshal Albert Kesselring, who had been commanding the German armies in Italy. Five junior officers who had been in command around Remagen were tried by field court-martial for dereliction of duty, and four were shot. Two days after the bridge was captured, Nazi Propaganda Minister Josef Goebbels recorded in his diary: 'It is quite devastating . . . In fact it is a raving scandal that the Remagen bridge was not blown in good time.'

Meanwhile, Patton had been making spectacular progress farther south. During the first week of March he had broken through the wooded Eifel region and cleared German forces from the north bank of the Mosel (Moselle), taking 5000 prisoners in the first $2\frac{1}{2}$ days of his attack alone. Reaching Koblenz on the 10th, only to find the bridges there blown up, he swung south-east across the Mosel, cutting off large numbers of German troops defending the Siegfried Line in the Saarland. By contrast, Lt General Alexander Patch's US Seventh Army, to Patton's south, was making slow progress. It attacked north-east through the Siegfried Line between Saarbrücken and Karlsruhe on March 15. But, helped by hilly terrain and stiffened by SS troops, resistance was unexpectedly fierce.

Patton, meanwhile, had reached the Rhine between Mainz and Worms. Ever mindful of personal publicity, he was determined to wrest the limelight from Hodges by making his own crossing at once. 'We have put on a great show,' he recorded in his diary on March 21, 'but I think we will eclipse it when we get across the Rhine.' Scarcely pausing for breath, he ordered his men to cross at the town of Oppenheim. The operation, during the night of March 22/23, using specially designed assault craft and amphibious motor vessels, was a complete success. The Germans were taken totally by surprise. Patton later claimed that most men of the panzer division holding the east bank had been caught in bed.

CROSSING AT WESEL

In the north, meanwhile, Montgomery remained unmoved by the dramatic events farther south. He had fixed the date for his own crossing and was not prepared to bring it forward. Simpson's US Ninth Army had reached the Rhine near Düsseldorf as early as March 3, but the British commander steadfastly refused the American's pleas to cross there and then.

By March 23 he had assembled no fewer than 250 000 men. Every possible German resistance point on the east bank had been bombed. That evening, 195 RAF Lancasters and 23 Mosquitoes struck the unfortunate town of Wesel. Their attack was followed by a short, sharp artillery bombardment.

'The enemy possibly thinks he is safe behind this great river obstacle,' Montgomery told his men that day. 'We all agree that it is a great obstacle, but we will show the enemy that he is far from safe behind it. This great Allied fighting machine, composed of integrated land and air forces, will deal with the problem in no uncertain manner. And having crossed the Rhine, we will crack about in the plains of Germany, chasing the enemy from pillar to post.'

The assault began at 9 pm on March 23. British commandos in Buffalo amphibious vehicles crossed the river and established a bridgehead just west of Wesel, meeting little opposition from the dazed German defenders. The RAF bombers now returned for one final devastating attack. According to the diary of one Commando officer: 'It seemed as if more than mortal powers had been unleashed.' During the bombardment the 15th and 51st Scottish Divisions crossed at Xanten on the commandos' left. Men of the Royal Tank Regiment, manning the Buffaloes that carried the Scots across, took with them the flag borne by their regiment when its men were the first British troops to cross the Rhine in December 1918.

The crossings continued all night, and by 9.45 the following morning Montgomery's tank and infantry troops were all across. Then at 10 am they saw a huge armada of aircraft flying east. The next moment paratroops of the British 6th and US 17th Airborne Divisions were dropping on the high ground north-east of Wesel. German anti-aircraft gun emplacements beneath inflicted heavy casualties on the paras and their aircraft. BBC correspondent Richard Dimbleby, flying with them, gave a graphic running report: 'On our right-hand side a Dakota has just gone down in flames . . . Ahead of us, another pillar of black smoke marks the spot where an aircraft has just gone down, and – yet another one; it's a Stirling – a British Stirling; it's going down with flames coming out of its belly.'

Nonetheless, the airborne troops quickly established themselves and linked up with the ground forces. The last German troops were driven out of Wesel on March 25, and Churchill himself watched the final mopping up. Three days later the bridgehead had advanced 45 km (28 miles) on a 40 km (25 mile) front.

The entire west bank of the Rhine from Switzerland to the North Sea was now in Allied hands, and three substantial bridgeheads had been established on the east bank. Victory was clearly in sight. But how to achieve it in the shortest possible time was still the subject of bitter argument among the commanders.

LAST OF THE FLYING BOMBS

The last two V-2 rockets landed in England on March 27, 1945. One struck a block of flats in Stepney, in London's East End, killing 134 people; the other landed at Orpington, Kent. Two days later the last V-1 – a modified long-range version – was shot down by anti-aircraft guns in Suffolk.

For months the number of attacks had been declining as the Allies pinpointed and eradicated the major launch sites and supply depots, bombing disrupted the German rail and road network, and fuel for the weapons became scarce. Finally, on April 11, US troops captured the underground factory near Nordhausen in central Germany – emptying it before the Russians occupied the area on June 1.

In February, the V-2's inventor Wernher von Braun and his staff had fled south from Peenemünde on the Baltic to escape the Russians. They hid 14 tonnes of archives, with vital information on the rockets, down a disused mineshaft north of the Harz mountains. This was to be in the British occupation zone, but the Americans 'liberated' the booty from under their ally's nose. Von Braun later headed the US space programme.

In all, 10 500 V-1s and 1115 V-2s were launched against England – though over a third of the V-1s were shot down before they hit their targets. They caused some 33 000 civilian casualties and much damage to property – but were too late to have any effect on the course of the war.

Advance to the Elbe

Once across the Rhine, the Allies fanned swiftly over Hitler's crumbling Reich and encircled its industrial heart, the Ruhr valley. On April 25 they linked up with the Russians at the Elbe river. Soon after, British troops reached the Baltic and Americans pushed into Czechoslovakia and Austria.

RUHR ROUNDUP Soldiers of the US Ninth Army search the ruins of the Krupps steel works in Essen for 'werewolf' snipers – members of a rumoured resistance group of fanatical young Nazis supposedly ready to harry the Allies.

Capturing the Remagen bridgehead on the Rhine in early March 1945 put General Eisenhower in a quandary. As Supreme Commander of the Allied forces on the Western Front, he was tempted to order his troops to make a bold thrust through central Germany to Berlin – 480 km (300 miles) away – ahead of the Russians, who were still held up on the east bank of the Oder river, only 56 km (35 miles) from the German capital. Eisenhower faced German forces weakened by the Ardennes campaign and by transfers to the Eastern Front, and the Red Army was not yet ready for its final push to the capital of the Reich.

Military considerations had to be weighed against political ones. In the postwar carve-up of Germany agreed at the Yalta conference of Allied leaders in February, the eastern part of the country surrounding Berlin was to become the Soviet Zone. To encroach too far on this now might entail heavy Western casualties in fighting for areas not earmarked for Western control and therefore difficult to justify at home. It might also jeopardise the Anglo-American alliance with the USSR, and Eisenhower was in any case under pressure from Washington to leave Berlin to the Red Army.

Military factors included the need to mop up enemy positions in central Germany to prevent a flanking attack on the thrust in the north. It was military considerations that eventually prevailed, and Eisenhower made it his chief priority to link up with the Russians around the city of Dresden on the Elbe river – thus dividing Germany across the middle and preventing its armies from regrouping.

MANNA FROM HEAVEN A Flying Fortress bomber flies a mission of mercy, dropping medical and food supplies to the Dutch at Schiphol Airport, Amsterdam. In Operation 'Manna', American and RAF bombers, flying very low, dropped 7000 tonnes of supplies in seven days.

So he decided to make the main thrust of the Allied attack from the Rhine across central Germany by the US forces of General Omar Bradley's 12th Army Group. These included General George Patton's Third Army, General Courtney Hodges' First Army and General William Simpson's Ninth Army (transferred from Field Marshal Sir Bernard Montgomery's 21st Army Group). Montgomery and his British and Canadian forces were given the secondary task of clearing the north German plain and securing the north German ports to cut off German armies in Norway and Denmark.

When the British heard Eisenhower's proposals they were aghast. Winston Churchill, whose mistrust of the Soviet leader Joseph Stalin had been growing over the past year, had long considered it vital for the Western Allies to take Berlin before the Russians got there. He believed, as he stated later in his memoirs, 'that Soviet Russia had become a mortal danger to the free world . . . that a new front must be immediately created against her onward sweep . . . that this front in Europe should be as far east as possible . . . that Berlin was the prime and true objective of the Anglo-American armies'. Montgomery, until now under the impression that he was to have the major role in the final drive into Germany, was also deeply upset by Eisenhower's plans.

However, neither the British nor the Americans wanted a major rift at this eleventh hour. The British, whose fighting forces were by this time massively outnumbered by the Americans, were obliged to climb down, although Montgomery continued to pester Eisenhower over the need to press on for Berlin.

REDUCING THE RUHR

The Allies' first task after the main Rhine crossing at Wesel in late March was to capture the 'forge of Germany', the Ruhr valley. This was Germany's most important coalfield and heavy industrial region, home of the great Krupp arms factories and Thyssen steelworks. It had been battered into rubble by months of incessant Allied bombing but was held by German Army Group B under Field Marshal Walther Model, whom Hitler commanded to defend the region to the last man.

Model's task was desperate. By April 1 the Ruhr was completely encircled by American armies; Simpson's Ninth coming from the north and Hodges' First from the south had linked up at Lippstadt, east of the valley. Nevertheless, the Germans continued to resist the Americans for 18 more days. In some towns the Germans surrendered without firing a shot, the mayor in many cases meeting the approaching Americans with a white flag. Elsewhere resistance was fierce, especially in the steep hills and valleys of the Sauerland, south of the Ruhr river, where every stream, village and defile was defended. By the time their resistance had at last been crushed, the Americans had taken no fewer than 325 000 prisoners, greater than the number captured by the Red Army at Stalingrad in 1943. Model committed suicide on April 21.

Meanwhile, other Allied forces were advancing rapidly east and north. The British Second Army under Lt General Sir Miles Dempsey, to the north of Simpson, captured Osnabrück on April 4 and reached the Weser river the following day.

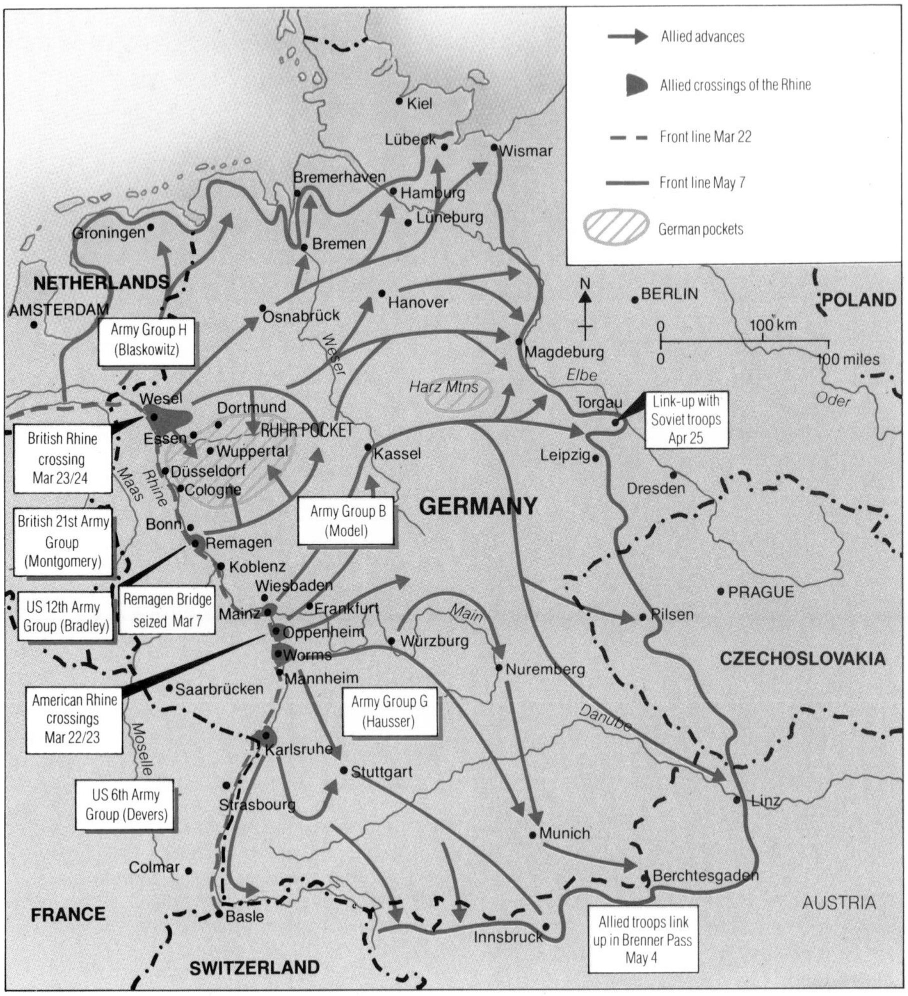

ALLIED BLITZKRIEG Once established in bridgeheads east of the Rhine, American, British and Canadian armies swept swiftly across the crumbling Third Reich. The Ruhr was encircled in classic blitzkrieg style.

The British then turned north, and on April 17 entered the suburbs of the port city of Bremen; but another nine days' fighting was needed to capture it. On April 19 British troops reached the Elbe opposite Lauenburg, east of Hamburg, then began to close up to the river farther south.

North of the British, the Canadian First Army under Lt General Henry Crerar was given the task of liberating the northern Netherlands. The people of this region had suffered from acute starvation and cold during the winter, following the Allied failure to break through at Arnhem. In retaliation the Germans had refused to move food, and by November many Dutch subsisted on only 1650 kJ (400 calories) a day, while fuel supplies had dwindled to nothing.

On April 2 the Canadians broke out of their bridgehead across the Waal at Nijmegen and secured Arnhem on April 15, after three days' savage fighting. They then made rapid progress, capturing Groningen, over 145 km (90 miles) to the north, by the end of the following day. This left the German Twenty-Fifth Army, centred on Amsterdam, still virtually intact. On April 28 Lt General Walter Bedell Smith (Eisenhower's chief of staff) arranged a ceasefire with the Germans, who from the next day allowed Allied bombers to drop food and medical supplies to the starving Dutch in the aptly named Operation 'Manna'. One aircrew member recalled: 'Children ran out of school waving excitedly . . . The roads were crowded with hundreds of people waving.'

PATTON'S PRIVATE CAMPAIGN

The Americans were also moving swiftly east. On April 10, while their fellow GIs were still fighting in the Ruhr, parts of Simpson's army reached Hanover. The following day his tanks arrived at the Elbe near Magdeburg and secured a bridgehead across it. They were now just 120 km (75 miles) from Hitler's Chancellery.

Patton's Third Army in the meantime struck north-east from their bridgehead over the Rhine at Oppenheim. On March 29 they took Frankfurt, where German resistance was initially fierce, so Patton allowed his tanks to bypass the city, leaving his infantry to capture it. He linked up with Hodges at Kassel on April 4, then turned east towards Leipzig.

During this drive, on the night of March 26/27, Patton may have indulged in a little private campaigning of his own. He sent an armoured column deep behind the enemy lines to a prisoner-of-war camp at Hammelburg, 65 km (40 miles) east of Frankfurt. The column reached the camp but was destroyed on the way back. Patton claimed that the point of the operation was to confuse the Germans. However, his son-in-law, Lt Colonel John K. Waters, who had been captured at Kasserine in Tunisia in early 1943, was an inmate of the camp, and most people believed that Patton's principal purpose was to rescue him. Waters was badly wounded and recaptured by the Germans during the operation.

Farther south, Lt General Alexander Patch's US Seventh Army, part of 6th Army Group, crossed the Main river at Würzburg on April 5. The group's other wing, the French First Army under General de Lattre de Tassigny, crossed the Rhine north of Karlsruhe on March 31, then turned south towards the Swiss border.

The progress of the Western Allies by mid-April had exceeded all expectations, despite occasional pockets of fierce German resistance – in the Ruhr, for example, and at Bremen. The Russians were still not ready to move out from the Oder, and the Anglo-Americans could still probably have beaten them to Berlin. But Eisenhower remained adamant that the German capital was a Russian responsibility and refused to move beyond the Elbe.

At the same time he was increasingly concerned by reports that the Nazis were planning a dramatic last stand in a 'National Redoubt' in the Alps. In order to forestall this, Eisenhower now made Munich the principal objective for his armies in the south. Patton – at the time heading across central Germany for Leipzig – therefore turned south-east instead, down the Danube valley into Bavaria, while Patch drove down on Patton's right through Nuremberg and into western Austria to link up with the US Fifth Army, which was advancing through northern Italy.

WHAT IF EISENHOWER HAD TARGETED BERLIN?

By mid-April 1945, the lightning advance of the Anglo-American armies had thrown the Germans into complete confusion, and Eisenhower's troops could almost certainly have reached Berlin ahead of the Russians – even though they were advancing on a broad front rather than making the single thrust attack advocated by Montgomery.

However, once the British and Americans reached Hitler's capital the resistance would have become altogether more formidable. The Germans, stiffened by several fanatical SS units, would probably have defended Berlin as fiercely as they did against the Russians. The resulting Allied casualties would have been high, since street fighting is always costly in lives.

The Russians would undoubtedly have closed in from the east before the Western Allies could secure the whole city. Indeed, Stalin – always mistrustful of British and American intentions – would have accelerated the attack to ensure that he held at least part of Berlin before the final German surrender.

There might also have been clashes, deliberate or not, between Anglo-American troops and their Russians allies. These would not have provoked a major conflict, since both the Western Allies and the USSR wanted the war to end, but they might have resulted in an earlier start to the Cold War – and acrimony would have marred victory over the Third Reich.

CAMPS OF HORROR

During the sweep across Germany the troops of the Western Allied armies saw for the first time the most horrific face of the Third Reich. On April 12 a German officer bearing a flag of truce arrived at the forward position of the British 11th Armoured Division on the Aller river north of Hanover. He asked that the area around a concentration camp at Belsen, just to the north, should be declared neutral. There had been an outbreak of typhus in the camp, he said, and the Germans were anxious that it should not spread.

The British agreed and sent a party of men to secure the camp. They arrived at mid-morning on April 15. The Russians had liberated the horrific extermination camps in Poland, such as Majdanek as early as July 1944 and Auschwitz in January 1945, but none of the censored reports received in Britain – dismissed as Russian propaganda – had prepared the soldiers for what they now found. Many will bear the mental scars of the experience to their dying day.

The organisation of the Belsen camps (there were in fact two – one for men, the other for women) had broken down completely. According to the young captain put in charge of the men's camp: 'I had a precinct littered with corpses, disease rampant, people dying of starvation, no light or water and enormous overcrowding, and I had no doctor, no medical supplies, no surplus food above our own rations and no idea of what was available in the camp.' The SS camp guards still lurked in their quarters – and despite intense revulsion for them the British soldiers had to protect them from the prisoners. There were similar scenes when the Americans liberated Buchenwald near Erfurt on April 13 and Dachau near Munich on April 29 – although at Dachau some SS men were summarily executed by GIs.

Coming across these monstrous sights spurred the men of the Allied armies to yet greater efforts to finish the war. History was made on April 25, 1945, near Torgau on the Elbe, when the Americans of Hodges' First Army rushed forward to meet Russian troops from Marshal Koniev's 1st Ukrainian Front. The two superpowers of East and West had linked up, for the first time, in the heart of war-devastated Europe.

In the north the British closed on Hamburg and Lübeck, and in the south Patch's US Seventh Army seized Munich on April 30. The French entered western Austria the day after. Patton drove into Czechoslovakia determined to reach Prague before the Russians, but was halted on May 5 by Eisenhower who did not want a clash with Stalin's troops. Patch pushed on south towards Innsbruck, in Austria.

Meanwhile, fighting had come to an end in Italy and the Russians had closed in on Berlin, where they were now clearing the last German resistance. The war in Europe would be over in a matter of days.

END OF THE NIGHTMARE An emaciated Buchenwald inmate poses for the cameras after the liberation of the concentration camp by the Americans in April 1945. Earlier in the month thousands of his fellow inmates had been piled into sealed trains by their SS guards, and with no food were shunted around what was left of the Third Reich in order to conceal their pitiful plight from the Allies. The intervention of the International Red Cross prevented many more being sent off in this way, but many of those who remained were too smitten with disease and starvation for their lives to be saved. Disguised SS men tried to escape.

LINK-UP ON THE ELBE

No one quite knew what would happen when Russian and Western Allied troops made contact. No mutual stop line had been agreed, but Eisenhower ordered his men not to advance beyond the Elbe river. When Hodges' US First Army took Leipzig on April 19 a more westerly limit of the Mulde river was imposed for fear of a clash with the Russians.

Six days later, Hodges was told that he could send patrols forward 8 km (5 miles) towards the Elbe, but no farther. On April 26 a group set out under the command of 1st Lieutenant Albert Kotzebue of the US 69th Infantry Division. The lieutenant met a number of Germans who wanted to surrender, but could not resist moving beyond the 8 km limit. At about 11.30 am, when 1.5 km (1 mile) from the Elbe, he spotted a Soviet cavalryman who regarded the Americans with suspicion; when asked through an interpreter where his commander was, the Russian merely waved to the east.

Kotzebue's patrol continued to the village of Strehla, near Torgau on the Elbe, where he found the remains of a pontoon bridge. There were figures on the far bank whom he identified through his binoculars as Russians. It was just after midday. Kotzebue could not raise the Russians on his radio, so he fired the agreed recognition signal of two green flares. The figures opposite approached the water's edge and stared back. Kotzebue shouted 'Amerikansky!' but there was still no positive response. He then spotted four small boats moored to the bank and quickly rowed across the Elbe with a small party.

When he told the Russians that he wanted to meet their commander, they broke into smiles and began slapping the Americans on the back. Shortly afterwards Lt Colonel Alexander Gardiev of the 175th Rifle Regiment appeared, shook hands with Kotzebue and said that it was a proud moment for both countries. Gardiev then told Kotzebue to take his party farther upstream where the rest of his men could cross by a hand-drawn ferry, and he would then take him to meet his superior, the commander of the 58th Guards Rifle Division.

When Kotzebue and his patrol reached General Vladimir Rusakov's headquarters a banquet had been laid out. Soon a party was in full swing with many toasts in vodka. The Third Reich was split in two.

The end in Italy

For nearly six months Allied and German armies had faced each other across Italy in near-stalemate. Then, in April 1945, the Italian front suddenly broke into life. Just one month later, all German troops in Italy surrendered.

THE WINTER OF 1944-5 was particularly grim in northern Italy. There were heavy snowfalls and freezing temperatures. Morale was dangerously low among troops of the Allied 15th Army Group, because of exhaustion after the hard fighting of 1944 and the widespread feeling that Italy was merely an unimportant sideshow of the war. By January 1945 they were holding a line from north of Viareggio on Italy's west coast across the mountainous spine of the Apennines and down to the east coast along the south bank of the Senio river. Then in February their fighting strength was seriously reduced after the Canadian I Corps was transferred to north-western Europe.

In December 1944 Field Marshal Sir Harold Alexander, Supreme Allied Commander in the Mediterranean theatre, decided to give his men a break from battle until April. He then planned to mount a final decisive push to drive the Germans back to the Alps. In the meantime the men would be kept busy patrolling the front line and preparing their jump-off positions – and with a strenuous training programme, practising everything from river crossings to street fighting.

If Allied morale was low, the position of the German Army Group C in Italy – which included five low-calibre Italian Fascist divisions – had become increasingly serious. In March General Heinrich von Vietinghoff took over command after Hitler promoted Field Marshal Albert Kesselring to Commander in Chief on the Western Front. Vietinghoff's troops occupied good defensive positions opposite the Allies along fortified river lines in the east and in mountains in the west, but they lacked strong reserves, which had been transferred to the main Eastern and Western Fronts. His only sensible course therefore was to continue the fighting withdrawal that Kesselring had conducted the previous year, using the Po and Adige rivers to cover his rear, then make a last stand in the Alps.

Kesselring, still Vietinghoff's commanding officer, supported this plan, but Hitler vetoed it. The Führer insisted that Army Group C must stand and fight where it was. Vietinghoff's position was further weakened by the Allies' overwhelming air superiority, which devastated his communications and made it almost impossible to bring his few tank reserves into play.

Around this time SS General Karl Wolff, head of the SS and police in German-occupied Italy and an even more powerful figure in the region than its nominal ruler Benito Mussolini, became convinced that the war was lost. At the end of February 1945, without the authorisation or knowledge of the Nazi leaders in Berlin, he opened secret negotiations with Allen Dulles, representative in Switzerland of the US Office of Strategic Services (predecessor of the CIA). Wolff tried to persuade the Western Allies to sign a separate peace with Germany, whose hands would then be freed to deal with the Russians.

FIRE AND FRATERNITY On Highway 64 near Bologna the 17-pounder (76.2 mm) guns of M10 tank destroyers blast German positions fighting a rearguard action against the advancing US Fifth Army. Baby-kissing (below) makes a welcome change from fighting for the infantry of the British Eighth Army passing through the streets of the newly won town of Ferrara in the Po valley.

BATTLE BEGINS

Alexander's spring offensive opened on the night of April 1/2. In a surprise attack, British commandos seized a wedge of land on the southern shore of Lake Comacchio, immediately north of the Allied lines on the east coast. In follow-up operations over the next few days, the commandos also took islands on the lake and a further stretch of its southern shore. One hero of these operations was Major Anders Lassen, a Dane in the British Army, who won a posthumous Victoria Cross for giving his life when covering the withdrawal of his men after a raid on the town of Comacchio.

The main attacks began on April 9. Because the Allies only had enough air power to give overwhelming close support to one major attack at a time, Alexander had decided that the British Eighth Army in the east under Lt General Sir Richard McCreery should attack first. It would head north-west across the Senio and Santerno rivers towards Ferrara, just south of the Po river. During the winter the Germans had flooded the low-lying country north of the Senio and Santerno, and the only dry route across was the main road from Ravenna to Ferrara through the town of Argenta – the so-called Argenta Gap. According to McCreery's plan, commandos would make an amphibious attack across Lake Comacchio to tie down German defences east of Argenta, while the main attack would be made from the south-east through the Argenta Gap.

The amphibious assault was launched in difficult circumstances. Weeks of drought had lowered the water level of the lake so much that the storm boats could not be launched from the shore. According to the Commando brigade major who took part, 'For hours men heaved and dragged and pushed unwieldy craft across more than a mile of sticky glutinous mud . . . It was a nightmare mixture of Venice by moonlight and the end of the Henley Regatta'.

FREEDOM FIGHTERS Italian soldiers earned a poor reputation in North Africa, but when Italy changed sides in 1943 and declared war on Germany, its troops acquitted themselves well alongside the Allies to free their homeland from the Nazi occupation.

Despite these problems, the attacks were a complete success. By April 17 the Eighth Army was in Argenta which one participant found to be 'a hideous heap of rubble, the civilian dead piled in pathetic masses and Germans still holding out in cellars and strongpoints'. By nightfall the town had been taken, and two days later the fighting was within 25 km (16 miles) of Ferrara. On April 14 the other wing of 15th Army Group, Maj General Lucien Truscott's US Fifth Army, had also opened its attack from the mountains south of Bologna. It met fierce resistance at first but by April 20 had broken through east of the city, which was taken unopposed the following day by Polish troops from the Eighth Army.

By now the Germans were under impossible pressure. For days Vietinghoff had been begging Hitler to let him withdraw beyond the Po – but in vain. On April 20 the German commander decided to take matters into his own hands and ordered a withdrawal without the Führer's approval. Three days later most of his men were across the river, but they had to leave behind almost all their heavy equipment.

SURRENDER

At this point Vietinghoff realised that Army Group C was doomed. On April 22 he met Wolff and other German commanders in Italy at Recoaro Terme in the foothills of the Alps. Here they agreed to surrender, regardless of orders from Berlin. On April 29, at Alexander's headquarters at Caserta near Naples, their representatives signed a document for the unconditional surrender of all German troops in Italy from 2 pm on May 2 – almost a week before the main German surrender. Meanwhile the Allies overran northern Italy and by May 6 were through the Brenner Pass and into Austria.

The campaign in Italy had achieved its objective of tying down large numbers of German troops. It was unique for the number of nationalities fighting in the Allied armies; besides British and Americans, there were Canadians, New Zealanders, Australians, South Africans, Poles, Italians, French, Belgians, Indians and even, from late 1944, a Brazilian corps. In addition, Italian partisan brigades harried German lines of communication.

WOLFF – THE POWER BEHIND MUSSOLINI'S THRONE

Exceptional charm, suave good looks and elegance helped Karl Wolff (1900-84) rise rapidly through the ranks of the SS. Having served as an under-age officer in World War I, he joined the Nazi party in 1931. Three years later he became principal aide and chief of staff to SS boss Heinrich Himmler – who is said to have seen in Wolff all the social poise and assurance that he himself lacked.

In September 1943 Wolff became senior SS and police commander in German-occupied northern Italy, nominally ruled by Mussolini, and later military governor and Hitler's personal plenipotentiary to Mussolini. His secret negotiations with Allied representatives led to the German surrender in Italy on May 2.

Wolff escaped prosecution at Nuremberg, though he appeared as a witness. But a German court later sentenced him to four years' hard labour for complicity in war crimes. He was released after only a week and went on to become a highly successful advertising agent. In 1962 he was rearrested by the German authorities after evidence emerged that he had sent Jews from eastern Europe to their death at the Treblinka extermination camp in Poland. He was sentenced to 15 years' penal servitude but was released in 1971.

THE DEATH OF 'IL DUCE'

After his rescue in September 1943, Mussolini was no more than Hitler's puppet. He ruled in name a state from Salò, beside Lake Garda, but northern Italy's real rulers were the Germans. In April 1945, as the Axis armies began to collapse in the Po valley, Mussolini left Salò for Milan, where he was joined by his mistress, Clara Petacci. Rejecting advice to flee to Spain, he was determined to join the Nazis in a dramatic last stand in the Alps. On April 25 Mussolini, Clara and a German escort left Milan for Como at the edge of the Alps, where Alessandro Pavolini, a loyal Fascist, had arranged to meet them with 3000 Blackshirts.

When they reached Como that night, however, there was no Pavolini. The party drove farther north, and near Menaggio Pavolini at length caught up with them. He brought just 12 men. Mussolini and his group had no option but to join a German convoy heading north into Austria.

At about 7 the next morning the convoy was halted by partisans, who agreed to allow the Germans through the roadblock, but no Italian Fascists. Mussolini was arrested with Clara. The next two days, while the partisans awaited instructions from the Committee for National Liberation, Mussolini and his mistress were kept in a small farmhouse. On the afternoon of April 28 a Communist partisan, Walter Audisio, arrived and bundled Mussolini and Clara into a car. After a short drive the car stopped. Audisio ordered them out, then shot them.

Their bodies were then taken to Milan and dumped in front of a garage in the Piazzale Loretto, where partisans had been shot in reprisal by Fascists a year before. Both were strung up by their ankles. People hurled filth and spat at the already disfigured corpses. Some laughed hysterically. One woman fired five shots into Mussolini 'to avenge her five dead sons'.

FASCIST FINALE Benito Mussolini, between Clara Petacci and a Fascist follower, on grisly display.

The battle for Berlin

After weeks of preparation the Red Army broke across the Oder for its long-expected attack on the German capital, and within ten days had completely encircled it. But the city fell only after bitter fighting, street by street.

STALIN'S ARMIES were launching out across the Oder river for the final attack on Berlin. But Hitler was determined to fight to the end. 'For the last time, the deadly Jewish-Bolshevik enemy has started a mass attack,' the Führer declared in a written order to his troops on April 15, 1945. 'He is trying to reduce Germany to rubble and to exterminate our people. Soldiers of the East! You are already fully aware now of the fate that threatens German women and children. While men, children and old people will be murdered, women and girls will be reduced to the role of barrack-room whores. The rest will be marched off to Siberia . . .'

Since early February Hitler had been preparing to defend his capital against the huge Soviet armies poised only 56 km (35 miles) away. He had three massive defensive lines – with anti-tank ditches, gun positions and other means – constructed to the east of the city, stretching 320 km (200 miles) from the Baltic in the north to the Sudeten Mountains along the German-Czechoslovak border in the south. Key to the first line was the rugged Seelow Heights, which ran north-south some 8 km (5 miles) west of a major Soviet bridgehead on the west bank of the Oder opposite Küstrin (now Kostrzyn). All villages and towns along the lines were converted into fortresses able to meet attacks from any direction.

ARMIES IN LINE

To defend Berlin Hitler had the Third Panzer Army and Ninth Army of Army Group Vistula, commanded from March by the highly capable General Gotthard Heinrici. They covered the Eastern Front from the Baltic to the junction of the Neisse and Oder rivers. Ninth Army under General Theodor Busse was given the task of blocking the Russians' direct route to Berlin while Third Panzer Army, under General Hasso von Manteuffel, was positioned farther north.

Facing the Soviets in the south, from the Neisse junction to the Sudeten Mountains, was Lt General Fritz Gräser's Fourth Panzer Army, left wing of Field Marshal Ferdinand Schörner's Army Group Centre. In operational reserve for the fighting east of Berlin were the six divisions of General Karl Weidling's LVI Panzer Corps. Also available was General Walther Wenck's Twelfth Army, eight divisions flung together from raw recruits and others without time to develop any cohesion. In the Berlin area itself there were some 100 *Volkssturm* (Home Guard) battalions, and north of the capital SS General Felix Steiner had some troops who were optimistically called by Hitler the Eleventh Army – though, in fact, they consisted of little more than an SS police division. In all, Hitler had around a million soldiers facing the Russians.

His men were massively outnumbered. Together Marshal Georgi Zhukov's 1st Belorussian Front on the Oder opposite Berlin and Marshal Ivan Koniev's 1st Ukrainian Front on the Neisse to the south had some 2.5 million confident, well-equipped soldiers. Farther north was the 2nd Belorussian Front under Marshal Konstantin Rokossovsky.

Yet Hitler – isolating himself more and more with his closest followers in his vast underground shelter, the Führerbunker – had deluded himself that Germany would still win. 'This time the Bolshevist will experience the old fate of Asia,' he told his troops on April 15. 'He must and shall fall before the capital city of the Third Reich.'

MARCHING ORDERS

On April 1 Stalin summoned Zhukov and Koniev to Moscow to give them their orders for the capture of Berlin. Zhukov's 1st Belorussian Front would make the main attack on the German

WHAT IF THE NAZIS HAD MADE A LAST STAND?

Disturbing reports began to reach General Eisenhower in February 1945: Intelligence sources suggested that the Nazis were planning to withdraw the cream of their forces to a 'National Redoubt' in the Alps of southern Bavaria, western Austria and northern Italy, where, in well-nigh impregnable positions, they would make a last stand.

In early 1945, Hitler did have the idea of creating such a stronghold and even appointed Field Marshal Schörner to command it, but it was never much more than an idea. Hitler simply did not have the troops or resources left to make it feasible. Nevertheless, Allied anxieties were increased in mid-April when Hitler ordered the hitherto little-known General August Winter to set up headquarters in the Alps. In fact, this had nothing to do with the National Redoubt; Hitler was merely establishing headquarters in both north and south to prepare for the imminent splitting of Germany when the Russians and Western Allies met on the Elbe. Grand Admiral Dönitz set up a similar headquarters, OKH North, at Flensburg near the Danish border.

If the Nazis had established an Alpine stronghold it would have presented the Allies, even assisted by the Russians, with a massive problem. The mountains would have favoured the defence, and persistent bad weather and high altitudes would have limited the effectiveness of the Allied air forces. The defence, too – probably mainly by Waffen-SS troops – would have been fanatical and casualties high.

FINAL PINCH A three-pronged attack from the Oder river by Zhukov's and Koniev's fronts (army groups) sealed the fate of Berlin, while Rokossovsky made for the Baltic.

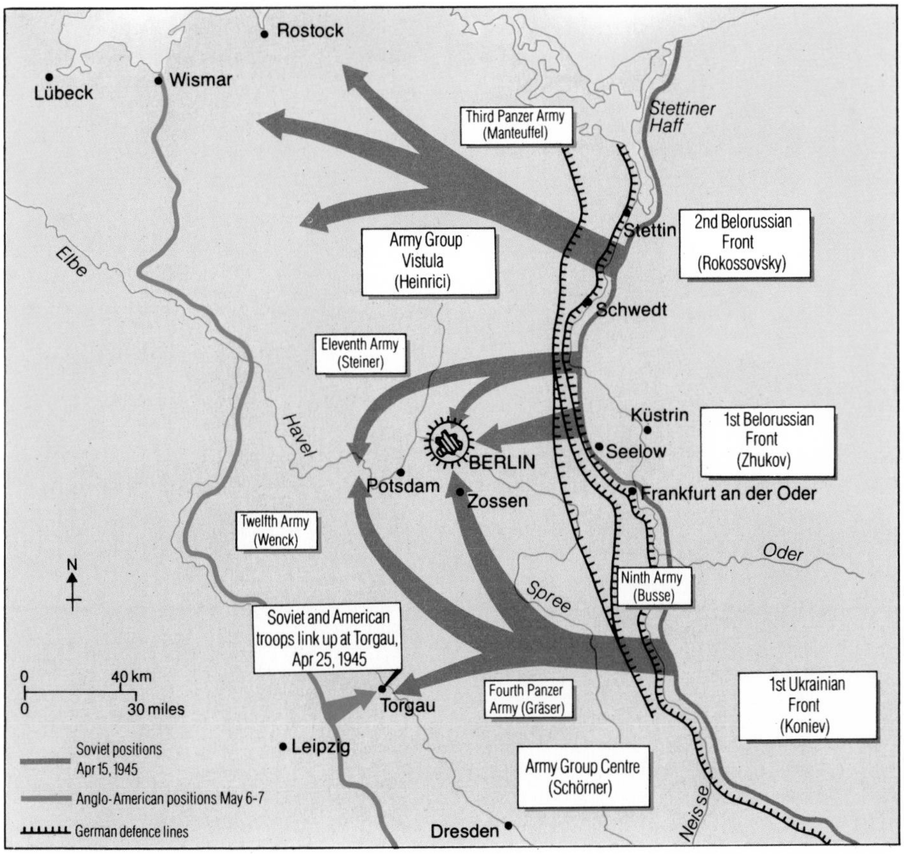

capital from the Küstrin bridgehead. Koniev's 1st Ukrainian Front to the south would support him but was also given Leipzig and Dresden as objectives. To the north Rokossovsky's 2nd Belorussian Front was to clear Pomerania and try to reach the German Baltic ports before the Western Allies.

Zhukov's attack was preceded before dawn on April 16 with a massive artillery barrage against the German positions opposite the Küstrin bridgehead; the Soviets had one gun for every 4 m (13 ft) of the 90 km (55 mile) front line. When Zhukov's troops advanced they soon came up against the Seelow Heights. Here the German resistance was fierce and the Russians did not capture the heights until late on April 17. Almost immediately they came up against the Germans' second defence line, where they again suffered severe casualties. This quickly put Zhukov behind the timetable laid down by Stalin.

To the south Koniev had better fortune. After a short artillery bombardment in the early hours of April 16 his troops crossed the Neisse with little difficulty. The more open terrain in this sector was favourable to tanks, and Koniev's men made rapid progress compared with Zhukov's. On the evening of April 17 Stalin ordered Koniev by telephone to turn two of his tank armies northwards to help Zhukov. Shortly afterwards Zhukov managed to break through opposite Berlin and by April 19 had reached the city's northern outskirts.

As the two Soviet fronts converged on Berlin, they trapped Busse's Ninth Army and much of Gräser's Fourth Panzer Army in a pocket south-east of the German capital – with the result that neither could contribute much to its defence. At the same time Rokossovsky's thrust north of Berlin had similarly trapped Manteuffel's Third Panzer Army against the Stettiner Haff, a large lake near the mouth of the Oder.

BIRTHDAY IN THE BUNKER

Since mid-January, when Hitler returned from his western headquarters at the 'Eagle's Nest' in the Taunus mountains, north-west of Frankfurt, at the end of the Battle of the Ardennes, he had not once left Berlin. Although based in the Reich Chancellery, he began to spend more and more time in the Führerbunker, where his faithful mistress Eva Braun vowed to stay with him to the end. His 56th birthday, on April 20, saw the last great gathering of the Nazi hierarchy, who came to offer Hitler their congratulations in the bunker. The day was also marked by the last Anglo-US air raid on Berlin. By now the city's electricity, gas and sanitation had broken down. There was little food, and street hydrants were the only source of water.

Hitler had intended to leave Berlin immediately after his birthday, planning to move to his summer retreat at Berchtesgaden in the Bavarian Alps, around which the Nazis would establish a 'National Redoubt' for their last stand (see box). After the birthday gathering there was a wholesale departure of Nazi leaders, including Himmler and Göring, from Berlin. But Hitler, now obsessed with the possibility of a decisive counterattack against the Russians north of his capital, decided to stay on.

More and more a victim of self-delusion, he had convinced himself that Steiner's largely illusory Eleventh Army could link up with Manteuffel north of Berlin, strike south and rescue the city from the Russians. He was encouraged in this delusion by visits from the fanatical Schörner of Army Group Centre and Wenck, who announced that his Twelfth Army would attack and tie down the Americans closing in on the Elbe, to the south-west.

But Steiner did not move. Attacks from Rokossovsky's and Zhukov's fronts left him in no position to mount a counteroffensive. Hitler, furious at Steiner's failure, decided to take personal charge of the city's defence, and a radio broadcast on April 22 announced that the Führer would stay in his capital to the last.

BERLIN ENCIRCLED

Meanwhile the Russian net was closing around Berlin. On April 21 Zhukov's armies had managed to break across the autobahn ring north of the city, although resistance in the east was still fierce. Koniev to the south continued to make good progress, capturing Zossen, about 35 km (22 miles) south of Berlin, on April 20. The following day his infantry were penetrating the capital's southern suburbs. His simultaneous drive to Dresden, though, was being held up by savage German counterattacks.

Realising that Berlin was about to be encircled, Hitler ordered his armies fighting the Western Allies towards the Elbe to come to the rescue – but it was too late. On April 24 Koniev's and Zhukov's forces met south-west of the city; the day after, US and Russian troops met for the first time near Torgau on the Elbe river. All efforts to break through to the beleaguered German garrison from the west were thwarted.

The final Russian assault on Berlin began on April 26, preceded by heavy air attacks – but it took a week of savage street fighting to destroy the last German resistance. Remnants of Wehrmacht, Volkssturm (*continued on p. 423*)

DAY OF RETRIBUTION In Berlin's fashionable Hohenzollernstrasse Soviet tank crews, some mere boys, receive the orders that will send them into the final phase of the battle for Germany's capital. Then, with grim memories of Moscow, Stalingrad and Leningrad, the avenging Russians roll relentlessly into the heart of the city – part of a 4000-strong armada of tanks moving in to crush the last remnants of German resistance. Smoke and fumes wreathe the shattered ruins of the Brandenburg Gate, Berlin's most famous landmark and once the scene of Hitler's great military parades. Rubble litters the shell-torn streets and shocked Berliners watch helplessly as their Führer's Third Reich crumbles to dust. Amid the ruins of Berlin (bottom), a Hitler Youth and a soldier wait for the advancing tanks.

Battle for the Reichstag

The Reichstag building in Berlin became the symbol of last-ditch resistance in the last days of the Nazi regime. In 1933 the building had been set on fire, and the Nazis blamed it on the Communists; now, ironically, Stalin's Red Army would turn it into a blazing inferno once again.

The assault began on April 30, with an artillery bombardment and Katyusha rockets, and the building was eventually stormed by infantrymen of the 380th, 574th and 756th Infantry Regiments. Nazi fanaticism, however, was to make it a long and bloody task. More than 5000 SS men, Hitler Youth and *Volkssturm* (Home Guard) members resisted desperately, fighting for every room, corridor, staircase and storey. It took the Russians two days to overcome the last vestige of resistance, and some 2500 of the Reichstag's defenders died, with 2600 taken prisoner.

VICTORS AND VANQUISHED Russian soldiers smile happily as the defeated Germans emerge from below the streets and lay down their arms.

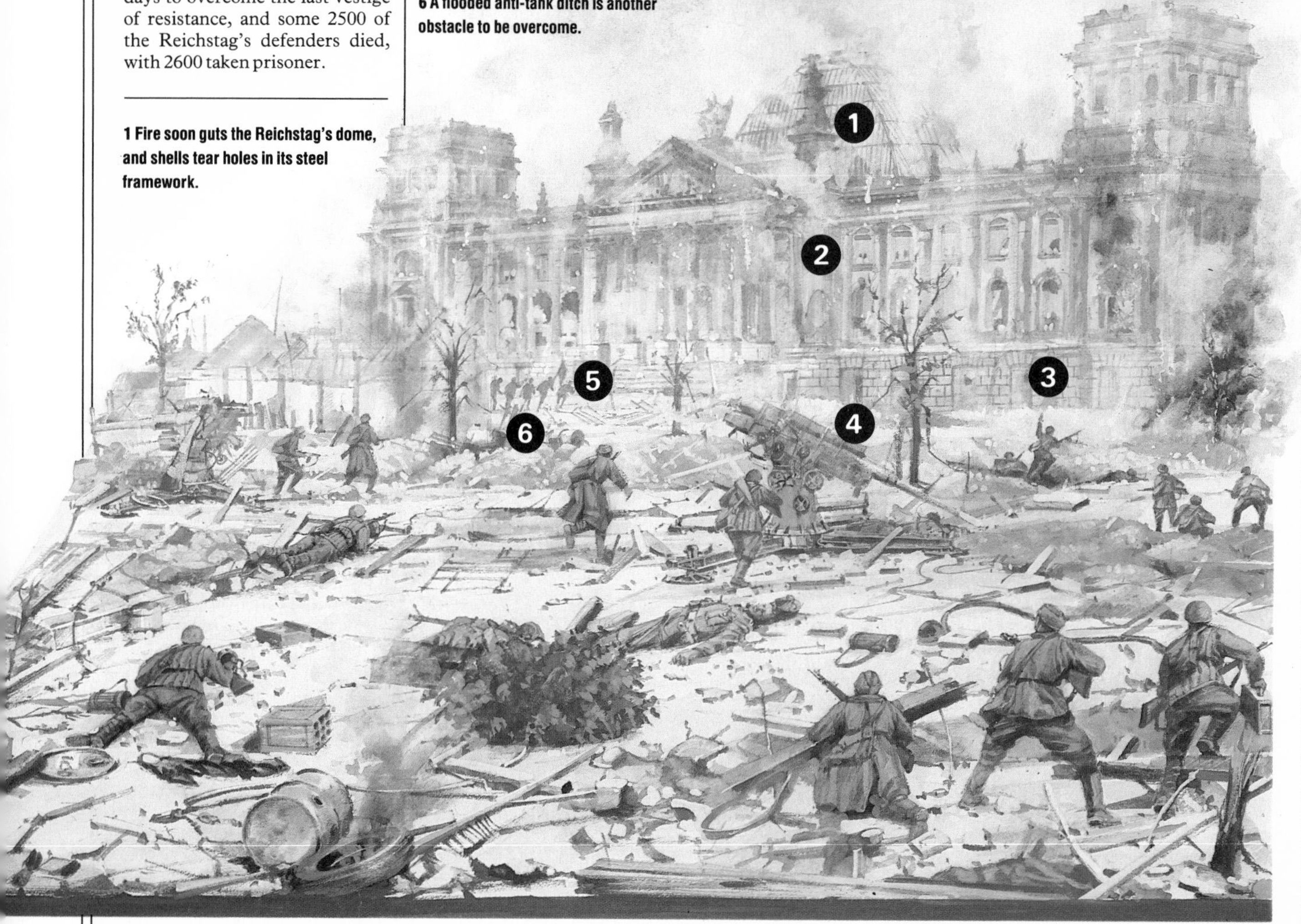

1 Fire soon guts the Reichstag's dome, and shells tear holes in its steel framework.

2 From the upper windows the defenders hurl grenades and keep up a constant barrage of machine-gun and automatic fire.

3 The lower storeys, reinforced with steel rails and concrete, turn the Reichstag into a fortress. Doorways and windows have been bricked up except for small firing slits.

4 In the square, 88 mm guns, brought in to hold off the Russian attack, have been abandoned as the Red Army infantrymen advance on the building.

5 One party, led by Captain S.A. Neustroyev, runs the gauntlet of machine-gun fire to attach the Red Flag to a column at the main entrance.

6 A flooded anti-tank ditch is another obstacle to be overcome.

and SS units fought desperately to stem the Russian tide. SS teams were everywhere to see that no soldier left his post. Any who did was immediately shot or hanged. Berlin's civilian inhabitants took to their cellars – their sense of time confused by the death and destruction around them – and waited fearfully for the Russian soldiers. Their fears were by no means groundless, for as the Russians overran more and more of the city, the rape of German women became more common. What remained of Berlin's infrastructure – from newspapers to public transport – collapsed, and looting was widespread.

By the evening of April 27 the Berlin garrison was confined to a narrow east-west corridor between 1.5 and 5 km (1 and 3 miles) wide and 16 km (10 miles) long. Hitler still desperately believed that Berlin would be relieved either by Wenck or by Busse's Ninth Army – but both were under heavy attack and could do nothing. By April 29 the Russians had broken across the corridor in two places, leaving three small pockets of German resistance.

HITLER BETRAYED

On April 23 Hitler received one of the cruellest blows of his last days. That evening Göring sent him a telegram from Bavaria in which he suggested that, since the Führer had decided to stay on in the beleaguered capital, Göring should take over 'complete leadership' of the Reich. If he received no reply by 10 pm, Göring went on, 'I shall take it for granted that you have lost your freedom of action . . . and shall act for the best interests of our country and our people.'

The Führer was beside himself. 'An ultimatum!' he screamed. 'A crass ultimatum! Now nothing remains. Nothing is spared to me. No allegiances are kept, no honour lived up to, no disappointments that I have not had, no betrayals that I have not experienced – and now this above all else. Nothing remains. Every wrong has already been done me.' He ordered that Göring be arrested and stripped of all his offices – but Hitler was no longer in a position to see that his orders were carried out. An even crueller blow came on April 28 when he learnt that SS chief Himmler, who had fled north to Lübeck, had been trying to negotiate an armistice with the Western Allies through the Swedish Count Bernadotte.

The same day General Weidling, now Battle Commandant of Berlin, reported to the Führer that there was only enough ammunition left for two days' fighting and that food was virtually unobtainable. The following evening his report was even bleaker – no ammunition, no chance of outside help, no hope left. Then even Hitler began to realise that the end had come, and he spent much of the day composing his last will and political testament. He confirmed that Göring had been stripped of all his offices, as had Himmler. He appointed as his successor as head of the Reich the commander of the German Navy, Grand Admiral Karl Dönitz, whom he had previously ordered to Schleswig-Holstein to take command of all German forces in the north. He blamed the Jews for the Reich's misfortunes and ordered his army commanders to 'set a shining example of devotion to duty unto death'.

THE END IN BERLIN

By now the Russians were approaching the Reichstag (National Assembly) building at Berlin's heart. In the early hours of April 30 they took the Gestapo headquarters, just 460 m (500 yds) away. One Russian officer who took part in its capture described the fighting: 'We had to work in small groups, and fight literally for every room. Smoke, smoke, smoke . . . It was stifling.'

At 1.30 pm, after an artillery bombardment, the Russians launched an attack on the Reichstag itself. The German defenders repulsed the first attack but the Russians made a second at 6 pm and got inside. The defenders fought desperately for every room and corridor – even after Sergeants Yegorov and Kontary, of the Red Army's 756th Infantry Regiment, raised their victory banner on the Reichstag's roof at 10.50 pm.

Meanwhile, little more than 200 m (220 yds) away in the Führerbunker, Hitler and Eva Braun – whom he had finally married the day before – had committed suicide (see box). The next day, May 1, Goebbels and Hitler's secretary Martin Bormann sent General Hans Krebs, since the end of March the Army Chief of Staff, to attempt to negotiate a ceasefire, at the same time informing the Russians that Hitler was dead.

The Russians insisted that only unconditional surrender by Germany as a whole was acceptable. Goebbels and Bormann gave no reply until that evening, when they rejected the Russian demand; the Soviet attacks therefore resumed. Later that evening Goebbels also committed suicide and during the night Bormann disappeared.

Early the next day Weidling decided to take action into his own hands. Further resistance now seemed pointless, and he let the Russians know by radio that he was willing to surrender. German troops began to surrender shortly afterwards and by 3 pm the fighting in Berlin was over.

There are no certain figures for casualties during the battle for Berlin. However, it is estimated that up to 100 000 German troops lost their lives as well as perhaps an equal number of civilians. Around the same number of Russian soldiers were killed. As for Berlin itself, hardly a building was intact by the end. The streets were strewn with rubble, knocked-out tanks and guns, and the city was covered with smoke and dust. Through it wandered Zhukov's and Koniev's men, savouring the thought that the long journey from Moscow was now at an end.

THE FÜHRER'S END

On the night of April 28/29, after hearing that Himmler had opened peace negotiations with the Western Allies, Hitler finally realised that defeat was inevitable. In the early hours of April 29, in a civil ceremony performed by one of Goebbels' staff, he married his longstanding and devoted mistress Eva Braun.

After the midday conference in the Führerbunker on Monday, April 30, with the Russians now beginning to attack the Reichstag, Hitler took lunch, then went to summon Eva in her room. His chauffeur in the meantime had been ordered to obtain some cans of petrol. Hitler and his wife bade farewell to Goebbels, Bormann and others who had remained in the bunker. Hitler's beloved Alsatian bitch Blondi had been put down in the early hours of the morning. After the farewells, Hitler and Eva retired to the Führer's suite.

A few minutes later a shot rang out. It was 3.30 pm. Hitler had apparently shot himself, and Eva – and some say Hitler too – had taken cyanide. Their bodies were taken outside into the rubble-strewn grounds of the Chancellery. Petrol was poured over them and they were set alight.

RED FLAG OVER BERLIN **The Soviet flag is fixed to a column on the Reichstag roof by two Red Army soldiers. The next day it was removed, to fly proudly over the city from the Reichstag's shattered dome.**

Victory in Europe

Hitler was dead, Berlin had fallen to the Russians and in Italy all German forces had surrendered. By May 2, 1945, it was clear that the war in Europe could last only a few more days. But Hitler's appointed successor was determined to postpone final surrender as long as possible.

HITLER'S HEIR, Grand Admiral Karl Dönitz, broadcast a solemn message to the German people on May 1, 1945. 'My first task is to save Germany from destruction by the advancing Bolshevik enemy,' he told them. 'It is to serve this purpose alone that the military struggle continues.'

Immediately before, to the sombre accompaniment of the slow movement of Brückner's Seventh Symphony, he had broken the news of Hitler's death the previous day. Keeping from the Germans the fact that their Führer had taken his own life, he proclaimed vaguely that Hitler had died 'a hero's death' in Berlin.

By now total German defeat was inevitable. On May 2, all German troops in Italy surrendered to the Western Allies and the last defenders of Berlin yielded to the Red Army. Other Soviet forces in northern Germany were closing steadily on the Elbe, already reached by the British and American troops of Field Marshal Montgomery's 21st Army Group. Also on May 2, troops under Montgomery seized the base of the Schleswig-Holstein peninsula, just ahead of the Russians, and Hamburg was about to surrender.

At the same time the German Twenty-Fifth Army was cut off in the north-western Netherlands and, since January, two other armies had been isolated in East Prussia and Courland on the Baltic. In the far south the 900 000 men of Field Marshal Ferdinand Schörner's Army Group Centre continued to fight desperately around Prague in Czechoslovakia – but he was trapped on three sides by the Russians, and the US Third Army under General George Patton was closing in from the south-west. In Austria, Army Group South under General Lothar Rendulic was similarly caught between Soviet and US armies.

Only in Scandinavia was the picture slightly brighter. During the winter, Russian and Free Norwegian troops had driven the Germans from Finnmark in the far north of Norway. But the Germans still held the rest of Norway and Denmark. Their forces here, however, could hardly turn the overall tide of defeat.

WINNING TIME

In his will Hitler had designated Dönitz, since 1943 Commander in Chief of the German Navy, his successor as Reich President, as well as naming him War Minister and Supreme Commander of the German Armed Forces. Unlike the leaders of the Wehrmacht and Luftwaffe, Dönitz had shown neither treachery nor incompetence in the war's last year. Since April the admiral had been based in the port city of Flensburg near the Danish border, commanding all German troops in the north of the country.

The new president's chief task now was to save as many of his people as possible from the Russians, who were wreaking a terrible vengeance for the German invasion of Russia. Dönitz had learnt – from a map captured in January 1945 at the end of the Ardennes battle – the boundaries of the postwar occupation zones agreed by the Allied leaders at the Yalta conference (p. 446). He was desperate to postpone total surrender as long as possible in order to win time for German civilians as well as members of the armed forces to escape from the Russian zone.

For this he needed the sympathetic cooperation of the Western Allies. So early on May 3 he sent Admiral Hans von Friedeburg, now Commander in Chief of the Navy, and three other officers to Montgomery's headquarters – three battered caravans parked on Lüneburg Heath, south-east of Hamburg. The Germans arrived at breakfast time, and 'stood to attention under the Union Jack', recalled Lt Colonel Trumbull Warren, Montgomery's Canadian personal assistant.

'They faced the three caravans with the doors all closed. How long they stood there I do not know but it seemed like ages – it was probably four or five minutes, and they never moved. Quietly the door of the centre caravan opened and there stood a rather short Anglo-Irishman [Montgomery], wearing khaki trousers and battledress.' Standing in a characteristic posture with his hands behind his back, Montgomery wore his familiar black beret with two badges – the field marshal's crossed batons and the Royal Tank Regiment badge.

FROSTY NEGOTIATIONS

After cold introductions Friedeburg offered the surrender of all German forces in the north of the country, including the two armies of Army Group Vistula retreating before the Russians. Montgomery replied that the troops fighting the Russians must surrender to the Russians – and demanded instead the unconditional surrender of all German forces in north-western Germany, the Netherlands and Denmark.

The Germans refused, then raised their concern about the civilian population. They asked Montgomery for assurances that civilians would be properly cared for as the German forces withdrew. Montgomery snapped back that it was a little late to express this concern, reminding them of the concentration camps and also of the devastating German air raid on Coventry of November 1940.

After a break for lunch, which the German delegation ate in a separate tent, there was another meeting. Montgomery repeated his demand for unconditional surrender, pointing out the overwhelming Allied superiority in the air and on the ground. Finally realising that Montgomery would accept no compromise, Friedeburg agreed to take his demands back to Flensburg.

Early the next day Dönitz and his staff held a conference to discuss Montgomery's demands. They eventually decided to accept them and Friedeburg went back to Lüneburg to sign the surrender document that evening (see box, *The*

THE MAN WHO SENTENCED HIMSELF TO DEATH

Until the Third Reich's last days, Hans Georg von Friedeburg (1895-1945) was a little known senior staff officer. He joined the Imperial Navy in World War I, serving in U-boats.

Later, on the staff of Hitler's War Ministry, Friedeburg formed a close association with SS chief Himmler. He rose rapidly, remaining in staff positions, until succeeding Dönitz as Naval Commander in Chief after Hitler's suicide and becoming one of the new president's chief negotiators with the Allies.

On May 23, 1945, the day the British finally arrested the Dönitz government, Friedeburg poisoned himself. He probably feared that many of his countrymen would later vilify him, as they had done the German delegates who had signed the Treaty of Versailles in 1919.

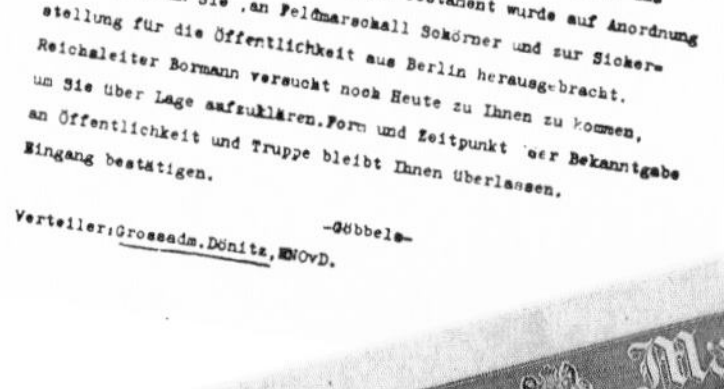
Marinenachrichtendienst

1446/1/ ... 32

F R R Grossadmiral Dönitz

--Gkdos Chefsache --Nur durch Offizier--

Führer gestern 1530 verschieden.Testament vom 29.4. überträgt ihnen das Amt des Reichspräsidenten,Reichsminister Dr.Goebbels das Amt des Reichskanzlers.Reichsleiter Bormann das Amt des Parteiministers,Reichsminister Seys-Inquart das Amt des Reichsaussenministers.Das Testament wurde auf Anordnung des Führers an Sie ,an Feldmarschall Schörner und zur Sicherstellung für die Öffentlichkeit aus Berlin herausgebracht. Reichsleiter Bormann versucht noch Heute zu Ihnen zu kommen, um Sie über Lage aufzuklären.Form und Zeitpunkt der Bekanntgabe an Öffentlichkeit und Truppe bleibt Ihnen überlassen. Eingang bestätigen.

-Göbbels-

Verteiler:Grossadm.Dönitz,MNOvD.

Daily Mail

FOR KING AND EMPIRE

No. 15,265 ONE PENNY WEDNESDAY, MAY 2, 1945

LATE WAR NEWS

HITLER DEAD, GERMAN RADIO TELLS WORLD

Admiral Doenitz is new Führer: 'The battle goes on'

ADOLF HITLER is dead. Grand Admiral Doenitz, Commander-in-Chief of the German Navy, has been appointed his successor. The German radio gave this news to the world at 10.25 last night in the following words: "It is reported from the Führer's headquarters that our Führer, Adolf Hitler, has fallen this afternoon in his command post in the Reich Chancellery fighting to his last breath against Bolshevism."

V DAY The full official plans

Nazi radio kept world in suspense

NO NEWS FROM HIMMLER, BUT Surrender begins on three fronts

REPORTS received in London late last night indicated that, while no fresh offer of capitulation has been received from Himmler, large German forces on widely separated fronts have begun to surrender piecemeal to the Allies with or without his authority.

Here is the latest position:

DENMARK.—German occupation forces were reported from Stockholm to be evacuating the country with all speed.

NORWAY.—Negotiations are said to be going on for the German garrisons to lay down their arms at the Swedish frontier.

CZECHO-SLOVAKIA: A delegation of German and Czech industrialists was reported by Luxemburg radio to have left Prague to meet representatives and hand over the ter...

Busmen to strike to-day

FOOD SHIPS FOR DUTCH

FÜHRER DEAD The news of Hitler's death, and of his own appointment as Reich President, reached Dönitz in a telegram from Goebbels. Britain first heard the news from Hamburg Radio, and the next day, May 2, newspapers carried the headlines the world had been waiting so long to read.

night that Monty drank champagne). Meanwhile, Dönitz had sent orders to all U-boats still at sea to return to port to surrender. At the same time he was using all ships left to him to evacuate as many troops as possible from the armies cut off in East Prussia and Courland.

SURRENDER AT RHEIMS

The Lüneburg surrender covered only those troops opposing Montgomery's 21st Army Group. Elsewhere the fighting continued – even at Dunkirk, whose German garrison had been holding out since the previous August. Dönitz's next task was to open negotiations with the Supreme Allied Commander, General Dwight D. Eisenhower, and he sent Friedeburg directly from Lüneburg to Eisenhower's headquarters at Rheims in northern France.

Eisenhower, however, was adamant that there should be no compromise with the Germans. When Friedeburg and his delegation arrived in Rheims on May 5, the Allied Commander refused to speak to them until they had signed a surrender document. In the meantime he left the negotiations to his chief of staff, Lt General Walter Bedell Smith. He also insisted that Maj General Ivan Susloparov, the Soviet representative at his headquarters, should be present during the negotiations to allay any suspicions in Moscow that the Western Allies were making a separate peace with Germany.

Friedeburg started by offering just that – the separate surrender of German forces in the west. When the Allies rejected this offer, Dönitz sent General Alfred Jodl, his chief of operations staff, to join the delegation at Rheims. Jodl was to offer a two-stage surrender. All hostilities would cease at the beginning of the first phase, but German troops would still be free to move at will – and so could escape the Russians. Then during the second phase the Germans would no longer have freedom of movement.

In the meantime, unofficial surrenders were taking place. Two armies opposite the US Ninth on the Elbe broke into small groups and surrendered to the Americans on May 5-7, while in the south parts of Army Group G surrendered en masse to US General Devers' 6th Army Group.

Jodl met with no better success than Friedeburg. Impatient at the Germans' delaying tactics, Eisenhower announced that he would close his lines so that no Germans could escape through them to the western sector 48 hours from midnight that night. Until then, though, the Germans would be free to move at will. This at least offered a breathing space – and Dönitz gave permission to surrender on these terms.

In the small hours of the morning of May 7 the German and Allied negotiators gathered in a former school room at Eisenhower's headquarters. At 2.41 am Jodl signed the unconditional surrender on all fronts that would end the war in Europe. It was to take effect from one minute past midnight, German time, on May 9. Bedell Smith signed for Eisenhower and Susloparov for the USSR, while Lt General Sir Frederick Morgan (for Britain) and General François Sèvez (for France) signed as witnesses.

'The mission of this Allied Force was fulfilled at 0241, local time, May 7, 1945,' Eisenhower signalled the British and US Chiefs of Staff.

VE DAY

Shortly after hearing news of the surrender, Churchill and the new US President Harry S. Truman decided that the following day, May 8, should be celebrated as Victory in Europe (VE) Day. They were about to broadcast this to their nations when news of Soviet objections reached them. Stalin, ever suspicious of his allies, was insisting on a Russian surrender ceremony to take place in Berlin, also on May 8. The Western leaders postponed their broadcasts – but news of VE Day had already leaked out through a German broadcast. They had to go ahead with the victory celebrations on May 8 (see box, p. 427), even though hostilities did not cease until that night.

The ceremony in Berlin took place in the morning of May 8. Hitler's former Chief of Staff Field Marshal Keitel, General von Stumpff representing the Luftwaffe and the luckless Friedeburg had been brought to Berlin to sign for Germany. Marshal Georgi Zhukov, commander of the Soviet 1st Belorussian Front, and Eisenhower's deputy, Air Chief Marshal Sir Arthur Tedder, signed for the Allies, with the US General Carl Spaatz and the French General Jean de Lattre de Tassigny as witnesses. Only then did the Russians recognise the German surrender.

Meanwhile, German troops fled desperately

THE NIGHT THAT MONTY DRANK CHAMPAGNE

The formal surrender of Germany's north-western armies – the first of several surrender ceremonies covering all German forces – took place in a tent at Field Marshal Montgomery's Lüneburg Heath headquarters, near Hamburg, on May 4, 1945.

After confirming to Montgomery that they were prepared to surrender unconditionally, the German delegation were escorted into the tent. In the centre was a simple trestle table covered with an army blanket, an inkwell, an army dip pen and two BBC microphones. Outside, representatives of the world's press and members of Montgomery's headquarters staff clustered around the tent.

Montgomery read out the surrender document, finishing with a warning that unless the Germans signed it there and then hostilities would be resumed. This was translated into German and the Germans, led by Admiral von Friedeburg, signed it. Montgomery also signed, stating that he was doing so on behalf of the Supreme Allied Commander, General Eisenhower. It was 6.30 pm; hostilities were to end within 21st Army Group's area of operations the following morning at 8.

That night the Germans slept at the British headquarters, and next morning travelled on to Eisenhower's headquarters at Rheims to open negotiations there. For Montgomery the Lüneburg surrender was the culmination of his career; that night, though normally strictly teetotal, he even drank a little champagne at dinner.

MOMENT OF TRUTH Admiral Friedeburg, with Admiral Wagner on his right, listens grimly as Montgomery reads them the Allies' surrender terms at Lüneburg Heath.

THE NAZIS' LOOT

LIBERATED ART A GI holds up a work by the French painter Fragonard from Göring's private art collection. The Nazis looted 10 890 paintings, many by famous artists, from France alone.

American soldiers from General Patton's Third Army discovered a fabulous treasure trove on April 6, 1945. Down a large, deep potash mine at Merkers, near Mühlhausen in Thuringia, they came across a hoard of art treasures and gold, later valued at US$315 million. Such was their astonishment that even Eisenhower took time to have a look.

The hoard was the result of systematic looting of art treasures and gold from occupied countries, much of it at the express orders of Hitler and Göring, who built up huge collections. As Allied bombing intensified, many of the treasures were moved to safety at Merkers, along with Reichsbank gold and currency reserves.

That summer the Americans tracked down another hoard of gold, hidden in caches in the hills above the town of Mittenwald in southern Bavaria. This was the Reich's last gold reserves whipped out of Berlin by the SS. But little of it reached the US Treasury. No one has ever been put on trial, but some believe much of the gold ended up in the hands of US Military Government officials. It remains the biggest robbery on record.

The art treasures collected by the Allies were returned to the countries from which they were stolen. As far as possible, so was the gold, but the international commission responsible still holds vast reserves whose rightful ownership remains unresolved.

FREEDOM FOR 'OUR DEAR CHANNEL ISLANDS'

Through much of Europe in 1945, newly liberated peoples were rejoicing in their freedom. But in Britain's Channel Islands there was a mood of black disappointment. Occupied by the Germans in June 1940, they had been bypassed when the Allies invaded nearby Normandy and were still under Nazi rule. They were also short of food. Allied plans for landings on the islands had been shelved as likely to cause too many civilian casualties. The German garrison would have to surrender unconditionally.

Then on May 1 hope blossomed for the islanders, when they heard on the radio of Hitler's death. Union Jacks began to appear on some buildings. But still they had over a week to wait for freedom. At noon on May 8, VE Day, two British destroyers, *Bulldog* and *Beagle*, rendezvoused off Guernsey with a German vessel; a German officer went on board *Bulldog*. But the meeting was fruitless, for the German was only empowered to discuss surrender terms, not agree them.

The German commander, Vice Admiral Friedrich Hüffmeier, maintained that he had received no orders to surrender and would not do so without them. He even threatened to fire on the destroyers, which retired. But the islanders were cheered to hear Churchill's VE Day broadcast in which he promised that 'Our dear Channel Islands are also to be freed today'.

Finally, early on May 9, the Germans signed a surrender document on *Bulldog*, now in the harbour of St Peter Port, Guernsey. Later that day, the first British troops landed on Jersey and Guernsey. Alderney, however, was only liberated on May 16. On Sark, the Dame – the island's redoubtable feudal ruler, Sybil Hathaway – was left in charge of a 275 man German garrison until May 17. But they caused her no trouble. On June 7 the King and Queen paid a special visit to Guernsey and Jersey.

westwards. Allied commanders had feared that the Waffen-SS might ignore the surrender and fight on. But the SS, even more than Wehrmacht troops, were terrified of falling into Russian hands. By midnight on May 8/9, nearly 2 million German troops – around 55 per cent of those on the Eastern Front – had escaped into the Western sector. Generally the Western Allies accepted their surrender – but most of the notoriously brutal SS *Totenkopf* ('Death's Head') Division were handed straight over to the Russians. Few of these ever returned home.

FIGHTING TO THE LAST

Some hostilities, however, had dragged on. As late as the afternoon of May 9 the German Commander in Chief South, Field Marshal Albert Kesselring, had to repeat a signal to the Sixth SS Panzer Army under General 'Sepp' Dietrich in Austria, reminding him that the surrender order was equally binding on his men.

In Czechoslovakia, Schörner's Army Group Centre continued fighting long after the official

THE BITTER END Looking pale and gaunt, Grand Admiral Karl Dönitz is arrested by a British officer at his Flensburg headquarters, where his government has continued briefly to function. His reign as Hitler's successor has lasted a mere three weeks.

ending of hostilities. In Prague, patriots had risen against the Germans in the first days of May. On the 5th, they broadcast urgent appeals for help, in both English and Russian, over captured Radio Prague transmitters. Then the city was plunged into a two-day bloodbath, as patriots – backed by Russian defectors under General Andrei Vlasov, who had fought for the Germans but switched sides once more – battled with crack SS units.

When it became clear, however, that the Americans were leaving Prague to the Red Army, Vlasov and his men fled west to the US lines – to be handed over later to the Russians and almost certain death. Some German units also surrendered, but others fought on. On May 9, Soviet troops, determined that they, not the local Resistance, should be seen as Prague's liberators, broke through into the city from the north-west. Schörner's last forces – in a large pocket north-east of the city – surrendered only on May 11.

Meanwhile, the Allies had allowed Dönitz's rump government at Flensburg to remain in office for two weeks after the surrender – to help ensure that the surrender terms were carried out. During this time Dönitz attempted to distance himself from Nazi crimes by asserting that he and the German armed forces had merely done their duty.

The former SS chief Heinrich Himmler tried to escape south, disguised as a policeman, but was captured by the British at Lüneburg and poisoned himself. Other SS men cast off their distinctive black uniforms and pretended to be ordinary soldiers and sailors – so that the Allies had to screen at great length their hundreds of thousands of prisoners. Hermann Göring, meanwhile, had surrendered to Americans in Bavaria on May 8.

On May 23, 1945, Dönitz's brief spell of government came to an end. British troops arrested him with Jodl, former Armaments Minister Albert Speer and other Nazi leaders at Flensburg and carried them off to prison first in Luxembourg, then at Nuremberg. The Third Reich had finally ended after just 12 years and two months of the 1000 years promised by Hitler.

DENMARK AND NORWAY LIBERATED

The Danish capital, Copenhagen, gave Maj General Richard Dewing an uproarious welcome when he flew in on the afternoon of May 5, 1945. The British general, accompanied by British paratroops, was head of the Allied Mission to Denmark. German forces in the kingdom had been part of those that surrendered to Montgomery at Lüneburg Heath the day before. On the evening of the 5th, more British troops crossed into Denmark from Schleswig-Holstein – to an equally rapturous welcome.

Most German troops in Denmark were happy to lay down their arms – but on the island of Bornholm, to the east of the rest of the country, there were problems. For the 20 000 German troops there, the surrender demand came from the Russians. The German commander stated that he would surrender only to the British, but the Allies had already agreed that Bornholm was to be a Russian responsibility. Eventually, on May 9, the Russians had to land and forcibly remove the Germans. The Russians stayed until April 1946, when they handed it back to the Danes.

In Norway, the Allies feared that the German commander, General Franz Böhme, would fight on. They tried unsuccessfully to contact him by radio throughout May 6 and 7, then late in the evening of May 7 Böhme made a broadcast over Radio Oslo acknowledging the surrender at Rheims early that morning and ordering a ceasefire. The Norwegian Resistance now came into the open, arresting local Nazis, while the Germans stood back.

On May 8 the official Allied mission landed in Oslo and Böhme signed a surrender document. Allied troops, mainly the British 1st Airborne Division, gradually arrived in Norway – and on May 12 Crown Prince Olav, together with members of the Norwegian Government-in-Exile, arrived in Oslo on British warships. On June 7 King Haakon returned to his country from Britain to a rapturous welcome, choosing to come back on the fifth anniversary of his departure in 1940.

LAY THAT PISTOL DOWN German troops disarmed.

CELEBRATION

Delirious crowds mobbed Churchill in London's Whitehall on VE (Victory in Europe) Day. The 71-year-old premier was on his way to Parliament and a service of thanksgiving at St Margaret's, Westminster. Earlier, he had broadcast to nation and empire: 'The evil-doers are now prostrate before us. Our gratitude to our splendid allies goes forth from all our hearts in this island and throughout the British Empire.'

From the day before (Monday, May 7) most British people had known that fighting in Europe was about to cease. Many had learnt of the Nazi surrender from lunchtime broadcasts on German radio, and Union Jacks began to appear on housefronts. The news was then confirmed on the BBC and a public holiday, VE Day, announced for Tuesday.

VE Day dawned with dull skies and slight drizzle. But, even so, boisterous, rejoicing crowds began to fill London's streets from an early hour, singing, drinking, many with red, white and blue rosettes in their buttonholes. Then in the afternoon the sun came out. That evening street lights all over Britain were switched on for the first time since the war began. Searchlights and floodlights came on too. For many children, used only to the blackout, it was like a fairyland. There were fireworks, bonfires and more revelling.

In London the King let the Princesses Elizabeth and Margaret mingle with the crowds outside Buckingham Palace. As he wrote in his diary that night: 'Poor darlings, they have never had any fun yet.'

There were similar scenes in Paris, the Hague and other recently liberated capitals and towns throughout continental Europe. In Moscow captured German trophies, such as Nazi standards, were piled at the feet of the Russian leaders in Red Square. In New York offices emptied as people descended to the streets while tickertape rained from above. In the Canadian east coast port city of Halifax celebrations got frighteningly out of hand. Thousands of sailors, aided and abetted by local petty criminals, rampaged through the city's streets, looting liquor, jewellery and clothes shops, setting some alight and drinking themselves senseless.

The British celebrations continued more soberly the next day, then petered out. People were exhausted after almost six years of war and many feared what lay ahead. 'We may allow ourselves a brief period of rejoicing,' Churchill had said in his broadcast. 'But let us not forget for a moment the toils and efforts that lie ahead. Japan, with all her treachery and greed, remains unsubdued.' Or, as one Australian – in whose country, as in New Zealand and India, celebrations had been more subdued – put it: 'Wait until all the fellows are home and the men of the 8th Division swing down Martin Place [at Sydney's heart]. That will be the day!'

27: JAPAN'S LAST GASPS

1945 – and it is time to step up the bombing and close in to strike at Japan's failing heart.

Into the inferno of Iwo Jima

By capturing Iwo Jima, the Americans would be one step nearer Japan's home islands and would remove a menace to US bombers attacking Japanese cities.

WHEN THE FIRST American marines scrambled ashore onto Iwo Jima, just after 9 am on February 19, 1945, they stormed into a hell they had not bargained for. For one thing, they could scarcely see their objectives; the tiny, 21 km (8 sq mile) surf-lashed island, shaped like a pork chop, was shrouded in smoke and dust from a massive three-day naval barrage that had preceded the assault. For another, as they leapt from their landing craft, the Americans sank shin-deep in the ash and cinders of the beaches. Even their amtracs (amphibious tracked vehicles) became bogged down.

Finally, the marines did not realise that behind the smoke screen lurked a deadly, 21 000-man force of fanatical adversaries in an 18 km (11 mile) maze of caves, tunnels, crevices, carefully camouflaged pillboxes and bombproof underground hideouts. What is more, the Japanese had been ordered to hold fire after the landings so that their positions would not be given away. The 4th and 5th US Marine Divisions made the initial assault. In command was Lt General Holland M. ('Howling Mad') Smith, with Maj General Harry Schmidt in charge on the ground.

It was 20 minutes after the first Americans hit the beach below the 168 m (550 ft) peak of Mount Suribachi that the Japanese opened up with all their artillery and mortars. The marines – a mere 180-275 m (200-300 yds) inland – were pinned down and many died there and then, their vehicles stuck in the ashy ground. Small-arms fire lashed them from camouflaged pillboxes and

Storming the volcanic fortress

For 75 days before the American assault on Iwo Jima, B-24, B-25 and some B-29 Superfortress bombers from Saipan, along with naval guns, 'softened up' the tiny island. In the final three days before the landings they let loose the longest and heaviest bombardment of the entire Pacific war. Guns alone rained almost 40 000 shells onto it.

Then, on the morning of the 19th, the largest collection of ships so far used in a Pacific operation – 450 vessels of the US Fifth Fleet – gathered offshore. At the same time, the 30 000 men of the 4th and 5th Marine Divisions transferred to landing craft, ready to begin the assault. But, despite destroying 100 Japanese naval aircraft, the softening-up had hardly touched the defenders. They were dug in deep inside a labyrinth of cunningly disguised gun and mortar positions, hollowed-out hills and underground pillboxes, all ready to fight to the death. The battle for Iwo Jima would be the bloodiest – and the most heroic – operation in the history of the US Marine Corps.

MOUNTAIN-TOP MASS Catholic marines celebrate the conquest of Suribachi.

SUPPLIES ASHORE With the beaches secure at last, US marines can concentrate on bringing ashore ammunition and other stores.

harmless-looking hummocks of sand. There was almost no protection. Frantically they scrambled behind stranded vehicles and the bodies of dead comrades. Howard Connor, V Marine Corps' official historian, later described the nightmare: 'Wounded men were arriving on the beach by the dozen, where they were not much better off than they had been at the front . . . The first two boats bringing in badly needed litters were blown out of the water. Casualties were being hit again as they lay helpless under blankets awaiting evacuation.'

For those who lived to fight on, there were other horrors, as author-historian William Manchester – then a sergeant (although not on Iwo Jima) – recounted in his autobiography: 'You tripped over strings of viscera 15 feet long, over bodies which had been cut in half at the waist. Legs and arms and heads bearing only necks lay 50 feet from the nearest torso. As night fell the

INCH BY PAINFUL INCH Slowly and painfully, US marines of the first wave ashore work their way up one of Iwo Jima's 1.5-5 m (5-18 ft) high volcanic-ash beach terraces. They meet a resistance more determined and devastating than anything they had expected.

1 About 8000 marines land on Iwo Jima between 9 and 10 am on February 19. Their landing craft and amtracs are followed by landing ships, with tanks, artillery and bulldozers. Aircraft and ships offshore bombard the island.

2 Gigantic tongues of fire leap from US flamethrowing tanks. Fighting is desperate. Defenders in skilfully camouflaged positions can wait until the Americans are on top of them before opening fire. There is also hand-to-hand fighting with bayonets and knives. Some Japanese make suicidal charges, wielding sabres.

Even so, by late morning, marines have crossed Iwo Jima, cutting off Mount Suribachi on their left.

3 The volcanic mountain bristles with enemy fortifications – and takes Lt Colonel Chandler W. Johnson's 2nd Battalion, 28th Regiment, three days to conquer. A 'foot-by-foot crawl, with mortars, artillery, rockets, machine guns and grenades making us hug every rock and shell-hole' is how one veteran was later to describe the battle. Eventually, at 10.20 am on the 23rd, 'Old Glory' flutters at the mountain top – though the men raising the flag suddenly have to confront some desperate Japanese.

4 With Suribachi taken, the Americans turn to the north of the island, which includes two completed Japanese airfields. The going is tough. Within two days, tank battalions have lost more than half their Shermans and many combat units are reduced to 50 per cent efficiency. By the end of the 25th, the Americans have captured about a third of the island, but Iwo Jima is not pronounced cleared until a month later – and mopping up continues into May.

TURNING THE TABLES Two resourceful US corporals turn a captured Japanese machine gun on its former owners. Their own gun was knocked out.

beach-head reeked of the stench of burning flesh.' On that first day, some 2420 Americans lost their lives.

The island-hopping strategy of Admiral Chester W. Nimitz, Commander in Chief of the US Pacific Fleet, meant closing in on the Japanese home islands, with Iwo Jima a key objective on the way – and Okinawa next on the list. Once taken, Okinawa would provide a base for the amphibious invasion of Japan proper.

The Americans needed first to capture Iwo Jima in order to protect the flank of their attack on Okinawa. Iwo also lay close to the route taken by the Marianas-based B-29 Superfortresses on bombing missions over Japan. The Japanese operated a radar station on the island, and Japanese fighters based at its two airfields were taking a heavy toll. Iwo Jima, just 1220 km (760 miles) from Tokyo, would also provide a base for US fighter escorts for the bombers.

On the Japanese side, meanwhile, the High Command could do little except wait for the American blows to fall. Their only hope was to sell territory so dear that Washington would offer suitable surrender terms. In summer 1944, they talked of 'sinking' Iwo, or cutting it in half with explosives, rather than let it fall into American hands. But after an inspection by Lt General Tadamichi Kuribayashi they decided to fortify it. Kuribayashi became garrison commander.

'OLD GLORY' Joe Rosenthal's picture of the raising of the US flag on Mt Suribachi was used on stamps commemorating the Iwo Jima victory. It also inspired the US Marine Corps memorial in Washington.

TO SURIBACHI'S PEAK

Despite the astonishingly fierce Japanese resistance on February 19 and the appalling American casualties, the marines did make progress. By late morning that day, men of the 1st Battalion, 28th Regiment, had crossed the island, cutting off Mount Suribachi. Within another 24 hours, the 2nd Battalion under Lt Colonel Chandler W. Johnson – reinforced by men of the 1st and 3rd – had made it to the volcano's base.

The job of organising the climb to the rim of Suribachi's craggy crater went to Lt Colonel Johnson. For three days, his men, backed up by constant air and naval bombardment, clawed their agonising way up the steep pitted slopes. Offshore, a *kamikaze* attack on February 21 sank the escort carrier *Bismarck Sea* and put the carrier *Saratoga* out of service. But the barrage was effective; early on the 23rd a patrol reported that all was quiet on the mountain.

Before the final assault began, Johnson handed the commander of the platoon assigned to the job, 1st Lieutenant Harold Schrier, a folded American flag. The 40 marines frequently had to pause for breath as they climbed. Below, men around the foot of the mountain watched their progress through binoculars. When they reached the rim of the crater, Schrier spotted a few battered gun emplacements and cave openings, but there was no Japanese fire. He ordered the men to file over the crater's edge. There was still no fire – not even when one man made the insulting gesture of urinating down the mountain's slope.

Then, as half of the patrol was checking the crater, a Japanese began to climb out of a deep hole. He was shot by a marine. Schrier and his men now prepared to raise the US flag. Two of them found a piece of discarded water pipe to use as a pole, and at 10.20 am on February 23, the Stars and Stripes was fluttering in the wind above the mountain. Marines below yelled, 'There goes the flag!' Men cheered, others wept with joy; offshore, ships sounded their whistles in tribute.

Then a Japanese soldier emerged from a cave and fired a rifle at Marine Chick Robeson and a photographer, Staff Sergeant Louis R. Lowery. He missed – and Robeson shot him. An officer now leapt out, angrily brandishing a broken-bladed sword. Some marines opened up with a volley of rifle fire – and the officer fell. Next came a series of hand grenades from a cave with several entrances. The marines answered in kind, blasted the openings with flamethrowers and sealed them with explosives. Lowery, trying to dodge a grenade in the skirmish, fell 15 m (50 ft) down the volcano's rim, breaking his camera.

Three hours after the raising of the original flag, it was replaced by a larger one brought ashore from a tank landing ship – and Associated Press photographer Joe Rosenthal took the celebrated photograph which became a model for the US Marine Corps War Memorial at Arlington, Virginia. A few days after Suribachi had been captured, a search of the summit cave revealed about 150 dead Japanese.

TAKING THE AIRFIELDS

On February 24, the Americans turned north, where the Japanese were holed up seemingly everywhere. Sherman tanks and artillery supported the marines, but there was no room for flanking movements. Each fierce assault was a bloody frontal affair.

'It takes courage to stay at the front on Iwo Jima,' wrote a marine in his diary, '. . . to push out ahead of those lines, against an unseen enemy who has survived two months of shell and shock, who lives beneath the rocks . . . It takes courage to crawl ahead, 100 yards a day, and get up the next morning, count losses, and do it again.'

So bitter were the battles, that the Americans began to give sectors of the rugged terrain such names as 'Bloody Gorge' and 'The Meat Grinder'. Nonetheless, by the end of the 25th they had captured about a third of the island, including the major airfield. Meanwhile, the reserve 3rd Marine Division had landed, and on February 27 the Americans captured the island's second airfield. On March 1, they reached the construction site of a third; now 82 000 men were ashore.

On March 8, near Tachiwa Point, on the south-east corner of the island, the 4th Division faced a virtually suicidal *banzai* charge by the Japanese – 650 of their bodies were found and later counts brought the total to around 800. Three days later the remaining defenders were pinned into a small area of the north-west. From then on, it was largely a mopping-up operation in the island's hills and gullies.

On March 4, the first American bombers made emergency landings on the main airstrip. On April 7, P-51 Mustang fighters operating from Iwo Jima escorted a daytime bombing raid on Tokyo. The island was to see 2251 landings by damaged Superfortresses in five months, saving the lives of nearly 25 000 American airmen.

But the cost had been horrendous: by the end of March, the Americans had lost 6821 men killed and nearly 18 000 wounded. Of General Kuribayashi's 21 000 defenders only 216 were taken prisoner; the rest fought to the death. According to some reports, Kuribayashi died leading a last suicidal attack on the night of March 25/26. His body was never found.

Twenty-six marines who fought on Iwo Jima won America's top award – the Medal of Honor. As Nimitz later commented: 'Among the Americans who served on Iwo Island, uncommon valour was a common virtue.'

In Japan's home islands, meanwhile, the people were preparing to resist the now inevitable invasion. Air and naval *kamikazes* prepared to batter the invasion fleet, while a fanatical citizenry-in-arms would back the army. All were ready to die in the defence of the 'sacred soil' of Japan and the 'sacred person' of the Emperor.

A SAMURAI'S SACRIFICE

'Have not eaten or drunk for five days,' ran the last signal from Tadamichi Kuribayashi (1891-1945) on Iwo Jima on March 21, 1945. 'But fighting spirit is running high. We are going to fight bravely to the last moment.' From a *samurai* ('warrior') family, and arguably the war's ablest Japanese general, Kuribayashi masterminded the defences that made Iwo Jima so hard to take. He was promoted a full general on March 17, but no one knows if he received the message sent to inform him.

AMPHIBIOUS EXPERT

Holland M. 'Howling Mad' Smith (1882-1967), nicknamed for his temper as well as his initials, was the best known US Marine Corps general of World War II. He was in charge of training marines in the USA from 1939 to 1943, then went to the Pacific and led the ground forces in the invasions of the Gilberts, Marshalls, Marianas and Iwo Jima.

Smith's relationship with the Army and War Department was not happy. The department disapproved of marine generals commanding army units. But Smith was the most successful American amphibious operations commander.

Okinawa – 'history's greatest madhouse'

Even before Iwo Jima fell, plans were afoot for the invasion of Okinawa. While desperate and bloody fighting raged ashore, the full fury of 'human bomb' *kamikaze* swarms battered the massive American fleet offshore.

APRIL FOOL'S DAY 1945 – Easter Sunday, as it happened – dawned brilliant and clear in the East China Sea as a gigantic armada of warships and troop carriers assembled off the mountainous, scimitar-shaped island of Okinawa, about 100 km (60 miles) long and 525 km (330 miles) south-west of Japan. An invasion force of 172 000 soldiers and marines, led by the tough 'do it by the book' Lt General Simon Bolivar Buckner, was poised to storm the last bastion before mainland Japan.

It promised to be no easy task, for the island was defended by 100 000 men of the formidable Thirty-Second Army, under one of Japan's ablest commanders, Lt General Mitsuru Ushijima. The Japanese also had what they believed would be a trump card – nearly 2000 *kamikaze* pilots had vowed to give their lives in the attempt to blow the invasion fleet out of the water.

All during the previous week, air and naval bombardments had pounded Okinawa to soften up the defences. Carrier-based planes had already hit the *kamikaze* bases on the southernmost Japanese home island of Kyushu. Then, on March 26, the 77th Infantry Division had gone ashore on the Kerama islands, off Okinawa's south-west coast, to secure a supply and repair base for the 1500 ships of Operation 'Iceberg'.

The invasion fleet included 430 landing craft and assault ships, 40 carriers, 18 battleships and some 200 destroyers. William Manchester, later to become an author and historian, but then a sergeant in the Marines, summed up the feelings of the men: 'This Easter happened to be my twenty-third birthday. My chances of becoming twenty-four were, I reflected, very slight.'

QUIET RECEPTION

At around 8.30 am on April 1, the first wave of assault boats began to churn their way ashore near the village of Hagushi, on Okinawa's west coast. The covering bombardment reached a crescendo as bombs, rockets and napalm rained down from US strike aircraft. Meanwhile, shellfire from 16 in (406 mm) battleship guns down to 40 mm Bofors blasted away at Japanese positions.

Marine Maj General Roy Geiger's III Amphibious Corps struck at the northern end of the beach front, while infantry of Maj General John R. Hodge's XXIV Corps splashed ashore to the south. Meanwhile, the 2nd Marine Division, under Maj General Thomas E. Watson, staged a diversionary 'landing' on the opposite coast – then reversed course and headed back to their parent ships. They repeated the procedure the next day.

By midday, tanks and artillery were rumbling ashore on the west coast, as the infantry pushed inland. Their main objectives were Okinawa's two major airfields, Yontan and Kadena. Within two hours, the infantry had secured Kadena and

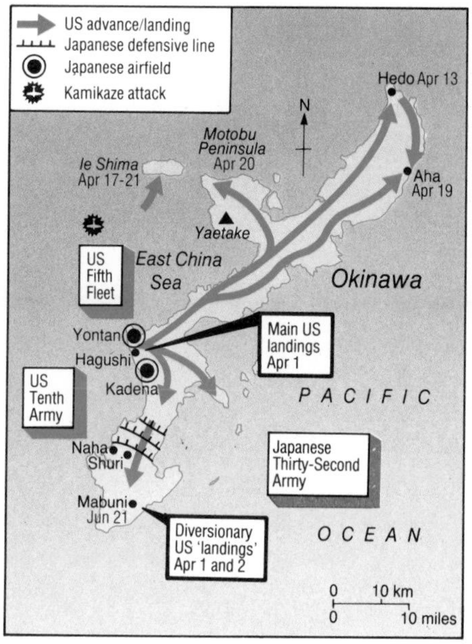

OBSTINATE OUTPOST The Americans had to capture Okinawa, Japan's last key Pacific stronghold, before turning north for the Japanese home islands. They attacked in massive numbers, but had underestimated enemy strength. The battle lasted three long, bloody months.

an hour later the marines overran Yontan, both meeting little resistance. By the evening of the first day, more than 60 000 American troops were ashore, on a beach-head now 13 km (8 miles) long and up to 3 km (2 miles) deep.

The first stages of the assault were deceptively easy. Ushijima's forces did not even try to defend the beaches or airfields. Tokyo had assured him that *kamikaze* attacks would smash the US fleet. Then, short of supplies and denied reinforcements, the Americans could be annihilated. Ushijima's men, well armed and firmly entrenched, waited for the Americans to come to them.

HONEYCOMBS OF DEATH

Ushijima, whose troops included 20 000 *Boetai*, native members of the Okinawa Home Guard, placed his main defences around the 13th-century castle town of Shuri in the south. They were arranged in a series of concentric lines based around rugged escarpments running east-west across the southern part of the island. He had also built a formidable honeycomb of interconnecting natural and man-made caves and tunnels in those encircling southern ridges. The largest served as barracks, command posts and field hospitals.

'None of us could have known,' Manchester was to write, 'that the battle would last nearly three months, becoming the bloodiest island fight of the Pacific war . . . We were all psychotic, inmates of the greatest madhouse in history, but staying on the line was a matter of pride.'

When Buckner sent the 6th Marines northwards over the narrow neck of the island, the only stubborn resistance was met on the Motobu Peninsula, in the north-west. The sheer, craggy and wooded terrain was dominated by the Katsu and Yaetake mountains, where two Japanese battalions were entrenched. In the bloody assault on Yaetake, the Americans lost 970 men.

By mid-April, marines had captured the northern two-thirds of Okinawa, and on April 16 the 77th Division landed on the offshore island of Ie Shima, needed as an air base. But here again the Japanese had dug in and were beaten only after six days of savage fighting. In the south of Okinawa, where Ushijima concentrated his main forces, it had been a different story for the US infantry. Kakazu Ridge, overlooking a deep gorge, and Nishibaru and Tanabaru ridges farther inland, were the first major battlegrounds. To capture Kakazu, the Americans had to cross the gorge under a terrific barrage of machine-gun, artillery and mortar fire.

The battle for the three ridges raged back and forth from April 9 to 14. On the lower slopes and in the gorge, tanks unprotected by covering infantry were subjected to repeated suicidal attacks in which Japanese carrying packs of explosives flung themselves at the vehicles. Once they had fought their way around the first line of ridges, the battle-worn troops pushed south to the next east-west fortress escarpment, Urasoe-Mura. To its east, where the cliffs grow steeper, it is known as Maeda Ridge and ends in a high, prominent rock, which the Americans, by now joined by the 77th Division, called Needle Rock.

This was the scene of vicious, hand-to-hand fighting, and it was on the ridge that an unarmed medical orderly, Private Desmond T. Doss, earned a Congressional Medal of Honor. Doss, a Seventh-Day Adventist, refused to carry a weapon. During a fierce Japanese counterattack, the enemy killed or wounded most of the soldiers

USHIJIMA – A FEARSOME ADVERSARY

A formidable opponent to the overwhelming American invasion forces on Okinawa, Mitsuru Ushijima (1887-1945) was a professional soldier who had served in the invasion of Burma in early 1942. He was appointed to the key post of Commandant of Japan's Military Academy later the same year.

His capable handling of the battle on Okinawa was possibly the best example of his country's defensive tactics of 1944-5. Ushijima continued to direct the battle almost to its end. Then, on the evening of June 21, as men of the 7th Infantry Division approached his command cave at Mabuni, he and his chief of staff ate a lavish dinner. Before daylight on June 22, dressed in full field uniform with medals, he committed *hara-kiri* with a ceremonial knife. At the same moment, General Cho severed his bowed head with a sabre. Cho then also committed ritual suicide.

CRAWLING THROUGH THE CANE Gleaming Johnson light machine gun in hand, 20-year-old US Marine Corporal George W. Wright creeps into the attack.

on top of Maeda, and Doss stayed behind to tend the injured while his surviving comrades pulled back down the steep cliffs. Under heavy fire, Doss managed to carry 50 wounded men to the edge of the 11 m (35 ft) cliff and lower them on ropes.

'BLOWTORCH AND CORKSCREW'

The three-month Okinawa campaign started in fine weather, but torrential rain soon blew in from the East China Sea, turning the ground into mud. Guns, jeeps and even bulldozers became bogged down; only amtracs and amphibious DUKWs managed to struggle on. Soldiers and marines found themselves permanently sodden, while the Japanese emerged from their hideouts dry.

Enemy tactics followed a pattern. Each defence line was stubbornly held until almost overwhelmed – then the Japanese soldiers would withdraw to new prepared positions, leaving snipers to pick off the advancing Americans. In dealing with the holed-up pockets of Japanese, the US troops found what General Buckner called the 'blowtorch and corkscrew' method most effective. A cave or dugout entrance would be blasted by a flamethrower – hand-held or tank-mounted – and then sealed with a grenade or a satchel charge (pack of explosives). By the end of April, the first two lines of Japanese defences – Kakazu and Urasoe-Mura with Maeda – had been captured.

FURY AT SEA

Offshore, men of the *kamikaze*-spotting picket lines of radar-equipped destroyers and destroyer escorts had not had an easy time – they themselves had become prime targets for waves of *kamikazes*.

The Japanese High Command had ordered a coordinated attack, called Operation *Ten-ichi* ('Heaven 1'). On April 7, 700 aircraft, many obsolescent and half of them suicide bombers, hurled themselves against the American fleet. Of these, the Japanese lost 335, but they sank three destroyers, a tank landing ship and two ammunition ships, as well as damaging 24 other vessels.

The *kamikazes*, packed with as much as 2 tonnes of explosives, would swarm in like hornets out of the misty haze to the north, then scream down on the American ships. The only way to stop them was for the Combat Air Patrol (CAP) of Marine Corsair fighters to shoot them down before their final dive, or for shipboard guns to blow them apart with a large calibre shell.

As *kamikaze* attacks intensified, the strain on the men of the Fifth Fleet took its toll through constant radar alerts, lack of sleep and the prospect of sudden, flaming death. The Japanese also sent in speedboats packed with high explosives, which damaged two destroyers and a few merchant ships. Some *kamikaze* pilots flew *Ohka* ('Cherry Blossom') rocket-powered missiles that carried a 1200 kg (2650 lb) warhead and struck home at more than 930 km/h (580 mph). Their first success came on April 12, when an *Ohka* sank the destroyer USS *Mannert L. Abele*.

For the sacrifice of half their *kamikaze* force of 1815 planes at Okinawa, the Japanese sank 32 American ships, killing 5000 seamen and wounding 4800. A total of 368 ships were damaged. These were the heaviest US Navy casualties in any single campaign of the war.

AMERICAN 'BANZAI' CHARGE

As the naval battle raged, the men on Okinawa continued their bitter step-by-step struggle. The Japanese counterattacked on May 4 across the neck of southern Okinawa, from Maeda in the centre to Ouki in the east. Violent fighting raged, but the only gain for the Japanese was in the central Tanabaru area, where the 24th Division broke through between the US 7th and 77th Divisions. The advance petered out by midnight the following day, when General Ushijima had lost more than 5000 of his crack infantry.

Despite pressure from his Marine generals to make an amphibious landing behind the Japanese lines, to relieve pressure on the fighting front, Buckner chose to continue the bitter, bloody

HE LED FROM THE FRONT

The son of a Confederate general in the American Civil War, Simon Bolivar Buckner (1886-1945) was head of the force that recaptured the Aleutian Islands in 1943. In June 1944 he was chosen to lead the newly formed US Tenth Army in the assault on Okinawa. A strict disciplinarian and a field soldier rather than a pen-pusher, he worked well as part of an inter-service team. However, his tactics in the closing stages of the Okinawa campaign came under some criticism for being over-cautious. He was killed three days before organised Japanese resistance on the island ended, cut down by shrapnel from a shell, and was buried there. After the war his body was flown back to his home state of Kentucky.

HONEYCOMBED HILLS A desolate-looking river bank on Okinawa is pitted all over with cave and tunnel entrances. As on Iwo Jima, the Japanese had built an elaborate underground defence system, near impossible to penetrate and subdue. Two US marines clamber up another war-devastated slope. One carries an entrenching tool, the other a detonator, ready to blast open enemy dugouts.

END OF THE BIGGEST BATTLESHIP

To coincide with the first *kamikaze* assaults on the American Fifth Fleet off Okinawa, the Japanese sent the pitiful remnants of its Combined Fleet on what amounted to a suicide mission. All that could be mustered were eight destroyers, the light cruiser *Yahagi* and the giant *Yamato*, the largest battleship ever built, with only enough fuel for a one-way trip. Their task was to smash through the American offshore armada and mop up any remaining ships.

'The fate of our Empire depends upon this one action,' Combined Fleet Commander in Chief Admiral Soemu Toyoda told his sailors. 'I order the Special Sea Attack Force to carry out on Okinawa the most tragic and heroic act of the war.' It set sail on April 6.

Just after 10 am the next day, two US air strikes, of 280 and 106 aircraft, from Vice Admiral Marc A. Mitscher's Fast Carrier Task Force, were airborne, ready to take on the Japanese. Fifth Fleet's Admiral Spruance had told Mitscher to steer clear of *Yamato*, but Mitscher was determined to have a go. Once his aircraft were in the air, he asked Spruance's permission to attack, and was told: 'You take them.'

The Japanese ships stood little chance as the American planes bore down upon them; all available Japanese fighters were providing *kamikaze* escorts and the force had no air cover. The first attack wave sealed the fate of the Japanese force in a raid that lasted barely 25 minutes. *Yamato* was struck by two bombs and two torpedoes; *Yahagi* suffered two torpedo hits, which stopped it dead. The destroyers *Asashimo* and *Hamakaze* were quickly sunk.

With scarcely a let-up, the next attack wave of planes scored two more bomb hits and no fewer than five torpedoes on *Yamato*. Its hull ripped open, the huge battleship lost speed and developed a dangerous port-side list, until another torpedo hit to starboard caused counter-flooding and the giant levelled off. *Yahagi* suffered another pounding and lay shattered and smoking, while the destroyers *Kasumi* and *Isokaze* were badly hit – and later scuttled.

The third American attack came half an hour later and swiftly sank the wallowing *Yahagi*. Three more bomb hits slowed *Yamato* and set it listing again to port. After yet more bomb and torpedo hits it finally blew up in a vast fireball that could be seen on the coast of Kyushu, 160 km (100 miles) away. Apart from one minor battle a month later, the Imperial Navy's war was over.

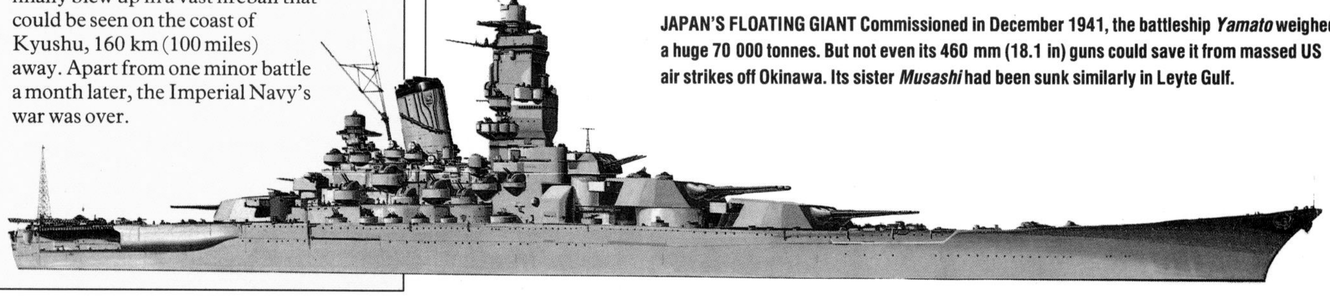

JAPAN'S FLOATING GIANT Commissioned in December 1941, the battleship *Yamato* weighed a huge 70 000 tonnes. But not even its 460 mm (18.1 in) guns could save it from massed US air strikes off Okinawa. Its sister *Musashi* had been sunk similarly in Leyte Gulf.

forward push, at great cost in dead and wounded. Manchester wrote: 'You could smell the front long before you saw it; it was one vast cesspool . . . It was hideous, and it was also strangely familiar, resembling, I then realised, photographs of 1914-1918 . . . The two great armies, squatting opposite one another in mud and smoke, were locked together in unimaginable agony.'

In nine days of fighting against the line of defence at Dakeshi, Wana and Ishimmi ridges, in front of Shuri Castle Hill, the 7th Marines suffered 1249 casualties. Western hills of this line, used by the Japanese as mutually supportive bastions, were named Sugar Loaf, Half Moon and Horseshoe by the US forces. Major Henry Courtney, executive officer of the 2nd Battalion, 22nd Marines, said of the hollowed-out Sugar Loaf: 'The only way we can take the top . . . is to make a Jap *banzai* charge ourselves.'

Marines of 6th Division remembered the day of the assault, May 14, as the bitterest of all the fighting. Tanks came under fire around the west slope, marines on the opposite side were unable to climb the slope because of fire from the nearby hills, and the marines fighting for those hills were in turn held up by Sugar Loaf's own defences. A total of 2662 marines were killed or wounded in the grim fight for Sugar Loaf. Around the same time, the 77th and 96th Infantry Divisions had been assaulting hills to the east.

RETREAT FROM SHURI

On May 26, all roads heading south from the old capital of Shuri were plugged with retreating Japanese soldiers and civilians: in an exceptionally heavy downpour, Ushijima had decided to pull the Thirty-Second Army out of his last defence line. On the 29th, the Americans occupied the rubble-strewn remains of Shuri Castle. Pursuit troops followed the retreating enemy southwards, to a sheer ridge line rising to a 52 m (170 ft) pinnacle which the 96th Division called 'The Big Apple', some 5 km (3 miles) from the southern tip of the island.

To take the final escarpments of 'Big Apple', Yuza Dake beyond it and Kunishi Ridge, the Americans had to approach in the open, with no protection. Soldiers and marines who entered the valley were cut down easily from the Japanese defence positions, while tanks too were easy prey. To the east, Captain Tony Niemeyer of the 7th Infantry Division scrambled up Hill 69, spraying liquid flame into gullies and caves from a 60 m (200 ft) hose he had rigged up.

On June 18, Buckner visited the 8th Marine Regiment on the southern battlefield at an observation post near Mezado Ridge. Peering towards enemy positions from between two rocks, he was hit in the chest and killed by flying shrapnel

SPRING SURPRISE The attractively named *Ohka* ('Cherry Blossom') was a fearsome *kamikaze* weapon – a piloted, rocket-powered flying bomb that was launched from the belly of a medium or heavy bomber.

when six anti-tank shells exploded in the rocks.

By June 22, Okinawa had fallen. General Geiger raised the American flag at Tenth Army headquarters near Kadena Airfield. It had ranked as some of the bloodiest and most sustained fighting of the Pacific war. Japan's casualties totalled 131 000 dead, including some 42 000 civilians. In addition, about 11 000 Japanese were taken prisoner. American land forces suffered 15 500 killed and 51 000 wounded.

Admiral William D. Leahy estimated that, at this rate, the US could expect 250 000 dead in an invasion of Japan. These thoughts offered the Japanese some hope that Washington would seek peace instead of invading. But they had not bargained for Washington's ultimate blows – the world's first and only atomic bomb attacks.

A NEW PRESIDENT

When US President Franklin D. Roosevelt died of a cerebral haemorrhage at Warm Springs, Georgia, on April 12, 1945, it hit the Americans hard. The only US president to be re-elected three times – he died less than five months into his fourth term – Roosevelt had dominated events for a decade. His death devastated civilians and the armed forces alike, but the American high command coped well with the loss.

He was succeeded by Harry S. Truman (1884-1972), a former World War I artillery officer, failed small businessman, and US Senator since 1934. He was chosen as Roosevelt's running mate only in the 1944 election, and the new president had not been briefed on the war effort. Yet he did little that his predecessor would have done differently. His most momentous decision was undoubtedly to use the atomic bombs on Japan. He also had the daunting task of leading the USA and Western world into the postwar era.

US subs cut Japan's lifeline

Without its seaborne imports, Japan could not survive. From the start, strikes by American submarines played a key role in pushing Japan towards defeat.

FOR FIVE HOURS the United States submarine *Barb* had been shadowing a southbound Japanese convoy first located around noon at the northern end of the Formosa Strait. At last *Barb* manoeuvred into position to unleash six torpedoes at the convoy. As four struck home, a massive expanding ball of white fumes, brilliantly lit within, burst from the sea and *Barb* rolled violently. The crew gasped for breath, feeling the air siphoning out of their lungs. They had been hit, not by an enemy depth charge, but by the shock waves of an explosion caused by their own torpedoes.

Lt Commander Eugene B. ('Lucky') Fluckey described one of the hits as a 'stupendous, earth-shaking eruption. A high vacuum resulted in the boat. Personnel in the control room said they felt as if they were sucked up the hatch'. Fluckey gave the order to pull away at full speed and *Barb* made off safely while debris hurtled into the water. One of the torpedoes had hit *Shinyo Maru*, with its load of ammunition.

The strike, on January 8, 1945, added to the already impressive tally scored by *Barb*, a star performer among the US submarines. By the end of the war, *Barb* had sunk 98 000 tonnes of enemy shipping – though not all with satisfaction. Two of the ships it helped to cripple on September 15, 1944, were carrying British and Australian prisoners of war. *Barb* managed to pick up only 14 survivors – after they had been adrift for five days on life rafts.

Japan depended desperately on imports: rice from south-east Asia to feed the densely populated home islands; coal and iron ore from Manchuria for its industry; rubber from Malaya and oil from the East Indies to keep its armed forces on the move. So from the very beginning of the Pacific war in December 1941, the US Navy launched a policy of ruthless submarine strikes at Japan's merchant shipping. They attacked any *Maru* (Japanese merchant ship) or warship they could get in their sights.

With little else at the time with which to attack Japan – the Americans had yet to push across the ocean and secure island air bases – the submarines of the Pacific and Asiatic Fleets went into action. The first 'kill' was the 8800 tonne *Atsutusan Maru*, sunk by USS *Swordfish* on December 15, 1941, a week after Pearl Harbor.

The standard US submarine, of which 195 were built, was the *Gato/Balao* class – 95 m (312 ft) long, 8.3 m (27 ft) in the beam, capable of 20 knots (37 km/h) on the surface and 9 knots (16.5 km/h) submerged, and armed with ten 21 in (533 mm) torpedoes. They did not make much impact at first. The submarines were fitted with radar only during 1942, so until then they worked 'blind'. Worse than that, their torpedoes were faulty: sometimes they would pass under the target or would simply fail to explode.

This was a depressing period for the crews, who did their work but had little to show for it. The submarines, with a range of 16 000 km (10 000 miles) and carrying 60 days' supplies, were at sea for long periods, with nearly 80 men crammed in the often stiflingly hot quarters.

In 1943 – the year the torpedo faults were put right – the success rate improved and Japan's big merchant fleet began to shrink. The submarines used bolder tactics, cruising on the surface (therefore quickly), attacking escorts head-on and on the surface (instead of diving to avoid confrontation), and attacking from the rear. The submarines hunted in small 'wolf-packs' of three to five. US codebreakers could often tell them where to look, and radar enabled them to home in.

The Japanese vessels sailed in small convoys and were inadequately defended, often by old destroyers. The submarines had a blitz against these – and against the oil tankers coming from the East Indies. In the first half of 1944, US submarines and bombers between them cut Japan's oil imports by 75 per cent to only 305 000 tonnes. The future was looking grim for Japan.

During 1944, the subs sank 2.7 million tonnes of Japanese shipping. The major killing ground – dubbed 'Convoy College' by the submariners – covered the East China and Yellow Seas. Top scorer in tonnage terms was USS *Tang*, under Commander Richard O'Kane, which sank ten ships in 12 days and had a total of 24 'kills'. *Barb* also did well. On one patrol from Midway starting on May 21, 1944, it scouted between the towering ice floes in the freezing waters round the Kuril Islands and sank seven Japanese ships before returning to base on July 5. It had evaded bombs from aircraft, and machine-gun fire and depth charges from escort vessels.

SHORTAGE OF TARGETS

By the end of 1944, so many ships had been sunk that targets were becoming hard to find. Attackers outnumbered potential victims and had to beware of getting in a sister-sub's line of fire. The surviving Japanese vessels were clinging to the coasts, sticking to water they hoped was too shallow for the submarines. In 1945, the offensive continued but the subs had to look even harder for targets, hunting in the more easily defended Sea of Japan and preying on small coastal vessels.

As well as destroying 1178 merchant vessels and tankers (totalling 5 million tonnes), the submarines sank 214 Japanese naval ships; served as supply ships and as transports to put commando forces and agents ashore; laid mines and rescued downed pilots. But their major achievement was to cut Japan's supplies of raw materials.

Because imported metals ran out, the Japanese people traded in their aluminium yen and were allowed only one metal cooking vessel and one bucket per household. Because food imports ended, they grew rice in their parks, pumpkins along their streets, and were half-starved on acorns, thistles and chickweed. Because oil imports were slashed, they did without motor transport and heating fuel. Industry was starved.

There were still some 5 million Japanese fighting men and 11 000 planes when the war ended – but where could they go without fuel?

BITTER END The death throes of a Japanese patrol boat after being torpedoed by USS *Seawolf* off Formosa. (Inset) US submariners plot the course of their target.

Superfortresses eclipse the Rising Sun

The Allies finally had a strategy and a bomber for blasting Japan out of the war – but would the devastation make its leaders accept the inevitable?

JAPANESE CITIZENS felt prepared. At home the broom and tank of water stood ready to beat or douse flames from incendiaries. Outside, there was earth in a box to smother fire, and a dug-out shelter bridged with earth-covered planks. Leaders of the *tonarigumi* – neighbourhood associations – insisted on the fire precautions. Along with troops and students, they made sure that great tanks of water were placed along the streets, ditches were dug as shelters in shopping areas and lines of buildings were torn down to create firebreaks. They organised plane spotters, air-raid wardens, strict blackout – and frequent air-raid drills. Municipal firefighting equipment was negligible and public shelters were few – enough for only 5000 people in Tokyo. Cities would be proof against fire damage, the authorities claimed, if every family stayed close to home and put out flames in their own property.

SUPERFORT NEMESIS

The B-29 Superfortress prototype flew on September 21, 1942, but many modifications had to be made before squadrons got it in 1944. Nearly 4000 were built, and the B-29 flew into the late 1950s. It was a high-level precision bomber, and had a range of 5200 km (3250 miles) with a 2270 kg (5000 lb) load; range was later increased to 6560 km (4100 miles) by adding extra fuel tanks. It cruised at 320-350 km/h (200-220 mph) and had a maximum speed of 585 km/h (364 mph). The ten (later 12) 0.5 in (12.7 mm) machine guns and one 20 mm cannon (later removed) were remote controlled, and bombing and navigation were radar assisted. The cabin was pressurised. The 'Superfort' epitomised the USA's technological lead over Japan.

Enough planes and trained crews were ready by early 1944 to form two bomber commands under General Henry H. ('Hap') Arnold: XX to be based in India and China, and XXI in the Pacific. But the planes' new fuel-injected engines were prone to catch fire, and those that reached their targets often missed because of cloud. In September 1944, Maj General Curtis LeMay brought new skills learned in Europe to XX Bomber Command. He introduced new formation-flying and bomb-aiming techniques – but still without great success. Losses were high: 147 B-29s to the end of 1944.

In January 1945, LeMay moved to XXI Bomber Command in the Marianas. After three more months of high-level precision raids in daylight, the switch to low-level night-time fire raids brought success.

DELUSIONS OF SAFETY

Tiresome though the drills were, they generated a spirit of togetherness – and false notions of having things under control. In the Doolittle raid of April 1942, citizens followed the routines they had practised, and the fires were put out with only 12 lives lost and a few houses burned down.

On the night of June 14/15, 1944, some 50 B-29 Superfortress bombers – soon to be christened 'B-san' by the Japanese – flying from the USAAF base at Chengtu (Chengdu) in south-western China, rumbled over the southern Japanese island of Kyushu to the Imperial Iron and Steel Works at Yawata. The raid showed that Japan was now within reach, but it was a failure. Only one bomb landed within 1.2 km (¾ mile) of the target.

There was even complacency when B-29s from the Mariana Islands first appeared over Japanese cities early in November 1944. They came to take reconnaissance photographs and to test the defences. On November 24, 111 of them took off from Saipan to bomb Tokyo. But engine troubles forced 17 back, and only 48 bombs hit the main target, the Nakajima aircraft engine factory which made one-third of all the engines needed by Japan's air force.

Over the next three months a series of missions against industrial targets in Tokyo, Nagoya and elsewhere failed to give the results the Americans expected. The technique used, as in Europe, was high-altitude precision bombing. But, also as in Europe, bombing accuracy suffered because of constant heavy cloud over the targets. Jetstream winds – blowing at 185 km/h (115 mph) or more at the altitude of some 9000 m (30 000 ft) where the B-29s were operating – made accuracy worse. Sometimes a bomber flying into the jetstream was blown backwards. If the jetstream was following, a B-29 could approach 800 km/h (500 mph).

The Americans were also surprised by the effective Japanese fighter defences – notably the *kamikaze*-style ramming attacks which first struck the B-29s over Tokyo on November 24. The loss rate of aircraft – each with 11 highly trained crew members – crept up to 6 per cent, and while aircraft could rapidly be replaced, trained men could not. Such a loss rate meant that a crew could not expect to survive beyond 16 raids. Crews were being pushed harder, too. A raid on Japan from the Marianas involved 15 hours' flying. Five such raids a month was the normal workload, but now this had been increased by one-third to 100 hours a month. Survival prospects were shrinking and morale sagged.

Among the Japanese, however, spirits were still high. The early raids had achieved so little that the citizens, as reporter Masuo Kato recorded, 'went through those early bombings in a spirit of excitement and suspense. There was even a spirit of adventure, a sense of exultation'. People assumed that nothing worse would befall them, but after a few weeks it was all to change.

The way towards greater American success was shown on December 18, when 84 B-29s from

LEMAY – FIRE BOMBER

One of the youngest-ever US generals – at 37 – Curtis LeMay (1906-) joined the US Army Air Corps in 1928 and worked on the development of bombing techniques. It led to his posting to England with the Eighth Air Force, leading B-17 raids over Germany during 1942-3. Nicknamed 'Iron Ass' or 'Iron Pants' by his men, LeMay originated the defensive box formation flying technique.

In 1944-5, as commander of XX, then XXI Bomber Command in China and the Pacific, he rapidly improved the B-29s' effectiveness. He took command of the whole of Twentieth Air Force in July 1945, and rose to high rank in the independent US Air Force after the war, eventually becoming its Commander in Chief.

Chengtu, commanded by Maj General Curtis LeMay, made a daytime raid on the dockyard at Japanese-held Hankow on the Yangtze river (Chang Jiang). For the first time LeMay's planes flew at a rather lower altitude – 6000 m (20 000 ft) – and four out of every five bombers carried incendiaries. Hankow's dock area was gutted. In another daylight high-altitude attack on the Japanese port of Kobe on February 4, 1945, 69 B-29s dropped over 150 tonnes of incendiary bombs, burning five of the city's 12 important factories and halving the capacity of its shipyard.

DESTRUCTION BY FIRE

The Joint Chiefs of Staff in Washington knew that the densely packed, largely wooden-built Japanese cities were vulnerable to fire. They also knew that much of Japan's industry was spread over wide areas in small workshops. Yet they had persisted with the high-explosive raids on specific industrial and military targets. On January 20, 1945, LeMay moved to the Marianas to take command of the USAAF's B-29s based there. He ordered a change in tactics to incendiary attacks on Japanese industrial and urban centres. The Superfortresses were stripped of all guns except that in the tail, to allow the maximum bomb load – a gamble on the ineffectiveness of Japanese defences. The attacks were still to be in daylight and from high altitude.

The first fire raid to hit Tokyo was on February 25. Another tactical change was made for the raid of March 9/10. It was at night and from low level – 1500 m (5000 ft) – so that the jetstream could not blow the bombers off course. The raid was devastating (see box, *Firestorm in Tokyo*), while only 14 US aircraft of the 325 that took off were lost over the target.

The next low-level fire raid – against Nagoya on March 11/12 – burned out 5 km² (2 sq miles) of the city. Attacks on Osaka, Kobe and Nagoya during the following week were even more successful in burning factories and housing. During April, May and June, strikes of up to 500 bombers attacked every other day. In June the China-based B-29s moved to the Marianas, and in July raids were even more frequent. Sometimes five different cities were being attacked on one day. Over 150 000 tonnes of bombs had spilled over Japan, killing nearly half a million Japanese and making 13 million homeless in 26 cities.

The fire raids all followed a similar pattern. A

FIRESTORM IN TOKYO

Radio warnings came at 10.30 pm and the sirens wailed soon after. Then, towards midnight, the deep bass rumble of 280 'B-san' bombers reached the ears of Tokyo citizens. It was an unfamiliar sound, for in previous raids the giants had been silent silver midgets glinting high in the daytime sky. Now on the clear, breezy night of March 9/10, 1945, the pathfinders put down napalm markers on the working-class suburb of Shitamachi. Wave after wave of bombers followed, dropping a torrent of incendiary bombs.

Within half an hour the flames were far beyond the endeavours of the firefighters. The wind fanned the fires into towering fireballs that whooshed across canals and firebreaks. The wind grew stronger in the intense heat, reaching 65 km/h (40 mph) and pushing along the walls of fire to outstrip running feet. People suffocated for lack of oxygen or collapsed with lungs seared by hot gases. Many plunged into the river – but drowned as crowds pressed in on them. Fusako Sasaki wrote later: 'As I ran, I kept my eyes on the sky. It was like a fireworks display as the incendiaries exploded . . . People were aflame, rolling and writhing in agony, screaming piteously for help, but beyond all mortal assistance.'

More than 2000 tonnes of incendiaries were dropped that night, concentrated on a 30 km^2 (12 sq mile) area. The glow could be seen 240 km (150 miles) away. The all-clear sounded about 5 am, but the last fires were not extinguished for four days. By then 40 km^2 (16 sq miles) of the city had been destroyed. The piles of dead took 25 days to clear. Most were unrecognisable charcoal bodies, some inseparably fused in the clasp of their final companions.

They certainly numbered more than 80 000, perhaps as many as 200 000. Many of the 1.8 million shocked, emaciated and terribly burned homeless survivors tried to find safety outside Tokyo. In hospitals swamped by the injured there was no plasma, no painkillers, not even bandages.

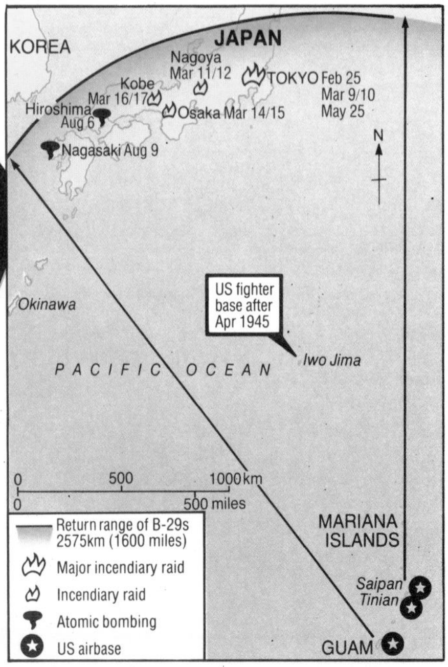

JAPAN ABLAZE Almost all of Japan was within range of B-29s based in the Marianas. (Left) An aircraft spotter keeps watch, but there was virtually nothing anyone could do to stem the fire raids, which left piles of charred corpses (below) in Tokyo after the March 9/10 raid.

pathfinder dropped a canister that exploded 30 m (100 ft) from the ground, spewing out dozens of napalm cylinders. The myriad small fires they started marked the target for the bombers behind. These dropped 6 lb (2.7 kg) oil-filled incendiaries which burst open overhead, releasing fountains of oil that caught fire from the shooting napalm flames. Wave after wave of bombers enlarged the area of destruction. The flimsy board walls, wooden floors, paper partitions and straw mats of the houses flared quickly into an incandescent mass, briefly caged in the more solid framework before the whole collapsed into a spread of hot embers that eventually died and powdered. Firefighting drills proved not the slightest use against such a holocaust.

JAPAN CRIPPLED

The destruction wrought by the incendiaries altered the role for which the B-29 had originally been designed. Now area bombing raids were just as frequent as precision attacks. Once Iwo Jima fell on March 26, American fighters based there could escort the B-29s and cut down bomber losses. The attackers were on the upswing, and LeMay believed that he could smash Japan without the need for an invasion. However, he also had some 'tactical' targets to deal with – notably the enemy airfields on Kyushu to prevent air (and especially *kamikaze*) attacks on the US fleet. Between March 27 and May 11, B-29s reduced the Kyushu airfields to rubble.

When the largest industrial areas had been crippled, LeMay struck at secondary industrial targets. The raids even continued for a week after the atomic bombs destroyed Hiroshima and Nagasaki in August. The B-29s also blew up oil installations and mined Japanese sea lanes and harbours. By the summer of 1945, these mines were sinking more Japanese shipping than US submarines. Bombers from US and Royal Navy carriers were also making devastating raids on Japanese aircraft and ships. On July 14 alone, 1391 sorties by carrier-based planes destroyed 11 warships and 20 merchantmen.

Normal life had been brought to an end, and Japan was incapable of carrying on the war – yet its military leaders were in no mood to surrender. They had not reckoned with the atomic bombs and the Soviet invasion of Manchuria.

The apocalypse bomb

'Little Boy', a four-tonne torpedo-shaped atomic bomb packing the power of 12 700 tonnes of high explosive, destroyed a city and changed the world. Along with 'Fat Man', another type of atomic bomb dropped three days later, it killed many thousands and helped to end the war.

IN HIROSHIMA, a medium-size city beside Japan's Inland Sea, August 6, 1945, was a quiet Monday morning. The early rising population were going about their affairs on a sunny, clear day that promised to become uncomfortably hot. At 7.09 am Japanese time an air-raid warning sounded. Most people took little notice – this was the time when an American weather plane routinely flew over – and 22 minutes later came the all-clear.

Then, at 8.16 am, history was made as the age of atomic warfare dawned. Just 43 seconds earlier, the innocuously named 'Little Boy' bomb had been dropped from a B-29 Superfortress – named *Enola Gay* after the mother of its pilot, Colonel Paul W. Tibbets – flying 9467 m (31 060 ft) above the city. The bomb went off 580 m (1900 ft) above ground, near a bridge over the Ota river.

The ground temperature immediately beneath the explosion was later estimated to be at least 5000°C (9000°F), and thousands of people were vaporised within an instant. The blast tore skin and clothing from others farther from the epicentre, and the shock wave flattened office blocks, factories and homes, leaving thousands more buried under blazing rubble. Tramcars flew through the air, trains were up-ended, the grass and trees of parklands blazed like dry kindling.

Overturned charcoal cooking stoves fuelled fires that raged through the city, blown by a fierce whirlwind. Many who sought refuge in the river were drowned as powerful winds whipped up high waves. Soon, black raindrops as large as marbles began to fall – vaporised moisture from the fireball condensing as a vast mushroom-shaped cloud rose above it and cooled. They carried the deadly, silent radiation that would claim many more victims.

PEEP INTO HELL

Enola Gay, suddenly 4 tonnes lighter, shot upwards when 'Little Boy' was released, and Tibbets made a rapid 155 degree right-hand diving turn to avoid the blast. Tail gunner Bob Caron, asked to report what he saw, was so stunned by the purple flash that penetrated even his special protective goggles that he could scarcely speak. 'A peep into hell' was how he later described it. Then the crew of ten and two ordnance experts on board felt a double shock. They thought it was anti-aircraft fire but Tibbets, briefed to expect shock waves, reassured them.

Looking back at the soaring mushroom cloud, co-pilot Robert A. Lewis gasped, 'My God, look at that son-of-a-bitch go!' according to other crew members. Later he recorded his reaction as, 'My God, what have we done?' They were 14.5 km (9 miles) from Hiroshima, and the crew could clearly see the gigantic fireball and the swirling cloud of thick white smoke. Below it, the city was shrouded in a grey-black dust pall which flashed with red and orange flame. 'We were at 33 000 ft [about 10 000 m] and the cloud was up there with us, rolling and boiling,' Tibbets recalled. 'Below, the surface was like a black, boiling barrel of tar . . . where once there had been a city.' The crew could see the awesome mushroom cloud until they were 580 km (360 miles) into the 2500 km (1550 mile) flight back to Tinian, in the Marianas.

President Harry Truman, hearing news of the successful attack on board the cruiser USS *Augusta*, returning to the USA from the Potsdam conference, commented: 'This is the greatest thing in history.' But could it win the war?

INDIANAPOLIS – ORDEAL IN THE PACIFIC

The American heavy cruiser USS *Indianapolis* had the task of transporting a vital, cup-shaped chunk of uranium-235, encased in a lead cylinder, from San Francisco to the island of Tinian in July 1945. The former flagship of Admiral Raymond A. Spruance had been undergoing repairs after a *kamikaze* attack on March 31.

The uranium was the main fissile component of 'Little Boy', the atomic bomb destined for Hiroshima; three smaller lumps had already been delivered, each on a different plane. Any one of the smaller lumps would be enough to prime the bomb but the larger piece was unique. The two special couriers in charge of it had strict orders: if the cruiser were to sink, their consignment had first priority for a motor launch or life raft.

The bomb material was safely delivered to Tinian on July 26, and *Indianapolis* sailed off for operations in the Philippines. But the unescorted cruiser was torpedoed four days later by ace Japanese submarine commander Mochitsura Hashimoto, and the veteran ship went down without even sending an SOS. Three days passed before Pearl Harbor's naval nerve centre realised that *Indianapolis* was overdue. As a result the 800 who managed to abandon ship spent a gruelling 84 hours in the sea, facing thirst, fatigue and, worst of all, sharks. When help at last arrived, only 316 of *Indianapolis*'s total crew of 1200 were picked up alive.

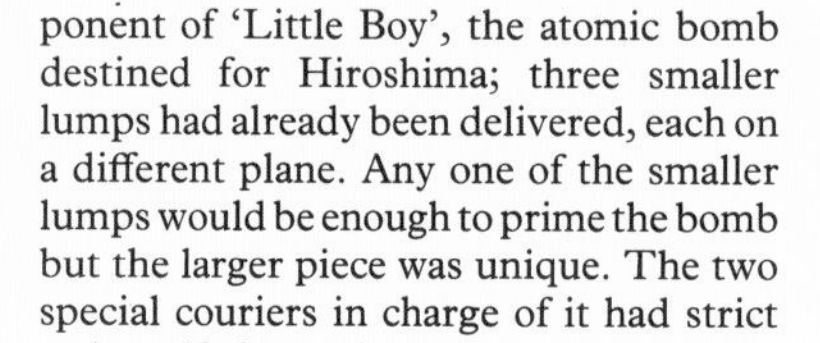

'Little Boy'

CHOOSING THE TARGET

For three years, thousands of Allied scientists, engineers and technicians had toiled in utmost secrecy to produce the atomic bomb. It was the largest weapons project ever yet undertaken (see feature, '*I am become death*', p. 441). But even before anyone knew whether it would work, doubts had been raised about using it. Hungarian-born physicist Leo Szilard – who did much to initiate the atomic programme – and his colleague James Franck, as well as Albert Einstein, were among those who argued, on moral, humanitarian and practical grounds, that it should not be used against a prostrate if unyielding Japan.

The recommendation to go ahead was issued in Washington by a committee of scientific, military and political advisers, chaired by Secretary of War Henry Stimson. They considered setting off a 'demonstration' explosion on unoccupied territory. But finally they recommended to the President that the 'ultimate weapon' should be used as soon as possible, without warning, and on a military installation or war depot.

Hiroshima had large military and supply bases, shipyards and industrial plants. Its population of 380 000 had been reduced to less than 300 000 through evacuation and the demolition of about 70 000 homes to create firebreaks, but its centre was still densely populated and it had so far escaped serious damage from conventional bombing. It fitted the bill. Other cities on a target list included Nagasaki, Kokura, Niigata and Kyoto – but Kyoto was deleted for cultural and humanitarian reasons. It was Japan's ancient capital and a treasure-house of the nation's culture.

Two bomber crews and their back-up teams began training in America in the summer of 1944. Tibbets formed the self-contained 509th Composite Group, built around 393 Squadron. Only he knew the secret of the bomb – none of his men was told the exact nature of their intended task. The 509th moved to Tinian in May 1945 and flew practice missions against the major Japanese base on Truk island, dropping 10 000 lb (4540 kg), TNT-filled, orange-painted bombs nicknamed 'Pumpkins' because of their shape and colour.

As August came, the 509th was well prepared and two bombs – 'Little Boy', containing uranium, and the rotund 'Fat Man', based on a different principle using plutonium – were ready to drop. After five days of unsuitable weather, *Enola Gay* took off at 2.45 am Tinian time on August 6 for the 13 hour round trip to Japan. Two B-29s with cameras and instruments followed.

HIROSHIMA FLATTENED

At about 1430 m (4700 ft), the in-flight armourer, Captain William S. Parsons of the US Naval Ordnance Division, who had fronted development of the uranium bomb's gun-like detonator mechanism, descended into the bomb bay to arm 'Little Boy'. He had persuaded his superiors that it was wiser to risk blowing up the B-29 in flight than perhaps destroying the entire island of Tinian – along with 'Fat Man' – in the event of a crash during takeoff. After passing Iwo Jima, the bomber cruised at around 2800 m (9200 ft) for most of the flight, climbing to 9467 m (31 060 ft) for the bombing run.

By 8.15 am Japan time the bombardier, Major Thomas W. Ferebee, had the Aioi Bridge aiming point in his sights, and released the bomb. 'Little Boy' – 710 mm (28 in) in diameter, 3.6 m (12 ft) long and weighing 4080 kg (9000 lb) – left 10 km^2 (4 sq miles) of Hiroshima's (*continued on p. 442*)

DESTRUCTION OF A CITY

The first atomic bomb caused less physical destruction and fewer casualties than the fire raids on Tokyo, but the horror of Hiroshima and its aftermath and the long-lasting psychological effects were devastating.

People standing by concrete walls near the epicentre of the explosion left no trace except their silhouettes, fused into the concrete by the heat blast, which was blocked for an instant by their bodies before they were vaporised. Others were horribly burnt and lacerated by storms of flying glass, wood and metal fragments.

Estimates vary, but between 75 000 and 100 000 people are believed to have died in the fireball and blast wave, while about 68 000 were injured. That was not all: from two to 15 days after the bombing, people who had been within 460 m (500 yds) of the explosion, even though shielded by buildings, began to show symptoms of deadly radiation sickness – vomiting, spitting of blood, lack of appetite and a breakdown of white blood cells. Most of them died within weeks.

Still the effects did not stop. New cases of radiation sickness occurred long after the blast, and leukaemia and other cancers attributed to radiation are still arising. Three Japanese scientists who went to study the aftermath in Hiroshima and Nagasaki died of radiation-linked cancers.

The novelist John Hersey was sent to Hiroshima by *The New Yorker* magazine in May 1946, to interview survivors. 'The eyebrows of some were burned off and skin hung from their faces and hands,' he wrote. 'Others, because of pain, held their arms up as if carrying something in both hands. Some were vomiting as they walked. Many were naked or in shreds of clothing. On some undressed bodies, the burns had made patterns – of undershirt straps and suspenders [or of] the shapes of flowers they had had on their kimonos . . . Almost all had their heads bowed, looked straight ahead, were silent and showed no expression whatever . . .

'To Father Kleinsorge [a German Jesuit priest], the silence in the grove by the river, where hundreds of gruesomely wounded suffered together, was one of the most dreadful and awesome phenomena of his whole experience. The hurt ones were quiet; no one wept, much less screamed in pain . . . none of the many who died did so noisily; not even the children cried . . .'

In 1968, the Japanese Broadcasting Corporation concluded that between 240 000 and 270 000 citizens of Hiroshima had either been killed outright or had died of radiation sickness within five years.

ATOMIC WASTELAND As the deadly cloud rises over Hiroshima, the city is in ruins. Bricks and tiles melt and twist, anything wooden bursts into flames. The only building to survive in the fireball area is the domed city exhibition centre (top right in inset) – today the 'A-Bomb Dome', a monument.

SILENT SUFFERING Numb with shock after the second atomic blast, wounded survivors wander among the debris of Nagasaki with expressionless faces, some clutching emergency rice rations. Ironically, the port city was the most Westernised in Japan before the war. Allied planners believed that it would take a double atomic shock to force Japan's rulers to surrender – and so it proved.

'I am become death' – the Manhattan Project

At dawn on July 16, 1945, a gigantic fireball, brighter than several suns, seared the arid wastes of the New Mexico desert, fusing sand to glass and exploding with a force equivalent to 20 000 tonnes of TNT. As the fireball died away, a mushroom cloud towered more than 12 000 m (40 000 ft) into the sky – a cloud that was to become the symbol of the Atomic Age. Physicist Robert Oppenheimer, who led the team that created the bomb, was reminded of a stark line from a sacred Hindu text, the Bhagavad Gita (Song of God): 'I am become death, the destroyer of worlds.'

As early as 1934 Leo Szilard, a Hungarian-born Jewish refugee physicist working in London, realised that the nuclei of certain atoms could be split by bombarding them with atomic particles called neutrons. This in turn would release more neutrons, which would split more nuclei and so on in a chain reaction. And according to Albert Einstein's Theory of Relativity, this would produce enormous amounts of energy. But what element would produce such a chain reaction?

In the same year, the Italian Enrico Fermi bombarded the element uranium with neutrons, wrongly thinking he had produced a new element. In fact, he had split the uranium nuclei, though without producing a chain reaction. That process was discovered in 1938 by two German physicists, Otto Hahn and Fritz Strassman. It became clear that uranium might be used in a devastating atomic bomb.

These discoveries were made under Fascist regimes whose oppression and persecution of Jews caused many of their leading scientists to flee to Britain and the United States. Fermi and Szilard went to America. Two German refugees in Britain, Otto Frisch and Rudolf Peierls, discovered that for an instantaneous, explosive chain reaction, the rare form of uranium called uranium-235 would have to be purified from the natural mineral. Frisch and Peierls were joined by French scientists who had found that a newly discovered man-made element, plutonium, might also make an atomic bomb.

In America, Szilard persuaded Albert Einstein – the most eminent physicist of the time – to write to President Roosevelt proposing a research programme to develop a bomb. It was coolly received; in 1940 America saw no need for such a weapon. The Japanese attack on Pearl Harbor on December 7, 1941, changed all that. Soon the scientists from Britain joined their American colleagues in what they feared was a race to beat Germany to produce the new weapon.

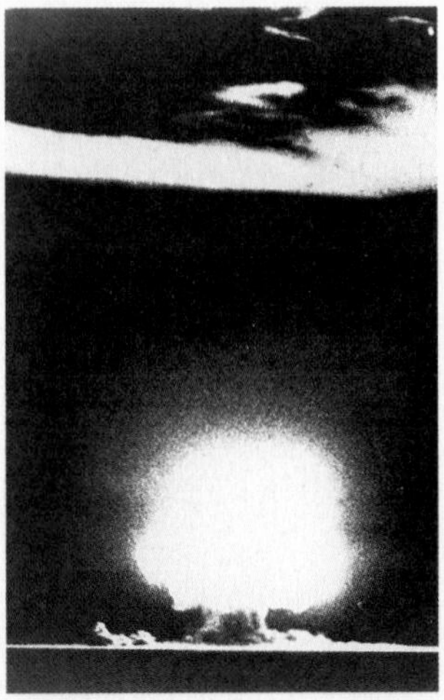

NUCLEAR DAWN An atomic fireball over the New Mexico desert (above) heralds a new age. (Right) Afterwards, bomb-makers Oppenheimer (on left) and Groves inspect their handiwork – the remnants of the steel test tower.

BEST BRAINS

In 1942, construction of laboratories and factories began for the bomb project – code-named the 'Manhattan Project', because initial work took place at Columbia University in Manhattan, New York. A US Army engineer, Brig General Leslie R. Groves, was put in overall charge. Robert Oppenheimer became scientific director, and gathered many of the Allies' best brains to a specially built laboratory complex at Los Alamos, New Mexico. At Oak Ridge, Tennessee, the world's biggest factory produced uranium-235 – and plutonium was made in nuclear reactors at Hanford, Washington state.

Meanwhile, at Los Alamos, scientists worked on the biggest problem – how to explode the bombs. Two methods had to be devised, for the uranium and plutonium bombs. The uranium bomb had a wedge of U-235 fired down a gun barrel by conventional high explosive into a ball of U-235 at the other end, to form a critical mass which then exploded. The plutonium bomb had a hollow sphere of plutonium surrounded by high-explosive charges which, when detonated, crushed the sphere into a critical mass. The scientists were pretty sure that the uranium bomb would work, but they had to test the plutonium device.

In the summer of 1945, after an expenditure of 2000 million dollars, a plutonium bomb was finally ready for testing. It was mounted on a steel tower in the desert, and a switch was thrown in a control bunker 9 km ($5\frac{1}{2}$ miles) away to detonate it. A fraction of a second later the tower had vanished, vaporised by the intense heat. An awesome new weapon had been born. Three weeks later it was first used in anger.

HEART-SEARCHING

Had there been a race for the bomb, as Szilard and his fellow-refugees feared? It turned out that no other country had managed to achieve a chain reaction. Hitler, despite German experiments using so-called 'heavy water' (which were sabotaged by the Allies), had not been prepared or able to set up the long-term effort required. No word of the 'Manhattan Project' was ever leaked to the Axis, but another refugee physicist, Klaus Fuchs, betrayed its secrets to the USSR.

However, there was much heart-searching among the scientists involved over what they had created. Szilard and others feared an arms race leading to nuclear annihilation, and tried to persuade Presidents Roosevelt and Truman not to use it. Oppenheimer, who had left-wing associations prewar, resigned two months after the bombs were dropped. Summoned before the 'Un-American Activities' committee during Senator Joseph McCarthy's anti-communist witch hunts of the early 1950s, he was asked if he had moral scruples about the loss of life the A-bombs would cause when used. 'Terrible ones', he replied. He died at 63 in 1967; Szilard died three years earlier, aged 65.

busy industrial, commercial and residential centre a flattened wasteland. The blast was later estimated as equivalent to 12 700 tonnes of TNT (see box, *Destruction of a city*, p. 439).

When *Enola Gay* finally touched down at Tinian, officers and enlisted men swarmed around the bomber in welcome. General Carl Spaatz, commanding the US Strategic Bombing Force, pinned the Distinguished Service Cross on Tibbets' overalls. Later, every airman taking part was decorated. Truman broadcast news of the bombing to the nation on August 7 and added: 'If they [the Japanese] do not now accept our terms they may expect a rain of ruin from the air, the like of which has never been seen on this earth.'

NAGASAKI NEXT

However, no Japanese surrender was forthcoming, and on August 9 'Fat Man' was dropped on the major military port and shipbuilding centre of Nagasaki. The bomb was bulbous, about 3.25 m (10 ft 8 in) long and 1.5 m (5 ft) in diameter, weighed 4540 kg (10 000 lb) and was even more destructive than the uranium bomb – the equivalent of over 20 000 tonnes of high explosive.

Major Charles W. Sweeney took off at about 3.45 am Tinian time – and his run was dogged with problems. Shortly before takeoff, it was discovered that his borrowed B-29 *Bockscar* – named for its original commander, Captain Frederick C. Bock – had a faulty fuel pump. But it was too late to delay the mission, so about 2730 litres (600 gallons) of fuel in an auxiliary tank could not be used. When Sweeney reached the southern island of Yakoshima, where *Bockscar* was to rendezvous with two observation aircraft, one of them – carrying the British scientist Dr William Penney and RAF Group Captain Leonard Cheshire – failed to arrive on time.

The B-29 circled for some 15 minutes, then Sweeney headed for the primary target, Kokura, at the northern tip of Kyushu, with its huge military arsenal. But heavy cloud over Kokura ruled out visual bombing, which had been ordered. After three abortive runs, using even more precious fuel, *Bockscar* headed south-west 160 km (100 miles) for the secondary target, Nagasaki. There Sweeney found a break in the cloud and dropped the bomb at 11.01 am from 8800 m (28 900 ft). Then he headed for Okinawa, rather than far-distant Iwo Jima as planned, on his little remaining fuel.

An alert had sounded in Nagasaki at 7.50 am after a weather plane flew over, and again five minutes before 'Fat Man' fell. But few people bothered to seek Nagasaki's ample hillside shelters. The bomb exploded about 500 m (1650 ft) over the industrial and residential district of Urakami, smashing the sprawling Mitsubishi works. Despite its greater power, the bomb caused less damage than 'Little Boy' had at Hiroshima, because hills around and within the city contained the blast. Nonetheless, the bomb flattened the northern part of Nagasaki and killed 35 000 people according to US estimates, although the Japanese later put the toll at 87 000.

There were horror scenes similar to those in Hiroshima, but expanses of water prevented a firestorm. An elderly woman, Matsu Moriuchi, emerged from Yamazato Grade School's air-raid shelter to find near-naked people lying around its entrance. Their bodies were hideously swollen and their skin was peeling off in ragged strips. Leaving the same shelter, Sadako Moriyama saw what she thought were two grotesque, reptilian monsters, croaking as they tried to crawl inside. Only when they moved into the light did she realise that they were people; their flesh was burnt raw red and their bodies smashed and broken as the blast had flung them against a wall.

Damage extended over a roughly oval area 4 by 2 km ($2\frac{1}{2}$ by $1\frac{1}{4}$ miles) at its widest, in which virtually every building was demolished or rendered uninhabitable. But the city was not as congested as Hiroshima and emergency services were not as seriously hampered.

SHOCK POWER

The message that a new dimension in devastation had arrived was not lost on Japan's rulers. Combined with the Soviet invasion of Manchuria on the same day as the Nagasaki strike, it provided the shock needed to turn the divided Japanese government towards peace. Emperor Hirohito and his peace-inclined ministers were able to convince the 'fight-to-the-death' faction that there was no option but to accept American surrender terms. In this sense, the bombs had justified their development and use. They had been dropped primarily to knock Japan out of the war and prevent Allied casualties – a million according to one estimate – which would inevitably follow an invasion of Japan.

Plans were ready. In Operation 'Olympic', 11 US Army and three Marine Corps divisions – a total of 650 000 men – would land on Kyushu, the southernmost main island, on November 1, 1945. Fighting as fierce as that at Iwo Jima and Okinawa was expected. On March 1, 1946, a million more men – including British, Australian and Canadian divisions – would land on the largest island, Honshu, in Operation 'Coronet'. Again total Japanese resistance was expected – including *kamikaze* attacks and long-term guerrilla activities. Japanese losses could hardly be estimated.

It could well have happened, for 'Little Boy' and 'Fat Man' were part of a gigantic bluff. By implication, Japan faced the choice of capitulation or annihilation. Yet in fact, America had no more atomic bombs immediately available; the earliest a third could be dropped would be August 24. Fortunately for both Japan and the Allies the bluff worked, and surrender negotiations began within hours of the Nagasaki explosion.

THE MAN WHO DROPPED THE FIRST A-BOMB

Colonel Paul W. Tibbets Jr (1915-) was 29 years old when he was chosen to train the 509th Composite Group, formed to deliver the first two atomic bombs. Decorated many times as a bomber pilot in Europe, he commanded the B-17 Fortress *Butcher Ship* on the first Eighth Air Force raid – on Rouen in 1942 – and went on to complete a tour of 25 missions.

Tibbets was briefed from the beginning on the nature of the highly secret weapon, so it was fitting that he should himself pilot the B-29 Superfortress that dropped 'Little Boy'. However, overall tactical command of the mission lay with the in-flight armourer, Captain William S. Parsons, though Tibbets played a part in selecting targets. He retired in 1965 as a brigadier general and became president of an executive jet aircraft company.

Japan bows in total surrender

Japan's leaders knew that they could not win the war, but to some, total surrender was unthinkable. Then the Emperor was asked for his opinion . . .

ON THE HOT SUMMER NIGHT of August 9/10, 1945, Japan's six most powerful men sat with Emperor Hirohito in an air-raid shelter within the leafy, wooded gardens of the Imperial Palace in Tokyo. Only hours before, the second atomic bomb had fallen on their country. That very day, Russian troops had stormed into Manchukuo, the Japanese puppet state in Manchuria. The decision facing the Supreme War Council now was whether to accept Allied surrender terms or to fight on to the death – all hopes of winning the war having vanished in the fireballs of Hiroshima and Nagasaki.

But even now the six were deadlocked – three for peace, three for fighting on. For the Allied terms were starkly uncompromising: surrender was to be unconditional, as laid down at Casablanca in 1943 and reaffirmed at Potsdam as recently as July 26, 1945. Never before defeated in war and steeped in the *samurai* warrior 'death before dishonour' tradition, the three 'hawks' on the council simply could not envisage delivering their country, themselves and their god-emperor into the hands of the enemy.

They were the War Minister, General Korechika Anami; Army Chief of Staff General Yoshijiro Umezu; and Admiral Soemu Toyoda, Navy Chief of Staff. Though conceding inevitable defeat, they were insisting on four conditions for peace: no Allied occupation, self-disarmament, self-conducted war-crimes trials, and no change in the status of the Emperor. Those for peace were the Prime Minister, Baron Kantaro Suzuki; his deputy, Navy Minister Admiral Mitsumasa Yonai; and Foreign Minister Shigenori Togo. However, while accepting the Allied terms, Togo also wanted the Emperor's position preserved.

HIROHITO SPEAKS

The arguments ground on into the early hours, then Suzuki made a totally unprecedented move. He asked the Emperor for *his* opinion. By tradition Hirohito had always remained silent at such meetings, merely acting as an observer. Now he said that he thought Togo's proposal – preservation of the ruler's status – should be accepted and that on that single condition Japan should surrender. Suzuki asked if anyone opposed the Emperor's opinion. No one dared. Anami simply asked that if the Americans refused, the Japanese should fight to the last man.

This was agreed and at 7.33 am on August 10 the necessary cables were sent. US Secretary of State James Byrnes replied that only unconditional surrender was acceptable – and the Emperor would be subject to the Supreme Commander of the Allied Forces, his status to be confirmed by public ballot.

This restarted arguments in Japan's War Council and Cabinet, which dragged on for four days while American air attacks continued and Russian troops were rampaging in Manchuria and northern China. On August 14, the Americans sent a message saying that the Imperial constitution would not be abolished, and pointed out that in previous centuries emperors had frequently been 'subject to' the *shogun* military rulers.

Asked once more for his opinion, Hirohito ordered the Cabinet to 'endure the unendurable' – and accept the terms. And to guard against any army rebellion or backing out, he made a recording explaining the surrender terms, to be broadcast to the nation next day, August 15.

FINAL BLOODY DRAMA

The Americans were informed of the acceptance, but before the surrender broadcast was transmitted, one last bloody drama was played out in Tokyo. On the night of August 14/15, a group of fanatical officers confronted General Takeshi Mori of the Imperial Guard, and proposed that Hirohito should be isolated from peace-seeking advisers and persuaded to carry on the war. Mori said he would pray for guidance – at which one of the ringleaders, Major Kenji Hatanaka, drew a revolver and shot him, while an accomplice hacked down through Mori's collarbone with a sword. Using the dead man's seal, the rebels forged orders giving them authority over troops stationed in the palace compound. They searched for the Emperor's recording and members of the peace faction.

They failed – the recording was locked in a wall safe in the palace administration building. Hatanaka also failed to persuade radio announcer Morio Tateno to let him broadcast news of the rebellion. General Seiichi Tanaka, commander of the Eastern Army District, reached the palace and persuaded the rebels to give up. Hatanaka shot himself in the palace grounds, and the others committed *hara-kiri*. Though not involved in the plot, War Minister Anami, despairing for the future of his country, also committed suicide with a ceremonial knife.

THE BROADCAST

Hirohito's radio broadcast, which went out as planned, stunned his people. Although he had reigned for 20 years, they had never even heard his voice. And how much of it they understood is debatable, since he spoke in archaic court Japanese. 'The war situation has developed not necessarily to Japan's advantage . . .', he said. 'The enemy has begun to employ a new and most cruel bomb . . . Should we continue to fight, it would not only result in the ultimate collapse of the Japanese nation, but also . . . the total extinction of human civilisation.'

As a result of the Emperor's broadcast, the surrender passed without untoward incident. The tradition of loyalty proved strong enough to prevent *kamikazes* attacking Allied forces, although some committed *hara-kiri*, while other pilots crashed deliberately into the sea. A new caretaker government was formed under Prince Naruhiko Higashikuni, Hirohito's uncle, and occupation troops were airlifted in.

On the overcast morning of September 2, the formal surrender document was signed on the quarterdeck of the battleship USS *Missouri* in Tokyo Bay. A scratchy recording of *The Star-Spangled Banner* blared out from *Missouri*'s loudspeaker system. Then Foreign Minister Mamoru Shigemitsu signed with General Umezu

DEFEAT! Japanese Foreign Minister Shigemitsu, solemn-faced and top-hatted, stands with Army Chief of Staff General Umezu and their entourage on *Missouri*, ready to sign the surrender. US officers and men look on. Shigemitsu's false leg made balancing on deck precarious.

RUSSIA CRASHES IN

Ten minutes after the Soviet Union's midnight declaration of war against Japan on August 8/9, 1945, a million and a half Russian troops began to storm into Manchuria and northern China, along an enormous front stretching over 5000 km (3000 miles). (See map, p. 135.)

The defending Japanese Kwantung Army, though still over a million strong, was simply overwhelmed. Once the cream of Japan's land forces, it had lost many of its best units and equipment, transferred to reinforce the armies in the Pacific. Men wore a ragged mixture of 'civvies' and uniforms, and often boots had given way to straw sandals. They were short of ammunition, fuel and explosives. Even so, many fought with the customary Japanese ferocity and dedication.

The Russians had spent over a year building up for the invasion. They had 5500 high-quality tanks and armoured vehicles, about 3900 planes and over 25 000 guns and mortars. Many of their troops were experienced veterans of the war in Europe, and they rapidly pushed parts of the Japanese forces back through Manchuria and into Korea.

News that Tokyo had accepted Allied surrender terms on August 14 led the staff of the Japanese Third Area Army (Army Group) in central Manchuria to issue a ceasefire order. But because it did not carry authorisation from the Kwantung High Command it was quickly rescinded. Even when the Kwantung Commander in Chief, General Otozo Yamada, heard the Emperor's broadcast on August 15, he insisted on waiting for written verification. And on August 16 he and his staff voted to fight on. Hirohito's personal order finally reached him on the 17th.

Even so, many of his units remained in ignorance of the surrender and continued fighting. So did the Russians, who smashed their way on, intent upon occupying territory. In the central and southern defiles of the Hingan mountains, tanks of the 1st Far East Front (Army Group) drove the Japanese down into the Central Manchurian Plain. On August 20, General Issa Pliev's Soviet-Mongolian Mechanised Cavalry Group emerged just north of Peking (Beijing) after a remarkable 560 km (350 mile) crossing of the Gobi Desert. On the same day, Marshal Rodion Malinovsky's Trans-Baikal Front captured Mukden (Shenyang), then drove on to take Port Arthur (now Lüshun). To the east, units of General Maxim Purkayev's 2nd Far East Front captured southern Sakhalin and the Kuril Islands.

Stalin finally called a halt on August 23, but it took the Russians months to round up and disarm hundreds of thousands of dispersed Kwantung Army troops – who were then put to forced labour. The Russians claimed 87 000 enemy dead (the Japanese said 21 000) and 594 000 taken prisoner; their own casualties were 8000 killed and 22 000 wounded.

for Japan. (Togo had resigned once the surrender terms were agreed.) General Douglas MacArthur signed as Allied Supreme Commander, Admiral Chester W. Nimitz for the USA, Admiral Sir Bruce Fraser for Britain and General Sir Thomas Blamey for Australia. A massed flypast of about 2000 Allied planes roared overhead. World War II was officially over.

MacArthur said: 'It is my earnest hope and indeed the hope of all mankind that from this solemn occasion a better world shall emerge out of the blood and carnage of the past – a world dedicated to the dignity of man and the fulfilment of his most cherished wish – for freedom, tolerance and justice.'

However, the surrender of Japanese forces in outlying areas had been delayed, at MacArthur's orders, until after the Tokyo Bay ceremony. This caused considerable chaos. It was not until September 12 that Admiral Lord Louis Mountbatten accepted surrender at Singapore. Similar ceremonies took place at Hong Kong and in China and Indochina.

Yet even that was not the end of the story. All over eastern and south-east Asia, Japanese garrisons had to be returned to Japan and Allied prisoners and internees collected up and repatriated – a process that took well into 1946. The long transition caused problems for the returning colonial powers, who often faced determined and well organised nationalists who in some areas such as the East Indies had large caches of Japanese arms. The war may have ended, but the prewar colonial era would never permanently return.

THE WAR IS OVER – OR IS IT?

In 1975 a Japanese soldier, Private Teruo Nakamura, was found living on a tiny Indonesian island to which he had been sent by the army 33 years before. He had no idea that World War II was over. He was 57. A year earlier 2nd Lieutenant Hiru Onoda, a Japanese officer sent to the Philippine island of Lubang in 1944 to gather intelligence, was finally persuaded that his country had surrendered. He was first sighted in 1972 when he and another soldier, Private Kinishi Kozuka, fought a gun battle with a police patrol. Kozuka was killed but Onoda escaped into the jungle. Only when his former commander, Major Yoshimi Tanaguchi, flew to the island to countermand his original order never to surrender did Onoda give up.

He and Nakamura were only two out of scores of Japanese fighting men who never heard – or refused to believe – that the war had ended. Left marooned on remote Pacific islands and in jungle hideouts by the retreating tide of battle, they began emerging in the late 1940s and 50s.

In 1951, for example, 19 Japanese on Anataten in the Mariana Islands surrendered only when the US Navy bombarded the island with leaflets. 'We are very sorry,' said their spokesman, Usui Tatsusaburo. 'We did not know . . .'

In 1978 the Japanese launched Operation 'Cherry Blossom' to try to flush out any remaining 'castaways' and convince them that the war is really over. It is possible that some still remain.

THE BITTER END In Burma, Major Wako Lisanori of Japan's 28th Army acknowledges defeat. He gives up his sword to Britain's Lt Colonel O.N. Smyth.

WHEN THE KISSING HAD TO START . . .

Air-raid sirens howled in San Francisco shortly after 4 pm Pacific Time on August 14, 1945. But instead of seeking shelter, people took to the streets in tens of thousands – wild with joy. For the banshee wail was signalling the end of the war with Japan. Car horns, factory whistles, ships' hooters and church bells joined in, and in scenes mirrored throughout the United States, traffic was brought to a halt by singing and cheering, kissing and carousing crowds.

In Washington, military police were called to keep an enthusiastic crowd out of the White House grounds – and had to be rescued by more troops as they were crushed against railings and walls. New Yorkers converged on Times Square, and exhausted cops later estimated the crowds in the area at a staggering 2 million.

Australia's new Prime Minister Joseph Chifley, like Britain's Clement Attlee and US President Harry Truman, proclaimed a two-day holiday celebration. (John Curtin, Chifley's predecessor, had died six weeks earlier.) At the peak of festivities, a million people were cheering, singing and dancing in the streets of Sydney, where an effigy of a Japanese soldier was burned near the Cenotaph. Girls mobbed army lorries and jeeps, snatched off servicemen's hats and swapped kisses for autographs. Loudspeakers blared *Roll Out the Barrel* and *Rule Britannia*, and 'snowstorms' of shredded income tax forms cascaded from office windows.

But amid the frenzy, thousands knelt solemnly in churches to give thanks, seek solace or pray for missing loved ones.

BRITAIN GOES WILD

In Britain, it was midnight on August 14/15 when Attlee broadcast the news, and bonfires were lit in many parts of the country. In London there were fewer than a hundred people in Piccadilly Circus when the announcement was made, and barely a dozen outside Buckingham Palace. But by 2 am there were thousands everywhere, shouting, singing, dancing, kissing and hugging one another.

American servicemen marched joyfully to their Grosvenor Square embassy; jeeps roared up and down Oxford Street and a great cacophony of car horns, klaxons, police whistles, drums, bells and dustbin lids rang out along the famous shopping thoroughfare. A great line of servicemen and women was joined by civilians in a giant conga – headed by a kilted Scotsman – which snaked from Marble Arch, through Grosvenor Square and on to Piccadilly. By 3 am the Piccadilly Circus crowds were as great as on VE Day, and in Trafalgar Square people climbed onto the lions and sang to a piano accordion.

In stark contrast, the shattered people of Tokyo gathered before the Imperial Palace and wept.

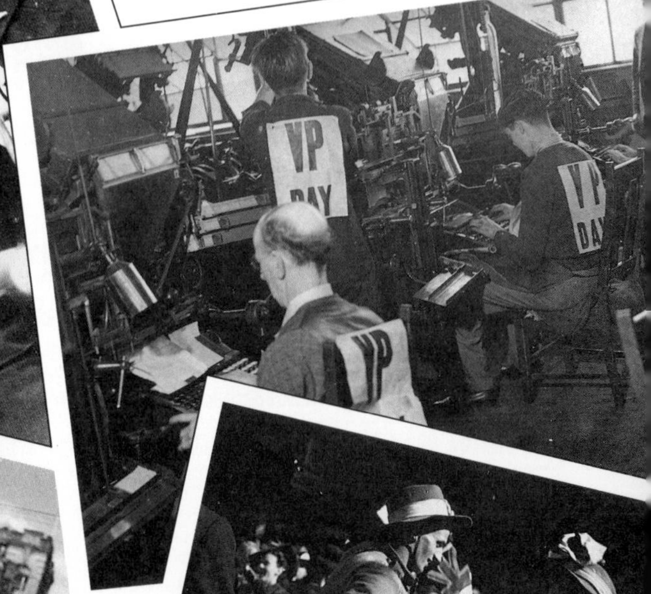

TIME TO LET RIP It's VJ (Victory in Japan) or VP (Victory in the Pacific) Day – and everyone is celebrating. A sailor in New York indulges in a long kiss. Three others find liquid satisfaction. In Australia, all is smiling girls' faces, cheeky messages for General Tojo and jigs in the street. Newspaper compositors in Perth, Western Australia, celebrate in their own way.

28: OUT OF THE FLAMES

Both victors and vanquished faced a huge task in trying to build a better postwar world.

Shaping the new Europe

After Hitler, what? That was a question the Allied leaders had to face even before the defeat of Nazi Germany seemed certain. Their answer was worked out in a series of conferences that altered the map of Europe.

EUROPE'S FUTURE increasingly figured in Allied discussions as the war drew to a close. Poland's postwar frontiers had been mapped out in rough and ready fashion when the 'Big Three' Allied leaders met in the Iranian capital, Tehran, in November and December 1943. There, as always, Stalin knew what he wanted. This time it was a slice of eastern Poland up to 300 km (185 miles) wide, an area traditionally claimed by the Russians. Poland was to be compensated by gaining a slice in the west – a slice cut from Germany's eastern boundary and extending Poland to the Oder and Neisse rivers.

However harsh for individuals, on balance this arrangement would be to Poland's advantage: the 114 000 km^2 (44 000 sq miles) of new territory had markedly better agricultural and industrial resources than the old, and the shorter frontier with Germany would be easier to protect.

SPHERES OF INFLUENCE

Less than a year later, Soviet advances into south-eastern Europe were both pleasing and disturbing to Churchill. He met Stalin in Moscow in October 1944 and with an approach based on the old imperial concept of 'spheres of influence', casually suggested to Stalin a trade-off. The Soviet Union should have 90 per cent influence in Romania, 10 per cent influence in Greece, 75 per cent in Bulgaria and 50 per cent in Yugoslavia, with the remaining percentages controlled by Britain.

Churchill scrawled these figures on a piece of paper and passed it to Stalin, who simply ticked it and passed it back. Churchill said that the paper should be burned, as it might be thought 'rather cynical if it seemed we had disposed of these issues . . . in such an offhand manner'. To this Stalin replied: 'No, you keep it.'

Stalin was content to keep his side of the bargain when it came to Greece, and did not intervene in the six-week Greek civil war in the winter of 1944-5 – though the same was not true when fighting resumed in 1946. But Churchill's scrap of paper – ironically reminiscent of that signed in Munich in 1938 – bore no relation to the reality on the ground in much of eastern Europe. There, the Red Army called the tune: between the summer of 1944 and spring of 1945, it occupied all eastern Europe and the Balkans with the exception of Greece, Albania and Yugoslavia.

By the end of the war, the Soviet Union reoccupied the Baltic states of Lithuania, Estonia and Latvia, which it had first seized in 1940; annexed much of East Prussia; took the ice-free port of Petsamo and part of the Karelian isthmus from Finland; acquired the Ruthenian region from Czechoslovakia, and Bessarabia and parts of Bukovina from Romania; and occupied eastern Poland. All these lands were to become integral parts of the USSR. Beyond the Soviet borders would stretch a protective buffer of eastern European nations that the Soviet Union had either liberated (Poland and Czechoslovakia) or invaded (Romania, Hungary and Bulgaria). Stalin gave his view in a speech in July 1944: 'Everyone imposes his own systems as far as his army can reach. It cannot be otherwise.'

DISUNITY AT YALTA

In February 1945, with the German Army on the retreat and the Red Army inside the frontiers of the Reich, it became an urgent matter for the Allies to settle the future of Europe. They met at

ALLIED LEADERS CONFER Russian soldiers present arms to Churchill whose host, Stalin, has laid on a ceremonial greeting for his arrival at Moscow airport in October 1944. Molotov, whose role was to play the inflexible hard man at Allied conferences, walks (in civilian clothes) a pace or two behind Stalin. At their meeting, Churchill and Stalin made plans for their roles in the postwar Balkan states. At Tehran (inset, near right) the previous winter, Stalin had insisted to Roosevelt and Churchill that Poland should be, in effect, pushed farther west, yielding territory to the Soviet Union but gaining from Germany. By the time the three met in February 1945 at Yalta in the Crimea (top inset, far right), Roosevelt was sick and gaunt, more wary of Churchill than of Stalin. During the Potsdam Conference in July and August (lower inset, far right), Clement Attlee was elected in Churchill's place; Roosevelt had recently died. Only Stalin remained in power of the wartime 'Big Three'.

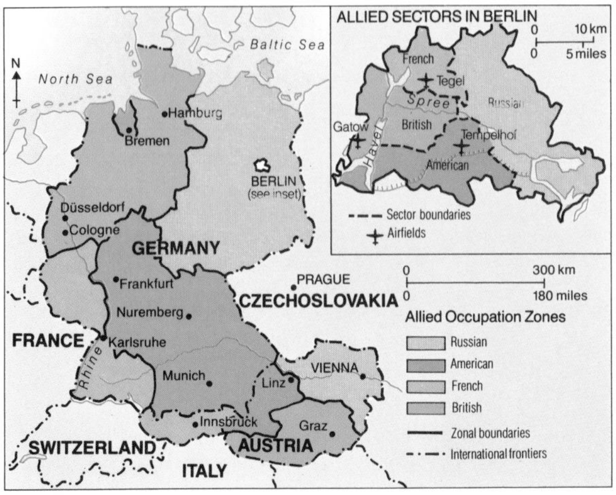

POSTWAR GERMANY 'Rankin C', the British proposal to divide control of Germany between the Allies, was first put forward in 1943 and signed and sealed at Potsdam in June 1945. Berlin was stranded in the Russian zone – with road, rail and air links to the west guaranteed by the Soviet Union – but the division was, at that time, seen as temporary. Moscow controlled East Germany and Poland, giving Stalin what he wanted – a docile buffer between his country and potential invaders from the west. The Allies, who went to war for Polish independence, were prevented by the reality of Red Army possession from giving democracy to Poland.

Yalta in the Crimea, and disagreements quickly surfaced. The Americans – under great pressure to bring the GIs home quickly once the war was over – were less forceful than the British.

Roosevelt, as chairman, was perhaps more conciliatory to the calm, unshakable Stalin than he would otherwise have been. He reserved most of his suspicion not for Stalin but for the old-fashioned imperialist notions of Churchill.

One of the first arguments was over the Tehran proposals for the German-Polish border. Had Poland been allotted territory up to the eastern branch of the Neisse – as Churchill and Roosevelt believed – or to the western branch 100 km (62 miles) nearer Germany, which was the Russian interpretation? A decision was put off until an eventual European peace conference – which never took place. In any case Stalin was determined that in Poland, a traditional invaders' route into Russia, any future government must be a 'friend of the USSR'.

At Yalta, the Americans submitted a 'Declaration on Liberated Europe'; among its provisions was the right of all peoples to choose the form of government under which they wanted to live. In reality, Poland's prospects of democracy had long since been shattered. When the Polish government-in-exile in London called for a Red Cross inquiry into the massacre of more than 4000 Polish officers at Katyn, revealed in 1943, the Soviet Union immediately broke off relations with the London Poles and set up their own Polish provisional government in Moscow. From then on, they backed the Polish National Liberation Committee, a Communist-controlled underground military organisation in Poland, rather than the London-backed Polish Home Army. The provisional government moved to Lublin in 1944 and to Warsaw in 1945. Many exiled Poles chose to remain in exile rather than return to a distrusted regime.

In Yugoslavia the situation was rather different. Marshal Tito's Communist-led partisans had liberated Yugoslavia with little outside help, and by the end of the war had established a self-confident Communist regime of their own. They saw no reason to exchange German occupation for Russian domination. Much the same happened in Albania; at first the new Communist regime there was friendly to Moscow, but after Stalin's death in 1953 it switched its allegiance to China. However, over the few years following the war the Russians made sure that subservient regimes were installed in Bulgaria, Romania, Hungary and Czechoslovakia.

DIVIDING UP GERMANY

As well as settling boundaries – and recognising realities – in eastern Europe, the Allies had to decide what to do about Germany itself. As early as 1943, the British had been working on a plan for a three-way division of Germany and joint occupation of Berlin, code-named 'Rankin C'. The Allies did not plan to make the division long-term, but better a divided Germany than an energetic nation of 79 million at the heart of Europe with the potential to become a Fourth Reich. The plan gave Moscow control of almost 40 per cent of Germany's postwar area, 36 per cent of its population and 33 per cent of its resources.

At Yalta, the Big Three formally agreed to the zones outlined in 'Rankin C', with the addition of a smaller French zone in the Saarland, carved from the British and American areas. Berlin was divided into four sectors and was to house the Allied Control Council for supervising the occupying powers. Moscow gave informal guarantees of access by air, road, canal and rail through their zone to the parts of Berlin occupied by the Western powers. Austria was split up in similar fashion, with Vienna providing the headquarters for a four-power commission.

The Allies met at Potsdam in the southern suburbs of Berlin in the summer of 1945 for their final great conference. Germany, now surrendered, was the main subject for discussion. On August 2 the leaders signed an agreement which put into effect the zoning arrangements agreed at the Yalta conference.

Roosevelt had died on April 12, 1945, and his successor Harry Truman was untried in the international arena. However, Truman held a trump card. During the conference, on July 23, he announced that the United States' new secret weapon, the atomic bomb, had been successfully tested at Alamogordo, New Mexico. Churchill's reaction was: 'It gives the Americans the power to mould the world. If the Russians had got it, it would mean the end of civilisation.' Stalin was impassive at the news – he no doubt knew that the Soviet Union would also in time have its own nuclear arsenal.

Stalin was now in a position of great strength. With Churchill replaced by Attlee on July 27, after Britain's general election, Stalin was the only one of the original Big Three still in office. He was the one constant factor during all the planning of postwar Europe – at the height of his power at home and unfettered by the democratic process. The outcome, settled by war and words, was that his Red Army – immensely powerful and with no other major strategic commitments – garrisoned central Europe and held one of Germany's greatest industrial areas.

TITO SUPREME The Communist partisan hero who liberated Yugoslavia shares the honours with smaller portraits of Lenin and Stalin at a Belgrade hotel where a meeting is to be held. Tito's independence of Moscow was emphasised two days later when only his portrait was on show and the others were removed.

Punishment and purge

The Allies had spent their blood and effort to rid Europe of the plague of Nazism. Now in the wake of their victory it was Germany's turn to pay. But not all the guilty men were to be punished.

WHO SHOULD PAY for the war? That was one of the most far-reaching decisions facing the Allies as events began to turn in their favour in 1943-4. Should they punish the entire German nation, or exact vengeance on only the most guilty Nazis? Stalin was in no doubt. Germany must be stripped of its industries, he argued. Even watchmaking demanded skills that could be put to military use, so watchmaking should be prohibited. Roosevelt too, for a time, favoured breaking up not just Germany's war machine, but its entire industrial potential. When he met Churchill in Quebec in September 1944, he put forward a plan prepared by his Secretary of the Treasury, Henry Morgenthau, that would have made Germany a preindustrial, farming society. The Morgenthau Plan proposed to demolish Germany's factories, especially steel plants, and to flood its mines. The people would have to live on whatever crops and livestock they could raise.

Churchill was at first opposed to the plan, but later accepted it, possibly because he wanted favours from Roosevelt in the form of continued Lend-Lease. But the cabinets of both leaders saw the folly and inhumanity of a scheme that would condemn millions of Germans to starvation. The Morgenthau Plan was hastily abandoned soon after it was leaked to the public. To some extent, it played into Nazi hands by stiffening their resolve. Josef Goebbels, the German Minister of Propaganda, noted in his diary: 'Germany is to be turned into a potato field, German youth of military age is to be compulsorily deported abroad as slave labour and reparations are to be paid – in short anyone can see that it would be preferable to be slaughtered.'

If the German people were not to be punished, justice still demanded that they should pay in some way, but the Western Allied leaders did not want to repeat the crippling of Germany that had followed World War I. Then, Germany could neither pay nor recover. Worse, the country's plight had fanned the spark of militarism.

There was little agreement among the Allies about how or how much Germany should pay. The Russians – who had already seized from Romania US$2000 million worth of vehicles, raw materials and machinery – insisted that German reparations of US$20 000 million had been agreed at Yalta, and that they should receive half. The Western Allies countered that the Soviet annexation of German and Polish territory was itself a form of reparation. Eventually they agreed to the Russians extracting reparations from the zone they occupied, plus 25 per cent of all industrial equipment from the Western zones.

There was no shortage of machinery. Although Allied bombing had halted industrial production, much of the equipment remained intact under the debris. Even in the heavily bombed Ruhr, only about 20 per cent was beyond repair; in fact Germany had more industrial plant in 1946 than in 1936. Trainload after trainload of dismantled equipment trundled eastwards, where, in the economic chaos of the Soviet Union, most of it rusted away in remote railway sidings.

RIDDING GERMANY OF NAZIS

'Don't Get Chummy With Jerry . . . In Heart, Body and Spirit Every German Is Hitler.' So the American forces newspaper *Stars and Stripes* exhorted the troops. The first American occupying troops had been issued with pamphlets forbidding contact with any German outside of their duties. The punishment for fraternisation was a fine of US$65, a month's pay for a GI. British soldiers, too, were liable to fines and loss of rank for fraternisation.

Once Germany had been occupied, denazification began. The Nuremberg trial of the major Nazi leaders (see box) was the centrepiece of the Allied attempts to fix the guilt for the horrors and suffering of World War II, but the process was extended throughout the occupied zones, in numerous local trials.

The Soviet Union had no qualms about carrying out swift denazification – shooting all government officials down to *Bürgermeister* (mayor) or below was their standard procedure. The Western Allies were less determined. The Nazi party in Germany had at its height numbered some 8 million members. Among them were the academic, industrial and bureaucratic managers and leaders, who would be needed if a semblance of economic order was to be restored. In the British and American zones, the authorities went stolidly through the motions. The Americans issued 12 million forms containing 131 questions about the subject's past life and associations. In the Western zones, just under 170 000 individuals were tried for their wartime activities, but many received only token punishment. Indeed there was something of a race among the Allies to take German rocket scientists, such as Wernher von Braun.

Alfried Krupp, whose father Gustav was considered unfit to stand trial at Nuremberg, had taken over as head of the largest Nazi arms organisation – 'employer' of huge numbers of slave-workers – in 1942. He was sentenced to 12 years in prison by a US court in 1948; it also ordered the confiscation of all his property. Within three years he was released and back at the head of Germany's federation of steel manufacturers. Of its 361 top executives who had been members of the Nazi party, only 33 were brought to trial. The rest stayed in their old jobs.

With the right connections and a degree of luck, a wanted Nazi could obtain a false International Red Cross passport, an entry visa to a foreign country and, ultimately, a job in an emigré community. From 1947, senior Nazis were aided with contacts and escape routes, often to South America, by ODESSA (*Organisation der SS Angehörigen*), a group of and for former SS members which posed (*continued on p. 450*)

ON TRIAL AT NUREMBERG

It was fitting that leading German war criminals should be brought to book at Nuremberg, for during the 1930s the city's destiny had marched closely in step with that of Germany's Führer. In the vast Nuremberg arena, built by Albert Speer, Hitler had roused his audiences to new fervour, their eyes shining back at him in the firelight from thousands of torches. There were practical reasons for the venue, too. Although pulverised by Allied bombing, Nuremberg still had a jail and a courthouse, the Palace of Justice, big enough to accommodate a major trial.

The 21 defendants, representing the German General Staff, government and Nazi party, were charged with crimes against peace, war crimes, crimes against humanity and conspiracy. Three more had been indicted but Martin Bormann, Hitler's secretary, had eluded capture; Robert Ley, leader of the Labour Front (the Nazi workers' and employers' organisation), had committed suicide; and armaments magnate Gustav Krupp was unfit to stand trial. The prosecutors and judges were drawn from the 'Big Four' – Britain, France, the USA and USSR.

In the dock Rudolf Hess stared fixedly into space, Julius Streicher was sweating and decrepit, Field Marshal Keitel sat stiff-backed. Göring, weaned off morphine and now too thin for his uniform (stripped of all insignia), dominated the trial with a bravura defence of Nazism.

The trial continued, with short recesses, from November 1945 until the end of August 1946. The evidence seared the names of places such as Belsen, Buchenwald and Dachau into the conscience of the world. The defence, more often than not, was 'I was only obeying orders'. The judges' findings were delivered on September 30 and the sentences on the following day. Ten went to the gallows in the Nuremberg prison gymnasium in the early hours of October 16. Göring forestalled the hangman the previous evening by taking cyanide. His body and those of the other executed Nazis are said to have been incinerated in the freshly lit ovens of Dachau concentration camp and their ashes scattered in the Isar river. Fritzsche, von Papen and Schacht were later tried on lesser charges and imprisoned.

It was unthinkable that the Nazis should go unpunished, but doubts have been expressed as to the legality of the trial. The League of Nations resolution of 1927 that 'a war of aggression' was an 'international crime' had not proposed punishments or blame for individuals. Perhaps the need to deter future aggressors weighed heavily, but the impression lingered that at Nuremberg the Allies dispensed 'victors' justice'. No mention was made of the Soviet invasion of Finland or the Italian invasions of Ethiopia, Albania and Greece.

THE NUREMBERG JUDGMENTS

Sentenced to death: Martin Bormann (Hitler's secretary; *in absentia*); Hans Frank (governor of Poland); Wilhelm Frick (Interior Minister; later governor of Bohemia-Moravia); Hermann Göring (Luftwaffe chief); Alfred Jodl (chief of staff to Keitel); Ernst Kaltenbrunner (security chief); Wilhelm Keitel (Chief of Staff); Joachim von Ribbentrop (Foreign Minister); Alfred Rosenberg (Minister for Occupied Eastern Territories); Fritz Sauckel (in charge of slave labour); Arthur Seyss-Inquart (governor of the Netherlands); Julius Streicher (owner of anti-Semitic newspaper *Der Stürmer*).

Sentenced to imprisonment: Karl Dönitz (U-boat and navy chief; Hitler's successor; 10 years); Walther Funk (president of Reichsbank; life); Rudolf Hess (Hitler's secretary to 1941; life); Konstantin von Neurath (governor of Bohemia-Moravia to 1941; 15 years); Erich Raeder (navy chief to 1943; life, commuted to 10 years); Baldur von Schirach (Youth Leader and Gauleiter of Vienna; 20 years); Albert Speer (Armaments Minister; 20 years).

Acquitted: Hans Fritzsche (radio propaganda chief); Franz von Papen (Chancellor in 1932; Vice-Chancellor in Hitler's first government); Hjalmar Schacht (Economics Minister in 1930s).

EVIL STAR Göring commands attention still, holding forth to Schirach, Sauckel and Rosenberg who lean in on his left (top to bottom). Hess is at his right, Dönitz listens behind while Raeder turns away. Ribbentrop is at Hess's back with Keitel (in uniform) and Jodl to his left.

as a charitable body. More than 20 000 Nazis made their escape in this way.

One who lost himself in a new life was Franz Stangl, the former commandant of the extermination camp at Treblinka, near Warsaw. He had been arrested automatically in 1945 as an SS officer, but his American interrogators did not discover that he had been at Treblinka. After two years in an American prisoner of war (POW) camp, he was transferred to Linz prison in Austria. He escaped from a prison working party in 1948 and made his way via Syria to Brazil.

Adolf Eichmann, the chief Gestapo official responsible for carrying out the 'Final Solution', was another. He had been imprisoned in an American POW camp after the war but not identified. He escaped in 1946, worked as a lumberjack near Hamburg for four years and then found his way to Rome. There a sympathetic priest gave him a refugee passport in the name of Ricardo Clement, enabling him to reach Buenos Aires where he lived until discovered and kidnapped by Israeli secret agents in 1960.

Eichmann was put on trial in Israel in 1961 and condemned to death for war crimes. He was executed on May 31, 1962. The evidence that came out at his trial made young Germans profoundly sceptical of their elders' claims to be ignorant of the terrible fate of the Jews.

MARK OF SHAME Armed French Resistance workers enjoy the humiliation of a compatriot who has slept with a German during the occupation. As punishment, her long hair is shaved off. Her visible guilt will take months to grow out. More serious collaborators faced summary execution.

'JUSTICE' FOR COLLABORATORS

Hand in hand with the process of denazification went the punishment of collaborators in the countries that Germany had occupied. Ironically, collaborators accused of relatively minor crimes soon after liberation frequently received harsher sentences than more serious offenders tried when pent-up passions had been dissipated.

In France, the purge of collaborators – known as *l'épuration* ('purification') – lasted from September 1944 to the end of 1949. According to official figures, there were 170 000 cases – ranging from the Vichy head of state Marshal Philippe Pétain to the entertainers Maurice Chevalier, Sacha Guitry and Tino Rossi. The trials resulted in 120 000 sentences; 4785 were death sentences, of which almost 2000 were carried out.

All death sentences on women and minors were automatically commuted by General de Gaulle, who was president of liberated France until January 1946. But the partisans settled old scores without legal trial by executing many thousands of collaborators, particularly in the Midi, for the south was a stronghold of the Resistance. The official figure for known executions is 4500, but the real figure may be 50 000. Lesser offenders were not let off. Women who slept with German soldiers had their heads shaved.

On July 23, 1945, the 90-year-old Pétain, a World War I hero, was arraigned on a charge of treason. The trial, in the Palais de Justice in Paris, was not strictly a legal process, but an elaborate ceremonial, aimed at symbolic condemnation of the Vichy government's policies.

In court Pétain wore the simplest uniform of a marshal of France and the Médaille Militaire, the only decoration shared by simple soldiers and great commanders. When his lawyer begged him to take his marshal's baton into the court, Pétain replied scornfully: 'That would be theatrical.' In his last words to the court before sentence Pétain said: 'My thought, my only thought, was to remain with them [the French people] on the soil of France, according to my promise, so as to protect them from and to lessen sufferings.' He was sentenced to death, but de Gaulle commuted the sentence to life imprisonment on the Ile d'Yeu in the Bay of Biscay. In June 1951, enfeebled and rambling, Pétain was freed. He died a month later.

Pierre Laval, the Vichy prime minister, also stood trial in Paris in the autumn of 1945. He was given no chance to defend himself, and the proceedings were frequently interrupted by abuse from the public gallery and even the jury. He was sentenced to death. On the day of his execution, October 15, Laval took poison. He did not die, and was revived by doctors to be dragged retching and crying for water to the firing squad – where he died with dignity.

The severity of the purges elsewhere varied. In Austria, where Nazism was deep-rooted, only 9000 stood trial, and there were just 35 death sentences. In Belgium 634 000 cases were opened after the liberation, a colossal figure for a nation of 8 million people. Eventually, nearly 90 000 were tried, of whom 77 000 were sentenced; although more than 4000 death sentences were passed, only 230 were carried out, but some 16 000 received long prison sentences. In Denmark, the Third Reich's showcase 'protectorate', the death penalty – which was never brought back during the occupation – was restored for the worst collaborators, and 46 were executed out of 112 initially sentenced to death.

In the Netherlands 35 special courts, each consisting of five judges, were set up to deal with the major cases of collaboration, while a host of tribunals handled smaller fry. By the autumn of 1945, there were 96 000 Dutch collaborators behind bars, and the tribunals were facing an insurmountable backlog of cases. A system of 'out-of-court' settlements was introduced. If the accused did not agree to the proposed settlement – normally a fine in the case of minor offenders – he would stand trial. About 80 per cent settled.

The Norwegians were the most systematic and vigorous in pursuing collaborators. In France 93 out of every 100 000 citizens were imprisoned for collaboration; in Norway 633 out of every 100 000 were punished. Among those tried was 83-year-old Knut Hamsun, Norway's greatest living writer, but the charges were dropped because of his senility. The leader of the Norwegian Nazi party, Vidkun Quisling, underwent a long trial. During it he was subjected to a 'severe' physical and psychological examination. His final defence speech, made without notes, lasted eight hours – after which he was sentenced to death. He was executed on October 24, 1945, in Oslo.

HUNTING THE ESCAPERS

Denazification, clear enough as a policy, proved difficult – even haphazard – in application. In the case of Klaus Barbie it failed signally. Barbie, the 'Butcher of Lyons', had been responsible for the torture and execution of many captured members of the French Resistance. After the war, Barbie fell into the hands of American Intelligence, which used his information against French Communists who fought in the Resistance. The United States blocked all efforts to extradite Barbie to France, and in 1950 assisted his flight to Bolivia. Only in 1983 was he extradited, at France's request, to stand trial in Lyons. He was found guilty of 'crimes against humanity' and sentenced to life imprisonment in July 1987.

The denazification fever in the immediate postwar years cooled, as punishments were meted out and peacetime problems took over. But Jews in particular never forgot the guilty Nazis. Simon Wiesenthal, an Austrian Jewish concentration camp victim, devoted much of his life to hunting down more than 1000 Nazi war criminals from his Jewish Documentation Centre in Vienna. He played a major role in the capture of Eichmann.

Marshall Aid saves half a divided Europe

Battered and exhausted by the war, western Europe was set on the path to recovery by a remarkable gesture on the part of the United States – the Marshall Plan. But the Soviet Union would have none of it. An alliance forged in the heat of war could not survive the chill of peace.

THE SPECTRE OF FAMINE stalked Europe as the war ended. Huge tracts of land had been devastated by bombing, flooding and shelling. Desperate shortages of labour, machinery, fertiliser, seed and livestock combined with a severe drought to produce a disastrous grain harvest in 1945, with crops down to half the prewar level across the continent. In Britain, bread was rationed – a measure never imposed during the war, but introduced as late as July 1946 because of the obligation to feed people in the British-occupied zone of Germany.

Europe's economic situation was daunting. The continent's coal production, for example, was only 42 per cent of the prewar level. Road, rail and canal networks were shattered. In the British and American zones of Germany, 740 of the 958 major bridges were down. Demolished bridges and flooding in the Netherlands paralysed the principal Dutch and Belgian canal systems for six months. France had lost two-thirds of its railway locomotives. Ports such as Calais, Bordeaux and Dunkirk were clogged with wreckage.

In Hungary and Greece, the currency collapsed. Belgium and Norway avoided a similar fate only with swingeing devaluations. Britain's finances had been drained by 1941 but, during the war, this decline had been concealed by the flow of goods and raw materials from the United States under the Lend-Lease agreement. When Lend-Lease ended in 1945, it became clear that Britain had external debts of US$14 000 million. The prewar gold and dollar reserves had disappeared, along with overseas investments worth US$4500 million. Collapse was avoided in December 1945 only by an emergency loan of US$4400 million from the United States; even so, in 1947 the pound sterling had to be devalued by 30 per cent against the US dollar.

In contrast, the United States boomed during the war years, and emerged as the powerhouse of the non-Communist world. The war also proved a springboard for economic development in Australia, New Zealand and Canada – all virtually unscathed. On the other hand, a quarter of all buildings in the Soviet Union had been destroyed, including 30 000 factories, and the economy was in ruins. Food output was down by 60 per cent and some people ate cats and dogs.

In continental Europe, the immediate need was emergency relief – which was undertaken by UNRRA (the United Nations Relief and Rehabilitation Administration), set up in November 1943 to help refugees of the nations then fighting the Axis. This became one of the agencies of the fledgling United Nations Organisation that was born at the San Francisco conference in April-June 1945.

UNRRA, financed primarily by the United States, supplied raw materials and equipment for rebuilding industry, agriculture, communications and essential services. Its other task was to care for refugees in camps and resettle them. By late 1945, every fifth inhabitant of the western zones of occupied Germany was a refugee, known then as a 'displaced person' or DP. Millions of Germans were forced to leave eastern Europe. Two million of them died of exhaustion, disease and starvation during the trek westward.

QUEUING FOR LEFTOVERS

About 20 000 refugees a day were arriving in Berlin's British sector. German soldiers also trudged into Berlin, now prisoners of war. Food was short: the ration was cut to only 3750 kJ (900 calories) a day. Women queued outside Allied billets for the troops' leftovers. Medical supplies were few; typhoid and dysentery spread rapidly.

An equally dismal life awaited the eastward-bound migrants – 5.5 million Russians who had been prisoners of war or slave labourers, or who had deserted to the enemy. At Potsdam, Britain and the USA had agreed to the forcible repatriation of all Soviet citizens who had been living within the Soviet Union's borders in 1939. Even though many of those repatriated were the enemy, having fought for Hitler, the British troops handing them over were sickened by their pitiable distress at being delivered into Russian hands.

A few thousand did manage to escape, but of the returning Soviet citizens, about 20 per cent were sentenced to death or to 25 years' hard labour. Many others died in transit, and only 15 per cent were allowed to return straight home. The rest were sentenced to internal exile or forced labour to help to rebuild the country's devastated cities.

MARSHALL AID A German poster declaring 'We are building a new Europe' shows a new nest tended by the doves of peace in a sturdy tree growing from the ERP – European Recovery Program, or 'Marshall Aid'. This 1947 plan offered aid to all European countries.

WHERE NOW? A trainload of refugees leaves eastern Germany for a new life in the west. They are some of the millions of ethnic Germans forced out of the countries of eastern Europe. Those who travelled by train were the lucky ones. Many walked. Ill-fed and poorly clothed, they trudged halfway across the continent.

In 1947, the responsibility for wartime refugees, and for postwar refugees from Communist eastern Europe, passed to a new United Nations agency, the International Refugee Organisation (IRO). By 1948, the number of refugees in Europe had fallen to 550 000, most of them housed in camps in Germany. Among them were thousands of pathetic children, many not even knowing their names.

Many Jewish survivors from all over Europe managed to resettle in Palestine, despite the attempts of Britain (which governed the area under a League of Nations – later UN – mandate) to restrict immigration. In November 1947 the UN voted to partition Palestine, and separate Arab and Jewish states were founded. The British departed in May 1948 – and Israel was born in the bloodshed of the first Arab-Israeli war.

Europe had become financially dependent on the United States and showed no sign of getting back on its own feet. Indeed European countries had by 1947 run up debts of US$5400 million with the International Monetary Fund (set up in 1944) and the World Bank (set up in 1946). The USA underwrote both these financial agencies.

OUR HERO The joyful wife and an excited son who hardly knows him run to greet a returning British soldier. 'Welcome home' signs went up with the bunting for VE Day. The first troops were demobilised in a month, a few not until more than two years later. For some, home had been blitzed and life began anew in a prefab. Joy was shadowed also by partings from comrades and by qualms about fending for oneself in Civvy Street, although the gratuity helped – £99 (US$395) for a British married private with three years' service. At the demob centre, release papers and ration books were issued. Men got a complete outfit of clothing; women, money and extra clothing coupons instead.

Europe needed more than normal lending. On June 5, 1947, General George Marshall, US Secretary of State, suggested possible American aid for Europe. Within hours, British Foreign Secretary Ernest Bevin seized on the suggestion as a firm offer and cabled acceptance. The idea was quickly fleshed out as the European Recovery Program, popularly called Marshall Aid. It offered aid to all European countries. By 1951, when it was wound up, 16 of Europe's non-Communist states had received US$13 000 million, plus another US$1000 million in low-interest loans. Except in Italy and Germany, industrial and agricultural output had returned almost to prewar levels. Spain, Finland and the Communist states had refused aid.

CURTAIN ACROSS A CONTINENT

Marshall Aid saved western Europe, but it confirmed the division between West and East. Stalin would not join a programme aimed at reviving capitalist economies and applied pressure to the Soviet satellite states to refuse it.

Churchill saw that Russia was consolidating a vast empire. During a speech at Fulton, Missouri, on March 5, 1946, he declared: 'From Stettin in the Baltic to Trieste in the Adriatic, an iron curtain has descended across the Continent. Behind that line lie all the capitals of the ancient states of Central and Eastern Europe.'

The communisation of the Soviet Union's satellites was piecemeal. One constant factor in the satellites was that everywhere the Communists were the minority. Terror tactics, bogus Fascist plots, trumped-up treason charges and direct intervention were used to oust the non-Communist leaders. Eventually in Bulgaria, Romania, Poland, Hungary and Czechoslovakia the all-party coalitions established after liberation were replaced first by 'Popular Fronts' in which Communists held the key positions and then by one-party Communist regimes.

Only one hole remained in the Iron Curtain. In East Berlin, people could buy an underground railway ticket to West Berlin and thence to West Germany. Berlin became the focus of the Cold War struggle for the control of central Europe.

In March 1948, Ernest Bevin persuaded France and the three Benelux countries to join the United Kingdom in the Brussels Treaty to form the Western European Union, a permanent military alliance. First on its agenda was the establishment of a West German government.

Almost at once, the Soviet Union withdrew from the Allied Control Council governing Germany. The three Western powers merged their zones into a single unit of 48 million people and reformed the currency of their zones, introducing the Deutschmark. The economy leapt back to life: within a month, production rose by a quarter and the shops began to fill with consumer goods. The Soviet Union faced the prospect of a strong West German state dangerously attractive to Soviet zone citizens.

Its reaction was to threaten the survival of West Berlin, first cutting the road and rail routes to it and then stopping electricity, coal, food and other supplies to its 2.25 million inhabitants. The Western powers overcame the blockade with a remarkable airlift that began on June 26, 1948. American, British and French pilots flew more than 277 000 flights into West Berlin, supplying the city with 2.3 million tonnes of cargo – coal, food and other supplies – at a cost of 65 lives. On May 12, 1949, the Russians admitted defeat by lifting the blockade, although the airlift continued until September to build up stocks.

One lasting effect of the Berlin blockade was to convert the Western European Union, in April 1949, into the North Atlantic Treaty Organisation (NATO), a defence alliance of the United States, Canada and ten Western European states. In the uneasy peace after 1945, Europe's Eastern and Western blocs were divided – and have remained so – virtually along the frontier established in the dying days of World War II.

THE CIGARETTE ECONOMY

Overwhelmed by total defeat, the German people were desperate for food, desperate for homes, those with homes desperate for warmth. All were searching for jobs in cities where the inhabitants scrabbled among the rubble to salvage usable or saleable objects.

The occupying powers imposed strict monetary controls, under which a hidden economy spurted into life – a black market that became the chief means of survival and involved occupiers as well as occupied.

The basic unit of exchange was the cigarette. With cigarettes men could buy anything from the services of a prostitute to luxuries such as Leica cameras. For 25 cartons of cigarettes a GI entrepreneur could buy a camera and sell it in the United States for US$600, with which he could buy 750 cartons of cigarettes – and so on. Fortunes were made in this way.

A new profession sprang up among the Germans, that of *Kippensammler* – a collector of cigarette ends. Seven butts made one cigarette and gained entry into a topsy-turvy world where a Persian rug would buy a sack of potatoes, or a fur coat a box of basic rations. For many Germans, a 'Persil Certificate' clearing them of any complicity in Nazism was the prize item.

The black market kept a substantial part of the population on the move, in crowded trains in search of scarce items of exchange. The 'Nicotine Line' took traders to the tobacco fields of the Rhineland. Because of its cargo, the train from Osnabruck, near the North Sea, to Berlin was the 'Fish Express'; on the return journey it became the 'Silk Stocking Express'.

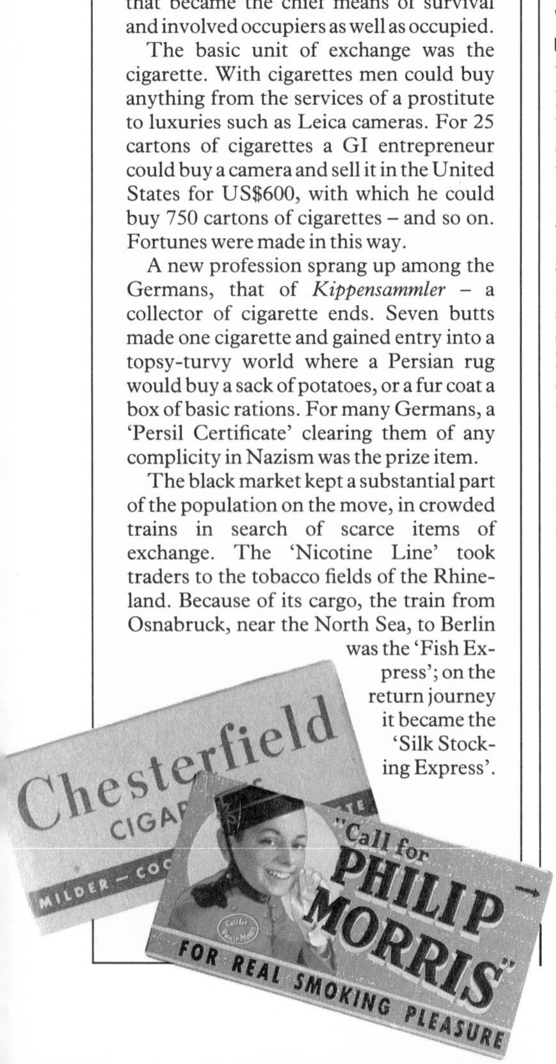

A new sun rises

The capitulation of Japan dealt its people a deep psychological blow. To a nation never before defeated in war, headed by an Emperor regarded as a god, unconditional surrender was the ultimate disgrace. But in only five years, Japan was transformed into a trusted ally of the West.

JAPAN'S OCCUPATION began in the small hours of August 28, 1945, when the first US soldiers landed at Atsugi airfield, a former *kamikaze* training base. Beyond it lay Yokohama and Tokyo, half-flattened, a wasteland of charred wood and rubble in which thousands of homeless squatted in makeshift shelters.

The same fate had overtaken much of Japan, whose highly combustible cities had been levelled by American B-29 bombers. Those Japanese with no money to enter the flourishing black market wore clothes made from a papery, pressed wood pulp which fell apart in the rain. Housewives scanned charts of edible weeds in the newspapers for ideas to fend off starvation.

The seven-year occupation was almost exclusively American, an acknowledgment of the fact that victory in the Pacific had been overwhelmingly achieved by the United States. Britain contributed a brigade to occupation duties and a few Dominion troops were there.

The occupation was intended to last until the Japanese had established a 'peacefully inclined and responsible government'. Presiding over it was the dominating figure of General Douglas MacArthur, Supreme Commander Allied Powers (SCAP). President Truman gave him sweeping powers that made him free to ignore the Allied Council, supposedly his advisers. From his headquarters in the Tokyo offices of the Dai-ichi Insurance Company, MacArthur embarked on the 'demilitarisation' of Japan – which was really an attempt at social engineering, to refashion Japan along Western lines.

US policy was to steer Japan at one remove, through Japanese officials, without altering the basic structure of the nation's government. MacArthur needed Hirohito to remain Emperor if Japan was to be easily controlled, but he was determined that the Emperor should no longer be regarded as a living god. To foster this new 'humanised' image, Hirohito was photographed swimming in the rain and the Imperial princesses were shown washing up in their summer villa.

The first practical stage in demilitarisation was to dismantle all of Japan's industries that were directly geared to war. Japanese industry and trade were to function at a level only sufficient to keep the population employed and prevent total collapse of the economy.

Great emphasis was also placed on psychological demilitarisation. The education system was reformed, with great stress being placed on individuality. Shinto was abolished as the state religion. Banknotes were withdrawn if they bore 'undesirable' images such as Shinto symbols or portraits of military leaders or national heroes. The press was heavily censored. There was no mention of the atomic bombs in case they should 'disturb public tranquillity'.

Most important of all was the new constitution imposed by MacArthur in 1947. It provided for independent judges and courts, guarantees of political and civil liberty, universal adult suffrage

JAPAN UNDER AMERICAN RULE Douglas MacArthur, virtual ruler of occupied Japan, arrives at Atsugi airfield (left) near Yokohama on August 30, 1945. In the empty stretches that were once Tokyo streets (below left), customers watch over their precious shoes that are being repaired yet again. A new pair would be impossible to come by in their postwar poverty, and a pair left with the shoemender could be stolen or sold as treasure. Japan was to enjoy Western democratic values. MacArthur's decree of equal voting and property rights for women brings them to the polling station (below) to vote for the first time.

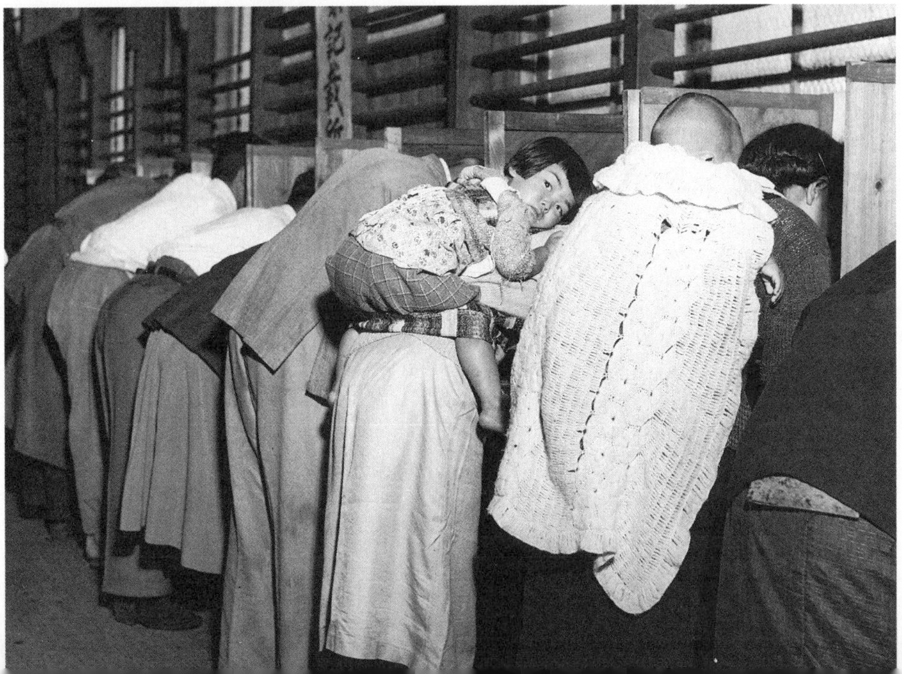

and equal property rights for women. Article 9, the most significant, declared Japan's intention of 'forever renouncing war as a sovereign right of the nation and the threat of use of force as a means of settling international disputes'.

HALF-HEARTED PURGE

Accompanying these measures was the elimination of undesirable elements – right-wingers, extreme nationalists and the military. To MacArthur, Japan's elite were 'war potential'. By May 1948, more than 200 000 principal citizens – from cabinet ministers to village leaders – had been removed from public life. In spite of its scale, the purge was relatively easy to avoid, principally because American policy was that the Japanese should be seen to carry it out themselves.

In May 1946, the Allies brought 28 people accused of major war crimes to trial in Tokyo. The trial lasted for 30 months and produced 48 412 pages of transcript, including 4336 exhibits and the testimony of 1198 witnesses. Seven defendants were sentenced to death (see panel). Among them was General Hideki Tojo, Premier and War Minister until the war's final year, who had tried to poison himself before his arrest. At the trial Tojo mounted a telling defence of his actions and showed little remorse. His cross-examination was badly conducted by the chief prosecutor, the American Joseph Keenan – a noted prewar 'gangbusting' attorney but now a hopeless alcoholic. Despite Keenan's incompetence, the case was proved. Tojo and six others were hanged in Sugamo Prison on December 23, 1948; 18 more were imprisoned.

'Minor' war criminals were tried in Yokohama under the aegis of the US Army. More than 1000 were brought to trial, of whom 200 were acquitted, 124 sentenced to death and 62 to life imprisonment. Throughout Asia, another 5700 Japanese were tried by Allied tribunals; 4405 were convicted and 984 sentenced to death. Cynicism occasionally replaced retribution: the US government concealed some prison-camp atrocities – such as bacteriological experiments on inmates (some of them American servicemen) – to gain information on biological warfare.

Most of the 594 000 Japanese survivors of the Kwantung Army, Tokyo's occupying force in Manchuria which surrendered to the Russians on August 15, 1945, were deported to prison camps in Siberia, although some were kept to work. But elsewhere Japanese troops were disarmed and then allowed to go home. Within ten months of surrender, 4.5 million troops returned home. In addition, more than 3 million Japanese civilian colonists of occupied territories in south-east Asia were repatriated. At the same time a million non-Japanese who had been forced into slave labour were repatriated from Japan.

NEW VENTURES

In the economic field, MacArthur was determined to break the grip of the *zaibatsu*, the immensely powerful financial combines that controlled the greater part of Japan's industry, trade and commerce. However, collusion between the combines and Japanese bureaucracy made it difficult, and in 1948 American policy changed. More successful were the moves to set up a strong trade union movement and a far-reaching series of land reforms, which turned Japan's peasant farmers into owner-occupiers. By the end of the 1940s, these petty capitalists farmed 89 per cent of Japan's arable land.

TOKYO WAR-CRIMES JUDGMENTS

Sentenced to death: Kenji Doihara (Kwantung Army commander; later ran POW camps in Malaya and East Indies); Koki Hirota (Foreign Minister then Premier in 1930s); Seishiro Itagaki (War Minister; chief of Army General Staff; later responsible for POW camps); Hyotaro Kimura (Vice War Minister, 1941-3, then army commander in Burma); Iwane Matsui (commander in China during 'Rape of Nanking'); Akira Muto (commander in Sumatra, then Philippines); Hideki Tojo (War Minister, 1940-4; Premier, 1941-4).

Sentenced to life imprisonment (survivors paroled 1954-5): Sadao Araki (War Minister, 1930s); Kingoro Hashimoto (influential pro-war army officer); Shunroku Hata (commander in China; War Minister, 1939-40); Kiichiro Hiranuma (Premier, 1939); Naoki Hoshino (Chief Cabinet Secretary); Okinori Kaya (Finance Minister); Koichi Kido (Hirohito's closest adviser); Kuniaki Koiso (governor of Korea; Premier, 1944-5); Jiro Minami (Kwantung Army commander, then governor of Korea); Takasumi Oka (chief of Naval Affairs Bureau; deputy Navy Minister); Hiroshi Oshima (ambassador to Germany); Kenryo Sato (chief of Military Affairs Bureau; commander in Indochina, 1945); Shigetaro Shimada (Navy Minister; responsible for massacre of POWs); Toshio Shiratori (diplomat); Teiichi Suzuki (cabinet minister); Yoshijiro Umezu (Kwantung Army commander, then Army Chief of Staff).

Others: Yosuke Matsuoka (Foreign Minister, 1939-40; died during trial); Osami Nagano (Navy Chief of Staff, 1941; died during trial); Shumei Okawa (influential warmonger; freed); Mamoru Shigemitsu (Foreign Minister and diplomat; 7 years but paroled 1950; Foreign Minister again, 1954); Shigenori Togo (diplomat and Foreign Minister; negotiated with USA just before Pearl Harbor; 20 years but died 1950).

TOJO'S FATE The wartime premier was executed.

The occupation entered a new phase in the autumn of 1947. No more reforms were made; the priority now was reconstruction. Japan was to be built up as an ally – a recognition of Japan's strategic position in the western Pacific. Control of Japan made safe the perimeter of the United States' sphere of influence. In Russian hands, Japan would threaten US Pacific bases.

In addition, Japan offered a large overseas market for the United States, but could afford to buy only if its own economy prospered. From 1948, aid and advisers were poured into Japan. The speed of its return to wealth and favour was hastened by events on the Asian mainland. In December 1949, Chiang Kai-shek's Nationalist Chinese forces were forced to withdraw to the island of Formosa (Taiwan), leaving Mao Tse-tung's (Mao Zedong's) victorious Communists in control of mainland China, where the People's Republic had been proclaimed in October.

Crisis quickly followed in Korea, where the 38th Parallel (38°N) had been established at the Potsdam conference of Allied leaders as the line dividing the US and Soviet zones of occupation. Soon this line became a frontier between two rival Korean republics – Chinese and Soviet Communist-backed in the north and US-supported in the south. When war broke out between the two Korean states in 1950, Japan became an essential supply and staging base, repair centre and rest area for US troops (who fought under the United Nations flag).

The Korean War also brought a change of thinking by Washington about Japanese rearmament, despite Article 9 of the new constitution. On July 8, 1950, 13 days after the invasion of South Korea, MacArthur ordered the formation of a Japanese National Police Reserve of 75 000 men, to be equipped and trained by the United States. Japan's 'Self-Defence Forces' today have the eighth largest arms budget in the world.

EMPIRES CRUMBLE

World War II did much to spur on the movement for independence among colonial countries in Asia. Japan's victories had destroyed the colonial powers' prestige in a continent where 'face' was so important. While Japan ruled, the Allies supported resistance movements that later turned on the colonial powers, using the large stocks of Japanese arms that they took over.

Among Britain's colonies, the Indian subcontinent won independence in August 1947, divided into India and Pakistan. Burma became independent in January 1948, and Ceylon (now Sri Lanka) in February. The Malay states formed a federation in February 1948, but a Communist guerrilla campaign delayed its independence until 1957. British influence waned also in Australia and New Zealand, which now looked increasingly to the United States for security in the Pacific.

The Philippines, an American-ruled semi-independent state, was granted full independence in July 1946. Indonesia, formerly the Dutch East Indies, became independent in November 1949 after four years of guerrilla warfare. The French lost Indochina: Laos became independent in October 1953, Cambodia in November. In 1945 the Communist leader Ho Chi Minh had claimed independence for Vietnam and after an exhausting struggle the French withdrew in July 1954. But the country remained divided and, like Berlin and Korea, became the arena for a bitter confrontation between the postwar enemies – the Communist world and the West.

REFERENCE SECTION

World War II year by year

1918

Nov 11: Armistice ends World War I

1919

Jan 5: German Workers' Party founded in Munich by Drexler
Jan 5-11: Spartacist (Communist) rising in Germany
Jan 18: Paris Peace Conference opens
Mar 23: Benito Mussolini forms first *Fascio di Combattimento* ('Combat Group') – forerunner of Fascist party
Apr 28: League of Nations founded
Jun 21: German fleet scuttles itself at Scapa Flow, Orkney
Jun 28: Treaty of Versailles signed by Allies & Germany
Aug 14: Foundation of Weimar Republic in Germany
Sep 16: Hitler joins German Workers' Party
Sep 10: Treaty of St-Germain signed by Allies & Austria
Nov 27: Treaty of Neuilly signed by Allies & Bulgaria

1920

Feb 24: German Workers' Party becomes National Socialist German Workers' (Nazi) Party
Mar 1: Admiral Horthy becomes regent & head of state of Hungary
Jun 4: Treaty of Trianon signed by Allies & Hungary
Aug 10: Treaty of Sèvres signed by Allies & Turkey
Nov 9: Danzig proclaimed a free city

1921

Apr 27: German reparations for World War I fixed at 200 million gold marks (about US$40 000 million)
May 15: Italian elections; Fascists win only 22 seats
Jul 29: Hitler becomes president of Nazi party

1922

Feb 6: Washington Naval Treaty limits numbers & size of major warships
Apr 16: Treaty of Rapallo: Germany & USSR agree measures of economic cooperation
Aug: German mark begins to collapse
Aug 3-4: Fascists seize control of Milan city council
Oct 24: Fascists demand resignation of Italian government & formation of Fascist cabinet
Oct 28: 'March on Rome' by Italian Fascists
Oct 30: Mussolini becomes Italy's prime minister
Nov 25: Mussolini granted dictatorial powers, at first until end of 1923

1923

Jan 11: French & Belgian occupation of the Ruhr after Germany declared in default on reparations
Nov 8-9: Munich ('Beer Hall') Putsch attempt by Nazis
Nov 11: Hitler arrested
Nov 30: Rentenmark replaces old German mark, now worthless

1924

Jan 21: Death of Lenin leads to power struggle in USSR
Apr 1: Hitler sentenced to term of imprisonment for part in Munich Putsch
Apr 6: Italian elections marked by violence; large Fascist majority
Aug 30: Dawes Plan for economic aid to Germany

1925

Apr 26: Hindenburg becomes German president
Jul 18: Publication of *Mein Kampf* Vol I
Aug 27: French troops leave Ruhr
Dec 1: Locarno treaties signed by European powers

1926

Sep 8: Germany admitted to League of Nations
Dec 10: Publication of *Mein Kampf* Vol II
Dec 25: Hirohito becomes Emperor of Japan

1927

Dec 27: Final victory over Trotsky faction confirms Stalin as Soviet leader

1928

Aug 27: Kellogg-Briand Pact: 15 nations (including Britain, France, Germany, Italy, Japan, USA – & later most members of League of Nations) agree to renounce war as a means of settling international disputes; but agree no means of enforcing the pact

1929

Mar 24: Official (ie, Fascist) candidates receive almost 100% of votes in Italian election
Oct 29: New York stock market crash

1930

Jan 21-Apr 22: London Naval Conference leads to agreement limiting size of fleets
Jun 30: French troops leave Rhineland
Sep 14: Nazis win 107 seats in German elections

1931

Sep 18: Japanese invade Manchuria, occupying Mukden, Changchun & Kirin ('Mukden Incident')
Sep 21: China appeals to League of Nations over events in Manchuria
Dec 12: Saarland evacuated by French troops

1932

Jan 9: Germany defaults on reparations payments
Jan 28: Japanese planes bomb Shanghai
Feb 18: Japanese set up puppet state of Manchukuo in Manchuria
Feb 29: Pu Yi named provisional president of Manchukuo
Mar 13; Apr 10: Hitler close runner-up to Hindenburg in German presidential elections
May 15: Assassination of moderate Japanese Prime Minister Inukai; government henceforth dominated by armed forces
Jun 2: Papen named chancellor of Germany
Jun 16-Jul 9: Lausanne Conference agrees to end German reparations
Jul 31: Nazis win 230 seats in German elections
Aug 13: Hitler refuses to serve as vice-chancellor under Papen
Aug 30: Göring elected president of Reichstag
Nov 6: Fresh German elections
Nov 8: Roosevelt elected US president
Dec 2: Defence Minister Schleicher becomes German chancellor

1933

Jan: Deadlock in Reichstag; new elections called, marked by violence
Jan 30: Hitler becomes German chancellor in Nazi-Nationalist coalition
Feb 23: Japanese occupy China north of Great Wall
Feb 27: Reichstag fire
Feb 28: Emergency decree suspends civil liberties in Germany
Mar 5: German elections give Nazis 44% of vote & 228 seats
Mar 21: First concentration camp opened at Oranienburg, outside Berlin
Mar 23: Reichstag passes Enabling Act, giving Hitler dictatorial powers
Mar 27: Japan announces decision to quit League of Nations after report on Manchurian invasion
Apr 7: German Civil Service Law bars anyone with a Jewish grandparent from civil service employment
May 2: Dissolution of Socialist-led trade unions in Germany; Nazi-directed Labour Front to replace all trade unions
May 28: Nazis gain majority in elections in free city of Danzig
Jun 22: German Social Democratic party outlawed
Jul 20: Concordat signed between Vatican & German government
Jul 14: Nazi party declared only political party in Germany
Sep 2: Italy & Germany sign pact of friendship, non-aggression & neutrality
Oct 14: Germany withdraws from League of Nations

1934

Jan 27: Fall of French government, brought down by revelations of corruption (Stavisky Affair)
Mar 1: Pu Yi crowned emperor of Manchukuo
Jun 14-15: Hitler & Mussolini meet in Venice
Jun 29/30: 'Night of the Long Knives': Hitler purges SA leadership
Jul 25: Attempted Nazi coup in Vienna; Chancellor Dollfuss of Austria assassinated
Aug 2: Death of President Hindenburg; Hitler becomes German president
Aug 19: Hitler affirmed as president as well as chancellor, taking title *Der Führer* ('The Leader'); also Supreme Commander of German Armed Forces
Sep 18: Soviet Union joins League of Nations
Oct 1: General strike in Spain; rebellions in Madrid, Catalonia, Asturias
Dec 5: Troops clash on disputed border of Ethiopia & Italian Somaliland
Dec 19: Japan renounces Washington & London Naval Treaties

1935

Jan 13: Saarland plebiscite favours reunion with Germany
Mar 16: Hitler denounces disarmament clauses of Versailles Treaty, introduces conscription & accelerates German rearmament
Apr 11-14: Stresa Conference: Britain, France, Italy discuss steps to counter militant Germany
May 2: Franco-Soviet Mutual Assistance Pact signed
Jun 18: Anglo-German Naval Agreement
Aug 20: Seventh World Congress of Communist International calls for creation of 'popular fronts' to combat tide of fascism
Aug 31: Roosevelt signs Neutrality Act
Sep 15: Nuremberg Laws deprive Jews of rights of German citizenship
Sep 28: Government control imposed over German Protestant Church
Oct 3: Italy invades Ethiopia
Oct 19: League of Nations votes for partial sanctions against Italy after invasion of Ethiopia
Dec 23: Italians begin using mustard gas in Ethiopia

1936

Feb 16: Spanish elections: Leftist Popular Front wins narrow majority
Feb 26/27: Attempted coup by ultra-nationalist army officers in Japan
Mar 7: Hitler denounces Locarno pacts; German troops march into Rhineland demilitarised zone
Mar 25: USA, Britain & France sign London Naval Agreement placing 35 000 ton limit on new warships
May 5: Addis Ababa falls to Italians; Ethiopian resistance collapses
May 9: Italy formally annexes Ethiopia
Jun 5: Blum forms Popular Front government in France
Jul 17: Army revolt at Melilla, Morocco: outbreak of Spanish Civil War
Aug 4: Coup makes Metaxas dictator of Greece
Oct 1: Franco named by rebel officers as leader & head of Spanish state
Oct 25: Pact establishes Rome-Berlin Axis
Nov 18: Germany recognises Franco
Nov 25: Germany & Japan sign Anti-Comintern Pact
Dec 10: George VI becomes British king on abdication of Edward VIII

1937

Apr 27: German Condor Legion destroys Spanish town of Guernica
May 28: Chamberlain becomes British prime minister
Jun 11: Stalin begins purge of Red Army generals
Jul 7: Marco Polo Bridge (Lukouchiao) incident: fighting between Japanese & Chinese troops near Peking marks start of Sino-Japanese War; Japanese troops invade China
Jul 28: Peking falls to Japanese
Jul 30: Tientsin falls to Japanese
Oct 13: Germany guarantees Belgium's integrity
Nov 6: Italy joins Anti-Comintern Pact
Nov 12: Shanghai falls to Japanese
Nov 20: Chiang Kai-shek sets up new Chinese capital at Chungking
Dec 11: Italy withdraws from League of Nations
Dec 13: Nanking falls to Japanese, followed by brutal 'Rape of Nanking': up to 200 000 Chinese massacred (to Feb 5, 1938)
Dec 12: US gunboat *Panay* sunk by Japanese planes in Yangtze river

1938

Feb 4: Nazis tighten grip on German Army & Foreign Ministry: Hitler takes command of War Ministry; Ribbentrop becomes foreign minister.
Feb 12: Austrian Chancellor Schuschnigg forced by Hitler to include Nazis in his cabinet or face invasion
Feb 20: Hitler demands self-determination for Germans in Austria & Sudetenland (western Czechoslovakia). British Foreign Secretary Eden resigns in protest at Chamberlain's 'appeasement' policy
Mar 9: Schuschnigg announces plebiscite on Austrian independence
Mar 11: German troops mass on Austrian frontier; Schuschnigg resigns; Seyss-Inquart, a Nazi, becomes Austrian chancellor
Mar 12: German troops invade Austria
Mar 13: *Anschluss* – union of Austria with Germany – proclaimed
Apr 10: Daladier becomes French premier. Austrian plebiscite: 99.73% vote in favour of union with Germany
Apr 24: Sudeten Germans demand full autonomy
May 3-9: State visit of Hitler to Rome
Jul 11-Aug 10: Japanese & Soviet troops clash on frontier of eastern Siberia & Manchukuo
Jul 19-21: State visit of King George VI & Queen Elizabeth to Paris
Sep 12: Hitler again demands self-determination for Sudeten Germans, leading to widespread disorder & martial law in Czechoslovakia
Sep 15: Chamberlain meets Hitler at Berchtesgaden
Sep 22-23: Chamberlain has second meeting with Hitler at Godesberg
Sep 24-29: International crisis over Czechoslovakia
Sep 29-30: Munich Conference to resolve Sudeten Crisis: agreement by Britain, France, Germany & Italy to transfer Sudetenland to Germany
Oct 1: German troops occupy Sudetenland
Oct 5: Czechoslovak President Beneš resigns
Oct 6: Slovakia becomes autonomous state within Czechoslovakia
Oct 21: Canton falls to Japanese
Oct 25: Hankow falls to Japanese
Nov 3: Announcement of Japanese 'New Order in Asia'
Nov 9/10: *Kristallnacht:* 200 German synagogues wrecked by Nazis, 20 000 Jews arrested; Jewish community 'fined' 1000 million marks

JANUARY 1939

26: Franco's troops take Barcelona

FEBRUARY 1939

27: Britain & France recognise Franco's government

MARCH 1939

10-16: Czechoslovakia dismembered: German troops annexe Bohemia & Moravia; Slovakia remains nominally independent under German 'protection'; Hungary annexes Ruthenia
19: Daladier speeds up French rearmament & mobilisation
21: Lithuania forced to give up Memel & the Memelland to Germany; Germany demands cession of Danzig & access to Danzig across Poland
28: Surrender of Madrid; end of Spanish Civil War
31: Britain & France guarantee Polish independence; end of appeasement

APRIL 1939

6: Formal British-Polish Agreement
7: Italian troops occupy Albania
13: Britain & France guarantee Romanian & Greek security
26: Bill for limited conscription introduced in British Parliament
28: Hitler renounces 1934 non-aggression pact with Poland & 1935 Anglo-German Naval Agreement; renews demands on Poland over Danzig

MAY 1939

3: Molotov replaces Litvinov as Soviet foreign minister
12: Start of four months of fierce fighting between Japanese & Soviet troops in Outer Mongolia
22: Italy & Germany sign Pact of Steel

JULY 1939

26: US renounces 1911 Commercial Treaty with Japan

AUGUST 1939

20: Polish crisis breaks, with public demands from Nazi leaders in Danzig
20-21: German-Soviet trade pact agreed
20-25: Heavy fighting between Soviet & Japanese troops in Outer Mongolia; Japanese defeated at Nomonhan
23: Chamberlain warns Hitler that Britain will fulfil guarantees to Poland. German-Soviet Non-Aggression Pact signed in Moscow; secret protocol agrees to partition of Poland, Soviet occupation of Baltic states
24: Roosevelt appeals for conciliation over Poland. British Parliament approves Emergency Powers Bill
25: Japan protests at German-Soviet pact. Britain & Poland sign mutual assistance treaty; converts earlier agreements into formal alliance.
31: Hitler orders attack on Poland.

SEPTEMBER 1939

1: German troops invade Poland & occupy Danzig. Evacuation of women & children from British cities begins
2: Britain & France issue ultimatums to Germany over Poland. Italy declares non-belligerence in war between Germany & Poland, & calls for international conference
3: Britain & its colonies, France, Australia & New Zealand declare war on Germany after ultimatums ignored. War Cabinet formed in London; Churchill appointed First Lord of the Admiralty. British passenger ship *Athenia* sunk by German U-boat; 112 die, including 28 Americans
4: First RAF attacks on German Navy at Wilhelmshaven & Brunsbuttel; 8 out of 29 British bombers shot down
5: USA proclaims neutrality in European war. German troops cross the Vistula
6: South Africa declares war on Germany
7: Introduction of Atlantic convoys
10: Canada declares war on Germany. BEF begins to move to France
14: First U-boat sunk (*U-39*)
17: Russian troops invade Poland from east; Polish government escapes into Romania. British carrier *Courageous* sunk off Ireland by German U-boat
21: Romanian Prime Minister Calinescu murdered by Fascist Iron Guard
23: German troops in Poland withdraw to demarcation line agreed with USSR
25: Heavy German air attacks on Warsaw
27: Warsaw surrenders to Germans
29: Treaty between USSR & Estonia allowing USSR to use Estonian naval bases. Soviet-German Boundary & Friendship Treaty signed
30: Polish government-in-exile set up in Paris

OCTOBER 1939

5: Fighting ends in Poland. Treaty between USSR & Latvia allowing USSR to use Latvian sea & air bases
6: Hitler puts forward peace proposals to Western powers; rejected by French (Oct 11) & British (Oct 12)
10: Treaty between USSR & Lithuania allowing USSR to use sea & air bases
11: Stalin presents territorial demands to Finns
14: HMS *Royal Oak* sunk by U-boat in Scapa Flow
26: Frank becomes Governor General of Poland

NOVEMBER 1939

4: 'Cash & Carry' clause introduced in US Neutrality Act to permit British & French to purchase arms
8: Hitler escapes assassination attempt, leaving Munich beer hall 20 minutes before bomb explodes
9: Venlo Incident: British MI6 agents Stevens & Best kidnapped by Germans. Finns reject Soviet demands
29: USSR breaks diplomatic relations with Finland
30: Soviet troops invade Finland: start of 'Winter War'

DECEMBER 1939

13-17: Battle of the River Plate
14: USSR expelled from League of Nations
17: *Graf Spee* scuttled by its crew just outside Montevideo harbour. Canadian troops begin to arrive in Britain. Empire air training agreement signed
26: First squadron of Australian airmen arrives in Britain

JANUARY 1940

8: Butter, bacon, sugar & meat rationed in Britain
10: Allies obtain German invasion plans after Luftwaffe staff officer crash-lands in Belgium
13: Belgium & Netherlands order 'state of readiness' in expectation of German invasion

FEBRUARY 1940

12: Finnish defences in Karelian Isthmus begin to crack
16: *Altmark* incident: HMS *Cossack* rescues 299 British prisoners from German ship *Altmark* in a Norwegian fiord; Norwegian government protests at breach of neutrality
24: Germans revise plan for attack in west to include panzer assault through Ardennes

MARCH 1940

12: Treaty of Moscow between Finland & USSR ends 'Winter War'; Finns have to give up Karelian Isthmus & part of eastern Karelia
16: First British civilian bombing casualty as Germans attack Scapa Flow naval base
18: Hitler & Mussolini meet at Brenner Pass
20: Daladier's cabinet in France resigns; succeeded by Reynaud
28: Allied War Council decides to lay mines in Norwegian waters
29: Molotov announces Soviet neutrality
30: Japanese set up puppet Chinese government under Wang Ching-wei in Nanking

APRIL 1940

5: Chamberlain tells Conservative party that 'Hitler has missed the bus'
8: British destroyer *Glowworm* sinks off Norway after ramming German cruiser *Hipper*
9: German troops invade Denmark & land in five places in Norway – Oslo, Kristiansand, Bergen, Trondheim, Narvik. Danish government capitulates
10: First Battle of Narvik: two German destroyers sunk by British flotilla
13: Second Battle of Narvik: seven German destroyers sunk
16-19: Anglo-French troops land in southern Norway; British troops occupy Faeroes
27: Himmler orders construction of Auschwitz concentration camp in Poland
30: Lodz Ghetto in Poland established by the Germans – first such closed & guarded ghetto

MAY 1940

10: German troops invade Netherlands, Belgium, Luxembourg & France; fall of Fort Eben-Emael; heavy air attacks on Rotterdam. Churchill becomes British prime minister, replacing Chamberlain; forms coalition government
12: RAF bombers attack bridges over Albert Canal
13: German troops cross Meuse at Sedan. Churchill's 'blood and toil' speech. Dutch queen & government flee to London. Liège falls to Germans
14: Rotterdam falls after heavy air bombardment. German breakthrough near Sedan. Recruitment begins in Britain for Local Defence Volunteers (later renamed Home Guard)
15: Dutch forces surrender to Germans
16: BEF begins withdrawal west of Brussels
17: Brussels falls
17-19: French tanks under de Gaulle attempt counterattack near Montcornet
18: Antwerp falls; Germans cross Sambre river to reach Amiens. Pétain becomes French vice premier
20: Abbeville and Amiens fall; German troops reach English Channel at Noyelles. Weygand becomes Allied Commander in Chief. Seyss-Inquart becomes Reich Commissioner for Netherlands
21: British & French tanks counterattack near Arras, stalling German advance
24: Hitler orders Guderian to halt before Dunkirk; German advance continues toward Paris
25: Boulogne falls; Allies fall back on Dunkirk
26-Jun 4: Operation 'Dynamo': evacuation of Allied troops from Dunkirk; 338,226 men saved
27: Germans take Calais
28: Belgian Army capitulates; King Leopold III surrenders to Germans; Belgian cabinet-in-exile in Paris repudiates surrender. Allied troops capture Narvik

JUNE 1940

3: Paris bombed by Germans
4: Churchill's speech: 'We shall fight them on the beaches.' Allied troops begin withdrawal from Narvik
7: King Haakon & Norwegian government leave Norway for London
8: British aircraft carrier *Glorious* plus two destroyers sunk off Narvik by *Scharnhorst* & *Gneisenau*. Last Allied troops leave Norway
9: Norwegian High Command orders ceasefire
10: Italy declares war on Britain & France. Roosevelt says that USA will 'extend to the opponents of force the material resources of this nation'
10/11: French government leaves Paris for Cangé, near Tours
11: Australia, New Zealand & South Africa declare war on Italy. First Italian bombing raid on Malta
12: 51st Highland Division surrenders at St Valéry
14: Germans enter Paris; French government moves to Bordeaux
15: USSR occupies Lithuania
15-20: Operation 'Ariel' - evacuation of British & French troops from Cherbourg, Brest, St Nazaire
16: Churchill offers 'indissoluble union' of Britain & France; turned down by French cabinet. Reynaud resigns as French premier; succeeded by Pétain
17: Pétain asks for armistice terms; French units in Alsace-Lorraine encircled. Liner *Lancastria* sunk off St Nazaire; 3000 perish
18: De Gaulle broadcasts first message to French from London. Hitler & Mussolini meet in Munich
20: French allow Japanese military mission into Indochina. USSR occupies Estonia
22: Franco-German armistice signed at Compiègne; French government keeps control of two-fifths of France & of navy & army (to be neutralised). USSR occupies Latvia
23: De Gaulle issues proclamation to 'Free French' from London
24: Franco-Italian armistice
24/25: First British commando raid (on Le Touquet)
27: Romania forced to cede Bessarabia and northern Bukovina to USSR
28: Britain recognises de Gaulle as Free French leader
30: Göring orders aerial blockade of Britain; Germans begin occupation of Channel Islands

JULY 1940

1: Beginning of U-boats' first 'Happy Time': between July & October, 217 merchant ships sunk in Atlantic. Pétain's government set up in Vichy
2: Hitler issues orders for Operation 'Sea Lion'
3: British naval squadron sinks French naval vessels at Mers El Kébir, Algeria
4: Italians attack Sudan
5: Vichy government breaks off relations with Britain
9: British ships engage Italian fleet off Calabria
10: First large-scale German bombing raid on Britain, on docks in South Wales; marks beginning of first phase of Battle of Britain
11: Pétain becomes Vichy French head of State
16: Konoye becomes Japanese premier; Tojo becomes war minister
18: British close Burma Road on Japanese demand, isolating China
19: Hitler's final peace appeal – 'a last appeal to reason' – in speech to Reichstag
21: Czechoslovak government-in-exile formed in London
22: SOE (Special Operations Executive) created in London to aid European resistance
25: USSR annexes Estonia, Latvia & Lithuania, incorporated as republics within USSR
26: Laval becomes Vichy French vice premier. First US embargo on war trade with Japan
29: Luftwaffe attacks Dover Harbour

AUGUST 1940

4-21: Italians occupy British Somaliland
12: Portsmouth bombed; radar stations in southern England hit
13: *Adlertag* ('Eagle Day') – first day of German bombing offensive against British airfields & aircraft factories
15: Heaviest air battles of Battle of Britain
17: Hitler declares total blockade of British Isles
20: Churchill's speech: 'Never in the field of human conflict . . .'
23/24: First bombs on central London
24: Bombing raids on RAF command centres at North Weald & Hornchurch; marks beginning of second phase of Battle of Britain
25/26: First RAF raid on Berlin

SEPTEMBER 1940

3: US-British agreement: USA to supply Britain with 50 destroyers in return for naval bases in Caribbean, Bermuda & Newfoundland
7: Beginning of London Blitz
11: Italian attack on Egypt begins
15: Massive German bombing raids on London, Southampton, Bristol, Cardiff, Liverpool & Manchester; Germans lose 56 aircraft, RAF only 23
16: Italian troops occupy Sidi Barrani
17: Operation 'Sea Lion' postponed 'until further notice'. Liner *City of Benares*, evacuating children to Canada, sunk by *U-48*; 260 killed
22: Japanese troops enter northern French Indochina
23-25: Abortive Free French & Royal Naval attack on Dakar
25: All Norwegian political parties, except Quisling's Nazi-style National Samling, dissolved
27: Germany, Italy & Japan sign Tripartite Pact – agreement for mutual military & economic assistance

OCTOBER 1940

4: Hitler & Mussolini meet at Brenner Pass
7: German troops enter Romania
12: Hitler postpones Operation 'Sea Lion' until following spring
18: British reopen Burma Road
22: Expulsion of Jews from Alsace-Lorraine & Rhineland begins
23: Hitler meets Franco at Hendaye; unable to persuade him to join Axis.
24: Hitler meets Pétain at Montoire; agree 'in principle' on collaboration. Belgian government-in-exile formed in London
27: De Gaulle forms French National Committee in London
28: Mussolini's ultimatum to Greece; Italian troops invade Greece. Hitler & Mussolini meet in Florence
29: British troops land in Crete

NOVEMBER 1940

3: RAF units arrive in Greece
6: Roosevelt elected to third presidential term. German pocket battleship *Admiral Scheer* attacks convoy HX84, sinks escort *Jervis Bay*
7/8: RAF raid on Krupp works at Essen
8-10: Major Italian defeat in Pindus Mountains in Greece
11/12: Three Italian battleships sunk at Taranto by Fleet Air Arm planes from carrier HMS *Illustrious*
12-14: Molotov confers with Hitler & other Nazi leaders in Berlin
14: Start of Greek counteroffensive against Italians which drives Italians back into Albania
14/15: German bombing of Coventry; 568 civilians killed, cathedral destroyed
19/20: RAF bombs Skoda armament works in Czechoslovakia
20: Hungary joins Tripartite Pact
23: Romania joins Tripartite Pact. Last Italian troops retreat from Greece
24: Slovakia joins Tripartite Pact
24/25: Bristol bombed
27: Naval battle off Cape Spartivento, Sardinia; Italian fleet retreats from Royal Navy force
28/29: Heavy Luftwaffe raid on Liverpool

DECEMBER 1940

6: Hitler sends Fliegerkorps X to Sicily to step up air attacks on Malta & British Mediterranean Fleet

DECEMBER 1940 cont

9-10: British victories at Nibeiwa & Sidi Barrani: beginning of Wavell's offensive against the Italians in Western Desert; British take nearly 40 000 prisoners
12/13: Heavy Luftwaffe raid on Sheffield
13: Laval dismissed by Pétain
16/17: RAF raid on Mannheim
17: British occupy Sollum on Egypt-Libya border
18: Hitler issues directive for the invasion of Russia
20/21: Heavy Luftwaffe raid on Liverpool
23: Eden becomes British foreign secretary, replacing Lord Halifax (named ambassador to USA)
29: Roosevelt's 'arsenal of democracy' speech
29/30: Heavy incendiary raid on City of London

JANUARY 1941

1-4: RAF bombs Bremen three nights running
6: Bardia, North Africa, surrendered by Italians; 30 000 Italian prisoners taken
10: Carrier *Illustrious* & convoy reach Malta. Klisura, Albania, falls to Greeks. Lend-Lease Bill introduced in US Congress. Heavy air raids on Malta
19: British & Empire troops under Platt invade Eritrea
22: Italian garrison in Tobruk surrenders to British
29: Death of Metaxas, Greek dictator
30: Derna, North Africa, occupied by British & Empire forces

FEBRUARY 1941

3: *Scharnhorst* & *Gneisenau* pass through Skagerrak into North Sea
3-Mar 27: Battle of Keren (Eritrea)
6: Benghazi (capital of Cyrenaica) taken by Australian troops
7: Battle of Beda Fomm; British take 20 000 Italian prisoners & Agedabia; all Cyrenaica in British hands
9: El Agheila, on border of Cyrenaica & Tripolitania, taken by British. Royal Navy bombards Genoa
11: Cunningham's troops invade Italian Somaliland from Kenya
12: Rommel arrives in Tripoli, to be followed by Afrika Korps
14: German units arrive in Tripoli
22: British agree with Greek government to send forces to Greece
25: Mogadishu (Italian Somaliland) falls to British African troops

MARCH 1941

1: Bulgaria joins Tripartite Pact
2: German troops move into Bulgaria
4: British Commando raid on Lofoten Islands, Norway
7: British force under Maitland Wilson begins to arrive in Greece
9: Italians open offensive in Albania, but it soon fails
11: Roosevelt signs Lend-Lease Act
24: Rommel launches first offensive; his troops reoccupy El Agheila
25: Yugoslavia joins Tripartite Pact despite strong local protests
27: Coup in Yugoslavia overthrows pro-Axis government of Prince Paul; new Simovic government repudiates policy of previous government. US Congress approves Lend-Lease appropriation of US$7000 million
28-29: Battle of Cape Matapan: three Italian cruisers & two destroyers sunk
30: Rommel launches offensive in Cyrenaica
30/31: RAF attacks *Scharnhorst* & *Gneisenau* in Brest

APRIL 1941

1: British Indian troops capture Asmara (capital of Eritrea)
2: Agedabia recaptured by Axis troops under Rommel
3: British driven from Benghazi; beginning of Rommel's counteroffensive from Agedabia. Revolt in Iraq: Raschid Ali sets up pro-Axis regime
6: Germany invades Yugoslavia & Greece; Belgrade bombed. Addis Ababa taken by British & Ethiopian forces
7: Rommel captures Msus & Mechili; O'Connor taken prisoner. Derna retaken by Rommel
8: British forces take Massawa, Eritrea
8/9: RAF raid on Kiel
9: Germans take Salonika
9/10: RAF raid on Berlin; Luftwaffe raid on Birmingham
10: Italian & Hungarian troops enter Yugoslavia
11: Bardia captured by Axis troops; beginning of Rommel's siege of Tobruk (holds out until relieved Dec 10)
12: Belgrade falls to the Germans. RAF begins daylight sweeps over Europe. British & Empire forces form front at Mt Olympus, Greece
13: Japan & USSR sign neutrality pact
17: Yugoslavs surrender to Germans; King Peter II & government flown out by British
17/18: RAF raid on Berlin
21: Greek Army surrenders to Germans
22: British begin withdrawal from Greece
23: Greek king & government flown to Crete
24: Germans defeat British & Anzac forces at Thermopylae
26: German paratroops & glider-borne forces land at Corinth
27: Germans enter Athens
30: Iraqi troops attack British bases & embassy in Baghdad

MAY 1941

1: Axis attack on Tobruk repulsed
1/2: Liverpool bombed
2: British complete evacuation of Greece. British occupy Basra, Iraq
5: Emperor Haile Selassie returns to Addis Ababa
9/10: RAF raid on Mannheim
10: Hess flies to Britain
10/11: Heavy German bombing raid on London; Houses of Parliament, Westminster Abbey & British Museum damaged; end of the night Blitz. RAF raid on Hamburg
11/12: RAF raid on Bremen
12: 'Tiger' convoy docks in Alexandria with 238 tanks for Desert Army
15: Wavell launches Operation 'Brevity' in Egypt
18: *Bismarck* & *Prinz Eugen* leave Gdynia harbour
19: Italian troops in Ethiopia under Duke of Aosta surrender to British at Amba Alagi
20: German airborne troops begin attack on Crete
21: Germans capture Maleme airfield, Crete, after heavy fighting
21/22: German seaborne assault on Crete fails
22: *Bismarck* & *Prinz Eugen* leave Kors Fiord in Norway
24: Sinking of *Hood* by *Bismarck*
27: Sinking of *Bismarck*. Rommel reaches Egyptian frontier. Germans capture Khania (Canea), capital of Crete
28-Jun 1: Evacuation of British & Empire troops from Crete
30: Iraqi revolt collapses

JUNE 1941

1: British troops enter Baghdad
2: Greek government-in-exile formed in Egypt
4: New pro-Allied government installed in Iraq
8: Allied troops including Free French invade Syria & Lebanon
12: Allied governments pledge that none will conclude separate peace with the Axis
14: US freezes Axis assets
15: Wavell launches Operation 'Battleaxe' – to relieve Tobruk
17: Rommel forces British back towards Egypt
21: Damascus captured by Allies
22: Operation 'Barbarossa' – German attack on USSR – begins; Italy & Romania declare war on USSR
23: Germans cross Bug river
24: Vilnius (Vilna) & Kaunas, Lithuania, fall to Germans
25: Finland declares war on USSR
27: British military mission arrives in Moscow. Japan proclaims 'Greater East Asia Co-Prosperity Sphere'. Hungary declares war on USSR
28: German encirclement of Minsk; Finnish troops cross into Russia
29: *Stavka* – new Soviet High Command – established
30: Germans capture Lvov

JULY 1941

1: Auchinleck replaces Wavell as Commander in Chief Middle East; Wavell appointed Commander in Chief India. Finns reoccupy Karelian Isthmus. Riga (Latvian capital) falls to Germans
3: Stalin orders 'scorched earth' policy
7: US marines take over British bases in Iceland, Trinidad & British Guiana.
9: Capture of Vitebsk & liquidation of Minsk pocket – Germans take 324 000 prisoners; German tanks cross Dniepr
12: Pact of mutual assistance between Britain & USSR
14: Vichy French in Syria sign ceasefire
16: Germans capture Smolensk
20: Stalin becomes People's Commissar for Defence
21: Japanese forces start to occupy southern French Indochina, with consent of Vichy
21/22: First German air raid on Moscow
22: 100 000 Soviet troops encircled near Smolensk
26: Roosevelt freezes Japanese assets in USA, suspends all financial & trading relations; Britain & Dutch government-in-exile follow suit
30: Russian pocket at Bialystok liquidated by Germans. Hitler halts advance on Moscow; diverts Hoth north towards Leningrad, Guderian south towards Kiev
31: Göring orders Heydrich to plan measures for 'the desired final solution of the Jewish question'

AUGUST 1941

1: US oil embargo against 'aggressors'
2: US lend-lease extended to USSR
3: 100 000 Soviet troops encircled in Uman pocket
5: Russian resistance in Smolensk pocket liquidated; 310 000 Soviet troops taken prisoner
7: Stalin becomes Supreme Commander of Soviet armed forces
9-12: Atlantic ('Argentia') Conference, Placentia Bay, Newfoundland: Churchill & Roosevelt meet at sea; issue Atlantic Charter, germ of United Nations
12: Hitler stipulates Donets coal basin & Crimea, not Moscow, as prime targets to be gained before winter
17: Germans take Novgorod
20: Germans overrun Leningrad's outer defences – beginning of 890 day siege
25-29: Joint British & Soviet occupation of Iran
25-Sept 3: Raid on Spitsbergen by British commandos, Canadians & Norwegian troops

SEPTEMBER 1941

3: Gas chambers first used at Auschwitz – on Russian prisoners of war
4: Germans start shelling Leningrad
6: By German government order, all Jews to wear Star of David as 'mark of shame'
11: Roosevelt orders US navy to 'shoot on sight' any Axis vessel that threatens a ship or convoy in 'waters under US protection'
12: First snowfall on Eastern Front; German advance slows in mud
16: Some 750 000 Soviet troops are encircled in pocket east of Kiev
19: Kiev falls to Germans
20: Italian midget submarine attack on Gibraltar
27: First Liberty Ship, *Patrick Henry*, launched in Baltimore. Heydrich becomes Deputy Reich Protector of Bohemia
28: First convoy to USSR leaves Iceland for Archangel
28-29: Massacre of 33 000 Jews at Babi Yar outside Kiev

29-Oct 1: Conference between Russian, US & British representatives in Moscow: assistance for USSR planned

OCTOBER 1941

2: Beginning of Operation 'Typhoon' – German advance on Moscow
3: Guderian captures Orel
6: Soviet troops encircled in pockets near Bryansk & Vyazma, & around Melitopol. Curtin becomes Australian prime minister
14-16: Liquidation of Soviet pockets near Vyazma & Bryansk; rain & mud impede German advance
16: Tojo becomes Japanese prime minister after resignation of Konoye. Soviet government officials & diplomats evacuated from Moscow to Kuybyshev. Soviet spy Sorge arrested in Tokyo. Odessa falls to German & Romanian troops after nine-week siege
16/17: US destroyer *Kearney* torpedoed off Iceland but reaches port
20: Stalin proclaims state of siege in Moscow
24: Kharkov falls to Germans
30: German troops reach Sevastopol
31: US destroyer *Reuben James* torpedoed off Iceland; first US vessel sunk by enemy action

NOVEMBER 1941

3: Germans capture Kursk
9: Germans capture Tikhvin, cutting rail line into Leningrad; supplies must now cross Lake Ladoga
13: Aircraft carrier HMS *Ark Royal* torpedoed & damaged off Gibraltar by German U-boat; sinks next day. Temperature near Moscow drops to -22°C (-8°F)
16: Kerch, in Crimea, falls to Germans
18: British open 'Crusader' desert offensive. Brooke becomes Chief of Imperial General Staff
19: Australian cruiser *Sydney* is sunk by – & sinks – German raider *Kormoran* off Australian coast
20: Rostov falls to Germans. Japan warns USA not to aid Chiang Kai-shek, demands free hand in China & Indochina
21-23: Tank battles around Sidi Rezegh
24-25: Rommel advances towards Egyptian frontier
25: HMS *Barham* sunk off Sollum, North Africa, by German U-boat
26: Ritchie replaces Cunningham as Eighth Army commander
27: Rostov retaken by Russians. USA rejects Japanese demands of Nov 20

DECEMBER 1941

1: German Army is only 38 km ($23\frac{1}{2}$ miles) from Red Square, Moscow
5: German attacks on Moscow called off. Britain declares war on Hungary, Finland, Romania
6: Red Army launches counteroffensive all along front
7: Japanese attack on Pearl Harbor. Hitler issues 'Night & Fog' decree, permitting 'disappearance' without trace of 'persons endangering German security'
7-8: Japanese raids on Malaya, Manila, Hong Kong, Guam, Midway, Wake; Japanese planes attack US bases in the Philippines; Japanese troops invade Hong Kong, land at Kota Baharu (Malaya) & Singora (Thailand)
8: 27 000 Jews massacred in Riga. USA & Britain declare war on Japan
9: Chiang Kai-shek's government declares war on Japan, Germany & Italy. Red Army recaptures Tikhvin
10: Red Army attacks along whole front. Japanese troops land in north Luzon, beginning invasion of Philippines; Cavite naval base, near Manila, bombed. British battleship *Prince of Wales* & battlecruiser *Repulse* sunk by Japanese off Malaya; destruction of Alor Star airfield in northern Malaya. Guam falls to Japanese. British Eighth Army relieves Tobruk garrison
11: Italy & Germany declare war on USA & vice-versa
12: Japanese land at Legaspi in south-east Luzon
15: First Japanese merchant ship sunk by US submarine
16: Kalinin retaken by Russians. Japanese invade Borneo & occupy Victoria Point, southernmost tip of Burma. British Foreign Secretary Eden meets Stalin in Moscow
17: Nimitz appointed Commander in Chief US Pacific Fleet. British advance to Gazala Line – Rommel in retreat
18/19: Italian midget submarine raid on Alexandria harbour – two battleships sunk. Japanese cross from Kowloon to Hong Kong island
19: Hitler replaces Brauchitsch as Commander in Chief of German Army. Japanese capture Penang, Malaya
22-Jan 7, 1942: 'Arcadia' (First Washington) Conference: Churchill, Roosevelt & military advisers set up Combined Chiefs of Staff; 'United Nations' declaration issued
22: Heavy Axis air raids on Malta. Japanese land in Lingayen Gulf, Luzon
23: Wake Island falls to the Japanese
24: Japanese land at Lamon Bay, on east coast of Luzon
25: British, Indian & Canadian troops surrender Hong Kong to Japanese.
27: Commando raid on Vaagso, Norway
29: Japanese capture Clark Field air base in Philippines
31: Rommel halts his withdrawal at El Agheila

JANUARY 1942

1: Representatives of 26 Allied nations sign Declaration of the United Nations
2: Japanese enter Manila
3: ABDA (American, British, Dutch, Australian) Command set up in Far East under Wavell
7: Wavell arrives in Singapore. Second stage of Soviet counteroffensive begins; formation of Demyansk Pocket
10: Japanese land on Tarakan (off Borneo) in Dutch East Indies; enter Kuala Lumpur, Malaya
11: Soviet troops reopen narrow supply corridor to besieged Leningrad
11-12: Japanese capture Manado (on Celebes)
13: U-boat offensive along US East Coast begins
14: Australians stall Japanese advance through Malaya, at Gemas. German battleship *Tirpitz* moves to Norway
16: Japanese advance from Victoria Point up southern Burma
17: Axis forces surrender Sollum & Halfaya to British
18: Timoshenko begins offensive in the Ukraine, intended to recapture Kharkov
19: Russian counteroffensive retakes Mozhaisk, west of Moscow
20: Wannsee Conference under Heydrich plans 'final solution of Jewish question'. Beginning of main Japanese attack on Burma, towards Moulmein.
21: Beginning of Rommel's counteroffensive from El Agheila. Stilwell appointed chief of staff to Chiang Kai-shek & head of US military mission in China
22: Rommel retakes Agedabia. Russian breakthrough between Smolensk & Lake Ilmen. Japanese breach Abucay Line on Bataan Peninsula, Luzon
22-24: Japanese land on New Britain, New Ireland & Bougainville (Solomon Islands)
24: Japanese land at Balikpapan, Borneo. Naval Battle of Makassar Strait: first US surface action since 1898
26: First US troops arrive in Britain
29: Rommel recaptures Benghazi
30-31: Battle of Moulmein: British pushed back in Burma
31: Last British & Empire troops withdraw from Malaya to Singapore

FEBRUARY 1942

1: Quisling made 'minister president' of Norway. US carrier aircraft raid Japanese bases on Gilbert & Marshall Islands
3: Japanese bomb Port Moresby, New Guinea
7: Rommel halts near Gazala. Speer appointed head of Todt organisation & German armaments minister
8/9: Japanese land on north-west of Singapore island
9: Japanese capture Makassar (Celebes) & Banjarmasin (Borneo)
11: Anti-conscription riots in Montreal, Canada
11/12: *Scharnhorst* & *Gneisenau* leave Brest for dash through English Channel
12: British aircraft attack *Scharnhorst* & *Gneisenau* in Channel
13: *Scharnhorst* & *Gneisenau* reach German North Sea ports
14: British Air Ministry issues 'area bombing' directive. Japanese paratroops land at Palembang, Sumatra
15: Singapore falls to the Japanese; 130 000 British & Empire troops captured. Japanese land on Sumatran coast north of Palembang
18/19: Naval Battle of Lombok Strait
19: Japanese carrier raid on Darwin, Australia. Japanese land on Bali
20: Timor invaded by Japanese
22: Harris appointed Commander in Chief, RAF Bomber Command
23: Sittang bridge disaster, Burma
25: ABDA Command dissolved
25-28: *Gneisenau* crippled by bombing in dock at Kiel
27/28: Naval Battle of Java Sea: Allied force destroyed. British paratroop raid on Bruneval, northern France, to capture *Würzburg* radar
28: Naval Battle of Sunda Strait
28-Mar 9: Java invaded by Japanese

MARCH 1942

1: Soviet offensive in the Crimea
2: Japanese land on Mindanao, Philippines
5: Japanese capture Batavia, Java
8: Japanese capture Rangoon, Burma
9: Japanese complete capture of Java
10: US carrier planes attack Japanese bases at Salamaua & Lae, New Guinea
11/12: MacArthur leaves Corregidor, Philippines, for Mindanao then Australia
12: Dutch East Indies administration in Sumatra capitulates
14: US troops arrive in Australia
16: Soviet counteroffensive around Moscow ends
17: MacArthur flies to Darwin, Australia; promises 'I shall return' [to Philippines]
18: Mountbatten appointed Chief of Combined Operations
22: Naval Battle of Sirte, off Libya
23: Japanese capture Andaman Islands
27/28 Royal Navy & commando raid on St Nazaire docks, France
28: First group of Parisian Jews sent to Auschwitz
28/29: Destruction of Lübeck by RAF
30: MacArthur appointed Commander in Chief, South-West Pacific Area

APRIL 1942

1: Japanese begin landings on Dutch New Guinea
5: Japanese planes attack Colombo, capital of Ceylon
6/7: Japanese break through Samat Line on Bataan Peninsula, Luzon
9: US forces on Bataan surrender; siege of Corregidor begins. Japanese planes raid Trincomalee, Ceylon, sinking carrier HMS *Hermes*
10: Bataan Death March begins
14: Under German pressure, Laval reappointed French premier
15: King George VI awards George Cross to island of Malta
17: Low-level daylight attack on Augsburg by RAF Lancasters
18: Doolittle leads first US bomber raid on Tokyo
21: Germans relieve Demyansk pocket
23/24: Luftwaffe raid on Exeter: beginning of 'Baedeker' raids
29: Japanese capture Lashio – southern end of Burma road to China. Hitler & Mussolini meet at Salzburg

MAY 1942

U-boats sink many Allied ships in Gulf of Mexico
1: Mandalay, Burma, falls to the Japanese

MAY 1942 cont

2: British troops in Burma withdraw from Irrawaddy river
3: Japanese seize Tulagi in Solomon Islands
4-8: Battle of the Coral Sea – first naval battle fought entirely with aircraft from carriers out of each other's sight
5: British force lands on Vichy French ruled Madagascar. Japanese advance into China along Burma Road
6: US & Filipino troops on Corregidor surrender to Japanese
8: US carrier *Lexington* sunk in Coral Sea. Germans begin summer offensive in the Crimea
10: US troops in central Philippines surrender to Japanese
12-28: Abortive Russian offensive to regain Kharkov
17: Germans counterattack at Kharkov
20: Last British troops retreat from Burma into India; Japanese have almost complete control of Burma
23: Two Soviet armies encircled east of Kharkov – 70 000 killed, 200 000 captured
26: Britain & USSR sign 20 year treaty of mutual assistance
26: Start of Rommel's offensive against Gazala Line
27: Heydrich assassinated in Prague (dies Jun 4)
28: Mexico declares war on Axis powers
30/31: First RAF 1000-bomber raid on Cologne

JUNE 1942

2-11: Siege of Bir Hacheim (held by Free French)
3: Japanese diversionary attack on Dutch Harbor in Aleutians
4-6: Battle of Midway: Japanese carrier fleet crippled as four carriers sunk
5: USA declares war on Bulgaria, Hungary & Romania
6-7: Japanese capture Kiska & Attu islands in Aleutians
7-Jul 3: Heavy fighting at Sevastopol
9-10: Czech village of Lidice wiped out in reprisal for assassination of Heydrich
11: Rommel breaks out of the 'Cauldron' south of Gazala (where temporarily contained by British); drives British back beyond Tobruk
16: Supply convoy reaches Malta
17: Heavy fighting at Sidi Rezegh, near Tobruk
18: Beginning of second siege of Tobruk by Axis troops
20: Rommel attacks Tobruk
21: Germans take Tobruk; Allied forces surrender
24: Czech village of Lezaky wiped out in reprisal for assassination of Heydrich
25: Auchinleck takes direct command in desert, replacing Ritchie
27: Germans reach Mersa Matruh
28: Germans open Operation *Blau* – summer offensive in USSR, aimed at oil-rich Caucasus
30: Rommel reaches El Alamein, under 100 km (60 miles) from Alexandria

JULY 1942

1-30 First Battle of El Alamein: Auchinleck stops Rommel's advance
2: Churchill wins vote of confidence in House of Commons (476-25) following fall of Tobruk
3: Sevastopol falls to Germans
4: Convoy PQ17 to Archangel ordered to scatter, following Luftwaffe attacks
5: End of Soviet resistance in Crimea
5-8: Two-thirds of convoy PQ17 sunk by German U-boats & aircraft
6: Voronezh falls to Germans during summer offensive in southern USSR
9: German drive towards Stalingrad begins
12: Australian force arrives at Kokoda, New Guinea
14: Congress Party passes 'Quit India' resolution, demanding immediate British withdrawal from India
16: Mass round-up of French Jews begins
21-22: Japanese land near Gona, New Guinea, in attempt to reach Port Moresby via Kokoda Trail
22: Treblinka extermination camp opened by Germans to gas Jews from Warsaw Ghetto
24: Rostov (for second time) & Novocherkassk fall to Germans
29: Japanese take village of Kokoda, on Kokoda Trail
31: Germans cross the Don on 240 km (150 mile) wide front

AUGUST 1942

3: Churchill goes to Cairo to reorganise command structure in North Africa
7: US troops land on Guadalcanal
8: Alexander appointed Commander in Chief Middle East; Montgomery to command Eighth Army. US marines take Henderson Field on Guadalcanal
9: Battle of Savo Island, off Guadalcanal. Arrest of Gandhi, Nehru & other Indian leaders; India convulsed by rioting. Maikop & Krasnodar oilfields in Caucasus taken by Germans
10: 'Pedestal' convoy leaves Gibraltar for Malta, hoping to break siege
12-15: First Moscow Conference: Churchill & Stalin, plus US & Free French representatives, discuss opening of second front; Stalin told that, instead of invading France in 1942, Western Allies would invade North Africa
13: Japanese take main pass over Owen Stanley Range, on Kokoda Trail, threatening Port Moresby
13-15: After heavy German & Italian attacks, 5 ships of 'Pedestal' convoy, including tanker *Ohio*, reach Malta
17: US Eighth Air Force's first independent attack on a European target – marshalling yards at Rouen
18/19: First use of RAF's Pathfinder Force
19: Disastrous Anglo-Canadian raid on Dieppe
21: German troops reach summit of Mt Elbrus in Caucasus Mountains
22: Brazil declares war on Germany & Italy
23: German troops reach Volga north of Stalingrad; massive air raid devastates Stalingrad, killing 40 000
23-24: Naval Battle of the Eastern Solomons
26-Sep 6: Battle for Milne Bay, New Guinea
31: Germans reach outskirts of Stalingrad
31-Sep 2: Battle of Alam Halfa: Rommel tries to break through British line but is driven back.

SEPTEMBER 1942

10-29: Further British & South African landings on Madagascar
12-14: Battle of 'Bloody Ridge' on Guadalcanal
13: Japanese land reinforcements on Guadalcanal. Battle of Stalingrad begins
16: Japanese reach Ioribaiwa Ridge, 51 km (32 miles) from Port Moresby, New Guinea – greatest extension of Japanese Empire
18: British land on east coast of Madagascar
21: British Indian troops open offensive into Arakan, Burma
23: Heavy Japanese attacks on Guadalcanal
26: Germans capture main Volga ferry landing in Stalingrad. Japanese begin withdrawal down Kokoda trail

OCTOBER 1942

3/4: British commando raid on Sark, Channel Islands
4: Start of German 'final offensive' against Soviet positions in Stalingrad
9: Systematic air attacks on Axis supply routes & bases in Italy & Libya
11-12: Naval/air Battle of Cape Esperance, off Guadalcanal
15: Japanese land further reinforcements on Guadalcanal
18: Hitler issues Commando Order: all British commandos taken prisoner to be executed
22: Clark arrives in Algeria by submarine for secret talks with pro-Allied Vichy French
23/24: Second Battle of El Alamein opens with Operation 'Lightfoot'
26: Naval Battle of Santa Cruz, off Guadalcanal: US carrier *Hornet* sunk; 100 Japanese aircraft destroyed. Intense air attacks on Malta

NOVEMBER 1942

1-2: Operation 'Supercharge' begins: Allied forces break through Axis lines at El Alamein
2: Australians recapture Kokoda village
4: Axis troops begin retreat from El Alamein
5: Vichy French forces on Madagascar surrender
8: Operation 'Torch': Allied landings under Eisenhower in Morocco & Algeria
11: Last Axis forces driven out of Egypt. French authorities in North Africa sign armistice with Allies; German & Italian troops march into unoccupied Vichy France
12-15: Naval Battle of Guadalcanal
13: Eisenhower & Darlan meet in Algiers; Darlan pledges that French Africa will side with Allies
19: Russians open counteroffensive north & south of Stalingrad
20/21: Heavy RAF raid on Turin: most devastating raid of war on Italy
23: Soviet units link up at Kalach, encircling German Sixth Army in Stalingrad
27: French fleet in Toulon scuttles itself rather than fall into German hands; German troops occupy Toulon
30/31: Naval Battle of Tassafaronga, off Guadalcanal

DECEMBER 1942

2: Beveridge Report on Social Security issued in Britain. Enrico Fermi activates first atomic pile in Chicago – birth of nuclear age
4: First USAAF air raid on mainland Italy (Naples)
9: Australians take Gona, New Guinea
11/12: British commando ('Cockleshell Heroes') raid on Bordeaux
12: Manstein opens counteroffensive to try to relieve Sixth Army at Stalingrad. Eighth Army begins attack on German defensive line at El Agheila
13: Axis troops begin retreat from Al Agheila
16: Second stage of Russian winter offensive begins; Italians routed on Don
17: Eden reveals to House of Commons that Jews from occupied Europe are being 'worked to death in labour camps', or 'deliberately slaughtered in mass executions' – first official Allied statement about Nazi extermination of Jews
20/21: First use of 'Oboe' navigation & bombing aid by RAF
24: Manstein's attempt to relieve Sixth Army stopped. Darlan assassinated in Algiers
25: Eighth Army occupies Sirte, Libya
28: Kleist begins withdrawal out of the Caucasus into Taman Peninsula
31: Naval Battle of Barents Sea

JANUARY 1943

1: Hitler decides to scrap most of German surface fleet. Russians launch offensive towards Rostov
2: Buna, New Guinea, taken by Australian & US troops
3: Germans begin general withdrawal from the Caucasus
10: Soviet offensive on Germans in Stalingrad begins
12-18: Russians establish corridor around south of Lake Ladoga, breaking worst of siege of Leningrad
14: Red Army captures Pitomnik airfield, outside Stalingrad
14-24: Casablanca Conference, Morocco: Churchill & Roosevelt agree to prepare for invasion of France & meanwhile (once North Africa is conquered) to invade Sicily. Issue demand for 'unconditional surrender' of Axis. De Gaulle & Giraud also attend
15: British Eighth Army starts drive to Tripoli
16: Iraq declares war on Axis powers
21: Sanananda, New Guinea, taken by Australians

22: Japanese resistance in Papua collapses
23: Tripoli taken by Eighth Army
25: Red Army completes capture of Voronezh
27: First USAAF attack on Germany – daylight bombing of Wilhelmshaven
30: Dönitz replaces Raeder as Commander in Chief of Kriegsmarine. In Berlin, Nazi 10th anniversary celebrations disrupted by low-level RAF Mosquito raid
30/31: Over Hamburg, first operational use of 'H2S' radar by RAF bombers
31: In Stalingrad, Paulus captured by Russians; surrenders southern half of Sixth Army

FEBRUARY 1943

1-8: Japanese evacuate Guadalcanal
2: Last German troops in Stalingrad surrender
3: In Arakan, Burma, Indian troops attack Rathedaung but are repulsed
4: Eighth Army enters Tunisia
6: Russians reach Sea of Azov, isolating German Army Group A
8: Kursk retaken by Soviet troops
13: Chindits cross Chindwin river into Burma
14: Rostov falls to Russians
14-25: Battle of Kasserine Pass, Tunisia: Rommel delays Allies
15: Voroshilovgrad falls to Russians
16: Kharkov retaken by Russians
18: In speech in Berlin, Goebbels declares 'total war'
27/28: British commandos raid heavy-water plant in Norway

MARCH 1943

1: Demyansk retaken by Russians
1-4: Battle of Bismarck Sea: Japanese convoy for New Guinea destroyed by Allied aircraft
3: Rzhev retaken by Russians.
5/6: RAF bombing raid on Essen marks beginning of Battle of the Ruhr
6: Battle of Medenine, Tunisia
9: Arnim takes over command of Panzerarmee Afrika from Rommel
12: Vyazma retaken by Russians
13: Time bomb in Hitler's aircraft fails to explode
15: Kharkov retaken by Germans after savage fighting
16-20: Climax of Battle of Atlantic: 38 U-boats attack two convoys, sinking 21 merchant ships
19-21: Belgorod retaken by Germans
20: Second bomb attempt on Hitler's life fails in Berlin
20-27: Battle of Mareth Line, Tunisia
25: Wingate orders Chindits to retire to India

APRIL 1943

5: In Burma, Japanese approach Indin near Indian frontier
6/7: Eighth Army makes night attack on Wadi Akarit Line in Tunisia, but fails to break through; Axis forces retire towards Enfidaville
7: British & American forces in Tunisia link up near Sfax
7-10: Hitler & Mussolini meet in Salzburg: Mussolini wants separate peace with Russia in order to concentrate Axis Forces in North Africa; Hitler persuades him to hang on
7-16: Major Japanese raids on US shipping & airfields in Solomons; sink US carrier but lose heavily in air battle
10: Axis forces in full retreat towards Enfidaville Line; British Eighth Army takes Sfax
11: British Eighth & First Armies link up in Tunisia
12: Axis troops dig in on Enfidaville Line, Tunisia
13: German radio announces discovery of mass graves of Polish officers in Katyn Forest near Smolensk
14/15: RAF raids Stuttgart
16/17: RAF raids Mannheim & Skoda works, Pilsen
18: Yamamoto killed when his aircraft shot down by US planes over Bougainville
18-19: Axis airlifts to Tunisia destroyed by Allied fighters
19: Warsaw Ghetto uprising begins
19-23: Eighth Army attacks Enfidaville Line but fails to break through
20: Warsaw Ghetto massacre of Jews begins: 56 000 are killed by May 16
21: German counterattack on centre of Allied line in Tunisia driven back
22: Eighth Army halts attack on Enfidaville Line, but First Army attacks towards Tunis
23: Anglo-American planning staff set up under Morgan for landings in northern Europe
25: Koga succeeds Yamamoto as Commander in Chief of Japanese Combined Fleet
26: US ships shell Attu island in Aleutians
26/27: Massive RAF raid on Duisburg
28-May 6: Battle of convoy ONS5: 42 ships attacked by 42 U-boats; 12 ships & 6 U-boats sunk
30: Body of 'the man who never was' – 'Major Martin' – deliberately released by British onto Spanish coast to deceive Germans about future plans

MAY 1943

6: Enfidaville Line breached
7: Tunis & Bizerta fall to Allies
11-30: US troops recapture Attu island in Aleutians
12: Maungdaw evacuated by Indian troops retreating north: end of first Arakan offensive
13: Axis troops in North Africa surrender
13-25: 'Trident' (Second Washington) Conference between Churchill & Roosevelt: set provisional date of May 1944 for invasion of France
16: Destruction of Warsaw Ghetto completed
16/17: RAF raid on Ruhr dams: Möhne & Eder dams breached, Sorpe damaged
18: Heavy bombing of Pantellaria island, south of Sicily, begins
23/24: RAF raid on Dortmund – heaviest to date
24: Dönitz orders U-boats in Atlantic to break off operations

JUNE 1943

10: Combined Chiefs of Staff issue 'Pointblank' directive allotting strategic aims to US & British bomber forces
11: Himmler orders liquidation of all Polish ghettos. Wilhelmshaven attacked by USAAF. Pantellaria captured
16: Large air battles over Solomons
18: Wavell appointed Viceroy of India
21-Aug 25: Allies take New Georgia, Solomon Islands
29/30: Australian & US troops land at Nassau Bay, New Guinea
30: US troops land on Rendova, Solomon Islands

JULY 1943

2: In New Guinea, Australians from Wau link up with Americans from Nassau Bay
4: Polish leader Wladyslaw Sikorski killed in plane crash while taking off from Gibraltar
5: Germans launch Operation *Zitadelle* to eliminate Kursk salient – start of Battle of Kursk
5/6: Naval Battle of Kula Gulf, Solomon Islands
9-10: Allied landings on Sicily
12: Huge tank battle at Prokhorovka, south of Kursk. Battle of Kolombangara, Solomon Islands
12-17: Red Army offensive from Smolensk to Black Sea
13: German *Zitadelle* offensive ends
19: Hitler & Mussolini meet at Feltre in northern Italy. Rome heavily bombed by Allies: about 2000 people killed & Basilica of San Lorenzo destroyed
22: US Seventh Army captures Palermo
24/25: First big bombing raid on Hamburg, beginning Battle of Hamburg (to Aug 3); first use of 'Window' to confuse German radar
25: Mussolini overthrown & arrested; new Italian government under Badoglio
25/26: RAF raid on Essen
26: Italian Fascist party dissolved
27/28: Heavy bombing causes firestorm in Hamburg
28: Japanese evacuate Kiska island in Aleutians

AUGUST 1943

1: USAAF planes bomb oil refineries at Ploesti, Romania, from bases in North Africa; 54 bombers lost
5: US troops take Munda airfield on New Georgia. Red Army captures Orel & Belgorod
6-7: Battle of Vella Gulf, Solomon Islands
14-Aug 24: 'Quadrant' (First Quebec) Conference between Churchill & Roosevelt: plans for invasion of France
15: Americans land on Vella Lavella, Solomon Islands. US & Canadian troops land on Kiska, in Aleutians
17: Allies enter Messina – Sicily is cleared. First US raid on Regensburg & Schweinfurt: 60 US aircraft lost
17/18: RAF raid on German V-weapon research centre at Peenemünde
23: Kharkov retaken by Russians
24: Himmler appointed German minister of interior
25: Mountbatten appointed Supreme Commander South-East Asia
28: Japanese resistance on New Georgia ends. Danish government resigns in protest at German demands for repressive measures against Danish saboteurs. Death of King Boris III of Bulgaria; succeeded by son Simeon.
29: Martial law in Denmark; Danish king seized by Germans – becomes virtual prisoner

SEPTEMBER 1943

3: Italians sign secret capitulation to Allies in Sicily. British Eighth Army lands at Reggio di Calabria, toe of Italy
4-5: Allied amphibious & paratroop landings near Lae, New Guinea
8: Eisenhower announces unconditional surrender of Italians
9: Main Allied landings on mainland Italy at Salerno; British take Taranto. Iran declares war on Germany
11: Italian fleet surrenders at Malta; Germans occupy Rome. Kesselring announces that Italy now under German military government
12: Allies take Salamaua, New Guinea. Mussolini rescued by German paratroops under Skorzeny from Gran Sasso in Abruzzi mountains
14-Oct 4: Free French liberate Corsica
15: British forces land on Aegean islands of Kos, Samos, Leros
16: Allies take Lae, New Guinea
17: Bryansk retaken by Soviet forces
21/22: Russian troops cross Dniepr at Bukrin; by end of month have established several small bridgeheads
22: Australian landing near Finschhafen, New Guinea. British midget submarines attack *Tirpitz* in Altenfjord, Norway
23: Foundation of German-backed Italian Social Republic at Salò
25: Russians recapture Smolensk. US lend-lease extended to Free French
27: Germans seize Corfu from Italians
29: Badoglio signs official Italian surrender

OCTOBER 1943

1: Allies enter Naples
2: Finschhafen, New Guinea, taken by Australians
3-4: Germans land on Kos in Aegean; British garrison captured
4-5: Round-the-clock air attacks on Frankfurt
5/6: Russians cross Dniepr near Zaporozhye
13: Italian government declares war on Germany. US Fifth Army crosses Volturno river, north of Naples
14: Second US bombing raid on Schweinfurt; 60 bombers shot down. Red Army captures Zaporozhye
19-30: Second Moscow Conference of British, US & Soviet foreign ministers: set up European Advisory Commission to look at postwar problems & express wish to found an international organisation to preserve peace (ie, United Nations)

OCTOBER 1943 cont

27: US marines raid on Choiseul, Solomon Islands

NOVEMBER 1943

1: US marines land on Bougainville, Solomon Islands; Japanese never completely flushed out, but after March 1944 are no longer a threat
1/2: Naval Battle of Empress Augusta Bay, off Bougainville
2-11: US carrier & land-based aircraft attack Rabaul, New Britain
3: Over 17 000 Jews killed at Majdanek concentration camp
6: Russians recapture Kiev
9: United Nations Relief & Rehabilitation Administration set up
12-16: Germans retake Leros
16: Eighth Army establishes first bridgehead across Sangro river
18/19: First major RAF bombing raid on Berlin begins Battle of Berlin (to March 1944)
20: British evacuate Samos
20-23: US troops take Tarawa & Makin, Gilbert Islands
21: British & Indian troops launch new offensive in Arakan region of Burma
22-26: 'Sextant' (First Cairo) Conference, between Churchill, Roosevelt & Chiang Kai-shek: discuss Far East war & particularly plans for Burma campaign
28-30: Teheran Conference: first 'summit' conference of Big Three – Churchill, Roosevelt & Stalin – discusses need for second front in Europe & postwar division of Europe

DECEMBER 1943

3-7: Second Cairo Conference, between Churchill, Roosevelt & President Inönü of Turkey
4: Bolivia declares war on Axis powers
15: US landings on Arawe peninsula of New Britain
24: Eisenhower appointed Supreme Commander, Allied Expeditionary Force (for invasion of France)
24-26: Russian offensives on Ukranian front launched
26: Battle of North Cape: *Scharnhorst* sunk.
26-30: Allies capture Cape Gloucester on New Britain
28: Canadians take Ortona, Italy, breaking Gustav Line
31: Red Army captures Zhitomir

JANUARY 1944

2: US troops take Saidor, New Guinea
5: Koniev launches offensive in southern Ukraine
8: Red Army captures Kirovograd
9: British Indian troops retake Maungdaw in Arakan
10: Malinovsky & Tolbukhin launch offensive aimed at Odessa & the Crimea
14: Red Army launches offensive to relieve Leningrad
16: Eisenhower begins duties as Supreme Commander, Allied Expeditionary Force
17: First attack towards Cassino (Italy)
19: Novgorod retaken by Soviet troops
22: Allied landings at Anzio (Italy)
24: Soviet attack on German salient at Korsun in Ukraine
26: Russians clear last enemy troops from Moscow-Leningrad railway. Liberia declares war on Axis powers
27: Russians declare end of siege of Leningrad – first of USSR's ten victories of 1944
28: Korsun pocket encircled by Red Army

FEBRUARY 1944

1-7: US marines capture Kwajalein atoll in Marshall Islands
4-24: Japanese launch Operation *Ha-go* in Arakan; 7th Indian Division holds out at Sinzweya
5-8: Russians take Rovno, Apolostovo & Nikopol
13-15: Allies counterattack in Arakan
15: New Zealand troops land on Nissan, in Green Islands, east of Rabaul
15/16: RAF makes heaviest raid of war on Berlin
15-18: Freyburg's attack on Monte Cassino, preceded by massive aerial bombardment that destroys monastery
16/17: After Germans attempt breakout, remainder of Korsun pocket liquidated – second of USSR's ten victories of 1944
17-18: Japanese naval base at Truk, Caroline Islands, destroyed by US carrier-borne aircraft
17-22: US troops assault Eniwetok & Engebi, Marshall Islands
18: RAF Mosquitoes bomb Amiens prison, breaching walls & allowing French Resistance prisoners to escape
20: Ferry carrying heavy water destroyed by Norwegian Resistance
22: Krivoy Rog taken by Red Army
29: In Italy, German counterattack against Anzio beach-head. US troops land on Los Negros, in Admiralty Islands. Soviet General Vatutin mortally wounded in attack by Ukrainian guerrillas; dies April 15

MARCH 1944

1: Chindits cross Chindwin again into Burma
4: Soviet offensive on Belorussian front begins. First major USAAF raid against Berlin
5: Chindits drop behind Japanese lines in Burma
7/8: Japanese in Burma open Operation *U-go* into Assam
15: Japanese launch offensive towards Imphal & Kohima
15-23: Renewed Allied attempt to take Monte Cassino
18/19: RAF raid on Frankfurt
20: US troops occupy Emirau island, completing encirclement of Rabaul. German troops occupy Hungary
22/23: RAF raid on Frankfurt
24: Air crash in Burma kills Chindit leader Wingate
25: Russians reach Romanian frontier
29-Jul 8: Battle of Imphal, Assam
30: Chernovtsy taken by Russians; German breakout from pocket near Proskurov in southern Ukraine
30/31: RAF raid on Nuremberg; 95 out of 795 bombers lost

APRIL 1944

3: *Tirpitz* damaged by British carrier aircraft
5-Jun 3: Battle of Kohima, Assam
8: Red Army launches offensive to liberate Crimea
9: Yeremenko captures Kerch
10: Odessa retaken by Russians
17: In China, Japanese launch *Ko-go*, first phase of Operation *Ichi-go*
22: Allies land at Hollandia & Aitape, New Guinea. Japanese capture Chengchow in China's Honan province

MAY 1944

9: Sevastopol retaken by Russians
10: Chinese/US Yunnan army crosses Salween river into Burma
11: Allied attack on Gustav Line near Cassino
11-17: French North African troops break through Gustav Line by crossing Aurunci Mountains
12: Germans in Crimea surrender – third of USSR's ten victories of 1944
15: Beginning of deportation of Hungarian Jews
17: Myitkyina airfield falls to Stilwell's Chinese/US troops
18: US forces land on Wakde, off New Guinea. Polish troops capture ruins of monastery of Monte Cassino
23: US Fifth Army launches offensive to break out from Anzio beach-head
27: US landing on Biak, off New Guinea. *To-go*, second phase of *Ichi-go*, is launched in China

JUNE 1944

4: Allies enter Rome
6: D-Day: Allies invade Normandy
7: Allies reach Bayeux
9: Panzer attack on Normandy bridgehead fails. Russians launch offensive against Finns in Karelian Isthmus
10: SS massacre of inhabitants of Oradour-sur-Glane. Red Army breakthrough in Karelian Isthmus
13: First V-1 raid on Britain. German counterattack at Villers-Bocage halts British attack on Caen
14/15: First B-29 Superfortress raid on Japan from China: Yawata steelworks on Kyushu island bombed
15-Jul 9: US troops take Saipan, Mariana Islands
16: In Normandy, 'Mulberry' artificial harbours completed
18: Japanese take Changsha in Hunan province
19-20: Battle of the Philippine Sea: Japanese lose about 400 aircraft in 'Great Marianas Turkey Shoot'
19-22: Great Channel Storm destroys US 'Mulberry' & damages British one; delays Allied build-up in Normandy
20: Russians take Viipuri, Finland: decisive point of campaign against Finns – fourth of USSR's ten victories of 1944
21: Massive USAAF raid on Berlin; some aircraft land at Poltava in USSR
22: Start of enormous Red Army summer offensive on central front – Operation 'Bagration'
22-29: Cherbourg taken by US troops
25: Five German divisions trapped by Soviet encirclement of Vitebsk
26: Russians take Vitebsk. British launch drive west of Caen – Operation 'Epsom'

JULY 1944

1: Rundstedt resigns as German Commander in Chief West; replaced by Kluge
3: Minsk retaken by Russians. In Normandy, US forces attack south to Coutances & St Lô, leading to 'Battle of the Hedgerows'
4: Canadian troops capture Carpiquet
8: Operation 'Charnwood' – frontal assault on Caen. Japanese withdrawal to Chindwin from Imphal begins. Japanese capture Hengchow
9-10: Caen taken by British & Canadian troops.
11: Americans recognise de Gaulle's French Provisional Government in liberated areas. 35 000 Germans in Minsk pocket surrender
13: Russians take Vilnius (Vilna), Lithuania; Belorussia is now free – fifth of USSR's ten victories of 1944. Koniev launches offensive in north Ukraine
17: Wounded in air attack, Rommel gives up command of Army Group B in France
18: Tojo resigns as Japanese prime minister following US capture of Saipan. St Lô taken by US troops
18-Jul 20: Operation 'Goodwood' in Normandy to bypass Caen to south towards Falaise plain
20: Stauffenberg's bomb fails to kill Hitler. Russians reach Bug river
21: US marines land on Guam, Mariana Islands
22: Creation of Soviet-backed 'Polish Committee for National Liberation'
24: Russians take Lublin; overrun Majdanek concentration camp. US Marines land on Tinian, Mariana Islands
25: Goebbels named Reich Minister for Total War. Launch of US Operation 'Cobra' to break out in Normandy
26: US troops break out from St Lô
27: Russians take Lvov & Stanislav in western Ukraine: liberation of western Ukraine – sixth of USSR's ten victories of 1944 – nearly completed
28: Russians take Brest-Litovsk. US troops take Coutances. First use of German Me163 rocket fighter
30: British Second Army tries to take Caumont. US troops take Sansapor, New Guinea. US First Army reaches Avranches
31: Russians are just 13 km (8 miles) from Warsaw, but are later pushed back

AUGUST 1944

1: Warsaw uprising begins. End of fighting on Tinian
2: Patton's Third Army breaks through

Avranches Gap into Brittany
3: Russians cross Vistula at Sandomierz. Myitkyina, Burma, falls to Stilwell's Chinese/US troops after 2½ month siege
6: Allies seal off Brest Peninsula
7: Germans begin counterattack towards Avranches
7-9: Canadian troops attack towards Falaise in attempt to seal Falaise pocket
8: US troops reach Le Mans
10: End of fighting on Guam
12: Allies take Florence. Failure of German Avranches counterattack. Churchill confers with Tito in Italy
15: Operation 'Dragoon': Allied landings in south of France
15-20: Germans caught in Falaise-Argentan pocket
17: St Malo falls to US troops; Falaise taken by Canadians & Poles
19: Paris uprising by FFI (Resistance); US troops cross Seine at Mantes-Gassicourt. Suicide of Kluge
19-20: Russian troops attack Tiraspol area in Romania – beginning of Russian offensive in Balkans
20: Allies close Falaise Gap; 40 000 Germans escape
21-29: Dumbarton Oaks Conference: meeting of US, British, Russian & Chinese diplomats, which puts forward proposals for a United Nations organisation
22: FFI takes control of Paris; Allied troops enter Marsailles & Toulon
23: Pro-Axis Antonescu government overthrown in Romania; new government surrenders unconditionally
24: Grenoble liberated by Allied troops
25: US & Free French troops enter Paris; German garrison surrenders. 'Red Ball Express' set up to supply US units in France. Romania declares war on Germany. In northern Italy, Alexander starts offensive against Gothic Line
26: Bulgaria announces withdrawal from the war – ignored by Russians
28: German garrisons in Toulon & Marseilles surrender.
29: Partisan uprising seizes large areas of central Slovakia
30: Nice captured by US troops. Russians take Ploesti, Romania
31: British capture Amiens. Red Army enters Bucharest: decisive point of Soviet campaign in Moldavia and Romania – seventh of USSR's ten victories of 1944

SEPTEMBER 1944

1: Eisenhower establishes HQ in France. Allies liberate Arras, Verdun, Dieppe & Abbeville
3: Brussels liberated by British troops. Lyons liberated
4: Ceasefire agreed between Finland & USSR. Antwerp liberated by British
5: USSR declares war on Bulgaria – & invades. Hitler re-appoints Rundstedt Commander in Chief West
5/6: US troops under Patton cross Moselle.
8: Bulgaria declares war on Germany. First V-2 rockets fall on London
9-14: US planes raid Japanese bases in central & southern Philippines, destroying 478 Japanese planes & sinking 59 ships
11: French/US troops from south of France make contact with US troops from north near Dijon
12: Armistice signed between Romania & Allies
12/13: RAF incendiary raid on Frankfurt
12-16: 'Octagon' (Second Quebec) Conference between Churchill, Roosevelt & chiefs of staff: agree to start work on permanent United Nations organisation
13: US troops breach Siegfried Line
14: US troops enter Hürtgen Forest; heavy fighting to Dec 5
15: RAF Lancasters bomb *Tirpitz* in Kaafjord, Norway
15-19: US forces take Morotai, Molucca Islands
15-Oct 14: US forces take Peleliu, Palau Islands
16: Russian troops enter Sofia
17: US troops land on Angaur, south-west of Peleliu
17-26: Operation 'Market Garden': bridges at Veghel, Grave & Nijmegen in Netherlands captured, but only temporarily at Arnhem
18: 'Pluto' pipeline from Isle of Wight to Cherbourg operational
18/19: RAF incendiary raid on Bremerhaven
19: Brest falls to US troops. Armistice signed between Finland & Allies in Moscow
21: Canadians & Greeks enter Rimini
22: Tallinn, Estonia, falls to Russians. Soviet troops enter Yugoslavia
25-27: Withdrawal from Arnhem

OCTOBER 1944

1: Finns attack Germans
2: End of Warsaw uprising: Polish Home Army surrenders. US troops begin assault on Siegfried Line at Aachen
4: British landings in Greece
4-9: Germans raze Warsaw to ground
5: Russian offensive against Hungary & eastern Czechoslovakia begins
6: Canadian assault on Breskens Pocket, on Scheldt Estuary
7: Russians launch attack on German forces in northern Finland
9-20: Third Moscow Conference between Churchill & Stalin (with US ambassador representing USA): agree on postwar 'spheres of influence'
10: Red Army reaches Baltic north of Memel
10-29: Huge tank battle near Debrecen, central Hungary
12-14: Allied air attacks (from carriers) on Formosa
13: Riga, Latvia, falls to Russians: decisive point of liberation of Estonia and Latvia – eighth of USSR's ten victories of 1944. Germans launch V-1 & V-2 bombs against Antwerp. Athens occupied by British & Greek troops
14: Rommel commits suicide
14/15: RAF raid on Duisburg
15: Russians drive Germans from Petsamo, northern Finland; Germans withdraw to Kirkenes, Norway
15-16: Horthy announces Hungary's request for armistice terms; Hungarian government arrested by Germans
18: Creation of *Volkssturm* (German Home Guard): every able-bodied man 16-60 drafted to defend Germany. Stilwell recalled to Washington; replaced as Chiang Kai-shek's adviser by Wedemeyer
20: MacArthur & US troops land on Leyte, Philippines. Liberation of Belgrade by Tito's partisans & some Russian troops: high point of Russian campaign in Hungary, Czechoslovakia and Yugoslavia – ninth of USSR's ten victories of 1944
21: Germans surrender in Aachen
22: Canadian First Army completes occupation of Breskens Pocket
23-25: Naval Battle of Leyte Gulf, Philippines
25: Soviet troops capture Kirkenes, in Norway, rounding off Petsamo campaign – tenth of USSR's ten victories of 1944. Major *kamikaze* attack on US ships off Leyte Gulf.
28: Armistice signed by USSR & Bulgaria
30: Last use of Auschwitz gas chambers

NOVEMBER 1944

1: Canadian & British troops land on Walcheren island, in Scheldt Estuary
7: Roosevelt elected to fourth term as US president; Truman elected vice-president. Soviet master spy Sorge executed in Tokyo
8: Last Germans surrender on Walcheren
10: Japanese take US air bases at Liuchow & Kweilin in southern China
12: Sinking of *Tirpitz* in Tromsø Fiord by RAF bombers
16: US First & Ninth Armies open offensive to clear Roer plain; second US attack in Hürtgen Forest
19: US troops occupy Geilenkirchen
20: French troops reach the Rhine through 'Belfort Gap'
21: Tirane liberated by Albanian Resistance
22: Metz falls to US troops
23: French troops capture Strasbourg
24: First B-29 Superfortress raid on Tokyo from bases in Mariana Islands
26: Port of Antwerp opened for Allied shipping
27: End of fighting on Palau Islands
28: First Allied convoy docks at Antwerp; V-2 attacks on port intensify

DECEMBER 1944

3: Tokyo bombed. British Home Guard demobilised
4: Athens placed under martial law, as civil war breaks out. Allies establish bridgeheads across Chindwin river in Burma. Canadian troops enter Ravenna
5: End of fighting in Hürtgen Forest
7: US landing at Ormoc, Leyte
9: British Eighth Army suspends offensive in Italy
10: Fall of Ormoc on Leyte, Philippines, to US troops
12: British begin general advance in Arakan, Burma
15: US landings on Mindoro, Philippines. Bhamo, Burma, falls to Chinese troops
16: Germans launch offensive in the Ardennes – start of Battle of the Bulge
17: Massacre of US prisoners near Malmédy by SS troops of Kampfgruppe Peiper
18: B-29 daylight incendiary raid on dockyards at Hankow, China
22: US troops under McAuliffe encircled at Bastogne refuse German surrender terms
25: German Ardennes offensive halted
26: Budapest encircled by Red Army. Patton relieves troops at Bastogne
29: Hungary declares war on Germany

JANUARY 1945

1: Last major Luftwaffe attacks in the West, against Allied airfields in France, Belgium, Holland: 270 German planes lost. Germans launch Operation *Nordwind* against US Seventh Army in the Vosges
2: Germans counterattack to attempt relief of Budapest
2-8: *Kamikaze* attacks on US convoy approaching Lingayen Gulf
3-4: Germans try unsuccessfully to take Bastogne
4: Akyab, Burma, occupied by British
9: US landings at Lingayen Gulf on Luzon, Philippines
11: Pact ends fighting between Communists & Royalists in Greece
12: Opening of major Red Army offensive across the Vistula.
14: British Indian crossing of Irrawaddy north of Mandalay
16: Operation 'Blackcock': British & Canadian troops attack Roermond Triangle. US First & Third Armies link up at Houffalize to split 'Bulge' in the Ardennes
17: Warsaw falls to Red Army
19: Cracow, Lodz & Tarnow fall to Russians
20: LeMay takes command of Far East bombing offensive. Hungary signs armistice with Allies. French First Army attacks Colmar Pocket
26: Auschwitz liberated by Soviet troops. Elimination of Roermond Triangle. East Prussia sealed off as Soviet troops reach Gulf of Danzig near Elbing
27: Last Japanese troops driven from Ledo Road, reopening supply route from Burma to China
30/31: Liner *Wilhelm Gustloff* torpedoed off Gdynia – at least 5000 German civilians & soldiers killed
31: Red Army establishes bridgehead over Oder, less than 80 km (50 miles) from Berlin. Further US landings on west coast of Luzon

FEBRUARY 1945

2: Ecuador declares war on Axis
3: US forces reach Manila; start of month-long battle

FEBRUARY 1945 cont

4-11: Yalta Conference: second 'Big Three' summit between Churchill, Stalin & Roosevelt; Stalin agrees to enter war in Far East three months after Germany defeated; discussion of postwar Polish borders & government
8: Operation 'Veritable': Canadian & British troops launch offensive near Nijmegen to capture Reichswald area
8-Mar 4: Paraguay, Peru, Venezuela, Turkey, Uruguay, Egypt, Syria, Lebanon and Saudi Arabia declare war on Germany & Japan. Chile & Iran declare war on Japan. Finland declares war on Germany as from Sep 15, 1944
9: Ramree, Burma, falls to British. Colmar Pocket cleared by French forces
13: Armistice signed in Greece between government & Communist guerrillas. Budapest falls to Red Army
13-15: RAF & USAAF bombing raids cause firestorm in Dresden
14: British Indian forces cross Irrawaddy at Nyaungu
16-26: US troops take Corregidor, Philippines
19: US marines land on Iwo Jima after 72 day bombardment
22: Massive Allied air attacks on German transport lines
23: Operation 'Grenade': US troops launch drive towards Ruhr valley. German pocket at Poznan falls
25: First incendiary raid on Tokyo
28: US troops land on Palawan in south-west Philippines

MARCH 1945

2: Communist government set up in Romania. Trier falls to US troops. Further USAAF raid on Dresden
3: Manila falls to US & Filipino troops. British Indian forces take Meiktila, Burma
4: US bombers begin to use airfield on Iwo Jima; USAAF raid on Tokyo
6: British troops reach Mandalay, Burma
6-16: German offensive in Hungary to defend oilfields – last German offensive of war
7: US troops establish bridgehead across Rhine at Remagen. Cologne falls to Allies. Lashio, Burma, falls to Chinese/US troops
9/10: Incendiary bombing raid on Tokyo kills 84 000
10: Allies close up on Rhine at Wesel and Koblenz. US landings at Zamboanga on Mindanao, Philippines
11/12: USAAF incendiary raid on Nagoya
12: Red Army captures Küstrin on the Oder
13/14: Incendiary raid on Osaka
16/17: Incendiary raid on Kobe
18: US landings on Panay, Philippines
20: Mandalay, Burma, falls to Allies
21: Japanese launch offensive to seize US air bases at Laohokow & Ankang, in China
22: US Third Army makes second crossing of Rhine, at Nierstein. Kesselring replaces Rundstedt as Commander in Chief West
22/23: Patton's troops cross Rhine at Oppenheim
23/24: Allied troops under Montgomery cross Rhine around Wesel
25: US Third Army captures Darmstadt
26: End of fighting on Iwo Jima. US troops land on Cebu, Philippines
27: Allies capture Wiesbaden. Last V-2 attack on London. Argentina declares war on Axis powers
27-May 11: Heavy raids on airfields on Kyushu, southern Japan
28: Eisenhower orders Allied advance beyond Rhine to concentrate on central & southern Germany, leaving Berlin to Russians. Gdynia falls to Russians. Krebs replaces Guderian as German Chief of the Army General Staff
29: Frankfurt falls to US troops under Patton. Last V-1 attack on London. US landings on Negros island in Philippines
30: Danzig falls to Soviet troops

APRIL 1945

1: US troops land on Okinawa. US Ninth & First Armies meet, encircling Ruhr & over 300 000 German troops
1/2: In Italy, first part of Allied offensive launched around Lake Comacchio
2: Hungarian oilfields captured by Red Army
4: British troops capture Osnabrück. Patton & Hodges link up at Kassel
5: US troops cross Main at Würzburg. Japanese government resigns; Suzuki forms a new, less militant, cabinet
6: Start of mass *kamikaze* raids on Allied warships off Okinawa; 32 ships sunk, 368 damaged to Jul 30
6-13: Battle of Vienna between German & Soviet armies
7: Battle of East China Sea: Japanese giant battleship *Yamato* sunk
9: Main part of Allied spring offensive in northern Italy begins
10: US troops take Hanover. Germans surrender Königsberg to Red Army
11: US troops reach Elbe river near Magdeburg
12: Death of President Roosevelt; Truman takes over
13: US troops liberate Buchenwald concentration camp near Erfurt. Vienna captured by Red Army
15: British troops enter Belsen, US troops Nordhausen concentration camps. Arnhem liberated by Canadians
16: Beginning of Red Army offensive against Berlin. US troops reach Nuremberg; POW camp at Colditz Castle liberated
17: Main US landing on Mindanao in southern Philippines
18: US forces complete operations in Ruhr. Cebu secured by US troops. US forces enter Czechoslovakia
19: British troops reach Elbe at Lauenburg
20: Hitler celebrates 56th birthday
21: Allied forces in Italy break into Po Valley. Bologna falls to Polish troops of British Eighth Army
23: Himmler meets Count Bernadotte of Swedish Red Cross without Hitler's authority; offers surrender of German forces to Western Allies, but not to USSR. Göring offers to assume control as Hitler's designated successor; Hitler orders his arrest. US Fifth & British Eighth Armies reach the Po river
25: US & Soviet troops make contact at Torgau on the Elbe. Berlin surrounded by Soviet troops
25-Jun 26: San Francisco Conference attended by delegates from 50 nations complete Charter of United Nations
26: Mussolini captured by partisans near Lake Como. British enter Bremen
27: Britain & USA reject Himmler's offer of armistice
28: Mussolini killed by partisans
29: German commanders in Italy sign unconditional surrender, to take effect May 2. Heavy fighting in Berlin: German garrison is split into three pockets. US troops liberate Dachau concentration camp (near Munich)
29/30: US Seventh Army captures Munich
30: Hitler & Eva Braun commit suicide; Dönitz designated Hitler's successor. Red Army reaches Reichstag. Ceasefire in Netherlands to allow food deliveries to civilian population. Turin & Milan occupied by Allies

MAY 1945

1: Australian troops land on Tarakan, off Borneo. Hitler's death announced. Goebbels & family commit suicide
2: German troops in Italy surrender. British troops reach the Baltic at Wismar. Berlin commandant surrenders city to Russians. British amphibious attack on Rangoon
3: Last German resistance in Berlin liquidated by Soviet troops. Hamburg falls to British. Rangoon, Burma, taken by Indian troops
4: Japanese attempt offensive on Okinawa. US armies advancing from Italy & Austria link up in Brenner Pass. Salzburg & Innsbruck fall to US troops. German forces in north-west Europe sign surrender at Lüneburg Heath – to be effective May 5
5: Army Group E in Bavaria accepts Allied surrender terms: immediate ceasefire & formal surrender on May 6. British airborne troops land in Copenhagen. Resistance forces in Prague rise against the Germans
6: British forces from Mandalay link up with those from Rangoon
7: Unconditional surrender of all German forces to the Allies, signed at Eisenhower's HQ at Rheims, but some troops in Czechoslovakia, Austria & Croatia continue fighting. Breslau falls to Red Army after 82 day siege
8: VE Day. German surrender to USSR signed at Karlshorst. Last Japanese cleared from Leyte, Philippines. Allies land in Norway
9: Prague falls to Soviet troops. Germans surrender in Channel Islands
11: Australians take Wewak, last Japanese base in New Guinea. New US offensive on Okinawa. Last Germans in Austria & Czechoslovakia surrender
12: Crown Prince Olav, with members of government, return to Norway
18: Chinese occupy Foochow
20: Japanese begin pulling back from Chinese bases
23: German High Command & Provisional Government arrested at Flensburg. Himmler commits suicide after arrest by British
25: US invasion plan for Japan issued. Incendiary raid on Tokyo
28: William Joyce (Lord Haw Haw) captured near Flensburg

JUNE 1945

5: Allied Control Council assumes government of Germany
6: Brazil declares war on Japan
7: King Haakon returns to Norway
10: Australian troops land in Brunei Bay, west Borneo
14: Ribbentrop arrested in Hamburg
19: British & Indian troops invade Thailand from Burma
22: Capture of Okinawa completed by US Tenth Army
26: United Nations Charter signed by representatives of 50 Allied nations attending San Francisco Conference
30: Official end of Luzon campaign – but mopping up continues to war's end. Mindanao declared secure

JULY 1945

1: Australian troops land at Balikpapan, eastern Borneo
4: Four-power occupation of Berlin takes effect
5: General election in Britain; Churchill loses to Labour party, but result not announced until Jul 26. Death of Australian Prime Minister Curtin. Philippines declared liberated
10-18: Allied carrier-based aircraft mount massive attacks on Japan
16: First atomic bomb tested at Alamogordo, New Mexico. B-29 raids on Honshu & Kyushu
16-Aug 2: Potsdam Conference – third & last wartime summit – attended by Churchill (replaced by Attlee after election result), Stalin & Truman: agree on postwar division of Germany & reaffirm demand for unconditional surrender of Japan
23: Trial of Pétain opens in Paris
30: US heavy cruiser *Indianapolis* sunk by Japanese submarine after delivering atomic bomb parts to Saipan – last major Allied ship to be lost
31: Laval extradited from Spain; US troops hand him over to French Provisional Government

AUGUST 1945

6: First atomic bomb dropped on Hiroshima
8/9: USSR declares war on Japan
9: Second atomic bomb dropped on Nagasaki. Red Army invades Manchuria
10-15: Heavy air attacks on Tokyo
14: Pétain sentenced to death – later commuted to life imprisonment
15: Emperor Hirohito's radio broadcast, accepting Allied surrender terms. VJ (VP) Day

17: Indonesia (Dutch East Indies) declares independence
21: Truman orders lend-lease to end
23: US occupation troops land in Japan. Stalin announces Russian victory in Manchuria
30: British naval force arrives in Hong Kong to reoccupy colony

SEPTEMBER 1945

2: Japanese & Allies sign surrender agreement aboard USS *Missouri* in Tokyo Bay; Japanese troops in Philippines surrender. Vietnam (French Indochina) declares independence
5: British troops land in Singapore
9: Japanese surrender in China signed
11: British troops land in Indochina
12: Japanese forces in south-east Asia surrender to Mountbatten
29: British & Dutch forces land in Java

OCTOBER 1945

15: Execution of Laval
24: United Nations Organisation comes formally into existence. Execution of Quisling, Norwegian Nazi leader. Last Japanese forces in Burma surrender

NOVEMBER 1945

20-Sep 30, 1946: Nuremberg war crimes trial
29: Yugoslavia declared a 'Federal People's Republic'

1946

Jan 1: Japanese Emperor Hirohito disclaims divine status
Jan 10: First meeting of General Assembly of United Nations in London
Mar 5: Winston Churchill's 'Iron Curtain' speech at Fulton, Missouri
Mar 6-July 20, 1954: First Indochina War
Apr 10: Tokyo trial of major Japanese war criminals opens
Oct 16: Execution of principal German war criminals; Göring commits suicide just beforehand
Nov 3: New Japanese Constitution promulgated (effective May 3, 1947)

1947

Feb 10: Peace treaties signed by Allies with Italy, Romania, Bulgaria, Finland, Hungary
Jun 5: Marshall Plan for European recovery proposed
Jul 4: Philippines granted full independence
Aug 15: India & Pakistan granted independence

1948

Feb 25: Communist coup in Czechoslovakia
Mar 17: Brussels Treaty, signed by United Kingdom, France, Belgium, Netherlands & Luxembourg, leads to formation of Western European Union
May 14: Creation of Israel
Jul 24: Soviet blockade of West Berlin begins
Jul 26-Sep 30, 1949: Berlin airlift overcomes Soviet blockade
Dec 23: Execution of principal Japanese war criminals

1949

Apr 4: North Atlantic Treaty signed by USA, Britain, France, Italy, Belgium, Netherlands, Luxembourg, Portugal, Denmark, Norway, Iceland & Canada in Washington – creation of NATO
May 23: Federal Republic of Germany (West Germany) comes into existence
Jul 14: First Soviet atomic test
Oct 1: People's Republic of China officially proclaimed in Peking
Oct 7: German Democratic Republic (East Germany) established
Dec 27: Indonesia granted independence from Netherlands
Dec 30: France grants independence to Vietnam (formerly Indochina)

1950

Jun 25-Jul 27, 1953: Korean War

1955

May 14: Creation of Warsaw Pact
May 15: Austrian State Treaty: Soviet withdrawal from Austria; Austria neutral

Human cost of the war

During six years of fighting, some 24 million sevice personnel, Allied and Axis, were killed. Even more civilians – perhaps more than 40 million – died in fighting on the ground or in bombing raids, in forced-labour or extermination camps, of starvation or disease, or executed as hostages or partisans.

In Europe, the Eastern Front saw the heaviest losses, both military and civilian. Brutal treatment of local populations – especially Jews – by their own governments swelled the numbers. The military losses of the Italians were almost equally of fighters for the Axis and for the Allies. Luxembourg's fighters were almost all forced to serve in the German Army – and a quarter deserted.

The armed forces of Poland were at peak size before the German blitzkrieg of September 1939. A Polish army-in-exile grew first in France, then in Britain, numbering over 100 000 by 1942 and over double that by the end of the war. The French story was similar. The armed forces were at peak size before the German occupation of June 1940. By December that year, a Free French force of 35 000 had formed, which doubled by mid-1942 and swelled to well over 300 000 by the war's end.

In the Philippines, a US possession, 11 000 Philippine Scouts were part of the US Army and more than 160 000 Filipinos fought in the Philippine Army. No reliable records exist, but some claim a million Filipinos, soldiers and civilians, died at Japanese hands.

The numbers of armed forces wounded listed in the chart gives only an indication of what the troops suffered, not an accurate count. The wounds recorded might vary from slight to permanently disabling. Some people were injured more than once, or died subsequently and were recorded among both wounded and dead.

Country	Approx wartime population	Peak size of armed forces	Total armed forces killed/missing	Total armed forces wounded	Total civilians killed/missing
Australia	7.1 million	680 000	34 000	181 000	Under 100
Belgium	8.1 million	800 000	10 000	15 000	90 000
Brazil	41.4 million	200 000	1000	4000	None recorded
Britain	47.8 million	4.7 million	420 000†	377 000‡	70 000
Bulgaria	6.7 million	450 000	19 000	22 000	Not known, but large number
Canada	11.4 million	780 000	43 000	53 000	None recorded
China	541 million	5 million	1.5 million	2 million	Enormous number, perhaps 20 million
Czechoslovakia	15.2 million	180 000	7000	8000	310 000
Denmark	4 million	15 000	4000	Not known	3000
Finland	3.9 million	250 000	79 000	50 000	11 000
France	41.9 million	5 million	245 000	390 000	173 000
Germany*	79.4 million	10 million	3.5 million	2 million	2 million
Greece	7.2 million	150 000	17 000	47 000	391 000
Hungary	14 million	350 000	147 000	Not known	280 000
India	388.8 million	2.4 million	48 000	65 000	None recorded
Italy*	45.4 million	4.5 million	380 000	225 000	180 000
Japan*	73.1 million	6 million	2.6 million	326 000	953 000
Luxembourg	297 000	12 000	2000	Not known	5000
Netherlands	9 million	500 000	14 000	2000	242 000
New Zealand	1.7 million	157 000	12 000	16 000	None recorded
Norway	3 million	25 000	5000	400	8000
Poland	35 million	1 million	600 000	530 000	6 million
Romania	20 million	600 000	73 000	49 000	465 000
South Africa	10.7 million	140 000	9000	15 000	None recorded
USA	132 million	16.4 million	292 000	675 000	Under 10
USSR*	193 million	20 million	13.6 million	5 million	7.7 million
Yugoslavia	16.3 million	3.7 million	305 000	425 000	1.4 million

* Figures include colonial, annexed or mandated territories; German figures include Austria.
† Includes 22 000 colonial forces killed; ‡ includes 7000 colonial forces wounded (both excluding India).

Glossary

air force USAAF equivalent of an army.
air group The full complement of planes stationed on an aircraft carrier.
Allies Powers opposed to Germany, Italy and Japan – chiefly Britain, its Empire and Dominions, France (until 1940 and after 1944), China, and the USSR and USA (from 1941).
armoured Of vehicles, covered with protective armour; of army units, equipped with armoured vehicles.
artillery Large-calibre ground-based guns, including cannon and howitzers.
Axis Powers allied to Germany – chiefly Italy (until 1943) and Japan.
banzai '[May you live] 1000 years!' – Japanese war cry or patriotic cheer.
bar Insignia added to a medal – usually a bar across the ribbon – showing that it has been won a second time.
battlecruiser Warship of battleship size, but with less heavy armour and speed of a cruiser.
battle group Naval task force led by a battleship or battlecruiser.
battleship Largest type of warship, usually of at least 30 000 tonnes, with the largest and greatest number of guns, and clad with the heaviest armour.
beach-head Position on enemy shoreline captured by advance troops.
BEF British Expeditionary Force, sent to France 1939-40.
bombardier USAAF bomb-aimer; British artillery corporal.
Bomber Command Arm of the RAF operating bombers; in the USAAF, a bomber unit equivalent to a corps.
bridgehead Position captured on the enemy's side of a river or pass.
cannon Any large-calibre artillery piece; also an automatic gun (eg, in an aircraft) firing shells rather than bullets.
capital ship Warship (eg, battleship or aircraft carrier) of the largest class.
carbine Light rifle with short barrel.
carrier group Naval task force led by a fleet carrier.
chief of staff Senior staff officer of a formation. *Chief of Staff:* the most senior staff officer of an armed service.
Chief of the Imperial General Staff (CIGS) Chief of Staff of the armed forces of Britain, its Empire and Dominions.
Combined Chiefs of Staff Committee of senior US and British chiefs of staff.
commander in chief Supreme commander of a major force.
Commando British unit trained for amphibious raids against enemy territory.
corvette Small, lightly armed warship used mainly as convoy escort.
creeping barrage Artillery barrage whose point of aim moves forward.
cruiser Fast, long-range warship, usually of 4-15 000 tonnes, with less armour and firepower than a battleship.
cruiser tank Fast tank designed to chase and engage enemy tanks.
depth charge Explosive charge that detonates at a pre-set depth of water.
destroyer Highly manoeuvrable medium-sized warship armed with guns, torpedoes and depth charges.
detachment Unit of troops or ships separated and sent on a special task.
DFC Distinguished Flying Cross.
DSO Distinguished Service Order.
Duce, Il 'The Leader': Mussolini's title.
E-boat German torpedo boat.
elevator On aircraft carrier, lift to move aircraft between hangars and flight deck.
escort carrier Small aircraft carrier providing air cover for convoys.
field gun Mobile artillery weapon.
Fighter Command Arm of the RAF operating fighter aircraft; in the USAAF, a fighter unit equivalent to a corps.
fire control computer Mechanical device controlling the aiming and firing of guns, particularly on warships.
flagship Headquarters ship of a fleet or squadron commander.
flak Bursting anti-aircraft shells; also German anti-aircraft artillery.
Fleet Air Arm Royal Navy's air arm.
fleet carrier Largest type of carrier.
flight Air force unit, part of a squadron, consisting of four or more aircraft.
frigate Ship smaller than a destroyer in Royal Navy but larger in US Navy.
front Most forward line of a combat force; also, Soviet army group.
Führer, Der 'The Leader': Hitler's title.
Gauleiter Nazi district governor.
GC George Cross: Highest British civilian decoration for gallantry.
Gestapo *Geheime Staatspolizei* ('Secret State Police'): German secret police.
GI US serviceman, usually a soldier.
group RAF administrative unit covering a particular area.
hara-kiri Japanese ritual suicide by disembowelment, also called *seppuku.*
HMAS His Majesty's Australian Ship – ie, Royal Australian Navy ship.
HMS His Majesty's Ship – ie, Royal Navy ship.
hollow charge Shaped explosive charge designed to pierce armour.
howitzer Heavy gun that fires shells at a high angle.
hull down Of a tank, dug in so that only the turret shows.
Imperial Navy Japanese Navy.
infantry tank Heavily armoured tank designed to support infantry attacks.
Iron Cross German military decoration, awarded in eight classes under the Nazis: Great Cross of the Iron Cross (given only to Göring); Knight's Cross of the Iron Cross with Golden Oak Leaves, Swords and Diamonds, with Oak Leaves, Swords and Diamonds, with Oak Leaves and Swords, and with Oak Leaves; Knight's Cross of the Iron Cross; and Iron Cross, 1st Class and 2nd Class.
Joint Chiefs of Staff Committee of senior US Army and Navy chiefs of staff.
kamikaze Japanese suicide pilot/plane.
Kampfgruppe 'Combat group': Specialist Luftwaffe (eg, pathfinder) or German Army unit.
Knight's Cross See *Iron Cross.*
Kriegsmarine German Navy.
landing circle Queue of aircraft circling to land on a carrier.
landing craft Flat-bottomed ship, opening at one end, for amphibious landing of troops and/or equipment.
landing ship Assault ship for carrying troops and equipment long distances.
Légion d'Honneur High French military and civilian decoration.
Luftflotte 'Air fleet': Luftwaffe arm roughly equivalent to a USAAF air force.
Luftwaffe German Air Force.
machine gun Automatic gun that fires repeatedly and rapidly.
machine pistol Repeat-firing pistol.
MC Military Cross.
mechanised Of army unit, equipped with motor and/or armoured vehicles.
Medal of Honor Highest US military decoration for bravery.
mine Explosive device designed to destroy ships, vehicles or men, laid under water or (land mine) just underground.
minesweeper Ship for destroying, removing or neutralising mines.
MM Military Medal.
mortar Muzzle-loaded weapon, usually portable, used to fire shells at short range.
MTB (British) Motor Torpedo Boat.
NCO Non-commissioned officer: Serviceman above the rank of private but below warrant officer – eg, sergeant.
OKH *Oberkommando des Heeres:* German Army high command.
OKW *Oberkommando der Wehrmacht:* German armed forces high command.
order of battle Disposition of a military force, its organisation, weaponry, etc.
panzer General term for German tank or armoured unit, from *Panzerkampfwagen* ('armoured fighting vehicle').
panzergrenadier Mechanised infantryman serving with a panzer unit.
para Paratroop; battalion of paratroops.
partisan Member of an armed resistance group in occupied territory.
petty officer Naval equivalent of warrant officer.
pom-pom Rapid-firing automatic anti-aircraft cannon.
proximity fuse Electronic device that detonates a shell etc near its target.
PT-boat (US) Patrol Torpedo boat.
RAAF Royal Australian Air Force.
RAF Royal Air Force.
Red Air Force Soviet Air Force.
Red Army Soviet Army.
Regia Aeronautica Italian Air Force.
regimental combat team US unit consisting of elements of all arms put together for a specific mission.
Reich 'Empire': Nazi Germany, or the whole area it regarded as 'home' territory.
RN Royal Navy.
salient Part of a front line that bulges.
samurai Member of traditional Japanese warrior caste.
sapper Military engineer.
sloop British convoy-escort warship, smaller than a corvette.
sortie Single attack or operation by an aircraft or small army unit; one aircraft may make several sorties in a day.
squadron Air force unit, consisting of two or more flights, usually totalling 10-20 aircraft; or a subdivision of a fleet; also an armoured army unit equivalent to a company.
staff officer Officer aiding a commander but not taking part in combat.
star shell Artillery shell that explodes in mid-air with a shower of lights.
Stavka Soviet high command.
strafe Attack ground targets from the air with machine-gun fire, rockets or bombs.
submachine gun Lightweight machine gun fired from the shoulder or hip.
Third Reich Name give to the period of Nazi rule in Germany (1933-45). The First Reich was the Holy Roman Empire (9th century to 1806), the Second Reich the empire of the Kaisers (1871-1919).
torpedo boat Fast naval boat equipped to launch torpedoes.
U-boat German submarine.
USAAF United States Army Air Force.
USMC United States Marine Corps.
USN United States Navy.
USS US Ship – ie, US Navy vessel.
VC Victoria Cross: Highest British decoration for gallantry in action.
WAAF Women's Auxiliary Air Force.
Waffen-SS 'Armed SS': Combat arm of the SS – part of Nazi party.
warrant officer Officer without a commission, but holding a warrant and above NCO rank – eg, sergeant major.
Wehrmacht German armed forces other than the Waffen-SS.
wing Air force unit consisting of three to five squadrons.
WRNS Women's Royal Naval Service.

Army formations

Main groupings are listed here in descending order of size, with approximate number of men (varies very widely) and usual rank of commander.

army group A number of armies grouped together – often over a million men – under a field marshal or general; called 'front' in Soviet Army.
army A number of corps – usually 250-450 000 men – under a general or lieutenant general.
corps A number of divisions – usually 75-150 000 men – under a lieutenant/major general.
division A number of brigades – usually 9-20 000 men – under a major general.
brigade A number of regiments or battalions – usually 4-8000 men – under a brigadier or brigadier general.
regiment A number of battalions – usually 2-3000 men – under a colonel. (In the British Army, a regiment is an administrative, not field, unit.)
battalion Mainly infantry formation – usually 600-1000 men – under a lieutenant colonel; organised in companies.
company Group of soldiers – usually 100-150 men – under a major or captain; called 'squadron' in some units; organised into platoons.
platoon Group of soldiers – usually 25-30 men – under a junior officer; called 'troop' in some units.
section Smallest tactical fighting formation – usually 8-10 men – under an NCO; called 'squad' in US Army.

Index

Page numbers in *italics* refer to captions and boxes.

A

B

E

F

G

H

N

S

T

ACKNOWLEDGMENTS

The illustrations in *The World at Arms* were supplied by the following sources. Names printed in *italics* refer to work commissioned by Reader's Digest. Where ambiguous, the position of an illustration on the page is indicated by letters in brackets.
Abbreviations: T = top; C = centre; B = bottom; L = left; R = right; IWM = Imperial War Museum; * = from private collection.

Inside front cover: Hulton Deutsch Collection. 1 US Army*. 2-3 Camera Press/IWM. 4 (TC) Popperfoto; (CR) Associated Press; (rest) IWM. 5 (TR) Popperfoto; (rest) IWM. 6 (TC) Suddeutscher Verlag; (CR) © 1943 The Curtis Publishing Company/printed by permission of the Estate of Norman Rockwell – copyright © 1943 Estate of Norman Rockwell; (rest) IWM. 8-9 *Gary Hincks*. 10 Hulton Deutsch Collection. 11-12 Suddeutscher Verlag. 13 (BL) *Paul Hannon*; (BR) Hulton Deutsch Collection. 14 (BC) Hulton Deutsch Collection; (BR) Bundesarchiv. 15 (Hitler reading) Hulton Deutsch Collection; (rest) Bundesarchiv. 16 Bundesarchiv. 17 (L) Bundesarchiv; (TR) Hulton Deutsch Collection. 18 (TR) Suddeutscher Verlag; (BL) Bundesarchiv. 19 (BC) John Frost Historical Newspaper Service; (rest) Suddeutscher Verlag. 21 Hulton Deutsch Collection. 22 (BL) Suddeutscher Verlag; (BR) Bundesarchiv. 23 (TR) *Paul Hannon*; (CL) Associated Press; (rest) Bundesarchiv. 24 (TR) *Eugene Fleury*; (CR) Bundesarchiv. 25 Hulton Deutsch Collection. 27 (BC) Australian War Memorial, no. 42817; (rest) Hulton Deutsch Collection. 28 (TL) Associated Press; (BL) by permission of International Music Publications/John Frost Historical Newspaper Service; (rest) IWM. 29 (BL) Popperfoto; (BC) *Paul Hannon*; (BR) Lehtikuva Oy. 30 Suddeutscher Verlag. 31 (photo) IWM; (map) *Eugene Fleury*. 33 Hulton Deutsch Collection. 34 (CL) IWM; (rest) Hulton Deutsch Collection. 35 *Paul Hannon*. 36 Suddeutscher Verlag. 37 (TL) *Malcolm Porter*; (BC) *Paul Hannon*. 38 (TR) Bundesarchiv; (BL) Suddeutscher Verlag; (BR) IWM. 40 (main picture) Associated Press; (BL) Popperfoto; (BR) 'Daily Mirror'/Syndication International/John Frost Newspaper Collection. 41 (BR) IWM. 42 (TL) Suddeutscher Verlag; (TR) National Archives*. 43 (BL) Hulton Deutsch Collection; (BR) Robert Hunt Library. 44 Hulton Deutsch Collection. 45 (BL) *Paul Hannon*; (BR) *Malcolm Porter*. 46 (TL) John Batchelor; (TCL) *Mick Gillah*; (BCL) John Batchelor; (BL) *Mick Gillah*. 46-47 (main picture) Hulton Deutsch Collection; (inset) IWM. 48 (TL) Camera Press/IWM; (C) Robert Hunt Library/IWM; (B) *Malcolm Porter*. 49 (CR) Bundesarchiv; (rest) IWM. 50-51 (B) Wing Commander T.F. Neil; (rest) IWM. 52-53 (diorama) Marshall Editions; (rest) Hulton Deutsch Collection. 54 (TL) Ullstein; (BR) John Frost Historical Newspaper Service. 55 Popperfoto. 56-57 Hulton Deutsch Collection. 59 IWM. 60-61 (BL) *Paul Hannon*; (C) Suddeutscher Verlag; (rest) Bundesarchiv. 62 (TR) IWM; (BR) John Batchelor. 64 UPI/Bettmann Newsphotos. 66 (CL) Associated Press; (diorama) Marshall Editions; (rest) IWM. 68-69 IWM. 70-71 (main picture) Hulton Deutsch Collection; (rest) IWM. 72-73 Keystone, Paris. 74 (TR) John Batchelor; (BL) IWM. 75 (TR) IWM; (BL) *Paul Hannon*. 76 (TR) *Eugene Fleury*; (CL) Farabola; (BL) IWM. 77 (TR) *Eugene Fleury*; (BR) IWM. 78 IWM. 80 (BL) Farabola; (BR) *Eugene Fleury*. 81 (TR) Farabola; (TL) Associated Press; (BL) private collection. 82 IWM. 83 Bundesarchiv. 84 (CR) Bundesarchiv; (BL) *Paul Hannon*. 85 (TR) *Malcolm Porter*; (CR) Bundesarchiv; (BL) IWM. 86 (TC) *Paul Hannon*; (BC) Hancock & Co; (BR) IWM. 87 (BL) Bundesarchiv/Manolis Korellis; (rest) IWM. 88 (BL) Suddeutscher Verlag; (BR) *Paul Hannon*. 89 Suddeutscher Verlag. 90 (T) *Malcolm Porter*; (BC) IWM. 91 (CR) Hulton Deutsch Collection; (rest) IWM. 92 (BR) *Paul Hannon*; (rest) IWM. 93 IWM. 94 (main picture) Bundesarchiv; (inset) IWM. 95 IWM. 96 (BR) *Paul Hannon*; (rest) IWM. 97 (TR) IWM; (BL) *Paul Hannon*. 98-99 (medal) Spink & Son Ltd; (rest) IWM. 100 IWM*. 101 (TR) *Malcolm Porter*; (BC) 'Daily Express'/John Frost Historical Newspaper Service; (rest) Bundesarchiv. 103 (TR) *Malcolm Porter*; (BL) IWM. 104 Bundesarchiv. 105 Topham Picture Library. 106 *Malcolm Porter*. 108-9 (TL) *Paul Hannon*; (BC) Tass; (rest) Novosti. 110 *Paul Hannon*. 111 (C) IWM; (BR) John Batchelor. 112 *Eugene Fleury*. 113 (BR) IWM; (rest) Tass. 114 Novosti. 115 (TL) J. Piekalkiewicz; (rest) Bundesarchiv. 117 National Archives*. 118 Novosti. 119 *Paul Hannon*. 120-1 (main picture) Bibliothek fur Zeitgeschichte; (inset) Hulton Deutsch Collection. 122 (BL) *Eugene Fleury*; (BR) IWM. 123 (CR) *Paul Hannon*; (BR) John Batchelor. 124 IWM. 125 *Eugene Fleury*. 127 (T) Novosti; (CL) Bundesarchiv. 128-9 *Gary Hincks*. 130-1 Private collection. 132 (B) Mainichi Newspapers; (CR) National Archives*. 133 (BL) US Air Force; (BR) private collection. 134 IWM. 135 (TL) *Eugene Fleury*; (CR) IWM. 136-7 National Archives*. 138-9 (diorama) *Ivan Lapper*; (TL) National Archives*; (TR) *Eugene Fleury*. 141 (TR) *Paul Hannon*; (BL) US Army. 143 IWM. 144 *Malcolm Porter*. 145 IWM. 146 US Army*. 147 *Eugene Fleury*. 148 UPI/Bettmann Newsphotos. 149 (TL) *Paul Hannon*; (CR) UPI/Bettmann Newsphotos; (B) Hulton Deutsch Collection. 150 *Malcolm Porter*. 151 Mainichi Newspapers. 153 *Malcolm Porter*. 154-5 (BR) IWM; (rest) private collection. 156 Australian War Memorial; no. 13190. 157 IWM. 158 National Archives. 160 (TL) National Archives/Navy Department*; (rest) US Air Force*. 161 National Archives. 162-3 (TL) *Malcolm Porter*; (B) National Archives*; (TR) *Paul Hannon*; (medal) IWM/Eileen Tweedy. 165 (TR) National Archives/US Air Force; (CL) National Archives; (B) Marshall Editions. 166-7 (TL) National Archives*; (TC) IWM; (TR) National Archives/Naval History; (rest) National Archives. 168 *Paul Hannon*. 169 (panorama) *Malcolm Porter*; (rest) Australian War Memorial, nos. 13755, 13971, 14028 & 26854. 170 Australian War Memorial*, no. 14211. 171 (CR) Australian War Memorial*, no. 14002; (BL) Australian War Memorial*, no. 13754/21. 172-3 (TC) US Army*; (TR) IWM Department of Documents; (BL) Associated Press; (BR) Australian War Memorial, no. 15429; (rest) IWM. 175 (C) Mrs J. Rayfield; (BL) IWM; (rest) Hulton Deutsch Collection. 176 (C) Macdonald Publishers; (CL) 'Daily Mirror'/Syndication International/John Frost Newspaper Collection; (CR) Hulton Deutsch Collection; (George Formby) Associated Press; (rest) IWM Department of Documents/Chris Barker. 177 (TC, TR) D.C. Thompson Publishers/Dennis Gifford; (C) Hulton Deutsch Collection; (BR) E.T. Archive; (rest) IWM. 178 (CL) Australian War Memorial, no. 3393; (BL) Africana Museum; (BR) National Film Archive. 179 UPI/Bettmann Newsphotos. 180 (TC) Popperfoto; (TR) by permission of International Music Publications/Denis Gifford; (rest) Hulton Deustch Collection. 181 (TR) IWM; (C) Hulton Deutsch Collection; (BR) UPI/Bettmann Newsphotos. 182 (CR) Macdonald Publishers; (BR) Suddeutscher Verlag. 183 (BC) Ullstein; (BR) Suddeutscher Verlag. 184 Hulton Deutsch Collection. 186 Editions Tallandier. 187 (B) Bibliothek für Zeitgeschichte; (rest) Roger Schall. 188 ADN-ZB. 189 Bundesarchiv. 190 (TR) Ullstein; (rest) Wiener Library/Chris Barker. 191 (TL) Wiener Library/Chris Barker; (TR) Robert Hunt Library; (BL) Bundesarchiv; (BR) Robert Hunt Library/Bundesarchiv. 192-3 (TL) copyright © 1988 by Cosmopress Geneva & Anne Frank-Fonds; (rest) Wiener Library. 194 (BL) Topham Picture Library; (rest) John Hillelson/Erich Lessing/Magnum. 195 (CR) J. Piekalkiewicz; (BR) IWM/Chris Barker. 196 IWM. 197 Novosti. 198 Ron Baybutt/Johannes Lange. 199 (TC) Camera Press; (CC) Associated Press; (BC) IWM; (rest) Ron Baybutt/Johannes Lange. 200 Suddeutscher Verlag. 201 Australian War Memorial, nos. 19199 & 132935. 202 (BC) Colorific/'Life' copyright © Time Inc, 1942; (rest) IWM. 203 (TL) IWM; (TR) Royal Commonwealth Society; (CR) Chuang-hui-tsuan Collection. 204 Mainichi Newspapers. 205 (BC) Bundesarchiv; (BR) Robert Hunt Library. 206 (CR) The Auckland Collection; (rest) 'Daily Mirror'/Syndication International/John Frost Newspaper Collection. 207 (BL) Takizo Sata; (BC) Tass. 208 (C) National Film Archive; (rest) The Kobal Collection. 209 (T) The Ronald Grant Archive/still from the film 'In Which We Serve' by courtesy of The Rank Organisation Plc; (CR) Library of Congress/still from the film 'Jew Süss' by courtesy of The Rank Organisation Plc; (C) The Kobal Collection. 210 (BL) Library of Congress; (rest) The Museum of Modern Art Stills Archive. 213 Popperfoto. 214 (BL) Bundesarchiv; (BR) Colonel Otto Wagner. 215 Frau Elyesa Bazna. 217 (BL) Private collection; (BR) Toftunislap Pgrabiska, Warsaw. 218 (BL) 'Daily Mirror'/Syndication International; (BR) National Archives. 219 (C) Trustees of the Science Museum, no. 186-80 (Crown Copyright); (BR) Smithsonian Institution. 220-1 *Gary Hincks*. 222-3 IWM. 224 (TR) IWM; (BR) Bundesarchiv. 225 John Batchelor. 226-7 (BL) Bundesarchiv; (diorama) Marshall Editions; (map) *Eugene Fleury*; (rest) IWM. 228-9 (main picture) Popperfoto; (map) *Eugene Fleury*; (rest) IWM. 231 IWM. 232 (CR) Hulton Deutsch Collection; (BL) IWM. 233 (TL) Suddeutscher Verlag; (CR) IWM. 234-5 (BC) *Paul Hannon*; (rest) IWM. 236 *Eugene Fleury*. 237 IWM. 238 Tass. 239 *Malcolm Porter*. 240 Hulton Deutsch Collection. 241 *Malcolm Porter*. 242-3 (TL) Bundesarchiv; (TR) IWM. 245 Hulton Deutsch Collection. 246-7 (BL) Tass; (main picture) Suddeutscher Verlag; (insets) Ullstein; (BR) Robert Hunt Library. 248 Novosti. 249 (T) Novosti; (C) Marshall Editions; (BL) *Eugene Fleury*. 250 Novosti. 251 *Malcolm Porter*. 252 IWM. 253 (TR) John Batchelor; (BL) Bundesarchiv. 254-5 (main picture) Public Archives of Canada*; (TR) IWM; (rest) National Archives. 256 Popperfoto. 257 (TR) *Paul Hannon*; (rest) IWM. 258 (B) John Batchelor; (rest) IWM. 259 IWM. 260 John Batchelor. 261 (T) Associated Press; (CR) IWM. 262 IWM. 263 (T) IWM; (CR) Crown Copyright/reproduced by permission of RSRE; (BR) BBC/David Ashby. 264 Associated Press. 265 (TR) John Batchelor; (B) IWM. 266 (TR) *Paul Hannon*; (BL) Robert Hunt Library; (BC) IWM; (BR) IWM Department of Documents/Chris Barker. 267 Carl Werner Schmidt-Luchs, Hamburg. 268 US Air Force*. 269 (BR) *Paul Hannon*; (rest) US Air Force*. 270-1 (BL) Smithsonian Institution; (C) IWM. 272 IWM. 273 (TL) Gary M. Valant/Confederate Air Force Museum, Harlingen, Texas; (TC) Popperfoto; (rest) John Batchelor. 274 (TR) *Eugene Fleury*; (B) IWM. 275 IWM. 276 (T) UPI/Bettmann Newsphotos; (C) IWM. 277 (BC) National Archives*; (BR) Bundesarchiv. 279 (TL) US Army*; (B) IWM. 280-1 (TR) US Army*; (rest) IWM. 282-3 *Malcolm Porter*. 284-5 (main picture) US Army*; (map) *Malcolm Porter*; (BC) IWM; (leaflets) The Auckland Collection. 286 (TR) *Malcolm McGregor*; (rest) The Auckland Collection. 287 (TL) IWM; (TR) W.H. Agnew/Public Archives of Canada/DND/PA-136204; (CL) Bundesarchiv. 288-9 (C) Hulton Deutsch Collection; (rest) IWM. 290 IWM. 291 (TR) *Paul Hannon*; (B) IWM. 293 (TR) 'Dieppe Raid' by Charles Fraser Comfort/Canadian War Museum/National Museums of Canada/12276; (B) Bundesarchiv. 294 IWM. 295 John Batchelor. 296 Bundesarchiv. 297 (C) Popperfoto; (BR) IWM. 298-9 IWM. 300-1 (panorama & map) *Malcolm Porter*; (figures) *Paul Hannon*; (BC) Robert Capa/Magnum Photos; (TR) US Army*. 302-3 IWM. 304-5 (C) IWM; (BR) Robert Hunt Library. 306 *Eugene Fleury*. 307 IWM. 308 IWM. 309 (TR) US Air Force*; (B) Popperfoto. 310-11 (photo) National Archives of Canada*; (map) *Eugene Fleury*. 312 US Army*. 313 *Paul Hannon*. 314 US Army*. 315 IWM; (C) Robert Capa/Magnum Photos. 316 *Paul Hannon*. 317 (photo) IWM; (maps) *Eugene Fleury*. 318-19 (diorama) Marshall Editions; (BR) Robert Hunt Library/IWM; (rest) IWM. 320-1 IWM. 322 (BL) IWM; (BR) Suddeustcher Verlag. 323 *Eugene Fleury*. 324 *Eugene Fleury*. 325 (BR) National Archives; (rest) US Army*. 326-7 (TL) National Archives; (BL) Bundesarchiv; (TR) US Army*; (CR) IWM. 328 (BL) Bundesarchiv; (BR) IWM. 329-30 IWM. 331 Novosti. 332 Bundesarchiv. 333 *Eugene Fleury*. 334 IWM. 335 (TR) National Archives; (CR) Robert Hunt Library/IWM. 337 Novosti. 338 (TL) *Eugene Fleury*; (BR) *Paul Hannon*. 339 (BC) IWM; (figure) *Paul Hannon*; (BR) Novosti. 340 Bundesarchiv. 342-3 IWM. 344-5 *Gary Hincks*. 346 *Paul Hannon*. 348-9 (main picture) US Marine Corps*; (inset) US Army*. 350 *Malcolm Porter*. 351 (TR) *Malcolm Porter*; (BL) IWM. 352 (TL) US Army*; (B) National Archives*. 353 (TL) Associated Press; (BR) IWM. 354 (CR) IWM; (BL) John F. Kennedy Library. 355 IWM*. 356 (T) *Eugene Fleury*; (BR) US Air Force*. 358 Australian War Memorial*, nos. 16020 & 16983. 359 (BL) *Paul Hannon*; (BR) US Navy*. 360-1 US Marine Corps*. 362 US Coast Guard*. 363 (C) US Army*; (BL) National Archives*. 364 IWM. 365 National Archives*. 366-7 National Archives. 369 (TL) National Archives*; (TR) *Paul Hannon*; (B) US Marine Corps*. 370-1 National Archives*. 372 Robert Hunt Library/US Army. 373 *Paul Hannon*. 374 *Malcolm Porter*. 375 *Paul Hannon*. 376-7 (TL) National Archives; (TR) private collection; (diorama) *Ivan Lapper*; (BL) *Paul Hannon*. 378-9 (TL, TC) US Army*; (BR) National Archives*. 380 *Malcolm Porter*. 381-2 National Archives. 384 National Archives*. 385 (TL) *Malcolm Porter*; (BC) *Paul Hannon*. 386 *Malcolm Porter*. 387-9 IWM. 390 (CR) US Air Force*; (BR) John Batchelor. 392 IWM. 393 US Army*. 394-5 (TL) Hulton Deutsch Collection; (TR) US Army*. 396-7 (CL) *Malcolm Porter*; (CR) IWM; (CB) private collection. 398 *Paul Hannon*. 399 Marshall Editions. 400 *Malcolm Porter*. 401 IWM. 402 US Army*. 403 (TR) IWM; (CL) US Army*; (BL) *Paul Hannon*. 404-5 (L) Tass; (BC) US Air Force*; (L) US Army*. 406 *Malcolm Porter*. 407 (TR) Pictorial Press; (BL) Bundesarchiv. 408 (R) Suddeutscher Verlag; (BL) *Paul Hannon*. 410 IWM. 411-12 US Army*. 413 John Hillelson/Robert Capa/Magnum Photos. 414 (TL) US Army*; (BC) Kryn Taconis/National Archives of Canada/PA-164611. 415 *Eugene Fleury*. 416 (TL) Editions Tallandier; (TR) Hulton Deutsch Collection. 417 (CR) US Army*; (BR) IWM. 418 (TC) National Archives*; (BR) F. Goldsworthy. 419 *Eugene Fleury*. 420-1 (main picture) Novosti; (TR) Pictorial Press; (BR) Ullstein. 422 (TR) Tass; (B) Marshall Editions. 423 Tass. 424 (CL) National Archives; (BL) 'Daily Mail'/John Frost Historical Newspaper Service. 425 (TR) National Archives*; (BL) IWM. 426 (TC) Associated Press*; (BR) Hulton Deutsch Collection. 427 Topham Picture Library. 428-9 (BL) National Archives*; (BC) Marshall Editions; (rest) US Marine Corps. 430 (TR) Robert Hunt Library; (CL) Smithsonian Institution. 431 *Malcolm Porter*. 432-3 (main picture) US Army*; (TR) IWM; (rest) US Marine Corps. 434 John Batchelor. 435 National Archives. 437 (TL) US Air Force*; (TC) Black Star, New York; (TR) *Malcolm Porter*; (CR) Koyo Ishikawa. 438 IWM. 439 (main picture) US Air Force*; (BR) US Army*. 440 (figures) Yosuke Yamahata; (rest) US Army*. 441 (TC) US Army*; (TR) UPI/Bettmann Newsphotos. 442 US Air Force. 443-4 US Army*. 445 (TC) The Herald & Weekly Times Ltd, Melbourne, Australia; (TR) West Australian Newspapers Ltd; (BC) Colorific/Alfred Eisenstaedt/'Life' copyright © Time Inc, 1945; (BR) private collection; (rest) courtesy of Queensland Newspapers Pty Ltd. 446 (main picture) Pictorial Press; (inset) Camera Press. 447 (TL) *Eugene Fleury*; (CL inset) US Army*; (BL inset) IWM; (BR) Popperfoto. 448-9 National Archives. 450 Hulton Deutsch Collection. 451 (TR) Library of Congress; (BL) Popperfoto. 452 (BL) US Army Quartermaster Museum, Fort Lee, Virginia; (rest) Hulton Deutsch Collection. 453 (CL) National Archives; (rest) private collection. 454 Popperfoto. Inside back cover: Associated Press.

The publishers acknowledge their indebtedness to the following books, which were consulted for reference.

The Abwehr by Lauran Paine (Robert Hale); *Aces High* by C. Shores & C. Williams (Neville Spearman); *Afrika Korps* by George Balin (Arms & Armour); *Afrika Korps* by Kenneth Macksey (Pan); *After the Battle* (Battle of Britain Prints International; quarterly); *Aircraft Carriers* by Anthony Preston (Bison); *Aircraft of the Royal Air Force since 1918* by Owen Thetford (Putnam); *Alamein* by C.E. Lucas Phillips (Heinemann); *Albanian Assignment* by David Smiley (Chatto & Windus); *Alex* by Nigel Nicolson (Weidenfeld & Nicolson); *Alexander of Tunis: A Biographical Portrait* by Norman Hillson (W.H. Allen); *All Hell on the Irrawaddy* by John Finnerty (Anchor); *The Armed Forces of World War II* by Andrew Mollo (Orbis); *Armed Truce* by Hugh Thomas (Hamish Hamilton); *The Army Air Forces in World War II* by W.H. Craven &

J.L. Cate (Chicago; official history series); *The Artful Albanian* by Enver Hoxha (Chatto & Windus); *Atlas of the Second World War* edited by Thomas E. Griess (Avery Publishing; two vols); *Atlas of World War II* by Richard Natkiel (Bison); *Auchinleck* by John Connell (Cassell); *Australia Goes to War 1939-45* by John Robertson (Doubleday, Australia); *Australia in the War of 1939-45* edited by Gavin Long (Australian War Memorial; official history series; various authors).

Barbarossa by Alan Clark (Hutchinson); *Battle of Britain* by Len Deighton (Jonathan Cape); *Battle of the Bulge* by John Pimlott (Bison); *Battle over Britain* by Francis Mason (McWhirter); *Battles of the Great Commanders* by Anthony Livesey (Michael Joseph); *Beyond the Chindwin* by Bernard Fergusson (Collins); *The Big Lie* by John Baker White (Evans); *The Biography of General George S. Patton* by Ian Hogg (Hamlyn); *The Black Angels* by Rupert Butler (Arrow); *Black Lamb and Grey Falcon* by Rebecca West (Viking); *Bodyguard of Lies* by Anthony Cave-Brown (W.H. Allen); *Bomber Command* by Max Hastings (Michael Joseph); *The Bomber Command War Diaries* edited by Martin Middlebrook & Chris Everitt (Viking); *The Bombers* by Robin Cross (Bantam); *The Book of Alfred Kantor* (Piatkus); *A Bridge Too Far* by Cornelius Ryan (Hodder & Stoughton); *Burma-Siam Railway: The Secret Diary of Dr Robert Hardie* (Jane's).

The Camera at War by Jorge Lewinski (Octopus); *Capitulation: 1945* by Marlis Steinert (Constable); *Cassino: Anatomy of the Battle* by Janusz Piekalkiewicz (Orbis); *Changi Photographer: George Aspinall's Record of Captivity* by Tim Bowden (Australian Broadcasting Corporation); *Checkmate at Ruweisat: Auchinleck's Finest Hour* by D.G. Brownlow (Christopher); *Children of the Blitz* edited by Robert Westall (Penguin); *Churchill's Private Armies* by Eric Morris (Hutchinson); *City of Fire* by J.W. Kunetka (Prentice-Hall); *Classic Aircraft Fighters* by Bill Gunston (Hamlyn); *Colours of War: War Art 1939-45* by Alan Ross (Jonathan Cape); *Commandant of Auschwitz* by Rudolf Hoess (Weidenfeld & Nicolson); *Corregidor* by Eric Morris (Hutchinson); *Cunningham of Hyndehope* by Oliver Warner (John Murray); *Curfew in Paris* by Ninetta Jucker (Hogarth).

Dawns Like Thunder by Alfred Draper (Leo Cooper); *Day of the Bomb* by D. Kurzman (Weidenfeld & Nicolson); *Deception in World War II* by Charles Cruickshank (OUP); *Decision of Destiny* by W.S. Shoenberger (Ohio); *The Desert Generals* by Corelli Barnett (Allen & Unwin); *Desert Rats at War* by George Forty (Ian Allan); *The Desert War* by Alan Moorehead (Hamish Hamilton); *Diary of a Nightmare* by Ursula von Kardorff (Hart-Davis); *Dictionary of National Biography* (OUP); *Dönitz: The Last Führer* by P. Padfield (Gollancz); *The Doodlebugs* by Norman Longmate (Hutchinson).

Eagle against the Sun by Ronald Spector (Viking); *Eastern Front* by J.D. Westwood (Bison); *Eclipse* by Alan Moorehead (Hamish Hamilton); *Encyclopedia of World History* edited by W.M. Langer (Houghton Mifflin); *Encyclopedia of World War II* edited by John Keegan (Bison); *Encyclopedia of World War II* edited by T. Parrish (Secker & Warburg); *England under Hitler* by Comer Clarke (NEL); *Enigma* by Wladislaw Kozaczuk (Arms & Armour); *Europe of the Dictators* by E. Wiskemann (Fontana).

Fighters over the Desert by C. Shores & H. Ring (Neville Spearman); *Fighters over Tunisia* by C. Shores, H. Ring & W. Hess (Neville Spearman); *Film and Radio Propaganda in World War II* edited by K.R.M. Short (Croom Helm); *The First Casualty* by P. Knightley (Quartet); *'44 and '45* by Charles Whiting (Century); *Four Samurai* by Arthur Swinson (Hutchinson); *The Fourth Arm* by Charles Cruikshank (Davis-Poynter); *From Pyramid to Pagoda: The Story of the West Yorks Regiment* by E.W.C. Sandes (Parsons).

GCHQ: The Secret Wireless War 1900-86 by Nigel West (Weidenfeld & Nicolson); *The German Air Force versus Russia 1943* by H. Plocher (Arno); *The Goebbels Diaries* edited by Louis P. Lochner (Hamish Hamilton); *Goodbye Darkness* by William Manchester (Michael Joseph); *'The Good War': An Oral History of World War Two* by Studs Terkel (Hamish Hamilton); *Great Battlefields of the World* by J. McDonald (Michael Joseph); *Great Battles of World War II* by J. McDonald (Michael Joseph); *Great War Speeches* by Winston Churchill (Corgi); *Guilt at Versailles* by A. Lentin (Methuen).

Haile Selassie's War by Anthony Mockler (OUP); *Heraldry of War* edited by Bernard Fitzsimons (Phoebus); *Hiroshima* by John Hersey (Penguin); *A History of Modern Japan* by Richard Storry (Penguin); *History of the Second World War* (HMSO; official history series; various authors); *History of the Second World War* (Purnell; partwork); *History of the Second World War* by Basil Liddell Hart (Cassell); *History of US Marine Corps Operations in World War II* (US Marine Corps; official history series; various authors); *History of US Naval Operations in World War II* by Samuel Eliot Morison (Little, Brown; official history series); *The History of World War II* by E. Bauer (Galley); *Hitler* by John Toland (Doubleday); *Hitler: A Study in Tyranny* by Alan Bullock (Penguin); *Hitler Moves East* by Paul Carell (Bantam); *Hitler's Elite: Leibstandarte SS* by J. Lucas & M. Cooper (Macdonald & Jane's); *Hitler's Englishman: The Crime of Lord Haw-Haw* by Francis Selwyn (Routledge); *Hitler's Gladiator: Sepp Dietrich* edited by Charles Messenger (Brassey's); *Hitler's Luftwaffe* by Tony Wood & Bill Gunston (Salamander); *Hitler's Personal Security* by P. Hoffmann (Macmillan); *Hitler's Secret Life* by Glenn B. Infield (Hamlyn); *Hitler's War* by D. Irving (Hodder & Stoughton); *Hitler's Young Tigers* by Rupert Butler (Arrow); *The Holocaust* by Martin Gilbert (Collins); *Home Front USA: America during World War II* by Allan Winkler (Harlan Davidson); *How We Lived Then* by Norman Longmate (Arrow); *The Hut Six Story* by G. Welchman (Allan Lane).

The Illustrated Encyclopedia of Military Vehicles by Ian Hogg & John Weeks (Hamlyn); *The Impact of World War II on the Soviet Union* edited by Susan Linz (Rowman & Allanheld); *The Imperial Japanese Navy 1941-45* by Paul S. Dull (Patrick Stephens); *An Infantry Company in Arakan and Kohima* by L.A. Lowry (Gale & Poulden); *In Hitler's Germany* by Bernt Engelmann (Methuen); *Inside the Third Reich* by Albert Speer (Weidenfeld & Nicolson); *I Saw Tokyo Burning* edited by Robert Guillan (John Murray); *Is Paris Burning?* by Larry Collins & Dominique Lapierre (Gollancz); *The Italian Campaign 1943-5* by G.A. Shepperd (Praeger); *It Happened in our Lifetime* by John Phillips (Michael Joseph); *I was Monty's Double* by M.E. Clifton James (Rider).

Japan's Last War by Ienaga Saburo (Blackwell); *Japan's War* by Edwin P. Hoyt (Hutchinson); *J. Robert Oppenheimer: Shatterer of Worlds* by Peter Goodchild (BBC); *June 1944* by H.P. Willmott (Blandford).

Kaputt by Curzio Malaparte (Panther); *Kesselring: The Making of the Luftwaffe* by Kenneth Macksey (Batsford); *The Knights of Bushido* by Lord Russell of Liverpool (Cassell).

The Last Battle by Cornelius Ryan (NEL); *The Last Führer* by L.W. Seagren (Naval Institute; USA); *Die Leibstandarte* by Rudolf Lehman (Munin Verlag, Osnabruck); *Life in the Third Reich* edited by R. Bessel (OUP); *Life in Wartime Britain* by E.R. Chamberlin (Batsford); *Life of my Choice* by Wilfred Thesiger (Collins); *Lilliput Goes to War* edited by Kaye Webb (Hutchinson); *London at War* by Joanna Mack & Steve Humphries (Sidgwick & Jackson); *The Longest Day* by Cornelius Ryan (Gollancz); *Lord Haw-Haw: The Full Story of William Joyce* by J.A. Cole (Faber); *Love, Sex and War: Changing Values 1939-45* by John Costello (Collins); *The Luftwaffe War Diaries* by C. Bekker (Macdonald).

The Making of the Atomic Bomb by Richard Rhodes (Penguin); *Mein Kampf* by Adolf Hitler (Hutchinson); *Memoirs* by Albert Kesselring (William Kimber); *Memoirs* by Viscount Montgomery of Alamein (Collins); *Mighty Eighth* and *Mighty Eighth War Diary* by Roger Freeman (Jane's); *MI6* by Nigel West (Weidenfeld & Nicolson); *Modern Greece* by J. Campbell & P. Sherrard (Benn); *Modern Greece* by C.M. Woodhouse (Faber); *Modern Small Arms* by Major F. Myatt (Salamander); *Monty: The Making of a General* and *Monty: Master of the Battlefield* by Nigel Hamilton (Hamish Hamilton); *Moscow in World War II* by Cathy Porter & Mark Jones (Chatto & Windus).

Narvik by Donald MacIntyre (Evans Bros); *The Naval Air War 1939-45* by Nathan Miller (Conway Maritime); *Nazi Germany's War against the Jews* (American Jewish Congress); *New Guinea 1942-44* by Timothy Hall (Methuen, Australia); *New Zealanders at War* by Michael King (Heinemann, New Zealand); *The 900 Days* by Harrison E. Salisbury (Macmillan).

On Borrowed Time by Leonard Mosley (Weidenfeld & Nicolson); *Once There Was a War* by John Steinbeck (Heinemann); *Operation Husky: The Allied Invasion of Sicily* by S.W.C. Pack (David & Charles); *The Order of the SS* by Friedrich Raeder (Foulsham); *Overlord* by Max Hastings (Michael Joseph); *The Oxford Book of Military Anecdotes* edited by Max Hastings (OUP).

Panzer Leader by Heinz Guderian (Michael Joseph); *Panzers in Normandy Then and Now* by Eric Lefèvre (Battle of Britain Prints International); *Patle: Supreme Fighter in the Air* by E.C.R. Baker (William Kimber); *Patton: The Man behind the Legend* by M. Blumenson (Jonathan Cape); *Patton: Ordeal and Triumph* by Ladislas Farago (Ivan Obolensky); *The People's War: Britain 1939-45* by Angus Calder (Jonathan Cape); *P.G. Wodehouse* by Frances Donaldson (Weidenfeld & Nicolson); *Photographs* by Robert Capa (Faber); *The Pictorial History of Air Warfare* by Chris Chant (Octopus); *Pictorial History of Australia at War 1939-45* edited by Charles Meeking (Australian War Memorial); *The Pictorial History of World War II* by Charles Messenger (Gallery); *The Politics of Propaganda* by Allan Winkler (Yale); *Prelude to Overlord* by H. Wynn & S. Young (Airlife); *The Price of Admiralty* by John Keegan (Hutchinson); *Prisoners of War: Australians under Nippon* by H. Nelson (Australian Broadcasting Corporation); *Propaganda: The Art of Persuasion* by Anthony Rhodes (Wellfleet); *Propaganda in War 1939-45* by Michael Balfour (Routledge).

Red Sun Setting by William T. Y'Blood (Naval Institute; USA); *The Right of the Line* by John Terraine (Hodder & Stoughton); *Rise and Fall of the Third Reich* by William L. Shirer (Secker & Warburg); *The Road to Berlin* and *The Road to Stalingrad* by John Erikson (Weidenfeld & Nicolson); *The Rome-Berlin Axis* by E. Wiskemann (Fontana); *The Rommel Papers* edited by B.H. Liddell Hart (Collins); *Rommel's Army in Africa* by Dal McGuirk (Stanley Paul); *Russia at War 1941-45* by Alexander Werth (Pan).

The Scourge of the Swastika by Lord Russell of Liverpool (Cassell); *Scramble: A Narrative History of the Battle of Britain* by Norman Gelb (Michael Joseph); *The Second World War* (Larousse); *The Second World War* by Winston S. Churchill (Cassell; series); *The Second World War* edited by Thomas E. Griess (Avery Publishing; two vols); *Second World War Posters* (Imperial War Museum); *The Secret War* by Brian Johnson (BBC); *Selling the War* by Zbynek Zeman (Orbis); *The Semblance of Peace* by J. Wheeler-Bennett & A. Nicholls (Macmillan); *Shoah* by Claude Lanzmann (Pantheon); *A Short History of Yugoslavia* by Stephen Clissold (CUP); *Short Stories from the Second World War* edited by Dan Davin (OUP); *Siege: Malta 1940-43* by E. Bradford (Hamish Hamilton); *Signal: Hitler's Wartime Picture Magazine* edited by S.L. Mayer (Bison); *Singapore: An Illustrated History 1941-1984* edited by Daljit Singh & V.T. Arasu (Ministry of Culture, Singapore); *Softly Tread the Brave* by Ivan Southall (Angus & Robertson); *South Pacific Handbook* by D. Stanley (Moon); *The Struggle for Europe* by Chester Wilmott (Fontana); *The Struggle for Greece* by C.M. Woodhouse (Hart-Davis); *Survey of International Affairs 1939-45: The War and the Neutrals* by A. & V. Toynbee (OUP).

Take These Men by Cyril Joly (Buchan & Enright); *Tanks Across the Desert* by George Forty (William Kimber); *Tanks and Other Fighting Vehicles of World War II* by B.T. White (Peerage); *Tarawa* by Charles Gregg (Stein & Day); *The Times Atlas of World History* edited by Geoffrey Barraclough (Times); *The Times Atlas of the World* (Times); *To Lose a Battle* by Alastair Horne (Macmillan); *A Trial of Generals: Homma, Yamashita, MacArthur* by L. Taylor (Icarus); *Triumph in the West* and *The Turn of the Tide* by Arthur Bryant (Collins); *2194 Days of War* by Cesare Salmaggi & Alfredo Pallavisini (Windward).

U-Boat Commander by Gunther Prien (Tandem); *Ultra Goes to War* by Ronald Lewin (Hutchinson); *The Ultra Secret* by F.W. Winterbothom (Harper & Row); *US Army in World War II* (Center of Military History, US Army; official history series; various authors).

VE Day by Robin Cross (Sidgwick & Jackson); *Victims of Yalta* by Nikolai Tolstoy (Corgi); *Victory in Europe* by Max Hastings (Weidenfeld & Nicolson); *The Volga Rises in Europe* by Curzio Malaparte (Panther).

Waffen SS: The Asphalt Soldiers by John Keegan (Ballantine); *The War against the Jews 1933-45* by Lucy Davidowicz (Weidenfeld & Nicolson); *War and Society in Europe 1870-1970* by Brian Bond (Fontana); *The War Artists* by Meirion & Susie Harris (Michael Joseph); *War Maps: Great Land, Sea and Air Battles of World War II* by Simon Goodenough (Macdonald); *War Report: D-Day to VE-Day* edited by Desmond Hawkins (BBC); *The War that Hitler Won* by Robert Edward Herzstein (Hamish Hamilton); *The War with Japan: A Concise History* by Charles Bateson (Ure Smith); *Webster's New Geographical Dictionary* (Merriam-Webster); *We'll Meet Again* by Robert Kee (Dent); *When Tigers Fight* by Dick Wilson (Hutchinson); *Who's Who in World War II* by David Mason (Weidenfeld & Nicolson); *Who Was Who in World War II* edited by John Keegan (Arms & Armour); *Winston Churchill: An Authentic Hero* by Piers Brendon (Methuen); *With the Foreign Legion at Narvik* by Pierre Lapie (John Murray); *World Aircraft* by E. Angelucci & P. Matricardi (Sampson Low; series); *The World Almanac of World War II* edited by Peter Young (Bison); *The World Atlas of Warfare* by Richard Holmes (Mitchell Beazley); *The World at War* by Mark Arnold-Forster (Collins); *World War 1939-45* by Peter Young (Arthur Barker); *World War II* (Time-Life; series); *World War II* by Ronald Heiferman (Octopus); *World War II Almanac* edited by Robert Goralski (Hamish Hamilton); *World War II Fact Book* by Christy Campbell (Macdonald); *World War II in Photographs* by John Pimlott (Orbis); *World War Two through German Eyes* by James Lucas (Arms & Armour).

The Years of MacArthur by D. Clayton James (Houghton Mifflin; two vols).

Reader's Digest thanks the following individuals and publishers for their kind permission to quote passages from the publications mentioned.

Arnoldo Mondadori for *2194 Giorni di Guerra* by A. Pallavisini and C. Salmaggi; © 1977 Arnoldo Mondadori Editore, Milan.
Barrie & Jenkins Ltd for *Russia at War 1941-45* by Alexander Werth.
Battle of Britain Prints International for their quarterly publication *After the Battle*.
British Broadcasting Corporation for *War Report: D-Day to VE-Day* edited by Desmond Hawkins.
Bison Books for *Encyclopedia of World War II* edited by John Keegan.
Century Hutchinson Ltd for *The Doodlebugs* by Norman Longmate and *Occupied Territory* by Polly Peabody.
William Collins for *The Rommel Papers* by B.H. Liddell Hart.
EMI Music Publishing Ltd for the song *A Thingamabob* by David Heneker.
The Imperial War Museum for *Arnhem Spearhead* by James Sims.
Norman Longmate Esq for *How We Lived Then* (Hutchinson, 1971; Arrow Books, 1979).
James Lucas for unpublished material on the Eastern Front.
Macdonald & Co for the partwork *Purnell's History of the Second World War*.
Macmillan Publishers for *Hitler's War 1939-42* by David Irving.
Michael Joseph Ltd for *Goodbye Darkness* by William Manchester.
Penguin Books for *Hitler, A Study in Tyranny* by Alan Bullock and *Hiroshima* by John Hersey.
Sidgwick & Jackson for *The Making of Modern London 1939-45: London at War* by Joanna Mack and Steve Humphries.
Time-Life Books for their series *World War II*.
Weidenfeld & Nicolson for *Who's Who in World War II* by David Mason, and for *The Road to Stalingrad* and *The Road to Berlin* by John Erikson.

Typesetting: Elite Typesetting Techniques, Southampton, England
Separations: Colourscan Co Pte Ltd, Singapore
Paper: Mead Paper Co, Escanaba, Michigan, USA
Cloth: Holliston Mills Inc, Kingsport, Tennessee, USA
Printing & binding: Rand McNally & Co, Indianapolis, Indiana, USA

40/186/1

44 St
LEBLANG-GRAY
50 FACTORY STORES
PUBLIC TELEPHONE CENTER for the ARMED FORCES
ER TOBACCOS
DINE-DANCE
EWMAN'S HEATRE ICKETS
Marlboro
SCHRAFFT'S
VICTORY GIFT SHOP
LONDON SHO